W9-CTW-433

Twentieth-Century Literary Criticism

Guide to Gale Literary Criticism Series

For criticism on	Consult these Gale series
Authors now living or who died after December 31, 1959	*CONTEMPORARY LITERARY CRITICISM (CLC)*
Authors who died between 1900 and 1959	*TWENTIETH-CENTURY LITERARY CRITICISM (TCLC)*
Authors who died between 1800 and 1899	*NINETEENTH-CENTURY LITERATURE CRITICISM (NCLC)*
Authors who died between 1400 and 1799	*LITERATURE CRITICISM FROM 1400 TO 1800 (LC)* *SHAKESPEAREAN CRITICISM (SC)*
Authors who died before 1400	*CLASSICAL AND MEDIEVAL LITERATURE CRITICISM (CMLC)*
Black writers of the past two hundred years	*BLACK LITERATURE CRITICISM (BLC)*
Authors of books for children and young adults	*CHILDREN'S LITERATURE REVIEW (CLR)*
Dramatists	*DRAMA CRITICISM (DC)*
Hispanic writers of the late nineteenth and twentieth centuries	*HISPANIC LITERATURE CRITICISM (HLC)*
Native North American writers and orators of the eighteenth, nineteenth, and twentieth centuries	*NATIVE NORTH AMERICAN LITERATURE (NNAL)*
Poets	*POETRY CRITICISM (PC)*
Short story writers	*SHORT STORY CRITICISM (SSC)*
Major authors from the Renaissance to the present	*WORLD LITERATURE CRITICISM, 1500 TO THE PRESENT (WLC)*

ISSN 0276-8178

R

Volume 57

Twentieth-Century Literary Criticism

**Excerpts from Criticism of the
Works of Novelists, Poets, Playwrights,
Short Story Writers, and Other Creative Writers
Who Lived between 1900 and 1960,
from the First Published Critical
Appraisals to Current Evaluations**

Joann Cerrito
Editor

Pamela Willwerth Aue
Christine M. Bichler
Laurie Di Mauro
Nancy Dziedzic
Jennifer Gariepy
Thomas Ligotti
Lynn M. Spampinato
Associate Editors

 **Gale Research Inc.**

An International Thomson Publishing Company

NEW YORK • LONDON • BONN • BOSTON • DETROIT • MADRID
MELBOURNE • MEXICO CITY • PARIS • SINGAPORE • TOKYO
TORONTO • WASHINGTON • ALBANY NY • BELMONT CA • CINCINNATI OH

STAFF

Joann Cerrito, *Editor*

Pamela Willwerth Aue, Christine M. Bichler, Laurie Di Mauro, Nancy Dziedzic, Jennifer Gariepy, Thomas Ligotti, Lynn M. Spampinato, *Associate Editors*

Marlene H. Lasky, *Permissions Manager*
Margaret A. Chamberlain, Linda M. Pugliese, *Permissions Specialists*
Susan Brohman, Diane Cooper, Maria Franklin, Pamela A. Hayes, Arlene Johnson, Josephine M. Keene,
Michele Lonoconus, Maureen Puhl, Shalice Shah, Kimberly F. Smilay, Barbara A. Wallace, *Permissions Associates*
Edna Hedblad, Tyra Y. Phillips, *Permissions Assistants*

Victoria B. Cariappa, *Research Manager*
Eva M. Felts, Mary Beth McElmeel, Donna Melnychenko, Tamara C. Nott, Tracie A. Richardson, *Research Associates*
Maria E. Bryson, Michele McRobert, Michele P. Pica, Amy Beth Wieczorek, *Research Assistants*

Mary Beth Trimper, *Production Director*
Mary Kelley, *Production Associate*

Cynthia Baldwin, *Product Design Manager*
Barbara J. Yarrow, *Graphic Services Supervisor*
Sherrell Hobbs, *Macintosh Artist*
Willie F. Mathis, *Camera Operator*

Library of Congress Catalog Card Number 76-46132
ISBN 0-8103-2439-3
ISSN 0276-8178

Printed in the United States of America

10 9 8 7 6 5 4 3 2 1

Contents

Preface vii

Acknowledgments xi

Preface

Since its inception more than fifteen years ago, *Twentieth-Century Literary Criticism* has been purchased and used by nearly 10,000 school, public, and college or university libraries. *TCLC* has covered more than 500 authors, representing 58 nationalities, and over 25,000 titles. No other reference source has surveyed the critical response to twentieth-century authors and literature as thoroughly as *TCLC*. In the words of one reviewer, "there is nothing comparable available." *TCLC* "is a gold mine of information—dates, pseudonyms, biographical information, and criticism from books and periodicals—which many libraries would have difficulty assembling on their own."

Scope of the Series

TCLC is designed to serve as an introduction to authors who died between 1900 and 1960 and to the most significant interpretations of these author's works. The great poets, novelists, short story writers, playwrights, and philosophers of this period are frequently studied in high school and college literature courses. In organizing and excerpting the vast amount of critical material written on these authors, *TCLC* helps students develop valuable insight into literary history, promotes a better understanding of the texts, and sparks ideas for papers and assignments. Each entry in *TCLC* presents a comprehensive survey of an author's career or an individual work of literature and provides the user with a multiplicity of interpretations and assessments. Such variety allows students to pursue their own interests; furthermore, it fosters an awareness that literature is dynamic and responsive to many different opinions.

Every fourth volume of *TCLC* is devoted to literary topics that cannot be covered under the author approach used in the rest of the series. Such topics include literary movements, prominent themes in twentieth-century literature, literary reaction to political and historical events, significant eras in literary history, prominent literary anniversaries, and the literatures of cultures that are often overlooked by English-speaking readers.

TCLC is designed as a companion series to Gale's *Contemporary Literary Criticism,* which reprints commentary on authors now living or who have died since 1960. Because of the different periods under consideration, there is no duplication of material between *CLC* and *TCLC*. For additional information about *CLC* and Gale's other criticism titles, users should consult the Guide to Gale Literary Criticism Series preceding the title page in this volume.

Coverage

Each volume of *TCLC* is carefully compiled to present:

- criticism of authors, or literary topics, representing a variety of genres and nationalities

- both major and lesser-known writers and literary works of the period

- 8-15 authors or 4-6 topics per volume

- individual entries that survey critical response to each author's work or each topic in literary history, including early criticism to reflect initial reactions; later criticism to represent any rise or decline in reputation; and current retrospective analyses.

Organization of This Book

An author entry consists of the following elements: author heading, biographical and critical introduction, list of principal works, excerpts of criticism (each preceded by an annotation and followed by a bibliographic citation), and a bibliography of further reading.

- The **Author Heading** consists of the name under which the author most commonly wrote, followed by birth and death dates. If an author wrote consistently under a pseudonym, the pseudonym will be listed in the author heading and the real name given in parentheses on the first line of the biographical and critical introduction. Also located at the beginning of the introduction to the author entry are any name variations under which an author wrote, including transliterated forms for authors whose languages use nonroman alphabets.

- The **Biographical and Critical Introduction** outlines the author's life and career, as well as the critical issues surrounding his or her work. References to past volumes of *TCLC* are provided at the beginning of the introduction. Additional sources of information in other biographical and critical reference series published by Gale, including *Short Story Criticism, Children's Literature Review, Contemporary Authors, Dictionary of Literary Biography,* and *Something about the Author,* are listed in a box at the end of the entry.

- Most *TCLC* entries include **Portraits** of the author. Many entries also contain reproductions of materials pertinent to an author's career, including manuscript pages, title pages, dust jackets, letters, and drawings, as well as photographs of important people, places, and events in an author's life.

- The **List of Principal Works** is chronological by date of first book publication and identifies the genre of each work. In the case of foreign authors with both foreign-language publications and English translations, the title and date of the first English-language edition are given in brackets. Unless otherwise indicated, dramas are dated by first performance, not first publication.

- Critical excerpts are prefaced by **Annotations** providing the reader with information about both the critic and the criticism that follows. Included are the critic's reputation, individual approach to literary criticism, and particular expertise in an author's works. Also noted are the relative importance of a work of criticism, the scope of the excerpt, and the growth of critical controversy or changes in critical trends regarding an author. In some cases, these annotations cross-reference excerpts by critics who discuss each other's commentary.

- **Criticism** is arranged chronologically in each author entry to provide a perspective on changes in critical evaluation over the years. All titles of works by the author featured in the entry are printed in boldface type to enable the user to easily locate discussion of particular works. Also for purposes of easier identification, the critic's name and the publication date of the essay are given at the beginning of each piece of criticism. Unsigned criticism is preceded by the title of the journal in which it appeared. Some of the excerpts in *TCLC* also contain translated material. Unless otherwise noted, translations in brackets are by the editors; translations in parentheses or continuous with the text are by the critic. Publication information (such as footnotes or page and line references to specific editions of works) have been deleted at the editor's discretion to provide smoother reading of the text.

- A complete **Bibliographic Citation** designed to facilitate location of the original essay or book follows each piece of criticism.

- An annotated list of **Further Reading** appearing at the end of each author entry suggests secondary sources on the author. In some cases it includes essays for which the editors could not obtain reprint rights.

Cumulative Indexes

■ Each volume of *TCLC* contains a cumulative **Author Index** listing all authors who have appeared in Gale's Literary Criticism Series, along with cross references to such biographical series as *Contemporary Authors* and *Dictionary of Literary Biography*. For readers' convenience, a complete list of Gale titles included appears on the first page of the author index. Useful for locating authors within the various series, this index is particularly valuable for those authors who are identified by a certain period but who, because of their death dates, are placed in another, or for those authors whose careers span two periods. For example, F. Scott Fitzgerald is found in *TCLC*, yet a writer often associated with him, Ernest Hemingway, is found in *CLC*.

■ Each *TCLC* volume includes a cumulative **Nationality Index** which lists all authors who have appeared in *TCLC* volumes, arranged alphabetically under their respective nationalities, as well as Topics volume entries devoted to particular national literatures.

■ Each new volume in Gale's Literary Criticism Series includes a cumulative **Topic Index**, which lists all literary topics treated in *NCLC, TCLC, LC 1400-1800,* and the *CLC* yearbook.

■ Each new volume of *TCLC*, with the exception of the Topics volumes, includes a **Title Index** listing the titles of all literary works discussed in the volume. In response to numerous suggestions from librarians, Gale has also produced a **Special Paperbound Edition** of the *TCLC* title index. This annual cumulation lists all titles discussed in the series since its inception and is issued with the first volume of *TCLC* published each year. Additional copies of the index are available on request. Librarians and patrons will welcome this separate index; it saves shelf space, is easy to use, and is recyclable upon receipt of the following year's cumulation. Titles discussed in the Topics volume entries are not included *TCLC* cumulative index.

Citing *Twentieth-Century Literary Criticism*

When writing papers, students who quote directly from any volume in Gale's literary Criticism Series may use the following general forms to footnote reprinted criticism. The first example pertains to materials drawn from periodicals, the second to material reprinted from books.

[1]T. S. Eliot, "John Donne," *The Nation and the Athenaeum,* 33 (9 June 1923), 321-32; excerpted and reprinted in *Literature Criticism from 1400 to 1800,* Vol. 10, ed. James E. Person, Jr. (Detroit: Gale Research, 1989), pp. 28-9.

[2]Clara G. Stillman, *Samuel Butler: A Mid-Victorian Modern* (Viking Press, 1932); excerpted and reprinted in *Twentieth-Century Literary Criticism,* Vol. 33, ed. Paula Kepos (Detroit: Gale Research, 1989), pp. 43-5.

Suggestions Are Welcome

In response to suggestions, several features have been added to *TCLC* since the series began, including annotations to excerpted criticism, a cumulative index to authors in all Gale literary criticism series, entries devoted to criticism on a single work by a major author, more extensive illustrations, and a title index listing all literary works discussed in the series since its inception.

Readers who wish to suggest authors or topics to appear in future volumes, or who have other suggestions, are cordially invited to write the editors.

Acknowledgments

The editors wish to thank the copyright holders of the excerpted criticism included in this volume and the permissions managers of many book and magazine publishing companies for assisting us in securing reprint rights. We are also grateful to the staffs of the Detroit Public Library, the Library of Congress, the University of Detroit Mercy Library, Wayne State University Purdy/Kresge Library Complex, and the University of Michigan Libraries for making their resources available to us. Following is a list of the copyright holders who have granted us permission to reprint material in this volume of *TCLC*. Every effort has been made to trace copyright, but if omissions have been made, please let us know.

COPYRIGHTED EXCERPTS IN *TCLC*, VOLUME 57, WERE REPRINTED FROM THE FOLLOWING PERIODICALS:

Ariel, n. 41, 1976. Both reprinted by permission of the publisher.—*Australian Literary Studies,* v. 11, May, 1983 for "Barbara Baynton: Woman as the Chosen Vessel' " by Kay Schaffer; v. 14, May, 1989 for "Gender and Genre in Barbara Baynton's 'Human Toll' " by Susan Sheridan. Both reprinted by permission of the respective authors.—*Cinema Journal,* v. XIV, Fall, 1974 for the "Evolution of Eisenstein's 'Old and New' " by Vance Kepley, Jr. © 1974, Society for Cinema Studies. Reprinted by permission of the publisher and the author.—*College English,* v. 26, March, 1965 for "Unlearned Lessons in 'The Secret Sharer' " by J.D. O'Hara. Copyright © 1965 by the National Council of Teachers of English. Reprinted by permission of the publisher and the author.—*Commentary,* v. 9, April, 1950 for "The Blue Piano of Else Lasker-Schueler" by Heinz Politzer. Copyright 1950, renewed 1978 by the American Jewish Committee. All rights reserved. Reprinted by permission of the publisher and the author.—*Conradiana,* v. III, 1971-72 for "Leggatt and the Promised Land: A New Reading of 'The Secret Sharer' " by Paul Bidwell; v. III, 1971-72 for " 'The Secret Sharer' and the Existential Hero" by P.L. Brown; v. VII, 1975 for "Comic Elements in Conrad's 'The Secret Sharer' " by Dinshaw M. Burjorjee. All reprinted with permission of Texas Tech University Press and the respective authors.— *Criticism,* v. XV, Winter, 1973. Copyright, 1973, Wayne State University Press. Reprinted by permission of the publisher.—*German Life & Letters,* v. XVIII, 1964-65. Reprinted by permission of the publisher.—*The German Quarterly,* v. XLIII, September, 1970. Copyright © 1970 by the American Association of Teachers of German. Reprinted by permission of the publisher.—*The Humanist,* v. XXXIV, March-April, 1974. Copyright 1974 by the American Humanist Association. Reprinted by permission of the publisher.— *The International Fiction Review,* v. 3, July, 1976 for "Friedrich Dürren Matt and Edgar Wallace" by Armin Arnold. Reprinted by permission of the publisher.—*The Midwest Quarterly,* v. VIII, Spring, 1967. Copyright, 1967, by *The Midwest Quarterly,* Pittsburgh State University, Reprinted by permission of the publisher.— *Modern Fiction Studies,* v. XIII, Spring, 1967. Copyright © 1967 by Purdue Research Foundation, West Lafayette, IN 47907. All rights reserved. Reprinted with permission.—*The New Republic,* v. 134, March 26, 1956. © 1956, renewed 1984 The New Republic, Inc. Reprinted by permission of *The New Republic.*—*New York Herald Tribune Books,* January 15, 1928. Copyright 1928, renewed 1956, New York Herald Tribune, Inc. All rights reserved. Reprinted by permission.—*The New York Review of Books,* v. XXVI, November 22, 1979. Copyright © 1979 Nyrev, Inc. Reprinted with permission from *The New York Review of Books.*—*The New York Times Book Review,* April 12, 1922; April 15, 1923; July 19, 1925; January 24, 1926; October 24, 1926; June 19, 1927; September 17, 1950. Copyright 1922, renewed 1950; copyright 1923, renewed 1951; copyright 1925, renewed 1953; copyright 1926, renewed 1954; copyright 1927, renewed 1955; copyright 1950, renewed 1978 by The New York Times Company. All reprinted by permission of the publisher.—*The New*

Yorker, v. XXVI, October 7, 1950. Copyright 1950, renewed 1978 by The New Yorker Magazine, Inc. Reprinted by permission of the publisher.—*The Pacific Spectator,* v. 6, winter, 1952. Copyright 1952, renewed 1980 by The Pacific Coast Committee for the Humanities of the American Council of Learned Societies. Reprinted by permission of the publisher.—*Partisan Review,* v. XLI, 1974 for "Anxious Energetics" by Frederick Crews. Copyright © 1974 by *Partisan Review.* Reprinted by permission of the publisher and the author.—*PMLA,* LXXIX, December, 1964. Copyright © 1964, renewed 1992 by the Modern Language Association of America. Reprinted by Permission of the Modern Language Association of America.—*Screen,* v. 12, Winter, 1971-72. © The Society for Education in Film and Television 1972. Both reprinted by permission of the publisher.—*The Sewanee Review,* v. LXX, Summer, 1962 for "A Diamond of Pattern: The War of F. Madox Ford," by Ambrose Gordon, Jr.© 1962, renewed 1990 by The University of the South. Reprinted with permission of the editor of *The Sewanee Review* and the author.—*Sight and Sound,* v. 43, Winter, 1973-74. Copyright © 1974 by The British Film Institute. Reprinted by permission of the publisher.—*Southerly,* v. 49, June, 1989 for "Barbara Baynton's 'Human Toll' : A Modernist Text? " by Shirley Walker. Copyright 1989 by the author. Reprinted by permission of the publisher and the author.—*Studies in the Literary Imagination,* v. XIII, Spring, 1980. Copyright 1980 Department of English, Georgia State University. Reprinted by permission of the publisher.—*Studies in Short Fiction,* v. II, Spring, 1965. Copyright 1965 by Newberry College. Reprinted by permission of the publisher.—*Twentieth Century Literature,* v. 16, April, 1970; v. 18 October, 1972. Copyright 1970, 1972, Hofstra University Press. Both reprinted by permission of the publisher.—*The Yale Review,* v. XL, September, 1950. Copyright 1950, renewed 1978, by Yale University. Reprinted by permission of the editors.

COPYRIGHTED EXCERPTS IN *TCLC,* VOLUME 57, WERE REPRINTED FROM THE FOLLOWING BOOKS:

Bergonzi, Bernard. From *Heroes' Twilight.* Second edition. The Macmillan Press Ltd., 1980. © Bernard Bergonzi 1965, 1980. All rights reserved. Reprinted by permission of Peters, Fraser & Dunlop Group Ltd.—Bradbury, Malcolm. From "The Denuded Place: War and Form in 'Parade's End' and 'U.S.A.' , " in *The First World War in Fiction: A Collection of Critical Essays.* Edited by Holger Klein. Macmillan, 1976. © The Macmillan Press Ltd. All rights reserved. Reprinted by permission of the author.—Briehl, Walter. From "Wilhelm Reich: Character Analysis, " in *Psychoanalytic Pioneers.* Franz Alexander, Samuel Eisenstein, Martin Grotjahn, eds. Basic Books, 1966. Copyright © 1966 by Basic Books, Inc., Publishers. Reprinted by permission of the publisher.—Cattier, Michael. From *The Life and Work of Wilhelm Reich.* Translated by Ghislaine Boulanger. Horizon Press, 1971. Copyright © 1971 Horizon Press. All rights reserved. Reprinted by permission of the author.—Cohn, Hans. From *Else Lasker-Schuler: The Broken World.* Cambridge University Press, 1974. © Cambridge University Press, 1974. © Cambridge University Press 1974. Reprinted with the permission of the publisher and the author.—Cohen, Ira H. From *Ideology and Unconsciousness: Reich, Freud, and Marx.* New York University Press, 1982. Copyright © 1982 by New York University. Reprinted by permission of the publisher.—Cox, C.B. From *Joseph Conrad: The Modern Imagination.* J.M. Dent & Sons Ltd, 1974. © C.B. Cox, 1974 All rights reserved. Reprinted by permission of the publisher.—Cunliffe, John W. From *Modern English Playwrights: A Short History of the English Drama from 1825.* Harper & Brothers, 1927. Copyright 1927 by HarperCollins Publishers, Inc. renewed 1955 by Guy S. Cunliffe. Reprinted by permission of HarperCollins Publishers, Inc.—Durchslag, Audri, and Jeannette Litman-Demeestère. From an introduction to *Hebrew Ballads and Other Poems.* By Else Lasker-Schüler, edited and translated by Audri Durschslag and Jeanette Litman-Demeestère. The Jewish Publication Society, 1980. Copyright © 1980 by The Jewish Publication Society, 1980. Copyright © 1980 by The Jewish Publication Society of America. All rights reserved. —Eagle, Herbert. From an introduction to *Nonindifferent Nature.* By Sergei Eisenstein, translated by Herbert Marshall. Cambridge University Press, 1987. © Cambridge University Press 1987. Reprinted by permission of the publisher and the author.—Eisenstein, Sergei. From "Image and Structure in 'Potemkin' , " in *The Classic Cinema: Essays in Criticism.* Edited by Stanley J. Solmon. Harcourt Brace Jovanovich, 1973. © 1973 Harcourt Brace Jovanovich, Inc. Reprinted by permission of the publisher.—Frost, Lucy. From "Barbara Baynton: An Affinity with Pain, " in *Who is She?* Edited by Shirley Walker. St. Martin's Press, 1983. © University of Queensland Press, St. Lucia, Queensland, 1983. All rights reserved. Reprinted by permission of St. Martin's

Reprinted by permission of New Directions Publishing Corporations.

PHOTOGRAPHS AND ILLUSTRATIONS APPEARING IN *TCLC*, VOLUME 57, WERE RECEIVED FROM THE FOLLOWING SOURCES:

Barbara Baynton

1857-1929

(Born Barbara Lawrence) Australian novelist and short story writer.

INTRODUCTION

Baynton was a novelist and short story writer whose works examine the alienation and isolation experienced by women in the Australian outback during the late nineteenth century. Contradicting the romantic ideals of independence and mateship popularized in Australian fiction of the 1890s, her works provide realistic depictions of the hardships of bush life while presenting a grim, subjective vision of a malevolent landscape and the sinister figures who populate it.

Biographical Information

Baynton was the daughter of John, a carpenter, and Elizabeth (Ewart) Lawrence, Irish immigrants to Australia. Her early childhood was spent in the Scone district of New South Wales before the family moved to Murrurundi in the 1860s. Baynton later became a governess in the Quirindi district and in 1880 married Alexander Frater, with whom she had three children. After Frater eloped with another woman, Baynton moved to Sydney and took a position selling bibles door-to-door. In 1890 she married Thomas Baynton, a wealthy physician nearly thirty years her senior. Dr. Baynton was an avid reader, and Baynton began writing fiction and poetry during their marriage. Her first story, "The Chosen Vessel," also known as "The Tramp," was published in 1896 in the *Bulletin*, the leading Australian literary periodical of the era. In 1902 six of her short stories were published together as *Bush Studies*. Following Dr. Baynton's death in 1904, Baynton spent much of her time in England and published little fiction. She remarried in 1921, and was divorced three years later. Baynton died in Melbourne in 1929.

Major Works

Baynton's literary reputation rests primarily on *Bush Studies*, her collection of short stories examining the hardships of bush life in Australia. In such works as "The Chosen Vessel," "A Dreamer," and "Squeaker's Mate" Baynton focused on the difficulties faced by women in the outback, and her stories are perceived as contradicting what A. A. Phillips has called the "robust nationalism" prevalent in Australian fiction of the 1890s. Each of Baynton's stories centers on the isolation and terror that often dominated women's lives in rural districts. In "The Chosen Vessel," for example, a bush wife is raped and murdered by a traveling swagman while her husband is away, and in "Squeaker's Mate," a paralyzed farm woman is confined to a shed when her husband brings home his new

"mate," a pregnant barmaid. Baynton's only novel, *Human Toll* continues in the grim mood of *Bush Studies* and shares its portrayal of the bush landscape as hostile and barren while presenting the bleak tale of an orphan in the outback. According to Shirley Walker, *Human Toll* is both "an exciting and disturbing text; exciting for its range of response to bush experience, for the passion of its presentation, and for the outrage of its tone."

Critical Reception

Baynton's works created a sensation among Australian readers but generated little interest abroad until English critic Edward Garnett championed the publication of *Bush Studies* in 1902. Called "stark" and "savage," her works have been chiefly valued for their unrelenting realism and uncommon vision of women's status in rural Australian life in the late nineteenth century.

PRINCIPAL WORKS

Bush Studies (short stories) 1902; also published as *Cobbers,* expanded edition, 1917
Human Toll (novel) 1907

CRITICISM

Vance Palmer   (essay date 1958)

SOURCE: "Barbara Baynton," in *Overland,* No. 11, January, 1958, pp. 15-16.

[*In the following essay, Palmer reminisces about his acquaintance with Baynton.*]

One of the most talented and original of our writers was Barbara Baynton, who created something of a sensation among readers by the daring and vigor of her ***Bush Studies*** at the beginning of the century. I very well remember the discussion aroused by her story, **"The Chosen Vessel",** which A. G. Stephens printed in his anthology, *The Bulletin Story Book.* It told of a woman left alone with her child on a remote selection and the night of horror she experienced when a crazy swagman appeared at sundown. The story was quietly told, but full of power, and reached its climax when the terrified woman escaped from her hut near morning and made through the dark bush to the road, throwing herself on the mercy of a solitary horseman coming home from the township. But this man, a superstitious fellow with a sense of guilt, had been drowsing half-drunkenly in his saddle; when he awoke to see the white-robed woman and her child he imagined it was a vision of the Madonna and galloped away in a panic, leaving her to her fate.

Other stories of Barbara Baynton's at the time were even more ruthless in their realism, but some had a robust masculine humor. How attractive and true to the spirit of the outback was that picture of the old hermit-shepherd apologising subtly to his dog for letting the ewe and lamb into the hut they shared. It was not the sort of writing you expected of a woman—especially in those days, when women were supposed to be concerned with little dramas of the drawing-room and the home. There was a good deal of curiosity about Barbara Baynton. What sort of a woman was she, people asked? Was she as mannish as her stories sounded? How had she gained her experience of this tough, primitive life which cut more deeply into the bone than anything written by Lawson?

My own curiosity was stimulated by a chance encounter with another boy a little older than myself, Bob Frater. We had been playing cricket in a little country town; we had missed the train home. And, sitting in a deserted park near the station, putting in time as best we could, we suddenly began talking about writing; or rather about the Bohemian world of Sydney which seemed a very dazzling place then to young people. Puffing at his cherrywood pipe (he was about eighteen) my companion spoke about it

with a casual familiarity that took my breath away. He knew all about it; he had already had paragraphs in the Bulletin; people like A. G. Stephens and Albert Dorrington had been calling in at the family home since he was a youngster. There was a doggy assurance about him when he told anecdotes of such men that made me feel terribly envious; he seemed to have been brought up in a world quite different from my own.

I had always been interested in writing, but had never met any writers. How had this Bob Frater managed to become familiar with so many of them? Well (it came out without any particular boastfulness on his part), his mother was a writer. She was, in fact, Barbara Baynton.

It was this fillip of personal contact that led me to make a special study of Barbara Baynton's stories. I didn't like them at first; there was something savage and remorseless about them; and yet they fascinated me by their unshrinking honesty. Such a woman, I felt, would never be daunted by anything.

Three or four years later when I was in London, trying to earn a living by free-lancing casting about for things that might interest editors, I wrote an article about Barbara Baynton's work, and though it was really about as unlikely a subject as could be imagined, it happened to gain publication in the *Book Monthly,* a journal that had some literary prestige at the time. One surprising result was an impulsive letter, written in a large, imposing hand that allowed very few words to a page.

> "Who are you that you know my work so well?" it asked challengingly. "Where do you come from? All the time I've been over here I've never had such encouragement. Won't you come and have dinner with me at my club?

It was an exciting letter for me to get in my little back room in Bloomsbury—exciting, but more than a little embarrassing. Could I screw my courage up to accept this warm invitation? How would this woman who talked of getting "encouragement" from me react when she found I wasn't a distinguished critic but a rather shy boy of twenty, battling for a few guineas? I thought of going to some obscure place and posting an answer from there, saying I was unable to come to London. I thought of a dozen desperate schemes for avoiding the invitation. But in the end I took my fate in my hands and went.

And I was glad I did, for Barbara Baynton was a large, generous woman who wasn't at all likely to humiliate a boy. In that fashionable club she still seemed like a bush-woman; there was an atmosphere of abundance about her. I was able to get on easy terms with her by talking about Bob Frater, that son of hers by her first husband. Her second husband, Dr. Baynton, had also died a few years before, but had left her a controlling interest in a law-book company that made her independent of writing as a means of earning a living; it was just as well, for her down-to-earth stories had had rather a chilly reception in England. She told me she had hawked her first book, ***Bush Studies,*** from one publisher to another and had had so many refusals that she thought of putting it in the fire.

"English readers are only interested in a background they

know," she said, "and Australia to them is more remote than Abyssinia. That's what I told the writers in Melbourne when I was home last. Don't come here. Stay at home where you can write about what you know for the people you know."

But luckily her stories had caught the eye of Edward Garnett, that very discerning critic who did so much for Conrad, Galsworthy, and D. H. Lawrence, and he persuaded Duckworth's to publish them. He also showed them to his friend, R. B. Cunninghame Graham, who pointed to them in rebuttal when some critic had written disparagingly of Australian writing; Barbara Baynton's stories bore comparison, Graham asserted, with the early work of Gorky. There was real penetration in this, for Barbara admitted to me that her models had been Russian and Scandinavian writers. She felt that the human condition in those countries was much the same as in our own; and that their peoples faced the same problems. She admired their starkness and simplicity. Most of the fashionable English writing of the day she regarded as mere confectionery.

In essence, for all the taste for high life she later acquired, she was a simple woman—gusty, forthright, robust—like Miles Franklin, but with more weight behind her. She had been brought up on the Hunter River when it was a more primitive place than it is now, and her mind was full of vivid little dramas of loneliness and people a little unhinged by isolation. Sometimes her writing rasped the nerves with its sheer violence, as in her description of a railway-train in plain country:

> Suddenly the engine cleared its throat in shrill welcome to two iron tanks, hoisted twenty feet, and blazing like evil eyes in a vanished face. Besides them it squatted on its hunkers, placed a blackened thumb on its pipe, and hissed through its closed teeth like a snared wild cat, while gulping yards of water.

But her conversation had a humor and a devastating wit—as instanced by her nickname, "Dingo Dell", for a certain Anglo-Australian club haunted by the sort of people who aped English habits and yet couldn't help emphasising their origins by cooeeing to one another across Regent Street. Dingo Dell! What a perfect combination of words for that hybrid place.

She and her daughter Jenny (now Lady Gullett) were figures in the Anglo-Australian world during and after the first World War, and I remember seeing her, in 1919, entertaining W. M. Hughes in her box at the theatre, looking a most imposing dowager. But she had given up writing; perhaps because her novel, **Human Toll,** into which she had put a good deal of herself, had no obvious success; perhaps because the harsh realities of the Bush that had nourished her talent were growing fainter in her mind. The life she was now leading—the life of country houses and great occasions—was not the sort she cared to write about, and I doubt whether she would have had the technique to cope with it. Anyone who reads the first page of **Human Toll** will see how far her imaginative world was removed from *Vanity Fair*. But she still cared deeply for literature. I remember her talking to me enthusiastically in 1919 about Knut Hamsun's *Hunger;* Knut Hamsun was

then a new writer whom few people had read. And I remember her at the same gathering listening to an elderly Anglo-Australian journalist who, because she was a writer, thought she would be interested in discussing the fashionable novel of the day. She listened, staring at him in what could only be called an explosive silence, till suddenly she let go:

> Man! Why do you waste your brains by troubling to read such stuff? It's not for grown-up men and women; it's for poor creatures who take just what's given them by the girl at the library.

The breath of vigor in her deep voice nearly blew him out of the window.

It was difficult to connect her robust realism with the airy artificialities of the society in which she moved. In her literary aspect she seemed as solid and substantial as one of the ironbark posts that fenced the selections of her native Hunter River. She was so fiercely determined to reveal the truth about life, no matter how bitter or brutal it might be. I often wondered if her society friends ever read her sketches, such as the one about **"Squeaker's Mate",** the battered bushwoman in clothes made of sacking, or that other sketch about the grotesque midwife who was called a "rabbit-catcher".

In 1921, she married Lord Headley, an English peer who had become a Moslem, and nine years later she died in Melbourne.

There are very few literary records of her, which is a pity. She wrote sparingly; she left, I believe, hardly any letters behind. But I treasure highly one in her big, round hand that she sent nearly fifty years ago to a boy who had, as she said, "given her encouragement" to go on writing.

A. A. Phillips　(essay date 1961)

SOURCE: "Barbara Baynton and the Dissidence of the Nineties," in *Overland,* No. 22, December, 1961, pp. 15-20.

[*In the following essay, Phillips assesses Baynton's works in the context of Australian writing of the 1890s.*]

In terms of the Legend, the Australian period of the nineties was distinguished by its fervent celebration of a robust nationalism, particularly manifested through its belief in the value of the Australian personality; but "periods" have an untidy habit of contradicting themselves, and there is also discernible in the writings of the nineties an undercurrent of revolt against the barbarous fate of being an Australian. The ambivalent attitude is admirably represented in A. H. Adams' poem "The Australian," with its attempt to reconcile the contradictions in the contemporary national perceptions.

The same tendency can be found elsewhere, sometimes surprisingly. Even so convinced a nationalist as Henry Lawson often shows a critical wryness when he is presenting typically Australian attitudes. That quality provides the cutting edge which makes a masterpiece of "The Union Buries Its Dead" and which intensifies the desolate scorn of "A Day on a Selection."

The attitude of revolt is plainly present in the Miles Franklin of *My Brilliant Career,* swinging her shillelagh against the stifling barbarities of cockiedom. The same tendency is revealed in the Norman Lindsay of *Redheap,* turning back after thirty years to attack the small-town puritans of the nineties. The book's weaknesses, even more clearly than its strengths, reveal the force of the rebellious tendency. Lindsay cannot achieve the detachment which his satire needs. Inner compulsions drive him to a wildness of caricature; he must flay his detested wowsers with improbable comic inventions—and he thereby reveals the headiness of an anger still effervescing after thirty years in the bottle.

Barbara Baynton represents this element of revolt against self-confident Australianism—less clearly perhaps than some others, partly because her fiction is intensely subjective, and partly because there is so little of it. Virtually all that survives of her writings is contained in two volumes. One is her novel **Human Toll,** which includes some of her most effective and characteristic writing, but which is too uncertain in the management of structure to be fully successful. The second is the little book called **Bush Studies** (1902), made up of the six short stories on which her claim to a place in the Australian canon mainly rests.

The bibliographies indicate the existence of a third volume called **Cobbers,** published by Duckworth in 1917; but this is, in fact, a re-publication of **Bush Studies,** with the addition of two other stories. The title is obviously a publisher's attempt to cash in on war-time sentimental interest in the Anzacs. No publisher is likely to achieve again a title so superbly unsuitable.

Perhaps we can best begin a consideration of the nature of Barbara Baynton's work by looking at the outline of the four stories in **Bush Studies** which are most characteristic of her writing methods. I regret this resort to so pedestrian an approach; but Baynton's work is so little known and so hard to come by that it would be unfair to assume the reader's familiarity with it—and some knowledge of the nature of its contents is necessary if the reader is to follow the implications which I find in it, and shall later discuss. Would that some enterprising publisher would restore **Bush Studies** to the availability which it deserves!

The first story in the book—**"A Dreamer"**—allows freer rein than her taut grimness usually permits to a sentimental tendency underlying Barbara Baynton's work. It is concerned with a woman returning to the bush-home of her childhood in order to see the mother from whom she has been long parted. She is surprised to find no-one at the station to meet her, so that she must make the three-mile journey on foot. Not a long distance, certainly; but the track is vague and difficult, the night is dark, rain is pouring down, and the creeks are in dangerous flood. The woman must fight every yard of the way, held to her task by the intensity of her desire to see her mother again and by the equally intense need to protect the child which she carries in her womb. Barbara Baynton's vivid practicality of description compels the reader to fight that journey almost step by step with her heroine. Eventually she battles her way to the right side of the creek, and reaches the

house—to find that her mother has died some hours before.

That is no snappy, O. Henry surprise-ending. A detail placed early in the story warns the reader what to expect. The tautness with which we follow the journey is intensified by our pre-knowledge of its futility.

"Squeaker's Mate" is concerned with a selector and his wife. The man is a repulsive creature—feckless, bone lazy, dull, callously selfish. The woman knows what he is but retains her love for him. She holds the farm together, fighting to establish residential claims to the selection by shouldering the main burden of the work. When the story opens the two are felling a tree with a cross-cut saw. The man soon wearies of the work, and wanders off on a transparent excuse. His wife, rather than waste the time of his absence, attacks the tree with an axe. As it topples, she lingers a moment too long in an attempt to free the trapped axe, and a snapped branch breaks her back.

The man on his return is too densely self-centred to realise what has happened. It is left to neighbors coming on the scene to get her to the house, to summon medical help, and eventually to make the husband recognise the situation. Even then he is indifferent. In a characteristic sentence, Baynton says "They (the neighbors) told him in whispers what they thought of him, and left."

Now the wife must lie on her bunk and know that the farm which she has heroically constructed is slipping through her husband's feckless hands. He sells off half his sheep to the local butcher. Then he disappears to the nearest town on a spree, leaving primitive food and a supply of water within reach of his wife. When he returns, he insists upon moving her from the shack to a near-by lean-to. Then he disappears again to town. He returns with a red-haired and pregnant barmaid whom he installs in the shack.

The wife's bitterness is the more intense because she has borne no child. With a characteristic irony, Baynton points out that, had she calculated the dates, she would have realised that the barmaid was not bearing the husband's child either.

Now there begins a long cold war between the couple in the shack and the wife and her fiercely loyal dog in the lean-to. It reaches a climax when the husband goes off after a bolting horse. He is away some hours. The day is hot and the barmaid exhausts her supply of water. She is too afraid of snakes to go to creek for more. She knows that there is water beside the wife, but she is afraid of her too. Eventually her thirst becomes too much for her, and she ventures into the lean-to. As she stoops for the water, the wife seizes her rival—even in her crippled condition, her work-toughened muscles are too strong for the flabby town-girl.

As they struggle, the man returns and frees his mistress by smashing a pole across his wife's arms. The barmaid rushes off in the general direction of town—the presumption is that she will be lost in the bush; and the wife's dog leaps to attack her assailant.

In an attempt to persuade her to call off the dog, the husband kneels on the bunk, assuring his wife that he cares only for her. The story ends with the dog fastening his teeth in the man's hand and dragging him back from the bunk.

"Scrammy 'And" begins with an affectionately humorous portrayal of eccentric character—a kind of writing which Baynton has essayed on one other occasion, in **Human Toll,** each time with notable success. The eccentric here is a hatter, brought alive for us through a long monologue with his dog—or, rather, a dialogue, for Baynton supplies the answers of the dog as his master interprets them.

In the course of this passage the situation is established for us. The hatter works for a selector to whom he is strongly attached, and whose wife he regards with a hostility bred from jealousy and the prejudices of the professional misogynist. The couple, when the story opens, have gone off to town, where the wife is to have her baby. They are due back at any moment, and the hatter awaits their return anxiously.

The sharpness of his anxiety is due to his fears of a sinister figure known as "Scrammy 'And"—the nickname refers to the hook which replaces one of his hands. This unprepossessing person has been lurking about the hatter's hut, and it seems likely that he has learnt the hatter's closely guarded secret of a hoard of sovereigns, his life's savings, which he counts over each night with lingering glee. The hatter has wishfully convinced himself that Scrammy 'And has gone off, but it is clear to the reader that the dog scents his presence in the shadows beyond the hut.

The hatter retires to his bunk, where he dies of a sudden heart attack—this episode is economically and dryly presented, with no nineteenth century licking-of-the-lips on the theme of death.

Now Scrammy 'And advances from the shadows, and a complex and vividly presented campaign follows, between the dog and the would-be thief. Eventually the thief forces an entry through the hut's roof, wounds the dog, finds the dead body, and flees in terror. For another day and a half, the dog remains on guard, protecting his master against the possible return of Scrammy 'And, and against the flies which he will not allow near the body.

His vigil ends when the selector and his wife re-appear. The man is at once aware of something amiss, for Scrammy 'And has released the sheep from their enclosure in an attempt to draw off the dog by the call of his pastoral duties. The selector goes to investigate, and the story ends thus:

> He entered the hut through the broken doorway, but immediately came out to assure himself that his wife had not moved. The sight inside of that broken-ribbed dog's fight with those buzzing horrors, and the reproach in his wild eyes, was a memory that the man was not willing that she should share.

"The Chosen Vessel" is certainly the most firmly built of Baynton's stories, and the best known, although most readers will have met it under the title of **"The Tramp,"** the name used when it was reprinted, towards the end of Barbara Baynton's life, in Dr. Mackaness' *Australian*

Short Stories (1928). In that version an incident has been excised, rendering the original title unsuitable.

The story begins with the wife of a shearer, who is away from his home, performing the task of penning the calf for the night—a frightening task for her (she is a town girl), because she must face the maternal anger of the cow, who disapproves of this separation.

On this day she is settling the calf earlier than usual, for she has been disturbed by the appearance at the hut of a tramp, who has not been deceived by stratagems designed to convince him that there is a man in the house, and whose eye has suggested lustful intentions. She proceeds to make the house as fast as she can. She forces the handle of a spade under the bar of the front door, and drives the blade deep into a crack in the floor, and similarly barricades the back door. Then she retires to bed with her baby, and waits.

Soon the tramp can be heard stealthily working his way round the hut. He finds the loose log in the wall, held only by a wedge, and attacks it with his knife. The woman throws her arms round the baby so as to shield its vital parts. The sound outside mysteriously ceases. Then a horseman can be heard galloping down the track. She picks up the baby and tries to rush out, but her own barricades delay her, and by the time she reaches the track, the horseman has passed; the tramp, who has foreseen her movements, is waiting in the shadows of the trees.

The scene is shifted to the home of a Catholic farmer who has just quarrelled with his mother. The electoral candidate favoured by the priest is too much a "squatter's man" to be accepted by the farmer, and for once he refuses to vote as a good son of the Church, despite his mother's persuasions. He rides down belatedly to the town to cast his vote. On the way he sees through the trees a woman draped in white carrying a baby. Obviously this is a vision of the Virgin Mary, sent to warn him. He rides on, casts his vote for the Catholic candidate, and then hurries to the priest to report the miracle. Having heard the tale, the priest bursts out: "Great God! and you did not stop to save her! Have you not heard?"

The viewing-point shifts again to a boundary-rider approaching the woman's house, observing eight sheep killed apparently by a dingo. Seeing the crows dipping towards earth and rising again, he deduces that there is a sheep destroyed there with a lamb still alive, for "even a dingo will spare a lamb sometimes." He is only metaphorically right. What he finds is the strangled body of the woman, her hand still clutching the dress of the babe, which is stirring from its sleep and beginning to grow frightened of the unnatural figure beside it.

> Many miles further down the creek a man kept throwing an old cap into a water-hole. The dog would bring it out and lay it on the opposite side to where the man stood, but would not allow the man to catch him, though it was only to wash the blood of the sheep from his mouth and throat, for the sight of blood made the man tremble. But the dog also was guilty.

In the anthologised version of the story, the episode of the

Catholic voter is omitted. It seems likely that either the editor or the authoress, looking back in a softened mood, felt that the sectarian assumptions of the episode were undesirably offensive to Catholic readers. One's first impulse is to regret this destruction of a strikingly devised incident, effectively echoing the story's rhythmic emphasis of the maternal instinct.

Yet, in fact, the excision improves the story. The incident weakens an important element in the tale's concentrated power, because it breaks from the claustrophobic setting of the hut in the bush; and its too-devised irony dissipates the tight-lipped terror of the tale's atmosphere.

This accidental remedying of a technical misjudgment interestingly illustrates the enormous difficulty of the storyteller's art. The episode is, in itself, a brilliantly imaginative touch; it fits snugly to the rhythm of idea underlying the story. Yet, for reasons that seem tenuous, it is wrong. What author, having been visited by so happy-seeming an inspiration, could have seen that it was wrong, without the intervention of chance?

This rehearsing of Barbara Baynton's plots cannot, of course, give much indication of the quality of her stories; indeed it may merely suggest a comically thumping emphasis on the gruesome and on melodrama—and that is not all the effect of the stories. Baynton's power arises from the controlled strength of her narration, and from the sense of truth built up by the rightness of her detail.

Occasionally—she is, after all, an Australian writer of the nineties—Baynton falls into cliche. Rather more often she is trapped by another common fault of her period; there is a too-obvious relishing of the intended well-turned phrase which is in fact conventional. These are, however, minor blemishes. More usually she writes with a spare muscularity, the weight borne firmly on verb and noun, with little of the dissipating flourish of adjective and adverb.

She has an unusually sure power of visualisation. She does not create her story in broad sweeps of the imagination, as writers of her type generally do; she sees it detail by detail with an assured concreteness. That spade driven in beside the door is typical of the practical firmness with which she grips her narrative. She does not obviously seek to build up atmospheric effect. She simply sees what is happening and conveys it with the austere directness of her style at its best; so that the reader must sit behind her eyes and see with their feminine, pouncing accuracy.

I have not, then, retailed the outlines of her plots in order to suggest the quality of her stories. I have been seeking rather to suggest something about their nature. Even from these outlines it should be clear that these stories are the literature of nightmare. They are akin to the stories of Algernon Blackwood and Richard Middleton, and other writers of a popular genre of the period. Perhaps they are more closely akin to the work of Emily Bronte—although there is no metaphysic of good and evil behind Barbara Baynton's stories, as there is behind *Wuthering Heights*.

It is noticeable that certain nightmare symbols tend to recur in these tales—and all of them recur again in the novel *Human Toll*. There is, for example, that lonely bush shack, besieged by a terrifying and invisible figure, who is also a terrified figure. There is the loyalty of the dog contrasted with the treachery of man. There is an insistent dwelling on the fierce, and often futile, power of the maternal instinct. A child's birth must be dragged in to **"Scrammy 'And"**; and in **"Squeaker's Mate"**, the bitterness of the barren woman must be underlined. There is a re-iterated emphasis on man's brutality towards woman. Sometimes this is an essential element in the story, as in **"Squeaker's Mate"**; more often it is an incidental detail forced into the story by some compulsion within the writer's mind. For example in the opening movement of **"The Chosen Vessel,"** Baynton writes:

> She used to run at first when the cow bellowed its protest against the penning-up of its calf. This satisfied the cow, also the calf, but the woman's husband was angry and called her—the noun was cur. It was he who forced her to run and meet the advancing cow, brandishing a stick, and uttering threatening words till the enemy turned and ran. "That's the way," the man said, laughing at her white face. In many things he was worse than the cow, and she wondered if the same rule would apply to the man, but she was not one to provoke skirmishes, even with the cow.

This is a story written with an obviously deliberate economy of style. There was no need to create the figure of the husband—his absence from the house is all the story demands of him. How vividly that passage does create him; and how significant is the unnecessariness of that creation, revealing a compulsive sub-conscious movement of Baynton's mind.

Observing these recurrent nightmare symbols, and the frequently slight need for their presence, one almost inevitably asks, "What would Freud make of this?" I don't care much what the answer may be; for I suspect that when the psychoanalyst reconstructs a writer's sub-conscious from the evidence of his published work, he is usually blissfully and unprovably wrong. The significant point is that we do ask the question, that we here feel that we are moving in Freudian country, that the essential motive behind Barbara Baynton's writing is some need to free a burdened subconscious by the relief of symbolic expression.

Although this is the literature of nightmare, it is, at one point, strikingly unlike the work of such writers as Blackwood or Middleton. With them the nightmare terror springs from the touch of unreality which they deliberately import into the story, the shiver of the supernatural vibrating from some slight detail which is nevertheless the core of the story's atmospheric effect. Barbara Baynton is an Australian writer, and she is true to the most persistent characteristic of that breed: she firmly roots her stories in the soil of the actual. She creates the line of the story, and its symbolic detail, from the pressure of nightmare impulse; but she creates the sort of things which do happen. Her episodes are the events of life-as-it-is. Her characters—at least her men—are often pushed to the limit of the probably evil; but they are not pushed over that limit.

They are not Heathcliffes, unacceptable on the level of the actual.

Moreover her episodes and her characters grow from the soil of the environment with which she is concerned. You can feel the Australian bush about them, shaping them into the forms which they assume. Baynton obviously knows bush-life with a deep intimacy and with something of the insider's pride—though perhaps she hates it, too. One can sense that she belongs to the freemasonry of the bush. One can feel her giving the lodge-grip, as she writes "The hospitality of the bush never extends to the loan of a good horse to an inexperienced rider," or as she relates the scorn of Billy Skywonkie for the city artist who had painted his horses drinking. The painter had called his picture "The Lake"—it wasn't a lake, it was a dam; and he had shown the horses sharing the water with frogs—fancy horses drinking water covered with frog's spit. Baynton loathes the abominable Billy—but surely she belongs to his lodge.

The terror and revulsion which Baynton is expressing belong, then, to the bush-life which is present in her work with a convincing actuality. What, then, are the qualities in that life which have pressed the writer into revolt against it? We can best pick up the clue to the answer to that question, if we look at the two remaining stories of **Bush Studies.** These are not terror stories, but simple farces of observation, almost without plot. Outwardly they are sardonically comic; inwardly they are filled with a savage revulsion of feeling.

"Bush Church" concerns a parson's visit to an isolated out-back settlement. The first person the parson falls in with happens to be the local loafer and joker, Ned. Scenting a leg-pulling opportunity, Ned offers to visit the selections in the district and advertise the parson's intention to hold a service at the squatter's homestead on the following day. Then Ned spreads the news that the squatter has brought up a Government inspector who is going to try to break the selector's claims, and that there is to be a meeting at the homestead. The selectors and their families duly turn up, armed with their papers and ready to battle for their rights—only to find that the waggish Ned has let them in for a church service. The subsequent proceedings are thoroughly farcical.

The feeling of the story can best be conveyed by quoting a few typical passages:

> An older girl, bare-footed and dressed in a petticoat and old hat, was standing near a fire before the wide opening that served as a doorway to the humpy. She had a long stick and was employed in permitting an aged billy-goat to bring his nose within an inch of the simmering water in the bucket strung over the fire . . . The thirsty billy was sneaking up again to the water, and she let him advance the prescribed limit before she made the jab that she enjoyed so thoroughly.

> . . . . .

> The clergyman gave out the text and the sermon began. Jyne's children commenced to complain of being "'ungry" and a fair-sized damper was taken from a pillow-slip. This, together with two

tin tots and a bottle of goat's milk was given to Jinny and she was told to do "thet sharin'".

> . . . . .

> For a short space only the voice of the preacher was heard, as, in studied stoicism, he pursued his thankless task. Occasionally they looked at him to see "'oo 'e wus speakin' ter," but, finding nothing directly personal, even this attention ceased.

> Liz leaned across to Tilly Lumber and asked, "Fowl layin'?"

> "Ketch 'em a-layin' at Chrissermus".

"Billy Skywonkie" is less comic and with bitterer undertones. A woman has accepted a post as housekeeper at an outback sheep-run. After a long train journey through desolate country in the company of drunken drovers, she is met at the siding by Billy Skywonkie, the rouseabout. (The nickname refers to the weather-prophecy in which Billy is reputedly skilled, but the present drought has proved too much for his prognostic powers.)

On the drive back to the homestead Billy makes a wide detour to visit the local wine-shop for refreshment and flirtation with the slut whom it houses. In all that rich gallery of sordid bush-shanties which is one of the glories of our national literature, this is the outright winner for sheer squalor.

They drive on with pauses for reference to the bottle which Billy has bought at the shanty. When they reach the homestead, it proves almost as sordid as the shanty. Soon the boss arrives, and indicates bluntly that the woman is too old for the real duties of the "housekeeper's" position.

Again the story's nature may best be conveyed by a few quotations:

> He shouted an oath of hatred at the crows following after the tottering sheep that made in a straggling line for the water . . . "They putty well lives on eyes! Blanky bush chinkies! I call 'em No-one can't tell 'em apart".

There is a reason for this violent Sinomania. Billy is married—de facto, at least—to a half-caste Aboriginal, and ashamed of it. So he compensates by a violent contempt for the Chinese and for the whites who make use of their girls.

" 'Know what I'll do to Lizer soon as she begins to start naggin' at me? . . . Fill 'er mug with this,' and the shut fist he shook was more than a mugful."

This is mere braggadocio. When Lizer does open up, Billy mutely accepts it. "On a block lay a flitch of bacon, and across the freshly-cut side the dog drew its tongue, then snapped at the flies. 'That dog will eat the bacon,' she said.

" 'No!' answered the [Chinese] cook. ' 'E no eat 'em—too saw.'

"It was salt; she had tried it for breakfast."

Whence arises the savage distaste which almost smothers the comedy of these stories? It is not, be it noted, the outsider's revulsion, the contemptuous snobbery of the town-ee towards the uncivilised rustic. Baynton does not look at that bush congregation through the eyes of the visiting parson; she has more contempt for his ineffectuality than for the selector's barbarity. Indeed there are moments of admiration, in these stories, for the bush-dwellers' steady stoicism and for their mastery of the practical crafts of their vocation. Barbara Baynton is a member of the Lodge. One senses that, if an outsider had attacked the bush-dwellers, she would have closed ranks in their defence.

But a strength of anger is plainly there, and it is directed against the peasant element in Australian bush life. Baynton is by no means the only writer who has been driven into an extremity of satiric rage, a compulsive thrashing contempt, when he or she has been confronted by the Australian peasant.

The force of the anger arises from the writer's feeling that the peasant element shouldn't be there. It is a denial of the Australian Legend; one of the articles of faith of that legend was the belief that Australian rural life was not a peasant's life, that the free and self-reliant Australian had broken away from the peasant's humilities and humiliations. When Furphy, for example, presents us with his contemptuous portraits of Sollicker, the feudal underling from Sussex, or the comic Chinese boundary-riders, he is clearly implying that they represent the peasant decadence from which native Australian life is free.

Now it is true that, on the stations and cattle-runs, the men of Australia had achieved an unpeasant-like initiative and independence. It is further true that on this rock the Australian pride is ultimately based. But it is not true that there was no peasant element in Australian rural life. It was there in the selectors of the dry country, in the near descendants of the convicts, in the Irish immigrants. When the Australian writer found himself confronted by this peasant survival he reacted with satiric fury, because it denied the Australian's proud vision of the sort of man he believed himself to be.

Once one has observed the obvious peasant element which Baynton satirises in **"Bush Church"** and **"Billy Skywonkie,"** one realises that the same element is present more subtly in the terror stories. It is there in the naked matter-of-fact violence of lust which these stories portray (the lusts—for women and money—are the lusts of all men; it is the naked matter-of-fact violence which has a peasant quality). It is there in the inevitable sordidness of extreme poverty, in the easy acceptance of cruelty, in the brutal masculine domination over women. One can find the same qualities recorded in other peasant literatures, but with this difference: the European delineator of peasant life accepts these qualities as a matter of course, and seeks the more imaginatively interesting qualities which underlie them. The Australian is so affronted by their recrudescence in the land of freedom that he cannot get beyond them.

The terror in Baynton's stories partly arises from these peasant qualities in the life she knows; but it partly arises from another element which is more exclusively Austra-lian—the sense of the crushing isolation of bush-life. It is noticeable that Baynton creates situations which emphasise that isolation. The recurrent image of innocence besieged in the islanded shack—surely through that image there speaks the authentic voice of the bush-woman, freeing her spirit of the fears and resentments which her isolation breeds.

There is something else too, I believe, less palpable, less easy to establish by documentation: a sense of spiritual darkness emanating from the land itself, a feeling of a primeval cruelty fed by the sunlight which glares instead of glowing, by the sombre grey of the bush which some obstinate Europeanism within us insists should be green, by the brown weight of the plains, by the harshness of man's struggle against nature.

That sense of a spiritual darkness emanating from the land itself touches Australian writing again and again; and almost always it seems to come from a deeper layer of the mind than the easy optimism, the simplicity of faith, which are more constantly present. There is a sense in which Patrick White is more traditionally Australian than is generally supposed. The feeling which I have been describing finds effective expression in the terror stories of Barbara Baynton.

You may claim that I am here guilty of a blatant contradiction. I have said that Baynton's terror-impulse comes from subjective and sub-conscious need; and I am now claiming that it represents some mystic emanation from the Australian land. You may reasonably object that I cannot have it both ways.

I believe that I can. I believe that sometimes the inner compulsions of a writer's individual need meet and mate with some element in the life and environment which he or she is interpreting; and I believe that when that happens, a propulsive imaginative power is generated. If you doubt that, if you feel that it is merely a Literary Gent's easy generalisation, I ask you to test it against the work of Emily Bronte, of Dostoievsky, of Herman Melville. For all her subjective compulsions, Barbara Baynton's power is an essentially Australian power; it is none the less so because she is also unique among Australian writers.

Sally Krimmer and Alan Lawson   (essay date 1980)

SOURCE: An introduction to *Barbara Baynton,* edited by Sally Krimmer and Alan Lawson, University of Queensland Press, 1980, pp. ix-xxxiii.

[*In the following excerpt, Krimmer and Lawson discuss themes and imagery in* Bush Studies *and* Human Toll.]

Barbara Baynton died on 28 May 1929 leaving one slim volume of short stories, a short novel, and a few poems and stories, some of which have never been collected. On her death her name was linked more closely with the world of fine china and antique furniture than it was with the literary world. Though her literary work has not gone without acknowledgment it is mainly in recent times that Baynton has emerged as an important figure in the history of Australian literature, and in her own right.

Principally a short story writer, writing in the 1890s, Baynton does not belong to the dominating legend which is supposed to have originated in that period. Her contribution to Australian literature is unique although she echoes in her writing much of what Lawson and Paterson felt. Like them, she too rejected the harshness of bush life. In seeking to offset, indeed to invert, the legend, Leon Cantrell argues [in *The 1890s: Stories, Verse, and Essays*] that the period shows a sense of alienation and loss as a principal literary hallmark. Baynton provides ample evidence for this theory, for nowhere in her stories can be found the characteristics often attributed to Australian literature in the 1890s. There is no nationalistic pride, no love of the bush and no feeling of mateship or affinity between the bush and its inhabitants. . . .

[The grim and often shocking stories of *Bush Studies*] seem to be written almost in revenge, as if provoked by the hardships of the bush. The stories can be seen also as a record of Baynton's quest for reality, expressed through her unifying vision of the bush. Although the six stories are separate, the recurrent themes, imagery and situations help to unify the book. The stories form a composite symbolic narrative to which each contributes a distinctive and memorable part. They are not limited in any way by their setting in the Australian bush: Baynton manages to make her studies reflect general human problems while she examines characteristically Australian bush situations.

Several themes can be seen running throughout *Bush Studies.* The landscape Baynton chose to write about was particularly brutal, as were its inhabitants. It is the brutalizing environment which her contemporary, Henry Lawson, described in "Crime in the Bush". More specifically Baynton shows men lacking in compassion in their attitude towards women. Lawson and even Steele Rudd wrote of a harsh landscape but Baynton studies the psychic effects of that landscape more explicitly. The bush is constantly portrayed as a lonely, hostile place, antagonistic to its inhabitants who depend on it for survival; Squeaker's Mate is felled by a tree, the Dreamer is impeded by water and whipped by the now "hostile" willows her mother had planted, Scrammy 'And is maimed, Billy Skywonkie's friends are deformed, and the landscape turns the chosen vessel into a ghastly parody of the Virgin Mary while offering her no refuge from her rapist and murderer. Here is found no noble sentiment but rather a savageness man has retained from his beginnings to enable him to cope with his brutal surroundings. But the land takes its toll, its "revenge" as Henry Handel Richardson put it. Always the sun is greedy, sucking any nourishment from the barren land. When man likewise becomes a predatory being, it can be seen that the landscape has moulded him in its own image. In **"Scrammy 'And"** Baynton writes of the primitiveness of a man who hangs on to life, with a primeval violence his only strategy for survival.

The absolute horror of the bush is introduced in the first story of *Bush Studies*, **"A Dreamer"**, where the trip which the pregnant daughter makes home to her mother belongs almost to the world of nightmare. Nature is depicted in this story in angry human forms: " . . . little Dog-trap Gully was proudly foaming itself hoarse"; the wind yelled

at the daughter and a "giant tree's fallen body said 'Thus far' and in vain the athletic furious water rushed and strove to throw her over the barrier". The woman's struggles with a cruel force are portrayed in the violent terms of a murderer fighting his victim. But despite the human qualities given to it in **"A Dreamer"**, the landscape is mostly unfeeling and unresponsive. The "sun-sucked" land in **"Bush Church"** parallels the arid spiritual life of the inhabitants. For Baynton, as for Lawson, Clarke, Richardson and many other Australian writers, the landscape is seen as having a direct effect on the spiritual and emotional, as well as on the physical, lives of its inhabitants: it is, as Lawson wrote in "The Bush Undertaker", "the nurse and tutor of eccentric minds".

If a malevolent landscape dominates *Bush Studies* so also does the man/woman confrontation where women, without choice, become acquiescent victims of men largely without realizing it. In most of the stories woman is shown as maternal, loving and peaceful while man is portrayed as brutally sexual. Man's natural home is the cruel landscape while woman is instinctively associated with civilization and the town. In **"A Dreamer"**, **"Squeaker's Mate"**, and **"Billy Skywonkie"**, town women arrive in the country and journey towards an inevitable fate. The woman in **"The Chosen Vessel"** is never in harmony with the bush, at least partly because of her city origins, and it is certainly from this base that her husband's cruel taunts arise. Knowing her fear he forces her to meet the advancing cow with nothing more than the phallically parodic stick. The woman's human, and explicitly female, vulnerability is a culmination of Baynton's studies of the bush. Removed from the social security of a town, she is anonymous (like all but one of Baynton's victims) and besieged by hostile predatory forces. In this story the psychological and symbolic rape is made scarifyingly actual. The woman is, from the beginning, a fourfold victim. Her husband's sexual sneer (intensified by being changed into direct speech in Baynton's revision printed here)—"Needn't flatter yerself, he had told her, nobody 'ud want ter run away with yew"—is of course ironic in terms of the plot, but more importantly it is a predatory male imposition of sexual value. Like the woman in **"Billy Skywonkie"** her sense of her identity is sexually assaulted. Secondly, she is also acutely aware of the vulnerability caused by her isolated situation. In a paragraph added after the story's first publication (in the *Bulletin* in 1896), Baynton draws attention to this in a way which also carries an irony of similar quality: "She was not afraid of horsemen; but swagmen, going to, or worse, coming from the dismal drunken little township, a day's journey beyond, terrified her". The fear of swagmen is, of course, well-founded but her confidence in horsemen is not. Indeed it is this confidence which leads her to run from her house when she hears Hennessey ride by and thus expose herself defencelessly to her attacker. Thirdly, she is also a victim of Peter Hennessey's appalling religious vision. Just as she is taken as a sexual object by the swagman so is she taken as religious object by Hennessey. The full horror of this conjunction is carried in the fact of his confusing a rape-victim with the Virgin Mary. Her fourth, and most obvious, vulnerability is to the exploiting male predator, the swagman, but this is compounded by the other three and given extra dimensions by her attempts to save herself from her fate. There is no point running to her husband—"in the past, when she had dared to speak of the dangers to which her loneliness had exposed her, he had taunted and sneered at her". The walls of her hut are easily breached and her potential saviour is instead preoccupied with his own spurious spiritual salvation over a political contest. The poverty of her resources is shown when she tries to bargain with the swagman by placing food and her one valuable object on the kitchen table. Her only defence is to bargain with him. Vulnerable when he first called she remains so even given time to assemble all her defences. For the lone woman in the bush there is no escape, no defence, no refuge and no rescue. A victim of man's carnal fervour in the first half of the story, she becomes a sacrifice to man's spiritual fervour in the second half. (This story affords an interesting comparison with Lawson's "The Drover's Wife" in which the woman protagonist is self-sufficient, but at a cost.)

Men are exploitative in all aspects of their activities. Nowhere is this more evident than in **"Squeaker's Mate"**, one of the most powerful stories in *Bush Studies.* Sombre human emotions of greed, violence, fear, anxiety, loneliness and quiet desperation combine to give the story an immediate impact. Here Baynton has written a stark but sympathetic study of a woman lying alone and isolated with a broken back, a woman formerly strong enough to do a man's job. Her previous strength confounded the difference of her sex, but even she finds that once strength is broken, anatomy is destiny. Nameless for most of the story—except as "Squeaker's mate", an appendage—she is identified at the end as "Mary", the archetypal maternal figure after her barrenness has been taunted by her realization of the obvious fertility of Squeaker's new mate. She alone of Baynton's victims is given a name and even hers is both generalized and ironic.

In **"Billy Skywonkie"** the familiar is inexorably inverted, and perverted. In what is a characteristic Australian pattern, the world is depicted "upside down". Mag and Biddy, for instance, are an obscene parody of the mother/daughter relationship. The landscape is a vivid realization of a wasteland and, as in T. S. Eliot, the landscape becomes an expression of the disunity between love and sex. The woman's role is made obvious through Billy's excessively delicate intonations and his remark that he had "promised ther 'Konk' t' leave 'im 'ave furst squint at yer". The sexual tension becomes more evident as boundary gates close, one after the other. The anonymous woman has no individuality apart from her sex, and remains unnamed throughout the story. Her intellectuality is emphasized in direct contrast to the baseness of the men, and thus implies another aspect of the cultural disjunction between the city and the bush. Her alienation and its effect on her ability to adapt to this new environment is expressed in a paragraph which is central to Baynton's vision of life in the bush. It is also remarkably close here, and on other occasions, to Lawson's. Like the old man in **"Scrammy 'And"**, the denizens of **"Bush Church"**, or Lawson's "Bush Undertaker", her perception of reality is distorted; her "normal" reactions inhibited:

> A giddy unreality took the sting from everything, even from her desire to beseech him to

> turn back to the siding, and leave her there to wait for the train to take her back to civilization. She felt she had lost her mental balance. Little matters became distorted, and the greater shrivelled.

That final sentence prepares us for the following story, the grim meaninglessness of **"Bush Church"**. The final image in **"Billy Skywonkie"**, that of the sheep ready for the slaughter, prefigures the meaningless sacrifice of the woman in the last story, **"The Chosen Vessel"**. The woman in **"Billy Skywonkie"**, suffering from the compound disadvantages of age, race, sex, and background is an unresponsive victim, an object, like the lamb, to satisfy man's hunger. Unlike Baynton's other victims she is away from secure surroundings. The others suffer in their homes and the fragility of that security is emphasized. This woman has not even that. Her isolation is complete.

Baynton, approached the basic situation of **"Billy Skywonkie"** again in a later story. . . . Published in an English weekly in 1921, **"Her Bush Sweetheart"** also combines the elements of a city woman whose youth is passing, a station-owner looking for a wife, and the Chinese. This time her view is less stark, there are fewer grotesques, but there is also less sympathy. The woman is predatory in a small but desperate way, the man limited and uninteresting, and the Chinese hostile. The bush is depicted with some sympathy but from a distance, and a poverty of circumstances and spirit takes its toll. Caroline Bell "was one who expected no friendship from women because she gave none to them".

The traditional bush values of mateship, hospitality and compassion are largely absent from the landscape of Baynton's stories. The bush community of **"Billy Skywonkie"** lacks humanity towards an "'alf chow", traditional bush hospitality is mocked at the beginning of **"Bush Church"** ("The hospitality of the bush never extends to the loan of a good horse to an inexperienced horseman") and at the end when food is withheld from those who have none. Squeaker's mate receives little sympathy from the other bush women—she had been "a woman with no leisure for yarning"—and her "uncompromising independence" becomes their excuse for indifference.

In contrast to the pervading vision of moral chaos and cruelty Baynton's images of motherhood emerge as a hope for humanity. Just as Baynton is aware of the inevitability of death, so is she keenly aware of the inevitability of birth, which ensures a continuity of life, and gives it meaning. In **"A Dreamer"** the daughter's own impending motherhood induces her to return home and know once more a mother's love. Amongst all of the destructive, environmental forces against which the daughter is doing battle, motherhood is the one creative element. The watchful mother bird's warning call gives security, just as "loving arms" and "a mother's sacred kisses" give a feeling of warmth and protection to the frightened, lost daughter as she imagines how her meeting with her mother will be. The daughter is anxious; she quickens her pace, but "did not run—motherhood is instinct in women". The supreme example of woman's instinctive desire to protect her young is found in **"The Chosen Vessel"**, where motherhood is presented as being the one quality which cannot be overwhelmed. The terrified mother constantly forgets her own safety in an effort to protect her child. When she calls for help, she does so in the baby's name, and her protectiveness continues even beyond her death: the boundary rider who finds her body has to cut the still-living child's gown from the persistent grasp of the dead mother.

As well as seeing an inherent goodness in maternity Baynton sees a value in the loyalty of the dog to its owner as Lawson does. Human loyalty between men and women may be non-existent but canine loyalty is present in several of the stories. Only the dog recognizes the returning daughter in **"A Dreamer"** and it is the dog which is the true mate in **"Squeaker's Mate"**. The dog has the qualities of humanity found lacking in Squeaker and it is this that Baynton constantly stresses against the greed and violence of Squeaker. The best example of devotion is perhaps found in **"Scrammy 'And"** where "Warderloo" is endowed with practically human qualities—Baynton achieves this effect by giving the dog answers to the man's questions and remembering past conversations, while the old man is silent. Even the dog's bark was "terribly human". The women in **"Billy Skywonkie"** and **"The Chosen Vessel"** are each without this loyalty and protection and so their vulnerability is correspondingly increased.

Religion on the other hand offers no such protection or succour. The bush society which Baynton depicts is one with no real use for it; in the class politics, and in the personal plight in **"The Chosen Vessel"** its interference is disastrous. In **"Bush Church"** religion comes under particular attack, as Baynton depicts the ineffectual relevance of a parson to the lives of people living in a land which offers scope only for the practical, and none for the spiritual. Throughout the scene depicting the service, Baynton's contempt is directed against the parson's lack of vision rather than at the barbarity of the listeners. Keogh, the government inspector, is a more relevant god figure to these bush people who have little sympathy for a stranger who visits the district once a year, demanding dates of birth from people who live by no calendars, Christian or otherwise. For people who are in continual conflict with the elements of the bush, the fact that the hen lays is more important than the ceremonial baptism of one of the children. The entire incongruity of religion, such as the parson offers, is climaxed in the subtle creation of absolute chaos at the bush service itself, as ten adults and eighteen children restlessly make their presence felt. Fear had been the only operating factor in getting these people to the service, so once the "gentle voice of the parson, and his nervous manner soon convinced them that they had nothing to fear from him" the scene became one of chatter and scrambling children.

Baynton's stories are powerfully expressed and closely unified. Her vision is communicated through a straightforward yet intense style. Each story has a clear, almost single-minded impulse and each contributes to a cumulative effect which is memorable and convincing. Her stories were first published in book form under the title of *Bush Studies* and it is as studies, and not just stories, that they

are best understood. Each sets out to investigate a particular situation, to explore a particular emotion, and to develop a particular motif. The characters are slightly developed but it is the situations which are given a symbolic resonance and which become interesting and involving. These qualities have induced critics to call the stories "universal", despite the clear and definitive way in which the stories express and diagnose Australian experiences. Each story has an inexorable progress towards a dire conclusion—death, rape, rejection or some combination of these—and the progress itself is in the form of an ordeal which serves to heighten the victim's (and our) perception of the horror of his or her vulnerability. The terrible logic of each study is increased by recurrent motifs, "light" in **"The Chosen Vessel"**, "death" and "motherhood" in **"A Dreamer"**, "decay from within" in **"Squeaker's Mate"**. A cumulative effect derives from the single-mindedness of each of the component stories, from a consistent style, from a consistent vision, and from a careful ordering of the stories. The last two stories of *Bush Studies* for instance can each be seen to take their direction from **"Billy Skywonkie"**. From its announcement that "little matters became distorted, and the greater shrivelled" we enter the chaotic wasteland of **"A Bush Church"**. From the final horrifying image of meaningless sacrifice in **"Billy Skywonkie"**—"the sheep lay passive, with its head back till its neck curved in a bow, and . . . the glitter of the knife was reflected in its eye"—we move unerringly towards the final story, **"The Chosen Vessel"**. The two elements of Baynton's vision of the bush—meaninglessness and malice—are finally separated and focused upon. The composite image of the besieged bush hut containing a defenceless, unnamed victim and a predatory, named attacker is created; human goodness is assailed and largely defeated, but a residue of goodness and hope remains, its fragility emphasized.

In 1917 *Bush Studies* was augmented by two new stories, **"Trooper Jim Tasman"** and **"Toohey's Party"**. . . . The first of these had appeared the previous year in the *British-Australasian*. The two new stories are of little interest in themselves, but while they lack the powerful impulse of the earlier ones they do offer a useful comparison helping to show where Baynton's strengths and limitations lie. In each she indulges her bent for recording dialect speech and her taste for a rather harsh form of social comedy. The new volume was given the unprepossessing title of *Cobbers* and seems to have been directed at the market composed of Australian soldiers on leave in London. The loose episodes of **"Trooper Jim Tasman"** derive from their experiences on leave. This story was also revised prior to publication in *Cobbers* and in the revision an interesting reference to Australia was omitted. After referring to the early pioneers she quotes Lord Salisbury (in a personal conversation) as having said "Courage is your inheritance; your forebears possessed it, or they never would have sailed far away to that great and unknown country". . . .

Like *Bush Studies*, *Human Toll* is based on Baynton's early experiences in the bush. However unlike the stories of *Bush Studies,* the novel lacks a firm plot structure and at times becomes discursive, only occasionally reaching the achievements of *Bush Studies.* Nevertheless *Human*

Toll excels in presenting short, compact and realistic scenes typical of bush life. While the stories in *Bush Studies* often refer to nearby bush towns it is only in *Human Toll* that Baynton portrays the life of bush towns in any detail. She seems to regard the small town as a minor civilizing influence (especially on the men) but while this restrains the malevolence it cannot remove the meanness and petty nastiness from people whose lives must be lived in such places. The narrative of the novel is interesting in that Baynton is clearly writing from personal experience, but how much of it is autobiographical is difficult to determine. The heroine of the story, Ursula Ewart, bears Baynton's mother's maiden name and Ursula is the name of one of her grandchildren. On several occasions in *Human Toll* Ursula expresses a desire to write. She feels, though, that she must wait until she moves away from the bush in order to distance herself from her experiences there.

The title *Human Toll,* like that of *Bush Studies,* points to Baynton's basic approach. The earlier book was a collection of "bush studies" not bush stories, the word "studies" implying a more serious observation. Similarly *Human Toll* focuses on the demands made of men and women who live in a harsh bush environment. Working within this framework, Baynton presents the familiar themes of *Bush Studies* again. She is concerned with the vulnerability of woman, the greed of man, the vapidity of religion, the vulgarity and ugliness of social life in the bush—symbolized as it is repeatedly in her work by the isolated bush hut. As with *Bush Studies,* the only positive value to emerge from the malevolence which pervades the book, lies in the powerful and instinctive response to maternity. The story line is a simple one. It follows the life of Ursula Ewart, an orphaned girl in the bush, who on the death of her father is taken away from the care of a reformed convict, Boshy, who adores her. She is brought up by people who lack real love or understanding and at this period of her life Andrew is her only friend. With the death of Ursula's guardian Boshy returns to the girl and she tends him in his last days. Ursula then returns to her former home with Andrew and Mina, a girl who has tricked Andrew into marrying her. Mina has a child and Ursula's attraction to Andrew suffers a further taunt: she is deprived of Andrew and of having his child. When Mina's ill-treatment of the baby culminates in attempted suffocation, Ursula "rescues" it and flees into the bush. The child dies and Ursula becomes delirious and hopelessly lost. On the last page the reader is tantalized with her "rescue" by Andrew and the Aboriginal Nungi, which may well be an hallucination.

Human Toll does not begin well, and the first chapter is confusing. The search for treasure has the appearance of being vital to the story but its significance soon diminishes and it becomes irrelevant to the narrative. This happens with many of the digressions throughout the novel, seeming to have no real function in either the story or the character development. The slow start of the novel may be attributed to Baynton's attempt to recreate the vernacular of the bush. Boshy is talking to his "Little Lovey" and the aborigines in a dialect that, at times, can be difficult to follow, impeding the flow of the action. Sometimes Baynton

has to resort to giving a translation of the dialect in brackets, a practice which is intrusive. Yet despite stylistic flaws early in the novel, *Human Toll* has scenes which recall Barbara Baynton's great ability as a short story writer. The bush town scenes, the sabbath at Mrs Irvine's, the drunken dance, and Ursula lost in the bush have a self-contained unity and intensity which echo the achievements of *Bush Studies.*

In Baynton's brilliant description of a Sunday at Mrs Irvine's, Mr Civil the parson is portrayed with the contempt found in *Bush Studies.* The visiting parson is also mocked. His reverberating "rs" and the repetition of key phrases—"The tears must flow—the tears must flow"—parody precisely a parson's evangelistic style, and emphasize the thin line between clergyman and salesman which Baynton contains in the words "alert showman". In contrast to the apathy in **"Bush Church"** the parishioners here prepare themselves for the church service with solemnity, but nevertheless the service still degenerates into a mere social routine. Ursie is ceremoniously washed, combed, and dressed in a ludicrous black hat and frock. Mrs Irvine's invitation for tea, which she extends to the vicar, is no more than a mark of her social stature. Only those without the social position, and without desire to perpetuate the existing order, such as Fanny, Jim and Boshy, can see Mr Civil for the harsh and hypocritical man that he is.

Whilst the sabbath at Mrs Irvine's is one kind of social event, the drunken dance is another. The male/female confrontation evident in *Bush Studies* again emerges in this scene, where the male once more establishes himself as an aggressive domineering character. Woman's value resides totally in her sexual role. Animal terms describe men as "colts" and "cattle", and women are seen by the men as "pieces of mutton". These terms effectively reduce man to a level of bestiality, appropriate for Baynton's purpose—her attack on man's animality. This can be seen in Hugh Palmer's sexuality, succinctly captured in the image "The bull on Keen's Mustard". Gus Stein's imitation of Hugh as the bull is wholly sexual; "He threw his body forward and sank his neck into his upraised shoulders". The physical nature of the dance is captured in the wine-frenzied faces of the dancers, with Andrew's eyes blazing excitedly. Ironically, the performers and participants in the dance dress for the occasion with the same ceremony as the Irvine household prepare for church. The finery produced for both occasions is juxtaposed derisively with flagrant passions at the dance. Sexual rivalry exists between Ursie and Mina who feels a sense of "malignant triumph" over Ursie when asked to dance by both Andrew and Hugh Palmer.

The last chapter of *Human Toll* is characteristic of Baynton at her best. Her writing is vibrant as she dramatically shows Ursie, lost in the bush, carrying Mina's dead child. Time and distance are not measured in any ordinary sense, but in terms of Ursie's mental state—she progresses from ignorance to self-knowledge, thereby conquering her fears. Behind Baynton's images lies a horror of universal isolation, of fundamental loneliness. In this last section, after the social battles and the personal confrontations, Ursie's basic conflict is within herself played out through a battle with the land. Her fear springs from her surroundings since "nature was frankly brutal". To her confused mind nature is grotesque—the spider's web becomes an "insidious circle", "trees shivered meaningly" and the sun "sent piercing tongue-shafts, till even the tough trailing vegetation drooped, showing the hot sand beneath". During her journey into madness, while wandering in the bush, Ursie never forgets the child as it was when alive and cares even more for it now that it is dead. Ursula's maternal possessiveness, surging "like the spring sap in a young tree", was the maddening irritant which drove Mina to murder the child—her own infant. Mina is continually described in terms of a serpent—her "venomous eyes" blaze with "green malignity"; she hisses; is "snake-head"; and her hands are "scaly". She is the symbolic embodiment of the evil which Ursula must overcome on her surreal journey through the wasteland.

Ursula's torment is shown by her constant questioning, and her answers, or the absence of answers, mirror the conflict of her internal and external predicaments. Her time in the bush is a struggle towards the light, her nightmare in the bush is a mystical dark night of the soul. Her strict religious upbringing had left her with a warped view of Christianity wherein her God was a God of Wrath and she associated herself with the ancient Israelites who sought guidance in the wilderness. The dead baby, referred to as "the lamb", was indeed her blood sacrifice in expiation for her sins. The traditional characteristics of an archetypal mystical experience are present, too, in her discarding all garments other than a "hair shirt"; in her fasting; and in her beholding a vision while in the wilderness. The sight of the devil, (the "gohanna"), and her trip to hell leave her begging for mercy. The vision of Christ in the gum tree, however, brings about her redemption. While she communes with Him she is found by the Aborigine Nungi and Andrew (the dark and fair centurions), and is saved. Ursula's dubious sanity though introduces an ambiguity into the ending. Is she saved, or is "Andree" another hallucination? Earlier incidents point to her being

---

Baynton on notable works of Australian literature:

While in London I read any Australian books I could get, and was much impressed by Leon Gellert's *Songs of a Campaign*. The earlier poets I read again, and could always go back to Henry Lawson's prose and verse. Lawson was the first to set forth Australian life, and his *Star of Australasia* deserves the highest praise. I remember thinking, after reading *While the Billy Boils,* that here for the first time a man had shown that the Bush was worth writing about, and it was a great encouragement to me when I started to write.

Barbara Baynton, in an interview in *Home,* September, 1920; reprinted in *Barbara Baynton,* edited by Sally Krimmer and Alan Lawson, University of Queensland Press, 1980.

---

sane, and the punctuation in the last paragraph seems to indicate that this is so. It is here that the stream of consciousness gives way to direct speech. . . .

Kay Schaffer   (essay date 1983)

SOURCE: "Barbara Baynton: Woman as 'The Chosen Vessel'," in *Australian Literary Studies,* Vol. 11, No. 1, May, 1983, pp. 25-37.

[*In the following essay, Schaffer analyzes "The Chosen Vessel."*]

When critics of Australian literature focus on the writers of the *Bulletin* school of the 1890s in terms of a tradition of democratic nationalism, they seldom mention women. A. A. Phillips however, in his 1966 revised edition of *The Australian Tradition,* includes a new chapter on Barbara Baynton, author of ***Bush Studies*** (1902). Phillips applies the label 'dissidence' to the character of Baynton's writing, along with that of Miles Franklin's *My Brilliant Career,* Norman Lindsay's *Redheap,* Arthur Adams' poem, 'The Australian', and some of the short stories of Henry Lawson, like 'The Union Buries its Dead'. He writes that they exhibit an 'undercurrent of revolt against the barbaric fate of being an Australian'. The issue is not woman's fate, but that of 'being an Australian'. Nonetheless, the manner in which this so-called dissidence is approached has relevance in the light of contemporary theoretical questions concerning the relationship between narrative and gender. Phillips' remark concerning Baynton's dissidence is relevant to both the production of 'woman's place' in the annals of Australian literature and to the processes of naming through critical exegesis. An examination of Barbara Baynton's short story, **'The Chosen Vessel,'** an abridged version of which originally appeared in the *Bulletin* in 1896 under A. G. Stephens' title, **'The Tramp',** and its critical reception by Phillips and others will serve to illustrate the nature of the problem. Focusing on the place of woman as sign in the short story and critical commentaries, keeping in mind the question of women's dissidence, I will trace the ambiguities of meaning within the original text and its more singular 'truth' as represented by the critical tradition.

Part One of the story introduces a woman and baby alone in the bush. When the story opens the woman is tethering a calf to prevent its wandering with the cow during the night. She is vaguely restless. As she works, she reflects on her fear of the cow, whose protests she has been taught to curb with a stick, and her husband's deprecation of her fears of both cow and bush. In anger at her fear, he has called her 'cur'. She wonders if the enemy who is her husband would run as does her enemy the cow if threatened by a stick: 'but she was not one to provoke skirmishes even with the cow'.

A swagman has been by earlier in the day looking for food, money, and something more by the look of his eyes as he gazed upon the mother with babe at her breast. In expectation of his return, the woman leaves some food and her mother's brooch, 'the only thing of value that she had', on the kitchen table. She then retires with her child to the barricaded house for the night. The sound of the returning swagman wakes her and she listens intently, careful not to wake the sleeping baby in her arms. In mounting terror, she watches his shadow circle the hut as he seeks a place of entry. When he is about to gain access through a fallen slab, the woman hears the sounds of horsehooves approaching and she runs from the hut, babe in arms, shrieking to the horseman for salvation. But she falls into the arms of the intruder as the horseman rides away, with curlews picking up her final cry of 'Murder', as they fly above his head.

Part Two details the discovery of the dead mother and her child by a boundary rider who initially misinterprets the scene as that of a lamb and ewe murdered by a dingo. 'By God', and then, 'Jesus Christ', he utters as he cuts away the infant's gown from the dead mother's grip.

Part Three recounts the story of the horseman, Peter Hennessey, who passed the woman and child without stopping to help them. A devout if superstitious Catholic, he had been riding that night to a nearby voting district to cast his ballot for a candidate of his own political persuasions but one not supported by the Priest. He contemplates his revolt, which 'had over-ridden superstition' as well as his mother's pleas, when the mother and child appear to him, calling 'For Christ's sake!' Peter misinterprets the scene as a holy vision sent to redeem him in answer to his mother's prayers. He proceeds to cast his vote for the Priest's squatter candidate and only learns the 'true' nature of his vision when he returns to the Priest to confess of his revolt and redemption.

Part Four depicts the swagman and his dog at the waterhole. The dog faithfully runs to return the swaggie's hat from the water but will not allow the man to wash the blood of sheep from its mouth and throat—blood which makes the swagman tremble. The original story and the 1917 final revision ends with the comment, 'But the dog also was guilty'. (This sentence has been omitted from the Angus and Robertson editions of **Bush Studies.** Krimmer and Lawson restore it to their edition of **Barbara Baynton.**)

If one accepts the opening as a distinct element in the story, what emerges is a five part structure which includes:

> *opening*—mother, called 'cur', isolated, fearful but passively resigned to the bush;

> *action*—her rape and murder by a non-descript swagman-as-Everyman;

> *discovery*—by boundary rider whose presence links natural (lamb and ewe), actual (mother and child), and supernatural ('By God', 'Jesus Christ!') levels of meaning;

> *action*—redeeming vision of the horseman which quells his revolt;

> *ending*—guilty swagman and his loyal dog.

This was the only story by Barbara Baynton to appear in the *Bulletin* (December 1896). A. G. Stephens, editor of the Red Page, thought her work 'too outspoken' for an Australian audience, but praised it for its realism. Six of her stories, including **'The Chosen Vessel'** were first published in England under the title **Bush Studies** in 1902.

Like **'The Chosen Vessel'**, all convey a hostile image of the bush as perceived by its victims—the old, the weak, the women. But the stories have been read in terms of the way in which they reflect the Australian tradition. Censorship of the stories to fit their assumed context began with first publication. Stephens cut the entire third section, concerning the Catholic voter/horseman, and he retitled the story **'The Tramp'**, possibly even changing Baynton's neutral pronouns for the man as 'he' into 'the tramp'. Baynton offered the title 'What the Curlews Cried', but it was rejected. Thus, from the outset, the religious theme of section three, which unites the sexual with the symbolic, the bush mother with the Virgin Mother, the silenced with the spoken theme, is censored. And the title was changed, thus shifting reader interest away from the murder, evoked on several levels of the text, and on to the male character, called a 'tramp', *not* bushman or swagman, by Stephens.

When A. A. Phillips writes of the story he comments that Stephens' judgements were 'sound' in these matters and suggests that even more could have been peeled away. He cites the opening episode, in which the text evokes a harsh image of the husband (not to mention the wife), as unnecessary as well. We only need to know, he says, that the husband was absent. The extra details are examples of Baynton's 'subjective obsession' about man's cruelty forcing its way into the incidental details of the story. Phillips is clearly bothered by Baynton's 'obsessions'; 'grim prepossessions' he calls them in another place. In reading the history of Phillips' association with the works of Baynton, and this story in particular, one begins to wonder whether the term might accurately be applied to him. Phillips is one of the few critics to take an interest in the works of Barbara Baynton. His major essay on her work, and **'The Chosen Vessel'** in particular, has been republished with slight revisions no fewer than seven times between 1961 and 1980.

But Phillips, like Stephens before him, explicates and situates the text on another terrain. He makes it meaningful on *his* terms. This involves a chopping and changing, a literal cutting up of the text, in the name of 'objective' literary and critical standards, to make it mean what he wants it to mean. The story in his hands is not about the murder of a woman at all, but about the bush legend. Once the critic has pared away all the superfluous details of the story and reduced it to the interaction between the mother and the tramp, he can interpret it in terms of his favourite obsession, the Australian tradition: the 'rock [upon which] the Australian pride is ultimately based'. Baynton is a 'dissident' because her writings pose a threat to that tradition. The critic's task becomes one of restoring the reader's faith in the legend by distinguishing between tramps and true bushmen and then ridding the bush of its tramps, both literal and figurative, even if they only appear in the 'intensely subjective' . . . 'nightmare obsessions' of a 'unique' Australian bush writer who was 'not . . . primarily moved by socially critical motives'. Reading these phrases, one asks: who speaks and for whom? Phillips' critical qualifications not only serve to rid the bush of its tramps but the tradition of its dissidents as well. *Whose* 'grim prepossessions' are being expressed in the defensive pattern of this rhetoric?

An analysis of Phillips' discourse on Baynton reveals a myriad of ways in which the writer is literally blind to women as writers/characters except as they reflect or challenge the bush ideal. The category 'woman' is empty and filled by shifting significations which mirror the place of woman in what might be called the Australian Imaginary (in the Lacanian sense of what we take to be real but is imagined with reference to a patriarchal symbolic order). The woman, herself, does not exist; she is absent from the discourse. For example, when Phillips delineates what he sees as Baynton's major themes, he says that they convey: 'the most intense effect . . . of the image of a lonely bush hut besieged by a terrifying figure who is also a terrified figure'. In **'The Chosen Vessel'** we recall that it is not the hut, but the woman in the hut, who is besieged. And the terrifying figure is certainly not 'also the terrified figure'. Here Phillips repeats Stephens' trick of shifting emphasis from victim to attacker. The second theme Phillips mentions is: 'the fierce power of the maternal instinct'.

Still there is no mention of the woman who possesses it. But later the text reads, 'the possessor of the maternal instinct is usually the victim of evil, which wreaks a terrible destruction'. The evil, we are assured, is 'essentially weak', while the maternal force 'has lasting strength'. So 'woman' as a central character, motif, theme in Baynton's fiction, has thus far been displaced as (1) the bush hut, (2) the terrifying figure of her attacker, (3) the maternal force, (4) the possessor of the maternal force, (5) the victim of evil, (6) the survivor (child or dog) which endures as the maternal representative. Where is the woman? Absent. How is she portrayed? Objectified into the unproblematical motif of 'the maternal'. This treatment is hardly justified given *both* of the author's designated titles: 'What the Curlews Cried', (that is, 'Murder!'), and **'The Chosen Vessel',** that is, the maternal mother/Mother ironically fused and, thus, destroyed.

Phillips' analysis aligns the maternal force, or instinct, or power, or what have you, with a 'bitter insistence on man's brutality to women'. He writes, 'One feels, perhaps without logical justification, that the two themes beat together in the pulse of Barbara Baynton's intuitions'. In this sentence the reader can begin to detect the workings of Phillips' imaginary, and the discursive transference to the symbolic order, in his juxtaposition of the logical with the intuitive. 'Perhaps without logical justification', for whom?

Phillips seems to be suggesting that *he* (the objective critic) has no logical justification for linking the two themes in her work. But as the sentence reads metonymically, he is also saying that perhaps *she* has none, that is, that there is no logical justification for linking the maternal instinct with man's brutality to women. This introduces a confusion between critic and writer, logic and intuition, objective truths and subjective obsessions, male and female. A battle, which is both sexual and textual, surfaces in the text.

From this point on the polarities between critic and writer, (analysis and its object), will vie for mastery. And the substance has more to do with woman's place in patriarchal discourse than with any content in Baynton's fiction—the ostensible 'subject'.

The strategy the critic will employ in his analysis to deal with this troublesome writer of dissident texts is to alternately praise and then condemn her writing by use of his categories, which are also *our* categories for establishing differences between "male" and "female" within the symbolic order of language. For example, Phillips concedes that Baynton is a powerful writer who conveys a sense of bush realism. In this she is 'one of the breed' of Australian writers. But, her 'nightmare visions' threaten to place her in the camp of melodramatic writers of 'popular genres of the period'. Her work is located on the border of nightmare visions and objective realism. What Phillips finds hard to deal with is her compulsion to detail man's cruelty to women ('perhaps without logical justification . . .'). In this she was 'obsessional', 'subjective'—in the country of the Freudian subconscious, the text dares to whisper. That is, the writer is seen as a possibly neurotic female, writing to assuage or cathect by revenge some emotional pain of her past. But if that (personal) theme is her weakness, which locates her among 'popular' writers, her strength, which locates her among Australian realists of the nineties, is her style. Her style is described in terms of its 'concrete detail' for portrayal of 'life-as-it-is', her 'bread-and-butter directness', the 'spare muscularity' of her prose, the power of her visualization, and, lastly, the 'austere directness' of her 'pouncing feminine accuracy' which mark her writings as 'masterly' works of 'thorough and effective craftsmanship'. What, one wonders, is 'pouncing feminine accuracy', and might it conflict with the 'masterly craftsmanship'? How does it pounce? For whom? On whom? Phillips is caught in the dilemma of trying to characterize a woman writer as an Australian writer of merit, without specific regard to her sex—in fact, with what often seems a deliberate suppression of the possible significance of her sex—and yet the analysis bristles with real and repressed gender-marked confusions. There appears to be a difficulty of viewing Baynton as a writer, and a good one, who is at the same time not-male. The arguments proceed, leaving a trail of unspoken assumptions concerning the difference between good and bad writers, differences which sound suspiciously like naïve critical assumptions concerning writers and women writers e. g.:

Writers	Women Writers
superior	inferior
objective	subjective
masterly	obsessional
logical	intuitive
thought	feeling
bush realism	melodrama/ nightmare vision
Australian tradition	popular genre
Phillips	?
?	Baynton

Where to locate 'Phillips' and 'Baynton' within these dichotomies is a repressed question in the essay. Although the critic might place himself on the positive side of the polarities, we often find him slipping into the negative mire. As the essay progresses, the author increasingly substitutes *his* intuitions and feelings for an objective analysis of Baynton's logic and craft. In relation to point-of-view, for example, Phillips writes:

'The reader is forced to sit behind her [Baynton's] eyes and see with their pouncing feminine accuracy'. He then corrects himself that in fact Baynton never writes from an 'uninventive' first person narration. The reader always follows her text through the vision of the characters. So, the critic denies what might be (but is not) a fault in her fiction by calling attention to it as if it were present in the stories. This repeated strategy links Baynton's style to all the attributes of an inferior, one might say 'female' fiction—the melodramatic, the subjective—making her guilty by association, and then shifting to praise the work for its superior, dramatic, symbolic and carefully controlled craftsmanship which marks Baynton as 'one of the breed'. Once Phillips makes a dubious case for the power of her creations, he concludes with the final thrust:

> Yet, *despite evidence* of alert and considered workmanship, I doubt if she *deliberately* chose the method of viewing the action through the character's eyes. *It seems more likely* that it grew *naturally* from her strong sense of actuality, her *intuitive* assumption that the essence of a story's effect lay in the reader's sense of involvement in event. (Emphasis mine).

In the end, the careful craftsmanship of the stories becomes the happy result of accidental circumstances. Her power is reduced to the intuitive, the natural; while *his* intuitions take on the air of critical logic.

In Phillips' argument there is a constant shifting of referents from Baynton's text to Phillips' text (the logical and the intuitive); from Baynton's bush to Phillips' bush; from her ambiguous naming of the 'maternal' to his reading of the 'fierce power of the maternal instinct'. The 'maternal' is constructed through a signifying chain of referents which exist outside of the text in the symbolic order of language but are also located within it. In the actual story **'The Chosen Vessel'** there is a conflation of the mother and the Maternal. The literal and the figurative meanings exist together. They cannot be separated. The 'maternal' is that which saves a child but kills a mother. But the mother is, inescapably, the maternal. The woman is an empty signifier which as mother/Mother stands for both sacrifice *and* redemption. It is not filled by woman, who can be absent in an absolute sense, but by religion, mythology, politics in the discourses of the symbolic order which supplement the image of woman-as-lack, disguise the imagined 'truth' of woman's castration by a denial of her absolute difference outside the orders of patriarchy. This operation of substitutions in which woman is defined as other in relation to a phallocentric norm is what gives rise to the concept of Identity—precisely what is at stake in Baynton's fiction as interpreted by the tradition—the rock upon which 'Australian pride is ultimately based'. Baynton's story appears to have threatened the rock's foundation. And all of Phillips' rhetorical devices, which include

attempts at balance, fusion, undercutting, veiling and replacement, have failed to heal the breach. Indeed, they trace a fault line which underlies all Western discourse in the name-of-the-father. In this case, they reveal how the Australian tradition is formulated with reference to a particular construction of 'femininity', herein represented as 'the fierce power of the maternal instinct'.

Phillips is not alone in his interpretation of Baynton's work. A majority of critics, including her most recent commentators, Sally Krimmer and Alan Lawson, assess the strength of her achievement in terms of her evocation of 'the maternal'. Krimmer and Lawson write [in their introduction to **Barbara Baynton,** 1980] that in her stories the 'malevolent landscape' is linked to a 'man/woman confrontation where women, without choice, become acquiescent victims of men, largely without realizing it'. They continue: 'the woman is shown as maternal, loving and peaceful while man is portrayed as brutally sexual'. They refer at length to **'The Chosen Vessel'** as a representative piece which shows 'motherhood as a hope for humanity. . . .' They conclude that 'the supreme example of woman's instinctive desire to protect her young is found in **"The Chosen Vessel"**, where motherhood is presented as being the one quality which cannot be overwhelmed'.

Is there not something ironic about the title **'The Chosen Vessel',** which in this case refers to a woman who is brutally raped and murdered but also and at the same time refers to the appellation for Mary, the Mother of God? Is the concept of the 'maternal' which defines and thus denies the 'real' woman, not problematic in its fusion of literal and figurative levels of textuality? Is the woman 'without choice' on both levels, or can we separate the two? Only when we do separate them can we register Baynton's irony in saying that which confers the power of the maternal as a concept, also demands the denial of the mother as a person. Baynton does not allow an unproblematic concept of 'the maternal' to dominate her text; the critics do. In fact, one could argue that it is the ironic handling of this concept which operates as a deconstructive force on the text. Lawson and Krimmer appear to avoid these ambiguities in relation to both the theme and form of her work. They conclude their introduction to Baynton with a few brief comments on her style which they characterise as a 'terrible logic', a 'singlemindedness', which renders her theme through a 'consistent style . . . a consistent vision . . . (and) a careful ordering'.

Perhaps we all need to look again at the text. Beginning with the ironic title and continuing through the development of theme, on a purely literal level, there are at least two contradictory messages. One, which I have already referred to, is the confusion between mother/Mother; another is the question of the woman's innocence or guilt. On the question of her fate, Krimmer and Lawson and a host of other commentators, maintain that the woman is innocent and has no choice. But the text reads ambiguously. Read thematically, with reference to metonymic associations conveyed through the narrative, one could conclude that the woman is implicated in the guilt which results from her murder. The problem with this reading is that there is no direct thematic evidence, aside from the final and disputed sentence, to support this conclusion. The woman does nothing 'wrong'; she is apparently guilty of no crime. She does not 'deserve' her fate. And yet, she is murdered while the swagman goes free. These events set up a problem in the text which critical interpretations attempt to resolve.

How is her guilt established textually? One recalls that the woman has no name except that which her husband has given her—'the noun was cur'—in relation to her fear of the cow. The nature of this naming relates to other networks of meaning in the text which work in at least two contrary directions. One linking chain of signifiers establishes a relation between the woman and the dog. As the attacker approaches the house, the woman hears a 'thud of something striking the dog's ribs, and the long flying strides of the animal as it howled and ran'. Violence to the dog (heard) precedes violence to the house (heard and felt, as if on the body of a woman): 'She heard his jerked breathing as it kept time with the cuts of the knife, and the brush of his clothes as he rubbed the wall in his movements, for she was so still and quiet, that she did not even tremble'. This violence to the house precedes the woman's own struggle with the attacker and describes by displacement her violent rape and murder, which is neither seen nor heard but represented by the cry 'Murder!' which is picked up and carried across the plains by the shrieks of the curlews who fly with the horseman. These connections echo back to the 'long flying strides of the animal [dog, now woman] as it howled and ran'. The final evocation of the dog occurs at the end of the story which depicts the dog's unswerving loyalty to the man who has been its and the woman's attacker. The final sentence, which appeared in the first and in the 1917 revised edition of the story, reads, 'But the dog also was guilty'. Having registered the various links between dog and woman from the opening to the conclusion, the reader is forced to rethink the message of the text. Why divert attention, in the final sentence, from murderer to victim, from man to dog? On a literal level the dog is guilty of killing sheep (he has blood on his mouth and throat which makes the man tremble); but one normally assumes that the action arises out of instinct, to which no blame is attached. Perhaps it might be said that on a moral level the dog is guilty by association with the man to whom it is loyal; but loyalty is usually taken to be a virtue, not a fault. Now, the woman exhibits both these characteristics: the 'instinct' of a mother to protect her child and the 'loyalty' to a man who abuses her. In this she is like the dog; but unlike the dog, she is a human agent, capable of making decisions for herself and thus culpable in the creation of her situation. In other words, if one accepts moral arguments concerning the agency of the human will for which there is some textual evidence, she had choice. She could have left the house and her vulnerable situation in the isolated bush and returned to her former home in the town. Her passive acceptance of the situation makes her an accomplice in her fate.

On the other hand, if one traces the links set up between the woman and the cow—the fear of which earned her the appellation 'cur', one comes to a quite different set of conclusions. The cow, in its relation to the calf (as the ewe in relation to the lamb, later) figuratively represents the ma-

ternal instinct. The cow bellows whenever the woman tries to tether its calf and she fears that it might turn on her. She 'was afraid of the cow (that is, the maternal) but she did not want the cow to know it'. This suggests that she fears something in herself, that which is called the maternal and the demands of its authority over her existence. Now, the woman does not impose demands. She is content to let the animals run free. Her husband insists on their control. His authority is represented (no doubt ironically) by the slight stick which he has given her to brandish at the cow and thus subdue the 'enemy'. Why must she do this if not to protect his property? She stands in for the absent father, both concretely and symbolically. Thus the imposition of rules for which there is no effective escape and the repressed impulse toward revolt are two contradictory directions in the text which are opened up in the first paragraph and yoked together throughout the tale. Although never made explicit within the text, by metonymic links and metaphoric referents, the woman paradoxically is what she fears. She embodies 'the maternal' in the symbolic order. She belongs to the same economy which brings about her murder.

The father's law limits the otherwise unlimited relationships between cow and calf, mother and child. It severs a 'natural' relationship, making the mother the enemy of the maternal even as it transforms her into its agent. The first sentence reads: 'She laid the stick and her baby on the grass'. The stick represents the father's law; her baby represents her entrance into that law as the maternal, as defined by the symbolic order. This first instance sets up a series of relationships between the actors and the acted upon, the dominant and the dependent, those who have the power to name and to act, and those to whom such power is denied. As the story progresses this dimension is conveyed through a conjunction of the literal and the figurative, the mother and the Maternal. But, to paraphrase Lacan, the images and symbols *of* the woman cannot be separated from the images and symbols *in* the woman. She is constituted by the patronym which binds her existence to the name-of-the-father.

And the patronym by which she is constituted and possessed extends well beyond the actual domain of the husband. A series of influences 'act' upon the woman. They effectively deny her herself, that is her difference outside of a relation to Man in the symbolic order she inhabits with him. These influences subdue her and locate her in a relational place. Firstly, there is the 'natural' order of calves and cows, lambs and ewes, dogs and masters; then, by order of appearance, there is the husband whose verbal abuse establishes the law and the woman's inferior relation to it. 'Needn't flatter yerself . . . nobody'ud want ter run away with yew', he tells her ironically. Then there is the swagman who steals 'the only thing she had of value', referring specifically to her mother's brooch, prefiguring the loss of her sexuality and ultimately her life, that is, her legacy from the mother. Then the horseman acts upon the woman by confusing her actual presence with an imagined vision of the Madonna and Child. Lastly, the Priest acts upon the woman. His religious doctrines translate the mother and child into an image which offers redemption and salvation for Man, but only by a displacement of woman into a religious mythology of the sacred Mother. She is sacred because she nurtures and protects the Child and guarantees the succession of authority from father to son, God to Christ, Priest to Peter. This final evocation of the woman as Madonna represents the ultimate denial of woman outside of the patriarchal order.

It is important to note that the text links the sacred to the profane through the effect of the male gaze, that is, on the level of the Imaginary. When the swagman first approaches the woman to ask for tucker, we are told, 'She feared more from the look of his eyes, and the gleam of his teeth, as he watched her newly awakened baby beat its impatient fists upon her covered breasts, than from the knife that was sheathed in the belt at his waist'. The man first possesses the woman with his gaze. The specular appropriation of the woman-as-mother by the swagman, who captures her as an object of desire, contains the image of both Virgin and whore. It links male incestuous desires to the castrating image of the mother as corrupted, that is, tainted by her sexual relation to the father. In the Imaginary, with its links to the Oedipal triangle, endemic to Western culture, the mother is not only guilty, but the source of the crime. She is to blame for having been desired. She becomes the cause of his crimes against her. The sublimation of mother as Madonna and Virgin, freed from sexual taint, acts as a powerful defence against that which has been repressed. In **'The Chosen Vessel'** the Priest and Peter represent these dynamics of repression, and in each case the operations are effected through the gaze. Peter imagines a vision of the Madonna and Child as he rides out his attempted revolt against paternal authority. He confesses his assumed crime (revolt against the Priest) under a painting of the Mother and Child which beams down on him in the Priest's study. 'Her eyes seemed to beam with the forgiveness of an earthly mother for her erring but beloved child'. Thus, the 'woman', read at once as mother/Madonna, is not only the source of the crime(s), actual or imagined, but also the agent, spiritual and physical, for forgiveness.

The religious connections which link the two levels of the story of a mother/Madonna, given the 'reality' to which they refer, are almost heretical. Each prayer spoken in the text becomes a profanation. And Peter, the horseman who does not stop to help the screaming woman, is the only character to have a name, a signature within the text. What is his importance? Like the biblical Peter, he too sins in a denial which saves himself. We recall that he is on his way to cast his ballot for a candidate the priest does not support. His revolt against the priest's authority is played out under the 'glorified sky of earliest spring', that is, according to biblical referents textually invoked, Easter. The dialogue he imagines as he rides through the night invokes the presence of Mary as the Mediatrix between father and son. He recalls his mother's praying 'Mary, Mother of Christ, save my son', at the same time as he hears the woman 'calling loudly in despairing accents, "For Christ's sake! Christ's sake! Christ's sake!"' He interprets the image of the real woman as a vision conjured up by a pre-existent and pre-ordained vision of woman which literally blinds him to the real. He sees her not; she is nothing to him; and yet she is the source of his 'blessed vision'. He returns to relate his redeeming vision to the priest as the curlews pick up the mother's cry of 'Murder!' We are reminded of Peter the Apostle's denial of Christ before the cock crowed thrice. Both Peters are forgiven, and both the Christ and child retain their authority. But a woman has been violently murdered. She is 'murdered' not only by the swagman, but by the various levels of signification which deny her existence—the 'natural' world of ewes and lambs, the domestic world of male dominance and female submission, the religious world of the Madonna and Child. The evocation of 'the maternal' also causes the death of woman by negating any sense of her difference from man's law. Peter is forgiven, but the woman is dead. Nevertheless, or by the same stroke, 'order' is restored. Yet the woman, like the Virgin Mary, retains the hallowed title **'The Chosen Vessel'**. We recall that Mary was a 'vessel' because she received the spiritual semen of the Holy Spirit (i. e. Jesus). The woman in Baynton's story becomes the 'vessel' of the swagman's semen. His possession effects her death; she becomes Everywoman.

The conflation of referents which blend literal and figurative meanings, denying as they uphold the 'fierce power of the maternal', exist together, at every point of text. But they work most explicitly with reference to the third section—that which both A. G. Stephens and A. A. Phillips deemed unnecessary to the unity of plot, character, action. In the third section a doubling takes place. The main action is repeated in a way that transforms murder into redemption, revolt into acquiescence, the absence of woman into the insistence of the maternal power, the transference of the literal into the figurative, the imaginary into the symbolic. If one reads through the contradictions, woman is not guilty at all—she is wholly absent. She takes no part in the actions of the story except to represent male desire as either Virgin or whore. Her 'lack', disguised as maternal power, enables 'him' (husband, son, horseman, priest) to attain or maintain an identity. She has been named, captured, controlled, appropriated, violated, raped and murdered, *and then* reverenced through the signifying practices of the text. And these contradictory practices through which the 'woman' is disseminated in the text are made possible by her very absence from the symbolic order except by reference to her phallic repossession by Man. Baynton's text, in its deliberate irony, calls attention to these facts while it calls into question the idealization of the bushman as the embodiment of the Australian personality.

The text, as our 'chosen vessel' comes to contain these contradictions. In its deliberate irony, it functions to deconstruct the 'place' of women in the (male) Imaginary. The writer mimes the role imposed upon women by pointing to it from the stance of a dissident, speaking to a tradition from its dangerous margins. But critics like Phillips, Krimmer and Lawson, by reducing the text to determinate meanings and singular visions, reproduce what the text deconstructs. The critics therefore reify a foreknown law—whether it is Phillips' bush ideal, the bedrock principle on which the Australian legend has been built, or Krimmer and Lawson's motherhood-as-the-hope-for-humanity ideal. One critique works through repression, the other through sublimation—both deny differences. They censor and repress the very aspects which Baynton's irony calls to our attention. A deconstructive reading also establishes a critical position. But it challenges interpretations which would posit 'a truth'. It insists that texts disseminate meaning which can never be reduced or determined, given the rich referentiality of language. The text calls attention to the complex constitution of woman in patriarchy through the discursive practices of language which name her as other in relation to man. By analysing the text as a *question,* by asking *how* it means by way of its constitution of the place of woman through its discursive practices, we can also begin to represent what has been unrepresentable all along. That is, woman not as other (in relation) but as Otherness itself in her radical resistance to all her specular representations to which the text calls our attention: the non-sense of the unspoken, the unrepresented, the absence whose place is filled by the phallic mother who can be at once our 'damned whore and God's police'.

Through our examination of Baynton's text as it attempts to deconstruct the place of woman we can register her dissidence, not only as interpreted by A. A. Phillips as that which denies the legend but also, and more fundamentally, as imagined by Julia Kristeva in her insistence [in *Polylogues*] that woman is the perpetual dissident. 'Woman is here to shake up, to disturb, to deflate masculine values, and not to espouse them. Her role is to maintain differences by pointing to them, by giving them life, by putting them into play against one another'. This surely has been one of the functions of Baynton's short story, **'The Chosen Vessel'**. Its re-presentation here, by way of this analysis, may help to restore to the vessel a richness and multiplicity of meanings which have been lost through repeated critical attempts at phallic mastery.

Lucy Frost (essay date 1983)

SOURCE: "Barbara Baynton: An Affinity with Pain," in *Who Is She?* edited by Shirley Walker, St. Martin's Press, 1983, pp. 56-70.

[*Frost is an American educator and critic. In the following excerpt, she identifies emotional pain as the primary inspiration for Baynton's works.*]

In these days when pain is fashionable Barbara Baynton is widely admired for writing accurately about the terrible lives endured by women in the bush. She is commended for having fractured the rose-coloured lenses through which Australians peered reverently at their pioneer mothers. However understandable this version of Barbara Baynton may be, it is also highly ironic. The woman herself was no truth-sayer. Her grandson H. B. Gullett put the matter charitably: "she was a highly imaginative woman with no strict regard for truth. She told her children many conflicting stories of her early years and of her parents, and it rather seems as if the truth to her was what she chose to believe it ought to be at any given moment, and of course it would vary with her moods". Such a woman makes a strange feminist icon.

It is not just the impulse towards falsifying that makes her difficult to come to terms with, but the direction that impulse took. She seems to have spent the second half of her life pretending away the experiences which made possible the writing of **Bush Studies** and **Human Toll.** By the time her grandson knew her, she had become a *grande dame* with an English title and antique-filled houses, first in London's Connaught Square and later in Melbourne's exclusive Toorak. When Gullett wrote his memoir of her for the Angus and Robertson reprint of **Bush Studies** in 1965, he drew from her "conflicting stories" a highly romantic tale which accounted for her childhood in the bush without allowing her to be contaminated by the harrowing squalor and bleakness of her fictional worlds. According to Gullett's version, Barbara was the daughter of a couple who had foresworn respectability and lived their love. Her mother Penelope Ewart sailed to Australia with her delicate cousin-husband Robert Ewart, the younger son of a leading merchant house established for several centuries in Northern Ireland.

When the ship called at Bombay, the handsome Captain Kilpatrick—formerly of the Bengal Light Cavalry—joined the voyage. Penelope met the Captain: passion conquered Ulster Presbyterianism, and the pair eloped on arrival in Sydney. Placed "outside decent society" by their illicit liaison, they retreated to the bush where "for the rest of her days" Penelope "led a life of impeccable rectitude". Three years before the birth of Barbara, the Kilpatricks' sixth and final child, Penelope's lawful husband died and she could at last marry her Captain. Until the advent of Barbara, the parents "were not primarily interested in their children" who "would grow up no better than their neighbors". Barbara was different. She was legitimate, "an attractive child", "certainly the favourite of both her parents", and therefore she "associated with them more than her brothers and sisters did". The company of her cultivated parents ameliorated Barbara's bush environment. From them she acquired taste in books, silver, and jewellery. Her father's library extended to the best in Russian novels. On Barbara Baynton's death certificate, her father is listed as "landowner". It sounds as though he had no occupation, just lived on his property in the manner of an Irish country gentleman.

These origins are fittingly appropriate background for a *grande dame,* but no *grande dame* wrote **Bush Studies.** The credibility of the stories relies on knowing the bush from an angle entirely different. It is not simply that the stories feel painful whereas life with the Kilpatricks does not. The problem lies more in a particular relationship between pain and detail. At its most evocative Baynton's prose specifies emotion within fact. The result is a heightened sense of immediacy as the reader responds directly. No interpreter, whether author or self-reflecting character, intervenes:

> She went towards the buggy, but as she neared
> it the driver got in and made to drive off. She ran
> and called, for when he went she would be alone
> with the bush all round her, and only the sound
> of the hoarse croaking of the frogs from the
> swamp near, and the raucous "I'll—'ave—'is—
> eye—out", of the crows.

The reader is not told explicitly what the new housekeeper in **"Billy Skywonkie"** is feeling when the train leaves her at the Gooriabba siding. Two details of sound establish the terror of being abandoned there. Those frogs and crows say more than a paragraph of explanation could. Barbara Baynton can pick out the revealing details because she *knows* the sources of sensation and emotion in that environment. Of course she might have known what drought does to a sheep station even if she had been brought up with the cultivated Kilpatricks, but would she have understood intimately the daily lives of those people like the housekeeper who inhabit her stories? Why would she have written about the bush as though it were a world of abiding terror? The stories have nothing at all to do with the déclassé household of Captain Kilpatrick.

Neither did Barbara Baynton herself, as Sally Krimmer discovered when she looked for the documentation. In 1976 Krimmer published her findings in an article appropriately entitled "New Light on Barbara Baynton". The "new light" should caution us against embracing Baynton as a heroic feminist truth-sayer. It may, however, make her more sympathetic as a nineteenth-century Australian woman struggling out of grim circumstances. Certainly it illuminates the potency of **Bush Studies** and suggests why she failed to sustain a literary career. The stories were written at the turn of the century when Barbara Baynton had escaped the bush and was quite probably feeling secure and self-confident for the first time in her life. In 1890 she had married the well-to-do and cultivated Sydney doctor, Thomas Baynton, who at seventy was twice her age. Nothing suggests that the marriage was passionless social climbing, but whatever benefits married life may have bestowed upon the fledgling author, it did not provide the material for her fiction. When she wrote, she went back to a past still close enough for its emotions to be raw, and when she wrote out of those emotions her stories were powerful.

Even with the still sketchy information now available, the emotional sources of **Bush Studies** have grown evident. Barbara Baynton's early life was far from romantic. Her father was no dashing Captain Kilpatrick. His name was John Lawrence and he was a carpenter in the Scone district in New South Wales. Barbara was the seventh child of a family who doubtless could ill afford to keep such a brood. Her older brothers and sisters were not illegitimate, although an eight child was. The social standing of the family is suggested by the fact that the brothers learned trades and went to work in the immediate vicinity, while Barbara was sent to a station in the Quirindi district as a governess, an unglamorous job likely to do little for a young woman's sense of prestige or self-esteem. Perhaps the fact that in 1880 the twenty-three-year-old Barbara married a son of her employer's family proves that she made the most of the severely limited opportunities open to her. This first husband, Alexander Frater, was a selector in the Coonamble district. By the time he took up his selection, the best land in that area was gone. As a selector's wife, Barbara probably lived on a small, second-rate piece of property where life was far from gracious, especially for a woman bearing and then caring for three children. Before the marriage was ten years old, Alexander Frater had run off with their servantwoman, Sarah Glover. In similar circumstances, even today, a woman might well go home to her parents. Instead, Barbara went to

Sydney, perhaps for the first time in her life. How she managed to sustain herself and her three young children is not clear. She may have sold bibles from door to door. Certainly she had no easily transferrable skills. Her jobs must have been menial, and with three children to look after, it is difficult to imagine her life as other than harassed and precarious. Marriage to Dr Baynton must have seemed heaven-sent. Tantalizing questions about that marriage remain unanswered. How did she meet Dr Baynton? Was she initially his housekeeper? How did she manage to marry him in a church the very day after her divorce was official? How could she have been sure enough of that date to have her banns announced? How did a divorced woman obtain a church wedding? Presumably because she claimed herself to be a widow on her marriage certificate, but did she lie only to the official or to Dr Baynton as well? Why does the marriage certificate alter truths about her background?

Whatever the specific answers to these questions, it is easy to feel sympathy for the woman. After an impoverished childhood, which the birth-certificate of her illegitimate younger brother leads one to suspect must have been emotionally fraught as well; after an unattractive job as a governess where she could be easily exploited; after a marriage which looks like a physical and emotional strain; after fending for herself and the children in an unfamiliar urban setting, she came to rest at last amidst the books and fine antiques of a man who could introduce her to a congenial circle of people. As Mrs Baynton, Barbara had come in from the cold and for the rest of her life she would remain warmed by the fires of the wealthy and the socially respectable. Surely no one can pass moral judgment on her for that. Literary judgments are another matter, and here the evidence is clear-cut: she wrote best when she was writing about people left out in the cold.

Her sensitivity to their plights even lends imaginative force to **"A Dreamer"**, with its mawkish plot characteristic of soppy fiction written for women's magazines. Here the central figure is a young pregnant woman left out in the cold quite literally. She has arrived late at night in a one-street country town to pay her mother a long overdue visit. Finding no one at the station to meet her, she walks three miles through a storm. After almost losing her way in the dark bush and nearly drowning in a flooded river, she gets home only to find her mother dead. The rank melodrama of the plot spreads out to infect the prose. Breathlessness abounds. Exclamation marks are everywhere. The natural world is treated as personally vicious. Even the ordinarily gentle willow trees have branches animated to become antagonists threatening death:

> The wind savagely snapped them, and they lashed her unprotected face. Round and round her bare neck they coiled their stripped fingers. Her mother had planted these willows, and she herself had watched them grow. How could they be so hostile to her!

Such overstated gestures abound. Yet, in a story clogged with literary trivia, with outmoded language and discredited fictional devices, there is genuine insight and power. The story is a remarkable rendering of a rarely treated subject: a woman's struggle to come to terms with feelings she has for her own mother at a time when she is about to become a mother herself.

The struggle engenders psychic disarray. The woman's passage through the storm becomes a metaphoric journey through a landscape experienced as nightmare. The physical world is shaped by a dreamer's fears, not by the laws of nature. The "feel" and the logic of the story belong to the world of nightmare. This is why willows are more than willows; they are personally hostile antagonists. To animate nature as if it were an extension of the perceiver is an epistemological fallacy in a waking mind (and the pathetic fallacy when it invades literature). For the dreaming mind, however, such animation is the arena of psychological truth, and this is why **"A Dreamer"** is truthful, against all literary odds. The narrative achieves insight into the confused state of a woman for whom motherhood is an issue compounded of violence, guilt and sentimentalized love.

In the dreamer's conscious mind motherhood is a stereotype with one basic characteristic: mother protects. This notion is offered early in the story when the daughter begins her walk through "the wind and rain and darkness . . . to her mother's home":

> From the branch of a tree overhead she heard a watchful mother—bird's warning call, and the twitter of the disturbed nestlings. The tender care of this bird-mother awoke memories of her childhood. What mattered the lonely darkness, when it led to mother. Her forebodings fled, and she faced the old track unheedingly, and ever and ever she smiled, as she foretasted their meeting.
>
> 'Daughter!'
>
> 'Mother!'
>
> She could feel loving arms around her, and a mother's sacred kisses.

Throughout the long dark walk, the daughter clings to this mindlessly sentimental image, and then as she struggles desperately in the flooded river, she hears her mother's "sweet dream-voice" whispering "Little woman". It's as though a spell were broken, and the nasty world had magically become kind and soothing:

> Soft, strong arms carried her on. Weakness aroused the melting idea that all had been a mistake, and she had been fighting with friends. The wind even crooned a lullaby.

This is the make-believe mother of our childhood hopes who can make everything right for the daughter she loves. Knowing her child is in danger, her disembodied voice whispers, and nature changes character. The enemy is suddenly the friend—and a friend distinctly mother-like when the wind, instead of savagely snapping willow branches, croons a lullaby. This is the miraculous logic of fairytales, clear and straight-forward. But what is one to make of it? And what about the "melting idea that all had been a mistake, and she had been fighting with friends"? Are friend and foe two aspects of mother, just as they are

of the natural world in which the trees are first hostile and then saving?

This question complicates the story's attitude toward the stereotyped mother-protector. That attitude has already been complicated by introducing the issue of guilt. For unexplained reasons, the daughter has not been to see her mother for a very long time. She feels this absence as neglect, bringing with it guilt, and so welcomes her long walk through stormy darkness because "there was atonement in these difficulties and dangers". The natural world, offering violent retribution as its role in her psychic drama, gives her the punishment she craves:

> Still she would not go back. Though the roar of that rushing water was making her giddy, though the deafening wind fought her for every inch, she would not turn back.
>
> Long ago she should have come to her old mother, and her heart gave a bound of savage rapture in thus giving the sweat of her body for the sin of her soul.

Why should she feel so guilty? She has done what many daughters do. She has married and moved from mother's territory. Specifically, she has moved to a "far up-country" town, just as Barbara did when she married Alexander Frater and moved up country to the Coonamble district. Once married, the daughter's loyalties have divided. Her husband is a "tie that had parted" mother and daughter; now, the mother is a tie accepted at the price of separation from her husband: "She battled instinctively, and her first thought was of the letter-kiss she had left for the husband she loved. Was it to be his last?" The story answers that question by getting her safety across the river. Because she has not died, she will presumably go home to her husband, bearing their child in her body. This is in fact the only option she will have. Although she has done her best to get back to her mother, has risked her life in the flooded river to be a daughter again, her quest has been futile because her mother's power is finished. This is what the daughter discovers in the revelation offered by the story's last sentence:

> The daughter parted the curtains, and the light fell on the face of the sleeper who would dream no dreams that night.

It's not just that the mother is dead, but that her dreaming is finished. With it goes her protective magic. The "sweet dream-voice" is stilled.

And that's not a bad thing, the story implies. The dreamer has reached her destination even though not the one expected. Just because she will be no mother's daughter again doesn't mean she has been abandoned. Her mother's house is not empty. Other women are there, one a mother who now in her turn is comforting a disturbed child awakened in the night, and if these women are strangers, they can still be sympathetic and helpful. The tone of the story's last lines is serene. The understated prose, which plays down even the revelation of death, contrasts with the over-excited language of nightmarish storm. The fearful dream world seems to have gone, relieving the dreamer of those uncertainties which plagued her journey. After the noise of the wind and rain, after the battle to survive, after the darkness, there is quiet and a light, something warm to drink, recognition by the old dog. It is as if the woman had stepped over a magical line protecting an impervious domestic tableau from the chaotic world of nature. The tense opposition between safety and vulnerability is resolved in favour of safety, even though there is certainly a sense of loss.

This patterned movement has shaped images as well as narrative. Concern with sources of sustenance and security is contained in images of face, including mouth, voice, and sound. On the side of safety are ranged the "watchful mother-bird's warning call"; "a mother's sacred kisses"; the words of the mother's prayer—"Bless, pardon, protect and guide, strengthen and comfort!"; and the "sweet dream-voice" in the river whispering "Little woman". On the side of terrifying vulnerability are images having to do with the external world. The train tunnels "in the teeth of the wind. Whoof! whoof! its steaming breath hissed at her. She saw the rain spitting viciously at its red mouth". The "Bendy Tree" stands as a melodramatic reminder of hideous death and "her childhood's fear came back", as childhood fear persistently does throughout Baynton's fiction. The river "roars". The wind is described by verbs such as "deafens", "yells", "shrieks"; it fights her "malignantly" and lashes "her unprotected face". As the woman struggles desperately in the river, she opens "her lips to call. The wind made a funnel of her mouth and throat, and a wave of muddy water choked her cry."

These images focus the story's obsession with the daughter's vulnerability and need for protection. Sounds, heard or unheard, dramatize the search for security. At the railroad station, the daughter returns to the porter hoping for a message from mother but receiving only the conventional and unhelpful words, "Wet night!". "More for sound she turned to look up the straggling street of the township"; what she hears is the "swift tapping" of the coffin-makers. Thrust into the violent natural world she cries to God "protect me" and utters "her child-cry, 'mother!' " but neither God, nor mother, nor her own efforts save her. She would have drowned if "a giant tree's fallen body" had not "said, 'Thus far!' " and held her so that "the back-broken water crept tamed under its old foe" and she could "get her breath". Thus delivered, she reaches the cottage where "not a word was spoken". The women she finds there are strangers, not the looked-for mother who would "smile her grave smile and stroke her wet hair, call her 'Little woman! My little woman!' and tell her she had been dreaming, just dreaming". The unknown women can nourish her nevertheless: "something warm was held to her lips". Now as a woman, not the child who was a *little* woman, she can return to the home she left with a "letter-kiss". When she dared the river with a "resolute, white face", "her mouth grew tender, as she thought of the husband she loved, and of their child".

It is of course appropriate that images of face, connected as they are with nourishment and protection, should dominate a story about "the instincts of motherhood". They concentrate intensity and contribute psychological cohesiveness. They also point up problems in the story. On a simple level they heighten our awareness of contrived, melodramatic prose. That in itself is a signal of something more deeply wrong with the whole endeavour. The images convey feeling without analyzing it. This is a difficulty with the story as a whole. Too many questions are left unanswered. If the storm with its images of danger and violence is a projection of psychic disarray occasioned by the daughter's unresolved tensions with her mother, what are we to make of the "sweet dream-voice" and its attendant magic? What makes "the giant tree's fallen body" eventually say "Thus far"? Why should the natural world which has attacked her suddenly turn "defender"? What does this have to do with the woman's psychological predicament? And why should the mother be dead? This seems extraordinarily convenient. Matters would have been much more complicated if she had lived. As it is, the daughter does not have to resolve her own daughter-mother relationship because the mother has magically disappeared. True, this means that the daughter must live without her mother's comforting protection, but the actual nature of that protection must be suspect anyway because the mother is implicated in the river's assault: the strangling willows are hers, not the rescuing tree. By dying the mother forestalls any searching question about complicity. She also absolves her daughter from guilt. Filial neglect ceased to be an issue once the parent dies.

The story does not resolve the issues it engages. It evokes the situation powerfully—and then evades it. The failing offers some insight into Barbara Baynton's art. By looking solely at the text, it has been possible to conclude that the fictional situation and the language are inadequate vehicles for the complex psychological material. The empirical world has been used symbolically, but because Baynton lacks the special skills of a writer like Kafka, she has effected the symbolic transformation by falling back on a banal plot and artificial language which she then tries to manipulate from her authorial position. The rawly felt emotion belongs to the writer. It is not engendered by the details of the fictional world. Barbara Baynton's talent does not extend to symbolism.

Why then did she write **"A Dreamer"** in this uncharacteristic mode beyond the range of her talent? The answer may well lie in her penchant for concealment. This story engages troubling personal issues. Of course any sensitive woman who has felt bonded to her mother will encounter difficulty with that bond when she marries and becomes a mother herself. In Baynton's case there were reasons to feel the dilemma with peculiar acuteness. We know from the certificate of her marriage to Dr Baynton that she had already begun to rewrite the story of her background. She advanced her father from carpenter to "clerk in holy orders". She changed the class implication of her own name by discarding the simple "Barbara Jane" of her christening in favour of a pretentious "Barbara Janet Ainsleigh". The success of this social upgrading surely depended on relegating parents to paper. If the "clerk in holy orders" had actually appeared in Dr Baynton's parlour, he might have spoken and behaved suspiciously like a carpenter from the backblocks. No wonder Barbara Baynton wrote a story permeated with guilt for the neglect of an old mother. Once having moved to Sydney, she probably never saw Elizabeth Lawrence again. This neglect may explain why the storm scene in **"A Dreamer"** is written with such nightmarish urgency. It also raises questions about the story's evasive conclusion. Is the mother's death a projected wish of the dreamer whose emotions look suspiciously close to the writer's own? The death is an easy way of finishing off the daughter's obligations. The serene tone of the prose suggests that the ending may have been psychologically consoling to the writer, even though it solved her personal dilemma no more truthfully or persuasively than it did the fictional daughter's. The serenity, like the nightmare, belongs to dreaming.

Barbara Baynton may well have been blind to these implications. Her critical judgments look like hit and miss affairs. True, either Baynton or an editor realized that **"Squeaker's Mate"** should not be ruined by hospitalizing the mate and having her die with God on her mind, as happens in two existing manuscript versions. On the other hand, for *Bush Studies* Baynton badly distorts a stark tale of sexual violation and murder already published in the *Bulletin* as **"The Tramp"**. Abandoning the editorial deletion made by A. G. Stephens, she re-introduces a silly counterpointing story of Peter Hennessey's Catholic conscience and changes the title to **"The Chosen Vessel"**. A more sophisticated writer would not have embraced the resulting melodrama. Baynton relies more on instinct than on critical awareness. In order to write well she needs to write honestly out of intuitive understanding. Given her almost morbid self-protectiveness she cannot locate that understanding in anything mistakable for autobiography. One might speculate, for instance, that filling **"A Dreamer"** with stilted literary language and clanking narrative devices is a way of claiming, perhaps unconsciously, "this guilt-ridden daughter might look like me, but I'm not writing about life at all—mine or any one else's—this is just a fanciful story—look at the title!" As psychological concealment, the persistent artificiality may have been effective. As art, it makes for failure, however peculiarly haunting that failure may be. I doubt whether Baynton, with her unusually low level of critical awareness, recognized this. Otherwise, she surely would not have opened her collection with one of its weakest stories.

Whether she knew what she was doing or not, the fact remains that she needed to objectify her intuitive knowledge by creating characters and circumstances clearly separate from her, and then writing about them from the dispassionate authorial stance she could assume once emotions were embedded directly in details. This she does in **"Squeaker's Mate"**, **"Scrammy 'And"**, **"Billy Skywonkie"**, **"Bush Church"**, the part of **"The Chosen Vessel"** dealing with the woman, and some sections of *Human Toll,* particularly the last sequence in which the desperate woman wanders lost and hallucinating in the bush with the baby she tries vainly to protect. With the exception of **"Bush Church"**, this fiction shares a second characteristic. It is located in a zone of consciousness where terror abides and the self is constantly under threat. Barbara Baynton has an imaginative affinity with pain.

In her most famous story, **"Squeaker's Mate"**, Baynton dramatizes the plight of a woman whose "uncompromis-

ing independence" is eroded by forces beyond her control. This seems an appropriate subject for a woman with Baynton's background, and the emotional shape of the story feels personal. The details do not. No one would identify character with author. The mate has her own special circumstances. Like the housekeeper in **"Billy Skywonkie"**, she is a woman of no sexual lure. As a consequence she does not fit comfortably into the rigid pattern of bush life as Baynton portrays it. The housekeeper is sent right back to Sydney because she is not the "young piece" the boss is expecting. In this story permeated with an aura of sexual humiliation, the boss takes one look at the woman "ghastly with bilious sickness". She "saw curiosity and surprise change into anger as he looked at her. 'What an infernal cheek *you* had to come! Who sent you?' he asked stormily."

Squeaker's mate has managed to protect herself against being similarly mortified. Within a community of small selectors and their families, she has made from hard steady work a reasonable life. Strong and reliable, she has won honorary mateship from men who discard her vulnerable-sounding female name, "Mary", and in deference to her "manly" virtues, " 'Squeaker's Mate', the men called her, and these agreed that she was the best long-haired mate that ever stepped in petticoats". So placed, the mate has aligned herself with the men in an environment where sexual expectations are narrowly defined: "the selector's wives pretended to challenge her right to womanly garments".

This alignment fractures when a falling tree branch transforms worker into paralytic. At first the men (other than her "lawful protector", Squeaker) are solicitous. Red Bob, the honey dealer, was "in a business way, greatly concerned, when he found that Squeaker's mate was "avin' a sleep out there 'cos a tree fell on her' ". He mounts a mercy mission. Later he and the other men who gather to hear the doctor's verdict sympathize with the mate's disaster as though it were their own, discussing "in whispers, and with a look seen only on bush faces, the hard luck of that woman who alone had hard-grafted with the best of them for every acre and hoof on that selection". They give Squeaker a piece of their minds and then grow like him: "with a cowardly look towards where she lay, but without a word of parting, like shadows these men made for their homes". After this they react to the mate as a woman, not as one of them. They yield her up to their wives. That means abandoning her. Baynton's laconic narrative voice does not hide the bitterness:

> Next day the women came. Squeaker's mate was not a favourite with them—a woman with no leisure for yarning was not likely to be. After the first day they left her severely alone, their plea to their husbands, her uncompromising independence. It is in the ordering of things that by degrees most husbands accept their wives' views of other women.

In fact the mate's independence has been irrevocably compromised by a tree, although she denies this truth and, ignoring the medical diagnosis, keeps her mind on the future when she will again define life through work. Meanwhile she struggles to keep what hold she has on the property.

This means accommodating herself to Squeaker's self-indulgence. The effort is doomed. She has lost power. Without grounds from which to negotiate, she can only acquiesce step by step, fearful that Squeaker will sell up. She stops pestering him about daily chores; she silently watches her pet sheep being sold to buy "a flash red shirt", silk handkerchief, and the like. Eventually she submits to being moved to the old hut on condition that "he put a bunk there for himself, keep out of town, and not sell the place". He agrees eagerly, shifts her, and immediately breaks his promise by riding off to town. He rides beyond the fears of his mate with her mind fixed on the selection: he rides to fetch another woman. This threat the mate had not considered. This time she is "stunned". She has assumed Squeaker as a given, with their farm as the variable. When she feels threatened as Squeaker's "mate", in the sense of being Squeaker's woman, she reacts with deeply felt jealousy. Her sexual possessiveness comes as a surprise. Clinging to the selection is one thing—but why she should want to keep Squeaker is "among the mysteries".

It is a mystery, however, only because in turning "Mary" into "mate", people have regarded this woman of "uncompromising independence" as though she were sexless. They were wrong to do so. The story's climax is a tale of sexual rivalry. The mate is jealous. It does not matter that the new woman is ugly, with thick lips and red hair hanging "in an uncurled bang over her forehead" on a face in which the lower part seems to have "robbed the upper". This unattractive creature has the upper hand. She is pregnant, whereas the mate is "barren", and "bitterest of all to women—she was younger". These grounds for sexual rivalry are bad enough. Even worse, the mate can be treated as though she doesn't exist, kept alive only to prevent people talking. Her diminishing power is reflected in the story's changing perspective and tone. From the first, the prose has been controlled by a sense of the mate, of what happens to her, how she reacts, what she feels. The story's values have been the mate's values—its experience is her experience. Consequently, the tone has been sombre, critical of Squeaker, sympathetic to the terrible plight of his back-broken mate. With the new mate's arrival, focus shifts. The woman from town, vulnerable in her ignorance about the bush, is a figure of comic incongruity. She and the utterly useless Squeaker are portrayed as fools, each conning the other and being conned in turn. Their life together is a collage of farcical vignettes. The story stands back from farce, however: that silent immobile witness in the old hut transforms comedy into the grotesque.

Squeaker does not realize that while his old mate has been losing power, he has been losing control. One of the stupidest men in all fiction, his mind is literal, lazy and evasive. In the weeks after his mate's accident he behaves like some particularly obnoxious child who avoids work, refuses all responsibility and is cruel without compunction:

> She wearily watched him idling his time; reminded him that the wire lying near the fence would rust, one could run the wire through easily, and when she got up in a day or so, she would help strain and fasten it. At first he pretended he had done it, later said he wasn't goin' t' go wirin'

or nothin' else by 'imself if every other man on the place did.

> She spoke of many other things that could be done by one, reserving the great till she was well. Sometimes he whistled while she spoke, often swore, generally went out, and when this was inconvenient, dull as he was, he found the 'Go and bite yerself like a snake', would instantly silence her.

Words are weapons for Squeaker. They fend off anything he wants kept away from him. They lack moral content and play no role in making of life a reasonable venture. The mate learns this step by step, although the lesson is hard. Even after Squeaker has broken every promise and has humiliated her with a sexual rival, she lies in bed listening to the trees fall as Squeaker does a little burning-off, and "at times, the practical in her would be dominant, for in a mind so free of fancies, backed by bodily strength, hope died slowly, and forgetful of self she would almost call to Squeaker her fears that certain bees nests were in danger". Of course she does not call to him. It is not that she denies the power of language to keep life in some sort of civilized shape, but rather that she has relinquished speech because Squeaker will not suit his actions to his words. His behaviour forces the mate back upon physical strength as the last refuge for self-esteem. Confronted with her violent attack on his new woman, Squeaker disintegrates into the grovelling pipsqueak who appeals to a womanliness in the mate he has taunted as refuse. Beseeching her as "Mary", he pleads for an intimacy long destroyed. In his desperation he falls back on the appeasing gesture—"to rouse her sympathy, he would have laid his hand on her". But she has taken the dog as companion by default, and now the dog attacks the man who withdrew his companionship. Squeaker has forfeited the rights belonging to mateship between man and woman. He has robbed his mate of her role in a way the tree could not, but together the man and the tree have compromised her independence and reduced her spirited integrity to that of the "wounded, robbed tigress" who attacks to punish.

"Squeaker's Mate" is an angry story of a woman who will not accept defeat. Its emotional contours surely found their genesis in Baynton's life with Alexander Frater among the selectors of the Coonamble district. Being displaced as wife by another woman in the same household, particularly by a servant, would have been mortifying, whatever contempt Barbara may have felt for Frater. Like the mate, she refused to turn her face to the wall and conveniently die. Fury maintained self-esteem. Barbara Frater left the demeaning bush life and took her children to Sydney. As Barbara Baynton, she could extract through her fiction the revenge of the tigress.

Barbara Baynton certainly took her revenge on the bush. Never for a moment in ***Bush Studies*** does it seem a genuinely desirable home for a woman. Everywhere the experience of the housekeeper in **"Billy Skywonkie"** is underlined:

> A giddy unreality took the sting from everything, even from her desire to beseech him to turn back to the siding, and leave her there to

wait for the train to take her back to civilization. She felt she had lost her mental balance. Little matters became distorted, and the greater shrivelled.

Bush life threatens to overwhelm the self. Barbara Baynton's problem as a writer was an inability to push beyond this insight. She needed pain to impel her imagination. Without pain, she seems to lose focus, as she does in most of *Human Toll,* or to write sentimentally, as she does in most poems and the later stories. In **"Trooper Jim Tasman"**, for example, the cause of neither soldier nor mother is well served when the narrator intones piously:

> I saw those silent bush women. Early pioneers, who had left father and mother, and sister and brother and friends, to face the great unknown as mate to their man, and of silent courage had bred those Anzac heroes.

The tough-minded prose of **"Squeaker's Mate"** has vanished. Without pain, and pain personally felt while objectively rendered, both truth and imaginative vividness are lost. Security and an easeful existence served the *grande dame* well, but not her fiction.

Susan Sheridan   (essay date 1989)

SOURCE: "Gender and Genre in Barbara Baynton's *Human Toll,*" in *Australian Literary Studies,* Vol. 14, No. 1, May, 1989, pp. 66-77.

[*In the following essay, Sheridan discusses* Human Toll *in the context of nineteenth-century women's fiction and in the tradition of realistic narrative.*]

It is not surprising that **Human Toll,** which was recently reprinted for the first time since its original publication in 1907, should have received little critical commentary; but what there does exist by way of comment is remarkably homogeneous. Beginning with A. G. Stephens' review in the *Bulletin,* and continuing through H. M. Green in 1930, Arthur Phillips in 1961, up to the editors of the 1980 reprint, there is clear agreement that Barbara Baynton's one and only novel, while it manifests the same grim vision of malevolence and victimisation as her **Bush Studies,** is severely flawed by her poor management of structure. One obvious conclusion to be drawn from this unanimous judgement of the novel's failure is that Baynton's *forte* was the short story after all. Thus Sally Krimmer and Alan Lawson, editors of the Portable Australian Authors **Barbara Baynton,** rescue the novel by granting it the virtues of Baynton's short stories—vivid scenes of rural town life and, in the final chapter, intense psychological conflict. Yet to conclude thus is to leave unquestioned notions of the well-made realist novel against which **Human Toll** has been measured and found wanting. Questions of narrative strategy, then, form one branch of my subject in this discussion.

The other branch concerns women writers and the ways in which they are read. It originates in the common assumption among critics that **Human Toll** is disguised autobiography. Krimmer and Lawson find the novel interesting, despite its many digressions, in that 'Baynton is

clearly writing from personal experience, but how much of it is autobiographical is difficult to determine'. In this, they echo A. G. Stephens: '**Human Toll** bears the impress of an autobiography loosely held together by a plot of hidden treasure that is lost sight of long before the end of the book'. Certainly it has autobiographical elements—the central character is a young girl growing up in the bush, who occasionally expresses the desire to become a writer or an actress, and other characters may be loosely linked with people from Baynton's youth. But the assumption that it is autobiographical deflects attention from the novel's textuality—as if the assertion that it was all 'true' and that writing it was a necessary catharsis could account for its strangely-wrought prose and obscure dynamics of desire. Moreover, the novel lacks the usual characteristics of autobiographical fiction. The narrative point of view does not stay consistently with the heroine, nor does it grant the reader privileged access to her consciousness, except in the final chapter. What we are faced with here is the patriarchal assumption that when a woman writes—and particularly when she writes in an unfamiliar and difficult manner—she is artlessly unburdening herself of her own experiences. It is an assumption made more attractive, perhaps, in cases when the writer's life is thought to have been more interesting than the sensationalist or domesticated romance plots often favoured by women novelists. Yet an acquaintance with the substantial body of nineteenth-century 'women's fiction' suggests that **Human Toll** can profitably be read as a contribution to that tradition, and a subversion of certain elements in it.

Nineteenth-century 'women's fiction' (which was not exclusively produced by women, nor exclusively read by them) has at its centre the pattern of a young woman's growth to adult femininity. Sometimes this includes an ambitiously female version of the *Bildungsroman,* the novel of formation, within an elaboration of social rites of passage, courtship and marriage. According to Ellen Moers [in *Literary Women,* 1977], the major conventions of this tradition are an orphaned (or at least motherless) girl, whose guardians are socially unsuitable or cruel persecutors, or both, who suffers in extreme forms the usual experiences of initiation into femininity: masculine cruelty and feminine malice, restraints on her freedom (including physical ones), mysterious and unexplained social rituals, the terrible need always to appear, as well as to be, virtuous, and the danger of slipping from the respectable to the unrespectable class of womanhood. There are usually two suitors, one true and one false; there is often a bad or mad woman who functions as the heroine's double; and there is frequently, as the means of securing her freedom to choose the true lover as her husband, an inheritance, which has been lost or kept from her.

'Reader, I married him' is the outcome, conventional in both senses: *Jane Eyre* is perhaps the prototype of this tradition. But its conventions are found early and late, in the Gothic form of Mrs Radcliffe's *The Mysteries of Udolpho* as well as in staid domestic romances. Nina Baym has studied the rise and fall of popularity of these domestic romances in the United States during the nineteenth century as a barometer of changes in the social definitions of femininity and argues that many of these novels are protofeminist in that their heroines are granted moral independence, at least. Baynton's Australian predecessors, including Catherine Spence and Ada Cambridge, wrote variations on the domestic romance which range from the novel of ideas to the comedy of manners. Feminist critics Sandra Gilbert and Susan Gubar have discerned behind many of the conventional romantic narratives in this tradition 'another plot, hitherto submerged in the anonymity of the background', which tells the story of the woman writer's struggle for self-definition, and which involves the heroine's close and ambiguous relationship with the figure invoked in their title, *The Madwoman in the Attic*. For them, too, *Jane Eyre* is the prototype. Yet there is a sub-group of women's novels in which the outcome for the heroine herself is madness or death. Often this is the heroine who harbours ambitious wishes more conventionally appropriate to the male protagonist of a *Bildungsroman* (Maggie Tulliver in *The Mill on the Floss*) or strong aggressive and erotic passions that break through the bounds of the courtship-and-marriage plot (Catherine in *Wuthering Heights*). This tragic (sometimes Gothic) version of the woman's novel can be distinguished from both the heroic novel of development and from the staid or comic domestic romance. I want to argue here that *Human Toll* is confusing (but not confused) because it mixes these modes. It directly confronts the conventions of the heroic women's novel by invoking them and then blocking their operation. The dominant mode, finally, is the Gothic/tragic.

Keeping in mind the major conventions of the woman's novel, let's look at the events and relationships that are set in action in *Human Toll.* The novel opens with the death of the heroine's father on a poor selection. Boshy, an old lag who has been employed there, wants to take care of the four year old orphan, but she is whisked away by the neighbour, Cameron, to be 'schooled' in town, along with his own son, Andrew, under the guardianship of his widowed sister. Chapters 3 to 9 see the child, Ursula, through various childhood experiences, mostly unpleasant. The widow has remarried and her parson husband, Mr Civil, plays the part of persecuting stepfather to Ursula and Andrew. After a period of absence at school (arranged by Boshy) Ursula is called back to town, to Mrs Civil's deathbed. Now, in adulthood, she and Andrew are estranged. Boshy returns, and she nurses him in *his* terminal illness. He has talked a lot about leaving Ursula his money, but dies without telling her where it is hidden. Again she is persecuted by Civil, who has declared himself her guardian. Andrew appears to be caught up with a girl from a nearby farm, Mina Stein. Ursula appeals for help to Hugh Palmer, Cameron's widowed son-in-law, who is fascinated by her but is actually, it appears, having an affair with Mina. Mina tricks Andrew into marrying her, is thrown out of home, and goes to live, with Ursula accompanying her, in the selector's hut which is now part of Cameron's property (though legally, perhaps, it belongs to Ursula). Andrew and Palmer both work there, and visit the hut now and then. An indeterminate period of time passes. Mina gives birth to a child, which she abuses. Ursula, who adores it, finally runs out into the scrub with it, to save it from Mina, but it dies. She wanders about with the dead child in her arms for several days, lost in the scrub. She suffers terribly from thirst and hallucinates a vision of

Christ hanging on a tree. Spurred on by the desire to succour Him, she finds water at last. Then she sees two figures, which seem to be part of the hallucinated crucifixion scene, but the last word of the novel is her childish cry of recognition, 'Andree!'.

The tragic or at least ambiguous redemptive ending (comparable to Olive Schreiner's *The Story of an African Farm*) follows from the ways in which Baynton has subverted the tradition's usual representation of male power and female struggle. Usually (taking *Jane Eyre* as prototype) the heroine develops, through experiences of rebellion against and reconciliation to patriarchial power, her own 'moral sense' and this, together with the freedom granted by the acquisition of material or social resources (e.g. being 'adopted' by a respectable family), enables her to choose the man who is loving, reliable, and socially appropriate for her to marry. In **Human Toll** this process is blocked at several points.

None of the adults in Ursula's and Andrew's world is reliable. Though Jim and Fanny, the servants, are kind to them, they are powerless to defend the children against Mr Civil. Similarly Boshy, and later the Aboriginal couple on the selection, are powerless in the social world of the novel—moreover their protectiveness (e.g. withholding information from Ursula) is actually harmful. All the father-substitutes, even Boshy, and her brother-figure in Andrew, fail to support Ursula; she is confined in her isolation. While it is quite usual for all the adult women in these novels to be represented as venal, malicious or frivolous, it is rare for there to be no protective male figures— even in *The Story of an African Farm* there is the old German uncle. It would seem that, with the death of her father, the possibility of a benevolent paternal god disappears.

Ursula is particularly isolated, passive and silent. Two incidents in her girlhood are marked as decisive. On her first Sunday in town the little girl learns a sense of her own wickedness together with a fear of certain punishment, and she ends the fateful day hiding in the brick oven in terror of God's wrath in the form of a thunderstorm. 'Since the Sunday of the storm', we are told in a rare explanatory comment from the narrator, 'she had met all dangers silently'. Later, when Ashton's circus visits the town, she loses her heart to 'these light-hearted folk of the tinsel and spangles' and 'that great world beyond these hills and near the sea' where they belong. Her small attachments to people and places are loosened as she grows older.

Her strongest relation to others is a protective one. For instance, having identified Aunt Civil as the heroine of *Maria Monk*, a cautionary tale, she resolves to 'guard' her from danger, and this prefigures Ursula's relationship to Boshy, to Andrew, and to Mina's baby. (Also, it is reminiscent of the faithful dogs in the **Bush Studies** stories.) There is a strong element of rivalry in her relation to Mina, most dramatically demonstrated in the Hardyesque incident of the pig's blood. Later this rivalry over Andrew is suppressed in a complex of Christian submission and silent vigilance (also rather dog-like) which, of course, is met by escalating victimisation from the sadistic Mina.

This relationship between the two young women conforms to the heroine-and-her-double type: they are opposites, yet their fates are inextricably bound together. Whatever virtue Ursula represents is sheer negativity, the failure or refusal to act, and so in contrast to this, Mina's predatory sexuality, cruelty, sloth, drunkenness and so on seem to represent Ursula, inside out. Her anger, for instance: 'Looking at Ursula's terrible little face, Hugh Palmer thought there was little to choose between the suppressed tempest of Ursie's now and Mina's unsuppressed passion earlier'. Just as Mina could be said to enact all Ursula's suppressed passions of anger and desire, so Ursula takes on the role of conscience, or watchdog over Mina, when she realises that Mina is 'muckin' around with Boss Palmer'. 'I will never leave you out of my sight, day and night', she storms, 'You are Andrew's wife, Mina; remember, Mina, you are Andrew's wife!' The narrator comments laconically: 'This was the beginning of an espionage of Ursula that bespoke the mettle of martyrdom'.

It is a strange martyrdom, though, as she continues to suffer shame and guilt over her unacknowledged passion for Andrew, as if Mina's sins had been her own. Ursula identifies with Mary Magdalene, that 'picturesque sinner' who 'had waited through the long night, then "very early while yet it was dark" had come: He, though knowing, was gone'. The reference recurs at the height of Ursula's literal martyrdom at the end of the novel: Magdalene is cast as the woman abandoned by Christ, the faithful keeper of the vigil by His body. Unlike the great majority of nineteenth-century heroines, Ursula is not only powerless and oppressed but also passive and purposeless—unless her purpose be the suppression of her love. The suppression of desire and the guilt which accompanies it, renders her mute and incapable of decision. Her actions are frequently described, as the narrative draws to its climax, as those of an automaton: 'spurred by an indefinable impulse', 'the mist of her ever-recurring sub-consciousness', 'spellbound with a compelling sense of waiting', 'an uncontrollable impulse mastered her'. 'Moral sense' fades before the power of the 'sub-conscious', and the discourse of psychology takes over from that of ethics.

Even more striking than her variations on the established theme of the young woman's moral development is Baynton's treatment of the inheritance motif. There are several strands to this. First, there is the inheritance from her father, which Boshy fears she will be denied, either because she is a girl or because her parents may not have been married; other characters deny that such an inheritance exists; when Ursula finally receives a copy of her father's will, Mina steals it before she has read it. The heroine shows no interest in it whatsoever. Baynton thwarts our readerly expectations of the heroine's triumphant reinstatement in respectability and (some) independence. Then there is the matter of the hidden treasure, the 'plot' that seems to lose its relevance to the narrative. It is elaborately introduced in the opening scene of the novel, when Boshy discovers a hoard which readers of **Bush Studies** will recognise. The 'gold-lined belt' which he drags out of the fat-can (a wonderfully anal image) is certainly 'Mr Baldy's hoard', the object of 'Scrammy 'And's' attention in the story of that name. In the tale, the hidden hoard is not found, the

threatened murder not committed, despite all the suspense engendered by both possibilities. In the novel, its function is not (as we might expect) suspense, but rather as a bargaining position. Boshy drops hints about it to gain himself credit of more and less tangible kinds in town; after his death, when Ursula is supposed to have inherited it, or at least to know its whereabouts, everyone is greatly interested in her, and her persecutors Civil and Mina redouble their attacks; finally it is discovered and stolen from the grave where Boshy buried it, presumably by Mina. So, again, Baynton plays with the expectations set up by what looks like a familiar plot. It is not so much that the hidden treasure plot becomes irrelevant, as that its significance shifts. The hidden treasure becomes synonymous in the public eye with Ursula's value as a marriageable woman—but it remains hidden from her, and she is indifferent to it.

The likelihood that she will be made to suffer for this indifference, or carelessness of her 'value' as an object of exchange, is prefigured in Chapter 1, in the ballad of the 'Three Golden Balls' taught to the child by Boshy. In the ballad, the daughter who loses the golden ball given by her father must be hung, unless the ball can be found. She asks each relation and friend in town, but none can help. They have only come to see her hung 'upon this iron gallows tree'. At last, however, comes the 'one true lover' who can give her back her golden ball and save her life from her father's wrath. The patriarchal transaction around female value/virtue is crudely clear. But Ursula does not ask for masculine protection, and none is offered her. The ballad's implications for the novel's ambiguous last-minute rescue scene at the 'crucifixion tree' are interesting, too, in that Ursula the martyr is associated with the Christ figure as well as with Magdalene. This is certainly a subversion of conventional representations of women.

The heroine's indifference to her possible material inheritance, which would enable her to function as an object of exchange in the patriarchal economy of marriage, seems almost sublime. It is no accident that her story ends on this sacrificial note. Her martyrdom is directly associated with the repression of her erotic longings and not with her egotistic and ambitious wishes. These, the expressed desires to write or to act, are precisely what Ursula gives up when, 'following some indefinable impulse', she accompanies Mina to the selector's hut in pursuit of Andrew and Palmer:

> 'Good God! What is life here!' she groaned, and covered her eyes. Unrestrained mentally she faced reality—instead of world wide fame—'Mina's Keeper', 'detecter', visualising the attitude of intense hatred of the sometimes thwarted and baffled Mina. [sic]

She is most of the time paralysed and mute, trapped in this conflict. It is only in a state of terror and madness that her desires and fears can be represented in the narrative. In the final chapter, as she wanders crazed with thirst, grief and exhaustion, she becomes haunted by a sense of her own 'lawlessness' and, 'because of her strenuous repression, Andrew was multiplied' among the images of people crowding her mind. Yet Nancy Miller's reading of the 'plots and plausibilities' of women's fiction [in her 'Emphasis Added: Plots and Plausibilities in Women's Fiction', in *The New Feminist Criticism*, edited by Elaine Showalter, 1985] leads her to suggest (*pace* Freud) that 'egoistic and ambitious wishes' are also repressed along with 'erotic longings' in young women, and that these wishes are figured in the sufferings of the victimised heroine which mark her ultimate superiority to her victimisers and take her beyond love and 'erotic longings'. It is this kind of martyred exaltation that marks Ursula's final trial and spiritual union with the composite figure of Christ/Andrew. *Human Toll* belongs to the melodramatic/tragic version of the 'women's fiction' plot.

I have been concerned so far to show that when *Human Toll* is situated in relation to the major nineteenth-century tradition of women's fiction it makes much more sense as an extended narrative structure. I hope that, in doing this, I have not re-familiarised Baynton's text. I would not want to deny that it is very peculiar, but rather to suggest some ways in which its peculiarities may be read as narrative strategies in accord with and in subversion of the genre of the 'women's novel', rather than the incompetence of that chimera, the 'born short story writer'. The qualities which I want to discuss now, however, can also be found in *Bush Studies.* They are to be found at the points where the writing draws attention to itself, to its own textuality, frustrating expectations that writing should provide a transparent window onto an unproblematic, already-constructed reality.

Baynton is usually read as a realistic writer, but one who offends by drifting out of control into melodrama and sentimentality or who distracts from the Gothic mode by being too satirical. As Rosemary Moore has pointed out [in " 'Squeaker's Mate": A Bushwoman's Tale', *Australian Feminist Studies,* Summer 1986], to read Baynton as a realist is to be faced with the problem of morally justifying her negative vision of men's inhumanity to women: 'Readers have comforted themselves by constructing the "maternal instinct" in Baynton's stories as providing the necessary "human value" ', affirming the continuity of life despite the death of female figures. Kay Schaffer goes on [in her *Women and the Bush: Forces of Desire in the Australian Cultural Tradition,* 1988] to read the contradictory constructions of femininity in Baynton's ironic texts as the mark of her dissidence from the Australian bush legend. The days of reading these texts in terms of realism and unified moral vision are surely numbered. In the discussion which follows I want to focus in particular on the narrative positioning of the reader as the major source of disorientation and dissidence.

Disorientation is the predominant state induced in the reader by Baynton's writing, in the stories as well as the novel. The opening chapter of *Human Toll* is a case in point. Krimmer and Lawson call it 'confusing', and object not only to the introduction of the hidden treasure plot referred to earlier, but also to 'Baynton's attempt to recreate the vernacular of the bush': the reader's difficulty in following dialect speech 'impedes the flow of the action'. These comments demonstrate readerly expectations of classic realist narrative in two respects.

First, the implied criterion is one of narrative *flow* and *accumulation* of significant information; that is, an organicist notion of narrative development, with its latent metaphor of a stream becoming a river in full flood—a notion particularly apt, it might seem, for a novel of development which can be expected to follow the life of the protagonist from childhood through adult crisis to resolution. But I need only recall the opening chapter of *Great Expectations* (Pip's encounter with Magwitch in the graveyard) to suggest the counter-view that not all such novels flow smoothly along without holding their readers up in dialect speech and entangling us in plots that make no promise of unravelling themselves gradually.

Secondly, Baynton's 'attempt to recreate the vernacular of the bush', while it frustrates our eagerness to get on with the story, forces us to notice that the actors in this scene are, in fact, an 'old lag', a very young child and three aborigines, a couple and an old man—not a standard literary pattern of social relationships. What used to be called 'standard English' is noticeably absent, for the authoritative voice of the white Boss is silenced. He lies dead in his hut. On this morning after his death Boshy, the one-eyed ex-convict, quite literally steps into the Boss's boots and attempts to control this remote domain in his place. What follows is a scene of Misrule, a parody of authority. Nungi, the Aboriginal rouseabout, rebels, threatening sabotage and murder:

> 'Urgh!' grunted Nungi, now at a safe distance from whip or even missile. 'Fat lot you can see, old Bungy-Blinkey-eye, ole one-eye! Couldn' see er butterfly nur anythin' else, yur ole blather skyte! 'Oo cares fur you? Nut me!'

> This sudden outburst shocked and surprised Boshy into fatal weakening, and he stood for parley.

> 'N-N-Nungi,' he stammered, 'W'ats come over yer ter go orn like thet? Nungi,' coaxingly, 'look 'ere now, ole man, yer know well w'at I gut ter do ter day. Go orn now an' get ter yer work an' water them yeos an' lambs, like ther w'ite man w'at yer are.'

> 'Not be meself,' said Nungi, but less aggressively, till, turning to take a look at the well, and catching sight of the rising sun, he grew at once savagely and cunningly courageous.

> Boshy's discomfiture increased.

> 'Go on now, Nungi; don't be a slinker on a day like that.'

> 'Nut fer you nur no one like yer, b—old blinky Boshy, ole splay-foot! Lars night I collared a bag er yer wool, an' ter smornin' I'll take it into Tambo, sell it, an git on ther plurry spree, sneak back ter night, plenty matches me,' drawing one from his trouser-pocket and striking it along the bare sole of his foot. 'Budgeree fire that feller, cobbon fire that feller,' pointing to the house 'See ole plurry one-eye Boshy burnin' like blazes! See old splay-foot runnin' 'ell for leather!'

Not unexpectedly, Boshy's appeal to Nungi to co-operate and 'act like the white man what you are' fails. His response to Nungi's insubordination is to threaten Old Jimmy with violence—kicking the one beneath him on the ladder. The verbal battle is then interrupted by one of those precisely worded but strangely hard-to-visualize descriptions often found in a Baynton text: '[Jimmy] slid down from the logs, and burrowing a hip into the ground, resolved into a rapidly-revolving four-spoked wheel, his hands and feet actively protecting his threatened hub'. It is a grotesque image, and a distinctly unfamiliar instance of cause-and-effect in the representation of human behaviour. The narrator's interpolation in this Tower of Babel scene provides no reassurance beyond a calm tone of voice.

All this dialect speech in the first chapter constitutes a denial of direct communication, in several senses. It is a mimetic denial, in that it frustrates at the same time the reader's anticipation of action and the character, Ursula's, desire to know what is going on—for Boshy's talk and singing is intended to distract the child from knowing that her father is dead. It is also, then, a symbolic denial: it confirms Boshy's often-repeated maxim, 'Ask no questions and ye'll be told no lies', advice that she fatefully takes to heart. And Boshy is trapped in his own maxim, in his inability ever to give up his long held secret, that is, his knowledge of the treasure-hoard's whereabouts.

The position of the narrator, here and in most of the first section of the novel, is that of a direct observer and reporter, providing little reassurance and no authoritative explanation of events. In this position, however, there is room for irony: the reader is invited to compare versions, as it were. We are placed somewhere between the child's bewilderment and the maxims, the threats and the mockeries imposed on her by a series of adult figures: Boshy, Cameron, Mr Civil, Jim and Fanny, the shopkeepers, the Chinese gardener. But in the later section of the novel, the return to the Bush when Ursula is an adult, this position changes significantly. Now the narrator's position is close to the heroine, but still observing without explaining. So we, as readers, share the position—it can hardly be called the consciousness—of a passive, almost-silent protagonist, who is opaque to herself. The space where irony could operate is now closed, and what we experience is the anxiety of paranoia. It is a position well described by David Punter in *The Literature of Terror:*

> The reader is placed in a situation of ambiguity with regard to fears within the text, and in which the attribution of persecution remains uncertain and the reader is invited to share in the doubts and uncertainties which pervade the apparent story.

Paranoia is also foregrounded in the text by the proliferation of spies and eavesdroppers. There is Ursula herself in her self-appointed roles as Mina's 'keeper' and the baby's guardian, as well as her several deathbed vigils. In return she suffers Mr Civil watching her like a jailer, Andrew and Boshy benevolently but unsuccessfully protecting her, Mina watching her with the child, Palmer observing her lustfully, and so on.

The position of listening or watching in mute fear or anguish marks almost all the moments of greatest tension and suspense in Baynton's writing. This is a feature which links it closely with the narrative mode of the fantastic as Rosemary Jackson describes it [in her *Fantasy: The Literature of Subversion* 1981]:

> The fantastic exists as the inside, or underside, of realism . . . The fantastic gives utterance to precisely those elements which are known only through their absence within a dominant 'realistic' order . . . [It] introduces areas which can be conceptualised only by negative terms according to the categories of nineteenth century realism: thus, the im-possible, the un-real, the nameless, formless, shapeless, un-known, in-visible.

And, it must be added, in Baynton's text the un-utterable: key scenes are marked by the muteness and paralysis of the protagonists. There is a curious instance of this phenomenon of muteness and paralysis in the farewell scene between Ursula and Andrew outside the selector's hut:

> Would he go in the night, as he did before from Stein's, without a word? Ursula's heart quickened agonizingly, though she lay still, tingling with the thought. Suddenly, an uncontrollable impulse mastered her; she rose and, shrouded with the counterpane, passed barefooted, without sound, into the night.
>
> The moon had almost sunk to a level with the stockyard, where her eyes turned. Standing near the old myall logs, she saw Andrew. He was bare-headed, but otherwise ready for his journey. He stood motionless, though he had seen and known her first, but from his eyes came beams of light as though to guide and draw her to him.
>
> At the head of his shadow she stopped, her eyes fixed on his, and blazing as though fed by the same flame. All about her fell the dazzling moonlight, greedily enveloping her lest his shade, stretching towards her, should dull its gleaming power on her face, throat, and bare feet. Her hands were out-stretched to him, his to her, yet both were motionless, for about them was a stillness, stagnant and omnipotent as death—and it was Death's moment, thought, and desired the girl—when suddenly, from a far point in the river, with the solemnity and clarity of Gabriel's trumpet, came that Bush-call, which few, even of its chosen, are privileged or fated to hear. In a span of sound it floated high over them, mournfully dying as it sank towards the lagoon, miles away in the scrub.
>
> Both had followed the sound with their eyes, but the light had died in Ursula's when they again sought Andrew's, and his shadow had conquered the moonlight. She raised her fallen hand in voiceless farewell, and in the same way his went out to her.

Like the example from chapter one of Jimmy rolling on the ground, it is a detailed description but strangely difficult to imagine. The 'Bush-Call' and other ghostly phenomena such as the sound of the pick and shovel outside Boshy's deathbed are not explained (though in several of her stories Baynton uses the eerie cry of the curlew to signal death). The ordinary senses of sight and sound are inadequate to meet this evocation of the supernatural, the uncanny. The man's figure signifies death (the enveloping shadow) as well as desire—the beams of light suggesting an Annunciation scene. The imagery of death is counterposed with that of desire, in a silent struggle in which death conquers.

There is a strong suggestion that the union of Ursula and Andrew, even if it is only symbolic, is fateful, and fateful because forbidden. The heroine's unexplained and apparently inexplicable guilt in relation to her de facto brother may be read, with the Gothic lens provided by the narrative here, as the guilt of incestuous desire. The elimination of the desire together with the guilt in death ('it was Death's moment, thought, and desired the girl') is the logical end of her muteness and emotional paralysis. This desire for union with the brother in a single self, effecting an imaginary relief of the pain of separation, of sexual differentiation, can often be discerned in women's texts, especially those drawing on the Gothic mode (*Wuthering Heights,* for one).

The Gothic, the fantastic, the literature of terror: all these terms invoke traditions of writing which disappear in the historical amnesia produced by criticism based on the assumption of realism. They are also traditions which have proved hospitable to the imaginations of women writers. Neither the genre nor the gender is readily accorded a place, even now, in the mainstream of Australian literary criticism. The recent spate of reprints of nineteenth-century women's texts and the publication of critical commentaries upon them raises the questions of whether the current task for feminist criticism is to gain mainstream recognition for women writers, or to establish a separate women's tradition, or to divert mainstreams and dismantle canons altogether. As for genre, however, in most of this recent criticism the assumptions of realism remain solidly in place.

Shirley Walker   (essay date 1989)

SOURCE: "Barbara Baynton's *Human Toll:* A Modernist Text?" in *Southerly,* Vol. 49, No. 2, June, 1989, pp. 131-48.

[*In the following essay, Walker focuses on Modernist narrative techniques in* Human Toll.]

Although Barbara Baynton's short stories have attracted considerable critical attention, her novel *Human Toll,* first published in 1907, but largely inaccessible to modern readers until the Krimmer and Lawson *Barbara Baynton* (Portable Australian Authors) in 1980, is usually either disregarded or dismissed as a flawed anti-climax to the controlled savagery of the stories of *Bush Studies.* For instance Sally Krimmer, in her introduction to the 1980 edition, criticises the novel for its discursiveness and lack of a firm plot structure. A. A. Phillips too comments on Baynton's "unsure management of structure" and is also uncomfortable about the melodramatic tendencies in the novel and the overt emotionalism of its final chapter. What the critics do seem to value is the novel's realism. The *Oxford Companion to Australian Literature,* for in-

stance, praises its "grim realism", its authenticity achieved by "the accumulation of detail" and "the accuracy of the idiom her characters use" and there is ample justification for a realistic reading of at least some portions of *Human Toll.* The novel fulfils the expectations of classical realism: it is bleak and pessimistic, it portrays the sordidness of working class life as a realistic novel ought to do, and it certainly gives that impression of verisimilitude which results from the use of realistic visual and social detail and of the vernacular. The geography of the selection Merrigulandri with its key reference points—the homestead, the wim, the hut with its broken roof and the ominous graves beneath the myall trees—is accurately realized, as is the layout of the small town with its flour mill beside the river:

> All week long the puffing and panting throat of the flour-mill belched vapour-columned arches, which, telescoping airily, spanned the river from bank to bank, as if purposefully linking the mill with Fireman Foreman's dwelling on the opposite side . . . But now, in the unillusioned light and broody quiet of a Sabbath morn, the cold, silent mill, shorn of its nebulous halo, looked old and worn—an aged actor off the stage.

Baynton's vivid miniatures, such as that of the "dawn-rising Chinamen" who "shogged with nimble bare feet under their yoke-linked watering-cans" add to the realism:

> These busy brethren, meeting sometimes on the same narrow track, would pause, ant-like, seemingly to dumbly regard one another and their burdens, then, still ant-like, pass silently to their work.

while her rendition of the church service and the dance at Stein's are masterpieces of social reportage. The use of the vernacular, though sometimes laboured, conveys a vivid sense of the idiom of the bush—of "Pat the dry sixpence" and the property "Gi' Away Nothin' 'All"; of a man "too slow to trap maggots" or another, Hugh Palmer, who resembles "the bull on Keen's mustard" and acts like one. Given Baynton's undoubted mastery of the techniques of pictorial and social realism, it is safe to assume that the digressions of the first two chapters and the circumlocution of the final two are less a failure of form on her part, than a deliberate experiment; an attempt in the former to set the scene in symbolic as well as literal terms, and in the latter to capture a different kind of realism, the psychological realism of disintegration.

There are elements too which would favour a naturalistic reading, for instance the deterministic progress to destruction of both Andrew and Ursula; the sense of the meaninglessness of individual effort in a world governed by greed and self-interest; and the depiction of the natural world as predatory. Realistic and naturalistic readings however are partial; they fail to account for the unique qualities of the novel, and even its earliest detractors were aware of, and disturbed by, its uniqueness. Modern readers immediately perceive that *Human Toll* is an exciting and disturbing text; exciting for its range of response to bush experience, for the passion of its presentation, and for the outrage of its tone. It is clearly a dissident text; one which challenges through a woman's experience the whole ethos of the nineties—of mateship, of bush community and of Australian nationalism. *Human Toll* is also an exciting technical experiment. If we view it not as a realistic novel which fails because of a lack of control, but rather as a proto-modernist text where a variety of techniques, many of them far in advance of their time, are employed in order to create a powerful account of the physical and psychic destruction of a young female in an Australian bush town and in the bush itself, then we may come to a clearer appreciation of Baynton's achievement. In these terms, for instance, Baynton's persistent use of the melodramatic is not a return to the tropes of Victorianism, but a means of conveying, by excess, the suffering and despair of her heroine and of condemning the spiritual poverty of bush society. Moreover, the incoherence of events and the impressionism of certain sequences can be seen as a totally appropriate means of portraying the disintegration of personality under extreme stress. It will be shown that this text is a subversive text, both thematically and structurally, in that it consistently utilizes conventional modes, forms and techniques, only to circumvent them in order to demonstrate that disintegration which is its major theme.

In a text of the sort which I'm proposing—that is a proto-modernist text which deals with psychic disintegration—there is no use looking, as the critics have done, for conventional structure. Nevertheless *Human Toll* does have its own structure, and it is one which is wholly appropriate to its overall vision. The first chapter, for instance, with its preoccupation with lost or hidden treasure, not only forms a link with Baynton's previous work (the lost treasure of the story **"Scrammy 'And"**), it introduces the theme of inheritance/disinheritance which is a major structural element in the text. Ursula, an orphan child, will be disinherited of her treasure. The association between treasure and death is also established in this chapter. The dead man's treasure, found, is buried in his grave for later retrieval while the boss dies and leaves his treasure, Ursula, a motherless lamb, to be claimed by false shepherds. This initiates the pastoral metaphor of lost and motherless lambs and false shepherds which is so important throughout the novel. Boshy's dialect, too, is important despite its tediousness. An ex-lag and rouseabout, he is naively ignorant of Ursula's legal position and will be no match for the squatter family, the Camerons, or the semi-educated cleric. This imbalance of power is established early by the use of dialectical difference. Meanwhile the digressions in the first two chapters are thematically and structurally important. The poems and ballads which the child recites in chapter one are all appropriate to the themes of family betrayal and the loss of love. Not only does the ewe refuse to accept her "liddle lamb", but the mangy pup is hung, as is the child in the ballad who loses her golden ball, while her family taunt her and gather round to watch her hang. A young man dies for love of Barbara Allen and, in another ballad, the bird (a cock which crows an hour too early) proves false. This anticipates several ominous crowing cocks later in the text, and the appearance of Mr Civil as a "black bird of ill omen" immediately before the marriage of the false lovers Andrew and Mina.

The impression of betrayal is overwhelming. It sets the scene for the long discussion in chapter two of who is to take the orphaned "liddle lamb" Ursula. The Camerons' claim appears to be more rational than Boshy's, but neither is ideal. Ursula is eventually destroyed almost as much by Boshy's loving impracticality as by the Camerons' greed, and the inevitability of her destruction is suggested early. Meanwhile the slapstick comedy of Baynton's Aborigines, stock figures of fun and ridicule in the first two chapters as they whine for food, flee from Debbil-debbils and speak in a degraded gibberish, though offensive to the modern reader, is redressed in the final chapters where the Aborigines provide Ursula's only support. Nungi is shown to be more upright than the pommy jackeroo Palmer, and Woona, a competent midwife, is more maternal and compassionate than Mina.

The first two chapters then are an indispensable introduction to the text. They are followed by the circular structure of chapters three to thirteen. This involves Ursula's departure from the lonely selection at the end of chapter two and her return to it, defeated, at the end of chapter thirteen, two chapters from the end of the narrative. There is a basic symmetry here as the circular journey is framed, at beginning and end, by two introductory and two concluding chapters. Such framed circularity would normally give a sense of completion, but this is subverted by the uncertainty of the final chapter. Each of the intervening chapters—from three to thirteen—deals with a further aspect of the Ursula's socialization as she develops from child to adult; what might be seen as her progressive initiation into the unfairness and hypocrisy of bush society. These chapters contain some of Baynton's best writing in the realistic mode; they are both comic and wickedly satiric as all the cruelty and hypocrisy of small-town society—especially its religious pretensions—are ruthlessly exposed. The motivating force for Ursula's victimization is invariably that of greed as her inheritance (Merrigulandri, Boshy's treasure and, eventually, Andrew's love, which is shown to be hers by right) attract predatory attention. At the same time her own compassion and sensitivity stamp her as both outsider and victim.

The last two chapters are more than an extraneous addition to the circular movement of chapters three to thirteen. They have their own circularity, as Ursula wanders in circles in the bush, and her mind circles ever in to the centre, the seeming religious experience which heralds either deliverance or madness and death. Ursula is now trapped and the seeming incoherence of the narrative closely mirrors her disintegration. The changing technique of the novel provides a further structural element as the movement from overt realism to impressionism and a narrated stream of consciousness parallels Ursula's inward regression under the stress of cruelty and deprivation. In the long final chapter the structural movement of the novel—into the suffering mind, into the punishing wasteland of the bush—is completed.

Human Toll has a deeper organizing structure, that of the *Bildungsroman*, the pattern, familiar in male novels, of the coming to maturity within a certain culture of a young hero. This structure is based upon the concept of *Bildung*, of the attainment of personal fulfilment within a culture. It involves, according to Annis Pratt [in *Archetypal Patterns in Australian Literature,* 1982], both social and psychological maturation. The hero (the traditional structure is a male one) must not only learn to make moral choices within the framework of his society; he must also realize and exercise his inner powers. The female *Bildungsroman* however is significantly different, for the female hero, according to Pratt, is alienated from the outset from her society. Because society's demands upon the woman are stunting to the self, she inevitably grows *down* rather than *up.* The female hero's development, in Pratt's terms, is less "a self-determined progression *towards* maturity than a regression *from* full participation in adult life". It is, moreover, characterized by imagery of suffocation and enclosure and by a nostalgic longing for the "green world" of nature which, for the female hero, has a special meaning as a "place of epiphany, of solace and renewal". Growing up will involve, for many female heroes, a choice between "secondary personhood" and "sacrificial victimization, madness, and death". Ursula's problems, in her progress to maturity, are as intense and destructive as Pratt suggests, in that she is within a society so mean and hypocritical that there is no question of her coming to terms with it in any way. Her desire to escape that constriction and enclosure which Pratt sees as part of the pattern of female maturation is focused upon a brief experience of Ashton's Circus which then recurs in her thoughts throughout the novel: "Her mighty had flown, but they had taken her heart with them to that great world beyond these hills and near the sea". The ephemeral nature of this longing is one measure of its impossibility. Baynton does gesture towards the goals of *Bildung* in her depiction of Ursula's moral education and her artistic aspirations, yet both gestures are unconvincing. Ursula's moral progress, for instance, consists in her learning not to be cruel, not to pull the legs and wings off insects, yet Baynton has created her so loving and compassionate that this deviation into childish naughtiness seems quite false. Ursula's aspirations for artistic fulfilment are equally unconvincing. Her vague ambition to write a book, for instance, is unjustified by anything else in the text; perhaps the minimilization of this ambition and its formlessness says something about the impossibility of achieving any artistic integrity in the bush. Certainly the achievements of the bush artist, the Fuchsia, the predilection in musical circles for Moody and Sankey's hymns, and the trashy romances which are the staple reading matter for young women in the town, bear this out.

It seems that Baynton's attention is focused upon emotional maturity rather than moral or artistic aspirations. That personal fulfilment within a society which *Bildung* implies can only be achieved in Ursula's case by a development of her feminine power to love, to protect, to sustain; those maternal powers which, according to the critics, are the only affirmative element in Baynton's works. Yet this release is impossible of achievement within the bush society which is obsessed with greed for her inheritance. Moreover, as if to demonstrate the impossibility of the development of Ursula's maternal powers in such a society, the concept of maternity in *Human Toll* is as ambivalent as it is, to my mind, in Baynton's earlier stories. When Sally Krimmer says of *Bush Studies* that "the only posi-

tive value to emerge from the malevolence which pervades the book, lies in the powerful and instinctive response to maternity", she ignores the way in which maternal love, throughout the *Studies,* is compromised. The pregnant woman in **"A Dreamer"**, for instance, risks her life to get to her mother, only to find her dead, and on the way she has been exposed to the destructive power of nature, which is traditionally seen as maternal and sustaining, and almost destroyed by it. The mother in **"The Chosen Vessel"** is powerless, and dies because the male passerby is engrossed in a vision of the Virgin Mary, and the woman in **"Squeaker's Mate"** is able to function as she does at the beginning of the story, that is with equal power to the male, only because she is childless.

There is the same ambivalence about maternity in **Human Toll,** and the novel is full of mothers who are either inept or false and hypocritical. These include Margaret who hands Ursula over to Aunt Maria (Mrs Civil). Aunt Maria—"A childless woman who has been a doll-less child"—is a creature of public hypocrisy and private gluttony (for food and sex). Her marriage to Mr Civil and subsequent death, from either poison or over-indulgence, leaves the girl vulnerable to Civil's sexual advances. Mina's mother is a pragmatist who plots Mina's marriage to the well-off Andrew, then casts her off with a great deal of relief, while Mina herself attempts to suffocate her illegitimate child. Moreover, this ambivalence about maternity is reinforced by a systematic symbolic reference to lost and betrayed young animals and young children. The children in the novel are either conniving and work-worn like "Lizarixon", or else under threat from either human or natural agencies. Ursula (Lovely) is seen early in the book as a "poor liddle motherless, fatherless lamb" and this is universalized by numerous references to lambs deserted by either their keepers or by unnatural ewes. This sense of familial betrayal is reinforced by the ballad, "Three Golden Balls", which Ursula recites to Boshy with relish in chapter one. Three girls are given golden balls by their father on condition that if a ball is lost, its owner is to be hung. The child who has lost her ball and is about to be hung cries out:

> "Oh, 'angman, stop the rope. I think I see me
> dear mother comin—"

The mother's vicious response sets the tone for the treatment of children throughout the text:

> "No, I haven't got yer goldin ball. Nor I haven't
> come t' set yer free. But I 'ave come t' see yer
> 'ung upon this iron gallers tree."

This same response is given by other family members, and the discussion concludes with an attempt by Boshy to define a "terue" lover; a definition which prefigures Andrew's later behaviour: "Terue lover . . . 'e iden a feller wot goes a-smellin' an' a-sniffin' an' a-sneezin' roun' after every rag orn every bush".

Even Ursula's maternal yearnings, though powerful, have dubious results. She inadvertently breaks her doll's leg (Mina also viciously destroys a doll by swinging it around until the sawdust falls out), her pet lamb is killed in excruciating circumstances (crushed to death by Palmer as he exits from Mina's chamber), and her efforts on behalf of Mina's baby are doomed—it probably dies as much from exposure in Ursula's wild rush into the bush to save it as from Mina's efforts to suffocate it.

The young stand little chance in Baynton's world and the father figures are as evil or ineffective as are the mothers. Mr Civil is cruel, grasping and sexually predatory; Andrew is well-meaning but weak and easily trapped; and Boshy, though true, is too unsophisticated to be a match for Ursula's enemies. Perhaps this is why Baynton has created him one-eyed, that is with half the seeing power of those who are ranged against him. Meanwhile so many are motherless, abandoned and disinherited in the text that this becomes a major thematic and symbolic factor in the presentation of the bush society as a loveless waste land which Ursula must negotiate. Within this loveless society Ursula progresses, not to female fulfilment, but through a series of experiences which teach her that her compassion and maternal love simply place her in the power of individuals such as Mr Civil and Mina.

Ursula's education into the society of the bush town takes up the central section of the text, from chapters three to thirteen. In despair after her defeat by this society Ursula, together with Palmer and Mina, retreats to Merrigulandri and, later, to the bush itself, where she tests the reality of Annis Pratt's "green world" of nature under the most extreme conditions. According to Pratt the "green world" of nature has a special meaning for the female hero as a place of naturistic epiphany and refuge; "a place from which she sets forth and a memory to which she returns for renewal":

> In most women's novels the green world is present in retrospect, something left behind or about to be left behind as one backs into the enclosure—a state of innocence that becomes most poignant as one is initiated into experience.

This departure from the "green world" of innocence and initiation into experience is much more intensive for Ursula. It is not simply that the Australian bush is significantly more hostile than the "green world" of Pratt's female heroes; Baynton's ultimate signification for the bush is an existential one: it stands for the meaninglessness of the spiritual cosmos, as well as that of the natural world. Therefore a clear progression—from innocence to knowledge; from the bush as joyous possession and refuge, to the bush as a meaningless space onto which Ursula projects her nightmares—is established.

The little child Lovey sees nature as benign and delights in its fruits and flowers—the five-corners, geebungs, wattle and clematis on Merrigulandri. The bush is a refuge too from cruelty, from the reality of her father's death, from the injustice of the Civil household and, as a young woman, from the sight of Mina with Andrew. However the association of death with nature is established early. The child's last sight of her home is that of myall grove sheltering the graves, and the same sight gives an ominous completion to her return as an adult. The association of nature with death is reinforced by the drowning of the boy Henry in the "snaggy hole"—one of her first experiences in the little bush town—but here her reaction is falsified

by the intense religious indoctrination to which she has been subjected. She now sees nature as in the service of a vengeful God, wreaking a "righteous revenge" for Henry's desecration of the Sabbath. The furious storm which breaks immediately afterwards extends this vengeance to herself and she hides in terror in the brick oven. She ignores the fact that nature itself—as clearly demonstrated by the hornet and the swallow—merrily rejects the Sabbath. The young Ursula persists in projecting a human meaning onto the bush: "the distant rock-garrisoned hills became castles—homes for angels. From their breath, the clouds, she peopled the sky—for to hold her there must be a human strain."

She is morbidly sensitive to the destructive and threatening aspects of nature. The storm and the onset of autumn both have a death-like quality for the child. Meanwhile the geography of the small town and the bush around it is suffused with the religious intensity of her childhood indoctrination:

> In a fertile hollow between river and hills were the remains of an aforetime vine-garden, full of old-world fruit and flowers . . . Near it a forgotten family vault, gaping and mouldering: as if to hide its neglect, a tangle of rank creepers climbed over and above it. This had been her childhood's Garden of Gethsemane, and this the tree beneath which Christ, lonely, had wept. Today, through the fullness of years, she stood possessed with the right time and place, still she hallowed the old memories.

Ursula's long-time habit of humanizing the bush and reading religious significance into it is a dangerous one which divorces her from reality. In the final chapter, lost in the bush with the dead child, Ursula is face to face with the truth of the Australian bush—it is a trackless, featureless and meaningless place. The circularity of her wandering images both the meaninglessness of the bush and the breakdown of her mind, and her attempts to project meaning onto its features is a symptom of her psychological breakdown. Her most significant and central projection—that of the crucified Christ—though justified in the context of hallucination, is a capitulation to religious fantasy, an evasion of truth rather than a confronting of it. Ursula's flight into the bush with the dead baby and her experiencing of a dark night of the soul, or a *rite de passage* in her confrontation with nature, is not a "naturistic epiphany" in Pratt's terms, a confrontation with the deep mythic force of nature, but an experience of terror and martyrdom.

The ending of **Human Toll** has been considered to be indeterminate. Ursula either achieves her *passage* and is reunited with Andrew (now free of Mina) or his appearance is an hallucination, a prelude to her death from thirst. Nothing in the novel has prepared us for a happy ending, and in terms of what has preceded it such a conclusion would be quite false. Meanwhile if Ursula does indeed (with the dead baby) die in the uncaring bush, this completes a deeply pessimistic and indigenous version of the *Bildungsroman*. It also provides yet one more example of an Australian archetype, that of the lost child, in which the usual features—the vain circling about the same spot and the eventual death from thirst with attendant hallucination—are present. However this example stands alone because of its use of the literary techniques of disintegration—impressionism and (narrated) stream of consciousness—and because of its religious sensationalism, which sets it quite apart from the literature of the bush.

Human Toll **is clearly a dissident text; one which challenges through a woman's experience the whole ethos of the 1890s— of mateship, of bush community and of Australian nationalism.**

—*Shirley Walker*

The way in which Baynton uses the pattern of the *Bildungsroman* with devastating unsubtlety in order to completely crush her hero is typical of the genre, the melodramatic, in which she is writing. In this sense the realism of the text is superficial, a matter of visual and social detail, while the aesthetic orientation of plot, characterization and symbolism is wholly melodramatic, as is the moral *schema*—of virtue assailed by the forces of evil— which underlies the plot. The melodramatic is a mode of excess which is appropriate to Baynton's presentation of the excessive suffering of her hero, and should not necessarily be viewed in a denigrating manner. Peter Brooks in *The Melodramatic Imagination,* for instance, sees the melodramatic as a serious and dynamic art-form, which works through flamboyance and hyperbole to project a Manichaean vision of the world as a battlefield, the setting for a cosmic conflict between polarized forces of good and evil. Brooks allows for a mixture of realism and the melodramatic, such as Baynton employs, when he says of certain novelists:

> Within an apparent context of "realism" and the ordinary, they seemed in fact to be staging a heightened and hyperbolic drama, making reference to pure and polar concepts of darkness and light, salvation and damnation.

Because of its concern with moral absolutes the melodramatic excludes the middle ground of inner conflict or psychological complexity. In fact the melodramatic hero, in contrast to the hero of tragedy, exists in a state of "monopathic" wholeness, "undivided, free from the agony of choosing between conflicting imperatives and desires. He greets every situation with an unwavering single impulse which absorbs his whole personality." Because the melodramatic mode exteriorizes conflict the forces with which the hero has to contend are invariably external rather than internal. According to James L. Smith [in his *Melodrama,* 1973] "it is this total dependence upon external adversaries which finally separates melodrama from all other serious dramatic forms". The perennial popularity of the melodramatic can be explained not only by our vicarious enjoyment of its emotional indulgence but also, in psychological terms, by "our need for fully externalized, personalized and enacted conflict, and for its clarifying resolution". This too explains that affinity which Brooks has proposed between the melodramatic and psychoanalysis. Each is concerned with expressing the repressed; with the bringing up out of the unconscious of primal or archetypal personifications and conflicts and their subsequent projection, clarification and resolution. Brooks suggests too an affinity between the melodramatic and the rhetoric of dreams or nightmares and, more importantly, recognizes the melodramatic mode as "a central fact of the modern sensibility" in that it is "constructed on, and over, the void" vacated by conventional theology, and yet insists that "behind reality, hidden by it yet indicated within it, there is a realm where large moral forces are operative, where large choices of ways of being must be made". Such a discussion is obviously of relevance to *Human Toll* and Baynton's use of the melodramatic mode, with all its artificiality and excess, is highly consistent with her outrage at the moral blindness, grotesquerie and evil to be found in the society of the bush. It is appropriate, then, to re-examine the text in terms of the melodramatic, with its projection of the conflict between moral absolutes, its personifications of virtue and evil, and its stylistic features of "monopathia" and of hyperbole.

The plot line of *Human Toll* is consistently melodramatic, being concerned with an orphan child, wicked stepparents, a lost treasure hidden in a grave, a will concealed from the rightful heir, and true love thwarted by wickedness. Its presentation is interspersed with red-hot speeches, dramatic gestures and expressions of despair, the true material of melodrama. Many of the characters too are "monopathic", that is they are the embodiment of moral absolutes and are defined as such by clearly visible characteristics. Mina's wickedness, for instance, is absolute, and is demonstrated constantly in her flashing green eyes and saw-like teeth, her freckled scaly hands, her hairy arms and (a surprising indication of Baynton's prejudice) her big womb! The symbolism too, though remarkably consistent, is excessive and extravagant. Though the pastoral imagery is based upon the actual, the life of the sheep-station Merrigulandri, and its further biblical reference to bad shepherds and lost sheep is justified by Ursula's orphanhood and the religious pretensions of those who look after her, the repetition of images of lost, abandoned, bleeding and dead lambs is extravagant. So too is the overwrought parallelism concerning injured dolls and dead children, little mothers and adult mothers deprived of dolls and babies respectively, a drowned boy and a strangled baby, and the parallel and horrible deaths of Ursula's two surrogate children, the pet lamb and Mina's baby. Such imagery can only be justified in terms of a melodramatic vision of the vulnerability of the young innocent in what Baynton sees as the extreme conditions of bush society. This becomes more complex in scenes such as that where Ursula, having suffered a slight rebuff from Andrew, stirs the pig's blood for Mrs Stein and, "a willing sacrifice", inhales the "steaming odour" of blood until "blindly lurching forward, with an inward heave, she plunged both hands into the warm blood". Here and in a later scene with Andrew, when this experience recurs to her, starved sexuality and frustrated maternity become confused with religious mysticism and the mode becomes that of religious melodrama, with its connotations of blood-sacrifice and martyrdom. Here it becomes clear that Ursula's name—that of St. Ursula, patron saint of virgins, martyred by the Huns—is well chosen in terms of her involuntary virginity, of her morbid impulse towards self-sacrifice, and her victimization by the barbarians of the bush community.

Much of the sensationalism of the text derives from its melodramatic treatment of religion. On one level the practice of religion in the bush town is dealt with realistically, and is the object of cutting satire. This is directed not only at the hypocrisy of religious observance, the contrast between the profession of Christianity and the cold repressive morality of its practitioners, such as Aunt Maria and Mr Civil, but also at the bitter sectarianism, between Protestant and Catholic, which divides the small town. The opportunism of both preachers in the small bush church is satirized with a great deal of humour. The relieving preacher not only fails to observe the convention of praising the incumbent, he uses the sermon to purvey his quack cures. Meanwhile the incumbent, Mr Civil, greedily eyes off the rich widow, who is herself a model of self-indulgent hypocrisy, while both of them attempt to prey on Ursula financially, and eventually Mr Civil attempts her sexual conquest. It is little wonder then that Ursula actively rejects the patriarchal religion of the strict Wesleyan church, but is drawn to the religion of a suffering Christ, and to the fascination with cruelty and death which has dominated the imagery of the novel. In this she is greatly influenced by the religious reading of her childhood and by the symbolism of Christianity, both of which she interprets in sensational terms.

The reading matter in her aunt's household is of a predictable nature: Shakespeare's works, *Pilgrim's Progress,* a *History of Jerusalem*—all three of which Ursula rejects—and the *Awful Disclosures of Maria Monk,* a small volume published [anonymously] in Philadelphia in 1836, which had a great vogue in bigoted Protestant families of the nineteenth century and which Ursula finds completely absorbing:

> *Maria Monk.* Maria! Her aunt's name was Maria, and even the preface of this wieldy little book owned that Maria was a girl. Lying on the sloping river-bank, hidden from the household, she spent hours daily absorbing the, to her, absorbable in Maria's ugly story. Summing up her facts and fancies finally, she was convinced that her aunt had been poor Maria, and earnestly she hoped that those in search of her very visible and incautious aunt would never succeed in kidnapping her. Lest they should, from that moment she constituted herself her aunt's body-guard, and she went home instantly to duty. She found her in the dining-room with Ann Foster, the little dressmaker.

Apart from the impropriety of allowing a small girl access to such a salacious book, there is a delightful irony here. The *Awful Disclosures of Maria Monk* ("as exhibited in a narrative of her sufferings during her residence of five years as a novice, and two years as a black nun, in the *hotel du nunnery* in Montreal") is an account of the systematic rape and torture of young novices in a Montreal convent by scheming priests, all in the guise of religious practice; the babies born in the convent being strangled and thrown into a well. Maria Monk eventually escapes but hides for the remainder of her life, for if found she would be killed. Aunt Maria's situation is significantly different; she actively seeks the embraces of the scheming priest, Mr Civil, under the guise of religious observance, and her appointment with the dressmaker is for the purpose of sewing her trousseau, a fact of which Ursula is blissfully aware. *Maria Monk* is shown to have had a significant influence on Ursula's developing mind, for she returns to it often during the course of the narrative and consistently views life in the same melodramatic terms of victimization and suffering. It also seems to have significantly influenced Barbara Baynton who would almost certainly have known it well. Elements from *Maria Monk,* such as debauched priests and illegitimate and murdered babies, have their parallel in the plot-line of **Human Toll,** while the tone of outrage and hysteria which informs **Human Toll,** particularly in the final chapters, is close to that of *Maria Monk.* Both texts share a sensational and melodramatic view of a world of rapacious men, martyred virgins and unwanted and strangled babies.

Whatever the conclusion of **Human Toll,** whether defeat by the bush or rescue by Andrew, Baynton remains consistently within the melodramatic mode, yet expands its possibilities in order to allow for that psychological disintegration which is her major concern, and which is communicated by the literary techniques of modernism. The allowance to the reader of a choice of alternative endings is curiously modern, yet either closure—triumph or defeat—is valid within the melodramatic mode, for [according to Smith] triumph and defeat are "simply alternative formulations of the same conflict, opposite extremes of the same melodramatic spectrum". The essence of melodrama is not necessarily the triumph of virtue but a catharsis which is achieved by working the basic emotions of melodrama—triumph, despair and protest—to the highest pitch, and this Baynton certainly does. If my conjecture is correct—that the finding of the lagoon, of Mina's body, and the rescue, are meant to be read as hallucinatory—then Baynton's choice of melodramatic defeat is consistent with the wasteland themes and the concentration upon self-sacrifice and death which have been so pervasive throughout the text. Meanwhile Baynton is at her most experimental in the last two chapters, where she moves to a degree of inner conflict which is usually incompatible with the melodramatic.

The shift from outer to inner which is a major feature of modernism is attempted by Baynton with varying degrees of success, mainly because it is so difficult for her to detach herself from the rhetoric of melodrama which has, so far, dominated the text. Thus in the penultimate chapter, which is largely concerned with the tensions of jealousy and distrust between the three characters left on Merrigulandri—Ursula, Palmer and Mina—there is some strain. Communication between the three is still conveyed through melodramatic gesture and speech:

> "Don't come a-nigh me, Ursie! If you're bit, there's no cure for snake-bite!" "I will—I will!" stormed Ursula. "I will never leave you out of

my sight, day and night. You are Andrew's wife, Mina; remember, Mina you're Andrew's wife!"

At the same time the groundwork for Ursula's disintegration is carefully laid through effects which convey the dislocation of her sensory perception—"She saw him tower, then shrink"—and in Lawrentian moments which, in overwrought symbolic terms, emphasize her morbid commitment to death.

> At the head of his shadow she stopped, her eyes fixed on his, and blazing as though fed by the same flame. All about her fell the dazzling moonlight, greedily enveloping her lest his shade, stretching towards her, should dull its gleaming power on her face, throat, and bare feet . . . yet both were motionless, for about them was a stillness, stagnant and omnipotent as death—and it was Death's moment, thought, and desired the girl.

At the same time Ursula is unable to absorb the significance of objective facts, such as the disturbed grave and the receipt of her father's will in the mail, which are perfectly obvious to the reader. The narrative moves increasingly into her consciousness as she retreats into an obsessive concern with the war between virtue and what she sees as the moral outrage (the adultery between Mina and Hugh Palmer) taking place within the bush homestead.

In the final movement into the bush in the concluding chapter, when Baynton is unimpeded by the demands of personal relationships or of complexity of plot and is able to concentrate exclusively on inner disintegration, her experimental techniques are much more successful. One such technique is the use of impressionism, where the progression of discrete impressions before the mind of the reader suggests the detachment of Ursula's consciousness from any idea of chronology or of relationship between events. The other is the circuitousness of Ursula's wanderings which pattern the increasing solipsism of her thoughts as they become detached from outer reality and move inexorably into madness and obsession. Her refusal to believe that the baby is dead, her obsessive burying and excavation of its body, her projection of the Christ figure, her fight with the vines which she mistakes for burning snakes (symbolising both evil and her repressed sexuality) and her mistaking of the "gohanna" for Satan, are all evidence of mental disintegration as well as a projection of the "moral occult" which is the main concern of the melodramatic mode. Here we enter the realm of dream and nightmare where primal forces and their archetypal personifications—the Christ and the gohanna—are drawn from the subconscious and projected in dramatic form (the aesthetic affinity between nightmare and the melodramatic mode has already been noted). Meanwhile the use of an insistent, repetitious and often hysterical voice, a narrated stream of consciousness, dramatizes the obsessive nature of Ursula's mental breakdown as traumatic events from her childhood—her cruelty to the hornet, the drowned boy, religious guilt—recur to her and direct her current interpretation of events. Such hysteria and excessive mental suffering are compatible with both the melodramatic mode and psychological realism, but the degree of mental conflict and the techniques which Baynton uses

to convey it take the text beyond the "monopathic" characterization of melodrama, and beyond the simplistic moral *schema* of that genre, into a province which is unmistakenly that of modernism.

The text is modernist too in its use of wasteland themes. There is no incompatibility between these themes and the melodramatic for, according to Brooks, melodrama "marks the final liquidation of the traditional Sacred" and "comes into being in a world where the traditional imperatives of truth and ethics are questioned", and this is certainly the case in *Human Toll.* Baynton's themes are those of the twentieth century; of a secular world deprived of love, of the failure of spirituality and the rejection of all traditional sources of spiritual comfort. In this sense the theme of maternity denied is all-important, for the bush township has cut itself off from all values except materialism and has perverted its religious heritage. The move to the bush itself, the natural world which Eliot was later to use to signify his existential wasteland, is significant too. The arid yet overgrown bush provides Baynton with waste-land imagery of drought and thirst, of burning sand instead of life-giving water, and of an overgrowth of foliage which threatens, impedes and "shuts out heaven" when it should nurture and protect. Meanwhile the tracklessness of the bush images its existential meaninglessness as well as the inner circling of the solipsistic consciousness which seeks spiritual refuge there and finds none. It is this search for a spirituality which has disappeared from the land—projected in Ursula's vision of the blind and crucified Christ upon the gum-tree—which confirms the orientation of *Human Toll* towards the twentieth rather than the nineteenth century.

The theme of disinheritance is important too in respect of the text itself. *Human Toll* may be seen as a disinherited text in that it rejects and deconstructs both the dominant literary traditions which precede it—that of bush nationalism and that of domestic romance. In its challenging of bush traditions, its use of a female figure to embody the suffering of women and children in the bush, and its total condemnation of organized religion, *Human Toll* challenges the whole bush tradition of the 'nineties with its easy optimism and confidence about the Australian character. Baynton's bush is a mean and violent place, of ex-lags, illiterate rouse-abouts, of Chinese and Aborigines, of grasping Germans, penny-pinching Scots and a drunken English jackeroo (probably a remittance man) who, in the midst of Ursula's torment, persists with Shakespearean comparisons as if to demonstrate the total irrelevance of an English literary tradition to the reality of the bush. Moreover the novel is as clearly disinherited from the other dominant literary tradition of the time; that of female romance. The plot certainly nurtures the expectations of the romance tradition. For instance Andrew is designed by Baynton as the perfect match for Ursula: and a marriage between them would neatly solve Ursula's legal as well as her emotional problems. Andrew is, for Ursula, her true inheritance in terms of the romance tradition; but the expectations of that tradition are subverted, not only by Andrew's defection, but by the careful rejection, within the text, of the artificiality of the "lovely Muriels, Daphnes, and Gladys, with their titled, but snubbed suitors" who inhabit the pages of romance: "Ursie closed the book. The contrast was too cruel, the matter hopeless." The text, it seems to me, takes up these traditions yet subverts them, for Baynton's concern is clearly with those larger moral issues which, for her, underlie the reality of bush life and which she dramatizes in the extravagant terms of the melodramatic. The true provenance of **Human Toll** is the world of melodrama (a comparison with popular stage melodramas of the time would probably be a fruitful one); its impulse is towards the definition of a world of moral absolutes which stands against and condemns Australian society; and many of its techniques are those which, in the twentieth century, are used by modernists to define the drift towards spiritual chaos and disintegration. This spiritual disintegration might well be seen to be the ultimate consequence of the Australian society which Baynton depicts.

The mixture of modes and techniques and the excessive experimentation of **Human Toll** possibly detract from its success, even for the most dedicated of readers. However the novel should be seen, not as a deviation from the Australian literary tradition from which it springs, but as a proto-modernist text which is well before its time.

FURTHER READING

Bibliography

Krimmer, Sally. "A Bibliography of Barbara Baynton." *Australian Literary Studies* 7, No. 4 (October 1976): 430-33.
    Includes primary and secondary material.

Biography

Krimmer, Sally. "New Light on Barbara Baynton." *Australian Literary Studies* 7, No. 4 (October 1976): 425-30.
    Corrects earlier romanticized accounts of Baynton's life.

Criticism

Kirkby, Joan. "Barbara Baynton: An Australian Jocasta." *Westerly* 34, No. 4 (December 1989): 114-24.
    Examines evocations of maternity in Baynton's fiction.

Webby, Elizabeth. "Barbara Baynton's Revisions to 'Squeaker's Mate'." *Southerly* 44, No. 4 (December 1984): 455-68.
    Discusses differences between the manuscript and printed versions of "Squeaker's Mate" and reprints the manuscript version.

"The Secret Sharer"

Joseph Conrad

The following entry presents criticism on Conrad's short story "The Secret Sharer" (1912). For information on Conrad's complete career, see *TCLC*, Volumes 1 and 6. For discussion of Conrad's novella *Heart of Darkness*, see Volume 13; for criticism on the novel *Nostromo*, see Volume 25; and for commentary on the novel *Lord Jim*, see Volume 43.

INTRODUCTION

Considered among Conrad's most significant works, "The Secret Sharer" is widely praised for the richness of its symbols and allusions. In this story of a young ship captain on his first voyage in command, Conrad uses the device known as the double, or doppelgänger, to portray the maturation of his central character. The allusive quality of the narrative has led to lively critical debate concerning the specifics of Conrad's intent in the story, yet critics agree that "The Secret Sharer" represents Conrad at his best. Conrad himself agreed with this assessment, writing to his friend Edward Garnett: "the 'Secret Sharer,' between you and me, is *it*. Eh? . . . Every word fits and there's not a single uncertain note."

Plot and Major Characters

Based loosely on Conrad's experience in the 1880s, when he was forced by an emergency to assume command of a ship in a Far Eastern port, "The Secret Sharer" concerns a young captain, anxious about his first voyage in command of a ship. During the first night of the voyage, the young captain discovers a man named Leggatt in the water near the ship and, although the man admits to being a fugitive accused of murder, helps him evade capture by bringing him on board and hiding him. A close relationship develops between the two men, and the young captain, convinced that Leggatt's crime was justified, takes him to a secluded island where he will ostensibly be beyond the reach of authorities. Afterward, the young captain commands his ship with a newly discovered sense of confidence.

Major Themes

Critical interpretations of "The Secret Sharer" vary, due largely to uncertainty about Leggatt's function in the story. Critics agree that the basic theme of the story lies in the young captain's need to come to terms with himself in light of the enormous challenges of his new role; they further agree that the young captain's relationship with Leggatt serves as the symbol of that struggle. However, while some have contended that Leggatt represents an ideal to be emulated by the young captain because of his firm actions in the face of great danger, others have argued that he displays cowardice, murderous instincts, and irra-

tionality, and therefore represents that which is evil within the captain and humankind. According to this latter reading, Leggatt serves to show the young captain the dark side of his own nature, which must be confronted and accepted before he can truly take command of his vessel. Recent commentators have suggested that both views can be reasonably inferred from Conrad's narrative, and note that the textual richness that has led to such controversies is one of the elements that makes "The Secret Sharer" a major achievement.

CRITICISM

Robert Wooster Stallman (essay date 1948)

SOURCE: "Life, Art, and *The Secret Sharer*, in *Forms of Modern Fiction: Essays Collected in Honor of Joseph Warren Beach*, edited by William Van O'Connor, University of Minnesota Press, 1948, pp. 229-42.

[*Stallman is an American educator, poet, essayist, and critic. In the following excerpt, he interprets "The Secret Sharer" as an allegory of Conrad's artistic struggle.*]

One measures an author's talent by his ability to apprehend "the full potentiality of the material," and to achieve that potentiality it takes great technical talent to recognize and single out from a myriad of memoried scraps the single consequent image, to select and place in their proper niche the character which fits, the incident which fits, the setting which fits—to find and fashion the exact image and the exact word. Conrad, in a letter to a friend, said of **"The Secret Sharer"**: "Every word fits, and there's not a single uncertain note. Luck, my boy! Pure luck!" But *was* it? To the contrary, the quality of intelligence inherent in **"The Secret Sharer"** got in there by virtue of intelligence—conscious scheming. It wasn't by pure luck that the bricks in that mosaic of meaning fell into place. For how could it be otherwise with any work that has meaning than that the meaning was executed brick by brick, built into the mosaic by the laboring intellect of the artist?

The novelist writes about imaginary things, happenings, and people; but writing about them, so Conrad contends, the novelist is only writing about himself. The letters Conrad wrote Mme Poradowska, says Morton D. Zabel, "reveal that almost every fundamental problem of his later fiction was sketched or suggested in that correspondence [between 1890 and 1900] and applied there with remorseless intimacy not to fictitious characters but to his own plight and state of mind. They also reveal that during those critical years of his life, when he was making a harassed transition from maritime service to the profession of novelist, he was already groping for the means and courage to translate these experiences into fictional form, to objectify them dramatically, and thus to come into an intellectual realization of their meaning which might save him, as he expresses it, 'from the madness which, after a certain point of life is reached, awaits all those who refuse to master their sensations and bring into coherent form the mysteries of their lives' " [*Sewanee Review,* Winter, 1945].

Conrad wrote **"The Secret Sharer"** in order to resolve a certain personal crisis. Writing it served him as a neurotic safety valve. Nevertheless, whatever the crisis motivating him to the act of creation, that personal crisis is by no means identical with the imagined crisis confronting the sea captain in **"The Secret Sharer."** The one crisis cannot be equated with the other. For the motivating situation of the author has become objectified in a dramatic framework of meaning that is impersonal and universalized. This point has critical significance. . . .

"The Secret Sharer" is the microcosm of Conrad's imaginative work—in plot, in structure, and in theme. The plot and structure and theme which are basic to the concept of Conrad's fiction are these: (1) The plot of a double conflict, external and internal: the one a conflict between an estranged individual and his hostile universe, the other a clash between an isolated soul and his ethical or esthetic conscience; (2) the structure of an impending crisis, a moment of crisis in which the individual is put to an inescapable test of selfhood and compelled to recognize anew his destiny; (3) the theme of spiritual disunity and moral or esthetic isolation. This is the theme of *Lord Jim, The Secret Agent, Under Western Eyes, Chance, Victory,* and

"The Secret Sharer." Among modern novelists, Morton D. Zabel points out, Conrad and Kafka have achieved the most successful dramatic versions of this theme of isolation and spiritual recognition; "and this for the reason which I believe distinguishes Conrad's contribution to modern fictional method: his imposition of the processes and structures of psychological experience (particularly the experience of recognition) on the form of the plot." Kafka's "Hunger-Artist" and Conrad's **"Secret Sharer"** allegorize (though not exclusively) the problem of the spiritual disunity of the isolated artist. The psychological and moral meaning of **"The Secret Sharer"** can hardly be missed, but what is not so obvious—it has eluded all the interpreters—is that circle of esthetic meaning which intersects the psychological and moral circles and almost coincides with them. I mean the allegory of the plight of the artist.

The story, to summarize it in brief, is about a newly appointed sea captain who feels a stranger both to his ship and to himself. It is his first voyage and therefore it is a test. Leggatt, who has committed a murder, escapes from the nearby *Sephora* and takes refuge under the cover of night on the captain's ship. The captain, sensing at once a "mysterious communication" with the stranger, hides him in his cabin, guesses his guilt, and shares his conscience. Leggatt becomes the subconscious mind of the narrator-captain. The captain cannot attain perfect command of his ship until his alien self is deposited into the sea. And so the captain takes his ship (it is an unnamed ship) close into shore, shaves the land as close as possible ("on my conscience, it had to be thus close—no less"), and, while Leggatt swims for the shore of Koh-ring (it is an unknown island), he watches in terror the approaching mass of land shadows which threatens to engulf the ship. What saves him in this moment of crisis is the warning marker left by the swimmer: It is the captain's own hat ("the saving mark for my eyes"), by which he knows that the ship has gathered sternway. At last he has established perfect communion with his ship. He is fitted for his task.

The allegory of the plight of the artist, that is one of the concentric circles of meaning in **"The Secret Sharer."** Stated thus the theme is impersonal. Stated in terms of the personal element, what is allegorized is the personal crisis which the artist Conrad confronted and triumphed over in creating his art—in particular, this piece of art. One of Conrad's critics has argued that a more "real" Conrad is revealed in the fiction, rather than in the autobiographical writings (that is, *A Personal Record,* the letters, and that book which Conrad called "my book, the soul of my life"—*The Mirror of the Sea*). But the fact is that during our reading of the imaginative work we forget this "real" Conrad, if he is present at all. We no more expect to bump into an author in his fiction than we expect to encounter his characters in life. The secreted personality having been transmuted into a depersonalized and anonymous thing, nothing exists but the work itself. To what extent is **"The Secret Sharer"** personative? Of course, the sea captain is not literally the man Conrad. The only "literal" equation is the one that figures in the relationship of the captain and the fugitive. It is the secret self of the captain that is "exactly the same" as the fugitive, who, dressed in "the ghostly gray of my sleeping-suit" (the garb of the unconscious life), remains always concealed from the eyes of the world. Were anyone to see them, "he would think he was seeing double." "Anybody would have taken him for me." But no one sees them. In darkness Leggatt appears and disappears out of, and into, that symbolic sea. Neither he nor the captain ever hears "each other's natural voice." The captain is hinting at the symbolical existence of Leggatt when he remarks that "an irresistible doubt of his bodily existence flitted through my mind. Can it be, I asked myself, that he is not visible to other eyes than mine? It was like being haunted." The captain sees it all going on as though he were himself "inside that other sleeping-suit." There is this psychic identity, and there is the physical identity: Leggatt's similarity in appearance, in accidents of age, background, and experience. "And it was as if the ship had two captains to plan her course for her." But there is a third captain, another "gray ghost," to plan her course. The sea captain's other double, allegorically, is the author himself.

Conrad's role, like that of Leggatt, is the role of an invisible participant. This other metaphorical identity the captain never quite senses, but he might be hinting at the thing, unwittingly, all the while that he is identifying himself with Leggatt. "I was so identified with my secret double that I did not even mention the fact in those scanty, fearful whispers we exchanged." What each of the trio says to the other is "something that a ghost might have said." "A mysterious communication was already established between us two [among us *three*]—in the face of that silent, darkened, tropical sea." Two whispering ghosts haunt the captain's cabin.

Fidelity is for Conrad the crux of moral integrity. "All a man can betray is his conscience," he writes in *Under Western Eyes.* The same dictum holds for the artist. **"The Secret Sharer"** is a double allegory. It is an allegory of man's moral conscience, and it is an allegory of man's esthetic conscience. The form of **"The Secret Sharer,"** to diagram it, is the form of the capital letter L—the very form of the captain's room. (It is hinted at, again, in the initial letter of Leggatt's name.) One part of the letter L diagrams the allegory of the captain's divided soul, man in moral isolation and spiritual disunity. The other part of the letter represents the allegory of the artist's split soul ("the man who suffers and the mind which creates"). The captain stands at the angle of the two isolations and the two searches for selfhood. "Such was my scheme," says the captain, "for keeping my second self invisible."

It is the captain, but it might also be Conrad, who says: "My strangeness, which had made me sleepless, had prompted that unconventional arrangement, as if I had expected in those solitary hours of the night to get on terms with the ship of which I knew nothing, manned by men of whom I knew very little more." To get on terms with his ship—that is Conrad's problem quite as much as it is the captain's. Conrad, in the hushed voice of the captain, is speaking of his own ship: "In this breathless pause at the threshold of a long passage we seemed to be measuring our fitness for a long and arduous enterprise, the appointed task of both our existences to be carried out, far from all

human eyes, with only sky and sea for spectators and for judges." The artist, of necessity estranged from normal everyday life, isolated with his vision, begins in self-doubt his newly appointed task. Sky and sea and "all that multitude of celestial bodies staring down at one"—the entire external world seems hostile to his secret enterprise. Everything threatens a perfect communion with his ship. Alone with his ship ("alone on her decks"), the artist is overwhelmed by self-doubt. He knows that this voyage will be a test. He cannot count upon "pure luck" to see him through. Being faced by "the breath of unknown powers that shape our destinies" (as the young captain in *The Shadow Line* says), he anticipates the possibilities of failure. It is his secret self, it is his creative conscience which he must not betray. "Everything was against us in our secret partnership," the captain complains. Everything—the elements, the men, even the ship; and "time itself—for this [this tension between the artist and his vision] could not go on forever." Conrad's secret partnership with the captain has its parallel in the captain's secret partnership with Leggatt. It is through the captain that Conrad establishes communion with *his* ship, even as it is through Leggatt that the captain establishes command over his. That is why the captain risks everything of his future ("the only future for which I was fit") for Leggatt's sake. Leggatt's appearance is the answer to the captain's question: "I wondered how far I should turn out faithful to that ideal conception of one's personality every man sets up for himself secretly." Leggatt provides him the utmost test. The captain, by virtue of fidelity to his vision of Ideal Selfhood, triumphs in the decisive moment of his destiny, and at that moment when he measures up to it a new existence, a spiritually unified one, begins. The artist, Conrad admits in his preface to *The Nigger of the "Narcissus,"* "the artist descends within himself, and in that lonely region of stress and strife . . . finds the terms of his appeal." Conrad's problem—the problem which every creator confronts—is resolved, no less than is the captain's, by the trial he imposes upon his ship. She weathers the crisis—the crisis which every creator risks. That **"The Secret Sharer"** comes round is by virtue of Conrad's fidelity to his vision. He has measured up to that ideal of artistic integrity, that ideal conception of one's esthetic conscience, which every artist "sets up for himself secretly." She comes round, she succeeds! Nothing can stand between them after that. "Nothing! No one in the world should stand now between us, throwing a shadow on the way of silent knowledge and mute affection, the perfect communion . . . "—of an artist with his ship. Having mastered "the feel of my ship," now like that other invisible stranger, he is at last "a free man, a proud swimmer striking out for a new destiny."

Albert J. Guerard   (essay date 1958)

SOURCE: "The Journey Within," in *Conrad the Novelist,* Cambridge, Mass.: Harvard University Press, 1958, pp. 1-59.

[*An American novelist, short story writer, biographer, and critic, Guerard is also the author of two studies of Conrad,* Joseph Conrad *(1947), and* Conrad the Novelist *(1958).*

In the following excerpt from the latter work, he offers his interpretation of "The Secret Sharer."]

"On my right hand there were lines of fishing-stakes resembling a mysterious system of half-submerged bamboo fences, incomprehensible in its division of the domain of tropical fishes . . . " The strange first paragraph of **"The Secret Sharer,"** with its dream landscape of ill-defined boundaries between land, air and sea, prepares us for this most frankly psychological of Conrad's shorter works. Even at a quite explicit level it is the story of a personality test: "I wondered how far I should turn out faithful to that ideal conception of one's own personality every man sets up for himself secretly." The narrator-captain is insecure at the start; he looks forward to leaving "the unrest of the land." The story moves from his sense of being stranger to his ship, and to himself, to a final mature confidence and integration: "And I was alone with her. Nothing! no one in the world should stand now between us, throwing a shadow on the way of silent knowledge and mute affection, the perfect communion of a seaman with his first command." This is the end of the experience. But he must give up, almost at its beginning, his illusion of the sea's great security and "untempted life." For the temptation appears on the very next page in the guise of Leggatt, fugitive from the *Sephora* because he had killed a member of his crew. Whatever test occurs, or whatever change in the narrator's personality, must be due to his relationship with Leggatt. For that relationship is the whole story.

He knows that the test must be faced in solitude: "far from all human eyes, with only sky and sea for spectators and for judges." Hence, in marked defiance of custom, he takes the anchor-watch himself, sending the other officers and men below. The direct result of this departure from routine is that the rope side-ladder is left hanging: the ladder up which Leggatt will climb moments later. The captain sees at the bottom of the ladder, when he tries to haul it up, a "headless corpse," "ghastly, silvery, fishlike." There is no way of knowing whether Conrad here intended the sea from which Leggatt climbs as a symbol of the unconscious, or whether he intended a reflexive reference to his opening sentence. What the scene does insist upon is that the captain is *responsible* for the dangling ladder and for Leggatt's coming. He has in a sense summoned Leggatt, who later remarks that it was "as if you had expected me." Even before the fugitive has a chance to reveal his crime, a "mysterious communication was established" between the two. The captain fetches a sleeping-suit, which is just the right size, and on the next page refers to Leggatt as his "double" for the first of many times. "It was, in the night, as though I had been faced by my own reflection in the depths of a sombre and immense mirror." He at once leaps to the most charitable interpretation of Leggatt's crime. He suggests it was due to a fit of temper.

It would be improper to forget, while preoccupied with the psychological symbolism, that Leggatt is substantial flesh and blood. The story dramatizes a human relationship and individual moral bond at variance with the moral bond to the community implicit in laws and maritime tradition. The narrator at once makes his decision to hide and protect the fugitive and at no time remotely considers betraying him. Leggatt must be hidden from the captain's own crew. And he must be kept hidden from the captain of the *Sephora* (with his fidelity to the law) on the following day:

> To the law. His obscure tenacity on that point had in it something incomprehensible and a little awful; something, as it were, mystical, quite apart from his anxiety that he should not be suspected of "countenancing any doings of that sort." Seven-and-thirty virtuous years at sea, of which over twenty of immaculate command, and the last fifteen in the *Sephora,* seemed to have laid him under some pitiless obligation.

We do not need to go to the biography and letters to discover Conrad's respect for "immaculate command" and "pitiless obligation," or for such a traditional figure; it is implicit in much of his fiction. The narrator's sympathy, however, is wholly for the criminal Leggatt.

The reader too incorrigibly sympathizes with Leggatt. But it is well to recall that Leggatt appears to be a rather questionable seaman: a man who had got his post because his "people had some interest" with the owners, who was disliked by the men, who "wasn't exactly the sort for the chief mate of a ship like the *Sephora.*" His crime was, like most crimes in Conrad, a marginal one. His order and his actions had saved the ship in a crisis; the same "strung-up force" had within the same hour fixed the foresail and killed a man. But still more essential (from an officer's point of view) is his contempt for law, his feeling that innocence and guilt are private matters. "But you don't see me coming back to explain such things to an old fellow in a wig and twelve respectable tradesmen, do you? What can they know whether I am guilty or not—or of *what* I am guilty, either?" It is entirely wrong to suppose, as some readers do, that Conrad unequivocally *approves* the captain's decision to harbor Leggatt. The reasons for the narrator's act are defined as "psychological (not moral)." Who knows what Conrad the responsible master-mariner might not have done, had he so connived in a fugitive's escape? The excellent captain of the *Cutty Sark* committed suicide four days after letting Leggatt's prototype go free.

This then is the situation in its purely human and material terms—a situation Conrad will dramatize again and again: the act of sympathetic identification with a suspect or outlaw figure, and the ensuing conflict between loyalty to the individual and loyalty to the community. It is, at our first response, a dramatic outward relationship. But as double Leggatt is also very inwardly a secret self. He provokes a crippling division of the narrator's personality, and one that interferes with his seamanship. On the first night the captain intends to pin together the curtains across the bed in which Leggatt is lying. But he cannot. He is too tired, in "a peculiarly intimate way." He feels less "torn in two" when he is with Leggatt in the cabin, but this naturally involves neglect of his duties. As for other times—"I was constantly watching myself, my secret self, as dependent on my actions as my own personality, sleeping in that bed, behind that door which faced me as I sat at the head of the table." He loses all "unconscious alertness," his relations with the other officers become more strained, and in the navigational crisis of Kohring he realizes that he does not know how to handle his ship.

He has been seriously disoriented, and even begins to doubt Leggatt's bodily existence. "I think I had come creeping quietly as near insanity as any man who has not actually gone over the border." The whispering communion of the narrator and his double—of the seaman-self and some darker, more interior, and outlaw self—must have been necessary and rewarding, since the story ends as positively as it does. But it is obvious to both men that the arrangement cannot be permanent. Nor would it do for Leggatt *to come back to life* in his own guise.

The narrator therefore takes his ship close to the land, so that Leggatt can escape and swim to the island of Koh-ring. But he takes the ship much closer to that reefed shore than necessary. He is evidently compelled to take an extreme risk in payment for his experience. "It was now a matter of conscience to shave the land as close as possible . . . perhaps he [Leggatt] was able to understand why, on my conscience, it had to be thus close—no less." Before they separate he gives Leggatt three pieces of gold and forces his hat on him, to protect him from the tropic sun. And this act of "sudden pity for his mere flesh" saves the ship. At the critical moment when the captain must know whether the ship is moving, in that darkness as of the gateway of Erebus, he sees his hat, a saving mark, floating on the water. Now he can give the order to shift the helm; the ship at last moves ahead and is saved. The final sentence refers to Leggatt: "the secret sharer of my cabin and of my thoughts, as though he were my second self, had lowered himself into the water to take his punishment: a free man, a proud swimmer striking out for a new destiny." Leggatt is perhaps a free man in several senses, but not least in the sense that he has escaped the narrator's symbolizing projection. He has indeed become "mere flesh," is no longer a "double." And the hat floating on the black water now defines a necessary separateness.

"The Secret Sharer" is at once so closeknit in texture and so large in suggestion as to discourage interpretation. We know that in Jungian psychology a hat, in dreams, represents the personality, which can be transferred symbolically to another. But what are we to make of this hat floating on the night sea—that a wished transference of personality has luckily failed? In psychological terms the positive end of the introspective experience is incorporation not separation and split. But such an end would have required Leggatt to remain on board indefinitely, an absurdity in dramatic if not psychological terms. The truer significance of the ending would seem to lie in a desperate hope that both sides of the self might live on and go free, neither one destroyed. In Jungian terms, again, integration of personality cannot occur until the unconscious has been known, trafficked with, and in some sense liberated. And we do feel this to be the general burden of the story, whatever the logic or illogic of the ending. The outlaw has had his innings, yet the captain has emerged a stronger man.

In any event, general deductions are more rewarding than dogmatic paraphrase. What can we say in very general terms? First, I think, that the story reflects insecurity and a consequent compulsion to test the self; or, a willingness to engage in the "heroism of self-analysis." In broad terms "The Secret Sharer" concerns the classic night journey

and willed descent into the unconscious. But even broader terms may be as true: that Conrad apparently detected in himself a division (possibly damaging, possibly saving) into a respectable traditional rational seaman-self and a more interior outlaw-self that repudiated law and tradition; and again, a division into a seaman-self operating from "unconscious alertness" and an introspective, brooding-self of solitary off-duty hours. In *Dejection: An Ode* Coleridge would doubtless have liked to prove that the introspective "abstruse researches" had not crippled his faculty for feeling. But he couldn't. Does not the positive ending of "The Secret Sharer" seek to prove that the self-analytic, introspective bent (reflected on every page of the story itself) has *not* crippled the seaman and active human being? The great danger of introspection is neurotic immobilization, and this is still another area "The Secret Sharer" touches upon. But Conrad deals with it more directly in *The Shadow Line.*

It might be objected that such an interpretation pays scant attention to the "work of art." On the contrary, the art of "The Secret Sharer" consists in its having conveyed so much human material so briefly and with such absolute authenticity. Its triumph is to have made one uninterrupted human relationship and story render so much: the suspenseful and sympathetic plight of Leggatt, the insecure narrator's resolution of his conflict, the deep human communion between the two men, the profound human experience (incorporating all the preceding) of the introspective night journey. We can say after the fact that a story attempting so much would be likely to split apart into its several themes. What holds it together? Partly, I think, a rigid economy and willed art of omission. The narrator, aside from his insistence that Leggatt is his "double," almost never adopts the language of psychological abstraction. He wisely makes no attempt to convey the hysterical immediacy of near-insanity (as Marlow in *Heart of Darkness* does); he avoids, as wisely, reporting the conversations of the two men at length. But most of all the story is saved and held by the narrator's grave, quiet, brooding voice, by the meditative seriousness of his tones. That voice commits us, from the beginning, to the interior resonance of the story. The point of view is not, as it happens, Conrad's usual one when employing the first person. His normal manner is to employ a retrospective first person, free to move where he wishes in time, and therefore free to foreshadow his conclusion. "The Secret Sharer," which carries us consecutively from the beginning of the experience to its end, is Conrad's most successful experiment by far with the method of nonretrospective first-person narration. The nominal narrative past is, actually, a harrowing present which the reader too must explore and survive.

(We may note, parenthetically, the way in which Conrad associates a famous crime with his first voyage as a captain—two crimes to be exact—and from the association derives this most subjective of his stories. And the story of the *Cutty Sark* suggests one of the reasons why *Lord Jim* and "The Secret Sharer"—in their marginal crimes, sympathetic identifications, and introspective concerns—belong to the same fictional and moral worlds.)

The incidents on which the two stories were based—the

abandonment of the *Jeddah,* the killing of a rebellious member of the crew on the famous *Cutty Sark*—both occurred in the summer of 1880. The chapter "A Hell Ship Voyage" in Basil Lubbock's *The Log of the "Cutty Sark"* [1924] provides certain details on the prototype of Leggatt, a "bucko mate" named Sidney Smith. He had vented his spite on three Negroes and especially on the incapable John Francis. When Francis refused to obey an order and the mate rushed upon him, the Negro raised a capstan bar. Smith wrested it away and struck the Negro with it, who on the third day afterward died. The mate persuaded "his kind-hearted captain" to let him escape, and at Anjer he was passed secretly to the American ship *Colorado.* Apparently only the crew of the *Cutty Sark,* though disliking both Francis and the mate, wanted to see justice done. The near-mutiny on board the *Narcissus* shows this pattern. Some years later Smith was apprehended, tried for murder on the high seas, and sentenced to seven years' hard labor.

Conrad's use of this material in **"The Secret Sharer"** and elsewhere suggests how an imagination both moral and sympathetic transforms a raw reality:

1. The character of Leggatt is made less brutal than that of Smith, but his crime has as much or as little justification.

2. The lawless act of sympathy was committed by the captain of the *Cutty Sark*—though he too, like the captain of the *Sephora,* had a fine reputation to uphold. He apparently regretted his act, for on the fourth day after leaving Anjer he committed suicide in a manner that reminds us of Brierly's suicide in **Lord Jim.** He called the helmsman's attention to the course, then jumped overboard. The apparent motive for Brierly's suicide was his sympathetic identification with Jim; though an assessor at the trial, he had wanted Jim to run away. Captain Wallace of the *Cutty Sark* thus enacted in real life one of the essential Conradian dramas: the torment of the conscientious man who has been guilty of a lawless sympathy, and of following an individual ethic in conflict with the "ethic of state."

3. The captain of the *Colorado* received Smith, according to Lubbock, because he was "only too glad to get hold of a manhandler of such reputation." Thus the narrator of **"The Secret Sharer"** combines both the sympathy of the *Cutty Sark's* captain and the formal receiving role of the *Colorado's.* Lubbock's book suggests, incidentally, that life on board the sailing-ships of that time could be at once more brutal and less disciplined than Conrad's novels and autobiographies indicate. At one time, earlier in the voyage, Francis and the mate had fought for fifteen minutes before being stopped by the captain.

4. However inhumane, Smith had "plenty of grit." He emerged from prison with his certificates gone but slowly worked his way up to command of an Atlantic tanker, and died in 1922, at the age of seventy-three. Did Conrad know what happened to Smith after the trial and imprisonment? In any event his sympathy must have been stirred, as it was with Lord Jim, by the spectacle of the man who wanted to go on living. One wonders, too, whether Sidney Smith read **"The Secret Sharer"** before he died?

The *Cutty Sark's* trials were far from over, and some of them may have suggested other scenes to Conrad. The ship worked its way back to Anjer after the captain's suicide, encountering such difficulties that a seaman given to gloomy prophecies claimed she was bewitched, and would have no luck until the murderous mate was under lock and key—which reminds us of Mr. Burns in **The Shadow Line** and of Singleton in **The Nigger of the "Narcissus."** Some of the crew felt that the prophet himself was "the Jonah at the root of all the trouble." When the *Cutty Sark* reached Singapore on September 18, it was to find the city "already all agog with the *Jeddah* disaster" which lies behind **Lord Jim.**)

Osborn Andreas   (essay date 1959)

SOURCE: *"The Secret Sharer,"* in *Joseph Conrad: A Study in Non-conformity,* Philosophical Library, 1959, pp. 135-38.

[*In the following essay Andreas discusses Conrad's treatment of the individual versus society in "The Secret Sharer."*]

Official society, represented by government officers and those in authority charged with law-enforcement, [had] been appearing at least in the background of several Conrad stories immediately preceding **"The Secret Sharer"**. In this story, however, official society and its opposite, the outlaw, take the foreground. Conrad's earlier stories dealt with outcasts in conflict with orthodox groups, but a progression has occurred from Almayer and Willems through Lord Jim, Gaspar Ruiz, Verloc and Razumov to Leggatt, the murderer and outlaw of **"The Secret Sharer."**

This is of course a natural progression, since the archetype of all groups is the ruling governmental society of any land, and the extreme type of the outcast or the deviant individual is the outlaw. With this story Conrad has finally isolated his antinomies, the individual who is a law unto himself, and the authority of law and order which stands for organized mankind.

The inescapable fact about **"The Secret Sharer"** is that in this story Conrad himself, the ship-captain in the story, chooses to conceal a murderer from his pursuers and assists him to escape capture by the legal authorities. Furthermore, this man who helps a fugitive from the law is himself an officer of the law, having just been appointed captain of a ship, his first command, and this act of law-evasion is his first act in his new post. Knowing that a crime has been committed, the captain assists and shelters the offender with the intent to defeat justice and in doing so he becomes an accessory after the fact.

The murderer, Leggatt, and the captain had held identical jobs as mates on separate ships until a few weeks previous to Leggatt's criminal act and the captain's promotion to his first command. And the captain realizes that the crime that Leggatt had committed was a crime that in similar circumstances he himself might have committed, and instead of becoming a member of the ruling class on the high seas he easily might, like Leggatt, have deviated into the class of the hunted outlaw. He therefore identifies himself with the murderer rather than with the judges who would condemn Leggatt should he be brought before them in a court of law.

The young ship-captain meets Leggatt for the first time during his first night as captain. He has a feeling of inadequacy in facing up to his new duties and he therefore spends his first night in performing the duties of the night watchman whom he has sent to bed. He hopes to accustom himself to his new and elevated status by spending the night in solitude and contemplation on the deck of the ship of which he is the new master. The ship is anchored outside a harbor in the Java sea and is ready to sail on the following day.

During the night he notices that a rope ladder is hanging over the side of the ship, goes to pull it in, and finds a naked man floating in the water and clinging to the rope's end. He invites the swimmer to climb aboard.

The stranger, a young man, introduces himself by the name of Leggatt and tells his story in a low voice, after he has put on the sleeping suit which the captain has fetched for him. Leggatt says he had been swimming for a couple of hours and had come from the ship across the bay. He had been mate of that ship until seven weeks ago, when he had been confined to his cabin for having killed a member of his crew, a worthless wastrel of a sailor who had exasperated him by insolence after a long hard storm. Leggatt had grabbed the sailor by the throat just as a huge wave broke over the deck. When the water disappeared, Leggatt's fingers were still grappling the sailor's throat, and the sailor was dead. The captain had locked Leggatt in his cabin and had intended to turn him over to the land authorities. Leggatt, however, had this evening, the first time that the ship has approached land, escaped from his cabin and jumped overboard. He had intended to swim until he sank, rather than face the routine of an Official Inquiry, but had come upon this neighboring ship in the dark, noticed the rope ladder and decided to cling to it for a short rest.

The captain, who narrates the story, and Leggatt seem to understand each other perfectly. The captain feels that under the same circumstances he himself would have done what Leggatt did, and he cannot disapprove of Leggatt's wish to disappear rather than face the Court of Inquiry. He himself has often been tempted to take some worthless sailor by the throat and no doubt would have done so had he been provoked to the same extent as had Leggatt. He proceeds to hide the refugee in his cabin and protect him from pursuit. It is as though he were protecting himself from the consequences of something which he himself might very well have done.

The next morning the captain of Leggatt's ship arrives and tells his story. He is astonished and suspicious at not finding Leggatt on board, but he accepts the assurances of the narrator-captain that none of his men had seen the runaway mate.

Several nerve-wracking days follow this event. Leggatt hides in the captain's shower-room when the steward is making the stateroom tidy; he and the captain converse only in whispers and only at night; the captain notices that the crew has begun to show in their behavior towards him that they think he is acting queerly. He comes upon groups of sailors whose sudden dispersal upon his approach indicates that they have been discussing him.

Leggatt soon decides that they have sailed far enough down the Java coast to be out of reach of the port authorities, who had undoubtedly been notified of his escape, and he therefore asks the captain to put his ship within swimming distance of the shoreline after dark. The captain is reluctant to do so, since he wishes to remove the secret sharer of his cabin as far as possible from the danger of recapture, but he agrees to Leggatt's proposal because the danger that some member of the crew will accidentally discover Leggatt's presence on shipboard is becoming too great. That night, on the pretext that he wants to pick up some land breezes with which to augment the ship's speed, the captain pilots his ship dangerously close to the shore line; Leggatt slips over the side in the dark and makes his getaway unseen.

The captain is now a changed man. His feeling of inadequacy has entirely vanished and he takes charge of his ship and crew in full confidence that he can body forth in his own person the full authority which his position of captain demands of him. It is as though the young captain before he could exercise authority convincingly to himself and to his men, had had first to take the law into his own hands and symbolically flout the authority of those above him before he could exert authority over those under him. The first use to which he put his newly acquired authority was that of shielding a fleeing outcast from a punitive society. The captain-narrator, Conrad himself, stands for the official group, and Leggatt stands for the deviant individual; and by protecting him from the other members of his group, Conrad here takes Leggatt's sin on his own shoulders and thereby admits not only his own moral complicity but that of society as well.

> "The Secret Sharer" is an uncommon tale for Conrad, rare in its power of affirmation, and, because of its optimism, an uncommonly cheerful phosphorescence in the rather gloomy sea of Conrad's work.
>
> —*Mark A. R. Facknitz, in* The Journal of Narrative Technique, *1987.*

Louis H. Leiter   (essay date 1960)

SOURCE: "Echo Structures: Conrad's *The Secret Sharer*," in *Twentieth Century Literature,* Vol. 5, No. 4, January, 1960, pp. 159-75.

[*Leiter is an American educator and critic. In the following essay, he illustrates how repetition of images and actions and parallels to biblical stories affect meaning in "The Se-cret Sharer."*]

For the most part critics agree that the narrator of Joseph Conrad's **"The Secret Sharer"** is a double for the protagonist, that actions and gestures of this newly appointed captain are reflected in the movements and behavior of the recently escaped Leggatt, and that each man echoes the most private thoughts and sentiments of the other. A series of echoes established by means of image, metaphor, symbol, and mime consistently suggest to the reader the manner in which he should interpret the roles of Leggatt and the captain-narrator. Although they are one person figuratively, the inner and the outer, the unconscious and the conscious, they are split for didactic and aesthetic reasons into two characters. What has escaped notice, however, is that echo structures similar to those which portray character have been employed for other reasons as well as this throughout the short novel. Structures not only of character but also of narrative action, parable, metaphor, and the like, become a fundamental means for achieving aesthetic and thematic effects.

The echo structure: An echo structure implies one or more structures similar to itself. The tautology which is the echo structure may be a repeated symbol, metaphor, scene, pattern of action, state of being, myth, fable, or archetype. If viewed within the perspective of Biblical story or classical myth, either directly stated in the text of the story or implied, that perspective may suffuse the echo structures of similar construction with additional meanings. If seen from the vantage of imagery alone, an echo structure is what has been called the principle of reflexive reference [Joseph Frank, "Special Form in Modern Literature," *Sewanee Review,* Summer, Autumn, and Winter, 1945]. It evokes thematic meaning when the total pattern of images has been examined in the context in which it appears. The thematic significance of echo structures will be demonstrated in the course of this essay.

Image cluster as echo structure: In this essay an image is any word which creates a relatively concrete "picture" in or presents some configuration to the reader's mind. Almost any word may be used for this purpose. Clusters of images occur when certain groups of words fall together recurrently so that we identify them as somehow significantly related. Thus Conrad's short novel opens with these lines:

> On my right hand there were *lines of fishing stakes* resembling *a mysterious system* of *half-submerged bamboo fences, incomprehensible* in its division of the domain of tropical fishes, and *crazy of aspect* as if abandoned forever by some *nomad tribe of fishermen now gone to the other end of the ocean;* for there was no sign of human habitation as far as the eye could reach.

In isolation these opening lines accomplish little more than the establishing of an appropriate atmosphere of mystery and the underlining of the narrator-captain's solitude as a stranger to his ship, to his men, and to himself. A few hours later, however, as the narrator paces the deck of his first command after sending all his men to rest, he suddenly discovers the ladder hanging over the side:

> Then I reflected that I had myself preemptorily dismissed my officers from duty, and by my own act had prevented the anchor watch being formally set and things properly attended to. . . . Not from compunction, certainly, but, as it were, mechanically, *I proceeded to get the ladder in myself.* Now a side ladder of that sort is *a light affair* and comes in easily, yet my *vigorous tug* which should have brought it flying on board merely recoiled upon my body in *a totally unexpected jerk.* What the devil! . . . I was so *astonished* by the immovableness of that ladder that I remained stock-still, trying to account for it myself *like the imbecile mate of mine.* In the end, of course, I put my head over the rail. . . . I saw at once *something elongated and pale floating very close to the ladder.* Before I could form a guess a faint flash of phosphorescent light, which seemed to issue suddenly from the naked body of a man, flickered in the sleeping water. *As he hung by the ladder,* like a resting swimmer, the sea lightning played about his limbs at every stir; and he appeared in it *ghastly, silvery fishlike. He remained as mute as a fish, too.*

In this passage the imagery cluster of the opening lines is echoed. However the original cluster has been modified into another cluster which resembles the first one but with certain significant changes. What is described as a seascape in the first passage is echoed in the second, and we shall see it once more in a third, with a more personal significance for the narrator. The "half submerged bamboo fences" for catching fish suggest the "ladder," that "light affair," which the narrator annoyed with his own negligence, "proceeded to get in." The "tug" and "jerk" of the second passage further suggest the idea of the narrator's fishing with something like a bamboo fence which has undergone a transformation into a ladder. "Mysterious" of the first passage echoes in "astonished" of the second, while "crazy of aspect" in the first appears as "imbecile mate" in the second. And "fishermen" of the former echoes in "fishlike" of the latter, reinforced by Leggatt's being "mute as a fish."

This first cluster of images along with the second, somewhat modified cluster appears once more in **"The Secret Sharer."** Toward the end of the story when the narrator relates that he must rid himself and his ship of Leggatt, he thinks:

> *Whoever was being driven distracted, it was not he. He was sane.* And the proof of his sanity was continued when he took up the whispering again. "It would never do for me to come to life again. . . . What does the Bible say? *'Driven off the face of the earth.'* Very well, I am off the face of the earth now. As I came at night so I shall go."

Once more the cluster of images echoes in this passage. We perceive that the two earlier structures are here somewhat shortened, some elements eliminated, and others echoed more strongly in modified form. "Distracted" and "sane" and "sanity" echo one set of images, while the Biblical quotation, "Driven off the face of the earth," transforms the image of "nomad tribe" into something more mysterious and frightening.

What the second and third passages accomplish is to charge the first passage with meanings which it does not possess when first read. Only after reading the second passage, and especially after reading the third, do we see that the first is a symbolic seascape corresponding point by point to the central thematic tensions of the novel and to the narrator's lack of knowledge of his own untested psyche. What we perceive through the narrator's eyes as he describes the setting is the projected, unexplored, unknown seascape of his own mind plucked, as it were, inside out and superimposed on the sea and land; but neither the narrator nor the reader becomes fully aware of this until much later. For the reader this occurs at the moment he perceives that the imagery clusters in the two widely separated echo structures have already appeared in the introductory passage.

The setting at the beginning is mysterious, atmospherically strange and unknown. Gradual revelation of and coming to terms with self throughout the novel is accompanied by a gradual change in and transformation of the imagery clusters parallel to the awakening to self knowledge. The bamboo fence belonging to the strangers becomes the narrator's own ladder, the means by which he "hooks" and brings to the surface his own secret self, that strange being who seems to live beyond the pale of human laws and who does indeed circumvent human punishment. The imagery in "fishing stakes . . . crazy of aspect" echoes in the narrator's being "astonished" when he pulls at the ladder with the creature, "mute as a fish," at its end, and in his description of his Chief Mate as an "imbecile." What this identification by means of imagery suggests is that somehow the three men, Leggatt-narrator-mate, are one person, or that certain aspects of their personalities are to be identified as similar.

Leggatt performs the role of the narrator's inner self, the possibility of the defections of the unconscious mind, its lawless (libidinous) forces breaking forth and overpowering law and order. Since they are identified through the imagery cluster, however, a specific aspect of the narrator's personality must be embodied in his Chief Mate. The narrator becomes more and more certain throughout the novel that he is losing his mind, that he is insane, that perhaps he is only imagining that he shares his cabin with Leggatt whom no one else has seen. In this way he gradually drifts toward the "imbecility" which he attaches so violently to his Chief Mate. Then in the third echo structure, the narrator confirms his own dangerous psychic condition when he seriously hints at his gradual loss of sanity, "Whoever was being driven distracted, it was not he. He was sane. And the proof of his sanity was continued when he took up the whispering again."

Conrad, I believe, wants us to see here that both men are indeed different aspects of the narrator's personality. The Chief Mate in many respects is just as dangerous as Leggatt. It is he who goes to pieces during the narrator's supreme test. Like Leggatt and like Captain Archbold of the *Sephora* he loses control of himself when in danger. Unlike Leggatt but still like Captain Archbold, the Chief Mate is obtuse. This very insensitivity, lack of trust, unawareness of the possible strength of personality, leads to his break-

down. But it also contributes to the narrator's demonstration of control over that very weakness of his own personality during the final trial scene in which he seizes the blubbering Chief Mate and transfers his strength to that man. Through this gesture (a mime repeated from the sail locker scene where he had gripped Leggatt just before consigning him to the deep) the narrator symbolically conquers the obtuseness of his own personality. The imagery cluster identifies the three men as one person and imagistically suggests that "insanity" and "imbecility" are symbolic of weakness or obtuseness. That part of the first cluster which is not echoed in the second cluster but appears in the third cluster of images, "some nomad tribe of fishermen now gone to the other end of the ocean," suggests the fate of Leggatt and the fate of the narrator himself. The biblical echo, "Driven off the face of the earth," is identified throughout **"The Secret Sharer"** with the Cain and Abel story, to which I shall return later in this essay. The first time the imagery appears, it is impersonally attached to "nomad tribe"; it does not affect the narrator in any way, although when we glance back at it we see it as part of the symbolic construction in that first passage to which "meanings" may be attached. Then suddenly a stranger, a wanderer, a swimmer really, appears at the ship's side. The absence of this part of the cluster of images in the second echo passage suggests the absence of knowledge as to who the stranger is or what he represents. But when the cluster appears again in the third echo passage, the narrator-captain has already gained knowledge of himself, of Leggatt, of his Chief Mate, and of the perilous situation on board his ship; he knows that he must help Leggatt, the Cain aspect of his personality, escape back into the sea (come to terms with or repress his inner self). The imagery cluster consequently from its introduction (nomad tribe) to its final echo (the Cain as wanderer reference) describes a movement from the superficial to the profound, from lack of knowledge of personality to penetrating awareness of what that part of the personality is capable of accomplishing-victory over moral disorder and victory over obtuseness.

Parable as echo structure: Parable, a short, simple story or observation, usually but not always an allegory, may serve as an echo structure. In the beginning of **"The Secret Sharer,"** as the narrator stands on the deck of his first command, watching the departing tug, which brought him to the harbor, he observes:

> Here and there *gleams as of a few scattered pieces of silver* marked the windings of the great river; and on the nearest of them, just within the bar, *the tug steaming right into the land became lost to my sight, hull and funnel and masts, as though the impassive earth had swallowed her up without an effort, without a tremor.* My eye followed the light cloud of her smoke, now here, now there, above the plain, according to the devious curves of the stream, but always fainter and farther away, till *I lost it at last behind the miter-shaped hill of the great pagoda.* And then I was left alone with my ship, anchored at the head of the Gulf of Siam.

This parable of the tug is echoed later in the novel when Conrad expands it into a major action, the most important one of the novel. As the tug steams into the land, so does the narrator's ship steam into the land when he sails in shore to rid himself of Leggatt. The identity of the echoed structures is made clear through the use of corresponding images. The water in both passages is silvery; a tug appears in one, a ship in the other; the "mitre-shaped" hill in the first, the mountain "Koh-ring" in the second. This is strengthened in the echo structure at the moment of climax when the narrator says of his ship, "Already she was, I won't say in the shadow of the land, but in the very blackness of it, already swallowed up as it were, gone too close to be recalled, gone from me altogether." The "silver" marking the passage of the river from the land into the sea will be reversed in the final structure into the "white hat" which marked the passage of Leggatt towards the land, with a reversal of the action included in the structures "from land to sea" to "from sea to land."

The major difference between the parable and its tautological echo in the latter structure is one of expansion and substitution; the dozen lines of the parable become the half dozen pages of the dilated action. Similarly that which the twenty-seven year old narrator impassively narrates in the first structure becomes that in which he is intimately even passionately involved in the echo structure. He speaks in the parable of the land as "impassive"; but in the structure of the echoed parable, the land becomes a place of "unrest" and "disquiet." The echo suggests, consequently, not only a structural principle operative in the novel, but also the result of "involvement" in experience, an experience which the narrator, untried in his new command, has never undergone previously, one which he observes in the parable's structure and one which he suffers through most intimately in the echo structure. The echoed, symbolic parable suggests that impassivity becomes disquietude when impersonality, lack of dedication to knowledge of self, becomes conscious dedication to a course of behavior leading to self-knowledge. "I wondered how far I should turn out faithful to that ideal conception of one's own personality every man sets up for himself secretly." As such this echoed parabolic structure establishes thematic meanings.

One more example of this principle will contribute to our understanding here. When thinking of his new Chief Mate, the narrator describes him in these terms:

> He was of a painstaking turn of mind. As he used to say, he "liked to account to himself " for practically everything that came in his way, down to *a miserable scorpion he had found in his cabin a week before. The why and wherefore of that scorpion-how it got on board and came to select his room rather than the pantry (which was a dark place more what a scorpion would be partial to), and how on earth it managed to drown itself in the inkwell of his writing desk*-had exercised him infinitely.

The extended actions of Leggatt in **"The Secret Sharer"** are an echo structure of the parable of the scorpion. As a matter of fact, the parable is almost a brief allegory of the entire action of the novel itself. The scorpion appears from the sea and enters the Chief Mate's cabin only to fall into the ink. Leggatt rises from the sea, enters the narrator's cabin, and then returns to the black waters of Kohring. Both scorpion and Leggatt are identified with light. The latter appears beside the ship all flashes of fire and phosphorescence; the former seeks the light of the Chief Mate's cabin. And Captain Archbold of the *Sephora* repeating the allegory once more, appears over the side of the ship in daylight and disappears over her side a short time later with his red whiskers twitching.

As in the instance of the tug-ship parable, the scorpion-Leggatt parable structure is expanded into many times its former, brief form and is modified and told in human terms. The echo structure of the scorpion parable appears a fourth time when after Captain Archbold of the *Sephora* departs, the narrator's Chief Mate tells him that the crew of the *Sephora* suspected Leggatt was aboard:

> "There was some little dispute about it. Our chaps took offense. *'As if we would harbor a thing like that'* they said. *'Wouldn't you like to look for him in our coal hole?'* Quite a tiff. But they made it up in the end. *I suppose he did drown himself. Don't you, sir?*"

Comparison of the scorpion parable and the echoing structures suggests the significance of the echo technique. Thematically the parable symbolizes something about the echoing action. The scorpion, mysterious, poisonous, inexplicable, provides meanings for Leggatt's actions, meanings for the consequences of those actions, which are not explicitly stated. Leggatt's arrival on the ship is as mysterious as that of the vermin and as dangerous to the narrator if he remains on the ship. The deadly quality of the scorpion is precisely that danger the captain experiences in his intercourse with Leggatt, the gradual but continuous poisoning of his relationship with his crew. Thus in another brief echo of the scorpion parable, Leggatt tells the narrator of the steward and second mate of the *Sephora* who hated him "like poison." And in still another the poison is at work in the narrator's ship:

> I was not wholly alone with my command; for there was that stranger in my cabin. *Or rather, I was not completely and wholly with her. Part of me was absent. That mental feeling of being in two places at once affected me physically as if the mood of secrecy had penetrated my very soul.*

Drowning of the scorpion signified not only the return of Leggatt to the black waters of Koh-ring but also the metaphorical death of the captain's "secret-sharer," the inner, uncontrollable, unconscious self, which vermin like, must return into the great sea of the unconscious from which it arose.

As the consequence of the use of parable as a structure which is echoed again and again in the novel, multiple thematic and symbolic dimensions are created which contribute to total meaning.

Action as echo structure: Action may also create echo structures. When Leggatt tells the young narrator of the man he has murdered, he says:

> There are fellows that an angel from heaven— and I am not that. He was one of those creatures that are just simmering all the time with a silly

sort of wickedness. Miserable devils that have no business to live at all. He wouldn't do his duty and wouldn't let anybody else do theirs. . . . *He gave me some of his cursed insolence at the sheet. I tell you I was overdone with this terrific weather that seemed to have no end to it.* Terrific, I tell you—and a deep ship. *I believe the fellow himself was half crazed with funk. It was no time for gentlemanly reproof. So I turned around and felled him like an ox. He up and at me. We closed just as an awful sea made for the ship.* All hands saw it coming and took to the rigging, but *I had him by the throat, and went on shaking him like a rat, the men above us yelling 'Look out! look out!'* Then a crash as if the sky had fallen on my head. They say that for over ten minutes *hardly anything was to be seen of the ship*-just the three masts and a bit of the forecastle head and of the poop all awash driving along in a smother of foam. It was a miracle that they found us, jammed together behind the forebits. *It's clear that I meant business, because I was holding him by the throat when they picked us up.* He was black in the face.

Later when the narrator takes his untried ship into shore, ostensibly to catch the land breezes, the following transpires between him and his Chief Mate hard upon a description of the "very blackness" of the mountain Kohring:

> Then stillness again, with the great shadow gliding closer, towering higher, without a light, without a sound. Such a hush had fallen on the ship that she might have been *a bark of the dead floating in slowly under the very gate of Erebus.*
>
> "My God! Where are we?"
>
> *It was the mate moaning at my elbow. He was thunder struck, and as it were deprived of the moral support of his whiskers.* He clapped his hands and absolutely cried out, "Lost!"
>
> "Be quiet," I said sternly.
>
> He lowered his tone, but I saw the shadowy gesture of his despair. "What are we doing here?"
>
> *He made as if to tear his hair, and addressed me recklessly.*
>
> *"She will never get out. You have done it, sir.* I knew it'd end in something like this. She will never weather, and you are too close now to stay. She'll drift ashore before she's round. O my god!"
>
> *I caught his arm as he was raising it to batter his poor devoted head, and shook it violently.*
>
> "She's ashore already," he wailed, trying to tear himself away.
>
> "Is she? . . . Keep good full there!"
>
> "Good full, sir," cried the helsman in a frightened, thin, childlike voice.
>
> *I hadn't let go the mate's arm and went on shaking it.* "Ready about, do you hear? You go forward"—shake—"and stop there"—shake—

"and hold your noise"—shake—*"and see these head sheets properly overhauled"*—shake, shake—shake.

And all the time I dared not look toward the land lest my heart should fail me. *I released my grip at last and he ran forward as if fleeing for dear life.*

The dramatic actions of the two passages are analogous: both Leggatt and the narrator, caught in perilous situations, attempt to save their ships; both have an encounter with someone who opposes their will; both come to grips with that person; both save their ships; but both face tests which they solve differently. Clearly the second of the two structural units is an echo of the former with certain very important changes. Thus in the latter structure, it is not the disobedient sailor's face which is black, that miserable devil "who had no business to live at all." That color has been transferred to the threatening land. Likewise, Conrad transfers in the echoed passage Leggatt's epithet for the recalcitrant sailor to the land, "the very gate of Erebus."

What Conrad achieves by shifting images from the sailor to the land is a transference of symbolic meaning, so that instead of the Chief Mate's being the threat, it is the land which threatens the ship and crew with evil and annihilation. To come to knowledge of self is a hellish business; the seeking of the winds of self knowledge and reconciliation with self and the world is full of terror, fraught with danger to life and soul. The new captain's Chief Mate does not resemble the murdered sailor in action as we might expect; for the land because it assumes the epithet, symbolizes cursedness, hellishness, and deadliness, the meaning also of the storm of the original passage in which Leggatt was involved in murder. In the echo structure, it is not a noisy typhoon which releases destruction; it is the silence of the ship and land and the Chief Mate's fear of the narrator's lack of experience, youth, and strange behavior, which unsettle him. Similarly, as Leggatt makes clear, the roles in the echo structure are a reversal of those of the earlier structure. Speaking to the narrator, Leggatt says of Captain Archbold during the typhoon:

> I assure you he never gave the order. He may think he did, but he never gave it. *He stood there with me on the break of the poop after the maintopsail blew away, and whimpered about our last hope—positively whimpered about it and nothing else—and the night coming on!* To hear one's skipper go on like that in such weather was enough to drive any fellow out of his mind.

The meaning of the technique of the echo action in these passages is somewhat elusive but not impossible to establish. Analogous scenes suggest by means of similar images and similar mimeing that the two scenes are essentially the same scene, something like archetypal initiations or tests. The first of the two scenes creates a kind of order, for good or for evil, against which the second tautological structure must be judged and evaluated. The difference between the two scenes, those dissimilarities which appear in the echo structure, when evaluated within the framework of the former scene, suggest the meaning of the latter scene. Both men, Leggatt and the young captain, undergo the same experience; Leggatt seizes the man by the throat at the climax of his archetypal trial by storm and kills him in a fit of uncontrolled passion; the narrator also seizes his Chief Mate under similar circumstances, his archetypal trial by silence, but by controlling himself, controlling the frightened, disbelieving man, he controls the ship and consequently saves her from destruction, while saving his reputation and winning the respect of his crew. The action of the echo structure implies, it seems to me, a moral judgment of Leggatt, although it does not state the judgment openly. It dramatizes it and by doing so makes the reader psychologically aware of it. At the same time the echo scene declares the moral superiority of the consciously aware narrator-captain who has come to face his secret inner self, to conquer it, and to control it.

Archetype, myth, or Biblical story as echo structure: A course of action, a metaphor, a symbol, an image, and the like, repeated often enough to assume traditional meanings and to be recognized as ritualistic is what is meant by archetype or archetypal pattern. The life and death of Christ is archetypal in these terms. It has certain similarities to the life, death, and resurrection of pagan gods, Dionysus, Tammuz, Adonis, the passing of the seasons, the rising and setting of the sun, and the phases of the moon, all recognizable as archetypes. The cross is an archetype which contains in it the entire Christian story. "Miserable devils," "hellish spell of bad weather," and "gate of Erebus" are conceivable as archetypes of the demonic in **"The Secret Sharer."** Archetypes may be obvious at once if they have not undergone complex disguise, or they may be distorted, disguised, fragmentary, inverted, or merely implied.

In Conrad's novel several direct references to the Cain and Abel archetype draw our attention to its relation to the Leggatt story. Leggatt describes his experience to the narrator-captain in these words:

> Devil only knows what the skipper wasn't afraid of (all his nerve went to pieces altogether in that hellish spell of bad weather we had)—of what the law would do to him—of what his wife, perhaps. Oh, yes! She's on board. Though I don't think she would have meddled. She would have been only too glad to have me out of the ship in any way. *The "Brand of Cain" business, don't you see. That's all right. I was ready enough to go off wandering on the face of the earth—and that was price enough to pay for an Abel of that sort.*

Later the captain reminds us of the story when he thinks, "The very trust in Providence was, I suppose, denied to his guilt." And once more it is echoed when the narrator and Leggatt search the map of the Gulf of Siam for an appropriate place for Leggatt's escape:

> He looked thoughtfully at the chart as if surveying chances and distances from a lofty height—*and following with his eyes his own figure wandering on the blank land of Cochin-China, and then passing off that piece of paper clean out of sight into uncharted regions.*

This is re-echoed in the structure of Leggatt's word when he decides to return to the sea, "What does the Bible say? *'Driven off the face of the earth.' Very well, I am off the face of the earth now. As I came at night so I shall go.*" The obvious references to the Cain and Abel archetypal structure are paralleled, as Leggatt suggests, in his relationship with the murdered sailor. As such they dictate a major structure of the novel, a ritual of murder, guilt, judgment, banishment or escape, and wandering, corresponding to the narrative course of Leggatt's story. But that is not all because the brother-murder-banishment-wandering archetypal structure echoes most of the principal relationships in the story. Leggatt and the murdered man; the narrator and Leggatt; the captain of the *Sephora* and Leggatt; the narrator and his Chief Mate and crew. Although Leggatt suggests the archetypal relationship between himself and the murdered man and the Cain and Abel story, the archetype is not complete because the captain of the *Sephora* also becomes the Cain figure who wants to kill Leggatt by turning him over to the law for trial. Because he is jealous of Leggatt's having saved the ship with the reefed sail, the *Sephora's* captain plays in an ironic reversal the Cain role to Leggatt's Abel. The Cain-Abel archetype circumscribes the narrator-Leggatt relationship as well, the longest pattern of action and most important relationship of the novel, for the narrator in a role comparable to that of Cain, figuratively kills his Abel-Leggatt when he consigns him to the sea. But the meaning of this archetypal action is symbolic and thematic because this Cain recognizes that he must destroy his Abel personality, an inversion of the Abel roll, by sending him back to the sea. That the narrator will wander the face of the earth like Cain is made clear in the last sentence of the novel. But by shifting our perspective slightly, we observe that the relationship of the narrator to his Chief Mate and crew and ship is also a fragment of the echoing Cain and Abel archetype. The narrator may have killed the hysterical Chief Mate, as Leggatt killed the mutinous sailor, and as Cain killed Abel, but he does something else. By transcending and controlling the Abels on the ship, Leggatt, the chief mate, the crew, he avoids the Cain role and, incidentally, transforms the archetype even as he completes it.

The echoed archetypal structures suggest the multiplicity of similar experiences. They suggest that every man may be his brother's killer wittingly or unwittingly. The captain of the *Sephora,* for instance, wishes to preserve law and order by turning Leggatt over to the courts, but how much of jealousy and shame lie behind his decision he never admits. To what degree does he maintain morality and responsibility and to what degree does he demand the death of Leggatt to free his own conscience from accusations of cowardice during the typhoon? How strong is the narrator's Chief Mate who likes to account for everything, and how much of the Cain does he have in him when he goes to pieces under the blackness of Koh-ring? Precisely this kind of ambivalence characterizes the use of the echoed archetypal structure in **"The Secret Sharer."** Thus the narrator as Cain *must kill* Abel-Leggatt in order that he may come to mature moral terms with his ship, crew, and self; and as Abel he *must not kill* or shame his first mate and crew in order that the trial be successfully passed.

The echo structure, by identifying various members of the ship's company now as Cain and now as Abel, suggests that all men in the ship-world are both Cain and Abel, that the Cain-Abel personality dwells in every man. "I wondered," says the narrator, "how far I should turn out faithful to that ideal conception of one's own personality every man sets up for himself secretly." And as the final structure in the novel suggests, the narrator meets his Cain personality in the form of Leggatt and in the form of his own blubbering Chief Mate and conquers both, dramatically answering his own question. Seeing Leggatt's phosphorescent flash pass under the white hat he wears into the water, the narrator thinks, "But I hardly thought of my other self, now gone from the ship, to be hidden forever from all friendly faces, *to be a fugitive and a vagabond on the earth, with no brand of the curse on his sane forehead to stay a slaying hand . . . too proud to explain.*"

Less explicit than the Cain-Abel archetypal structure is that of the Jonah archetype which appears in somewhat shadowy form in **"The Secret Sharer"** but which creates an echo structure nevertheless. During the fierce typhoon Leggatt kills the mutinous sailor, as he reminds us, a "miserable devil." Then he describes the mounting fury of the storm which follows hard upon his act:

> *And the ship running for her life, touch and go all the time, any minute her last in a sea fit to turn your hair gray only a-looking at it.* I understand that the skipper, too, started raving like the rest of them. The man had been deprived of sleep for more than a week, and to have this sprung on him at the height of a furious gale nearly drove him out of his mind. *I wonder they didn't fling me overboard after getting the carcass of their precious shipmate out of my fingers.* They had rather a job to separate us, I've been told. A sufficiently fierce story to make an old judge and a respectable jury sit up a bit.

This first part of the structure is about one half of the Jonah archetype: the fierce storm, the cursed or pursued or immoral person whose actions are intimately connected with the howling typhoon, the breach of a moral code, the suggestion of being thrown overboard, the hint at judgment. The final half of the archetypal pattern appears many pages later when at the end of the novel the echo structure completes the archetype. The narrator-captain has made a decision to put Leggatt overboard:

> "Now," I whispered, loudly, into the saloon— too loudly, perhaps, but I was afraid I couldn't make a sound. He was by my side in an instant— *the double captain slipped past the stairs— through the tiny dark passage . . . a sliding door. We were in the sail locker, scrambling on our knees over the sails.* A sudden thought struck me. *I saw myself wandering barefooted, bareheaded, the sun beating on my dark poll.* I snatched off my floppy hat and tried hurriedly in the dark to ram it on my other self. He dodged and fended off silently. I wondered what he thought had come to me before he understood and suddenly desisted. Our hands met gropingly, lingered united in a steady, motionless clasp for a second. . . . No word was breathed by either of us when they separated.

Returning to the deck, the narrator looks about on the sea for some marker which will indicate the position of the ship as it begins its turn from the land:

> All at once my strained, yearning stare distinguished a white object floating within a yard of the ship's side. White on the black water. A phosphorescent flash passed under it. What was that thing? . . . I recognized my own floppy hat. It must have fallen off his head . . . and he didn't bother. Now I had what I wanted—the saving mark for my eyes.

Thus at the last moment before the turn toward resolution in the novel, the second half of the echo structure is completed when Leggatt leaves the ship so that she may save herself and he himself. But the novel suggests more than this. Since Leggatt is to be saved from immediate death, since the suggestiveness of the sail locker scene evokes the atmosphere of the belly of the whale into which Jonah descended and from which he was to be released, since the ship releases him into the waters of freedom, and since the narrator himself is released from his Cain (Leggatt) personality in the sail locker scene ("I saw myself wandering barefooted, bareheaded, the sun beating on my dark poll"), the echo part of the structure seems to identify the ship as an archetypal image of Jonah's whale. At the same time the Cain-Abel archetype passes through the Jonah archetype when the narrator thinks of himself as wandering unprotected over the face of the earth. The significance of this crossing of archetypes lies, I believe, in the identification of common elements between Jonah as wanderer and Cain as wanderer. The former refused to carry out the commands of his God; the latter broke the commandments of his God by killing his brother.

What then is the significance of the Jonah archetype which we have seen is split into several parts, the first appearing near the beginning of **"The Secret Sharer,"** the second part, the echo structure, appearing on the last page of the novel? The archetype, for one thing, gives meaning to experience, those traditional meanings which cluster about the Cain and Abel story and, in the immediate situation, the Jonah story. The echoed archetype especially gives a kind of continuity to fragmentary, splintered, or shattered actions, movements, or partial patterns of behavior. It makes sense out of the meaninglessness of disparate experiences by giving recognizable form to discontinuous, perhaps chaotic experiences. The Biblical archetypes establish a moral climate within whose atmosphere the actions of the story may be judged. The archetype ritualizes, congeals, makes cohere, for instance, those scattered, almost senseless actions of men. To this, however, it brings its own meaning from the tradition of which it is a part. The way Leggatt is significantly identified as Jonah and the way the narrator is also identified as Jonah must now be examined.

Aboard the narrator's ship, Leggatt gradually poisons the relationship between the narrator and his crew. In the becalmed sea, a direct reversal of the typhoon scene, the threat of the presence of this Jonah to the narrator and his ship is as great as the threat to the *Sephora* and Captain Archbold in the howling storm. Jonah's moral weakness arose from his disobedience; Leggatt's moral defection lies

The Otago, *on which Conrad served as captain in 1886.*

in his murderous disposition, his inability to live within the strict confines of a moral atmosphere, and his essentially nihilistic attitude toward inferiors: "Miserable devils that have no business to live at all." Jonah flees his Lord; Leggatt flees from the captain's retribution and from the threat of law. Jonah, after spending three days in the whale, is coughed up and reconciled with his God; Leggatt after spending a number of days in the narrator's cabin, bathroom, and sail locker, is lowered into the water signalizing the reconciliation of the narrator with that other part of himself, the moral, controlled, ethical forces with the threatening, amoral forces of his personality.

The Jonah archetype like the Cain-Abel archetype contributes another dimension to the novel and reinforces its central thesis by suggesting in "other words" the very same thing that the Cain-Abel archetype suggested. Every man potentially *is* Cain and *is* Abel or every man *is* Jonah (Cain and Abel in one configuration); every man must come to terms with the other personality lurking within the human flesh. But, and this is most important, the Cain-Abel archetype suddenly crosses or is superimposed on the Jonah archetype in the sail locker scene. As suggested, this correspondence of archetypes seems to hint that essentially the two are one archetype told in different terms. Thus murder and disobedience are deliberately confused by means of the fusion of the archetypes, and they become, in terms of the thematic development of the novel, symbolic of any moral weakness which would not

permit man to know his most secret self and the constant threat which that inner self imposes on personality. Leggatt does not have the brand of Cain on him, the echo structure suggests and the narrator says at one moment near the end of **"The Secret Sharer,"** "with no brand of the curse on his sane forehead to stay a slaying hand." Leggatt does swim from the ship-whale, however, identified as the Cain who is condemned to wander the earth even if incognito "now gone from the ship to be hidden forever from all friendly faces, to be a fugitive and a vagabond on the earth." At the moment the two archetypes cross, while the men are in the darkened sail locker, Leggatt assumes his role once more in the Cain-Abel archetype; and the narrator assumes the role of Jonah in the second archetype. Symbolically this transference is achieved when the narrator claps his hat on the head of the reluctant Leggatt and when their hands meet for a final identification and farewell. The narrator arises to pace the deck of his ship-world no longer the disobedient Jonah within the punishing whale. He returns to the deck in the symbolic role of the obedient Jonah from that sail locker-belly to assume full command of himself, of his men, and of his ship.

Anyone familiar with archetypal structures will observe immediately that another archetype complicates the two discussed here by overlaying them with suggestions of Leggatt as scapegoat. As Kenneth Burke describes the archetypal function of this device, the scapegoat is "the 'representative' or 'vessel' of certain unwanted evils, the sacrificial animal upon whose back the burden of these evils is ritualistically loaded . . . the tendency was to endow the sacrificial animal with social coordinates, so that the goat became replaced by the 'sacrificial King.' " The conditions for becoming the archetypal scapegoat are any of these:

> (1) He may be made worthy legalistically (i.e., by making him an offender against legal or moral justice, so that he "deserves" what he gets).

> (2) We may make him worthy by leading towards sacrifice fatalistically (as when we so point the arrows of the plot that the audience comes to think of him as a marked man, and so prepares itself to relinquish him). . . .

> (3) We may make him worthy by a subtle kind of poetic justice, in making the sacrificial vessel "too good for this world," hence the *highest* value, hence the *most perfect* sacrifice (as with the Christ theme, and its secular variants, such as little Hanno Buddenbrooks, whose exceptional sensitivity to music made him worthy to be sacrificed to music).

Clearly Leggatt is the scapegoat for Captain Archbold and for the narrator as well. In the case of the captain of the *Sephora* Leggatt fulfills the first of the three conditions. By offending against legal justice when he kills the devilish sailor, Leggatt becomes "worthy legalistically" for sacrifice. But his guilt is complicated and mitigated because of his relation with Captain Archbold, for the captain uses him as a "vessel" for his own lack of bravery, for his own going to pieces when the ship appeared lost, and for his sense of guilt in front of his crew and wife. In the latter sense, then, the damning legal condemnation must be ameliorated and Leggatt, the legal murderer, must be seen as something less than a criminal. This scapegoat does, after all, save the *Sephora* and the lives of everyone on board including that of Captain Archbold, who performs the sacrifice of his scapegoat by putting him down a suicide.

For the narrator Leggatt serves as a scapegoat by fulfilling the two final conditions of the archetypal structure. Leggatt is led "towards sacrifice fatalistically" because the reader is constantly reminded that he represents Cain, that he destroys the harmony of the narrator's ship, that he prevents order from being established, and that he is the metaphorical scorpion threateningly present. It is not guilt or a sense of guilt or jealousy or evil which the narrator transfers to him as he places his hat on his head in that sail locker scene. It is something more subtle and more elusive. This scapegoat is a reminder to the narrator at the outset of his taking command of his first ship that all men have within them the very great possibility of another "presence" which in times of trial will defeat the outer self, the social mask constructed for our relationships with other men, unless the presence and its threat is met and conquered. The "secret self," Leggatt, struggles for a moment in the darkness of the sail locker (whale's belly), trying to fend off the hat, but the narrator defeats him there and places it firmly on his head. In the same way he will defeat his own threatening obtuseness when he returns to

deck and seizes and shakes strength into his bewhiskered Chief Mate.

As a fulfillment of the final condition, Conrad draws Leggatt as worthy of the sacrifice, with overtones of great reluctance on the part of the narrator. First, he is identified with the narrator whose own personality we admire. Then through a piling up of detail, Conrad builds a case for our admiration of Leggatt, and this in spite of the murder. He is, for instance, "a strong soul"; his father is "a parson"; he and the narrator are "Conway" boys. The narrator thinks, "And I knew well enough also that my double there was no homicidal ruffian." Leggatt does not despair nor does he think of suicide when he is certain that he is lost, although Captain Archbold will make him a suicide to clear his records and conscience. Leggatt refuses to try to break out of the *Sephora* in a violent manner because, "somebody would have got killed for certain, and I did not want any of that." The narrator marvels "at that something unyielding in his character which was carrying him through so finely." And, finally, the last statement of the novel, a deliberate ambiguity referring to both the narrator and Leggatt, "A free man, a proud swimmer *striking out for a new destiny.*" In this way and because he frees the narrator from the threat of defections of self, Leggatt is the most perfect sacrifice, the scapegoat of the highest value.

The sail locker scene is crucial to an understanding of the functioning of archetypal patterns. Here the three patterns suddenly coalesce and when they separate thematic relevance has been resolved. Until the transfer of the hat, Cain, Abel, Jonah, and scapegoat relationships are mingled and fused into each other. Then the hat is pushed down on Leggatt's head, the three archetypes separate, and the story plunges toward its climax, each archetypal role clearly distinguishable from all others.

The fundamental thematic tensions in **"The Secret Sharer"** embodied in and conveyed by these overlapping archetypal patterns. The knowledge which the narrator must gain, that he has lurking within the possibilities of moral corruption, represented by Leggatt and his attitude towards humanity, and the narrator's being tested, is carried in the Cain-Abel archetype which creates for the narrator a situation similar to that created for Leggatt. But by failing to pass his initiatory test successfully, Leggatt remains a Cain figure. By passing his test successfully the narrator faces his Cain characteristics and subjects them to his will. The Jonah archetype is introduced to suggest reconciliation by showing the two figures re-united in one person who carries with him the moral background of the Biblical tradition from which the archetype came. The possibility of danger and threat to those intimately related to Jonah as he seeks to flee is suggested by Leggatt's flight from the *Sephora* and his gradual disruption of the narrator's relationship with his men. But the possibility of salvation through a period of suffering and willingness to admit to and rid oneself of certain defections, and the possibility of undergoing a test of the reintegrated personality is portrayed in and symbolized by the narrator's shifting to the leading role in the Jonah archetype. As the reborn Jonah arose from the belly of the whale successfully reconciled with his God, so too the fully reintegrated narrator climbs from the sail locker a new person to face and pass his test victoriously.

Jocelyn Baines   (essay date 1960)

SOURCE: "Achievement without Success, III," in *Joseph Conrad: A Critical Biography,* Weidenfeld and Nicolson, 1960, pp. 346-78.

[*Baines was an English editor and critic. In the following excerpt from his* Joseph Conrad: A Critical Biography, *which has been acclaimed as the definitive study of Conrad, he argues that the text of "The Secret Sharer" does not support the often-proposed interpretation of Leggatt as a symbol for the narrator's unconscious desires.*]

Conrad wrote **'The Secret Sharer'** some time during the end of November and early December [1909]—exceptionally quick for him. It is undoubtedly one of his best short stories, but certain critics, notably Albert Guerard [in *Conrad the Novelist,* 1958] and Douglas Hewitt [in *Conrad: A Reassessment,* 1952], have claimed for it a position as a key story in Conrad's work and attributed to it a significance which I do not believe that it can hold. It is intensely dramatic but, on the psychological and moral level, rather slight.

The story is based on an incident which happened on board the *Cutty Sark* in 1880. The *Cutty Sark* had put in to Singapore on 18 September, three days after the chief officer of the *Jeddah* (the *Patna* in **Lord Jim**) had arrived there. In Conrad's adaptation of the *Cutty Sark* incident, Leggatt, the mate of the *Sephora,* kills a disobedient member of the crew during a storm and is put under arrest by his captain. But he escapes and swims to another ship of which the narrator of the story is captain. The captain is a young, comparatively inexperienced man who has just been given his first command—here Conrad seems to draw on his own experiences on the *Otago*—'a stranger to the ship' and 'somewhat of a stranger to myself'. He had taken the anchor watch himself and thus spots Leggatt in the water, clinging to a rope ladder; without calling anyone, for 'a mysterious communication was established already between us two', he lets Leggatt come on board and fetches some clothes for him.

> In a moment he had concealed his damp body in a sleeping-suit of the same grey-stripe pattern as the one I was wearing and followed me like my double on the poop.

When the captain has heard Leggatt's story he decides that he must hide him in his cabin. He does this at great risk and strain to himself and at the cost of becoming somewhat estranged from the rest of the crew because of the precautionary antics he has to go through to prevent Leggatt being discovered.

After some eventful days which include a visit from the captain of the *Sephora* he is able to come in close to shore and allow Leggatt to escape.

Constantly throughout the story it is emphasised that the young captain regards Leggatt as his double, and in a letter to Pinker Conrad suggested for titles of the story 'The Second Self', 'The Secret Self', 'The Other Self' (these three phrases, without the definite article of course, occur in the text); he also suggested **'The Secret Sharer'**, but wondered whether it might not be too enigmatic. The point of this, apart from heightening the dramatic effect, and the point of the story, is to suggest that the fates of these two men were interchangeable, that it was quite possible for an ordinary, decent, conscientious person to kill someone or to commit some action which would make him 'a fugitive and vagabond on the earth'. Thus Leggatt takes his place alongside Jim and Razumov. There is no suggestion of a transcendental relationship between Leggatt and the captain or of the 'double' being a psychological manifestation of an aspect of the original as there is in Poe's vulgar, trashy 'Richard Wilson' or Dostoevsky's obscure nightmare, 'The Double'.

But that is the way in which Guerard interprets the story. For him the 'hero' is the young captain: 'The real moral dilemma is *his,* not Leggatt's'. He, and Marlow in **Heart of Darkness,** 'must recognise their own potential criminality and test their own resources, must travel through Kurtz and Leggatt, before they will be capable of manhood . . . and moral survival'. The story will bear this interpretation, as long as it is realised that such was no part of the author's conscious intention. However, Guerard goes on to assert that Leggatt is not merely an 'other self', he is a 'lower self', 'the embodiment of a more instinctive, more primitive, less rational self'. I believe that this misses the whole point. Leggatt is not a symbol of the unconscious but a man on precisely the same level as the young captain; their selves are interchangeable (the epithet 'secret' might imply the opposite but its context and the whole tone of the story show that the word was intended in its literal sense: Leggatt was 'secret' because he had to be kept secret or hidden). Guerard's interpretation makes nonsense of the last sentence of the story, in which Leggatt departs, 'a free man, a proud swimmer striking out for a new destiny'. This is no way for a symbol of the unconscious to behave; Guerard's answer is that Leggatt is both a symbol and a 'man of flesh and blood'. He continues: 'By seeing his own dilemmas and difficulties in Leggatt, the captain has turned this man into symbol and spirit. . . . But at the end, emerging from his self-examination, the captain can see Leggatt as a separate and real human being.' But there is no indication in the story, explicit or implicit, that the captain sees any of his dilemma or difficulties in Leggatt or that he performs any self-examination. Nor is there any 'moral dilemma'.

Guerard's interpretation is based partly on what I believe is a mistaken assessment of the narrator's, or Conrad's, attitude to Leggatt's action. He claims that, for Conrad, 'a crime on shipboard . . . was simply and irrevocably a crime'. But there is no suggestion that Conrad or the captain-narrator condemns Leggatt's action; quite the contrary. At the start the captain says that he knew Leggatt was 'no homicidal ruffian'; and when the foolish mate comments on the event as 'A very horrible affair. . . . Beats all these tales about murders in Yankee ships', the captain snaps back: 'I don't think it beats them. I don't think it resembles them in the least.' His own opinion is summed up: 'It was all very simple. The same strung-up force which had given twenty-four men a chance, at least, for their lives, had, in a sort of recoil, crushed an unworthy mutinous existence.'

In this connexion it is interesting to see that Conrad softened the crime, if it can be called a crime, which took place on the *Cutty Sark* and also softened the character of the mate. The mate of the *Cutty Sark* was apparently a despotic character with a sinister reputation. An order which he gave to an incompetent negro named John Francis was twice disobeyed, and when he went forward to deal with Francis the insubordinate seaman attacked him with a capstan bar; after a struggle the mate got hold of the bar and brought it down on Francis's head so heavily that he never regained consciousness and died three days later. Nonetheless the captain of the *Cutty Sark,* who was by no means a hard man, is supposed to have said that it served Francis right, and he helped the mate to escape from the law. When the mate was eventually captured and tried, he was acquitted of murder and the judge, 'with great pain', sentenced him to seven years for manslaughter.

Leggatt was, however, clearly an exemplary sailor, and his provocation was greater; it was in the middle of a storm when the fate of the ship was at stake and the captain had lost his nerve. Leggatt was in the process of performing an action, which probably saved the ship, when one of the sailors was insubordinate; Leggatt 'felled him like an ox. He up and at me. We closed just as an awful sea made for the ship. All hands saw it coming and took to the rigging, but I had him by the throat, and went on shaking him like a rat, the men above us yelling, "Look out! look out!" Then a crash as if the sky had fallen on my head.' Although Leggatt says, 'It's clear that I meant business, because I was holding him by the throat still when they picked us up,' his action was far less deliberate than that of the mate of the *Cutty Sark.*

The object of this digression is to show that Conrad had no wish to condemn Leggatt but considered him an honourable man who had done something that other honourable men might equally well have done under similar circumstances. He was in fact 'simply knocked over' when a reviewer described Leggatt as 'a murderous ruffian', and certainly had no intention that he should be a symbol of the dark impulses of human nature.

Although his interpretation is not so extreme, Hewitt also regards Leggatt as a symbol, 'an embodiment of his [the captain's] original feeling of being a "stranger" to himself, of that fear that there are parts of himself which he has not yet brought into the light of day', and this 'strangeness' is finally exorcised with the departure of Leggatt. But this is again reading a meaning into the story which the text neither explicitly nor implicitly warrants; and despite the young captain's initial feeling of 'strangeness', the passage at the end where he says 'Nothing! no one in the world should stand now between us, throwing a shadow on the way of silent knowledge and mute affection, the perfect communion of a seaman with his first command' can be countered by a similar passage, before Leggatt turns up, where the captain is alone in 'quiet communion'

with the ship, his 'hand resting lightly on my ship's rail as if on the shoulder of a trusted friend'.

Although I do not believe that Conrad intended '**The Secret Sharer**' to be interpreted symbolically, it is easy to discover an unconscious symbolism which has no direct literary relevance but is important psychologically and autobiographically. Conrad had just left off writing his reminiscences for the *English Review,* in which he had been particularly concerned to justify his action in leaving Poland and to answer charges of desertion. It is tempting to identify Conrad with Leggatt and to see the implicit justification of Leggatt's action as a justification of Conrad's own, which metaphorically had made him too 'a fugitive and a vagabond on the earth, with no brand of the curse on his sane forehead to stay a slaying hand—too proud to explain'. It seems that in the twelve months which saw the completion of the reminiscences, the writing of '**The Secret Sharer**' and the finishing of *Under Western Eyes,* Conrad finally succeeded in coming to terms with his sense of guilt with regard to Poland. It is thus that the last sentence of '**The Secret Sharer**' acquires an added significance as an expression of Conrad's desire to be:

> a free man, a proud swimmer striking out for a new destiny.

Robert A. Day   (essay date 1963)

SOURCE: "The Rebirth of Leggatt," in *Literature and Psychology,* Vol. XIII, No. 3, 1963, pp. 74-81.

[*Day is an American educator, editor, and critic. In the following essay, he maintains that "The Secret Sharer" contains a double narrative that depicts both the maturation of the narrator and the rebirth of Leggatt.*]

Whenever possible, we like to see a work of art from a single point of view, as a harmonious whole. Anything extraneous to the desired pattern leaves us uneasy. Thus the mysterious figure of Leggatt has been a stumbling block for critics of Conrad's **"The Secret Sharer."** For example, [in an introduction to *Heart of Darkness and The Secret Sharer,* 1960] Albert J. Guerard, Jr., sees the story as a dramatization of the archetypal "night journey," in which the protagonist makes a "provisional descent" into darkness and the primitive, emerging with a new self—knowledge and a new maturity. Guerard finds Leggatt "the embodiment of a more instinctive, more primitive, less rational self," and he feels that the captain "both sympathize[s] with and condemn[s]" this image. But this interpretation raises a new problem. How shall we account for the fact that this symbolic lower self is also "a free man, a proud swimmer striking out for a new destiny"—for the captain's (and Conrad's) favorable view of Leggatt? Elsewhere Guerard finds the symbol "wrenched" at the end—"Theoretically, Leggatt should have remained on the ship;" the "proud swimmer" passage is a distortion—"the darker self . . . is in no sense such an heroic figure of freedom"—and the conclusion, he says, "is the chief area of incomprehensible feeling in the story." He attempts to solve this problem by suggesting that the captain, having profited from the contemplation of the Leggatt-image, is now able to see Leggatt as a mere man of flesh and blood, and therefore to part with him [*Joseph Conrad*, 1947].

Carl Benson, who is concerned solely with Conrad's known artistic intentions, takes issue with Guerard's view of Leggatt. Benson sees him rather as a "model of assured courage," supporting this position with Conrad's own views, as expressed in an indignant letter. If such an interpretation answers the previous question, Benson presents another one; he feels that the captain's initiation is "humanly abortive," and points out that meanwhile the captain has neglected his duty and his ship; furthermore, that he has measured up to his ideal image "only in a limited, egocentric way" [*PMLA*, 1954].

R. W. Stallman considers the story on the literal level, and also as an "allegory of the plight of the artist," but does not analyze the links between the story and the allegory; therefore the question whether the actions and character of Leggatt fit consistently into a symbolic pattern does not arise. On the literal level, the appearance and disappearance of Leggatt are perfectly acceptable; Stallman points out that Leggatt "provides [the captain] the utmost test . . . of his fidelity to his vision of ideal selfhood." Furthermore, Stallman emphasizes the captain's "doubt of Leggatt's bodily existence; Leggatt is an invisible participant" [*Forms of Modern Fiction*, 1948].

These approaches see the story as concerned chiefly with an experience of initiation. They tend to minimize the importance of Leggatt, and they see the action *through* the captain, or from his point of view. This last is of course entirely natural, because of Conrad's angle of narration. I suggest, however, a wider approach—the examination in detail of certain symbols in the story, and an attempt to view the narrative as it surrounds Leggatt rather than the captain—and this approach is justified by our knowledge of how Conrad reworked the facts on which he based **"The Secret Sharer."** Such an approach offers a solution of the problems mentioned above; it provides evidence that Conrad, whether consciously or unconsciously, created a double narrative, in which the captain's initiation into maturity is paralleled and complemented by a symbolic presentation of the archetype of rebirth—the rebirth of Leggatt.

Conrad's works, and **"The Secret Sharer"** in particular, were written more "intuitively" and with less purely logical planning than much modern fiction. This intuitive method gives the author's imagination free rein, not merely planning what may be effective for the reader, but also promoting the introduction of details which the author somehow feels to be "right." Such a writer may allow the wider area of his unconscious mind to influence his creations very freely, and in his fiction we shall find a better key to the workings of his unconscious than in that of an author who meticulously revises with an eye coldly fixed upon artistic effect.

Furthermore, **"The Secret Sharer"** could not have been subjected to the pruning which may have altered the original drafts of Conrad's more artful works. His wife writes [in *Joseph Conrad and His Circle*, 1935] that the story, a long one by ordinary standards, was conceived, composed, finally typed, and sent off to the printer within the space

of a week, and without Conrad's telling her any details about the incident which had inspired it, or the process of its creation. He told her, "It is pure fiction, my dear." However, the *Sephora*-Leggatt part of the story is based on incidents which took place on the clipper *Cutty Sark* in 1880, and which were familiar to Conrad. In short, **"The Secret Sharer"** gives us an example of Conrad's seizing on a fragment of remembered material, taking his distinctive psychological and moral sight upon it, and reworking it into a satisfactory artistic whole very rapidly, without the correction and hindsight which would have modified a more laborious and slowly executed work. Such a story may well contain symbols and thought-patterns of whose existence the author himself was only partially conscious.

A close reading of **"The Secret Sharer,"** if it is seen as the tale of the greatest crisis in Leggatt's life, reveals a linking of details with archetypal patterns seen in many classic narratives of men and the sea. It is a critical commonplace that the sea represents the unconscious, primordial elements in man's mind, that it is the great mother of life, and so forth; some such associations may have been in Conrad's thoughts. But the presence here of the "night journey" theme reminds one especially of famous sea-tales in which the theme is prominent. *The Ancient Mariner* comes at once to mind, and a comparison of **"The Secret Sharer"** with *The Ancient Mariner,* as analyzed in Maud Bodkin's pioneer work on poetic archetypes, is particularly illuminating. In both an untried innocent, held by a mysterious attraction or bond, receives instruction from one who has sinned, been cast out, and is a wanderer. The vicarious experience of sin and its consequences has a powerful effect, and the hearer grows in wisdom. Many discrepancies are apparent; yet if the two narratives are viewed with reference to the rebirth archetype, the discrepancies are bridged and the "plots" are seen to be essentially similar both in general and in detail.

Miss Bodkin presents the essence of the rebirth-pattern as follows:

> Within the image-sequence examined the pattern appears of a movement, downward, or inward toward the earth's centre, or a cessation of movement—a physical change which . . . also appears as a transition toward severed relation with the outer world, and, it may be, toward disintegration and death. This element of the pattern is balanced by a movement upward and outward—an expansion or outburst of activity, a transition toward redintegration and life-renewal [*Archetypal Patterns in Poetry,* 1948].

This pattern clearly parallels Leggatt's abandonment of society—the *Sephora* and the order of life it represents—his descent into the sea (darkness, oblivion, death), his passivity and inertness in the cabin, and his final burst of activity and entrance into a new order of existence—wandering over the earth. Leggatt's experience resembles even more closely the account of a dream which Miss Bodkin associates with her pattern: a man dives from a crowded steamer; the water becomes warmer as he descends (the tropic sea of **"The Secret Sharer,"** whose temperature has something to do with Leggatt's preservation); he ascends and finds at the surface a little boat which saves him.

Miss Bodkin stresses two other elements in the archetypal pattern of *The Ancient Mariner:* the quickening of the wind, which she equates with new life or artistic inspiration, and the figure of the man who expiates a crime by wandering endlessly—Cain, The Wandering Jew, the Mariner. Leggatt sees himself as Cain on several occasions and he knows well that he is forever doomed to wander, an outcast from society. Likewise, Leggatt has the lesson of his crime to teach. And his arrival on the ship is followed by an end to the dead calm that has prevailed. Activity begins, the wind rises, and the ship proceeds on her way.

The problem of relating Leggatt's crime to the Ancient Mariner's is more difficult, but not insoluble, for we know that Conrad went out of his way to mitigate Leggatt's action as much as possible. Guerard, who remarks that Leggatt is "outcast and more primitive . . . a rather dubious hero," says elsewhere:

> No symbol was ever less abstract than the poignant Leggatt, doomed to a life of wandering for the slight defect of a manly temperament,

thus emphasizing the disproportion between crime and punishment, as in *The Ancient Mariner,* where it is thought to point up the symbolic nature of the Mariner's sin. Leggatt is sure that society will inevitably condemn him, that it cannot properly judge him, and that he must escape from society if he wishes to survive. He does not repent his crime, though he deplores it; he excuses himself on a number of grounds—that he saved the *Sephora,* that the murdered man was utterly worthless, that the attack occurred in a fit of passion under great stress. Nor does the captain do his duty and clap him in irons or turn him over to the captain of the Sephora—a curious sort of behavior if he truly condemns Leggatt, or if Conrad does, as Guerard would indicate.

Moreover, if we compare Leggatt with the *Cutty Sark's* mate Sydney Smith, on whom Conrad based his character, we find a number of significant changes. We cannot determine precisely what Conrad knew of the events on the *Cutty Sark;* he mentions only that the story had been common among merchant seamen for years, and he is uncertain about the date. (Probably, however, he got the detail of the captain's white hat from remembering that the owner of the *Cutty Sark* habitually wore such a hat.) But if we assume that Conrad was fairly well acquainted with the story, we can find much of interest in the differences between **"The Secret Sharer"** and its source. Smith did not have Leggatt's calm confidence; there was no notion that he was a superior being—he was a good officer, and that was all. Some gave him a bad character, and he was said to be too ready for a fight. An insolent seaman, against whom Smith had a long—standing grudge, clumsily let go a rope and threatened Smith with a capstan bar when Smith started after him to punish him—hardly provocation to murder or manslaughter for a competent officer surrounded by subordinates.

Conrad altered details with interesting effect. Smith was smuggled aboard a nearby ship by his own captain (who committed suicide by jumping overboard later on the voyage); and while a search for Smith was made, the crew of the *Cutty Sark* was not allowed aboard the ship concealing him. Moreover, the mate did not swim from one ship to the other, although later tall stories sometimes credited him with a heroic feat of long-distance swimming. And the symbolic and literal importance to Conrad's story of the "proud swimmer's" astonishing powers in the water can hardly be overemphasized.

We cannot explain Conrad's modification of these facts unless we suppose that in some sense he approved of the conduct he had assigned to Leggatt and wished to mitigate his guilt while retaining the artistically useful parts of the original account. One doubts whether Conrad or his fictional captain could have exonerated the real Sydney Smith. Thus Leggatt is like the Ancient Mariner in that his punishment—being cast out to wander forever—is disproportionate to his crime, though the disproportion is admittedly less.

Furthermore, one remembers the universal condemnation which the Mariner receives from his shipmates (suggesting the figure of Jonah, a classic example of the rebirth archetype); he who is to be reborn is first rejected. Leggatt is likewise an outcast on the *Sephora.* Its captain regards him with fear and abhorrence, and at one point he says, "I wonder that they didn't fling me overboard." Thus Conrad emphasizes Leggatt's role as outcast, making it clear that his position in "society" is quite hopeless—his pleas to be allowed to escape are refused, unlike the friendly and criminal assistance given to his prototype. Leggatt's only alternatives are certain death imposed by law or a voluntary flight to death and oblivion. His preservation, if it is hardly supernatural, is brought about by a combination of circumstances so unusual as to verge on the miraculous.

The unnamed captain's importance to **"The Secret Sharer"** as narrator overshadows Leggatt's importance to it as part of the source material; but since the captain may have been made up of whole cloth and Leggatt was not, our viewpoint as readers necessarily differs from Conrad's as writer. Conrad has included many significant details about Leggatt, his appearance, his actions, which the captain (and we) pass over in favor of more important matters. They are in the story, nevertheless, and contribute to Conrad's intended effect. They include statements, comparisons, and situations, and the symbolic pattern they form might be called the "secondary description" of Leggatt—remarks about him other than the more obvious ones such as his remarkable identification with the captain. The elements of this pattern are images—images of conception, gestation, and birth. Let us first consider Leggatt's journey from this point of view.

Like the male element in procreation, Leggatt is cut off from his source, and faces destruction unless the one chance in a million happens—as it does. He is saved by blind chance, by the presence of the ship, the trailing ladder, and the captain's being on deck alone—though again, like the male element toward the female, he is attracted by the ship and makes for it on a vague impulse. But the captain (who in this context would play the role of the female element or act as its symbol) is actually responsible for all these saving factors. Now Leggatt goes into a fetus-like state—his passive crouching in the dark cabin, completely helpless, protected and nourished by the captain, without movement or responsibility. At length, with regret and hesitation on both his part and the captain's, he escapes, as does the fetus, from his imprisonment into liberty, but also into danger and responsibility for himself. The whole experience, culminating in the perilous feat of seamanship involved in Leggatt's departure, like the agony of birth, has given the captain a new maturity and added a new dimension to his character.

This interpretation of the story not only fits the facts, but is borne out by a number of relevant statements. Some of these are conditioned by the physical facts of the shipboard setting; others are completely gratuitous, and therefore of more significance. But even of the necessary passages one might ask why these details should be spelled out; why might Conrad not just as well have omitted them?

According to this interpretation, the captain and the ship would play the feminine role. And the captain early displays himself as not merely hesitant, which is only natural in his first command, but singularly passive and anxious to avoid trials and difficulties—a "feminine" attitude, as our civilization regards it. In contrast to this passivity, one of the first impressions we have of Leggatt is that "the voice was calm and resolute," and we hear of his thoroughly aggressive and vigorous (or "masculine") conduct in his escape. Appropriately to his role of fetus, however, he is naked, and the captain must clothe him and lead him to shelter, where he seems almost instinctively to choose the long and concealed part of the L-shaped cabin; the captain finds him there on returning. The idea of Leggatt as fetus is reinforced by several detailed descriptions of his immobility and his posture.

> I . . . saw the naked man from the sea sitting on the main-hatch, glimmering white in the darkness his elbows on his knees and his head in his hands.

> I saw him far back there, sitting rigidly on the low stool, his bare feet together, his arms folded, his head hanging on his breast—and perfectly still.

> [While telling his story] he did not stir a limb.

> He reclined on the floor, his legs bent, his head sustained on one elbow.

Having been established in the cabin and having told his story, the "amazing swimmer" is suddenly so exhausted as to need help in climbing into the (recessed) bed; and the captain, after assisting him, is "extremely tired in a peculiarly intimate way." This curious wording, at such a point in the story, suggests allusion to post-coital or post-parturient lassitude.

It seems impossible to get food to Leggatt from outside—although Conrad might well have surmounted this difficulty—and all of his nourishment except for the captain's morning coffee comes from within the cabin, and from the captain's own private stock—"all sorts of abominable sham delicacies out of tins." At this point we have an amplification of the womb-imagery: the food Leggatt consumes is not a man's food, but a soft, prepared diet which has its source in the cabin, his refuge and prison.

The identification of Leggatt with the captain, and the inevitability of their meeting, are significant, though less importantly, in this interpretation. The idea—commonplace in all cultures—of the physical and mental bonds linking the mother and the child she carries is easily connected with the preternatural sympathy of the captain and Leggatt.

When the time for Leggatt's release comes, the captain is reluctant, and even Leggatt falters briefly, but they realize that the "birth" is necessary and inevitable; it cannot be delayed beyond a certain point. The captain says reflectively that he quickly realized that his hesitation to part with Leggatt "had been mere sham sentiment, a sort of cowardice." Leggatt has a moment of panic when the captain is guiding him toward his place of escape; he worms his way through a porthole, and he uses a rope's end to lower himself into the water. To see a suggestion of the birth canal and the umbilical cord here may seem fanciful, but the actual need of the rope is questionable; at a moment of such great tension on deck the crew would hardly hear or give attention to a splash over the side.

Leggatt is given a chance to live twice; his old life is wiped out, and after a symbolic conception and gestation he is liberated from the womb of the ship and born to a new life; again he must undergo the penalties of human existence.

> [He] had lowered himself into the water to take his punishment; a free man, a proud swimmer striking out for a new destiny.

The closing lines of the story are concerned not with the captain-narrator, but with the release and "baptism" of the reborn Leggatt. The captain, having been the agent of this symbolic birth, has received fulfilment, a new depth of character, new confidence, knowledge of a new kind, and is now secure in his ability to cope with the problems of maturity.

Granted that the rebirth archetype and the imagery of birth are present in **"The Secret Sharer,"** are they intrinsically significant to its total effect as a work of art? Do they exist organically, or do they merely crop up now and again in a confused and fragmentary manner? If we compare **"The Secret Sharer"** to *The Ancient Mariner* or to the Book of Jonah, we at once observe a difference in the order of events. It is this different order, and certain technical elements of story-telling which inevitably claim the reader's primary attention, that so obscure the pattern. In the "classical" pattern, the sinner commits his crime, is reprehended and cast out, makes his descent toward death, repents, rises and is reborn, wanders to expiate his crime, and teaches others. But in Conrad's story this order has been modified by the grafting on of the captain and his role. He is at once the agent of the rebirth and the man who learns from the sinner; thus paradoxically the agent of salvation is the innocent (as with Parsifal), and the redeemed pays for his salvation by instructing his savior.

Both profit simultaneously. The captain, by his intuitive understanding and material help in a hostile society, has given Leggatt courage and the incentive toward a new life (Leggatt himself is decisive about escaping), and Leggatt, by being at once a model of courage and a symbol of the potentialities of evil, has expanded and enriched the captain's character and self-knowledge. The captain now feels that he must pay his mentor—"It was now a matter of conscience to shave the land as close as possible"—and what better payment than by having fostered him in helplessness and by engineering his rebirth into a new life?

The problem of repentance is a more difficult one. How can Leggatt properly teach before he has repented? Yet the machinery for repentance has been set in motion by Leggatt's acceptance of the inevitability of punishment and his determination to suffer it, perhaps to atone—one might adduce as a parallel the situation in *Lord Jim.* Furthermore, the nature of the "lesson" must be considered. If the teachings of the Mariner and of Jonah's experience may be simplified to injunctions against hate, pride, and impiety, then Leggatt has fulfilled his function as teacher by making the captain recognize his own evil potentialities, as is hinted when he uses violence on the mate. If we decide that Leggatt is simply unconscious of guilt, or refuses to admit it, then we may question whether conscious repentance must be included in the basic pattern of death to one life and rebirth to and integration with another.

The rebirth archetype is demonstrably present in **"The Secret Sharer,"** though masked by telescoping and realignment of its elements. That it is so obscured as to be almost unrecognizable is due also to more concrete factors in the story. Conrad was not one to present the bare bones of his fable, and the reader is so gripped by the dramatic details of the surface narrative that only by close study can he become aware of their rich background of symbol and image. The dramatic arrival of Leggatt, his dangerous concealment, the continual narrow squeaks with the steward, the officers, and the *Sephora's* captain, the nerve-wracking approach to Koh-ring, force attention away from the line-by-line detail of the story. The reader focuses on the captain, strained to the breaking point by constant fear, watchfulness, and the need for clever improvising. But even the casual reader must be struck by Conrad's final image—the proud, confident Leggatt, triumphantly quitting the scene.

Conrad has written a double narrative of rebirth and initiation, by both direct and indirect means. To see the captain as a mere initiate and Leggatt as a mere "lower self" is to find inconsistent presentation and twisted symbolism. The rebirth pattern fills out the seeming gaps in characterization, symbol, and moral process. The characters meet and interact; each performs a vital service to the other, which only he can perform; each is learner, teacher, protector; and each, after a violent wrenching apart, in which both prove their new maturity, goes on his way with confidence in himself and the future. Conrad did not, I think, intend the story to cover a vast moral area, but rather to be a complex dramatization of a particular experience which comes to many—the profound modification of character, amounting almost to a new life, which may

come through an accidental, brief, but profoundly important association with a stranger. The significance of such an encounter is vigorously underscored if it is labeled a true rebirth, and Conrad seems unconsciously to have planted such an implication beneath the surface of **"The Secret Sharer."**

Porter Williams, Jr. (essay date 1964)

SOURCE: "The Matter of Conscience in Conrad's *The Secret Sharer,*" in *PMLA,* Vol. LXXIX, No. 5, December, 1964, pp. 626-30.

[*In the following essay, Williams interprets "The Secret Sharer" as an exploration of the narrator's capacity for immoral behavior and his rescue from the consequences of that behavior.*]

In spite of the critical attention that it has received, Conrad's **"The Secret Sharer"** continues to present mysteries that usually affect our understanding of the story's climax in which Leggatt, the murderer and fugitive, is given his chance to escape while the ship hovers on the edge of disaster. Clearly enough, in its broadest aspects, the story is framed by a question and its answer. The narrative opens by presenting an uninitiated captain, a stranger to his ship and to himself, wondering how far he "should turn out faithful to that ideal conception of one's own personality every man sets up for himself secretly." It closes with the answer that through self-knowledge and self-mastery the captain has achieved "the perfect communion of a seaman with his first command." But between these two points, knowledge and self-mastery are won only after the disconcerting ordeal of protecting Leggatt and the strange exposure of the ship to near destruction, for the dangers from which the captain is allowed to extricate himself seem unnecessary ones of his own making. In turning towards the rocks of Koh-ring, he has done what he "certainly should not have done . . . if it had been only a question of getting out of that sleepy gulf as quickly as possible." Moreover, in shaving the land "as close as possible," he has approached disaster far closer than necessary if it had been only a question of testing his authority or granting Leggatt a reasonable chance to escape. He did not even turn his ship until he could answer his question about being "close enough" with the words, "Already she was, I won't say in the shadow of the land, but in the very blackness of it, already swallowed up as it were, gone too close to be recalled, gone from me altogether." Even after swinging the mainyard, while the fate of the ship "hung in the balance," the captain could do nothing but wait "helplessly." Obviously Leggatt could have made his escape long before this; "half a mile" would have been easy for this powerful swimmer. Why, then, was the ship about to enter "the gates of everlasting night"? And why was Leggatt being given so much more than the reasonable distance that he had asked for? Unquestionably this was beyond an absolute limit for any responsible mariner, even though it involved an act of compassion.

It is true that without a supreme test of his authority, the captain might never have experienced that "perfect communion" with his first command, but this reward came afterwards, almost by accident. What we are actually told at the moment of rashness is something quite different: "It was now a matter of conscience to shave the land as close as possible—for now he must go overboard whenever the ship was put in stays. Must! There could be no going back for him." Ostensibly, this means that beyond the kindness of giving Leggatt the opportunity to escape, the captain had created a situation which gave Leggatt no other rational choice but to go. But Leggatt already knew this and had earlier convinced the captain of this very fact. Something new was obviously disturbing the captain's mind when he expressed the hope that "perhaps he was able to understand why, on my conscience, it had to be thus close—no less." This is more than an effort to embarrass a guest into leaving by providing a suitable opportunity— all this had been agreed upon and the guest stood ready, hat upon head. There is here a new matter of "conscience" that Leggatt would "perhaps" be able to fathom. Was he to understand that the captain needed to face his supreme test alone with his first command, in which "Nothing! no one in the world should stand now between us, throwing a shadow on the way of silent knowledge and mute affection". Obviously this assertion of independence is crucial, but there is also something more that involves the character of Leggatt.

In evaluating Leggatt, there is always the danger of representing him as nothing more than some dangerous but potentially useful manifestation of the captain's suppressed alter ego. In this role he is seen as the mysterious source of the captain's strength and courage. Conrad often describes him as a "strong soul," appearing always "perfectly self-controlled, more than calm—almost invulnerable." But Leggatt is also a human being in his own right, fully aware of the danger he faces as an outlaw and suffering from terrible loneliness and the need "to talk with somebody" before going on. Even as the captain's other self, he represents this weakness as well as strength, and depends upon the captain to provide the same kind of moral support that the captain found in him. In their roles as doubles or as separate individuals, "the two become interchangeable, and the success of one depends upon the success of the other" [Frederick R. Karl, *A Reader's Guide to Joseph Conrad*, 1960]. Outward events as well as inner psychology have brought them together to share strength and weakness, and nowhere is this sharing more essential than at the moment of parting.

It is near the climax of the story that we learn most clearly that just as the captain received strength from his double, so Leggatt found in the captain what he needed most, someone who had "understood thoroughly" and who had declined to make a judgment about his guilt. It was precisely this understanding that had given Leggatt the courage to accept exile and to persuade the reluctant captain to recognize the truth of his warning, "You must maroon me." Unfortunately, such sympathetic understanding had become for each a sustaining bond, a union with a second self. Shortly before the moment of parting, the captain "for the first time" had observed in Leggatt "a faltering, something strained in his whisper," which had ended in Leggatt's clutching the captain's arm. For the first time the captain had been made aware of the intensity of Leg-

gatt's emotional attachment, occurring at a moment when the captain had already overcome his own reluctance and was prepared to let Leggatt go. Leggatt too had made his decision, but at the heart of it lay the need for an absolute assurance, expressed by his words to the captain, "As long as I know that you understand." Regardless of what was behind Leggatt's faltering, whether it was a weakening of this assurance or a reluctance to leave its source, the captain sensed it and now realized that Leggatt's dependence upon this emotional bond had to be broken, by shaving the rocks of Koh-ring if necessary. It was a matter of conscience, ultimately, to offer Leggatt a compelling demonstration of absolute understanding and sympathy by indulging in an act of supreme daring, rash enough to convince a hesitant Leggatt of the sincerity of the captain's moral support. In essence, this matter of conscience was a demonstration of sympathetic understanding that momentarily involved the risk of sharing Leggatt's doom in order to justify deserting him. When the ship's "very fate hung in the balance," the captain waited "helplessly" in the darkness, unable to detect movement and hence unable to act. It is essential to realize that at this moment the captain had almost put his ship beyond rescue, for there was not time enough to get the marker he needed. He was almost as committed to the consequences of rashness as his outcast secret sharer had been, for he knew he was on the verge of sharing Leggatt's exile: "I realised suddenly that all my future, the only future for which I was fit, would perhaps go irretrievably to pieces in any mishap to my first command." If Leggatt had needed the assurance of some final demonstration of sympathy, he now had it. It can be assumed that he understood why the captain's rashness was a "matter of conscience," just as the obligation to go was now also a matter of conscience. Ironically enough, the rash act designed to force Leggatt into the water also provided the "saving mark" for the captain's eyes—the floppy hat given for Leggatt's protection against the sun. That the captain was allowed this saving mark, a symbol of compassion, was presumably a fortunate accident "which counts for so much in the book of success." Competence alone had not saved the ship. On this basis, Leggatt the murderer had at least as much right to become "a free man, a proud swimmer striking out for a new destiny" as did the rash captain to feel "the perfect communion of a seaman with his first command." In saving a ship, Leggatt has unnecessarily stepped beyond acceptable moral limits by violently killing a man, and he accepts the punishment of becoming an outcast, though along with this punishment stands the opportunity for a new destiny. Likewise, the captain, while saving a fugitive and winning back his command, daringly exposes his ship to possible destruction. The truth that he was not also a fugitive, if this defines a moral difference between them, was a mere accident having little to do with degrees of innocence or guilt. In fact, had the ship gone upon the rocks, more than the blood of one man might have been upon the captain's hands. There would have been nothing marginal about his guilt in the eyes of a British court. Leggatt's murderous rage and the captain's decision to risk his ship, though not alike in terms of motivation, came surprisingly close to having the same destructive consequences in terms of human life.

Having thus placed emphasis upon the captain's desperate manner of freeing himself from Leggatt's hold, there is danger of forgetting that other problems remain. Even if the sensing of Leggatt's hesitation justifies the risk of going beyond a convenient distance to a daring and absolute limit, it does not explain the logic of placing the ship so nearly "beyond recall" that there was serious doubt about saving her. Above all it does not explain why Conrad leaves us with the impression that there is no need to condemn what appears as the shocking behavior of reaching the point where the loss of the ship and much of its crew seemed so nearly certain. We can only marvel why such rashness is rewarded with a clear conscience and serene self-assurance. It can be assumed that it is not usual for Conrad to approve of a captain who risks a ship to remove a troublesome passenger, just as it can be assumed that Leggatt's punishment implies that we are not to approve of a chief mate who murders to subdue a rebellious seaman. We need think only of MacWhirr's admirable concern for the lives of those aboard the *Nan-Shan* and of how he subdued his mutinous second mate without killing him. In contrast stands the shame that haunted Jim even after he had learned of the rescue of the pilgrims he had abandoned. Naturally it is made clear in **"The Secret Sharer"** that punishment awaited the captain if he had lost his ship; nevertheless, in any exacting moral sense his miraculous escape hardly seems to lessen his guilt. As Carl Benson protests, from the viewpoint of those endangered, the captain has still "demonstrated the power of authority in a needlessly fear-inspiring way" ["Conrad's Two Stories of Initiation," *PMLA*, March, 1954]. The judgment of the terrified mate verifies the statement: "You have done it, sir. I knew it'd end in something like this . . . She'll drift ashore before she's round." The captain's own thoughts during the crisis support the accusation.

In the light of such severe judgments, it would appear that Conrad has indulged in a specious argument that the miraculous escape has cleared the record and given his captain an honorable place beside such conscientious men as MacWhirr and the young captain in **The Shadow-Line.** Yet we know from a letter to Garnett how Conrad felt that he had luckily achieved the exact effect intended when he wrote, "Every word fits and there's not a single uncertain note." The reader can only assume that the text of the story somehow supplies the additional evidence needed to help us "accept" the near disaster. As the narrator in **"Falk"** saw the alternatives, to overcome obstacles standing in the way of efficient command "a skipper would be justified in going to any length, short of absolute crime." How, then, in spite of appearances, has Conrad kept the actions of his captain within acceptable moral bounds?

The most obvious device that Conrad uses, of course, is to suggest through parallels that it is actually possible to understand the captain as sympathetically as he has understood Leggatt. Although Leggatt is condemned as a murderer by the captain and crew of the *Sephora* and admits his kinship to Cain, he wins his protector's sympathy and understanding by making him aware of very genuine extenuating circumstances, including the exhausting strain of the storm, the heroic action of saving the *Sephora*, and the savage though not entirely unprovoked attack of a "half-crazed" seaman. Through the captain's feelings of identity, the reader is persuaded to understand how Leggatt's heroism so easily turns into unnecessary violence. Similarly, from the moment the fugitive is offered shelter, we are made aware of how the pressure of unforeseen consequences tightens about the captain until we are ready to admit the need for desperate remedies if there is to be any escape at all.

The necessity of compelling Leggatt to leave becomes crucial only when it is understood how desperately the captain needed to establish his authority. Just as any mishap to the ship would have wrecked the captain's career, so also would the mere discovery of Leggatt's presence. Either way, the proper management of the ship and the captain's career are in jeopardy. Added to this are the inevitable complications, the intensity of the strain and the certainty of defeat even if nothing is done, which must surely be included in any evaluation of Conrad's stories of initiation. The test of character must be made while body and spirit are being crushed and death or defeat is imminent. Just how desperate the captain's predicament became receives constant attention until it is made clear that the captain came "as near insanity as any man who has not actually gone over the border." Extreme fatigue, the unrelieved "strain of stealthiness," the "confused sensation of being in two places at once," and above all the dread of "accidental discovery" were distracting "almost to the point of insanity." It is entirely to the captain's credit, however, that his greatest concern was over the manner in which his seamanship was affected: "I was not wholly alone with my command . . . not completely and wholly with her. Part of me was absent." Final emphasis is placed upon the manner in which the captain's physical sensitivity is deadened, for this complication enters with a vengeance at the climax of the story: "But I was also more seriously affected. There are to a seaman certain words, gestures, that should in given conditions come as naturally, as instinctively as the winking of a menaced eye. A certain order should spring on to his lips without thinking; a certain sign should get itself made, so to speak, without reflection. But all unconscious alertness had abandoned me. I had to make an effort of will to recall myself back . . . to the conditions of the moment." Thus it is from all these crushing consequences of his predicament that the captain must save himself if he is to win back the command he is losing. Removing Leggatt is the key. Gaining absolute control of his ship is the commendable goal.

It is the "self-controlled, more than calm" Leggatt, with his "sane forehead," who shows the captain the way of escape. The "sanity" of the advice is insisted upon. Leggatt forces the captain to realize that further "hesitation in letting that man swim away" would have been "a mere sham sentiment, a sort of cowardice." Leggatt thoughtfully releases the captain from any further moral obligations to his fugitive once the ship is brought within reasonable distance from the shore—"I want no more." But unquestionably Leggatt gets much more when the effort to compel him to act ends in the rashness of taking the ship momentarily beyond control. This fact is hard to deny. Even if it be magnanimously granted that the captain had exaggerated when he expressed the fear that his ship was "beyond recall," "gone from me altogether," the fact remains that the ship would have been lost without the "saving mark" of Leggatt's hat. This kind of escape could not have been part of the plan. Put in this way, there is still the crux of explaining away what normally should have ended in responsibility for a wrecked ship.

Surely critical evaluation and not Conrad has erred at this point. The redeeming fact is simply that any genuinely courageous action involves a risk of error and failure, and while taking such a risk the captain unintentionally found himself at the mercy of an error, a moment of ignorance, that nearly made failure certain. In making this error a part of the record, Conrad excludes any question of wilful destruction, even if the ship had been lost and the question of taking unpardonable risks remained. For it is also a part of the record that the captain had conscientiously set for himself practical limits that were always included in his plans. For example, on the evening he was to depart, Leggatt was told, "I'll edge her in to half a mile, as far as I may be able to judge in the dark"; and later, "I shall stand in as close as I dare and then put her round." There was never any plan to include difficulties that might make it impossible to "come about." Even as the ship began to approach the dangerous windward side of the island and the captain first formulated the idea that it was a matter of conscience to "shave the land," there was still the reservation as close "as possible" and the plan to come about by putting the ship "in stays" at the last moment. The maneuver, criticized by the mate, was understood to be a dangerous one, but the captain insisted that "She will weather." The nautical details are important here because more than anything else they record the exact moral significance of what the captain thought he was doing.

Unfortunately, at some moment in the maneuver, a moment during which the captain lost touch, the ship was nearly wrecked. When the captain suddenly assumes that he had "gone too close to be recalled," he skillfully impresses his will upon the alarmed crew and presumably upon Leggatt as he enforces the orders to bring the boat around, doing exactly what he had intended doing all along except for one thing. In spite of all the planning, one crucial factor, forgotten as the captain's will was being exerted upon Leggatt, again enters the pattern of unforeseen consequences. As the ship hangs in the balance, only half about and poised near the rocks, the captain recalls what he should never have forgotten: "And now I . . . remembered only that I was a total stranger to the ship. I did not know her. Would she do it? How was she to be handled?" It was essential for the captain to know that the ship had gathered sternway, but in spite of all his skill "it was impossible to feel the ship coming-to." This important failure, repeated in three consecutive paragraphs, is surely a reminder of the earlier passages already quoted in which the captain had been concerned about how "unconscious alertness" had abandoned him. But in the shadow of Koh-ring, with "no time" left to compensate for a weakness, the captain was paying for what an earlier alertness would have given him—instinctive knowledge of his ship. Again the narrator in **"Falk,"** also a stranger to his ship, explains the difficulty: "A misunderstanding between a man and his ship, in a difficult river with no room to make it up,

is bound to end in trouble for the man." If he had understood his ship better, our captain, even in "that smooth water and light wind," would have known what his ship was doing and hence what should be done to complete his stalled maneuver.

Even at this point in the crisis, the ship near ruin and the captain waiting "helplessly" in his ignorance, the margin for error that was turning daring skill into disaster was a matter of a few feet or a few seconds only, measured against the time that could not be spared to "run down" for some object to throw upon the water as a mark. When Leggatt does not "bother" to retrieve the dropped hat, he provides just in time the only means of learning that the ship had ceased moving forward, had gathered sternway, and would then finish coming about and start forward again *only* if the helm were shifted. Had the helm not been shifted, and without knowledge of the drift sternward the captain would have seen no reason to shift it, the rudder would have begun to swing the bow back towards the rocks, and there would have been no room for a second try. With these unexpected consequences of his inexperience to explain how the captain exceeded his own absolute limits and survived, Conrad leaves himself free to record how his reprieved captain can be left to enjoy his new command amid the "cheery cries" of his crew. Both sharers, the exiled murderer and the lucky navigator, have been given a second chance. In the light of all the difficulties that had to be overcome, if the questionable decision to come about at the last possible moment should not weigh upon the captain's conscience, neither should the moment of ignorance that placed the ship at the mercy of an abandoned hat.

The verdict for the captain (and Leggatt) is something very near to a suspended sentence. "What can they know whether I am guilty or not—or of *what* I am guilty, either?" A fugitive has been sheltered, a dangerous maneuver attempted in a bid for full authority, and a slight miscalculation about instinctive skills nearly proven fatal. It can always be said that such risks should never have been taken in a private matter of conscience, but then the degree of guilt and the kind of guilt become matters for debate, preferably among master mariners. In weighing honorable intentions against faulty execution, Conrad has tried to counter the easy verdict of guilty with just enough evidence on the other side to cast a shadow of doubt: not quite murder for Leggatt, not quite unforgivable risk for the captain, but an ambivalent realm where guilt and innocence, selfishness and compassion, inexperience and skill all overlap. In short, we are left with the thoughts of an earlier story: "I had no desire to judge—which is an idle practice anyhow."

Conrad, then, has hinted at a theme that is central to *Heart of Darkness.* As Guérard expresses it, "Conrad believes, with the greatest moralists, that we must know evil—our own capacities for evil—before we can be capable of good" [Introduction to *Heart of Darkness and The Secret Sharer,* 1958]. Likewise, Marlow's words about Kurtz may be applied to Leggatt: "True, he had made that last stride, he had stepped over the edge, while I had been permitted to draw back my hesitating foot. And perhaps this is the whole difference . . . That is why I have remained loyal . . . to the last." The captain had remained loyal to his fugitive, but in spite of the worthiness of his motives, he had all but stepped over the threshold of disaster. If in some way the compassion for Leggatt was responsible for the gift of the "saving mark," then Leggatt also, as a secret sharer, should be permitted something for his own compassionate concern for the captain and the sincere warning to "Be careful." But at crucial moments, neither one had been careful enough, and so the whole difference lay in the permission, granted by an accident, to draw back a hesitating foot. With this wisdom about life's uncertainties, a gift of the sea brought by Leggatt, the captain was prepared for his first command. He now understood the precarious terms upon which success is won.

J. D. O'Hara (essay date 1965)

SOURCE: "Unlearned Lessons in *The Secret Sharer*," in *College English*, Vol. 26, No. 6, March, 1965, pp. 444-50.

[*In the following essay, O'Hara asserts that the narrator of "The Secret Sharer" fails to absorb the lessons of Leggatt's experience.*]

There are only three major hindrances to navigation in **"The Secret Sharer"**—the narrator, Leggatt, and Captain Archbold of the *Sephora*—but scarcely a critic has avoided coming to grief on one of them. Leggatt was once the major hazard. Albert J. Guerard has now warned most readers, however, by pointing out that "it is entirely wrong to suppose . . . that Conrad unequivocally *approves* the captain's decision to harbor Leggatt" [*Conrad the Novelist*, 1958]. We must regard Leggatt as a criminal, Professor Guerard points out, even though the narrator sympathizes with him. In skirting this Scylla of sentimentality, however, Professor Guerard is sucked in by Charybdis when he concludes that the story's narrator experiences "the profound human experience . . . of the introspective night journey." Conrad and the narrator differ widely. For clear sailing, we must always remember this disagreement. When the story is read with skepticism (surely the proper attitude when the narrator's values differ from the author's) we will discover that Leggatt is indeed a criminal and that Captain Archbold is the moral center of the story. More significantly still, we find that the narrator, at the end as at the beginning, is neither remarkably admirable nor remarkably bright.

Captain Archbold is unattractive. Critics agree that he behaved badly during the storm, and they seem to feel that his pursuit of Leggatt, though legally justifiable, is undertaken in order to make him a scapegoat for Archbold's own sins. If we keep in mind the narrator's obvious bias and Leggatt's dubious moral character, however, we will find these opinions of Archbold less tenable than they seem.

We are first encouraged to side with Leggatt against Archbold by Leggatt's description of the storm. But this description is introduced by some details that ought to warn the reader against Leggatt. His father is a parson, and he puts himself on the side of the angels against "miserable devils" like the man he killed. We cannot accept so easily

the moral values implied by "angel" and "devil," however, especially since Leggatt's comments ("Do you see me before a judge and jury on that charge? For myself I can't see the necessity") reveal his arrogant feeling of moral superiority to other men. The narrator's sympathetic comment also betrays the weakness of Leggatt's position. "I knew well enough," he tells us, "the pestiferous danger of such a character [as the murdered sailor] where there are no means of legal repression." But there *are* legal means aboard ship, as Conrad surely expects us to realize and as the narrator certainly ought to know.

With these slight touches to keep our sympathy at a distance, Conrad introduces Leggatt's description of the storm. Leggatt stresses the idea of madness: the crew were "screaming 'Murder!' like a lot of lunatics"; Captain Archbold "started raving like the rest of them"; "to have this sprung on him at the height of a furious gale nearly drove him out of his mind." But when we look closely at this description, we can see that it is completely untrustworthy. In fact, if anyone went mad it was Leggatt himself. As the fight began, a huge wave approached the ship, he tells us, but he would not or could not let go of the sailor. For more than ten minutes, as the sea washed over the deck, Leggatt clung to the sailor's throat. He continued to cling to it while being dragged aft; and he admits that the crew "had rather a job to separate us." We must conclude that he was in no condition to appraise his shipmates' sanity. In fact, he didn't even see them, apparently. From the time when he grappled with the sailor until he came to himself in his bunk, the story of the storm is told at second hand: "they say" that the ship was covered with water for ten minutes; "it seems" that they brought him aft; "I understand that" the captain raved; "I've been told" that it was difficult to separate the murderer from his victim. From whom did Leggatt learn these details? Archbold probably told Leggatt about his own actions, but there is no reason to believe that anyone told him about Archbold's madness or the crew's. We must suspect that Leggatt invented the story himself.

Archbold is crazy, not cowardly, as Leggatt first tells the tale; and Leggatt doesn't claim to have originated the idea of rigging the reefed foresail. He only says, "it was I that managed to set it". Even that modest claim is unconvincing. The fight broke out before the sail had been completely set—the insolent sailor was "at the sheet"—and Leggatt obviously did nothing admirable after the fight. It would seem more reasonable to say that the sail was set despite the homicidal madness of the officer in charge. When Archbold comes aboard, looking for Leggatt, the reader recognizes that Archbold's story of the storm contradicts Leggatt's. The narrator recognizes it too; he tells us that "it is not worth while to record that version. It was just over two months since all this had happened, and he had thought so much about it that he seemed completely muddled as to its bearings. . . ." Clearly the comment applies to Leggatt's "version" with even more force.

When Archbold leaves the ship, Leggatt—perhaps fearing that the narrator had been turned against him by Archbold's story—immediately accuses Archbold of cowardice and claims that Archbold "never gave the order" to set the sail, but "positively whimpered about it and nothing else." The matter is never cleared up, but surely Conrad has not encouraged us to think of Archbold as the whimpering type; he is too much like Captain MacWhirr in *Typhoon.* Even the narrator, though basically hostile, reveals no doubt of Archbold's honesty, and his summation of Archbold's motives is radically different from Leggatt's. Leggatt had accused Archbold of fear—fear of the law, fear of his crew, fear of his second mate, and fear of his wife. The narrator ignores all this; he tells us instead that "seven and thirty virtuous years at sea, of which over twenty of immaculate command, and the last fifteen in the *Sephora,* seemed to have laid him under some pitiless obligation."

In short, it would seem that we must take Leggatt's charges against Archbold with several grains of salt. As Professor Guerard says, "we do not need to go to the biography and letters to discover Conrad's respect for 'immaculate command' and 'pitiless obligation,' or for such a traditional figure; it is implicit in much of his fiction." We must conclude that Captain Archbold's actions are respectable. "He always seemed very sick when he came to see me," says Leggatt, "—as if he could not look me in the face"; and "he was shaking like a leaf " when he refused to let Leggatt escape. To the scornful Leggatt these are signs of fear, but we are more likely to conclude that Archbold's acceptance of his responsibility as Leggatt's jailor

was indeed a painful duty and one that he genuinely regretted. But, as Conrad suggests, the law's obligation is necessarily pitiless—or, more accurately, obliges one to pity the mass of men, not the individual. Conrad therefore sets Archbold's "obscure tenacity" to his duty against Leggatt's tenacity in clinging to the sailor's throat. Small details lend weight to this interpretation: in his conversation, Archbold refers three times, "impressively" and "fervently," to God; and the narrator's description of Archbold's "pitiless obligation" is given moral overtones by references to his "awful" and "mystical" tenacity, his "virtuous" years at sea, and his "immaculate" command of the *Sephora.* Archbold, then, far from being the villain of the piece, is a man not so much insensitive as disciplined; a man who, unlike the narrator, has fully accepted his moral position as captain—"a position of the fullest responsibility."

When Archbold's character and Leggatt's are correctly understood, we can see that he and Leggatt are the poles between which the narrator fluctuates; and we see that the narrator finally sides with Archbold, more or less, after several days of unpleasantness and indecision. Some readers have described this experience in most serious terms, speaking of a rite of passage or a night journey into the darkness of the soul. In fiction as in real life, however, the participants in such rites seldom profit as they should.

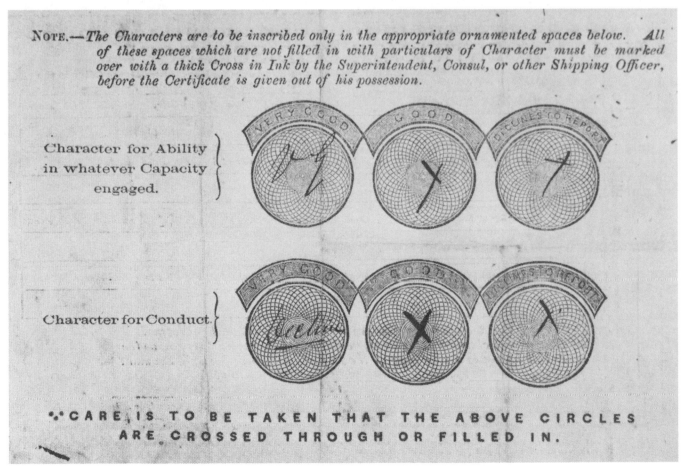

Captain's report on Conrad's performance as second mate on the Riversdale, *1884.*

Odysseus and Aeneas learned nothing very profound in Hell. Huck Finn, who should have lighted out from the Phelps farm for the Injun Territory, took a steamboat back up the river to St. Petersburg and the materialistic glory of a torchlight parade. (See *Tom Sawyer Abroad*.) Even Marlow, despite his portentousness, gained no apocalyptic knowledge from his trip into the heart of darkness. And the narrator of **"The Secret Sharer,"** I suggest, learns just barely enough to save himself from Leggatt's fate.

The specific nature of the testing must be understood if we are to judge the narrator, and Conrad takes pains to state his subject clearly. At the beginning of the story the narrator tells us, "The youngest man on board . . . , and untried as yet by a position of the fullest responsibility, I was willing to take the adequacy of the others for granted. They had simply to be equal to their tasks; but I wondered how far I should turn out faithful to that ideal conception of one's own personality every man sets up for himself secretly." Most critics fasten tenaciously onto the last sentence. In so doing, they are likely to miss half the story's theme. The other half is rather hidden in the passage above, but it becomes clear a little later as the narrator pictures the coming voyage. "All its phases were familiar enough to me," he says, "every characteristic, all the alternatives which were likely to face me on the high seas—everything! . . . except the novel responsibility of command." The narrator's initiation into life, then, is a specific, limited test—an initiation into the fullest responsibility, the responsibility of command. By making this theme clear, Conrad emphasizes the standards by which we must judge the narrator, Leggatt, Captain Archbold, and the narrator's ideal conception of himself. It is impossible by these standards to disapprove of Archbold or to approve of Leggatt—and Leggatt seems to embody the narrator's ideal conception of himself.

If Archbold has been exposed to some harsh and unmerited critical scorn, the narrator has received some remarkably sentimental approval. To clear the air, let us regard him through other eyes—the eyes, for instance, of a master mariner. As master mariners, let us judge the narrator's fitness for responsible command.

In the beginning, his attitudes toward command and responsibility are almost ludicrous. Though he knows that "exactitude in small matters is the very soul of discipline," he dismisses the crew for the night with their work unfinished, and he takes the anchor watch himself. These actions receive their proper comment in such words as *unusual, unconventional, astonishment,* and *caprice.* The crew's dismissal causes the ladder to be left over the side; if it had been hauled in, Leggatt—anticipated by the scorpion image—would never have come on board. Exhausted by his swim to the ship, he says that he "wasn't capable of swimming round as far as your rudder-chains. And, lo and behold! there was a ladder to get hold of." Even before his arrival, though, Conrad had pointed up the narrator's irresponsibility. The anchor watch's job is to observe anything approaching the ship. He must not leave his post, of course. The unwatchful narrator, however, hardly notices even the ship itself. He mentions that "I had hardly seen her yet properly"; but after a cursory glance over the main

deck he retreats into his thoughts, "my mind picturing to myself the coming passage." Later, he leaves his post and goes below for a cigar. A small detail calls our attention to the significance of the act: "as I passed the door of the forecastle I heard a deep, quiet, trustful sigh of some sleeper inside." The sigh leads the narrator to rejoice in "the great security of the sea"; but we are surely expected to recognize that the security, such as it is, has been violated. Despite the trustful sigh, the narrator is untrustworthy. During the time he was dreaming on deck and getting his cigar below, Leggatt has approached and has reached the ship unchallenged. Things go from bad to worse; after a chat that looks mild enough on the page but is wildly improbable as a description of an English captain coping with such a strange visitor in a foreign land, the narrator lets Leggatt climb the ladder unwatched while he goes below for some clothes. Once again an apparently irrelevant detail reminds us of the narrator's neglect of duty: "a faint snore came through the closed door of the chief mate's room."

We master mariners can see that the narrator's first actions in the story, though they pass unnoticed by most landlubbers, are meant to warn us against adopting the narrator's point of view, especially on such subjects as the responsibility of command. The warning is conveyed in other ways, too.

While standing his anchor watch, for instance, the narrator tells us that "I took heart from the reasonable thought that the ship was like other ships, the men like other men, and that the sea was not likely to keep any special surprises expressly for my discomfiture." Within minutes, the sea presents him with the extremely discomfiting Leggatt. The sleeper's trustful sigh, also ironic, leads the narrator to rejoice "in the great security of the sea as compared with the unrest of the land, in my choice of that untempted life presenting no disquieting problems [what would Lord Jim say?], invested with an elementary moral beauty by the absolute straightforwardness of its appeal and by the singleness of its purpose." The smug ignorance of tone here verges on caricature. Earlier, the narrator struck a romantic pose with his ship, only to be disconcerted by eavesdropping stars: "with all that multitude of celestial bodies staring down at one," he complained, "the comfort of quiet communion with her was gone for good."

This characterization of the narrator is, after all, a necessary one. A mature and sensible captain, no matter how new to his position, would not have invited a floating stranger aboard so readily nor sympathized with a murderer so whole-heartedly; but Leggatt's egotism and his Byronic melodrama make an understandable appeal to this young narrator's naive heart, as do Leggatt's carefully distinct murmur about being a Conway boy and his repeated reference to his parson father—which the narrator oddly calls "this important fact."

Conrad begins the story, in short, by urging us to look rather askance at the narrator and his double. Notice the sly wit, for example, in this decorative and thematic detail: "Two bunches of bananas hung from the beam symmetrically, one on each side of the rudder-casing." His next task is to initiate this youngster in the responsibilities of command. Once Leggatt is aboard, the narrator quickly begins to see the difficulties involved in clinging to his secret self. As he soon recognizes, "there are to a seaman certain words, gestures, that should in given conditions come as naturally, as instinctively, as the winking of a menaced eye. A certain order should spring on to his lips without thinking." In short, responsibilities should be met unconsciously. Almost the only proper action performed by the narrator before Leggatt's arrival, the attempt to raise the rope ladder, is significantly described as a mechanical act. Once Leggatt comes aboard, the narrator loses this mechanical rightness. The first example of his new self-consciousness verges on slapstick. The steward comes in early the morning after Leggatt's arrival; he wishes to close the captain's port because the deck above is being washed. The narrator sends him away, saying that the port is already closed; then in his confusion he immediately opens it. The consequence, we must assume, is that the sleeping Leggatt is awakened by a faceful of dirty water; but Conrad has moved soberly on to other matters.

The narrator's slow dislodgement from his position of identification with Leggatt is barely perceptible. Conrad keeps us from hearing the narrator discuss matters with himself, and the change of position is only slight. We are given some hints, however, especially in connection with Archbold, that the narrator is capable of appreciating responsible attitudes. When Archbold first comes aboard, for instance, he is "densely distressed"; and the narrator comments, "perhaps I should have sympathized with him if I had been able to detach my mental vision from the unsuspected sharer of my cabin." It is true, of course, that when Archbold leaves, the narrator reasserts his approval of Leggatt by claiming that "the same strung-up force which had given twenty-four men a chance, at least, for their lives had, in a sort of recoil, crushed an unworthy mutinous existence." This gross oversimplification is even introduced with the naive assertion that "it was all very simple." Apparently, however, the narrator was by no means completely convinced. His next comment suggests that he was about to set Archbold's story against Leggatt's when Conrad interrupted him with a person-from-Porlock device: "But I had no leisure to weigh the merits of the matter—footsteps in the saloon, a heavy knock."

The wind has risen; the ship gets under way; and the narrator covers four or five days of sailing with a few anecdotes. These call our attention to the growing wretchedness of the steward and the uneasiness of the crew. Meanwhile the narrator, himself a nervous wreck, notices Leggatt's quietness more and more: "he looked always perfectly self-controlled, more than calm, almost invulnerable." By the time Leggatt is ready to go over the side, this quality has become decidedly distasteful to the narrator: "to find him sitting so quietly was surprising, like something against nature, inhuman."

But the incident that affects the narrator most and leads him to let Leggatt go, occurs when the narrator is dining with the mates and the steward goes into the bathroom where Leggatt is hiding. "I expected to hear a yell of surprise and terror," the narrator tells us. "Had my second self taken the poor wretch by the throat?" Significantly,

it is the steward who is pitied as the poor wretch here, not Leggatt. The narrator has been forced to admit, despite his own and Leggatt's rationalizations, that he does after all suspect Leggatt of being a murdering brute.

To be sure, the narrator makes no comment on the incident. We can guess that it affected his attitude toward his secret ideal only because his narrative turns immediately to the scene in which Leggatt asks to be set ashore and the narrator, after hesitation based on "a mere sham sentiment, a sort of cowardice," agrees. This agreement is the sign of a new maturity in the narrator and of a shift in his attitude toward Leggatt. But the change is not radical. Conrad lets us know that the narrator has not acquired any dazzling insight into life and truth—not even unconsciously; he lets us know by his handling of the series of events in which Leggatt leaves the ship.

If we interpret the sleeping suits as symbolic, then it is significant that the narrator would not have made the course change that he did make "if it had been only a question of getting out of that *sleepy* gulf as quickly as possible" (my italics). There are more obvious indications of the narrator's backwardness, however. Despite a new authority in his dealings with the crew, he is still engaged in a basically foolhardy action—bringing his ship dangerously and unnecessarily close to an unknown shore. Myth-and-ritual critics speak at this point of night journeys and descents into Hell. Conrad the mariner would surely make a distinction between solitary descents into the maelstrom and the unnecessary risking of a crew and ship. In any case, the event—whatever its potential significance—is not treated profoundly.

This series of incidents reaches its climax when the chief mate loses his nerve and the narrator grabs him: "I hadn't let go the mate's arm and went on shaking it. 'Ready about, do you hear? You go forward'—shake—'and stop there'—shake—'and hold your noise'—shake—'and see these head-sheets properly overhauled'—shake, shake—shake. And all the time I dared not look towards the land lest my heart should fail me. I released my grip at last and he ran forward as if fleeing for dear life." Many critics have noticed that this incident parallels the one in which Leggatt strangled the sailor. The mate is in despair; the sailor was "half crazed with funk." Leggatt would not take his eyes off the sailor to look at the approaching wave; the narrator "dared not look towards the land." Leggatt had the sailor "by the throat, and went on shaking him like a rat"; the narrator shakes the mate at length and uncontrollably. The sailor died; the mate "ran forward as if fleeing for dear life."

How should this event be interpreted? We may emphasize the difference between Leggatt and the narrator: the narrator only scares the mate; the narrator keeps his sanity and completes his task successfully. For Conrad, however, the incident was surely more than a neat contrivance, nicely echoing and lightly altering an earlier incident, just as it was more than a Jamesian *donnee,* indifferent in itself. Over thirty years of life at sea surely required Conrad to take such incidents realistically and seriously. For him, then, the resemblance between the narrator and Leggatt must have been more important. He makes the narrator's shedding of his secret sharer as foolishly romantic and ir-responsible as his reception of him; the chapter of accidents (such as the floating hat), rather than any deep understanding of life, saves the narrator from wrecking his ship and his career.

Certainly he has not learned from his experience. The reader may have been changed, but the narrator is essentially the man he was before he met Leggatt. The reader, comprehending the symbolic and parabolic implications of the story, may have matured immensely; the Eliotic narrator has had the experience but missed the meaning. We may therefore expect that the story will end as it began. It does. The narrator's heroic concluding description of Leggatt as "a free man, a proud swimmer striking out for a new destiny," can only be taken ironically. Leggatt's freedom is surely an illusion; even the narrator himself has already predicted that Leggatt's pride will get him in trouble. But the most obvious sign that the narrator is essentially the same is that he still speaks of his ship and his command in a tone of fatuous overconfidence: "Already the ship was drawing ahead. And I was alone with her. Nothing! no one in the world should stand now between us, throwing a shadow on the way of silent knowledge and mute affection; the perfect communion of a seaman with his first command." We have already heard him grumble that "with all that multitude of celestial bodies staring down at one, the comfort of quiet communion with her was gone for good"; we are not likely to believe in the unrealistic perfection of this present communion, nor can we share the assumption that life holds no more problems. We *are* likely, however, to conclude that the narrator still has much to learn.

In conclusion, then, Conrad is working less profoundly and more cheerfully in this story than many critics believe, even though he develops here themes that, in other stories, he treats with seriousness and complexity. In this regard a comparison between **"The Secret Sharer"** and *The Nigger of the 'Narcissus'* is striking. In both stories, Conrad criticizes the sentimentality that exalts the individual at the expense of the group. Both set the solitary against the crowd, the self-centered man against the selfless man, the emotions against reason, sentimentality against pitilessness, the natural life against the moral life, the development of the self against the welfare of the group, and self-awareness against happiness. But the relative values of these qualities are developed thoroughly and "argued" artistically in *The Nigger of the 'Narcissus'*; they are assumed or treated sketchily in **"The Secret Sharer."** The characters—especially Leggatt—are given no subtlety of perception or strength of conviction, and we are never taken far into the narrator's confidence. The story seems to have interested Conrad primarily as a technical exercise, a stylistic experiment in communicating through an unsympathetic point of view. And unsympathetic the narrator certainly is, from his strangely irresponsible actions at the beginning of the story to his complacent assurance at the end.

J. L. Simmons (essay date 1965)

SOURCE: "The Dual Morality in Conrad's *The Secret Sharer*," in *Studies in Short Fiction*, Vol. II, No. 3, Spring, 1965, pp. 209-20.

[*In the following essay, Simmons argues that the character of Leggatt represents an ideal of morality in the context of maritime discipline.*]

"The Secret Sharer" Remains one of Conrad's most enigmatic works in spite of the large bibliography which it has collected. The basic critical problem, of course, concerns the moral nature of Leggatt and his relationship with the narrator-captain. The more widespread opinion is that Leggatt represents the "outlaw self," allied with instinctive evil and violence, which the captain acknowledges as a part of himself and then exorcises. This interpretation has been most forcefully and influentially advanced by Albert J. Guerard [in *Conrad the Novelist*, 1958]; and, though there have been modifications in recent years, the culpability of Leggatt has never, with the exception of an essay by Daniel Curley, been pointedly refuted ["Leggatt of the Ideal," in *Conrad's "Secret Sharer" and the Critics*, 1962]. The nature of the publication in which this refutation appeared has no doubt blunted some of the force it should exert in the necessary re-examination of one of Conrad's most widely read short novels. The following essay, like Curley's, insists upon the ideal nature of Leggatt and will deal with a fundamental theme of the story which has been overlooked: an operative dual morality which creates the conflict of both Leggatt's external situation and the captain's internal one, a duality growing out of the special conditions which distinguish life on the sea from that on land.

G. H. Bantock, [in "The Two 'Moralities' of Joseph Conrad," *Essays in Criticism* III, 1953] though he does not mention **"The Secret Sharer"** specifically, finds the conflict between two moralities to be crucial in Conrad's work:

> We become aware, then, in the work of Conrad of the co-existence of two "moralities": that derived from a simple tradition of "Westernness" which still served, in the total scheme of things, to validate a limited "placing" of the characters; and that derived from an awareness of the force, and indeed, necessity of *"égoïsme"* in a decaying order which contained within itself no general principle of moral being to cope with the profounder metaphysical apprehensions of highly self-conscious individuals.

I recognize that the distinction made in my analysis between the two moralities is not to be equated with Bantock's, not to be defined, that is, in terms of internal and external morality, so that we are left with the old romantic conflict between the individual morality and that of society. There is here a more Classical conflict, one which the Greeks and Shakespeare knew so well, that conflict between two external moralities and the destruction one invites in making the necessary total commitment to one. But Bantock makes clear that the conflict of moralities is very much present in Conrad's work and therefore encourages one to examine Leggatt's "crime" in light of it. Even Curley has done little more than justify in a negative way his killing the mutinous sailor, since the killing, in terms of the land law, could *not* be positively justified. But Leggatt's act can be shown to follow unquestionably and instinctively the morality of the sea which Conrad dramatizes throughout the work.

Leiter has referred to Leggatt as representing the libidinous forces in the captain, ["Echo Structures: Conrad's 'The Secret Sharer,'" *Twentieth Century Literature,* 1960] and many critics have equated the secret sharer, if only tacitly, with the amoral subconscious. But if one is to employ Freudian terminology, then the more accurate name for Leggatt's function, as far as the narrator is concerned, is the super-ego. The first break in the story, after Conrad has set up the narrator's insecurity with himself, ship, and crew, ends with the following, much noted, passage: " . . . but I wondered how far I should turn out faithful to that ideal conception of one's own personality every man sets up for himself secretly." Not only the key position of the passage but the last word of it, echoing unmistakably the title, reveals this to be a foreshadowing of the story's development. The story is *about* a man trying to live up to his ideal, and immediately this ideal is dramatized in the person of Leggatt. If after the climax, as is generally agreed, the captain has become essentially his super-ego, then a viewing of Leggatt as this ideal would return the story to the kind of simplicity and explicitness which the texture urges. More important, we must view Leggatt as the narrator does if we are to take his maturity at the end as being worth anything. No critic has ever managed to

cite a passage which shows the narrator's opinion of Leggatt to be anything but one of admiration—the stark admiration, in fact, with which one would view the ideal one aspires to be. As for Guerard's comment that "the reader too incorrigibly sympathizes with Leggatt," no doubt criticism has overstepped its bounds when it negates the basic impressions with which it must work. The common reader had better have his say here.

Since this ideal is one which the narrator has at the outset of the story, enabling him to communicate immediately with Leggatt on his appearance, two passages before this communion begins are of vital importance in the dual morality theme. The opening of the story gives, as Haugh points out, "a beautifully realized view of sea and shore. . . . It is significant that in the opening images the captain can scarcely tell where one element begins and the other starts"[*Joseph Conrad: Discovery in Design,* 1957]. Then, after the narrator is alone with his ship, the first differentiation between the judgment of action on land and on sea occurs:

> In this breathless pause at the threshold of a long passage we seemed to be measuring our fitness for a long and arduous enterprise, the appointed task of both our existences to be carried out, far from all human eyes, with only sky and sea for spectators and for judges.

The appointed task is of course to get the ship to its destination, an act which must fundamentally insist that the ship stay afloat. If this task is obvious, it is no more obvious than a basis for morality usually is—love of God, fear of the law, respect for order. The second passage, occurring at the beginning of the captain's watch when once more he is alone, amplifies and simplifies further this basis for morality in quite explicit terms:

> And suddenly I rejoiced in the great security of the sea as compared with the unrest of the land, in my choice of that untempted life presenting no disquieting problems, invested with an elementary moral beauty by the absolute straightforwardness of its appeal and by the singleness of its purpose.

The contrast with land morality is made definite. It has been frequently pointed out that this passage is ironic, but the distinction must be made between that which is ironic and that which is not: "The great security . . . presenting no disquieting problems" is not what the narrator has or is likely to get. His mistake at this point is in the confusion of a simple morality with a simple life, in the thought that if one knows what to do and what not to do, moral action becomes effortless. But the distinctive basis for morality is here, to keep the ship afloat, and it follows that acts which work toward that purpose are in themselves moral. If there is a question of judgment, "only the sky and sea" can give it, a point which Leggatt stresses again and again:

> "But you don't see me coming back to explain such things to an old fellow in a wig and twelve respectable tradesmen, do you? What can they know whether I am guilty or not—or of what I am guilty, either? That's my affair."

Life on the shore is more often than not confused in its

moral life—"the unrest of the land"; and God, law, and order can never offer the clear-cut line of action, "the absolute straightforwardness," which the sea does. Theologians, lawyers, and philosophers write tomes on morality; landsmen debate issues endlessly: but there is not the time for this debate on the sea. Conrad dramatizes this obvious fact brilliantly in the scene after the *Sephora's* captain's visit when Leggatt completes his version of the killing. The narrator of course understands Leggatt's point of view:

> It was all very simple. The same strung-up force which had given twenty-four men a chance, at least, for their lives, had, in a sort of recoil, crushed an unworthy mutinous existence.

> But I had no leisure to weigh the merits of the matter—footsteps in the saloon, a heavy knock. "There's enough wind to get under way, sir." Here was the call of a new claim upon my thoughts and even upon my feelings.

Of course there is no leisure to weigh the merits: the voyage has begun and with it the moral life of the sea. Judgment must be simple; more than simple, it must be instinctive. An object is loose upon the water with a purpose and lives at stake; the natural force that keeps that ship above the water rather than below it is so subject to sudden change that a moment can mean defeat and destruction. The lives of the "old fellow in a wig and twelve respectable tradesmen" never are so tenuous. Certainly Leggatt is right in feeling that they could never understand and that their judgment is not applicable.

Having set up the narrator's dim understanding that there is a basic difference between the moral life of the land and that of the sea, Conrad introduces the captain of the *Sephora* to dramatize further this duality. Guerard uses this abject man to throw doubt on Leggatt's capabilities, but to take this captain's word that Leggatt "wasn't exactly the sort for the chief mate of a ship like the *Sephora*" requires the reader to overcome not only incorrigible sympathy for Leggatt but incorrigible pity and antipathy for a man so unimpressive that the narrator cannot even remember his name. For we have in the captain of the *Sephora* one of Conrad's brilliant portraits of a miserable failure, the man who has failed to meet the test. True, he has spent thirty-seven "virtuous years at sea, of which over twenty of immaculate command"; but there is an evident failure of perception if one is to view his record as a sign of "Conrad's respect." It is "not the routine action of ordinary seagoing, but action of some extraordinary kind," the crisis, which proves the ideal seaman [Leo Gurko, *Joseph Conrad: Giant in Exile,* 1962]. And in the moment of crisis this captain fails. Like Lord Jim, after his failure, the captain attempts rationalization. It becomes with him an *idée fixe* that Leggatt be turned over to the law of the land:

> To the law. His obscure tenacity on that point had in it something incomprehensible and a little awful; something, as it were, mystical, quite apart from his anxiety that he should not be suspected of "countenancing any doings of that sort."

The reason is obvious. His "pitiless obligation" for turning Leggatt over to the authorities is nothing more than an attempt to justify his own failure: for if he can have his first mate declared guilty in terms of the land's morality, his own failure in losing control of the ship, his own immorality in terms of the sea, is obscured. He, not Leggatt, is the guilty man: "He always seemed very sick when he came to see me," Leggatt tells the narrator, "as if he could not look me in the face." Leggatt is his greatest accuser: the captain knows that he has failed, and the face of the ideal is unbearable to him.

This captain is totally lacking in self-knowledge. The narrator tries to make him see that, in spite of the killing, the reefed foresail which Leggatt put up saved the ship. Even though the captain falsely asserts that he gave the order for putting it up, he stubbornly refuses to give the credit to the man who, in the face of the crisis, did in fact put it up: "It was by a special mercy," he tells the narrator. "God's own hand in it." The lack of logic here punctures everything that the captain reports. It does not take much sympathy to believe Leggatt when he assures the narrator that the captain did not even give the order.

The captain fails out of a lack of commitment to the moral life which he chose to follow. He is, in short, too committed to the land. What other reason for the striking detail, which has I think completely escaped notice, of his wife's presence on board? Thirty-seven virtuous years are wiped out by the one moment of crisis, the moment which reveals the man for what he is. Opposed to him is Leggatt, who is instinctively a saint as far as life on the sea is concerned: he has thoroughly given up worldly considerations to achieve his canonization.

The narrator is thrown between the two and placed in the position of making a choice. Conrad enforces this triangular situation through the use of parallel, an element in the structure which has not gone unnoticed. But one parallel which has not been stressed is that between the narrator and the captain of the *Sephora*. Both men lack self-knowledge. Both men are insecure with their crews, insecure to the point of fear. "He was afraid of the men," Leggatt tells the narrator, "And also of that old second mate of his who had been sailing with him for years—a grey-headed old humbug; and his steward, too, had been with him devil knows how long. . . . Those two old chaps ran the ship." There is no doubt that the narrator is afraid of his first and second mates. And which member of the crew strikes greatest terror in him (in the scene in which Leggatt is almost discovered) if not the steward? This insecurity, this division within the crew, represents potential disaster to the ship, even though thirty-seven years of easy sailing might pass. The *Sephora's* captain is captain only in name, the narrator's situation exactly: "Of course, theoretically, I could do what I liked, with no one to say nay to me within the whole circle of the horizon. . . . " But only theoretically. The reality of the narrator's situation is that his crew runs the ship through the power which impudence, sarcasm, and cynicism exert on the untried man.

The most revealing scene in which the narrator's likeness to the other captain is drawn is in the interview between them: "He was densely distressed—and perhaps I should have sympathised with him if I had been able to detach my mental vision from the unsuspected sharer of my cabin as though he were my second self." Without the ideal, he would be drawn to the nature of the pathetic man before him. And even at this point the choice is not firmly made-rather, it cannot meet the *test:*

> But there was the danger of his breaking through my defence bluntly. I could not, I think, have met him by a direct lie, also for psychological (not moral) reasons. If he had only known how afraid I was of his putting my feeling of identity with the other to the test!

It is towards this test, then, that the story begins to build. It is not enough for the narrator to perceive even the embodiment of the ideal: the ideal must be translated into terms of action or it is worth little pragmatically, as *Lord Jim* proves.

During this time of uneasy sailing, after the ship heaves anchor and before the crisis is precipitated, the narrator goes through the period of introspection which brings about the integration of ego and super-ego. This period of introspection, during which effective action is impossible, has been held up as proof of the harm which Leggatt exerts on the narrator. Again, a serious failure in critical perception.

> He [Leggatt] provokes a crippling division of the narrator's personality, and one that interferes with his seamanship. . . . The whispering communion of the narrator and his double—of the seaman-self and some darker, more interior, and the outlaw self—*must have been necessary and rewarding,* since the story ends as positively as it does [Guerard, *Conrad the Novelist*].

There is almost a *prima facie* admission, revealed in my italics, that the critic does not understand the function of this section of the story. Other critics, more sympathetic to Leggatt, also imply a *blame* which can be placed on him—the cause of the "crippling division." But such commentators fail to see that this period of introspection is necessary even while it results in a dangerous position for the ship. The narrator's actions had been unorthodox (in dismissing the night watch) and uncertain before Leggatt came aboard; and if his peculiarity is heightened for the crew after the secret intrigue begins, it is only an intensification of the narrator's self-division which already existed. To see the situation otherwise is to see the narrator as having no problem at all while the ship is waiting for the wind, nothing, at least, which a few days of experience and adjustment would not take care of. It is to overlook the narrator's own admission that he lacks knowledge of ship, crew, and himself. Even Leo Gurko, who achieves a sympathetic interpretation of Leggatt by agreeing to see him not as what he is but as what the narrator thinks him to be (a view which if strictly followed would prevent an understanding of Conrad's intention altogether), finally avoids interpretation: "By saving the fugitive and releasing him into freedom, he [the narrator] is *somehow* achieving his own maturation, and for it he is willing to pay a heavy price." Again I have italicized the dismissing word. Self-knowledge, which is necessary before knowledge of ship and crew can come, does not come through action but

through the introspection which Leggatt forces upon him through his ironic personification of what the narrator desires to be.

No doubt, already in 1909, Conrad had in mind the Hamlet dilemma, which he would use again with even greater effect in *Victory:* the impossibility of acting effectively while a mental conflict rages. Like Hamlet, the narrator gives the appearance of being mad. He whispers in his mate's ear; he gives inexplicable orders. He alternates between strange silences and sudden ejaculations until the mate taps his finger on his forehead. But all the while there is an essential health beginning to emerge. The narrator's first appearance on deck after the silent communion begins shows him asserting himself:

> I watched him [the chief mate] coming with a smile which, as he got into point-blank range, took effect and froze his very whiskers. I did not give him time to open his lips.

> It was the first particular order I had given on board that ship; and I stayed on deck to see it executed, too. I had felt the need of asserting myself without loss of time.

This assertion grows even before the discharge of Leggatt. He sternly reprimands the second mate, "that intolerable cub," for shuffling about in "a slack, improper fashion"; and when he gives the strange order to open the quarter-deck ports, he tells the incredulous sailor: "The only reason you need concern yourself about is because I tell you to do so." And yet the ship still has "two captains," and the crew still lacks respect for him.

The captain is, in short, capable of self-conscious action, but he lacks the ability to act instinctively. And from the instinct must come all action and judgment in a life so precarious as that of the sea:

> There are to a seaman certain words, gestures, that should in given conditions come as naturally, as instinctively as the winking of a menaced eye. A certain order should spring on to his lips without thinking; a certain sign should get itself made, so to speak, without reflection.

This instinctive action was typified by Leggatt when he killed the mutinous sailor. Guerard and others have seen in his act a proof that he is "criminally impulsive"; but Curley has pointed out the basic error of confusing the instinctive with evil. "Conrad himself explicitly includes instinctive action among the necessary virtues of the ideal seaman."

As in the case of Hamlet, the narrator's difficulty, the break between thought and act, is caused by a lack of moral certainty and the attending failure in commitment. The narrator, like Marlow and Heyst, is no doubt naturally disposed toward the contemplative, the reflective side at the expense of action: he does not instigate the act which will bring him forth as the man of action; again like Hamlet he has the situation thrust upon him. Leggatt insists that it is time for his escape, and the reluctant narrator replies with superb unconscious irony: "Maroon you! We are not living in a boy's adventure tale." But he knows that the time has come for him to get along without Leggatt, to see whether the ideal self is a part of him truly, not merely hidden away in his cabin or set up in his mind secretly.

It should not, as Guerard urges, be necessary to remember "while preoccupied with the psychological symbolism, that Leggatt is substantial flesh and blood." There are not two levels in the story: the story is given to us only through the narrator's point of view, and his sophistication as far as symbols and psychology are concerned gives us the literal rendering of the story in the only interpretation that makes the story a story. Such a complaint as [Marvin] Mudrick makes [in "Conrad and the Terms of Modern Criticism," *The Hudson Review,* 1954], that Conrad is too obvious in the narrator's awareness of the psychological and symbolic aspects, becomes irrelevant: what if the narrator (not Conrad) is intelligent enough to recognize, at least afterwards, the significance of his dilemma? The story is important to him only because an external event happened to reflect and finally resolve his psychological and moral difficulty. "The dual working of my mind distracted me almost to the point of insanity," he says soon after the communion begins. "I was constantly watching myself, my secret self, as dependent on my actions as my own personality." The recognition here fuses the literal and the symbolic.

The resolution lies in the narrator's full understanding of the total commitment which he must make to the morality of the sea. If that commitment results in the punishment which Lord Jim inflicted upon himself, a man whose commitment failed, it is the price one must pay; and the irony of the result's being the same is simply another of Conrad's trenchant observations on the life of men who seek absolutes in a world full of men like the crew of the *Sephora*. Leggatt's humble acceptance of his fate is the final comment one could make on the ideal nature of his character: "I don't blame anybody. I was precious little better than the rest. Only—I was an officer of that old coal-wagon, anyhow—". The moral overtones that critics have heard in "a good swimmer" are certainly here in the word *officer*. He was the ideal captain, but he happened *not* to be the captain. So, refusing the judgment of land, he takes on the punishment which God dealt to Cain: he leaves the world he was meant to inhabit. But that we are not to see the parallel as a valid one is made clear in the closing pages: "But I hardly thought of my other self, now gone from the ship, to be hidden for ever from all friendly faces, to be a fugitive and a vagabond on the earth, with no brand of the curse on his sane forehead to stay a slaying hand . . . too proud to explain." It is not, I think, a quibble to point out that without the mark of Cain, the analogy, which has always been made by Leggatt, hardly holds. That Leggatt has used the analogy simply shows how clearly he recognizes the conflict into which the dual morality has brought him. He *is* concerned with morality: his incredulous repetition of the "important fact" that his father is a parson, the representative of absolute morality on the land, proves his concern, as well as his consternation at finding that the conflict of two moralities can cause one's destruction.

One of the things which the narrator has "understood thoroughly" is that one must be prepared to face exactly what Leggatt now faces. ". . . I realized suddenly that all my future, the only future for which I was fit, would perhaps go irretrievably to pieces in any mishap to my first command." But such a realization of what is at stake must not lead to compromise, to timidity, to a lack of self-confidence. So it is "a matter of conscience" that the narrator sail as close as he does to that black place where one may find either destruction or self-realization.

Exactly why it is a matter of conscience is a tricky question. But the answer is not to be found in such a response as the following:

> He has conquered his feeling of insecurity, and he has demonstrated to the crew that he is firmly in command of the vessel. Certainly the establishment of authority is necessary. But it should be said, too, that (from the point of view of the crew) he has demonstrated the power of authority in a needlessly fear-inspiring way, by taking the ship far too close to the rocky coast.

> **"The Secret Sharer,"** in short, is not a story of full initiation into mature responsibilities; it is the beginning of the initiation, but it does not portray . . . the passage from egocentric youth to human solidarity [Carl Benson, "Conrad's Two Stories of Initiation," *PMLA,* 1954].

One can, first of all, object to Benson's use of the word *initiation*: initiation *is* the beginning. But, more important, human solidarity is exactly what is swiftly portrayed in the closing paragraphs. For the first time we have a "cheery" crew, functioning under the command of the first mate, now subdued, watched over in the perfect hierarchic pattern by the captain. For the first time, in fact, he is the captain—no longer only in theory. And yet a problem remains in the climax, but the kind of problem which proves the story's lasting quality as literature. The motivation is plural, not singular, and, as in Shakespeare, character and event are all the more alive because of their ineluctable nature.

Certainly the most important function and explanation of the event is the dim awareness on the part of the narrator, the decisive one on the part of the reader, that there is a clear case of symbolic re-enactment. Both in the Leggatt episode and in the episode here, the ship is in imminent danger. In both instances the men highest in command other than Leggatt and the narrator "go to pieces," both men who as far as appearances were concerned were expert seaman of strong temperament. The first mate, in his distracting cries which hinder the narrator, also offers a striking parallel to the man Leggatt killed. As Leggatt did with the mutinous sailor, the narrator seizes the first mate and forces him under control. Fortunately the narrator has a hold on the man's arm instead of his neck, but the effect is the same.

If the ship is put in extreme danger, it is a necessary danger and merely forces to an issue the danger the ship would have been under until a crisis appeared. Without the dramatic moment there would be little chance that the captain could change the nature of his relationship with the crew. The captain must meet the test; and the moment that the secret ideal is leaving the ship is the perfect time for him to turn the ideal into action, to prove that it is literally dependent upon his own personality. That his hat, the Jungian symbol of the personality, gives him the needed guide is appropriate: he has, before he spies the marker, forgotten Leggatt; his victory belongs to him alone: he has become the ideal.

But one cannot overlook the most conscious motivation that comes through in the narrator's actions leading up to the crisis. The well-planted detail that Leggatt is an excellent swimmer must not obscure the fact that the narrator is extremely concerned for the safety of the departing man, and Leggatt's aquatic prowess does not lighten his sense of responsibility. Though Conrad has told his story along the two lines of a dual morality, both moralities finally operate upon this respect for human life. If Leggatt's "crime" was a simple matter of one man for twenty-four, the climax becomes the offering of twenty-four for one. The difference in value is, of course, that the one in the former was a mutinous sailor and the one in the latter is the ideal. It is not the narrator alone who is grateful but, though they will never know, the crew of the ship. They are in safe hands now; previously, the ship was every moment a potential disaster, a ship without a captain.

Conrad did not use the sea and the life it offers as something basically different from the common experience of humanity, but rather as a distillation of it. The elements of experience, including the morality, are more simple, straightforward, and elemental; but Conrad's final concern, as we know so well, lay in his reverence for "the heat of life in the handful of dust" which grows out of all his ironies.

Edward W. Said　(essay date 1966)

SOURCE: "The Craft of the Present," in *Joseph Conrad and the Fiction of Autobiography,* Cambridge, Mass.: Harvard University Press, 1966, pp. 120-36.

[*Said is a prominent American educator and critic who has written widely on modern critical theories. In the following excerpt, he analyzes autobiographical elements in "The Secret Sharer."*]

The much-discussed **"The Secret Sharer"** (completed in 1909) most skillfully dramatizes Conrad's concerns at this time. It is important to say at once that I am not considering the story as a Jungian fable. **"The Secret Sharer"** seems more interesting to me as a study in the actualized structure of doubleness—thus I treat it as an intellectual story of qualified emotional force. The story's opening is quite similar to the openings of its precursors, differing from them only in the young narrator's intuition of his ship's power, her strong part in his existence.

> In this breathless pause at the threshold of a long passage we seemed to be measuring our fitness for a long and arduous enterprise, the appointed task of both our existences to be carried out, far from all human eyes, with only sky and sea for spectators and for judges.

In *The Mirror of the Sea* Conrad had told his readers that a ship is like a man's character,—made and tested by experience and hence a work of art. The young captain, whose "ideal conception" of himself is to be tested with his ship, is like Conrad, the writer who is about to test his character in a projected course of his own making. The background of this endeavor is the sea:

> And suddenly I rejoiced in the great security of the sea as compared with the unrest of the land, in my choice of that untempted life presenting no disquieting problems, invested with an elementary moral beauty by the absolute straightforwardness of its appeal and by the singleness of its purpose.

When Leggatt comes aboard and begins to tell his story, the narrator realizes that what he is hearing "was no mere formula of desperate speech, but a real alternative in the view of a strong soul". Leggatt's youth apparently guarantees him the ability to confront clear issues, and the narrator's immediate understanding of this is in marked contrast to the circuitous way, in Conrad's earlier stories, by which the deeply problematic aspects of the past had been evoked to trouble the present. Reality and unmistakable clarity are important new additions to the erupting past; consequently, the narrator has powers of sympathetic intuition and "mysterious communication." Leggatt, in other words, must be rescued in no uncertain way and for no uncertain reason. There is a bond of simple, uncomplicatd sympathy, one man for another.

This seems to be the point that grants the Jungians license to interpret the story as the progress toward the integration of the unconscious self. But surely "integration" in some manner is a feature of all fiction anyway; moreover, this story possesses a number of deliberate details whose interest extends beyond their use as prescriptions for psychic good health. The bond of sympathy between the narrator and Leggatt, for instance, is sudden, just as an action is impulsive, and the explanation for that bond is given afterwards. Thus Conrad's psychological bias is preserved, with thought following action. The amorphous sea, upon whose surface nothing can remain reflected for long, yields to Leggatt, whose function as a mirror, it appears, is secure in the narrator's consciousness. Conrad is no longer hopelessly trying to establish causal relations between past and present. Instead, he summons a person out of the past whose restless flight embodies an old "secret action" that seeks sympathetic recognition in the present. While Leggatt is a real person, he is also an image according to which the young narrator can see himself in an extreme intellectual and moral perspective. Discrete rather than indeterminate recollection, courageous self-identification rather than shameful retreat—these are the benefits that Leggatt brings to the becalmed young captain. In **"Youth"** Conrad had worried about the feeling that might disrupt the narrative. In **"The Secret Sharer"** Leggatt is like a feeling of rebelliousness that has become both intrinsic to and alive in the narrative. In still different terms, Leggatt is an economy for the benefit of the narrator's understanding of himself, just as the sailor-become-writer is an economy for Conrad's benefit.

But why, then, is Leggatt introduced as a fugitive outcast?

Why was Conrad anxious to make Leggatt and the narrator aware of crime's enormity as well as its supposed justification? It would be too easy to say that Conrad's sympathy with Leggatt provoked a temporizing moral attitude. There is a trace of slightly embarrassed zeal in Leggatt's narrative, which may convey a poignancy that Conrad himself felt. Like Leggatt, Conrad had covered the artistic failures he felt as an author with a pose of aggressive self-assertion. The conventional opprobrium attached to murder haunts Leggatt's crime. Yet Leggatt's attitude toward what he has done lies somewhere between shame and pride, between guilt and righteous vindictiveness. And so does Conrad's. Consequently, the morality of **"The Secret Sharer"** moves within a self-consciously aesthetic framework of values that is not sustained by universal imperatives like "my station and its duties." Whatever imperatives pertain now are eminently personal and temperamental: Leggatt is like the *poète maudit* who supplants conventional morality with the power of his personality. All in all, some of Leggatt's traits are motifs in a dramatic paraphrase of the peculiar mismatch between Conrad's scrupulous self-commentary and his public pretenses.

The reason for the narrator's sympathy is explained a few moments later: "It was, in the night, as though I had been faced by my own reflection in the depths of a sombre and immense mirror". There are two important points to make about this sentence. One is that intruder from the past, for the first time in Conrad's short fiction, is not sought out as an instrument for magically reordering things, as a symbol for the use of the narrative consciousness (as Mrs. Hervey is for Hervey). On the contrary, Leggatt is a direct reflection of the narrator; he is a person in whom the young narrator can see himself, clearly and directly. In the second place, we must remember that the large mirror of the sea, heedless and immense, had already established itself in Conrad's mental cosmology; so we see that Leggatt, in spite of his extenuating crime, first defies and then replaces the larger sea mirror with himself.

Evidence of mismatch continues to appear in the tale as the two young men gradually adjust to each other's trials. Leggatt's interpretation of his escape appeals to the young narrator because of its familiarity. The relaxed entreaty of "the 'brand of Cain' business" is not at all like the disquieting strangeness of Kurtz's moral exile. The results of Kurtz's outrages upon convention had required endless, inconclusive elucidation. In Leggatt's narrative, however, "there was something that made comment impossible . . . a sort of feeling, a quality, which I can't find a name for." Nevertheless, all is not well. It is significant that at an important point in his narrative Leggatt says that he had been swimming in what seemed to be a thousand-foot cistern, from which there was no escape. Is this not a deliberate recollection of Conrad's own struggle in the black cave? A short time later the young narrator, having accepted Leggatt as his secret sharer, says:

> and all the time the dual working of my mind
> distracted me almost to the point of insanity. I
> was constantly watching myself, my secret self,
> as dependent on my actions as my own personal-
> ity, sleeping in that bed, behind that door which
> faced me as I sat at the head of the table. It was

very much like being mad, only it was worse because one was aware of it.

The young narrator's consciousness has absorbed the full import of the masquerade, and from now on we can assume that *his* mind, displacing Leggatt's, is really at the center of the tale. He too, like Conrad, feels the effects of the imposture.

In the second half of the tale, it is the captain of the *Sephora*, Leggatt's ship, who represents the general fear of being taken to task for the game of disguise and concealment. Perhaps it is too bold a speculation, but I like to think that in some ways the captain's "spiritless tenacity" is distinctly reminiscent of Conrad's publishers, and even of his public, always curious, always demanding to have and know more. The narrator says:

> My lack of excitement, of curiosity, of surprise,
> of any sort of pronounced interest, began to
> arouse his distrust. But except for the felicitous
> pretence of deafness I had not tried to pretend
> anything. I had felt utterly incapable of playing
> the part of ignorance properly, and therefore
> was afraid to try. It is also certain that he had
> brought some ready-made suspicions with him,
> and that he viewed my politeness as a strange
> and unnatural phenomenon. And yet how else
> could I have received him? Not heartily! That
> was impossible for psychological reasons, which
> I need not state here. My only object was to keep
> off his inquiries. Surlily? Yes, but surliness might
> have provoked a point-blank question. From its
> novelty to him and from its nature, punctilious
> courtesy was the manner best calculated to re-
> strain the man. But there was the danger of his
> breaking through my defence bluntly. I could
> not, I think, have met him by a direct lie, also
> for psychological (not moral) reasons. If he had
> only known how afraid I was of his putting my
> feeling of identity with the other to the test! But
> strangely enough—(I thought of it only after-
> wards)—I believe that he was not a little discon-
> certed by the reverse side of that weird situation,
> by something in me that reminded him of the
> man he was seeking—suggested a mysterious si-
> militude to the young fellow he had distrusted
> and disliked from the first.

This is an excellent example of what Sartre would call refuge from an unbearable situation; the evasion of the narrator is mercifully helped along by the captain's stupidity. Nevertheless, the captain's effect on the course of the tale is considerable, since through his questions Leggatt and the narrator learn that the supposedly dead fugitive from conventional punishment must remain "dead." Leggatt must remain secret and obscure. This is again a transformation of the "obscurity" and "mystery" so prevalent in Conrad's earlier work. Whereas previously the desire to illuminate obscurity led one only into more obscurity, here the elucidation of obscurity is accomplished, even though it is only the narrator who finally possesses the secret he shares with Leggatt. Surely this is an illustration of Baudelaire's dictum that all the phenomena of the artist's double nature are possessed by the artist. When Leggatt reminds the narrator that "we are not living in a boy's adventure tale," he is prohibiting implications that would make of the whole episode a simple question of sensation or adventure, or even one with a conventional explanation.

The narrator ironically affirms Leggatt's reminder by admitting to himself that he would be very glad if the fugitive left the ship. Having created in his life a dual image of himself, like Conrad, the young captain must launch it with a daring navigational exploit; this is the exercise of art, as James would have said, flying in the face of expectations. Conrad's remark to Garnett that "every truth requires some pretence to make it live" is also pertinent. Truth resides in the young captain's determination to free himself by mastery of his métier, to prove himself a good sailor. The analogy is close at hand: Conrad desires the exultant freedom of the acclaimed novelist. The ship is suddenly put about (Conrad defiantly altering the course of his work) and Leggatt whispers, " 'Be careful' . . . I realized suddenly that all my future, the only future for which I was fit, would perhaps go irretrievably to pieces in any mishap to my first command." There is now a period of "intolerable stillness," a return to the opening mood of pervasive calm. But now the narrator is armed with objective knowledge of the past and can use it to *create* a convincing show of craft and self-mastery. Leggatt leaves the ship; the captain is left "alone with his command." Swimming off, Leggatt, is "a free man, a proud swimmer striking out for a new destiny."

"The Secret Sharer" contains, then, the double working out and rescue that Conrad now saw as the momentary salvation for his embattled self. Leggatt rescue the captain and the captain rescues Leggatt—an apparently straightforward interchange administered with "piety." Moreover, the acceptance of a fact of past experience is taken in and used to alleviate an unrelieved tension in the present. Lastly, a convincing image of human kinship, modally altered to one expressed in terms of action and sympathy as opposed to action and thought, sends the figure from the past back into the unknown, free from constricting troubles, and sends the present consciousness into the future, armed with reassured mastery.

Leonard Gilley   (essay date 1967)

SOURCE: "Conrad's *The Secret Sharer*," in *The Midwest Quarterly,* Vol. VIII, No. 3, Spring, 1967, pp. 319-30.

[*In the following essay, Gilley maintains that the action of "The Secret Sharer" is implausible.*]

Joseph Conrad wrote **"The Secret Sharer"** in November of 1909. It is a story about a bond between the narrator and the fugitive Leggatt; at the same time, it is the story of the narrator's response to his first command; and finally and more briefly the story of Leggatt's saving the *Sephora* and strangling a man.

In this tale the narrator is in a unique, though illusory, position of freedom. Whether it was a happy accident of his seafaring life or whether it was a more conscious choice of the artist, Conrad employs the young captain in **"The Secret Sharer"** to examine the personality of a partially free man in the great universe. Not only examine, but also

test. This narrator is uninitiated; he holds his first command—unlike another captain, Ahab in *Moby-Dick,* who is old with the ways of the sea and who attempts, unsuccessfully, to pierce the secret mask of the universe itself.

Here in **"The Secret Sharer"** it is not the universe that is to be examined, but the mystery in a man's mind. The universe, the world is present, a dark, nearly black, brooding presence against which, in quiet but not particularly fearful isolation, the narrator is tested. He tells us he is not only a stranger to the world of the ship, but also that "I was somewhat of a stranger to myself." And we find that when, at the end of the story, the strangeness in the narrator's mind is gone, so too is gone his sense of strangeness in the world. The human mind is the seat of mystery and reality, not the external world-mask that Ahab is attempting to pierce. The mask that the narrator of **"The Secret Sharer"** is concerned about is the one that covers his own face. The dark oriental world outside is only a symbolic reinforcement of the strangeness within himself.

Alone with his ship, his first command, "under the enormous dome of the sky" and with "no sign of human habitation as far as the eye could reach," the young captain dreams of his journey, which will begin the next morning, a journey homeward toward the known. At that precise, almost stationary instant in which the story begins, the narrator is acutely aware of the coming test, says of himself and his ship, "we seemed to be measuring our fitness for a long and arduous enterprise, the appointed task of both our existences to be carried out, far from all human eyes, with only sky and sea for spectators and judges." And further, "I wondered how far I should turn out faithful to that ideal conception of one's own personality every man sets up for himself secretly." Soon we are to see in Leggatt a man who, in the eyes of the narrator, is the ideal toward which the narrator aspires.

But even from the beginning of the tale the narrator's aloneness is an illusion, the result of "some glare in the air to interfere with one's sight"; for easily within view is another ship with people on it, not to mention the other human beings on his own ship. Finally the narrator does see the other ship, and he mentions it to his mates at supper. Neither of these men is the ideal toward which the young captain can aspire; it will have to be an outsider who is elevated to the ideal. But since he is writing a realistic tale, Conrad is confronted with the problem of how to get that outsider onto the ship in a believable way. As preparation—to accustom the reader to the unlikely—we read the amusing account of the scorpion finding its way to death in the chief mate's inkwell. A second odd happening immediately follows: The second mate's inexplicable delay in relating his knowledge of the *Sephora.*

Now we are supposed to be prepared for a key implausible event. The narrator sends everyone to bed so that his crew can get extra rest before raising anchor and so that he himself can be alone with his ship. He says, "I felt painfully that I—a stranger—was doing something unusual." Possibly we too find it painful, especially if it is obvious carpenter-work in order to lift Leggatt up out of the water.

Everyone except the narrator is asleep and the narrator is

pacing the deck dreaming of the fine figure his ship will cut sweeping homeward before the wind. He descends to his cabin for a cigar and his sleeping suit:—he has cast off the wide-awake conscious self, freed the dreamer. He sees his position this way: "And suddenly I rejoiced in the great security of the sea as compared with the unrest of the land, in my choice of that untempted life presenting no disquieting problems, invested with an elementary moral beauty by the absolute straight forwardness of its appeal and by the singleness of its purpose."

Does the narrator offer this moral beauty as a truth—or illusion, just as his alleged aloneness was an illusion? Certainly the other aspect of his evaluation—namely, that sea life is secure, that there are no disquieting problems at sea—is a momentary illusion. Men at sea have problems, and the tale itself turns upon mysterious unrest in the narrator's mind, possibly doubt regarding his ability to live up to his deep ideal of himself. Yet the symbolic light in the forerigging is clear, untroubled, confident, bright.

After this dreamy passage, the narrator's mind focuses upon a practical matter: The rope ladder which, conveniently for the plot, was not hauled in some hours earlier. In life coincidence seems to play a role, although it might not if we could see relationships in a wider perspective. Generally in realistic fiction, if the author uses coincidence to solve for him the development and resolution of the problems he is examining, we as readers have a right to be skeptical.

In reply, the narrator of **"The Secret Sharer"** voices contempt for the cause-effect mind of that "imbecile mate of mine"; by associating stupidity with rationality, the narrator attempts to convince us that reason cannot account for all the happenings in the world. Still, it just may be that Conrad has played tricks in order to get the reader to accept a set of too slick circumstances.

Whatever the case may be, Conrad as soon as he has secured the swimmer to the rope ladder can return the responsibility for the story to the narrator. The swimmer says, "My name is Leggatt." "The voice was calm and resolute," comments the narrator. "A good voice. The self-possession of that man had somehow induced a corresponding state in myself."

Immediately, the narrator discovers a quality—self-possession—in Leggatt that he wishes to emulate. The relationship is established. Leggatt dons a sleeping suit that duplicates the one the narrator is wearing and so becomes the narrator's double—the mirror image of what the narrator aspires to become. And yet there is a problem because Leggatt has killed a man. Curiously, the narrator is not disturbed by this news. Even before he hears the somewhat ambiguous circumstances surrounding the killing, the narrator offers an excuse for Leggatt. " 'Fit of temper,' I suggested."

Leggatt seems to nod in agreement and the narrator writes, "It was, in the night, as though I had been faced by my own reflection in the depths of a somber and immense mirror." Many critics read this passage as meaning that the narrator realizes that he too might have killed—

and this possibility welds the bond between the two men. I think this reading is correct.

What I cannot accept so readily is the justification of the killing which the narrator (but not necessarily Conrad) offers and which so many critics buy. The argument runs this way: The man killed was, according to Leggatt, one of those "miserable devils that had no business to live at all."

The narrator concurs: "I knew well enough the pestiferous danger of such a character where there are no means of legal repression." The narrator reasons here like a television detective hero—a man is justified in taking direct extralegal action, even to the extent of killing. The death, at least we are told, was no accident. Leggatt says, "It's clear that I meant business, because I was holding him by the throat still when they picked us up." At the same time there is more than a hint of temporary madness—although Leggatt turns the thing around and accuses the rest of the crew of madness. Still, the killing does occur in extremely trying circumstances. Leggatt and everyone else on the *Sephora* have been pushed by the storm beyond the limits of human endurance and control; and so Leggatt strangles the pestiferous seaman. Leggatt has been tested; he passed the test when he saved the *Sephora*. Then, however, he failed when he lost control and struck the seaman and strangled him. But this is not the view of the narrator who attempts to convince the reader that Leggatt has done an almost admirable deed in ridding the world of the sailor.

And for some reason, a number of critics say that Leggatt killed the man in order to save the *Sephora*. Certainly the saving of the *Sephora* must be recorded in Leggatt's favor, although he himself is a bit too insistent in telling about it. The point is that the narrator sees the saving of the ship as justification for the killing. Perhaps the critics, having difficulty with this justification, solved the problem by misstating the facts of the story; *i.e.,* Leggatt killed in order to save.

Now if that had actually been the case (justifiable homicide), then much of the ambiguity of the situation would have been washed away. But Conrad did not want a clear case. Conrad wished to show that life is not simple. Thus, possibly one failing of the tale is that it is all too easy for even the perceptive reader to be won over by the narrator's arguments. Beyond the narrator is Conrad, and it is his point of view that is not clear. I hesitate to solve the problem the way so many critics do; namely by assuming Conrad's viewpoint can be equated with the narrator's—or, to go further, to say the narrator is Conrad: Conrad took over his first command under similar circumstances, etc.

The narrator does stack the facts in Leggatt's favor—is there a critic anywhere who does not agree? But to conclude that the reader should accept this bias as truth is quite another matter. Always with a first person narrative the reader must be careful about the reliability of the reporter.

Next comes an interlude in the story that at first glance seems irrelevant: Leggatt's detailed account of his escape from the *Sephora*. Actually the purpose is soon clear. The account provides another example of noble behavior for the narrator to admire. In his escape, Leggatt displays courage, intelligence, and self-control—all combined with incredibly good luck.

At the same time, Leggatt gives his reasons for escaping. He believes that judge and jury in England would be unfair to him, that he has the right to decide his own case, and that he has rid the world of an "ill-conditioned snarling cur." The narrator quite agrees with these assertions. What I object to is the ubiquitous critic who is so sure that the evidence tips entirely and absolutely in favor of Leggatt—largely because the narrator says so. Never do we like to rely on the evidence of one witness, and in this case not even an eye-witness. Thus, Conrad indirectly is obligated (or isn't he?) to give the reader at least one other point of view. This he does, but apparently he should have been more heavy-handed about it.

Meanwhile the narrator has poured the exhausted Leggatt into bed and fallen asleep himself on the couch, to be awakened by the steward bringing morning coffee. Now a nightmare begins for the narrator. He must hide this fugitive Leggatt; he must court danger and pass the test. He, by odd behavior, must disguise or hide his own secret, but real, self. Only after passing the test can he be free—and only then can Leggatt be free, too.

Regarding his freedom, the narrator says, "Of course, theoretically, I could do what I liked, with no one to say me nay within the whole circle of the horizon; but to lock my cabin door and take away the key I did not dare." The narrator's freedom is limited; he feels the pressure he is under; and we need to remember that if anyone finds out about the fugitive, the career of the narrator will be demolished. He is a worried young man. He says, "all the time the dual working of my mind distracted me almost to the point of insanity," and it "was very much like being mad, only it was worse because one was aware of it."

This pressure mounts when the captain of the *Sephora* comes aboard to attempt to find Leggatt. The irony is excellent in that they proceed immediately to the narrator's cabin, the hiding place of Leggatt. This visiting captain is portrayed unsympathetically—the narrator's delineation of the man's physical characteristics is anything but flattering; and the captain is said to be unintelligent and to exhibit a spiritless tenacity. The narrator is employing an old trick. By painting one character, here the captain, as repulsive and stupid, by simple contrast another character—Leggatt—acquires a stature of integrity without having to demonstrate that integrity. Suppose, for example, the captain—whose name the narrator cannot even remember since the captain is such a nonentity—suppose the captain had been portrayed as an intelligent, sensitive, reasonable man. This would have had a reverse effect, and rather severely so: It would have diminished the stature of Leggatt, again without any real revelation of character.

The narrator tells us that there was "something incomprehensible and a little awful" in the captain's sense of obligation to apprehend the killer. By implication, Leggatt must be right—if we compare him with this evil old captain. Beyond this, the narrator cannot betray Leggatt to the cap-

tain because to betray Leggatt would be to betray himself and his career in a very practical sense; but the narrator means a betrayal in a mystical sense, a betrayal of his ideal and, at the same time, dark vision of himself.

It is a curious fact that Leggatt is ideal only to the narrator. When the narrator's own officers and crew hear about the killing, they do not side with the noble Leggatt. According to the narrator, we are supposed to believe that all the men on shipboard except Leggatt and the narrator are senseless beasts. Only Leggatt and the narrator are men of refined sensibilities. Many critics see it this way, too.

After the captain of the *Sephora* departs, Leggatt rails against him and glorifies, justifies, himself again in an outburst to the narrator. Before the narrator can really evaluate the character of Leggatt who at once is capable of saving a foundering ship and of killing a man, conveniently footsteps are heard:—with the departure of the captain of the *Sephora* a wind conveniently has arisen and it is time to get busy, to set sail for merry England, and so the narrator rationalizes, "I had no leisure to weigh the merits of the matter." The narrator has his excuse for not examining the case against Leggatt. Rather, the narrator tells us he is caught up in his concern to make a proper impression on his mates and crew. But he is not successful and the crew decides he is mad. He is disturbed, but not Leggatt, who, the narrator reports, "looked always perfectly self-controlled, more than calm—invulnerable."

Ironically, the presence of the ideal secret self fails to enable the narrator to emulate that ideal. Instead, the narrator's behavior becomes increasingly quixotic, forcing the mates and crew to become even more fearful. The narrator himself says, "I think I had come creeping quietly as near insanity as any man who has not actually gone over the border." Again in contrast, he admires Leggatt, "marveling at that something unyielding in his character which was carrying him through so finely. . . . He was sane." The narrator especially admires Leggatt's sane assertion, "What can they [a jury] know whether I'm guilty or not—or of *what* I'm guilty either? That's my affair." Perhaps this is what the narrator meant when he spoke of the moral beauty of the sea. Or is the moral beauty the unnecessary risking of destruction of the ship and the lives of the mates and crew?

In any case, the narrator is impelled to bring the ship nearly to destruction. Leggatt is an excellent swimmer; his safety cannot be the reason. What then is the reason for this foolish maneuvering of the ship? As good a one as any is that the narrator believes he must risk destruction of the ship before he is competent to command. He must do a foolhardy or, more euphemistically, a dangerous act to test himself, and if he can pass that test he will be fit for command. The analogous situation occurred when Leggatt saved the *Sephora*. But is nearly running the ship aground deliberately, almost destroying it rather than saving it in a storm, an intelligent test to prove the fitness of command? Many critics believe it is. The owner of the ship, the mates and crew might not agree.

Even after nearly a week at sea, the narrator says, "I was

a total stranger to the ship." He pushes the ship almost aground and says "her very fate hung in the balance" and a moment later "I had not learned yet the feel of my ship." If he was this slow-witted about learning to handle his command, then it was doubly foolish to point the ship at the land to appease his conscience or whatever was troubling him. He sees moral obligation only to himself and Leggatt, none to his ship and crew. If this mad sailing of a dangerous course will cleanse his soul and give him courage, then no matter; for he is far more important to himself than are the responsibilities of command.

Neatly, by accident, the ship is saved. It is not the skill of this young captain, but his hat, given to Leggatt, that, drifting upon the water, rescues the ship from destruction. Because the ship accidentally eludes crashing, the narrator believes he has passed the examination. He says, "Already the ship was drawing ahead. And I was alone with her. Nothing! no one in the world should stand now between us, throwing a shadow on the way of silent knowledge and mute affection, the perfect communion of a seaman with his first command." From another point of view, his master's license should be revoked.

As the ship glides safely back out to sea, the narrator walks to the rail to salute his second self, Leggatt, whom he defines as "a free man, a proud swimmer striking out for a new destiny." Here, some critics discover themselves a bit astonished, for they do seem to recall that Leggatt killed a man and they object now to the idealized final statement. After all, it is not quite right to call the fugitive free and proud. But the narrator must say this. It is thoroughly consistent with his values throughout the tale.

Leggatt, earlier, said, "There's nothing of a boy's tale in this"—but he was wrong. Not only is this story built on the convenient coincidence of cheap adventure fiction, but also the narrator's moral stance is of dubious worth. Leglatt's reward for killing and running away is a shiny new destiny; and the narrator's reward for hiding Leggatt and for nearly wrecking the ship is to prove himself fit for command.

Writing of this tale, Conrad said, "Every word fits, and there's not a single uncertain note." If he really believed this statement, and there is no reason to think that he did not, then perhaps he had an imperfect understanding of what he had written.

On the other hand, the universe may not be an Aristotelian one. Investigations in physics and in human behavior point in this direction; and in much contemporary fiction the argument presented is that human life does not proceed by rational cause and effect. Although the Aristotelian reader may want the world explained by rational principles, the writer often scatters chaos on his pages. From this viewpoint, it might be possible to justify, at least partially, "The Secret Sharer."

Yet I still urge that the method of the tale—ridicule of and contempt for the rational—is suspect; this is not the way to give validity to contrivance and *deus ex machina*. When all is said and done, no amount of finely phrased criticism can deny the fact that Conrad has here played tricks in order to get the reader to acquiesce to a set of preposterous circumstances.

Daniel Curley   (essay date 1967)

SOURCE: "The Writer and His Use of Material: The Case of *The Secret Sharer*," in *Modern Fiction Studies*, Vol. XIII, No. 1, Spring, 1967, pp. 179-94.

[*Curley was an American educator, novelist, playwright, short story writer, and critic. In the following essay, he examines Conrad's use of historical and autobiographical materials in "The Secret Sharer."*]

Several years ago I became involved in a controversy over the nature of a character in Joseph Conrad's story **"The Secret Sharer."** The question was this: Is Leggatt, the escaping murderer, a good man or a bad man? Symbolically, as everyone agrees, Leggatt stands for the captain's other self, but is that other self good or evil, his higher or his lower nature? I felt then—and I feel now—that Leggatt represents the higher nature of the captain, his ideal self in fact, and that everything in the story points in that direction. In working out my case, I used as part of my evidence certain changes Conrad made in adapting the actual historic events on which the story was based. At the same time, I noted in the story other uses of historical and autobiographical materials which were then irrelevant to my purpose but which might some day be worth investigating to see exactly how it is that a writer uses the raw material he has at his disposal.

There are really three sets of data which we must keep in mind during this discussion: the story itself, the autobiographical materials relating to Conrad's first voyage as a sea captain, and the historical materials relating to the disastrous voyage of the ship *Cutty Sark*.

Although **"The Secret Sharer"** is very well known, it is long and complicated; so I shall make brief narrative summaries where they seem necessary to focus attention. For the moment, at least, the relevant facts are simply these. A young officer has just taken command of his first ship, and the story opens as the ship lies at the head of the Gulf of Siam waiting for a breeze. The action of the story continues through several days as the ship makes its passage down the Gulf.

The bare circumstances of a young man's first command and the geographical location are easy to pin down as autobiographical. Conrad passed his master's examination at the end of 1886, but he was unable for some time to get a command. In January of 1888 he determined to return to Europe where his luck might be better, and he was in Singapore waiting for a ship to give him passage when he was offered exactly the opportunity he wanted. The captain of the barque *Otago* had died at sea, and the *Otago* was in Bangkok expecting a new captain. Although the dead captain does not come into **"The Secret Sharer"** in any way, he is noteworthy as an example of the sort of thing the writer must contend with in his raw material. There is a vivid sketch of him in G. Jean-Aubry's *Life and Letters*:

> [The late captain of the *Otago*] had been a man

of somewhat singular character. From the second officer [Conrad] learnt that he had been sixty-five years old, and that he had spent the last weeks of his life playing the fiddle day and night in his cabin, without paying the smallest heed to the ship's course,—except to prevent her touching at a port; that he had seemed not so much indifferent to the welfare of his officers and crew, as desirous of seeing them all perish some day of hunger and boredom. One day, feeling himself to be ill, he had thrown his fiddle overboard and allowed himself to die; to the last completely indifferent to his crew.

This sketch clearly suggests the kind of self-control a writer must exercise in selecting his material. It would have been easy to start the story a little earlier in order to include this beguiling interlude. The temptation is certainly great. But Conrad was not distracted. He recognized exactly what his story was about and where it began. The story is not about the difficulties of taking over a ship from a mad captain, who wrote dirty poems in the ship's account book and never deigned to let the owners know where he was or what he was doing. That is a story—in fact it is two stories, and the name of one is *The Shadow Line* and the name of the other is **"Falk."** In **"The Secret Sharer,"** however, Conrad dismisses all this with a line: "In consequence of certain events of no particular significance, except to myself, I had been appointed to the command only a fortnight before."

The story that is of significance now is the classic life-voyage story, and Conrad quite rightly starts it at the beginning of the voyage. The second paragraph of **"The Secret Sharer"** makes this clear: "She floated at the starting-point of a long journey, very still in an immense stillness, the shadows of her spars flung far to the eastward by the setting sun. At that moment I was alone on her decks. There was not a sound in her—and around us nothing moved, nothing lived, not a canoe on the water, not a bird in the air, not a cloud in the sky. In this breathless pause at the threshold of a long passage we seemed to be measuring our fitness for a long and arduous enterprise, the appointed task of both our existences to be carried out, far from all human eyes, with only sky and sea for spectators and for judges."

There is no place in this beginning for a mad captain. Conrad knows he will keep and be usable another time. As already indicated, this is not a story of the difficulties of taking over command, a story of one's relationship with others. It is, rather, a story of a private test of worthiness to command, a story of a man's relationship with himself: " . . . I wondered how far I should turn out faithful to that ideal conception of one's own personality every man sets up for himself secretly."

So far we have located the source of several important elements in the story. First, is the general circumstance of the first command, begun suddenly when the ship has been long at sea. This follows the pattern of events in Conrad's own first command. Second, the setting of the story is also taken from that same autobiographical incident. The opening description of the area around the mouth of the Meinam River and the later description of the island Koh-

ring are both from Conrad's direct perception at that time. And, third, the very idea of a sea captain leads to the moral center of the story, the problem of responsibility.

Although we now have situation, setting, and moral center, we still have no story whatever. Something has got to happen. A test has got to be devised to determine the young man's worthiness of his new position, not only as captain of his ship but also as captain of his soul.

Of course, Conrad could have devised some kind of storm or shipwreck to test the mettle of the young captain. He knew all that sort of thing. He has the captain say when he narrates the story: "[I pictured] to myself the coming passage through the Malay Archipelago, down the Indian Ocean, and up the Atlantic. All its phases were familiar enough to me, every characteristic, all the alternatives which were likely to face me on the high seas—everything! . . . except the novel responsibility of command. But I took heart from the reasonable thought that the ship was like other ships, the men like other men, and that the sea was not likely to keep any special surprises expressly for my discomfiture."

The captain quite rightly calculates that ship and crew and sea are as they have always been and have no special surprises for him, but he does not properly weigh the most important thing of all: that he himself is something he has never been before and that he holds in store the very special surprise each person has for himself as he takes his position as a morally responsible individual. And it is because of his desire to focus on the moral nature of the story that Conrad declines the suggestion that he test his new captain with some maritime spectacular.

There is no end to the material he might have used, for he was, of course, familiar with the lore of his trade. He must have lived in a world very much like that of his characters, who constantly give the impressions that they know about each other and enjoy a constant flow of rumor and gossip; and we can be sure from this alone that he would be familiar with the story of the *Cutty Sark,* an unlucky ship much in the news about eight years before he himself took over the command of the *Otago.* But if we have any doubt at all, we need only look at the beginning of **"Falk,"** the story dealing with the period of his life immediately preceding the events on which **"The Secret Sharer"** is based—in fact, **"Falk"** is the story of the captain of that very tug we catch just a glimpse of at the beginning of **"The Secret Sharer"**: "steaming right into the land . . . hull and funnel and masts, as though the impassive earth had swallowed her up without an effort, without a tremor."

At the beginning of **"Falk,"** as often happens in Conrad's stories, we have a group of men sitting around. We know that one will shortly begin a story, but for the moment the talk is rather scattered. "We talked of the sea and all its works. The sea never changes, and its works for all the talk of men are wrapped in mystery. But we agreed that the times were changed. And we talked of old ships, of sea-accidents, of break-downs, dismastings; and of a man who brought his ship safe to Liverpool all the way from the River Platte under a jury rudder. We talked of wrecks, of short rations and of heroism—or at least of what the newspapers would have called heroism at sea—a manifestation of virtues quite different from the heroism of primitive times."

This fanciful speculation merely outlines what must have been at Conrad's disposal for the writing of his story. When it comes to the facts of the case there is simply this: in the Author's Note to *'Twixt Land and Sea,* Conrad says that he was familiar with the story of the *Cutty Sark* and used it in **"The Secret Sharer."** We cannot be sure what version of the story Conrad heard on his travels, but we do know that he was in England during the summer of 1882 when the mate of the *Cutty Sark* was tried for murder, and we do know that in the same Author's Note he speaks of the affair's having "got into the newspapers about the middle eighties." It seems reasonable to suppose that he read the accounts in the papers, perhaps this in the *London Times,* August 4, 1882:

> John Anderson, 31, seaman [alias Sidney Smith], was indicted for the wilful murder of John Francis. . . .
>
> The accused, it appeared, was chief mate on board a tea clipper called the Cutty Sark, which sailed from the port of London in May, 1880. The deceased, who was a coloured man, shipped as an able seaman, and it was stated that he soon afterwards incurred the displeasure of the prisoner in consequence of his incompetency. About the 9th or 10th of August, 1880, the vessel had just rounded the Cape, and at a quarter to 9 o'clock the prisoner was in command of the watch. The night was dark and dirty, and the watch was occupied in hauling the sail round. The deceased not being competent to perform seaman's duty, had been placed on the forecastle on the look out. The watch on hauling the ropes found that the "fore lazy tack" was fastened, and the prisoner called out to the deceased to let the tack go. The deceased replied "Very well" or, according to the prisoner's version, "Go to the devil." Immediately afterwards the deceased let go the lazy tack, but instead of doing so as an able seaman would, he let the end go overboard. The prisoner said, "That—has done that out of spite." The deceased retorted, "Well, you told me to let it go," and the prisoner exclaimed "I will come on the forecastle and heave you overboard, you nigger." The deceased replied, "If you come up here I have got the capstan bar waiting for you." The prisoner then went on the forecastle and was seen to raise the capstan bar, with which he struck the deceased on the head. The blow knocked the man over the forecastle on to the deck, and he never spoke again. . . . The account given by the prisoner was that he did it in self-defence. . . . Before the arrival of the ship at Anjer the accused, with the connivance of the captain, made his escape. The vessel proceeded thence to Singapore, and during the passage the captain committed suicide by jumping overboard, having previously dropped into the sea the capstan bar used by the prisoner. At Singapore the matter was reported to a magistrate, who, in due course, instituted an inquiry. The prisoner was arrested in London.

. . .

> The learned counsel addressed the Court in mitigation of punishment, pointing out that the vessel had been under-manned, and that at the time in question the accused had had an important manoeuvre to perform with respect to the sail. The deceased behaved in an insolent and "lubberly" manner, and it was absolutely necessary that the prisoner should assert his authority.
>
> Numerous witnesses were then called on the part of the defence to show that the prisoner bore an excellent character and was a man whose disposition was humane and kindly.
>
> The jury, by his Lordship's direction, then returned a verdict of manslaughter against the accused.
>
> MR. JUSTICE STEPHEN, in passing sentence, told the prisoner he had considered the case with anxious attention and with very great pain, because the evidence which had been given showed that he was a man of good character generally speaking and of humane disposition. He was happy to be able to give full weight to the evidence given in his favour. The deceased had certainly acted in a manner which was calculated to make the prisoner very angry, but it must be clearly understood that the taking of human life by brutal violence, whether on sea or on land, whether the life be that of a black or a white man, was a dreadful crime, and deserving of exemplary punishment. He sentenced the prisoner to seven years' penal servitude.

In his book *The Log of the Cutty Sark,* Basil Lubbock, however, gives quite a different picture of the mate. According to Lubbock, Smith, although Scotch, was a bucko mate in the best Yankee tradition. He drove the men so hard as they coasted down to Wales that the crew deserted *en masse,* and the *Cutty Sark* had to put to sea with a pick-up crew. Even so, they had a remarkably fast run, only sixty-nine days from Wales to Java. We learn, for example, in **"The Secret Sharer"** that the *Sephora* took 123 days.

The actual murder was not the only instance of violence between Smith and Francis. Things actually came to such a pass at one time that the captain felt obliged to force a show-down fight between them. They battered each other inconclusively for a quarter of an hour while the captain stood by brandishing a revolver to discourage any sailor who might be tempted to take advantage of the occasion and slip a knife into Smith.

Having established the facts in the historical voyage of the *Cutty Sark,* it is now time to return to the new captain, sitting on his first ship waiting for the wind and waiting also for a labor which will test his manhood, a rite which will initiate him into the great world of adult moral responsibility.

One thought which might have occurred to Conrad is simply to place the events of the *Cutty Sark* on board the new captain's ship. He was, after all, totally unfamiliar with his officers. One of them could easily have turned out to be

Mr. Bucko Smith. Events then take their course. A man is killed, and the captain must act in a morally responsible manner. What, however, is the captain's responsibility?

Taking into consideration Conrad's rigid conception of sea morality, I think there can be little doubt that he would have felt the captain to be faced with the same kind of obligation as Captain Vere in *Billy Budd* to honor the laws under which he held command of his ship and to turn the mate over to the shore authorities. That this solution is unsatisfactory can be seen by a glance at **"The Secret Sharer"** where the captain of the *Sephora,* the ship on which the "murder" actually took place, is depicted as being anxious to follow exactly this course of action. The young captain of the unnamed ship holds the captain of the *Sephora* in contempt because, in refusing to allow the mate to escape, he has yielded to public pressure and has refused to accept his role as a morally responsible individual, preferring instead to cower behind the forms of legality. On the other hand, the historical captain of the *Cutty Sark* behaved exactly as the young captain wanted the captain of the *Sephora* to behave: he released the mate, but when he had done that he was unable to face the consequences of his action and committed suicide.

We can see from the cases of the captain of the *Sephora* and the captain of the *Cutty Sark* that, if Conrad had placed his young captain in command of the ship on which the murder took place, the situation would have been virtually impossible to resolve in any satisfactory way. Conrad would have been unable to guide his young man safely to a new destiny, for he could only make him refuse responsibility like the captain of the *Sephora* and live on "densely distressed," or he could make him accept responsibility like the captain of the *Cutty Sark* and forfeit his career and his very life. The problem is actually insoluble. The captain must make up his mind whether he is going to slight his legal responsibility to the ship or his moral responsibility to his subordinate. This may be a decision an established man—Captain Vere—can make, but it is not the kind of decision to demand of a young man in an initiation ritual story.

Clearly, therefore, it would not do to give the young captain command of a ship like the *Cutty Sark;* but the story of the *Cutty Sark* itself suggests another possibility, and that is to have the murderer escape to the young captain's ship. In this way, the captain is freed from any legal responsibility for the death and can apply himself solely to the moral aspects of the case.

Even as the story is finally constituted, the young captain's problem is not an easy one. It takes its most obvious form in regard to his handling the ship during the final escape of Leggatt, the fugitive mate of the *Sephora.* He must bring the ship close enough to shore to allow Leggatt to escape safely, and he must stay far enough away from shore to keep from wrecking the ship. He could stay so far from shore that the ship was absolutely safe and leave Leggatt to drown—an obvious betrayal of Leggatt and of himself because Leggatt is, of course, himself—or he could give Leggatt absolute safety and wreck the ship—a betrayal of the crew, the owners, and himself, because, as he himself says, " . . . all my future, the only future for which I was

fit, would perhaps go irretrievably to pieces in any mishap to my first command." But in the end he proves himself able to judge nicely in balancing against each other the dual risks of responsibility to self and responsibility to society, and he has good luck. Leggatt was as good a judge, but his luck was bad.

Having come this far and established the broad lines along which *Cutty Sark* material is to be used, we must next turn our attention to the character of Leggatt alias Smith alias Anderson. Concerning the mate of the *Cutty Sark* we know little, and even that little is contradictory. The evidence at Smith's trial lays stress on his good character and humane disposition, whereas Lubbock's account, drawn from the log of the *Cutty Sark* itself, presents him as a regular hellion mate. Human nature and the courts being what they are, perhaps we should give less weight to the character testimony of defense witnesses than to the account of a journalist, who might at worst tend to heighten the dramatic elements of his material.

In neither account, however, is there any suggestion that Smith is a gentleman or in the least educated above the requirements of his position. He is certainly a violent and hardbitten man in both versions, and very far from being recognizable as related in any way to Leggatt, of whom even the captain of the *Sephora* says, " 'He looked very smart, very gentlemanly, and all that.' " Leggatt is, as a matter of fact, the son of a parson and a graduate of the training ship *Conway,* both of which facts grant him a definite class position. He is a gentleman, son of a gentleman, educated and trained to the best tradition of the sea. He is as far as possible from being a murderous ruffian, although he is involved in a violent death.

In spite of Conrad's care in adapting his material to his own purposes, many critics have interpreted Leggatt as being much closer to Smith than Conrad obviously intended. Conrad himself made two direct references to **"The Secret Sharer."** Both are maddeningly inconclusive, but they are all we have. The first is in a letter to John Galsworthy:

> Dearest Jack, . . . I can't tell you what pleasure you have given me by what you say of the **"Secret Sharer,"**—and especially of the swimmer. I haven't seen many notices,—three or four in all: but in one of them he is called a murderous ruffian,—or something of the sort. Who are those fellows who write in the Press? Where do they come from? I was simply knocked over,—for indeed I meant him to be what you have seen at once he was. And as you have seen, I feel altogether comforted and rewarded for the trouble he has given me in the doing of him, for it wasn't an easy task. It was extremely difficult to keep him true to type, first as modified to some extent by the sea life and further as affected by the situation.

In order to understand this completely, we need to have the Galsworthy letter Conrad is responding to, but we can see at once that Conrad intended above all that Leggatt should not be a murderous ruffian and that he should be true to the type he belonged to before going to sea: he was the son of a parson with all that implies.

Konrad Korzeniowski (later known as Joseph Conrad) in Marienbad, 1883.

The second reference occurs in the Preface to **The Shorter Tales,** some ten years later. This time he says, "The second story deals with what may be called the *'esprit de corps,'* the deep fellowship of two young seamen meeting for the first time." Here again the author, although not indicating the exact nature of the fellowship, seems specifically to exclude the possibility that it is a fellowship of violence or evil.

It might be objected that in making these changes Conrad was simply re-arranging things to make a better story. He was, of course, doing this; however, it can be demonstrated that in shaping his material he made changes of a consistent pattern intended to produce not just any better story but a specific better story—a story, furthermore, which can be properly understood only in terms of the answer to a very specific question: Why does the hellion mate of the *Cutty Sark* become the gentleman of the *Sephora,* a man who is by birth, education, and his own acts to be known as "one of us"?

The changes in the mate's character show that Conrad was trying to increase the identification between him and the captain and to establish unmistakably the nature of that "deep fellowship" and that " *'esprit de corps'* " re-

ferred to in the Preface already quoted. It cannot be too strongly insisted on that no such changes would have been necessary if Conrad had intended the fellowship to be based on a secret bond of criminal impulsiveness. The bucko mate of the *Cutty Sark,* just as he was, would have served admirably for that purpose; but instead of using the mate as he was, Conrad carefully removed from his character all the elements which could have supported the interpretation commonly forced on the story, that Leggatt represents the evil potentiality of the captain. The result of these changes is that it is not the mate of the *Cutty Sark* but Leggatt whom the captain recognizes as an extension of himself, and it is not merely a possible extension but an actual extension. The very closeness of the identification indicates that Conrad was after something other than a recognition of possibility, because he proceeds quite differently when he is presenting a character who is being led to penetrate the darkness of his own heart. A case in point is that of Captain Brierly in **Lord Jim,** who apparently has nothing whatever in common with the disastrous Jim but who, because of an insight into possibility, is driven to commit suicide in a manner strikingly reminiscent of the suicide of the captain of the *Cutty Sark.*

Before going further it is necessary to take another look at the autobiographical material in order to see what was available on that side for Conrad's use in testing the young captain's mettle. Conrad's own voyage down the Gulf of Siam in the *Otago* was surely adventurous enough to try the nerve of any captain, young or old. The ship was becalmed. The crew were all down with fever, dysentery, and cholera. Becalmed in the middle of the Gulf, Conrad discovered that the late captain had, among his other eccentricities, sold the quinine out of the medicine chest, the one thing Conrad had counted on to keep at least some of the crew on their feet.

This is all very trying indeed, but it is lacking in one element which makes **"The Secret Sharer"** a successful story of a young man's passage into maturity. The thing which is missing is the element of choice. The young Conrad had every reason to be proud of his endurance and his ability, and the whole episode can very well take its place, as Conrad says of the voyage, among " . . . such events of one's life as one has no reason to be ashamed of." Still, on the *Otago* there was no alternative. Conrad was stuck with the ship and had to get it into port somehow. There was no point at which he could accept or reject responsibility and no point at which he had to face anything other than staggering material odds. He thought of not going on, to be sure, but that was only in passing, and no great moral courage was required for him to do his simple and obvious duty. The only moral pressures which were on him urged him to behave correctly and honorably. His course was automatically imposed by his situation and his tradition.

But in the case of the young captain, faced with the problem of the escaped Leggatt, Conrad has taken care to eliminate the possibility of an automatically imposed correct solution. The captain must create out of the tradition of his life and his profession an individual moral choice to meet the totally unexpected situation, and he must do it in the face of the counter moral pressures of his own crew and of the captain of the *Sephora.* It would be easy for him to act in a way which would win him social approbation, to make a choice which would be universally acknowledged moral, but it requires a fully developed moral being to make a choice which he alone knows to be moral and which appears to everyone to be criminal or mad.

These observations apply equally to Leggatt. His steadiness throughout the story is the result of the moral strength he has already won by the choice he has already made, and the circumstances of Leggatt's choice involve the second major change in the *Cutty Sark* material, the change which has made the original form of death impossible to his new character. The story demands, however, that there still be something which looks like a murder; that Leggatt be made to appear to do something which his character will not allow.

It must not be supposed that the choice Leggatt makes is the choice of violence; for his choice, like the captain's, is a choice of responsibility. Further, it is a choice made under trying circumstances when the natural source of authority, in the captain of the *Sephora,* has totally failed. Leggatt is, in effect, in command of the ship, thereby underlining Conrad's parallel of two morally responsible individuals. The death is merely the by-product of the choice and affects neither its correctness nor its effectiveness: "It was all very simple," the captain thinks when he has heard Leggatt's story. "The same strung-up force which had given twenty-four men a chance, at least, for their lives had, in a sort of recoil, crushed an unworthy mutinous existence." Within the story itself Leggatt twice rejects violence as a way out. He refuses to break out of his cabin on the *Sephora,* for, he says, " . . . I did not mean to get into a confounded scrimmage. Somebody else might have got killed—for I would not have broken out only to get chucked back, and I did not want any more of that work." Later he says, "Do you see me being hauled back, stark naked, off one of these little islands by the scruff of the neck and fighting like a wild beast? Somebody would have got killed for certain, and I did not want any of that."

If there is anybody in the story who recognizes violence as a possibility in himself, it is Leggatt, not the captain; but Leggatt specifically renounces violence when only his personal freedom or his life is at stake. He labels it "fighting like a wild beast," and in the second instance quoted above, he does not say, "I didn't want any *more* of that," but "I didn't want any of that." The omission of *more* seems to indicate that he makes a clear distinction between what happened when he saved the ship and what might happen in a struggle to save himself. It is quite clear that Leggatt's resolutions are not those of a "criminally impulsive man," nor do they fit with the one action which is charged against him.

It is now desirable to look again at the *Cutty Sark* material to see the original action out of which Conrad created Leggatt's action. In both the version in the *Times* and the version in Lubbock, the sailor is brained with a capstan bar, a device rather more potent than a baseball bat. In the *Times* version, the episode is reported as follows: "The deceased replied, 'If you come up here I have got the capstan

bar waiting for you.' The prisoner then went on to the forecastle and was seen to raise the capstan bar, with which he struck the deceased on the head. The blow knocked the man over the forecastle on to the deck, and he never spoke again. The prisoner said to the watch, 'Did you see that nigger lift the capstan bar to me,' but the men replied that they did not."

The only difference in Lubbock's account is a rather cautious "apparently the darkey met him not only with an insolent tongue but a raised capstan bar." It really makes little difference whether the sailor got first cracks or not; Smith's blow was not the act of a humane and gentle man, and Smith did not have the excuse of being under undue strain, for the maneuver was a simple change of tack in a "nice wholesail breeze," a scene of very low dramatic value.

In **"The Secret Sharer"** the death takes place in a towering storm. The emotional intensity of the scene is reflected in the storm, but Conrad generates a further tension by making Leggatt tell the story in a whisper in a dead calm at night. His version goes like this, and we can see that it is a great improvement over the original.

> "It happened while we were setting a reefed foresail, at dusk. Reefed foresail! You understand the sort of weather. The only sail we had left to keep the ship running; so you may guess what it had been like for days. Anxious sort of job, that. He gave me some of his cursed insolence at the sheet. I tell you I was overdone with this terrific weather that seemed to have no end to it. Terrific, I tell you—and a deep ship. I believe the fellow himself was half crazed with funk. It was no time for gentlemanly reproof, so I turned round and felled him like on ox. He up and at me. We closed just as an awful sea made for the ship. All hands saw it coming and took to the rigging, but I had him by the throat, and went on shaking him like a rat, the men above us yelling, 'Look out! Look out!' Then a crash as if the sky had fallen on my head. They say that for over ten minutes hardly anything was to be seen of the ship—just the three masts and a bit of the forecastle head and of the poop all awash driving along in a smother of foam. It was a miracle that they found us, jammed together behind the forebits. It's clear that I meant business, because I was holding him by the throat still when they picked us up. He was black in the face. It was too much for them. It seems they rushed us aft together, gripped as we were, screaming 'Murder!' like a lot of lunatics, and broke into the cuddy. And the ship running for her life, touch and go all the time, any minute her last in a sea fit to turn your hair grey only a-looking at it."

The total effect of this scene is to commit Leggatt to an action which he cannot control and which the reader cannot easily evaluate. Some of the difficulties are suggested by the conduct of the judge who tried the much more clear-cut case of the mate of the *Cutty Sark.* In the first place, the judge allowed the reduction of the charge from murder to manslaughter. He also gave full weight to testimony of good character and to the fact that the mate had an important maneuver to perform and needed to assert his authority. He accepted all these points in arriving at a sentence, for indeed there can be no standard by which they are not relevant.

If we consider the infinitely greater complexity of Leggatt's case and the fact that Leggatt's skill and courage had just succeeded in setting the sail which saved the ship, the question of his guilt becomes almost impossible to settle. In fact, to the young captain there is no question, because he concludes "it was all very simple." In a sense, however, Conrad has made it simple for the reader too—at least simpler than it is often made out to be—because Leggatt in asserting his authority had no intention of harming the man. He just wanted him out of the way, so he felled him like an ox. Certainly under the circumstances the action was not only not wrong but actually the standard thing to do and of no more importance than throwing a glass of water in the face of a screaming child. But when the sailor came at him again, Leggatt was forced to adopt stronger measures and began to throttle him into submission—on Captain Vere's ship the sailor would have been liable to execution. When the wave broke over the ship, Leggatt's reflex led him to hold fast to anything. Unfortunately he happened to have hold of a man's throat, and what we now have is something which is a murder in form but not a murder in fact. Leggatt's own remark, " 'It's clear that I meant business,' " is not at all an expression of guilt, because the business which he meant was far from the business which resulted.

The total pattern of changes Conrad made in adapting the *Cutty Sark* material effectively removes the episode of the death from the area of ordinary legality. The meaning of this removal can perhaps be made more clear by further reference to *Billy Budd*, in which there is a similar conflict of legality and morality, but in which, in contrast to **"The Secret Sharer,"** the decision has to be made in purely legal terms and in complete disregard, as far as the action goes, of the obvious moral implications of the case. Captain Vere, on whose ship the death occurs, is sure that Billy is morally innocent; but there is no doubt that he struck and killed his superior officer, and no circumstances can be effectively offered in mitigation of punishment of that crime. The manifest evil of the victim, the colossal provocation are irrelevant to the level on which the case must be tried. Captain Vere, like the captain in **"The Secret Sharer,"** recognizes the superiority of the moral law over the civil or military law, recognizes Billy as innocent under one law and guilty under another. Unfortunately the law under which he is guilty leaves Captain Vere no choice but to hang him, and the young captain in **"The Secret Sharer"** would likewise have had no choice but to turn Leggatt over to the shore authorities if the death had occurred on his own ship.

I suggested earlier that Conrad might have made more use than he did of the actual events of his own voyage on the *Otago*. In truth, he did at another time make very complete use of them. In the novel *The Shadow Line* he started the action in Singapore, where he himself had once waited for a ship to take him to England and where he unexpectedly received his first command. The story takes the new captain to Bangkok and goes into all the difficulties of get-

ting the ship ready for sea and then through all the voyage down the Gulf of Siam and back to Singapore. **"The Secret Sharer,"** in contrast, utilizes only a few days at the beginning of the voyage down the Gulf. These two uses of the same material can give further insight into the possibilities among which the writer must choose in telling his story, and in no story element is this more clear than in Conrad's handling of the two points of view.

"The Secret Sharer" is an unusual story for Conrad. It lacks the retrospective element commonly found in his work, and for that reason is uncommonly immediate and youthful. It is the story of a moment as a short story must be, but it is the story of a young man's moment unqualified by the wisdom of age and experience. Conrad's moments are usually those of men who are looking back over a considerable period of time and have the advantage of being able to see themselves as they once were. Perspective is the meaning of that older man's moment, not immediacy. For example, when Marlow, one of Conrad's favorite mouthpieces, speaks of his own youth, he is able, while in the very act of glorifying it, to see it as made up of ignorance, folly, and hope.

Considering the evidence of setting, characterization, and plot, the theme of "The Secret Sharer" might be stated as follows: Because of the dangerous and chaotic world in which mankind lives, it is imperative that men of wisdom control and protect the lives of their fellows.

—*John Howard Wills, in* The University of Kansas Review, *1961.*

In **"The Secret Sharer"** there is no such perspective. There is no suggestion that the captain has meditated on what he is talking about. He might be telling the story the next day, and what comes through, raw and immediate, is the special arrogant ruthlessness of youth. We hear Leggatt saying in so many words, " 'He [the victim] was one of those creatures that are just simmering all the time with a silly sort of wickedness. Miserable devils that have no business to live at all.' " In a narrative commentary on Leggatt's remark, the young captain expresses his agreement: "He appealed to me as if our experiences had been as identical as our clothes. And I knew well enough the pestiferous danger of such a character where there are no means of legal repression." The captain's own earlier remark will stand for both of them: "I should have gathered from this that he was young; indeed, it is only the young who are ever confronted by such clear issues."

In *The Shadow Line* there is a similar conversation, but with the different pace and the different perspective of the novel Conrad is able to include the voice of an older man, the voice we expect of Conrad himself. The young captain has just allowed himself the luxury of righteously throwing a mortal scare into a minor official who illegally tried to keep him from getting that coveted first command. The older man, Captain Giles, hearing of it, humanely goes to put the official's mind at ease. When he returns, the young man says,

> I looked up with surprise. But in reality I was indifferent. He explained that he had found the Steward lying face downwards on the horsehair sofa. He was all right now.
>
> "He would not have died of fright," I said contemptuously.
>
> "No. But he might have taken an overdose out of one of them little bottles he keeps in his room," Captain Giles argued seriously. "The confounded fool has tried to poison himself once—a couple of years ago."
>
> "Really," I said without emotion. "He doesn't seem very fit to live, anyhow."
>
> "As to that, it may be said of a good many."
>
> "Don't exaggerate like this!" I protested, laughing irritably.

We are here in a very different world, the world of the novel, a world in the process of becoming, not the world of the story, a world of the moment of truth or the epiphany.

Both **"The Secret Sharer"** and *The Shadow Line* are stories of a young man's passage into maturity. In both cases he learns important things about himself. In **"The Secret Sharer"** he learns splendid youthful things. He measures up in every way to that ideal conception everyone sets up for himself secretly. But, as I have already pointed out, Conrad is well aware that life is not a series of Boy Scout tests. It is a far more complicated and tragic business than that. This total knowledge is what makes Conrad reduce the consciousness of the narrator to a young man's consciousness in order to allow him to reproduce the splendor of a young man's moment, and to allow him to end his story with a good ringing phrase applicable both to Leggatt and to himself: "a free man, a proud swimmer striking out for a new destiny."

In *The Shadow Line,* however, the consciousness is not reduced, and the effect of the passage into maturity is, logically, to make the young captain stop being young. Observe the new captain's relationship with Captain Giles after he has brought his ship back to Singapore. Captain Giles is speaking:

> ". . . a man should stand up to his bad luck, to his mistakes, to his conscience, and all that sort of thing. Why—what else would you have to fight against?"
>
> I kept silent. I don't know what he saw in my face, but he asked abruptly:
>
> "Why—you aren't faint-hearted?"
>
> "God only knows, Captain Giles," was my sincere answer.
>
> "That's all right," he said calmly. "You will

learn soon how not to be faint-hearted. A man has got to learn everything—and that's what so many of them youngsters don't understand."

> "Well I am no longer a youngster."
>
> "No," he conceded. "Are you leaving soon?"
>
> "I am going on board directly," I said. "I shall pick up one of my anchors and heave in to half-cable on the other as soon as my new crew comes on board and I shall be off at daylight tomorrow."
>
> "You will?" grunted Captain Giles approvingly. "That's the way. You'll do."
>
> "What did you expect? That I should want to take a week ashore for a rest?"
>
> I said, irritated by his tone. "There's no rest for me till she's out in the Indian Ocean and not much of it even then."
>
> He puffed at the cigar moodily, as if transformed.
>
> "Yes, that's what it amounts to," he said in a musing tone. It was as if a ponderous curtain had rolled up disclosing an unexpected Captain Giles.

This sudden insight into Captain Giles is the real mark of this young man's growing up; but, like the young man in **"The Secret Sharer,"** he is a free man striking out for a new destiny. However, his conception of the destiny is entirely different, for he senses that the freedom is the terrible freedom of responsibility. The immediate point of view of **"The Secret Sharer"** would not do here at all, and Conrad in the opening sentence of *The Shadow Line* establishes his perspective when he says, "Only the young have such moments." We know at once that it is no young man speaking, and we have a different world of possibilities from that dictated by the point of view of **"The Secret Sharer."**

It has been impossible to talk about Conrad's use of his material without giving a reading of the story, although adding yet another reading to the literature on **"The Secret Sharer"** was by no means my intention. Neither was it my intention to discuss his sources, for they are already well known. What I hope I have been able to do is to cast some light on the way in which a writer goes about his work, where his material comes from, how he uses it, and what choices he must make in using it.

Lawrence Graver (essay date 1969)

SOURCE: "Stories During the Years of the Great Novels," in *Conrad's Short Fiction,* University of California Press, 1969, pp. 123-71.

[*Graver is an American educator, biographer, and critic. In the following excerpt, he asserts that the psychological aspects of "The Secret Sharer" are widely overemphasized and the story's greatest significance is its emphasis on moral conflict.*]

In 1903-1904, while working on *Nostromo,* Conrad had

gone two years without writing a short story, and only a request from the *Strand* magazine brought him back to the form. In 1909 a similar situation developed.

Except for the revision of his first story, **"The Black Mate,"** he had not written a short work since the spring of 1907. Then, without warning, he received a visit from Captain C. M. Marris, recently back from the Malay Seas. As Conrad explained to [his agent, J. B.] Pinker:

> It was like the raising of a lot of dead—dead to me, because most of them live out there and even read my books and wonder who the devil has been around taking notes. My visitor told me that Joshua Lingard made the guess: "It must have been the fellow who was mate in the Vidar with Craig." That's me right enough. And the best of it is that all these men of 22 years ago feel kindly to the Chronicler of their lives and adventures. They shall have some more of the stories they like.

This liberating stroke forced Conrad to write about personal experience (or at least personal memories) for the first time since **"The End of the Tether."** The three stories inspired by the visit of Marris (**"The Secret Sharer," "A Smile of Fortune,"** and **"Freya of the Seven Isles"**) are notable because they blend qualities drawn from both periods of Conrad's working life. They are based on first-hand experience (his most reliable source) and they explore substantial themes; but they are also full of the conventional devices of bad magazine fiction. Since they draw from the best and the worst of Conrad, it is possible to account for their peculiar strengths and weaknesses only by recognizing their divided nature.

The supreme case in point is **"The Secret Sharer,"** widely acclaimed as a psychological masterpiece, and the subject of more fanciful interpretations than any of Conrad's other stories. Yet no one who has written on this problematical tale has given a wholly reliable sense of its peculiar distinction. Polemical and highly selective, the average reading of **"The Secret Sharer"** is easily open to charges of partiality or distortion.

Take, for instance, the argument about Leggatt's representative status. Because there is ample evidence to suggest his symbolic nature, critics have been trying for years to explain what he stands for. In the 1940s R. W. Stallman insisted that Leggatt represents both the captain's moral consciousness and the world that lies below the surface of our conscious lives. But, as J. L. Simmons and others have pointed out, Leggatt can hardly be both at the same time. Moreover, when Stallman follows this contradiction with a third, aesthetic allegory, his essay sinks under its own extravagance. Albert Guerard, in several influential discussions of the story, then tried to establish Leggatt as the embodiment of the criminal impulse in the narrator's personality. According to Guerard, Conrad's story dramatizes the act of sympathetic identification with an outlaw and the achievement of self-mastery when the secret self is exorcised. But, lately, this interpretation has been convincingly undermined by several writers, the most thorough of whom is Daniel Curley. In his essay, "Leggatt of the Ideal," Curley has brought together all the evidence

against Leggatt's putative viciousness. First, Conrad recast the *Cutty Sark* source material to make Leggatt more agreeable; if he had wished to create a character in some ways disreputable, he need not have made any changes at all. Second, there are many details in the story itself to counter the argument that Leggatt is lawless. And third, Conrad protested vigorously when he read a review calling the mate a "murderous ruffian—or something of the sort."

But, as if unable to leave well enough alone, Curley and others have argued that Leggatt represents not a lower but a higher self, the captain's image of the ideal. Yet, just as there is adequate evidence to deny Leggatt's villainy, so there is proof to smudge his status as an ideal figure. As I shall suggest later, the captain does not want to model himself on Leggatt; he wants to be able to show some of his traits of manliness in a time of crisis. One thing can be said with certainty about Leggatt: he is neither higher nor lower, only different.

Similar assertions, either mutually exclusive or self-contradictory, have been made about other teasing elements in the story. Is the floppy hat a symbol of the human personality or of the captain's compassion or is it merely a floppy hat? And why does the captain bring the ship so dangerously close to shore? According to several recent critics, he shaves the coast because (1) he wants to make Leggatt's departure as safe as possible; (2) he considers it a matter of conscience to prove to Leggatt that he understands his predicament; (3) he wishes to pay Leggatt for his self-knowledge; (4) he needs an exceptionally forceful gesture to "change the nature of his relationship to his crew"; (5) he must symbolically reenact an extreme situation resembling Leggatt's crisis on the *Sephora;* (6) he hopes to lay the ghost of his secret sharer, as Marlow laid the ghost of Kurtz. Remarkable motivation for a character who rarely thinks deeply about his own situation!

In reaction to such strenuous analysis, some critics—most notably Frederick Karl and Jocelyn Baines—have argued that on the psychological and moral level **"The Secret Sharer"** is rather slight: "the surface in this case *is* the story." Although this is more persuasive than the so-called alchemical readings, it is not wholly satisfactory either. To say that **"The Secret Sharer"** is a straightforward tale implies that the mysterious symbolism is not there, a fact belied by quotation and the experience of the common reader. Usually, in the face of a work improperly understood, critics blame one another; but in this case the work itself is at fault. Although **"The Secret Sharer"** is a fascinating and provocative story, its details are at times so vaguely portentous that readers are seduced into hunting for a complex symbolic consistency which the work does not possess.

None of the famous interpretations (like Guerard's night journey or Stallman's aesthetic allegory) can be supported without tampering with the text, either by omitting relevant material or by bending it out of recognizable shape. Because the darkness, the headless figure, the sleeping suit, and the idea of a secret self all have persuasive connections with the unconscious, Guerard's reading has, at first, a genuine appeal. But in addition to the dubious argument about Leggatt's criminality, there is nothing in the story to support Guerard's belief that the captain gains self-control by coming to terms with the dark side of his nature. On the contrary, Leggatt's attractiveness is based less on some sinister appeal than on an obvious self-possession and strength. Seeing him as a man of action who saved his ship by courageously setting the foresail, the captain dismisses the killing as a trifling accident: "it was all very simple. The same strungup force which had given twenty-four men a chance, at least, for their lives, had, in a sort of recoil, crushed an unworthy mutinous existence." By the end, the captain has learned nothing about his own capacity for evil; he has learned only to assume confident command of his ship.

True enough, the identification between the captain and Leggatt is conveyed with such overwhelming insistence (the words "double," "other self," "secret sharer" occur nearly forty times) that an interpretation resting on the singular appeal of manliness appears to rob the story of its celebrated allusiveness. However, on close examination, much of that allusiveness will not bear looking into. Instead of developing the complex psychological implications of the events, Conrad frequently makes tantalizing rhetorical promises that he later fails to keep. Because it touches on some of the characteristic subject matter of modern literature, **"The Secret Sharer"** has often been praised as profound. But despite an intensely dramatic plot, the story is a flawed piece of work, psychologically static, and symbolically consistent only on a rather obvious level. As Ian Watt has argued in another connection, Conrad's symbolism is not a matter of obscure and esoteric secrets but only of extending and generalizing the implications of his "things, events and people" [*Critical Quarterly,* Summer, 1960]. The best way to appreciate the quality of **"The Secret Sharer"** is to establish which of its implications can be extended and which cannot.

The opening tableau, with its self-conscious emphasis on solemnity and loneliness, helps define the conditions of the test. A stranger both to his ship and to himself, the narrator wonders whether he will measure up to the "ideal conception of one's own personality every man sets up for himself secretly." Although the crew is briefly differentiated at the start, the main emphasis is on the captain's relationship to the ship. Compare this to the opening of *Heart of Darkness,* in which the brooding silence also serves to introduce the story of a test, and certain dramatic differences become obvious. From the start, Marlow's story has an elaborate social and historical context. He speaks to an audience and his earliest remarks link his adventures to those of Romans in ancient Britain. In **"The Secret Sharer,"** the captain's situation more closely resembles that of Marlow in **"Youth,"** for both men are natural egoists anxious to prove themselves against an exacting private challenge. The captain is, of course, more reflective than the young Marlow; but by admitting his willingness to take the adequacy of the crew for granted, he defines his self-absorption and the narrow range of the test.

Leggatt's spectacular entrance raises the first interpretive problem of the story. Faced with a "green cadaverous glow," a body that resembles "a headless corpse" and a

"ghastly, silvery fish," the Captain feels "a horrid, frost-bound sensation" grip his chest. This, however, passes quickly and the two men talk with the quiet assurance of well-bred strangers at the boat harbor of a fashionable club. Although the identification is established immediately (and reinforced beyond bearing for the rest of the tale), it is not easy to define the factors on which the tie is based. Because the captain alternates between an insistent, incantatory rhetoric and prosaic understatement, readers seem to find a mandate to look for analogues either in Jung or in the Seaman's Code. Primal symbolism seems to count for a good deal. The double comes up like a fish from the dark sea to wear the captain's sleeping suit; and yet the men communicate on the basis of experiences as mundane and "as identical as our clothes"—on one hand, primitive archetypes and, on the other, Conrad's statement that the story "deals with what may be called the 'esprit de corps,' the deep fellowship of two young seamen meeting for the first time." Yet, if the captain's responses are studied closely, the teasing symbolism turns out to be decorative, suspenseful, and inconclusive; at times, rather Poe-like. The less esoteric reading accounts more satisfactorily for the main thrust of the tale, if not for all its details.

The first two conversations between the captain and Leggatt establish sympathetic identification and provide clues to the nature of the crime. In every conceivable way, the murder is minimized. The victim had been a peevish malingerer, "half-crazed with funk," and by killing him Leggatt acted instinctively to help save the ship. No doubt crosses the narrator's mind, and Leggatt himself refers casually to the murder as a disagreeable necessity. His insistence that the price of exile is enough to pay "for an Abel of that sort" gains the admiration of the captain and should gain ours.

By minimizing the murder in these opening scenes, the narrator introduces a major theme of the story. When catastrophe threatens aboard ship, the life of someone who seriously interferes with seamanship may be legitimately sacrificed for the safety of the crew. Situations in which certain basic imperatives emerge as stronger than the traditional codes of the law are common in Conrad's fiction. A similar predicament faces the crew of the *Narcissus,* and Leggatt himself resembles Falk, who committed cannibalism in order to survive. In the context of their particular dilemmas, both men win respect for the ruthless force of their natural egoism. Oddly enough, a passage from the early part of **"The Secret Sharer,"** which is usually read ironically, can be seen to have literal truth. Despite the anxiety caused by Leggatt's arrival and concealment, the drama of the *Sephora* does strike the captain by its "elemental moral beauty" and the "absolute straightforwardness of its appeal."

Once the captain has heard the facts of the case, he pays little attention to the murder. Nor, it should be emphasized, does he reflect at any length on the similarity between himself and the fugitive. Although he strains excessively to convey the drama of the identification, he fails to probe its meaning, concentrating instead on hiding Leggatt and assuming responsibilities on the ship. The fright of constantly seeing double does not prevent him from giving his first order and staying on deck to see it carried out. Leggatt's presence may be worrisome, but his self-possession continues to "induce a corresponding state in myself."

The opening scene of Part II, in which the captain plays host to Archbold with Leggatt hiding a few feet away, further strengthens the loyalties already established. Archbold, skittish and easily out of temper, is a foil to Leggatt and to the captain as well. Throughout the interview, he gives off an air of fussy distraction, and in his most authoritative act sticks out his tongue to imitate the death mask of Leggatt's victim. Archbold's solemnity is contrasted with the playfulness of the captain, who fakes being deaf and happily leads his guest on a futile search of the ship. For a man quick to confess his dislocation, the captain is remarkably self-assured. In a revealing exchange, he catches Archbold distorting his own action during the crisis on the *Sephora*:

> "That reefed foresail saved you," I threw in.
>
> "Under God—it did," he exclaimed fervently. "It was by a special mercy, I firmly believe, that it stood some of those hurricane squalls."
>
> "It was the setting of that sail which—" I began.
>
> "God's own hand in it," he interrupted me. "Nothing less could have done it. I don't mind telling you that I hardly dared give the order. It seemed impossible that we could touch anything without losing it, and then our last hope would have been gone."
>
> The terror of that gale was on him yet. I let him go on for a bit, then said, casually—as if returning to a minor subject:
>
> "You were very anxious to give up your mate to the shore people, I believe?"
>
> He was. To the law. His obscure tenacity on that point had in it something incomprehensible and a little awful; something, as it were, mystical, quite apart from his anxiety that he should not be suspected of 'countenancing any doings of that sort.' Seven-and-thirty virtuous years at sea, of which over twenty of immaculate command, and the last fifteen in the *Sephora*, seemed to have laid him under some pitiless obligation.

According to the scale of values sketched earlier, Archbold is clearly the villain of **"The Secret Sharer."** Personally inadequate against the pressure of the storm, he refuses to admit Leggatt's heroic role and retreats to an unthinking reliance on Providence. Instead of responding flexibly to the exceptional circumstances of the murder, he becomes increasingly more rigid and more mystical. Archbold's failure of imagination, his inability to see that the moment called for charity not intransigence, testifies to the correctness and decency of the captain's response. Conrad, often scathing about sentimental benevolence, here gives Leggatt the benefit of every doubt and makes him worthy of pity in a way that a James Wait is not.

When the captain hears Leggatt confirm Archbold's fecklessness, he makes his final judgment of the affair: " 'I quite understand,' I conveyed that sincere assurance into

his ear. . . . It was all very simple. The same strung-up force which had given twenty-four men a chance, at least, for their lives, had, in a sort of recoil, crushed an unworthy mutinous existence." His response follows a familiar pattern. After a forceful conversation with Leggatt, he can spare "no leisure to weigh the merits of the matter," but goes out "to make the acquaintance of my ship."

Despite this renewed effort, the captain's self-mastery remains for a time incomplete. Unable to forget Leggett or the suspicions of his crew, he admits that he requires deliberation to perform acts that for a confident commander would be instinctive. At each new threat of exposure, he becomes increasingly apprehensive, while Leggatt continues "perfectly self-controlled, more than calm—almost invulnerable." When the steward opens the door of the bathroom in which Leggatt is hiding, the captain nearly swoons with terror; and before he learns of Leggatt's safety, he automatically stresses the inexplicable, nightmarish quality of the events. But once again, when he learns the mundane truth, he marvels at "something unyielding" in Leggatt's character "which was carrying him through so finely."

Much has been made of the severity of the captain's self-division at this point in the tale, though not enough, I think, of the comic quality of the action. The adventures that throw the Captain into fits of nervous anxiety are hardly sinister. He startles the steward who thought he had been below and then sends him around the ship on incomprehensible errands. How can one speak solemnly about dark nights of the soul when the antic disposition is so reminiscent of *Room Service?*

Following the narrow escape in the bathroom, Leggatt asks to be marooned, and after an initial protest the Captain accepts the challenge. There is no need to probe the unconscious to understand his ambivalent motives: he recognizes the value of getting rid of Leggatt, but is frightened of losing the man who so vividly inspires confidence. Once he accepts the inevitability of Leggatt's departure, the captain begins to conform more closely to the ideal of the perfect commander. Decisiveness becomes a matter of instinct as he fulfills Coleridge's formula for maturity: "act spontaneously, not with reflection; but it is your duty to study, inform yourself, and reflect so that you progressively become the kind of person whose spontaneous reflection is wise." Just before the climactic moment, he gives the fugitive three sovereigns and, on "sudden thought," rams his floppy hat on Leggatt's head to protect him from the sun. To insure Leggatt's safety, and as a gesture of self-assertion, he sails dangerously close to shore. As Leggatt goes over the side, the Captain—with the hat as a marker—executes the daring maneuver which puts him back on course, in "perfect communion" with his first command.

What, then, has Leggatt meant to the captain? Exemplary but not necessary ideal, Leggatt represents a kind of behavior, a physical stance so to speak, which inspires the captain to act boldly himself. Having profited from his presence, the captain is now a better and luckier man than Leggatt, who—despite the declamatory ending—is faced with an uncertain future. The description of the fugitive in the final lines is still another index to the weakness of **"The Secret Sharer."** To call Leggatt "a free man, a swimmer striking out for a new destiny" is a triumph of grandiloquence over the facts of the case. Whatever one might say about Leggatt's resolution in the past, his future can hardly at this point be cause for celebration. An exile, swimming in the darkness toward an unknown island, his destiny may be new but not exactly enviable. The pretentious romanticism at the close has a revealing analogue in a later Conrad story. When Geoffrey Renouard, in **"The Planter of Malata,"** commits suicide by swimming out to sea, the narrator remarks: "Nothing was ever found—and Renouard's disappearance remained in the main inexplicable. For to whom could it have occurred that a man would set out calmly to swim beyond the confines of life—with a steady stroke—his eyes fixed on a star!" The high-coloring here and in the last line of **"The Secret Sharer"** recalls **"Gaspar Ruiz,"** not *Heart of Darkness.*

Some of the rhetorical embroidery in **"The Secret Sharer"** is surely temperamental (none of Conrad's major works is wholly free from it); but some is due to the uneasy relationship between Conrad and the magazine audience. The story's excessive length may have been the result of *Harper's* rigid yardstick (it fit neatly into two issues in the summer of 1910); and the three dozen synonyms for "double" seem designed to accentuate a dramatic point for fear of having it missed. Although the repetition reassured readers in 1910, it has proven fatal to critics since then. Because of its insistent promptings and seductive detail, **"The Secret Sharer"** has become everybody's Rorschach test. But its psychology remains elementary; its finest effects are explicit and traditionally moral.

P. L. Brown   (essay date 1972)

SOURCE: "*The Secret Sharer* and the Existential Hero," in *Conradiana,* Vol. III, No. 3, 1971-72, pp. 22-30.

[*In the following essay, Brown illustrates how Leggatt exemplifies the ideals of existentialism.*]

Discussions of Conrad's **"The Secret Sharer"** have emphasized that the narrator's sympathy for his double, Leggatt, represents a rapprochement with his own irrational self. Prominent symbols in the story—the sea and such objects as islet, fence, and boat half submerged in the sea—clearly represent the unconscious. Leggatt himself, emerging from the sea to wear the narrator's sleeping suit and hide in his cabin, is hardly flesh and blood at all but the narrator's unconscious self, more specifically the id. [Albert] Guerard [in his *Conrad the Novelist,* 1958], for example, speaks of a communion between "the seamanself and some darker, more interior, and outlaw self." However, there are limitations in such an interpretation. If Leggatt is only the darker side of the narrator, we would expect him to personify exclusively those repressed destructive impulses and those amoral and asocial drives which we associate with the id. It is true that he kills a man, and this violent action is symbolic. But it symbolizes the single act by which a man asserts his freedom and authenticates himself as a person, not a habitual murderous proclivity. His behavior is vigorous and impulsive but not compulsive

and obsessive like, for instance, Captain Ahab's. And he certainly is not the destructive degenerate that Kurtz becomes. He lacks the secretive, guilt-ridden demeanor of most of those tormented souls we identify with the unconscious; he appears calm, self-possessed, frank, and open to the narrator. He asks his captain's permission to escape. He presents an honest appearance in his first exchange with the narrator, returning his stare unperturbed even as a lantern is flashed in his face. In a similar situation Ahab reacts violently. "What art thou thrusting that thief-catcher into my face for, man? Thrusted light is worse than presented pistols." Then, of course, there is the problem in the conclusion of the story. It is difficult to understand why the personification of the narrator's id should be swimming away from him as "a free man, a proud swimmer striking out for a new destiny."

These limitations of the psychological interpretation can be overcome by expanding the frame of reference in which the relationship of the narrator and Leggatt is seen so as to include the common ground of existential action which the two men share. Leggatt becomes a part of the narrator's subjective self because both men have common philosophical goals: both rebel against traditional values and desire to develop freely their own existential self-reliance, to prove themselves, and to gain mastery over themselves and their world. Both face worlds that are uncongenial to freedom if not actually absurd. Leggatt came to terms with such a world in a storm at sea. The situation was desperately frustrating, the frightened captain being able only to whimper about "what was their last hope," and the crew, apparently, was even worse. Leggatt realized, as he fought both the storm and later the insubordinate sailor, that there were no universals and no higher ethic to sanction a course of action by which he could cope with the situation in which he found himself. Realizing that he must choose either to assume command illegally and order the men to help him set the sail or to accept probable shipwreck, he decided on a course of action independently and vigorously. "I just took it in my own hands and went away from him boiling. . . . Do you think that if I had not been pretty fierce with them I should have got the men to do anything?" He acted in a way Sartre would approve—freely, individually, responsibly. However, as is frequently the case in the modern world, Leggatt found it difficult to complete the course of action he had initiated. The additional frustration of an insubordinate sailor forced on him another decision, whether to put aside law and kill the man who was hindering the setting of the sail or to reason with him and risk failure through delay. He decided that reason does not avail in an absurd world. His second decision is another example of his defiance of traditional values and of his assertion of the self in an absurd situation. In the first he defied law by assuming command; in the second he defied it by choosing to kill a man. He dispatched the sailor with the same impulsive, but also deliberate, energy that he had displayed in his initial act. "It's clear that I meant business, because I was holding him by the throat still when they picked us up." The entire incident resolves on an absurd dilemma, to invite shipwreck by remaining within the law or to invite execution by defying it.

Leggatt justifies his putting aside law to save the ship and men by his own system of values. The crew interpreted his individuality and defiance as madness and criminality. "God only knows why they locked me in every night. To see some of their faces you'd have thought they were afraid I'd go about at night strangling people." His own reaction towards the members of his crew was a sense of his own superiority over their irresponsibility, weakness, and cowardice. They rushed him and the dead sailor aft "screaming murder and broke into the cuddy" while the ship was "running for her life, touch and go all the time, any minute her last in a sea fit to turn your hair gray only a-looking at it." They seemed to him like "a lot of lunatics" in their irrational response to what he felt was a rational act. In his Nietzschean way he had refused to submit, as they had submitted, to the petty virtues and petty policy, to "the sand-grain consideration, the ant-hill trumpery" of ordinary men [Friedrich Nietzsche, *The Philosophy of Nietzsche*, 1954]. His comment that the sailor he killed was one of those "miserable devils that have no business to live at all . . . a sort of ill-conditioned snarling cur" shows the same Nietzschean contempt for the weak which a student puts into words for Raskolnikov: "Don't you think that thousands of good deeds will wipe out one little, insignificant transgression? One death, and a hundred lives in exchange—why it's simple arithmetic! What is the life to that stupid, spiteful, consumptive old woman weighed against the common good?" The narrator's sympathy with Leggatt as he listens foreshadows the similar act of self assertion he will perform when he takes the ship dangerously close to Koh-ring. And his feeling that the crushing of one mutinous existence is worth twenty-four lives saved shows the same Nietzschean contempt for the weak and faith in the extra-legal rights of the higher man that Leggatt has shown.

The parallel between the narrator and Leggatt becomes a contrast in the case of Archbold. Archbold is committed to a traditional higher ethic instead of existential or Nietzschean values. Thus J. D. O'Hara's contention [in *College English*, February, 1965] that Archbold is the moral center of the story has relevance in a different perspective. It is true that Archbold's "obscure tenacity" is to duty, but a traditional duty to the masses rather than to the individual. The narrator's use of such expressions as "virtuous years," "immaculate command," and "pitiless obligation" does indeed refer to the captain's moral commitments. However, it is difficult to accept O'Hara's view that the narrator sympathizes with Archbold and rejects Leggatt's description of him as weak and cowardly. There is implicit in the narrator's description of Archbold a negative assessment of his sensitivity and strength of character. He describes his smeary, unintelligent eyes, forever looking vaguely around. "A spiritless tenacity was his main characteristic, I judged. . . . He mumbled to me as if he were ashamed of what he was saying . . . in the manner of a criminal making a reluctant and doleful confession."

In his exchanges with Archbold the narrator repeatedly tries to elicit the implications of an individual act. He interrupts the captain's description of the hasty sea burial. " 'That reefed foresail saved you,' I threw in. 'Under God—it did,' he exclaimed fervently. 'It was by a special

mercy, I firmly believe, that it stood some of those hurricane squalls.' " Ignoring the reference to divine intervention, the narrator again attempts to force the captain to consider the impact of that individual act " 'It was the setting of that sail which—'I began.' " Again, Archbold appeals to a higher order. " 'God's own hand in it,' he interrupted me. 'Nothing less would have done it.' " Twice the narrator has returned to the deed of one man which saved the ship. After letting Archbold talk on a bit about the terror of the storm, the narrator remarks, casually, "as if returning to a minor subject, 'You were very anxious to give up your mate to the shore people, I believe?' " In the first two exchanges with Archbold the narrator has emphasized Leggatt's act of individual responsibility. In this last exchange he is subtly trying to make Archbold accept responsibility for his own action toward Leggatt. But Archbold again appeals to a higher order, the law. "His obscure tenacity on that point had in it something incomprehensive and a little awful; something as it were mystical, quite apart from his anxiety that he should not be suspected of 'countenancing any doings of that sort.' " That the tenacity is obscure and has something incomprehensive about it implies that Archbold does not have a clear sense of what his duty and responsibility are. At least it is clear that he feels responsible to an abstraction and not to the human necessities of any person in a concrete situation. It would seem in light of these remarks by the narrator that his reference to Archbold's "seven and thirty virtuous years at sea, of which over twenty [were] of immaculate command" is ironic. Archbold's virtue is conformity and his immaculateness lack of involvement. After years of unthreatened conformity his response to an extraordinary situation is a sense of obligation which entails no sympathy for the lives of his crew or the motivation of Leggatt.

Neither Leggatt nor the narrator sympathizes with Archbold's refusal to commit himself as an individual and a social being. Both he and his crew fail to seize upon the opportunity provided by the storm to "legitimize [one's] behavior "[Jean Paul Sartre, "Existentialism as Humanism"]. In Leggatt's eyes and those of the readers of the story, Archbold is a non-individual who lacked even enough control and self-will to give the order to set the sail. Leggatt, on the other hand, "makes a choice not of violence but of responsibility, a choice made under trying circumstances, when the natural source of authority had totally failed" [*Modern Fiction Studies*, Summer, 1967]. He epitomizes Sartre's existentially motivated man who is "nothing else but what he purposes . . . nothing else but the sum of his actions, nothing else but what his life is."

Leggatt does not habitually resort to violence. His rejection of it in refusing to break out of the cabin and in wanting to avoid the struggle that would result from being discovered on one of the islets illustrates that he understands the kind of commitment he made during the storm. For Leggatt violence, either killing or dying, should be the culmination of some vigorous meaningful action, or at least a movement towards something no matter how indefinable. He does not wish to kill in a futile bid for freedom. He explains to the narrator why he did not smash in his door or push Archbold aside and bolt out. The crew would have been alerted, and there would have been a struggle.

"Somebody else might have got killed—for I would have not broken out only to get chucked back, and I did not want any more of that work." This time the violence would have been meaningless. Again, when he explains why he did not want to run the risk of being "hauled back off one of these little islands by the scuff of the neck," he stresses that "somebody would have got killed for certain, and I did not want any of that." He is equally concerned with the way in which he himself faces death. He does not wish to face possible execution at the judgment of a jury. He does not want to commit suicide by drowning or to swim around in circles like a crazed bullock or finally be forced, in despair, to swim back to his ship. Instead, he wishes to swim until he sinks, in the hope of encountering "something to swim for." In explanation of his swimming up to the ship's ladder he tells the narrator, "I don't know—I wanted to be seen, to talk with somebody, before I went on." It is not that he has definite goals or plans. There is in the swimming incident much that is impulsive, but there are still a deliberateness, an obstinacy, and a sense of purposefulness in this as in everything he does. When Leggatt comments that he had weeks to think about his situation, the narrator imagines "perfectly the manner of this thinking out—a stubborn if not a steadfast operation."

Not only does Leggatt seek to avoid useless violence, but he also accepts responsibility and punishment for the violent acts he does commit and considers justified. However, he has his own concept of just punishment for himself as he has his own concept of the acts themselves. Thus, he had no intention of coming before "an old fellow in a wig and twelve respectable tradesmen" with his parson father looking on. Instead, he chose to be allowed to swim to the nearest land the ship would come to: "I was ready enough to go off wandering on the face of the earth—and that was price enough to pay for an Abel of that sort." Moreover, he sees his killing of the sailor not so much as a violation of the rights of an individual but as a violation of the ethic established by a society to protect its members. Therefore, he considers it fitting that he be isolated and outcast both from society as a whole and from the community of the ship. In addition, he feels that Archbold refused his request to be allowed to swim not out of conscience but out of fear of the community on his ship and out of fear of the law they symbolized. "This thing must take its course. I represent the law here." He accepts the external brand of a criminal, a Cain, realizing that he is in fact alone in his existential life style and that no one on the *Sephora* knew the internal man and what motivated him the night of the storm. He makes light of the Christian ethos of being one's brother's keeper by making the "snarling cur" he killed his Abel.

Leggatt's swimming away is carried out with the same vigor as his action during the storm but has an additional quality of absurdity. When his room was left unlocked after a meal (perhaps by unconscious intention?), a sudden temptation came over him as he was strolling on the deck. He kicked off his slippers and jumped into the water before, as he explains, his mind was completely made up. The act was gratuitous. Only after he was in the water did he decide to swim until he sank; he is quite explicit in his explanation to the narrator that he had no intention to commit suicide by drowning. The riding light then provides him with a destiny, something to swim for and an occasion for another choice between life and death. As the narrator speaks to him over the side of the ship, he gets the impression that Leggatt is on the point of letting go the ladder and swimming away. "He seemed to struggle with himself, for I heard something like the low, bitter murmur of doubt. 'What's the good.'" Fortunately, in this, the penultimate step in his fight for freedom, Leggatt confronts a being anxious to assert his individuality and willing to act rebelliously, defiantly, committedly.

For the reason the narrator hides Leggatt and identifies with him is precisely the same reason he dares to come so close to Kohring: he wants to prove himself. He wants the kind of freedom, independence, courage, and self-reliance he senses in this mysterious sailor who becomes an objectification of his own existential ideal. "The voice was calm and resolute. The self-possession of that man had somehow induced a corresponding state in myself." When the narrator praises his swimming, Leggatt presents to him what he feels is now his choice: "The question for me now is whether I am to let go this ladder and go on swimming till I sink from exhaustion, or—to come on board here." The narrator intuitively feels that this comment is "no mere formula of desperate speech, but a real alternative in the view of a strong soul." The narrator has already shown himself capable of independence in a small way—he has defied the normal, conventional pattern of command by taking the watch himself in spite of the disapproval of his crew. He has the same choices between conformity and individuality, submission and freedom, self-delusion and responsibility as Leggatt had although his world is static and uncertain rather than hostile as is Leggatt's.

The narrator's subjective description of his external world, especially the land, which symbolizes to him the condition of human existence, suggests insecurity. The islets are barren and resemble ruins; the fishing stakes, looking like a bamboo fence half submerged, suggest all that is abandoned and are crazy in aspect. The horizon is monotonous. Groves of trees look almost as insignificant as the barren islets. The impassive earth seems to have swallowed the tug as it followed a devious stream. He turns away from the land and tries to find security in his ship and the sky and the sea, but the death-like stillness and aloneness does not bode good. "She floated at the starting point of a long journey, very still in an immense stillness. . . . There was not a sound in her—and around us nothing moved, nothing lived." The most essential similarity of his position to Leggatt's is his aloneness. He is a stranger to his ship, to his crew, and to the world around him. His attempts to relieve his feelings of insignificance and dread of failure by establishing some mystical communion with the sea and his ship are a form of romantic self-delusion which he momentarily indulges. He naively rejoices in what he feels is the great security of the sea as compared with the unrest of the land, in his choice of a life that offers "no disquieting problems." This quiet communion is easily broken by the sight of a strange ship, by the multitude of stars seeming to stare down on him, by a ladder carelessly left out, and finally by the appearance of Leggatt.

That "horrid frost-bound sensation" the narrator experiences upon seeing Leggatt is the result of more than simply the surprise of seeing a man swimming near his ship. What is crucial here is that Leggatt from the very beginning becomes an ambiguous symbol for the narrator. His courage in swimming from nowhere, his confident air, his absurd audacity in asking such astonishingly ordinary questions as the time of day suggest a strong, unique individual. But Leggatt also appears deathlike to the narrator. In the dark, glassy glimmer of the sleeping water, he looks like a floating dead body—pale, livid in a greenish cadaverous glow, looking like a headless corpse. The narrator's frightened reaction is representative of what existentialists feel modern man fears most—the death of the soul, the loss of self. "Man is anxious because he is agonizingly aware of the threat of annihilation to his precious individuality, a threat from which there is no final and positive escape except death "[Davis D. McElroy, *Existentialism and Modern Literature*, 1963]. Paradoxically, then, Leggatt becomes a symbol of both life and death—the proud swimmer at the end of the story who swims toward a new destiny, but also towards Erebus. He is, on the one hand, a symbol of the narrator's own fear of life, his self-doubts and insecurities, and, on the other, of his desire to live actively and freely. As he looks down at Leggatt at the foot of the ladder, he thinks it "inconceivable that he should not attempt to come on board, and strangely troubling to suspect that perhaps he did not want to." He cannot conceive that anyone would choose death over life, yet he senses that this mysterious swimmer might actually be strong willed enough to choose death over a life of nothingness. At this point the vitality and independence Leggatt represents are as "strangely troubling" as the death he also symbolizes.

To his crew the narrator is as surely a stranger as Leggatt was to his. In his preoccupations with himself and the man who shares his psychological and philosophical values, in his self-doubts and sufferings, he alienates himself from his crew. In their own traditional way they could not understand why any captain would upset routine by taking a watch, and they are so far removed from his rebellious position that they are ready to fight anyone who suggests that perhaps they are hiding Leggatt on the ship. The narrator's torment of himself and of his crew reminds one of such tortured existential heroes as Dostoevsky's Underground Man. Especially painful and deliberate are his "frigid dignity" in presiding over dinner with his two mates, his shouting conversation and elaborate search of the ship with Archbold, and his various altercations with his steward. Indeed, his patronizing, almost contemptuous remarks make of his first mate, whom he calls "Bless my soul," a double of Leggatt's Archbold. The narrator is as unsympathetic to his first mate's "painstaking turn of mind" and "earnest considerations" as Leggatt was to Archbold's "obscure tenacity." Like Leggatt, at a critical moment he stands alone. His impatience at his mate's numbed fear in the face of Koh-ring parallels Leggatt's own frustration at Archbold's impotent panic and whimpering during the storm. And his increasing hostility to-

ward his second mate, "that sneering young cub," suggests Leggatt's explosive reaction to the insubordinate sailor, the "snarling cur."

The narrator identifies with Leggatt, whose ethical code is made to provide an answer to the narrator's psychological conflict. In the very act of sheltering Leggatt, which entails repudiation of convention, defiance of law, and disrespect for the authority of his own office, he imitates the existential commitment of the man whose accomplice he becomes. He ridicules Archbold absurdly and defiantly by playing games with him—pretending he is deaf, and forcing the unfortunate captain to inspect every inch of his ship. His ignoring Archbold's pious comment that it was God's hand that had set the sail parallels Leggatt's own defiance of Christian ethics in his allusions to his parson father and his identification of himself with Cain and of the mutinous sailor with Abel. His act at the end of the story is his ultimate attempt to prove himself. He places the self above the community by endangering the lives of his crew to perform this final test. The hazardous close approach to Koh-ring, unnecessary not only for navigational purposes, but even for the escape of Leggatt, who could swim ashore from farther out, is a defiance of his crew and of his own better judgment as a commander. Finally, he defies death itself, for Koh-ring provides him with as ambiguous a symbol as Leggatt has become for him. In that it is land and Leggatt is swimming toward it to a new destiny, it represents life. However, in that is also "Erebus," it represents death as well. It provides the narrator with a most appropriate test of his ability to gain mastery over himself, his ship and his world, over life itself.

Paul Bidwell   (essay date 1972)

SOURCE: "Leggatt and the Promised Land: A New Reading of *The Secret Sharer*," in *Conradiana*, Vol. III, No. 2, 1971-72, pp. 26-34.

[In the following essay, Bidwell discusses parallels to the biblical story of Moses in "The Secret Sharer."]

Of all Conrad's stories none word-for-word has generated more comment and confusion than **"The Secret Sharer."** Although readers have differed about many aspects of the tale it is particularly a fair judgment of Leggatt, the fugitive "killer" from the *Sephora*, which has proved most contentious. That a correct understanding of Leggatt is crucial to one's conception of the sea captain who narrates the tale has never been doubted, yet interpretations of Leggatt confusingly oscillate between the view that he represents man's dark, evil impulses to the opinion that he is an ideal model for moral conduct. While it is probable that the mate of the *Sephora* symbolizes neither pure violence nor pure innocence, it is surprising that there has been no consensus as to which element of his personality is thematically salient. The purpose of the present argument is to re-open Leggatt's trial in the light of new evidence. The defendant would undoubtedly look upon the proceedings with some scorn, yet since a trial *in absentia* has not deterred others, there is considerable precedent for what follows.

Of the many explications of **"The Secret Sharer"** perhaps

the most impressive is Louis H. Leiter's demonstration that the ultimate meaning of the story depends upon Conrad's technique of creating "echo structures" [*Twentieth-Century Literature,* January, 1960]. Leiter bases his analysis on previously unnoted parallels involving narrative, parable, myth, scene, and archetype. In particular, he examines Conrad's echoing of two biblical stories which have strong archetypal reverberation, the careers of Cain and of Jonah. Since the present discussion is in the nature of special pleading on Leggatt's behalf to the effect that not two but three Old Testament stories provide the significant archetypes for Conrad's tale, it becomes necessary at this point briefly to review Leiter's evidence.

In unravelling Conrad's intricate use of the Cain-Abel motif Leiter argues that its relevance is not limited to establishing a familiar context for Leggatt's "fratricide," but that it provides "a major structure of the novel, a ritual of murder, guilt, banishment or escape, and wandering," which echoes most of the significant human relationships in the story. Thus, even though it is the mate of the *Sephora* who identifies himself with Cain, the reader soon discovers that Leggatt is not alone in his impulse to eliminate a "brother." It is only his relationship to the dead sailor which associates Leggatt with Cain; considered in relation to Captain Archbold or to the ship captain who harbors him he recalls the threatened victim, Abel. Only a slight shift in perspective is required for the reader to identify Archbold's zeal for vengeance with Cain's jealous crime. Again, the narrator's recognition of Leggatt as a danger to his position as ship captain suggests a pattern in which Leggatt is closer to Abel than to Cain.

In part it is the subtly chosen phraseology of the story which establishes such allusive relationships. After Leggatt finally leaves the narrator's ship the captain reflects: "I hardly thought of my other self, now gone from the ship, to be hidden forever from all friendly faces, to be a fugitive and a vagabond on the earth, with no brand of the curse on his sane forehead to stay a slaying hand. . . . " Such an identification as is suggested by the phrase "my other self " demands a reading in which both men, the secret shares of a mutual identity, become at once the wandering criminal and the exposed victim. Leiter concludes that the importance of this echoed biblical motif is its implication that "all men in the ship-world are both Cain and Abel, that the Cain-Abel personality dwells in every man." We are encouraged to respond to Leggatt with moral ambivalence. Guilty? Innocent? Next witness.

The story of Jonah, although not so explicitly or persistently evoked, is undeniably pertinent to Conrad's intended meaning in **"The Secret Sharer."** The life and death struggle of the storm-tossed *Sephora* echoes the situation and dramatic atmosphere of the ship in which Jonah fled from the wrath of his God. Leggatt's bewilderment that "they didn't fling me overboard" for killing his shipmate is a recognizable echo of Jonah's fear of the same fate. Noting these parallels Leiter then explicates the sail-locker scene as a symbolic journey through the belly of the great whale sent by God to rescue Jonah. The Jonah archetype thus reorchestrates what the Cain-Abel archetype suggests, that the capacity for good and evil, obedience or

disobedience, is shared by all men. Leggatt, then, is both criminal and victim, guilty and innocent, in whichever biblical context we view him.

Leiter's evidence is valuable, his presentation sound. Yet because it overlooks the presence of a third Old Testament scheme in Conrad's tale we cannot rely solely upon it in rendering a verdict upon the accused. Most of the important events in the life of Moses closely reflect and help to give significant pattern to the basic elements of Leggatt's dilemma and its counterpart, the narrator's attempt to manage his difficult new role as commander of ship and crew. A close examination of the Book of Exodus in conjunction with **"The Secret Sharer"** reveals, moreover, that Conrad consciously and cleverly exploited the parallel in order to evoke a more complex and yet more precise response to the subtleties of the relationship between the two men.

The second chapter of Exodus records the first of Moses' adult adventures, an incident which has marked similarities to Conrad's donnee:

> 11 In those days after Moses was grown up, he went out to his brethren: and saw their affliction, and an Egyptian striking one of the Hebrews his brethren.
>
> 12 And when he had looked about this way and that way, and saw no one there, he slew the Egyptian, and hid him in the sand.
>
> 13 And going out the next day, he saw two Hebrews quarrelling; and he said to him that did the wrong: Why strikest thou thy neighbour?
>
> 14 But he answered: Who hath appointed thee prince and judge over us: wilt thou kill me, as thou didst yesterday kill the Egyptian? Moses feared, and said: How is this come to be known?
>
> 15 And Pharaoh heard of this word and sought to kill Moses: but he fled from his sight, and abode in the land of Midian.

From this passage it is apparent that Moses was responsible for an ambiguous act of violence, a crime of passion committed to protect others from serious harm. In both Exodus and **"The Secret Sharer"** it is made quite clear that the victim, whether an oppressive official or a disobedient underling, deserved his fate because he posed an immediate threat to the killer's community. In this respect Leggatt is a truer reflection of Moses than of Cain, the murder of Abel conveying none of the social extenuation relevant to the incident aboard the *Sephora.* The very word "murder" must be legally qualified in referring to the actions of Moses and Leggatt. Moreover, Leggatt recalls Moses, but not Cain, in that he is forced to flee in order to escape an unjust punishment. Cain's exile, of course, was imposed upon him by God as his punishment. Again, we may see in Leggatt's summary confinement an antecedent to the misunderstanding and lack of gratitude expressed by Moses' countrymen after he had killed to protect them.

The evidence introduced thus far being largely circumstantial the connection between Leggatt and Moses may still seem tenuous and artificial. A firm and unequivocal link must be forged before we proceed to examine similar parallels between the two men. That Conrad was exploring the relationship between his own fictional creation and the Hebrew patriarch becomes more than simply an interesting speculation when we consider the following passage:

> "There's a ship over there," [Leggatt] murmured.
>
> "Yes, I know. The *Sephora*. Did you know of us?"
>
> "Hadn't the slightest idea. I am the mate of her—"
>
> He paused and corrected himself. "I should say I *was.*"

And who is the original mate of the *Sephora?* Again, Leggatt's comment is a biblical echo, for, after killing the Egyptian who threatened his countrymen, Moses fled from the wrath of Pharaoh and was received by by Jethro, a priest in Midian. Jethro gave the escapee the hand of his daughter in marriage. Her name was Sephora.

It might be objected that while there may be a case for equating Leggatt with Moses in that both men are "mates" to Sephora, the violation of sequence in **"The Secret Sharer"** renders the biblical allusion meaningless. Moses, after all, ran from the law to Sephora, whereas Leggatt escaped *from* the *Sephora* and the arbitrary justice represented by her master. As a symbol the word *Sephora* would seem to carry contradictory impressions which cannot be reconciled within the context of Conrad's tale. Here, however, a curious fact concerning the earliest part of Moses' celebrated life becomes illuminating and significant.

Moses' first "crime" was, of course, not the killing of an Egyptian, but the very fact of his own birth. The general outline of the adventure is familiar to all. Pharaoh's injunction to the midwives, whereby all male children born to Hebrew women were to be killed, was often defied. Enraged, Pharaoh ordered his entire nation to slaughter newborn Israelite sons, thus forcing Moses' mother to place her child in an ark and to conceal him among the bulrushes banking the Nile. Here he was later discovered by Pharaoh's daughter but saved from the general decree because of her immediate affection for the infant. Moses' mother, her identity unknown, was enlisted to care for the foundling.

The broad parallels between this biblical story and Leggatt's dilemma are clear. Leggatt, like Moses, finds it necessary to escape an inexorable law by entering the water. Both fugitives are saved by accidental and sympathetic discovery by one who might normally be expected to prove an enemy. Once again, however, the specific details of the Bible indicate that the link is substantial rather than simply circumstantial. Exodus 1:15 records that, "The king of Egypt spoke to the midwives of the Hebrews: *of whom one was called Sephora*" (emphasis added).

The irony thickness. Sephora was not only wife and haven to Moses but also an early threat to his life. Exploiting the kind of paradox which snares many of his characters (Jim, Razumov, Hirsch), Conrad echoes the motif of inadvertently running towards what one is trying to escape. Leggatt's dilemma aboard the *Sephora* thus carries subtle overtones of Moses as threatened, helpless infant. Captain Archbold's function in such a pattern again encourages the reader to associate his attitude with that of an oppressive ruler. Symbolically, the threat which the Israelites represented to Pharaoh is reorchestrated as the threat which Leggatt poses to Archbold's authority over his ship and crew.

Once we begin to see the shadow of Moses fall across the pages of **"The Secret Sharer"** certain details of Conrad's presentation gain significance and pattern against the backdrop of Exodus. The effect begins (on a second reading), with Conrad's first sentence: "On my right hand there were lines of fishing-stakes resembling a mysterious system of half-submerged bamboo fences, incomprehensible in its division of the domain of tropical fishes, and crazy of aspect as if abandoned forever by some nomad tribe of fisherman now gone to the other end of the ocean; for there was no sign of human habitation as far as the eye could reach." Later, as the narrator-captain tries to pull in the ladder which has been left hanging over the side of his ship, he extends his original angling image by indirectly associating the ladder with the fishing-stakes already described. Leggatt is discovered, "ghastly, silvery, fish-like"; he is pulled from the water as one would land a fish. Leiter's identification of echo structures in the story connects the "nomad tribe" with Leggatt's own role as a wandering Cain, "driven off the face of the earth." A Leggatt-Moses identification would suggest the nomad tribe as an allusion to the wandering Israelite nation: The vertical fishing-stakes recall the bulrushes in which the infant Moses was concealed.

The unusual nature of the relationship between the story's narrator and Leggatt has been the subject of continuing debate. The very title of the tale underlines the central importance to Conrad's design of their strange intimacy. Regardless of whether Leggatt is to be interpreted as a sign of good or evil, as a physical character or a psychic state, it is clear that neither the Cain-Abel story nor that of Jonah offered Conrad a framework which could account for the mutual identification and feeling of emotional alliance which makes it impossible for the reader to understand either the narrator or Leggatt separately. The career of Moses, however, does offer such a framework, a fraternal alliance which, when considered in conjunction with **"The Secret Sharer,"** clarifies several key images which are otherwise blurred or obscure. Indeed, the bond between Moses and Aaron is central to a full comprehension of the narrator's imaginative sympathy for the fugitive from the *Sephora*. Aaron, it will be remembered, was enlisted by God to support Moses in his attempt to persuade Pharaoh to let the Israelites worship in the wilderness. He was also to act as spokesman for Moses in order to convince the children of Israel of Moses' divine commission for his authority over them. The need for Aaron sprang from Moses fear that his people would not trust and believe him.

This basic idea reappears in Conrad's plot. Indeed, the crucial and suspenseful scene in which Archbold invades the narrator's cabin in search of Leggatt supports the likelihood that Conrad had the Moses-Aaron brotherhood in mind as an informing context for the "double" in **"The Secret Sharer."** The technique is complex. As with the allusions to Cain and Abel the biblical roles are subtly interwoven so that both men function as Moses, both as Aaron. By this technique Conrad imaginatively suggests the merging of identities which the narrator's admitted empathy indicates is the story's central psychological force.

When Captain Archbold comes aboard the narrator's ship in search of the escaped killer he is, as a matter of diplomacy, brought to the captain's cabin, the very place where Leggatt is concealed. The strained interview which follows very much suggests that the host is acting as a spokesman for Leggatt. The narrator's stratagem of feigning partial deafness is a transformed but clearly recognizable parallel to God's instructions to Moses: "Thou shalt speak to [Aaron] all that I command thee; and he shall speak to Pharaoh, that he let the children of Israel go out of his land" (Exodus 7:2). The effect of the narrator's deceit is to include Leggatt in the conversation, but only as a listener. Archbold's inflexibility excludes the fugitive from pleading his own defense. Yet he has in his protector, as Moses had in Aaron, a competent and friendly advocate. After suggesting to Archbold that perhaps the "sheer weight" of the sea could account for the death aboard the Sephora, the narrator takes a new rhetorical tack by reminding his unwelcome visitor that the nautical procedure of setting a reefed foresail, accomplished by Leggatt, was what saved the ship from disaster. Like Pharaoh, however, Archbold is adamant.

Many other details from **"The Secret Sharer"** guide the reader towards the atmosphere and symbolism of the biblical Exodus. In the opening sequence the narrator, alone with his new command, echoes the misgivings expressed by Moses upon being told to take charge of his people. Moses' reply to God's command, "Who am I that I should go to Pharaoh, and should bring forth the children of Israel out of Egypt" (Exodus 3:11), is echoed in the narrator's concern that he "turn out faithful to that ideal conception of one's own personality every man sets up for himself secretly." He also recalls Moses in stressing the personal importance of his first journey as leader: "In this breathless pause at the threshold of a long passage we seemed to be measuring our fitness for a long and arduous enterprise, the appointed task of both our existences to be carried out, far from all human eyes, with only sky and sea for spectators and for judges." The impression of biblical influence is made even stronger by the first scene in the narrator's cabin. He explains to his "secret sharer" that he "had been appointed to take charge while I least expected anything of the sort," and that, "as to the crew, all they knew was that I was appointed to take the ship home." Both of these explanations reflect the feelings of surprise and uncertainly articulated by Moses upon being told by God to lead His chosen people "home."

Another probable echo involves an important image from Exodus which reappears neatly within Conrad's narrative.

After the children of Israel are liberated from their subjection to the Egyptians, Moses dutifully leads them towards the promised land. The Bible emphasizes God's guidance with a striking symbol in double from: "And the Lord went before them by day in a pillar of a cloud, to lead them the way; and by night in a pillar of fire . . . " (Exodus 13:21). The pillar of cloud appears in Conrad's first paragraph as the newly-appointed captain surveys the view from his ship: " . . . the tug steaming right into the land became lost to my sight, hull and funnel and masts, as though the impassive earth had swallowed her up without an effort, without a tremor. My eye followed the light cloud of her smoke, now here, now there, above the plain, according to the devious curves of the stream, but always fainter and farther away, till I lost it at last behind the mitre-shaped hill of the great pagoda." The religious associations of "mitre-shaped" and "pagoda" lend credence to the suggestion that the tug-smoke is meant to carry symbolic weight. The pillar of fire is evoked by the narrator in his description of the ship's light immediately before he discovers Leggatt clinging to the ladder: "The riding-light in the fore-rigging burned with a clear, untroubled, *as if symbolic,* flame, confident and bright in the mysterious shades of the night" (emphasis added). The point of this "symbolic" light is made clear when Leggatt twice tells his rescuer that the riding-light gave him something to swim for. The ship's light represents hope to the fugitive from the *Sephora* (he would otherwise have continued swimming until he sank), just as the biblical pillar of fire assured the Israelites, led by the original "fugitive from Sephora," that they were on course for the promised land.

One final parallel seems inescapable. If we attend carefully to the version of Leggatt's actions aboard the *Sephora* given by Captain Archbold, the story begins to take on a much greater significance than would seem to be called for by the purely rhetorical question of who it was that ordered a reefed foresail. Archbold's very words seem to have been chosen by Conrad to suggest that the storm through which the *Sephora* struggled derives from the Old Testament:

> "That reefed foresail saved you," I threw in.
> "Under God—it did," he exclaimed fervently.
> *"It was by a special mercy,* I firmly believe, that it stood some of those hurricane squalls."
>
> "It was the setting of that sail which—" I began.
>
> "God's own hand in it," he interrupted me. *"Nothing less could have done it!"* (emphasis added)

Moses too, it will be remembered, saved his people from a watery death. One of the most famous stories in the Old Testament involves the dramatic escape of the Israelites, led by Moses, from the pursuing Egyptian chariots. The Red Sea was miraculously parted, and again, as the biblical account makes clear, "God's own hand" was in it. The subtle echoing of this adventure in **"The Secret Sharer"** points to a far more heroic and worthwhile "crime" for Leggatt than has so far been suggested by the story's critics. That it is through Archbold's words that the hint is conveyed to the reader is a fine tribute to Conrad's ironic powers.

One can only speculate as to how consciously Conrad exploited in detail the potential parallels between Moses' career and Leggatt's misfortunes. Of all biblical stories, however, Moses' destiny must surely have meant most to Conrad's imagination. The dilemma of a man who is celebrated for having brought to his people a law which said, "Thou shalt not kill," and yet who had himself been forced to kill, is a particularly Conradian irony. Not only Leggatt, but Jim and Razumov, illustrate his fascination for the man who, although trusted and responsible, had to live with the memory of a past scarred by a trust broken and a responsibility failed. If, then, we cannot render a verdict of "innocent" in Leggatt's case, neither can we ignore the enormous mitigating circumstances which Conrad's complex imagination has woven into the tale. Unlike **Under Western Eyes** and **Lord Jim** the accent in **"The Secret Sharer"** is on youthful optimism. It is not surprising to find its final words describing Leggatt, in terms which evoke Moses setting out for the promised land, as "a free man, a proud swimmer striking out for a new destiny."

Mary-Low Schenck   (essay date 1973)

SOURCE: "Seamanship in Conrad's *The Secret Sharer,* in *Criticism,* Vol. XV, No. 1, Winter, 1973, pp. 1-15.

[*In the following essay, Schenck examines "The Secret Sharer" as the story of the narrator's development as a ship's captain, asserting that earlier criticism of the story lacks sufficient analysis of the story's "physical details" and "surface action."*]

Since its first appearance in 1910, **"The Secret Sharer"** has elicited critical reading focused primarily upon psychological or symbolic aspects of the story. On the other hand, a number of critics have perceived that the surface as well as the symbolic aspects are worthy of examination. Nevertheless, although this story has received a large number of readings and explications, not a single critic appears to have fully understood and exploited the actual physical action of the story. Although R. W. Stallman argues that the "meanings which attach to the narrative or surface level are less likely to be missed" [*The Art of Joseph Conrad,* 1960] than the symbolic meanings, I shall try to show that indeed critics *have* overlooked or failed to understand significant surface activity. Instead, they have plunged, like pearl divers, into the dark recesses of the captain's mind, preferring to believe and interpret what he tells and hints, rather than to examine what he actually does. Indeed, it is the startling dichotomy between the captain's thoughts and his actions, between inner and outer reality, that makes **"The Secret Sharer"** the rich yarn that it is. It is interesting to speculate that the old salts, had they read the story when it first appeared in *Harper's,* would have had a better insight into certain of its complexities than many of the modern critics now publishing in learned journals.

When one follows carefully the captain's activities and the maneuvering of the vessel as the climactic moment of Leggatt's escape approaches, there emerges a rather different story from that normally presented by the critics. For example, the commonly-held opinion is that the captain's seamanship and abilities are crippled by Leggatt's presence and that only when Leggatt leaves can the captain regain control of his situation. Such a view, however, is incorrect. As I will demonstrate, the captain is completely in control of both ship and crew as the dark mountain of Koh-ring is approached, and it is only in the final inshore tacking maneuver that he momentarily loses his grasp on his situation for perfectly valid psychological reasons. Leggatt is not primarily the "dark" or "violent" side of the captain as some critics suggest. He is what his name implies, a legate, an envoy or messenger, or something coming from an ancestor or predecessor, and what he brings or bequeaths to the captain is nothing less than the authority of command. **"The Secret Sharer,"** then, is, as many critics have noted, a story of initiation, but here, the initiation is into captainship—the very specialized occupation of master of a square-rigged vessel. **"The Secret Sharer"** is extraordinarily elitist in its view, but its real fascination is in the insight that it gives us into what Conrad thought was the making of master—or at least one component of that process.

"The Secret Sharer" begins with the introspective captain ruminating on himself, his crew, and his impending journey. At supper with his mates, he makes conversation about another ship he has noticed inside the islands. But this first attempt at familiarity fails when the first mate foolishly blurts out "Bless my soul, sir!" and the second mate attempts to enlist the captain, by glance, in poking fun at the first mate. The second mate after allowing the captain and first mate to speculate on the strange ship, finally gives its name and particulars, "thus overwhelming us with the extent of his information." The important point of this scene is that in attempting to be familiar with his officers, to establish human contact, the captain is rebuffed and produces an entirely different effect.

Next he decides to take the watch himself since "the crew had had plenty of hard work . . . " But here again, his motives are misunderstood and his officers astonished; indeed, the young captain wonders if "my action might have made me appear eccentric."

Throughout and surrounding these two scenes we are treated to the captain's inner ruminations. His Hamlet-like questionings and the tentativeness of his dealings with his officers are in concert in these first few pages. The captain reassures himself, "the ship was like other ships, the men like other men . . . " yet he also is "vexed" with himself at his failure properly to set the anchor-watch and thus insure the rope-ladder's being brought aboard. It would be ridiculous to suggest that these modest difficulties and oversights presage disaster in the captain's long journey, nor does Conrad appear to urge this. What the young captain lacks is more than a sense of ease with his officers. Rather, it is that essential component of captainship that might be described as self-assurance, that emotional coolness that permits one to act with complete independence.

Captain Archbold from whose ship, the *Sephora,* Leggatt has escaped, despite his thirty-seven years at sea and his twenty years of "immaculate command," has never (his name notwithstanding) gained this independent sense, this mastership, yet he has made many safe voyages. But in a crisis, Conrad is suggesting, a master without this confidence is lost, as Archbold, his ship, and his company would have been without the intervention of Leggatt's boldness in setting the sail during the storm.

The turning point in the captain's tentativeness occurs once Leggatt has come aboard, as the captain's words reveal: "The self-possession of that man had somehow induced a corresponding state in myself." Moreover, in contemplating Leggatt, the captain becomes aware of what he lacks—the very traits required of the good captain: "And I could imagine . . . a stubborn if not a steadfast operation; something of which I should have been perfectly incapable." The brush with the steward in the cabin is enough to convince the captain that his actions are suspect, and he reflects wisely, "I must show myself on deck." At this point a crucial change occurs in the narrative. The captain's speculations, musings, and inner doubts continue with little or no change; he seems at times the classic neurotic afraid even to imagine the next moment. But *outwardly,* in his actions as master and seaman, the shift is dramatic. First, he cuts the grinning first mate with "the first particular order I had given on board that ship," and he "stayed on deck to see it executed too." Such actions see the "sneering young cub [get] taken down a peg or two." During breakfast, far from making vague and friendly attempts at conversation with his crew, the captain presides "with such frigid dignity that the two mates were only too glad to escape from the cabin as soon as decency permitted." Now, when the steward comes unexpectedly to the cabin, the captain, instead of starting and turning red, responds with a peremptory " 'Well!' " and coolly orders the steward to get the ladder over for the approaching Captain Archbold.

In the extended conversation with the older man, the captain betrays no outward panic, even though his mind is racing with questions and alarms: "From its novelty to him and from its nature," says the captain, "punctilious courtesy was the manner best calculated to restrain the man." In addition, the captain cleverly feigns partial deafness. This episode with Captain Archbold shows us that the captain has an inaccurate view of his own actions. Despite his impression that he is attracting attention, the captain is totally cool and collected. When Archbold indicates that he will report a suicide, the captain's retort shows masterly self-control: " 'Unless you manage to recover him before tomorrow,' I assented dispassionately. . . . 'I mean alive.' " Yet only a few lines further on, the captain asserts that he "felt utterly incapable of playing the part of ignorance properly, and therefore was afraid to try." Propelled by his fear—"fear, too, is not barren of ingenious suggestions"—the captain dissembles smoothly and convincingly, despite his protestations to the contrary.

The same observation holds true for his behavior in front of his crew. Here again, the two threads of the narrative are sharply diverging. In his mind, the captain is agonizing: "I felt I was producing a bad impression . . . I felt less torn in two when I was with [Leggatt]." And later: "I was not wholly alone with my command." No wonder

that so many critics have misread the events after the sails are set. The captain himself says, "There are to a seaman certain words, gestures, that should in given conditions come as naturally, as instinctively as the winking of a menaced eye. . . . But all unconscious alertness had abandoned me. I had to make an effort of will to recall myself back (from the cabin) to the conditions of the moment. I felt I was appearing an irresolute commander to those people who were watching me more or less critically." What we are seeing here is a somewhat paranoid reaction produced by the captain's guilty feelings about harboring Leggatt. He is convinced that the crew is talking about him and remarking his strange behavior:

> My nerves were so shaken that I could not govern my voice and conceal my agitation. This was the sort of thing that made my terrifically whiskered mate tap his forehead with his forefinger. I had detected him using that gesture while talking on deck with a confidential air to the carpenter. *It was too far to hear a word, but I had no doubt* that this pantomime could only refer to the strange new captain (emphasis mine).

We have only the captain's words for the reaction of the crew to his behavior, and it may well be that they remark nothing at all. In any event, the captain's actual ability to function is not impaired in the slightest. In fact, the very presence of Leggatt is forcing the captain towards independent decision and action, precisely as the storm and Captain Archbold's irresoluteness forced Leggatt to save the *Sephora,* and, in so doing, to kill a recalcitrant seaman. Leggatt's fierce and unique example and his actual presence "educate" the young captain in two steps. The first effect is to force the captain to stand apart from his crew, even to the point of treating them with coldness, rudeness and hostility. But this, of course, is only part of the captain's voyage to mastership. This hard-won loneness must next be applied to its logical use: the welding of ship and underlings into a perfect tool with which the captain can accomplish whatever he chooses. Thus the Leggatt-captain relationship cannot continue indefinitely. Continuous rigidity and elitism by the captain toward his mates and crew can only result in as much difficulty as his former vagueness and pointless good fellowship has done. Thus, after Leggatt has forced the captain to share his command only with him, he next insists that he be put ashore. It is in this putting ashore that the captain must assemble the several skills that Conrad is suggesting are required of a sailing master: independent aloofness, a cool head in the face of danger, total control of the men under him, and seamanship.

The ship is proceeding down the eastern side of the Gulf of Siam. The wind is blowing lightly from the south and the captain is making slow tacks against it, running close-hauled. At midnight of the fourth day, having decided to move in close enough to the eastern shore of the Gulf to put Leggatt off, the captain puts his ship on starboard tack; that is, the wind is blowing over the right side of the ship and the vessel is moving about southeast. At noon, when the captain might be expected to change tack and head back out into the Gulf, he fails to do so, explaining that he is looking for the "land breezes." After dinner he makes his final plans with Leggatt: " 'It's got to be Koh-ring. . . . It has got two hills and a low point.' " Koh-ring is evidently an island running roughly north and south with hills on each end. " 'She will clear the south point as she heads now,' " says the captain to Leggatt, but a bit later it becomes evident that he has no intention of passing south of the island and heading in to the mainland shore.

The captain explains the scheme to Leggatt, " 'I shall stand in as close as I dare and put her round. . . . when the ship's way is deadened in stays [a ship's forward motion stops as she changes tacks in a light breeze] and all hands are aft at the main braces you will have a clear road to slip out and get overboard through the open quarter-deck port.' "

The captain has been badgering the steward for several days whenever he approached the captain's cabin and the hidden Leggatt. This background of authoritarian treatment now enables the captain to send the steward on a pointless errand for hot water while he smuggles Leggatt into the sail locker, which communicates to the open quarter-deck ports.

The captain next goes on deck and sees the southern hill of Koh-ring bearing off his port (left) bow and close by. The "wise" young second mate is on watch and the captain coolly deceives the young man as to his intent, " 'She will weather' " to which the mate replies incredulously, " 'Are you going to try that, sir?' " The captain, ignoring the mate, speaks to the helmsman, " 'Keep her good full.' "

What is going on here is simply this: the captain might if he chose "weather" Koh-ring island, that is, stay on starboard tack and by keeping as close to the wind as possible, pass by the island close to its southern point on a long south-east diagonal. We know that such a course is possible: the captain has told Leggatt, " 'She will clear the south point as she heads now.' " But, of course, the captain has no intention of weathering. On the contrary, he has explained to Leggatt that he will put the ship about onto port tack (in layman's terms, change from the zig to the zag in his zig-zag course) when he gets as close to the land as he dares. Moreover, his next order, " 'Keep her good full' " makes it highly unlikely that the ship could weather. Nor would he issue such an order if he hoped or intended to weather. In order to weather the point, the helmsman would have to steer the ship more nearly into the southerly wind with the result that her sails would spill some of their wind. On the other hand, if the helmsman is to keep the sails full, as ordered by the captain, he must steer more to port, that is, in an easterly direction, off the wind, and directly toward, rather than just past, the southern tip of Koh-ring so that it would be impossible to weather the point. Thus, the captain's intent is to deceive the mate, and he is essentially lying, because immediately after speaking the words, " 'She will weather,' " he issues the order that makes the statement false. As will be shown later, the tacking maneuver is essential to the captain's plan for putting Leggatt off without detection by the crew.

There is a crucial reason for this deliberate and cool manipulation of the second mate. The captain is dealing with a conceited and "sharp" young man, but one probably lacking in experience and the judgment that stems from experience. To have explained that he was going to sail inshore to a desperately short distance and then to tack would have not only disturbed the young second mate but might have produced some sort of semi-mutinous action. Yet inshore tacking is the only course of action that will allow Leggatt's escape to go undetected. The captain's problem is that he cannot possibly give any plausible reason for putting the ship about so close to the southern hill of Koh-ring as he wishes to do. He must pretend that he plans to weather in order to account for going in so close. His strategy is to confuse the second mate on a matter of sailing judgment. The mate's judgment is that the ship will not weather, but we know that there is sufficient doubt about this to inhibit the young second mate's intervention in the matter when he is, himself, not sure whether the vessel will pass the island or not.

The intriguing thing about this scene is that the captain has no inner qualms whatever about his manipulation of the second mate. Indeed, it is his lack of introspection at this point that has deceived many critics who have built their readings of the story on the captain's inner thoughts and psychological reactions. In his earlier scene with Captain Archbold, the young captain says, "I could not, I think, have met him by a direct lie, also for psychological (not moral) reasons. If he had only known how afraid I was of his putting my feeling of identity with the other to the test!" Yet here, though he is lying now to his mate, he feels no qualms or doubts whatever. There are two factors in operation to produce this change in the captain. First, his days of hiding Leggatt have toughened him in his relationships with his men. Second, Archbold is a captain, an equal member of the select society into which the young captain is being introduced. If, as I maintain, Conrad is dealing in this story with the rather specialized way in which a sailing master is made, then this second possibility is the most interesting. Essentially, we are seeing that captains do not lie to each other, but captains lie, without hesitation, to underlings.

The deception cannot continue indefinitely. As the southern mountain looms blackly, the second mate speaks again in an "unsteady voice," " 'Are you going on sir?' "

The captain refuses to answer but speaks to the helmsman, " 'Keep her good full. Don't check her way. That won't do now.' " Up to this point the captain has maintained the pretense that he intends to pass close by the southern tip of Koh-ring keeping on starboard tack, but with this order he drops this pretense and makes it evident that he intends to tack the ship close to the shore. The most typical error of a beginning sailor or a nervous helmsman coming in on a lee shore (a shore toward which the wind is blowing) is to ease his vessel into the wind (away from the shore) and thereby check her forward progress. The reason this is a dangerous error is that if a ship does not have sufficient speed she will not respond to her rudder when it is put over for the tacking maneuver. The captain, aware that such an error is instinctive, warns against it, and in so doing effectively notifies the second mate that he intends to tack momentarily and needs as much speed as possible.

By now, however, the second mate is too awed by the nearness of the mountain to attempt any action. Further, there is no sensible action available to him at this juncture other than the one being pursued by the captain. Essentially, the captain has been manipulating the second mate as a puppeteer dangles a puppet. When indirection was required to lull him, the captain used it, and when the truth of the captain's intention became obvious, it was too late for the mate to react in any harmful way.

The final scene is not only the climax of the story, but the rock on which the bulk of criticism of the story shatters. Most critics founder at this crucial action over two questions: First, why does the captain take the vessel in so close to shore? And second, what, exactly, is the risk involved?

On the first point, the commonest reading seems to be that the captain is proving something in a psychological sense to himself, his crew, and/or Leggatt. But a more reasonable understanding of the situation becomes available if one accepts the captain's thoughts as meaning exactly what they say: "There could be no going back for him." The captain is responsible for Leggatt's life. The only way to insure that this life will be preserved is to take the vessel as close inshore as a capable seaman dares. Many critics have noted that Leggatt can swim several miles so that the ship could have comfortably tacked much further offshore. But the captain's contention that there could be no going back for Leggatt is exactly true in at least two senses. First, if Leggatt cramps or is unable to make a nearby landing because Koh-ring's rocky side falls sheerly into the water, the captain cannot go back to retrieve the swimmer. Further, if Leggatt cannot get into the water because of a near-by crew member or some other last minute hitch, he cannot get back from the quarter deck to the captain's cabin without considerable risk of discovery. But there is more to the captain's problem than this. While the on-deck business is going forward, Leggatt must go from the sail locker, to the lobby, and thence overboard through the quarter-deck port. For this is to be carried out, it is essential that the below-decks area be completely clear of men—men who have already bridled at the thought that they might be harboring a murderer. On a quiet night, only a single watch would be needed to accomplish a tacking maneuver. Square riggers normally kept two watches, port and starboard, with the first and second mates going on duty with their respective watches. But this would mean that half the crew would be below or lounging around who knows where during the time the vessel was coming about. Double watchstanding is normally resorted to only in foul weather or conditions that require extra hands. What then is the captain to do? Clearly, he must create an "artificial" emergency, so paralyzing as to bring every man on deck and then transfix their attention away from the quarter-deck area while Leggatt is escaping. In meeting this requirement, the captain is fortunate that the mountain of Koh-ring admirably fills his needs. The entire crew is on deck when he calls for the second watch— " 'And turn all hands up' " and we can be sure that every man is looking up at the black mountain.

The question of wilfully taking the ship into danger still remains, and bothers several critics. Even if the captain

must "shave the land" to insure Leggatt's safety, this is still an ignoble decision if it condemns many sailors to death, or even risks such a tragedy. But again, critics have failed to penetrate that what actually is at stake is only the captain's reputation as he notes himself: "I realized suddenly that all my future, the only future for which I was fit, would perhaps go irretrievably to pieces in any mishap in my first command." And "mishap" is exactly what is being risked here. At most a minor injury to the vessel, and a blot on a young captain's record. There is no surf and no sign of the rocks that the first mate mentions when the captain runs easterly toward the Cambodje shore ostensibly seeking the land wind (which, indeed, he might in part be doing). The captain presumably does have an Admiralty chart of the area which, while it might have been sketchy on inshore soundings, would surely show any above-water rocks. But even if the vessel did strike a rock (and this would be the worst disaster that could befall it) it seems unlikely that she would be badly holed, much less that she would sink. From the description, it appears she is moving at barely a knot, since at any greater speed she would presumably have come about more handily than she does. The first mate, certainly not the most optimistic member of the crew, speaks out: " 'She'll drift ashore before she's round. O my God!' " But this is hardly a disaster to make maritime history. If the ship did ground, it is to be expected that the longboat would be lowered, a kedge anchor taken out westward from Koh-ring, and the anchor capstan worked to pull the ship into deep water. The point is, *no one's life is in danger here except Leggatt's.* He is the one who must swim to a dark and strange shore, avoiding even the slightest noise that would attract instant attention by those on board. The only real casualty from a grounding would be the captain's reputation, for the incident would appear in the log and attract attention, especially if sufficient damage were done to force the ship back into a local port. The captain is gambling his reputation on assuring Leggatt's safety. This seems a fair trade—a reasonable moral equation. The other human actors in the drama are involved in only a peripheral manner.

The first mate is more of a problem for the young captain. He is older and more experienced, less easily fooled on questions of seamanly judgment. We recall that "his dominant trait was to take all things into earnest consideration." He is also cautious. The best way of handling this man, while the ship slides under Koh-ring's bulk, is to let him sleep, off watch. But the captain cannot very well call the other watch without calling its chief and so the first mate arrives on deck at the crucial moment and promptly has hysterics. There is certainly a similarity between this scene, where the captain shakes his mate and orders him forward, and the scene described by Leggatt when he strangled a mutinous sailor, but Conrad is too subtle a writer to suggest that the correspondence is one-to-one. Actually, the captain-first mate confrontation is a kind of parody of the more serious and violent business on the *Sephora.* The bewhiskered first mate is simply not as important to the captain, or his story, as the mutinous sailor was to Leggatt. The young captain is a puppet-master controlling all his men, mates and seamen. He confuses the second mate by coolly lying about his intention. He controls the first mate by steadiness and disciplined violence and he manipulates the crew members with the help of the awesome blackness of Koh-ring. The point to recognize here is the considerable discrepancy between the captain's thoughts, which are chaotic and disturbed and his actions, which are purposeful, economic, and sound in both a psychological and seamanship sense.

Whether one believes Leggatt is an ideal or a dark force, it is a critical commonplace to represent his effect on the captain as detrimental. The fact is, however, that it is not until Leggatt goes over the side that the captain slips seriously. Until he puts his vessel about, he is completely in control of his situation. But at this moment psychology and seamanship come together. The captain's mental confusion finally overwhelms his nautical judgment. It is not Leggatt's being on board that almost destroys the captain, it is his leaving.

To understand this final moment of the story, it is necessary to know what is going on vis-a-vis the nautical situation. The vessel is moving very slowly in a southeasterly direction on starboard tack (wind over the right bow). The captain gives the order to put the rudder over to the right so as to bring the ship around, " 'Hard alee!' " She has so little way, however, that she hangs "in stays" (that is, stops in the midst of the turn). This happens when the turning motion of the ship is so slow that the wind and water-drag resist and stop it, usually when the ship is pointing dead to windward. The ship then begins to move backward. But the captain must know whether the ship is still moving ahead in order to steer correctly: "And then I watched the land intently. In that smooth water and light wind it was impossible to feel the ship coming to. No! I could not feel her." If the captain had reversed his rudder (turned it to the left) before the forward motion had ceased, the ship would have tended to fall back off on her original tack and again point directly toward Koh-ring, probably drifting onto the shore before she could get way again. If, on the other hand, the forward motion had ceased and the ship had started to drift backward because of the wind pressure on her square sails and upper works and the captain had failed to reverse the rudder the effect would have been equally troublesome. When a ship moves backward, the stern becomes the front in terms of steering and a right rudder will move the stern to the right and the bow to the left, toward Koh-ring in this case. Thus, the captain must know exactly when his vessel gains sternway so as to reverse the rudder at that critical instant. When the captain sees the hat "drifting forward" he knows that the ship has gathered sternway and that he must reverse the rudder. " 'Shift the helm,' " he says, and now the left rudder moves the stern to the left toward Koh-ring and moves the bow to the right toward open water. As soon as the ship has fallen far enough off on the port tack her sails will fill and the very slight rearward motion will be stopped. She will then draw ahead out toward the middle of the Gulf of Siam.

The important thing to understand about this situation is that it is one of the most essential considerations in large-ship sailing. The great bulk of lost sailing vessels foundered because they could not come about when being driven down on a lee shore and could not, in the vernacular, 'claw up to windward.' On a dark night and in a strange vessel, it is inconceivable that a master who has shown the planning and operational skill that our young captain has exhibited would not have anticipated the essential point: that he would have only one try at coming about, and it must work. Furthermore, his own words to the helmsman—" 'Don't check her way. That won't do now.' "—prove that he is aware of the necessity of either getting her around or reversing the rudder if she hangs in stays, as proves to be the case. Yet when the crucial moment comes, the captain is totally unprepared: "Had she [stern] way on her yet? . . . It was impossible to tell. . . . What I needed was something easily seen. . . . To run down for it I didn't dare."

At this point I must, like the other critics, leave the certainties of seamanship for the ambiguities of psychological motivation. Whereas the captain does behave (whatever his thoughts) cleverly and surely until the final moment, he suddenly muffs a completely obvious and predictable emergency. The reason, I submit, lies in the meaning of Leggatt to the captain. Leggatt is not only a kind of model or example but he is also the problem which forces the captain to make his way towards mastership. Leggatt not only *teaches the captain how* to treat the first mate with fierce discipline and to overawe the crew, but his presence *forces the captain actually to do* these things. The hitch is that the captain has not thought beyond the moment when Leggatt goes over the side. He has so closely identified himself with Leggatt, that this parting has almost the trauma of the surgical parting of Siamese twins. Thus the very common critical reading of the story, which assumes the captain is crippled when Leggatt is aboard and only becomes whole when Leggatt has gone, actually has the situation backward.

At this critical juncture, Leggatt providentially "returns" through the intervention of that most interesting and controversial symbol, the floating hat. The captain had given Leggatt the hat to "save his homeless head from the dangers of the sun," but it fell off or Leggatt discarded it and the captain was able to assess the moment when his ship gained sternway by watching the relative motion of the ship and hat. Although my reading of "The Secret Sharer" leans heavily away from inner psychological complexities and symbolic interplay, it would be an error to avoid the clear symbolic importance of the hat. Leggatt is certainly that "ideal conception of [the young captain's] personality" and, as such, he transmits to the young captain the attitudes and aptitudes that befit a commander. When the young captain falters at the end, because his model has left, the model provides, unwittingly but importantly, a final "saving mark for [his] eyes." The hat is then a kind of crown which Leggatt is symbolically passing to the captain. Leggatt has exhibited his boldness in saving his vessel, the *Sephora*. The young captain has yet to meet such a stern test. His handling of the inshore run and tacking maneuvers cannot be compared, either in importance or personal ability, to Leggatt's setting of the sail during a hurricane. Yet Leggatt's career has now turned to different channels and it is reasonable to assume that whatever coolness and bold decision he possessed has somehow passed to the young captain. The crown symbol is especially apt, since what Leggatt has passed is a rather elitist and authoritarian standard. The true master makes moral decisions that may disturb the academic critic. To be sure, a vessel's safety is worth more than a single man's life. But a man's life is more important than the chance of a minor wreck. Lying and bullying are acceptable when required to work the ship properly. Above all, the important thing is to act decisively. Skill without this coolness and nerve can lead to many years of "immaculate command" (witness Captain Archbold) but will not triumph at that critical moment.

C. B. Cox (essay date 1974)

SOURCE: "Mirrors in *The Secret Sharer* and *The Shadow Line*," in *Joseph Conrad: The Modern Imagination*, J. M. Dent and Sons Ltd, 1974, pp. 137-58.

[*Cox is an English educator, editor, and critic. In the following excerpt, he suggests that critical debate over "The Secret Sharer" is due in part to the fact that the story raises questions about the narrator but does not seek to provide answers.*]

> Now I am a lake. A woman bends over me,
> Searching my reaches for what she really is.
> Then she turns to those liars, the candles or the
>   moon,
> I see her back, and reflect it faithfully.
> She rewards me with tears and an agitation of
>   hands.
> I am important to her. She comes and goes.
> Each morning it is her face that replaces the
>   darkness.
> In me she has drowned a young girl, and in me
>   an old woman
> Rises toward her day after day, like a terrible
>   fish.
>
>   Sylvia Plath, 'Mirror'

To peer too long into a mirror may prove disconcerting. We may recognize aspects of our personality we prefer to forget, and we may become uncomfortably aware that our identity is composed of numerous secret selves. If we stare hard enough we may wonder whether the reflection is completely under our control, and suspect that it might begin to form grimaces and attitudes of its own.

The fear of reflected images, common among primitive peoples, is described at length in Robert Roger's *The Double in Literature*. There is a widespread belief that shadows, reflections, and portraits of the body are the same as souls, or are at least vitally linked with the well-being of the body. The folk custom of covering mirrors or turning them to the wall after someone has died in a house is based on the idea that the soul reflected in the mirror may be seized by the ghost of the departed. It is thought especially dangerous for sick people to see themselves in a mirror. Even today people can suffer from catoptricophobia—fear of mirrors and reflections—and the superstition that breaking a mirror brings bad luck is a sign that these primitive feelings still run deep. The same fears are often occasioned by pictures. There are still places in Africa, even in a comparatively civilized community such as Khar-

toum, where it is unwise to take photographs in the street. It is assumed that the photographic image is an extension of the self, and that the camera may thus steal a man's soul from his body. The best-known example of the use of this motif in literature is presumably Oscar Wilde's *The Picture of Dorian Gray*.

A novelist who writes about heroes like himself is creating just such mirror-reflections; indeed it has even been suggested that fictional characters may all be projections of the author, all images of potential selves. Flaubert wrote: 'Madame Bovary, c'est moi'; and it has been argued that Dostoevsky's brothers Karamazov are all different facets of the novelist. Freud has commented on the tendency of modern writers to split up their ego by self-observation into many component egos, and in this way to personify the conflicting trends in their own mental life in many heroes.

Henry James, E. M. Forster, James Joyce, D. H. Lawrence and Virginia Woolf are among the many twentieth-century writers who use fiction to explore their own mirror-images. I am thinking of obvious examples, such as 'The Beast in the Jungle', *The Longest Journey*, *Portrait of the Artist*, *Sons and Lovers* or *The Waves*. The writing of such fictions may help the artist to master anxiety, or exorcize psychological conflicts, to achieve maturity through self-recognition. But the mirror may reveal more than the author intends. We may discern a morbid preoccupation in the writer with his own essence, and a submission to dangerous elements in his make-up. In the case of D. H. Lawrence there is the vicarious participation in sadistic killing in *The Plumed Serpent*. In *Sons and Lovers* the treatment of Miriam and Mrs Morel reflects double standards. Behind the supposed events, explanations and evaluations, as recounted by the narrator, the reader discerns that Paul's fixation on his mother accounts for more of his problems than the author consciously realizes. Lawrence's own psychological condition looks out from behind the story like some irrepressible ghost.

Conrad's **'The Secret Sharer'** (1910) is one of the greatest examples in fiction of the use of the mirror-image. The device enables him to explore the conflicts in his personality between seaman and artist, loyalty and betrayal, sanity and insanity. The story brilliantly exemplifies the problems of the modern imagination. . . . In **'The Secret Sharer'** he draws on his memories of his first command on the *Otago,* when he, like the captain-narrator, felt a stranger on his ship. He thus creates an image of himself in the captain, who is then confronted with a second mirror-reflection in Leggatt, the criminal doppelgänger who appeals for help after he has killed a man on board his own ship. Through the two mirrors, both in some way reflections of Conrad, both in some way reflections of each other, he identifies and examines a number of possible roles. Leggatt is both a real flesh-and-blood seaman as well as some kind of alter ego for the captain, and Conrad handles most delicately this double function. But the clue to interpretation of the story is that the mirror-reflections are multiple in meaning rather than simply dual. The story's imaginative success, as I hope to show, is that the dramatic situation bewilders and disturbs the reader, leaving him unsure where he should approve and where disapprove. As the two mirrors, captain and criminal, confront each other, their roles resist clear definition. As soon as we think we have grasped the true meaning of the symbolism, we are startled by some contradictory effect. The story expresses Conrad's sense of the variety of identities available to each intelligent individual. The captain is supposedly being initiated into maturity and responsibility, but we may wonder at certain moments whether the narrator, presumably telling his story years later, is a sane man. The mirror images are used to express rather than resolve the tensions in Conrad's personality, and he refuses to provide the reader with definitive judgments about the value of the identities on offer.

The story was published in 1912 in the volume *'Twixt Land and Sea* together with **'A Smile of Fortune'** and **'Freya of the Seven Isles'**. In a letter to Garnett, Conrad confessed how much he admired **'The Secret Sharer'**, how much it satisfied him:

> I dare say Freya is pretty rotten. On the other hand the Secret Sharer, between you and me, is *it*. Eh? Every word fits and there's not a single uncertain note. Luck my boy. Pure luck. I knew you would spot the thing at sight. But I repeat: mere luck.

As the two young men, narrator and Leggatt, put their heads together in whispered colloquies, both dressed in identical sleeping suits, the image unsettles the reader, like some secret dream from the depths of the unconscious. Conrad was right to think he had found a highly stimulating idea from which his imagination could extract a wealth of effects. But he too might have wondered whether the mirrors revealed more than he intended. In this story, as in *Under Western Eyes,* he seems to use fiction as a kind of exorcism. He creates a drama in which the captain by a supposedly heroic act rids himself of the dark side of his consciousness. The meaning of the end is not so easy to figure out as some writers on Conrad have suggested. I feel that as Leggatt swims away into the darkness it is as if Conrad is saying farewell to some essential element in his artistic identity. The reflection in the mirror bears the soul away.

Both Freudian and Jungian interpretations throw some light on the symbolism of **'The Secret Sharer'**. Robert Rogers gives a clear account of the Freudian approach. The captain on a ship has almost unlimited authority, and is easily associated with the psychological father. Leggatt's crime against discipline aboard ship thus becomes a symbol of the primal crime of the son: rebellion against authority. The captain-narrator associates himself with the crime because he feels guilty and inadequate at this moment when he is assuming the responsibility of his first command: 'In Eriksonian terms, the story portrays the new-made captain as undergoing an "identity crisis", an identity crisis which in Freudian terms harks back to the earlier oedipal crisis.' He is anxious whether he has the ability to fulfil his new role, and so fears he is a usurper. The tension between subconscious guilt and a confident sense of responsibility is symbolized in Leggatt's story. His crime is against the established laws of discipline, yet committed in the interests of maintaining order among a crew berserk with fear, and with the purpose of saving the ship: 'Leggatt has, *in extremis,* usurped the role of his commander in both a maritime and a psychological sense.' By helping the outlaw, the captain proves himself competent and resolute, and he eventually succeeds in getting rid of his scapegoat double. This justifies the happy ending, for he is now secure in his professional role, and no longer feels anxiety and guilt.

The Jungian interpretation is argued most cogently by Albert Guerard. According to this approach, the story, like *Heart of Darkness,* concerns an insecure and morally isolated man who meets and commits himself to a man even more isolated. In whispered, unrepeatable conversations, he holds communication with his secret self, and this represents a symbolic descent into the unconscious. The real moral dilemma for the captain-narrator is that he must recognize in Leggatt his own potential criminality, his own lower or more primitive self, and so through a new self-awareness initiate himself into true manhood. Integration of the personality occurs when the unconscious has been known, trafficked with and in some sense liberated. In Jungian psychology, as in dreams, the captain's floppy hat represents the personality, which can be transferred symbolically to another. The captain's gift of his hat to Leggatt demonstrates that he now accepts the unconscious self; this generosity saves the ship, and symbolically his own psychic health, when the hat is used as a marker to determine whether the ship has gathered sternway.

Jocelyn Baines treats these symbolic interpretations with some exasperation. In his view, the story is intensely dramatic, but, on the psychological and moral level, rather slight. He specifically attacks Guerard's arguments, and asks how the Jungian interpretation can make any sense of the last sentence, in which Leggatt departs 'a free man, a proud swimmer striking out for a new destiny'. This is no way for a symbol of the unconscious to behave. Baines argues that there is no indication in the story, explicit or implicit, that the captain sees any of his difficulties in Leggatt, or that he performs any self-examination. Nor is there any moral dilemma. There is no evidence in the plot that the captain would have failed as a seaman if Leggatt had not appeared. He realizes his own mistake in abandoning routine to take the anchor watch, and asks himself whether it is ever wise to interfere with the established routine of duties even from the kindest of motives. This occurs before he finds Leggatt at the bottom of the ship's ladder.

In *A Reader's Guide to Joseph Conrad,* Frederick R. Karl adopts a similar no-nonsense approach. Like Baines, he attacks those who find some kind of cosmic significance in the story: 'The surface in this case is the story, and the surface is the arrival of the Captain at a degree of maturity in which he gains self-respect and confidence.' Karl argues that **'The Secret Sharer'** deals principally and simply with the theme of growing up that Conrad dealt with in so many other stories and novels. The captain does not betray the outlaw (as Razumov does), and by arranging his escape proves his own manhood. The story is one of Conrad's best, a microcosm of his major themes, 'but for all its suggestiveness, it is, paradoxically, one of his most straightforward and obvious works. Its narrative is a model of clarity, like those uncomplicated narratives **"Youth"** and *The Shadow-Line.*' According to Karl, the story is psychologically shallow, and the theme of the alter ego is laboured to excess.

Baines and Karl have a case which needs answering. Neither the Freudian nor the Jungian interpretations can provide a complete explanation for every important detail of the story. Leggatt possesses several characteristics which unfit him for the role of symbol of the unconscious. He is a sane, determined man who, when immersed in the destructive element of the sea, swims purposefully towards the distant light of the captain's ship; he would never commit suicide. The Freudian analysis fits quite well, but takes attention away from the actual cause of the tension in the captain's mind. He almost breaks down because of the strain imposed by the very real problem of keeping Leggatt's presence hidden from the crew. It is difficult to accept that this is a symbol of his secret oedipal guilt, when he has every reason to fear exposure. Discovery might mean death for Leggatt, and the captain himself might have to stand trial for assisting a murderer to escape. Such rational explanation of his anxiety seems more to the point

than a supposed sub-conscious identification with Leggatt's crime.

Yet Baines and Karl ignore many features of the story which do not fit in with their simple interpretations. Guerard is particularly successful in describing the symbolic reverberations of the landscape, the apparition of the headless swimmer, the business with the hat, or the blackness of Koh-ring. Although we may reject any one symbolic interpretation as incomplete, the method of narration suggests hidden meanings, and Freudian or Jungian ideas are inevitably aroused in the reader's mind. Also, the reading that sees this as only a forceful dramatic tale ignores several extraordinary incidents. Neither Leggatt nor the captain is a straightforward character. The various accounts of the murder include elements that suggest that Leggatt is not just an honest Conway boy who killed a man in a fit of justified temper. The captain's behaviour is at times so astonishing that we must look for sources additional to the strain of secrecy. And so we come to the great crux of the narrative, which neither Baines nor Karl considers. Why does the captain sail his ship so near to the black hill of Koh-ring? The obvious reply is that he wishes to give Leggatt every chance to swim safely ashore; but Leggatt has proved himself an excellent swimmer, and so there is no necessity for the ship to shave the land so dan-

Conrad in 1912.

101

gerously close. The captain admits that his heart was in his mouth, and under any other circumstances he would not have held on a moment longer. The crew are convinced they are doomed. The plain fact is that for moral or psychological reasons the captain endangers his ship and the lives of his men unnecessarily, and they are only saved by the lucky accident that the floppy hat, dropped in his escape by Leggatt, serves as a marker in the water. Is this irresponsible piece of daring a sign of maturity, of his competence to assume the role of captain of the ship? It could be said he behaves like a madman. Why? Baines and Karl are clearly wrong to think there is anything simple about this story.

The story begins with a description of landscape whose delicate symbolism is not easy to define:

> On my right hand there were lines of fishing-stakes resembling a mysterious system of half-submerged bamboo fences, incomprehensible in its division of the domain of tropical fishes, and crazy of aspect as if abandoned for ever by some nomad tribe of fishermen now gone to the other end of the ocean; for there was no sign of human habitation as far as the eye could reach. To the left a group of barren islets, suggesting ruins of stone walls, towers, and blockhouses, had its foundations set in a blue sea that itself looked solid, so still and stable did it lie below my feet; even the track of light from the westering sun shone smoothly, without that animated glitter which tells of an imperceptible ripple. And when I turned my head to take a parting glance at the tug which had just left us anchored outside the bar, I saw the straight line of the flat shore joined to the stable sea, edge to edge, with a perfect and unmarked closeness, in one levelled floor half brown, half blue under the enormous dome of the sky. Corresponding in their insignificance to the islets of the sea, two small clumps of trees, one on each side of the only fault in the impeccable joint, marked the mouth of the river Meinam we had just left on the first preparatory stage of our homeward journey; and, far back on the inland level, a larger and loftier mass, the grove surrounding the great Paknam pagoda, was the only thing on which the eye could rest from the vain task of exploring the monotonous sweep of the horizon. Here and there gleams as of a few scattered pieces of silver marked the windings of the great river; and on the nearest of them, just within the bar, the tug steaming right into the land became lost to my sight, hull and funnel and masts, as though the impassive earth had swallowed her up without an effort, without a tremor. My eye followed the light cloud of her smoke, now here, now there, above the plain, according to the devious curves of the stream, but always fainter and farther away, till I lost it at last behind the mitre-shaped hill of the great pagoda. And then I was left alone with my ship, anchored at the head of the Gulf of Siam.

The fishing stakes are 'mysterious', 'incomprehensible' and 'crazy', suggesting perhaps man's failure to impose his patterns of work on nature. The islets, like ruins, have their foundations in a blue sea whose 'solid', 'stable' quality we know to be an illusion. There is already a hint of

menace, of man's isolation in a dangerous and inexplicable universe. Land, sea and sky merge together in a moment of stillness, a kind of dream-landscape, typical in Conrad as the hero approaches his test. The objects he perceives appear beyond his control, for there will be no consolations for his lonely mind in the monotonous sweep of Nature. The tug seems to have been swallowed up by the impassive earth, as all man-made things will eventually return to the non-human neutrality of the primal forms of matter. In *Joseph Conrad: The Imaged Style*, Wilfred S. Dowden argues that the insignificant twin clumps of trees suggest the dyadic aspects of the captain's personality, and that the pagoda represents the higher ground of self-knowledge. Conrad's symbolic landscapes rarely convey such precise connotations. Indeed, it is the *lack* of significance which is being stressed. As the captain's eye watches the smoke of the tug gradually disappearing along the river, the scene suggests how little the eye can know, understand or control. The main impression is of insubstantiality. Later in the story the hill of Koh-ring and the stars above appear to move while the ship stands still; human reference points have no absolute validity. The ordeal takes place in a 'phantom' sea, a 'sleepy gulf', as if the captain and Leggatt inhabit an area of consciousness on the borders of dreams. This insubstantiality of the physical universe is for Conrad a simple fact which has to be accepted. The captain's quest for self-identification will not be helped by his perceptions of exterior objects. He must seek to find himself in his subjective consciousness, where sense-impressions never entirely lose the aspect of hallucination.

The captain admits he lacks self-confidence. The crew have been together for eighteen months; he is a stranger and, except for the second mate, the youngest. We begin to wonder what sort of man he is when he tells us: 'I was somewhat of a stranger to myself.' After his foolish decision to take the anchor watch, he enjoys introspective ruminations under the stars. He has not integrated himself into his appointed role, has not merged his separate identity into the functions demanded of a captain. We may sympathize with this imaginative side to his temperament, and conclude that this suggests he is superior to a conventional captain such as MacWhirr. But in the opening paragraphs he shows his inexperience of life. He rejoices in the great security of the sea as compared with the unrest of the land, in his choice of an untempted life presenting no disquieting problems, 'invested with an elementary moral beauty by the absolute straightforwardness of its appeal and by the singleness of its purpose'. Events are to prove that the sea can make confusing claims, and we may recall Jim's similar feeling of security just before the *Patna* collision.

Leggatt's self-confidence contrasts with the self-questioning, Hamlet-like behaviour of the captain. He first appears in the water at the bottom of the ladder like a headless corpse. It is the captain's fault that the ladder has been left overboard, as if he had subconsciously willed that Leggatt should come from the depths of the sea. In the phosphorescent flash caused by summer lightning on the water, Leggatt appears like a denizen from another world. What the captain draws up from the sleeping waters corresponds with his own dream of an ideal personality, or at first appears to do so. Leggatt is active, energetic and self-possessed, and has proved himself in dangerous extremities. Throughout the ensuing days the captain must confront this ideal image in living reality, must try to keep up to Leggatt's standards by successfully organizing the rescue. He must establish that his own head could properly be worn by Leggatt's body, that he has the right to recognize himself in his brave alter ego. But in this confrontation between extrovert and introvert, the ideal and the actual, the captain is torn apart by inherent ambiguities and tensions in both roles. On the one hand his own active imagination induces a collapse of self-control, and a submission to neurotic strain. On the other, Leggatt's courageous service to the ship apparently involves a primitive, savage determination to survive.

After Leggatt has come on board and is hiding in the captain's cabin, many of the narrator's actions can be explained as legitimate devices to hide the outlaw from the crew. But soon the reader who has been vicariously identifying with the captain starts to feel uneasy and embarrassed. The captain's response to the crisis suggests extreme neuroticism. On the first morning, when he can eat nothing at breakfast, he already has to confess 'the dual working of my mind distracted me almost to the point of insanity'. The mental experience of being in two places at once affects him physically, 'as if the mood of secrecy had penetrated my soul'. He so far forgets himself that having occasion to ask the mate, who is standing by his side, to take a compass bearing on the Pagoda, he reaches up to his ear in whispers. A little later he startles the helmsman by moving to look at the compass with a stealthy gait as if he were in a sick room. He admits he had crept 'quietly as near insanity as any man who has not actually gone over the border'. Such lack of self-control hardly justifies those commentators who deduce that through the ordeal he proves his manhood. His reaction to the test is extraordinary, quite different from that of a brave man tackling a dangerous adventure. On one occasion he says of Leggatt: 'But there was nothing sickly in his eyes or in his expression. He was not a bit like me, really.' This is a surprising admission from the narrator. It implies that the captain has something sickly in his temperament; his antics with the mate and helmsman suggest confrontation with his alter ego shocks his soul to its very depth.

Leggatt claims the murder was justified. In a letter to Galsworthy, Conrad expressed shock that anyone should consider Leggat to be a murderous ruffian. Baines describes how Conrad deliberately toned down the details of the crime which he took from an actual incident on the *Cutty Sark.* The mate of the *Cutty Sark* was a despotic character with a sinister reputation, who killed an incompetent negro with a blow of a capstan bar. In contrast, Leggatt seems a model officer, whose bravery when he set the reefed foresail saved the ship. He strangled the insubordinate member of the crew in a fit of blind rage, dazed and eventually unconscious of what he was doing under the force of the huge wave that came over the side. The captain-narrator ascribes the murder to a justifiable sense of desperation: 'The same strung-up force which had given twenty-four men a chance, at least, for their lives, had, in a sort of recoil, crushed an unworthy mutinous existence.'

At sea it is arguable that any act, even murder, committed to the end of keeping the ship afloat is moral. Leggatt has proved adequate where the true captain, Archbold, failed, and Archbold tries to cover up his weakness, his immorality in terms of the sea, by committing Leggatt to be hanged by the law of the land. Leggatt correctly judges that twelve respectable tradesmen in England will never comprehend the violent extremities necessitated by the morality of the sea.

And yet Leggatt's crime is not presented as just a fit of temper, and there are certain peculiar aspects to this outburst of violence. Leggatt behaves like a man possessed. He takes the insolent seaman by the throat, and goes on shaking him like a rat. When the great wave comes overboard, ten minutes are supposed to elapse before the two men are found together jammed behind the forebits. Leggatt tells the narrator: 'It's clear that I meant business, because I was holding him by the throat still when they picked us up. He was black in the face.' The crew are at first unable to prise Leggatt's fingers loose from around his victim's neck, and it is some time before he recovers consciousness. It is as if at this moment of heroic trial and endeavour his will has been abandoned to primitive, destructive urges. For a moment we may recall Kurtz, the apostle of the Savage God. Both Captain Archbold and his crew react to the killing as an event of unnatural horror, as though these ordinary, unexceptional seamen had been granted a glimpse of another dimension of being. Leggatt compares the crash of the wave to the sky falling on his head. The sea had gone mad: 'I suppose the end of the world will be something like that.' Like Kurtz, Leggatt is a man whose courage has carried him outside civilized restraints, to confront a moment of ultimate truth beyond the ken of normal social conventions.

Leggatt's case suggests that human survival depends on energetic self-assertion, and that men of his exceptional calibre may find themselves taken over by the desire for criminal violence. He admits that if he had tried to break out of his cabin when he was imprisoned on the *Sephora* he might have been forced to kill again. He explains that after his door had been left unlocked, and he had swum away from the ship, he was determined not to be dragged back 'fighting like a wild beast'. He is compared to Cain, and however much we sympathize with him, we must acknowledge that he is a man who would always kill to save himself from death. When the captain narrator himself is forced to act, and to make the crew comply with his orders to turn the ship about, he shakes the mate's arm violently, and goes on shaking it, rather as Leggatt shakes the seaman he kills. This story conveys no simple faith in the values of the good seaman. As in *Heart of Darkness,* the man of action submits himself to the ambiguous claims of the destructive element.

And so we come to the climax of the story, the captain's decision to sail his ship dangerously and unnecessarily close to the shore of Koh-ring. As usual in Conrad, we are given hints and possibilities rather than one clear motive. The captain sympathizes with Leggatt's isolation after the murder, and by the rash act of sailing close to the shore tries to give him a convincing demonstration of moral support. As Leggatt swims away he will appreciate the reason for this gesture, and this will console him later as he wanders barefoot under the alien sun. Is this what the captain means when he reiterates that 'it was now a matter of conscience to shave the land as close as possible'? But was such an extraordinary risk essential merely to encourage Leggatt with an expression of sympathy? If we take this as a sign of the captain's commitment to a fellow human being, then we must also accept that he endangers the lives of his crew in the process.

We must deduce that the captain sails close to Koh-ring because of some psychological necessity in his own being. He needs to prove his manhood by this act of self-assertion. He wants to behave in a daring and apparently irrational manner because of deep subjective needs he himself never seems properly to understand. Two contradictory attitudes are possible to this decision. We might argue that the captain identifies himself with Leggatt as an exceptional man who has courageously demonstrated that greatness involves the breaking of the social conventions, the law of the land. The captain proves to himself that he is not a rigid automaton, blindly obeying the seaman's code, but that he too in exceptional circumstances will take exceptional measures, wherever they may lead. But does this argument mean that action outside social conventions involves a submission to violence and irrationality? Is not the captain proving himself a dangerous lunatic who should never be given charge of a ship again? What evidence is there that he will never behave so foolishly a second time? And if we approve of his daring act, then do we agree that he would be right to repeat it on a comparable occasion? Anyone who holds that argument should be asked if he would like to travel as a passenger with the captain-narrator on the bridge.

As usual, this ambiguous treatment of heroic action reflects the tension in Conrad's own mind between loyal service to the seaman's code and a sense that his artistic nature and beliefs involve repudiation of social conventions. This imaginative obsession determines the symbolism of Koh-ring. The hill hangs over the crew 'like a towering fragment of the everlasting night'. The ship glides towards this enormous mass of blackness like 'a bark of the dead floating in slowly under the very gate of Erebus'. Once again Conrad depicts the journey towards the moment of truth, of self-recognition, as a voyage into the country of the dead. Just as in the opening description the tug appears swallowed up by the land, so the captain feels his ship is about to be 'swallowed up' by the shadow of Koh-ring. He confronts fearlessly the ultimate extinction of the subjective consciousness, the annihilation of human forms. By sailing as close as possible to the blackness, he proves that, unlike Lord Jim, he will never be rendered impotent by the vision of an ultimate meaninglessness. After this initiation, the man of imagination is fit to rule as captain. He forgets the secret stranger as he attends to the business of taking his ship away from danger: 'Already the ship was drawing ahead. And I was alone with her. Nothing! no one in the world should stand now between us, throwing a shadow on the way of silent knowledge and mute affection, the perfect communion of a seaman with his first command.'

And yet there is a sense of loss. The captain has enjoyed a special relationship with Leggatt which now is ended (and there is no need to support this argument by finding hints of homosexuality). The Freudian interpretation is that the ship is feminine, and the captain can now accept a mature sexual role, having purged the guilty shadow of the father. But Leggatt's status as hero and criminal, and his disappearance towards Koh-ring, the country of the dead, arouse other responses in the reader's imagination. The daring act of sailing the ship too close to shore seems to act like an exorcism for the captain. Leggatt has involved him in experiences which have brought him close to insanity, and which have demonstrated that his secret imaginative life might throw him completely off balance. He rids himself of this area of experience by depositing Leggatt at the very gate of Erebus. Is it possible that the efficient captain of the future will have forfeited the imaginative side of his nature which made him exceptional?

The last line rings out with apparent confidence, yet only adds to our uncertainties. Our last glimpse of Leggatt is of a man lowering himself in the water to take his punishment: 'a free man, a proud swimmer striking out for a new destiny'. Is the captain in future to live a life confined and circumscribed by the seaman's code? Should we in contrast prefer to admire the free man who in isolation, carrying his knowledge of guilt, makes a new destiny outside the security of civilization? Is it perhaps true that this story meant so much to Conrad because it enacted his own need to exorcize his mirror-image, to jettison those fantasies of alienation and suicidal loneliness which were disturbing his own balance of mind?

Dinshaw M. Burjorjee (essay date 1975)

SOURCE: "Comic Elements in Conrad's *The Secret Sharer*," in *Conradiana*, Vol. VII, No. 1, 1975, pp. 51-61.

[*In the following essay, Burjorjee demonstrates the presence of comic elements in* "The Secret Sharer."]

> Ere Babylon was dust,
> The Magus Zoroaster, my dead child,
> Met his own image walking in the garden.
> That apparition, sole of men, he saw.
> For know there are two worlds of life and death:
> One that which thou beholdest; but the other
> Is underneath the grave, where do inhabit
> The shadows of all forms that think and live
> Till death unite them and they part no more . . .
>   *Prometheus Unbound*

The Earth's adjuration to Prometheus in Shelley's lyrical drama reflects the solemnity of much of the criticism on Joseph Conrad's **"The Secret Sharer."** Certainly, the best of these criticisms are oriented towards, and succeed in, eliciting those psychological, symbolical, and metaphysical dimensions in **"The Secret Sharer"** which give it complexity and depth. Yet, unfortunately, such exegeses of an exclusively high seriousness inevitably relegate to the shadows a vital element in this work—comedy.

Unquestionably, Conrad's **"The Secret Sharer,"** written sixty years ago, is a work which still satisfies the modern reader because of its complex integration of a number of enduring themes—the young Captain faces up to a delicate moral problem; he tests himself in a self-initiation in his quest for identity; and he exercises the greatest humanity toward a fugitive from a system in which he is himself an archetypal figure of isolated authority quite easily susceptible to dehumanization. Besides, its elements, cohering in the relationship of the young Captain and Leggatt, inspire it (intentionally or otherwise) with a relucent quality which responds to the darker rays of psychological illumination. These psychological considerations, including the abnormal, are the heavy interest of those who wish to penetrate the "darkness thrown by a towering black mass like the very gateway of Erebus." Their claim to do so cannot be denied, but for those who prefer to bask in the sunlit expanses of **"The Secret Sharer"** the signpost is "Comedy."

Few will deny that there is a current of humour in this perhaps most happily civilized and youthfully exuberant of his sea stories which Conrad has imbued with, one might say, a Meredithian spirit. **"The Secret Sharer"** rebuts the charge against Conrad, typified in H. G. Wells's doubly-barbed report of Conrad's first encounter with G. B. Shaw, that he lacked the native feeling for English humour:

> When Conrad first met Shaw in my house, Shaw talked with his customary freedoms. "You know, my dear fellow, your books won't *do*"—for some Shavian reason I have forgotten—and so forth.
>
> I went out of the room and suddenly found Conrad on my heels, swift and white- faced. "Does that man want to insult me?" he demanded.
>
> The provocation to say "Yes" and assist at the subsequent duel was very great, but I overcame it. "It's humor," I said, and took Conrad out into the garden to cool. One could always baffle Conrad by saying "humour." It was one of our damned English tricks he had never learnt to tackle.

It is true that in his earlier work the same Conrad who wrote with "brilliant rhetorical effects" was also, and understandably, so uncertain of the commonest English syntax that he wrote such sentences as "I understood, then, what meant this illusion of ghostly murmurs. . . . " However, by the time **"The Secret Sharer"** was written, there were very few traces of foreign infusions, if any, in Conrad's phrases. The English language had by that time completely adopted Conrad, who, unlike the *métèque,* never strained after merely startling effects of style. Of **"The Secret Sharer"** Conrad himself said, "Every word fits and there's not a single uncertain note," and this confident assertion cannot be seriously questioned. Indeed the understatement in this perfect cameo among stories about the "double" is quite English and, if read with the right inflections, it imparts to **"The Secret Sharer"** the comic tone of which its unmistakably comic devices are adjuncts.

The more obvious comic devices in **"The Secret Sharer"** are its concealments and "disguises" which, beside the happy ending, are the stock-in-trade of the earliest comedies of intrigue. Dramatic situations which rely heavily, if not entirely, on suspenseful concealments or manipulat-ed encounters, assumed disguises or unsuspected resemblances, mistaken identities or changeling substitutions and the like are still used both on the stage and in literature. The double has, of course, been directed with varying degrees of intensity and success, to psychological purposes in the literature of a particular genre—for instance Poe's *William Wilson* (perhaps the great single influence on Oscar Wilde's *Picture of Dorian Gray*), Dicken's *A Tale of Two Cities,* Stevenson's *Dr. Jekyll and Mr. Hyde,* Haggard's *She,* Stoker's *Dracula,* and Dosteovsky's "The Double." Nevertheless, both devices—disguises and doubles—are the ancient appurtenances of comedies such as Plautus's *Menaechmi* and the principal dramaturgical props in Shakespeare's *Comedy of Errors* (and others of his plays), Sheridan's *School for Scandal* (as much a comedy of intrigue as it is a comedy of manners), Gilbert and Sullivan's *H.M.S. Pinafore* (and others of their operettas), Wilde's *The Importance of Being Earnest,* and Beerbohm's "The Happy Hypocrite," to instance a few. The devices of concealment and the double are put to serio-comic use in **"The Secret Sharer."** The whispered confabulations between the doubles, Leggatt's snatched meals of *pâté de foie gras* and asparagus, a sort of "musical chairs" between the stateroom and the bathroom in the young Captain's quarters to escape detection (over some six days), and the confrontation of the young Captain by the Captain of the *Sephora,* are redolent of a blending of *The Prisoner of Zenda* and *Box and Cox* (or *Charley's Aunt*).

The comic elements which are not so obvious are the action of **"The Secret Sharer,"** the caricatured oddity of its characters, and the eccentric diction in both its descriptions and its dialogues. First of all, the genesis of **"The Secret Sharer"** harks back to the *Cutty Sark* affair of 1880. This analogue for Conrad's story is, if anything, rather tragic, for it concerns an incident off the Straits of Sunda in which Sidney Smith, a "bucko mate" of the famous clipper (but very efficient and seaman-like), killed a member of the crew, a somewhat troublesome negro seaman named John Francis. This homicide was occasioned when, instead of executing Smith's orders smartly in Bristol fashion, Francis raised a capstan-bar to the mate. In the ensuing struggle Smith, wrenching the bar from Francis, hit him a blow on the head which killed him. The crew immediately became sullen, and made clear their desire for legal action against the mate. The skipper, Captain Wallace, however, felt that Smith had acted within his rights, and helped him jump ship at Hongkong, the next port. Thereupon, on the next leg of the voyage (to Yokohama) the crew, who suspected their Captain's connivance, became semi-mutinous in their resentment. Captain Wallace, a humane and cheery sort before this, was deeply affected by his crew's behaviour. In his depression, knowing that his crew were determined to get justice at Yokohama and would name him as an accomplice, the poor man became quite psychotic and committed suicide by walking off the deck of his ship into the sea.

Conrad could have treated his analogue quite tragically. Melville before him had transformed the sordid *Somers* mutiny of 1842 into his multi-dimensional tragedy, *Billy Budd.* Conrad had read, and written about, Melville but unlike that other great writer of those who go down to the sea in ships, he took a different tack and, in **"The Secret Sharer,"** gave his readers something also many-faceted and many-layered, but quite distinctly not tragic. A reading of the facts in the *Cutty Sark* affair establishes clearly the salient differences in Conrad's story which modulate in it the harshest elements of the action in its analogue.

One of the most important differences is that in **"The Secret Sharer"** Leggatt has killed a mutinous seaman "half crazed with funk," during the critical reefing of the foresail which, on the admission of Captain Archbold ("Under God—it did"), saved the *Sephora* from being pooped. There is no such storm in the *Cutty Sark* affair; according to Basil Lubbock there was "a nice wholesail breeze from the south-east." The exigencies of a violent storm which demanded the sternest seamanship so extenuate Leggatt's act that it cannot be classified unreservedly as murder. Leggatt's crime, *if it is a crime at all,* is not so heinous that it must ineluctably prohibit the young Captain from harbouring his double. Besides, Leggatt, unlike Smith in the analogue, has had to make his own escape. In the *Cutty Sark* affair Captain Wallace was, with far less cause, sympathetic enough to help his subordinate officer jump ship. In **"The Secret Sharer,"** however, Captain Archbold's prejudice in the case ("Mr. Leggatt, you have killed a man. You can act no longer as chief mate of this ship") and his fear of the crew ("He was afraid of the men") determine Leggatt to take other chances by going overboard. He had asked his Captain to help him, but Archbold's reply was " 'This thing must take its course. I represent the law here,' " and the representative of the law begins "shaking like a leaf." Even more amusing is his escape after the quivering representative of the law has confined him for nearly seven weeks. The *Sephora's* steward ("a dogmatic sort of loafer who hated me like poison") inadvertently leaves Leggatt's door unlocked, and he just "strolled out on the quarter-deck . . . kicked off [his] slippers and was in the water before he had made up his mind. . . . " When someone heard the splash, Leggatt says, "they raised an awful hullabaloo. 'He's committed suicide! No, he's swimming.' . . . I landed on the nearest islet before the boat left the ship's side." If the humour in this passage must be explained, it might be done perhaps in terms of the cry-harrow in Chaucer's "Nun's Priest's Tale" or the hullabaloo which, without fail, preceded the bumbling chases of the Keystone Cops. Finally, at the close of Conrad's story Captain, unlike the unfortunate Captain Wallace of the *Cutty Sark* whose suicide put an end to career and all, saves his double for a "new destiny," asserts his own new-found identity, and establishes "the perfect communion of a seaman with his first command." The action of **"The Secret Sharer"** is comedy inspirited with the "cheery cries" of the young Captain's crew which, in a hand less deft than Conrad's would have been the huzzas that bring the curtain down on *H.M.S. Pinafore.*

The characterization in **"The Secret Sharer"** is consistent with the comic element in its action. The young Captain is, in his own words, "the only stranger on board," and he wonders "how far [I] should turn out faithful to that ideal conception of one's own personality every man sets up for himself secretly." Anyone who is in new surroundings is at first all at sea. The actions, let alone idiosyncracies, of a newcomer in a group, which are seldom closely scrutinized after familiarity, lend themselves to exaggeration and caricature, especially when the newcomer, or *stranger,* assumes a position of near-absolute authority, as with the captain of a ship. The humour lies in the disparity between his crew's public conception and the young Captain's private self-appraisal of his personality. The romantic understands at once just why, after his ship has been anchored, the *young* Captain should direct the Chief Mate "to let all hands turn in without setting an anchor watch." He wishes to enjoy the solitude of his ship "till one o'clock or thereabouts," but such behaviour is alien to his entirely unimaginative crew, and the Second Mate, as much as the Chief, is astonished at this "unheard-of caprice." The ship's officers amuse the reader no less than the young Captain, because it is in their myopic vision that the apparent eccentricity of the skipper—the result of Leggatt's advent, the young Captain's decision to succour him, and his actions in so doing—is compounded.

As the young Captain says, "My action might have made me *appear* eccentric," but his Chief Mate is in fact eccentric. He is "absurdly whiskered," and to the simplest questions or statements—such as "Are you aware that there is a ship anchored inside the Islands?"—responds (with his "usual ejaculations"): "Bless my soul, sir! You don't say so!" The Chief Mate visibly evinces the "effect of collaboration on the part of his round eyes and frightful whiskers" in an attempt "to evolve a theory of the anchored ship." He is of "a painstaking turn of mind" and problems, such as the scorpion which drowned itself in the inkwell of his writing desk, "exercised him infinitely." Yet, later on, this figure of fun—"the whiskers" as the young Captain calls him—steals glances at his skipper "from below—for signs of lunacy or drunkenness. . . . "

If the Chief Mate is a caricature of elderly and ineffective first officers who cannot be depended upon by their skippers, the Captain of the *Sephora*—"his name . . . was something like Archbold"—is a literary creation with inheritances from Dickens, Cruikshank, and Daumier. "I represent the law here," he had said to Leggatt, and one might remark here, with Bumble in mind, that "the law is a ass!" The young Captain characterizes him by "a spiritless tenacity." Archbold's tenacity is parody of, say, Inspector Javert's in Hugo's *Les Misérables,* and he provokes laughter with his ponderous comment on Leggatt's crime: "I've never heard of such a thing happening in an English ship," as though such incidents were confined to merchant ships not flying the Red Duster. He does not question the obvious "mysterious similitude to the young fellow he had distrusted and disliked from the first," but is full of silent "mistrust" till the young Captain takes him through his stateroom. Archbold is the result of "seven-and-thirty virtuous years at sea, of which over twenty of immaculate command, and the last fifteen in the *Sephora, "* but he is a fool who will not admit that he could not, and did not, give the order to reef the foresail, and that Leggatt had saved his ship by giving it. For all his name, Archbold is a quavering ancient mariner and a parody of the self-confident young Captain after he has been initiated.

The actions and attitudes of the crews in both ships are no less humorous than those of the Chief Mate of the young Captain's ship and the skipper of the *Sephora.* The Second Mate, who is also young, shares his skipper's professional estimate of his First Mate—"I detected a slight quiver on his lips. I looked down at once. It was not my part to encourage sneering on board my ship"—but, unlike his youthful Captain, he is altogether too earnest. Later in the story "the lip of that confounded young cub quivered visibly" at the Captain himself and, when his Captain orders the opening of the quarter-deck ports, he makes "some jeering remark to the carpenter as to the sensible practice of ventilating the ship's quarter-deck." Persons of this sort, who are know-alls, are another species of ass which is lacking in good humour, who in comedies usually gets "taken down a peg or two." However, he is of less consequence than that "busily ministering spirit," the young Captain's Steward, "that harmless man" who poses the greatest threat to the young Captain's and Leggatt. Under happier circumstances (perhaps after the young Captain's success), he is usually a type of nautical Jeeves, but in **"The Secret Sharer"** the Steward scuttles about when "thundered" at. Comically, however, it is the young Captain who is just as "terrified at the sight" of him making for his cabin with his coat on his arm. The Steward is constantly in and out of the Captain's stateroom, and what is most humorous in the maneuverings to avoid discovery is that the poor man is subjected to "a maddening course of being shouted at, checked without rhyme or reason, arbitrarily chased out of [the Captain's] cabin, suddenly called into it, sent flying out of his pantry on incomprehensible errands, that accounted for the growing wretchedness of his expression." The Steward is demented in a Pavlovian situation given over to the Comic Muse.

Likewise, with regard to the crew of the *Sephora,* the keynote is dementia intensified. As Leggatt recounts it, the mutinous seaman was "half-crazed with funk"; the crew were "screaming 'Murder!' like a lot of lunatics"; the skipper, too, was "raving like the rest of them"; and when Leggatt came to himself the first thing he heard was "the maddening howling of that endless gale." Captain Archbold's manner reflects clearly that "the terror of the gale was on him yet." He is so unnerved that he can neither see, nor admit, the truth of the young Captain's explicit assertion that Leggatt had saved the *Sephora.* Instead, turning the remark—"That reefed foresail saved you"—which is distinctly intended to establish the correctness of Leggatt's actions, Archbold attributes the "setting of that sail" to "a special mercy" which had "God's own hand in it." As one once of those who invoke that particular Providence that "maketh the storm a calm," it is not my intention to denigrate Captain Archbold's exaltation of that "special mercy," but rather to focus attention on his ludicrous preoccupation with it at the cost of his ship and crew. On his own admission, he "hardly dared give the order," and one can scarcely expect Divine Providence, however well disposed, to reef a foresail in a storm. Archbold's failure of nerve sets off a chain of events which, despite the seriousness and urgency of its concerns, creates a darkly humorous situation in a lunatic *cosmos*—a parody of the storm in *The Tempest,* lashing a world peopled by characters who belong to the frenzied finales of some of Ionesco's plays and are brought to chaos by their human inanities.

Much of the diction in **"The Secret Sharer,"** especially in the dialogues, is indisputably comic. The verbal exchanges between Leggatt and his double are fraught with the psychological stresses of their peculiar predicament and the lurking danger of discovery, but they are invested with humour. Leggatt is possessed of a dry wit which manifests itself immediately upon his advent. No pathetic weakling, he is capable of badinage with the young Captain even about his own fate. The question "whether I am to let go this ladder and go on swimming till I sink from exhaustion, or—to come on board here" is *Hamlet* parodied. Later, when he recounts (with some relish) the commotion of his going over the *Sephora's* side—"Somebody heard the splash and they raised an awful hullabaloo. 'He's gone! Lower the boats! He's committed suicide! No, he's swimming.' "—he displays the same robust humour: "Certainly I was swimming. It's not so easy for a swimmer like me to commit suicide by drowning." The parson's son is capable of giving his biblical allusions—"The 'brand of Cain' business, don't you see"; "What does the Bible say? 'Driven off the face of the earth.' Very well, I am off the face of the earth now": and "Not naked like a soul on the Day of Judgement. I shall freeze on to this sleeping suit. The Last Day is not yet"—comic inflections by an associated remark like "It would never do for me to come to life again," an oblique, but palpable, hit at Archbold's spiritless piety.

When Leggatt asserts, rather than asks, "I suppose your captain's turned in?" the young Captain's reply is oddly flippant: "I am sure he isn't." Leggatt's response to his double's question, "Something wrong?" is only slightly less so: "Yes. Very wrong indeed," and he concludes his account of the *Sephora* incident with the remark, "Nice little tale for a quiet tea party." Of course it is not nice, not "a pretty thing to have to own up to for a Conway boy." However, the grimhumoured understatement in "a nice little tale for a quiet tea party" is quite intentional, as it is in Leggatt's remarks about his fate as a Cain, which in contrast is realistically, if hyperbolically, defined by the young Captain as being "hidden forever from all friendly faces, to be a fugitive and a vagabond on the earth, with no brand of the curse on his sane forehead to stay a slaying hand." Yet Leggatt is unconscious of the absurdity of his logic in "My father's a Norfolk parson. Do you see me before a judge and jury on that [murder] charge?" which is no less cross than Captain Archbold's in his strictures on the incident: "What would you think of such a thing happening on board your own ship? I've had the *Sephora* for these fifteen years. I am a well-known shipmaster." In both instances the ridiculous *non sequiturs* make one smile, if not laugh outright.

It is Leggatt who provides the solution for his own disposition: "You must maroon me as soon as ever you can get amongst these islands off the Cambodje shore." The idea of marooning a man in order to save him is quaintly ironic, but it also makes the opportunity for his double to interject rather vehemently, "Maroon you! We are not living in a boy's adventure tale." The young Captain's comment is of significant literary importance, since it is patently intended to steer the reader away from the shallower waters of a "boy's adventure tale." The heedless, largely comic, excitement in this story is contrapuntal to its sober initiation into command and its responsibilities which the young Captain had lost sight of until he "realized suddenly that all my future, the only future for which I was fit, would perhaps go irretrievably to pieces in any mishap to my first command." The young Captain, who we must not forget is also the narrator, is at pains to point out that this is not merely a "boy's adventure tale," but in so doing he cannot help drawing closer attention to the comedy which warms with a youthful human glow the coldly realistic illumination of what he stands to lose.

The conversation between the young Captain and Archbold is likewise underlaid with a rich vein of humour. **"The Secret Sharer"** obviously has great cinematic possibilities, and any one of the veteran English actors—Miles Malleson, Cyril Cusack, John Le Mesurier, etc.—would catch and exploit fully the lumbering comic inflections in Captain Archbold's phrases, such as "Painful duty," "Such a young man, too!" "God's own hand in it," and "Sui-cide! That's what I'll have to write to my owners directly I get in." Practically all of Archbold's lines beg the same kind of delivery, for instance "What would you think of such a thing happening on board your own ship? I've had the *Sephora* for these fifteen years. I am a well-known shipmaster"; "I have been at sea now, man and boy, for seven-and-thirty years, and I've never heard of such a thing happening in an English ship. And that it should be my ship. Wife on board, too;" and "He looked very smart, very gentlemanly, and all that. But do you know—I never liked him, somehow. I am a plain man." He may be "a plain man," but there is a "unique, guilty conscientious manner of sticking to the point," and in his inability to complete his parting remark to the young Captain, "I say . . . you . . . you don't think that—" Archbold ends with a comic whimper.

The "Bless my soul, sir! You don't say so's" of the "whiskers" conjoin with Captain Archbold's fatuous ponderosities to provide the comic conversational element which throws into sharp relief the *Leitmotifs* of capability and responsibility in **"The Secret Sharer."** In addition, the Chief Mate's real eccentricity, a foil to the young Captain's apparent "lunacy or drunkenness," gives the Second Mate ("that unplayful cub") the occasions for lip-quivering criticisms, tacit and overt, of his senior officer's capacities, a foretaste of those moments when the young Captain orders the ship closer inshore (ostensibly to catch the land wind). The tension of those crucial minutes is given a comic dimension by the Chief Mate's lamenting distrust of the young Captain's seamanship. He makes "as if to tear his hair," and addresses his skipper recklessly: "She will never get out. You have done it, sir. I knew it'd end in something like this. She will never weather, and you are too close now to stay. She'll drift ashore before she's round. O my God!" The helmsman responds to his Captain's commands with "a frightened, thin, childlike voice," while the Chief mate "wailed" that the ship is "ashore already." The young Captain shakes the older man as if he were a fractious child: "I hadn't let go the

mate's arm and went on shaking it. 'Ready about, do you hear? you go forward'—shake—'and stop there'—shake—'and hold your noise'—shake—'and see these head-sheets properly overhauled'—shake, shake—shake." The naughty boy is silenced till the ship comes about to "the cheery cries" of the crew and only after, regaining his lost composure, "the frightful whiskers made themselves heard giving various orders." The Chief Mate's lugubrious dissuasions are the last obstacle which the young Captain overcomes, so that he can declare confidently that "Nothing! no one in the world should stand now between us, throwing a shadow on the way of silent knowledge and mute affection, the perfect communion of a seaman with his first command."

The major criticism which evaluates **"The Secret Sharer"** as a stroy of initiation, or an account of an interior psychological journey, or a quest for identity, freedom, moral values and so on, almost without exception neglects the vital constituent of its comedy. When Conrad ignored the intensely tragic potential of his analogue, the *Cutty Sark* affair, he may have felt, with [W. K.] Wimsatt, that "tragedy has always had the crippling limitation of being only *high*," whereas "comedy (or at least a range of several things called 'comedy') can be either high or low" [*The Idea of Comedy*, 1969]. The result, at any rate was felicitous. The happy ending is by no means mawkish. Despite the deterministic rigours of life, men do have their successes and are clearly able to demonstrate that they are not all creatures of circumstance. Indeed, like Nicky Garnet in Somerset Maugham's short story, the young Captain (who also could have "burnt his fingers") triumphs over "The Facts of Life." Is not there even a suggestion that, as the narrator, the young Captain is thumbing his nose while telling his story? He certainly revels in telling it and detailing the humours of its characters. Their humours (including his own apparent eccentricity) and their drollness, as he depicts them, provide the comic counterpoint throughout the action.

This comic counterpoint, far from damaging the action, brings into sharper relief the psychological effects of the Doppelgänger in the story. At the same time it alleviates the sombre Dostoevskian bitterness of its moral thrust with a Meredithian vision of life which is "humane" and "an achievement of man as a social being." Albert J. Guerard, who has collected in a slim volume just two of Conrad's stories and no other—*The Heart of Darkness* and **"The Secret Sharer"**—says in its introduction that the two stories belong together because they "alike exploit the ancient myth or archetypal experience of the 'night journey,' of a provisional descent into the primitive and unconscious sources of being." There is surely a more obvious reason why they belong together. If *The Heart of Darkness* is, as Guerard maintains, Conrad's most "intense expression of [his] mature pessimism," then **"The Secret Sharer"** is a good-humoured and joyful paean to youthful idealism, its optimistic aspirations, and its not infrequent success. In this respect, it certainly "beats all these tales we hear about murders in Yankee ships."

Joan E. Steiner on Conrad's use of the "double" in "The Secret Sharer":

While the doubling here is, in some respects, less complicated than that in some of Conrad's other works, such as *Heart of Darkness* and *Victory,* it confirms his thorough mastery of a convention that had already undergone considerable development in the hands of his nineteenth-century predecessors. By using the double as the central image in a tale exploring a number of ostensibly clear-cut dualities and, simultaneously and paradoxically, as the focus of persistent ambiguities that blur those dualities, Conrad transforms the device into one peculiarly his own.

Joan E. Steiner, in her "Conrad's 'The Secret Sharer': Complexities of the Doubling Relationship," in Conradiana, *1980.*

Steve Ressler (essay date 1988)

SOURCE: "*The Secret Sharer*: Affirmation of Action," in *Joseph Conrad: Consciousness and Integrity,* New York University Press, 1988, pp. 80-97.

[*In the following excerpt, Ressler offers his interpretation of "The Secret Sharer," noting that the exploration of individual morality is Conrad's major concern in the story.*]

In late November, early December 1909, Conrad put aside the unfinished *Under Western Eyes,* which he had been working on for the past two years, and began **"The Secret Sharer,"** completing it in less than a month. He then resumed *Under Western Eyes* and brought it to an end; the typescript is dated "End. 22 Jan. 1910." Even more than the overlapping period of composition, internal evidence suggests a special relationship between the short story and the end of the novel. For psychological and creative reasons, to relieve the burden of consciousness and find release and inspiration in self-affirming action, it was essential for Conrad to compose **"The Secret Sharer"** before he could finish the unsparing, artistically inevitable *Under Western Eyes* to which his major themes point. The Russian novel is a resolution of major proportions, a working out in ultimate terms of fundamental conflicts, particularly the themes of betrayal, guilt, punishment, and redemption. In **"The Secret Sharer,"** Conrad's treatment of these concerns is open-ended, resulting in a future for the two comrades that is problematic but to which Conrad extends a deserved hope. In *Under Western Eyes* Conrad carries these fictional ideas to their limit, stamping them with a sense of conclusiveness. Furthermore, Conrad realizes in Razumov his maturest conception of integrity, central to which is growth of consciousness, a quality noticeably absent in the captain. The unsentimental but questionable affirmation which closes the sea tale is better understood if **"The Secret Sharer"** is seen as the romantic counterpart to the tragic *Under Western Eyes.* Other elements in these contiguous works contribute to this sense of complementarity: the maritime sphere and the problems of leadership as against the urban milieu and the realm of politics; up-

holding a direct appeal for trust in contrast with Razumov's cowardice and infidelity to Haldin. But the most telling difference is in their respective endings: youth advancing confidently into the future set against Razumov's terrible futurelessness. Two controlling factors in **"The Secret Sharer"** help account for Conrad's moral attitudes as well as this concluding note of hope, a rare feature in Conrad's best art. There is an absence of the usual Conradian skepticism, primarily because of Conrad's use of an "unintellectual" first-person narrator; by not exerting ironic or moral pressure on his spokesman, Conrad lessens the severity of his tragic vision. (Only Archbold suffers its full brunt.) And second, an impulse which flows from this absence, Conrad places a decided emphasis on courageous action to the subordination of moral consciousness.

At the outset of his initiatory journey, understandably anxious because of first command, the novice is profoundly unready for leadership. Beneath a posture of youthful assurance exist inexperience, doubt, a vague sense of self, and an imagination given to romanticizing and abstraction. Despite some resentment and suspicion, the crew cannot know and the captain himself cannot appreciate just how dangerously vulnerable he is. Protective self-ignorance, reinforced by vanity, is matched by a naiveté of outlook; he thinks reality safe and reasonable, the sea and men predictable and moderate. Other details more strongly call into question his moral fitness. It is hinted that this choice of a career of presumed moral simplicity is partly an evasion from the snares, duplicity, and uncertainty that the captain ascribes solely to the land. He is defensive about how he received his commission ("In consequence of certain events of no particular significance, except to myself, I had been appointed to the command only a fortnight before"), and this guarded tone suggests his uneasiness that factors other than deserved merit, the usual steady rise up the ranks, were instrumental in his assignment. (Leggatt was taken on through connections, and suspect circumstances were involved in the placements of Marlow and Kurtz in *Heart of Darkness.*) As he confesses to Leggatt, "I had been appointed to take charge while I least expected anything of the sort." Callowness is associated invariably with an unpreparedness for critical experience, but Conrad does not view such unreadiness leniently or absolve one from accountability because of youth. When do the weaknesses linked to callowness become the character flaws in an older person? For example, when does an adolescent self-absorption become blinding egotism, unsophistication of mind become willful ignorance or irresponsibility, inexperience become a calculated evasion of significant encounter? Conrad uses the unpreparedness of his heroes to set the stage for a radical test of character. In unreadiness, all past safeguards, of ordinary consciousness, of habitual responses, of vanity, prove unavailing; life seems to expose and bear down unerringly on just those facets of self which make the risk of failure most acute. For anyone with claims to integrity, the ensuing conflict is inescapable and total, and Leggatt's coming plunges the beginner into just such a trial.

Conrad provides numerous signs that Leggatt is to be regarded as a symbolic manifestation of the captain's unconscious, his being a physical double both suggesting and reinforcing unconscious connections. The night setting, the captain in sleeping grab, his mood of reverie and intro-spection evoke the world of dreams. Prompted by a feeling of strangeness, he dismisses the anchor watch and assumes the post himself, an unusual disruption of established routine which startles the crew. His unaccountable behavior is responsible for leaving the rope ladder over the side, the link of communication which brings Leggatt to him, and in this way the captain may be said to have invited his visitor. Leggatt remarks that the captain seemed to have expected him. The swimmer appears to rise from the depths of the sea, a universal symbol of the unconscious, to the surface, to conscious life. Feeling weight on the ladder, the commander peers over the rail and sees an eerie, ghostly-glowing shape. "He was complete but for the head. A headless corpse." And the observer's head completes the figure. Just from their initial exchange of words, the captain senses a "mysterious communication" established between them, suggesting an intuition of a special kinship. Leggatt is a messenger, a "legate," an emissary of the unconscious come to confront the apprentice with unrealized aspects of himself, a harbinger of the captain's future, an inspirer who helps promote the becoming of identity.

In the sense that the visitor corresponds uncannily to the wished-for male image, one might say that the captain has dreamed Leggatt into existence. To act forcefully when it matters most is what the tyro questions in himself, admires and envies in his confederate. On one level, as [Albert] Guerard argues [in his introduction to *Heart of Darkness and The Secret Sharer,* 1950], Leggatt is "the embodiment of a more instinctive, more primitive, less rational self," but simultaneously he is an ideal possibility for the captain, an inspiration and example, an epitome of leadership. As the stranger announces his name, the narrator thinks, "The voice was calm and resolute. A good voice. The self-possession of that man had somehow induced a corresponding state in myself." Later, the captain admires Leggatt's ability to plot his escape from the *Sephora* during his six-week captivity: "And I could imagine perfectly the manner of this thinking out—a stubborn if not a steadfast operation; something of which I should have been perfectly incapable." Significantly, when escape does occur, Leggatt describes it as his giving in to a sudden temptation as he dived off the ship and was in the water before he fairly made up his mind. The captain's marked agitation after the steward's near-discovery of the stow-away in the bathroom is in sharp contrast to Leggatt's steady self-control, a bearing that causes the observer to marvel "at that something unyielding in his character which was carrying him through so finely." That composure under duress can hearten another sympathetically is a truism, not at all unfamiliar to Conrad's pages. A simple expression of this effect, for example, is in *Typhoon.* Fearfully shaken during the hurricane, Jukes experiences a resurgence of confidence and self-belief at Captain Mac-Whirr's steadfastness, his conviction that the way to get through the worst seas is to run with the wind, to face it and keep a cool head.

In *A Personal Record,* Conrad describes a decisive episode during which the sight of "an ardent and fearless traveller" infused his demoralized adolescent self with re-newed spirit. On holiday in 1873, the fifteen-year-old Conrad saw a vigorous Englishman marching through the Furca Pass as he sat nearby dejected before his tutor's arguments against his taking to sea.

> Was he in the mystic ordering of common events the ambassador of my future, sent out to turn the scale at a critical moment on the top of an Alpine, pass, with the peaks of the Bernese Oberland for mute and solemn witnesses? His glance, his smile, the unextinguishable and comic ardour of his striving-forward appearance helped me to pull myself together. . . . I had been feeling utterly crushed. It was the year in which I had first spoken aloud of my desire to go to sea.

Conrad's epithet for him, "the ambassador of my future," even in name suggests Leggatt, another manly envoy come unexpectedly to inspire a youth in his vocation. In the memoir, Conrad gives an imaginative and life-shaping importance to the whole Furca Pass incident, rounding off the experience by noting that eleven years later he became a master in the British Merchant Service.

Both Leggatt's calm and capacity for spontaneous action are vital to the commander's ideal conception of himself. "There are to a seaman certain words, gestures, that should in given conditions come as naturally, as instinctively as the winking of a menaced eye. A certain order should spring on to his lips without thinking; a certain sign should get itself made, so to speak, without reflection." Experience and habitual performance help create the naturalness of professional conduct; such unity implies surety of self, a confident relation to the inner life. Obviously, as with the captain, dissociation from one's interior being can induce debilitating conflict. At the same time, Conrad suggests that stalwartness and self-command draw upon instinctive vitality, just as the demonic and savage have their source in primitive impulses. "The same strung-up force which had given twenty-four men a chance, at least, for their lives, had, in a sort of recoil, crushed an unworthy mutinous existence." This amoral energy can help carry a man through in a crisis, but it can also cause self-abandon. Leggatt strangles the mutineer in a "fit of temper" as a huge sea wave smashes over the pair, the chief mate's engulfing aggression paralleling the fury of nature. Leggatt has a forcefulness that can break through all restraint, and Conrad implies that the unconscious has the power to move a man into actions both brave and lawless. One intellectual advance from earlier works in Conrad's conception of the unconscious is a recognition of its beneficial potential, acknowledging it as a source of strength and not (as most notably in *Heart of Darkness*) as something primarily to be feared and repressed in civilized man, associated with the illicit and self-destructive.

On the face of it, the captain's protection of the escapee seems to present an acute conflict between Conrad's private and public values. An outlaw's appeal for trust and another chance is set in direct opposition to maritime law. That the captain acts out of "psychological (not moral) reasons" is entirely convincing. Not all commentators accept this line of argument. Consequently, the apparent merger of Conrad with his persona and what this effect means about Conrad's attitude toward Leggatt (the narrator takes no moral stance) leave many critics uneasy, if not baffled. For example, Donald Yelton writes [in *Mimesis and Metaphor,* 1967] that "the narrator does not pronounce against Leggatt's act; and I do not find that Conrad, by any device of irony or multiple perspective, implies any moral judgment beyond the judgment (or suspension of judgment) of the narrator." [H. M.] Daleski states [in *Joseph Conrad: The Way of Dispossession,* 1977] that critical readers cannot "unreservedly accept the captain-narrator's easy condonation of him [Leggatt]; but this is the judgment that the author, limited here to the point of view of his narrator and not having any recourse to irony, would appear to want us to make." The question is not made any less perplexing by the observable impression that conduct motivated by sympathetic identification *seems* like an expression of moral endorsement. What more could the captain do for Leggatt, one asks, if he sanctioned his actions throughout? An additional knot: if one grants an incapacitated moral sense during the actual experience, one must note that in recapitulating the events, the captain offers no moral perspective. Drawn to Jim, Marlow could criticize him simultaneously.

Though the young officer might not consider himself bound to confront the moral dimensions of his conduct, Conrad by no means evades those issues, which are dealt with implicitly. Doubtless, the law would not recognize the captain's psychological reasons as exculpatory, compelling as they are. However, Conrad forces us to weigh the question of illegality (harboring a fugitive) and reckless endangerment (the Koh-ring venture) against the possible consequences if the captain had not become Leggatt's ally. To say nothing serious need have happened is to disregard Conrad's terms: the novice's romantic misperceptions and self-ignorance, crew members verging on disrespect (slack authority led to the fatal eruption on the *Sephora*), inner defect (Archbold breaks after thirty-seven years of service, Leggatt kills a man), and nature's ferocity and treacherous calm. To the charge that the narrator is irresponsible in not getting to know the crew and ship, it can be answered that such intimacy is impossible in his present condition with Leggatt on board. And even if the runaway had not appeared, familiarizing himself with his command would not reach his depths of unease, would not rouse in him the urgency to act upon the real danger posed by his deficient knowledge. The strain of concealing Leggatt exacerbates a divisiveness he had from the outset, but to the crew he seems as peculiar as when he first boarded. He performs minimum duties and gets by because nothing demanding is called for. Enforcing a mood of indeterminacy and anxious waiting, the oppressive heat and faint breezes in the gulf invite the reader to suspend judgment as the captain retreats inwardly. Leggatt brings matters to a head, so to speak, and as a result the captain gains a psychological preparation and sense of crisis which enables him to initiate the Koh-ring maneuver and carry it through with disciplined authority.

The idea of acting for psychological and not moral reasons is critical to the story and helps clarify other important encounters of a similar nature in Conrad. For example, I see no moral content in Jim's release of an armed Brown.

Whatever ethical judgment Jim may have been capable of is corrupted by sympathetic identification with Brown, by a need to repress guilt, by cowardice and egotism. Similarly, to argue that Razumov aids Haldin initially out of "compassion"—which carries an aura of the moral—is to oversimplify and sentimentalize Conrad. Had Razumov a genuine belief in his convictions, clear-sightedness, and courage, he could—without regret and with unassailable justification—have ordered Haldin from his room once the assassin began explaining himself. Sympathetic identification, invariably with the outcast or law-breaker, derives its considerable power and complexity from unconscious connections. Indeed, when intellectual or moral affinity is absent, as in the Jim-Brown and Razumov-Haldin pairings where trust is misplaced, sympathetic identification can have the gravest consequences. Fidelity to the double has to do with remaining faithful to aspects of, and possibilities intrinsic to, oneself. The real difficulty arises when the leading character of the two harbors a corrupt element of self, e.g., unresolved guilt, masked cowardice, a form of morally ambiguous romanticism which he has not examined or is not prepared to repudiate. However, no such complication obtains in the captain's situation because he has not yet failed. The violative act in Conrad is a crime exposed to the public which simultaneously is an offense against conscience, often repressed. This condition does not apply to the captain. He has no reservations about his confederate (the story, however, dramatizes a moral distinction); trust is honored; and though the captain's psychological stress is increased drastically, the end result of the relationship is mutually beneficial. Leggatt's astonishing physical likeness to his rescuer makes the latter's identification with him immediate and serves to reinforce deeper bonds. Conrad is here making explicit the key feature of sympathetic identification: intense involvement with a part of self. One has only to recall Marlow's profound affinity for Kurtz to realize that physical similarity, while having a decided impact, is not essential to such a relationship. Leggatt and the captain are "doubles" regardless of looks. Nevertheless, their external resemblance, insisted upon by Conrad, reminds us constantly that the captain is in the grip of a compelling and unrelieved fascination, a mixture of passivity and wonder, which nullifies autonomy. Conrad's emphasis on doubleness is an important strategy for persuading us that moral judgment does not enter into the commander's conduct, encouraging us not to question his untroubled conscience over union with a fugitive.

Links of kinship exist other than appearance and background. I have already discussed Leggatt as the captain's ideal. An immediate point of communion is their common situation vis-à-vis their respective ship's company. The captain's position of being an isolated outsider regarded with suspicion is pushed to an ugly extreme in Leggatt's case. Though appointed through family influence and not engaged directly by Archbold, Leggatt faces an outright antagonism that has less to do with resentment engendered by nepotism than with the threat he poses to the unofficial governing arrangements because of Archbold's lapsed authority. "He was afraid of the men, and also of that old second mate of his . . . a gray-headed old humbug; and his steward, too . . . a dogmatic sort of loafer who hated me like poison, just because I was the chief mate. No chief mate ever made more than one voyage in the *Sephora,* you know. Those two old chaps ran the ship." Having his wife on board is a Conradian telltale of Archbold's unfitness. In such circumstances, Leggatt is substantially the responsible power of the ship. Flinching before the need to use the foresail is the dramatic culmination of Archbold's eroded leadership. Conrad's case against the aging married seaman is damaging indeed. The captain's grey-striped sleeping suit, a duplicate of which he gives Leggatt, resembles a convict's uniform and evokes the wearers' outcast and adversary status, implies that the captain is becoming increasingly a prisoner of his own fears, and signifies that in fact, if not in conscience, he is guilty of breaking the law. Up against the reality of a wrecked career, Leggatt is living out the captain's deepest insecurities. Protecting the symbolic failed self becomes a means of succoring himself in defeat, of warding off his own potential ruin, and of drawing sustenance from the living proof that spirit can remain unbroken despite crushing odds. Increasingly, the captain's fate, like his identity, begins to merge with that of the other. Obviously, discovery of the stowaway would all but destroy the captain professionally and expose to official inquiry his self-misgivings, but more subtly, if Leggatt cannot gain reprieve, this shutting down may in some essential way foreclose the future for the captain as well, strike fatally at his root sources of being. Both their destinies, it turns out, hinge on Koh-ring. In embracing the pariah, the captain has unconsciously begun to shape the crucial opportunity for himself, the decisive act of mastery and courage.

What the protagonist sees as injurious in his bonding with Leggatt is not the violent inner conflict it induces, the near-insanity of a divided nature, but rather his excessive dependency, which he recognizes as a form of cowardice. When Leggatt advances the idea that he must depart, the captain exclaims, "You can't!" Immediately, however, he catches himself and reflects:

> I felt suddenly ashamed of myself. I may say truly that I understood—and my hesitation in letting that man swim away from my ship's side had been a mere sham sentiment, a sort of cowardice.

The sentiment was false because self-indulgent, a clinging need for security and comfort springing from the fear of facing his ordeal alone. That wishes and feelings can take on the psychic equivalent of deeds is unarguable, but here Conrad implies that shameful feelings can have a private reality which is the moral equivalent of a deed. Such an extreme standard contains a streak of fanaticism, an exigency for a purified, heroic self. To sustain this lofty self against the assaults of experience is all but impossible. This romantic pursuit, however, is a rich imaginative inspiration for Conrad, and he follows it to its end point (cf. the fates of Marlow in *Heart of Darkness,* Jim, Gould, Nostromo, Haldin). Part of the urgency behind the daring hunt for land breezes is the captain's need to redeem himself from this lapse into cowardice. "It was now a matter of conscience to shave the land as close as possible—for now he must go overboard whenever the ship was put in stays. Must! There could be no going back for him." There

was never any doubt as to Leggatt striking out for freedom, and I think the imperative here is self-directed, an exhortation to make the necessary rupture, to authenticate self by severing the incapacitating dependency he has developed for his twin.

If one contends that the Koh-ring enterprise is "irresponsible," by the same token Archbold is "overly-cautious" in not ordering the foresail set during the hurricane. To shun risk would have doomed the *Sephora.* There is for a captain a critical area of initiative and personal decision beyond rule book procedure and conventional thinking. And even where suitable methods have been codified, the commander must be able to discern their applicability and bring himself to follow them. With resignation unthinkable, the story argues that the captain's uncertainties, a threat to reliability and performance, can only be overcome through action. It goes without saying that a leader's miscalculation about himself or lack of self-faith jeopardizes the men under him. For the terms of selfhood the captain wants and obviously needs, there is no prudent course: to let matters stand would doubtless worsen his condition and further strain ship morale; to remain alert for an eventual danger rather than force the issue would be psychologically wearing and a dubious strategy for confronting life. The captain is primed now, the moment is there to be seized. Desire converges with opportunity, aspiration rushes against fear. Conrad implies that in the field of action, with a participant caught up in the immediacy of experience, a standard of moral scrupulousness cannot be pressed. Abstract right in this in stance will not serve. The issue is not one of calculated pragmatism since the captain can hardly be said to have acted with premeditation. What the story rewards and what a favorable outcome hinges on are values of heroism, disciplined self-mastery, spirited engagement, virtues of a warrior's code. This same problem of reaching a moral judgment as to the protagonist's means and ends, his apparently "egotistical" behavior during the heat of charged experience, is evident in Gould's threat to explode the mine in *Nostromo.* Both episodes are similar in that necessity and success seem to outweigh moral reservation.

Fear grips the captains as he drives the ship landward, but with a Leggatt-like aggressiveness, he presses nearer, determined that the ship will weather. What begins as a controlled risk develops rapidly into a crisis. As Porter Williams, Jr., emphasizes [in *PMLA,* December, 1964], with the ship only half-about in her turn windward and poised near the rocks, the newcomer does not know whether she has gathered sternway. Without such knowledge, he is in effect blind and cannot give an informed command. This eventuality was of course unforeseen. What prevents shipwreck is the success made possible by the "favorable accident" of the floppy hat. During the emergency, the whiskered and sneering mate, a double to the bearded Archbold—tenacious, rational, dogmatic—and reminiscent in diminished form of the insolent mutineer who challenged Leggatt, is reduced to whimpering helplessness, paralleling Archbold's funk. This moment of peak stress for the captain, hovering on the precipice and utterly alone in his position of responsibility, when panic could sweep the crew and absolute discipline is crucial for survival, duplicates the conditions faced by Leggatt in the gale. Shaking the mate's arm (Leggatt shook his antagonist like a rat) to jar him from his fear and compel obedience to orders gives some indication of the "strung-up force" within the captain, but paralysis rather than violent outburst seems the greater danger for him. So formidable are the demands of Conradian selfhood that one must undergo a test where all is at stake, an ordeal that brings one within a hair's breadth of the horror, to the very gates of darkness (Erebus) that lead to the hell of unredeemable moral failure. With the peril of Koh-ring scant yards away, the captain spots his white hat and reacts with that part of himself which is aware, responsible, disciplined. "And I watched the hat—the expression of my sudden pity for his mere flesh. . . . behold—it was saving the ship, by serving me for a mark to help out the ignorance of my strangeness." Self-pity not moral approval prompted the captain to give Leggatt his hat to shield him from the tropical sun because he suddenly imagined himself suffering the exile's desolation. The return of the hat implies a moral separation between the two selves, though a profound affinity cannot be denied. The man who had once "lost his head" must leave behind the hat, which becomes in context an emblem of conscience. Leggatt must return as he came, a "headless corpse," a being primarily physical and instinctual. When the captain thrust his hat on Leggatt, he thought of it as a protective headpiece. Conscience of course is that part of consciousness which protects a man from losing restraint. Because he pulls back at the critical point, the narrator earns the name of captain, fusing self with professional role.

Needless to say, Conrad's attitude toward Leggatt is far from simple. Whereas Jim blamed circumstance and his own unpreparedness, Leggatt does not throw off responsibility for homicide, but he will not permit himself to be judged by the community, especially a parson father who could not possibly understand. Though the idea of standing trial is repugnant to Leggatt, the factors arrayed against a strong legal defense seem well-nigh insuperable: the crew's hostility to the outsider, the more so now with one of their own killed, the extreme circumstances which make for fragmentary and unreliable reporting, Leggatt's setting of the foresail without due authorization, as well as Archbold's character, distinguished record, and sense of his own faintheartedness if not malfeasance. These considerations have the effect of gaining favor for the criminal and his decision to choose exile. However, [in *Conrad the Novelist*] Guerard warns against an undue sympathy for the man, cautions against identifying Conrad's attitude with Leggatt's strong-willed egotism. "Essential (from an officer's point of view) is his [Leggatt's] contempt for law, his feeling that innocence and guilt are private matters." Nevertheless, my own conclusion is that guilt, judgment, and punishment *are* ultimately personal concerns for Conrad, and I appreciate the powerful resistance, often taking baroque forms, which this authorial conviction generates in his art. As with Jim, Conrad does remove Leggatt from the service and send him out of the civilized world, but in this story and elsewhere, what emerges as fundamental to Conrad's morality is the preeminence of conscience over the claims of external authority. Conrad's attitude expresses an unyielding individualism, even if it be noted

that conscience for him is more exact and terrible than the law. On this score, Conrad's work prompts troubling reflections. For instance, one can accept legal and even personal responsibility for a crime without feeling remorse: one's sense of guilt may be shallow or unconscious or one may feel one has not debased conscience. The illicit need not correspond with one's sense of the unethical. Guilt may be felt for neurotic reasons, for reasons which society would not deem immoral, or for hidden reasons not linked causally to any one act. This terrain is Kafka's rather than Conrad's but certainly relevant to any study of guilt. And most tragically in Conrad, conscience becomes the last measure of humanity in a country whose legal system is unprincipled, an instrument of politics. Nevertheless, from a social point of view, particularly in a democracy, individual morality superseding collective values is dangerous and arbitrary. It will be observed, however, that none of Conrad's protagonists/violators escapes punishment, though the effective penalty is not through law or public disapproval.

Clearly, psychological accuracy and moral content are Conrad's absorbing interests rather than legal or public accountability. One may suppress guilt like Archbold or distance oneself physically from its reminders like Jim or refuse institutional judgment like Leggatt, but no man with claims to integrity can truly escape its effects. Part of Conrad's complex moral judgment can be inferred from the presence of guilt feelings in his characters. Throughout the interview with the captain, Archbold mumbles, appears ashamed and distressed, recites the introductory facts "in the manner of a criminal making a reluctant and doleful confession," is desperately evasive about his own and Leggatt's role during the storm. Granted, we perceive Archbold through the eyes of someone who sides emotionally with Leggatt, but nothing contradicts, even by implication, this description of Archbold or Leggatt's version of the *Sephora* events, as there does, say, the captain's sure optimism at the end. If the reader does not accept the accuracy of the narrator's depiction of Archbold, his entire narrative becomes hopelessly tainted. Although the old skipper will be spared a trial, he appears guilt-ridden and self-condemned, an index of his failure and of the limitation—in its conventionality and rigidity—of the world he represents. His last years marred, deprived of the consolation of a faultless career, he cannot be a free man. Leggatt's disappearance into a wilderness "unknown to trade, to travel, almost to geography" differs from Jim's flight in that unlike his fictional predecessor, Leggatt is not seeking redemption and escape from disgrace. This parson's son does not feel dishonored—note his forthright manner of presenting the details compared with Jim's tortured account of the *Patna* experience to Marlow. The victim and the circumstances of the crime may help explain Leggatt's want of self-reproach, but to condemn him for not feeling remorse is presumptive; one cannot impose an obligation to feel. The absence of remorse is part of his character. One might say, in providing a neutral description, that Leggatt is not a man of thought, that what we see of him makes moral growth beyond him. At the same time, Conrad is abetting his survival by sparing him the inner rift that saps Jim and seems to afflict Archbold. Conrad wants us to see Leggatt's exile as simultaneous punishment and opportunity, as both payment and emancipation.

Colored by a young man's triumph, the ring of affirmation which closes the tale is emotionally stirring, but as an interpretation of events, the narrator's words require qualification. For reasons having to do mainly with the completion of *Under Western Eyes,* Conrad needed to win a confident rendering of life's possibilities that did not dilute his more deeply felt tragic knowledge. Dark elements verging on the tragic exist in **"The Secret Sharer"** as background, as implication, as a sufficient force of opposition to compel a more sophisticated, comprehensive, and sober perspective than that offered by the speaker. And while cause for self-assurance and promise is cut back, nevertheless, a basis for hope remains justified. That the text yields a less sanguine view of things than the conclusion would warrant is readily apparent. The sheer accident of the bobbing hat, far from being a flaw in the work, is its essential point. Daleski protests that the fortuity of the hat's appearance is a weakness, "for it makes his achievement of knowledge too much a matter of chance—and it turns the highest kind of seamanship into a tightrope of contingency." But to ponder the meaning and implications of this luck at the very edge of disaster is enough to shake one considerably, to chill the elation in any sense of victory. And when chance's role in this near-death escape is added to other unsettling realities—the fact that Archbold broke after a lifetime of laudable service, that in personal terms his one failure annuls an entire career and will spoil his remaining days, that Leggatt can be both hero and murderer, that the amoral, destructive, and unpredictable inhere in nature and human nature—a sense of trust in the world and in oneself is undercut sharply. The terms of existence register as harsh, precarious, and threatening. No guarantees are possible, no safeguards are sufficient. Anxiety becomes a constant of being, and a permanent element of uncertainty relating to all action enters consciousness.

Attuned to this skepticism, one can pursue a more "Conradian" reading of the narrator's final pronouncement: "[M]y secret sharer . . . had lowered himself into the water to take his punishment: a free man, a proud swimmer striking out for a new destiny." A painful and enduring deprivation, Leggatt's exile means to be lost to family and country, to leave behind a blackened reputation as murderer and suicide that he can do nothing to repair. Knowing that the captain has understood him, that his story will be remembered with sympathy as he has told it, is a heartening source of consolation. Slander and obloquy will inevitably attach to his memory with no one to speak in his name. The importance of upholding reputation (here, through the loyalty of a confidant), especially when made vulnerable through questionable failure, withdrawal, exile, death, is a recurring motif in the author's work and prompts one to reflect on Conrad's distress at those accusing Polish voices, real and internalized, that continued to assail his "defection." Leggatt's fate means also to be compelled to adopt a new name and identity—never without its costs for Conrad—to move into a future outside the bonds of white civilization (perhaps a symbolic way of Conrad bidding farewell to his exotic romanticism, burying it with Leggatt's "suicide"), to be denied the fra-

ternity of the craft and the attainment of his chosen profession. With this stark reality before Leggatt, how is one to understand the assertion that he is a free man with a virgin future? Elsewhere in Conrad, the notion of freedom never escapes the grip of his skepticism. As Marlow says of Jim's yearning to start afresh: "A clean slate, did he say? As if the initial word of each our destiny were not graven in imperishable characters on the face of a rock." The captain's "Impossible! You can't" to Leggatt's plan to go off the face of the earth echoes Marlow's reflection on Jim's hope to escape into a new life, though without Marlow's understanding of the impossibility of disowning the influence and deeds of one's past. By themselves, a change of place and name do not transform moral character; Leggatt carries memory and his ungovernable violence with him.

This much had to be said to correct any overstated optimism, but Leggatt's fate also contains promise. For those who rationalize wrongdoing like Jim and, in more complicated ways, Razumov, Conrad's method is to bring them to see the violative meaning of what they have done. If, as a matter of speculation, one were to place Leggatt in this pattern, the question arises whether he would be able to withstand emergent moral consciousness. Two factors in conjunction set him apart from Conrad's flawed heroes and lend support to the captain's hopeful projection for him: Leggatt's crime is not an act of cowardice (a point to be underscored), and he is thoroughly unromantic. Tough-spirited and tough-minded, he has none of Jim's callowness or the narcissistic weakness common to both Jim and Nostromo. Leggatt does not fear disrepute, poverty, or social neglect, and with some assurance one can envisage him establishing and maintaining a solid life in this remote region by his own efforts. At the same time, to give substance to the claim that Leggatt is a "free" man, a transgressor who has squared his accounts, Conrad must satisfy the demands of his artistic conscience for a higher sense of justice than legal prosecution. Punishment and redemption are integral to such demands. Leggatt's exile is sufficiently hard and exacting to warrant seeing it as punishment, though his suffering will not be the internal anguish of consciousness, conflicts engendered by guilt, self-scrutiny, disillusionment. However, with redemption the matter is subtle.

Conrad has split this theme and its resolution between two characters. Previously, with Jim and Monygham, Conrad grappled with this problem of winning integrity in the face of necessary punishment in a single figure, but in each case qualifications suggested an incomplete working out. In Conrad's terms, the crime must be redeemed by a reliving of an equivalent of the original deed and by an act of courage where once there was irresponsibility. In **"The Secret Sharer"** the chief mate's "legacy" is to inspirit his ally to rise up to his best self; in achieved captaincy, the initiate becomes an unfallen Leggatt. By living through a trial essentially similar to Leggatt's storm ordeal but by exerting restraint at the crucial instant where Leggatt lost himself, the captain has "redeemed" his double in the sense that the compulsive pattern is broken, the crime is not repeated. By suggesting redemption through the efforts of the captain, Conrad has taken the issue beyond Leggatt's subjectivity, for to the fugitive, his act does not admit of reparation; he suffers no psychic cleavage, and he accepts exile as punishment. Thus, Conrad would seem to have removed the need for redemption from Leggatt's future, and artistically the moral dimensions of Leggatt's case are settled within the story's confines. Like Marlow growing into an identity that has roots in Kurtz, becoming transfigured from seaman to "voice," the captain reincarnates Leggatt, who has died to the world. In both instances, a man capable of extremes bestows a legacy of spiritual paternity in that he is responsible for quickening to life a self in his own image latent in the other which emerges, however, as the morally stronger.

Conrad's granting favor to a pair of young men has much to do with his characterizing neither as a romantic egotist. Experience has cut through the captain's complacency and romantic glaze without the disillusionment that annuls self-image. A consciousness of leadership, not the pursuit of heroism or reputation or a transcendent private cause, is strong in both men. Duty compelled Leggatt to set the foresail, and later, as a prisoner, he chooses not to endanger the men on the *Sephora* by attempting a violent escape. Because the narrator's identity is bound to the values of the calling, the necessity impelling the Koh-ring challenge serves not individualism but maritime ideal. By way of contrast, professionalism merged with egotism distinguishes Brierly. The surety won by the captain is the kind that is absorbed in the blood; he has it in reserve, a knowledge and capacity he can call upon in the line of duty. But he cannot be said to have reached maturity because he lacks developed consciousness, those attributes of mind Conrad associates with moral acuity.

Neither introspective nor probing, the quality of the captain's intellect stands forth in the direct simplicity of his narrative. It is without the reflective commentary, the groping for clarity, the note of hesitancy and anxious brooding that characterize Marlow's yarn in *Heart of Darkness.* Such forthrightness reveals the untroubled mentality of a young captain just come into his own, markedly different from the moral philosopher Marlow of both the Congo story and *Lord Jim.* Using an uncomplicated first-person narrator of densely complicated material does more than heighten immediacy. There is no retrospective sense, no time gap between the original events and their recounting. In contrast, the effect of elapsed time in *Heart of Darkness* between Marlow's experience and its recital is important dramatically. The storyteller is substantially different from the man who underwent the journey; a breakthrough in consciousness has been painfully achieved, and this struggle knowledge is felt to be actively continuing. However, one detects no intellectual growth in the captain. Conrad does not give his young hero time or cause to meditate. By sparing him the onset of thought, Conrad preserves the captain's victory and secures for himself the vital sense of youth winning out, of life opening, of spirited effort rewarded that emerges dominantly from the story. This romantic necessity afforded Conrad imaginative strength, consolation, and sustenance as he returned to complete the searing ordeal of *Under Western Eyes,* whose stark finality inflicted an agonizing toll on its creator.

Ricardo J. Quinones　(essay date 1991)

SOURCE: " 'The Secret Sharer,' " in *The Changes of Cain: Violence and the Lost Brother in Cain and Abel Literature,* Princeton University Press, 1991, pp. 109-21.

[*Quinones is an American educator and critic. In the following excerpt, he examines Conrad's treatment of the Cain and Abel story in "The Secret Sharer," asserting that Conrad "expand[s] the psychic and moral dimensions of the story."*]

What Gessner's *Der Tod Abels* was to the second half of the eighteenth century (and beyond), Byron's *Cain* was to the nineteenth century: each was a work of some originality, signaling a change in sensibility that in turn helped to spawn generations of followers. Conrad's **"The Secret Sharer,"** rather than initiating a period of reinterpretation, actually caps a near-century of development (and in this, of course, Conrad remains, pre-modernist). Conrad carries on and develops the patterns and devices of regeneration that Byron introduced to the Cain-Abel story. These are (1) the continued elevation of Cain's character and motivation, and coordinately, and perhaps even more important, the further demotion of Abel; (2) the growing separation between those who adhere to the common level of understanding and the initiates in a special mystery, to which Conrad even adds the special cryptophasic language of twinship; allied to each of these, (3) Conrad's fascinating use of the double as co-conspirator and twin. All told, what Conrad has done is to expand the psychic and moral dimensions of the story, and in so doing he has added another page to the story of Cain as regenerate hero, Cain the Sacred Executioner, who, within the tight limitations of an intense moral drama, actually struggles to restore and revive a diminished social structure. Cain of **"The Secret Sharer"** continues to participate in a foundation sacrifice.

But in other ways Conrad's and Byron's versions of the story differ. For one, the disruptions in Conrad's story, although clearly matters of life and death, are not treated in as cosmically fundamental a style or design. Leggatt is not an intellectual rebel, a dissident and a disruptive character in a hopelessly divided world. He displays even less dark and savage grandeur than does Byron's Cain. Like Byron's Cain, he is an honorable person, but unlike Byron's Cain, his sternness of character does not show itself in hostility but rather in the severity by which he holds to his own destiny and is willing to accept his guilt. This temperamental roughness is the personal corollary to the essential facts of division and the hard choices that are part of the Cain-Abel story.

Where Byron introduced extenuations of motive, mitigating the act somewhat by its inadvertence, Conrad suggests even greater ambiguity around the event. It is never quite certain that Leggatt actually killed the surly mate (although the strong grip around his neck seems more than circumstantial). Moreover, in assertions that we are bound to accept as factual, his act of violence is actually responsible for saving the ship. That he is not a ruffian by nature is shown by his efforts to avoid further skirmishes. The Cain of **"The Secret Sharer"** is actually not divided but is a well-defined and integrated personality. Far from being subject to anguish and turmoil, he impresses the captain with his calm demeanor. If he is so well-contained and well-defined the importance of his coming obviously pertains to the young captain (whose name we never learn—an important indication that his personality is still in the process of formation).

Although the stories of regenerate Cain will create space around the event, that is, a moral space that makes room for greater complexities of judgment, the story itself requires a kind of physical closeness. Brothers themselves promote this kind of relationship, and suggest even further the nexus of involvement from which neither will ever be free. The physical setting of life on board a ship reinforces this requirement. Life at sea shows an isolated society, but one that in its very isolation seems to render more intense the gravest issues. Matters are stripped to moral fundamentals. Moreover, the very confinement suggests the unavoidability and even the fatal inexorability of the theme. Despite the moral expansion of the theme in Conrad's hands, the context itself suggests some of the grimmer aspects of the story. And indeed, while holding his ship at the head of the gulf of Siam, the young captain (also narrator) communicates some sense of the sheer momentousness of the journey involved: "In this breathless pause at the threshold of a long passage we seemed to be measuring our fitness for a long and arduous enterprise, the appointed tasks of both our existences to be carried out, far from all human eyes, with only sky and sea for spectators and for judges."

The young captain seems to have had some premonition of the implications of the passage. "I wondered how far I should turn out faithful to that ideal conception of one's own personality every man sets up for himself secretly." That he should have entertained these concerns would have of itself indicated his own complexity. Nevertheless, what he seems to enjoy about life at sea is its absence of complexity, in fact, its very regularity and straightforwardness: "And suddenly I rejoiced in the great security of the sea as compared with the unrest of the land, in my choice of that untempted life presenting no disquieting problems, invested with an elementary moral beauty by the absolute straightforwardness of its appeal and by the singleness of its purpose." This is almost too much: with the coming of Leggatt he will encounter the opposite of every single virtue he thought the sea represented.

We know of course that the coming of the double is as much a response as it is a summons. The young man is called, but there is something in his nature that initiates the calling. If the double is divisive, he is coming in response to an already existent division. While valuing straightforwardness, singleness of purpose, the untempted life, the greater security of the sea, the young captain shows evidence, muted and subtle though it may be, of being not quite reconciled to the life of security that his choice of the sea seems to promise. Not only is he a "stranger to the ship" (including, of course, the crew by virtue of his recent appointment—they had been together for eighteen months), but, more important, he is a stranger to himself ("and if all the truth must be told, I was some-

what of a stranger to myself"). That he assumes the anchor watch, where the fateful meeting occurs, is itself regarded as an irregular action for a captain. In short, the coming of Leggatt is not a gratuitous event, but rather in response to some maverick quality in the young captain. But it is more than maverick; it shows a higher responsiveness to the order of things.

From its origins in Genesis, where such fundamental divisions are described, to its role in the drama of Christian salvation history, the Cain-Abel story was invested with a sense of mystery. So, too, the double adds to the mysterious connections and resonances. The meeting takes place far from the scenes of domesticated society, in a kind of no-man's-land—the volume in which **"The Secret Sharer"** first appeared was called *'Twixt Land and Sea.* In the new, yet old, closed arena of the Cain-Abel story there is more than meets the eye. The evidence of the senses requires greater capacity for interpretation, for understanding. The slightly wayward, even fugitive, instincts of the young captain reveal his inner directions. This is why the double, the changed valuations of the Cain-Abel characters, with the greater emphasis on better awareness, and the sense of a momentous encounter, all come together in a sense of mystery.

The mystery is associated with Leggatt's coming and with the role he plays. The young captain is shocked enough at the apparition of a figure floating alongside his boat to let his cigar drop into the water. The captain's impression after a brief exchange was that Leggatt was about to swim away—"mysterious as he came." "A mysterious communication" establishes itself between the two. The phrase is used again and again. Leggatt later recollects the reassurance he felt in the captain's quiet voice—"as if you had expected me." When preparations are finally made for Leggatt to depart secretly, the young captain begins apologetically, "I won't be there to see you go." And then he resumes, only to cut himself short abruptly, an ellipsis that is rhetorically typical in the work, indicating an unexpressed but deeper understanding. "The rest. . . . I only hope I have understood, too." "You have," Leggatt reassures him, "From first to last."

From first to last. Although the young captain's understanding is not yet complete, his psychic life conveys him in the direction he wishes to go. His final understanding, with all that it implies of more fundamental division and separation, is that Leggatt has had imposed upon him the fate of Cain. This is not Citizen Cain, nor the Abhorred Other with monstrous progeny, but rather Cain as Sacred Executioner, who performs a violent act that is responsible for the salvation of the state (here the ship of state), but one that brings a terrible sentence and judgment upon himself. Moreover, it is not a doom that he wishes to elude or deny. It is simply one that he does not wish to have pronounced by the common understanding.

In this sense the division between awarenesses is a part of the creation of space around the event, and this creation of space—one can call it ambiguity—is the reason for Leggatt's arrival in the presence of a young captain, who, although unsettled himself and not partner to the responses of "Bless my soul," has nevertheless committed himself to a life of singleness and straightforwardness. There is then a greater meaning to Leggatt's coming, one caught up in the inner reserves and secret resources of the Cain-Abel story. The untempted life of security at sea that the young captain has chosen is essentially a life of undifferentiation. Leggatt's intervention is fatalistic in the sense that he separates the young captain from that undifferentiated and secure life forever. From within an illusory community—in which division had already occurred—a call is issued to break with unity, to venture out into a fundamental confrontation with the self. The double, while offering a partnership of soul, compounds but does not initiate a break that may be unrecognized. Finally, the young captain must sacrifice his saving double. As Dante did to Virgil, he must slay his companion-guide if he is to achieve his true identity. The hard fact of experience is that "the other" although psychically similar, is not "the same," or the self. Momentarily their two lines intersect, but they are obliged to resume their divergent paths.

In this way, **"The Secret Sharer"** shows its even greater appropriateness for the Cain-Abel story. In Byron's *Cain,* Lucifer is not symbolically slain, even though his message is finally not endorsed. Perhaps because his message is not congenial, he does not become a true double. Although partial soul mate he does not become enough of the better other, the lost brother, to enter sufficiently into a relation of doubleness that would therefore require the second slaying. It is sufficient that his message is regarded as incomplete in the larger quest of Byron's *Cain.* But in **"The Secret Sharer,"** the dimensions of the foundation sacrifice are more amply fulfilled. A dreadful, even awesome and mysterious, sundering must occur. If the young captain is to achieve his own identity, Cain must assume his traditional role as wanderer, take up his own destiny.

It is categorically impossible to understand **"The Secret Sharer"** without reference to the Cain-Abel story. This is not only because of crucial explicit allusions to the language of Genesis 4, but because such realization is part of the young captain's own dawning consciousness, and because so many of the exchanges, actions, and emotions are dependent upon the realization. Moreover, the so-called inner reserves of the theme help to explain the movements of Conrad's masterpiece (when he finished it, he is reported to have said, **"The Secret Sharer"** . . . is it!"), the separation from the crew, and ultimately the separation from Leggatt, as well as many of the specific concerns of the story itself (for instance, that with language).

There is no question that Leggatt in his calm and resolute and unspectacular way is aware of the role he is meant to fulfil. When he relates to the young captain the events that led to his imprisonment, he indicates that the wife of the captain of the *Sephora*—her presence is an exception to the normal actions of Cain at sea—would have been only too happy to let him escape: "The 'brand of Cain' business, don't you see. That's all right. I was ready enough to go off wandering on the face of the earth—and that was price enough to pay for an Abel of that sort." Later, in the most crucial exchange between Leggatt and the young captain, the fugitive explains why it is necessary for him to leave and why he cannot allow himself to be returned to stand trial:

> "But you don't see me coming back to explain such things to an old fellow in a wig and twelve respectable tradesmen, do you? What can they know whether I am guilty or not—or of what I am guilty, either? That's my affair. What does the Bible say? 'Driven off the face of the earth.' Very well. I am off the face of the earth now. As I came at night so shall I go."
>
> "Impossible" I murmured. "You can't."
>
> "Can't? . . . Not naked like a soul on the Day of Judgment. . . . I shall freeze on to this sleeping-suit. The Last Day is not yet—and . . . you have understood thoroughly. Didn't you?"

Intimations are necessarily obscure, as we shall see, in the allusive, cryptic style surrounding the mystery of Leggatt's nature. The captain recoils from accepting the harsh destiny that Leggatt must accept, but then chastises himself for succumbing to a "mere sham sentiment, a sort of cowardice." The Cain-Abel story enjoins such hard choices, and, particularly in the modern dramas of the regenerate Cain, inspires great resistance. A sentiment that Melville already expressed in *Billy Budd* is echoed in **"The Secret Sharer"**: there's nothing of a boy's adventure tale in this.

By a gradual process, Leggatt, the already-double, is assimilated into the captain's regimen. In fact, beginning with the moment when he puts on the captain's sleeping-suit, there are some ten references to this role as a double. What is of interest in this establishment of a spiritual twinship is the way it sets the cohorts off against the common understanding of the seamen whose lives adjoin but do not penetrate the closed circle, and the ways this relationship is sealed and insured by the secret language of twinship. After Leggatt recounts the harrowing details of the storm, the death of the first mate and his own imprisonment on that account, the link of communion between the two is tightened in obvious separation from the crew:

> We stood less than a foot from each other. It occurred to me that if old "Bless my soul—you don't say so" were to put his head up the companion and catch sight of us, he would think he was seeing double, or imagine himself come upon a scene of weird witchcraft: the strange captain having a quiet confabulation by the wheel with his own grey ghost . . .

In fact, in his self-imaginings he seems to relish the shock value this "discovery" would provide. "Anyone bold enough" to open his bedroom door "would have been treated to the uncanny sight of a double captain busy talking in whispers to his other self." When the search party from the *Sephora* comes on board, the young captain protects Leggatt, thus sealing their compact and sharing his crime. He senses that he, like Leggatt, would not measure up to the *Sephora's* captain's requirements for a chief mate.

Beyond the young captain's imaginings of how he and his double would appear to the less knowing, the second point that stands out in this fact of doubleness is their secret communication. Their language is cryptic, punctuated by ellipses, particularly when, in the passage already cited, Leggatt seeks reassurance as to the captain's right understanding. In the perfect understanding and communion of cryptophasic twins, the one does not need to complete his thoughts because the other is so finely tuned that he can complete the interrupted thoughts in his own mind. Their conspiratorial whisper further seals them and their secret knowledge from the rest of the world. Leggatt is finally gratified that the young captain has understood.

> "As long as I know that you understand," he whispered. "But of course you do. It's a great satisfaction to have got somebody to understand. You seem to have been there on purpose." And in the same whisper, as if we two whenever we talked had to say things to each other which were not fit for the world to hear, he added, "it's very wonderful."

Their communication in interrupted sentences and whispers becomes the ultimate in the communion of twins, it becomes aphasic. Finally, no words need be exchanged. Immediately prior to Leggatt's departure, the young captain, in a gesture of protective sympathy—one that will return to save him and his boat—forces Leggatt to accept his hat. This action is inspired by another imagining of the young captain, a fraternal one, as he sees himself in Leggatt's position: "I saw myself wandering barefooted, bareheaded, the sun beating on my dark poll." He has put himself in the place of the outcast, the wanderer, the dark one—like Cain. When Leggatt no longer resists the offered cap, their communication ceases to be verbal: "Our hands met gropingly, lingered united in a steady, motionless clasp for a second. . . . No word was breathed by either of us when they parted." From interrupted speech marked by ellipses, to cryptophasia, and finally to aphasia, the communion of twinship between them is established.

Conrad's Cain is self-possessed, even remarkable for his calm sanity, the clarity with which he weighs alternatives and then accepts his fate. This elevation of Cain was begun by Byron (although some higher motivation was already present in Gessner's Cain). Conrad's Cain even goes beyond Byron's however; there is nothing of turmoil or turbulence in him. This means of course that Abel suffers a corresponding demotion. Rather than simply pious, Abel becomes more and more typified by unawareness, even stupidity. But this very stupidity has within it the seeds of further demotion. In its unawareness it can come to represent a "mindless tenacity," the sheer instinct for survival that typified the station managers in *Heart of Darkness.* As Cain becomes more heroic, Abel moves from simple piety, to unawareness, to a stupidity that is self-protective; but in fulfilling this last-named instinct, the simpler Abel becomes passively evil, in essence, requiring Cain as a scapegoat in order to protect himself. Evil in this sense is ingloriously petty, not radical. Perhaps continuing the detheologized directions laid down by Gessner, the stories of a regenerate Cain do not partake of any "mystery of iniquity."

The great intellectual divisions of the nineteenth century had much to do with this reversal of roles and the demo-

tion of Abel, a process I refer to as the "conventionalization of the ethical." In this process, Abel moves from simplicity to professionalism, or, as Joyce expressed it in *Finnegans Wake,* he moves from being charming to being chairmanly. Abel becomes associated with positions of authority, while Cain, completing the tandem, represents the figure of the outlaw. Nevertheless, Cain, although violating the ethical, or seeming to—and we must remember the crucial ambiguity here—actually bears witness to an older, more fundamental law and moral principle. He comes to represent the highest consciousness of the age, and this represents a fundamental revolution in the theme. Cain becomes the spiritual adventurer, trying to overcome conventional understanding, to transcend the ethical (as Kierkegaard has required) by means of a higher consciousness, moving toward the religious and the tragic in such a way as not to abrogate the ethical. This, as I have repeated (here in other terms), represents the great suitability of Cain for the modern world.

The philosopher who enunciated this important change in values and characterization was Schopenhauer, who, as Ian Watt informs us, exerted a primary influence on Conrad. In a section called by his translator, "Ethical Reflections," Schopenhauer provides in expository from the specific bases for understanding this extraordinary change in values. "Innocence is in its very nature stupid," he begins one reflection.

> A golden age of innocence, a fools' paradise, is a notion that is stupid and unmeaning, and for that very reason is in no way worthy of respect. The first criminal and murderer, Cain, who acquired a knowledge of guilt, and through guilt acquired a knowledge of virtue by repentance, and so came to understand the meaning of life, is a tragical figure more significant, and almost more respectable, than all the innocent fools in the world put together.

The division between those who understand (the conspiring cohorts) and those who do not, between the irregular and the conventional, but more important, between a divided, struggling consciousness and a kind of simplemindedness becomes the main duality represented by Cain and Abel. The elevation of the Cain figure into a more significant figure was begun by Byron, but his elevation into a figure even more "respectable," that is, more meritorious and even virtuous, is a product of nineteenth-century German thought, of which . . . Hesse, is an even more direct heir. This development of course requires greater elaboration than the simple equation of the conventionalized ethical with stupidity. The conventional becomes the domain of the unenterprising bureaucrat whose purpose is not only not to commit an error but not to be perceived as having committed one. This also means that the purview of the law has been altered (and this division within the law itself will obviously enjoy great play in the modern versions of Cain). In the passage quoted above from **"The Secret Sharer,"** it is clear that Leggatt is making a distinction between the law of the State, which is purely passive and negative, one might say, and the moral law, which requires a more positive (and hence more dangerous) action.

The essential division in the story is completed by the

major contrast between the young captain and the older captain of the *Sephora,* who, I submit, embodies the qualities that have resulted in the degeneration of Abel. The conventional law as represented by the older captain is no longer moral or ethical, but is small-minded and mean-spirited as well. During the storm he actually defects. In words that we are obliged to take as record of fact, Leggatt assures the young captain that the older captain (whose correct name we never quite get) never gave the order to set the reefed foresail. Into this vacuum of authority Leggatt moves to take the burden upon himself, and in so doing saves the ship. It is important to note that Conrad specifically absents the structure of authority in this work, which is so devoted to the regeneration of Cain and the intervention of the double, and more important, which is so intent on using Cain to expand a limited moral code. The demotion of Abel in a work where the sustaining patriarchal structure is missing is also part of the pattern.

In **"The Secret Sharer,"** though, authority is worse than absent. It returns to reassert its preeminence, which means primarily to protect its record. The captain's aim is to deflect attention away from his own panicked ineptitude and to place it on Leggatt. Hence his unstinting emphasis on the event. His own nature cannot permit ambiguity or even recognition toward which the young captain wishes to direct him that Leggatt may indeed have saved the ship. "What do you think of such a thing happening on board your own ship? I've had the *Sephora* for these fifteen years. I am a well-known ship-master." The young captain reflects that this length of service and his "immaculate" command "seemed to have laid him under some pitiless obligation." The captain has created the scapegoat by means of an unconscious instinct for self-protection. He fails to recognize the provocation to which Leggatt responded, the possibility that Leggatt saved the ship and, more difficult to concede, the fact that these events took place as a consequence of his own defection.

What Schopenhauer and Conrad reflect is a genuine moral transvaluation that Byron helped initiate and that is perfectly legitimate. By any discerning higher law Leggatt (and following him the younger captain by contrast with the captain of the *Sephora*) is the more responsible and more virtuous soul. It is indeed a complicated matter, and that is the point of the regenerate Cain under the sign of the Sacred Executioner. Leggatt's role is that of a Sacred Executioner, whose virtue and whose crime—the saving action and the death of the first mate—are so intertwined that it is practically impossible to separate the one from the other. It is to this complicated interrelation that the young captain instinctively responds in his own receptivity to the double, finally now shown to be representative of ambiguity itself, and to which the unformed "Archbold" fails to respond. The more intricate weaving of destiny and circumstance is precisely the complication of understanding that Leggatt has brought with him, and it is the legacy he leaves.

All of this does not mean, of course, that Leggatt poses no risks for the young captain. The double is also divisive, separating the young captain from his ship, compounding the early sentiments of strangeness that he felt in regard to his first command. "Indeed," he confesses at one moment, "I felt more dual than ever." He realizes that "this sort of thing" could not go on for very long. The duality of his existence, the total identification with another self, the secret forms of communication, he sees literally as distractions pointing toward insanity. "I was constantly watching myself, my secret self, as dependent on my actions as my own personality. . . . It was very much like being mad, only it was worse because one was aware of it." The presence of the double, the intense self-consciousness that it provokes, separates the young captain not only from his ship and crew but also from himself, serving to block his instinctive life. And it is here that we approach the inner reserves and the critical ambiguities that make the Cain-Abel story so intriguing and appealing.

The intervention of the double represents a growth into self-consciousness, into awareness, and it is this awareness, prompted by the emergence of Leggatt, that separates the young captain from his shipmates as well as from the older captain of the *Sephora*. Yet, although necessary, this growth into self-consciousness can also jeopardize the fullest functioning of the self; its self-alienation can be an enemy to a reintegration of the divided resources of the personality. For this reason, Leggatt must depart if the captain is to be restored to himself. Alienation from the crew is harmful for a captain on his first command, but alienation from his most instinctive life is far more hazardous. This is they young captain's realization:

> But I was also more seriously affected. There are to a seaman certain words, gestures, that should in given conditions come as naturally as instinctively as the winking of a menaced eye. A certain order should spring on to his lips without thinking; a certain sign should get itself made, so to speak, without reflection. But all unconscious alertness had abandoned me.

We begin to see some of the real dimensions of the Cain-Abel story, the inner resources and psychic dimensions to which I referred at the beginning of this section. In post-Byronic literature the Cain-Abel story emphasizes the growth of awareness. Abel is demoted because in his innocence he lacks the possibility for such development. Part of this awareness is self-awareness. But to a certain extent, this consciousness of self represents a violation of primal innocence, of the sensed at-oneness of the individual with his environment. Hence the suitability of the violence, the sense of rupture, contained in the Cain-Abel story for the depiction of the psychic violence perpetrated when one splits up the primary self; a schism into consciousness has occurred, an act of estrangement from self and from other. This is why the character of Leggatt comes bearing identifications with Cain. As he is the force of social division, so he can also represent psychic division. In postromantic literature, in so far as this intervention of the double represents a growth in consciousness, Cain is a force for regeneration and expansion. But nevertheless, he still bears the marks of history and destiny. His calling is still a severe one. And just as he must accept his destiny, so the young captain must accept his identity. He can only do so by abandoning Leggatt-Cain.

Although the noted compliance of the double with the

Cain-Abel theme serves to expand the dimensions of that theme, it is also clear that the alliance with the theme drastically alters the nature of the double. The double might come offering a kind of freedom, a noncommitment that suggests the postponement of choice; this prospect of a free-floating being could be confused with wholeness, with completion. Caught in the grips of the Cain-Abel theme, the double, although at first offering each of these possibilities, ends by being involved in a drama of choice, of identity, of history, and even perhaps, of fatality. If a wholeness is achieved, it is not achieved by immortality, but rather by the recognition of separate destinies and identities, in effect, by mortality itself. The import of the double in the Cain-Abel story is that there is a fate worse than death, and that is to be unformed, to be always other, to be a stranger to one's own life. The danger, intellectual as well as personal, is that ultimate reality be attributed to the double, to that which is derivative, while the original source of the doubling is annulled.

Cain-Abel shows its roots in the foundation sacrifice—and in turn illuminates the meaning of that sacrifice—when it insists that the double himself must be abandoned, thus requiring not one but *two* slayings. This explains Cain-Leggatt's double function. In setting the reefed foresail he saves the *Sephora,* but in so doing he acquires a guilt that will always haunt him, and will always compel his destiny to be that of an eternal wanderer far from civilization. This is why he is a Sacred Executioner. His dutiful and heroic, risk-assuming act has made him a criminal. But then his role shifts. He is even more of a sacrifical figure within the personality of the young captain. The young captain experiences some of the pain of execution, when Leggatt becomes the sacrificed other, the lost brother who must be gone. He is the other half of the twinship, one that has brought illumination, consciousness, the sense of the higher complications of event and circumstance that in some ways have suited a deeper need of his personality— hence the coming of Leggatt. And yet, in order to save himself, to realize his own identity, intimately connected with his own instinctual life, the young captain must kill, as it were, be willing to shed the saving self. To refuse to do so would amount to a refusal of life itself. In this connection with the foundation sacrifice the Cain-Abel story becomes expressive of the conditions of existence. And just as the foundation sacrifice was required to secure the entity of the state, the rule of one, so the sacrifice of the double is needed to move from duality into identity.

This decision to accept separate destinies as well as identities—despite its ultimate acceptance of what the double may at first have come to deny, one's own death—is nevertheless a stirring resolution. Thinking back to the *Purgatorio,* one realizes that in abandoning Virgil, Dante experiences no diminishment of the self, but rather its fuller development. So it is that in **"The Secret Sharer,"** Leggatt, who needed to be abandoned so that the young captain could achieve his identity, had lowered himself into the water from whence he came, "a free man, a proud swimmer striking out for a new destiny." For his part, the young captain suffers no bereavement as he assumes now for the first time full command of his ship. "Already the ship was drawing ahead. And I was alone with her. Noth-

ing! No one in the world should stand now between us, throwing a shadow on the way of silent knowledge and mute affection, the perfect communion of a seaman with his first command."

What Conrad has effected is a brilliant reinterpretation of the Cain-Abel story. While Byron provided the larger frame for regeneration, Conrad made some highly intriguing personal adjustments. This is seen in the use to which he puts tow residual elements of the theme: the sentence placed on Cain and the much-discussed mark. The first murderer has not only become a revolutionary figure, but more importantly the upholder of a more significant moral law. Typical of the stern and complex regenerate Cain, he does not deny his guilt; he simply denies the competency of a court of law made up of twelve respectable townsmen to understand and hence to judge his fate. In so doing, he submits himself to a greater not a lesser moral law, to a greater not a lesser punishment. In fact, the fate he accepts falls under the interpretation of Ambrose: to prolong his life is to increase his punishment. And even more bravely, this modern Cain who assumes the burden of the old wanderer, does so with no special mark to ward off attack. The young captain, himself desperately engaged in trying to rescue his own ship, spares a thought for his erstwhile double: "his other self, now gone from the ship to be hidden forever from all friendly faces, to be a fugitive and a vagabond on the earth, with no brand of the curse on his sane forehead to stay a slaying hand." Cain, our true contemporary, bears no special mark, and this absence, or this unrecognizability, makes the acceptance of his portion all the more heroic. The pattern of the Sacred Executioner has a special relevancy for the Cain-Abel theme in the more modern versions intent on legitimizing Cain. But the difference between Conrad's version and the primitive ritual of blame and banishment is that society does not know that it has a redeemer in its midst. Society is ignorant, or rather, feels it in its interests to ignore the virtues of the executioner who is saving it. Leggatt makes a sacrifice that his society fails to recognize and he assumes a burden of which it is unaware. In the more modern versions of the Cain-Abel theme, and not only in those stories where Cain is a regenerate character, there exists a wide gap between the communal understanding and the agony undergone. The double contributes of course to the mystery of this discrepancy. With fuller understanding and with greater psychological realism than the useful but still schematic ideas of modern cultural anthropology, Conrad lays bare the true workings of the Sacred Executioner in human society.

This is not a story, as was *Heart of Darkness,* marked by an extreme split between unacceptable alternatives—a demonic energy and a depleted apathetic consciousness. By means of his double, the young captain enjoys a reintegration of forces that Byron had first anticipated in his *Cain.* What one might say is that, by moving out and then returning, the young captain has brought the conquest of rebellious psychic energy to his command. Formerly, as we have argued, the Sacred Executioner was utilized for purposes of public legitimation: the state was changed and preserved only by means of the historical burden assumed by the New Prince. The more modern versions of the regenerate Cain seem to promise a kind of psychic renewal. But what **"The Secret Sharer"** does is bring psychic renewal to the structure of authority. In this sense, it continues to allow for the more public dimensions of the Sacred Executioner. If the ethical has been conventionalized, and the demotion of Abel is associated with the decline in the structure of authority (witness the defection of the captain of the *Sephora*), then the role of the sacrificial Cain would seem to inspire a renewed association of that which is conventional (in this case the captaincy of a ship) with the more enterprising psychic energies. **"The Secret Sharer,"** with all of its intensely internal aspects, is still a poem of civilization because it tests civilization's capacity to absorb elements that are discordant and complex. In this sense, the aim of the story is to return suppleness to authority. In this, of course, **"The Secret Sharer"** succeeds brilliantly.

FURTHER READING

Bibliography

Teets, Bruce, and Gerber, Helmut E. *Joseph Conrad: An Annotated Bibliography of Writings about Him.* Dekalb: Northern Illinois University Press, 1971, 671 p.
Comprehensive primary and secondary bibliographies of Conrad's works.

Biography

Conrad, John. *Joseph Conrad: Times Remembered.* New York: Cambridge University Press, 1981, 218 p.
Reminiscences by Conrad's youngest son.

Karl, Frederick R. *Joseph Conrad: The Three Lives, A Biography.* New York: Farrar, Straus, and Giroux, 1979, 1008 p.
Detailed critical biography. Includes information regarding the milieu in which each of Conrad's works was written, the relationship between Conrad's inconsistent temperament and his literary output, and the influence of friends and collaborators on his works.

Meyer, Bernard C. *Joseph Conrad: A Psychoanalytic Biography.* Princeton, N.J.: Princeton University Press, 1967, 396 p.
Psychoanalytic study of Conrad's life, interspersed with discussions about his works.

Criticism

Benson, Carl. "Conrad's Two Stories of Initiation." *PMLA* LXIX, No. 1 (March 1954): 46-56.
Examines Conrad's treatment of the issue of initiation in "The Secret Sharer" and *The Shadow-Line.*

Boyle, Ted E. *Symbol and Meaning in the Fiction of Joseph Conrad.* London: Mouton & Co., 1965, 245 p.
Includes a section on "The Secret Sharer" in which Boyle analyzes the relationship between Leggatt and the narrator.

Cohen, Michael. "Sailing Through 'The Secret Sharer': The End of Conrad's Story." *Massachusetts Studies in English* 10, No. 2 (Fall 1985): 102-09.
Explains nautical details in the concluding scene of "The Secret Sharer."

Daleski, H. M. " 'The Secret Sharer': Questions of Command." *Critical Quarterly* 17, No. 3 (Autumn 1975): 268-79.
Asserts that Conrad's experiences at sea led to his exploration of the issue of "self-possession" in "The Secret Sharer."

Dazey, Mary Ann. "Shared Secret or Secret Sharing in Joseph Conrad's 'The Secret Sharer.' " *Conradiana* XVIII, No. 3 (1986): 201-03.
Explores the implications of the title of "The Secret Sharer."

Dilworth, Thomas R. "Conrad's Secret Sharer at the Gate of Hell." *Conradiana* IX, No. 3 (1977): 203-17.
Traces parallels between imagery in "The Secret Sharer" and imagery in works by other writers and artists, maintaining: "In this story, . . . the features and posture of a person, the relative positions of figures in a defined space, and more comprehensive, topological relationships are sometimes described with an exactitude and clarity that gives to them the specific significance of visual puns. Such precisely defined images, taken together, appear almost to pantomime aspects of the invisible, unconscious drama taking placed in the young captain's psyche. Furthermore, those allusive images establish for this interior drama a significant background of analogue and typology by reference to Conrad's known interests, notably works by Rodin, Dante, and Baudelaire."

Dobrinsky, Joseph. "The Two Lives of Joseph Conrad in 'The Secret Sharer.' " *Cahiers victoriens & edouardiens*, No. 21 (April 1985): 33-49.
Contends that "The Secret Sharer" "encompasses Conrad's 'two lives': the oft-quoted phrase by which in *A Personal Record*, [Conrad] linked his years at sea to his years at the desk."

Dussinger, Gloria R. " 'The Secret Sharer': Conrad's Psychological Study." *Texas Studies in Literature and Language* X, No. 4 (Winter 1969): 599-608.
Argues that "The Secret Sharer" is successful as a work of fiction only if read as a psychological study.

Foye, Paul F., Harkness, Bruce, and Marvin, Nathan L. "The Sailing Maneuver in 'The Secret Sharer.' " *Journal of Modern Literature* 2, No. 1 (September 1971): 119-23.
Discusses the blend of reality and symbolism in Conrad's works and provides a "literal explanation of the nautical facts in the last episode of 'The Secret Sharer.' "

Hamilton, S. C. " 'Cast Anchor Devils' and Conrad: A Study of Persona and Point of View in 'The Secret Sharer.' " *Conradiana* 2, No. 3 (Spring 1969-70): 111-21.
Provides an analysis of the narrative structure, use of point of view, and development of personas in "The Secret Sharer," contending that such an analysis provides a context within which the body of criticism on the story may be synthesized.

Harkness, Bruce. "The Secret of 'The Secret Sharer' Bared." *College English* 27, No. 1 (October 1965): 55-61.
Parodies radical interpretations of "The Secret Sharer" by illustrating that it is possible to support an argument that "the true archetype of the story is the Hyacinthine

and that its secret can consequently be summed up in one word: homosexuality."

Haugh, Robert F. "The Secret Sharer." In his *Joseph Conrad: Discovery in Design*, pp. 78-82, Norman: University of Oklahoma Press, 1957.

Plot summary and analysis of various dualities in "The Secret Sharer."

Hewitt, Douglas. "The Secret Sharer." In his *Conrad: A Reassessment*, third edition, pp. 70-9, Totowa, N.J.: Rowman and Littlefield, 1975.

Studies various influences on "The Secret Sharer," including Conrad's personal experiences at sea and his confrontation of his past in Poland.

Hoffman, Charles G. "Point of View in 'The Secret Sharer.'" *College English* 23, No. 8 (May 1962): 651-54.

Discusses the importance of the narrator's point of view in providing a psychological and thematic understanding of "The Secret Sharer."

Johnson, Barbara, and Garber, Marjorie. "Secret Sharing: Reading Conrad Psychoanalytically." *College English* 49, No. 6 (October 1967): 628-40.

Establishes a framework for psychoanalytic interpretation of literature and applies it to "The Secret Sharer."

Johnson, Bruce. "The Whole Man: 'The Secret Sharer.'" In his *Conrad's Models of Mind*, pp.126-39, Minneapolis: University of Minnesota Press, 1971.

Asserts that in "The Secret Sharer" Conrad "exploits [an] almost Freudian model [of the unconscious mind] at the expense of the all-too-painful sense of nothingness he had manfully confronted" in *Lord Jim, Heart of Darkness*, and *Nostromo*.

Jones, Michael P. "'The Secret Sharer': The Triumph of the Imagination." In his *Conrad's Heroism: A Paradise Lost*, pp. 101-12, Ann Arbor: UMI Research Press, 1985.

Analyzes Conrad's treatment of heroism in "The Secret Sharer."

Murphy, Michael. "'The Secret Sharer': Conrad's Turn of the Winch." *Conradiana* XVIII, No. 3 (1986): 193-200.

Asserts that the young captain in "The Secret Sharer" is an unreliable narrator. Murphy writes: "By this I do not mean, of course, that I think he is lying, but simply that he is not telling the whole story."

Otten, Terry. "The Fall and After in 'The Secret Sharer.'" *Southern Humanities Review* XII, No. 3 (Summer 1978): 221-30.

Examines Conrad's treatment of the "paradoxical nature of man's Fall, at once the loss of Innocence and the hope of what Blake called Higher Innocence" in "The Secret Sharer."

Steiner, Joan E. "Conrad's 'The Secret Sharer': Complexities of the Doubling Relationship." *Conradiana* XII, No. 3 (1980): 173-86.

Contends that Conrad used the literary convention of the double to create both "clear-cut dualities" and "persistent ambiguities" in "The Secret Sharer."

Williams, Porter, Jr. "The Brand of Cain in 'The Secret Sharer.'" *Modern Fiction Studies* X, No. 1 (Spring 1964): 27-30.

Discusses parallels to the biblical story of Cain and Abel in "The Secret Sharer," asserting that "the Cain story seems to be entering into the life of Conrad's tale as a precise symbol of Leggatt's predicament."

Wills, John Howard. "Conrad's 'The Secret Sharer.'" *The University of Kansas City Review* XXVIII, No. 2 (December 1961): 115-26.

Examines setting, characterization, plot, and theme in "The Secret Sharer."

Wyatt, Robert D. "Joseph Conrad's 'The Secret Sharer': Point of View and Mistaken Identities." *Conradiana* V, No. 1 (1973): 12-26.

Illustrates the unreliability of the narrator in "The Secret Sharer."

Additional coverage of Conrad's life and career is contained in the following sources published by Gale Research: *Contemporary Authors*, Vols. 104, 131; *Concise Dictionary of British Literary Biography, 1890-1914*; *Dictionary of Literary Biography*, Vols. 10, 34, 98; *DISCovering Authors*; *Major 20th-Century Writers*; *Short Story Criticism*, Vol. 9; *Something about the Author*, Vol. 27; *Twentieth-Century Literary Criticism*, Vols. 1, 6, 13, 25, 43; and *World Literature Criticism*.

John Drinkwater

1882-1937

English dramatist, poet, and critic.

INTRODUCTION

Known primarily for his historical dramas based on the lives of such figures as Abraham Lincoln, Oliver Cromwell, and Mary Stuart, Drinkwater is credited with popularizing verse drama in the early twentieth century. Seeking an alternative to realism in the theater, Drinkwater turned to historical events to create protagonists who display extraordinary qualities during periods of crisis.

Biographical Information

Drinkwater was born in Leytonstone, Essex. He spent his early years touring with his father, a professional actor, and occasionally substituted for other actors onstage. At the age of nine, Drinkwater was sent to Cornmarket near Oxford to live with his grandfather. After graduating from high school, he took a job with the Northern Assurance Company in Nottingham. He began writing for the *Ilkeston News*, and in 1903 paid a local bookseller to print his first book of poems. He continued his career in journalism, working for various newspapers throughout England. During this time, Drinkwater also acted in and directed plays produced by the Pilgrim Players. In 1911 his first serious work as a dramatist, *Cophetua*, was produced by the Pilgrim Players. Drinkwater achieved only moderate success with his subsequent plays, until 1918 when his *Abraham Lincoln* was produced and his reputation as a historical dramatist was secured. Drinkwater continued writing plays, poetry, and criticism, as well as giving lectures on literature, until his death in London in 1937.

Major Works

Early in his career as a dramatist, Drinkwater's major interest was to reintroduce verse drama to the English stage. His first plays, written in blank verse, often reflect his antipathy for war, a theme Drinkwater would explore throughout his career. *X=0: A Night of the Trojan War* is Drinkwater's most enduring play from this period. A critical and popular success, *X=0* is a one-act blank verse drama that centers on four soldiers in the Trojan War, two Greeks and two Trojans, shown in parallel scenes expressing regret, loss, and hope for the end of the war. Highlighting the similarities of the two sides, Drinkwater emphasized the futility and pain of war. Despite the success of *X=0*, Drinkwater abandoned verse in *Abraham Lincoln*, which is widely considered his best work. *Abraham Lincoln* uses the chronicle format to trace the development of its protagonist. Depicting Lincoln as a peace-loving man caught in the perils of war, the play was a popular success in both the United States and England. Drinkwater's next

play, *Oliver Cromwell*, is an expansion of his earlier epic poem on the controversial English politician. Although it is similar in form and tone to *Abraham Lincoln*, *Cromwell* achieved less success with audiences. *Mary Stuart* is considered more sophisticated than either *Lincoln* or *Cromwell*, but was not favorably received by audiences or critics. Concentrating on Mary's well-known relationships with her lovers Darnley, Riccio, and Bothwell, the play attempts to forward the notion that certain women are able to love several men at once without internal conflict.

PRINCIPAL WORKS

Poems (poetry) 1903
Cophetua (drama) 1911
The Pied Piper (drama) 1912
Rebellion (drama) 1914
The Storm (drama) 1915
The God of Quiet (drama) 1916
The Wounded (drama) 1916
X=0: A Night of the Trojan War (drama) 1917

Abraham Lincoln (drama) 1918
Mary Stuart (drama) 1921
Oliver Cromwell (drama) 1921
Robert E. Lee (drama) 1923
Robert Burns (biography) 1925
Bird in Hand (drama) 1927
Cromwell: A Character Study (biography) 1927
The Gentle Art of Theatre-going (nonfiction) 1927
Napoleon: The Hundred Days (drama) 1932
Shakespeare (criticism) 1933
A Man's House (drama) 1934

CRITICISM

Charles Lewis Hind (essay date 1921)

SOURCE: "John Drinkwater," in *Authors and I,* John Lane Company, 1921, pp. 86-90.

[*In the following excerpt, Hind praises Drinkwater's poetry and his play* Abraham Lincoln.]

There must be many dramatic authors who, in face of the success of *Abraham Lincoln: a Play,* are saying to themselves, "Why did I not think of this as a subject, why did not I write a play on Abraham Lincoln, why should an Englishman do it?" These be mysteries. Yet are they? Did not an Englishman, Lord Bryce, write "The American Commonwealth," which eminent Americans have called "the best treatise on American government?" Is it not because distance and aloofness from a subject give clearness and simplicity of vision? The man on a hilltop looking down upon a wood can write a better account of it than the man who is plodding through the undergrowth. The walker sees the trees; the man on the hill sees the shape of the wood, and its bearing on the country. Some Americans who saw the play in London were angry because the local colour was sometimes wrong, because there were anachronisms, because the "hired girl" was called a servant-maid, because General Grant was made to say, "My word!" instead of "By gad, sir," and so on. As if such ephemera matter. The shape and bearing of the wood is not affected because two or three of the trees are misnamed. I am reminded of the British colonel who protested that he would never read another word of Kipling "because, By gad, sir, the fellow is all wrong about the number of buttons on the tunics of the Heavy Dragoons."

Why was John Drinkwater, an English poet, not very well known, able to do it, when there are so many able dramatists who should have been able to write a play around Lincoln? Is it because he is a poet and an idealist, who had a vision of Lincoln as God's man, and kept that vision clear and clean?

In part that answers the question, but it is not the whole answer. Let us look at John Drinkwater's past. He was born a poet, not by any means a great poet, but one whom the Muse had called, touched lightly, and to whom she had also given the philosophic, spiritual, humanist outlook, say of Matthew Arnold and William Watson. That,

by itself, is not a very marketable equipment for life. Most poets of this kind earn a living in a government office, the Board of Trade, or the British Museum, and compose poems in the luncheon hour, or during week-ends, adding to their income by writing for the *Spectator* and *The Nineteenth Century.*

This John Drinkwater did; I mean he wrote for high-class weeklies and magazines; but he has also moved across a much more substantial and fertile background—the Theatre. He may be said to have been called cradled in the Theatre. His father was manager to Granville Barker; and although the early years of his life were spent clerking in Assurance companies (safety first is the way of fathers all the world over), he eventually stepped into his rightful niche as Co-Founder of "The Pilgrim Players," and eventually as Producer, etc., to the Birmingham Repertory Theatre. There he learnt practically and strenuously the business of writing, producing, and acting in plays. The poet in him had to face facts. Lucky poet!

One day he read Lord Charnwood's monograph on "Lincoln." He took fire, and wrote *Abraham Lincoln: a Play.* He was ripe for it. The poet in him dreamed the dream of Lincoln, the play wright and the actor in him curbed and directed the poet. It was all so natural; the circumstances synchronised; and the world, tired of self-seekers, of politicians masquerading as statesmen, of man-made dogmas masquerading as Faith, hungering for just such a play, found it in *Abraham Lincoln.*

He is a quiet poet. I can see why he could write the simple, unadorned dialogue of *Abraham Lincoln,* a style that looks so easy, but is so hard. He is a contemplative poet who walks serene pastures; who makes poems on places and on cloistral thoughts. How do you like this, called **"Reciprocity"**?

> I do not think skies and meadows are
> Moral, or that the fixture of a star
> Comes of a quiet spirit, or that trees
> Have wisdom in their windless silences.
> Yet these are things invested in my mood
> With constancy, and peace, and fortitude,
> That in my troubled season I can cry
> Upon the wide composure of the sky,
> And envy fields, and wish that I might be
> As little daunted as a star or tree.

Oh yes, a calm poet, a studious poet, who entirely forgets when he is writing poetry that there are such people as actors, and such places as Broadway and Leicester Square. Here are four lines from **"The Last Confessional"**:

> For all the beauty that escaped
> This foolish brain, unsung, unshaped,
> For wonder that was slow to move,
> Forgive me, Death, forgive me, Love.

And here is a fragment from a longer poem called **"To One I Love"**:

> I am thirty-six years old,
> And folks are kindly to me,
> And there are no ghosts that should have reason
>   to haunt me,
> And I have tempted no magical happenings

By forsaking the clear noons of thought
For the wizardries that the credulous take
To be golden roads to revelation.

Would you have thought that this kind of poet—reflective, gentle, companionable, trim—could write one of the most successful plays of the day, and himself, at one time or another, act all, or nearly all, the chief characters in the play?

Edmund Wilson, Jr.   (essay date 1921)

SOURCE: "After the Play," in *The New Republic*. Vol. XXVI, No. 331, April 6, 1921, p. 162.

[*A major twentieth century American literary and cultural critic, Wilson wrote several influential critical studies, including* Axel's Castle *(1931), which examined literary symbolism. In the following essay, he reviews* Mary Stuart.]

The great thing about John Drinkwater's **Abraham Lincoln** was that, unlike most historical plays, it dramatized an idea. The Disraelis and Paganinis and Sophies and Madame Sands have been merely attempts to dramatize picturesque personalities; one shuddered when one heard that Mr. Arliss was thinking of producing a Voltaire, because one apprehended a Voltaire like Disraeli and Paganini, a Voltaire reduced to a wig and a wicked grin, who would be shown, in spite of all his waspishness, to have had a heart full of wholesome sentiment. And the fiction inspired by Lincoln—*The Toy Shops* and *The Perfect Tributes*—had suffered especially from this deficiency: it had concerned itself mainly with the high hat, the homely manner and the kind deed. What Mr. Drinkwater dramatized for the first time was the idea of not taking vengeance on your enemies; and for this reason, largely, I believe, his play was a great success, in spite of its rather undistinguished style and the puppet-like quality of its characters.

The same thing is true of **Mary Stuart**, which has just been put on at the Ritz Theatre. In this case, the idea is that of the "great lover," the woman whose capacity for love is so great that she can love several men at a time and whose tragedy is that she finds about her no one worthy of her love; and Mr. Drinkwater has made of it an intelligent and interesting play. But it is not the great play it might be: the tragedy of the superwoman condemned to inferior men. In the first place, the story is burdened in its presentation with a distressingly clumsy apparatus. It opens with a modern prologue, in which two men in a library discuss what is supposed to be a case analogous to Mary Stuart's: the young man's wife has a lover and he is greatly distressed about it, but the older man advises him not to worry, because there are some kinds of women who can love two men at a time without being false to either. Mary Stuart, he says, was just such a woman. Whereupon the Queen herself appears as a phantom, declaring "I can tell you everything!"—the modern setting disappears and the real play begins. If this prologue was written to fill out the evening, because the real play was too short, I should think it would have been much better to have had a long curtain-raiser; if it was written to remind the audience that Mary was a not uncommon type and might still be met with today, I think it hardly serves its purpose; for the

point of the play is that Mary was longing for a lover as great as she and had to be content with lesser ones, whereas the point of the prologue is that a woman may love two men at once. This objection may be pedantic, but, at any rate, it would have been much better to have had it appear from the play itself that Mary is speaking not only for herself but for a whole class of women.

The play itself is a long episode which ends in the murder of Riccio. Mary's husband, Darnley, is a cad; Riccio is a shallow courtier; Bothwell is an equally shallow bully. Mary's tragedy lies in the fact that she cannot care enough about any of them for him to cause her a real tragedy. This sounds like an admirable theme, but Mr. Drinkwater muffs its possibilities for intense emotion. The trouble is that all the moral interest is dumped at the beginning of the play. In the first place, Mary's character and situation are explained as copiously as possible before the main drama even begins; and, as soon as the curtain has gone up on the main drama, Mary proceeds to explain herself even more elaborately. Some of her speeches in this early scene are thrilling,—in fact, they are the best thing in the play. The trouble with them is that they come too soon: when Mary has told of her fierce desire for a mate who will be her peer and her revolt against the ignoble intrigues with which she tries to satisfy her passion, there is nothing more to be said. You know the story before it is told: there is nothing left except incident. The climax of the action brings no moral climax with it. The interest is derived, not from the fact that Riccio is murdered: everybody knew all along that he was going to be; but in the fact that Mary does not care enough about him, after all, to be deeply moved even by his death. But this is surely not enough. One expects a great statement of the main theme; and this has now become impossible, because the fullest possible statement of the main theme has been given at the very beginning. I should think that the way to have made the play into a really effective drama would have been to let Mary's character and situation leak through from the incidents of the play and only at the very end have her declare herself in some magnificent passionate utterance.

The conclusion is further weakened by the dragging in of the machinery which blurred and encumbered the beginning. In the end, the voices are heard off stage of the two characters of the prologue repeating the same words with which the prologue closed. And Mary says again, as she hears them: "I can tell you everything!"—and the curtain goes down. This is too silly for a serious play: it is the sort of thing one expects of *As You Were* or *When Knights Were Bold*; it is purely a "trick" ending, which has no moral connection with the theme.

Miss Clare Eames, as Mary Stuart, is, I am sure, one of the most convincing queens ever seen on any stage; she looks as if she had been painted by Holbein. She has all the dignity and sculptural beauty of royalty, and not a little of its smooth coldness. She is perfect in all the scenes which require poise and authority (the scene with the Ambassador, for example), but Mary Stuart, as described in the play, she certainly is not. In the first place, it is impossible to imagine that she has lived a long time in France; there is nothing French about Miss Eames; she has very little lightness or gaiety. And then she is never really passionate or bitter; she gives no sign of the smouldering emotions which are supposed to be consuming her; in fact, she remains as imperturbed throughout as if she were the modern Queen Mary. When she gives herself up to Bothwell's embrace, you feel that something shocking has happened, as if you were a schoolboy looking in at the Superintendent kissing Teacher. It is disconcertingly uncharacteristic, where it should seem perfectly natural.

The three men are perhaps as well done as the text demands; the author has sketched them in rather simply, as types, without individualizing them. It seems to me the whole play is done on too slight a scale; Mr. Drinkwater has a fine instinct for dramatizing ideas, but a feeble dramatic imagination. His characters are always a little like flat colored pasteboard figures; they do not take independent life and precipitate their own tragedies; they are essentially illustrations for tragedies already provided by history. But if his plays are less a gallery of real creations than an historical picture-book, it is at least a picture-book by a man with something better than the usual eye for costume and romance; it is the work of an artist intelligent enough to understand the real issues of the past and to present his historical figures in terms of actual humanity.

Ashley Dukes (essay date 1923)

SOURCE: "Poets and Historians: John Drinkwater," in *The Youngest Drama: Studies of Fifty Dramatists,* Ernest Benn, Limited, 1923, pp. 150-56.

[*Dukes was an important English playwright and drama critic during the first half of the twentieth century. He is most noted for his works on modern European theater, particularly poetic drama, and introduced English audiences to the work of several French and German dramatists. In the following essay, he discusses Drinkwater's historical dramas.*]

Abraham Lincoln owed as much to President Wilson as to its own titular hero. It was a play of the hour, and in every line an allusion to the momentous issues of the hour could be heard. For large audiences (including returned soldiers among their number) it was the first drama to break the spiritual silence of five years. After the manner of plays with a message, it was open to more than one interpretation. Its sternness may have fortified those stalwarts who saw in the enemies of their country a band of moral outlaws and harbingers of slavery. Its sublimation of the passions was equally a reminder that other wars than that of North and South are wars of brothers, and its appeal to statesmanship was an invocation to Versailles. The play brought a new audience into the theatre. The Puritans (who are more numerous than the Nonconformists) found the author zealous in good works. Everywhere he was acclaimed by men of goodwill. In fine, the importance of *Lincoln* was ethical, political, social, and Mr. Drinkwater was not yet a biographer, but a prophet.

With the advent of *Mary Stuart* it was necessary to reconsider him as an artist. A historian, plainly, he was not. No historical dramatist is a historian. From Æschylus to Shakespeare and our day, historical drama has always

been a masquerade of the contemporary spirit. Nor was he in the narrower sense a biographer. A good portrait, it has been well said, is one in which we recognize the painter. A good play is one in which we recognize the author. What we shall look for in this *Mary Stuart* is a portrait of Mr. Drinkwater. Mary's own portrait (as in the prologue) may hang on the wall, and the incidents of her life may be reviewed for the sake of a young man smarting under the loss of a young wife's affection. But we shall not believe in Mary Stuart absolutely. We shall believe in her relatively, and it rests with the author to furnish the relation. We return always to what Mr. Drinkwater thinks about her, which is very much what he thought about Abraham Lincoln, and very much what he thinks about the world in general. This woman has distinction and beauty of character; she has courage and wit. Can it be truly said that she lives? It is foreshadowed in the prologue that at the heart of her history lies "the one glowing reality, a passionate woman." She lives as the illustration of her moral; she lives up to it, as people say. She explains herself satisfactorily. She coquets with Rizzio, she despises Darnley as we all despise him, she accepts Bothwell with a shrug; and the end of it is that she intellectualizes for us "the one glowing reality" of the modern prologue. She sets out deliberately to be an abstraction, and there she succeeds.

Abstractions, nevertheless, have their qualities. The best of this play is its quality of unexpectedness—the turning away from empty rhetoric that fills out dramatic situations, the turning inward to the idea behind the drama. In that respect Mr. Drinkwater belongs to his age, and is in touch with the movement that is surely spreading over the European theatre. He accepts no cheap appearances; he is for what he believes to be the inward truth at all costs. When Mary learns that the wretched Darnley, murderer of Rizzio, is himself about to be murdered by his rebel lords with Bothwell's knowledge, she mutters the few words: "Poison—this life—all of it. Barbs, barbs." No rhetoric here, no playing with smooth verses or smooth prose lines that round off the dramatic effect, but a concentration on the symbols that express emotion. "There are tides in me as fierce as any that have troubled women," says this Mary. And again, "I am wiser even than my blood." The urgent force of the idea is there. Its springs lie deeper than realism, deeper also than wit or what is conventionally called poetry (meaning the declamation of speeches). There is dynamic power in these words that gather up the thought, and are themselves gathered up and thrown like spray from a wave of feeling. It is only one step from this dynamic force to the last embodiment of the dramatic idea, which is ecstasy; but it is a long step for Mr. Drinkwater to take. The Puritans who are his natural audience mistrust ecstasy, rapture, poetic exaltation, or whatever it may be called that lifts men in a non-moral sense above themselves. If Mary Stuart were ever rapturous we might understand her better, and know why it was that she broke hearts and troubled kingdoms. She is always wiser than her blood—too much wiser, as we feel. Hers is a composite portrait. A little history and much philosophy and some poetry have gone to its making; but behind the lineaments of this spirited beautiful creature in ruff and farthingale a discerning eye may note the sterner features of Praise-God Barebones.

Oliver Cromwell is surely a play after the dramatist's heart. However fond Mr. Drinkwater may have grown of Mary Stuart, we feel that in the end he was glad to be rid of the minx, with her Renaissance airs and graces breaking in upon the solemnity of sermon-time. The clank of spurs and the thump of brass-bound Bibles are indeed manlier to the ear. And this play, more than the other, offers scope for the craft of the true biographer—the craft of reflected portraiture, the mirroring of mind in mind. "Mr. Milton has been reading to me this afternoon," says old Mrs. Cromwell as she lies abed. What Mrs. Cromwell says may not be dramatic evidence, and yet it carries weight with the jury. John Milton, we may be sure, wasted none of his leisure hours in reading "Paradise Regained" at the bedside of the Stuarts. When Milton crossed a threshold and grasped a hand, the hand was clean and the hearth something more than Puritan. He came as the world's ambassador to the court of greatness. Oliver Cromwell was a plain country gentleman, but he was Milton's friend; he was a stern soldier, but he was also "our chief of men." As with Milton, who remains a hearsay witness, so it is with Hampden and Ireton, who appear. Their friendship transfigures Cromwell, illumines his sombre character, lends eloquence to his curt speech. So let Little Arthur rage, and W. G. Wills imagine a vain thing. This Cromwell has his faults, but he is still "our chief of men."

His biographer also is a dramatist. He makes no pretence of aloofness, but himself speaks with friendly warmth. Upon the whole he speaks well, though his literary silences are hard to endure. It is in the nature of the subject that Cromwell should at times overwhelm us by his nobility. If presbyter be priest writ large, we must accept the pontifical immensity of the Arch-Independent, or Lord High Nonconformist, in the full blast of benediction upon friends and malediction upon enemies. It is in the nature of the subject that Cromwell should sometimes appear to address himself to our particular pew; and we leave the theatre with a feeling of surprise that the singing of the Doxology, or at least of the Old Hundredth, should not bring the proceedings to a close. Puritanism belongs to the spirit of the man; it is a ray of the light of character that streams from him.

And *Robert E. Lee*? We who are not moral biographers, but common hero-worshippers, may be pardoned for grudging to the great Southern general a degree of nobility that was proper to the characters of Lincoln and Cromwell. The pedestal we have each of us privately built for greatness is threatened with overcrowding at the summit. We admit a new claimant with the utmost unwillingness. We yearn secretly for a Frederick the Great or a Machiavelli who will lend stability to the lower portion of the structure. And yet, as his author proves, General Lee has an incontestable right to high place. We believe in him as a great soldier, a far-sighted citizen, a magnanimous enemy, a warm-hearted friend. We accept his strategy and his tactics, his victories and his defeats, his generous impulses and his sagacious reticences. We believe even in his sense of humour, for a twinkle seems to enliven that weather-beaten eye. If he have a fault, it is that of being over-rational. His wisdom flows too readily from the springs of action. He pauses in the midst of a natural gesture to utter the unnatural word. The roar of battle is suddenly hushed, and reason speaks. Our consolation must be found in the doubt whether the annals of history contain enough men both great and good to last Mr. Drinkwater for the rest of his natural life as a dramatist. One day he will have to start on the rogues. It will be a joyous occasion.

Frank Swinnerton on Drinkwater:

It was as a poet that John Drinkwater first became known to readers, and it was in Birmingham, as actor and as manager of the Repertory Theatre, that he made his stage reputation. The experience he had in Birmingham taught him the craft of playmaking; and *Abraham Lincoln,* the chronicle which was brought to London by the Birmingham Repertory Theatre, and afterwards went all over the world, was the distinguished result. He has never written novels; but his work, for the theatre has been supplemented by a number of biographies—one of Pepys, written in the old home of the Pepys family at Brampton, one of John Hampden, and a particularly good one of Charles James Fox—all of which have had their own qualities; and a charmingly equable autobiography must have made many friends for a man already possessed of a large circle of welcoming admirers.

That is a fact which must be remembered about Drinkwater: he was generally liked. He was so much liked that St. John Irvine, for example, when once forcibly engaged in that odd, unnecessary pastime of choosing which one man of your acquaintance you would rather have as a companion upon a desert isle, after winnowing his way through a multitude fixed upon John Drinkwater in preference to myself. And when I reported this fact to Hugh Walpole, Walpole answered:

"Oh, I'd *much* rather be wrecked with John than with you. In twenty-four hours I should be ready to murder you; but John's different. Yes, John, decidedly."

Frank Swinnerton, in his "An Ideal Companion,"
Mark Twain Quarterly, *Summer 1937*

Graham Sutton   (essay date 1925)

SOURCE: "John Drinkwater," in *Some Contemporary Dramatists,* Kennikat Press, Inc., 1925, pp. 53-72.

[*In the following essay, Sutton compares Drinkwater's historical plays to Greek drama.*]

Let us compare some passages:

> A wind blows in the night,
>   And the pride of the rose is gone;
> It laboured, and was delight,
>   And rains fell, and shone
> Suns of the summer days;

And dews washed the bud,
And thanksgiving and praise
    Was the rose in our blood.

And out of the night it came,
    A wind, and the rose fell—
Shattered its heart of flame.
    And how shall June tell
The glory that went with May?
    How shall the full year keep
The beauty that ere its day
    Was blasted into sleep?

Roses! O heart of man:
    Courage, that in the prime
Looked on truth, and began
    Conspiracies with time
To flower upon the pain
    Of dark and envious earth. . . .
A wind blows, and the brain
    Is the dust that was its birth.
What shall the witness cry,
    He who has seen alone
With imagination's eye
    The darkness overthrown?
Hark! from the long eclipse
    The wise words come—
A wind blows, and the lips
    Of prophecy are dumb.

And this—

Rude are the wills of princes: yea,
    Prevailing alway, seldom crossed;
    On fitful winds their moods are tossed:
'Tis best men tread the equal way.

Aye, not with glory but with peace
    May the long summers find me crowned:
    For gentleness—her very sound
Is magic, and her usages

All wholesome: but the fiercely great
    Hath little music on his road,
    And falleth, when the hand of God
Shall move, most deep and desolate.

Or again—

Or Greek or Trojan, all is one
    When snow falls on our summer-time,
    And when the happy noonday rhyme
Because of death is left undone.

The bud that breaks must surely pass,
    Yet is the bud more sure of May
    Than youth of age, when every day
Death is youth's shadow in the glass.

Beside us ever moves a hand,
    Unseen, of deadly stroke, and when
    It falls on youth—

And then—

But they within whose garden fair
    That gentle plant hath blown, they go
Deep-written all their days with care—
    To rear the children, to make fast
Their hold, to win them wealth; and then
    Much darkness, if the seed at last
Bear fruit in good or evil men!

And one thing at the end of all
Abideth, that which all men dread:
    The wealth is won, the limbs are bred
To manhood, and the heart withal
    Honest; and lo, where Fortune smiled,
Some change, and what hath fallen? Hark!
    'Tis death slow winging to the dark,
And in his arms what was the child.

Two of these passages are from Euripides: one from *X=O*; another from **Abraham Lincoln.** And I doubt whether many of us who have allowed our classics (including **Abraham Lincoln**) to rust for awhile would be quite sure of our ability to identify them. This is no superficial resemblance; nor is it confined to the quotations above. For behind all Euripides—behind all Greek tragedy, indeed—is an acute sense of the fragility of individual life, as against the continuity of human experience: or, as the Greeks would say, as against the decrees of the gods. Now this is precisely Mr Drinkwater's spirit: and it is this that raises such a play as **Lincoln,** or the *Alcestis,* or *Samson Agonistes* or the *Œdipus Rex* to the heroic level, as opposed to the mundane level of many excellent plays (O'Neill's *Diff'rent,* for example) whose horizon is limited to the individual fate. In most moods we may prefer the latter kind as the more humane, the less austere and exacting. But the levels are different.

Lincoln was not the first play in which Mr Drinkwater showed himself sensitive to the thought of the Greeks. *X=O* is Greek in spirit as well as in setting—more Periclean than Homeric, indeed. This was the last of five short plays with which the poet served his apprenticeship as dramatist to the Birmingham Repertory Theatre. It is planned simply, and with the same kind of exquisite austerity which we shall find later in the Chronicle plays; the Trojan sculptor with his friend who dreams of statecraft, the Greek poet with a similar friend: the common curse of war, that cares for none of these things: the death of the Trojan, barrenly compensated by the death of the Greek— there is nothing in **Abraham Lincoln,** in **Robert E. Lee,** in **Oliver Cromwell** that is not logically deducible from the philosophy of this stark little play. The rest are more obviously prentice-work, the poet remodelling himself as dramatist—not always successfully; they lack directness, confidence, and stage-presence; they are experiments and exercises rather than plays; parts of them are crude—in **The God of Quiet** especially; **The Storm** rings artificial, as it were Wordsworth trying to write like J. M. Synge; **Cophetua** sometimes vertiginates on the brink of bathos. And yet in thought and manner (as distinct from sense of the theatre) **Cophetua** has its moments: and the best of them Greek:—

SECOND WISE MAN. He has gone. He is fiery proud.

THIRD WISE MAN. He is King. It is well, it is well.

FOURTH WISE MAN. There is fear on my heart, and a cloud.

KING'S MOTHER. There is building a story to tell—

FIRST WISE MAN. He leaves the clear ways that are worn.

FIFTH WISE MAN. 'Tis the purpose of God—we must bend.

CAPTAIN. Not in vain shall he mock us and scorn.

KING'S MOTHER. A story—who knows of the end?

SECOND WISE MAN. This day is fulfilled my fore-telling.

THIRD WISE MAN. The stars are in counsel with kings.

FOURTH WISE MAN. There is gloom in the house of our dwelling.

FIFTH WISE MAN. To God be the shaping of things.

FIRST WISE MAN. The thread of the years now is broken.

CAPTAIN. To the edge of his sword be the shame.

KING'S MOTHER. What word of this day will be spoken? What song will be sung of our fame?

Here, with its delicate antistrophe and haunting rhyme, is a passage of word-music lovely to listen to. The matter is nothing much: the story is not advanced by it: before an audience insusceptible to verse-drama it must fail absolutely . . . Perhaps one of Mr Drinkwater's objects at this time was to discover whether an audience susceptible to verse-drama could be evoked or created; in five years he far outstripped *Cophetua* with *X=O*; then ceased to write verse-plays.

X=O may thus be regarded as a turning-point. The last of the verse-plays, it was also in some sort the first of the Chronicles—an embryonic *Lincoln* or *Lee*. And in choosing Chronicle Mr Drinkwater proceeded to apply the lesson he had learnt from the Greeks: namely, that in drama one of the interesting things, the *big* things, is the sense of history's continuity—the sense that great men may rise and fall, but that mankind goes on; side by side with this, the sense of our own fellow-humanity with bygone greatness. Chronicle again invokes the very potent stage-appeal or remembered glory, recreated for the physical eye; Lamb speaks of it—"Here was the court of Persia. It was being admitted to a sight of the past . . . I heard the word Darius, and I was in the midst of Daniel. All feeling was absorbed in vision." True, *X=O* presents no great epony-mous hero: though we hear the word Helen, and the name of Troy stirs our imagination as *Chevy Chase* did Sidney's, like a trumpet-call. But in the full-dress Chronicles this appeal is used to the utmost. It is used in—

"The President is coming up the stairs, sir."

Or in—

"What time is John Hampden coming?" "By nightfall, he said. Henry Ireton is coming with him."

Or in—

"Mr Milton was reading to me this afternoon."

Or best of all, in the Mayor of Ely's opening words—

"At Edgehill in Warwickshire, I hear?"

Simple and casual as such lines are, they arouse a thrill which makes them in each case memorable in the plays where they occur.

And yet this special appeal—this imaginative realism as we may call it—is not in itself enough to make good Chronicle. Nor will mere accuracy of detail suffice; *Lincoln* could not have gained, and might have lost considerably, had Mr Drinkwater turned pedant and made it as accurate as Hansard. Good Chronicle rests primarily on characterisation. These great men were of like passions with us, we must be made to feel the kinship. Wherefore, a certain accuracy for honesty's sake: as much realistic colour as the design will stand: but character first, because on the stage that which is merely accurate without being humanly convincing means nothing. *Lincoln* was not good Chronicle for showing Abe's devotion to Artemas, any more than it was bad Chronicle for letting him die in the wrong box; it was not even good by virtue of Mr Rea's extraordinarily convincing makeup: but because it made its great man not only credible, but somehow inevitable. One went into the theatre passively aware of Lincoln's greatness, one came out actively convinced that he was great in just that sort of way: so much so that when superior persons pointed out this flaw or that, one was apt to resent their information as an impertinence.

So much for Mr Drinkwater's technical achievement—his vision of character: his command of magnanimous simplicity: his creative faith in the power of untested audiences to respond to this kind of play. *Lincoln* owed much to workmanship. But it owed something also to the age that brought it to birth, and to its author's instinct for interpreting the "best magnificence" of his own time. It was a splendid instance for the theory. (not elsewhere justified to any great extent on the contemporary stage) that a great age produces great drama. In which connection it is significant, I think, to recall the English popularity of another Lincoln play, almost contemporary with Mr Drinkwater's—in its own field as great as his: one of the earliest "super" films, and still one of the few that have deserved that exuberant adjective—*The Birth of a Nation*. With both these our time was pregnant. We had thought previously of America in terms of comic-papers, perhaps—in terms of cowboys, or of sky-scrapers, or of Eldorado finance; and by "we" I mean the man in the street—dare I say, you and I? I, frankly: though I heard echoes of more vital things: traditions of southern courtliness: old wonderful heroic tales my father told me in childhood about the Civil War. . . . Then came the American attitude to our own war, and an ideal nailed to the mast. Our inspired journals knew what to make of that, of course; and indeed it was easy enough to crack jokes about a people "too proud to fight." But there was something more. . . . *The Birth of a Nation* first, **Abraham Lincoln** soon afterwards, touched the imagination with regard to that something more. The prologue of *Lincoln* would hold good for both of them—

> This is the wonder, always, everywhere—
> Not that vast mutability which is event,
> The pits and pinnacles of change,
> But man's desire and valiance that range
> All circumstance, and come to port unspent.

Both these were plays to dream over; and to see either for the first time was an unforgettable experience. In both, one beheld ideals forged and tested. In both, one felt one's own kinship with the bygone idealists, as well as the lasting splendour of the ideal. Both were interpretations of to-day in terms of yesterday: in a word, classics.

After *Lincoln,* with its immense success on either side of the Atlantic, the dramatist turned to Britain and his own narrower heritage in history for his next two plays. But the great epic of America still gripped him. Lee had stepped into the earlier play and out again—no more than a glimpse indeed, but of heroic stature. The play called after him deals with the Southern view, Lincoln appearing only as a name reluctantly honoured. The title was purest Drinkwater (would any other dramatist have ventured to call such a play by a name best known as that of a ragtime song? could any other have carried it off successfully?), but the play itself is a distinct variation of the Drinkwater type. Some of the shrewdest critics have found it better than *Lincoln.* For myself, diffidently and without contending too straitly that there is not room for several themes in a single play, I cannot help feeling that *Lee* loses something by its duality. It differs from *Lincoln* in that it is really two plays—first, the problem of Lee himself, a man forced by circumstances to fight for a cause in which he does not believe: secondly, an incident-story of four musketeers of the Virginian army. The author makes some show of combining these: the musketeers clamour to serve with Lee in person; in Scene 2 they echo Lee's misgivings on the rights of the case; after which, like him, they accept their part as something beyond argument: "Once thinking is over, it's worth it—we've just got to think one thing: hit and hit hard" (an idea still fresh in our memories from the late war: We shall meet it presently in Mr Monkhouse's *The Conquering Hero*). So Lee in the next scene: "We shall all have to believe that we are wise and just. That's the way of these things. Argument is over, and faith begins." . . . Faith, as expressed in action: for henceforward Lee the thinker seems to flag, dwindling to Lee the incident-character, the fifth musketeer of the tale; his personal problem disappears, to be recalled only by the rather formal, "They have died for Virginia . . . but we have now to live for America" at the end of the play. Perhaps this was Mr Drinkwater's intention; few ethical problems can stand up against the impact of personal action and danger (compare *The Conquering Hero* again: and observe, by way of contrast to the soldier Lee, that Lincoln's nose was kept continually against the grindstone of thought). The author, certainly, is at some pains to stress the physical side of the tale—witness Scene 5 where he contrives two deaths, a walking-casualty, and a broken banjo to bring home to us that Lee is in an exposed position; bullets drive like hail; there are alarums and excursions; there is less abstract argument than in *Lincoln,* there is more hot blood;

there is even humour, a quality of which the other play is rather destitute. But *Lee* lacks *Lincoln*'s spell of single-hearted austerity, sounding at times as though the author had decided, on the advice of "experts," to adapt and popularise himself; it is more fussed and episodic than *Lincoln,* less deep-toned; perhaps the very excellence of the musketeer scenes throws the rest out of focus. So the play threatens to fall between two stools, fine as it is. To say that it swaps horses in midstream were too harsh a metaphor; rather, it changes gear a shade unskilfully, and the cogs sometimes rattle.

Turning to British history, Mr Drinkwater courted more openly the dangers which beset the chronicler-dramatist, and which in *Lincoln* he had been able either to surmount or evade. These dangers are not so much historical (it were scarce paradoxical to say that history is what matters least in a history-play) as due to the preconceptions, prejudice, and half-knowledge with which we are apt to judge the type. "It is we who are Hamlet," said the critic. So are we Lincoln, Mary Stuart, Cromwell—and with a stubbornness that increases as we draw nearer home. To a new history-play we take each one of us his private portrait; and although each portrait is a little out of drawing (being composite of so much beside good history—of old errors, of prejudice and partisanship, of grotesque prints in nursery history-books), yet it has "damnable iteration" and will most likely defy the sincerest dramatist's attempts to supplant it. In *Lincoln* the danger had been less; for I suppose not one per cent. of audiences went to that play without being prepared to accept Lincoln as a great and admirable figure; whereas any number of people went to *Mary Stuart* and *Cromwell* (and came away too) in active hostility to the protagonists. Even so, prejudice alone will not account for *Mary Stuart*'s failure; there is less prejudice against the queen than against Oliver, whose story was much more favourably received. The trouble with Mr Drinkwater's portrait of Mary is that it is too small for the frame. For stage purposes her story is that of a light-o'-love, raised from the plane of common harlotry to that of admiration and sympathy by some greatness within herself (Shakespeare raised *Antony and Cleopatra* so.) Lacking that greatness she is nothing; there is no middle way; it is a story of grand passion, or it is farmyard stuff. . . . Objectively, Mr Drinkwater does what he can for Mary in the prologue by the mouth of old Boyd; but unless Mary vindicate herself there is no help here, promiscuity by the name of Stuart smelling no sweeter for all the old fellow's pontifications. And Mary lets Boyd down; there is no passion in the portrait of her (one may doubt whether passion is ever within this dramatist's range), only a green-sick, posturing pursuit of the *idea* of love; contrast with this the lovers whom she has to accept, and you receive an impression not so much of pathos (as the author intends) as of an irremediable deflation of dignity against which the play struggles in vain.

Oliver Cromwell is a better play. As a whole, it stands in the same ratio to *Mary Stuart* as *Lincoln* to *Lee*—that is to say, it has more dignity; it is more nobly sustained; its mood is more austere; and it would seem to echo a more authentic greatness. Piecemeal, the two plays do not bear out the *Lincoln-Lee* comparison; for there are scenes in

Lee as fine as any in *Lincoln*—the first war-episode for instance, and Duff Penner's death—whereas the best of *Mary Stuart* falls short of the *Cromwell* average, and the best of *Cromwell* might be by another hand. There is some noble prose—Cromwell's long speech in Parliament, for example: there is the exquisite tenderness of the Ely homestead: there is that brief and poignant scene during Charles's execution—bare as a board, five minutes of pauses and disjointed speech—which might stand in any text-book of dramatic craftsmanship as the model of "atmosphere" on the stage. Nothing in *Mary Stuart* can be classed with these; nothing in any of the plays excels them.

Cromwell is notable in another connection, being (together with *Lincoln*) a good instance of what may be termed the matriarchal tendency of modern drama. After its long glut of "womanly" women—clinging natures, like a well-knitted sock, as C. E. Montague once said—the stage is returning to the new-old fashion which Ruskin discerned in Shakespeare's plays, "Shakespeare has no heroes: he has only heroines. . . . The catastrophe of every play is caused always by the folly or fault of a man; the redemption, if there by any, is by the wisdom and virtue of a woman. . . . Infallibly faithful and wise counsellors, incorruptibly just and pure examples, strong always to sanctify even where they cannot save." These words cannot, of course, be applied wholesale to modern dramatists (Galsworthy stultifies them flatly, for one). Even Ruskin pleading his special case found himself gravelled by Goneril, by Regan, and by Lady Macbeth. But it does seem as though the modern stage were cultivating a type of woman, and of old woman especially, who conforms accurately to the Ruskin idea. Crones are out of date, and comic old women failing fast. The new type is motherly and philosophic: sharp-tongued but golden-hearted: schooled in experience: a looker-on at the queer game of life, and seeing the best of it: as it were the beacon of the restless folk in the play, and the touchstone of their ideas. One need only mention Mr Shaw's old ladies, about whom a monograph must surely be written some day; there is Miss Dane's Mrs Farren too, the perfect type; Mr Ervine, strongly influenced by Shaw, abounds in them. His Jane Clegg, for instance, you would hardly call a ministering angel—rather an angel of wrath; but she towers head and shoulders above the rest of her play, nor am I sure that she has not saved even Henry Clegg by insisting that he shall lie in the bed of his own making; old Mrs Thurlow in *The Ship* is the best of her line, stronger even than the great man himself who needs her strength in the end; so Portia in *The Lady of Belmont*; so Mrs Rainey in *Mixed Marriage,* "strong always to sanctify" though she cannot save. After Shaw, no dramatist is richer than Ervine in this motherly type . . . . Drinkwater has but two of them, Mrs Lincoln and Mrs Cromwell. I have raised the point, however, *à propos* of him, partly because this is the only woman-type with which he is quite at home, partly because no dramatist has drawn the type better. Let Mrs Lincoln speak—

> You said this was a great evening for me. It is, and I'll say more than I mostly do, because it is. I'm likely to go into history now with a great man. For I know better than any how great he

is. I'm plain looking and I've a sharp tongue, and I've a mind that doesn't always go in his easy, high way. And that's what history will see, and it will laugh a little and say, "Poor Abraham Lincoln." That's all right, but it's not all. I've always known when he should go forward, and when he should hold back. I've watched, and watched, and what I've learnt America will profit by. There are women like that, lots of them. But I'm lucky. My work's going farther than Illinois—it's going farther than any of us can tell. I made things easy for him to think and think when we were poor, and now his thinking has brought him to this. They wanted to make him Governor of Oregon, and he would have gone and have come to nothing there. I stopped him. Now they're coming to ask him to be President, and I've told him to go.

> MR STONE. If you please, ma'am, I should like to apologise for smoking in here.

> MRS LINCOLN. That's no matter, Samuel Stone. Only, don't do it again.

So Mrs Cromwell, even more than Oliver, is the buttress and rock of the English play. Her last scene is full of a deep, tranquil beauty; and that is typical; for in such women we may divine the unseen foundation of the hero's strength. They are the hero's origin, and in a sense his end. They stand between him and priggishness. They are his ballast of commonsense, the base to which his heroics rally. Men strut and fret, racked by their passions and ideals, while these others look on; but in the end, the ideal gained or vanished, heroism accomplished or lost, the great men return to them; for to these too the line that Arnold chose from Dante is adaptable—"In their will is our peace."

Cromwell was better received than *Mary Stuart,* in spite of its more controversial nature. It was not everybody's Cromwell, of course—not mine by any means, may I say without arrogance? since I have made it clear, I hope, that such a play is bound to run counter to all sorts of prejudices, and to be judged more or less unfairly according to them. Reading the text some while after production, I found that it was the acting rather than the authorship which had upset my own particular crotchet. Prejudice dogs one's path. Mr Ainley's Cromwell, I am very sure, seemed to many playgoers as noble a thing as Mr Rea's Lincoln did to me. But in blunt truth, I disliked it greatly. It is not merely that I deprecate his speed (though in some scenes the alternate gabble-and-bleat between Cromwell and Hampden was of the drollest) and windy suspiration of full stops in the middle of sentences: his conception of Cromwell's presence seemed to me fundamentally wrong. There were no warts on it, physical or otherwise: no uncouthness, no roughness in the grain; it was theatric, unctuous, hail-fellow-well-met with God and man; its very bluntness was oratorical; it lacked yeoman stamina, the heroic chest of the character slipping down (I speak metaphorically) by unperceived degrees into a sort of spiritual *embonpoint.*

And yet a fine and moving performance, even to individuals who may not happen to see Cromwell quite in that way. One knows one's own private Oliver the better for having witnessed it. This man was an idealist: in his way, an artist: a dreamer of great dreams. And being so, he may after all have had something of the flamboyant and theatrical quality with which Mr Ainley invested him. A fresh stroke in the old portrait need not be a false one; Mr Ainley at all events "restored" with skill. The trouble is that in such a case each man must be his own restorer, and each honest critic will admit that his restoration is an entirely prejudiced and personal process. If you should say, in fair retort, "Very well! Let us have this idea of yours, this conception which Ainley was so far from fulfilling," I should reply with the King's line from the sixth scene: "Strangely, the fellow grows on me. But he's a fool, Neal. Brave, but a fool—" Just that. "Fool" is wrong, of course—tragically wrong, like the King's superb "We do not fear disaster" a few moments later. Yet for all its wrongness that line clove through the fuss and fret of staginess to lie nearer the mark than all the shafts of Mr Ainley's quiver—a plain goose-quill shaft, as one might say, against which the actor's armoury seemed somehow peacock-feathered.

Florence Mary Bennett   (essay date 1925)

SOURCE: "A Contemporary Renaissance?" in *Poet Lore*, Vol. XXXVI, Spring, 1925, pp. 126-35.

[*In the following essay Bennett discusses Drinkwater's plays in relation to Elizabethan drama.*]

Fundamental to all discussion of literature is the idea that the appeal of any art to the public should be real. The validity of this statement is probably most concretely illustrated in the arts of painting and sculpture, whose flowering, in the history of our culture, has always belonged to a time when there was a demand for their ministrations. For example, in the days when Greek sculpture reached its pre-eminence, the artists worked simply and earnestly and enthusiastically to fill the demand for statues for market-place, civic building, temple, and national precinct. This was no self-conscious cry of "art for art's sake." The demand of noble utility on the part of the public met the creative imagination of genius. Again, in the period when Italian painting was at its best, the artists were responding to a need for pictures for convent, church, and cathedral. I am sure that as inexorable as any of the laws of physics is this aesthetic canon,—and here I am speaking, of course, of all the arts, that of literature conspicuous among them: Great Art Exists Only in Response to a Sincere Demand.

No problem is as simple as its statement; naturally, room must be left for the play of various forces. Life always and everywhere is carried on in terms of the resultant of forces. In this instance, it will be objected that the presentation of good art stimulates popular taste, whence comes the demand; in other words, the artist creates the demand. I conceive a measure of truth to be here, but I believe that the greater truth lies in an opposite statement: artists, responsive to the needs of the moment, but equipped with powers more than commensurate with those necessities, fashion, more or less the taste of their age, objects of abiding beauty. By their achievement public taste is ennobled and the

demand becomes importunate. If you will, it is a case of discerning and computing the dominant force in the group out of which our resultant comes. The fact is clear that the artist, however unconsciously, interprets his age. Recall by way of illustration the truism that the kind of thing which Shakespeare executed was being done by numbers of his contemporaries, but he worked at the common task in a supreme way. In our own day the problem is confused by a self-conscious and sophisticated effort among coteries of devotees to the arts to educate the public.

That there is on the part of the people of our country a vivid interest in the drama is abundantly manifest. It is astonishing to note how many community-players' clubs and "little theatres" have sprung up in various cities, how keen is the enthusiasm for pageants and masques, how alert are minds everywhere for reviews and essays and text-books dealing with the modern theories and conventions, whether of presentation or of colour or of lighting, of the professional stage. I am strongly of the mind here, as I am with reference to certain other forms of literary art to-day, that there is a genuine *popular demand,* out of which, if we have patience, beautiful fruition will come.

Furthermore, I am inclined to think that poetic drama will enter into its own again, although I am not willing to prophesy regarding the variety. One has but to peruse current catalogues of publishers to be convinced that the output of plays in verse is steady, howbeit it is not this medium of expression which is in vogue now on the *professional stage.* Yet drama or masque served poetically flourishes in groups of serious non-professional players who command on occasion very large audiences; and in the annals of the commercial stage of this generation and the one before it the names of Maeterlinck and Rostand are not without savour of success. Moreover, certain conspicuously successful plays of our very own time and in our own language are poetic in their general conception, if not in actual diction.

Take Mr. Drinkwater's work for example. In his historical plays he invariably lifts the whole scene to the realm of the general. Hear the words of Aristotle on this point: —"Poetry is a more philosophical and a higher thing than history: for poetry tends to express the universal, history the particular." The best illustration of this in Mr. Drinkwater's dramatic writing is in his ***Abraham Lincoln.*** Observe, please, how the Prologue lifts the life of Lincoln to the plane of the universal, showing his accomplishment in terms of the grandly liberating achievement wrought in political government by the English race. For the moment, in quoting these lines, I wish to emphasize their content rather than their form.

PROLOGUE TO DRINKWATER'S LINCOLN

TWO CHRONICLERS.
THE TWO SPEAKING TOGETHER. Kinsmen, you
  shall behold
Our stage, in mimic action, mould
A man's character.

This is the wonder, always, everywhere—
Not this vast mutability which is event,
The pits and pinnacles of change,
But man's desire and valiance that range

All circumstances, and come to port unspent.

Agents are these events, these ecstasies,
And tribulations, to prove the purities
Or poor oblivions that are our being. When
Beauty and peace possess us, they are none
But as they touch the beauty and peace of men,
Nor, when our days are done,
And the last utterance of doom must fall,
Is the doom anything
Memorable for its apparelling;
The bearing of man facing it is all.

So, kinsmen, we present
This for no loud event
That is but fugitive
But that you may behold
Our mimic action mould
The spirit of man immortally to live.

FIRST CHRONICLER. Once when a peril touched
   the days
Of freedom in our English ways,
And none renowned in government
Was equal found,
Came to the steadfast heart of one,
Who watched in lonely Huntingdon,
A summons, and he went,
And tyranny was bound,
And Cromwell was the lord of his event.

SECOND CHRONICLER. And in that land where
   voyaging
The pilgrim Mayflower came to rest,
Among the chosen, counselling,
Once, when bewilderment possessed
A people, none there was might draw
To fold the wandering thoughts of men,
And make as one the names again
Of liberty and law.

And then, from fifty fameless years
In quiet Illinois was sent
A word that still the Atlantic hears,
And Lincoln was the lord of his event.

THE TWO SPEAKING TOGETHER. So the un-
   counted spirit wakes
To the birth
Of uncounted circumstance.
And time in a generation makes
Portents majestic a little story of earth
To be remembered by chance
At a fireside.
But the ardours that they bear,
The proud and invincible motions of charac-
   ter—
These—these abide.

The lines are metrical. I think that instinctively the author chose poetry rather than prose for the abstract present-ment of his theme, the prelude to the prose action. Each scene in the play is introduced by a similar foreword poeti-cally expressed. To read these in sequence gives the very soul of the drama. The whole play in the full illumination of its interpolated poetry is poetic in conception. I find it tremendously significant that a play of this type should have proved, in the most practical sense, successful. I will draw attention to one more detail indicative of the poetic mould of this drama:—Mr. Drinkwater introduces a ficti-tious character into Lincoln's Cabinet, *Burnet Hook,* in order that through this person he may generalize and ob-jectify the forces that were antagonistic to the hero. He de-fends the device thus:—"This was a dramatic necessity, and I chose rather to invent a character than to invest any single known personage with sinister qualities about which there might be dispute." No other artifice could more clearly show than this that Mr. Drinkwater ap-proached his theme with the poet's, not the historian's mind.

In another of his plays, one far less fine in construction and developed without the strand of interpolations in po-etry, he uses a Scotch street song of the sixteenth century as the main theme, a sort of thread on which the plot runs. I refer to the **Mary Stuart,** through which echoes the song attributed to the Queen herself. The first verse is:

> Ill names there are, as Lethington,
>   Moray, Elizabeth,
> By craft of these I am undone,
>   And love is put to death.

The theme itself is phrased thus in a line from the third verse:

> Mary the lover be my tale.

And the last verse has this key-note:

> Not Riccio nor Darnley knew
>   Nor Bothwell how to find
> This Mary's best magnificence
>   Of the great lover's mind.

The thesis, that Mr. Drinkwater's dramatic procedure in handling historical subjects is distinctly that of a poet, would be well worth full explication. I believe that it is highly probable that he will some day write a drama—a good, playing drama—cast in verse from first to last, albeit his most recent contribution *to the genre* under discussion, the **Lee,** is executed entirely in prose.

Few, I imagine, will be inclined to dispute the opinion that the **Lincoln** is this writer's masterpiece. It concerns the purpose of my present study to demonstrate that his use in this of poetic interpolations which sequentially convey the spiritual meaning of the play is a return to the old con-vention of the Chorus. Be it observed at the outset that the author handles the device so that it belongs vitally to his drama, seeming not at all anachronistic or archaistic. Those who have seen the **Lincoln** played can testify to the impressiveness of the device in actual use.

The Elizabethan stage received by literary inheritance from the Roman stage, which in many matters it closely followed, this convention of the Chorus: to wit, a single speaker appearing as the interpreter of the action. Shake-speare, for us the most familiar, and incomparably the greatest, Elizabethan, employs the convention in several plays. *Henry VIII* has Prologue and Epilogue, of which the function is more that of preface and after-word than that of interpretation. The Prologue starts thus:

> I come no more to make you laugh: things now,
> That bear a weighty and a serious brow,
> Sad, high, and working, full of state and woe,
> Such noble scenes as draw the eye to flow,

We now present.

Having defined several categories of plays and having classified his own, the poet concludes, after a complimentary appeal to his audience, with the often quoted couplet:

> And, if you can be merry then, I'll say
> A man may weep upon his wedding-day.

The Epilogue is in lighter vein, savouring, indeed, of advertising:

> 'Tis ten to one this play can never please
> All that are here: some come to take their ease,
> And sleep an act or two; but these, we fear,
> We have frighted with our trumpets; so, 'tis
>   clear,
> They'll say 'tis naught: others, to hear the city
> Abused extremely, and to cry 'That's witty!'
> Which we have not done neither: that, I fear,
> All the expected good we're like to hear
> For this play at this time, is only in
> The merciful construction of good women;
> For such a one we show'd 'em: if they smile,
> And say 'twill do, I know, within a while
> All the best men are ours; for 'tis ill hap,
> If they hold when their ladies bid'em clap.

In much the same vein Rosalind pronounces the Epilogue in *As You Like It*.

> It is not the fashion to see the lady the epilogue;
> but it is no more unhandsome than to see the
> lord the prologue. If it be true that good wine
> needs no bush, 'tis true that a good play needs
> no epilogue: yet to good wine they do use good
> bushes, and good plays prove the better by the
> help of good epilogues. What a case am I in then,
> that am neither a good epilogue nor cannot insinuate with you in the behalf of a good play! I
> am not furnished like a beggar, therefore to beg
> will not become me: my way is to conjure you;
> and I'll begin with the women. I charge you, O
> women, for the love you bear to men, to like as
> much of this play as please you; and I charge
> you, O men, for the love you bear to women—as
> I perceive by your simpering, none of you hates
> them—that between you and the women the
> play may please. If I were a woman I would kiss
> as many of you as had beards that pleased me,
> complexions that liked me and breaths that I defied not: and, I am sure, as many as have good
> beards or good faces or sweet breaths will, for
> my kind offer, when I make curtsy, bid me farewell.

The very words show how completely in vogue was the convention in the great playwright's day. A merry illustration may be found in *Midsummer Night's Dream*, where the "mechanicals" are planning their play which is to regale Duke Theseus and his Court. Bottom, having set forth certain difficulties that may interfere with their artistic enterprise,—notably that the ladies will never be able to abide Pyramus' drawing his sword and killing himself—assuages thus the anxieties aroused in his mates:

> I have a device to make all well. Write me a prologue: and let the prologue seem to say, we will
> do no harm with our swords and that Pyramus
> is not killed indeed; and, for the more better as-

surance, tell them that I Pyramus am not Pyramus, but Bottom the weaver: this will put them out of fear.

QUINCE. Well, we will have such a prologue; and it shall be written in eight and six.

BOTTOM. No, make it two more; let it be written in eight and eight.

SNOUT. Will not the ladies be afear'd of the lion?

STARVELING. I fear it, I promise you.

BOTTOM. Masters, you ought to consider yourselves: to bring in—God shield us! —a lion among ladies, is a most dreadful thing; for there is not a more fearful wild-fowl than your lion living; and we ought to look to't.

SNOUT. Therefore another prologue must tell he is not a lion.

The ridiculous prologue itself, an exquisitely comic satire on the poet's own art, belongs to the first scene of the last act. The second part of *King Henry IV* has for prologist, "Rumour, painted full of tongues," for epilogist one of the Dancers belonging to the final festive scene. The text for the latter, executed in prose, is close to that which Rosalind speaks as quoted above. Its tenor may be judged from this beginning: "First my fear; then my courtesy; last my speech. My fear is, your displeasure; my courtesy, my duty; and my speech, to beg your pardons." That of the former matches more nearly the conception of the Roman Chorus, being explanatory of the play:

> RUMOUR.—Open your ears; for which of you
>   will stop
> The vent of hearing when loud Rumour speaks?
> I, from the orient to the drooping west,
> Making the wind my post-horse, still
>   unfold
> The acts commenced on this ball of
>   earth:
> Upon my tongues continual slanders
>   ride,
> The which in every language I pronounce,
> Stuffing the ears of men with false reports.
>
>   . . . . .
>
>   Why is Rumour here?
> I run before King Harry's victory;
> Who in a bloody field by Shrewsbury
> Hath beaten down young Hotspur and
>   his troops,
> Quenching the flame of bold rebellion
> Even with the rebel's blood. But what
>   mean I
> To speak so true at first? My office is
> To noise abroad that Harry Monmouth fell
> Under the wrath of noble Hotspur's
>   sword,
> And that the king before the Douglas'
>   rage
> Stoop'd his anointed head as low as
>   death.

This have I rumoured through the
    peasant towns
Between that royal field of Shrewsbury
And this worm-eaten hold of ragged
    stone,
Where Hotspur's father, old North-
    umberland,
Lies crafty-sick; the posts come tiring
    on,
And not a man of them brings other
    news
  Than they have learn'd of me; from
    Rumour's tongues
They bring smooth comforts false,
    worse than true wrongs.

Thus the historical setting for the action is given. In *Henry V* the poet uses a Prologue before each act of the play and concludes with an Epilogue and he denominates the speaker "Chorus," the term itself being indicative of the ancestry of the device. Those who saw Mansfield's magnificent production of the play will remember the august effect of these solemnly timed appearances of the Spirit of History in the character of Chorus. The service thus rendered in this play is that of a narrator rather than that of an interpreter, the intention being to inform the audience of certain facts pertinent to the development of the plot, but not included within the action.

It has seemed to me important to illustrate amply this Elizabethan usage in the hands of the master-poet for from these examples one can define exactly the Chorus of this and of the earlier English stage. It was mainly that of Prologue and Epilogue,—at its furthest extension, that of narrator of events outside the action which the audience must understand for a full comprehension of the play. Shakespeare uses the Chorus in a minority of his dramas, and I gather, furthermore, from the burlesque in *Midsummer Night's Dream* and from a certain tone in his serious Prologues and Epilogues that the convention was irksome to him. Observe, if you please, how perfunctory the note is in the examples above of that which I may term the Chorus as Advertiser. Tastes change, and indubitably a transition time in this detail of the dramatic art is apparent here. —In passing, it may be noted that something in the nature of a Chorus, interlarding the narrative, belongs to the work of the early English novelists. Fielding's *Tom Jones* will probably offer the best known instance. George Meredith now and then goes back rather quaintly, with deliberately conscious effect of drollery, to this mannerism. The author's motive in such case is precisely that which lies behind a preface.

However, my chief point in illustrating the use of Chorus in Shakespearean drama is to show that essentially it is not that of Mr. Drinkwater in the *Lincoln.* He takes his suggestion rather from the Greek Chorus. His Chroniclers are not mere narrators of event, nor clever-spoken apologists for the playwright. They give a lofty poetic interpretation of the drama, the very thing which the Greek Chorus of the grand Fifth Century tragedies did, albeit here the service was performed more elaborately and with the co-operation of the arts of music and dancing. The Greek Chorus belongs more intimately to the action of the drama than do Mr. Drinkwater's Chroniclers. In other words,

Mr. Drinkwater uses the spirit of the Greek Chorus, but in the style of the Roman and later European drama. One further consideration should be given prominence here: Mr. Drinkwater divides his play into scenes, eschewing the stock English usage of act-division and following the Greek dramatic convention of episodes.

Another likeness between the *Lincoln* and the ancient drama of Greece emerges: the outline of the play is known to every spectator. The artistic contribution of the dramatist therefore must be his novel and exquisite handling of the theme, his soundly unified development of character. But reflect how rich were the resources at Sophocles' or Euripides' hand,—the tools of his craft, prepared and polished by custom,—when compared with those at the modern writer's disposal. The spectacle was enhanced by lofty music and the rhythmic motions of ritual dancing. Here was pure drama with the embellishments of the opera. Indeed, it must not be forgotten that modern opera itself is derived from an attempt in Renaissance times to reproduce in Italian the effect of ancient Greek plays. The sponsors of the new art, imperfectly understanding the old, created a new *genre*. The appeal of Greek drama at its height—and this I wish to make salient—was a complete aesthetic appeal to the intellect and to the emotions. Aristotle in the *Poetics* (ch. vi) enumerates the parts of Tragedy as PLOT, CHARACTER, DICTION, THOUGHT, SPECTACLE, SONG,—a goodly band. The Greeks, gifted with infallible taste, did whatever they had in hand completely, adjusting delicately the appeal to mind and sense. As perfect in its way was the artistic discretion of the Church when she built up her liturgy as a drama of emotional and intellectual appeal, summoning the various senses to share with the mind the stimulus. AEsthetics, of course, must be based on the laws of nature. Aristotle's clear discernment of the bearing of this fact on his discussion of the art of literature is recorded thus: "Imitation is one instinct of our nature. Next, there is the instinct for harmony and rhythm . . . Persons, therefore, starting with this natural gift, developed by degrees their special aptitudes, till their rude improvisations gave birth to Poetry."

It is somewhere along the lines of the restoration of lofty emotional appeal that I think the drama of the future will develop. I believe it will use song and dance and colour, prose probably for much of the diction, poetry inevitably for much,—in any case diction of artistic worth. Modern science has enormously enhanced the possibilities of the Spectacle *per se,* and artists will, I think, avail themselves of their opportunity. As I said at the outset, I am unwilling to prophesy regarding the *variety* of the poetic drama which shall be brought to us by the creative mystery of a *renaissance.* I am more than willing to express abundant hope and to indicate the direction in which I conceive the wind of the spirit to be blowing.

Be it remembered that no form of art is static. There is growth and there is decay in the things born of the imaginative genius of man. Art at its best does not repeat the past, although that which is aesthetically sound never is old, and although art always learns humbly of the past. Be it also remembered that art is a stern taskmaster, for him who creates and for him too who truly appreciates,—veritably a hard saying for our day and for our nation.

Arthur R. Ropes   (essay date 1926)

SOURCE: "History and Drinkwater," in *Contemporary Review,* Vol. CXXIX, May, 1926, pp. 613-20.

[*In the following essay, Ropes analyzes representations of historical figures and events in Drinkwater's plays.*]

Not very long ago the remarkable success of Mr. John Drinkwater's **Abraham Lincoln** made us wonder if we were to see a revival of historical drama. There seems no reason why the great Elizabethan tradition should remain merely a tradition. Here was a play presenting great political issues, summed up in the character and career of a great statesman—and one who, by a happy chance, was fitted to call forth laughter and tears together, to move in a mingled halo of reverence and ridicule. Uncouth and almost grotesque in some aspects, Lincoln was saved from vanity by his homely humour, and raised into dignity by the might of his unwavering yet never fanatical patriotism. This was the theme of the play; the Civil War was always present in thought, but there was no ineffectual bustle of stage battles, no vestige of the once inevitable "love interest." Yet the piece achieved a popular success. Was it to be the first of a new school of historical drama?

The author clearly intended it to be so. He wrote a drama on Mary Queen of Scots, whose fascination for poets after her death has been almost as great as for lovers during her life—and almost as unfortunate. He presented the stage with another view of Oliver Cromwell and, as a pendant to **Abraham Lincoln,** gave us Lee, the great soldier of the Confederacy. None of these plays met with much success. Partly, perhaps, the novelty of the historical play had worn off; but I think that the dramatist's method is more at fault.

"When I wrote **Abraham Lincoln,**" says Mr. Drinkwater in his preface to the collected plays, "I had in my mind a group of historical plays conceived on a more or less definite plan. It was not that chancing on Lincoln and Cromwell and the rest I thought they would be interesting characters to write about. It was that having deliberated a good deal on certain themes that I wanted to dramatise, I found in these figures a release, as it were, for my imagination." He goes on to say that what attracted him as a dramatic theme was "the problem of leadership." Lincoln was the leader who gave his life to preserve the Union; Lee was the leader fighting against odds for the cause of Virginia and the Confederacy. Cromwell, as Mr. Drinkwater sees him, is the leader who "was determined with a religious zeal to sweep away the old order and found a new one."

Now it is in no carping spirit that I say that Mr. Drinkwater's method, as set forth by himself, seems an almost perfect instance of putting the cart before the horse, both as to history and as to the drama. Poets generally are best without philosophical and critical theories; and when they try to carry such general ideas or methods out in their work,

> Even the heavenliest poet
> Sinks somewhere safe to prose,

or is still a poet in defiance of his doctrines. Milton set out "to justify the ways of God to man," and glorified the ways of Satan. Wordsworth wrote wearisome wastes of blank verse as he chose, and immortal lyrics because he could not help it. Poe professed to have written *The Raven* by a deliberate method; but he never wrote another noteworthy poem in that way, and most critics are agreed that he derived the theory from the poem, *après coup.* I strongly suspect that **Abraham Lincoln** came before the theory of historical drama that Mr. Drinkwater formulates; or at least that the dramatist, deceived by his success, ascribed it to his following out a central idea, and not to his good fortune in finding that idea embodied in a strong human personality. He proceeded to apply his method to other historical characters, with little more success than the gambler who plays on a "system."

In the case of Oliver Cromwell he chose an interesting figure; but his idea was almost as wrong as that of Victor Hugo or Wills. It is the tragedy of Cromwell's career that he was not a radical reformer, but a strong Conservative. He set out to restore the English State organisation to what he held to be its old and true form, corrupted and overlaid by the arbitrary innovations that the Tudors practised and the Stuarts formulated. Illegal and unjust acts that had been tolerated or even applauded as saving the State from greater evils, were now to be made part of a permanent system. The Star Chamber, formed to deal with offenders too powerful for the regular law courts, was to override those courts, now that they were stronger. The royal power that had carried through the compromise of the Reformation was now used to oppress the more Protestant section of Englishmen. Strafford in the State and Laud in the Church were shaping the temporary Tudor methods into a permanent system. Cromwell wanted to restore the constitutional, parliamentary government that had been the theory of the Lancastrian kings. He spoke and voted and fought, not for Liberty with the capital letter, but for "the liberties of England" as embodied in law from Magna Carta onwards. Revolutionary reformers, republican theorists, there were plenty in Cromwell's time, and he loathed them. "Oh, Sir Harry Vane, Sir Harry Vane! The Lord deliver me from Sir Harry Vane!" Strafford's "Thorough," an efficient despotism with himself as the Richelieu, Cromwell hated; and he was driven to be the Charles and Strafford, in one, of a more efficient and more despotic rule. He was always struggling to be a constitutional king, and always having to fall back on the support of the army. He was a Napoleon who had tried to be a Washington, or even a Lafayette.

If Mr. Drinkwater had begun with Cromwell, and tried to realise him as a man and a ruler, he might have grasped the obvious fact that he was a great man longing to be constitutional and legal and driven to be a military usurper—just as Cæsar began as a democrat and ended as an autocrat, or as the East India Company longed after trade and achieved empire. But the dramatist clung to his *à priori* theory, and hence he had to omit significant and important sides of Cromwell's character, because they did not bear out his idea. He almost petulantly protests in his preface that it is not his business to take any notice of the facts that "Cromwell wore dirty linen, and behaved like a maniac in Ireland." The "dirty linen" is obviously a reference to the story that when Cromwell was first noticed in Parliament, his "band" was not quite clean, and was even spotted with blood—a detail which Carlyle plausibly explains by "bad razors." Cromwell was careless about his dress, like many great men, but he was not usually slovenly. And his ruthlessness in Ireland was not the behaviour of a maniac, any more than that of Napoleon Bonaparte shooting the garrison at Jaffa, or Nicholson and Havelock refusing quarter to the Bengal mutineers. It was the merciless temper that most great soldiers have shown to rebels, mutineers, irregulars, bandits, and barbarians—the indignation that the disciplinarian feels against wretches who dare to fight without observing or even knowing the customs of civilised warfare. Nobody wants a dramatist to present Cromwell at the massacre of Drogheda, or on any of the occasions when he was merciless to enemies; but we do require the playwright to give us a man who could refuse quarter without being habitually cruel or intermittently insane.

Mr. Drinkwater, however, while claiming the right to omit any acts of his heroes that do not fit his dramatic scheme, admits that he is open to criticism if he makes them out to have been what they were not. I do not know whether he would consider the scene of Cromwell's (supposed) speech in support of the Grand Remonstrance of November, 1641, as such an instance; but he has made a bad and unnecessary blunder over the speech. Cromwell was undoubtedly a strong supporter of the Remonstrance; if it had not passed, he said, he would have sold his lands and gone to America. But Mr. Drinkwater makes him say, "Is there not ship-money? Is there not a Star Chamber?" and brings in a humble dependent of Cromwell's, mutilated by sentences of the Star Chamber (more barbarously than that Court ever dared), some four months after the Star Chamber had been abolished, and three after ship-money was declared illegal.

The well-known facts are that the Long Parliament had swept away the whole machinery of Charles's personal government, and attainted his ablest minister. Charles had given his assent to these measures, and moderate men were saying that he ought now to be given a chance of showing that he could reign as a constitutional king. The leaders of the Puritans did not believe in his sincerity—probably with justice. Accordingly they recapitulated the grievances and oppressions of the past in the Grand Remonstrance, in order to prevent the nation from forgetting and forgiving its wrongs. The narrow majority by which the Remonstrance was passed shows that there was already a reaction in favour of Charles; but with his usual fatal instinct for doing the wrong thing, he retaliated by the illegal and futile attempt to arrest the Five Members, and the Civil War was inevitable. Mr. Drinkwater's treatment of the Remonstrance reminds me of the wonderful drama that Villiers de l'Isle Adam wrote for the centenary of American Independence, in one scene of which a previously loyal American was driven into revolt by a sudden demand for heavy arrears under the Stamp Act.

In selecting Cromwell for his gallery of representative leaders of men, Mr. Drinkwater chose a great dramatic personality, but gave his hero the wrong central idea. In selecting Robert E. Lee for his next drama, he got the idea right, but failed to find a sufficiently dramatic hero. Apart from Lee's military genius, there was nothing salient about him. He was as rigidly loyal to his duty as Wellington, without any of Wellington's cold, stiff pride. He carried courtesy and consideration to his officers to a military fault. He allowed Jefferson Davis's half-knowledge of military matters to hamper him almost as much as Lincoln's ignorance hampered the Northern generals. But there is nothing in this to set on the stage. It is impossible to show on a few yards of platform the grapple of great armies over miles of tangled woodland and marsh. Mr. Drinkwater has realised that only Lee's military genius and the love between him and his officers and men had any great value for a drama. The central principle of Lee's loyalty to Virginia against the Union is no more fit to make a play than would be the loyalty to the Union of another Virginian soldier, George H. Thomas, who won for the North the most crushing victory of the Civil War.

In Lee's military career there are three great moments. There is his finest victory at Chancellorsville, gained against double odds and saddened by the death of Stonewall Jackson, his best general, at the hands of his own men. There is the failure of the great charge on the third day at Gettysburg, when the Army of Northern Virginia was fatally crippled. Lastly there is the surrender at Appomattox Court House.

Of these three dramatic moments, Mr. Drinkwater has omitted Gettysburg and left Chancellorsville to a few allusions in conversation, and Stonewall Jackson's end to a couple of telegrams. The surrender he had already shown in *Abraham Lincoln,* and hence could not treat it fully. Instead of either the fine victory or the fatal failure, he has, with extreme unhappiness, chosen to show Lee as a great general at the battle of Malvern Hill—by consent of all military critics, his very worst battle, in which his troops were flung away in uncombined assaults on an impregnable position. At Chancellorsville the dramatist could have shown Lee really directing his battle, could have given Jackson's death-bed, could have drawn touches of reality, perhaps, from the wonderful story of a Northern private in that battle, as told in *The Red Badge of Courage.* At Gettysburg he could have shown the broken survivors of the charge drifting back through the woods, and Lee, calm and smiling, with death in his heart, rallying and comforting the stragglers, taking the blame of defeat on himself, and holding off by sheer resolution of attitude the counter-attack that might have shattered his army.

A little study of the American Civil War, a little discussion with a student of military history, might well have led Mr. Drinkwater to these two fine dramatic scenes. But he seems to have found in such military detail as he does give, "a release, as it were, for his imagination." He makes his Lincoln resolve to replace McClellan by Grant, when it is notorious that McClellan was followed in command by three other selections, two of whom were the worst generals who ever sacrificed the patient Army of the Potomac. He makes Lee, during the battles of Spotsylvania, resolve to retreat to Petersburg, and hold out there against Grant, at a time when neither Grant nor Lee had any idea of going there. It was not till Grant's overland advance on Richmond was wrecked by the carnage of Cold Harbor, that he resolved to swing round to the south of the city, and Lee followed him. These technical details are dramatically unimportant, says Mr. Drinkwater. That might be an excuse for omitting them, but hardly for putting them in elaborately wrong.

One other historical drama Mr. Drinkwater has written, but it does not fall under the same formula as his other plays. Still, his *Mary Stuart* has a formula of its own—not to its advantage. Mary Queen of Scots has always been "the daughter of debate" in all senses of the word. Her enemies, in her own day and after it, have depicted her as a blend of Medea and Messalina; her advocates, as Swinburne caustically said, have made her out not only innocent, but "an innocent." In their defence, she is a mere passive victim of circumstances, as incapable of killing Darnley or loving Bothwell as Darnley or Bothwell was of behaving like a gentleman. And now Mr. Drinkwater shows her as a *femme incomprise,* with a magnificent but always disappointed capacity for loving and being loved, drifting through the sixteenth century like a premature Hedda Gabler, or Hilda Wangel, or any of those ladies who yearn to "live their own lives" and spoil everybody else's.

Swinburne, perhaps, could have come nearest to giving us a credible Mary, if he could have written real dramatic dialogue for more than a few lines together. But he could no more keep his lyrical exuberance out of his dramas than he could keep the redundant syllables out of his blank verse. Mr. Drinkwater can write terse and effective dramatic dialogue in prose, though his blank verse does not escape the lyrical invasion. But Mary Queen of Scots is even less to be reduced to formula than Oliver Cromwell. And Mr. Drinkwater's *Mary Stuart* is handicapped by the most perverse of prologues. A young modern Scotchman, by name John Hunter, comes for advice to his old friend Andrew Boyd, because Margaret (John's wife, whom we never see) has informed her husband that though she still loves him, she also loves a certain Finlay (unseen), who has written a book on Mary Queen of Scots, and is, thereby, qualified to appreciate Margaret, her modern counterpart. John Hunter is not unnaturally annoyed, but his friend finds Margaret's conduct perfectly proper, as she shares Mary Stuart's "magnificence" as a lover, and it takes a prince among men, or several princes, to appreciate her as she deserves. This thesis Mr. Boyd supports by quoting an old song about Mary, in which the unknown poet has successfully anticipated Mr. Drinkwater's own manner. At this, Mary herself appears on the balcony and offers to explain everything to the young man. Then he and his friends vanish and we have episodes in Mary Stuart's life. The only connection with the prologue (called Act I) is that Mary begins her first scene by waking from the dream in which she was offering to tell John Hunter "everything," and ends another scene by going out into the same dream again. Later, she alludes to the dream once more; and anyone who could disentangle this se-

quence would find it easy to rationalise the epilogue of *Saint Joan.*

What Mary Stuart told John Hunter, or would have told him if he would have listened, we are not privileged to hear, but we can guess from the play; for when Mary is not rallying Riccio or despising Darnley or half-yielding to Bothwell, she is explaining herself to Mary Beaton or Randolph or the audience. Nothing particular happens on the stage; we hear Riccio stabbed and Darnley exploded "off," and Mary finally goes off herself with Bothwell. Her verdict on the three men is "Riccio is nothing. Darnley is nothing. Bothwell—is nothing." Obviously she preferred Bothwell, as there was a certain dash about the man.

Here again Mr. Drinkwater has put the cart before the horse. He formed, independently or after Ibsen, the conception of a woman whose temperament demands a great lover—or lovers—a woman who wanders unhappily through life seeking affinities in vain. Having got this central idea, he thought that Mary Queen of Scots expressed it in her life. Thereby he unnecessarily hampered himself by having to conform, in some measure, to the main facts of Mary's life. Working backwards in this way, Mr. Drinkwater made Mary the anticipation of the modern Margaret Hunter, instead of (as he intended) making Margaret the reincarnation of Mary. His Mary Stuart is not only temperamental, which she was, but introspective, which she was not, and passive, which she assuredly was not. The one impression Mary left on foe and friend alike was that of high courage, strong loves and hates, intense and brilliant life. She could do anything, win any man; and by an ironic doom it was always the wrong thing and the wrong man. She was double-souled, Scottish and French; too much of a born Scot for France, too much of a Frenchwoman bred for Scotland. Mr. Drinkwater turns this flying-fish, playing or hunted in sea or air, into a jelly-fish, drifting helpless in the tide.

The critical moral to be drawn from Mr. Drinkwater's historical plays is that neither history nor drama can be properly developed from mere theory. Not a few philosophers have tried the method with history. Herbert Spencer, for instance, had assistants searching history for events that would bear out his political theories, or rather for the particular versions of those events that supported his views. Others have done the same; they have tried to frame a philosophy of history, and have merely added a chapter to the history of philosophy. Poets have followed this plan also. Robert Browning explained Strafford as mainly moved by personal affection for Charles I—he might almost as well have said that Richelieu's guiding principle was love for Louis XIII.

In the drama, and to a great extent in history, "a man is everything," as Napoleon said of war. The ideal historian must be a dramatist, if he is to thread his way through the labyrinth of conflicting first-hand evidence as to any event of modern history. What he wants is not a theory, not even a central principle; few men act consistently on one principle, and no man acts on theory. Robespierre held (after Rousseau) that men were naturally good, and that capital punishment was wrong. His practical methods, if unchecked, would have left him alone with Sanson the executioner. A historian will be able to understand Robespierre's actions if he has a concrete conception of a real, recognisable man; the theories will only serve to explain Robespierre's speeches. Had Mr. Drinkwater studied Cromwell as a man first, he would have discovered that the Protector was anything but a radical or a revolutionist. Had he studied Robert E. Lee as a man, he would have discovered that his career would not bear being made into a play. He began at the wrong end, and hence the many fine passages in his dramas go for very little.

In *Saint Joan* we see a great success, which might have been a failure if Mr. Bernard Shaw had followed the Drinkwater formula, and would have been an even greater success if he had not tried to work in theory at all. Studying the records of Joan's life, and particularly of her trial, he formed (being a born dramatist) a conception of her as a real, credible, and recognisable human figure. Having done this, however, he remembered that he was (at least to the Germans) a serious philosopher and a satirist of English life, and must needs drag in the Feudal System and British snobbishness, and other irrelevancies, thereby doing what he could (which happily was not much) to spoil a great play.

The old method is known and justified by its fruits. Make your characters, historical or imaginary, real men and women, and the rest will take care of itself. As for central theories, they are no better in a play than "the pictures" in a theatre—or the moth in the leading man's fur coat.

Hamlin Garland on Drinkwater

John Drinkwater was one of the most favored men of my acquaintance. Handsome, a delightful orator and a charming conversationalist, he would have been a notable figure had he never written a play or a poem. I recall an evening when he was announced to speak after a long program of dull and strident speakers had worn us all out, and those who knew his skill as an orator leaned back in their chairs knowing that something graceful was at hand. Taking his place on the platform with much of the quiet authority with which Augustus Thomas always addressed an audience, Drinkwater's fine voice and considered phrase combined to make an effect which I still vividly remember.

While riding with me in London, or rather while he was driving me down town, he told me that Lord Charnwood's *Lincoln* had started him on his study of our great war President. He asked how I liked his *Lincoln* and I told him that I had found it most appealing, and in saying this I was sincere, for while there were some shortcomings and a few misconceptions of pioneer life, it was a noble play. If he had written no other work this play would have made him memorable in America.

Hamlin Garland, in his "A Man Most Favored," Mark Twain Quarterly, *Summer 1937*

John W. Cunliffe (essay date 1927)

SOURCE: "John Mansfield and Other Poet-Dramatists," in *Modern English Playwrights: A Short History of the English Drama from 1825,* Harper & Brothers, 1927, pp. 180-207.

[*In the following essay, Cunliffe offers an overview of Drinkwater's major plays.*]

John Drinkwater is primarily a poet. He was associated with Rupert Brooke in the confident and successful effort to create a new poetic age which began in 1912 with the publication of *Georgian Poetry* and was almost brought to an end after the publication of *New Numbers* in 1914. In the latter enterprise, which would have been published quarterly if the outbreak of the War had not killed it after its first issue, Drinkwater was one of the four authors concerned, the other three being Wilfrid Wilson Gibson, Lascelles Abercrombie, and Rupert Brooke; and after Rupert Brooke's death Drinkwater enshrined his friend's memory in one of his **Prose Papers** (1917). The group had much in common in purposes and ideas, and came as near as is perhaps possible in England to forming a school—the new "Georgians."

It is not without significance that of the five plays preceding **Abraham Lincoln,** one, produced and printed privately in 1914, was entitled **Rebellion.** Its hero, Narros, gives voice to the protest against Victorian limitations and restrictions; to Drinkwater, as to his fellow-poet and dramatist, Lascelles Abercrombie, "prudence, prudence is the deadly sin." So Narros, not seeing that he will be ultimately victorious, recalls, in the hour of his temporary defeat, the Georgian desire for a full and unfettered life, unhampered by petty commercial consideration and dead conventions:

> When I was grown
> To man's full vehemence, there was fixed in me
> A will to know the sap of life, a will
> To live ungoverned by the prudent hands
> That are instruction. I watched this King and all
>   of you
> Spending the marrowy bounty of your days
> In lean and patchy argument, as who
> Should bear this right or that, who carry in
> And who go laden forth, what gain should be
> Marked for this trading, what forfeiture for that,
> How should the tithes be reckoned, should those
>   ships
> Be chartered so, divided so the spoils
> Of each man's labour. And I sickened then
> For a state should foster in a man the will
> For life not netted in these prudences;
> I saw life simple, and you peopled it
> With idiot ghosts that would not let me rest
> Till I too mouthed it, and denied myself.

Of the other four early dramas, published in 1917 as **Four Poetic Plays,** as has been pointed out by Professor Morgan, **The Storm** has much in common with the poems and plays of humble life done by Drinkwater's older comrade, Wilfrid Wilson Gibson. The scene is a shepherd's cottage in the mountains, to which comes a tourist who sees in the wind and snow only a magnificent exhibition of the powers of nature for him to enjoy and battle against successfully.

But to the shepherd's wife the storm spells tragedy and "it is not good to praise it." To her it seems "drenched in treachery and sin"—an outburst of the powers of evil. And the end justifies her foreboding, for her husband's life is lost in it.

X=0: A Night of the Trojan War (1917) is a War play, going for its inspiration to the greatest of anti-war dramatists, Euripides. In the first scene two Greeks, Pronax and Salvius, are sitting in camp at night outside Troy, and Pronax, not at all liking the job, goes out to slay one of his adversaries on the walls of the city; these walls are shown in the next scene, with Ilus leaving Capys to pick off some Greek straggler. Pronax, having accomplished his mission, returns to find Salvius dead; Ilus returning finds the body of Capys, slain by Pronax. Two young lives have been extinguished—cancelled out. Where is the gain? "X=0." And these young men had neither hate nor envy in their hearts. It is theirs "merely to die," and with them dies not only youth but beauty. "Beauty is broken."

Both the above plays were first acted at the Birmingham Repertory Theatre, and it was here, too, that ***Abraham Lincoln*** had its original production under the direction of the author on October 12, 1918. Drinkwater was uncommonly fortunate in his choice, for as the War was nearing its successful close, there was a strong feeling of gratitude in Great Britain for the help of the American soldiers, some of whom had marched through the cheering throngs of London on their way to the front, and a new and lively interest in the United States was aroused. Lincoln was one of the few heroes familiar to the British public—was there not a statue to him by an American artist outside the House of Commons?—and Lord Charnwood in his excellent biography had given the reading public some appreciation of the elevation of Lincoln's character and of the difficult issues he had to deal with; incidentally, the biography had also provided the dramatist with the necessary facts, in a striking and convenient form. Drinkwater was fortunate in the hour and also in the man, but it must not be forgotten that before him half-a-dozen American dramatists had done their best to put Lincoln effectively on the stage and had failed. With all allowances for the opportuneness of the moment, which made Drinkwater's tragedy a popular success on both sides of the Atlantic, it must be acknowledged that ***Abraham Lincoln*** is not only a craftsmanlike job but a moving play, rising to the height of its great argument. Lincoln's spirit of "malice toward none, charity for all" spreads angelic wings over the scene, but it is not so much as Drinkwater's earlier work a drama of ideas; it is a drama of character. The two Chroniclers, who serve in the play the same purposes as Shakespeare's Chorus in *Henry V,* make this clear in the Prologue:

> Kinsmen, you shall behold
> Our stage, in mimic action, mould
> A man's character.
> This is the wonder always, everywhere—
> Not that vast mutability which is event,
> The pits and pinnacles of change,
> But man's desire and valiance that range
> All circumstance, and come to port unspent.

The event is a mere agency: "the bearing of man facing it is all."

> So kinsmen, we present
> This for no loud event
> That is but fugitive,
> But that you may behold
> Our mimic action mould
> The spirit of man immortally to live.

Lincoln was great because he was "the lord of his event," and it is not his political struggles, much less the conflicts on the battle field—merely things of chance remembrance at a fireside,

> But the ardours that they bear,
> The proud and invincible motions of
>   character—
> These—these abide.

So, after an introductory scene presenting to us Lincoln in his modest home at Springfield, accepting the presidential nomination, the Chroniclers indicate that a year has gone by and invite us to contemplate

> A heart, undaunted to possess
> Itself among the glooms of fate
> In vision and in loneliness.

We see Lincoln struggling with his Cabinet, worried by pacifists and profiteers, signing the Emancipation Proclamation, and visiting Grant on the eve of Lee's surrender. Then the two Chroniclers foreshadow Lincoln's death under the similitude of the fall of the rose:

> And out of the night it came,
> A wind, and the rose fell,
> Shattered its heart of flame,
> And how shall June tell
> The glory that went with May,
> How shall the full year keep
> The beauty that ere its day
> Was blasted into sleep?
>
> Roses, oh, heart of man:
> Courage, that in the prime
> Looked on truth, and began
> Conspiracies with time
> To flower upon the pain
> Of dark and envious earth. . . .
> A wind blows, and the brain
> Is the dust that was its birth.

Finally come the short assassination scene and the reminder that "events go by":

> But, as we spoke, presiding everywhere
> Upon event was one man's character
> And that endures; it is the token sent
> Always to man for man's own government.

In many familiar touches the dramatist has helped us to remember the kind of man Lincoln was—homely, human, dominated in small things by his wife, in great matters controlled by no one, sympathizing with the simple-hearted, and not afraid to put an end sternly to the self-seeking of the ambitious and pretentious. Lincoln's great aim is clearly set forth in his own words, "My paramount object in this struggle is to save the Union." But along with this, we are made conscious of his hatred of slavery. In the first scene, he says to the delegation which brings the news of his nomination:

While we will not force abolition, we will give slavery no approval, and we will not allow it to extend its boundaries by one yard. The determination is in my blood. When I was a boy I made a trip to New Orleans, and there I saw them chained, beaten, kicked as a man would be ashamed to kick a thieving dog. And I saw a young girl driven up and down the room that the bidders might satisfy themselves. And I said then, "If ever I get a chance to hit that thing, I'll hit it hard."

The final scene makes use of a sentence or two from the Gettysburg speech. But through it all we are aware of Lincoln as a man, bearing in loneliness a terrific responsibility in order to "make as one the names again of liberty and law." His talks with the old negro and with the soldier condemned to death are perhaps the scenes which best illustrate his rich humanity, but this is the centre of Lincoln's character as Drinkwater conceived it, and we are never allowed to forget it. We see the man as he was— humorous, shrewd, kindly, gentle, hating force, but accepting the war "in the name of humanity, and just and merciful dealing, and the hope of love and charity on earth."

Behind all this is the thought, brought out especially in the poem of the rose quoted above, of the evanescence of all things human. At the height of his power and wisdom, just when his spirit of charity and forbearance was most needed, Lincoln is snuffed out by the revolver of a cowardly assassin.

> Disaster strikes with the blind sweep of chance,
> And this our mimic action was a theme,
> Kinsmen, as life is, clouded as a dream.

In an earlier scene the dramatist has recalled as one of Lincoln's favourite passages from Shakespeare the lines from *The Tempest:*

> We are such stuff
> As dreams are made on, and our little life
> Is rounded with a sleep.

In the Prologue above cited Drinkwater had named Cromwell as the one man fit to be put by the side of Lincoln as "lord of his event" and it was not surprising that after the success of *Abraham Lincoln, Oliver Cromwell* should quickly follow (written 1920, published 1921, acted 1922). The events of Cromwell's life do not arrange themselves so readily for dramatic presentation as those of Lincoln, and the play enjoyed only a *succés d'estime.* An even harder fate befell *Robert E. Lee* (1923) which was rejected at Richmond, Va., as giving "a false idea of the principles for which Southern people suffered and died" and "not worthy of the great name it bears."

In the preface to his collected plays Drinkwater, after replying to the critics who accused him of historical inaccuracies and insufficiencies, set forth his method as essentially that of a dramatist, not of a biographer; he endeavours to give a truthful and consistent picture of the man as bringing out certain principles and ideas the poet-dramatist wishes to illustrate; and he is at liberty to omit matters irrelevant to that theme. Lincoln, Cromwell, and Lee are all examples in Drinkwater's view of the qualities and aims of leadership:

> There was the man who, certain of his aims, had to face all the cunning and malice of unscrupulous intrigue in order to preserve what he conceived to be the only sure foundations of society as he knew it. This was leadership determined to preserve a great establishment. There was then the man who was convinced that society as he knew it was being destroyed by corruption and tyranny, and who was determined with a religious zeal to sweep away the old order and found a new one. Then again, there was the leader who felt, with absolute purity of heart, that loyalty to his own tradition was the first, and altogether becoming, duty of man. Here, then, were the three aspects of my problem, or perhaps one should say three of the aspects: the leader inspired by a great moral idea to the vindication of a system, the leader inspired by a great moral idea to the overthrow of a system, and the leader for whom a system became a great moral idea in itself.

It is not difficult to see why, for dramatic purposes, Lincoln was a much better subject than Cromwell or Lee—he is more human, more various, with a character and a cause that come home more directly to the hearts of the English-speaking peoples; and his sudden taking off gave a tragic ending which is lacking in the other two instances of leadership, notably in the case of Lee, who lived for many years after his defeat a comparatively obscure life as President of a Southern College; his complete abnegation so far as politics were concerned and his devotion to the educational interests of his people were nobly generous, but they could hardly be made effective on the stage. *Abraham Lincoln* remains Drinkwater's one masterpiece, and in the opinion of competent critics it is a masterpiece that will endure.

Perhaps a word should be said about *Mary Stuart,* which was of about the same period as *Cromwell* and was even less successful. The critics were more divided about it than the public. Professor Nicoll thinks it Drinkwater's subtlest drama, embodying the idea that "there are some women who have hearts so wide, who have ideals so high, that they cannot find any one man great enough to satisfy their soul's love. . . . Darnley and Bothwell and Rizzio are merely portions of that larger whole for which she craves. She desires strength and beauty and passion: perhaps she finds one of these qualities in one of her lovers, another in another, but never has she discovered all in one man. She is not fickle and faithless; it is simply that her ideal is too high for human attainments."

Admitting this as a possible frame for the portrait of Mary, E. Graham Sutton contends that the figure Drinkwater has drawn is too small for it; Mary should appeal to our admiration and sympathy by some greatness within herself, and she has not even true passion—"only a green-sick, posturing pursuit of the *idea* of love."

Drinkwater was apparently more encouraged by one success than dismayed by three failures, for the newspapers credit him with the intention of dealing dramatically with the character of Byron and also with that of Burns—neither of them, one would think, as promising as those he has tried already for the chronicle play centred about an idea. He is to be commended for his persistence in following a line of development which seems rarely to have the good fortune of winning public approval; and indeed for the lover of English drama one such success as **Abraham Lincoln** is consolation enough for many reverses, especially when the unsuccessful experiments involve such points of interest in characterization and philosophy as **Mary Stuart, Oliver Cromwell,** and **Robert E. Lee.**

Martin Ellehauge   (essay date 1931)

SOURCE: "John Drinkwater," in *Striking Figures among Modern English Dramatists,* Levin & Munksgaard, 1931, pp. 69-88.

[*In the following essay, Ellehauge examines Drinkwater's aesthetic philosophy.*]

John Drinkwater continues the conscious revolt against the problem-play. His strong aversion to this school leads him to substitute the themes of a remote time for the present day affairs. In his study of William Morris, 1912, he calls attention to the danger for a poet in a too close contact with contemporary problems because

> broadly speaking the things of immediate importance are the unimportant things.

Cognate feelings induce him to flee from the exterior world and take refuge in his own mind. His first poems and such plays as **Cophetua,** 1911, and **Rebellion,** 1914, extracted the following comment from his critics:

> . . . writing contemporaneously with others of his own generation, he was not yet a contemporary poet. [Mary Sturgeon, *Contemporary Poets*]

And he soon realises that he has chosen a wrong method of revolt. This recognition is accompanied with regret and repentance. In his spiritually autobiographical poem, **"The Fires of God"**, included in **Poems,** 1914, he promises amendment:

> I see the years with little triumph crowned
>
> . . . . .
>
> And weary-eyed and desolate for shame
> Of having been unstirred of all the sound
> Of the deep music of the men that move
> Through the world's days in suffering and in
>   love,
> Poor barren years that brooded over-much
> On your own burden, pale and stricken years,
> Go down to your oblivion, we part . . .

The practical value of art was pointed out by Morris in "The Earthly Paradise", where he argues that if man and his surroundings were made more artistic, all social evils would disappear, and life would become happier. In the purpose of making life artistic Morris and Wilde meet, in spite of their entirely different motives. We have seen Cannan attaching importance to art as a medium through which man may understand life, and as an embodiment of the ideal vision which practical politicians may imitate. From these points of view he quite logically infers that the aim of education must be to make children capable of understanding art.

To Drinkwater as to Morris art is a panacea with wonderful social effects. But his arguments are original. Morris accentuates the sweetening of life by art which will produce happiness, and happiness, he thinks, will produce love of one's neighbour. According to the theories of Drinkwater the supreme value of art does not lie in its being a source of happiness, but in its power to effect "a radical quickening of the spirit" of man. The sole source of social evils is, in the opinion of Drinkwater, injustice, injustice being identical with immorality. It is the result of mental inertia. As art has power to cure this, it becomes the universal and infallible social remedy. His syllogism put in a nutshell is this: art makes us alive, but to be alive is to be moral, consequently art makes us moral. From this point of view art is not a guide to life, it is the creator of life. But both Cannan and Drinkwater act logically on their theories in pleading the cause of art as a factor in education. Drinkwater not only proposes to give poetry a greater space on the time-tables of the schools, but also to send theatrical companies to the villages to play Shakespeare.

In this connection he turns against the old system of children's education in the schools and the system of adult education in theatres which prevailed during the preceding epoch:

> We must turn from the enunciation of moral principles—as assertion dulls consciousness—to the fostering of man's spiritual activity. If we can contrive this, moral principles may safely be left to take care of themselves. [**Prose Papers**]

The shortcoming of the problem-play Drinkwater finds in the following fact:

> If you show the ordinary lethargic human being the terror of the evil he is doing very vividly or directly in your drama or otherwise, you may occasionally shock him into perception, but in nearly every case the shock will be merely temporary and effect no radical quickening of the spirit.

For the negative aim of the problem-playwrights he then substitutes his own positive aim and trusts to achieve a more permanent effect.

On the same principles he solves the general problem of didacticism in art, or rather abstains from solving it, for it is a question that can "occupy but dull and unimaginative minds". He might make Cannan's remarks his own: "The purpose of the artist is so mightily passionate as to transcend consciousness". His study of the true nature of art, 1917, causes him to revoke his earlier principle of keeping aloof from his age. The question whether a poet should express his age or not, or whether he should choose his theme from his own time or any other time, proves too petty for a true poet to occupy himself with. He now accepts the theory of Oscar Wilde that a poet's vision is not related to any particular epoch; that it is not his business to express any age but to express himself. He is still conscious of the danger in being absorbed in petty ephemeral affairs, but he seeks contact with the vital current of contemporary life, and he is stirred by the great events which stir the minds of ordinary men.

The change in Drinkwater began before the war; but the war completed it. His despair at the waste of young lives, intensified by the death of his friend Rupert Brooke, April 23rd, 1915, wrung from him the cry of agony of which *X equals O* is the embodiment.

> Yet it is the bitterness for youth,
> When nothing should be but scrutiny of life,
> Making and building towards a durable fame,
> And setting the hearthstone trim for a lover's
>   cares,
> To let all knowledge of these things go, and learn
> Only of death, that should be hidden from
>   youth.

The tenor of Drinkwater's essays on art suggests that, speaking of art in general, his mind concentrates on two definite forms: poetry and drama. His writings also explain why he idealises these forms. In poetry he finds the best medium of expressing "passionate experience":

> When the impulse to express the thing seen passes beyond a certain degree of urgency, the expression takes a new quality of rhythmical force, shaping itself generally into verse.

The difference between prose and fine verse is thus "fundamentally one of urgency and intensity rather than of beauty".

Drama appeals to him as the means of getting the largest possible audience. He notices that the more familiar the image, the wider will be the audience. The image nearest and most familiar to man is his fellow man, and in a higher degree than in the case of any other art the dramatic image is man.

From such remarks it may be inferred that the ideal form of art, to Drinkwater, is the poetic character-drama.

His technique is also characterised by search and experiment. As in the initial stages of his career he turns to remote ages for subject, so he imitates ancient forms of technique. In *Cophetua* he introduces figures corresponding to the Greek chorus, distinctly separated from the acting characters. On the model of Thomas Hardy's "The Dynasts" the choric comment is divided into several points of view. The captain represents "the point of view of the massed and blind power of the people" and the wise men that of "absolute confidence in the tradition of kingship". The comment on the action of *Abraham Lincoln* is laid in the mouths of two chroniclers. In *Mary Stuart* the purpose of a chorus is accomplished by a peculiar device. A short poem conveying the author's conception of Mary is placed under her picture. It is first read by one of the characters, then sung by a mysterious voice, and at last sung by Mary herself. As a means of accentuating her chief characteristics and summarising her case in general it is effective:

> Not Riccio nor Darnley knew,

> Nor Bothwell, how to find
> This Mary's best magnificence
> Of the great lover's mind.

Swinburne's "Mary Stuart" opens Drinkwater's eyes to a danger which threatens the dramatists who treat the historical theme, the danger of mixing up dramatic art with historical scholarship. This danger Swinburne did not avoid. As a dramatist he was interested in the presentation of character, and as a historian he wanted to draw the epoch. The consequence was the extraordinary copiousness of his play.

> When a character speaks, he has not only to think of the utterance pertinent to the dramatic moment, which may need two lines, but also of the conduct of history to the next point, which may need thirty.

This is Drinkwater's criticism, and he is determined to keep clear of that error:

> Kinsmen, you shall behold
> Our stage, in mimic action, mould
> A man's character.
> This is the wonder, always, everywhere—
> Not the vast mutability which is event.

In harmony with this opening speech by the chroniclers in *Abraham Lincoln,* the dramatist announces, in a prefixed note, that his purpose is that of a dramatist, not of a historian. He does not traverse history, but he freely cuts and supplements with a view to constructing an effective character.

Character is, then, the predominant element in Drinkwater's drama. He never tires of emphasising the supreme importance of this dramatic element:

> As the image chosen by the truly imaginative artist is human character, the action which is subsequently invented is constructed, solely arising out of the natural demand of that character, and for the purpose of showing that character in operation, and never for its own isolated excitement.

The character-dramatist therefore limits himself to "those normal events which spring from character for the machinery of the drama"; and only decadent drama is constructed out of abnormal and sensational events. Drinkwater needs no events more exciting than such regular forms of everyday life as tea-parties, political conferences, rendez-vous between soldiers and officers, etc. The events have no interest in themselves; they are interesting only by their relevance to the psychological processes in the chief characters.

Abraham Lincoln may be chosen as an illustration of the author's constructional method. A definite character is selected for presentation. Next a series of events, suited to throw light successively on different sides of the central character, are linked together. The events are connected as closely as possible, but the author does not hesitate to insert isolated events to serve his main purpose. The tea-party in the third scene, and the confrontation of the condemned soldier with the president in the fifth scene have no apparent connection with the main action; but they give the president good opportunities of demonstrating his principles. This might seem disastrous to the unity of the play, but does not actually destroy it, as it is preserved by the dominating position of the central character. When the author makes character the unifying element of the play, he claims to observe the convention of native English drama:

> The unity of this depends . . . upon the cohesion of the fabric of character built above the foundation of events.

It is true that the events have always been subservient to a "cohesive fabric of character" in great English drama, and also that in certain periods the demand for a logical connection between the events has not been emphatic. Yet broadly speaking, up to the time of the problem-play school, the theory according to which the action in itself must form a unity was always officially accepted in England. William Archer, for instance, would never have tolerated the insertion of events irrelevant to the main action. nor the momentary introduction of people, for the sole purpose of illuminating certain sides of the central character.

The method followed by Drinkwater forms an exact parallel with the formula of the problem-play. A psychological motif is substituted for an intellectual motif as the chief factor to which the rest of the play is subordinated.

Drinkwater is not so original in practice as in theory. In spite of his opposition to the realistic intellectualism of the preceding epoch his relationship to it is conspicuous. When in *Cophetua* he throws the light of modern philosophy on an old theme, he acts like so many other authors of the intellectual school. When Cophetua asserts his right to choose his mate without regard to imperial politics, his arguments are based on theories advocated by Nietzsche, Wedekind and Bernard Shaw:

> . . . Shall a king then . . .
>
> . . . . .
>
> Be called a braggart and a knave
> That he dares no less than a thrall to save
> The shrine of his heart from shame?
>
> . . . . .
>
> You bid me mate. And shall it be
> To make adultery a thing
> Honoured from sea to shining sea
> For that the sinner is a king?

Cophetua here identifies the customary royal marriage with prostitution, and refuses to stoop to it. Nietzsche, Wedekind, and Shaw did something quite corresponding before Drinkwater. His firm determination to comply with the demands of pure love is almost the sole trait in the character of Cophetua.

Rebellion, Drinkwater's next play, is governed by a similar intellectual motif. Shuba, a Greek queen, and Narros, the leader of a rebellious party in her country, both recognise the supreme value of human life and insist on the necessary compromises in exterior circumstances to favour its growth. The King and the rebels quarrel on a trifling ques-

tion of wages, and it seems that blood is going to flow. Narros dissociates himself from his comrades, for although their cause may be just, the attainment of petty material advantages is unimportant compared with the enormous waste of lives which is its cost. "Some barren right, not worth a day's remembrance" is an inadequate excuse for releasing the "eagles of desire" that

> Cry up the wind in sinewy flight
> Not shamed of the immoderate fire
> That feeds the crucibles of lust,

with the consequence that

> The ploughs of reason rust
> In reason's night.

He does not succeed in dissuading the rebels, and in a moment of weakness promises to espouse their cause and lead them against the King's forces, and as Shuba is equally unsuccessful in her attempt to influence the King, the war is breaking out.

As the cause of life in itself requires opposition against such destructive forces as barren pride and justice, not to speak of vengeance and hatred, so those factors of life that are conducive to its growth need defence against forces tending to check growth. The central vitalising factor is found to be love, and consequently in the conclusive parts of the play the supreme right of love as compared with all other phenomena of existence is vindicated.

At the moment fixed for the attack, Narros is told that Shuba is prepared to grant him her favour and has gone to meet him in a certain place. Instantly he leaves the army to its fate and goes in search of Shuba. The plea of duty does not count:

> Now comes to me
> A call out of the life I spoke of then,
> And now must be my answer.
> A Captain objects: You are sworn.
> But Narros retorts: Light things are lightly
> sworn.

When Drinkwater in this play pleads the cause of life against an irrational ideal of justice and honour, and when he declares that love justifies the violation of the most sacred duties in other respects, he is in harmony with the central tendencies of Continental naturalism and rationalism. He stages a conflict of ideas rather than a character-conflict, and the conflicting ideas as well as the issue are customary.

Mary Stuart is closely related to *Rebellion* by its glorification of love in its naturalistic sense. Continental naturalism not only raises love above irrelevant duties, it also releases love from duties towards its objects, vindicates its right to change objects in accordance with its most unreasonable caprices, in short allows it to develop absolutely freely.

This theory is defended already in *Rebellion* in the relation between Narros and Shuba. But the figure of Mary Stuart is its chief embodiment. This play shows a fusion of problem-study and character-study, just as we may see it in English and Continental problem-plays.

On the analogy of a large section of English and Continental plays of the school which Drinkwater in theory attacks, the case of Mary is used as an illustration of a modern theory. Hunter complains that his wife has fallen in love with somebody else, yet without having ceased to love him. This is the answer:

> BOYD. Who are you, who should be glad of this woman's love, that you should presume to confine it, to dictate its motions?
>
> HUNTER. . . . I won't share.
>
> BOYD. Boy—will you not share the sun of heaven, the beauty of the world? What arrogance is this?

A moment later Mary appears in order to illustrate this typical naturalistic theory. Mary is a woman with a great capacity for loving, tied to an unworthy husband, in restless search of an object matching the dimensions of her love. Yet history forbids the author to make the illustration quite relevant, as there is no fit object within her reach. This is, from the point of view of the author, fortunate, for the consequence is that the personal tragedy of Mary becomes more effective than her illustrative significance.

In the portrayal of her character, irrespective of theories, the author again seems to look towards models in the dramatic literature of the past epoch. The woman whose tragedy arises out of spiritual and physical starvation in dwarfish environments is a common figure in Continental and English drama. Wedekind's Lulu, Synge's Pegeen, and Masefield's Nan, are typical examples. Mary is, according to Drinkwater, such a woman. Darnley, her husband, debases himself to the level of singing indecent songs outside her windows. She takes some comfort in the company of Riccio; but he is a poor substitute for a real lover, no more than a toy doll or a singing bird to her. The bold and virile Bothwell gratifies her senses, at least temporarily, but he has no food for her soul:

> BOTHWELL. You want my love, burningly you want it.
>
> MARY. I know—yes. But for an enterprise like this love must be durable. Yours would fail . . .
>
> . . . . .
>
> BOTHWELL. You have fires. Can you quench them? Mary, my beloved, I am stronger than you. Come. I bid it. (Mary stays a moment, bound in his arms. Then she slowly releases herself.)
>
> MARY. It is magnificent. But I told you. I am wiser than my blood.

After all there *is* a difference between Drinkwater and the Continental naturalists. In Drinkwater the passion of the soul, which weighs little with Wedekind and Schnitzler, is the absolutely predominant element of love. It is even questionable whether the vague and melancholy longing for an opportunity of showing the strength of her sympathies may properly be called a passion. At least, sexual passion she does not know. Sinking into the arms of Both-

well she quite coolly describes the feelings she experiences; but she does not even for a moment lose her self-control. When Bothwell declares that she has fires, we may trust his words. She does not show them. The figure suggested by the libellous songs which we learn through Darnley is not the Mary who acts in the play.

In the majority of his plays the author very wisely drops the subject of love as an isolated phenomenon, and pleads the cause of life in a general sense. In these plays he draws a series of quite effective characters who endeavour to create favourable conditions for the natural development of life, and who deeply regret the fact that they do not succeed. In these people the love for life grows to such a strength that "passion" is no improper designation.

The God of the Quiet includes two representatives of the passion for life: the King and the soldier. The soldier belongs to a besieged town, and the King has brought forces to relieve it. Both plead fervently against such destructive passions as pride and vengeance and greed for power, which produce the disastrous result of war:

> Poor clay that would excel in power,
> Made frantic by some silly pride.
>
> Anger blunts us and destroys.
> . . . though my friend is death, I will not go
> Courting a vain death for my renown.

War is entirely irrational:

> . . . much disputing is but foolishness—
> A ploughing of sown fields.
> We wake, a generation turns,
> We learn to love, and we have done . . .
> And shall we spend these little days
> Disputing till our veins are cold?

As resistance seems useless, the King and the soldier both are determined to stop fighting, but they are not even allowed to. "Cries and the noise of arms break out again as the Curtain falls". It seems that strife, although hostile to life, is inherent in life:

> . . . Not man
> But life it is that frets us till we die.
>
> . . . . .
>
> . . . life distract is savage in the throat,
> A blind uncaptained vigour, and remote
> From reason's airy palaces . . .

This propensity to destroy through fighting is a mysterious force in life:

> . . . I only see,
> Beyond disaster that I understand
> Darkly as men the process of a hand
> Obscure in heaven and hell, a little space
> For rest.

X equals O portrays a scene from the Trojan war. A few Greek and Trojan soldiers give vent to their longings for peace and express their acute sense of the absurdity of the life they are leading. One is looking forward to a time when he may devote his efforts to the prosperity of his country, another feels inspired with the poet's gift and is waiting for favourable opportunities of writing poetry, a third one is lost in dreams of a quiet life in the country enjoying the love of his family and engaged in productive work. Suddenly death strikes its fatal blow. Their hopes are never to be realised. Their talents are lost to the world. And what is the cause of this calamity?

> . . . There was some anger
> Some generous heat of the blood those years ago
> When Paris brought his Helen into Troy
> With Menelaus screaming at his heals;
> But that's forgotten now, and none can stay
> This thing that none would have endure.

A petty offence starts the process of war, and the war continues to rage long after the cause has been forgotten. The idea of the absurdity of war may possibly explain the enigmatic title *X equals O.* It need hardly be hinted that the author's thoughts are in places far from old Troy.

The insoluble problem of war recurs again in *Abraham Lincoln* and *Robert E. Lee.* When the southern States declare for secession from the Union Abraham Lincoln, who has a firm faith in imperial organisation, makes up his mind to declare war on them, and fights them for four years until they surrender unconditionally. It now appears that there are causes great enough to justify bloodshed, that the cause of life does not require the preservation of life absolutely irrespective of its conditions. On the other hand, the President's attention is firmly fixed on the aim, and he is determined to control the passions of vengeance and hatred, which, if loosened, are apt to blind the eyes of men to the real issue. There is to be no destruction of life beyond what is necessary for the cause to which he devotes himself.

Robert E. Lee reverts to the war started by a trifling offence. The Virginian government feels offended by the policy pursued by the central government of the States, and determines to secede in order to save national, or local, honour. Although being aware that the secession involves war, and fully conscious that this silly quarrel is an absolutely inadequate reason of starting a war, Lee lends himself to the provincial policy of Virginia, because he knows that opposition would be futile:

> PEEL. I can't help feeling that the quarrel, whatever it is, is so little beside the desolation that is coming.
>
> LEE. I know. But everybody feels that really. The trouble is that the world goes on without caring for our feelings. Only an adventurer here and there really wants war. But the strain comes, and men's wits break under it, and fighting is the only way out.

Not only in his imperial policy, but in his capacity of commander-in-chief also, the Virginian President is guided by the antiquated ideal of national honour:

> We stand for the honour of the South. It can be vindicated only by our complete success, or our destruction.

It is the idol that demands the last drop of blood, which he worships. But even this monstrosity does not induce Lee to desert him. At a certain time he informs the President that everything is lost. To go on fighting only means shedding blood uselessly. The President's reply is: "Go on!" and Lee obediently leads his regiment into death. The abstract theories which Lee practises in this case are suggested by the following passage:

> PEEL. You mean that you, or any of us, may be wiser than the state, and yet the state is the great good for which we must give all, life perhaps?
>
> LEE. . . . a tragic mystery. But inescapable.

It is a conflict very like the old conflict between traditional patriotism and a rational love of one's country, known from Strindberg, Tolstoy and Bernard Shaw, which repeats itself in this play, but with the opposite termination. It might seem that the principles of Lee involve his desertion of the great cause of life. When he complies with the headstrong policy of the President against better knowledge he sacrifices a great quantity of national blood to an empty ideal of honour. But it is not quite so. Lee considers himself an impotent instrument in the hand of fate.

Probably Drinkwater reasons as follows: The gospel of rational nationalism was preached during years by philosophers and essayists. The theories were staged by leading dramatists. Then the war broke out, and was conducted as if no word of this kind had ever been spoken. Might we not look for the actual cause in some irrational and uncontrollable force of life? And might not after all the benefits derived from the system of states be worth the sacrifice?

The characters of Abraham Lincoln and Robert E. Lee contrast on some points with the intellectual hero of the preceding epoch. Such figures as Wedekind's Bismarck and Shaw's Cæsar militate against the ideals of nobility, generosity, self-sacrifice, the exaggerated sense of duty, pompous gestures, etc., in short, the romantic ideal of heroism. They demonstrate their greatness by evading shams and maintaining a rational policy; they assert the authority of reason in defiance of the blind instincts of the masses.

Abraham Lincoln has many characteristics in common with these types. He keeps a straight course between the principle of revenging injuries and humiliating enemies and the principle of making peace on any terms. He is accused of thirst for blood when he refuses to desert his cause by a premature peace. He risks friendships by checking murderous passions. And when his triumph is settled his terms of peace are limited to what is necessary for the realisation of his policy.

But Lincoln as well as Lee and other figures of the plays also conforms to the heroic ideal. When Lincoln opposes political intrigues he not only acts wisely, but he shows that he is prepared to sacrifice himself to his cause, and when he saves the condemned soldier he not only prevents useless waste of life, but he reveals a noble mind. The magnanimous terms of peace which Grant presents to the defeated opponent not only prove his capability of steering straight, but they contribute to the glorification of generosity.

> GRANT. You have come—
>
> LEE. To ask upon what terms you will accept surrender . . .

GRANT. (taking the paper from the table and handing it to Lee):

They are simple. I hope you will not find them ungenerous.

LEE. (having read the terms): You are magnanimous, sir, May I make one submission?

GRANT. It would be a privilege if I could consider it.

. . . . .

(Lee unbuckles his sword, and offers it to Grant.)

GRANT. No, no . . . It has but one rightful place. I beg you. (Lee replaces his sword. Grant offers his hand and Lee takes it. They salute.) . . .

In this climactic scene ideal heroism in the romantic sense is extolled.

Lee resigns his illustrious post as imperial commander-in-chief to play a comparatively obscure part in the national defence. He sacrifices his personal principles to comply with the bloody policy of the Virginian President. He displays greatness by subjecting himself to the strictest mental discipline and fulfilling a national duty of the most unpleasant kind. In contrast to Bismark and Cæsar he deserts reason to identify himself with the collective will as represented by the President.

Yet Lee is no exact copy of the romantic hero. His eyes are open to the futility of the heroic ideal. He is conscious of acting irrationally, and he regrets that he feels forced to act thus. He is only an incarnation of fatal and destructive forces.

Drinkwater's plays express a fatalistic view of life. In the plays that have been surveyed an attempt is made to characterise the fatalistic forces. The early play **The Storm** suggests the destructive caprices of fate without any such attempt. A man is surprised by a snow-storm in the mountains. He is very well acquainted with the district and cannot reasonably be expected to come to any harm: yet his family is waiting for him in anxious suspense, they cannot explain why. Hours pass, and he does not arrive. At last his corpse is found. The atmosphere of doom suggests Maeterlinck and Synge. Specifically the presentiment of death parallels Sarah with the old man in *L'Intruse* and Maurya in *Riders to the Sea*. That side of fatalism which refers to nature is however frequently expressed in English poetry; the parallels may therefore be accidental.

The solemn, even somewhat pompous, tone in Drinkwater's essays on art is not quite justified by his practice. He is not nearly so original as he wants his readers to believe. In spite of his repudiation of the problem-play principles there is much intellectual reasoning and theorising in his plays. He does not always put the human element into the seat of honour which we might expect from his proclamation. He has constructed some effective characters; but often the characters subserve abstract thought. He admires Shakespeare, he quotes Shakespeare, and he attempts to imitate Shakespeare; we may even hear echoes of Shakespeare:

There is brain in you should be our piloting.

. . . . .

. . . Friends, let persuasion move
Not stripped of all its courtesy. May we not
Balance this issue with some temperate thought.

. . . . .

. . . It were enough
That love had made immortal one brief hour,
One period snatched out of the measured void
Men live by.

But Drinkwater has nothing like the Shakespearean felicity of phrase. He criticises Swinburne for monotony of style, but he does not himself escape this fault. His exaggerated solemnity tends to make him monotonous. And yet in spite of defects he maintains a fair standard. The student does not search in vain for passages of effective poetry.

John Drinkwater with Cyril Clemens (interview date 1932)

SOURCE: An interview in *The Sewanee Review,* Vol. XL, No. 4, Autumn, 1932, pp. 442-45.

[*In the following interview, Drinkwater discusses his life and literary career.*]

In the Highlands, on the outskirts of London, but a few doors from a house once inhabited by Coleridge, lives John Drinkwater, who cordially welcomed me one autumn afternoon. The poet is a stalwart Englishman, some six feet tall and correspondingly broad, and the possessor of fine, penetrating, gray eyes, heavy black hair, and a complexion inclined to be ruddy.

The poet led the way into his study, a glorious room where a log fire was brightly burning at one end, and, opposite, was an enormous window commanding a view of a flower garden of surpassing charm. A table littered with manuscripts stood before the fire, at which the poet had evidently been working recently. Around about were countless books, and various gifts from many famous men and women. The long high mantelpiece was decorated with an unusually striking bust of Walter de la Mare. After we had seated ourselves before the fire (for the autumn day was somewhat chilly) the poet remarked, motioning towards his manuscript,

"I am just putting the finishing touches on my biography of Samuel Pepys, which I have been working on all summer at Pepys' House, Brampton, near Huntingdon. This house, where Pepys was born in 1633, I bought several years ago."

I asked Drinkwater what part of the diarist's life he had concentrated upon.

"My biography deals with his whole career", the poet answered, "My feeling is that his entire career has never been adequately treated before. The diary, as you know, covers only nine years, from 1660 to 1669. I deal at considerable length with his early years. I believe with Bernard Shaw that the childhood and youth of an individual comprise perhaps, his most important period. It was a great inspiration for me working in the house where Pepys had actually lived. I felt always in the right mood for writing the biography. At times I could even imagine that he was standing by my side watching me write."

"What do you think of those modern authors who try to write in the style and manner of Pepys?" I asked.

"They have managed to imitate the old fellow's words and phraseology pretty neatly," he replied, "but they simply cannot catch his spirit which is the chief thing in Pepys, and the sole reason for his great popularity. Consequently I find all Pepys' modern imitators stale and flat. Why read a pale and insipid disciple, when the hale and hearty master waits in your library?"

After a discussion of Pepys for a few minutes more, the conversation turned upon hobbies.

"I have two hobbies", commented Drinkwater, lighting a cigarette, "collecting Confederate stamps and medals. I have had these two hobbies almost as far back as I can remember. Just the other day my stamp collection won a gold medal at the International Exhibition in Antwerp, and it is now being exhibited in Berlin."

Drinkwater showed me some of his very interesting stamps of the Confederacy and continued,

"Do you know, it is a peculiar thing, but collecting these stamps first aroused my interest in the history of the United States. Before that the history of your country meant little or nothing to me. In the early twenties and thirties of last century they had a sort of mail service along the Mississippi, and throughout several of the Southern states. Some stamps were issued locally, just as so many bank bills were at that period, and it is these local issues that have become especially scarce, and of late years exceedingly so, due to the manipulations of stamp dealers. The service and arrangement of some of these mail routes were similar to the Pony Express of a later date."

After stirring the fire for a moment or two Drinkwater went on,

"Naturally, my interest did not end with the stamps. I became interested in the Western settlement of America, and then in that mighty conflict of tendencies that resulted in the Civil War. It was not unnatural that my interest should especially be attracted to the most outstanding characters of that period, Robert E. Lee and Abraham Lincoln—hence my two plays dealing with these men. But if it hadn't been for my interest in postage stamps I almost certainly never would have written *Abraham Lincoln* and *Robert E. Lee.*"

While Drinkwater was being summoned to the telephone my attention was attracted by a rather unusual pen and ink drawing of Napoleon that was hanging on the wall. And on a small table near by, stood a bust of the emperor. When my host returned, I asked him about the drawing.

"Oh, that is the artist's original drawing for the jacket cover of Hardy's *The Dynasts.* I am a good friend of the man who first illustrated the famous poem."

In the course of our conversation the poet told me that he had no "especial regard" for Bonaparte, but, considering the drawing and the bust, one cannot help feeling that the great Napoleon is numbered among his heroes. I would not be at all surprised if some day Napoleon appeared upon the boards in the same brilliant way that Abraham Lincoln and Robert E. Lee have done. At this point we adjourned to a sort of breakfast room exceedingly prettily furnished for tea. Like the study this apartment commanded a captivating view of the garden. A delicious tea was spread out for us on a little table, consisting of sandwiches, seed cake, and some toothsome apple tarts, not to mention fine buttered toast. In one corner of the room there was a revolving bookcase of miscellaneous volumes, and opposite to where I sat stood a fair sized bookcase containing all the books that Mr. Drinkwater had written. A shelf or two hardly held his various volumes of poems, such as *Swords and Ploughshares, Olton, Tides, Loyalties* and so forth. Another shelf had his plays, among them being *Abraham Lincoln, Mary Stuart, Oliver Cromwell,* and lower down were the shelves holding his various biographies.

I asked the poet what was his favorite of his own books. He smiled a moment and then replied,

"I have no favorite among my own children. But if any at all it is usually the last book I have written. Now it is my life of Pepys. Next year it will probably be some new work that I will have finished by then."

Other authors, notably G. K. Chesterton and Fannie Hurst, have told me that their last book is the one that they hate the most. It has cost them so much drudgery and eyestrain that they never want to see it again, much less read it. The conversation then shifted to early recollections. To the question how far back he could remember, Drinkwater answered,

"I don't remember as far back as some writers do, certainly not as far back as Penelope Anne's age, for instance." Penelope Anne was the poet's little one year old girl who had just been brought into the room by the nurse.

After a while the subject of America came up for discussion, as it always does when Americans and English talk together.

"I have made two visits to the United States," said Drinkwater with a smile of pleasant recollection, "and admire its energy and its knack of always getting the thing accomplished that it sets out to do. In the things of the spirit you are also well advanced. I have a great admiration for your literary men, such as E. A. Robinson, Edgar Lee Masters, and Carl Sandburg."

Drinkwater told how from his earliest years Mark Twain had been one of his favorite authors, and that the days he devoted to his first perusal of *Tom Sawyer* and *Huckle-Berry Finn* were red letter days of his boyhood. At my request he gladly sent the following message to his fellow members in the United States.

I like that word, "let us now praise famous men", and am proud to belong to a Society that in praise remembers a man so justly famous. And Mark Twain, I think, was the sort of man who would like to be praised in this way by after years. —All good wishes to the Mark Twain Society.

Highgate.

September 22.

JOHN DRINKWATER.

As I bade goodbye to the poet I thought of the poem of his called **"Passage"** that advises us in reading history to

> Remember then that also we,
> In a moon's course are history.

Graham Greene (essay date 1934)

SOURCE: A review of *A Man's House,* in *The Spectator,* Vol. 153, No. 5535, July 27, 1934, p. 129.

[*An English literary figure, Greene is generally considered the most important Catholic novelist of the twentieth century. In his major works he explored the problems of spiritually and socially alienated individuals living in corrupt and corrupting societies. In the following essay, he reviews Drinkwater's* A Man's House.]

Every generation has *The Sign of the Cross* it deserves, but Mr. Drinkwater's version [*A Man's House*] has suffered a little from the time-lag. Although this story of a Jewish family in Jerusalem in A.D. 33 is written in, roughly speaking, contemporary English, it has the air of an older, more frankly melodramatic day. The blind girl miraculously healed after a rather abrupt conversion and courted by a Roman centurion, bow-armed in a breastplate; the handsome young convert with Renaissance hair who elopes with his girl to Bethany (an oddly romantic interpretation of the command, "Leave all and follow me"); all these have their sources almost as far back as *The Sign of the Cross* itself. The mixture of romantic love and religious history belongs to the evangelical school, and the old poet Nathan (how one pitied Mr. Scott Sunderland, who played this tremolo part) is only more modern in the sense that in his rapture and innocence he might have been a contributor to Mr. Marsh's Georgian anthologies.

Mr. Drinkwater's idea was a good one: to show the effect of Christ's entry into Jerusalem, His crucifixion and resurrection, on a prosperous middle-class family of Jews. Salathiel, a rich merchant, liberal as old men are liberal, finds himself, from the moment that the new preacher reaches Bethany, no longer master in his own house. Nathan, his brother, Rachel, his daughter, both go to Bethany; and his son Mathias, a strong, intolerant, agreeably acid character, takes control of the business and the household. The times are revolutionary; there is no room for the tolerance of old men; they must be pushed aside. The shades of Fascism and National Socialism move ominously in the background, and the first few minutes of the play promise exciting and legitimate contemporary parallels. Christ is at Bethany; He is planning His entry; the streets are unnaturally quiet. All the discontented in Jerusalem are waiting a chance to demonstrate: "gossip, strange faces, furtive figures in the shadows, keys being turned in doors." Christ, the agitator: "He, who at midwatch came, By the starlight, naming a dubious name": seen only through the unsympathetic eyes of the bourgeois Jew: this would have been a subject of great interest.

But Mr. Drinkwater has compromised; the struggle in the household between Christian daughter and Jewish father has a formal banality; it is as if a prentice playwright had been reading his textbooks on the subject of conflict in drama. Religious inspiration must not be dealt with superficially; the theme in Mr. Drinkwater's play seems banal because it is too great for him. The dialogue, pleasantly concrete in the case of Mathias, the young business man, becomes vague and sentimental in the case of the Christians: Rachel, the servant Jacob, Nathan, Esther, the blind daughter. "He made me feel somehow that I—I mattered, if you understand. Not grand, or anything like that—but—somebody": so the boy Jacob. "You can't describe it. There is something about this man that is quite new": so Nathan. "What is it tonight, Uncle Nathan? Something seems to be moving—everywhere": so Rachel. Something, somebody, somewhere, inarticulacies, abstractions: you cannot make a play out of these any more than you can make a faith. There were moments of poetic writing or of tense looks and brooding silences which I found peculiarly embarrassing. In the stillness one became painfully conscious of the irreverent creaking of one's shirt.

But unreserved praise can be given to Mr. Paul Shelving, who designed the scenery and dresses, and to most of the cast, especially to Mr. Basil Radford in the long and rather monotonous part of Salathiel, the father, to Mr. Reginald Tate as Mathias, and to Mr. Stanley Lathbury, who shared with Mr. Tate the best dialogue in the play. The production was not as satisfying as the acting; there was no reason why two Roman soldiers should have been statuesquely present while Salathiel and Mathias discussed the most intimate of their family affairs, and the last ten minutes of the play were amazingly clumsy and a quite unfair strain upon the actors. The stage was crowded like a railway platform with people saying good-bye; some of the characters were off to Damascus and some to the Adriatic; hurried handclasps, hurried kisses, hurried embraces, and then the flag is not waved, the whistle is not blown; with acute embarrassment one prolongs the handclasp, the embrace, beyond the limits of sincerity.

FURTHER READING

Bibliography

Berven, Peter. "John Drinkwater: An Annotated Bibliography of Writings about Him." *English Literature in Transition* 21, No. 1 (1978): 9-66.
     Comprehensive secondary bibliography.

Pearce, Michael. *John Drinkwater: An Annotated Bibliogra-

phy of His Works. New York and London: Garland Publishing, 1977, 157 p.

> Bibliography of Drinkwater's writings, including contributions to periodicals and anthologies and film scripts.

Criticism

Abercrombie, Lascelles. "The Drama of John Drinkwater." *Four Decades of Poetry, 1890-1930* 1, No. 4 (July 1977): 271-81.

> Appreciative essay on Drinkwater's work by his friend Abercrombie, originally presented as a lecture at the Malvern Festival on 23 July 1934.

Mark Twain Quarterly 1, No. 4 (Summer 1937): 1-5, 8, 15, 24.

> Recollections of Drinkwater by friends and literary figures, including Frank Swinnerton, Hamlin Garland, John Masefield, John Cowper Powys, and Sherwood Anderson.

Wood, Frederick T. "On the Poetry of John Drinkwater." *The Poetry Review* 24 (January-February 1933): 27-51.

> Overview of Drinkwater's poetry.

Additional coverage of Drinkwater's life and career is available in the following sources published by Gale Research: *Contemporary Authors*, **Vol. 109; and** *Dictionary of Literary Biography*, **Vols. 10, 19.**

Sergei Eisenstein

1898-1948

Russian director, scriptwriter, and film theorist.

INTRODUCTION

Eisenstein was an innovative filmmaker whose aesthetic theory and visual technique helped to revolutionize film as an art form throughout the world. Among his best known works are *Bronenosets "Potyomkin"* (*The Battleship Potemkin*), *Aleksandr Nevskii* (*Alexander Nevsky*), and *Ivan Groznyi* (*Ivan the Terrible*).

Biographical Information

Eisenstein was born into an upper-middle-class family in Riga, a Baltic port city in Latvia. His father was a civil engineer, and Eisenstein himself studied architectural engineering at the School of Public Works in Petrograd from 1914 to 1917. While in school he became interested in the aims of Bolshevism, and he joined the Red Army at the age of twenty. During his time in the military he also helped to promote communist ideology through his work as a poster painter and theatrical designer. After the establishment of the Soviet Union, Eisenstein moved to Moscow, where he worked in the theater as a set and costume designer, and ultimately a director, at the Proletkult, a government-sponsored theater. Eisenstein's stage work convinced him that live drama was too limiting for his visual imagination, and that only film could provide Soviet communism with the revolutionary art form that it needed to further its ideology of collectivism. His early films, *Stachka* (*Strike*) and *Potemkin*, were generally well received in the Soviet Union, but the director was forced to alter or abandon several of his later films for political reasons: while Eisenstein defined himself as a patriot loyal to the goals of the communist revolution, his artistic individualism was considered suspect by the Soviet government. From 1929 to 1931, Eisenstein visited the United States with the intention of directing films in Hollywood, but Paramount studios, to whom the director was under contract, failed to produce any of Eisenstein's proposed film scenarios, including one for a film version of Theodore Dreiser's *An American Tragedy*. Abandoning Hollywood, Eisenstein traveled to Mexico and shot footage for a historical drama about the struggles of Mexican peasants, but the film was never completed. In 1932 Eisenstein returned to the U.S.S.R., where he spent some time teaching at the Film Institute in Moscow before returning to filmmaking. He went on to complete *Staroie i novoie* (*Old and New*), *Alexander Nevsky*, and parts I and II of *Ivan the Terrible*. Despite the small number of films he actually completed, Eisenstein's work and his theories of filmmaking made him one of the foremost directors in the world. He died in 1948.

Major Works

Eisenstein's second and most important film, *Potemkin*, which is based on a 1905 mutiny aboard a Russian battleship, earned the director international acclaim. This work has been praised both for its compelling narrative and for its use of the editing technique Eisenstein called montage. The term has since come to refer to many types of editing, but Eisenstein's concept of montage referred specifically to the juxtaposition of images in order to create dramatic and visual tension. He theorized that film viewers watching a montage sequence would absorb a single, composite impression that was synthesized from separate images and which altered the individual meaning of single shots. After the enthusiastic reception of *Potemkin*, Eisenstein began work on several other film projects, many of which were suppressed by the Soviet government or altered in order to conform to Communist Party ideology. *Old and New*, which began its production under the title "The General Line," was re-edited and retitled in order to bring the film's ideology into agreement with Joseph Stalin's agricultural policy. During the latter part of his career, after he was forbidden by Stalin's government to use the montage technique he pioneered, Eisenstein turned his attention to ornate costume dramas with elaborate sets. These works include *Alexander Nevsky*, which interprets a medieval Russian folk hero as a precursor of the communist revolution, and *Ivan the Terrible*, an uncompleted trilogy.

Critical Reception

Despite his persecution by the Soviet government, Eisenstein remained an enthusiastic supporter of collectivism throughout his life. All of his works sought to express this Soviet ideal and to build a mythology around it. While some critics dismiss Eisenstein as a simple propagandist, most admit that his visually striking and intellectually complex approach to making films helped to raise the status of the motion picture from simple entertainment to complex art form. His aesthetic theory, expressed in his many written commentaries on filmmaking and visual art in general, continue to influence both filmmakers and critics.

PRINCIPAL WORKS

Stachka [*Strike*] (film) 1924
Bronenosets "Potyomkin" [*The Battleship Potemkin*] (film) 1925
Oktyabre [*October: Ten Days That Shook the World*] (film) 1927
Staroie i novoie [*Old and New*] (film) 1929
Aleksandr Nevskii [*Alexander Nevsky*] (film) 1938
The Film Sense (essays) 1942
Ivan Groznyi [*Ivan the Terrible, Part One*] (film) 1944
Ivan Groznyi: Boyarskii zagovor [*Ivan the Terrible, Part Two: The Boyars' Plot*] (film) 1945
Notes of a Film Director (essays) 1947
Film Form: Essays in Film Theory (essays) 1949
Que Viva Mexico! (screenplay) 1951
Izbrannye proizvedeniaa v shesti tomakh. 6 vols. (autobiography, criticism, essay, and scenarios) 1964-71
Film Essays with a Lecture (essays) 1968
The Complete Films of Eisenstein, Together with an Unpublished Essay by Eisenstein (screenplays and essay) 1974
Immoral Memories: An Autobiography (autobiography) 1983

CRITICISM

O. Brik (essay date 1929?)

SOURCE: An excerpt from *Movies and Methods: An Anthology,* edited by Bill Nichols, University of California Press, 1976, pp. 17-20.

[*In the following essay, which first appeared in the Soviet journal* New Lef, *Brik charges that Eisenstein's* October *falsifies historical facts.*]

Sergei Eisenstein has slipped into a difficult and absurd situation. He has suddenly found himself proclaimed a world-class director, a genius, he has been heaped with political and artistic decorations, all of which has effectively bound his creative initiative hand and foot.

In normal circumstances he could have carried on his artistic experiments and researches into new methods of film-making calmly and without any strain: his films would then have been of great methodological and aesthetic interest. But piece-meal experiments are too trivial a concern for a world-class director: by virtue of his status he is obliged to resolve world-scale problems and produce world-class films. It comes as no surprise therefore that Eisenstein has announced his intention to film Marx's *Capital*—no lesser theme would do.

As a result there have been painful and hopeless efforts to jump higher than his own height of which a graphic example is his latest film, **October.**

It would, of course, be difficult for any young director not to take advantage of all those material and organisational opportunities that flow from the title of genius, and Eisenstein has not withstood the temptations.

He has decided that he is his own genius-head, he has made a decisive break with his comrades in production, moved out of production discipline and begun to work in a way that leans heavily and directly on his world renown.

Eisenstein was asked to make a jubilee film for the tenth anniversary of October, a task which from the Lef point of view could only be fulfilled through a documentary montage of existing film material. This is in fact what Shub has done in her films, *The Great Road,* and *The Fall of the Romanov Dynasty.* Our position was that the October Revolution was such a major historical fact that any 'play' with this fact was unacceptable. We argued that the slightest deviation from historical truth in the representation of the events of October could not fail to disturb anyone with the slightest cultural sensitivity.

We felt therefore that the task that Eisenstein had been set—to give not the film-truth (*kinopravda*), of the October events, but a film-epic, a film-fantasy—was doomed in advance. But Eisenstein, who in some areas has moved towards the Lef position, did not share the Lef viewpoint in this instance—he believed that it was possible to find a method of representing October, not as documentary montage, but through an artistic 'play' film. Eisenstein of course rejected the idea of straightforward historical reconstruction from the start. The failure of [Boris Barnet's 1927 film] *Moscow in October*—a film based purely on the reconstruction of events—showed him to be right in this regard. What he needed was an artistic method for the representation of October events.

From the Lef standpoint such a method does not exist and indeed cannot exist. If Eisenstein had not been loaded down by the weighty title of genius, he could have experimented freely and his experiments might have brilliantly demonstrated the impossibility of the task set him. Now however, alongside pure experiment, he was obliged to create a complete jubilee film, and therefore to combine experiments with form and trite conventions in a way that sits curiously in one and the same work. The result is an unremarkable film.

While rejecting straightforward reconstruction, Eisenstein was obliged one way or another to deal with Lenin, the central figure of the October Revolution, in his jubilee film. To do so he resorted to the most absurd and cheapest of devices: he found a man who resembled Lenin to play the role of Lenin. The result was an absurd falsification which could only carry conviction for someone devoid of any respect or feeling for historical truth.

Eisenstein's film work on the heroic parts of his film is analogous to the operations of our cliché painters, like Brodsky or Pchclin, and these sequences have neither cultural nor artistic interest.

Only in episodes fairly distantly related to the development of the October Revolution is his work as a director apparent and it is to these episodes that any discussion of the film has to be limited.

The Women's Battalion. This theme is given much greater prominence in the film **October** than the women's battalion had in the actual historical events. The explanation for this is that women in military uniform represent rich material for theatrical exploitation.

However, in structuring this theme Eisenstein has committed a crude political mistake. Carried away by his satirical portrayal of the woman soldier, he creates, instead of a satire on the women who defended the Provisional Government, a general satire on women who take up arms for any cause at all.

The theme of women involving themselves in affairs that don't concern them draws further strength in Eisenstein's work from juxtapositions in a metaphorical relation of the women soldier and images like Rodin's The Kiss and a mother and child.

The error is committed because Eisenstein exaggerates the satirical treatment of the women without constructing a parallel satire on the power which they were defending and therefore no sense of the political absurdity of this defence is conveyed.

People and things. Eisenstein's search for cinematic metaphors gives rise to a whole series of episodes which intercut the lines of objects and people (Kerensky and the peacock, Kerensky and the statue of Napoleon, the Mensheviks and the high society dinner plate) and in all these constructions, Eisenstein commits the same error.

The objects are not given any preliminary non-metaphorical significance. It is never made apparent that these objects were all to be found in the Winter Palace, that the plate, for instance, was left in the Smolny by the Institute originally housed there. There is therefore no context for their sudden and inexplicable emergence in a metaphorical relation.

While the verbal metaphor allows us to say 'as cowardly as a hare' because the hare in question is not a real hare, but a sum of signs, in film we cannot follow a picture of a cowardly man by a picture of a hare and consider that we have thereby constructed a metaphor, because in a film, the given hare is a real hare and not just a sum of signs. In film therefore a metaphor cannot be constructed on the basis of objects which do not have their own real destiny in terms of the film in which they appear. Such a metaphor would not be cinematic, but literary. This is clear in the sequence which shows a chandelier shuddering under the impact of October gunfire. Since we have not seen this chandelier before and have no sense of its pre-revolutionary history, we cannot be moved by its trembling and the whole image simply calls up incongruous questions. . . .

The unthought out linkage of objects and people leads Eisenstein to build relations between them which have no metaphorical significance at all but are based purely on the principle of visual paradox; thus we have tiny people alongside huge marble feet, and the overlap from earlier metaphorical structures leads the viewer to look for metaphorical significance where none proves to exist.

The opening of the bridge. As a film director Eisenstein could obviously not resist filming the raising of the bridges in Petrograd, but this in itself was not enough. He extended the episode with piquant details, women's hair slipping over the opening, a horse dangling over the Neva. It goes without saying these *guignol* details have no relation to any of the film's themes—the given sequences are offered in isolation, like some spicy side dish, and are quite out of place.

Falsification of history. Every departure from historical fact is permissible only where it has been developed to the level of grotesque and the extent of its correspondence to any reality is no longer relevant. . . .

When departure from historical fact does not approach the grotesque, but remains somewhere halfway, then the result is the most commonplace historical lie. There are many such instances in **October.**

1. The murder of a bolshevik by women in the July Days: There was a similar incident which involved the murder of a bolshevik selling *Pravda* by junkers. In an attempt to heighten the incident, Eisenstein brings in women and parasols—the result is unconvincing and in the spirit of trite stories about the Paris Commune. The parasols prove to have no symbolic value, they function as a shabby prop and distort the reality of the event.

2. The sailors' smashing of the wine cellars: Everyone knows that one of the darker episodes of October was the battle over the wine cellars immediately after the overthrow and that the sailors not only did not smash the wine cellars, but looted themselves and refused to shoot at those who came after the wine. If Eisenstein had found some symbolic expression for this affair, say, demonstrating some kind of eventual resolution between proletarian consciousness and the incident, the sequence might have had some justification. But when a real sailor energetically smashes real bottles, what results is not a symbol, not a poster, but a lie. Eisenstein's view as it has been expressed in his most recent articles and lectures is that the artist-director should not be the slave of his material, that artistic vision or, to use Eisenstein's terminology, the 'slogan'

must be the basis of cinematography. The 'slogan' determines not only the selection of material, but its form. The Lef position is that the basis of cinematic art is the material. To Eisenstein this seems too narrow, too prone to nail the flight of artistic imagination to the realm of the real.

Eisenstein does not see cinema as a means of representing reality, he lays claim to philosophical cinema-tracts. We would suggest that this is a mistake, that this direction can lead no further than ideographic symbolism. And *October* is the best proof of this.

From our point of view, Eisenstein's main contribution lies in his smashing the canons of the 'play' film, and carrying to the absurd the principle of creative transformation of material. This work was done in literature by the symbolists in their time, by the abstract artists in painting, and is historically necessary.

Our only regret is that Eisenstein, in the capacity of a world-class director, feels obliged to construct 80 per cent of his work on the basis of worn-out conventions which consequently considerably lower the value of the experimental work he is trying to carry on in his films.

Sergei Eisenstein   (essay date 1949)

SOURCE: *Film Form: Essays in Film Theory,* edited and translated by Jay Leyda, Harcourt Brace Jovanovich, 1949, pp. 115-20, 163-66.

[*In the following essay, Eisenstein discusses* Battleship Potemkin.]

To return anew to the question of purity of film form, I can easily counter the usual objection that the craft of film diction and film expressiveness is very young as yet, and has no models for a classic tradition. It is even said that I find too much fault with the models of film form at our disposal, and manage with literary analogies alone. Many even consider it dubious that this "half-art" (and you would be surprised to know how many, in and out of films, still refer to the cinema in this way) deserves such a broad frame of reference.

Forgive me. But this is the way things are.

And yet our film language, though lacking its classics, possessed a great severity of form and film diction. On a certain level our cinema has known such a severe responsibility for each shot, admitting it into a montage sequence with as much care as a line of poetry is admitted into a poem, or each musical atom is admitted into the movement of a fugue.

There are plenty of examples that may be brought in from the practice of our silent cinematography. Not having the time to analyze other specimens for this present purpose, I may be allowed to bring here a sample analysis from one of my own works. It is taken from material for the conclusion of my book *Direction* (Part II—*Mise-en-cadre*) and concerns *Potemkin.* In order to show the compositional dependence between the plastic side of each of the shots, an example has been intentionally chosen not from a climax, but from an almost accidentally hit-upon place: four-

teen successive pieces from the scene that precedes the fusillade on the Odessa steps. The scene where the "good people of Odessa" (so the sailors of the *Potemkin* addressed the population of Odessa) send yawls with provisions to the side of the mutinous battleship.

This sending of greetings is constructed on a distinct cross-cutting of two themes.

1. The yawls speeding towards the battleship.

2. The people of Odessa watching and waving.

At the end the two themes are merged. The composition is basically in two planes: depth and foreground. Alternately, the themes take a dominant position, advancing to the foreground, and thrusting each other by turns to the background.

The composition is built (1) on a plastic interaction of both these planes (within the frame) and (2) on a shifting of line and form in each of these planes from frame to frame (by montage). In the second case the compositional play is formed from the interaction of plastic impressions of the preceding shot in collision or interaction with the following shot. (Here the analysis is of the purely spatial and linear directions: the rhythmic and temporal relations will be discussed elsewhere.)

The movement of the composition takes the following course:

I. The yawls in movement. A smooth, even movement, parallel with the horizontals of the frame. The whole field of vision is filled with theme 1. There is a play of small vertical sails.

II. An intensified movement of the yawls of theme 1 (the entrance of theme 2 contributes to this). Theme 2 comes to the foreground with the severe rhythm of the vertical motionless columns. The vertical lines foreshadow the plastic distribution of the coming figures (in IV, V, etc.). Interplay of the horizontal wakes and the vertical lines of both sails and columns. The yawl theme is thrust back in depth. At the bottom of the frame appears the plastic theme of the arch.

III. The plastic theme of the arch expands into the entire frame. The play is effected by the shift in the frame's content—from vertical lines to the structure of the arch. The theme of verticals is maintained in the movement of the people—small figures moving away from the camera. The yawl theme is thrust completely into the background.

IV. The plastic theme of the arch finally moves into the foreground. The arc-formation is transposed to a contrary solution: the contours of a group are sketched, forming a circle (the parasol emphasizes the composition). This same transition in a contrary direction also takes place within a vertical construction: the backs of the small figures moving towards the depth are replaced by large standing figures, photographed frontally. The theme of the yawls in movement is maintained by reflection, in the expression of their eyes and in their movement in a horizontal direction.

V. In the foreground is a common compositional variant:

an even number of persons is replaced by an uneven number. Two replaced by three. This "golden rule" in shifting the *mise-en-scène* is supported by a tradition that can be traced back to the principles of Chinese painting as well as to the practice of the *Commedia dell'arte*. (The directions of the glances also cross.) The arch motive is again bent, this time in a contrary curve. Repeating and supporting it is a new parallel arch-motif in the background: a balustrade—the yawl theme in movement. The eyes gaze across the whole width of the frame in a horizontal direction.

VI. Pieces I to V give a transition from the yawl theme to the watcher's theme, developed in five montage pieces. The interval from V to VI gives a sharp returning transition from the watchers to the yawls. Strictly following the content, the composition sharply transforms each of the elements in an opposite direction. The line of the balustrade is brought swiftly into the foreground, now as the line of the boat's gunwale. This is doubled by the adjacent line of the water's surface. The basic compositional elements are the same, but counterposed in treatment. V is static; VI is drawn by the dynamics of the boat in motion. The vertical division into "three" is maintained in both frames. The central element is texturally similar (the woman's blouse, and the canvas of the sail). The elements at the sides are in sharp contrast: the dark shapes of the men beside the woman, and the white spaces beside the central sail. The vertical distribution is also contrasted: three figures cut by the bottom horizontal are transformed into a vertical sail, cut by the upper horizontal of the frame. A new theme appears *in the background*—the side of the battleship, cut *at the top* (in preparation for piece VII).

VII. A sharply new thematic turn. A background theme—the battleship—is brought forward into the foreground (the thematic jump from V to VI serves somewhat as an anticipation of the jump from VI to VII). The viewpoint is turned 180: shooting from the battleship towards the sea—reversing VI. This time the side of the battleship in the *foreground* is also cut—but by the *lower* horizontal of the frame. In the depth is the sail theme, developed in verticals. The verticals of the sailors. The static gunbarrel continues the line of the boat's movement in the preceding shot. The side of the battleship would seem to be an arch, bent into an almost straight line.

VIII. A repetition of IV with heightened intensity. The horizontal play of eyes is transformed into vertically waving hands. The vertical theme has moved from the depth into the foreground, repeating the thematic transfer to the watchers.

IX. Two faces, closer. Speaking generally, this is an unfortunate combination with the preceding shot. It would have been better to have brought between VIII and IX a shot of three faces, to have repeated V with a heightened intensity. This would have produced a 2:3:2 structure. Moreover, the repetition of the familiar groups of IV and V, ending with the new IX, would have sharpened the impression of the last shot. This error is somewhat remedied by the slight change in plane, coming closer to the figures.

X. The two faces change to a single, closer face. The arm is thrown very energetically up and out of the frame. A correct alternation of faces (if the suggested correction were made between VIII and IX)—2:3:2:1. A second pair of shots with a correct enlargement of the dimensions in relation to the first pair (a proper repetition with a qualitative variation). The line of odd numbers differs both in quantity and quality (differing in the dimensions of the faces and differing in their quantities, while retaining the common direction of the odd numbers).

XI. A new sharp thematic turn. A jump, repeating that of V-VI, with new intensity. The vertical *up-throw* of the arm in the preceding shot is echoed by the vertical *sail*. In this the vertical of this sail rushes past in a horizontal line. A repetition of the theme of VI in greater intensity. And a repetition of the composition of II with this difference, that the horizontal theme of the moving yawls and the verticals of the motionless columns are here molded into a single horizontal movement of the *vertical* sail. The composition repeats the *sequence's theme* of an identity between the yawls and the people on the shore (before moving on to the concluding theme of this reel, the fusion of the yawls and the battleship).

XII. The sail of XI is broken up into a multitude of vertical sails, scudding along horizontally (a repetition of piece I with increased intensity). The little sails move in a direction opposite to that of the large single sail.

XIII. Having been broken up into small sails, the large sail is newly reassembled, but now not as a sail, but as the flag flying over the *Potemkin*. There is a new quality in this shot, for it is both static and mobile, —the mast being vertical and motionless, while the flag flutters in the wind. Formally, piece XIII repeats XI. But the change from sail to banner translates a principle of plastic unification to an ideological-thematic unification. This is no longer a vertical, a plastic union of separate elements of composition, —*this is a revolutionary banner, uniting battleship, yawls and shore.*

XIV. From here we have a natural return from the flag to the battleship. XIV repeats VII, with a lift in intensity. This shot introduces a new compositional group of *interrelationships between the yawls and the battleship*, distinguished from the first group, *yawls and shore*. The first group expressed the theme: "the yawls carry greetings and gifts from the shore to the battleship." This second group will express *the fraternization of yawls and battleship*.

The compositional dividing-point, and simultaneously the ideological uniter of both compositional groups, is the mast with the revolutionary banner.

Piece VII, repeated by the first piece of the second group, XIV, appears as a sort of foreshadowing of the second group and as an element linking the two groups together, as though the latter group had sent out a "patrol" into the territory of the first group. In the second group this role will be played by shots of waving figures, cut into scenes of the fraternization between yawls and battleship.

It should not be thought that the filming and montage of these pieces were done according to these calculations, drawn up *a priori*. Of course not. But the assembly and distribution of these pieces on the cutting table was already clearly dictated by the compositional demands of the film form. These demands dictated the selection of these particular pieces from all those available. These demands also established the regularity of the alternation of these pieces. Actually, these pieces, regarded only for their plot and story aspects, could be re-arranged in any combination. But the compositional movement through them would hardly prove in that case quite so regular in construction.

One cannot therefore complain of the complexity of this analysis. In comparison with analyses of literary and musical forms my analysis is still quite descriptive and easy.

. . . . .

From a tiny cellular organism of the battleship to the organism of the entire battleship; from a tiny cellular organism of the fleet to the organism of the whole fleet—thus flies through the theme the revolutionary feeling of brotherhood. And this is repeated in the structure of the work containing this theme—brotherhood and revolution.

Over the heads of the battleship's commanders, over the heads of the admirals of the tzar's fleet, and finally over the heads of the foreign censors, rushes the whole film with its fraternal "Hurrah!" just as within the film the feeling of brotherhood flies from the rebellious battleship over the sea to the shore. The organic-ness of the film, born in the cell within the film, not only moves and expands throughout the film as a whole, but appears far beyond its physical limits—in the public and historical fate of the same film.

Thematically and emotionally this would, perhaps, be sufficient in speaking of organic-ness, but let us be formally more severe.

Look intently into the structure of the work.

In its five acts, tied with the general thematic line of revolutionary brotherhood, there is otherwise little that is similar externally. But in one respect they are absolutely *alike:* each part is distinctly broken into two almost equal halves. This can be seen with particular clarity from the second act on:

II. Scene with the tarpaulin → mutiny

III. Mourning for Vakulinchuk → angry demonstration

IV. Lyrical fraternization → shooting

V. Anxiously awaiting the fleet → triumph

Moreover, at the "transition" point of each part, the halt has its own peculiar kind of *caesura.*

In one part (III), this is a few shots of clenched fists, through which the theme of mourning the dead leaps into the theme of fury.

In another part (IV), this is a sub-title—"SUDDENLY"—cutting off the scene of fraternization, and projecting it into the scene of the shooting.

The motionless muzzles of the rifles (in Part II). The gaping mouths of the guns (in Part V). And the cry of "Broth-

ers," upsetting the awful pause of waiting, in an explosion of brotherly feeling—in both moments.

And it should be further noted that the transition within each part is not merely a transition to a merely *different* mood, to a merely *different* rhythm, to a merely *different* event, but each time the transition is to a sharply opposite quality. Not merely contrasting, but *opposite,* for each time it *images exactly that theme from the opposite point of view,* along with the theme that *inevitably grows from it.*

The explosion of mutiny after the breaking point of oppression has been reached, under the pointed rifles (Part II).

Or the explosion of wrath, organically breaking from the theme of mass mourning for the murdered (Part III).

The shooting on the steps as an organic "deduction" of the reaction to the fraternal embrace between the *Potemkin's* rebels and the people of Odessa (Part IV), and so on.

The unity of such a canon, recurring in *each act* of the drama, is already self-evident.

But when we look at the work as a whole, we shall see that such is the whole structure of **Potemkin.**

Actually, near the middle, the film as a whole is cut by the dead halt of a *caesura;* the stormy action of the beginning is completely halted in order to take a fresh start for the second half of the film. This similar *caesura,* within the film as a whole, is made by the episode of the dead Vakulinchuk and the harbor mists.

For the entire film this episode is a halt before the same sort of transfer that occurs in those moments cited above within the separate parts. And with this moment the theme, breaking the ring forged by the sides of one rebellious battleship, bursts into the embrace of a whole city which is topographically *opposed to the ship,* but is in feeling fused into a unity with it; a unity that is, however, broken away from it by the soldiers' boots descending the steps at that moment when the theme once more returns to the drama at sea.

We see how organic is the progressive development of the theme, and at the same time we also see how the structure of **Potemkin,** as a whole, flows from this movement of the theme, which operates *for the whole* exactly as it does *for its fractional members.*

David Sylvester   (essay date 1958)

SOURCE: "Strike," in *New Statesman*, Vol. LVI, No. 1439, October 11, 1958, pp. 490-91.

[*In the following excerpt, the critic describes* Strike *as cinematic poetry and likens its symbolism to that used by T. S. Eliot in* The Wasteland.]

Minor poetry is often met with in the cinema, and now and then major poetry, for the duration of a sequence. **Strike** stands apart from other films: it hammers the nerves and exalts the spirit as intensely as *Oedipus* or *Lear,* and it goes on so doing as relentlessly.

If the sustained empathy which *Strike* induces is like that induced by the great tragedies, it is, of course, quite unlike any tragedy of the stage in that it has neither a hero nor a coherent narrative. Its method is closely analogous to that of a poem with which it is almost exactly contemporary—*The Waste Land*. It is alike in that it operates through the rhythmic relationship of scattered images, each of them precisely concrete yet also symbolic, the juxtaposition of which startles and surprises, yet not because the connection is purely irrational (as in surrealist montage) but because it reveals itself only as the whole thing works itself out, which it does, not in a continuous narrative, but symphonically, in a series of self-contained but thematically related movements. It is, again, like *The Waste Land* in that it has no hero and heroine but only, so to speak, supporting characters, some of whom reappear from time to time and with each reappearance are more meaningfully involved in the complex of the action as a whole—characters whose death is foreshadowed and then seen (like Eliot's Phoenician sailor and Eisenstein's little girl), characters sketched in as grotesque caricatures (like Eliot's plebeian women in a pub and Eisenstein's 'riff-raff' living in holes in the ground), and characters kept carefully in view for a time to be minutely, lingeringly, sardonically observed (like Eliot's queenly woman at her toilet and Eisenstein's company chairman with his port).

Basically the likeness resides in the fragmentation of the language, in the fantastic width of reference of the fragments, in the freedom and diversity of the rhythms with which the fragments are assembled. The tone, the tempi, the message of the two works could scarcely, needless to say, be more different. Yet there is one respect in which they are alike in content as well as form—in their obsession with the blind movement of helpless crowds.

The helplessness of the crowd, its inevitable helplessness, is, indeed, the main theme of *Strike* (thus there is more emphasis on the crowd as such, and on its suicidal impulse, than in the Odessa Steps sequence of *Potemkin*). This is, of course, one of the recurrent themes of Russian art: think of Moussorgsky's *Boris*. It is also a theme which the cinema is better equipped than any other medium to deal with. It is not by chance that the cinema's greatest contribution to the corpus of tragedy should be a film in which the crowd is the tragic hero.

Jay Leyda   (essay date 1959)

SOURCE: "Two-Thirds of a Trilogy," in *Film Quarterly*, Vol. XII, No. 3, Spring, 1959, pp. 16-22.

[*Leyda is an American critic, filmmaker, and the translator of several of Eisenstein's works on film theory. In the following essay, he analyzes Eisenstein's political goals and influences as reflected in his two films about Russian czar Ivan the Terrible.*]

Eisenstein's several aims in making *Ivan the Terrible* have continued and will continue to be defined and argued. The theories find no common ground and do little to resolve the many questions the film evokes. For more than a decade we had only three pieces of evidence—the released version of *Ivan*, Part One; the published script of the

whole two-part (later three-part) film; and denunciations and rumors of the unreleased *Ivan*, Part Two. On this basis were formed the political interpretation (Ivan IV shown as a prototype of Stalin), the psychological interpretation (explored, in detail, through Chapter XV of Marie Seton's biography of Eisenstein), the artistic interpretation (usually presented as the formal freezing of a too deliberate artist), and other side issues or private phobias. Now we have another important piece of evidence, the released version of *Ivan*, Part Two. (The sequences filmed for Part Three will probably remain uncut and unshown.) A last piece of evidence will, I hope, become generally available soon: Eisenstein's notes and drawings in preparing the entire work. Weighing these materials brings one to the conclusion that the best perspective on *Ivan the Terrible* is still that given by Eisenstein in an introductory article on his approach to the historical place and complex character of Ivan IV:

> And thus, concealing nothing, smoothing over nothing in the history of the actions of Ivan Grozny, —detracting nothing from the formidably impressive romanticism of that splendid image of the past, it has been our wish to present it in all its integrity to the audience of the world. This image,—fearful and wonderful, attracting and repelling, utterly tragic in Ivan Grozny's inner struggle along with his struggle against the enemies of his country, —can be comprehensible to the man of our day. ["Ivan Grozny," *VOKS Bulletin*, 7-8, 1942]

A reading of the whole scenario together with a viewing of both parts—the only just way to experience Eisenstein's last film—shows a scrupulous execution of this large program that he set for himself. Ivan's historical "mission" is never lost sight of, nor are the human contradictions in his motives and behavior, along which the main dramatic line is built. The separation of the two parts by the film's critics is a fault for which they are not entirely responsible, for Eisenstein could not have foreseen how many years would pass between the appearance of Parts One and Two (nor that Part Three would remain a project). Seen together at last, the majestic, ceremonial qualities of Part One, growing more passionate toward its conclusion, are transformed into the flaming bitterness and violent malice of Part Two. The calculated stylistic growth of the whole drama could only be guessed by the disgruntled critics of Part One, including the outraged Hollywood audience at its Academy preview. To see Part Two by itself must have been equally a shock to the private political viewers in 1946—here was the intrigue and carnage of *Hamlet's* conclusion without the preparation and artistic justification of the first two acts, or the torture and storm of *Lear* without the introductory dramatic mask of ceremony and hypocrisy that Shakespeare spent scene by scene stripping away. If any of the Kremlin viewers had some parallel in mind with Stalin, or even felt the need to change the popular concept of the *Terrible*, one can imagine how personally insulting Ivan's drama appeared. The keenest of those viewers must have been worried by the mystery play episode (was this a hint that the whole film was a fable? —with what moral?), and by the more explicit passage in which Ivan permits someone else to assume the responsibility for his bloodiest acts.

For a project of such complex magnitude Eisenstein was just as intent on efficiency of schedule and budget as in the simpler *Nevsky,* regardless of the problems of war-time filming in the Palace of Culture in remote Alma-Ata—and only at night, when munitions factories were not using the electric power. Within a year after filming was begun in April 1943, almost all of Part One was in the cutting room, along with much of Part Two; these later scenes had often been filmed early, to take advantage of standing sets and actors' commitments. The photography was divided between Tisse, who took the exteriors (including the siege of Kazan and the thrilling "shots in depth" at the end of Part One), and Andrei Moskvin, who filmed all the studio sequences, the larger part of the film (in Part Two the camera rarely leaves the studio).

An error, possibly fatal for both the work and its creator, may have been made in the wartime decision to divide Part Two, as published, into two parts—to produce a trilogy. Several scenes planned for the original Part Two required northern exteriors (and Tisse) that could not be adapted to the studio work in Alma-Ata. (In any case, it is difficult to see how all the material and ideas for Part Two could ever have been crowded into a film of normal length.) The resulting trilogy plan thus concluded with a Part Three of great mass movement, battle, breadth, etc., transforming the new Part Two into a purely "interior" dramatic interlude between grander and more open sec-

tions. This doomed Part Two to a concentration on psychology and on intrigue, the most dangerous elements in any "social" treatment of Ivan's reign.

The tasks that Eisenstein gave to the actors caused more friction than in any of his previous experiences with trained actors, for their training had not prepared them for the heroic Elizabethan manner, the startling "noble" style invented for *Ivan.* The staging of Shakespearean tragedy had grown increasingly realistic in the Soviet theater; the works of his more extreme contemporaries, Marlowe and Webster, impossible to play realistically, were almost unknown in actual performance there (though beloved by Eisenstein); and the one Russian "Elizabethan" drama, Pushkin's *Boris Godunov,* was unthinkable except on a realist stage. The most resistance to Eisenstein's demands came from the most trained actors; up to Eisenstein's death Nikolai Cherkasov, who played Ivan, complained bitterly [in his *Notes of a Soviet Actor*] of the compositions he had been twisted into, the aching positions he had been forced to maintain:

> Carried away by his enthusiasm for pictorial composition, Eisenstein moulded expressive, monumental *mises-en-scène,* but it was often difficult to justify the content of the form he was striving to achieve. In some of his *mises-en-scène,* extremely graphic in idea and composition, an actor's strained muscles often belied his inner feelings. In such cases, the actor found it difficult indeed to mould the image demanded of him. Eisenstein insisted that his ideas be carried out. This insistence infected us . . .

> My confidence in the film waned and my worries grew with each passing day. After watching scenes of the second part run through I criticized some episodes, but Eisenstein brushed my criticism aside, and in the end stopped showing me edited bits altogether. In films, it is the director who has the last word.

For his "romanticism" Eisenstein had no need for the shadings and delicate indications that Cherkasov had learned with such psychological "truth." When Michael Chekhov saw the film in America, he could not believe that his former colleague, Serafima Birman (who plays the hawklike boyarina), could have accepted such a "betrayal" of all their lessons without her protest. On the other hand, younger actors—such as Ludmila Tselikovskaya (playing Ivan's bride) and Pavel Kadochnikov (Vladimir)—enjoyed the new problems Eisenstein gave them.

> The grandeur of our subject called for monumental means of presentation . . . This was how the style of the film was determined, a style that ran counter to many of the traditional methods to which we have grown accustomed . . . The general custom is to try to make the historical personage "accessible," to portray him as an ordinary person sharing the ordinary, human traits of all other people—to present him "in dressing-gown and nightcap."

> But with Ivan we wanted a different tone. In him we wished chiefly to convey a sense of majesty, and this led us to adopt majestic forms. We had the actors speak in measured tones, frequently

Eisenstein with his parents, c. 1900.

accompanied by music . . . [Eisenstein, "How We Filmed *Ivan the Terrible*," *Cinema Chronicle,* February, 1945]

The unified "deliberate" film, especially the film that does not conceal its maker's calculation, has always been the least popular film anywhere in the world—in and out of the film industry. A *Rashomon* or *Cobweb Castle* will always have a harder life than a *Gate of Hell;* a Murnau or a Dreyer will always suffer more than a Lubitsch or a Huston. The rare film artist who defies the spontaneous, to show that the medium can invent as well as mirror, has as much to contribute to the future of cinema as do all the great artists—including Chaplin, Dovzhenko, Fellini—who treasure the *effect* of improvisation. Since the release of *Ivan,* Part One, there has been some slight use, by Soviet and foreign film-makers, of the lessons it teaches, but full use of *Ivan's* art apparently waits for the future.

In January, 1946, close to the completion of the cutting of Part Two, I heard from Eisenstein that his theoretical work advanced throughout the production of *Ivan:*

> I was (and still am for about 3 weeks) busy like hell: just finishing to shoot and cut the second part of *Ivan.* This part includes two reels made in color [the banquet before the murder of Vladimir]. Color used in quite different a way, than it is usually done—so that it gives a big additional chapter to what is nearly ready in book form. [In a footnote, the critic adds: "This was to have been a sequel to *The Film Sense:* it was unfinished at the time of his death."] If everything is all right here with the picture I expect to take a vacation and finish the book—3/4 of which are ready for print. Most of the stuff is unpublished (part of it even-unwritten yet!) and is mostly concerned with the development of the principles started by *Potemkin* during these 20 years in different media (is that the way to say it?) —treatments of sound, music, color. The way of composing ecstatic scenes, etc. *Ivan* in connection with *Potemkin.* I will send you a detailed plan as soon as the film goes to the laboratory to be printed. . . .

Part Two was completed under a great lift of morale; the postponed Stalin Prizes of 1943 and 1944 were announced in early February, 1946, and they included awards to the artists responsible for the high quality of *Ivan the Terrible,* Part One.

The final work on the editing of *Ivan,* Part Two, was done on the day that Part One's prize was to be celebrated. Eisenstein left the cutting room, for the last time, at 10:30 P.M., went directly to the celebration dinner, and while dancing, at about 2 A.M., collapsed to the floor with a heart attack. Five weeks later, lying in the Kremlin Hospital, he described the next few horrible moments to Brooks Atkinson:

> They told him to lie still; they told him not to move, that they would carry him to the hospital.
>
> "But I was temperamental," Mr. Eisenstein continued. "I insisted on getting up and walking to the car unassisted."

According to the doctors, that is when he died. . . .

> "I am dead right now," he said mischievously. "The doctors say that, according to all rules, I cannot possibly be alive. So this is a postscript for me, and it's wonderful. Now I can do anything I like. I am going to have a good time." [*New York Times,* March 11, 1946]

His "good time" was to read the accumulation of old and new books that *Ivan* had kept him from; his cable to me of March 21 renewed the writing promise: " . . . looking forward long reconvalescence entirely devoted writing books." And on April 18, 1946: " . . . trying hard to recover . . . working on opus two." At the end of May he was transferred to a sanatorium outside Moscow, and in June, to his cottage in the country. I do not know for how long the news was concealed from him that the Central Committee was extremely critical of Part Two. Unless he was allowed no papers he must have seen the attack in *Sovietskoye Iskusstvo* (a weekly he always read), of August 16, 1946:

> The second part of *Ivan the Terrible* provides a very clear illustration of the results to which a lack of responsibility, a disdainful attitude toward the study of essential material, and a careless and arbitrary treatment of historical themes may lead. (An editorial, "Increase the Sense of Responsibility Amongst Film Experts"; I quote a translation made by the British Films Officer in Moscow.)

One of the most negative periods in Soviet film history was introduced by the Central Committee's resolution of September 4, 1946. The particular target of its detailed attack was the second part of *A Great Life,* a film about the postwar restoration of the coal mines of the Donbass, directed by Leonid Lukov—but the second part of *Ivan the Terrible* was also unequivocally condemned:

> Eisenstein . . . showed his ignorance of historical facts by portraying the progressive force of the oprichniki [bodyguards] as a band of degenerates similar to the American Ku Klux Klan, and by portraying Ivan, a man of strong will and character, as a man of no will and little character, resembling Hamlet.

For a while Eisenstein's physical condition prevented either defense or revision of his film, and at that time there was no one else brave enough either to defend or to revise it. But in the following months Eisenstein made two careful moves, calculated to bring his *Ivan* back to life. In *Culture and Life* he published a reply to the resolution's criticism; agreeing for the most part with the condemnation, even going further in some details, there is yet one ambiguous passage that has a flavor of defense:

> We know Ivan Grozny as a man with a strong will and firm character. Does that exclude from the characterization of this tzar the possibility of the existence of certain doubts? It is difficult to think that a man who did such unheard of and unprecedented things in his time never thought over the choice of means or never had doubts about how to act, at one time or another. But

could it be that these possible doubts overshadow the historical role of historical Ivan as it was shown in the film? Could it be that the essence of this powerful sixteenth-century figure lies in these doubts and not in his uncompromising fight against them or unending success of his state activity? Is it not so that the center of our attention is and must be Ivan the builder, Ivan the creator of a new, powerful, united Russian power, Ivan the inexorable destroyer of everything that resisted his progressive undertakings? [*Kultura i zhizn,* October 20, 1946; I quote the translation used in Marie Seton's biography of Eisenstein]

Alexandrov later told Marie Seton of another move this winter. Eisenstein wrote to Stalin, asking for a discussion of the banned film, and Stalin invited him and Cherkasov to talk with him about their plans. The result was a compromise: as soon as Eisenstein was well enough to work, he should complete Part Three, incorporating in it the least offensive sequences from Part Two. It was just after this that he cabled me (March 14, 1947): "Everything okay continue working Ivan." But, so far as we know, he was never well enough to again enter a sound-stage or a cutting room.

Ten years after his death, the night of February 10-11, 1948, and five years after Stalin's death, moves were made to bring *Ivan,* Part Two, to the world film audience, and it was finally released to Soviet audiences in September. A month later it had its "western" première in the setting of the Brussels Exposition where, if any hero were to be named for the week there of The Best Films of All Time, it would certainly be Sergei Eisenstein, the creator of *Potemkin* and *Ivan.*

The curious irony of this delayed exhibition of *Ivan,* Part Two, is that we are seeing it in exactly the version in which Eisenstein left it, without any of the revisions demanded by the angered or worried censors of 1946. This extremely significant fact was revealed in the statements of two distinguished Russian visitors to Brussels at the time of *Ivan*'s showing there—Cherkasov and Kozintzev, a colleague and lifelong friend of Eisenstein—"This is the film as Eisenstein showed it to me." There are a few roughnesses in the cutting of Part Two that may be accounted for by recalling that he completed his work-print only, without an opportunity to make a final polished version before the negative was cut, posthumously, to match his work-print. The content and arrangement of scenes do not always correspond to that of the known scenario, but such an exact correspondence would be extraordinary in the case of any finished film, and surely in the case of one that was completed two years after its scenario was published.

The only flaw in the Brussels and subsequent London screenings of Part Two was that the color sequences were shown in black and white, for Moskvin was dissatisfied with the process he had used, compared with his later successes in color. Two months later, however, the persistence of the Cinémathèque Francaise achieved a Paris showing of the last reels as intended by their makers—a world of difference in the total effect of the film. In Brussels Kozintzev had told us how Eisenstein had treated

color as another instrument, and of his occasional unreal manipulation of colored light; but the actuality surpassed all expectation. After a generation of discreet film color it is a new stimulation to see it used indiscreetly, boldly, and with ideas. Like another group of instruments, it heightens every purpose it is applied to, and you can hear Prokofiev orchestrating for it, with the same unreal dramatic enhancement that you hear in the boyarina's ambitious lullaby when her exultation is suddenly supported chorally. Though the cathedral climax between the two color passages was filmed earlier in black and white, the transitions between color and monochrome were turned ingeniously to the film's advantage. And it was good to see Eisenstein enjoying a taste of color before his career closed.

We have not yet seen the whole of Eisenstein's trilogy, and it is now sadly clear that we never shall, for the passages intended for Part Three are too fragmentary for editing or judgment (though its sketches may be complete). But we now have an hour and a half more of *Ivan the Terrible* than we had before, and this is a great deal to be thankful for. It means this much more of Eisenstein's ideas and inventions, plus this much more of Prokofiev's music—prepared for us thirteen years ago by two great artists who are now dead.

In Eisenstein, the genius of an artist and the fervour of an inspired scholar were united; and his six completed films, though they represent but a fraction of his creative activity, reveal him as one of the most important artists of the 20th century.

—Marie Seton, in her Sergei M. Eisenstein: A Biography, *1978.*

William S. Pechter (essay date 1961)

SOURCE: "The Closed Mind of Sergei Eisenstein," in *The Kenyon Review,* Vol. XXIII, No. 4, Fall 1961, pp. 687-94.

[*In the following essay, Pechter questions the validity of Eisenstein's reputation as a great filmmaker.*]

The great success of the 1925 Moscow film season was not *Potemkin,* but some undistinguished Hollywood colossus; some thirty-five years later, Eisenstein had his season in New York. His huge presence looms even larger now than then; somehow, the twilight casts a more enhancing shadow than the dawn. The Museum of Modern Art Film Library is perforce becoming a mausoleum. Where will one today find a work so vast, so ambitious, as to challenge the pre-eminence of the early classics? Is it only twilight that descends, or some more permanent darkness?

Which is, perhaps, a somewhat elaborate way of saying that things are not so good, and, perhaps, suggesting that they were not ever so good as it may now seem. The Museum of Modern Art's retrospective Eisenstein exhibition struck me as being as significant of our past excesses as of our present dearth. We still do not really know what has been genuinely important in the brief, tragical history of the film; at least, we seem incapable of discriminating it from the flamboyance of mere specious success. It is not the forest that the trees obscure; rather, the other trees, those closer to the center. The presence looms large; with the Soviet Union's release of *Ivan the Terrible,* Part II, for cultural export, the recent rediscovery of *Strike,* his first and previously almost forgotten film, and the present availability of his writings, Eisenstein stands before us whole. The figure imposes upon our imagination, demanding judgment. There once was a man named Sergei Eisenstein, and, somehow, we must attempt to come to terms with him.

Eisenstein once called *All Quiet on the Western Front* a good Ph. D. thesis, and Dwight Macdonald has described *The Film Sense* as a bad Ph. D. thesis. Events have now, I suppose, come full circle; Eisenstein is dead, Macdonald a regular film reviewer for *Esquire,* and Milestone is still making movies. Even those for whom Eisenstein was a modern Shakespeare (always excepting the Jay Leydas, for whom, presumably, Shakespeare was a premature Eisenstein) have tended to dissociate Eisenstein the filmmaker from Eisenstein the theoretician. Even Eisenstein himself, whose sympathies are rather more with the Jay Leydas, remarks, with his customary heavy-handed wit, upon his deficiency as a literary stylist. And, certainly, what could be further from the stunning virtuosity of *Potemkin* than the gnomic phraseology and leaden pedantry of *The Film Sense,* or, for that matter, *Film Form* as well. Eisenstein on *pars pro toto* is a hilarity too good to be missed. One is tempted to say, as Eric Bentley has remarked of another artist become theoretician, that Eisenstein begins a new paragraph every time he does not have a new idea, which is usually a good many times per page. Yet this kind of writing is what George Bluestone has found to be related to Susanne Langer's analysis of symbolic thinking, and to Merleau-Ponty's application of phenomenological psychology to cinema. I am reminded of the famous, if, perhaps, apocryphal, doctoral dissertation on *The Function of Cleaning the American Living Room,* in which it was discovered that there was a Definite Correlation between the Spatial Relationships Factor of the area in question and the Furniture Quantity Factor in determining the Cleaning Time Function.

Perhaps the most likable quality which Eisenstein displays in his writings is an honest admiration for his own films. With some justice, he treats *Potemkin* as a classic; it is nothing if not that. *Alexander Nevsky* receives similar reverence, perhaps somewhat less deservedly. Less honest is the vein of disingenuous self-congratulation that runs through his writings, usually expressed in rallying cries in praise of the Soviet cinema in general. More disturbing still is the impersonal way in which he speaks of his "mistakes." Thus of *Strike:*

> . . . our enthusiasm produced a one-sided representation of the masses and the collective; one-sided because collectivism means the maximum development of the individual within the collec-

tive, a conception irreconcilably opposed to bourgeois individualism. Our first mass films missed this deeper meaning.

Thus a sequence in *October* was an "error." Is this a man, not to say an artist, or a committee speaking?

And Eisenstein is not above urging that the cinema is the greatest of arts, an extravagance scarcely inclined to diminish his own reputation.

> Here we shall consider the general problem of art in the specific example of its highest form—film.

> The inexhaustible potential of all art, having achieved its highest level of development in the form of cinema . . .

He quotes Lenin's famous remark that "the cinema is the most important of all the arts to us," leaving off the "to us." He devotes one article to a condescending consideration of the limits of all other arts, explaining how the older arts are subsumed and augmented by cinema.

> Moreover, the cinema is that genuine and ultimate synthesis of all artistic manifestations that fell to pieces after the peak of Greek culture, which Diderot sought vainly in opera, Wagner in music-drama, Scriabin in his color-concerti, and so on and on. . . .

> How narrow is the diapason of sculpture. . . . How frustrated have been those efforts by composers. . . . How bound is literature. . . . How imperfect and limited, too, is the theater in this respect! . . .

> As for their expressive means, escape here lies in a transition to a more perfected stage of all their potentialities—to cinema.

He will speak patronizingly of Joyce in order to establish a point in favor of cinema.

> When Joyce and I met in Paris, he was intensely interested in my plans for the inner film-monologue, with a far broader scope than is afforded by literature. . . .

> The most heroic attempt to achieve this in literature was made by James Joyce in *Ulysses* and in *Finnegan's Wake.* . . .

> . . . None of the "previous" arts has been able to achieve this purpose to the full.

He carefully explains that the film-maker must necessarily be a supreme master of all the arts.

> No one, without learning all the secrets of mise-en-scene completely, can learn montage.

> An actor who has not mastered the entire arsenal of theater craft can never fully develop his screen potentialities.

> Only after mastering the whole culture of the graphic arts can a cameraman realize the compositional basis of the shot.

> And only on a foundation of the entire experience of dramaturgy, epos, and lyricism, can a

writer create a finished work in that unprece-
dented literary phenomenon—film-writing,
which includes in itself just such a synthesis of
literary forms as the cinema as a whole comprises a synthesis of all forms of art.

The least one might hope for in reading Eisenstein on film
theory is a clear exposition and definition of montage. For
those who share Eisenstein's belief that there are such
things as knowable "fundamental laws of art," there may
be some accomplishment in his positing five categories of
montage—metric, rhythmic, tonal, overtonal, and intellectual—but certainly this is only the prelude to a definition. And when that definition comes it is either absurdly
self-evident:

> Example 3 (from ***Potemkin***): . . . In the thunder
> of the *Potemkin's* guns, a marble lion leaps up,
> in protest against the bloodshed on the Odessa
> steps. Composed of three shots of three station-
> ary marble lions at the Aluppka Palace in the
> Crimea: a sleeping lion, an awakening lion, a ris-
> ing lion. The effect is achieved by a correct cal-
> culation of the length of the second shot. Its su-
> perimposition on the first shot produces the first
> action. This establishes time to impress the sec-
> ond position on the mind. Superimposition of
> the third position on the second produces the
> second action: the lion finally rises.

or densely metaphysical:

> An example: the "fog sequence" in ***Potemkin***
> (preceding the mass mourning over the body of
> Vakulinchuk). Here the montage was based ex-
> clusively on the emotional "sound" of the
> pieces—on rhythmic vibrations that do not af-
> fect spatial alterations. In this example it is inter-
> esting that, alongside the basic tonal dominant,
> a secondary, accessory *rhythmic* dominant is
> also operating. This links the tonal construction
> of the scene with the tradition of rhythmic mon-
> tage, the furthest development of which is tonal
> montage. And, like rhythmic montage, this is
> also a special variation of metric montage.

You have to admit that's a lot of . . . montage. The fog
sequence remains one of the most beautiful passages in
Eisenstein—significantly, one without people—reminiscent of a Ryder mystical seascape, and, perhaps, a reminder of how much the best in Eisenstein owes to Tisse,
his photographer. What Eisenstein claims for it, however,
is quite simply beyond human ken. Probably, no statement
is so frankly revealing on the subject of the mystique of
montage as Eisenstein's casual reference, in another context, to "Fira Tobak, my wonderful, long time montage assistant"—like Shakespeare and his wonderful, long time
dialogue assistant! With characteristic bureaucratic bluntness Hollywood has reduced "montage" to a special effects sequence. In France and Italy, it just means editing.

There is, of course, behind all of Eisenstein's theoretical
writing, a dazzling display of erudition. But what is one
finally to say when he cites Flaubert, Kabuki, haiku, the
whole of Japanese culture, Plato, Dante, Spinoza, Newman, Michelangelo, Rembrandt, Delacroix, Debussy,
King Lear, the fundamental principles of thought and
speech, Polynesian birth customs, Milton, Leonardo, El

Greco, and Walt Whitman in order to establish precedent
for . . . montage! All extant culture becomes fair game
when a point must be proved. At this point, however, one
must distinguish between the intellectual, the mind which
is open, free, inquiring, and skeptical, and the idealogue,
the mind which is closed, committed, and intent on mar-
shalling all knowledge only toward the end of ratifying its
own preconceptions.

As Robert Warshow has observed, the real hero of the
classic Russian movies was neither the individual nor the
masses, but, as every good Hegelian knows, history. (Always, of course, excepting Peter, Nevsky, Ivan, and Stalin,
Riders of the Purple Zeitgeist.) When history is the hero,
the best the individual can hope for is to recognize the
forces at work, and, if he is lucky, sacrifice himself to them
when the right opportunity arises. Vakulinchuk, the martyr of ***Potemkin,*** simply senses the tremor of revolutionary
excitement in the air, seizes upon it, and sets inevitable
events into motion. His individual destiny is simply to die
at a good time, and in a good cause. More important, he
makes a good symbol, and lies in state with the legend
"For a spoonful of soup" pinned to his chest. His death
has meaning only as it serves higher purposes: provoking
a mass demonstration, and providing Eisenstein with a
good montage sequence. It is occasionally difficult to tell
which of these consequences is the more important; it is,
perhaps, not inapposite to note that the Peoples' State
came to suspect it was the latter. Reading Eisenstein on
the sequence of the Odessa steps is, in this respect, particularly illuminating. For him, the famous moment in which
the woman with a pince-nez is wounded in her eye is a
good instance of Example 2: an illustration of instanta-
neous action (under) Capital Letter A. Logical (under)
Roman Numeral II. *An artificially produced image of motion* (under) Heading: *a tentative film-syntax.* Photographs
of the trampled child and the mother carrying the dead
child advancing to meet the soldiers are reproduced above
the captions "Graphic Conflict" and "Conflict of Planes,"
respectively. His detailed analysis of the "pathos" and
"organic-ness" of the entire sequence concludes:

> Then the *chaos* of movement changes to a de-
> sign: the *rhythmic* descending feet of the sol-
> diers. . . .
>
> Suddenly the tempo of the *running crowd* leaps
> over into the next category of speed—into a *roll-
> ing baby-carriage.* It propels the idea of rushing
> downward into the next dimension—*from roll-
> ing, as understood "figuratively," into the physi-
> cal fact of rolling.* This is not merely a change in
> levels of *tempo.* This is furthermore as well a *leap
> in display method* from the figurative to the
> physical, taking place within the representation
> of rolling. . . .
>
> *Chaotic* movement (of a mass)—into *rhythmic*
> movement (of the soldiers). . . .
>
> Stride by stride—a leap from dimension to di-
> mension. A leap from quality to quality. So that
> in the final accounting, rather than in a separate
> episode (the baby-carriage), *the whole method of
> exposing* the entire event likewise accomplishes
> its leap: a *narrative* type of exposition is replaced

(in the montage rousing of the stone lion) and transferred to the concentrated structure of *imagery.* Visually rhythmic prose leaps over into visually poetic speech.

Need one be a socialist realist to cry "Formalism!" Eisenstein's approach to his material is supremely that of a *metteur en scene.* Masses enter on left—"then the *chaos* of movement changes to a design"—and arrange themselves in stunning patterns; soldiers come on and perform an exquisite massacre—"*chaotic* movement (of a mass)—into *rhythmic* movement (of the soldiers)." And so another montage is born. What is this if not the conception of a *decorator?* Now a healthy art has a place for its decorators (e. g. Stuart Davis, Jackson Pollock); sometimes, as in the case of a René Clair, the decorator may combine taste, wit, sensitivity, and elegance to a point at which he may, occasionally, become indistinguishable from a complete artist. But it is one thing to decorate with Labiche, even Goethe, and quite another to arrange human beings and catastrophic events into merely pleasing or exciting pictorial patterns. To reduce *Faust* to pretty pictures may be merely frivolous, but to make a beautiful arrangement of terror-stricken, dead and dying people is, in addition, aesthetically and morally irresponsible. Robert Warshow has called the films of Eisenstein and Pudovkin "a triumph of art over humanity." Perhaps, it should be added, the remark was not intended as praise.

Montage: it has so long been the shibboleth of intellectual enthusiasts of the cinema, for whom attendance at a silent Russian film is in the nature of a sacrament, that one who similarly considers himself a partisan of the medium cannot but utter the word without stirrings of pride. At last, irrefutable, invincible proof that the film is an art. And so we behold a massacre of peasants intercut with the butchering of a bull in *Strike.* ("As a matter of fact, homogeneity of gesture plays an important part in this case in achieving the effect—both the movement of the dynamic gesture within the frame, and the static gesture dividing the frame graphically.") And so the famous sequence intercutting shots of stock exchange and battlefield in Pudovkin's *The End of St. Petersburg.* A bridge is raised in *October,* and a dead woman's hair hangs over the edge, while a dead horse dangles limply from its harness over the river below. To what extent do such sequences enlarge and illuminate the human experience? Rather, to what extent do they simplify and diminish such meaning? Don't ask! It's montage! Perhaps as significant a comment as one can make on such episodes is merely to note that, in *lieu* of "movie magic," a real bull and horse were slaughtered for their occasions. One need not respond sentimentally to this fact, but one might reasonably wonder if, given the opportunity, Eisenstein wouldn't mind similarly slaughtering a few extras, providing they might "die" better.

"Down to feed the maggots," flashes the title, while the image is of a pince-nez belonging to the *Potemkin*'s doctor dangling from a rope along the ship's side. The title is adequate to the image; another bourgeois has been disposed of, and by an ingenious display of *pars pro toto* (which Eisenstein enthusiastically submits to protracted analysis) we don't even see the body. Another life has been adequately converted into a slogan. In a sense, it is no differ-

ent from Vakulinchuk's motto, "For a spoonful of soup." All grist for the same revolutionary mill, in which all experience is relieved of its individual dignity and meaning outside of its value to a cause. History is our hero, and for history one individual is pretty much like another, only the slogans change. It really *is* the triumph of art over humanity. In the cinema, it is always impolitic to talk politics. But pinning a slogan to a corpse would have equally been an act of moral crudity, emptiness, and barbarism in democratic Athens. Only it wasn't done in democratic Athens. Even Socrates was allowed to possess his own death. For human beings, individuals, change but one slogan is pretty much like another.

And so, in the West, where the notion of the individual is given some currency, however debased, it was possible to regard Eisenstein's political circumstances as a "tragedy," albeit in the modern mode of "unheroic tragedy." In Russia, it must have seemed more nearly just another comedy, bureaucratic comedy. Eisenstein was no Meyerhold, and no one had the right to ask him to be. And so the dismal chronology of public declarations.

> The intellectual cinema . . . is too vulgar to consider. *The General Line* was an intellectual film. [1935]

Eisenstein as a child.

There was a period in Soviet cinema when montage was proclaimed "everything." Now we are at the close of a period during which montage has been regarded as "nothing." Regarding montage neither as nothing nor everything, I . . . [1938]

The formalist temptations left me. The Gordian knots untied themselves. [1939]

We artists forgot . . . those great ideas our art is summoned to serve. . . . We forgot that the main thing in art is its ideological content. . . . In the second part of **Ivan the Terrible** we committed a misrepresentation of historical facts which made the film worthless and vicious in an ideological sense. . . . We must fully subordinate our creations to the interest of education of the Soviet people. From this aim we must take not one step aside nor deviate a single iota. We must master the Lenin-Stalin method of perceiving reality and history so completely and profoundly that we shall be able to overcome all remnants and survivals of former ideas which, though long ago banished from consciousness, strive stubbornly and cunningly to steal into our works whenever our creative vigilance relaxes for a single moment. This is a guarantee that our cinematography will be able to surmount all the ideological and artistic failures . . . and will again begin to create pictures of high quality, worthy of the Stalinist epoch. [1946]

As Robert Warshow has observed, "if there is one thing we should have learned from history—and from the history of the Russian Revolution above all—it is that history ought to be nobody's hero."

And so in the year 1958, a dismal body described as "117 film historians" (everyone knows there just *aren't* 117 film historians) solemnly, and to the surprise of no one, put its collective head together, reaffirmed the opinion of thirty-three years' abdication of intellect, and cast its ballot for **Potemkin** as The Best Film of All Time. And so it goes with an audience that still cannot distinguish what is merely brilliant and clever from what is great; that mistakes its innovators for its creators, its artisans for its artists, its hacks for its geniuses. So it goes with an audience for whom historical and aesthetic importance are synonymous, committed irrevocably to the notion of a cultural hit parade. Such an audience always gets its Eisensteins. It always gets what it deserves.

Eisenstein always treated *Potemkin* as the benchmark of his career. His detractors had to grant the power of this film, which would remain the most famous Soviet contribution to world cinema.

David Bordwell, *in* **The Cinema of Eisenstein,** *1993.*

Paul Seydor   (essay date 1974)

SOURCE: "Eisenstein's Aesthetics: A Dissenting View," in *Sight and Sound,* Vol 43, No. 1, Winter, 1973-74, pp. 38-43.

[*An American educator and critic, Seydor is the author of a study of the westerns of director Sam Peckinpah. In the following essay, he contends that Eisenstein was a purveyor of doctrine whose films manipulate through excessive emotionalism, and whose aesthetic deliberately "keeps reality at arm's length."*]

Everybody 'seriously interested' in film pays obeisance to Sergei Eisenstein in one way or another. Even those few critics, scholars and knowledgeable lay moviegoers who don't like his work feel compelled to preface or conclude unfavourable remarks about even its gross defects by praising his style, his craftsmanship, his cinematic sophistication and—this always—his genius (although some of the less generous among this dissenting contingent may qualify that with 'misguided' or similar euphemisms). Many *auteuristes* and other self-appointed taste-makers are more certain: Eisenstein is simply the greatest filmmaker who ever lived, *Potemkin* the greatest film ever made. And so by the time one gets round to seeing *Potemkin,* the first of his movies one usually does see, one is suitably prepared. James Agee, among others, found parts of it 'as brilliantly organised as a movement in a Beethoven symphony.'

What one may be unprepared for is an efficiently engineered political cartoon posturing as an epic, with admitted moments of 'brilliance' even if the comparison with Beethoven is too flattering and wildly misleading. One doesn't think of Beethoven as an 'organiser', while it is hard to think of Eisenstein as anything else. Thus one comes away feeling that if *Potemkin* is what film professors and other experts insist on touting as a cinematic masterpiece, perhaps it is not altogether a bad thing that most people become interested in movies long before they see any Eisenstein; for if the latter experience were to precede the former interest, it might also preclude that interest.

The objection to this could of course be that one is led to expect too much. True enough, perhaps—Eisenstein's admirers are nothing if not ardent—but one is led to expect scarcely less, since pretentious comparisons are in order, from Beethoven's own *Eroica,* Shakespeare's *Winter's Tale* and Renoir's *La Règle du feu.* None of which disappoint; all of which, quite to the contrary, far exceed anticipation. Perhaps the problem is that Eisenstein's admirers are afraid to let the man and the work speak for themselves, which may explain why so many of the panegyrics to each have little to do with the actual experience of reading the one and seeing the other. Another objection, especially relevant to works whose greatness is no longer questioned or hardly even reassessed, is that the unconvinced are simply expressing preferences as to taste. Although this, too, may be true enough, short of wilful idiosyncrasy questions of taste and judgment almost always are inextricably associated with and lead inevitably to questions of aesthetics and ideology. Could the deficiencies in Eisenstein's work, literary and visual, be less in the eye that receives than in the mind that conceived? Certainly there are deficiencies in his aesthetic theories, the most telling of which are probably his method of exposition and line of reasoning ('lines' is perhaps more accurate here, for Eisenstein hardly ever hands the reader a *single* line).

Conflict is the basis of Eisenstein's aesthetics; and dialectical conflict in particular is the informing principle of montage as he first enunciated it in his early essays **'The Cinematographic Principle and the Ideogram'** and **'A Dialectic Approach to Film Form'**. In the latter essay he set the ground-work for his theory:

> In the realm of art, this dialectic principle of dynamics is embodied in
>
> CONFLICT
>
> as the fundamental principle for the existence of every artwork and every art-form.
>
> *For art is always conflict:* (1) according to its social mission, (2) according to its nature, (3) according to its methodology.

Let us take these in order. There is a long and salutary tradition of sociopolitically oriented art that goes at least as far back as the Greeks and includes such diverse works as *Paradise Lost, Leaves of Grass,* the novels of Zola and Dos Passos, the operas of Janáček and some of the symphonies of Shostakovich. But from another point of view, everyone is in some kind of conflict with his society, even artists like Mozart, Shakespeare and John Ford, whom we don't think of as being socially committed in the narrow political sense. It is therefore necessary to distinguish between that kind of conflict by which the artist desires only improvement of an existing social system he is otherwise happy with, and that kind of conflict aimed at revolution.

For all the social criticism in Shakespeare's plays, he was not in *dialectical*—that is to say, in Eisenstein's terms, opposing, revolutionary—conflict with Elizabethan England. Yet it is precisely dialectical conflict which Eisenstein posited as the social basis of art. He insisted on this on almost every page of **'A Dialectic Approach to Film Form'**, the title itself an example of that insistence; and he implied it in his criticism of other film-makers, such as Griffith, of whom he said, 'nowhere in his films is there sounded a protest against social injustice' (which, by the way, is incorrect). One wonders what Eisenstein would do with, say, a poet like Dante, who wanted to reconcile his readers to an existing order (an order he didn't want to alter, only purify)? Or, alternatively, what he would do with his own **Potemkin** and **October.** If the social basis of art is always conflict, then how could he have made these two movies, which were made after the revolution and within a social order he presumably approved of?

This raises the major ramification of his first premise: namely, if an art work is always the result of an artist's conflict with his society, what becomes of art once socialism is realised? (Some of the more extreme Marxists, it is said, believe that art is only an interim activity vaguely necessary to orient consciousness towards the desired social state but unnecessary thereafter. Marx and Engels, it should be noted, did not share this belief.) If the implica-

tions of this first premise are thoroughly pursued, after the revolution art is left with only one function—that of legitimatising the new order, a function which, however valid in and of itself, is inherently limited and ultimately stifling. It is not incidental to add that in fact legitimation was the only function the Stalinist regime recognised and permitted its artists.

The second premise is that the nature of art is 'a conflict between natural existence and creative tendency.' Is Eisenstein stating here anything more than the truism that an artist must work his materials into a form that will clarify and communicate what he wants to say? To the extent that his materials in their raw state are more than likely not in the finished form he desires, then there is of course some conflict. But the term needs to be more precisely defined. Many artists, especially those of the romantic period and virtually all those who are genuine exponents of the organic tradition, experience nothing like dialectical conflict with their materials, mainly because nature and artistic genius are not conceived of as being essentially at odds. More exactly, the problem for the organic artist is not that of bending what Eisenstein characterised as 'passive nature' to the 'active industry' of the will, but of discovering the latent forms which an all too active nature takes.

Perhaps it is because Eisenstein, referring so often to the dynamism of his movies, fancied himself in the organic tradition that many people just took his word that he was part of it. There are enough similarities between his aesthetics and those of the organic tradition. Both involve dialectical thought; both are against 'art for art's sake', although Eisenstein, as will be shown, only nominally so; both are aware of the importance of historical continuity ('a usable past,' van Wyck Brooks called it); both ground aesthetics firmly in ideology and insist upon the social commitment of the artist. But these similarities are largely superficial. Organic artists translated social commitment, for example, mainly as a concern for relating to and expressing the on-going, *living* life of their society. For them dialecticism meant recognising and resolving, not preserving, conflict; it was a way of expressing the belief that the universe is endlessly shifting, protean, active. Their metaphors, like André Bazin's, are usually biological and botanical. ('Give me the out-of-doors. It is a metaphor, infinite of interpretation, this out-of-doors,' wrote the great architect Louis Sullivan in *Kindergarten Chats*.) Eisenstein's metaphors, on the contrary, are mostly mechanistic, as when he said, 'I would approach the making of a film in much the same way that I would approach the equipment of a poultry farm or the installation of a water system.'

The differences are not merely rhetorical but suggest differing world views, the machine as opposed to the garden. When Eisenstein wrote, 'We are seeking a definition of the whole nature, the principal style and spirit of cinema,' he evidently believed that he was discovering eternal laws governing the making of movies. This is something a truly organic artist would never have thought to do or even thought could be done, because the belief is that there are no abiding principles in the arts. Like the universe itself, the arts are continually in flux, in transition, developing and adapting. Even Sullivan's famous axiom 'form follows function' was intended less as a dictum than as a guiding suggestion to indicate that every new art work presents a new set of problems which demand new perspectives, new solutions, new means, new forms.

Consider, for contrast, Eisenstein, who in **'Film Language'** wrote:

> For those who are able, montage is the most powerful compositional means of telling a story.

> For those who do not know about composition, montage is a syntax for the *correct* construction of each particle of a film.

> And lastly, montage is simply an *elemental* rule of film-orthography for those who mistakenly put together pieces of a film as one would mix ready-made recipes for medicine, or pickle cucumbers, or preserve plums, or ferment apples and cranberries together. [emphases added]

Here is Eisenstein's own ready-made recipe. An expression is an *'inter-relation of the three phases: Conflict within a thesis* (an abstract idea)—*formulates* itself in the dialectics of the subtitle—*forms* itself spatially in the conflict within the shot—and *explodes* with increasing intensity in the montage-conflict among the separate shots.' This, he found, is 'fully analogous to human, psychological expression', 'which can also be comprehended in three phases': 'Purely verbal utterance,' 'Gesticulatory (mimic intonational) expression,' and 'Projection of the conflict into space.'

And he rarely deviated. In his essays he usually first formulated his theme, then juxtaposed it with other themes, and finally projected it into 'space' by calling on all of culture past to shore up his argument. (The difference between Eisenstein's use of the past and an organic artist's—say Renoir's—is the difference between building upon and therefore expanding the past, and appropriating it for one's own ends and thereby diminishing it. Eisenstein would have translated Brooks' phrase as 'an exploitable past'.) He constructed his movies as he did his essays. *October,* for example, begins with an awkward formulation of revolution as a statue of the Czar falls to pieces. This is in turn later reversed (literally: the opening footage is run backward) as the Provisional Government is seen to offer more of the same. Finally the theme is projected into space by a detailed look at the ten days that led to the October Revolution. (One of the last effects is a figurative explosion: the moment the Winter Palace is taken, Eisenstein cuts in shots of clocks showing the relative hour all over the world.)

Now could anything be less organic in principle, nature, or fact than this method which Eisenstein repeatedly impasted on his movies and essays alike, or more resemble what he specifically criticised linkage as being—'bricks, arranged in series to *expound* an idea'? Shots are selected and combined in such a way that the montage sequence expresses what he wills it to express. What could Eisenstein possibly have been thinking of when he wrote, 'Expressionism left barely a trace on our cinema'? Certainly German expressionism wasn't to make its 'trace' manifest until the days of *Ivan the Terrible;* but *Strike, The General Line, Potemkin* and *October* are so clearly intended to express specific, paraphrasable theses that it ill behove Eisenstein to criticise the work of other film-makers as mere 'exposition' or 'a good PhD thesis'.

Eisenstein once quoted with approval a remark by Goethe to the effect that we never experience things in isolation but in spatial and temporal relationships. Superficially, it is easy to infer from this that montage is organic because its meanings depend on the relationship of its components. And Eisenstein's much-quoted rallying cry 'Away from realism to reality' seems to corroborate the organic reading of his work, because organic artists also wanted to return to life for their materials. But Eisenstein's statement needs closer examination.

For one thing, as a serious aesthetic injunction it makes no sense because he is trying to compare incomparables. Realism is a technique (at most, a genre) of expression; reality is an object of expression and can just as effectively be expressed by realism (O'Neill) as by, say, deliberate artifice (Cocteau in *La Belle et la Bête*). For another, by realism Eisenstein does mean a technique, the slavish reproduction of the external world in the theater; by reality he means not some para-reality, as the neo-Platonic romantics did and as many of his admirers seem to think, but quite bluntly the material world. Furthermore, even that isn't absolutely certain, for he appears to think of the term as a technique of expression, and in so far as he persists in this, it becomes for him a simple extension of realism: displacing the reconstruction of the thing with the thing itself—in other words, virtually location shooting. Thus he once staged a play set in a gas factory in an actual gas factory. And as his admirers are forever pointing out, 'the sailors in *Potemkin* are real sailors . . . the heroine of *Old and New* is really a milkmaid . . .'

Admittedly, this aspect of Eisenstein's aesthetics was at least partially tenable for the silent film, and for the Russian silent film in particular (because it de-emphasised the role of the individual in favour of the masses). Purely as visual objects non-actors can carry considerable conviction because we don't have to listen to them speak. The moment Eisenstein began using sound and playing up the individual, he was forced to employ actors. Well, was there another solution, especially for the costume dramas that were his later stock in trade? A 60-year-old man may indeed, as Eisenstein once said, have had sixty years experience being sixty; but it does not follow that he has the technique and sensibility to express what it means and how it feels to *be* sixty.

It can be said that Eisenstein first wants to escape from theatrical art as imitation. The real thing is better. Yet when he moves into the material world, he finds himself dissatisfied with that reality and betrays it by imposing his own meanings upon it. When, in *October,* he cuts together shots of workers in a cannon factory with people starving in a wintry street, the obvious point is that war consumes resources that could be used to clothe and feed the populace. But Eisenstein has merely stated an idea, not conveyed a felt reality, because the awesome weight of the symbolic construct crushes any potential feeling. We respond to the construct, not to the human misery that it in part wants to express.

In a sense, the problem is that Eisenstein has realised his intentions rather too well. The creation of dramatic art works, approached dialectically, involves a kind of distortion that tends to gross simplification of idea or of character on the one hand, or to abstraction on the other, or to both. Whether the dialectical dynamic is twofold, threefold or manifold, the artist is nevertheless imposing a preconceived design on his material. All dialectical art is not necessarily the worse for this, just as all organic art is not necessarily the better for its openness (Antonioni, for example, is sometimes so open as to be formless, structureless and pointless). However, Eisenstein's peculiar combination of an abstract final cause arising out of a materialistic material cause seemed doomed to failure from the outset because the natural world, as we shall see, will almost always undercut, even contravene, the world of insistent ideology.

For the moment we can only observe that by the end of his career, Eisenstein not only had replaced non-actors with actors, but had also replaced the gas factory with the reproduction of the gas factory. He set himself to reproducing, in the best fake grand manner of which David Lean is now the exemplar, ancient castles, costumes, rooms and characters, with slavish attention to surface detail. In short, for Eisenstein, reality was just a circular route back to realism.

Yet there is no contradiction here; and maybe those who insist that Eisenstein's late work is a continuous development from his early work are right after all. The later aesthetics of slavish reproduction and heavy artifice is the logical extension of montage in general and of what Eisenstein called 'montage of attractions' in particular. For Eisenstein, nature is static and industry is active, the synthesis of this dialectic producing the dynamism of montage. But does it? Is not in fact the opposite the case—that montage, by conferring a fixed meaning on the things of nature, by carefully isolating them with the camera and then recombining them in unnatural ways in the cutting room, moves so far from dynamism as to become the very epitome of *stasis*?

Despite what he said, Eisenstein's big problem was always that nature is too fluid, too elusive, to remain in his grasp for very long. By formulating the theory of 'montage of attractions', in which all the elements at the film-maker's disposal are reduced to the same level of importance or non-importance as the case may be, Eisenstein hoped to strip things of their intrinsic meanings, which stem from the place they occupy in integral space and their relationships with other things in that space. He wanted complete control over the meaning of his films. Nature, indeed the material world in general, must of course forever be the enemy of such an aesthetic; for things do not, especially in a medium like film, readily relinquish their own character and the meanings attendant to that character.

Confronted thus with the reluctance of fact to be completely distorted, Eisenstein faced the choice of giving up either the aesthetics or the real world. He chose to give up

the latter, as his later work shows; yet the solution was implicit from the beginning. For dialectical montage displaced the natural relationship things enjoy in the world with an artificial, contrived relationship which tried to impose alien meanings. This is what André Bazin meant by his devastating observation that Russian montage does not so much give us events as allude to them, and in so doing keeps us at one remove from reality.

Later, when Eisenstein was forbidden to employ montage, he found other ways to escape reality. *Nevsky* and *Ivan* have temporal settings deep in the past; while the spatial settings moved either outside Russia (the Mexican fiasco) or, once more, away from the contemporary urban settings which distinguished his first films. Similarly his actors came to resemble people less and less, to the point that even his admirers became dubious. For James Agee, Cherkassov's Ivan is made up 'with a chin and cranium which becomes ever more pointed, like John Barrymore as Mr. Hyde.' And Dwight Macdonald observed that, 'the leading characters are men become beasts: Ivan is a lean, tired old wolf; the boyars are great fat bears billowing in furs; the two leaders of Ivan's Oprinchina police are bulls with curls low on their brutal foreheads; the wicked Efrosinia is a beaked hawk.'

The usual response to such criticism is to refer to Eisenstein's interest in cartoons, at which he was adept; or to bring up his theory of 'typage', which, as Jay Leyda pointed out, was a way of creating stock figures 'based on the need for presenting each new figure in our first glimpse of him so sharply and completely that further use of this figure may be as a known element. Thus new, immediate conventions are created.' If we discard Leyda's euphemistic description, as we confidently may, typage is revealed as nothing more sophisticated than a kind of instant stereotyping, pure caricature; and such references therefore serve to confirm rather than to deny the criticisms. *Ivan* especially is less grand opera *sans* singing, as it has been called, than an elaborate cartoon world of fantastic sets and sharp contrasts of light and shadow and ludicrous posturing by the actors. And one means to be neither facetious nor derogatory when suggesting that such celebrated sequences as the rising stone lion in *Potemkin* and the numerous icons and statuettes in *October* juxtaposed to make them appear to move, are essentially creations of a cartoon sensibility. That is, a mind more interested in creating motion (and commotion) by symbolising movement than in observing movement by allowing animate objects freedom to move. Here is Eisenstein:

> I claim that every object is a dead object even though it has moved before the camera. For movement before the camera is not movement before the screen. It is no more than raw material for the future building up of *real* movement [emphasis added], which is obtained by the assemblage of the various strips of film.

Although as he grew older, Eisenstein wrote more and more about synchronising the senses, his films, despite the rather conventional use of sound, relied so heavily on visual expression that Pauline Kael could remark quite accurately of *Ivan*, 'It's a great collection of stills.' And in the final analysis it *is* the visual style which tells all. Eisenstein's was always a style that relied heavily, and to some tastes excessively, on the close-up. But in the early films there is some balance among the kinds of shots so that there is a moderately varied dynamic range. In the later films, however, and especially in *Ivan,* close-ups dominate to the point of making the work monotonously intense, which is perhaps the other side of being intensely monotonous. They not only press us closer to the film, but more significantly they eliminate space.

Whereas film-makers as stylistically dissimilar as Renoir, Welles, Peckinpah and Kurosawa use close-ups to italicise or otherwise detail aspects of a larger world the integral sense of which is never lost, Eisenstein used them to dissolve spatial relationships—to dissolve, in other words, that reality which, as Bazin pointed out, is the one 'common denominator between the cinematographic image and the world we live in': 'the reality of space.' This is true of *Ivan* despite the archly framed and artfully composed full and long shots. For in them the objects, especially the characters, achieve another kind of anonymity, where they go and how they stand being determined less by who they are and what they do than by how they'll look once they get there.

But it was no different in the early films, only differently achieved. What unites the early and late films is the absence of integral space. What separates them is Eisenstein's conception of montage and the way the films are experienced. His first formulation of montage was thoroughly dialectical: montage was the conflict between two or more dissimilar shots placed side by side, giving rise to an 'invisible' movement or space supplied by the viewer. Editing was *the* central device without which dialectical montage could not exist. 'Conflict within the shot is [only] potential montage,' Eisenstein warned. The effects depended upon the obliteration of space, on the very absence of integral space, because the viewer was, ideally, expected to make the desired connections between shots, these connections in turn becoming the context (*i. e.,* displacing integral space) in which relationships would be seen and evaluated. Eisenstein's early cinema is quintessentially a cinema of (though not necessarily for) the mind. Space and movement are not literally seen, that is, are not on the screen: they exist only in the viewer's imagination, his eye serving to register the details with which his mind will make the 'proper' points.

Subsequently Eisenstein broadened montage to include conflict within the shot, and then to include virtually every conceivable relationship of elements in a film (*e. g.,* sound to image, object to camera, and so forth), which only broadened its meaning right out of existence. Since every art work must have internal relationships, film-makers as disparate as Godard, Wyler, Hitchock and Vigo, indeed, anyone who makes movies, become exponents of montage. Moreover, Eisenstein's original montage could be achieved only through dissonance; later, presumably even harmonious relationships qualified as montage. It is no wonder that, as William S. Pechter has observed, 'Hollywood reduced the meaning of "montage" to a special-effects sequence. In France and Italy, it just means editing.'

The implications are, however, more far-reaching than merely semantic. No one would deny that contrasts of lighting, volume, plane and size are in some sense conflicts, but are they *felt* as such? When they are combined in a single shot, they are generally experienced as contrasts that contribute to a unified composition. This is because the eye is, as McLuhan has shown us, a neutral organ and works to unify and resolve tensions in a single image. The eye needs a stimulus to jar its inherent neutrality, and cutting was originally that stimulus and was what gave Eisenstein's early films their particular energy and occasional attention-riveting suspense. In the later films, without the dialectical cutting and without a larger world fully imagined by the director, there is just about nothing for the viewer to do but sit in awe as a seemingly endless series of impressive photographs is paraded before him.

When Eisenstein abandoned his original conception of montage, he just kept on using his painterly style of within-the-shot composition, apparently unable to develop a fluid, open, flexible approach that would replace the excitement of dialectical montage with another kind of excitement, more exploratory and searching, allowing the eye to roam about the frame and to follow observed movement. These days it doesn't seem to matter much, then, whether one prefers the stupefied amazement of watching *Ivan* or the coercive nervousness of watching *Potemkin;* in one we're given nothing to do, in the other we're always being forced to do something. Ironically, the actual result of Eisenstein's late montage is about the same as that of his early montage: an expressionism that expressed nothing so much as maniacal formalism.

Still, there is no denying the great moments. The disfiguring by a bullet of a woman's face in *Potemkin* is truly shocking; and the most celebrated sequence of *October,* the July Days demonstrations, works spectacularly well, perhaps because the montage techniques genuinely serve and grow out of the material. For example, the rapid cutting between shots of the machine-gun barrel, the gunner, and a fuller shot of the gunner, really does achieve an aural effect of clatter. And the dead horse-drawbridge sequence is certainly impressively staged and brilliantly organised. One may admire such effects for their obvious artistry and yet feel shamed at the same time, as Robert Warshow did, for the readiness with which Eisenstein was willing to appropriate the deaths of real people and the actuality of historical events for his own purposes.

And one could question as well the glaring disparity between the naturalism of what is in the shots and the artifice of their combinations. One could ask, for example, why we see only one horse-drawn carriage during the demonstrations, while there are thousands of people milling around and while we are in the centre of the city. Why do both the horse and the girl's hair span the jointure of the drawbridge? How is it that the bourgeois soldier and his girl friend are able to continue making love oblivious to the panic and shooting and screaming around them? Why is the background in the close-up of the gunner black when he is firing in broad daylight?

The obvious answer is that Eisenstein could not have created his effects and racked up his polemical points without such discontinuities, inconsistencies, contradictions and contrivances. The raising of the drawbridge would be seen as a simple and logical tactical procedure instead of as this enormous ideological hyperbole contrived to express the oppression and brutality of the bourgeoisie and the hero- ism and dignity of the masses—meanings all tacked on by that flaxen hair gradually slipping away and that horse dangling over the edge. If one has any feel for this sort of thing, one knows as soon as the drawbridge begins to be raised and the horse slumps over the edge that the beast isn't going to drop loose until the bridge reaches the zenith of its ascent. One may know this, yet sit there responding helplessly in breathless anticipation. Eisenstein was a bril- liant organiser.

But the real question to be asked of these effects is: what is the operative logic, the organising principle, behind them? The answer is that it is fundamentally not humanis- tic or ideological or political or socialistic—although it may be any of these in passing. Fundamentally, it is aes- thetic. Primary value is placed upon, everything is swept before, purely formal beauty. Stalin had some cause to be concerned, given the prevailing notion of what art was supposed to do in Russia, a notion Eisenstein paid fre- quent lip service to. And his admirers rarely helped mat- ters by raving less about what he did than about how he did it. Dwight Macdonald wrote, 'Mob scenes have never been so convincingly done as here,' adding, 'the propagan- distic bias is unimportant alongside [the] fidelity to art and nature.'

Well, less faithful to truth perhaps than to beauty, Eisen- stein's aestheticism being most clearly evidenced by the extent to which the two can be separated in his movies. He is usually never less convincing than when he is trying to do something else than create a purely beautiful sequence. Thus in **October** we are subjected to such witless japery as Kerensky becoming a peacock and then a Napoleon. Or consider the Kerensky-Kornilov sequence which Eisen- stein said is supposed to express General Kornilov's 'mili- tarist tendency', which 'could be shown in a montage that would employ religious details for its material.' Does any- body but the most dogged specialist—say, a biographer of Kornilov, if he ever had one—infer that from the se- quence? In fact this sequence, as a whole the most compli- cated and opaque in the film, is also the one which receives the most gingerly treatment by the film's enthusiasts.

Much easier to deal with, if only because so embarrassing- ly clear in meaning, are such effects as the Mensheviks jux- taposed with the harpists, an effect Eisenstein himself de- nounced as too literary; and the conversion of the cycle corps depicted by an 'abstract' shot of several suspended spinning bicycle wheels, an effect he was rather pleased with. Although neither one is especially pleasing, the for- mer, despite its clumsiness, is much closer to Eisenstein's notion of transferential montage because there is a genuine transfer of meaning between dissimilar objects; whereas with the latter, neither new meaning nor new information is added by the inserted abstract image.

If a rampant aestheticism was the result of montage, it was not its motivation. Eisenstein elected expressionism over impressionism because he wanted to create 'a purely intel- lectual film'. His greatest ambition was evidently to film *Das Kapital,* and to that end he moved away from realism to reality and then away from reality too. Yet what other direction could he take to realise such a cinema, 'freed from traditional limitations [since Eisenstein wrote this in 1929, one wonders what 'tradition' he has in mind], achieving direct forms for ideas, systems and concepts, without any need for transitions and paraphrases,' except that by which he could completely transcend the material world with its copious and distracting associations, intru- sions, surprises, mysteries and ambiguities?

Eisenstein desired as well a completely visceral cinema. He once said he wasn't interested in 'kino-eye', he was after 'kino-fist'. And in one essay declared: 'The film's job is to make the audience "help itself", not to "entertain" it. To grip, not to amuse. To furnish the audience with car- tridges, not to dissipate the energies that it brought into the theater.' To which faintly fascistic end he studied Pav- lov, hoping to discover a system of system of infallible stimuli that would make audiences salivate, and in which he was at least somewhat successful. Aware as we may be of how we're manipulated, it's nevertheless difficult not to respond to his early films. Eisenstein knew how to work on our nervous systems, and we react to each mercilessly placed cue.

These twin emphases on cerebral and visceral response have evidently puzzled many of his admirers, who try des- perately to reconcile the two by saying that we're sup- posed to respond emotionally first and then to think about it later. But within the terms of Eisenstein's aesthetics, this is impossible. By making us respond first, he has made us act; and an act is an irrevocable commitment that cannot be reneged upon. **Potemkin** and **October** and **Nevsky** are less intellectual machines designed to make us think (much less to 'make manifest the contradictions of Being') than celebrations of key events in the formation of the so- cialist state. Like their analogous pageants in primitive so- cieties, in which the people 'understood', say, the creation of the world by re-enacting it as a ritual, these movies are meant to involve the spectator at the most instinctual, sub- intellectual level. For what are these movies anyway but socio-political legitimation, and not to the ends of under- standing and awareness but to force assent and affirma- tion?

In this sense, one could take issue with Macdonald and argue that far from being unsuited to a totalitarian society, Eisensteinian montage is uniquely suited to it; for its latent message is to act as we are told, no, *made,* to act. (Could this be what Lenin had in mind when he said that of all the arts cinema was the most important to the revolution?) Think about it later if we must, which of course means don't think about it at all, for there never is any 'later' since we have already symbolically acted by responding. In any case, even if we were disposed to think about it later, we couldn't do so except by going outside the frame- work of the films because they are closed systems. The only context for evaluation is the network of associations drawn by dialectical montage, which eliminates potential ambiguities and along with them the possibilities for scepticism and doubt. This is why Eisenstein's cinema can be called a cinema of but not *for* the mind.

Ultimately, Eisenstein discovering montage is not unlike T. S. Eliot rediscovering classicism. Each artist's aesthetic represents a search for authority—Eisenstein's political, Eliot's religious—in the face of an overwhelming fear of the individual and his freedom. Especially feared is the artist and his creative imagination, which must forever be subversive of all systems and all imposed authority. Thus we find Eisenstein, in the most significantly revealing of his many painful apologies to the Stalinist government, admitting that he forgot to 'fully subordinate [his] creations to the interest of the education of the Soviet people.'

> From this aim we must take not one step aside nor deviate a single iota. We must master the Lenin-Stalin method of perceiving reality and history so completely and profoundly that we shall be able to overcome all remnants and survivals of former ideas which, though long ago banished from consciousness, strive stubbornly and cunningly to steal into our works whenever our creative vigilance relaxes for a single moment.

In this light it is of course not flattering to Eisenstein to see him as the cinematic equivalent to Eliot, for it makes him less the great revolutionary artist of the screen than one of the most repressive, conservative and—there's no other word—genteel. Eisenstein wants to realise no ideals; rather he wants to idealise the real, which may be why Warshow called his films 'a triumph of art over humanity'. Eisenstein's attempts to move us emotionally are virtually without exception sheer bathos. He is never more pathetic than when he is desperately trying to open his heart; far from infusing the screen, it remains firmly attached to his sleeve, which is perhaps the best place for it, safely divorced from mind and body.

Scenes like the death of Vakulinchuk, the slaughter of the demonstrators, the trampling of the little boy on the Odessa steps, the martyred horse and girl and the starving workers in *October,* are either so aggressively sentimental or so ruthlessly didactic that one sits unmoved and suspicious. For sentimentality is rarely more than an excessive display of feeling where little or none exists to begin with; and, as Leavis has shown us, the form of an art work almost always offers the clearest indication of its sincerity. When Eisenstein pins the note 'for a spoonful of soup' to Vakulinchuk's body, he forfeits all claims to sensitivity: this is life, and death, in the service of art, and ideology.

Not that life will be cheated of the last word. A movie is inevitably a record of some aspect of nature, even if, as in Eisenstein's later movies, it is reduced to walk-on status in the form of a few exterior shots and the faces of the actors; and it will always subvert the attempts of directors to impose meanings that are not there or to remove meanings that are there. The most obvious, at least the most revealing, instance of this subversion in Eisenstein's films is the scene in *October* where a Bolshevik soldier enters the Czarina's bedroom. He sees some trinkets and knick-knacks on a night stand, a silly painting of Christ blessing the Czar and his family, some bed-clothes, presumably made of silk or other fine cloth. For a moment he is transfixed, uncomprehending and dazed by the splendour, richness and suffocating beauty of the room. He stares at a pillow pierced by the end of his bayonet; feels it; then, with a look of disgust, begins to tear it to shreds.

Doubtless Eisenstein meant us to respond sympathetically, to approve when the young soldier smashes and tears and rages at this corrupt, decadent opulence. But the scene suggests more than that. The soldier's revulsion is not directed only at the spectacle of ill-gotten wealth, and it is not motivated only by a sense of social injustice. It is, rather, directed at *all* finery and grace and delicacy; and what is revealed is less the cheerful solidarity of the masses than their ugly philistinism—manifested here as a frightening ignorance become stupidity that destroys what it cannot understand. Life takes its revenge, all right. It was this same philistinism in the Union of Soviet Socialist Republics, the inception of which Eisenstein had so lately celebrated in *October,* that would not long afterwards censure, conscript and ultimately squelch 'difficult' artists like himself in the name of history.

Vance Kepley, Jr.   (essay date 1974)

SOURCE: "The Evolution of Eisenstein's *Old and New,*" in *Cinema Examined,* edited by Richard Dyer MacCann and Jack C. Ellis, E. P. Dutton, 1982, pp. 185-201.

[*In the following essay, originally published in 1974 in* Cinema Journal, *Kepley examines Eisenstein's reworking of his film* Old and New *in compliance with the demands of evolving Soviet agricultural policy.*]

Soviet cinema is often shaped by Communist Party politics rather than audience tastes, and when the dictates of the Party leadership change, the film industry may be left in a difficult position. From Lenin's death in 1924 to Stalin's ultimate triumph in the power struggle that followed, the Soviet Union experienced a period of uncertainty, and Bolshevik policy was subject to radical alterations. Sergei Eisenstein's *Old and New* is an example of a film caught in the complexities of changing Soviet agricultural policy. [In a footnote, the critic adds: "For those who have not seen the film, a plot synopsis is in order. Marfa Lapkina, a peasant woman in a poor village, is determined to overcome the backward farming methods of the area. The local kulaks refuse to help her. When a Soviet agriculture specialist proposes the formation of a dairy cooperative, Marfa is an enthusiastic supporter, but most peasants are suspicious and refuse to join. The backward peasants try to fight a drought by forming a religious procession, but they fail. When a cream separator is introduced to the villagers, it proves a success and wins many converts to the cooperative. After some difficulty the peasants save enough money to purchase a cooperative bull, Fomka, but jealous kulaks poison him. The cooperative seeks to acquire a tractor, but bureaucratic inertia delays its delivery. Due to Marfa's efforts, it finally arrives; the pompous tractor driver is humbled, and the villagers are united in their efforts for a successful cooperative."] Originally, the film was to be a simple lesson on the need for the Soviet peasantry to join collective farms, but it was in production from 1926 to 1929, the very years in which Soviet farm policy was undergoing major changes. Eisenstein responded to the fluctuating political climate, and the finished film emerged as a sophisticated examination of ancient Russian tradition and Marxist modernism.

In order to understand the complexities of Eisenstein's subject and the difficulties he faced during production, some historical background is necessary. Russia has always been a land of dichotomies. The vast Russian plain, one-sixth of the world's land surface, stretches into both Europe and Asia. Forces of Western European civilization have been at odds with Slavic and Eastern Orthodox traditions, resulting in the split between the Westernizers and the Slavophiles. An additional schism exists between the urban-based, autocratic government and the rural peasantry, which has always resisted interference from far-off St. Petersburg or Moscow. The primary concern of the peasants has always been their attachment to the land, reflected in the myth of "Mother Russia." When the Bolsheviks gained power in 1917 they were an essentially urban movement with Western European intellectual roots. They would have preferred immediate nationalization of all farmland, but Lenin understood the old peasant suspicion of governments. Since the government was too weak at that point to enforce collectivization, Lenin sanctioned the system of individual land holdings of the peasants, and he recognized that the ideal of collectivization would have to wait until the new socialist state was on more solid footing.

Lenin's New Economic Policy (N.E.P.), initiated in 1921, was an additional concession to practical considerations. N.E.P. was a semi-capitalist system designed to allow the Soviet Union time to recover from the economic chaos of the Civil War. N.E.P. permitted the peasants to solidify their private holdings and sell grain on the open market. The wealthier peasants, the kulaks, became even stronger as a result of N.E.P. concessions, and the Bolsheviks recognized them as a threat to the future of socialism. The Bolsheviks, however, intended N.E.P. to be a temporary measure, and they realized that eventually socialism would have to be taken into the countryside.

All these historical and economic factors came to a head at the same time that Eisenstein was making *Old and New.* The middle and late 1920's was a period of serious dissension within the Bolshevik Party, and from this struggle Stalin emerged as the unchallenged power in the Soviet Union. Even before Lenin's death in 1924, Stalin had begun laying the groundwork for his ascension by forming a triumvirate within the Politburo with G. E. Zinoviev and L. B. Kamenev. Within a year after Lenin's death, they had forced Trotski to resign as Commissar of War, thus ending any potential danger of a Bonapartist movement. With Trotski weakened, Stalin could direct his energies against other Politburo members who might represent threats to his power, and the sham nature of the triumvirate became apparent. In striking at his fellow Politburo members, Stalin exploited the debate over Soviet agriculture within the party.

The inner circles of the Communist Party were divided into two groups on the rural issue. The left wing of the Po-

litburo was represented by Stalin's allies, Zinoviev and Kamenev. They believed that a stable socialist state could not be maintained unless the countryside was modernized. They urged the government to encourage the rapid collectivization of farmland to coincide with immediate industrialization of the Soviet economy. A rightwing opposition soon crystallized headed by N. Bukharin, M. Tomski, and A. Rykov. While they accepted the principle of modernization of the economy, they opposed collectivization for the immediate future. They felt that the state should continue to encourage individual farm holdings and appease the kulaks in order to meet the pressing need to supply grain to the cities.

With the lines clearly drawn, Stalin was able to play one side against the other while trying to find a practical solution to the farm problem. Stalin decided that it would be necessary to delay collectivization until the Soviet economy was more fully revived under N.E.P. This also gave him the chance to undermine the positions of the other two triumvirs, who were identified with the left-wing, pro-collectivization faction of the Politburo. Stalin threw his support to the rightist faction, but he was careful to appear as something of a conciliator. The issue came to a head at the important Fourteenth Party Congress in 1925. The resolution on agriculture which was outlined at the preliminary Fourteenth Party Conference in October called for continued support of the individual efforts of the peasants, with a provision warning against the kulaks gaining undue power included as a concession to the leftist faction. When the full Congress met in December, the leftists were denounced by Stalin and it was obvious that collectivization was defeated.

In the aftermath of the Congress, Stalin was able to cripple the left wing. When Zinoviev and Kamenev recognized that Stalin had abandoned them, they sought to form an alliance with Trotski to protect their position. Stalin had already removed several Zinoviev supporters from key party positions, and when he saw the alliance forming around his arch-enemy Trotski, he moved swiftly against it. By October, 1926, Stalin had forced Zinoviev, Kamenev, and Trotski out of the Politburo. When Trotski led a counter-demonstration on the tenth anniversary of the November Revolution, he was banished to Alma A ta and Kamenev and Zinoviev were forced to issue renunciations of their views. Stalin had shattered the illusion of the triumvirate and asserted his personal authority.

The defeat of the leftist group allowed Stalin to direct his energies against the right wing of the party, and again the agriculture issue provided the opportunity. Although some cooperative farms had been established under N.E.P., 97 percent of the sown acreage was still in individual holdings. A crisis occurred when the cities experienced a serious grain shortage in the winter of 1927-8. The grain shortage was partly the result of a work slowdown by peasants and withholding measures by the kulaks. The rightist faction of the Politburo, Bukharin, Rykov, and Tomski, was identified as the pro-kulak group, and the grain shortage left them in public disfavor. This was the opportunity that Stalin needed. Although Stalin had supported the rightist faction, he had been careful not to be identified too closely with them. Stalin claimed that the kulaks, and, by implication, the prokulak faction, were to blame for the grain shortage. He initiated emergency measures to extract grain from the countryside, and he declared that it was time to "strike hard" against the kulaks. By the beginning of 1929, Stalin had forced the rightist faction to issue confessions of ideological guilt, and Trotski had been banished from the Soviet Union. Stalin had triumphed over friend and foe alike.

The four-year period from 1925 to 1929 was thus a time of crisis for the young socialist state. The split within the party and the question of the future of the Soviet economy resulted in a general uncertainty about what lay ahead. Stalin was playing at power politics in his maneuvers on the agriculture issue, but he was also responding pragmatically to legitimate economic factors. In 1925 Stalin recognized the need to give N.E.P. additional time. By 1929, however, Stalin could not continue to concede to the wishes of the kulaks, who were demanding higher grain prices, without losing the crucial support of the urban proletariat. The grain shortage of 1928 had been a timely crisis which precipitated a necessary shift in policy. Before 1929 was out Stalin announced both the First Five-Year Plan for industrialization and the collectivization of the farms. In doing so he made the ominous statement, "We must smash the kulaks, eliminate them as a class . . . After four years of debate, the turmoil of collectivization was about to begin.

When Eisenstein undertook his film on Soviet agriculture, he had to come to terms with the various historical forces which shaped the lives of the peasants. The peasant relationship to the land, the old dichotomies and struggles in Russian life, and the complex process of forming Soviet agricultural policy in the 1920's were factors influencing Eisenstein's handling of his subject.

There was little in Eisenstein's background to qualify him as an authority on Russian agriculture. He was born of well-to-do parents in Riga, an old Hanseatic city which was closer to Western Europe in culture than to old Russia. He spent much of his youth in another city modelled on Western standards, St. Petersburg, and like many products of gentile Russian families, he learned French and German as a child. His thoroughly urban background and training as an engineer would seem to preclude his grasping the nuances of peasant culture, but he was a man of enormous intellectual curiosity. His voluminous reading and his capacity to do thorough research were his qualifications for undertaking *Old and New.*

When Eisenstein initiated the project, he was determined to do exhaustive research on both the economic aspects of farming and the culture of rural Russia. As Marie Seton said, "scientific fever possessed him," and he searched through documents of the Commissariat of Agriculture, examining records and reports. He hunted through newspapers and books on Soviet agriculture to the point of consulting A. A. Zorich's brochure, *About Cauliflowers.* He cited the resolution on agriculture of the Fourteenth Party Congress, and from what he assumed was the party line on agriculture, he took the original title for the film, *The General Line.* A very important source was a book of

sketches of a rural village, O. Davydov's *Maklochania.* The book includes a discussion of a dairy cooperative which served as a prototype for the one depicted in *Old and New.* Davydov tells of the farm acquiring a cream separator and pooling funds to purchase a cooperative bull, and both incidents appear as episodes in *Old and New.* In fact, the cream separator as a symbol of modernization so fascinated Eisenstein that he kept an advertisement of an American separator on the wall of his Moscow apartment. In addition to this intellectual research, Eisenstein was anxious to get a sense of the visceral quality of village life. In order to do this, he, his co-director Grigori Alexandrov, and their cameraman Eduard Tisse went to live in a village for a month before beginning production.

Although Eisenstein's preparation for the film acquainted him with the history and culture of the Russian peasantry, he could not have anticipated the shifts in agricultural policy within the party. He began work on the film in the spring of 1926, but did not complete it until the fall of 1929, the exact period in which the debate over Soviet agriculture was being waged. The inability of the artist to contend with changing historical forces is evident in the history of *Old and New.*

Eisenstein and Alexandrov began work on their agricultural film, then referred to as *The General Line,* in May, 1926. They completed the first draft on May 23 and reworked that into a more concise scenario which they submitted to their studio, Sovkino, on June 30. They then worked out a contract with Sovkino which specified that shooting should begin on October 1, 1926, and terminate on February 1, 1927. Eisenstein began shooting *The General Line* on schedule, and shooting progressed through the winter of 1926 at Rostov-on-Don, Baku, and the northern Caucasus. But in January, 1927, Sovkino instructed Eisenstein to stop shooting *The General Line* in order to begin making *October* for the tenth anniversary of the November Revolution. For the rest of the year Eisenstein was involved in his celebrated race to finish *October* before the November 7 anniversary date and before Pudovkin presented *The End of St. Petersburg.*

The chronology of the first phases of production of *The General Line* indicate that work was progressing smoothly on the film until the order came to begin production of *October.* The anniversary was certainly a memorable occasion for the young socialist regime, and it is not surprising that Sovkino would want to have its famous young director involved in a commemorative film. On the other hand, recalling a film crew from location on a moment's notice was not a matter to be taken lightly by a film industry which was not abundantly wealthy. It seems very likely that Sovkino was concerned about the shape of the Communist Party's agricultural policy at the time. When the order to postpone *The General Line* was given, Stalin was still adhering to a policy of encouraging individual farm production and appeasing the kulaks. A film calling for collectivization and depicting kulaks as incorrigible villains could represent an embarrassment if Stalin's stance became the long-range policy, and at that point there was no indication that Stalin would change his position. A film in honor of the November Revolution must have seemed much safer to Sovkino; it would rally public support for the film industry and allow the regime to maintain an image of unity even while Stalin was trying to undo Trotski and others within the party.

In fact, the title, *The General Line,* was one of the most ironic misnomers in the history of cinema. It was precisely the dissension within the inner ranks of the Bolsheviks which precluded the establishment of a general line on agriculture. Although Eisenstein considered the decision on agriculture of the Fourteenth Party Congress to be the inspiration of the title, this was a curious claim. The Congress did not endorse collectivization; it sanctioned individual holdings. *The General Line* was on unstable ground from the beginning.

After *October* was finished, Eisenstein returned to *The General Line* in the spring of 1928. Again the date is significant. This was after the winter grain shortage which had inspired Stalin's shift in attitude toward the peasants. Kulaks were once again officially labelled as villains, and there was no worry about portraying them as such in the film. Eisenstein returned to the film with a second scenario which he and Alexandrov completed in April of 1928, and shooting on the film continued from July to November of that year. The film was then edited and presented to Sovkino, where it was given approval in February, 1929. But the authors were still not satisfied, and they decided to do more work on the film. They travelled to the collective farm "Giant" near Rostov-on-Don, where they shot additional footage. This material was then incorporated into the film, and it was ready for release before the spring was out.

Eisenstein and Alexandrov considered the production completed and were preparing to travel to the West when an additional delay occurred. They received a call from none other than Joseph Stalin asking them to drop in for a chat. Stalin complained that the conclusion of the film was in-appropriate. He told them, "Life must prompt you to find the correct end for the film. Before going to America, you should travel through the Soviet Union, observe everything, comprehend, it, and draw your own conclusions about everything you see. As a result of this request, a shooting crew was assembled, and they travelled through rural areas for the next two months shooting location footage. The additional work done on the film may not have greatly altered the shape of the film, but it did delay its release until October of 1929.

Why did Stalin choose to interfere personally at this point? Was it worth the added delay and expense to incorporate some more rural footage into the film? Had Stalin determined at that point to announce collectivization in the fall, and did he want the film's release delayed until that time? This is difficult to determine, but there is some interesting circumstantial evidence. The film opened on October 7, 1929, and it had been retitled *Old and New* so as not to be identified with the agriculture policy of the Fourteenth Party Congress. Besides opening in three Moscow theaters, the film was shown simultaneously in 52 other cities throughout the Soviet Union in areas as widely separated as Sevastopol, Archangel, and Vladivostok. This distribution indicates that it was recognized as an important and timely film which should be widely seen. More importantly, the film was designated to be shown in conjunction with an official event scheduled for October 14. This was "Collectivization Day," an all-out public relations effort to sell the idea of collectivization, and *Old and New* was part of this campaign. Assuming Stalin knew in May that he would be announcing collectivization in the fall, he may then have decided that a more timely premiere of the film would be advantageous.

Back in December of 1928, before the final revisions in the film had been made, Eisenstein and Alexandrov noted that of the 10 months invested in production of the film, there had been only 120 working days. They claimed that 180 days had been lost to bad weather, moving, and the "struggle for the existence of *The General Line.*" They are not clear on what that struggle entailed. There may or may not have been factors that militated against the continuation of one film project over such a long period of time; there may have been interference from Sovkino during production. Soviet critic Viktor Shklovski recounts an incident in which Eisenstein had to contend with outside interference during production, although the subject was economic rather than political. The financial overseers of the film industry had to check on Eisenstein's progress before they would allocate additional funds for production. With an impish rebelliousness, Eisenstein concocted a "carnival film about abundance" to show the economists. Footage of plentiful harvests, cattle, sheep, and milk was thrown together and presented to the economists as representative of Eisenstein's work on the film. They were apparently impressed by Eisenstein's little joke, as they promptly approved the additional funds.

Whether there was any interference beyond this apparently routine checking is unclear. But Eisenstein was certainly aware of the debate over collectivization, and that this put his film in a potentially vulnerable position. How did he respond to the evolution of Soviet agricultural policy over the three-year period in which *Old and New* was in production? The answer to this lies in the changes that he made in the conception of the film, reflected in the various scripts that he and Alexandrov prepared. The script versions indicate that he maintained the same general shape and intent of the film, and most of the original scenes are retained from the earliest version. The alterations that he did make are significant, however, because they often reflect compromises that Eisenstein made with the changing political environment.

The first script version that Eisenstein and Alexandrov submitted to Sovkino in June, 1926, suggests a more dramatic depiction of the material than the finished film. The script opens by establishing an immediate tension between the peasants and the prosperous landowners.

> 120 million peasants—and . . .
>
> A few thousand landowners.
>
> MUCH land to the landowners—
>
> LITTLE to the peasants.
>
> Such cannot exist.

This situation erupts into violence as the peasants mass for an attack on the landowner's estate.

> The guns of the landowners tremble nervously. The enemy freezes, staring eye to eye. Hatred to hatred.
>
> A light breeze blows open the door.
>
> The landowners shudder.
>
> The peasants don't falter.

In the ensuing battle, the central character, a peasant girl named Evdokiia Ukraintseva, loses her husband, and this later inspires her to work for the formation of a collective to overcome the landowners. The battle culminates with a Cossack charge reminiscent of the Odessa steps sequence in *Potemkin.* In fact, this similarity to *Potemkin* seems to have been conscious, as if Eisenstein intended the film to be a sequel to *Potemkin,* which he had completed only a few months earlier. The land struggle is treated as a manifestation of the same revolutionary ferment as the Black Sea mutiny. This relationship is further illustrated by the fact that Eisenstein had originally written this very scene, an attack on a landowner's mansion, for *1905,* the script from which *Potemkin* evolved. Also, the scene of the demonstration of the cream separator contains a direct reference to *Potemkin.* As the villagers wait to see whether or not the machine will function, their suspense resembles "the time of the battleship 'Potemkin' when the crowd waited for the encounter with the squadron." The success of a cream separator is as significant to the cause of revolution as the rebellion of a naval fleet.

The 1926 version was very specific on technical matters relating to agriculture. Soviet scientists are depicted working to improve breeding techniques by experimenting with flies imported from Texas, of all places, via the "Anikovski Experimental Exchange." As a result of this experimentation at a state farm, startling successes in breeding occur: "Chickens, cows, rams, guinea pigs, horses, pigs, rabbits, cats: they are perfected just as the automobile was perfected." The revolution as depicted in *Potemkin* progressed from maggots to the entire fleet; modernization of agriculture begins with the flies and progresses to include all forms of livestock. The prodigious rate of breeding of the collective bull, Fomka, necessitates that facilities for the calves be found. The old landowner's estate is converted.

> [The Society for] the Preservation of Ancient Monuments has sent a representative. The representative removes the count's memorial wreaths while the peasants bury skeletons from the coffins in a hole: from the sarcophagus they make feeding troughs, from a glass coffin found there they make containers for milk. In the well-lit, large premises of the burial vault the young animals are quartered.

The symbols of death and waste associated with the landowners are converted into utensils for life and productivity by the cooperative.

While this version shows the Soviets importing flies from Texas, an even more important American import central to the scenario is a Fordson tractor. The cooperative ap-
plies to the Soviet government for finances to purchase a Fordson, but the bureaucracy refuses them credit. The members of the cooperative compromise their position to raise funds for the tractor by agreeing to sell shares to the kulaks. Evdokiia reacts to this threat of a concession to the kulaks by insisting that the bureaucracy deliver the tractor, and she is successful. When the tractor finally arrives, the peasants celebrate "Fordzosha" (modernization), and the "Fordson stands like a monument."

If the process outlined in this section of the scenario suggests capitalism, it is because in 1926 N.E.P., with its free market and emphasis on private property, was still in operation. But why would Eisenstein make such a specific reference to Fordson tractors and their maker Henry Ford, the epitome of capitalist ideology? Surprisingly, Henry Ford was a hero to the Soviets in the 1920's. He had done what the Soviets had longed to do by perfecting the techniques of mass production, and he was thought of throughout the U.S.S.R. as a modern revolutionary. More importantly, the Soviets were heavily dependent upon the Ford Motor Company for machine imports. Before industrialization under the First Five-Year Plan, the U.S.S.R. imported nearly all of their trucks and tractors. In 1927 eighty percent of these came from the Ford Motor Company. Of 5,700 tractors in the Ukraine, 5,520 were Fordsons. The name was so magical that the process of mass production was referred to as "Fordizatsia."

The conclusion of this scenario has a dramatic depiction of Soviet prosperity. As a result of modernization, the Soviets go into battle against backwardness: "They go to battle on the front. / FOR THE RENOVATION OF THE EARTH!" Images of war abound in the climax.

> Tractors tear down fences, razing ditches, and the cross-field barriers.
>
> FOR A COMMUNE!
>
> They break down windmills; turn dilapidated huts inside out.
>
> Logs stand up like a fan from the tractor power.
>
> Individual windmills are smashed into dust.
>
> Locusts fall back from crop-dusting attacks.
>
> The war blazes up.
>
> DARKNESS RETREATS!
>
> Spiders seek refuge.
>
> The priests retreat from the atheists.
>
> The ravens fly away.

This violent imagery of attacks against the symbols of backwardness, from dilapidated houses to priests, again suggests the parallel with the violence and drama of revolution and the link to *Potemkin.* But the destruction is nicely counterpointed by images of productivity which grow out of this conflict.

> Grain grows only like it can in the cinema-in two minutes! And not only grain-young pigs are transformed in only half a minute into one-

thousand pound hogs, and a chick into masses of fifteen thousand.

The script concludes on a cheerful note with a shot of Michael Kalinin, ceremonial President of the Soviet Union, smiling and saying, "Eat your fill!" From the opening images of tension and violence, the scenario has progressed to a conclusion of prosperity and goodwill.

The version that Alexandrov and Eisenstein prepared after completing *October* was submitted to Sovkino in April, 1928. Although it has some significant alterations from the 1926 scenario, it is not by any means a completely new approach to the subject. This version is considerably more subdued and less dramatic than the 1926 script, and it is less directly related to *Potemkin.* The allusion to *Potemkin* in the cream separator scene is retained, but there is none of the open conflict of the first script which derived from the action scenes of *Potemkin.* The entire scene of the siege of the landowner's estate was deleted, as well as the later references to the conversion of the landowner's estate for use by the cooperative. Eisenstein apparently no longer felt the need to establish the direct historical link between the Potemkin mutiny and the building of a socialist state. *October* allowed him to render the violence of revolution, which was the logical link between *Potemkin* and *Old and New.* As a result of having made *October,* Eisenstein was free to deal with the question of perfecting socialism without the dramatic clashes of the first version.

The cooperative still relies on imports in the 1928 version. The Texas flies again are instrumental in perfecting breeding techniques. The tractor is still clearly identified as a Fordson, and bureaucratic inertia and kulak machination figure in the problem of obtaining the tractor. Images of the battle for a "Renovated Earth" recur in the coda, but they are much more subdued than in the 1926 script.

> The tractor tears down fences. It razes ditches and destroys the cross-field barriers.
>
> FOR A COMMUNE!
>
> They break down the windmills. Tear down old dilapidated cottages.
>
> Logs stand up like a fan from the tractor power.
>
> The one-legged mills and the kulak lairs are smashed to bits.
>
> A squadron of machines cultivate the conquered earth.

There is less emphasis on destruction here. Images of war, such as the image of the priests and spiders retreating like withdrawing armies, have been deleted. The new emphasis is on machines conquering the land, but the result is the same, as images of abundance are capped by the same shot of Michael Kalinin offering a toast. Except for a slight tightening of the script, the only major changes from the 1926 scenario were associated with the toning down of images of violence.

The alterations which appear in the 1928 version were made for artistic rather than political reasons, but changes in the third version, which is dated 1929 and based on the final version of the film, suggest that Eisenstein had practical political factors in mind. Not only is the scene of the attack on the landowner's mansion missing from the final version, but many of the topical references have been deleted as well. The scene of the demonstration at the state farm remains, but there is no longer a reference to flies being imported from America. The acquisition of the tractor is considerably different. The central character, now called Marfa, still must cope with bureaucratic inaction, but there is no financial arrangement with the kulaks. Instead, Marfa and a factory worker unite to present the demand for the tractor to the bureaucrats, and when they are finally spurred into action, a Soviet factory produces the tractor. There is no reference to importing a Fordson now.

The deletion of references to Soviet dependence on American science and technology is important. By the time of the final shaping of the film, it was clear that large-scale industrialization would accompany rural collectivization. The decree establishing Machine Tractor Stations, the political bureau which would distribute machines to the villages, was handed down on June 5, 1929. When Eisenstein was performing the final editing on *Old and New* in the summer of 1929, he wisely decided to pay a tribute to Soviet industrialization. But the tribute is undermined; the final version of the film still contains a close-up of the tractor's label, which clearly identifies it as a Fordson. Could this be an oversight, an unconscious admission that the U.S.S.R. still was not industrialized? Or could it be another example of Eisenstein's pixyish sense of humor? It may well be that the director who made a "carnival picture" to fool some snooping economists was offering a good-natured rebellion against the politics of film-making.

Another significant change Eisenstein made was in the conclusion. Perhaps as a result of Stalin's request, the final scenes of abundance were omitted. Gone also is the shot of Michael Kalinin offering a toast. After seeing how the winds of Soviet politics could change, Eisenstein must have recognized that too topical a reference could prove to be embarrassing later on. If Trotski could be declared persona non grata, could not Kalinin also? Since Kalinin had risen from a peasant to become President of the Soviet Union, an essentially symbolic post, his function in the script had been to represent the unity of the peasantry with the government. Without his image in the final version, Eisenstein had to devise another coda which accomplished the same end. This was done by the scene of Marfa, now a tractor driver, encountering the former tractor driver who has become a farmer. This was an homage to Chaplin's *A Woman of Paris,* but it was also an image of the unity of purpose under the new Soviet system.

Old and New could have been a direct, unambiguous propaganda film, or it could have been an example of the stagnation of the "girl meets tractor" films which characterized many Soviet films. Eisenstein, however, attacked the seemingly mundane subject of farming with all his creative intensity, and he sought to elevate his subject through a complex and dynamic treatment. Ironically, his research into Russian rural life taught him that this so-called mundane subject was very complex indeed. The difficulty lies in drawing all the cultural and historical threads together, and Eisenstein achieved this through a carefully worked out thematic structure. A brief discussion of theme indicates that elements of traditional Russian culture, ancient myths, and tenets of modern Marxism are subtly woven together in the finished film.

Old and New opens with long shots of the most important element in the film, the land. The great Russian plain, "Mother Russia," represents the central myth of Russian civilization, and spiritual attachment to the soil is a unifying force in Russian life. But we are shown agricultural methods which destroy this unity as the land is divided into individual peasant holdings. Division occurs within the family as well, as brothers split their inheritance to the point of sawing their father's house in half. The asymmetrical images of the fences dividing the land and the close-ups of the fences with their criss-crossing wooden posts suggest chaos as well. Within the context of this fragmentation, we are introduced to Marfa, the village woman who is determined to overcome these anachronistic practices. Marfa Lapkina has many of the traditional qualities of the earth mother figure; she is physically strong, and the vitality that she exhibits in her struggles identifies her as a life force. But she soon learns that determination is insufficient without the assistance of modernized methods.

In response to a drought, villagers form a religious procession to pray for rain, but the scene depicts the inadequacy of spiritualism and ritual in the face of material hardship. The drought, representing death and sterility, and the procession to counter it take on an ambiguously sexual flavor. The procession culminates in a prayer in which the participants display unusual passion. The tempo of the editing increases with the passion of the participants, suggesting a religious orgy. The marchers end their frantic prayer in a state of exhaustion, and their dishevelment lends them the appearance of having joined in some huge debauchery. The drought continues, however, and the frustration of the processioners implies the experience of sex without pleasure, or, more importantly, sex without fertility. The scene contains another interesting ambiguity. The icon of the Madonna and Child is intercut with shots of a lamb suffering from thirst. The lamb image could simply be a comment on the poor condition of Russian livestock, or it could represent a parody of the gullibility of the processioners who follow the dictates of the church like sheep. But the juxtaposition of the icon and the lamb is given added significance by the fact that the lamb is the traditional symbol of Christ. Perhaps the presence of the lamb intimates that the suffering of the peasants may result in a form of redemption. But the attack on mysticism that runs through the scene implies that this redemption must be material, not spiritual.

Many of these religious and erotic elements are further dealt with in the following scene in which the cream separator is introduced to the village. The cream separator is treated with near religious reverence. Eisenstein has stated that the handling of the separator is an allusion to the Holy Grail, the symbol of spiritual perfection. But in *Old and New* the Holy Grail surrogate is functional, a machine which is essential to the production of butter. The theatrical unveiling of the separator, and the fact that it dazzles the peasants, suggests an association with church iconography or art. When the machine is operated, we again see ritual, but, in contrast to the elaborate religious rites of the procession, the ritual here is work. The stylized cranking of the machine handle becomes a substitute for prayer, and the important theme of the replacement of religion by technology emerges. Recurring sexual implications also counter the scene of the religious procession. The prominence of the machine's spout (and Marfa's obvious admiration of it) along with the tempo of the editing give the scene a very erotic tone. Shots of the flow of the cream from the spout are intercut with shots of a fountain, a traditional symbol of the source of life. Thus the sexuality of this scene results in fecundity, and it serves as a foil to the sterility of the scene of the procession. Labor and technology are depicted as life-giving, while spirituality is useless.

The importance of the communal bull, Fomka, reinforces the theme of fertility. Marfa's rather Freudian dream of the bull looming up over a herd of cows is an image of this obsession with reproduction, as if Fomka was expected to render a Stakhanovite performance as a breeder. The wedding in which Fomka is mated with a cow is a comic, pagan celebration of life which signals the beginning of the cooperative dairy herd. When Fomka is poisoned by the kulaks, the villagers again revert to paganism as they carry out mysterious rituals in an effort to save him. Eisenstein intercuts the rituals with gloomy shots of skulls which symbolize the inevitability of death and the futility of trying to conquer death through mysticism. Death is conquered through the act of reproduction, however, as Fomka's offspring survive to replenish the herd.

The harvest scene is another example of the synthesis of tradition and modernization. The line of men moving through the field cutting wheat with their scythes recalls the famous harvest scene in *Anna Karenina,* and the harvesters seem to experience the same exhilaration of physical labor as Tolstoi's Levin. But a rivalry develops between two of the harvesters, an enormous man and a smaller, more energetic youth. As they race against one another, their competition becomes increasingly heated and they nearly come to blows. Eisenstein presents this rivalry as a conscious allusion to the ancient David and Goliath legend. Their competition is interrupted when their attention is drawn to a mowing machine which cuts wheat at such a rate that their dispute seems petty and is forgotten. Machinery is a unifying force, and David and Goliath join hands in homage to technology.

The theme of the beauty of technology culminates with the introduction of the tractor to the cooperative. The inertia of bureaucracy is satirized in grotesque images of huge typewriters, pencil sharpeners, and preening secretaries. The ultimate image of bureaucratic sloth is the official signature which is rambling and chaotic. When Marfa and a factory worker confront the bureaucrats and incite them to accelerated action, the sequence is punctuated by the stamp of an official seal, which is an abrupt and precise depiction of administrative action. It also introduces the circle image, which dominates the last scenes of the film. The circle is usually pictured in various close-ups of wheels. This is important, as the wheel, the first great technological invention, contains the implication of movement and progress. It is also significant that the circle is the traditional symbol of unity and perfection. From the chaotic criss-crossing fenceposts of the opening scenes, the imagery of the film has progressed to the symmetry of the circle, suggesting the progression of the peasants toward unity. Since the circle is also a Christian symbol, this reinforces the theme of the supplanting of religion by technology; production becomes the new peasant religion. The role of the tractor as a unifying force is also demonstrated by the fact that, while the horses panic and scatter the village wagons, the tractor is able to pull all of the carts in a long line. The train of carts symbolically unites the village behind the power of the tractor. Finally, the tractor smashes down the fences which have divided the Russian plain. The imagery returns to the original symbol of the film, "Mother Russia," free of barriers and the fundamental element of unity in Russian life.

The integration of tradition and modernism in *Old and New* is achieved in a structure suggestive of a Marxian dialectic. Ancient Slavic culture (thesis) encounters Marxism (antithesis) to create a collective farm (synthesis). The symbol patterns which emerge in the film indicate Eisenstein's fascination with peasant culture and mythology. Although he may not have been the closet Christian that Marie Seton suggests, he was certainly interested in the importance of religion in rural Russia. His intense research in preparation for the film and his interest in anthropological works such as J. G. Frazer's *The Golden Bough* indicate that he was interested in the mythological roots of religious doctrine. Eisenstein saw the religious symbols in *Old and New* as archetypes, and through them he hoped to penetrate to the subconscious of his audience. He and Alexandrov wrote that their film was a call for a "new man"; they were working to develop "the collectivized man and the collectivizing man." By using ancient archetypal elements, Eisenstein sought to make his modernistic, Marxist message more meaningful to his audience.

Eisenstein had made a propaganda film, but his fascination with the ambiguities of his subject and his complex presentation transcended the conventions of propaganda. A cubistic presentation of a cream separator, a subjective depiction of a bull's orgasm, a slapstick satire of bureaucracy, and a light-hearted parody of the American Western film in the scene of the tractor's wagon train are all evidence of an artist who refused to be restricted by his subject matter. Eisenstein seemed to enjoy raising the experiences of farm life to abstractions. He wrote of "emotive structures applied to non-emotive material" in reference to *Old and New.* Hence, a cream separator supplants the Holy Grail as a means to perfection. He has combined elements of the documentary and the fiction film, drama and slapstick with the same subtlety with which he had integrated themes of old and new. This mixing of genres and styles represents the ambitions of an artist who would not comply with the normal expectations of what constitutes a good propaganda film.

How then, was the film received? Critics responded favourably. The review in *Pravda* was enthusiastic; it spoke of "the great mastery, the tremendous emotion, the

sweep, and the pulsating tempo of life. . . ." Mordaunt Hall, in *The New York Times,* praised the film as "an enlightening cinematic study." But it is difficult to tell how the Soviet public responded to *Old and New.* It ran for only a week in the Moscow theaters where it opened. Marie Seton reported that a screening of *Old and New* for the Red Army Club at the time of release produced a negative response. If this evidence is indicative of the reaction of the larger Soviet public, it may be because the experimentalism of *Old and New* was disconcerting to its audience. Eisenstein's abstract and episodic film may have seemed out of place in its association with "Collectivization Day" propaganda.

Or more likely, the film was once again victimized by the forces of history. Not long after *Old and New* was released, it became an obsolete depiction of collectivization. Collectivization was undertaken, but it had none of the utopian flavor of Eisenstein's film. Rather than peasants voluntarily joining collective farms after seeing the benefits of Soviet methods, they were forced into collectives by Stalin's rapid and drastic measures. Bolshevik agents sent into the countryside to enforce the policy used harsh punitive measures against those who hesitated to give up their private claims. The peasants then resisted Soviet tactics by slaughtering their own livestock and wrecking property in outbursts of violence reminiscent of ancient peasant and serf rebellions under czarism. Also, Stalin's decision to "eliminate the kulaks as a class" was carried out via the order forbidding kulaks to join collective farms. Their property was confiscated and they were sent to forced labor camps or executed. By the spring of 1930, the turmoil in the countryside had grown so serious that Stalin had to issue a warning against "overzealousness" on the part of those executing collectivization policy. But the resistance continued through the next several years, and the cost in human lives was staggering. Famine, executions, and labor camp conditions took a human toll which, it has been estimated, ran into millions. The harsh reality of collectivization must have made *Old and New* look like a cruel joke for contemporary Soviet citizens.

Eisenstein could not have anticipated the consequences of Stalin's collectivization policies. Eisenstein had sought in *Old and New* to harmonize the dichotomies of Russian life between the Westernizer and the Slavophile, the city and the country, the state and the peasant. To Eisenstein, the collective farm represented the synthesis of the old institution of the peasant commune and the modern methods of Soviet rationalism. But the reaction to forced collectivization demonstrated that the animosities were too deeply imbedded in Russia to be overcome through one film. For Eisenstein, the political complications that he encountered in the making and release of *Old and New* were a foretaste of the difficulties that he and other Soviet film-makers would have to face in the later Stalin years.

Stanley Kauffmann   (essay date 1975)

SOURCE: "Potemkin," in his *Living Images: Film Comment and Criticism,* Harper & Row, Publishers, 1975, pp. 290-98.

[*Kauffmann is a noted American theater and film critic. In the following essay, he analyzes Eisenstein's* Potemkin *as an expression of the director's political and artistic vision.*]

Sometimes one imagines that there is a small but constant supply of genius throughout the world and that a particular juncture of circumstances in any one place touches the local supply to life. Otherwise, how explain the sudden flowering of Athenian architecture or Elizabethan drama or Italian Renaissance painting? Can one believe that there had been no previous talent and that geniuses were born on cue? It almost seems that the right confluence of events brings dormant omnipresent genius awake; without those events, nothing. Possibly the man with the greatest potential genius for symphonic composition lived in New Guinea five hundred years ago, but there was nothing in his world to make him know it.

This theory, admittedly fanciful, gets some support from what happened in Soviet Russia in the 1920s. A new revolutionary state was born as a new revolutionary art emerged, and that combination brought forth at least three superb creators in the new art: Vsevolod Pudovkin, Alexander Dovzhenko, and—the most important because the most influential—Sergei M. Eisenstein. Conjecturally, all of them might have had outstanding careers in other fields, but the Soviet Revolution and its need for film, one may say, made geniuses of them.

For all the joy and ebullience that attended the birth of Soviet film and Eisenstein's entrance into it, his career as a whole is a sad story, and it puts my comments on *Potemkin* in true, cruelly ironic light to have some of the biographical facts first. Sergei Mikhailovich Eisenstein was born in Riga in 1898, studied engineering in St. Petersburg, and entered the Red Army in 1918 to fight in the civil war. While in the army, says Yon Barna in his recent biography, Eisenstein became involved in amateur theatricals, which intensified an interest in the theater he had felt since he was a boy. He decided to abandon an engineering future for a theatrical career. In 1920 he was demobilized, got himself to Moscow, and found a job at one of the new workers' theaters as a scene designer. He went on to do some designing for the renowned theater director Vsevolod Meyerhold, whose anti-psychological, anti-"internalizing" views influenced him greatly; then in 1922-24 Eisenstein himself directed plays, including one called *Gas Masks*. But his impulse toward direction, as he later wrote himself, was much more cinematic than theatrical: he staged *Gas Masks* in a gasworks!

From there he moved quickly into film. He had already done a short film interlude for a theatrical production, and in 1924 he made his first feature, *Strike.* In 1925 he made *Potemkin,* which is sometimes known as *Battleship Potemkin* or *Armored Cruiser Potemkin.*

Absolutely congruent with his bursting film energies was his fervor for the Communist Revolution and the establishment of the Soviet state. These factors are integral in any talk of Eisenstein. To think of him as a director who just happened to be Russian or who (in those early days) was subservient to a state-controlled industry and managed to slip some good art into his films despite this subservience, is to miss the core of Eisenstein. His works in those days were cinematic exponents of his beliefs.

With his next completed film *October,* released in 1928, the complications begin. Originally the film had sequences showing Trotsky's part in the revolution of 1917, but while Eisenstein was finishing it, Trotsky went into disrepute and then into exile as Stalin ascended. Eisenstein had to revise his film to take account of this rewriting of history.

His troubles increased as time went on. The Stalin era was not exactly a continuation of the high, shining Bolshevik days. To sum it up: the rest of his career, until his death in 1948, is a story of frustration and frequent abortion. Out of numerous projects he completed only four more films. Even an expedition he made to the West ended abortively. He was allowed to go to America in 1930, discussed several projects with a Hollywood studio, made none, and then shot a lot of footage in Mexico for a film he never edited, although others have arranged versions of it.

He spent much of his time in his later years teaching at the Institute of Cinematography in Moscow, writing (most of these writings are not yet in English), and not complaining about the state. Still the facts speak for themselves: this furiously imaginative and energetic man left a total of only six completed films. One virtually completed film, *Bezhin Meadow,* was apparently destroyed by the Soviet government in 1938, although the official line is that it was destroyed by German bombs in World War II. (Isaac Babel worked on the final script of *Bezhin Meadow,* which was based on a Turgenev story that echoes the ideological difference between Eisenstein and his conservative father.) The USSR's waste of Eisenstein, melancholy in any view, is especially grim when seen in the light that blazes off the screen from *Potemkin.*

When it was first shown abroad in 1926, it was hailed by many, including such disparate figures as Max Reinhardt and Douglas Fairbanks, as the best film that had yet been made anywhere. Agree with that opinion or not; few can see this relatively short picture—five reels, eighty-six minutes—without being catapulted into an experience that is stunning in itself and illuminating of much that followed in film history.

During the mid-1920s the Soviets were busy trying to consolidate ideologically their political and military victories, and they called on the arts to help. Eisenstein was assigned to make a huge film called *The Year 1905,* dealing with the events of the earlier, failed, but momentous outbreak against Czarism. He and his script collaborator Nina Agadzhanova-Shutko wrote a scenario in which, says Barna, "the *Potemkin* mutiny took up a relatively tiny part." When Eisenstein went to Odessa to shoot that part, he decided to limit the film to that single *Potemkin* episode.

Here is the episode, as he presents it. While the warship is anchored in the Black Sea near Odessa in June 1905, the restive crew protest against the maggoty meat that they are served. The captain orders the execution of the dissenters. Instead of obeying orders, the firing squad joins the crew in mutiny, and they take over the ship. One of the leaders is killed; his body is taken ashore so that it may lie "in state." The sympathetic citizens of Odessa pay homage to him and support the sailors on the anchored vessel with gifts of food. When a mass of these citizens gathers on a huge flight of steps overlooking the harbor to cheer the *Potemkin,* the Czar's troops appear and march down the steps, scattering the crowd and killing some of them. The government sends a naval squadron to retake the *Potemkin,* which sails to meet them in battle. At the moment of encounter, the fleet allows the mutineers to pass through. In fact, the ship sailed to Constanta in Rumania, where the crew opened her seacocks, then sought refuge inland; however, Eisenstein leaves the story open-ended, with the *Potemkin* sailing onward through the friendly squadron, bearing the seed of revolution that was to bloom twelve years later.

Now, irrespective of the viewer's political beliefs, this story is a natural thriller. Nothing has more wide or direct theatrical appeal than resistance to tyranny, whether it is Spartacus or William Tell or the Boston Tea Party. Any competent Soviet director could have made the *Potemkin* story into an exciting film. But Eisenstein—and, to repeat, this is the core of his importance—was an *artist of revolution,* not merely a good director, not merely a gifted propagandist. That revolution was as central and generative for his art as, to cite a lofty precedent, Christianity was for Giotto. There are acres and acres of fourteenth-century Italian frescoes and canvases that present Christian ideas more or less affectingly, but the Arena Chapel in Padua is the work of a Christian genius and a genius that was Christian. In proportion, the same relation exists between Eisenstein's genius and Soviet communism.

The dynamics behind the particularity of his art can be traced to Marxist concepts and, I think, to none more clearly than to some in the *Communist Manifesto* of 1848 by Marx and Engels. I do not maintain that Eisenstein used the *Manifesto* as an explicit text, but he certainly knew it well and its ideas were certainly part of his intellectual resources. One idea in the *Manifesto* seems outstandingly relevant. In the second section, where the authors anticipate objections to their arguments, they write:

> Does it require deep intuition to comprehend that man's ideas, views, and conceptions—in one word, man's consciousness—changes with every change in the conditions of his material existence, in his social relations and in his social life?

Straight to this profound concept, that a changed world means a changed awareness of the world, Eisenstein struck in his film making, and never more deeply than in *Potemkin.* That he was following Marx perceptively I cannot say, but clearly he felt that a new society meant a new kind of *vision;* that the way people saw things must be altered; that it was insufficient to put new material before, so to speak, old eyes. Anyone anywhere could tell a story of heroic resistance in traditional style; it was his duty as a revolutionary artist, Eisenstein felt (and later wrote), to find an esthetically revolutionary way to tell a politically revolutionary story.

The prime decision was in the visual texture. He wanted

to avoid historical drama; he wanted to make a drama of history. He and his lifelong cameraman, Édouard Tissé, aimed at a kind of newsreel look: not coarse graininess (there is, indeed, a good deal of subtle black-and-white gradation), but not painterly chiaroscuro either, no imitation museum-look. He wanted the feeling, essentially, of extraordinary eavesdropping.

A recent scion of this approach was Pontecorvo's *The Battle of Algiers,* except for the difference that, in these earlier days, Eisenstein relied very much less than Pontecorvo on individual performances. That was Eisenstein's second decision; he used very few actors. Mostly, he used ordinary people whose faces and bodies he liked for particular roles—a furnace man as the ship's doctor, a gardener as the ship's priest—and each one was used for a relatively short performance that the director could control easily and heighten with camera angles and editing, in a kind of mosaic process. Eisenstein called this approach "typage," the casting of parts with such striking faces—often introduced in close-up, sometimes intense close-up—that our very first glimpse tells us most of what we need to know about him or her as an element in the mosaic. In his subsequent films **Alexander Nevsky** and both parts of **Ivan the Terrible,** Eisenstein blended the use of "typage" with large roles for professional actors, but in **Potemkin** human depths come from the combination of pieces rather than the exploration of any one piece.

The "typage" idea leads directly to the cinematic technique most closely associated with Eisenstein: montage. Basically, montage is editing: the selection and arrangement of bits of film to produce certain effects. Every film ever made, from **Potemkin** to TV commercials, literally contains montage. But Eisenstein's use of montage was different from any use of it before him, including the work of his acknowledged master D. W. Griffith, is immediately recognizable as Eisenstein's, and is the source of much that followed after him.

He wrote often on the subject, which for him was the heart of cinema. For him, there were five kinds of montage. Briefly put, these are: metric montage, which is simply a relation between the lengths of the various pieces; rhythmic montage, which is based on the contents, in movement and composition, of the various pieces; tonal montage, based on the emotional colors of the pieces; overtonal montage, which is the conflict between the principal tone of the piece and its overtonal implications; and intellectual montage, a conflict that arises when similar actions are seen in conjunction but have been performed for different reasons (e. g., a hammer blow by a blacksmith, a hammer blow by a murderer).

These were not academic formulations. These five kinds of montage were, for Eisenstein, organs of a vibrant, live art. With them, and combinations of them, he fashioned **Potemkin** into a kind of bomb that penetrates our customary "entertainment" appperceptions to burst below the surface and shake us from within.

The story itself he phrased into five movements: Part One, Men and Maggots; Part Two, Drama on the Quarterdeck; Part Three, An Appeal from the Dead; Part Four, The

Odessa Steps; Part Five, Meeting the Squadron. Each of these parts, like an act in a good drama, is a structure in itself, with its own cantilevered stress and tensions, that contributes to the structure of the whole.

Commentators have pointed out that both the montage in **Potemkin** and its five-part structure had their origins at least partly in practical considerations. Raw film stock was in very short supply in the early Soviet days. Most of what was available was in relatively short snippets, so directors had to work in short takes. Eisenstein developed the esthetics of montage out of an exigency. Also, most Soviet film theaters at the time had only one projector; there was a pause when one reel ended and another reel had to be put on the machine. The five parts of **Potemkin** are on five reels, so the pauses come at reasonably appropriate moments. But, as is so often true in the history of art, the practical needs were not constrictive but stimulating. Another great precedent: the *David* in Florence is huge because the city had a huge block of marble on its hands, left over from an unfulfilled commission, and asked Michelangelo to make use of it.

With the very opening moments of **Potemkin,** we know we are in the presence of something new, and the miracle is that we know it every time we see the film. The waves beat at the shore, the lookouts converse, the ship steams across the sea, and all this is modeled with an energy, controlled yet urgent, that bursts at us. Then, when we cut to the crew's quarters and we move among the slung hammocks, we know we are in the hands of an artist who sees the difference between naturalism and realism. The scene of the sleeping sailors is accurate enough, yet Eisenstein sees the arabesques that the hammocks form, and he uses these graceful, intersecting curves as a contrast to the turbulence of the waves earlier and the mutiny that is to come. Shortly thereafter, he uses the swinging of the suspended tables in the mess hall in the same way—another moment of irrepressible grace in iron surroundings.

Fiercely, electrically, the film charges forward into the confrontation between officers and men, the action caught in flashes that simultaneously anatomize and unify it—in Eisenstein's double aim to show things as they are yet make us see them as never before. One of his methods, which has been likened to cubism and is a forerunner of a technique used in *Last Year at Marienbad,* is to show an action and then repeat it immediately from a slightly changed point of view. A celebrated instance of this is the moment when a young sailor smashes a plate on which is inscribed "Give us this day our daily bread." We see his action twice in rapid succession, from two angles, and the effect is intensification, italicized rage.

Eisenstein shot the quarterdeck sequence on board *The Twelve Apostles,* the surviving sister ship of the *Potemkin,* which had to be altered somewhat but which nevertheless gives the sequence a steely verisimilitude. (Remember *Gas Masks!*) When the obdurate sailors are herded together and a tarpaulin thrown over them before they are to be shot—itself a simple, dehumanizing image—the firing squad prepares, and the film cuts away: to a close-up of two cannon, to a view of the ship at anchor, as if to implicate the environment. Of course it is D. W. Griffith's old technique of intercutting to distend a moment of climax, but it is used here for thematic as well as visceral effect.

At the last moment the firing squad goes over to the sailors' side, and in the fight that follows Eisenstein uses another of his favorite devices, which he himself called synecdoche. After the corrupt ship's doctor is thrown overboard, we see a close-up of his pince-nez dangling from the rigging—the same pince-nez with which he had inspected the maggoty meat and pronounced it edible. The man's corruption and what followed it are caught in that shot. And there is another such moment. Before the fight, we have seen the ship's priest, one of the clerics whom Eisenstein was constantly caricaturing in his films, lifting his crucifix and bidding the men obey. During the fight, after the priest has been knocked down a flight of steps, we see a close-up of the crucifix, an edge of its lateral bar stuck in the deck where it has fallen, like an axe plunged into wood—an axe (Eisenstein implies) that has missed the necks for which it was intended.

The most noted sequence in the film, without question the most noted sequence in film history, is the Odessa Steps. It is oceanic. With some hundreds of people, Eisenstein creates the sense of an immense, limitless upheaval. With the quick etching of a few killings, he creates more savagery than thousands of commonplace gory films. With crosscurrents of perspective and tempo, he evokes the collision of status quo and inevitable protest.

Here are two examples of Eisenstein's montage in this sequence that is a treasury of montage esthetics. First, as he himself noted, the recurring shots of the soldiers' boots coming down the steps toward the frightened and angry citizens are always in a different rhythm from the rest of the sequence, ideationally establishing a different political impulse, esthetically creating an exciting counterbeat. Second, he establishes, by typage, a woman with glasses protesting the soldiers' butchery. Shortly afterward, we see an officer swinging a saber at the camera; then we cut to her face, one lens of her glasses shattered, her eye streaming blood, her features frozen in shock. (The bank teller in *Bonnie and Clyde* who was shot through the car window is her direct descendant.) The suggestion of the blow's force by ellipsis is masterly enough; but in the brief moment in which we see the officer swinging his saber at us, totaling less than two seconds, there are *four different shots* of him, exploding his fury into a horrifying prism.

This episode raises one more point to be made about the whole sequence, the whole film. Even when one sees **Potemkin** without musical accompaniment, which is preferable to most of the scores that have been tacked on to it, when it is seen absolutely silent, the effect is of roaring tumult. One strong impulse to the development of montage in the days of silent film was the attempt to create visually the effect of sound: shots of train whistles or church bells or door knockers so that you could see what you couldn't hear. But in this film, by the way he counterpoises rhythms and faces, marching boots and guns and moving masses, Eisenstein draws from that silent screen a mounting and immense "roar" that has rarely been surpassed in sound films.

The double vision of *Potemkin,* subjectivized and also cosmic, is paralleled in its double effect throughout the world. Subjectively, it was made as a celebration for those already fervent in communism; but it was simultaneously intended as propaganda for the unconverted world. Emotionally and esthetically, if not politically, it unquestionably has had a great effect; but those who control the film have much less faith in it than its maker had. No important picture has been more seriously tampered with. Political messages have been tacked on fore and aft on some prints; some prints have been snipped internally; thirty-five years ago in New York the picture was given a filmed prologue and epilogue spoken by American actors. The only music that Eisenstein approved was written by an Austrian, Edmund Meisel, for the Berlin premiere, and this score has only recently been rediscovered. Most prints of *Potemkin* have some other music ladled on.

Eisenstein's career, in terms of its free growth, describes a curve that coincides with the rise and fall of world-wide radical hope for Soviet communism. But at the height of his faith, he created a film that both proclaimed his faith and transcended it, a work of political fire that lives because it is a work of art.

Edward Murray   (essay date 1978)

SOURCE: "Potemkin," in his *Ten Film Classics: A Re-Viewing,* Frederick Ungar Publishing Co. 1978, pp. 1-17.

[*Murray is an American critic and educator. In the following essay, he summarizes Eisenstein's theory of montage and analyzes the composition of* Potemkin.]

Sergei Eisenstein will be remembered not only as a major filmmaker—his *Potemkin* has often been called "the greatest film ever made"—but also as one of the most important theorists of the cinema. Although he had provocative things to say about acting, sound, color, and film as a synthesis of all the arts and sciences, Eisenstein's most significant contribution to film study centers on his conception of montage.

The word "montage" comes from the French; it means "mounting" or "putting together." Sometimes montage is used loosely as a synonym for editing. Among Western film-makers, montage often means an impressionistic sequence of short shots intended to convey a sense of time passing. For Eisenstein, however, montage had a wholly different signification.

As an engineering student, Eisenstein had learned the definite laws governing the construction of roads, bridges, waterways, and the principles involved in the management of machinery. With rigorous analysis, he maintained, one could also discover the laws which determined all forms of art. From the beginning, the Soviet film was linked to the 1917 Revolution. "Of all the arts," Lenin once announced, "the cinema is the most important for us." He was thinking of propaganda. In the nineteenth century, Hegel formulated his triadic dialectic of thesis, antithesis, and synthesis; later Marx and Engels transformed the Hegelian logical-metaphysical-idealist approach into what has come to be called dialectical materialism. Whereas

Hegel saw the movement of the dialectic in history as a phenomenal expression of the movement of absolute thought, Marx and Engels argued that the dialectical movement of human thought merely reflects the dialectical process inherent in "reality," or nature and history. The development toward a perfect communist world, then, is based on a series of contradictions, followed by contradictions of contradictions, leading to ever higher stages in the dialectical process.

Eisenstein sought to apply this philosophy to film. Two shots different in kind (the "thesis" and the "antithesis") collide to establish a new concept (the "synthesis"). In his essay **"A Dialectic Approach to Film Form"** (1929), Eisenstein explains that the relationship between the shot and the subtitle on the one hand, and between the shot and montage on the other, represents dialectical phases: "Conflict within a *thesis* (an abstract idea)—*formulates* itself in the dialectics of the subtitle—*forms* itself spatially in the conflict within the shot—and *explodes* with increasing intensity in montage—conflict among the separate shots." Eisenstein aimed for "pathos" in his dialectical form. He wanted to send the viewer into ecstasy, out of himself—out of passivity, and into action.

According to Eisenstein, there is a correspondence between montage and Japanese hieroglyphic writing. An ideogram results from the fusion of two separate hieroglyphs; for instance, the picture of a dog plus the picture of a mouth becomes "to bark." The ideogram is not the sum of two hieroglyphs but their product. By this distinction, Eisenstein intends that whereas each hieroglyph represents an object the ideogram stands for a concept—a value of another dimension. This, for Eisenstein, is montage—that is, the "combining [of] shots that are *depictive,* single in meaning, neutral in content—into *intellectual* contexts and series." The shot is not an element of montage but a cell which, so to speak, divides to form an entity of another order. Montage is characterized not by a simple chain of pictorially continuous images but by "shock attraction"—or the clash of images—which produces a new idea.

The shots, or montage cells, have no value as separate entities. As Eisenstein observes in **"Film Language"** (1934), the more arresting individual images are in themselves, the more a film becomes a series of beautiful but disconnected snapshots. Nevertheless, conflict exists within each specific cell; the same kind of conflict which can be found between shots can also be found within the single shot. In **"A Dialectic Approach to Film Form,"** Eisenstein distinguishes ten such types of conflict: 1) graphic conflict; 2) conflict of planes; 3) conflict of volumes; 4) spatial conflict; 5) light conflict; 6) tempo conflict; 7) conflict between matter and viewpoint; 8) conflict between matter and its spatial nature; 9) conflict between an event and its temporal nature; and 10) conflict in terms of audio-visual counterpoint. It is montage structure alone, however, which confers meaning on the individual shots.

In 1929, Eisenstein listed five kinds of montage (see **"Methods of Montage"**); in 1938, as a result of his work on *Alexander Nevsky* (1938), he added a sixth (see **"Synchronization of Senses"**). Metric montage depends on the "absolute lengths" of the film strips joined together in such a way as to resemble a musical beat Content is less important here than the fixed, mechanical relation of the film strips to one another. A Griffith last-minute-rescue sequence would serve as an example for this type of montage (which, by the way, Eisenstein did not regard highly). Rhythmic montage shows concern for the content of a shot. Here, the mechanical considerations of metric montage surrender to an ordering of the film strips according to their "actual lengths." In the Odessa Steps sequence of *Potemkin,* Eisenstein informs us, the rhythmic drum of the soldiers' feet as they descend the steps violate all metrical demands, since the movement of the soldiers remains unsynchronized with the tempo of the cutting. Tonal montage points to the "general tone" of a piece. If a film sequence is described as having a shrill quality, one should look for angle shots and angular shapes, inasmuch as some kind of "graphic tonality" is at work. *Overtonal montage* can be distinguished from tonal montage "by the collective calculations of all the piece's appeals." The superior film-maker seeks to present more than one emotional tone per shot; he calls upon the overtonal approach to reveal a number of feelings and ideas within a single image.

Metric, rhythmic, tonal, and overtonal are terms used to designate methods of montage. These methods can be described as montage constructions only when they are patterned into the duration of a shot and movement within the frame; similarly, tonal montage grows out of the clash between the rhythmic and tonal qualities of the work; finally, overtonal montage results from the clash between the major tone (its dominant) and the overtone. The four methods of montage work on the viewer at the affective—physiological level. *Intellectual montage,* however, is intended to make its appeal to the rational faculty in the viewer—it involves a conflict between ideas.

A re-viewing of *Potemkin* shows how very much the film-maker's theory remains relevant to an appreciation of his masterpiece.

In 1925, Eisenstein was instructed by the Soviet government to make a film about the abortive revolution of 1905—a film broad in scope. Only about forty shots of the 800 planned were to have been about the mutiny aboard the battleship *Potemkin.* However, when Eisenstein saw the Odessa Steps, he changed his plan and revised his script. Now, one mutiny would stand for the entire revolution. Although the 1905 rebellion failed, the Soviet authorities wanted Eisenstein to end the film optimistically.

The *Potemkin* was the pride of the Imperial Russian Navy. But poor food, including wormy meat, served to the sailors for months created a situation conducive to revolt. When a seaman complained about the food, an officer shot him; the officer, in turn, was shot by some crew members and tossed overboard. The captain and the other officers on the ship were also slain. Arriving at Odessa, the *Potemkin* received fuel and supplies from their comrades on shore. Other ships from the Black Sea fleet, however, did not join the *Potemkin* in mutiny. Later, the men on board the battleship argued among themselves and finally decided to surrender the ship to Rumanian authorities. Some sailors managed to escape, but others were executed. In the film, Eisenstein concludes the action by showing the *Potemkin* sailing past the Czar's fleet—sailing victoriously out to sea—without a shot fired by either side. According to Eisenstein, although the revolt aboard the real *Potemkin,* like the 1905 revolution as a whole, was not ultimately successful, it foreshadowed the later triumph of 1917. The optimistic conclusion to the film therefore seemed justified.

Eisenstein divides the structure of *Potemkin* into five parts, each part titled and numbered, the five parts representing a chronological series of events: I. Men and Maggots; II. Drama on the Quarter-Deck; III. The Dead Man Cries for Vengeance; IV. The Odessa Steps; V. Meeting the Squadron. *Potemkin* is a perfect example of fragmentation editing. Whereas the average film contains about 600 shots—and though 800 had originally been planned for a film about the entire 1905 revolution—the structure of *Potemkin* is made up of 1,346 shots.

"Men and Maggots" opens with five shots of waves crashing symbolically over a jetty, and shots of waves flowing over rocks on a shore. Cut to an insert title: "Revolution is the only lawful, equal, effectual war. It was in Russia that this war was declared and begun." The quotation is from Lenin. Two seaman are introduced: Matyushenko and Vakulinchuk. The former says: "We, the sailors of the Potemkin, must support the revolution with our brothers, the workers." Thus, conflict is presented immediately, and in a clear-cut fashion. Eisenstein works by contrast: the arrogant faces of the officers versus the angry faces of the crew; the well-cut uniforms of the officers versus the plain-looking garb of the crew; the authority of the officers versus the rebelliousness of the crew. As Vakulinchuk puts it: "What are we waiting for? All Russia is rising. Are we to be the last?"

The struggle commences when the men refuse to eat any more rotten food. Smirnov, the ship's doctor, appears and examines a carcass of meat. He folds his pince-nez in half to form a magnifying lens, and informs the men that there are no maggots in the meat, though the camera-eye shows them clearly in close-up.

Like most of the performers in *Potemkin,* Smirnov is played by a nonprofessional. During the twenties, Eisenstein's films were cast on the basis of what he called "typage" theory—or what Hollywood refers to as "type casting." Whether he used professional or nonprofessional actors, Eisenstein chose them on the basis of how they looked. They were thought of as simply plastic material to be shaped by montage. Eisenstein observed the general characteristics of doctors, formed a composite image of one, and then looked for the "type." Smirnov was played by a man who knew nothing of medicine; he was, in fact, a porter. The pince-nez became identified with the doctor. Later in the film, when Smirnov is tossed overboard, his eyeglasses get caught on one of the ship's cables. Eisenstein presents the pince-nez in a close-up, thus reminding us of the earlier scene, in addition to letting the part (the glasses) stand for the whole (Smirnov himself).

Although there is a confrontation between the crew and some officers in the first part of *Potemkin,* there is no bloodshed. "Men and Maggots" ends in the ship's galley. Sailors are washing and drying the officers' plates and setting the table for dinner. One sailor reads the inscription on a plate: "Give us this day our daily bread." Slowly, his anger rises. With great force, he smashes the plate and upsets the table prepared for the officers. This symbolic action is extremely important structurally and thematically. As a result, Eisenstein prolongs its impact visually on the screen. Normally, the breaking of a dish would take about two seconds. Instead of recording the action in real time with a single shot, Eisenstein substitutes filmic time by editing nine shots from various angles in an overlapping progression, so that the breaking of the dish takes longer than it realistically would have aboard the actual *Potemkin*. The technique marks the difference between life and art.

In Part Two: "Drama on the Quarter-Deck," the officers and crew of the *Potemkin* reach a turning point in their relationship. A bugle sounds, calling all hands to the quarter-deck. Commander Golikov roars: "All those satisfied with the food step two paces forward!" Throughout this scene, Eisenstein repeatedly shoots the action from a position in back of the two cannons which protrude threateningly over the men. The cannons symbolize the power of the government against which the men are revolting. Most of the sailors refuse to step forward. Furious, Golikov shouts: "Hang them from the yardarm!" Eisenstein cuts nervously back and forth between the men and the officers. An old sailor looks up at the yardarm. Here Eisenstein uses a subjective camera: the viewer sees what the old sailor imagines—six bodies swinging from the yardarm.

"Call out the marine guard!" cries Golikov. Just then, Matyushenko breaks rank and urges his comrades to join him at the gun-turret. The guard appears. "Now," shouts Matyushenko. "The time has come!" The majority of the sailors join him at the turret. With most of the men crowded on either side of the cannons, and with Golikov standing in the line of the cannons, Eisenstein visually suggests that the balance of power has begun to shift in favor of the men. Suspense remains, though, because we do not know how the marines will respond to Golikov's commands.

To the men who have not been able to escape from the prow of the *Potemkin*, Golikov warns: "I'll shoot you down like dogs . . . Cover them with a tarpaulin!" The order is carried out. An officer shouts: "Attention!," and the marine guard stiffens. Shot of a priest, standing with a cross raised before him: "Lord, show thyself to these unruly sinners." The sailors who are about to be shot wait in fear. "At the tarpaulin—" comes the command— "Fire!" But the marines hesitate to kill their fellow seamen. Close-up of the cross in the priest's hands; cut to a close-up of an officer's hand stroking the hilt of his dagger. The transition from one object to another, both of them shaped in a similar fashion, underlines the link between church and military in the Czarist regime.

From the first command given to the marines to fire, through their agony of indecision and the torment of the intended victims, to the moment when Vakulinchuk's cry: "Brothers!" finally wins over the guard, Eisenstein edits dozens of shots together in order to sustain the tension. When it becomes clear that the guard will not kill the un-

happy men, violence at last breaks out—and the tension is broken. In the battle the officers are overpowered, many of them slain, but Vakulinchuk is also killed.

Part Two ends with Vakulinchuk's body lying on the pier of Odessa, his clasped hands holding a lighted candle on his chest. A sign rests on his body: "For a spoonful of soup."

Part Three: "The Dead Man Cries for Vengeance" remains a relatively calm sequence, a bridge between the violence of both "Drama on the Quarter-Deck" and Part Four: "The Odessa Steps." At the heart of the third section is the mourning of the masses for Vakulinchuk; the mood, however, develops gradually from sorrow through anger to end on a happy, confident note. In time, the sequence moves from night to dawn.

"The Dead Man Cries for Vengeance" begins with an iris shot of Odessa as viewed from the sea. By opening with a technique which shows an image in only one small round area of the scene, Eisenstein "poetizes" his material; it is a signal that symbolism here will be more important than a documentary-like realism. Throughout **Potemkin**, Eisenstein combines realism (the film was shot on location, there are mostly non-professionals in the cast, much of the action is factual) with stylization (the extreme form of montage, with its fragmented editing, the expansion of time, and the showing of the same event more than once, such as in the Odessa Steps sequence). Tonal montage is apparent in Part Three as Eisenstein's shots are selected, initially, for their "mistiness," and later for their "brightness." In tempo, Eisenstein edits slowly at first, then builds to a brisker pace.

To symbolize the growing power of the masses' sentiments, Eisenstein shows more and more people filing past Vakulinchuk's body. Shot of rising steps empty of people (the right and left sides of the screen are blacked out). Dissolve to a shot of the steps crowded with people. Shot of the masses ascending stairs at the edge of the pier to view the dead hero's body; behind them can be seen a narrow jetty, filled with people, stretching beyond the frame of the picture. High-angle shot of a crowd surrounding Vakulinchuk's corpse. Slow pan from the masses—to the waters of the harbor. Nothing, Eisenstein suggests, can stop the advance of the workers. Waves of people move relentlessly across the curving stairways on either side of an enormous bridge. Almost everyone in Odessa seems to support the mutineers aboard the *Potemkin*.

Almost everyone . . . Speeches are made over Vakulinchuk's body. A sailor cries: "We will avenge ourselves! Death to the oppressors!" Three women sing out: "All for one . . . one for all!" Men and women continue to harangue the crowd. But one well-dressed man persists in cynically sneering at the impassioned speakers. "Down with the Jews!" he says. Close-up of a sailor's angry face. Shots of peasants and workers glaring at the well-dressed defender of the government. Suddenly the crowd attacks the man, beating him with their fists, driving him to the ground. "Shoulder to shoulder!" screams an agitator. Shot of men and women moving down two large stairways, advancing under the arch of a bridge. Shot of men and women streaming across the bridge, others pouring beneath the arch. All Russia seems to be rising against the Czar.

Cut to a shot of the *Potemkin.* "The enemy has been dealt a decisive blow!" a civilian tells the assembled sailors. "Together with the rising workers of our land we will be victorious!" The sailors fling their white caps in the air, cheering. Cut to a shot of the Odessa Steps, a huge stairway leading down to the harbor, where a crowd has gathered to stare across the water at the *Potemkin.* The sun is shining now, and many women shield themselves with parasols. Cut back to the *Potemkin,* where a forked flag is being raised as a symbol of successful rebellion . . . Fade out.

Part Four: "The Odessa Steps" is probably the most celebrated sequence ever filmed. The structure of the section clearly exemplifies Eisenstein's theory of dialectical movement. At the start of "The Odessa Steps," the film-maker establishes his "thesis" by cutting back and forth between the happy crowd on shore and the victorious sailors aboard the *Potemkin.* When the foot soldiers and Cossacks appear to put down the demonstration on shore, Eisenstein introduces the "antithesis." In response to the slaughter on the Steps, however, the sailors of the *Potemkin* fire their cannons at the headquarters of the attackers. This represents the "synthesis."

To film the massacre on the Odessa Steps, Eisenstein developed a number of strategies. He built a trolley for his camera on the Steps, so that it could move along with the action. In addition, he wanted to balance the objective presentation of the carnage with subjective shots. To do this, he strapped a camera to the waist of a technician and had him roll down the steps.

One test of a great director is how well he handles crowd scenes. Eisenstein was not only a master of orchestration where large numbers of people were concerned but he also had a genius for isolating individuals in the crowd in order to prevent the audience from merely being overwhelmed by the massive destruction. For example, in "The Odessa Steps" sequence he cuts back and forth between shots showing the soldiers shooting into the crowd and shots depicting the reactions of various persons in the crowd: a mother and her child, a student, a woman wearing pince-nez, a baby in a carriage. By showing us specific human beings up close, by forcing us to identify with them, Eisenstein makes us react emotionally to the sequence. "The Odessa Steps" is no dehumanized newsreel account of an atrocity—it is the high point of Eisenstein's artistry.

From beginning to end, the massacre on the Odessa Steps is masterly in its construction. The transition from the happy scene on the Steps to violence is abrupt and signaled by a title card with one word printed on it: "Suddenly . . ." Shot of a woman's dark hair which fills the screen. The woman pulls back from the camera, still caught in a close-up, her mouth open, screaming. Shot of a legless man hopping in panic down the Steps on blocks of wood held in his hands under his hips. Shots of the crowd fleeing down the Steps. Shot of the cripple gazing for a moment in horror up the Steps. Long shot of the

crowd, with the camera positioned at the top of the Steps, the backs of the citizens all that can be seen. There is a bronze statue in the foreground of the shot . . . Then, all at once, we finally see the cause of the panic. Moving underneath the outstretched arms of the statue is a line of soldiers, fixed bayonets on their rifles.

Throughout the massacre on the Steps, Eisenstein uses the various forms of conflict and methods of montage which he discusses in his theoretical writings. There is, for example, graphic conflict (shot of a body intersecting the Steps) and conflict of planes (shot of a line of soldiers shooting down the Steps at a mother holding a child in her arms). Within individual compositions there is conflict between the chaotic rush of the crowd and the mechanical, ordered movement of the soldiers; between light and shadow; between a lone mother moving up the Steps and the crowd fleeing down the Steps past her. As noted earlier, Eisenstein cites the sequence on the Steps as an example of rhythmic montage. The cutting is fast; it is not synchronized with the marching feet of the soldiers. "The final pull of tension," Eisenstein writes, "is supplied by the transfer from the rhythm of the descending feet to another rhythm—a new kind of downward movement—the next intensity level of the same activity—the baby carriage rolling down the Steps. The carriage functions as a directly progressing accelerator of the advancing feet. The stepping descent passes into a rolling descent."

As he did in Part One: "Men and Maggots," in the scene where the sailor breaks the plate on which is inscribed: "Give us this day our daily bread," Eisenstein again expands real time into filmic time in order to emphasize the importance of the slaughter by the Czarist forces. It would take about two minutes for the average person to run down the Odessa Steps. In *Potemkin,* it takes the soldiers almost ten minutes to clear the Steps, because Eisenstein keeps intercutting to show isolated bits of action in conjunction with an overall view of the massacre. Furthermore, time is expanded because Eisenstein presents the same event more than once. At one point, the Steps are swept clean of all the living as the soldiers march relentlessly forward, their rifles smoking. Then a woman carrying her child moves up the Steps to confront the seemingly inhuman soldiers. She is shot down. Once again, the Steps are filled with people and the soldiers are firing at them. We are so involved in the action, however, that during a viewing of *Potemkin* we never ask ourselves where the second wave of people have come from. We simply accept the fact—emotionally—that for the people trapped on the Steps the carnage seems to be going on and on and on. Eisenstein's expansion of time and violation of logic are perfectly justified aesthetically.

The slaughter on the Steps ends with an excellent illustration of what Eisenstein means by montage. Shot of a Cossack swinging his sword, his eyes looking down into the camera. Three more rapid shots—all close-ups—of the Cossack's snarling face. Then a shot of an old woman wearing pince-nez, in close-up, blood spurting from her right eye. We never see the sword as it strikes the eye. Through "shock attraction," Eisenstein takes shots of the Cossack and a shot of the woman—shots which in themselves are "single in meaning"—and combines them to form a new concept; the woman has been slashed by the Cossack.

Immediately, Eisenstein cuts from the woman to the guns of the *Potemkin*. The rebellious sailors fire upon the Odessa Theater, in which the Czar's officers are housed. Once again, Eisenstein provides a memorable example of montage. Three quick shots of marble lions appear on the screen: the first lion is sleeping; the second waking up; the

The awakening of the stone lion in Battleship Potemkin.

third rising. Individually, the shots are "neutral in content," but the sum of the shots—through the illusion of a single lion jumping to its feet—produces a new idea: the Russian masses are fighting back against the inhumanity of the Czarist government.

"Meeting the Squadron"—the fifth and last part of *Potemkin*—is inevitably a letdown after "The Odessa Steps." However, Eisenstein does his best to end the film in a dramatic way. Suspense is achieved by establishing the possibility that the bulk of the Russian fleet will sink the *Potemkin*. In order to build up tension, Eisenstein edits dozens of shots of the sailors waiting, water splashing against the ship, the dark sky, dials on pressure gauges, the guns of the *Potemkin*. Suddenly the tension is broken—the squadron is sighted—and activity commences. The sailors of the *Potemkin* prepare themselves for combat, knowing that they are doomed if their fellow seamen on the other ships decide to follow orders. Title: "Will they fire . . ." Eisenstein cuts to the faces of anxious men aboard the *Potemkin*. Title: ". . . or . . ." Cut to shots of more faces, pistons moving furiously below deck. And then, finally, the title: "Brothers!" The sailors aboard the opposing vessels refuse to fire on the *Potemkin*. Overjoyed, the rebellious sailors, cheering, toss their caps in the air. The film ends with a close shot of the *Potemkin's* prow heading straight into the camera, and continuing on to freedom.

One can see that the structure of *Potemkin* also illustrates Eisenstein's concept of progression according to the dialectic. The sailors and the civilian population revolt against authority. This is the "thesis." In response, the government shoots down the civilians on the Odessa Steps. Here we have the "antithesis." Finally, the Russian fleet refuses to fire on the *Potemkin* and allows it to escape unharmed. The massacre has created an even stronger solidarity. This is the "synthesis."

After more than fifty years, *Potemkin* still represents an unforgettable cinematic experience. Vividly photographed by Eduard Tisse (one of the greatest cameramen in the history of cinema), brilliantly conceived and edited by Eisenstein, strong in content, the film has lost none of its power to delight our eyes with its pictorial compositions or hold our attention with its violent actions. The massacre on the Odessa Steps remains an unsurpassable accomplishment.

Eisenstein's conception of himself as both a film artist and a propagandist for the Russian Revolution creates, however, an uneasy tension in *Potemkin.* For example, the characters are over-simplified representations of humanity; they are black (the officers on the ships) and white (the sailors and the workers). At times, *Potemkin* comes perilously close to resembling a cartoon strip, with the "good guys" battling the "bad guys." Joseph Goebbels, propaganda director under Hitler, looked upon Eisenstein's film as a model which Germany would have to surpass . . . a sentiment which prepared the way for Leni Riefenstahl's *Triumph of the Will* (1934), which celebrates the annual Nazi Reich Party Day rally in Nuremberg.

In his essays, Eisenstein often speaks of realism and reality. Unfortunately, he never defines his terms. At the survival level, "reality" seems to be whatever Marx and Engels and Lenin and Stalin say it is. At the artistic level, "reality" is merely something to be put into montage form to fit the revolutionary aims of the film-maker. Truth here is totally dependent on the purposes of the artist, since it is just *as if* things did not exist at all. Now, every artist in cinema transforms reality; he creates, for instance, a new filmic space and time. However, a film like, say, Fellini's *La Strada*, though it reflects the artist's rearrangement of life—that is, his subjectivity (*not* subjectivism)—nonetheless remains a window on the real world. The artist's ideas and attitudes coexist with a reality which—except at the submoral or subethical level—is no mere unspecified stuff.

According to Eisenstein, film can only become art through montage. We know, however, that when a director (for instance, Hitchcock) plans every shot in advance of filming, when, during filming, the shot is lighted this way, composed that way, the actors placed thus and so, artistry is involved in the entire process. Eisenstein tended to place too much stress on the conceptual work of editing, while insufficiently emphasizing *what* the camera sees. "*Primo*: photo-fragments of nature are recorded; *secundo*: these fragments are combined in various ways," he writes. "Thus, the shot (or frame), and thus, montage . . . The minimum 'distortable' fragment of nature is the shot; ingenuity in its combinations is montage." Because the shot does not distort the real world as much as montage, Eisenstein attaches less significance to it.

We turn now to a film classic which, in its artistry, represents an alternative to Eisenstein's approach in *Potemkin*.

Richard Taylor   (essay date 1979)

SOURCE: "October" and "Alexander Nevsky" in his *Film Propaganda: Soviet Russia and Nazi Germany*, Croom Helm, 1979, pp. 92-102, 116-30.

[*In the following excerpt, Taylor analyzes the content and structure of Eisenstein's* October *and examines* Alexander Nevsky *as a study in film technique and Soviet propaganda.*]

> After *Battleship Potemkin, October* is bad.
>
> Soviet critics, 1928

> *October* is without doubt a film of great revolutionary and artistic importance. It is good in its revolutionary content, good in its execution.
>
> Krupskaya, 1928

These two comments are typical of the reception that greeted Eisenstein's third film and typical of the arguments that surrounded the film maker's career as a whole. Eisenstein was commissioned to make a film of the revolutionary events of 1917 to commemorate the tenth anniversary of the Revolution: similarly Pudovkin was commissioned to make *The End of St Petersburg* and Shub made *The Fall of the Romanov Dynasty* and *The Great Way*. Eisenstein had already completed *Strike,* which had been attacked for its experimental nature and its obscure symbolism, and *Battleship Potemkin* which, despite its immense popularity in Berlin, had failed to move Soviet au-

diences in large numbers, probably for similar reasons. When approached to make the film that was to become *October,* Eisenstein was already engaged in filming *The General Line.* He deferred this project to make his revolutionary film. He had little choice, and there is no evidence to suggest that he had any doubts; none the less it was a decision that was to have serious consequences for his career. *October* (if we allow for the earlier start on *The General Line*) was Eisenstein's last silent film, and the last film he was to complete for over ten years. After *October* Eisenstein was always on the defensive: in 1929, for instance, he announced that *The General Line* was 'an experiment comprehensible to the millions'.

October was made in a hurry. Filming began in mid-April 1927 and did not finish till October. Editing began in September and a preliminary version of the film was shown to a selected audience in the Bolshoi Theater, Moscow, on 7 November, the actual date of the tenth anniversary of the October Revolution. The film was then re-edited, some of the more 'intellectual' sequences were removed, and it was given a general release on 14 March 1928. Like *Potemkin, October* was shown in Berlin, where it was retitled *Ten Days that Shook the World,* after John Reed's famous account, to increase its popular appeal. Nevertheless, *October* never achieved the fame or notoriety of *Potemkin* and never attracted the same degree of political acclaim outside the USSR. Inside the Soviet Union its reception was, as we have seen, mixed. On the one hand it was attacked for being obscure: one of the speakers at the first Party Conference on the Cinema in March 1928 remarked:

> In the countryside many films are not understood . . . And it must be said that the more widely the Soviet cinema develops, the greater will be the percentage of films that are completely incomprehensible to the peasantry. I am talking about a film like *October.*

On the other hand, Krupskaya, Lenin's widow, felt that *October,* despite its faults, marked a turning-point in the development of Soviet film art: 'Now an art is emerging that is near to the masses, that depicts the fundamental experiences of the masses. This art has a colossal future. The film *October* is a fragment of this art of the future.

I am inclined to agree with Krupskaya, although for different reasons: despite its weaknesses *October* is of fundamental importance, both in the Soviet context in terms of the transition from artistic pluralism to the straitjacket of socialist realism, and in the general context in terms of the development of the propaganda film, especially in the field of the heroicisation of reality.

Almost no film exists of the October Revolution or of the most important event of the February Revolution, the abdication of the Tsar. The reality of the Revolution does not therefore exist on film and it was thus necessary to create it. The Bolsheviks had to establish a basis of historical legitimacy for their regime and the absence of adequate documentary evidence gave Soviet film makers a golden opportunity for the re-creation of the realities of Russian history, and for some improvement on them. Eisenstein was in the forefront of the projection of this revolutionary realism at the expense of the actual historical reality. In *Battleship Potemkin* he had highlighted the oppression of the masses by inventing the episode on the Odessa Steps. In *October* he was to present the Bolshevik view of the elemental nature of the October Revolution, culminating in the storming of the Winter Palace. Ironically enough, the very absence of documentary material which made this possible has also meant that subsequent historians and film makers have turned to *October* as their source material, and Eisenstein's fictional re-creation of reality has, because of its very realism, acquired the legitimacy of documentary footage. That is a measure of its success as a propaganda film.

October begins with a sequence showing the toppling of the statue of Tsar Alexander III. the symbol of the worst aspects of autocracy, who ruled Russia from 1881 to 1894 after Alexander II, emancipator of the serfs in 1861, had been assassinated. Alexander III epitomised the depths of reaction and repression and the massive machinery of tsarist oppression is conveyed by his immense statue. In his hands he holds the traditional symbols of power, the orb and sceptre, while the pedestal is adorned with eagles. The film shows these symbols in closeup. To us the meaning of this sequence may be abundantly clear, but a Soviet peasant in the 1920s would have found the symbolism incomprehensible, and the necessary process of explanation (which was attempted with this and other 'difficult' films) would have destroyed much of the vivid effect of the film: it was for this type of relative obscurantism, for the 'intellectual cinema' in which he so fervently believed, that Eisenstein was constantly criticised. Workers rush up towards the statue, echoing the Odessa Steps sequence in *Potemkin:* but on that occasion they were mown down by the Tsar's soldiers, whereas this time they will, ultimately, gain their revenge. They erect a ladder against the statue's head and tie ropes around the Tsar: autocracy is doomed and helpless. The film then cuts to a crowd of peasants angrily wielding their scythes: the peasantry too is in revolt and, by implication, in alliance with the workers and soldiers in the overthrow of the *ancien régime*. The first title appears: 'FEBRUARY'. For those of us in the know, this is a warning, but only if we do know the subsequent history of the Revolution. The statue is toppled hesitantly and in parts: first the head, then the arms and legs, with the orb and sceptre, and finally the throne itself. The workers', soldiers' and peasants' Revolution is apparently accomplished, the autocracy is overthrown. But then Eisenstein's warning is made explicit: the Revolution is greeted by the bourgeoisie and blessed by the Church. It is *their* Revolution, although it was effected by the masses. As such, February is but a prelude to the *real* Revolution, that of October, and the aptly named Provisional Government is more provisional than even it anticipated.

From the Revolution the masses expect land, peace and bread, fundamental human demands that date back to the Old Testament and beyond. The soldiers at the front abandon their rifles and fraternise with the 'enemy': we see an Asiatic Russian soldier trying on a German helmet, while the German tries on his fur cap. The solidarity of the international working class is thus underlined, the artificiality of the concept of patriotism in an imperialist war empha-

sised. Then, suddenly, the tsarist eagle is intercut with the abandoned rifles: the threat to the Revolution is now direct. A lackey crosses a tiled floor, bows low and proffers a silver platter with the government's note: 'THE PROVISIONAL GOVERNMENT HONOURS ITS OBLIGATIONS TO ITS ALLIES.' There is a violent shellburst, the war is resumed, the working class betrayed. In the cities bread rationing is introduced. We see women and children queuing for bread in heavy snow. As the ration is gradually reduced, Eisenstein introduces a metaphor: we see a press being lowered as if to squeeze the workers. Finally their situation becomes intolerable, they are desperate - but a saviour is at hand.

The scene switches to the Finland Station. Searchlights flash frenetically across the roof, the crowd is turbulent, a sense of eager anticipation prevails. The tension reaches its climax with the heroic, liberating arrival of: 'ULYANOV . . . LENIN.' There is a storm of enthusiasm and Lenin speaks from an armoured car. Flags and banners fluttering dramatically in the background and the flickering searchlights increase the sense of urgency. He denounces the Provisional Government and pledges a socialist Revolution: he offers the masses hope in their hour of utmost trial. None the less, despite this elaborate heroicisation, Lenin does not appear in *October* as an individual but as an embodiment of the elemental power of the mass, of the collective will. Eisenstein was severely criticised by many of his contemporaries for the portrayal of Lenin in this film: the poet Mayakovsky attacked the superficiality of the characterisation: 'It is revolting to see someone striking poses and making movements like those of Lenin, when behind this exterior you can feel complete emptiness, the complete absence of life.'

The Soviet critics quoted at the head of this chapter also had their doubts about the characterisation of Lenin:

> Lenin has turned out badly. The audience is faced with a rather brisk and fidgety little man. Ilyich's characteristic dash and liveliness have given way to an improbable fussiness. Antonov-Ovseyenko grows into the gigantic figure of the leader of the whole uprising.

The part of Lenin was played by an unknown worker by the name of Nikandrov. Eisenstein was averse to the use of professional actors, at least as far as his silent films were concerned, feeling that greater realism was to be achieved by using ordinary workers and peasants. In the case of Lenin, having the part played by a worker emphasised the revolutionary's role as representative of the mass. It was perhaps inevitable that, if Lenin were to be portrayed in this impersonal way, he would fail to come alive for audiences as a human being: his function is as a leading symbol in a film full of symbols. Indeed Krupskaya conceded that if the film had a fault, it lay in the director's use of symbolism that would not in fact be 'comprehensible to the millions':

> In the film *October* there is a great deal of symbolism. There is some symbolism that is accessible and comprehensible to the mass: the toppling throne, the idols from St Basil's, etc. These symbols are very good: they help the viewer to make

sense of the film, they provoke him to thought. But in the film there is much symbolism that will be little understood by the masses, and this is particularly true of the symbolism embodied in the statues - all the Napoleons and so on. The following symbol is probably also incomprehensible: a sea of scythes that appears before the toppling of the thrones. To someone who had not seen pictures and sculptures that symbolise the mass peasant movement by scythes this image would probably be incomprehensible and it would pass right over him.

Krupskaya was thus agreeing with the implied criticism of other reviewers that Eisenstein was, in effect, producing a pedant's film for a peasant audience.

The symbolism however was only just beginning. The action of the film moves now to July 1917. Workers and soldiers are seen streaming across a bridge bearing placards and banners calling for: 'ALL POWER TO THE SOVIETS!' The Provisional Government loses its nerve and the demonstrators are machine-gunned. Bolsheviks are denounced, attacked and beaten up. There is a particularly gory sequence of a young worker being stabbed to death by bourgeois ladies in their finery using their umbrellas as offensive weapons. Their hatred is quite clear, as is the nature of their allegiance to the Revolution. We then see a functionary of the government speaking on the telephone. The order is given to raise the bridges, thus cutting off the workers' quarters from the centre of the city. The martyrdom of the working class is symbolised, rather sentimentally, by the images of the dead girl and the dead horse, both lying across the middle of the bridges, both in a sense torn apart by the decision to raise them. The horse eventually drops into the river, thus linking with the next scene, where the bourgeoisie are throwing copies of *Pravda,* the Bolshevik paper, into the same river, the Neva. The banners of the demonstrators are also seen floating down the river: the Revolution is being literally washed away. The First Machine-gun Corps is 'disarmed for solidarity', the Bolshevik Party headquarters is ransacked. The Revolution would seem to be in ruins.

Then for the first time we see inside the Winter Palace. Kerensky climbs the stairs. He is in fact climbing the same flight of stairs over and over again, but the sequence is filmed to imply that he is climbing a single endless staircase, metaphorically speaking as well, for his ascent is interspersed with titles proclaiming his different positions: 'DICTATOR/SUPREME COMMANDER/AND SO FORTH . . . AND SO FORTH . . . KERENSKY.' Finally, both metaphorically and actually Kerensky reaches the Tsar's apartments. His figure is overshadowed by a statue holding a crown, and he is attended by the Tsar's footmen. We are shown his elaborate boots and gloves: he is fascinated by the external trappings of power. By contrast with Lenin, Kerensky is a dilettante, playing at revolution, alone and isolated from the mass. Whereas Lenin has been shown in an active and decisive posture, Kerensky vacillates. At this point Eisenstein introduced another of his 'intellectual' metaphors: a golden peacock, a gift from Tsar Nicholas to his wife Alexandra, preens itself. Kerensky hesitates again and then enters the Tsar's apartments.

To underline the contrast with Lenin the scene then switches to the latter's thatched hideout in the misty marshes near Razliv. There could be no greater contrast. Back in Petrograd Kerensky broods now in the Tsarina's apartments. Eisenstein uses the caption 'ALEXANDER FYODOROVICH IN THE APARTMENTS OF ALEXANDRA FYODOROVNA': by playing on the fact that Kerensky's first name and patronymic share the same root as those of the Tsarina he is able to imply a continuity and a close resemblance. This resemblance goes beyond the shared imperial heritage, for in showing Kerensky in the Tsarina's bedroom, surrounded by all her finery, he is also able to suggest a degree of unmanly weakness and indecisiveness both on the part of the Prime Minister and his government. His one decisive action is a reactionary one, the reintroduction of the death penalty. This action leads into the scene criticised by Krupskaya. We see first Kerensky, then a statuette of Napoleon. To an audience that knows its history the inference is clear: Kerensky is a second Napoleon and, like his mentor, he will usurp and betray the ideals of the Revolution. His intentions are symbolically clarified as he plays with a set of decanters, moving them into different positions and finally bringing them into place, fixing them together with a stopper that is shaped like a crown. Kerensky, like Napoleon, wishes to be emperor. But he is not alone in this ambition. A factory hooter sounds a warning: 'THE REVOLUTION IS IN DANGER!' While Kerensky busies himself changing the monogram on the Tsar's bed from A III (representing the autocrat whose statue has been toppled in the opening sequence of the film) to A IV, thus confirming his own imperial ambitions, General Kornilov is approaching the city with British tanks, French aeroplanes and the notorious 'Wild Division' of Cossack horsemen. He stands 'FOR GOD AND COUNTRY'. His values are expressed through a sequence of religious images from the Russian Orthodox through the Muslim and Buddhist back to primitive tribal masks. This sequence served partly to indulge the director in one of his particular artistic interests but in the context of the film it has a more immediate importance in demonstrating that the significance of the appeal to religion is a universal one, just as the significance of the Revolution will be universal. Further, the universal appeal of religion, even in its diversity of forms, serves to point up the universal appeal of patriotism in its diversity of forms. Both religion and patriotism are, in the Marxist terminology, opiates of the people, both are spurious focal points for popular allegiance: only the Bolsheviks represent the true demands and needs of the mass for bread, peace and land. The religious masks fade into epaulettes and military decorations: the Tsar's statue is restored by montage and the nadir of the Revolution's betrayal has been reached.

Kornilov and Kerensky are compared with two statuettes of Napoleon: both are traitors and counter-revolutionaries, both megalomaniacs. The one, Kerensky, lies motionless and helpless face down-wards on a couch, not knowing what to do: he has the trappings of power but not the power itself. The other, Kornilov, advances on revolutionary Petrograd. The Provisional Government, in the hands of the ineffectual Kerensky, is powerless to defend the city and this task is left to the Soviet. For the first time we see the Bolshevik headquarters at Smolny. Arms are being distributed to the proletariat, agitators harangue the fighting men by the light of bonfires and torches. The darkness enhances the sense of anticipation. The camera cuts to Kornilov's Wild Division: a close-up tells us that their swords are inscribed with the motto 'God is with us'. Bolshevik agitators arrive, distribute leaflets and address the 'enemy': they offer bread, peace, land. The Cossacks sheath their swords, dance and fraternise: the Wild Division has changed sides. Kerensky takes refuge under the Tsarina's cushions as his power ebbs away.

Eisenstein then indulges in an effective piece of trick photography. In a series of stills a rifle is assembled from its constituent parts. Symbolically this sequence denotes the need for proletarian self-help: the mass must make the best of the materials it has available, it must literally forge its own weapons to defend the Revolution that nobody else will save. The next title reiterates this: 'PROLETARIAT, LEARN TO USE ARMS.' We see the serried ranks of the Petrograd Soviet training on a makeshift parade ground. The scene shifts again, to the smoke-filled room in which the Bolshevik leaders are deliberating. With Stalin at his side Lenin designates 25 October as the date for the seizure of power. The deadline for the victory of the Revolution has now been established: progress can be measured against that deadline and the tension that leads to the climax of the film can therefore be created.

Eisenstein then intersperses a shot of the cruiser *Aurora* which is to fire the shot that signals the storming of the Winter Palace. The bridges reappear: they are raised, then lowered. The functionary on the telephone is beside himself. Kerensky is desperate: he phones for the Cossacks but the phone is answered by a Bolshevik sympathiser and his message is not passed on. He flees to Gatchina in a car flying the US flag. The comparison with Napoleon is continued by the stance that Kerensky takes in the car, and by his gestures. As the captain leaves his sinking ship, the gates of the Winter Palace are closed on the outside world. The Provisional Government is now completely isolated, devoid of outside support, and the final confrontation is drawing near. The Palace itself is defended by a remarkable group of rather Brechtian women called the Shock Battalion of Death. They are largely drunk and disorderly. There are shots in which the women admire a Rodin statue of an embracing couple and another sculpture of a mother and child: by these devices Eisenstein suggests that the Shock Battalion of Death has been driven to its reactionary political stance by sexual frustration. The scene switches to Smolny, a complete contrast, a hive of frenzied activity as the Bolsheviks enthusiastically report for duty, while the Mensheviks spy on them treacherously. The darkness of the surroundings serves to heighten the tension: the storm clouds are gathering.

The Second Congress of the Soviets is in session. If the seizure of power is not effected soon, the Mensheviks, Social Revolutionaries and Constitutional Democrats will gain control and the Bolsheviks will have lost their historic opportunity. Lenin waits in the corridor, disguised as a man with toothache: there is a tension-heightening diversion as we wonder whether he has been recognised by his enemies. Meanwhile Kerensky's car speeds towards Gatchina and

the Provisional Government sits waiting, the Prime Minister's chair conspicuously empty. The contrast of extremes between Lenin and Kerensky, Soviet and government, is once more underlined by the juxtaposition of the imagery. *Aurora* appears again: it represents the new element that will upset decisively the present balance of authority between the two. The Congress of Soviets, like the government, waits and tension mounts. The Bolshevik appeal is distributed, the Red Army surrounds the Winter Palace and presents an ultimatum. The government still waits. Some of the women soldiers defending the Palace lay down their arms and join the Revolution, while others remain undecided. Their indecision is echoed by the owl clock that moves its head first one way and then the other. Bolshevik agitators penetrate the Winter Palace, sailors arrive on the roof. The Bolsheviks take over the Congress of Soviets, their banner adorns the platform as the Revolution gathers its momentum. A messenger enters: 'THE CYCLE CORPS IS WITH US!' There is a montage of cycle wheels accelerating in tempo and heightening the tension still further. Sailors drop a grenade through the Palace roof, breaching its defences. The government sleeps as history slips beyond its reach. At the Congress a Menshevik speaker urges caution: a montage of harps suggests that these tired arguments have been heard once too often. A Bolshevik takes the rostrum and announces: 'THE TIME FOR TALK IS PAST.' Action, not words. The guns open fire on the Palace, now virtually undefended The Provisional Government is like the emperor without his clothes. Eisenstein makes this visual comparison by showing the ministers' empty suits.

This is the climax of the film *October*—the storming of the Winter Palace. It is midnight on 24 25 October 1917. Crowds of workers, soldiers and sailors stream across the square and up the stairs. This time they will be victorious, this time they will avenge *Potemkin* and the betrayal of February. When this vanguard of the masses penetrates the Palace, when ordinary workers and soldiers see the ornate splendour of the royal bedchamber and the size and scope of the royal wine cellars, they are amazed. Their amazement soon turns to something less passive and they begin to loot the Palace. But property, especially royal property is theft and the sailors take disciplinary action. To prevent the looting of the wine cellars, they start to smash the bottles. This time the liquid that flows across the screen is not the workers' blood but the Tsar's wine. In the bedroom soldiers find religious images, Fabergé eggs and a box containing thousands of the medals that have been used to reward bravery at the front. The truth of the imperialist war finally dawns on them: 'IS THIS WHAT WE FOUGHT FOR?' The hollow façade of imperial power is then underlined by a shot of a small boy sitting on the Tsar's throne, swinging his legs. The soldiers, led by Antonov-Ovseyenko, burst into the Cabinet Room and arrest the Provisional Government. The film quotes Lenin's declaration that the government is overthrown. A series of clocks indicates this historic moment in the different time zones of the world: Petrograd, Moscow, London, Berlin, Paris, New York and other places. The boy on the Tsar's throne is asleep: history has passed him by and made the throne irrelevant. The Congress of Soviets applauds Lenin's declaration and the montage of clapping hands merges into a montage of the clock faces. Finally, Lenin speaks to the Congress. Again he is bursting with vitality and movement—a leader, but of and with the mass: 'THE WORKERS' AND PEASANTS' REVOLUTION IS ACCOMPLISHED. LONG LIVE THE WORLD OCTOBER.' The victory that had been thwarted in **Strike** and **Battleship Potemkin** is now finally assured.

October, as I have already shown, had a mixed reception. One leading critic insisted that the film should be re-edited. Another, describing the film as 'not easily accessible', conceded that, 'In spite of all its defects. **October** is undoubtedly the best film that we have of the history of the October Revolution. The discussions provoked by the film in the columns of the journal *Zhizn' iskusstva* were perhaps most fairly summed up in the following words:

> **October** is unusual in theme and execution. It requires interpretation, careful preparation for its comprehension and the explanation of the enormous work and the enormous material which it contains. It deals with the great events of the proletarian revolution in a new cinema language, aimed not merely at the contemporary cinema audience, but also at the audience that will appear in the near future as the cultural level of the broad working masses improves. And we are entitled to say that, with all its particular and separate faults, **October** is our great achievement, preparing the way for the creation of a great Soviet cinema art.

But even this praise did not save Eisenstein from his critics. In June 1928 a rather unpleasant caricature of the film director appeared in the pages of *Sovetskii ekran* and Eisenstein's career never really recovered from **October.** It is ironic that one of the supreme examples of cinematic myth-making should have caused its creator to be denounced for obscurantism by the very people whose ideology he was attempting to popularise. However, when Pudovkin saw the film, he remarked, 'How I should like to make such a powerful failure.'

. . . . .

> 'Patriotism is my theme' was the thought immediately in my mind and in the mind of everyone in our creative collective during the shooting, the sound recording and the editing.

Sergei Eisenstein, 1939

Alexander Nevsky, made in 1938, marks a watershed in the development of Sergei Eisenstein as a film director. After completing **October** in 1927, in time for the celebration of the tenth anniversary of the October Revolution, Eisenstein returned to the studio to finish **The General Line,** his film statement on the problems confronting Soviet agriculture. Unfortunately, during the time he had spent making **October** the Party Line on agriculture had changed: for this reason **The General Line** had to be altered, and then re-titled as **The Old and the New.** He was then sent abroad on a delegation to investigate the possibilities of sound and stayed in the United States and Mexico to shoot **Que Viva México!** This project ran into difficulties and Eisenstein returned to the Soviet Union. But the Soviet film industry was now under the control of

Boris Shumyatsky, who proved to be unco-operative towards the director's proposals for a film involving Paul Robeson or one based on Marx's *Das Kapital.* Eventually, in 1935, Eisenstein was allowed to begin shooting **Bezhin Meadow** which dramatised the problems of collectivisation in a conflict between the generations. In March 1937 however, after two million roubles had been expended on the film, Shumyatsky ordered a halt to production, alleging that Eisenstein was wasting the resources that he had been given. Ironically enough, when Shumyatsky was dismissed in January 1938 these same charges were made against him and he was accused especially of squandering money by cancelling films like **Bezhin Meadow.**

It was Shumyatsky's dismissal that opened the way for Eisenstein to finish a film. **Alexander Nevsky** was to be his first completed film since **The Old and the New** in 1929 and his first completed sound film—the first opportunity therefore for the public to measure the practical application of the principles of 'orchestral counterpoint' enunciated by Eisenstein, together with Pudovkin and Alexandrov, in their statement of August 1928, in which they had inveighed against the use of sound for ' "high cultural dramas" and other photographed performances of a theatrical kind'. In his own writing [*Izbrannye proizvedeniaa,* vol. 1] Eisenstein made the political purpose of **Alexander Nevsky** abundantly clear:

> The theme of patriotism and a national rebuff to the aggressor is the theme that permeates our film. We have taken a historical episode from the 13th century when the forerunners of the present-day fascists—the Livonian and Teutonic knights—waged a systematic struggle for the conquest and invasion of the east in order to subjugate completely the Slavs and other peoples in the same way that contemporary fascist Germany is seeking to subjugate them with the same frenzied slogans and the same fanaticism.

The film then was to be an allegory, a projection of present events on to the past, an appeal to the example offered by Russian history:

> Reading the chronicles of the 13th century and alternating them with contemporary newspapers, you lose all sense of the difference in time, for that murderous fear spread by the conquering orders of chivalry in the 13th century is almost the same as that which is being spread in Europe today.

> And so the picture, telling of a completely historical epoch, of completely historical events, was made and is seen, according to audience testimony, as a completely contemporary picture, so close are the feelings that inspired the Russian people in the 13th century in repulsing the enemy to the feelings that inspire the Soviet Russian people now, and doubtless to all the feelings that inspire all those towards whom the grasping claw of German aggression is spreading.

This historical precedent was to be used to strengthen the resolve of those inside and outside the Soviet Union who were engaged in the struggle against fascism, to transform their passive opposition into active resistance:

We want our film not only to mobilise those who are in the thick of the fight against fascism on a world scale, but also to give heart, courage and conviction even to those parts of the world population to whom fascism appears as invincible as the orders of chivalry appeared in the 13th century. Let them not cringe before fascism, let them not kneel before it without protest, let them stop the unending policy of concession and appeasement towards this insatiable monster. Let the sceptics remember that there is no force of gloom and darkness that could stand against the combined efforts of all that is best, healthiest, most progressive and forward-looking in mankind.

These words were written early in 1939; like the film itself they were to fall foul of the Nazi-Soviet Pact of August 1939 and be temporarily suppressed in the Soviet Union. They do however confirm that *Alexander Nevsky* was both conceived and executed primarily as a work of political propaganda: the artistic considerations were therefore secondary.

In terms of both its content and its style *Alexander Nevsky* marks a break with Eisenstein's previous films and looks forward to his last film, *Ivan the Terrible.* The differences are only partly attributable to the advent of sound, for they also reflected developments in Eisenstein's technique and the changes that had occurred in the political life of the Soviet Union. His silent films had all been characterised by a use of free and rapid montage. This in itself had a dehumanising effect on the characters in the drama and underlined the director's deliberate policy of making the mass, rather than an individual, the hero of his work. The introduction of sound slowed the pace of visual montage even for a more experimental director like Dziga Vertov; it also enabled individual characterisations to be more fully developed on the screen for the characters could now voice their thoughts as well as demonstrate their actions. Instead of the workers in *Strike* or *October* or the sailors in *Battleship Potemkin,* we have the figure of *Alexander Nevsky* himself. Admittedly Eisenstein had also used an individual characterisation for the figure of Marfa Lapkina in *The Old and the New:* she came to symbolise the progressive peasant, just as Alexander was to symbolise the spirit of Russia and its resistance to the invader. However, Lapkina's limited individualism is the only trace of that characteristic in the film: *Nevsky,* on the other hand, also offers us the characters of Gavrilo Olexich and Vasili Buslai and their rivalry in love and war. It is in their characterisation above all that we see the break: for the first time in an Eisenstein film we see characters who display signs of individual human emotion and motivation, who behave as the audience might behave, rather than as symbols. This is also true of Vasilisa, whose ferocious participation in Alexander's army is inspired by the Germans' torture and execution of her father during the sacking of Pskov. It is of course true that the degree of individualism permitted by Eisenstein in *Alexander Nevsky* is no greater than that employed by Pudovkin in *Mother* twelve years earlier and in this sense he may be reacting to the criticisms levelled at his films in the late 1920s. However, in the emphasis given in the film to a powerful

leader figure, Eisenstein is following in the steps of other directors of the 1930s. In the 1920s the mass themselves had been the hero of the Soviet cinema, but now the mass had acquired a leader. Marc Ferro has amply demonstrated the function of *Chapayev,* made in 1934, in propagating the ideology of Stalinism, but other examples of the powerful and charismatic leader figure abound: Petrov's *Peter the First,* Pudovkin's *Minin and Pozharsky,* Dovzhenko's *Shchors* (made in response to Stalin's request for a Ukrainian *Chapayev*), even Vertov's *Three Songs of Lenin,* and films like *A Great Citizen, Baltic Deputy* and later *Bogdan Khmelnitsky* and *Ivan the Terrible.* But perhaps the simplest and most instructive comparison can be made between *October* and films like *Lenin in October* or *Lenin in 1918:* in the latter the role of the individual, and the role of Stalin in particular, is much enhanced.

It is against this background then that we must see *Alexander Nevsky.* When Stalin had distributed honours to the Soviet film industry in January 1935 Eisenstein had been ignored. In February 1939 both he and Nikolai Cherkasov, who played Alexander, were awarded the Order of Lenin. *Alexander Nevsky* was the film that rehabilitated its director: it also marked his major contribution to the Soviet war effort.

The screenplay for the film was written in collaboration with Pyotr Pavlenko and a first draft, under the title *Rus,* the name for mediaeval Russia, was published in December 1937. Several alternative titles were considered—*Lord Great Novgorod* and *Battle on the Ice* among them—but eventually *Alexander Nevsky* was chosen; in the light of Stalin's 'personality cult the choice is in itself significant. Filming began on 5 June 1938 and finished on 7 November. Eisenstein was determined to show that he could produce a film quickly if necessary, to rebut Shumyatsky's criticisms of *Bezhin Meadow.* He succeeded beyond his wildest expectations. The film divides into three major sequences: the first depicts the Russians uniting in the face of common danger. This sequence further divides into seven scenes: (1) on the shores of Lake Pleshcheyevo Alexander encounters the Mongols; (2) Gavrilo and Vaska rivals in love; (3) the Novgorod assembly debates its response to the German attack; (4) the sacking of Pskov; (5) emissaries from Novgorod come to Pereyaslavl to ask Alexander to lead the Russian forces; (6) a brief interlude showing the recruitment of the peasant army; (7) Alexander assumes command of the Novgorod forces. The second sequence marks the focus and the climax of the film— the Battle on the Ice. The third sequence, with which the film ends, consists of the victorious entry of Alexander's forces into Pskov and the reckoning with the invaders.

The opening scene of the film shows the devastation and humiliation suffered by mediaeval Russia at the hands of foreign invaders. In this case the invaders are the Mongols. It was Eisenstein's original intention to depict a Russia fighting a battle on two fronts—against the Mongols, symbolising the contemporary threat from Japan, and the Teutonic Knights, representing the Nazis. In an early draft of the screenplay Alexander, having defeated the Germans, was to have been poisoned by the Mongols, and his death was to have been avenged by his great-grandson,

Dmitri Donskoi, another legendary figure from the history of mediaeval Russia. But a battle on two fronts would have disturbed the simplicity of the story line and lessened the impact of the propaganda message. Eisenstein was therefore content to confine the Mongol presence to this opening episode. The scene is set on the shores of Lake Pleshcheyevo, near Alexander's home at Peryaslavl. It is a scene of peace and harmony, emphasised by the shots of the lake and the sky. Throughout the film there is a close relationship between man and nature and their respective moods. As Eisenstein wrote elsewhere: 'Everywhere the emotional landscape assumes the form of the mutual submergence of man and nature in one another.

In this scene the sky is open and bright, but the idyll is disturbed by the arrival of Mongol horsemen. They are dark and threatening figures, kicking and lashing the Russian peasants. The khan has sent an envoy to ask Alexander to join the Golden Horde. The contrast between the two men is instructive: Alexander is tall, composed and dignified, a fisherman and man of the people, a man among men, a Russian among Russians. The Mongol peers from behind a curtain; he is feared by his men and his whole position is unnatural and alien. Alexander refuses the offer: 'We have a saying: die on your native soil, do not abandon it.' The incident brings home to Alexander the plight of his country and its imminent need of his services: 'The Mongol can wait. We have an enemy more dangerous than the Mongol, closer at hand and more evil, one who cannot be bought off by tribute—the German. When we have beaten him we can attend to the Mongol.' This tentative call to arms leads into the next scene.

In a sense the next scene is a light interlude between serious affairs of state. The two characters Vasili Buslai and Gavrilo Olexich are seen together, joking and courting Olga: their friendly rivalry is established. Novgorod is busy and prosperous, with little outward sign of the impending danger. The sets for the Novgorod and Pskov scenes were reconstructed in the studio because the originals, in Eisenstein's eyes, were no longer sufficiently authentic. Over the centuries the old palaces and churches had sunk several feet into the ground and their visual proportions and perspective had therefore altered. Such was Eisenstein's sense of perfection that they were rebuilt in the studio according to their original proportions. But the idyll of Novgorod too is shaken as a bell calls the population to an assembly. We see carts bringing refugees from Pskov and a wounded soldier calls for vengeance. Tension mounts as he tells of the German atrocities and the crowd respond:

> *Soldier:* If they catch you with a sword, they beat you for having it! If they catch you with bread, they beat you for the bread! They've tortured mothers and wives for their sons and husbands.

> *Crowd:* The German is a beast! We know the German!

There are of course those who argue for compromise and collaboration with the invader, but they are confined to the merchants and the Church, both by now familiar actors in the demonology of Soviet propaganda. There is

confusion and shouting, emphasised by the music, but eventually the assembly decides to call on Alexander Nevsky to lead the forces of Novgorod. It seems that Russia may be saved.

The next scene brings us face to face with the confrontation between good and evil that has been hinted at in the opening sequence and the previous scene. The portrayal of the sacking of Pskov is itself a classic example of atrocity propaganda. The characters are all typecast in line with Eisenstein's concept of 'typage', and we revert briefly to the Eisenstein of the silent film era. The Russians are again open, human characters, 'real people'. The Germans are faceless, often hooded and frequently shot in profile, with cruel, animal-like features. In their meanness they are dwarfed by the massive solidity of the Russian buildings that surround them. The contemporary relevance of the film is underlined by a shot of a knight's helmet decorated with the swastika. Otherwise their symbol is the conventional Latin cross of Western Christianity, usually shot from below to increase the sense of its power. Russian Christianity, which obviously played a significant part in the life of the country in the thirteenth century, is represented in the first instance by its buildings. But these are portrayed as an integral, almost a natural, part of the Russian background. The only priests who appear on the Russian side play the part assigned to the monk Ananias, that of a traitor. The Russia presented on the screen is a secular state, religion is only a folk memory; in other words the portrayal reflects the official view of contemporary Soviet life. But the mayor of Pskov, Tverdilo, is a Russian who has betrayed his country: his character echoes the accusations of the purges and presages the role of Shuisky in *Ivan the Terrible.* He is contrasted with Pavsha, the good Russian, who is executed calling for vengeance. Similarly the traitor-priest Ananias, despatched to Novgorod to rouse the people there against Alexander, is contrasted with the beggar Avvakum, whose dying words at the stake become the clarion call for Russia's resistance:

> Arise, people of Rus,
> To glorious battle, mortal battle!
> Arise, men of freedom,
> For our fair land!

The next scene takes place in Alexander's hut near Pereyaslavl. The prince is pacing up and down; one of the men voices his thoughts: 'We ought to be fighting the Germans, not mending nets.' Emissaries from Novgorod arrive to ask Alexander to lead the army of resistance. He accepts the challenge with fighting words and plans to raise a peasant army. The scene changes to show the peasants joining Alexander's army in large numbers. They are seen largely in silhouette against the sky, and dominated by it. Again man is closely intertwined with nature: the Soviet cameraman, Anatoli Golovnya, has observed of this sequence:

> The movement of people is drawn across the bottom of the frame. The earth is at times completely absent from the frame and it looks as if people are walking across the sky. There is a certain convention at the basis of such composition. The white costumes show up effectively against a background of grey sky. With its indefinite colour the earth would only disturb the purity of

the tonal compositions . . . A realistic treatment of the action at times involves the sacrifice of decorative effect.

In the final shots of this sequence the peasants merge like streams flowing into one large river; there is something elemental in their urge to resist the invader.

In the original screenplay for *Alexander Nevsky* there followed a scene set in Novgorod showing two fighting camps, one supporting Alexander and the other, composed of merchants, arguing for peace. The material for this scene was shot at considerable expense but was not included in the final film. The critic Viktor Shklovsky has explained:

> Eisenstein was editing the picture . . . He edited and edited and lay down and fell fast asleep.
>
> One night there was a telephone call from the Kremlin. They said Stalin was asking for the film. They did not wake the director but took the cans and carried them away.
>
> The film was a great success, but one scene had not yet been edited and the can containing the sequence on the Volkhov bridge lay apart from the others.
>
> It was not shown. Nobody noticed and they decided not to mention that they had not shown the complete film, and that is how it was released. The absence of this sequence was not noticed by a single critic.

It is not known whether the missing sequence has been preserved in the archives. Eisenstein however considered the missing scene to be an integral part of the structure of the film and petitioned Dukelsky, Chairman of the Committee on Cinema Affairs to have it reinstated. He was unsuccessful. He described his feelings in his autobiographical notes:

> The eternal rush of the film world was the undoing . . . of the Novgorod bridge in *Alexander Nevsky.*
>
> On it we filmed the scene of the famous fistfights between the St Sofia and merchants' quarters of the ancient city.
>
> In terms of the story it is here that Vaska Buslai and Vasilisa have their first romantic encounter. And it is here in the midst of the scuffle that Vaska first shouts enthusiastically, 'What a fine girl!' after Vasilisa has hit him in the teeth.
>
> I grieve for this lyrical link in the relationship between the two romantic heroes. I grieve deeply for those desperate children who throw themselves from the bridge into the icy water in October . . .
>
> But I grieve most of all that this whole scene flew into the bin.

It is ironical that what was in some ways Eisenstein's most successful film should have been released in a form that he considered incomplete and unsatisfactory.

The film as released moves straight from the raising of the peasant army to the assembly where Alexander addresses the people of Novgorod. The cathedral broods over the proceedings. The orators are filmed against the sky, their heads on a level with the church cupolas. Only the doubting merchants are filmed from a higher angle, so that the buildings rise above and dwarf them. They are out of step with their environment and with the spirit of the times. Alexander calls for the defence of Russia and the crowd follow him, singing what has become their battle hymn, 'Arise, people of Rus!' The spearmakers vie with the smiths in their contributions to the armoury. Ignat distributes chain mail and weapons to all and sundry. Vaska and Gavrilo ask Olga to decide between them: she agrees to give her hand to the one who proves bravest in battle. Ignat is left with a chain-mail shirt that is too small for him: 'This shirt's on the short side!' The scene ends with the battle hymn once more.

The Novgorod scene is full of life and vibrant with activity. The next scene on the other hand, set in the Teutonic camp, reeks of death. In the background is the bishop's tent, adorned with the cross. The knights, with the Master of the Order at their head, are kneeling in prayer. Whereas Alexander, though a prince, is still a man of the people, here there is a clearly defined hierarchy and a remoteness from real life. They hear that Alexander's army is marching through the forest towards them. It is night and the snow weighs heavily on the trees. The Master believes that the Russians can be trapped and orders his men on to their horses.

In the middle of the forest the knights find a detachment of Russians: it is the advance party led by Vaska. Although taken by surprise, they do not run away. Battle is joined and the longest scene in the film begins. All in all the sequence of the Battle on the Ice lasts 37 minutes: it is both the climax and the focal point of the film. It was perhaps typical of Eisenstein that he should decide to shoot the most important scene in *Alexander Nevsky* first. But this desire conflicted with his wish to shoot the film very quickly. He could not wait until the winter of 1938-39 and so a battlefield of artificial ice and snow was created and the scene was shot in the middle of a Moscow heatwave. Shklovsky writes [in his *Eizenshtein,* 1973]:

> Winter scenes are very difficult to shoot, because winter is a gloomy season. They decided to reconstruct it without icicles, without steam, and without snow-covered trees. They constructed not winter but a battle. They felled a cherry orchard, dug up the roots, ploughed up a vast field and covered it with asphalt.
>
> Then they put a mixture of chalk and naphthalene on it. They dressed the Russian army and the Teutonic army and started filming.

But before we come to the actual Battle on the Ice there is a period of tense waiting. The sounds of battle are heard in the Russian camp, while Alexander and Gavrilo await the return of Vaska's detachment. Ignat entertains them with a story. The tension mounts. The tale of the hare and the vixen is an allegory for the fate that awaits the Teutonic knights on the field of battle. It is this tale that galvanises Alexander into action: the German troops are heavier and less mobile and he therefore decides to fight them on the ice of Lake Peipus, rather than on Russian soil. Just as the vixen in Ignat's story is trapped between two trunks because she is too fat, so the knights will be trapped on the breaking ice because they are too heavy. The plan is reminiscent of Kutuzov's strategy of allowing Napoleon deep into Russia, only to be worn down by the rigours of the winter climate. It is also a warning to the potential contemporary aggressor that he too will have to cope with the Russian winter, and it is a warning that Hitler and his generals ignored at their peril. One of the strengths of this pre-battle scene lies in the fact that the enemy is unseen and the tension is increased by the prolonged anticipation of their appearance. Here Prokofiev's score plays a very important part, although the relationship between the music and the visual image remains significant throughout the film. Viktor Shklovsky wrote [in "Aleksandr Nevskii," *Kino*, 2 November 1938] of the composer's part in *Alexander Nevsky*: 'For a long time music has remained on the fringes of the cinema. Now the cinema breathes music. This particular segment of the film, the scene leading up to the appearance of the invading army on the screen, has been analysed by Eisenstein in the fourth chapter of the collection of essays published in English as *The Film Sense*. Writing generally of the relationship between the director and the composer in this film and dealing in particular with the question of which of the two has the leading role, he observes:

> It makes no difference whether the composer writes music for the 'general idea' of a sequence, or for a rough or final cutting of the sequence; or, if procedure has been organised in an opposite direction, with the director building the visual cutting to the music that has already been written and recorded on sound-track.
>
> I should like to point out that in *Alexander Nevsky* literally all these possible approaches were employed. There are sequences in which the shots were cut to a previously recorded music-track. There are sequences for which the entire piece of music was written to a final cutting of the picture. There are sequences that contain both approaches. There are even sequences that furnish material for the anecdotists. One such example occurs in the battle scene where pipes and drums are played for the victorious Russian soldiers. I couldn't find a way to explain to Prokofiev what precise effect should be 'seen' in his music for this joyful moment. Seeing that we were getting nowhere, I ordered some 'prop' instruments constructed, shot these being played (without sound) *visually,* and projected the results for Prokofiev—who almost immediately handed me an exact 'musical equivalent' to the visual image of pipers and drummers that I had shown him.

Eisenstein goes on to explain how individual frames, and individual notes, achieve their power because of the uniqueness of their particular position in the sequence and their combined effect:

> The *farewell embrace* between Vaska and Gavrilo Olexich in *Alexander Nevsky* . . .

could only occur at one *precise* point in the musical score, in the same way that the close-up shots of the German knights' helmets could not be used before the point where they were finally employed in the attack sequence, for only at that point does the music change its character from one that can be expressed in long shots and medium shots of the attack to one that demands rhythmic visual beats, close-ups of galloping and the like.

> Alongside this, we cannot deny the fact that the most *striking* and immediate impression will be gained, of course, from *a congruence of the movement of the music with the movement of the visual contour*—with the graphic composition of the frame; for this contour or this outline, or this line is the most vivid 'emphasiser' of the very idea of the movement.

I would refer the reader to *The Film Sense* for the more detailed analysis of the 'dawn of anxious waiting' sequence with which Eisenstein justifies his statement that 'The audio-visual aspect of *Alexander Nevsky* achieves its most complete fusion in the sequence of the "Battle on the Ice" . . . The method used in it of audio-visual correspondence is that used for any sequence in the film.

The Russian forces wait. Alexander stands above the lake on Raven Rock, peering into the distance, against a background of open sky and storm clouds. There is little movement. At the base of the rock the Russian army waits; shots of its massed ranks are intercut with close-ups of Ignat and Vasilisa. The conflicting angles of pictorial composition add to the tension created by the music. Suddenly and almost imperceptibly the Germans appear on the horizon, marching across the lake that is to become their graveyard. At last we see the two opposing forces at their full strength. Gradually the camera moves from the Russians to the Germans: it is they who first fill the horizon, then move diagonally across the screen until their movement fills it completely. The final shot in this sequence sets the two armies in immediate confrontation: the camera is raised and the advancing Germans are seen through the heads of the Russian soldiers, through a forest of their spears. The opposing armies meet and the great battle begins.

The Battle on the Ice allows Eisenstein to realise to the full his concepts of montage and an orchestral counterpoint between sound and image. Visually the film cuts from general shots of the advancing armies and the battle to close-ups of the individual participants: Ignat, Vaska, Gavrilo and Alexander himself. The music too is a mixture, combining Russian and German themes until the point in the battle where the tide turns in favour of the Russians: then the Russian themes swamp the German. For much of the scene the music functions in counterpoint to the image, in places sound and vision run parallel, while on two occasions, with the image of the German horns and that of the Russian bugles, the music acts as a direct sound illustration of the image. By this variety of approaches Eisenstein and Prokofiev build up a sense of the confusion and the excitement of the battle. The Russian victory is confirmed by the man-to-man combat between Alexander and the Master of the Teutonic Order, which ends with the Master

Eisenstein in Chicago, 1930.

slipping from his horse. He is led away with a noose round his neck, defeated and humiliated. Vasilisa and Ignat tie up the German bishop, whose prayers for deliverance have remained unheard. Ananias is pursued and killed by Vasilisa. Tverdilo, whose treachery is underlined by his inability to decide whether to cross himself in the Latin or the Russian manner, is captured by Ignat. But at this moment the German war horn sounds, Ignat turns and is stabbed in the back by Tverdilo. He dies muttering, 'This shirt's on the short side!', taking us back to the scene in Novgorod when Alexander took command of the Russian forces. The battle is however won. The Germans crowd round their war horn and the ice covering Lake Peipus begins to crack beneath them. Like Napoleon and Hitler they are to fall victim to the Russian winter. Because of the lack of detailed evidence for thirteenth-century Russian history, Eisenstein was able to use poetic license in this fashion; indeed it was this freedom that attracted him to the story of Alexander Nevsky.

The next brief scene is known as the 'Field of Death'. It is night and there are corpses everywhere, but Vaska and Gavrilo find one another alive. Olga comes in search of them: each tries to convince her that the other has fought more bravely and the three stumble off into the foggy darkness.

The final scene in **Alexander Nevsky** marks the liberation of Russia and the triumphal entry of Alexander's forces into Pskov. First the dead heroes are brought in, then the captured Germans. Alexander displays his humanity by releasing the foot soldiers and holding only the knights for barter. Tverdilo is left to the mercy of the people he has betrayed. All that remains is for Olga to decide between Gavrilo and Vaska. It is Vaska who makes her decision for her: Gavrilo will take Olga and Vaska will have Vasilisa, the bravest warrior of all. The badinage over, the film comes to its serious conclusion. Alexander addresses his army and the people of Pskov: 'Go and tell all in foreign parts that Rus lives. Let people come to us as guests without fear. But he who comes with the sword shall perish by the sword. On this Rus stands and will stand forever!' His words merge with the shouts of the people and the film ends with the battle hymn:

> Arise, people of Rus,
> To glorious battle, mortal battle!
> Arise, men of freedom,
> For our fair land!

The filming of **Alexander Nevsky** was completed by the deadline that Eisenstein had set himself—7 November 1938, the twenty-first anniversary of the October Revolution. By 23 November the editing too had been completed and the film had its première. It was released to the general public on 1 December and was an immediate success, capturing, as it did, the spirit of the times. **Alexander Nevsky** brought Eisenstein the official recognition that he had for so long been denied: on 1 February 1939 he was awarded the Order of Lenin, the highest honour that the Soviet government can bestow, and on 15 March 1941 he received the State Prize, First Class. His film was withdrawn from distribution after the Nazi—Soviet Pact had been signed in August 1939, just as anti-Soviet films like *Frisians in Peril* were withdrawn in Germany, but it was released again after the German attack in June 1941. It is perhaps a tribute to the powerful role that the film played in strengthening the Soviet resistance that the government instituted a new battle honour, the Order of Alexander Nevsky.

To Eisenstein himself the success of what he regarded as his least satisfactory film remained an inexplicable mystery. In his archive there is a note, dated 24 December 1938 and entitled 'The Riddle of *Nevsky*':

Nevsky is *brazenly* effective despite *itself. Everyone* can see its defects: its staginess *avant tout,* its length, the rhythmic breaks and failures. *Everyone* can see them, not just the specialists. The persistence with which even those who were dissatisfied the first time go two or three times would make it seem that even the devil would go again if he didn't like it! And it is effective *quand-même*. Why? I think it's a matter of 'Shamanism': it's just like the Shaman's tambourine, there's only a single thought, and *everything* revolves around a *single* thought. There's not a word, a remark, an episode or a scene where the speech and the plot are not concerned with the enemy and the need to beat him: in the shots, designs, reminiscences, the very actions themselves. You do not, of course, have to search so openly for this *single-mindedness* through all the variety (and even diversity) of what is happening. It rivets you hypnotically.

Herbert Eagle   (essay date 1987)

SOURCE: An introduction to *Nonindifferent Nature* by Sergei Eisenstein, Cambridge University Press, 1987, pp. vii-xxi.

[*In the following essay, Eagle provides an overview of Eisenstein's critical writings and demonstrates how the director's theories were exemplified in his films.*]

Sergei Eisenstein dedicated **Nonindifferent Nature** to "poor Salieri," who, in Alexander Pushkin's dramatic poem, laments: " . . . True tone I smothered, dissecting music like a corpse; I test with algebra pure harmony. . . ." It was Eisenstein's intent, though, to vindicate Salieri by arguing that the spontaneous and intoxicating act of artistic creation *must* be followed by "ever-increasing, precise knowledge about what we do." Thus, **Nonindifferent Nature** not only represents the most advanced stage of Eisenstein's thinking on the structure of film, but it is the creator's attempt to demonstrate, once again, the validity of his own personal lifelong synthesis of creative art *and* theoretical analysis, a synthesis not always viewed positively by official Soviet criticism.

Eisenstein's films of the 1920s, *Strike, Battleship Potemkin, October (Ten Days that Shook the World), The Old and the New (The General Line)*, captured the attention of the world with their daring approach to film montage. Eisenstein clearly was not satisfied to represent the world from without, as if through an illusionist window on "reality"; he wanted to assault the viewer with his own particular perceptions, understandings, and emotions. The mental state to be produced *in the viewer,* and not the object to be represented, was at the center of Eisenstein's film practice and of his later theories. He broke down "reality" into signs and symbols and reassembled it into films that, to this day, represent a unique approach to the art.

By the late 1920s, however, Eisenstein's experimental work was no longer a preferred form for the conservative bureaucracy that ultimately prevailed in Soviet cultural policy and ushered in the officially sanctioned style of "socialist realism." Eisenstein remained a hero of Soviet culture on the international scene, but at home his planned films were delayed or shelved. Scholarship, theorizing, and teaching occupied his attention increasingly, as film scripts and projects awaited authorization. Beginning in late 1928, and for two decades afterwards, Eisenstein articulated and broadened the theories of montage for which he is now so famous. Because Eisenstein considered the cinema to be the highest stage of the arts, a complex synthesis of literature, drama, the visual arts, and music, his theoretical speculations, backed by prodigious reading, ultimately became a theory of culture and art as a whole. In his expositions and discussions, examples came from the works of writers, painters, sculptors, and musicians as often as they did from filmmakers, and his sources ranged from psychologists, natural scientists, and philosophers to theoreticians and historians of art, music, and theater. This breadth of interest, and Eisenstein's constant empha-

sis on art as communication through signs, led the Soviet linguist V. V. Ivanov to devote a major portion of his *Notes on the History of Semiotics in the USSR* (1976) to Eisenstein's thought.

Eisenstein's work on montage as a collision of signs began appearing in 1928 with an article on Kabuki theater and an afterword to a book on Japanese cinema. In these articles, Eisenstein drew close parallels between the principles of montage and the ideograms of Japanese writing, where separate signs, originally representational, are superimposed to create new signs whose meaning is the result of a metaphorical operation (for example, the ideographs for "knife" and "heart" are combined to form the ideogram "sorrow"). In Kabuki Eisenstein was fascinated by the "decomposition" of reality into independent visual and aural signs and their free recombination: A verbal text is read offstage; onstage an actor mimes, while elements of makeup represent character traits and emotional moods. In essence, Eisenstein was in agreement with the Russian formalist theoretician Yuri Tynyanov, who wrote: "The visible person, the visible thing, is only an element of cinema language when it is given in the quality of a semantic sign."

In his articles of the late 1920s (including the famous programmatic statement, signed by his colleagues the directors Pudovkin and Alexandrov, about the function of sound in cinema *not* being reduced to the mere recording of dialogue), Eisenstein emphasized the *collision* of disparate and conflicting elements in montage in order to produce, in the synthesis, new concepts and emotions. Eisenstein coined such phrases as "overtonal montage" to refer to modulations on such levels as lighting and color, and "intellectual montage" to describe collisions produced by the juxtaposition of objects with rich cultural implications (thus, Eisenstein, in *October,* seeks to discredit Orthodoxy by juxtaposing its religious icons and idols with Asian and African statues, which for his European audience would connote the primitive and the superstitious).

In the mid-1930s, Eisenstein turned increasingly to the problem of modeling "inner speech," of creating in cinema an analogue for both the "thematic-logical" and the "image-sensual" aspects of thought. According to Eisenstein, cinema could recover the organic and syncretic qualities of primitive culture, simultaneously integrating impulses along a number of different tracks. These concerns led Eisenstein to the problems of "*pathos* constructions" and of "vertical montage," which are the principal themes of **Nonindifferent Nature.**

Although the first outline for the entire monograph **Nonindifferent Nature** dates from 1945, the articles that clearly anticipate it appeared during 1939-41, the period of Eisenstein's collaboration with the composer Prokofiev on the film **Alexander Nevsky.** Three articles from that time were, in fact, revised and included in **Nonindifferent Nature**: **"On the Structure of Things"** [published first in the journal *Iskusstvo kino* (*The Art of Cinema*) in 1939], **"Once More on the Structure of Things"** (which appeared in the same journal in 1940), and **"Poor Salieri"** (written as an introduction to a planned edition of Eisenstein's articles but unpublished until its appearance in the posthumous *Collected Works* of Eisenstein in 1964). In 1940, Eisenstein also wrote three articles for *The Art of Cinema* entitled **"Vertical Montage,"** which form an important introduction to some of the considerations in *Nonindifferent Nature.* (These articles constitute most of the volume entitled *The Film Sense,* published in English in J. Leyda's translation in 1942.) The remaining portions of *Nonindifferent Nature,* which constitute the majority of the monograph, were written by Eisenstein in the years 1945-7, after his work with Prokofiev on *Ivan the Terrible.* The volume is thus highly representative of Eisenstein's most pressing artistic concerns during the very active and energetic final decade of his life. It also brings to the fore quite eloquently those central concerns that unify Eisenstein's work from the 1920s to the 1940s.

From the earliest period of his work in theater and film, Eisenstein wrote of techniques for causing the viewer to experience the emotions linked to a particular content; even then these techniques involved the use of separate elements of mise-en-scène, gesture, and sound to carry the chain of emotions to the audience. In his famous article **"Montage of Attractions,"** published in the journal *LEF* in 1923, he stated: "The attraction (in our diagnosis of the theater) is every aggressive moment in it, i. e., every element of it that brings to light in the spectator those senses or that psychology that influence his experience." In Eisenstein's directorial practice, as in that of his teacher Vsevolod Meyerhold, "leaps from one type of expression to another" were common—from elements of the set to features of costume to the acrobatic movements of the actors. The "vertical montage" that Eisenstein devised fifteen years later was an application of this same principle to the cinema. He wrote in 1939: "The juxtaposition of these partial details in a given montage construction calls to life and forces into the light that *general* quality in which each detail has participated and that binds together all the details into a *whole,* namely, into that generalized *image,* wherein the creator, followed by the spectator, experiences the theme."

In **"On the Structure of Things,"** Eisenstein designated by the term *"pathos"* the heightened emotional state produced by works of art. Such works must possess qualities that arouse passion in their receivers. Eisenstein asserted that this could occur only by means of "a compositional structure identical with human behavior in the grip of *pathos*" (taking the term in its original Greek meaning). Such behavior entailed a leap out of oneself, *ex stasis,* ecstacy: "To be beside oneself is unavoidably also a transition to something else, to something different in quality, to something opposite to what preceded it." The problem then was to fuse the structure of human emotional behavior with the receiver's experience of the content.

Eisenstein looked to both physiological and psychological manifestations of emotions, from irregular breathing, quickened heartbeat, and emphatic gesture to metaphorical and poetic speech. The structural elements of such phenomena would have to be recreated in the composition of the work of art. Seeking them, Eisenstein analyzed his own films *Battleship Potemkin* (1925) and *Alexander Nevsky* (1939), as well as Emile Zola's prose, Alexander

Pushkin's poetry, and the painting *The Boyarina Morozova* by V. I. Surikov. From these comparative studies, Eisenstein derived two key principles: organic unity and the leap to a new quality.

Although the notion of organicity might seem to be somewhat of a cliché, Eisenstein took the concept quite literally and specifically: "The organic unity of a work, as well as the sense of organic unity received from the work, arises when the law of the construction of this work corresponds to the laws of *the structure of organic phenomena of nature.*" In **Battleship Potemkin,** Eisenstein found that all five parts of the film, as well as the film as a whole, are governed by the same structural law (evidence of a general organic order). In each part, revolutionary brotherhood grows from a small incipient "cell" into a manifestation of greater intensity or larger scale, and there is a turning point (Eisenstein terms it a "caesura"), when the action "leaps over" from a quieter protest to a more angry and violent clash: The approaching execution under a tarpaulin of resisting sailors "leaps over" into the shipboard mutiny; the mourning for the martyred sailor Vakulinchuk "leaps over" into an angry demonstration; the peaceful fraternization between ship and shore turns suddenly into a massacre with the scream of a woman and the appearance of a rank of firing tsarist troops at the top of the Odessa steps. From the points of transition at these caesuras Eisenstein derived an important principle:

> And it is also remarkable that the jump at each point—is not simply a sudden jump to *another* mood, to *another* rhythm, to *another* event, but each time it is a transition to a *distinct opposite.* Not contrastive, but *opposite,* for each time it gives *the image of that same theme from the opposite point of view and at the same time unavoidably grows out of it.*

The caesuras in each of the film's parts echo a central caesura in the film as a whole: the sequence of mourning for the dead Vakulinchuk. At this point, the stormy actions of rebellion are replaced by near stillness, and the theme of universal revolutionary embrace must begin to build again to its climaxes in the second part of the film: the spread of the rebellion to the city, and then to the entire tsarist fleet.

It was "the leap to a new quality," however, that became for Eisenstein the most important characteristic of the *pathos* construction. It was to this subject that he devoted the series of chapters written in 1946-7, entitled "Pathos," which comprise most of the first half of *Nonindifferent Nature.* These studies constitute a detailed elaboration of the leap into a new and opposed quality (in particular, the leap from the literal into the metaphorical) and of the merging of opposites into the organic unity of the whole. Eisenstein points to instances of these structures in his films *The Old and the New* (1929) and *Ivan the Terrible* (1944), as well as in the work of various writers (Zola, Whitman, Zweig, Pushkin), performers (the actor Frédérick Lemaître, the poet Mayakovsky reciting his own verse), and artists (Claude Monet, Vincent van Gogh, El Greco, Leonardo da Vinci).

Eisenstein argues that in *The Old and the New,* his filmic

paean to collectivization and the mechanization of agriculture, *pathos* constructions per se are more distinguishable than they are in **Potemkin** where the theme of revolution itself already carries much of the *pathos*. The task in **The Old and the New** was to create the *pathos* of the machine through expressiveness and composition alone; Eisenstein's techniques led French critics of the day to refer to the film's "epic lyricism" over "those terrestrial gifts that derive their inspiration from the machine" and its rendering of "everyday phenomena . . . in themselves insignificant" with "Dionysian lyricism." Eisenstein focuses his attention on the sequence "Testing of the Milk Separator" in which he embodied, structurally, the property of continually leaping from one state to another of different quality. What played a crucial compositional role was the ability of the wide-angle lens to distort perspective, enabling objects "to go beyond themselves, beyond their natural bounds of volume and form." As the collective farmers wait to see if the separator will work, Eisenstein moves from group shots to two-shots to close-ups of faces. "Their movement is caught up by shots of spinning disks and the feed pipes of the separator, appearing all the more frequently at various angles." "Shots of intensifying hope" use gradually brighter lighting, whereas "shots of aggravated suspicion" gradually become darker. As the change from bright to dark frames occurs more often, the disks spin faster and faster. A drop at the end of the separator pipe begins to swell.

Finally the drop falls, hitting the bottom of the pail in a starlike spray. Eisenstein describes the ensuing montage as follows:

> And now unchecked, at furious pressure bursting from the body separator, a jet stream of thickened white cream thuds into the pail.
>
> By now, through editing, the spurts and spray pierce through the stream of enthusiastic close-ups with a cascade of snow-white streams of milk, a silvery fountain of unchecked spurts, a fireworks display of unceasing splashes.
>
> And then, as if in answer to the involuntary comparisons emerging on the screen, after the explosion resulting from the first spurts of milk, the sequence of these milk streams is interjected by what appears to be foreign matter flooded with light . . . Aquatic pillars of shooting fountains.

The fountains of milk then leap over into a new dimension, into images of an actual fountain, and then leap again into an image of fireworks, produced by coloring separate shots of the shooting water streams and intercutting them rapidly. The sequence finally reaches a purely formal climax: a totally black field with intermittent "lightening" flashes of white. As Eisenstein puts it: " . . . the structural system itself skipped over from the sphere of the *representational* to its opposite sphere of the *nonrepresentational*." Nonrepresentational leaps on the level of color also occur in **Ivan the Terrible (Part II),** where the sequence of the boyar conspiracy (in gray tones) leaps over into the banquet sequence wherein the tsar sets in motion his passionate and bloody response (in a color sequence dominated by reds and golds), and then leaps again into the murder in the ca-

thedral (almost entirely in stark contrasts of black and white).

In Zola, Eisenstein finds that the emotionally moving descriptions are produced by a hyperbolic multiplication of everyday objects possessing a particular quality—the descriptions seem to "eject out of one another" in a rising level of frenzy. The repetitions represent a diversity of manifestations of a single thesis. Then, suddenly, the metonymic accumulation of detail leaps into metaphor. Zola ends by describing not the literal event but his own emotional passion over it.

Eisenstein argues that the unity of opposites is strikingly portrayed in the style of the great nineteenth century French actor Frédérick Lemaître, the literal meaning of whose words was often completely contradicted by the emotional qualities of his delivery. Thus, the qualities that Lemaître could convey were often described by his contemporaries as, in fact, oppositional pairs: "energy and sensitivity," "cunning and good nature." Eisenstein terms this "the dynamic unity of mutually exclusive antithetical principles within a character." The same can be said of Dostoyevsky's heroes, for "one is often struck not only by the duality, but especially by the at times unmotivated collapse of a character into another extreme. . . ." This, says Eisenstein, is what inspired him in his creation of Ivan the Terrible: " . . . the construction of *pathos* effects by the direct charging of elements ecstatically exploding into each other with constantly increasing intensity. . . ."

Two of the most intriguing analyses in the *pathos* section of **Nonindifferent Nature** concern the art of El Greco and of Piranesi. In both cases, Eisenstein describes meticulously the structural "explosion" of an early variant to yield a more ecstatic (and justifiably more famous) later variant. He explores the harmonic transition of certain forms into other forms; a sequence of forms "overflowing" into new forms. Entire movements in art show a similar mechanism: The Gothic "explodes" the preceding features of Romanesque architecture; impressionism and cubism explode the contours and the spatial bounds of realism's objects.

Artists make such leaps, notes Eisenstein, when they themselves are overcome by ecstacy, obsessed by certain ideas. This ecstacy, which approaches madness (in El Greco and in Piranesi), is akin to the state induced by opiates, for "the dynamics of these construction elements overflowing into each other promote the feeling of emotional seizure."

Eisenstein, with his training in civil engineering and his early experience as a set designer, is himself obsessed by the symbolic meaning of architectural forms, a potential he utilizes so brilliantly in **Battleship Potemkin** and in **Ivan the Terrible.** He compares architectural composition to cinematic montage, sees in Gothic churches ecstacy embodied in stone, and in the buildings of the reign of Tsar Nicholas—"the image of absolutism." Architecture speaks in "the strongest figurative rhetoric of its epoch . . . of its system or of its inner aspirations."

Eisenstein's own personal ecstacy over Piranesi's work is

reflected in this discussion, where insights are expressed not only in structural diagrams of the spatial and graphic "explosions," but also in the poetic and metaphorical quality of Eisenstein's prose. The inspiration of Piranesi is evident as well in Eisenstein's set designs for *Ivan the Terrible,* where a system of receding "wings" forces our eyes deeper and deeper into the distance, while at the same time the foreground of shots is occupied by close-ups of parts of heads. All of this, Eisenstein asserts, is based on the effect of the telescope, of one thing thrusting out another. He draws analogies also to recent "accelerations upon accelerations" in science: nuclear chain-reaction explosions and multistage rockets, in which a new leap in magnitude accompanies each successive stage.

From architecture and science, Eisenstein returns again to literature (via Gogol's little known article in the miscellany *Arabesques* on "The Architecture of Our Time.") Gogol's preference for the ecstatic Gothic is no accident, states Eisenstein, for the very same process of forms metamorphosing into other forms, of contrastive metaphors leaping from one dimension to another, is as characteristic of Gogol's prose as it is of Gothic architecture.

Eisenstein finds the tendency of things to grow out of one another in a diversity of other cultural phenomena as well: in the structure of toys (like the chain of sticks that, in changing their angles, produce a jack-in-the-box thrust, or like the Russian *matrushka* dolls that emerge out of one another), in the practice of Yucatan cultures that built pyramids directly over previous pyramids, in the spiral repetition of features in design motifs in many cultures. Moreover, notes Eisenstein, there are important similarities between the structure of *pathos* and the structure of comedy. When there is a sign of growth, but, instead of a leap into a new quality, we get merely the repetition of the same thing, the effect is comic. Thus, concludes Eisenstein, the formula for construction of extreme versions of phenomena is the same, whether in science or in art: ". . . this formula is nothing but the moment (instant) of the culmination of the dialectic law of the transition of quantity into quality."

"Why are *pathos* constructions in all of these varied art forms essentially the same?" asks Eisenstein. Because they must correspond to a basic "formula for *pathos*" in the emotive (nonlogical) centers of the brain. They depend not on psychological factors, but on a psychic state. The basic laws governing change in natural phenomena are imprinted in this psychic state, which in turn determines the structuring of the material in an ecstatic work of art. The art work's ecstatic structures in turn produce a vivid experience in the receiver.

When the artist is first inspired by some object that produces in him an intensity of experience, his ecstacy, in itself, is objectless and formless; it cannot be described verbally. However, the artist reconstructs the process of ecstatic movement through his structuring of the material of his theme, thus communicating the very same *pathos* to his audience. Thus, the process, for Eisenstein, is rooted in the more primitive functions of the brain. Ecstacy is a state prior to thinking, and there is no means of expressing that state other than by simple signs, that is, either by an analogue of the state (in semiotics, an "icon") or by a recreation of a part of the state itself (the semiotic "index").

As a postscript to the "Pathos" study, Eisenstein concluded the first half of *Nonindifferent Nature* with a revised version of his article "Once Again on the Structure of Things," first written in 1940. The subject of the article is "the way the general dialectic position on the *unity* of opposites is applicable to the area of composition." As a twenty-six-year-old filmmaker, Eisenstein reminds us, he was faced with the challenge of surpassing the highly popular American films of the day, with their clever intrigues and their glittering "stars." Instead of using a direct assault, he went in the opposite direction: the rejection of traditional plot and the denial of the isolated individual as hero (the masses themselves become the basic dramatis personae). Of course, on a deeper level, these "formally" opposite solutions reflect basic ideological oppositions.

A decade later, in the film *Chapayev* (1934), which dates from the period of Soviet film's return to classical narrative, the *pathos* embodied throughout *Potemkin* by a leap away from plot and the hero is now accomplished by means of a reversal of the leap. The hero Chapayev, although the main protagonist, does not push forward ahead of the others; he remains a man of the people. What is conventionally spoken in elevated emotional speech, he, instead, talks in simple conversational words. If Eisenstein's style was a leap into the poetic, the Vasiliev brothers (directors of *Chapayev*), accomplish a leap from poetic expectations into conventional speech.

The second half of *Nonindifferent Nature,* actually written in 1945, consists of the extended study "**The Music of Landscape and the Fate of Montage Counterpoint at a New Stage.**" It is the culmination of Eisenstein's work on the subject of "vertical montage" and polyphonic structure, a study begun in a series of essays in *Iskusstvo Kino* during 1939-40 and published in English in 1942 as *The Film Sense.* Eisenstein used the term "vertical montage" to indicate the process of superposition and integration of the various structural levels of cinema: landscape and scenery, mise-en-scène, gesture, music, lighting, and color. In the articles on vertical montage, Eisenstein claimed that all of these levels should reflect the dominance of a unified theme, one which governs all the choices in all the participating "lines":

> The juxtaposition of these partial details in a given montage construction calls to life and forces into the light that *general* quality in which each detail has participated and which binds together all the details into a *whole,* namely, into that generalized artistic *image,* wherein the creator, followed by the spectator, experiences the theme. (*The Film Sense*)

Eisenstein's work with Prokofiev, with the cinematographers Tisse and Moskvin, and with the actors in *Ivan the Terrible* was to embody this process, for the architectonics of the set, the framing, the lighting, the camera angles, the costuming, the intonation and gestures of the actors, and the musical score all figured in a montage construction wherein integration had to take place not only horizontally (in collisions from shot to shot) but also vertically:

Through the progression of the *vertical* line, pervading the entire orchestra, and interwoven horizontally, the intricate harmonic musical movement of the whole orchestra moves forward.

When we turn from this image of the orchestral score to that of the audio-visual score, we find it necessary to add a new part to the instrumental parts: this new part is a 'staff' of visuals . . . where shot is linked to shot not merely through one indication—movement, or light values, . . . or the like—but through the *simultaneous advance* of a multiple series of lines, each maintaining an independent compositional course and each contributing to the total compositional course of the sequence. (*The Film Sense*)

In the last period of his life, with his work on *Ivan the Terrible,* on *Nonindifferent Nature,* and on a series of essays on the use of color in cinema, Eisenstein turned increasingly to the specific problems of vertical montage—the problems of identifying and elaborating the features according to which such a synaesthetic montage could proceed. In the second part of *Nonindifferent Nature,* Eisenstein is inspired by the use of nature in Soviet silent cinema, where it was hardly "indifferent," but served to create emotional mood through an "inner plastic music." This task fell to landscape because it was "the least burdened with servile, narrative tasks." Like music, it could express emotionally what was inexpressible by other means and, like later musical sound tracks, it could interweave with the narrative portions of the film.

Indeed, the silent films of Eisenstein, Pudovkin, Dovzhenko, and Kozintsev and Trauberg often began with a landscape "prelude," setting up certain motifs that would then resonate with landscape inserts later in the film. Eisenstein himself, in his writing on "overtonal" montage in 1929, had provided a detailed analysis of the "harbor mist sequence" in *Battleship Potemkin.* After the body of the martyred sailor Vakulinchuk (leader of the successful rebellion) is taken to shore and placed in a tent, there is a seascape suite consisting of shots of the fog-enshrouded harbor, with outlines of ships, buoys, and seagulls barely visible through the mist. Eisenstein analyzed the modulations of gray lighting, the vibrations of the light within the fog (echoed by the rippling motion of the waves), as homologous to the mood of sorrow.

In **"The Music of Landscape,"** Eisenstein parallels such cinematic techniques to those of Chinese and Japanese poetry, based on the calligraphy of symbols that are, in themselves, ideograms. It is not so much a poetry of sound as a poetry of graphics, "music for the eye." Just as words with different meanings and different sounds can rhyme *graphically* in this poetry, so elements of landscape or background can rhyme visually with one another, a process Eisenstein terms "plastic rhyme." Such "plastic" correspondences produce semantic effects; the images in which they occur stand in the same figurative relationship induced for rhymed words in poetry.

In Chinese landscape painting (scroll painting), one finds such "musical" composition, based on the interplay of a limited set of symbolic elements of nature (which correspond to the musical notes in Eisenstein's analogy) appearing in various combinations along the scroll (just as they would in the measures of a musical score). The art historians whom Eisenstein quotes consistently discuss these scroll paintings in musical terms, for the identical landscape motifs and elements are combined as they would be in a polyphonic composition: The theme goes through numerous variations, built upon resonances and "echoings."

The complementary principles of segmentation and continuity figure in Chinese landscapes as they do in a number of disparate cultural forms (Eisenstein cites, for example, Indian spiral painting and Greek "oxfurrow" writing). Elements that are distinct in their oppositions to one another are integrated into a continuous whole along a linear chain; they form a polyphonic stream. Film art, for Eisenstein, not only embodies these properties but raises them to the greatest complexity in terms of the number of different kinds of "lines" or different signifying systems that are integrated.

In all of these art forms, Eisenstein contends, it is the human personality and its attributes that are conveyed in metaphorical terms, whether through the details of landscape (as in Chinese painting), through the fantastic anthromorphism of nature (as in mythology), or through the disparate voices of narrators and characters (as in the "polyphonic" novel as analyzed by Bakhtin). Thus, the compositional devices themselves must also be rooted in the nature of the human mind and human behavior.

Eisenstein's excursions into anthropological theory are quite fascinating, for he contends that artistic syntax is dependent on two instinctive principles that provide the foundation for human culture: plot as pursuit (manifested early in culture as hunting) and interweaving (appearing in the construction of baskets). The hunt can easily be seen as the basis for adventure and mystery plots, but many other narratives retain the quest or riddle structure as well (somewhat later, the French structuralist theoretician Roland Barthes would also name the drive to answer questions, what he called the *hermeneutic code,* as one of the fundamental structures of literature). The inclination to interweave, that is to say polyphonic structure, Eisenstein locates in diverse human activities, from the tying and untying of knots, to the magician Harry Houdini's escapes, to the word weaving of poetry, to the plot complications of novels and plays:

Something of this longing of each knot to be unraveled corresponding to the yearning to tie knots, as we have seen, sits deeply in the psyche of man. . . .

It is all the same, whether it occurs in the graphic knots of Leonardo and Durer,

in the frequencies of vibrations of vowels that wind into the phonetic knots of Dante,

or in the peripeteias of the arrangement of the sequence of scenes that attract equally Pushkin, Joseph Conrad, and Orson Welles!

These are the methods that Eisenstein himself employed in *Ivan the Terrible,* developing the image of the tsar as a unity in variety, expressed through the integrated flow of his graphic contour and makeup, and the lighting and camera angles for the shots. The visual properties of the image (the "landscape" in the broadest sense of the term) echoes the emotional state of the tsar. Eisenstein indeed sees his work on *Ivan the Terrible* as the third (and culminating) stage of film montage. During the first historical stage, there was the shooting of long-shots, from one setup and with no editing; the second stage (exemplified by his own work in the 1920s) exhibited a separation of distinct signifying elements, but with a use of sharp divergence and opposition in their combination (Eisenstein's famous "collision montage"); only in the third stage (*Ivan the Terrible*) is there harmonious counterpoint that eschews "paradoxes and excesses." Eisenstein's disavowal of his work of the 1920s as excessive should be taken here with a grain of salt; because the "collision" theory of montage was related to the Russian formalist valorization of "making strange" as the basis of art, and because that formalism had been condemned with the onset of the Stalinist period, Eisenstein might be seen as politically circumspect in distancing himself somewhat from this "formalist" period. Thus, Eisenstein tells us in 1945 that many of the devices in *Battleship Potemkin* could be described as the "exposed nerve" of montage, whereas the "harbor mist sequence" represents "a fused structure of contrapuntal currents" that anticipates the polyphonic montage of *Ivan the Terrible.*

But Eisenstein does not want to completely disavow the shock tactics of his early "montage of attractions"; rather, he now sees those diverse sensual attractions as more primitive realizations of what can be achieved, in the third stage, through more subtle audiovisual means: "This is one more reason why we are not only interested in analyzing what has been done in *Ivan the Terrible,* but also in tracing retrospectively how what was done in this direction in *Ivan, is derived in method from what had been done in Potemkin.*" Thus, what Eisenstein in the 1920s termed collisions of opposed elements to form attractions, he now calls a "systematic unity of diverse components." The basic principle of an integrative montage structure, a synthesis of diverse "contrapuntal" stimuli, remains the same. Eisenstein simply expands and reformulates his ideas so as to put some distance between his theories of 1945 and his politically disreputable "formalist" past.

The centerpiece of Eisenstein's discussion of polyphonic montage is his analysis of the mourning scenes in *Potemkin* and *Ivan the Terrible.* In the latter film, Ivan is mourning the death of his beloved Anastasia. She has been poisoned by his aunt Ephrosinia Staritskaya, but Ivan does not know this. He sees the death as possibly a condemnation from God. He is subdued, repentant, depressed, and, at this scene's nadir, virtually crushed (he seems to cower below the funeral bier). Suddenly, from somewhere deep within himself, a resistance, a rebellion, a self-affirmation arises—at the scene's climax. This complex interplay of moods and drives is rendered by diverse levels of the audiovisual montage. The sharp camera angles (the sequence opens with a panning shot from above that reveals Ivan kneeling at the foot of Anastasia's catafalque), the graphic lines of the mise-en-scène, Ivan's ges-

tures, and a multivoiced sound track all contribute to the vertical montage. Eisenstein breaks down the movements of Ivan into a "distinctive orchestra of parts," a decomposition of the human figure into signs. The elements of mise-en-scène are a poetry of significant shapes, of light and shadow, which match the timbers, melodies, and rhythm of the sound track.

That track itself is very complex, interweaving several voices: a choir singing a funereal dirge, Metropolitan Pimen (Ivan's enemy) reading about man's hubris and insignificance (passages from the Book of Lamentations), Malyuta (Ivan's loyal servitor) reporting the defection of Ivan's "friend" Prince Kurbsky to the enemy, the encouraging words of Ivan's *oprichniki* (personal guard) the Basmanovs, and Ivan's own voice—which varies greatly in its modulations. The respective voices of Pimen and Malyuta ultimately constitute an antithesis that develops along two lines:

> The line of *death and constraint of will* enters with the immobile face of the dead Anastasia, passes into the constrained, immobile shots of Ivan, develops in the theme of Pimen's reading ("*exhausted* from wailing," "my throat *dried out,*" "my eyes grew weary"), and is crowned by shots of the vehicle of the theme of death and its actual culprit—the poisoner Staritskaya.

> The line of affirmation—Malyuta's line—is taken up by the Basmanovs (father and son), the inflammatory nature of the old man's speech passes into the fiery "Two Romes fell, and a Third stands" of the tsar, and ends with the flight of servants in the real fires of the torches.

Quite clearly, Eisenstein feels that every level of a physical manifestation can be broken down into distinctive features, systems of opposites. To grasp something, we might analyze and describe these oppositions (as the theoretician does) or we might extract a synthetic image, a gestalt that captures the basic tonality of the whole complex (as the artist does). The latter method underlines Eisenstein's theory of typecasting ("the process of selecting types"). He searched for faces where the expressive "resonance" is "absolutely *precise,* like a chord or note," and "this precision . . . expressed with maximum clarity and directness, so that a certain image of a completely defined human characterization could be formed from a short, momentary appearance to the viewer's perception." Thus, for example, in the "suite" of shots of grieving faces over Vakulinchuk's body, each face bears not only a note of grief but also a sign of social class and of other everyday life experiences. The effect of this suite is a portrait of the universality of the grief over Vakulinchuk's death.

Eisenstein stresses that vertical montage also affects linear montage to a significant degree, since each "line" must realize its own rhythmic pattern, must carry its own melody, while at the same time integrating itself with the other accompanying lines.

In discussing the vertical montage in *Ivan the Terrible,* Eisenstein also has frequent recourse to analogies with the structure of verse, strongly echoing the views of the Russian formalist theoretician Yuri Tynyanov, who in the

1920s compared the "turn" from one shot to the next with the turn from one compact verse to the next. Accents within each shot come from the various visual and audial lines (changes in light tonality, actor's abrupt gestures, sudden shifts in vocal intonation or music); these accents, in Eisenstein's view, are most effective when the visual accent counterpoints the musical accent, so that the pattern produced is analogous to that of bricklaying (where the junctures of the bricks at one level should not coincide with the junctures on the next). The effect is akin to enjambment in poetry, where the metrical and syntactic orders or organization do not coincide, thus producing the special semantic tensions of the verse form. In film editing where the accents on the various levels regularly coincide, states Eisenstein, the correspondence becomes mechanical and a comic effect is likely to be produced.

At the conclusion of *Nonindifferent Nature,* Eisenstein brings the two halves of his study together by identifying "emotional landscape" as another bearer of *pathos,* since it provides an image of "the mutual immersion of man and nature into the other. . . . in the miracle of a genuinely emotional landscape we have a total unity in the mutual interpenetration of nature and man with all the overflowing variety of his temperament." Such a total unity of a landscape with the soul of its creator is achieved in works such as El Greco's *Storm over Toledo.*

In the "Epilogue" to *Nonindifferent Nature,* Eisenstein sought to justify his own role in the development of Soviet cinema in the light of the theories he presented in the volume:

> Ancient writings contained a whole series of books under the general title "didactic."
>
> I also look on my films as being "didactic" to a certain extent; that is, those which, besides their immediate aims, always contain researches and experiments in form.
>
> These researches and experiments are made so that—in another interpretation and from another individual point of view—they could be used later collectively by all of us working on the creation of films in general.

Characteristically, Eisenstein admits, on the one hand, the validity of the criticism that he sometimes carried his structural passions too far; on the other, he asserts a much more important fact: Those very experiments and his postanalysis of them had an immense and indelible impact on the development of the cinema as an art form.

FURTHER READING

Bibliography

Leyda, Jay. "The Published Writings (1922-1964) of Sergei Eisenstein." In *Film Essays,* by Sergei Eisenstein, edited by Jay Leyda, pp. 188-216. London: Dennis Dobson, 1968.
     Comprehensive list of Eisenstein's published writings in Russian, with notes on their English translations.

———. "Bibliography of Eisenstein's Writings Available in English." In *The Film Sense,* by Sergei M. Eisenstein, translated and edited by Jay Leyda, pp. 269-76. New York: Harcourt, Brace, 1942.
     Annotated bibliography of Eisenstein's writings available in English.

Biography

Montagu, Ivor. *With Eisenstein in Hollywood.* New York: International Publishers, 1969, 356 p.
     Details Eisenstein's stay in Hollywood during the 1930s. This volume also includes scenarios for two of Eisenstein's unfinished film projects: *Sutter's Gold* and *An American Tragedy.*

Seton, Marie. *Sergei M. Eisenstein.* London: Dennis Dobson, 1978, 533 p.
     Biography of Eisenstein based on primary sources, including Eisenstein's own letters. Appendices include Eisenstein's introduction to the scenario for the uncompleted *Que Viva Mexico!* and his correspondence with American novelist Upton Sinclair.

Wilson, Edmund. "Eisenstein in Hollywood." In his *The American Earthquake,* pp. 397-413. New York: Farrar, Strauss, Giroux, 1958.
     Discusses details related to the making of *Alexander Nevsky, Ivan the Terrible,* and the uncompleted *Que Viva Mexico!* and *Behzin Meadow.*

Criticism

Aumont, Jacques. *Montage Eisenstein.* Translated by Lee Hildreth, Constance Penley, and Andrew Ross. Bloomington and Indianapolis: Indiana University Press, 1987, 243 p.
     Focuses on Eisenstein's theories of filmmaking as presented in the director's writings. Aumont calls Eisenstein "one of the great philosophers of art of our century" and attempts to "renovate the literature" on his work. This volume also includes detailed analysis of segments from *Old and New* and *Ivan the Terrible.*

Barthes, Roland. *Image, Music, Text.* New York: Hill and Wang, 1977, 220 p.
     Contains analytical notes on several Eisenstein stills and a chapter on the aesthetics of Eisenstein's visual composition.

Bordwell, David. *The Cinema of Eisenstein.* Cambridge, Mass.: Harvard University Press, 1993, 316 p.
     Examines Eisenstein's films and writings in an effort to define his impact on the history and development of film art. Bordwell provides an overview of previous critics' assessments of Eisenstein's work.

Christie, Ian, and Taylor, Richard, eds. *Eisenstein Rediscovered.* London: Routedge, 1993, 260 p.
     Collection of essays analyzing Eisenstein's importance to the history of cinema, his influences as a filmmaker, and his film theories.

Gerould, Daniel. "Eisenstein's Wiseman." In *The Drama Review* 18, No. 1 (March 1975): 71-6.
     Details Eisenstein's attempts to create a revolutionary kind of theatrical experience in the production of *The Wiseman,* which he directed at the Proletkult theater.

Goodwin, James. *Eisenstein, Cinema, and History.* Urbana: University of Illinois Press, 1993, 262 p.
> Survey of Eisenstein's career, with chapters devoted to each of his completed films.

Gordon, Mel. "Eisenstein's Later Work at the Proletkult." In *The Drama Review* 22, No. 3 (September 1978): 107-12.
> Discusses the political objectives and the production details of the stage plays *Do You Hear, Moscow?* and *Gas Masks,* both directed by Eisenstein.

Lary, N. M. "Eisenstein's Cinema of Cruelty." In his *Dostoevsky and Soviet Film,* pp. 85-110. Ithaca: Cornell University Press, 1986.
> Examines the influence of Dostoevsky's novels on Eisenstein's *Ivan the Terrible* and some of his other films.

Mayer, David. *Eisenstein's "Potemkin."* New York: Grossman, 1972, 252 p.
> A shot-by-shot analysis of Eisenstein's most famous film.

Murray, Edward. "Theodore Dreiser in 'Hooeyland'." In his *The Cinematic Imagination: Writers and the Motion Pictures,* pp. 116-23. New York: Frederick Ungar, 1972.
> Examines Eisenstein's unsuccessful attempt to turn Dreiser's *An American Tragedy* into a Hollywood film.

Nizhny, Vladimir. *Lessons with Eisenstein.* Translated and edited by Ivor Montagu and Jay Leyda. New York: Hill and Wang, 1962, 182 p.
> Memoir of one of Eisenstein's film students that attempts to capture both Eisenstein's method and content.

Solski, Waclaw. "The End of Sergei Eisenstein." *Commentary* 7, No. 3 (March 1949): 252-60.
> Examines the suppression of Eisenstein's work in the Soviet Union.

Thompson, Kristin. *Eisenstein's "Ivan the Terrible": A Neoformalist Analysis.* Princeton: Princeton University Press, 1981, 321 p.
> Detailed examination of the visual techniques used in Eisenstein's last film.

Wenden, D. J. "*Battleship Potemkin*—Film and Reality." In *Feature Films as History,* pp. 37-61. Knoxville: University of Tennessee Press, 1981.
> Analyzes the differences between the historic *Potemkin* mutiny and the way the revolt is portrayed in Eisenstein's film.

Additional coverage of Eisenstein's life and career is contained in the following source published by Gale Research: *Contemporary Authors,* **Vol. 114.**

Parade's End

Ford Madox Ford

(Born Ford Hermann Hueffer; also wrote under the pseudonyms Fenil Haig, Daniel Chaucer, and Baron Ignatz von Aschendrof) English novelist, poet, critic, biographer, historian, essayist, and autobiographer.

The following entry presents criticism of Ford's tetralogy *Parade's End*. For a discussion of Ford's complete career, see *TCLC*, Volumes 1 and 15; for a discussion of his novel *The Good Soldier*, see *TCLC*, Volume 39.

INTRODUCTION

A major figure of the Modernist movement in English literature, Ford was a prolific author who produced works in a variety of genres. His fiction is noted for its intricate structure and impressionistic rendering of characters and events. In *Parade's End* Ford presented his most comprehensive treatment of the dominant theme in his work: social decay and alienation in post-Edwardian England.

Plot and Major Characters

Parade's End comprises four novels: *Some Do Not, No More Parades, A Man Could Stand Up,* and *The Last Post.* The protagonist, Christopher Tietjens, is referred to as "the last Tory," because of his devotion to conservative Edwardian traditions of honor and propriety, despite what appears to be the systematic dismantling of his well-ordered, mannerly world. Annoyed by Tietjens' unflagging desire to do what he believes is right, his wife Sylvia often acts as his nemesis, attempting to destroy his credibility and security through deceitful plots and extramarital affairs. Although in love with the young suffragette Valentine Wannop, Tietjens refuses to compromise his moral principles and marriage vows. In *No More Parades* and *A Man Could Stand Up—*, Ford vividly depicts the devastation of war through Tietjens' experiences on the front lines in World War I. As the world of honor he values continues to erode, Tietjens suffers a breakdown and is nursed back to health by Valentine, who finally becomes his lover. *The Last Post* focuses on Tietjens' adaptation to the new order, represented by Sylvia's destruction of a tree at Tietjens' ancestral home. Symbolic of the conflict between tradition and progress, the felling of Groby Great Tree allows Tietjens to successfully move into the future with Valentine and their unborn child.

Major Themes

Written during the 1920s, *Parade's End* addresses the moral uncertainties of Ford's times, documenting the sense of disorder, degeneration, and chaos he believed were the fruits of "the first modern war," the end of the Edwardian era, and the emergence of a society notable for its superficiality and rejection of such traditional values as

loyalty and personal honor. Through Tietjens, who perseveres in spite of the relentless destruction of all that he values and has labored to protect, Ford suggested that humanity will survive political and social upheaval.

Critical Reception

Critics are divided on the question of whether the Tietjens series should be considered a tetralogy with four separate but equal elements, as supported by commentators Neil D. Isaacs, Robie Macauley, and William Carlos Williams, or a trilogy with a sequel, the position taken by such critics as Graham Greene and John Meixner. Even those who assert that *The Last Post* is an essential component of the Tietjens saga conclude that it is structurally inferior to the first three novels. Critics also dispute the function of Sylvia in the series. While some scholars believe she signifies an evil antithesis to Tietjens' values, others argue that she is a necessary impetus to Tietjens' ultimate acceptance of change.

CRITICISM

John W. Crawford (essay date 1926)

SOURCE: "Ford Madox Ford Adds a Volume to His Epic of the War," in *The New York Times Book Review,* October 24, 1926, p. 7.

[*In the following review of* A Man Could Stand Up, *Crawford characterizes Ford's Tietjens series as a modern-day epic.*]

Ford Madox Ford has now reached the third of his monumental series of novels. There are those who say the epic is a dead form which can never be made to function in such a complicated and rational and disillusioned age as ours. The epic is not dead, for its impulse has surely impelled the setting down, in passionate narrative prose, of the adventures of Christopher Tietjens. If the heartbreaking, quixotic Christopher is not of the stuff of great legends, a sort of contemporary Bayard, with much honest fear and many undeserved reproaches, then there is no heroism left. If the personal and public battles in which Christopher takes part are not action, in the strict epic sense, then contemplation and indecision and irresponsibility have been the lot of the twentieth century. The only point where Mr. Ford may possibly be conceded to have omitted to write an epic in fiction is in his language. The tone of these three novels is not elevated and noble. It is as if men, in a house about to be blown up, knowing that a time fuse has been set, calmly occupy themselves with getting their cigars well lighted and talk of ordinary things in the vernacular of the day.

This very quality of Mr. Ford's style is indubitably a chief factor in enabling him to speak directly to a reader where he lives. This series makes it apppear that literature is, after all, not a superfluous affair. Books, such books as these three, do matter, and matter enormously. It is incredible that a reading of them can leave a receptive mind untouched. It means a definite and ponderable gain in experience, a measurable and welcome deflection of the course of being. And it is all done with such simplicity and absence of exclamation that the full brunt of the thing is not felt until some time after the last page has been turned. *A Man Could Stand Up,* like its predecessors, lives on, happily, in the reader's mind, when the printed page is no longer before the eye, and the materials of the novel incite endless associations and recreations and suppositions as if it actually were a block out of the reader's own life.

That is not at all to say that Mr. Ford has been faithful to life. It is just his triumph that he has taken notable and identifiable landmarks, scattered them throughout his three books, and yet left them significantly books and nothing else. *Some Do Not—* dared to take the heated years of the woman suffrage militancy in England, boil them down to one intense passage on a golf course and present the first meeting of Valentine Wannop and Christopher Tietjens as a contact of personalities, which took on a little color from a political conflict. Yet that episode gave a more vivid picture of the suffragette fight than volumes upon volumes of more pretentious history. *No More Parades* called up a graphic vision of a civilian population and corridors upon corridors of intriguing Government officials behind a small outfit of men on their way to the front. *A Man Could Stand Up* gives a more complete picture of what fighting meant and what the war was about to the men actually in it than oceans of rhetoric might do or have done. It's all there in the title, in fact.

Mr. Ford has a felicitous knack for titles. The name of the present book calls up lines of stooping men, cramped in their lungs, soggy in their feet, waiting for a bit of "Morning Hate," ordered by their own superiors to surprise those boresome gray men over yonder, or by the German superiors to impress the Allies. The aching wish to stand up once more on a hill in the sunlight and the enforced duty, instead, of digging for two buried men in a pit of slime, with the roar of a shell still in the ears, is Christopher at war, and, somehow, entire armies of men at war with him, engaged with him in this tedious business of wearing away the patience of the adversary. There it is, the whole impact of a military tactic of attrition, of sitting, or standing, and waiting for something to happen and longing all the while for nothing more than "to stand up on a hill."

Of course, that would be Christopher's way of going to war—wanting with all his might to do something that he could not do, being a Major and the personal property of his King. Christopher is the indomitable Tory, still, abiding to the letter by an intricate code of conduct, resentful of infringement and invasion of his individuality, anxious to establish personal relations even with the enemy. Christopher, in *No More Parades,* passing thousands of men under review and trying to give each one what he wanted, and what he ought to have, instead of what the regulations prescribed, and getting into endless difficulties with his commanding officer, was a typical view of that tall, graying blond man with the meal-sack torso and the khaki tubes of legs. In the front-line trenches he continues to regard his men as his personal responsibilities and to receive as reward echoes of Sylvia's pursuing spite. That remarkable woman, his wife, who figured in the amazing scene with her mother and the priest in *Some Do Not—* and in the entanglement with three men, one Christopher's godfather and chief of staff, General Campion, in *No More Parades,* appears only indirectly in *A Man Could Stand Up.* But it is the same vindictive yet incredibly sympathy-provoking Sylvia.

To admirers of Christopher the re-emergence of Valentine Wannop in the present book will be a welcome item of news. Throughout the second book, whether Christopher is writing a sonnet in two and a half minutes, or wangling leave for a lovesick soldier, or making extraordinary wills, there runs through his mind as a sort of refrain: "Shall I send at least a picture postcard to Valentine Wannop?" He has left her in a desperate state of uncertainty, and he knows it. It is the act of a cad not to write, he cannot communicate without conveying too much, and it is the act of a cad to let her know how much he cares when he may "stop one" before the war is over.

It is delightful to meet Valentine Wannop again, and on the very first page. She is still in a Girl Scout uniform, acting as physical instructress in a girls' school. She is talking over the telephone to, of all unlikely yet inevitable people. Lady Macmaster, she that was Edith Ethel Duchemin, wife of the bawdy priest in *Some Do Not—* and hostess at that magnificently contrived breakfast party. Edith Ethel manages to hint to Valentine, over the din of the Armistice Day celebration, that some one has returned, mad, to his eighteenth century house; that his wife has been in a nursing home, that he has no furniture, and that he does not recognize the porter. It is, of course, Christopher. In this indirect, allusive fashion Mr. Ford establishes that much has happened to Christopher. He then gives a glorious cut-back of Christopher at the front and as fine a picture of a party of men during and just after the explosion of a shell as could be desired.

The book closes with a reunion of Christopher and some of his buddies from the front, all come to celebrate peace with the Major. Valentine is there, in the bare house which Sylvia has stripped of all its furniture and which Christopher has refurnished, frugally and austerely, as if it were his hut at the front. The next book may tell much of peace in England, and more, unquestionably, of Christopher and Valentine and of the wicked woman, Sylvia. Mr. Ford has promised four novels about Christopher, the last to deal with his demobilization. It will undoubtedly be different, yet continuous. Each of the three now issued is an entity, with a separate mode of development, and distinct climaxes and problems, yet each grows out of the preceding book or books, and all taken together are a whole and gradually enlarging and invincibly civilized vision of contemporary life. It is about the most exciting thing that has happened to the novel since *The Way of All Flesh* by Samuel Butler.

Perhaps the notable contribution of *A Man Could Stand Up* is its oblique picture of the horror of up-to-date war. Christopher stands on a ledge to look toward the Germans and a lark flies almost into his mouth, as a bullet might very well have flown into his mouth. There is this unreal menace become immediate, in terms of a common, everyday circumstance—a lark flying from its nest. Mr. Ford then uses that same lark to distinguish between the viewpoint of Christopher and of his men. The argument as to whether the lark is merely obstinate or filled with trust in humanity itself becomes an exposition of Christopher's way of diverting the strain from the minds of his men. That, of course, brings back overwhelmingly the nature and the quality of that tension under which these men at war are living and breathing. Further, the reader is led into the very stuff of this life by such imperceptible stages as this, until it is brought all but intolerably close. This series begins more and more to look like that fiction for which a lot of parsimonious, grudging superlatives have been saved. There is, however, one more volume to come.

William McFee (essay date 1928)

SOURCE: "Tietjens Once More," in *New York Herald Tribune Books,* January 15, 1928, p. 3.

[*McFee was an English writer best known for his tales of adventures at sea. In the following excerpt, he offers a mixed review of* The Last Post.]

Readers will have this opinion and that about these novels by Mr. Ford. They will be enthusiastic, and they will remain mildly indifferent to a very highly-specialized glamour. But they will all fail to agree with the announcement on the jacket-flaps of *The Last Post* that the novels deal with the lives of a small group of representative individuals. That word "representative" needs some qualification. Those individuals may be described as interesting and convincing and so on, but with the possible exception of Mark Tietjens, they are not representative English people. They are representative of Tory England only in their intense individuality, in their ability to do odd and shocking things without turning a hair.

Mark Tietjens, brother of the unhappy Christopher, holds the center of the stage in *The Last Post.* We find him, on page one, stretched out on a pallet beneath a roof of thatch in a Sussex garden on a hill where he can see four counties falling away below him. That is all he can do now—see, hear and think. Near by Christopher is living with Valentine Wannop, who is going to have a baby. They are in the antique furniture business, Christopher sending his finds to a partner in New York. Mark is being cared for by his wife, Marie Léonie, née Riotor, a big, blonde Norman woman with whom he lived for twenty years before he made her Lady Tietjens after the war.

It turns out, as one suspected while reading *A Man Could Stand Up,* that Mark Tietjens is a much more interesting man than Christopher. He is the real Tory. Christopher has the instincts of his class, but he is too self-conscious to be typical, or even quite credible, until he steps out of his class. Because a self-conscious Tory is almost a contradiction in terms. Christopher runs true to form, but Mark's form is much more true. He is the perfectly inarticulate Englishman, the man whose interests in life are limited to his horses, his women and his job. The trouble with such a character in an ordinary novel is that, as he never speaks in character, he cannot be exploited by the ordinary conventional machinery used in such a novel. He can only be caricatured. Dickens did this in *Dombey and Son* in the case of Mr. Toots, to whom everything in the world was "of no consequence." Mr. Toots was a genuine Tory of the old school. And so Mr. Ford really loses nothing by bringing on Mark Tietjens bedridden by a stroke that has robbed him of the powers of speech. A Yorkshire Tory never had any powers of speech. What we get in *The Last Post,* through Mr. Ford's fine art, is Mark's thoughts; his thought of Marie Léonie, of Sylvia and young Mark, son of Sylvia and Christopher, who comes from Cambridge full of acquired communistic ideas and ineradicable Tory instincts; of Valentine, and of the American woman, Mrs. Millicent de Bray Pape.

The action—if that is the Right word—covers a very brief period. That is the modern way of doing the novel. James Joyce took 400,000 words to deal with 24 hours in one man's life. Mr. Ford requires only 60,000 words for an afternoon. But once we are in the stream of consciousness time ceases to have much significance. This is the secret of Mr. Ford's art. He does not give us the almighty lift that came to us while reading *No More Parades,* but it is there. It may be—though this is not laid down as an iron law—

that the composition of Sagas, like the reading of them, is a tiring business. They have to be very good, these later volumes, because they inevitably invite comparison with their forebears, from which they are biologically descended.

Does this last of the Tietjens books, the fourth of the series, come off? The answer is that, so far as technique is concerned, it comes off extraordinarily well. That it is practically flawless. The question immediately arises, however, whether a flawless technique is the whole story. There is a rage among the upper crust of readers for flawless technique, for great reservoirs of memories of past events out of which pour streams of consciousness. But when all is said and done it is only what is in the author's brain that can come out in his book. The chances are that he has to invent his psychology at times just as he has to contrive and shape his plot, if he deigns to have one. And certainly the more flawless his technique the more convincing he can make that psychology. But whether mankind in general will ever cotton to these intricate word-patterns is doubtful. They are becoming a shade too stenographic. *The Last Post* at times is terribly like a psychopathic ward in some fabulous hospital for world-war wreckage. One is desperately sorry for these people, even though they had a superb time of it in England for a hundred and fifty years. But one is glad at least to get out into the open air again.

Robie Macauley (essay date 1950)

SOURCE: An introduction to *Parade's End* by Ford Madox Ford, Alfred A. Knopf, 1950, pp. v-xxii.

[*Macauley is an American author and educator. In the following introduction to the first edition of* Parade's End, *he affirms that the tetralogy should be considered as a single work rather than as four separate novels published together for the first time.*]

The year before he died Ford Madox Ford used to walk around the campus at Olivet College like a pensioned veteran of forgotten wars. We took him for a kind of vast, benevolent and harmless Uncle Toby, leaning on his stick in class or sitting in his dark little basement office and wheezing out his stories of Henry James as Toby might have spoken of Marlborough. His books seemed like medals achieved, perhaps, in the Crimea; and we read Auden, Kafka, Evelyn Waugh.

We were no different from the rest of the world. We knew vaguely that his Tietjens books were about the first World War and we suspected that they might be a good enough account of a soldier's disillusioning experiences—but we had read all that before. If any of us went far enough to look at the introductory letter to *A Man Could Stand Up—*, the third in the series, he would find Ford confirming it:

> This is what the late war was like: this is how modern fighting of the organized, scientific type affects the mind. If, for reasons of gain, or, as is still more likely out of dislike for collective types other than your own, you choose to permit your rulers to embark on another war, this—or some-

thing very accentuated along similar lines—is what you will have to put up with! I hope, in fact, that this series of books, for what it is worth, may make war seem undesirable.

A little afterward some of us went to war ourselves and later, coming back, took Ford's novels down from the shelf to see if his easy prediction had come true. It seemed impossible that we could have been so wrong.

For some peculiar reason of his own he had hoaxed us; he was neither benevolent nor harmless and his books were by no means a simple warning as to what modern warfare is like. To read the Tietjens story for that would be like going through Henry James to improve one's manners or through Conrad to learn how to navigate a ship.

Nevertheless, this is the way the novels were taken when they were first published. They were thought to be books of "experiences" and they sold well. The reaction came when Ford's readers discovered that what he had actually given them was not another *Under Fire* or *What Price Glory?* but something complex and baffling. There was a love story with no passionate scenes; there were trenches but no battles; there was a tragedy without a denouement. Ford was quickly and easily forgotten.

We are a little older now and perhaps a little less superficial. We have been living a little longer with the great, enveloping tragedy Ford set out to describe. Perhaps in this edition we can take a second look at the Tietjens story and discover that it is less about the incident of a single war than about a whole era, more about our own world than his.

"The two young men—they were of the English public official class—sat in the perfectly appointed railway carriage." So begins the Tietjens story. Everything is excellent, comfortable, predictable: the leather window straps are of virgin newness, the mirrors immaculate, as if they had reflected very little, the upholstery a luxuriant scarlet and yellow design, the air smelling faintly of varnish. The train runs as smoothly as (Tietjens thinks) British gilt-edged securities. Moreover, the two young men are of the class that administers the world. "If they saw a policeman misbehave, railway porters lack civility, an insufficiency of street lamps, defects in public services or in foreign countries, they saw to it either with nonchalant Balliol voices or with letters to the *Times,* asking with regretful indignation, 'Has the British This or That come to *this?*' " Under their care are manners, the arts, diplomacy, inter-imperial trade and the personal reputations of prominent men. They do not realize that their train has got on the wrong line.

Actually it is not running from London to Rye as they think, but from the past into the future, and ahead of them on their one-way journey is a chaotic country of ripped battlefields and disordered towns. Their fellow-passengers will grow hysterical and unpredictable, station masters will put up the wrong signals, troops will come aboard and get off again, the good furnishings of the train will get worn and broken, the schedule will go to pieces. And, experiencing all this, Christopher Tietjens will learn to expect that somewhere, beyond some bridge or tunnel, the tracks themselves will finally disappear into the dry sands of the wasteland.

But to begin where Ford did we must return to take a look at the unsuspecting passenger as he sits in his comfortable seat at the start of the journey. The beginning of the Tietjens story took form in Ford's mind just after the war. He had returned to France and was spending the summer in Harold Monro's villa on the deserted Riviera, a discharged officer, a cast-off writer immersed in a sense of disaster. As he walked in the garden of the Villa des Moulins, his ideas, cloudy at first but growing more precise, began to gather around the memory of an old friend, now dead.

Arthur Marwood had been enough of a paradox in himself to suggest greater ones. He was the son of a good Yorkshire country family, a mathematician of brilliance in the government office of statistics and Ford's associate in publishing *The English Review*. His mind was "acute and scornful" Ford says. "He possessed the clear Eighteenth-century English mind which has disappeared from the earth, leaving the earth very much the poorer." However, "he was, beneath the surface, extraordinarily passionate—with the abiding passion for the sort of truth that makes for intellectual accuracy . . . " In spite of his brilliance, Marwood had no career.

It was tuberculosis, actually, that forced him into a retired and inactive life, yet Ford, going beyond that, saw a tragedy of disinheritance. His kind of intelligence and what it represented passed through the metamorphosis of the author's imagination and became Christopher Tietjens. "I seemed," Ford says, "to see him stand in some high place in France during the period of hostilities taking in not only what was visible but all the causes and all the motive powers of infinitely distant places. And I seemed to hear his infinitely scornful comment on those places. It was as if he lived again."

So Marwood furnished the outline and the intellect, but there had to be more to Tietjens than that alone. Through the course of the four books the development of his personality is one of the most elaborate and singular accomplishments of modern writing.

His character is synonymous with the character of an ordered, bounded, and harmonious past. Socially, this means the England of gentry and farms before the middle classes built it into an empire. Morally, it means a code of honor and self-respect in contrast to business honesty and puritan habits. It means that Tietjens is humane in his relationships, feudal in his outlook, Christian in his beliefs, a classicist by education, a Tory in politics. He is, in fact, "the last English Tory." Mirrored in this "clear Eighteenth-century mind," the world is an equable and logical mechanism in which God, Man, and Nature have a balanced relationship. It is not specifically an English view; it has belonged to every Western nation.

In one place in **No More Parades** Tietjens concocts a kind of fable for himself. He sees:

> The Almighty as, on a colossal scale, a great English landowner, a benevolently awful duke who never left his study and was thus invisible, but

knowing all about the estate down to the last hind at the home farm and the last oak; Christ an almost too-benevolent land-steward, son of the Owner, knowing all about the estate down to the last child at the porter's lodge, apt to be got around by the more detrimental tenants; the Third Person of the Trinity, the spirit of the estate, the Game as it were, as distinct from the players of the game; the atmosphere of the estate, that of Winchester cathedral just after a Handel anthem has been played.

Tietjens means it as a semi-humorous comment on himself, but beyond that it is serious. Heaven is a Platonic reflection of earth, a place of feudal order and harmony and there are laws of science, morality, or theology to cover every event.

But Tietjens is out of his time in a world where the laws have lost their reality, the system has collapsed and the synthesis of knowledge and belief has lost its validity; under his feet he feels the great landslip. England (his specific example) once had a defined and integrated culture, but during the Nineteenth century it had become a kind of pseudo-civilization marked for export. Like cheap trading-goods, imitations, her morals, manners, and religion were shipped to every part of the world. It was a process of weakening, dilution, and overextension in more than a physical sense. Earning great paper profits, she had actually been spending her capital.

Ford saw the war as simply a dramatic heightening of the inevitable processes of ruin. England's victory was only an irony, a catalytic occurrence and she emerged from it into a social and intellectual chaos. The telling thing, Ford thought, was not that the world had changed physically to any great extent, but that the lines of communication had broken down. There was no longer a recognized continuity between past or present or present and future. The traditional modes of relationship among people had disappeared and there were no new ones to take the place.

We are likely to judge history as the blind men took the elephant; it is too big for us and too misleading in its various parts. The historian may offer a splendid, documented, analytical narrative; and yet we feel the lack of a plot. The novelist of history offers us a kind of mystery-play in which the great mass of ideas and events are concentrated into a sharp and comprehensible drama. Shakespeare's historical cycle and *War and Peace* are such mystery-plays. Though I do not wish to suggest a qualitative comparison—those two works are almost the grandest of their kind—Ford's Tietjens novel at least belongs in the same category. But with a difference. Ford was trying to define dramatically a thing that was only a direction or indication in his own time and his story includes the future. Looking at England today we can see more plainly what he meant. Tolstoy left the future out or, rather, he saw it as a twin-brother to the past and the cycle of his novel goes through the sequence of revolt and disorder back to order again. Chekhov, seeing differently, implied the future and we know now that the ring of the axe on the cherry tree outside the Ranevskys' windows was a more prophetic sound than the laughter in the Behuzovs' drawing-room at the end of *War and Peace*.

Therefore, Ford took as the scheme for his allegory the life of one man, Christopher Tietjens, a member of an extinct species, which, as he says, "died out sometime in the Eighteenth century." Representing in himself the order and stability of another age, he must experience the disruptive present.

I have been trying to give a bare idea of the abstract concepts which govern the development of the Tietjens novel, "the game," Ford says, "as distinct from the players of the game." One of Flaubert's important insistences was that the writer deal directly and exclusively with the explicit, leaving value judgments to implication. For a novelist whose abstract meaning is readily available this is not hard. The younger Flaubert, for instance, demonstrates just the right evidence to make the case of *Madame Bovary* clear. But it is a relatively simple case. The older Flaubert, dealing with the greater and more complicated issues of *L'Education sentimentale,* produces a story whose surface is difficult, contrasting, and perplexed. Ford went along the same path; the lucidity and perfect form of **The Good Soldier** was followed ten years later by the slippery indirections of the Tietjens story. (The comparison is even more exact if we remember that Ford's early enthusiasm was for *Madame Bovary* but that in later life, he said, he read *L'Education sentimentale* fourteen times.)

There is perhaps one central question arising from the events and circumstances of the Tietjens story that seems almost unexplainable in terms of the plot alone. It is one of the chief ambiguities that must exasperate and rebuff the unwary reader and yet it seems to lie in wait for him in almost every phase of the entire story. A workable answer to it should supply a great deal.

Why is Christopher Tietjens so endlessly persecuted? Nearly everyone else in the novel, consciously or unconsciously, tries to discredit, injure, attack, or betray him. He seems to be the object of a kind of compulsive hatred, yet in himself he is honorable, amiable, apparently a danger to nobody. In various ways this enmity appears in his friends, his acquaintances, fellow-officers, superiors, but most particularly and significantly in his wife. It is the last, his relationship with Sylvia, that offers the decisive clue to the seemingly purposeless affliction that he finds on every side.

At the beginning of **Some Do Not . . .** the domestic situation of the two is outlined. Sylvia has had a child whose paternity is doubtful and more recently she has run away to the Continent with another man. Then she has changed her mind and asked Tietjens to have her back again, a proposal to which he assents by cable. Sylvia, in Germany, is shown in a scene with a Socratic Irish priest, Father Consett, who draws from her the admission that what she hates most about her husband and what she can't live with is his essential and imperturbable goodness. In the meantime Tietjens has met a young woman named Valentine Wannop at Rye and taken a long ride in the fog with her. The first part is chiefly an establishment of character and the lines are drawn between Sylvia, an arrogant, reckless, and morally chaotic woman and Christopher, the wise and enduring man.

The antagonism gets dramatic exposition in the second part of **Some Do Not . . .** through a long scene which is built up by one of Ford's favorite devices, the *progression d'effet.* It is a psychological melodrama which gradually produces an intolerable pressure.

Tietjens, in the interval between the two parts, has been in the early battles of the war. A portion of his mind has been numbed by amnesia and he is wondering if this may be the first terrible sign. At the same time Sylvia is attacking his mental security in her own way. "I'll torment him," she has promised herself and she proceeds by accusation, sarcasm, lies, and open hatred. She has slandered him to his friends, whispered that he is keeping a mistress, that he has had a child by another woman; she has involved him in financial trouble. She is trying by all desperate means to reduce him to her own state of emotional anarchy—one sign of anger or weakness is all that she needs. "If," Sylvia went on with her denunciation, "you had once in your life said to me: 'You whore, you bitch . . . May you rot in hell . . . ' you might have done something to bring us together."

But Tietjens grows stronger under the assault. Bit by bit his memory is returning and with it the emotional and intellectual equilibrium that belongs to him. He treats her violence with his odd courtesy, dispassion, and forgiveness.

"There is only one man from whom a woman could take *'Neither I condemn thee'* and not hate him more than she hates the fiend!" Sylvia says, and finally gives her last furious thrust: Tietjens' father, she says, was driven to commit suicide by hearing the report that Christopher had got the daughter of his oldest friend with child.

Tietjens answers. "Oh! Ah! Yes! I suspected that. I knew it really. I suppose the poor dear knows better now. Or perhaps he doesn't . . . It doesn't matter." Instead of the expected explosion there has been a deflation and Sylvia has lost again.

Later on in **No More Parades** Tietjens's relationship with Sylvia is developed in another crucial scene. It is in France during wartime and Tietjens, now in command of a base camp, is suffering from enormous nervous stresses. Sylvia has managed to get there by unofficial means and they meet at a hotel during an engagement party. She is unable to explain to herself exactly why she has come; she confronts herself with the apparently insoluble paradox that Christopher, whom she detests so much, is actually the only man in the world she can love. But once there, she gives herself up to the luxury of torturing and trying to ruin him. Though she cannot quite see what it means, her memory furnishes her with an exquisite sadistic example of her motives in the anecdote of a white purebred bulldog (looking something like Tietjens) that she had once whipped raw and left out in the weather to freeze.

Sylvia has no difficulty raising all kinds of troubles, official, domestic, and personal, around Tietjens's head. She seems to arouse the hidden or latent antagonism of everyone else towards him. ("Christopher . . . A Socialist!" gasps General Campion when Sylvia tells him an absurd lie. "By God, I *will* have him drummed out of the service . . . ") It ends in a strange muddle in her hotel room and as a result Tietjens is transferred to the front lines.

The portrayal of Sylvia is as remarkable as that of Christopher. The unusual thing that Ford manages to transmit is not only Sylvia's insecurity and self-doubt, but her real terror at the idea of her husband. The intolerable fact to her is that he is sane.

And some of this terror at Tietjens is shared by everyone around. They are fragmentary people, uncertain, confused, without values. They sense that Tietjens belongs to a moral frame of reference that both makes the world intelligible and wards off its shocks. To their jumbled and neurotic lives he stands as a reproach, and they must destroy him if possible.

The two middle books of the novel, *No More Parades* and *A Man Could Stand Up—* might be described as concurrent with the war rather than about it. The scene is France during the hostilities and Ford manages to show a great deal of Tietjens's life, first as an administrative officer in charge of organizing drafts of replacements and later as commander of a front-line unit. It is often vivid, always well-observed and convincing; yet the mere fact of the war has a curiously secondary importance.

Fiction about war has always been, essentially, a kind of adventure fiction. With the older novelists it was an adventure of sides or armies seen from a high hill. How will the English (or the Scotch or the French) win this battle? was the question we were supposed to hang on. Victor Hugo's Waterloo is the most elaborate example. Then came Stendhal, the innovator, and wrote the adventure story of a single man lost in the tremendous confusion. How will Fabrizio escape? he asks. It seemed to be a much more interesting question.

Tolstoy and Crane followed his line and so did nearly all of Ford's contemporaries who wrote about the first World War. To it they added their own generation's contempt for illusion and made the point that such an adventure must turn out badly. War was a savage, hideous thing and had to be shown as such. Nevertheless, it was a kind of entity in itself, an unexplained adventure that had little to do with the normal course of the world.

Ford saw the war as a concentrated specimen of the whole history of his time, a bloody dumb-show imitating the bigger drama. If there is any adventure in Ford's war it is a cerebral adventure and if there is any danger it is psychological danger. Tietjens's question: "Am I going mad?" becomes a universal one and while protagonists of other war novels see villages wrecked, Tietjens sees a civilization going to ruin.

Ford always felt somewhat embarrassed in trying to explain his own work; the great artistic immodesty of James's prefaces was something he could not understand. Consequently, his prefatory remarks to these books might have been written by a mild, slightly deprecating friend who had little idea of their subject. In a typical understatement to be found in the dedicatory letter to *No More Parades* he says that the book is about Worry:

> That immense army was . . . depressed by the idea that those who controlled it overseas would—I will not use the word "betray" since that implies volition—but "let us down." We were oppressed, ordered, counter-ordered, commanded, countermanded, harassed, strafed, denounced—and, above all, dreadfully worried. The never-ending sense of worry, in fact, far surpassed any of the "exigencies of troops actually in contact with the enemy forces," and that applied not merely to the bases, but to the whole field of military operations. Unceasing worry!

This statement hints at something, but by no means expresses it. The more valuable idea that Ford's war is seen as something like a violent intensification of all the troubles of a foundering society comes out a little more clearly in his remarks concerning his "war books" in the autobiographical volume, *It Was the Nightingale*:

> A man at this point is subject to exactly the same disasters and perplexities as his temperament prepares him for in time of peace. If he is the sort of man to have put up with the treachery of others, his interest at home will suffer from treasons; if he is the man to incur burdens of debts, debts will unaccountably mass themselves; if he is a man destined to be betrayed by women, his women will betray him exaggeratedly and without shame. For all these vicissitudes will be enlarged by the strident note that in time of war gets into both speeches and events . . . And he is indeed then *homo duplex:* a poor fellow whose body is tied in one place but whose mind and personality brood over another distant locality.

In *No More Parades* the "disasters and perplexities" that haunt Tietjens have actually taken possession of those around him. Lt. McKechnie is the lunatic remnant of a brave officer, a classical scholar. His troubles with his wife are a wildly exaggerated version of Tietjens's relations with Sylvia and he has got to the point where he hears a kind of shelling within his brain. "The memory seemed to burst inside him like one of those enormous tin-pot crashes." For Tietjens he is like a horrible premonition.

There is the Welsh private, O Nine Morgan. His wife has gone off with a prize-fighter and when he applied for leave to go home Tietjens refused it in order to save him from being killed by the fighter. Morgan is a dispatch-runner; he is hit by a shell-burst in the street just outside the door of Tietjens's office and he falls inside to die in Tietjens's arms. "So he was better dead," Tietjens thinks. "Or perhaps not."

"Is death better than discovering that your wife is a whore and being done in by her cully? *Gwell angau na gwillth,* their own regimental badge bore the words. 'Death is better than dishonor.' . . . No, not death, *angau* means pain. Anguish! Anguish is better than dishonor. The devil it is! . . . He was born to be a blooming casualty. Either by shellfire or by the fist of the prize-fighter."

O Nine Morgan, the semi-anonymous man, is an example or a parable. He is truly *homo duplex,* born to be a casualty wherever he might go—either from fists at home or splinters of iron abroad, both of which, in the final view, are aspects of the same thing.

The war experiences, in a way, represent Tietjens's dark night. *No More Parades* piles injustice on injustice, but one of the things that helps Tietjens remain firm is the increasing realization that he is experiencing no simple personal nemesis but the total breakup.

"We were fitted neither for victory nor defeat," he thinks; "we could be true neither to friend nor foe. Not even to ourselves." He sees the clearest irony in his story of a visit to the War Office in 1914 where he had seen an official preparing the one ceremony of the war for which (Tietjens thinks) England was prepared—the disbanding of troops. It would close with the band's playing *Land of Hope and Glory*. The adjutant would then say, *"There will be no more parades."* And, Tietjens adds, "Don't you see how symbolical it was? . . . For there won't. There damn well won't. No more Hope, no more Glory, no more parades for you and me any more. Not for the country . . . Not for the world, I daresay."

A Man Could Stand Up— begins with a telephone message to Valentine Wannop in England, informing her that Tietjens has come home but that he seems to have lost his mind. With this ominous suggestion about him, the novel takes a step backward in time to show the history of one day in the trenches. The major part of it takes place in Tietjens's mind, an interior monologue that mingles a thousand fragments of the past with a thousand details of the present. Tietjens is second-in-command of a thinned-out battalion awaiting a German attack. As he goes about the routine business of the day Tietjens makes an effort of memory and imagination to hold off the gathering insanity he feels all about him. He must quiet the frenzied McKechnie and deal with his colonel who, losing control, has taken to drink. He tries to keep up the morale of his men.

Most important of all, he must keep his own balance. One night Tietjens had awakened to hear a voice coming from a mine almost beneath his feet, *"Bringt dem Hauptmann eine Kerze,"* it said. "Bring a candle to the captain." Was it real? he wonders. Or is his mind becoming a tangle of fantasy like all the others'?

But Tietjens has an amulet to carry him through. It is the recurring thought of George Herbert on a hill above Bemerton parsonage composing the line, *"Sweet day so cool, so calm, so bright, the bridal of the earth and sky . . . "* It is a vision of serenity and sanity. It serves to remind Tietjens that he belongs to a consistent system of belief, that there is or has been once a regular, logical, beautiful order to nature of which he is part. As long as that idea remains, as long as he can distinguish the song of the larks from the noise of the barrage, he will be safe.

The battlefield of *A Man Could Stand Up—*, thus, is more mental than physical and only one actual shell falls on it. It comes as a climax to the scene, burying Tietjens, a lance-corporal, and a lieutenant under a pile of earth. Tietjens crawls out, uncovers the others and carries the lieutenant away under fire. Immediately he is ordered to report to General Campion who, spic and span, is visiting the trenches on a tour of inspection. He is enraged that Tietjens has not reported before, that his uniform is dirty and that he has a hand in one pocket. The general relieves him of his command and with this unexpected little irony the war is over for Tietjens.

The third part of the book begins where the first left off, bringing Tietjens and Valentine together in his empty house in London. He is not mad, but just saved from madness. At last they are ready to admit they love each other, but as the horns and bells of Armistice Night sound, the crazy spectres from the trenches drift in one by one. Now that the ordeal is over, they seem simply harmless scarecrows and Tietjens and Valentine give them something to drink to celebrate the war's end.

Before looking at the final book of the Tietjens story, I should mention the matter of style. It is quite possible that Ford knew as many of the trade-secrets of writing as did any author of his time and a real discussion of his technique would be more extensive than an introduction allows. A few important methods and intentions, however, can be noted.

The language of the Tietjens story is one of simplicity and understatement. It is neither commonplace nor rhetorical and it manages to reveal exciting events without any surface theatricality of its own.

The chief strategems of narrative or dramatic style are somewhat more difficult to describe; they are the *progression d'effet,* the time-shift and the interior monologue. I have noted a good example of the first in the breakfast scene between Tietjens and Sylvia in *Some Do Not . . . ,* in which all the nerves are slowly drawn to the snapping point.

In the Tietjens novel the time-shift and interior monologue are employed simultaneously. Ford often translates the scene of his story into the mind of one character or another and then uses all the tenses of memory as if they formed a keyboard. A scene from the far past is juxtaposed significantly with a present incident; the happening of a year ago has some bearing on yesterday. The "stream-of-consciousness" techniques (Woolf, Joyce, Proust, Richardson) bear both similarities and differences, though Ford at this time had not read the work of his contemporary experimenters.

In all, Ford cannot be called a great stylistic innovator. Rather he tried to use the best techniques of others with great care and imagination. He himself called his style "impressionistic." If a term is needed, that word seems both sufficiently general and sufficiently descriptive.

The Last Post is the strangely inconclusive conclusion of the Tietjens story. In form it is the most oblique of any of the books, the most extreme example of what might be called Ford's "tangential relevance." Christopher Tietjens is present physically for only one moment at the end of the book and yet he is the most central being in it. The system of the book might be thought of as a temporarily eclipsed sun with a number of visible satellite consciousnesses surrounding and defining its position. There are nine relative and interconnected interior monologues representing several people in the general vicinity of the cottage to which Christopher and Valentine and Mark and his long-time French mistress (now his wife) have gone after the war.

Each one of these monologues is a digressive collection of commentary, gloss, footnote, addenda, and paraphrase of the whole Tietjens story. The mind of Marie (Mark's wife) is described as being like a cupboard, "stuffed, packed with the most incongruous materials, tools, vessels and debris. Once you opened the door you never knew what would tumble out or be followed by what." Nearly all of the incongruous material that tumbles out of each mind, however, is pertinent somehow to the life of Tietjens.

Each one of these minds floats in the atmosphere of time, crossing and recrossing the orbits of the others, yet there must be a binding device to connect each one with the here-and-now of the book and to remind the reader of real people in a real place. Ford introduces a certain amount of present incident into the story to effect this (a woman entering the garden, Marie making cider) and each present incident is viewed from a different perspective by several different characters. The whole book is like an immense juggling act of time and point of view.

In the fantastic trench-world, Tietjens had wished for peace: "to stand up on a hill." The post-war world seems to be an image of his hope—placid and rural. But when the minds are opened we realize that nothing has actually changed and that the chaos, disorder and combat are still there. It is a non-sequitur world just as the memories of its inhabitants are non-sequitur.

Christopher's elder brother Mark becomes the Tietjens symbol. He has been paralyzed by a stroke (the Tietjenses can no longer be an effective force actually, physically), but his mind is as active and perceptive as ever (the intellectual dominance remains). He lies on a cot under a thatch roof, staring out at a landscape. He knows that he will soon die. His consciousness is thus purified of all physical dross and from him we can expect some definition, a statement removed into the realm of the absolute and final by death itself.

To the other six mental discussions of the Tietjens story, which are ambiguous, unreliable, partial views, Mark's three sequences of thought stand as a kind of framework. He appears at the beginning, middle, and end. (The actual succession follows this order: Mark; Marie-Leonie, his wife; Cramp, a farmer; an American woman, a stranger; Mark again; Marie; Sylvia Tietjens; Valentine Wannop; finally, Mark.)

In Mark's thoughts the various puzzles of the Tietjens history are solved at last. He knows now that his father's "suicide" was really an accident, that Christopher's son is truly Christopher's son. Now that the ancient tree of Groby is to be cut down and the family estate passed into the hands of a Catholic, he knows that the traditional curse will be off the Tietjens—in effect, the dire but honorable curse of simply being what they are. Last night he had heard a rushing sound and had been "sensible of the presence of the Almighty walking upon the firmament." He is ready for death and sure of heaven.

He hears the people in the garden as voices from the past. "Damn it all could they all be ghosts drifting before the wind?" Christopher stands in front of his eyes for a moment with a chunk of the fallen Groby great tree in his hands and then Mark is dead; and the time of the Tietjenses is dead with him.

Mark's final statement is beyond emotion; the "curse" has always implied a future and it is now lifted. He presents both a summation of the Tietjens's case and a reconciliation with its destruction. Both their strength and their failure lie in the fact that they have been true to something in a world where no one is true to anything. They are an anachronism and, as an anachronism, must disappear. It is inevitable that one theory of Truth, one systematic idea of how man may lead a "good" life, will be swallowed up in a world of Untruth, but that is according to history's law—not its equity.

In his crotchety book on the English novel, Ford found much to complain of. He could see in its history no progressive intellectual maturation, no regular development of a tradition and no continuing attempt to uphold the artist's responsibility of "rendering" the life he saw. There were, however, a few writers here and there who understood that responsibility and lived up to it.

The difference between the general library of English novels and these few isolated achievements is partly a matter of method and partly of artistic integrity. Fielding, Smollett, Dickens, Thackeray—and most of the others we are inclined to call the major English novelists—failed, Ford thought, in the peculiar duty of an artist to his work. It resulted in, "mere relating of a more or less arbitrary tale so turned as to insure a complacent view of life." "Complacent" is the important word. It recalls, as a near-perfect example, the ending of *Tom Jones* when Tom, outcast and disinherited because of his honesty and courage, is welcomed back again simply because Fielding has performed the magician's trick of discovering his gentle birth. This complacency, this annihilating compromise with banality Ford thought to be a result of the English writer's continual urge to be considered "respectable" in a country where the artist had no honor and no social place.

The working toward ultimate conformity produced another commitment, which was one of method and viewpoint. The novelist presupposes a whole social scheme; within that circumference he arranges the smaller scheme of his plot and within the plot he assigns his characters various appropriate roles. When Fielding or Thackeray suddenly surprise us by showing their faces over the tops of their puppet theatres, we realize exactly what the novelist should keep us from realizing: that these are not self-directing people involved in a situation that seems to generate its own drama, but contrivances of cloth and wood assigned to their roles of good or evil.

According to Ford's view, the other kind of novel—in distinction it might be called the "intensive" novel—was produced intermittently during the eighteenth and nineteenth centuries by, first, Richardson, later Austen and Trollope, finally Conrad and James. (His own name belongs next.)

In France it became a tradition; in England it remained a series of singular performances.

This kind of novelist pursues an intense inquiry into the behavior of a certain group of characters both as unique beings and as part of an interweaving, interacting system of relationship. Finally he reasons, or suggests that we reason, from the particular to the general. All society, he declares, is simply a sum total of how human beings behave towards each other and if he is fortunate enough or gifted enough to select for his study circumstances of relationship that have a widespread application, he will have achieved, into his contemporary world, the most penetrating act of inquiry possible. In this kind of novel we surprise the individual situation in the very act of turning into the general circumstance.

We can imagine Mansfield Park as the geographical center of an early nineteenth-century culture and its concerns—love, money, manners, personal virtue—being pivotal to that culture. Visibly, things changed so little during the next seven decades that these could still remain preoccupations for that great pedant of the sensibilities, Henry James.

But geological shifts had been taking place in the culture and those values, by the end of the nineteenth century, no longer represented the same importance. Conrad had to deal with an expanding world and Ford an exploding one. In the Tietjens novel Ford had not only to consider a greater multiplicity of values (all of them changing, becoming ambiguous) but the greater question of value itself. If the quiet but intricate life of Mansfield Park is the proper symbol of one period, the wartime life of the Tietjens book is a symbol of our own destructive, inchoate time.

In this way Ford expanded the dimensions of the "intensive" novel to fulfill a more complicated assignment, yet he retained the central principle of precise moral-emotional-psychological investigation. The general argument or "meaning" of his book is not, of course, unique. In different ways and under different disguises it is one of the common motives of most important twentieth-century writers; Mann, Joyce, Gide, Eliot, Proust have all shared it and projected it in their various ways.

Each one of these writers has produced his response—Ford has not. It may be that the Tietjens novel demands a greater effort of self-recognition from the world, but if this effort can be made we shall not only have added a major novel to our literature but shall have performed a major act of understanding about ourselves and our era.

I have been referring to the Tietjens story as one novel divided into four different books and I think it can be comprehended in no other way. There is a misleading note in Ford's dedicatory letter to *The Last Post* which seems to indicate that he added this book as a kind of sequel to show "how things turned out." Addressing it to Isabel Paterson, he says:

> For, but for you, this book would only nebularly have existed—in space, in my brain, where you will so it be not on paper or between boards. But, that is to say, for your stern, contemptuous and almost virulent insistence on knowing "what be-

came of Tietjens" I never should have conducted this chronicle to the stage it has now reached.

Most likely, this should be taken more as a compliment to a literary friend than as exact truth. Without *The Last Post,* the novel would have been sadly truncated and though it could never "turn out" as an ordinary novel must turn out, the recapitulation and final statement of *The Last Post* is indispensable. In his book on Conrad, Ford explains that it was necessary for him to have a whole design in mind (contrary to Conrad's procedure) before he could begin.

The entire novel was written over a period of five years, *Some Do Not . . .* appearing in 1924, *No More Parades* in 1925, *A Man Could Stand Up—* in 1926, and *The Last Post* in 1928. It was begun at St. Jean Cap Ferrat, continued during Ford's wanderings from there to Paris, from Paris to Guermantes, to Toulon, Paris again, Avignon, and was finally finished in New York on November 2nd, 1927.

Previous to this edition it has not been published in its proper form, as a unit. *Parade's End,* the present title, was Ford's own choice as a designation for the whole.

It seems the most appropriate of any. With an immense sense of tragedy, Ford saw the long and splendid procession of the Western nations coming to an end and Tietjens is the ghostly voice of the adjutant at the final disbanding. He says, "There will be no more Hope, no more Glory. Not for the nation. Not for the world, I daresay. *There will be no more parades.*"

Paul Pickrel (essay date 1950)

SOURCE: A review of *Parade's End* in *The Yale Review,* Vol. XL, No. 1, September, 1950, pp. 189-91.

[*Pickrel is an American author, educator, and critic whose reviews have appeared in* Commentary, *the* New York Herald Tribune, *and* Book Week. *In the following excerpt, he suggests that* Parade's End *reflects Ford's belief that people will attempt to avoid loneliness and isolation at all costs.*]

The chief character in *Parade's End* is Christopher Tietjens, the younger son of a great Yorkshire family, a man who calls himself "the last Tory," who regards himself as a survival of the eighteenth century: a gentleman, a scholar, and (with a landlord's respect for the Biggest Landlord of them all) a Christian. Married to a beautiful, depraved woman whose object in life is to make him miserable, he falls in love with a younger and plainer girl and eventually, after he has served his country well in the First World War, sets up housekeeping with her, in a very humble way.

Ford's admirers have made much of Christopher Tietjens as a man with a code in a codeless society, but in truth this is the least attractive aspect of the story. The code is a shabby one which (for example) demands that a man afford the protection of his great name and wealth to a worthless woman ("a gentleman never divorces") but permits him to expose a far finer woman to the calumny of living out of wedlock and her children to the reproaches of illegitimacy. Surely a man, gentleman or otherwise, can and sometimes should sacrifice himself to his ideal of honor, but just as surely he cannot sacrifice others, including those still unborn.

Indeed, as you read *Parade's End* you realize that Ford's respect for the code is to a considerable extent simply his taking sides with those who have had power against those who are going to have it. But Christopher Tietjens himself points out, "The first Tietjens who came over with Dutch William, the swine, was pretty bad to the Papist owners." In other words, people who know how to behave are always being replaced by those who don't. That very eighteenth century which Tietjens admired so much saw some pretty considerable revolutions, and the seventeenth century (in which he would have liked to be a country parson like George Herbert) was not an entirely placid time, even for country parsons. No, this alignment with the social-class-that-was is the least attractive aspect of Ford's novel, and it accounts for most of its less pleasant characteristics, such as the smirking anti-Semitism and the sometimes tiresome display of upper-class information.

Happily, Ford's sense of the tragic went far beyond his anguish at a faulting in the social strata, and, as a result, his book is very much worth reading today. His subject—the subject of all that is finest in the novel—is the difficulty of "keeping in touch." This is the foundation of the book; it appears and reappears on the surface with almost endless variety. It unites in one sweeping metaphor the sections dealing with the war (surely some of the finest writing about war ever to appear in English) with the sections laid in peacetime.

"It was the dominant idea of Tietjens, perhaps the main idea he got out of warfare—that at all costs you must keep in touch with your neighboring troops." This is a narrow and practical statement of the great horror of trench warfare as Ford sees it: the feeling that one is being abandoned and betrayed—sometimes by one's superiors, sometimes by one's equals or inferiors, but always by those at home, those in charge. What should have been a mighty wave is just a collection of drops that will vanish into the unmarked sand. The feeling of separateness—from civilians, from home, from one's companions—increases until there remains only the single commandment: Thou shalt not go mad.

What is explicit in war is implicit in peacetime. The need to communicate with your neighbors is just as imperative and just as difficult to fulfill. When one man's appearance is the next man's reality, they cannot often be talking about the same thing. With marvelous—and perhaps excessive—dexterity, Ford surrounds Tietjens with layer after layer of misinterpretation, and on each layer one or another of the characters builds his life; and by an extraordinary command of the techniques of modern fiction, Ford makes the reader participate in the novel very much as the characters do, for the reader frequently builds on false premises and finds himself in the middle of a situation long before he understands it.

At the end, the whole story is gathered up in one daring symbol: Tietjens' brother Mark. As a Minister of Transport, Mark Tietjens has devoted his life to communication

of a sort, but he has given up the whole effort. Ill and resolved to speak no more, "wanting to be out of a world that he found fusionless," withdrawn like a dumb god while the mortals who still hanker after communication parade past him as in a frieze, he at last makes a little sense of his life. In the end, the Word was not.

Parade's End is a book of great brilliance and very little charm. There are scenes—such as one at a breakfast party—as dazzling as anything in modern English fiction; but those winning aspects of the world which at the same time heighten the tragedy of man's aloneness and go far towards reconciling him to it find no place in the novel. There isn't, for instance, a single child or even a likable dog in the whole 836 pages. And as long as human beings want to like life, charm will outlast brilliance in fiction.

Caroline Gordon   (essay date 1950)

SOURCE: "The Story of Ford Madox Ford," in *The New York Times Book Review*, September 17, 1950, pp. 1, 22.

[*Gordon was an American author and educator whose works include* The Good Soldier: A Key to the Novels of Ford Madox Ford *(1963). In the following excerpt from a review of* Parade's End, *Gordon contends that the work is best understood from a historical distance.*]

Ford's work—the body of it—may be compared to a huge stone cast into a pond; only the water which is displaced by its presence will have intimate contact with the stone, but the tiniest ripple will in time carry its impact to the shore. Ford was the best craftsman of his day; we are only now beginning to realize how widespread and pervasive such a literary influence can be.

The wielder of this powerful influence was born in London in 1873 (he died in 1939), the grandson of the pre-Raphaelite painter Ford Madox Brown. His youth was thus spent among the Rossettis and their circle. At 17 he published his first book. His international background gave him ready access to the leading literary and artistic movements of his generation: his finest short novel, *The Good Soldier* (1941), he himself rewrote in French. And, indeed, as John Rodker said of this book, it is the greatest French novel in English.

Breadth of view, immense knowledge of many literatures, and an unwavering loyalty to his great profession marked Ford as perhaps the last great man of letters in the nineteenth-century style. Whatever concerned the vitality of letters was within his province. He was one of the few great editors of this century. In reckoning his value one must not forget that as editor of *The English Review*, founded in 1908, he brought what we know now as "modernism" to England.

In the Knopf edition just published Ford's four war novels, commonly known as "the Tietjens series," appear at last for what they are: one great novel under the title *Parade's End.* The novels which make up the tetralogy were written at the close of World War I and achieved a brief popularity. They were held to be a not too realistic account of one soldier's disillusioning experience in that war. They are being published on what is perhaps the eve of a third world war, with a preface by Robie Macauley, a young writer whose own work will doubtless be better known later on than it is today.

Mr. Macauley points out in his preface that *Parade's End* begins, as many great works of fiction have begun, with a journey: two young men sit in a perfectly appointed railway carriage; everything in the carriage is of the best material; the window straps are of the finest leather, the mirrors immaculate, "as if they had reflected very little"; the air smells faintly of an excellent varnish. Christopher Tietjens, the hero, and his friend, Vincent Macmaster, are on their way to spend a week-end in the country. They are of "the class that administers the world." If they see anything wrong anywhere—a policeman misbehaving, an insufficiency of street lamps, a defect in public service—they feel it their duty to set the matter right. The train they are riding runs as smoothly (Tietjens thinks) "as British gilt-edged securities." However, it is running on the wrong track.

"Actually," Mr. Macauley; says in his brilliant preface, "it is not running from London to Rye as they think, but from the past into the future, and ahead of them on their one-way journey is a chaotic country of ripped battlefields and disordered towns. Their fellow-passengers will grow hysterical and unpredictable; station masters will put up the wrong signals, troops will come aboard and get off again, the good furnishings of the train will get worn and broken, the schedules will go to pieces. And, experiencing all this, Christopher Tietjens will learn to expect that somewhere, beyond some bridge or tunnel, the tracks themselves will finally disappear into the dry sands of the wasteland."

It is easier now to read the Tietjens novels than when they were first written. It is becoming apparent that when he wrote them Ford was writing history, as any novelist is writing history when he records faithfully the happenings of his times. (It was Henry James who observed that the novelist's obligation to record faithfully is as binding, "as sacred" as that of a Thomas Macaulay or an Edward Gibbon.) Ford was one of the most brilliant and faithful recorders of his time. There is no one, not even James, who can bring a scene before us with more vividness.

In some of Ford's writing, however, there is too much going on. If the reader relaxes his attention he will soon not know where he is. Then, too, he must pay attention with his ear as well as with his eye, for sound plays an important part in Ford's dramatic effects. The first part of the tetralogy ends with the words: "He had caught, outside the gate of his old office, a transport lorry that had given him a lift to Holborn." These cadences, which tell us that Tietjens' future life will be sober, if not mournful, fall on deaf ears if the reader has not read every word that precedes them.

Such demands were not made on English readers at the time when Ford began writing novels. They had not been made by Thackeray and were made only sporadically by Dickens; Arnold Bennett and Swinnerton and Galsworthy did not make them—and Joyce had only just been published.

It is easy to see why Ford's work was not popular in his own day, but it is hard to see why it has been neglected in our own, for he would seem, in these times, to have a special claim on our attention. He is a superb historical novelist, seeming as much at home in a medieval castle or in Tudor England as in Tietjens' twentieth-century railway carriage. At his touch some of history's driest, barest bones take on flesh. Yet he is comparatively unknown as a historical novelist in an age in which the historical novel enjoys the greatest vogue it has ever enjoyed.

It seems highly suitable that the preface to *Parade's End* should be written by a young, comparatively unknown writer, since Ford himself has as yet hardly been recognized as a writer. Or perhaps it is more exact to say that he has been recognized only intermittently. Certainly he lapsed after his two modest successes—the publication of the Tietjens series and *The Fifth Queen* trilogy—into obscurity greater than he had known before.

It has been fashionable to regard this obscurity, deeper and darker than that surrounding any comparable talent of our time, as no more than he deserved: the proper reward for a misspent life. Ford during his lifetime was often the subject of gossip, his actions often seemed ill-advised; he made powerful enemies. In his late fifties his powers failed him: he was no longer able to write fiction and kept himself going by writing over and over a sort of fictionalized autobiography.

Yet all this was part of one story, the same story he was all his life telling, for like most novelists he had only one story to tell. His novels are all either rehearsals for that story or variations of its pattern. The action is presented very vividly in the Tietjens series and it is possible that that is the version of the story by which Ford would prefer to be remembered.

Christopher Tietjens may be thought of as "the last Tory." Indeed Ford himself says that he so conceived him, a man who through no apparent fault of his own is at odds with his times. However, "he and she," as Chekhov sagely observed, "are the engine that makes fiction move." Tietjens is a fine fellow, but for all his virtues he is not at peace with himself; for one thing, he has made a bad marriage. Sylvia Tietjens, his wife, is a *belle dame sans merci*. Tall, beautiful, wealthy, she alternately hates and loves her husband and is hell-bent on his ruin. When she is not tormenting him she suffers from boredom. She is too fastidious to take a lover and, instead, practices on men "every variety of turning down."

As a novelist Ford is much preoccupied with those life-giving and death-dealing attributes of woman. Ford's heroes are all involved with some *belle dame sans merci* who looms to them a little larger than life.

The heroines who battle with these apparitions for the love of Ford's heroes are usually little, fair women, possessed of great filial piety, who have recently had reverses of fortune. In the earlier novels the white goddesses are triumphant. The hero and the woman who is attached to him are nearly always ruined.

Still, no matter how his fortune turns, Ford's hero stands always between two women whose natures are diametrically opposed, inclining a little toward the *belle dame sans merci.* Man naturally seeks his own ruination, the author seems to say, particularly if there is no exterior order to which his case can be referred. A priest usually broods over the conflict: in *Parade's End,* Father Consett; in *A Call,* a Greek Orthodox priest who sardonically points out to Robert Grimshawe what his own loss of faith has cost her. Man's plight, the novelist seems to say, is always the same: he must exercise his free will and choose between the good and the bad.

It does not seem to matter where or when Ford sets his stage; he is always able to make the action immediate and convincing. In *The Young Lovell* the young knight praying over his arms, "in the new French fashion," succumbs to the temptations of a sorceress, passes three months and a day in her company and thereafter finds his family, friends and fiancee unendurable. He finally follows her into barren pastures to spend his life in a long enchantment. In Ford's hands this variation of an ancient legend symbolizes the plight of the modern man; Tietjens' expensive railway carriage is heading for the same trackless wastes.

Lloyd Morris   (essay date 1950)

SOURCE: "Ford's Masterpiece Now Reappears," in *New York Herald Tribune Weekly Book Review,* October 1, 1950, p. 4.

[*Morris was an American biographer, critic, social historian, essayist, and pioneering educator who is credited with introducing contemporary literature courses to the American university system in the 1920s. In the following review of* Parade's End, *he suggests that Ford is the literary equal of James Joyce, Marcel Proust, and Franz Kafka.*]

Here, finally presented as its author wished, is one of the major English novels of the twentieth century. *Parade's End* brings together four books by Ford Madox Ford, first published between 1924 and 1928, and long out of print: *Some Do Not . . .* ; *No More Parades*; *A Man Could Stand Up* and *The Last Post.* Issued separately and at intervals, these books were read as a series of novels having the same central characters and a common theme. But Ford intended them to be read as a unit. The single massive novel which he conceived is now offered under the title he chose for it. *Parade's End* gives us—for the first time in its organic unity—his greatest achievements.

Ford died in 1939 at the age of sixty-six. Readers who were then middle-aged remembered him as a very distinguished writer and a remarkable literary figure. He was the contemporary of Joyce, Proust and Kafka, but he had won no fame comparable to theirs. As a result, he is virtually unknown by the rising generation of today. But publication of *Parade's End* should establish him, belatedly, in the company of the great trinity of his period. This novel, so curiously neglected for a quarter of a century, now emerges as one of the few real masterpieces of fiction that have been produced during our era.

In common with Proust, Ford portrayed a distintegrating society; his picture is large in scope and thickly crowded.

Like Joyce, he conceived his novel as an epic and made it the vehicle of a prophecy. Like Kafka, though not as explicitly, he designed his novel as an allegory, expressing abstract meanings through concrete, material forms. This indicates how far, in *Parade's End,* Ford deliberately transcended his own concept of the novelist's primary function. He wanted the novelist, he said, to assume "his really proud position as historian of his own time" and he declared that "fiction should render, not draw, morals." In the last twenty-five years, history has elaborately confirmed the prophecy contained in Ford's novel, so that the book has even more relevance to our world today than to the world which Ford was portraying. Yet, however impressive Ford now seems as the historian of his own time and the prophet of ours, *Parade's End* shows that he was something more important than either. He was one of the very few writers of his generation who understood the moral significance of the tragedy he attempted to record in dramatic narrative.

Parade's End deals with the private fortunes of Christopher Tietjens, an English gentleman, during the first world war, and thus appears to be a representative example of the psychological and social novel. It can be so read, and on this level it is an astonishing, magnificent achievement. The central characters of the story, Christopher and his wife Sylvia, are memorable both for their extraordinary complexity and their absolute convincingness. In rendering their domestic situation and the prolonged disastrous conflict of their personalities, upon which the story largely turns, Ford has given us a treatment of modern love as illuminating, in its exposure of the secret recesses of the heart, as that contrived by Proust. No less subtle in his insight, probing as deeply as Proust did, Ford used the dramatic rather than the analytical method of presentation. The long, intolerably painful luncheon scene which first reveals the relationship of Christopher and Sylvia is a characteristic and brilliant illustration of his method. For sheer intensity for cumulative dramatic power, the scene has few equals in the modern novel. Yet it is not a mere episode; it harvests an entire past and, as the reader discovers on finishing the story, it forecasts the outcome. Ford set his central characters in the midst of a society; he did not pose them against it as a background and it is this society, represented by the many other characters of the novel, which gives the cases of Christopher and Sylvia a significance far greater than that of individual circumstance. They are not only protagonists, but allegorical figures. They personify the civilization which Ford regarded as doomed to ruin and the chaos which he envisaged as succeeding it.

Ford portrayed English society as already in process of breakup, and the first world war, as it appears in the novel, is both the symbol and the consequence of that process. Christopher Tietjens, whom he described as "the last English Tory," is a surviving example of a species already extinct. He possesses the "clear eighteenth-century mind" that Ford admired. He exemplifies the kind of social order, the kind of world toward which Western civilization, after the Renaissance, appeared to be progressing. He illustrates the ideals of private honor, public responsibility, humane conduct, incorruptible justice, order and harmony that were intrinsic to Western culture. He regards his own life as, in essence, a moral career; convinced that all his choices are free, he knows that all of them must be decided by ethical principle. In the twentieth-century world, as Ford shows, Tietjens is an anachronism. His fundamental sanity and security inspire fear in those around him; his inherent virtue arouses hostility everywhere. His wife cannot endure his excellence; both loving and detesting him, she is obsessively bent upon accomplishing his ruin, and her successful enlistment of others in this destructive enterprise forms the plot of the novel. The society portrayed in *Parade's End* is the world of Sylvia Tietjens. It is becoming a world of moral chaos in which all principles will lose their validity, in which the great cultural tradition will be bankrupt, in which conduct will be motivated by the lust for power and dictated by expediency. Writing a quarter of a century ago, Ford made Sylvia prophetic of the future. She represents anarchy, terror and the sense of guilt.

Parade's End has an excellent introduction by Robie Macauley, who was a student at Olivet College when Ford, the year before his death, was "author in residence" on the campus. Ford's eagerness to serve youth never flagged during his long career and it seems singularly appropriate that an illuminating discussion of his art should come from a member of the last generation with which he was to have personal contact.

Hamilton Basso   (essay date 1950)

SOURCE: "Christopher Tietjens: His Life and Times," in *The New Yorker,* Vol. XXVI, No. 32, October 7, 1950, pp. 126, 129-30.

[*An American novelist, biographer, and critic, Basso is best known for* Sun in Capricorn *(1942), a novel which, like much of his work, explores the societal structure and cultural mores of the American South. In the following review of* Parade's End, *he calls the tetralogy "a minor performance," asserting that Ford was unable to create a convincing portrait of a politically conservative character.*]

Parade's End, by Ford Madox Ford, is an omnibus collection of four books that make up a single novel, along with an introduction by Robie Macauley. The titles of the books, as they originally appeared, over a period of five years (1924-28), are *Some Do Not . . . , No More Parades, A Man Could Stand Up—,* and *The Last Post.* The author, who died in 1939 and who was one of the younger members of the generation of writers that included Joseph Conrad, Henry James, Stephen Crane, and H. G. Wells, built his novels around a central character named Christopher Tietjens. The time encompassed was the period of the First World War—before, during, and immediately after.

When the Tietjens novels were first published, they were regarded collectively by many as being in the same category as *What Price Glory?* and *All Quiet on the Western Front*—another story, though longer than most, of a soldier's disillusioning experiences in modern warfare. Ford himself fostered the notion. "This is what the late war was like," he wrote, in connection with *A Man Could Stand Up—.* "This is how modern fighting of the organized, sci-

entific type affects the mind." But his actual purpose, as Mr. Macauley points out in his introduction, was infinitely more ambitious. Ford intended his four books to be a saga of a whole era; he was writing about what he saw as the collapse of modern society. Christopher Tietjens is not so much a character as a symbol of the old, comfortable, leisurely England that had the props knocked from under it by the first of this century's long series of wars. "His character," Mr. Macauley writes, "is synonymous with the character of an ordered, bounded, and harmonious past. . . . Tietjens is humane in his relationships, feudal in his outlook, Christian in his beliefs, a classicist by education." Ford at one point describes Christopher Tietjens as "the last English Tory"; Mr. Macauley, whose introduction is certainly the most sympathetic that Ford has ever had, agrees with this definition of him.

In his identity as the last English Tory, Tietjens finds himself entirely out of place in a disintegrating society. He undergoes one humiliation, embarrassment, and persecution after another. His friends, his acquaintances, his fellow-officers, and his superiors all attack, injure, discredit, or betray him. And most of all his wife, Sylvia. If Mr. Macauley is correct in his interpretation of Ford's symbolism, as I think he is, Sylvia is to be regarded as a personification of the moral anarchy of the new order. She and practically everybody else appear to look upon Tietjens as a kind of walking reproach. Driven by their individual varieties of compulsive hatred, they feel it necessary to destroy him. In the end they do.

There could hardly be a better theme for a novel than this. It suggests the dual note so often struck by Joseph Conrad—the individual's sense of moral isolation, and the fate of man, stripped of all the ordinary supports of friendship, love, and position, who is hunted to his doom. The size and nature of Ford's debt to Conrad, with whom he collaborated in his earlier years on three books, need not concern us here; more to the point is the use he made of his rather Conradian theme. Mr. Macauley feels that he completely succeeded with it. So does Graham Greene ("There is no novelist of this century more likely to live than Ford Madox Ford"), Glenway Wescott ("the most grievously neglected of the major works of fiction of this century"), and Granville Hicks ("a brilliance that was at times almost too dazzling"). These appreciations, which appear on the book's dust jacket, are bolstered by others in a similar vein, contributed by William Troy, Arthur Mizener, and Carl Van Doren. In the glare of such admiration, fierce enough to cause a sun tan, it is moderately discouraging to have to enter a contrary opinion. It is my notion, however, that Ford made pretty much of a hash of things. He had a theme and he had an ambition. What he did not have, as I see it, was the ability to measure up to their demands.

The entire book, as is apparent, rests on the person of Christopher Tietjens; if he doesn't hold it up, the whole thing is bound to collapse. Moreover, he has to carry conviction not only as a character in a novel but in the larger, symbolic role that Ford assigned to him—the last English Tory. Ford asks us to believe that all Tietjens' misfortune and misery come to him as a result of his being in possession of a particular set of standards and values. This is especially true of his relation with Sylvia, a chronically unfaithful woman who has presented him with a son whose paternity is most uncertain. Disintegrating epochs and social landslides to the side, the heart of the book lies in the conflict between Tietjens and Sylvia. She makes life a hell on earth for him; she makes it a hell for some eight hundred and thirty-six pages. Why, then, doesn't he divorce her? It is in this connection that some of the Toryism of this last English Tory comes into play. Here, for instance, are three examples:

> The lady was subsequently [after the birth of her child], on several occasions, though I do not know how many, unfaithful to me. She left me with a fellow called Perowne, whom she had met constantly at the house of my godfather. . . . My wife, after an absence of several months with Perowne, wrote and told me that she wished to be taken back into my household. I allowed this. My principles prevented me from divorcing any woman, in particular any woman who is the mother of a child.

> I have always held that a woman who has been let down by one man has the right—has the duty for the sake of her child—to let down a man.

> She had never been anything but unfaithful to him, before or after marriage. In a high-handed way so that he could not condemn her, though it was disagreeable enough to himself. . . . And now she was running about the world declaiming about her wrongs. What sort of a thing was that for a boy to have happen to him? A mother who made scenes before the servants! That was enough to ruin any boy's life . . .

These passages have their moments of comedy, but comedy was not even incidental to Ford's intention. In urging this fantastic point of view upon us as an integral part of the Tory faith, he is owl-solemn throughout. So is he in another place, when he writes about Tietjens' inner, secret character: "His private ambition had always been for saintliness: he must be able to touch pitch and not be defiled. . . . And his desire was to be a saint of the Anglican variety. . . . The desire of every English gentleman . . . A mysticism . . . "

It would be possible to fill up several pages with similar revelations of the Tory creed, but I hardly think it necessary. The truth of the matter is that all this huffing and puffing about Toryism caused Ford to blow his own house down; he ended up by making Christopher Tietjens more of a booby—because he is such a pretentious booby—than David Low's cartoon creation Colonel Blimp.

Reading Douglas Goldring's biography of Ford, *The Last Pre-Raphaelite,* one gets the impression that Ford's knowledge of the former ruling class in England was based largely on hearsay; the child of a professor-critic father and a painter-of-sorts mother, he moved all his life in what used to be called an artistic atmosphere. More important, it would appear that he stood in rather strenuous opposition—and this is borne out by some of his other books—to a large proportion of the established, conservative, traditional values that in his long novel he would have Christo-

pher Tietjens adhere to. Yet, despite these limitations, he attempted to write from the ruling-class point of view. That he failed is not surprising; what is surprising is that he thought he could bring it off. There are some good things in his novel—many of the war episodes, glimpses of the English and European countryside, an occasional bit of crooked humor—but these come about when Ford is writing about matters that he has known or experienced at first hand. As a matter of fact, there is a rather large element of autobiography in the book; Christopher Tietjens is best seen not as the last, or any other kind of, English Tory but as a spokesman for Ford Madox Ford. Even so, I have my doubts about the book's being anything but a minor performance. H. L. Mencken once wrote of Ford, "The high, purple spot of his life came when he collaborated with Conrad, and upon the fact, I daresay, his footnote in the Literature books will depend." It was one of Mencken's more pugnacious judgments, but I wouldn't be surprised if it should stand.

John R. Tobyansen   (essay date 1950)

SOURCE: A review of *Parade's End,* in *Shenandoah,* Vol. 1, No. 3, Winter, 1950, pp. 29-36.

[*In the following essay, Tobyansen offers a thematic overview of* Parade's End *and discusses the novel's principal characters.*]

Parade's End is a single volume containing four of Ford's earlier novels, ***Some Do Not, No More Parades, A Man Could Stand Up*** and ***The Last Post,*** and an introduction by Robie Macauley. The four novels, published originally over a five-year period (1924-1928), achieved only brief popularity. When they first appeared, they were considered as merely another group of "war novels." In the Knopf volume they appear as what they should be—one great novel—titled ***Parade's End.*** The whole volume is an accurate presentation of the personal and univeral histories of several people and a country in the years immediately before, during, and after the first great war. This was a period in which tradition, the British moral aristocracy, was perishing due to the strains imposed by modernism, the new statism, while both elements were at the same time allied in fighting a devastating war.

Tradition is wounded and then dies before the sniping power of modernism. The pathos of tradition's death is that modernism's weapons are usually being aimed by opportunists. Christopher Tietjens, the epitome of landed aristocracy, bends slowly before the fire of Vincent Macmaster, Mrs. Duchemin, and the interim-war officials who have sensed the inevitable social upheaval and who have joined "the new movement" to further their own ambitions. Valentine Wannop, representing the modernist element in ***Some Do Not,*** is actually closer to Tietjens than any other of his intimates. Although she represents the social change that is pushing him aside, she loves and admires him because of his respect for traditional decorum and pattern.

The immediate purpose of ***Some Do Not*** is to indicate the pattern that the four novels (often called the Tietjens series) follow. Ford did not write the four novels so that each one would stand as a complete story in itself. The Tietjens story is a "saga" with each of the four novels concerned with a particular phase of the saga. *Some Do Not* is a novel that must be read carefully, for in it Ford introduces his themes, his people, and their conflicts. The characters and their actions symbolize and predict the strains and changes England will undergo in the years from 1914 to 1926. Ford wrote a history of those fateful years as shown by the lives of Christopher Tietjens, one of the last great landed aristocrats; Valentine Wannop, one of the first suffragettes; Vincent Macmaster, a parasitic opportunist; and Sylvia, Tietjens' unfaithful wife, but ultimately savior of his estates. The richness of the four novels is augmented by the portrayal of several other well-drawn characters, but they, in their turn, all refer to the main characters. Thus there should be no confusion as to the basic pattern of the saga.

Mr. Ford's characters are actually too complex to serve as mere symbols—indeed it is their complexity that keeps the series from becoming a barren recital of history—but if we are to consider *Some Do Not* as the novel that will enable us to identify the clashing themes and conflicts in *Parade's End,* we must take the temporary liberty of labelling the main figures in the books. Once we have established the pattern by this means, then we will consider more fully the paradoxes within the principal characters.

The first meeting of Christopher and Valentine is symbolic of the respect the conflicting ideals permit each other. It also symbolizes the triumph that modernism will eventually enjoy. The setting is a golf course where Tietjens ("I loathe the beastly game") is part of a foursome which has a brush with a group of suffragettes. Valentine Wannop enlists his aid to help one of her friends escape the police. Tietjens succeeds in effecting her friend's escape. Valentine feels that she must explain herself to this man.

He rides in a dogcart through a dense fog with Valentine, and the dialogue symbolizes, again, a dawning realization of the fact that modernism might eventually triumph.

> . . . . He called out:
>
> "Are you all right?" The cart might have knocked her down. He had, however, broken the convention. . . . His last thought came back to him. He had broken their convention: he had exhibited concern: like any other man. . . . He said to himself:
>
> "By God! Why not take a holiday: why not break all conventions?"

When the war takes Tietjens from England, he is attacked socially by the opportunists at home, particularly by a banker named Brownlie. He is trapped into accepting this petty social attack because of the self-confining mores of his own traditional philosophy, the philosophy that forbids an active resistance to modernism.

> "That was quite proper, for if the ennobled family of Brownlie were not of the Ruling Class—who had to go (to war)!—they were of the Administrative Class, who were privileged to stay. . . ."

Mr. Ford establishes the underlying theme—the destruction of a system of life—by noting all the subtle ties, not by posting open notices of the fight due between the past and the present. But there are minor themes that are as capably handled as the major idea. In *Some Do Not,* love is the obvious motive of the story, not a simple love, but the triply-complex relationship between Tietjens and his wife; Tietjens and Valentine; and Sylvia and Valentine. Tietjens' wife, Sylvia, hates him because she understands him. Valentine loves Tietjens but understands him less than his wife. Tietjens endures his wife and yearns for Valentine, but can never bring himself to any overt demonstration of love for Valentine. But are traditionalism and modernism ever close enough to exist tranquilly together? Obviously not in the early stages of the clash between the two philosophies, and so it is that Mr. Ford never allows Christopher and Valentine to indulge their love for each other.

Some Do Not also leaves one with the impression that Ford is writing history. But the dialogue and actions of his characters give the history of these times a personal meaning. The history is so neatly connected with the characters that a reader finds himself wondering about the outcome of a story that has already been told.

No More Parades is concerned chiefly with what was referred to by GI's of the recent war as red tape and chicken. It is a recital of and report on the mounds of unnecessary paper work a base officer is buried under at a replacement depot. If there is a weak link in the series, this would be the novel to be inspected for lack of strength. Until Sylvia arrives in France and further demonstrates her determination to drive her always composed and superior husband to the breaking point, the novel is no more than a protest against military bureaucracy.

Sylvia's conduct results in Tietjens striking a fellow officer and insulting a General, both of whom have violated the privacy of their bedroom at the hotel where she and Christopher were preparing to retire for the night. The incident expands because of the many military and personal complications and misunderstandings involved, so that it is necessary to send Tietjens to the front in order to preserve the decorum of the depot where he is stationed.

The trenches, mud, and frustration are the backdrops for the third novel, *A Man Could Stand Up.* The greater portion of the book is taken up with a single day in the trenches. Ford uses the impressionist technique, the method in all four novels, more clearly here than in the preceding books. The characters react to a scene or action as they see it. There is little attempt at "descriptive" detail. He relates the subconscious association of images and symbols that his characters experience as a result of a situation. He does not depict the situation. His characters suggest it for him. The reality of Tietjens' situation, in the trenches, is forced again and again on Tietjens' reflecting mind. He hears voices from a German mining tunnel beneath his feet, "Bringt dem Hauptman eine Kerze"; then he is snapped back to his immediate circumstances. The officers with whom he associates are all suffering from monotony, fear, and frustration. Inconsequential items are given ludicrously passionate attention. Only the frayed nerves of these men have survived the sacrifice of minds in this macabre life in the mud. The last incident in the trench section illustrates the tragic-comic plight of these men. After being buried by a German shell and escaping, Tietjens is confronted by his commanding officer—who relieves him of his command because of his dirty uniform.

The last part of the novel takes Tietjens to London, to an empty house with Valentine Wannop. They are in love; they have decided to violate convention. It appears as if he has at last decided to cast off the outmoded mores that had him trapped. They are visited by the physical and mental ghosts from the war which used to annoy and confound Tietjens, but they no longer worry or affect his state of mind.

In *The Last Post,* Ford demonstrates even more fully that pure impressionist technique so clearly evident in the third novel. Ford accomplishes his denouement through the thoughts of Tietjens' brother, Mark, who, paralyzed in an outdoor bed, reflects on the Tietjens' estate called Groby. He considers Christopher's and Sylvia's child. This is the son who will inherit Groby and the tradition for which it stood. Mark ponders Sylvia's conduct and the events that have taken place in the preceding novels. Groby, Tietjens' son, and Sylvia sum up, in themselves, all the complexities of the preceding novels. The thoughts of Mark turn continually to Christopher Tietjens or to things which are concerned with him. Christopher appears only briefly at the end of the book. We see Christopher through the eyes and thoughts of other people, and these thought patterns are so skillfully woven that the intersection points never tend to destroy the novel's continuity and purpose.

In Mark's mind the events are reviewed from Tietjens' initial journey on a train with Macmaster ("A journey from the present into the future," according to Robie Macauley's brilliant preface to the volume) to the present fall of Groby into the hands of a Catholic. But Mark sees it all as no failure, rather as a retirement with honor. Virtue in the sense of adhering to the precepts of the Tietjens' traditional philosophy has been preserved. The series is resolved on a Faulknerian note of hope. The possibility of salvation lies in the exchange of the Groby tradition for the Catholic tradition. The hope for salvation is present despite the threat of modernism. Christopher Tietjens has been true to his own set of values and retires before the forces of moral anarchy and modernism, defeated outwardly, but inwardly proud and strong.

Having surveyed the history and major theme in *Parade's End,* let us take a closer view of the characters. Ford has drawn them almost too richly to permit an exhaustive analysis, but it is only by examination of the individual problems that the paradoxes within the people can be appreciated.

Christopher Tietjens possesses a brilliant mind—perhaps the most brilliant in all England. He has a tremendous knowledge of the classics, a remarkable talent for figures, and a fund of odd information and talents that enable him to entertain intelligent opinions on a variety of subjects. He is the past—a landed independent aristocrat in the most traditionally individualistic manner—and he is out

> **Ford's skill in drawing his characters prevents history from deciding which philosophy was the right one. Ford lures his readers into the lives of his people.**
>
> — *John R. Tobyansen*

of place in the present. He has a set of chivalric, humane rules that he applies to other men, nature, God, and women. Nothing can alter his determination to abide by these rules. He and his brother Mark are scornful of titles and ostentation. They remain above the petty court jealousies, secure in their identity as Tietjens of Groby.

Tietjens refuses to divorce his wife, Sylvia, despite her scandalous conduct. When she wires him, after running away with another man, that she is ready to return to him, he accepts. His rules require that a husband always provide a wife with a home. Despite Sylvia's repeated sins and infuriating actions, he never loses his composure. His rules require coolness in the face of calamity.

In one scene, at breakfast with Sylvia, Tietjens is presented as having an injured memory due to the effect of a shell burst in France. Sections of his vast knowledge are missing entirely. He confesses that he has been reading the encyclopedia to restore his knowledge. (This is a typical Fordian twist, England's greatest mind studying the encyclopedia.) His bank account is overdrawn. His wife tells him that her lies have driven his father to suicide, to which Tietjens replies: "I supoose the poor fellow knows better now. Or perhaps he doesn't. . . . It doesn't matter." Once again his standards of conduct and philosophy fail to tremble before the neurotic schemes and attacks of his treacherous wife.

Sylvia is the most fascinating of all the Ford people. She is dedicated to bringing her husband to his knees. She hates his composure, his tolerance, his code, his knowledge, and most of all, his indifference. Paradoxically, hating Tietjens as she does, she cannot divorce him. No other man can mean anything to her, yet she encourages these other men so that she can have the satisfaction of turning them down. She is a Catholic, but an example of the moral anarchy of the times. She exists to try to make Tietjens show emotion because that would be a sign of weakness. While she is so terrifyingly busy trying to destroy Christopher, she is actually, but accidentally, his savior. The old estate called Groby, which is the source of Tietjens' individuality, is fated by legend to return to the hands of a Catholic. It is Christopher and Sylvia's son, a Catholic, who lives to inherit Groby and its traditions. That Sylvia should accomplish the material salvation is again a Ford paradox.

Valentine Wannop, who loves Tietjens but never understands him as his wife does, presents another interesting paradox. She is a complete realist. With the collapse of her family fortunes, she goes to work as a maid. Later she supports herself as a physical education teacher. When the same group of fair weather friends who have rejected Tietjens reject her company, she accepts their action as an expected and practical one. She does secretarial work for her mother who attempts to earn a living by writing. She and her mother are always in dire economic straits, but neither of them complain or look for loans from Tietjens.

Despite Valentine's ardent desire for modernism, she is remarkably patient in waiting for Christopher, and trying to understand him. Outspoken and passionate in her opinions on social issues, she is tolerant and almost reticent about her man. Yet this failure to fight for him wins him for her, because his intimates drive him into her arms. She presents more of a problem to Sylvia because of her tolerance than she would if she had been more forward and had blatantly become Tietjens' mistress. She remains stoically above the jealous sniping gossip of the opportunists. She who should be opposed to the Tietjens' estate and all it stands for, is respectful of it, and her family is saved by it. (Christopher's father leaves the Wannops money.) Sylvia, who is of the Tietjens' "class," tries to destroy the estate and all it stands for, but inadvertently becomes its savior.

Ford had no choice as to the basic factual situation at the end of the volume. History had decided the end as Ford wrote the novels. But the facts are not only an evaluation of the value of Tietjens' individuality as opposed to Sylvia's moral anarchy. Nor are the facts only an evaluation of the landed tradition's death before the new statism. Ford's skill in drawing his characters prevents history from deciding which philosophy was the right one. Ford lures his readers into the lives of his people. At the end of the volume, history has its influence, but the evaluation is up to the reader in so far as the reader has, by means of the impressionist method, been led into a psychological identification of himself with one of the central characters.

Ford's very subtle interchanging of person and theme (or individual and historical attitude) gives both width of scope and depth of intensity to *Parade's End.* This is not to say that the impressionist method is the only method of encircling a subject from every possible point of view, but Mr. Ford refuses to over-simplify the paradoxes in his extremely British characters, and he refuses to lose sight of the dominant theme which binds the paradoxes together.

William Carlos Williams   (essay date 1951)

SOURCE: *"Parade's End,"* in *Selected Essays of William Carlos Williams,* Random House, 1954, pp. 315-23.

[*Williams was one of America's most renowned poets of the twentieth century. Rejecting as overly academic the Modernist poetic style established by T. S. Eliot, he sought a more natural poetic expression, endeavoring to replicate the idiomatic cadences of American speech. In the following essay, which was first published in 1951, he focuses on the significance of Sylvia in the transition of Christopher Tietjens throughout the novel, and suggests that Tietjens is not "the last Tory," but rather the first of a new, more enlightened generation of Englishmen.*]

Every time we approach a period of transition someone cries out: This is the last! the last of Christianity, of the publishing business, freedom for the author, the individual! Thus we have been assured that in this novel, *Parade's End,* we have a portrait of the last Tory. But what in God's name would Ford Madox Ford be doing writing the tale of the last Tory? He'd far rather have tied it into black knots.

In a perfectly appointed railway carriage, two young men of the British public official class, close friends, are talking quietly together. Back of their minds stands Great Groby House, the Tietjens' family seat, in Yorkshire, the north of England—its people, neighbors, and those associated with them just prior to the beginning of the First World War. It was a noteworthy transition period. It would be idle of me, an American, to try to recreate so highly flavored an atmosphere as that represented in this railway carriage. One of the speakers is Christopher Tietjens, younger son to Groby's ancestral proprietor; he is a blond hulk of a man, a sharp contrast to his companion, MacMasters, dark-haired and with a black pointed beard, a smallish Scotsman for whom the Tietjens family has provided a little money to get him through Cambridge and establish him in town.

Sylvia, young Christopher's beautiful wife, has four months previously gone off to the Continent with a lover. She has sickened of him and wants to be taken back. The two men on the train, thoroughly well bred and completely British, are discussing the circumstance and its profitable outcome—Christopher, defending his wife, has consented to let her do as she pleases. There begins now to unravel (you might almost say it is Christopher's ungainly bulk itself that is unraveling) as intimate, full, and complex a tale as you will find under the official veneer of our day.

Four books, *Some Do Not, No More Parades, A Man Could Stand Up,* and *The Last Post,* have been for the first time offered in one volume as Ford had wished it. The title, *Parade's End,* is his own choosing. Together they constitute the English prose masterpiece of their time. But Ford's writings have never been popular, as popular, let's say, as the writings of Proust have been popular. Yet they are written in a style that must be the envy of every thinking man. The pleasure in them is infinite.

When I first read the books I began, by chance, with *No More Parades*; as the story ran the First World War was in full swing, the dirt, the deafening clatter, the killing. So it was a little hard for me to retreat to *Some Do Not,* which deals with the social approaches to that holocaust. At once, in the first scenes of this first book the conviction is overwhelming that we are dealing with a major talent. We are plunged into the high ritual of a breakfast in the Duchemin drawing room—all the fine manners of an established culture. There's very little in English to surpass that, leading as it does to the appearance of the mad cleric himself, who for the most part lies secretly closeted in his own home. Beside this we have the relationship of the man's tortured wife with Tietjens' friend MacMasters; the first full look at Valentine Wannop and of Tietjens himself before he appears in khaki—the whole rotten elegance of the business; Sylvia, at her best, and the old lady's "You are so beautiful, my dear, you must be good." Then it shifts to Christopher and the girl, Valentine, in the fog, linking the land, disappointment, the yearning for fulfillment and—the ten-foot-deep fog itself covering everything but the stars of a brilliant sky overhead; we see Christopher in the carriage holding the reins, Valentine leaping down to find a road sign and disappearing from his view. Only the horse's head, as he tosses it, reappears to Christopher from time to time as the man sits there alone. Following that is the restraint and hatred in the scene between husband and wife, Christopher and Sylvia. He at table in uniform, she standing behind him, bored. Casually she flings the contents of her plate at the back of his neck, glad she hadn't actually hit him—but the oil from the dressing dribbled down on his insignia. He didn't even turn. It is their farewell as he is about to leave for the front.

This is the first of the four books. The war intervenes. *No More Parades.* The war ends. Tietjens is invalided home, his mind half gone. Valentine lives for him and he recovers. Mark, the present heir to Groby, the Correct Man, represents the family and England as a family. Living with his French mistress he suffers a cerebral hemorrhage and lies, during all of *The Last Post,* in a sort of summerhouse, where with his last breath, and as he holds the pregnant Valentine by the hand, the saga comes to an end.

Sylvia, through all the books, in her determination to destroy her husband, does everything a woman can, short of shooting him, to accomplish her wish. From start to finish she does not falter.

This is where an analysis should begin; for some, who have written critically of *Parade's End,* find Sylvia's extreme hatred of her husband, her inexorable, even doctrinaire hatred, unreal. I think they are wrong. All love between these two or the possibility for it was spent before the story began when Christopher lay with his wife-to-be, unknowing, in another railway carriage, immediately after her seduction by another man. It made an impossible situation. From that moment all that was left for them was love's autopsy, an autopsy and an awakening—an awakening to a new *form* of love, the first liberation from his accepted Toryism. Sylvia was done. Valentine up! A new love had already begun to shimmer above the fog before his intelligence, a new love with which the past was perhaps identical, or had been identical, but in other terms. Sylvia suffers also, while a leisurely torment drives her to desperation. It is the very slowness of her torment, reflected in the minutiae, the passionate dedication, the last agonized twist of Ford's style, that makes the story move.

In his very perception and love for the well-observed detail lies Ford's narrative strength, the down-upon-it affection for the thing itself in which he is identical with Tietjens, his prototype. In spite of all changes, in that, at least, the Tory carries over: concern for the care of the fields, the horses, whatever it may be; the landed proprietor must be able to advise his subordinates who depend on him, he is responsible for them also. That at least was Tietjens, that too was Ford.

> Tietjens is not the "last Tory" but the first in the new enlightenment of the Englishman—at his best, or the most typical Englishman.
>
> — *William Carlos Williams*

When you take those qualities of a man over into the new conditions, that Tietjens paradoxically loved, the whole picture must be altered—and a confusion, a tragic confusion, results, needing to be righted; it is an imperative that becomes a moral duty as well as a duty to letters.

Ford, like Tietjens, paid attention to these things. I'll not forget when he came to visit me in Rutherford, a town lying in the narrow sun-baked strip of good soil, land which the Dutch farmers cultivated so well in the old days, between the low Watchung Range and the swampy land of the Hackensack Meadows. It is one of the best tilled, you might almost say currycombed, bits of the Garden State, as New Jersey is still called. Old Ford, for he was old by that time, was interested. He asked me to take him out to see the truck farms. We spent the afternoon at it, a blistering July day when the sprinkler system was turned on in many of the fields, straight back into the country, about three or four miles, to the farm of Derrick Johnson, who personally showed us around. I was more interested in the sandpipers running through the tilled rows—birds which I hadn't seen up to then other than running on the wet sand of beaches as the water washed up and retreated, uncovering minute food. But on the farm they were nestling, here their eggs were laid and hatched in the heat between the beet rows on the bare ground. But Ford, who was looking around, questioned the farmer closely about the cultivation of the lettuce, carrots, dandelion, leeks, peppers, tomatoes and radishes which he was raising. It was all part of his understanding of the particular—and of what should properly occupy and compel a man's mind. He might have been Tietjens.

So far I have spoken in the main of Christopher and Sylvia, their relationship, their positions and their marriage. But there are other characters as important in the argument as they. Mark, Christopher's elder brother, the one man whom Sylvia has never been able to impress, should be put down as the first of these—as Ford, I think, recognizes, when he makes him the key figure of the entire last book, *The Last Post.* Mark, the perfectly cultured gentleman. Professor Wannop, old friend of the family, a studious recluse who has brought up his daughter, Valentine, in his own simple and profound ways, is gone. And there is, of course, Valentine herself, though she appears, generally speaking, little. She fills, however, a dominant place. *A Man Could Stand Up* is her book. General Campion, official England, is another to be named. He will carry off the girl, old as he is, at the close. At every turn he appears, often as Sylvia's instrument to thwart Christopher, triumphant officialdom.

But greater than he, Tietjens, are the men in the trenches, his special responsibilities, over whom he pains, a bumbling mother, exhausting himself to the point of mental and physical collapse.

Few could be in the position which Ford himself occupied in English society to know these people. His British are British in a way the American, Henry James, never grasped. They fairly smell of it. The true test is his affection for them, top to bottom, a moral, not a literary attribute, his love of them, his wanting to be their Moses, to lead them out of captivity to their rigid aristocratic ideals—to the ideals of a new aristocracy. Ford, like Tietjens, was married to them, and like Sylvia they were determined to destroy him for it. Even when he could help them, as Tietjens helped MacMaster, Ford got kicked for it and was thrown out of the paradise of their dying ideas—as much by D. H. Lawrence on one side, the coal miner's son, as by the others. He helped Lawrence but Lawrence soon backed out. And still no one grasps the significance of Tietjens' unending mildness, torn between the two forces—no one, really, but Valentine and Mark in the last words.

Sylvia's bitter and unrelenting hatred for Tietjens, her husband, is the dun mountain under the sunrise, the earth itself of the old diabolism. We sense, again and again, more than is stated, two opposing forces. Not who but *what* is Sylvia? (I wonder if Ford with his love of the Elizabethan lyric didn't have that in mind when he named her.)

At the start her husband has, just too late for him, found out her secret; and feeling a responsibility, almost a pity for her, has assumed a superior moral position which she cannot surmount or remove. She had been rudely seduced, and on the immediate rebound, you might almost say with the same gesture, married Tietjens in self-defense. She cannot even assure her husband that the child is his own. She cannot be humble without denying all her class prerogatives. Christopher's mere existence is an insult to her. But to have him pity her is hellish torment. She is forced by everything that is holy to make him a cuckold, again and again. For England itself in her has been attacked. But Valentine can pick up her young heels, as she did at the golf course, and leap a ditch, a thing impossible for Sylvia unless she change her clothes, retrain her muscles and unbend.

But there is a deeper reason than that—and a still more paradoxical—in that Tietjens forced her to do good; that as his wife she serves best when she most hates him. The more she lies the better she serves. This is truly comic. And here a further complexity enters. Let me put it this way: If there is one thing I cannot accede to in a commonality of aspiration, it is the loss of the personal and the magnificent . . . the mind that cannot contain itself short of that which makes for great shows. Not wealth alone but a wealth that enriches the imagination. Such a woman is Sylvia, representing the contemporary emblazonments of medieval and princely retinue. How can we take over our *Kultur*, a trait of aristocracy, without a Sylvia, in short as Tietjens desired her? What is our drabness beside the magnificence of a Sistine Chapel, a gold salt cellar by Cellini, a Taj, a great wall of China, a Chartres? The mind is the

thing not the cut stone but the stone itself. The words of a Lear. The sentences of *Some Do Not* themselves that are not likely for this to be banished from our thoughts.

Ford gave the woman, Sylvia, life; let her exercise her full range of feeling, vicious as it might be, her full armament of woman. Let her be what she *is*. Would Tietjens divorce her? When there is reason yes, but so long as she is truthfully what she is and is fulfilling what she is manifestly *made* to be, he has nothing but respect for her. Ford uses her to make a meaning. She will not wobble or fail. It is not his business. This is a way of looking at the word.

Ford's philosophy in these novels is all of a piece, character and writing. The word keeps the same form as the characters' deeds or the writer's concept of them. Sylvia is the dead past in all its affecting glamor. Tietjens is in love the while with a woman of a different order, of no landed distinction, really a displaced person seeking replacement. Valentine Wannop is the reattachment of the word to the object—it is obligatory that the protagonist (Tietjens) should fall in love with her, she is Persephone, the rebirth, the reassertion—from which we today are at a nadir, the lowest ebb.

Sylvia is the lie, bold-faced, the big crude lie, the denial . . . that is now having its moment. The opponent not of *le mot juste* against which the French have today been rebelling, but something of much broader implications; so it must be added that if our position in the world, the democratic position, is difficult, and we must acknowledge that it is difficult, the Russian position, the negative position, the lying position, that is, the Communist position is still more difficult. All that is implied in Ford's writing.

To use the enormous weapon of the written word, to speak accurately that is (in contradiction to the big crude lie) is what Ford is building here. For Ford's novels are written with a convinced idea of respect for the meaning of the words—and what a magnificent use they are put to in his hands! whereas the other position is not conceivable except as disrespect for the word's meaning. He speaks of this specifically in *No More Parades*—that no British officer can read and understand a simple statement unless it be stereotype . . . disrespect for the word and that, succinctly put, spells disaster.

Parenthetically, we shall have to go through some disastrous passages, make no mistake about that, but sooner or later we shall start uphill to our salvation. There is no other way. For in the end we must stand upon one thing and that only, respect for the word, and that is the one thing our enemies do not have. Therefore rejoice, says Ford, we have won our position and will hold it. But not yet—except in microcosm (a mere novel you might say). For we are sadly at a loss except in the reaches of our best minds to which Ford's mind is a prototype.

At the end Tietjens sees everything upon which his past has been built tossed aside. His brother has died, the inheritance is vanished, scattered, in one sense wasted. He sees all this with perfect equanimity—Great Groby Tree is down, the old curse achieved through his first wife's beneficent malevolence, a malevolence which he perfectly excuses. He is stripped to the rock of belief. But he is not really humiliated since he has kept his moral integrity through it all. In fact it is that which has brought him to destruction. All that by his upbringing and conviction he has believed is the best of England, save for Valentine, is done. But those who think that that is the end of him miss the whole point of the story, they forget the Phoenix symbol, the destruction by fire to immediate rebirth. Mark dead, Christopher, his younger brother, has got Valentine with child.

This is not the "last Tory" but the first in the new enlightenment of the Englishman—at his best, or the most typical Englishman. The sort of English that fought for and won Magna Carta, having undergone successive mutations through the ages, has reappeared in another form. And this we may say, I think, is the story of these changes, this decline and the beginning of the next phase. Thus it is not the facile legend, "the last Tory," can describe that of which Ford is speaking, except in a secondary sense, but the tragic emergence of the first Tory of the new dispensation—as Christopher Tietjens and not without international implications. *Transition* was the biggest word of the quarter-century with which the story deals, though its roots, like those of Groby Great Tree, lie in a soil untouched by the modern era. *Parade's End* then is for me a tremendous and favorable study of the transition of England's most worthy type, in Ford's view and affections, to the new man and what happens to him. The sheer writing can take care of itself.

Joseph J. Firebaugh   (essay date 1952)

SOURCE: "Tietjens and the Tradition," in *The Pacific Spectator*, Vol. 6, No. 1, Winter 1952, pp. 23-32.

[*In the following essay, Firebaugh contends that* Parade's End *is best read as an allegory.*]

Now that the extraordinary tetralogy, *Parade's End,* has been republished, we ought to reconsider it in the light of the message which Ford Madox Ford meant it to convey. For he did intend the "Tietjens Saga" to teach a lesson, although he was too much a product of his post-pre-Raphaelite times not to feel that he sinned against his literary gods by that intention. The meaning of the novels, however, is so much richer than his avowed purpose of denouncing warfare that he can have offended only the most dogmatic worshipers of artistic purposelessness.

The Tietjens cycle deals with the second decade of this century as those years were lived by Christopher Tietjens, "the last Tory." It is of some historical interest that in creating Christopher, Ford had in mind one Arthur Marwood, with whose financial help the *English Review* had been founded under Ford's editorship. Ford's literary achievement consists in his making of Tietjens and his circle a subtle allegory of social decay and reform. This he does through a story of personal disintegration and recovery which, both for technical accomplishment and allegorical treatment of a typical human situation, demands its place with the important literary works of our time. Readers who are approaching the series now for the first time

may be aided by a few suggestions as to how the story may be allegorically read.

Parade's End is an allegory of social decay. Christopher Tietjens, "the last Tory," is the England to which this decay is happening, and who must be saved if England is to be saved. He stands for the traditional virtues. The youngest son of his family, he has left the ancestral seat, Groby, for a berth in the Department of Statistics, where his brilliance would seem to augur a great career. But there is a certain fraudulence about the statistical profession—statistics can be made to mean many things; they deal with appearances, not realities. Fraud in its many forms is a dominant leitmotiv of the novel; it is against fraud that Tietjens-England must struggle.

Christopher has had the misfortune to choose a fraudulent wife as well as a fraudulent career. Sylvia is a beautiful, brilliant, neurotic young woman who embodies the chief symptoms of the contemporary social decay. A Catholic by birth, she retains the faith only superstitiously, superficially; thus she, too, has deserted her tradition. As the novel opens, she has deserted Christopher for another man, not because she loves the other man but because she wishes to hurt her husband. She has accepted the superficiality of her social circle, the group which gets itself photographed by the Sunday papers, which is constantly changing sexual partners, and which more than any other shows the decay of a stable, traditional social order. Tietjens she hates because he represents a stability to which she cannot attain. The only happiness of which her disordered mind is capable is the sadistic one of causing him pain. In one great symbolic scene she lashes to death a huge white bulldog which she identifies with Tietjens (and thus, in our reading, with England and tradition). For sheer horror, Sylvia is an almost unsurpassed depiction of beautiful female viciousness. Her neurosis is the neurosis of the modern world. Insanity and near-insanity make up another of Ford's persistent leitmotivs in *Parade's End.*

Sylvia's neurosis, though it impels her to create suffering for Tietjens, causes her to withdraw from the suffering world when the World War comes. She retreats to a convent, emerging from time to time with evil purpose toward her suffering husband, who as a member of the British aristocracy can only do his duty by entering the Army. Her humanitarianism is of the sort which withdraws in horror from the basic facts of human suffering, failing to see that suffering is involved in life, and that withdrawal creates even worse human agony. Sylvia is a kind of prototype of Munich, of the selfish avoidance of pain which leads only to its more violent affliction; Ford created Sylvia during the 'twenties, but in her he anticipated the fact that at the time of Munich he would seriously consider renouncing his English citizenship. Christopher Tietjens, by accepting his responsibility in the war, alleviates suffering in the very process of bearing it, and, inescapably, inflicting it. Thus, threatened with disintegration by Sylvia's conduct, he finds his way toward a new integration. Tradition, and England, is to be saved.

Tietjens and the tradition suffer not only from such neurotic dissenters as Sylvia, but also from those *arrivistes* who would become a part of the tradition: who aspire, through a certain coarse-grained ambition, to be received into the authentic tradition, but who understand it only in its superficial, apparent, aspects. These fraudulent persons offer another aspect of the decadent civilization which fascinated Ford so much. There are several representatives of this broad group, defeating traditional values by spurious emulation. One of the most important is Vincent Macmaster, a school friend of Christopher, whose university education has been paid for by Christopher's money, and who, though less brilliant than Tietjens, is so "circumspect and right" in observing the proprieties of the aristocratic class to which he aspires that he promises to have a fine career in the same Division of Statistics to which Tietjens belongs.

An amateur literary critic, Macmaster has just published a monograph of Rossetti. Ford, so closely related to the pre-Raphaelite group—his grandfather was the painter Ford Madox Brown—sees its members and imitators as fundamentally fraudulent—more concerned with appearances than realities. Macmaster sets up an elaborate establishment, chiefly paid for with money borrowed from Tietjens, and never repaid. His one stroke of official brilliance, which gains him a knighthood, he has stolen from Christopher, who threw it out playfully, as the sort of unscrupulous statistical juggling that could be done by an unprincipled man. Macmaster rises rapidly in the world while the more scrupulous Christopher falls. The "circumspect and right" classes, the career men, the *arrivistes,* continue to rise; the downright, forthright, honest Christophers of the world lose out. The world is topsy-turvy.

Macmaster is abetted by the "lady of his delight," who is "so circumspect and right," Edith Ethel Duchemin, a post-pre-Raphaelite beauty. She has been married to a former pupil of Ruskin, the Reverend Mr. Duchemin, who has long been afflicted in his clerical office with a scatological mania which is regularly brought on by overindulgence in communion wine. Here the theme of insanity again, to which is added the idea of a tradition perverted through the degeneration of a symbol. Edith Ethel becomes Macmaster's mistress long before her husband's death—always trying, however, to preserve appearances. When she can finally marry Macmaster, it is to preside brilliantly at the *salon* which she creates for him, to insist that he now desert Tietjens entirely, and to advance his career by methods of her own. We last hear of Macmaster as the victim of a nervous breakdown. Thus, to rise in the modern world is to lose one's integration. Insanity and neurosis nearly always accompany success, in the topsy-turvy world of *Parade's End.* To cross the lines of class, to embrace the goddess of getting on, as the *arriviste* does, is to spoil both the world and his place in it.

Adultery in *Parade's End* serves as a kind of symbol of social disintegration. We meet it both in Sylvia's affair and in the affair of Edith Ethel and Vincent Macmaster. It is later to befall Tietjens himself, but not until, after long years, it becomes, in a disintegrating world, a symbol not of decay but of salvation.

The girl with whom Christopher falls in love is Valentine Wannop, the daughter of his father's old friend. Valentine's allegorical part in the novel is that of the social radi-

cal: she is an active, demonstrating, suffragette, and a pacifist. One of Ford's ironies is that through Valentine, the Tory Christopher is to achieve his salvation. Although they realize at once that they are in love, they do little about it during the years of war. Partly this is because of a sense of abstract right, a feeling that "some do not"; partly also their restraint is due to the excesses of Valentine's brother, far more radical than she, who drunkenly comes between them—symbolically, I think—on a crucial evening. Both the radical Valentine and the conservative Tietjens are repelled by his youthful excess—repelled at least to the extent of renouncing their own indulgence. The conjunction of the two—Tory and social radical—cannot take place in the atmosphere which her brother creates, composed about equally of Communist principles and self-indulgence. Thus their love forms a nice contrast to the Vincent Macmaster–Edith Ethel affair—a contrast between their own forthrightness and the *arriviste* circumspection.

Christopher and Valentine are separated throughout the war years, Valentine teaching in a girl's school and Christopher filling the traditional aristocratic role of Army officer. As a captain he suffers with his men, agonizing when a decision of his deprives one of them of life, identifying himself with them as he tries to straighten out their problems—all of which, he observes, are essentially his own problems of money and women. In suffering for his men and identifying himself with them, he is a sort of Christ symbol, as indeed his name suggests. And in caring for them like a shepherd he fulfills—to borrow one of William Empson's insights—the pastoral function of the aristocracy.

Christopher's Army career is kept rather unsuccessful by the troubles Sylvia has made and continues to make for him. She seems deliberately to be trying to drive him to madness, and she nearly succeeds. Following him to the Front, she informs his commanding officer that he imagines himself to be Jesus Christ, and that he is a Socialist, either charge being enough to prejudice the conventional military mind of his superior. Confronted with the latter charge, Tietjens explains that he has "no politics that did not disappear in the eighteenth century": "Of course . . . if it's Sylvia that called me a Socialist, it's not astonishing. I'm a Tory of such an extinct type that she might take me for anything." He is so nearly of an extinct type, indeed, as to be quite indifferent to personal wealth, and seriously concerned with the welfare of the lower classes. Very early in the first novel Tietjens has discovered the similarity of his Tory program to a Labour minister's socialism:

> Over their port they agreed on two fundamental
> legislative ideals: every working man to have a
> minimum of four hundred a year and every
> beastly manufacturer who wanted to pay less to
> be hung. That, it appeared, was the High Tory-
> ism of Tietjens as it was the extreme radicalism
> Left of the Left.

Thus Ford prepares, early in the series, a synthesis of the Right and the Left. (One might note here, partly for those who think that "cradle-to-grave planning" is a heretical invention of modern socialists, that Arthur Marwood, Christopher's prototype in real life, had contributed to the

English Review, under Ford's editorship, an article called "A Complete Actuarial Scheme for Insuring John Doe against all the Vicissitudes of Life.")

Being a Tory of a nearly extinct breed, Tietjens dreams, at the Front, of the quiet seventeenth-century countryside. One morning, before a great German strafe, he hears a cornet player in the English trenches practicing an air of Purcell, to which Christopher fits a poem by George Herbert:

> Sweet day so cool, so calm, so bright,
> The bridal of the earth and sky.

The tune, a kind of symbol of sanity, of order, in a world gone mad, leads him into a reverie in which he imagines himself, like George Herbert, to be the occupant of Bemerton parsonage. That he may save what he can of the seventeenth century, he decides to order the musician's transfer to the rear lines. And before the strafe begins, he sees, at right angles to the trench, but leading to the left, a channel which he feels an almost overwhelming urge to follow, imagining in his reverie that it will lead him both to seventeenth-century peacefulness and to the quiet arms of the little radical, Valentine. Thus the synthesis of the Left and Right is anticipated.

The synthesis finally occurs when, after the war, in the last novel of the four, Christopher and Valentine go to live together in the country near Bemerton parsonage. Their life is complicated by Sylvia's continued troublemaking. She is now determined upon the destruction of Groby Great Tree, a symbol of the family, which

> had been planted to commemorate the birth of Greatgrandfather who had died in a whoreshop—and it had always been whispered in Groby, amongst the children and servants, that Groby Great Tree did not like the house. Its roots tore chunks out of the foundations and two or three times the trunk had had to be bricked into the front wall of the house.

Groby Great Tree, in commemorating an ancestor whose death had occurred under circumstances which showed a certain falling away of greatness, becomes a symbol of family decline. Not only has the great-grandfather died in a brothel; the Tietjens family has survived into a century which is very like a brothel—cultivating appearances rather than realities, preferring money to quality, glitter to worth.

Christopher, like his great-grandfather, has fallen prey to some of these attractions. Specifically, he has done so in marrying Sylvia. In deserting her for Valentine, he has deserted falsehood for truth. But his devotion to Groby Great Tree is a weakness—a pride of family, of even its least perfect monument. The tree is felled, and part of the house falls with it. The American tenant will have to pay for repairs to the house; but with the removal of the aristocracy, the establishment has been badly damaged; not even American wealth can restore it. Sylvia is able to gloat:

> She had got down Groby Great Tree: that was as nasty a blow as the Tietjens' had had in ten generations.

But then a queer, disagreeable thought went through her mind. . . . Perhaps in letting Groby Great Tree be cut down God was lifting the ban off the Tietjens'. He might well.

In uprooting the tree, Sylvia suddenly realizes, she has provided Christopher the way to salvation. For he has now achieved the full detachment for which he had longed: from lands, from money, from family. One had almost said from tradition. Rather, Tietjens' task, with Valentine, will be to re-establish tradition.

Tietjens has always had aristocratic respect for the lower classes. The last novel presents a specimen of these classes, Gunning, who has become a servant to Tietjens. Valentine's reverie reflects Christopher's attitude:

> The Gunnings of the land were the rocks on which the lighthouse was built—as Christopher saw it. And Christopher was always right. Sometimes a little previous. But always right. Always right. The rocks had been there a million years before the lighthouse was built, the lighthouse made a deuce of a movable flashing—but it was a mere butterfly. The rocks would be there a million years after the light went for the last time out.
>
> Gunnings had been in the course of years, painted blue, a Druid-worshipper, later, a Duke Robert of Normandy, illiterately burning towns and begetting bastards—and eventually—actually at the moment—a man of all works, half-full of fidelity, half blatant, hairy. A retainer you would retain as long as you were prosperous and dispensed hard cider and overlooked his blear-eyed peccadilloes with women. He would go on. . . .

During the war, Christopher has often expressed respect for the men serving under him, and has gone to considerable trouble for them, identifying their problems with his in a self-sacrificial manner. This is the aristocratic attitude toward the lower classes; the aristocrat is the protector and defender of his retainers—that is to say, of his own protectors and defenders. If, as William Empson thinks, one of the pastoral traditions has been the descent of the man of birth into the lower ranks, there to learn how better to rule, and if that descent can further be identified with the idea of the sacrificial god dying for his people, that they—and he—may be born again, we then see Tietjens performing the functions both of aristocratic defender and of sacrificial god. The close of the novel shows him and Valentine living together in peaceful frugality, in circumstances similar to those of their retainers. In one of her reveries, Valentine agrees with Christopher's position "that if a ruling class loses the capacity to rule—or the desire!—it should abdicate from its privileges and get underground." They must descend, to rise again. Groby Great Tree is felled. Tietjens is living a pastoral life, beginning as his ancestors had begun. The rebirth of the tradition is thus being prepared. It is dead, but it will rise again.

Specifically, it will arise again through the birth of Valentine's child, for whom she and Christopher have definite plans. Chrissie, as Valentine names him in her reverie, is to become the type of seventeenth-century country parson that his father would like to have been, reading Greek and watching his flock in the pastoral-aristocratic manner. His parents want, indeed, to buy a living for Chrissie, if possible at Bemerton, where George Herbert had been pastor. Through Christopher's *illegitimate* union with Valentine, then, one aspect of British tradition is to be reaffirmed and regenerated.

What of his other union? Through this *legitimate* union Christopher had allied himself with a woman who represents the decadent society of her day, the world of appearances. By Sylvia, he has become the father of a boy, Michael Mark, who, at his brief appearance in the novel, is a callow but charming student at Cambridge University, where he has embraced the political and economic doctrines of Marxian communism. As heir to Groby, Michael Mark will become owner of vast coal lands, which have once been primarily pastoral. But as a young Marxist, the boy chiefly represents the ideas of industrialism and progress. To be sure, Ford makes fun of his callow Marxism, his assumption of a belief in industrialism; but even undergraduate poses have their reality. England, like this youth, has followed an industrial program not in its tradition. This through its *legitimate* conduct, which is really *illegitimate,* because out of character.

The paradox exists also in the fact that the boy is both Catholic and Marxist. As Catholic, he is an authoritarian pastoral traditionalist; as Marxist, an authoritarian perfectibilitarian. That he can be both is, perhaps, due to their common basis in authority. Two aspects of English tradition are at war in Michael Mark's adolescent breast: tradition and progress, pastoral and industrial civilizations. In one particularly amusing scene, his reverie concerning the coming industrial society is interrupted violently when his agricultural sensitivities are wounded by a stupid American woman who clumsily walks through a field of standing hay. He may not for long, then, be a Marxist; but for the time being he is; and when he ceases to be, he no doubt will remain an industrialist. Chrissie, on the other hand, is to be prepared for the England that loves the old, that lives the traditional life of the shepherd and flock. Tietjens-England has sired both and will understand both; but there is no doubt that his sympathies will be with Chrissie, the child who, ironically, has for a mother a fine English girl who is also both a social radical and a pacifist. Even more ironically, Chrissie's birth has had to be achieved through *illegitimate* means—through, that is, a defiance of the world, which is at such sixes and sevens that only through illegitimacy can one achieve integrity.

Through *legitimate* capitalist-industrialism, then, the land is inherited by a person in whom there is conflict of the old pastoral tradition and the new proletarian-industrialist ideologies. The latter may win for a while. But the new synthesis is likely to be that achieved by an antithetical and *illegitimate* union, which is to produce Chrissie, the peaceful pastor, the lover of old books, who, for all his illegitimacy, may in fact prove to be the new legitimacy. Into his making have gone equal parts of the Left and Right; one was as essential as the other. Let who will have the coal lands and the industrial plants—for these, indeed, only *seem* to be England. Give Chrissie his living in Bemerton—he, with his Greek Testament and his

fundamental humanity—he will *be* England. Nor will his legitimate elder half-brother, Michael Mark, remain a stranger to him. Michael Mark is already wavering. He may someday desert his world of appearances for the world of realities, industrial acquisitiveness for pastoral humanity. The real is the human. Man is the synthesis, not goods, not goals. Man will suffer trials; he may die symbolically or actually; his fundamental value is the synthesis, the humanity, not the various partisanships or greeds to which he may be subject.

To partisans of the Left or Right this solution will be unsatisfactory, for they have always been drawn to the apparent differences which conceal fundamental humanity from view. To condemn or praise Ford Madox Ford as a conservative or as a man who moved in the direction of the Left would be equally beside the point. He moved in a more significant direction than either—toward a comprehension of human life in all its tragicomedy.

His fictional statement of this ambiguity is neither propagandistic nor didactic, whatever he himself may have said. Neither is it withdrawn from life; hence it is not "aesthetic" in the pejorative sense of that term. It is rather an able conjuction of fable and idea, symbol and concrete fact, allegory and event. It teaches, as literature somehow always does. It lacks both the preciosity of the self-conscious art-novel and the confident affirmations of those novelists who know all the answers. It embodies the tensions of its author's times, and it invites us to reflect upon them—for they are still with us. Ford's irony and humor draw us on with the sure charm of art to reflect upon the human problem. We are not likely much longer to ignore either his wit or his comprehension of mankind.

E. V. Walter   (essay date 1956)

SOURCE: "The Political Sense of Ford Madox Ford," in *The New Republic,* Vol. 134, No. 13, March 26, 1956, pp. 17-19.

[*Walter is an American author and educator. In the following essay, he disputes the critical opinion that a well-crafted novel cannot be a political novel, citing* Parade's End *as an example of both.*]

Ultimately, when critics write about Ford Madox Ford, they write about his technique, and since he is, if anything, a virtuoso of the well-made novel, it is appropriate that they insist on this side of his work. Still, in *Parade's End,* the Tietjens tetralogy (*Some Do Not . . .* ; *No More Parades*; *A Man Could Stand Up—*; *The Last Post*), he is also a political novelist.

This aspect is obscured by some of his admirers who make a fastidious effort to preserve the concept of the well-made novel from political defilement.

Facile conclusions have been drawn from this position, leading to a Manichaean view of the novel that conceives form and life as somehow antithetical and also implies a denigration of the concept of politics. The conception is not to be taken lightly, for, as Lionel Trilling has warned, "Unless we insist that politics is imagination and mind, we will learn that imagination and mind are politics, and of a kind that we will not like."

The well-made novel and the political novel are not mutually exclusive genres, as some would have us believe. The vitality of the Tietjens cycle as a political novel is achieved by its formal excellence, and the politics of the tetralogy is an aspect as essential to an understanding of Ford's authorship as is his craft.

Throughout the tetralogy, Ford's art breathes life into the ancient political truth that the state is the soul writ large and the self is the republic in microcosm. History, in the Tietjens cycle, plays a dual role, providing an emotional milieu that infuses the characters with motives for their dramatic movement and serving as a backdrop against which their lives are acted out. The terrible irony of world politics contrasts the goals of Empire with the sufferings of the men in the line, Imperial destiny with stupid official behavior, and strategic logic with tactical exigency. The lives of the characters explore for us the relation between inner and outer chaos and show how the pathology of the self is conditioned by "the public events of a decade."

Christopher Tietjens, Ford's hero and the incarnation of the aristocratic ideal, encounters the effete institutions of post-Edwardian England, and that world, sick unto death, tries to destroy him. Hating him because he is a symbol of the very ideal they have betrayed, his own people, the recreant ruling class, are his fiercest harrower. He survives their onslaught, endures the First World War, and escapes underground, hinting that in another day aristocracy will rise again. On the one hand, through the mind of Tietjens we perceive the aristocratic ideal from the inside; on the other, we have an allegory of the disintegration of the English governing class.

In the aristocratic imagination, there are four royal roads to the sublime life: the saintly, the wise, the heroic and the bucolic. Spiritual archetypes, these patterns are not necessarily aristocratic—the saint may be beggar as well as pope; the sage, poor or rich; the hero, worker or knight; the tiller of soil, peasant or squire—but they are perennial forms in which the aristocratic ideal appears. Since Tietjens represents, to some degree, all four, his destiny corresponds to the fate of the ideal. He is saintly, but is persecuted for his sanctity; he is sagacious, but the war almost destroys his mind; he is heroic, but his military career turns into a fiasco and he is all but drummed out of the service; he returns to the soil, yet not to find some creative power but only to flee the world and get underground.

As Irving Howe has pointed out, the 19th-Century political novel ruminated over the latent chaos in institutional life and the menacing subversion or destruction of order which lurked beneath the smooth surface, whereas the 20th-Century political novel accepts the destruction of the old order as a *fait accompli*. In one way, Ford stands between the two, watching English society as it comes apart.

In Ford's earlier book, *The Good Soldier,* the narrator had confided that behind the mask of appearances, below the surface of conventions, there are "broken, tumultuous, agonized and unromantic lives, periods punctuated by screams, by imbecilities, by deaths, by agonies." Later,

after his experience in the war, Ford was impelled to develop this vision as it is reflected in the collective life.

Collective disorder brings chaos to all forms of private life, including the sexual life. The pathology of Duchemin, the mad clergyman whose demon makes him hurl Latin obscenities; Sylvia, whose sex hunger demands violence; Edith Ethel, whose polite adulteries disintegrate into hysteria; and the rumors that almost overwhelm Christopher are part of the syndrome. Christopher and Mark, whose monogamy is grounded on principle, have an immunity. Christopher's own passion for Valentine, hinting at an image of *l'amour courtois,* is saved by its being an anachronism.

Ford had given the key to the problem of sexual chaos in *The Good Soldier.* There the narrator had observed:

> If everything is so nebulous about a matter so elementary as the morals of sex, what is there to guide us in the more subtle morality of all other personal contracts, associations, and activities? Or are we meant to act on impulse alone? It is all a darkness.

But if Christopher and Mark Tietjens stand for monogamy, the controlling irony again appears: not conventional but ideal monogamy. For Mark lives with his mistress whom he will not marry (until he is on his deathbed), whereas Christopher is married to a woman with whom he will not sleep and attached to another who is a mistress in idea only (until after Armistice Day). Monogamy must be based on principle, and principles are "like a map"— they let you know where you are. Especially in a world where there will be no more parades, no more hope, no more glory, no more respect.

Refusing to separate politics and morality, Tietjens pronounces heavy judgment on his class. It is proper, he reflects, that one's individual feelings be sacrificed to the necessities of a collective entity, but not if that entity is to be betrayed from above. The war convinces him that he must make a radical break with the world. In the army, he hopes to be out of it before the end of the war, for then, perhaps, he would be in time for the last train to the old feudal heaven. No longer is there a tidy universe—you'd think God would have arranged the war so Yorkshiremen could go to heaven with the other North Country fellows instead of with Cockneys and Portuguese. In the old days, you used to fight beside men from your own hamlet, led by the parson's son, but now the Feudal Spirit is broken and dying is a lonely affair.

The all but destructive effect of the war on the mind of Tietjens represents its effect on aristocracy and tradition itself. At one point, shell shock leaves him with a temporary memory loss, and he, who had once been an authority on almost everything and had despised books of reference, finds it necessary to read the entire Encyclopedia. His condition suggests Unamuno's formula: memory is to mind as tradition is to society. The dimension of time is highly significant for the Tietjens allegory, and Ford makes extensive use of the time-shift device to dramatize the interplay of time-memory-tradition.

The decline of the Tietjens family is the fate of the old governing class—the Good People who once ruled the nation and were responsible for its destiny. Their physical afflictions take on a larger meaning when one considers the ancient analogy between sickness in the body and injustice in the state. In the concluding book of the tetralogy, the abdication of the old ruling class is represented by the paralysis of Mark Tietjens. His immobility is the result of a stroke, but in his mind his silence is voluntary. Enraged by the behavior of his nation, he has vowed never to speak again. Thus, in the new world, aristocracy is impotent but secretly believes its condition self-imposed.

With the death of Mark, the passage of Groby to Christopher's papist son, the destruction of Groby Great Tree, and the escape of Christopher to the land near Bemerton parsonage, the ancient curse is lifted from the house of Tietjens and a new life begins for Christopher and Valentine. If a ruling class loses the capacity or the desire to rule, Tietjens had said, then "it should abdicate from its privileges and get underground." Frugality, temperance and industry regulate their lives as they live, without the convention of marriage, to remake "reality." Desiring to live hard, "even if it deprived them of the leisure in which to think high," and true to their anachronistic vision of the good life, they will be "jogging away to the end of time, leaving descendants to carry on the country without swank." Bemerton parsonage is the real England. Damn the Empire, it is England that matters, Tietjens had proclaimed, like a Cato denouncing orientalism, demanding a revival of the agrarian virtues and a return to the bucolic way of life.

The manner of his escape is a classical pattern of the aristocratic imagination. The pastoral idyll itself is protean and expressed by minds as diverse as Lao Tse, Theocritus, Rousseau, Jefferson and Tolstoy, but in its aristocratic form it is sometimes a reaction against chivalry that still retains the basic structure of the chivalric ideal. It is insufficient to tag this kind of agrarianism "romantic," for the chivalric romanticism of restraint is entirely different from its involution, the modern romanticism of impulse.

Even in times when the aristocratic view of life is the dominant image, the difference between ideal and practice cannot be concealed. Reality gives the lie to the illusions and pretensions of the chivalric view of society, and individual character determines the response to the shock of contradiction. Mockery is one way: in feudal times, the coarse satire of *les fabliaux* and the more polished raillery of a blasé court. Another way is the escape to innocence: to flee the hypocritical preciosity of aristocratic life, one could go to the soil and take refuge in uncorrupted nature. In the modern world, this escape is the way chosen by Tietjens. However, he must flee not only his own decadent circle, but the whole dying world.

In his flight, he corresponds to the figure of the contrite noble, not aware of any personal guilt but of the *culpa* of his class. In many ways he is like the Slavophil *narodnik,* sensitive to social anxiety and apocalyptic dread, who proclaims that when the ruling class isolates itself and a gulf appears between it and the people, then society totters on the brink of the abyss. Although they are worlds apart in their traditions, there are nonetheless certain affinities be-

tween the impulse of Tietjens to return to the land and the desire of Count Tolstoy to live as a simple muzhik.

Feudalism survives underground with Tietjens, but in the world it is finished. After Armistice Day, the places of men are taken by strangers, their settlements occupied by "a vindictive and savage tribe." Since the moribund governing class had lost control of the state, a transfer of power was inevitable. Marie Léonie reads in the papers of "the deeds of assassins, highway robbers, of the subversive and the ignorant who everywhere seized the reins of power." Also, in the place of true nobility there are unscrupulous nouveaux. The world, without manners, would be a tiring place run by tiring people.

The feudal mysteries of power are reduced by the official secrets of the bureaucracy. To Christopher's Tory mind, the old ruling class is responsible for the change. The indiscretions of the ruling class appear to him equivalent to scenes made before the servants. It follows that when the lower classes grow accustomed to such scenes, aristocracy loses its aura of sanctity and the arcanum of power is invaded. The new masters, it is implied, without Tory noblesse, would have little regard for the real welfare of the lower classes.

The lower classes are shadowy figures, and their indistinctness may be attributed as much to Ford as to the mind of Tietjens. Ford lacked the vision of Henry James, whose feeling for aristocracy did not obscure his penetration of souls, regardless of class. In his admiration of James, he freely admitted that although he had lived among agricultural workers, his knowledge of them did not measure up to that of the Old Man. Since he lacked the latter's perception of the emotional life of the poor, his lower classes remain lay figures.

They are all villeins: either faithful servants or "dirty . . . and with the mystified eyes of the subject races." In the army, faced with the breakdown of feudal categories, Tietjens had struggled with his image of the Other Ranks, worrying over the men in his command, reassuring himself that they were not just populations but "each man with a backbone, knees, breeches, a rifle, a home, passions, fornications, drunks, pals, some scheme of the universe, corns, inherited diseases, a greengrocer's business, a milk walk, a paper stall, brats, a slut of a wife." But in spite of his struggle to see them as real, they wear the faces of batmen and servants—underground figures and completely mysterious.

Some critics suggest that Tietjens represents a defender of the lower classes. On the contrary, he is merely a defender of their limits. It is true that noblesse breeds a tender regard for the tiller of soil, the shepherd, and the poor merchant, but only as long as their behavior conforms to the categories set up in the feudal mind. Behavior that exceeds these limits is interpreted as presumption, and, through it, villein becomes barbarian. In this mode of thought, the masses represent chaos—always a potential menace. The restraint of feudal conventions, it is assumed, gives them humanity.

The aristocratic mind withdraws from the terror of a world of changing forms; however, on an island of its own it can survive. In self-imposed exile, surrounded by faithful retainers (the "rocks" on which the "lighthouse" is built), Christopher and Valentine live their bucolic idyll, insulated from the world in ruins.

The war, like the industrial fog that had long hung over the countryside, had been only a symptom of a deadlier disease, and the perfidious nation merely a magnification of the untrue self. The premise of *Parade's End* is the same as that of *The Good Soldier*—that conventions are erected as restraints upon impulse—but it concludes that if the ruling class, the architect of morals, is itself not restrained, then it dies in the wreckage, its own house about its ears.

Yet, hidden in Yorkshire under the debris, Tietjens and Valentine are a new Adam and Eve, and Tietjens discloses his intransigent conviction that after a long, dark night of the collective soul, aristocracy (meaning true nobility, which is based on virtue) may be reborn. It is said that during the Deluge it was a Yorkshireman who stood on Mount Ararat with water up to his chin and shouted to Noah: It's bound to clear up!

Kenneth Young   (essay date 1956)

SOURCE: "The Tietjens Tetralogy," in *Ford Madox Ford*, Longmans, Green & Co., 1956, pp. 28-35.

[*Young is an English author and editor whose works include book-length studies of D. H. Lawrence and Ford Madox Ford. In the following excerpt, he focuses attention on the characters of* Parade's End *and their function in what he considers to be Ford's melancholy treatment of society in transition.*]

To pass from [Ford's novel] *The Good Soldier* to [his] *Parade's End* is to emerge from a room heavy with discharged passion into a city street full of vivid personalities. Up they pop like freshly painted jack-in-the-boxes: 'Breakfast' Duchemin, so called from his habit of giving lavish morning parties, the rich, cultivated parson who breaks without warning into loathsome Latin obscenities . . . '09 Morgan, the Welsh private in the trenches whose wife has run off with a pugilist . . . The sly, snobbish Macmaster rising suavely in the civil service and to a wartime knighthood for literary services . . . The Old Squire of Groby, master of vast acres, whose gardener lays out his filled pipes in the bushes every morning, for he is not allowed to smoke in the house . . . Lord Portscatho, the banker, whose world crumbles when one of his officials uses his position to injure an enemy . . . Miss Wanostrocht, the headmistress, 'her little fingers hooked together, the hands back to back: a demoded gesture . . . Girton of 1897'.

These minor characters are not accidentally so varied. In *Parade's End* it was Ford's aim to 'register my own time in terms of my own time'. His registrations of the period 1910 to 1920 are as accurate as are his backgrounds— country-house weekends, a golf course invaded by suffragettes, bachelor chambers in London, a trench in France and a hotel in the G.H.Q. area, and Groby estate in north Yorkshire. We pass briefly also inside Whitehall offices, a small cottage where a learned woman sits pounding out journalism for a livelihood, a great girls' school.

Amid these middle-class scenes ambles the central character of the four novels—Christopher Tietjens, a lumbering 'meal-sack' sort of man, his fair hair patched with grey, clad usually in too bulky tweeds, exchanged for some of the time for khaki uniform. He is the younger son of the squire of Groby, a brilliant mathematician, a good Latinist, of whom it is said that he passes dull train journeys in tabulating from memory the errors in the latest edition of the *Encyclopaedia Britannica*. He has a certain intellectual arrogance, an immense kindliness, even sentimentality, and he is a Tory—but a Tory whose principles were last heard of in the eighteenth century, that is to say, at a time when the Tory party was supported by the poor, the landowners and the 'clerks', in Julien Benda's sense of schoolmasters, parsons, and journalists.

Christopher has married Sylvia, a pale Society beauty and a hard, selfish and disloyal woman. He married her because, in his rather bumbling, high-minded way he believes he compromised her by chance kisses on a train in which they were returning from a weekend house party. Sylvia, of course, would never have looked at a younger son had she not been in a panic, believing she had become pregnant in one of her *affaires*. By chance Christopher learns of this. A child is born but, whether it is his own or not, he cherishes it. Sylvia leaves him for her lover; tires of the latter; confesses to her mother's friend, the Roman Catholic priest Father Consett, who has an important influence on Sylvia. She wishes to return to Christopher, and he, though having visions of 'certain Hell', agrees. And for all these things she hates him—for, as she tells a friend, it is 'his lordly full-dress consideration that drives me mad . . . He's the soul of truth like a stiff Dutch-doll . . . I tell you he's so formal he can't do without all the conventions there are, and so truthful he can't use half of them.'

She sets out to ruin him, by spreading stories of his living on her money, keeping mistresses and so on. This results in his being cut' in society and in various unhappinesses which he bears without saying a word in his own defence. His father, the old squire, 'accidentally' shoots himself when he hears that Christopher has seduced Valentine Wannop, the daughter of his great friend, Mrs. Wannop, the bluestocking. The seduction was one of Sylvia's rumours; but Christopher has in fact, in his slow way, fallen in love with Valentine, this clean-run girl, the best Latinist in England, athletic, a suffragette and something of a pacifist. The attraction is mutual; both recognize, however, that nothing can be done: Christopher has his duty to Sylvia; Sylvia, being a Catholic, will in any case never divorce him.

This insoluble situation haunts Christopher through three of the novels; it haunts him in France where he serves during the war, and so does Sylvia, still pursuing him with her malignity; and through her the disfavour of General Lord Campion, his godfather, also descends upon him, making his army life more miserable than it is of necessity.

The middle two novels—*No More Parades* and *A Man Could Stand Up*—provide one of the most vivid, yet calm, pictures of the First World War in France, from trenches to headquarters. There is nothing harrowing; the mud and blood, the muddle and heroism, is real enough, but it is

Ford, circa 1915, when he enlisted in the British Army.

lifted to that plane where the mind reacts with breathless absorption and with the pity that classical tragedy evokes. 'The poetry', as Wilfrid Owen, the true poet of that war, wrote, 'is in the pity . . . ' Ford, like Flaubert, looks at his characters from above; yet as Flaubert is half in love with his Emma Bovary though perceiving all her foolishness, so is Ford with his Christopher, his '09 Morgan, his little blinded lieutenant Aranjuez.

But the war changes Christopher. He returns to London to find that Sylvia has dismantled his flat and gone to Groby. In the flat he meets Valentine, but, before they can speak, former fellow officers arrive determined to celebrate the armistice with Christopher. Amid the laughter and noise Christopher realizes: 'That girl with the refined face, the hair cut longish, but revealing its inner refinement . . . That girl longed for him as he for her! The longing had refined her face . . . This then was the day! The war had made a man of him! It had coarsened and hardened him. There was no other way to look at it. It had made him reach a point where he would no longer stand unbearable things . . . What he wanted he was prepared to take. What he had been before, God alone knew. A Younger Son? A Perpetual Second-in-Command? Who knew? But today the world was changed. Feudalism was finished; its last vestiges were gone. It held no place for

him. He was going—he was damn well going!—to make a place in it for . . . A man could stand up on a hill, so he and she could surely get into some hole together!'

The room is furnished only with a camp bed. Valentine sees it as her nuptial couch: why then are those three officers, glasses in hand, jigging up and down on it? Then comes one of the most moving endings in all fiction:

> They were all yelling.
>
> 'Good old Tietjens! Good old Fat Man! Pre-war Hooch! He'd be the one to get it.' No one like Fat Man Tietjens! He lounged at the door; easy; benevolent. In uniform now. That was better. An officer, yelling like an enraged redskin dealt him an immense blow behind the shoulder blades. He staggered, smiling, into the centre of the room. An officer gently pushed her into the centre of the room. She was against him. Khaki encircled them. They began to yell and to prance, joining hands. Others waved the bottles and smashed underfoot the glasses. Gipsies break glasses at their weddings. The bed was against the wall. She did not like the bed to be against the wall. It had been brushed by . . .
>
> They were going round them; yelling in unison:
>
> 'Over here! Pom Pom Over here! Pom Pom!
>
> That's the word that's the word; Over here . . .'
>
> At least they weren't over there! They were prancing. The whole world round them was yelling and prancing round. They were the centre of unending roaring circles. The man with the eyeglass had stuck a half-crown in the other eye. He was well-meaning. A brother. She had a brother with the V.C. All in the family.
>
> Tietjens was stretching out his two hands from the waist. It was incomprehensible. His right hand was behind her back, his left in her right hand. She was frightened. She was amazed. Did you ever!
>
> He was swaying slowly. The elephant. They were dancing. Aranjuez was hanging on to the tall woman like a kid on a telegraph pole. The officer who had said he had picked up a little bit of fluff . . . well, he had! He had run out and fetched it. It wore white cotton gloves and a flowered hat. It said: 'Ow! Now! . . .' There was a fellow with a most beautiful voice. He led: better than a gramophone. Better . . .
>
> *Les petites marionettes, font! font! font! . . .*
>
> On an elephant. A dear, meal-sack elephant. She was setting out on . . .

One interesting aspect of *Parade's End* has been pointed out by Mr. Graham Greene: the four novels are, he writes, 'almost the only adult novels dealing with the sexual life that have been written in English'. There is nothing, in the relations of Sylvia and Christopher, Valentine and Christopher, Edith Ethel and Macmaster, Mark and Marie Leonie, of the mystical heights nor the crude depths of Lawrence; yet these thoughts of Christopher as he waits

> **Parade's End** is a moving study of human beings and a beautiful work of art; but through it, if we listen carefully, we shall catch a note of lament, of elegy. The bell tolls for the passing of old ways of living and thinking.
>
> —*Kenneth Young*

for the war to end are more like the sexual life as most men know it than Lawrence would ever admit, or perhaps could ever conceive:

> If they could go home he would be sitting talking to her for whole afternoons. That was what a young woman was for. You seduced a young woman in order to be able to finish your talks with her. You could not do that without living with her. You could not live with her without seducing her; but that was the by-product. The point is that you can't otherwise talk. You can't finish talks at street corners; in museums; even in drawing rooms. You mayn't be in the mood when she is in the mood—for the intimate conversation that means the final communion of your souls. You have to wait together—for a week, for a year, for a lifetime, before the final intimate conversation may be attained . . . and exhausted. So that . . .
>
> That in effect was love.

Mark Tietjens, Christopher's elder brother and heir to Groby, who has reached high position in the civil service, is the central character of the last of the four novels, **Last Post,** but until the final page he does not speak. For when the armistice drew near he as head of the Ministry of War Transport, is told that the Allies do not intend to pursue the Germans into their own country. To him this is so evidently a betrayal of France—indeed of all those who have fought—that he determines never to speak again. The doctors call it a stroke. So he lies in a thatched hut without walls in Groby grounds: the master of Groby, who never wished for the country life, has returned—paralysed and speechless. He wishes to give Christopher money, for Christopher to take over the estate. Christopher, being a stubborn Yorkshireman, refuses; he goes into business with a Mr. Schatzweiler, selling antique English furniture to the Americans. But when Sylvia, whose son will be the heir to Groby, tries to let the house furnished to some *nouveaux riches,* and has the great tree cut down, Christopher and Valentine go to live there. The son has been brought up by Sylvia and 'was by now a full fledged Papist, pickled and oiled and wafered and all'.

In the end, while Valentine is pregnant, Sylvia arrives—and relents. With the words of her son 'Be sporting, mother!' in her ears, she tells Valentine: 'They can all, soon, call you Mrs. Tietjens. Before God I came to drive out those people' (the *nouveaux riches* who came to view the property) . . . But I wanted to see how it was you kept

him . . . ' There is the old flash as she says: 'Damn it, I'm playing, pimp to Tietjens of Groby—leaving my husband to you!' But the influence of Father Consett is too strong; she will get her marriage dissolved by Rome.

So there is some light in the darkness, and as Mark dies he mutters to Valentine the old story about the Yorkshireman on Mount Ararat, his chin scarcely above the waters, who remarked to Noah that it was bound to clear up; and he adds: ' "Never let thou thy child weep for thy sharp tongue to thy good man . . . A good man! Groby great tree is down . . . " He said: "Hold my hand." '

Parade's End is a moving study of human beings and a beautiful work of art; but through it, if we listen carefully, we shall catch a note of lament, of elegy. The bell tolls for the passing of old ways of living and thinking. Christopher, the most obstinately Conservative and deeply virtuous of men, is forced to accept the new sexual morality and to install an unmarried woman as his and Groby's mistress. It was all very well to have mistresses hidden away and from the proper class: 'In their sardonic way the tenants appreciated that: it was in the tradition and all over the county they did it themselves. But not a lady: the daughter of your father's best friend! They wanted Quality women to *be* Quality.' Again, it was right for Mark to have his mistress; but not to marry her; yet marry Marie Leonie he does.

The *nouveaux riches,* the traditionless, are battering at the gates. Groby Great Tree is down—the tree that for centuries has been regarded by the country folk as having magical properties, and whose roots reach deep into ancestral consciences. 'A Papist at Groby and Groby Great Tree down . . . The curse was perhaps off the family!' Mark thinks. In some old families, whose property came to them as a result of Henry VIII's dispossession of the monasteries, a sense of guilt lingered through the generations. Groby had originally been monastic land; perhaps, now that a Papist would inherit, the crime would be expiated. It was an idea that had haunted Ford all his life: it was, it will be recalled, for the restoration of these properties that Katharine Howard had striven in **Fifth Queen Crowned.**

So there is interwoven in this strange and vivid story something of what Jung might call 'the collective unconscious' of the English nation. But the strangeness does not end with the last page of **Last Post.** Christopher, as we know, was based on a real person, Arthur Marwood, and long after the novels appeared Ford said that he felt him to be still alive:

> With him I set out on several enterprises—one of them being a considerable periodical publication of a Tory kind—and for many years I was accustomed, as it were, to 'set' my mind by his comments on public or other affairs. He was, as I have elsewhere said, the English Tory—the last English Tory, omniscient, slightly contemptuous and sentimental in his human contacts . . . And still I have only to say: 'Tell us what he would here have done!' and at once he is there. So you see I cannot tell you the end of Tietjens, for he will end only when I am beyond pens and paper . . . He will go jogging

along with ups and downs and plenty of worries and some satisfaction, the Tory Englishman, running his head perhaps against fewer walls, perhaps against more, until I myself cease from these pursuits.

But Mark was also based on a real person—Arthur's elder brother, Sir William Marwood, whose estate was called Busby and, like the fictional Groby, it lay on the Cleveland hills in north Yorkshire. *Last Post* was published in 1928: Sir William, the hale and hearty squire, did not read it, for Ford was held in somewhat bad repute in that house on account of the scandal over Violet Hunt and because he had had a difference of opinion with Arthur shortly before the latter's death during the war.

In 1934, Sir William Marwood was struck down with cancer of the throat. 'He lay', a member of his family wrote to me recently, 'without speaking for weeks unless he was desperate. The Great Tree at Busby is really a marvellous Spanish chestnut which is still there, but a huge cedar began to split the flags round the walls and had to be cut down when Sir William was ill. He died a few days later from grief about this, and at the end he said: "Hold my hand." '

Neil D. Isaacs   (essay date 1959)

SOURCE: "Ford Madox Ford and the Tietjens Fulfillment," in *The Lock Haven Review,* No. 1, 1959, pp. 58-65.

[*Issacs in an American author and educator. In the following essay, he contrasts* Parade's End *with* The Good Soldier, *evaluating the two works based on Ford's own criteria as a literary critic.*]

In the dedicatory letter to an American edition of *The Good Soldier* (1915), Ford Madox Ford says that he put into that novel everything he knew of the technical art of writing. He also says that he expects to be considered *homo unius libri* and that *The Good Soldier* is the one book. Elsewhere he claims that *The Last Post* (1928) was no more than an afterthought to the first three Tietjens books, *Some Do Not* (1924), *No More Parades* (1925), and *A Man Could Stand Up* (1926). These statements are mentioned first in order to get them out of the way. They are all equally untrue. The novels themselves refute them. Moreover, the testimony of all who knew Ford is that anything he might say at any time could be untrue. The truth is that *Parade's End* must be considered as a single aesthetic entity and that it is patently and demonstrably superior in many ways to the earlier, slighter work.

Two basic ideas went into everything Ford wrote, one aesthetic and one moral. The aesthetic idea is twofold, consisting of the importance of literature—"The only activity that has always been of extreme importance to the world is imaginative literature. It is of supreme importance because it is the only means by which humanity can express at once emotions and ideas . . . nothing that is not an art is of any lasting importance at all, the meanest novel being humanly more valuable than the most pompous of factual works" [in Ford's *Return to Yesterday,* 1932]; and the importance of the word, the *mot juste*—" . . . the exact use of words seems to me to be the most important thing in the world. We are, in the end, governed so much more by words than by deeds" [in Ford's *Between St. Dennis and St. George,* 1915].

The moral idea is that the major concern of life is moral, that the most important thing an individual does is to decide what he should do. This becomes the large concern of his novels. He inherited this theme, of course, from Henry James, whom he called *"cher maître."* But it was basic to Ford's technique of "impressionism" that no *specific* moral be drawn and that the author must not intrude into the work.

In evaluating the relative merits of Ford's works, then, it will not help to look for the philosophy of life which is revealed. Nor will it be useful to compare mood and tone, for his attitude toward his subjects was always sympathetic and serious, as, rightly or wrongly, he never failed to consider them important; and toward his readers he was at once apologetic and patronizing, as the simultaneous reaction to and product of the precocious dilettantism of his early career. His growth as a serious novelist from *The Good Soldier* to *Parade's End* can be seen, however, in the subject matter of the novels and the technical means of treating these matters.

Ford once said that *The Good Soldier* was the first of his works which was not a *tour de force.* Quite the contrary, it is very consciously, almost sickeningly, a *tour de force.* How else describe a novel whose author adopts as *persona,* narrator, and one of four principal actors, a character so far removed from himself or his experience as to be ridiculous? John Dowell is an independently wealthy American, without any knowledge of English society, literature, or any of the arts, without sensitivity in human relationships, and even without the ability to express himself interestingly. The only point of comparison between him and Ford is the naive sentimentalism which they share. The reader is made constantly aware of the great disparity between author and *persona* by the obvious artificiality involved. The repeated phrases, "Of course, I wouldn't know about . . . " and "This . . . was very new to me," serve to accentuate the painful presence of an author who intends complete absence and anonymity. Occasional fine turns of phrase, such as "cosmopolitan harpy," which are typical of Ford Madox Ford or Sylvia or Christopher Tietjens, are revealingly jarring when they come from John Dowell.

At first glance, the circumstances of the plot seem worthy of a Henry James treatment. Two couples are constant companions for the better part of ten years. The American's wife is the mistress of the Englishman with the complete knowledge of his wife and the equally complete absence of suspicion on the part of the American. In Ford's treatment, however, the effect is closer to that of a bad fourteenth-century French *fabliau,* with the dupers punished by death and the duped living to tell "the saddest story I ever heard." True to the spirit of the *fabliaux,* however, the dupers have had their fun, while the duped have earned their horns by their own ignorance. The presentation of the incidents of the plot seems like an elaborate exercise in the use of the time-shift device. This succeeds artfully in creating a degree of suspense which is, however, overshadowed by the improbability of the complication and resolution and the dramatic ineffectiveness of the entire plot.

Ford always recognized the fact, as did James, that character is the most important intrinsic element of a novel. It is strange, then, that he employed a remarkably unsuccessful method of characterization in *The Good Soldier.* Edward and Leonora Ashburnham and Florence Dowell are seen through the insensitive, indiscriminate eye of the narrator, and emerge as little more than two-dimensional caricatures, as does John Dowell himself. Leonora is the best of a poor lot, anticipating Sylvia Tietjens in her sex-viciousness and Catholicism, and suggesting Kate Croy in her coarse gentility. Edward is, perhaps, an embryonic Tietjens without honor, that is, without Christopher's most important trait.

Ford, then, has utterly failed in his twofold intention. A work of art has not been created in *The Good Soldier,* nor is the effect on the reader that of experiencing the decisions of people as to what they should do under their circumstances. These people, their circumstances, and their decisions are gauche and blatant in their unreality.

How Ford attained his amazing artistic maturity in the decade between *The Good Soldier* and *Parade's End* can never adequately be explained. His war experience certainly provided him with richer material and greater insight into human relationships and psychological operations. In addition, he must have been guided by some aesthetic intuition in combining his knowledge of the technical aspects of his art and his comprehension of people and the workings of their minds into the fine novel that the Tietjens saga is.

The fourth part, *The Last Post* (to dispose first of the one major fault of the book), is unsatisfactory in its partial reversion to the method of *The Good Soldier.* The events which make up the action of the novel are here viewed through the consciousness of a handful of minor characters, and the "centres," to use Jamesian terminology. Christopher, Sylvia, and Valentine, are seen only obliquely. Thus, much extraneous matter is brought in, such as Michael's multiple Freudian involvements (surprisingly overlooked in Robie Macauley's introduction), and such central matters as the fulfillment of the major characters are imaged forth from relatively dim reflectors.

The time-shift, which had been laboriously practiced in *The Good Soldier,* is used to such effect here that realistic concern with chronological time is obviated, and the dramatic use of time, à la Proust, appears natural and necessary. In addition, Ford uses here, with equal accomplishment, those "accoutrements and attributes of a work of art in all its glory," which he so admired in Flaubert— *progression d'effet, charpente, façade, cadences, mots justes.*

What is even more important to the success of *Parade's End* is the addition of what he called the chief factor in James' late work—"more and more detail, so that the exact illusions and the exact facts of life may appear." Thus, upon entering a room, the reader is not given a jour-

nalistic report of the entire room as in Dickens, but the room is seen in the infinite detail with which the particular observer would see it. In Christopher's eye, an old piece of furniture is observed, appreciated, categorized; in Sylvia's, the dust on the brandy decanter is noted and sardonically commented on; in Valentine's, a poor edition of Catullus is immediately and violently noticed on the bookshelf. Scenes, then, are vividly portrayed, not materially objective scenes, but scenes of the sensibilities and the psychologies of the observers.

These devices, along with much skillful use of interior monologues, produce a verisimilitude so complete that the probability of the work cannot be called in question, and the arrangement of the materials has a satisfying dramatic effect, with the exception of the resolution in *The Last Post.*

The development of character throughout *Parade's End* is the greatest accomplishment of the book. Christopher Tietjens is the most remarkable figure in English or American literature of the twentieth century. Christopher is observed by and revealed through the consciousness of people who love him, hate him, admire him, misunderstand him, sometimes all at once. His own consciousness accentuates the complexity of his character. He is the "soul of honor," but he sets up housekeeping with Valentine Wannop, who is to have his child. He is incapable of hurting a living being, yet is unconscionably cruel to his wife. He is a mathematical genius, but he loses much of his prodigious memory through his experiences at the front. He is, in short, unbelievable. Yet he becomes as real and warm as a father or an admired uncle. One knows what he has done and why, what he should do and must, what he can do and will. The reader's concerns become the novelist's concerns, which are Christopher's moral dilemmas. Moreover, the solution of the character, the author, and the reader, is one and the same. And the twofold intention of the writer is almost absolutely fulfilled.

In addition to being a novelist, Ford achieved some degree of notoriety, if not success, as a propagandist, an editor, an art critic, a writer of fairy stories, a poet and a literary critic. Literature was the great love of his life, and he devoted a large part of his tremendous energy to criticism. It would be interesting and fitting to examine, in conclusion, how *The Good Soldier* and *Parade's End* might fare under the scrutiny of Ford's own critical theory and under the terms of his own criteria.

In his system, an acceptance of certain classical and Aristotelian doctrines is evidenced side by side with strong idealistic tendencies. The attempt at combining these incongruous elements results in a hotchpotch which breaks down at every turn. In trying to be empirical, he gives himself away by the use of such terminology as "attuned," "pixy-like," "reöxygenation of the blood," and "aura in the air." And, in trying to be definitive, he often uses vague or loaded words such as "life," "lived," "pure," and "purely." He has pretensions to vast learning, but tries to be unlearned in his presentation. He is scientifically unscientific, dualistically empirical, and historically antihistorical. Nor do the antitheses end there. He proclaims himself a classicist and a realist, but in practice is a romanticist and an impressionist. Only his sentimentalism is acknowledged. His methods do not agree with his preconceived notions, and, since he fails to recognize the insurmountable difficulties in all these contradictions, his system has to be a failure. He is a dualist who calls Aristotle the most brilliant of philosophers and an idealist who says that Plato was the enemy of all the arts. Ford presents the strange phenomenon of a man who tries to combine opposites which he himself says are impossible of uniting—quaint observation and tranquil generalizings.

When not concerned with combining his idealism with Aristotelian classification, however, Ford achieves some degree of consistency by the rigorous application of certain criteria which he sets up for a good or great work.

1. The work must be a work of probability, or what Ford calls common sense.

2. The great work must have a dominating quality of omniscience.

3. A work of art must use stylistic devices in order to portray life, give verisimilitude, and take the reader out of himself.

4. A work cannot be good without a good style, founded on the vernacular, as near as possible to the common speech of the day without having a shocking, comic, or gross effect.

5. No moral should be drawn, nor should the author intrude into the work. This, the absence of the author, is what Ford calls "impressionism" and, in conjunction with criterion three, is the most important standard for the novel.

Ford's ideals of probability are the works of Turgenev and Jane Austen. That *Parade's End* stands up quite favorably and that *The Good Soldier* fails miserably under this test has already been shown.

By omniscience, Ford does not mean the technical term referring to the Thackerayan point of view. He means the quality, without regard to point of view, which a novel by James, or even by Conrad, has. The reader senses the author's complete and intimate knowledge of, and the overall rightness of, the created world of the novel. Once again, *Parade's End* is quite successful where *The Good Soldier* fails.

I have already spoken of Ford's successful use of stylistic devices in *Parade's End.* One has only to experience the complete lack of verisimilitude in *The Good Soldier* with all its devices to wonder whether they are indeed concomitants or if verisimilitude may be achieved in spite of artificialities. Nevertheless, the superiority of the later novel is apparent here, too.

On the question of style, it would appear that *The Good Soldier* is closer to Ford's criterion. The language is often common, while that of *Parade's End* is often unusual. The language, then, corresponds roughly to the characters, who in *The Good Soldier* are common types and in *Parade's End* are rare individuals. It is not the style of *Parade's End* which should be criticized here, but the criterion which sets up this Wordsworthian standard. The lan-

guage of *The Good Soldier* is flat, dull, and uninteresting, while that of *Parade's End* is alive and believable in its frequent novelty and infinite variety.

Neither novel draws a moral or seeks to generalize from particulars, although individual moral concerns are central to both. Author-intrusion is another matter, however. The disparity between Ford and Dowell, his *persona* in *The Good Soldier,* creates an unconscious intrusion not only of the author but also of the artificiality of his technique. Even fully accepting the narrator and the devices, the reader would still find irritating and intrusive his many digressions outside the area of the plot, which, after all, only serve to put in bold relief the obvious *tour de force.* The technique ought to be unobtrusive, as in *Parade's End,* and there Ford achieves his greatest success in keeping himself out of a book. There is only the barest suggestion of intrusion in the observations of Mark Tietjens in *The Last Post.*

This method of cross-comparison, however valid or invalid it may be, has served the function of a check to reconfirm the validity of judgments previously arrived at. But any consistent critical approach to these two novels must find as great a distance between them as there is between Christopher Tietjens, the powerful embodiment of Ford's humanistic and Christian ideals, and either Ashburnham or Dowell, who represent all that Ford came to mistrust and detest. The distance—surely it is a gap of quality—may be measured by the insensitive and weak souls at one pole and the "soul of honor" at the other.

Ambrose Gordon, Jr.   (essay date 1962)

SOURCE: "A Diamond of Pattern: The War of F. Madox Ford," in *The Sewanee Review,* Vol. LXX, No. 3, Summer, 1962, pp. 464-83.

[*Gordon was an American author and educator. In the following essay, he offers a structural and thematic overview of* No More Parades, *the second novel of the Tietjens tetralogy.*]

How we find any writer is so often a matter of where we first came in—of how we first encountered him, with what expectations and hopes. In the case of Ford Madox Ford there are over sixty wrong places for a first encounter and there is perhaps only one right one, since, as Ford knew, first impressions stick. The beginning reader should probably not begin with "This is the saddest story I have ever heard." Nor even with "The two young men—they were of the English public official class—sat in the perfectly appointed railway carriage." There is a better spot than either of these—another window that opens onto more of the garden.

Here as elsewhere, chance has something to be said for it as a guide. It was perhaps actually a slight advantage back when the novels that make up *Parade's End* were as yet uncollected, when *The Good Soldier* was still out of print—indeed when almost all Ford's books were out of print. One then read what came his way, hit or miss, and with a minimum of prejudice. The official opening of *Parade's End,* the first scene of *Some Do Not,* lies suspiciously close to cliché: the two unnamed gentlemen who are found sitting in the elegant railway "carriage" just pulling out of the station. Its Edwardian prose is right but not arresting. And, in the collected reissue, the thickness of the volume lying in wait (836 pages) may give the reader pause. Besides, he has probably just finished considering Robie Macauley's introduction, which announces that this novel's subject is "the last Tory," and he may have decided that he is not much interested in Tories, first or last. But if the reader was so fortunate as to come to Ford deviously, by way of chance references to "Hueffer," picking up *It Was the Nightingale* overseas and later forgetting most of it except for a strange anecdote about a dung beetle and a Corsican bandit, and another about a lone man making a stew, to be followed considerably later by Ford's little book on the English novel with its brave defiance and the occasional howlers (Ford talks about the personal friendship between Caxton and Chaucer), and if he came finally upon *No More Parades* simply because the title was attractive and with no knowledge of its subject or its relation to the other novels in the tetralogy—never having heard of Tietjens—then its opening page produces for him the true shock of recognition as it places him in a familiar, stiff, square, resonant, and (oddly) *brown* world. *No More Parades* opens with the words:

> When you came in the space was desultory, rectangular, warm after the drip of the winter night, and transfused with a brown-orange dust that was light. It was shaped like the house a child draws.

The scene is a hut in a replacement depot in France; the time is World War I. Outside there is an air raid going on. The brown light comes from "a bucket pierced with holes, filled with incandescent coke"; there is a gleam of brass in the background, two officers; two men squat by the brazier ("as if hierarchically smaller"); at one end of the hut two noncommissioned officers droop over tables "in attitudes of extreme indifference." The only sound is the murmur of the two men by the glowing bucket—they had been miners—talking "in a low sing-song of dialect, hardly audible" and the dripping from the eaves of the hut. But the brown light soon is irradiated by brighter colors.

> An immense tea-tray, august, its voice filling the black circle of the horizon, thundered to the ground. Numerous pieces of sheet-iron said, "Pack. Pack. Pack." In a minute the clay floor of the hut shook, the drums of ears were pressed inwards, solid noise showered about the universe, enormous echoes pushed these men—to the right, to the left, or down towards the tables, and crackling like that of flames among vast underwood became the settled condition of the night. Catching the light from the brazier as the head leaned over, the lips of one of the two men on the floor were incredibly red and full and went on talking and talking.

We catch the true Fordian note from the start. The prose is the quietest and suavest imaginable; to render noise the writer need not become noisy. Ford does not shout at us; rather, he is asking us to *contemplate* noise—battle noise. The tone is composed and the prose is composed; the noise is orchestrated for us. Two conversations are counter-

pointed: the miner and his comrade who went on talking; the immense tea-tray with the august voice, to which the numerous pieces of sheet iron replied, "Pack. Pack. Pack." The note of insanity and horror is all in one detail, the lips that were "incredibly red and full and went on talking and talking." Ford once said that the tone he sought in his prose was that of one English gentleman whispering into the ear of another English gentleman. The miners here, to be sure, are not gentlemen, quiet though they may be. And of H. M. officers one is crazy and is soon roaring:

> He began to talk, faster than ever, about a circle. When its circumference came whole by the disintegration of the atom the world would come to an end.

Here we are given a glimpse of violence in a matrix of quietness, of intimacy being violated by more than sound. *No More Parades* opens brownly upon a world in which gentlemen, alas, will no longer whisper.

The four Tietjens novels—*Some Do Not, No More Parades, A Man Could Stand Up, Last Post*—were written and published between the years 1924 and 1927 but were not brought together as a single book until a quarter of a century later. The collective title is Ford's (though there is some doubt as to whether he wished *Last Post* to be included). At the level of plot, *Parade's End* is the story of the relations between three principal characters: Christopher Tietjens, a mathematical genius and staunch Yorkshire squire, his estranged wife, Sylvia, and Valentine Wannop, a young suffragette he has come to love. In addition to these, there is Tietjens' godfather, who is a general under whom he will later serve (Campion), a mad Pre-Raphaelite Anglican clergyman famous for his breakfasts (Duchemin), an Irish priest (Father Consett), Sylvia's mother, Tietjens' brother Mark, and some other memorable lesser characters. Before their marriage Tietjens had seduced his future wife on a train; later when the child was born he learned from her that she did not even know whether he was its father. The husband and wife have become increasingly estranged. The first novel of the series, *Some Do Not,* introduces us to these characters a year or more before the outbreak of World War I, and shows them later at war, Tietjens being home on sick leave. In the second book, *No More Parades,* Tietjens is—as we have seen—back in France serving in a giant replacement depot. Into this already chaotic scene his erring wife, Sylvia, suddenly erupts, creating added embarrassments and confusion. The later volumes take Tietjens to the front (where Sylvia cannot get to him) and then bring him home again.

When the four novels appeared together in 1950 as *Parade's End,* they were widely—and on the whole favorably—reviewed. The reviewers were all united on one point: they seemed preoccupied with the peacetime sections of the book. No one appeared to be much interested in the war. Mr. Macauley in his introduction defined *Parade's End* as social history of a prophetic sort, explaining that England had for decades been slipping, the old social order was corrupted or corroded, *noblesse* no longer obliged; the war was merely the *coup de grace* for a moribund society. And when Ford had said that his tetralogy was a war book—as he had—he was (Mr. Macauley's words) "hoaxing us." Some of the reviewers discussed the novel's formal qualities and all, of course, its content. But no one seemed much concerned about where the two meet: in the unique angle of vision that danger, and especially war, creates. Or perhaps it would be better to say unique quality of vision, all that takes place under brown light.

Ford himself seems to have been in no doubt about his subject: it was war, and *No More Parades* was the germinal volume. In much the way that Strether's conversation with little Bilham in the garden was the nub from which *The Ambassadors* grew, Tietjens' monologue to distract the mad McKechnie contains the germ for *Parade's End.* In that monologue Tietjens tells Captain McKechnie how at the beginning of the war he had visited the War Office and found in a room someone devising the ceremonial for the disbanding of a Kitchener battalion.

> "You can't say we weren't prepared in one matter at least. . . . Well, the end of the show was to be: the adjutant would stand the battalion at ease: the band would play *Land of Hope and Glory,* and then the adjutant would say: *There will be no more parades.* . . . Don't you see how symbolical it was: the band playing *Land of Hope and Glory,* and then the adjutant saying *There will be no more parades?* . . . For there won't. There damn well won't. . . . No more Hope, no more Glory, no more parades for you and me any more. Nor for the country . . . Nor for the world, I dare say . . . None . . . Gone . . . Na poo, finny! No . . . more . . . parades!"

Ford's account of how his tetralogy was conceived is given in the autobiographical *It Was the Nightingale,* where he is discovered in postwar retirement—a sort of Cincinnatus-Henry James tending pigs.

> I was covered with mud to the eyes, in old khakis, shorts and an old khaki army shirt . . .
>
> A voice said over the hedge:
>
> "Didn't I once meet you at Henry James's?"
>
> Standing above me on the bank was the comfortable and distinguished figure of Sir Edward Elgar. I did not remember having met him at Henry James's but I knew him for the local great man—and of course as the composer of the *Dream of Gerontius*—and *Land of Hope and Glory.*
>
> There came into my mind suddenly the words: "The band will play: '*Land of Hope and Glory*'. . . . The adjutant will say: 'There will be no more parades . . .' "
>
> It worried me slightly that I could no longer be certain of all the phrases of that ceremonial for the disbanding of a battalion. Nothing in the world was further from my thoughts than writing about the late war. But I suppose the idea was somewhere in my own subconscious, for I said to myself:

> "If I do not do something about it soon it is possible I shall forget about the details." And I wondered how the common friend of myself and Sir Edward would have treated that intractable subject. I imagined the tortuous mind getting to work, the New England scrupulousness, the terrific involutions . . . and for the rest of the day and for several days more I lost myself in working out an imaginary war-novel on the lines of "What Maisie Knew. . . . "

> I found I still had by heart all the paragraphs of King's Regulations and Military Law that a regimental officer could be required to know. I went over in my mind every contour of the road from Bailleul to Locre, Locre-Pont de Nieppe, Nieppe down to Armentières—and of all the byroads from Nieppe to Ploegsteert, Westoutre, Dramoutre. And I found that I could remember with astonishing vividness every house left, in September 1916, along the whole road, and almost every tree—and hundreds of shell holes!

The contours, be it noted, came first; the primary motive of Ford's war novel was scenic—an assertion that may appear improbable to the reader who still thinks of the novelist's trade as "story-telling" or to the other, perhaps more sophisticated, reader who looks at every novel as symbolic action. Nevertheless, Tietjens, Sylvia, Valentine Wannop, General Campion and the rest—their whole complex, funny, and sad imbroglio, and *Parade's End*'s originality of form and style—all exist ultimately in order that Ford may penetrate and encompass that torn scene and recreate the particular kind of countryside that is called a battlefield. Tietjens' long parade begins and ends in a landscape.

Ford, incidentally, was never quite decided whether the resulting labor was one book or four—and with reason. The separate volumes follow one another more closely than sequels, yet each (with the exception of the last) is formally complete in itself, and, since much of what has happened is recapitulated in each new volume, they are best read with a certain interval of time between one and the next. In any case, to take in the whole tetralogy the critic must stand too far off. A look at a single volume reveals more, since each *in petto* reflects a pattern found in the whole. Of the four, *No More Parades* is probably the best. It also comes nearest to being central.

In structure, *No More Parades* is a strictly scenic novel. There is no general narrative: we are always locked up in a particular scene, but the scene in turn is locked up in a particular mind. It is a worrying mind, both anticipatory and mnemonic, since fragments of a remembered past and a looked-forward-to future are continually being filtered in. Henry James, in his preface to *The Awkward Age,* once explained the advantages he felt would accrue to the novelist who restricted himself, as nearly as possible, to the conventions of the stage-play. Ford's affinities, however, are more with the movies; his way of building up a scene—out of fragmented details, sudden "cuttings," shifts in "camera angle," etc.—closely resembles film montage. As a result we are if anything even more *in* the scene than James would have us—we are shut in, boxed in. In the opening scene of *No More Parades* there are stressed, almost to the point of claustrophobia, its indoor—even domestic—aspects. About all the doings in that hut there clings a suggestion of a monstrous tea party. The falling, and lethal, insides of shrapnel shells are called "candlesticks." Of the men by the brazier, one is muttering dejectedly about his unfaithful wife, one about a queer cow that "took a hatred for its cawve (up behind Caerphilly on the mountains)." The Canadian sergeant-major is worrying himself about a new pocket-book. The hut is shaped like the house a child draws. Inside, there is a curious air of false domesticity, into which the sounds of the outside come, appropriately, like the falling of a large tea-tray.

This depiction of soldiers under fire is (or ought to have been) the death of a noble cliché: war seen as outdoors living, active, virile. There is much cold, much wet, much mud in Ford's landscape, but there is very little action. Ford knew that war was mostly waiting. He also knew that in war one is always surrounded—if (please God!) not by the enemy, then by one's own side. Tietjens finds himself in a hut, in a depot, in an army, on a front, in a war—and in a whole cluster of tangled social situations, his own and others'. Outside, forward and beyond, is what? Unknown. Meanwhile, there is the waiting. Wait long enough and it will come. But when the outside does come in, when Death enters the hut, his appearance and manners are strangely domesticated and prove to be in keeping with the scene. The air raid has temporarily let up, the two runners have been sent out to see about candles and chow; but before long the planes return. There is more waiting. One runner re-enters with candles. There is now more light; the stage is set for someone's grand entrance. More talk takes place between the two officers, the younger becoming calmer—it is no longer his scene. As the elder officer (Tietjens) relaxes, his eyes play tricks on him; he has a piercing vision of his wife, "In a sheath gown of gold tissue, all illuminated, and her mass of hair, like gold tissue too, coiled round and round in plaits over her ears. The features very clean-cut and thinnish; the teeth white and small; the breasts small; the arms thin, long and at attention at her sides." More waiting. Then:

> A man, brown, stiff, with a haughty parade step, burst into the light. He said with a high wooden voice:
>
> "'Ere's another bloomin' casualty." In the shadow he appeared to have draped half his face and the right side of his breast with crape. He gave a high, rattling laugh. He bent, as if in a stiff bow, woodenly at his thighs. He pitched, still bent, on to the iron sheet that covered the brazier, rolled off that and lay on his back across the legs of the other runner, who had been crouched beside the brazier. In the bright light it was as if a whole pail of scarlet paint had been dashed across the man's face on the left and his chest. It glistened in the firelight—just like fresh paint, moving!

This is vivid writing and not easily forgotten. It is only possible when (as Ford would say) the novelist has prepared his effects, as we have seen him doing. But the technical problem raised by writing of this sort—with its hard cameo outlines—is a matter of continuity: how to get on, how to mediate between one scene and the next. The very

sharpness of impression prevents a flow, especially since anything like ordinary chronological continuity is avoided by Ford. Life does not narrate; it impresses itself upon our minds and senses; and that is what Ford sought through his brand of impressionism.

Ford once said that the tone he sought in his prose was that of one English gentleman whispering into the ear of another English gentleman.

— *Ambrose Gordon, Jr.*

Ford's solution to the problem is hinted at in his curious, and controversial, little book on Joseph Conrad. He warns against the novelist's reporting whole speeches—for example, by a long-winded suburbanite in his garden: "If you gave all those long speeches one after the other you might be aware of a certain dullness when you reread that *compte rendu*. But if you carefully broke up petunias, statuary, and flower-show motives and put them down in little shreds, one contrasting with the other, you would arrive at something much more coloured, animated, lifelike and interesting. . . ." The same principle, I believe, holds true for the large garden that is a battlefield: by laying down "in little shreds" such motives as blood, noise, mud, battle neurosis, relations between officers and men, thoughts of home, sexual excitement, interest in nature, etc., Ford creates an effect that might be thought of as fugal. Or—to alter the metaphor—like seeds, these motives will show a strong inclination to grow and force their way from one scene into the next, as they do so often, undergoing curious and interesting metamorphoses. They weave the parts of the book together—and do much more besides.

The image of dead O Nine Morgan will illustrate the method, whose blood "glistened in the firelight—just like fresh paint, moving!" The suggestions called to mind by fresh paint—its stickiness in particular—are horrible enough, but the last word caps them: *moving!* It sticks in our minds and Tietjens' (as the blood sticks on his shoes). Tietjens suffers a series of recalls. Particularly interesting is the way that death and his wife's sex mania are drawn together in most of these, as though the motive were a rope with strands in two different colors. The first recall comes the same evening when, tucked up in bed in his fleabag, Tietjens is writing—jotting down as coolly and deliberately as he can, like a military estimate of the situation, the salient facts of his marital situation, hoping to find the answers to certain questions: *Has* his wife left him? Does that mean he will be free to live with Valentine Wannop? Should he? His thoughts are interrupted by the orderly who is carrying on a doleful conversation with an officer in another part of the tent, concerning the evening's casualty. Tietjens hears the orderly say:

> "Poor–O Nine Morgan! . . . " and over the whitish sheet of paper on a level with his nose Tietjens perceived thin films of reddish purple to

be wavering, then a glutinous surface of gummy
scarlet pigment. Moving!

The second recall, coming two days later, is not of the
blood directly but of a slowly moving brass door handle.
The handle evokes a scene rather different from the replacement depot hut: a bedroom in an elegant hotel in the
nearby town, where we find Tietjens with Sylvia, half-
dressed, who has materialized in France with the same violence that Poor–O Nine Morgan had burst into the hut,
made his succinct report and dropped dead. To create
trouble Sylvia has left her bedroom door unlocked. An in-
toxicated M. P. colonel breaks in and is physically ejected
by Tietjens who, as a consequence, is placed under arrest
and confined to his quarters. But General Campion, wishing the whole thing hushed up, comes the next morning
to inspect Tietjens' unit and orders him to accompany the
inspecting party on its rounds. (The general and Tietjens
both know that this in effect releases him from arrest.)
Also, and compassionately, the general sends in by his aid,
Colonel Levin, a bottle of smelling salts since Tietjens is
understandably a bit shaky. But these do not have at all
the bracing effect desired:

> Tietjens asked himself why the devil the sight of
> that smelling-salts container reminded him of
> the brass handle of the bedroom door moving al-
> most imperceptibly . . . and incredibly. It was,
> of course, because Sylvia had on her illuminated
> dressing-table, reflected by the glass, just such
> another smooth, silver segment of tubing. Was
> everything he saw going to remind him of the
> minute movement of that handle?

The analogy between the two movements—the blood and
the door handle—and the two scenes apparently does not
occur to Tietjens the bond being an unconscious one.

In the painful interview with the general that follows,
Tietjens receives a movement order—to the front (to
which he desperately doesn't want to go). He has, after all,
been on his feet for two days and has suffered a series of
shocks. He panics rather badly. It is mud that particularly
upsets him, and with the news of his movement order
comes another involuntary memory—of the trenches.
Mud not only rhymes with blood, and is sticky like it, but
it also sometimes moves—horribly.

> In November . . . A beginning of some
> November . . . With a miracle of sunshine: not
> a cloud: the mud towering up shut you in inti-
> mately with a sky that ached for limpidity . . .
> And the slime had moved . . . following a
> French bombardier who was strolling along eat-
> ing nuts, disreputably, his shoulders rolling . . .
> *Déserteurs* . . . The moving slime was German
> deserters. . . . You could not see them: the
> leader of them—an officer!—had his glasses so
> thick with mud that you could not see the colour
> of his eyes, and his half-dozen decorations were
> like the beginnings of swallows' nests, his beard
> like stalactites. . . . Of the other men you could
> only see the eyes—extraordinarily vivid: mostly
> blue like the sky!

The final recall—coming late in the book—is, appropriately, undisguisedly, of O Nine Morgan, once again coming

by way of Sylvia. Near the close of the interview the general, now adopting a fatherly, or avuncular, tone, asks the
one question that for Tietjens is the most upsetting: "Why
don't you divorce?"

> Panic came over Tietjens. He knew it would be
> his last panic of the interview. No brain could
> stand more. Fragments of scenes of fighting,
> voices, names, went before his eyes and ears.
> Elaborate problems. . . . The whole map of the
> embattled world ran out in front of him—as
> large as a field. An embossed map in greenish *pa-
> pier mâché*—a ten-acre field of embossed *papier
> mâché*: with the blood of O Nine Morgan blur-
> ring luminously over it.

This motive of O Nine Morgan's blood is merely a single
instance; in *No More Parades,* and the tetralogy as a
whole, there are dozens of others. What Ford said looking
back at *The Good Soldier* applies also here: " . . . I will
permit myself to say that I was astounded at the work I
must have put into the construction of the book, at the intricate tangle of references and cross-references." And, in
Parade's End at least, it is a tangle that *moves*—and not
a tangle either but a fugue, as scene follows scene threaded
on not one string but many.

The war as seen by Ford Madox Ford is not quite the war
of Hemingway, or of Tolstoi, or Stephen Crane, or anyone
else—though it is tempting to suggest that it might almost
have been Henry James's ("a war-novel on the lines of
'What Maisie Knew' "). For other writers the key fact of
war and not-war (one hesitates to say peace) is their separation. The soldier is, in action and out, hardly the same
man. When Lieutenant Henry is busy retreating from Caporetto, he is busy retreating from Caporetto, winging de-
serters, dodging Austrians, and so on; when he is safe in
Milan eating midnight sandwiches with Catherine Bark-
ley, he is eating midnight sandwiches—and never the
twain shall meet. Not so with Ford's soldiers. Each is, as
Ford put it, *"homo duplex: a poor fellow whose body is
tied in one place but whose mind and personality brood
eternally over another distant locality."* It is this persistent
doubleness that controls the ranges of horror, of which
Ford presents quite a bit. And yet—and this is the point
I wish to stress—Ford's presentation of horror is not harrowing. Indeed, on reflection, his depiction of war seems
principally comic—though we may have to stretch our
conception of comedy and scrap some received ideas
about what subjects are intrinsically funny. Bedroom
farce, for example, is usually regarded as inherently
comic, dying not. And yet . . .

Consider Sylvia. Eros and thanatos, Venus bedded with
Mars—who is Sylvia and what is she? Though a pacifist
who hates war, Sylvia Tietjens has a curious affinity with
it. It is symbolically apt and right, I think, that, where Valentine Wannop is unimaginable in wartime France, Ford
should bring Sylvia across the Channel and develop her
line of destruction in counterpoint with that of the war.
Even Sylvia seems half to know that she and war are one
flesh, a single perverse will, when she realizes, as she puts
it, that she is "in the very belly of the ugly affair." In her,
peace and war meet, cruelly and absurdly.

Ultimately, Sylvia stands for the Ruling Classes and the established order of pre-war England—the order which led to, and collapsed in, the war. Though she hardly realizes this, she is its direct embodiment. She is a marvellously convincing depiction of tradition in decay, not the decay of paralysis and torpor but the decay of boredom, of keeping up appearances, which leads to endless restless irresponsibility; she is cruel, yet brave and noble, even at moments generous—not wholly distinct from Tietjens himself. That is one reason why Sylvia is so convincing. All of these characters are members of the same leisured society that Ford once described as "fairly unavailing, materialist, emasculated—and doomed." Sylvia is merely its most virulent—and in some ways most attractive—manifestation. Tietjens breaks with it only in his final break with her.

But by far the most important point about Sylvia, and one which might easily be overlooked, is that she is among other things a splendid comic heroine—or comic villainess rather. The embarrassments that she creates are nearly always funny and the humor is not lost on her. She has a keen wit and a sense of the incongruous, even at her own expense, as in the words with which she finally gives up Tietjens to the somewhat mousy though virtuous Valentine, who by now is his *de facto* wife. Sylvia says:

> "An the King will have my head I carena what
> he may do with my . . . "

The allusion is to the words of her fellow papist Fraser of Lovat just before he was executed in the 'Forty-five. Ford explains: "They had told him on the scaffold that if he would make some sort of submission to George II they would spare his body from being exhibited in quarters on the spikes of the buildings in Edinburgh. And Fraser had answered: 'An the King will have my heid I care not what he may do with my—,' naming a part of a gentleman that is not now mentioned in drawing rooms."

Sylvia, indeed, comes very close to being Ford's muse, since Ford's continual juxtapositions, the altercations he contrives for his characters, the "perspectives by incongruity," superimposing war on peace and peace on war, create a way of looking at things that can only be described as comic. Comedy permeates Ford's world at even its grimmest, even in the death of O Nine Morgan. In our last glimpse of him (in person, as distinct from the recalls) he is being carried "in a bandy chair out of the hut. His arms over his shoulders waved a jocular farewell."

Northrop Frye has observed [in his "The Argument of Comedy," *English Institute Essays,* 1948, 1949] that comedy "contains a potential tragedy within itself. With regard to the latter, Aristophanes is full of traces of the original death of the hero which preceded his resurrection in the ritual. Even in New Comedy the dramatist usually tries to bring his action as close to a tragic overthrow of the hero as he can get it, and reverses this movement as suddenly as possible." Certainly these ritual elements—of death and resurrection—might be looked for in such a novel as *A Man Could Stand Up,* Christopher Tietjens having about him much of the sacrificial hero (as Sylvia remarks to Sergeant-Major Cowley: "They used to say: 'He saved others; himself he could not save . . . ' "). This

is, however, not the path that I wish to follow at present. Rather, I would like to revert to certain consequences of the curiously closed-in quality of Ford's scene. Out there and a little beyond is unnamed horror: the horror of what lies beyond the front lines, of No Man's Land, of the unknown, from which for the most part we take cover with varying degrees of success. Were the action placed out there, as it is in much of the *Iliad,* it would necessarily be tragic. But Ford's characters remain enclosed, boxed-up, holed-in. We—the readers and the characters—await the inevitable intrusion, and when it comes it is horrid and macabre, but not tragic. It is more than anything absurd, since in this shut-in scene the social norms of a life of reason and common sense (or what passes for them) have, despite all, been preserved, in particular such matters as rank and class. These are simply incommensurate with the intruding horror, and it with them. So, when death enters in the guise of O Nine Morgan, for a brief time the social norms are shattered—for one thing his blood gets on an officer's shoes—but the normal is quickly re-established. It is perhaps this very quickness, indeed, which keeps the rhythm comic.

The phenomenon is of course not merely a wartime one. In peacetime the same is true; death, chaos, and madness being no respecters of our abstractions "war," "peace." This Ford knows as he shows us the same pattern working out quite early in *Some Do Not,* for example at the breakfast with the mad clergyman or, later, a road accident in the fog. Always the scene is an interior (though the walls may be only of vapor) into which there is a violent intrusion, a very brief dispersal, and a quick regrouping. The very recurrences of this pattern suggest a further structural principle: each such boxed-in interior—whether of hut, or hotel bedroom, or telephone booth on Armistice Day, or elegantly appointed railway carriage, or dugout at the front—comes to suggest all the rest. As the novel proceeds we are translated, as though by metamorphosis, from one interior to the next, and to the extent that we are aware of this strange transmogrifying process—this sliding-away of panels—we must find the whole process comic. Indeed, these rapidly shifting perspectives are implicit in the minutiae of Ford's writing and, as such, probably make themselves felt from the start.

The shadings of Ford's war comedy cover a wide range. Some of his queer juxtapositions, though they make their point, seem fairly obvious. There is Tietjens composing a sonnet in under three minutes to rhymes supplied by McKechnie while signing incredible numbers of papers for incredible numbers of soldiers of a draft that is on its way up the line. There is the highly efficient Sergeant-Major Cowley's penchant for sudden transformations: "The sergeant-major, now a deferential shopwalker in a lady's store, pointed out that they had had urgent instructions not to send up the draft . . . ," "the sergeant-major, now a very important solicitor's most confidential clerk, etc." There is the inappropriate name of the general's war horse, "Sweedle-pumpkins." But at its best the comedy is not obvious at all, as in this little glimpse of Sylvia's peculiar way of torturing her husband: "She warned him that, if he got killed, she should cut down the great cedar at the southwest corner of Groby. It kept all the light out of the principal drawing-room and the bed-rooms above it. . . . He winced: he certainly winced at that." And there are bits of battle-humor, so thoroughly a part of the atmosphere of an army at—or near—the front ("Do you know the only time the King must salute a private soldier and the private takes no notice? . . . When 'e's dead. . . .") From this, Ford modulates to something far more eerie and grotesque as the sergeant-major explains to Mrs. Tietjens how at Noircourt the captain had stumbled:

> "Caught 'is foot, 'e 'ad, between two 'ands. . . . Sticking up out of the frozen ground . . . As it might be in prayer. . . . Like this!" He elevated his two hands, the cigar between the fingers, the wrists close together and the fingers slightly curled inwards: "Sticking up in the moonlight. . . . Poor devil!"

Horrible? Haunting? Funny? Or terrifying? It is hard to say which this is. It is all and more, with its faint echoes of Dante; and it is not quite like any other writing about war that one can think of, nor like any other twentieth-century prose. It is a high and horrible comedy, with much compassion played off against an unrelenting pressure of the absurd.

The whole movement of Ford's tetralogy comes to a brief rest, as it should, in a fine scene at the end of *No More Parades,* a repetition of the familiar pattern of intrusion—if we can so characterize a general's inspection. The fall of France at this point appears imminent, and the fall of Tietjens with it; yet the ending Ford supplies is comic, light, and gay. It follows the disagreeable private interview between General Campion and Tietjens and serves both as a recapitulation and a comic coda. Tietjens, we are told, had earlier been given a moment to alert his cook-house of the approaching inspection.

> "You can do what you please," the sergeant-cook said, "but there will always be one piece of clothing in a locker for a G. O. C. I. C.'s inspection. And the general always walks straight up to that locker and has it opened. I've seen General Campion do it three times."
>
> "If there's any found this time, the man it belongs to goes for a D. C. M.," Tietjens said. "See that there's a clean diet-sheet on the messing board."
>
> "The generals really like to find dirty clothing," the sergeant-cook said, "it gives them something to talk about if they don't know anything else about cook-houses. . . . I'll put up my own diet-sheet, sir. . . . I suppose you can keep the general back for twenty minutes or so? It's all I ask."

At the conclusion of his interview with Tietjens the general said:

> " . . . You can fall out."

Tietjens said:

> "My cook-houses, sir . . . Sergeant-Cook Case will be very disappointed. . . . He told me that you couldn't find anything wrong if I gave him ten minutes to prepare. . . . "

The general said:

> "Case . . . Case . . . Case was in the drums when we were at Delhi. He ought to be at least Quartermaster by now. . . . But he had a woman he called his sister . . . "

Tietjens said:

> "He still sends money to his sister."

The general said:

> " . . . He went absent over her when he was colour-sergeant and was reduced to the ranks. . . . Twenty years ago that must be! . . . Yes, I'll see your dinners!"

Sergeant Case's situation, it is readily apparent, is analogous to Tietjens', but with a difference—he is a man who has been both ruined and not ruined by his woman. He keys us for the novel's finale. *No More Parades* began with the words "When you came in"; it ends with a locker door opening.

> The building paused, as when a godhead descends. In breathless focusing of eyes the godhead, frail and shining, walked with short steps up to a high-priest who had a walrus moustache and, with seven medals on his Sunday tunic, gazed away into eternity. The general tapped the sergeant's Good Conduct ribbon with the heel of his crop. All stretched ears heard him say:
>
> "How's your sister, Case? . . . "
>
> Gazing away, the sergeant said:
>
> "I'm thinking of making her Mrs. Case . . . "
>
> Slightly leaving him, in the direction of high, varnished, pitch-pine panels, the general said:
>
> "I'll recommend you for a Quartermaster's commission any day you wish. . . . Do you remember Sir Garnet inspecting field kitchens at Quetta?"
>
> All the white tubular beings with global eyes resembled the pierrots of a child's Christmas nightmare. The general said: "Stand at ease, men . . . Stand easy!" They moved as white objects move in a childish dream. It was all childish. Their eyes rolled.
>
> Sergeant Case gazed away into infinite distance.
>
> "My sister would not like it, sir," he said. "I'm better off as a first-class warrant officer!"
>
> With his light step the shining general went swiftly to the varnished panels in the eastern aisle of the cathedral. The white figure beside them instantly tubular, motionless and global-eyed. On the panels were painted: TEA! SUGAR! SALT! CURRY PDR! FLOUR! PEPPER!
>
> The general tapped with the heel of his crop on the locker-panel labelled PEPPER: the top, right-hand locker-panel. He said to the tubular, global-eyed white figure beside it: "Open that, will you, my man? . . . "
>
> To Tietjens this was like the sudden bursting out

of the regimental quick-step, as after a funeral with military honours the band and drums march away, back to barracks.

John A. Meixner (essay date 1962)

SOURCE: "Tietjens, the Great War, and England," in *Ford Madox Ford's Novels: A Critical Study,* University of Minnesota Press, 1962, pp. 190-256.

[*Meixner is an American author and educator. In the following excerpt, he analyzes* Some Do Not, *the first of the four Tietjens novels, and asserts that* Parade's End *should be considered a trilogy with a sequel rather than a tetralogy.*]

The four novels of the Tietjens series, although published separately, have in recent years been gathered together under the comprehensive title of *Parade's End.* But should Ford's work be considered, in fact, as a tetralogy? Or is it more accurately a trilogy, with *The Last Post* as sequel? Robie Macauley, in his introduction to *Parade's End,* has supported the first position, urging that the four should be considered as one book: "I think it can be comprehended in no other way. . . . Without *The Last Post,* the novel would have been sadly truncated." Acknowledging that the work could never "turn out" as an ordinary novel must, he asserts that the recapitulation and final statement of *The Last Post* are "indispensable." Support for Macauley's position, which he himself does not cite, may be found in the epistolary dedications to the books, in which Ford declares his structural intention. After observing, in the introduction to *No More Parades,* that his protagonist had been shown in the first volume at home during wartime and that in the second he is seen going up the line, he adds; "If I am vouchsafed health and intelligence for long enough I propose to show you the same man in the line and in the process of being re-constructed." And in the dedicatory letter to the next book, Ford wrote that *A Man Could Stand Up* is "the third and penultimate" of the series.

Nevertheless, despite Macauley's assessment and these observations from Ford, the sounder approach is to view the enterprise not as tetralogy but trilogy—with the fourth volume as a kind of after-thought, separate from the main design. For by the completion of *A Man Could Stand Up,* Ford, however he may have felt earlier, had clearly altered his intention. In his dedication to *The Last Post,* for example, we find him writing that if it were not for Isabel Patterson's "stern, contemptuous and almost virulent insistence" on knowing "what became of Tietjens," he never would "have conducted this chronicle to the stage it has now reached." Indeed, it is curious that his statement calling the third book the penultimate in the series is dated May 18, 1926, while the novel itself is not marked as finished until more than two months later, July 21. Still more decisive evidence that Ford considered the work a trilogy appears in a letter of 1930. In reply to a proposal that the Tietjens books be issued as an omnibus volume, Ford suggested the title, *Parade's End* (rejecting *The Tietjens Saga* as difficult, and liable to confusion with *The Forsyte Saga*), and added: "I strongly wish to omit *Last Post* from the edition. I do not like the book and have never liked it and always intended to end up with *A Man Could Stand Up.*" Nor was this significant judgment expressed only privately. Three years later in *It Was the Nightingale* Ford again indicated his view of the matter by referring several times to the Tietjens books as a "trilogy," and even quoting as its closing words: "On an elephant. A dear meal sack elephant. She was setting out. . . ."—the ending of *A Man Could Stand Up.*

To depart from Ford's final, definite judgment is unwise, particularly since the texts themselves support his verdict. As we have seen, the Tietjens cycle cannot be approached—even as a trilogy—as though it were conceived and executed as a perfect artistic whole, since commercial demands required that each volume stand separately. Nevertheless, between the first book and the end of the third there is a definite, clear unity of subject—the subject Ford himself said he had in mind—that of the "world which culminated in the war," presented through the focus of Christopher Tietjens, the central observer. *Some Do Not* begins symbolically in peacetime in a shiningly appointed railway car, and *A Man Could Stand Up* ends in a bare, stripped room on Armistice night among the damaged victims of the war. England itself has been stripped, and there will be no more parades. The over-all conception of the three books is gaunt, stark, and complete. After them, the action of *The Last Post* can only be considered an addendum, a fact signalized by Ford's removal of his central character from any prominent role. Unlike the first three volumes, the last, as Ford saw, does not come meaningfully under the banner of *Parade's End.* To include it there is only to obscure the force and impact of the basic conception.

Nor is the fourth volume consistent in its fundamental method. The approach of the earlier novels is essentially realistic. Although their characters and events possess a meaning beyond themselves, the significance is implicit, hinted through the texture of actuality. *The Last Post,* on the other hand, is only nominally realistic, its particularity of character and event the merest coloring. Rather, its method is symbolic: the characters and the action overtly serving Ford's *idea.* Less individuals than forces, the characters are like allegorical figures in a pageant. Valentine is motherhood impending, Christopher huntsman and family protector, Sylvia (described in one passage as "it") a diabolic marble statue, Marie-Léonie domesticity, and Mark the presiding magician and deity (willing against Sylvia's influence). The Groby Great Tree, finally, is the highly conscious symbol of the curse upon the Tietjenses. The note of unreality, of a primarily symbolic world, is in fact struck at the opening by the extreme peculiarity of Mark's personal withdrawal. *The Last Post* is a novel plainly of another style altogether from the first three.

Beyond this point the case against including *The Last Post* in the main plan need not go. Ford's own assessment and the disunity of subject and method are decisive. Yet a further argument perhaps may be offered—based on a critical judgment. The book should be excluded finally because it violates the essential spirit and master mood not only of the first three volumes but of Ford himself. . . .

Ultimately, however, the issue of trilogy or tetralogy is academic. Whether entitled *Parade's End* and *The Last Post* or called *Parade's End* alone, the Tietjens cycle as a whole will not stand importantly to Ford's credit as a novelist. The true achievement of his Tietjens creations is the first volume, *Some Do Not.* The succeeding books will not last. Where *Some Do Not* is a magnificent and rich work of the novelist's imagination in almost all aspects—characterization, narrative suspense, authoritative atmosphere, and emotional power—the rest are thin productions which peter out the vein. The larger conception of the trilogy, in brief, is splendid, but it is not filled out.

And essentially this judgment is also Ford's, given covertly and without detail but unambiguously in *It Was the Nightingale,* where he comments that after *Some Do Not* his works had considerably deteriorated. The reason, he said, was an attack of writer's cramp. After the completion of the book he "began at St. Jean Cap Ferrat" (*Some Do Not* from earlier reference), the cramp became so severe he could not hold a pen. And so he took to using a typewriter—"to the considerable deterioration of my work"—and "then, worst of all, to dictating." The typewriter and the stenographer, Ford remarked, made him too fluid. "It is as if they waited for me to write and write I do. Whereas if I have to go to a table and face pretty considerable pain I wait until I have something to say and say it in the fewest possible words."

The failure of the novels after *Some Do Not* lies precisely where Ford has indicated: in their excessive fluidity. Because they are not composed with scrupulous care or by a fully engaged mind, the imaginative vitality established for the Tietjens world in the first book is mostly lost. In writing these volumes, Ford had ceased to be an artist. Documentation of this point can be brief, for the same faults characterize all three.

The unfortunate consequences of Ford's hurried carpentry are evident in a variety of ways, but probably the central casualty is his management of the interior monologue, which (unlike *Some Do Not*) dominates all three books. The device, particularly fashionable at the time of their composition, possesses decided advantages for developing the inner life of a character. Its weakness, however, which follows from its associative principle, is an inherent looseness of structure. Like free verse, its very freedom makes it all the more difficult to do well. The author must not only render successfully the illusion of a character's flowing stream of thought, but he must also contrive, without harming that illusion, to maintain interest and excitement and to advance his narrative. And neither of these ends does Ford achieve in the later books. Too facilely exploiting the liberties of his method, he inevitably has come away empty-handed. Far too often the details which he puts into a thought process are not there to build his character inwardly but to explain the events of the earlier books. And since the exposition required is elaborate, the process can only become deadening. Converted into a garrulous expository machine, the character thus has insufficient life of his own. Similarly, thoughts occurring originally in the mind of one character are often repeated later in exactly the same words in another's, without justifica-

tion either in cause and effect or proximity—only in the needs of plot machinery. There is a tendency also to resort to a same few motives, the effect of which is to restrict the inner life of the characters. To Valentine, for example, Tietjens is always a bear, and the same tags of Latin and English poetry constantly reappear. Nor is any distinction made in the interior monologue between characters. Each sounds like every other, with the same tone, cadence, and recurrent mannerisms of speech—"Something like that," "oh, say—," "*call it*"—which are in fact the mannerisms of Ford's personal voice as a memoirist.

As a result, the characterizations in the three volumes are on the whole thin and unsuccessful. If, earlier, Ford was highly praised for creating in his Tietjens world so many first-rate, imaginatively compelling characters, the praise was thoroughly earned. He has done precisely that, and triumphantly, as any reader of *Some Do Not* must allow. But after the first volume these great characters unfortunately narrow into dullish stereotypes. Christopher becomes merely a burdened stoical figure with almost absurd tendencies toward *noblesse oblige.* Losing her complexity and style, Sylvia is reduced to an incredibly vulgar (and extremely unpleasant) monster. The same flattening out may be seen in other of the characters who reappear, such as Valentine, General Campion, Edith Ethel, and Mrs. Wannop. Permanently set, they do not change or grow. Whether in appearance, behavior, or mental configuration, Ford ceases to observe them freshly. In the first volume, the fact of Christopher's erudition and intelligence is convincingly demonstrated in his conversation; in the later books this brilliance is merely asserted, by the easy device of having someone utter an admiring: "You do know everything!" Nor is the deterioration of Ford's splendid characters compensated for by the fullness with which new ones are created. Those introduced in the later volumes—Captain Mackensie, General O'Hara, Colonel Levin, the line captain, the men in the trenches, the peasant Gunning, Millicent de Bray Pape—remain counters. Only Marie-Léonie has genuine charm and surprise.

No less unhappy is the effect of the interior monologue on the narrative strength of these three books. Very little in them is deeply engaging because the method is basically a non-dramatic prison—much of the "action" occurring posthumously, so to speak, in the mind of a character. And since the focus is not on the conflict itself but on the character's thoughts about it, the few dramatic scenes which do take place tend to be muffled and oblique. The method as implemented also makes for an over-all linear impression, in pale contrast to the rich and various world of *Some Do Not.*

Finally we should consider still another important casualty of this easy fluidity: the prose. Lack of genuine care is revealed by numerous tests. The same words recur again and again in brief space. Paragraph three of *No More Parades,* for example, repeats *hanging about* four times; the next does the same with *very annoying.* And although such a device might be defended as a calculated intensity, a demanding art recognizes (as in *The Good Soldier* and *Some Do Not*) that it is more truly expressive not to dissipate verbal power by repetition. Certainly it is difficult to justify the technique's being used in two successive paragraphs. Ford plainly was exploiting an easy trick, not artfully creating. . . .

That the last three volumes of the Tietjens cycle are inferior to Ford at his best needs to be acknowledged. Yet it would be a serious error, of course, to dismiss them out of hand. They are not without their admirable qualities. And a somewhat detailed survey of these qualities will be worth our attention.

Probably the best of the three is **No More Parades.** It is told with considerable skill and with an authentic power of feeling, especially in its depiction of the life of the army. Its finest section is at the beginning, at the wintry base depot, during which the complex pressures that weight upon Christopher are vividly created. The very first page strikes the note of the situation: inside Tietjens' sackcloth hut, with its blazing paraffin heater. The sound of shellfire is in the distance:

> An immense tea-tray, august, its voice filling the black circle of the horizon, thundered to the ground. Numerous pieces of sheet-iron said, "Pack. Pack. Pack." In a minute the clay floor of the hut shook, the drums of ears were pressed inwards, solid noise showered about the universe, enormous echoes pushed these men—to the right, to the left, or down towards the tables, and crackling like that of flames among vast underwood became the settled condition of the night.

And gradually the men in Tietjens' charge are sorted out, each with his own nagging private claim and worry: the two Welsh miners squatting on their heels at the fire, one of them angry at Christopher for not allowing him leave to see his wife who, he senses, has taken up with another man; the Canadian sergeant-major uncertain whether he had packed his new pigskin wallet—the one he had wanted to look very smart with on parade; the deranged, brave officer who may disrupt Tietjens' urgent work at any moment; the other ranks filing by and making out their sometimes complicated wills to be read and signed by Christopher, who is already burdened with an enormous amount of paper work. And beyond the immediate scene is the heavy image in Tietjens' mind of why all these creatures were assembled, and where they are going:

> He seemed to see his draft: two thousand nine hundred and ninety-four men he had had command of for over a couple of months. . . . He seemed to see them winding away over a great stretch of country, the head slowly settling down, as in the Zoo you will see an enormous serpent slowly sliding down into its water tank. . . . Settling down out there, a long way away, up against that impassable barrier that stretched from the depths of the ground to the peak of heaven. . . .

Vivid too is the later episode in the hotel ballroom at Rouen, with the wicker furniture, the dimmed lights, the gramophone playing, and the bombing—all as chorus to Sylvia's passionate willing that Christopher submit to her desire for him. Well presented also is the closing section at the base depot, in which Tietjens and Campion have a

final interview which emerges into trust. At its conclusion, the cook-houses are inspected, and a sense of military order is for the moment achieved, as seen in the passage which completes the book:

> The general tapped with the heel of his crop on the locker-panel labelled PEPPER: the top, right-hand locker-panel. He said to the tubular, global-eyed white figure beside it: "Open that, will you, my man? . . ."

> To Tietjens this was like the sudden bursting out of the regimental quick-step, as after a funeral with military honours the band and drums march away, back to barracks.

The most powerful incident in **No More Parades,** however, is the death of O Nine Morgan—the Welshman Christopher had protectively denied leave. "A man, brown, stiff, with a haughty parade step, burst into the light. He said with a high wooden voice: 'Ere's another bloomin' casualty.' " The streak of fatal injury to half his face and to his chest is depicted, and Tietjens is astonished that a human body could be so lavish of blood. As he bends over the figure—the heat from the brazier overpowering—Christopher hopes he will not get his hands covered with blood, "because blood is very sticky. It makes your fingers stick together impotently. But there might not be any blood in the darkness under the fellow's back where he was putting his hand. There was, however: it was very wet." The image is to recur again and again to Tietjens' mind, and beyond any other incident in these novels it catches Ford's deepest mood and vision. It is also a significant, appropriate echo of the episode with the injured horse in **Some Do Not,** which will be described later.

In **A Man Could Stand Up,** Ford's writing is again most compelling in the scenes involving the men and the effects of war. The episodes in the trenches, if not superlatively done (what Conrad would have made of such a setting!), are still interesting for their quiet, unheroic rendering of the details of such combat. There are one or two spectacular passages, of course—as the following virtuoso description, set under the theatrical lighting of the Verey flares:

> Tietjens became like a solitary statue of the Bard of Avon, the shelf for his elbow being rather low. Noise increased. The orchestra was bringing in *all* the brass, *all* the strings, *all* the wood-wind, all the percussion instruments. The performers threw about biscuit tins filled with horse-shoes; they emptied sacks of coal on cracked gongs, they threw down forty-storey iron houses. It was comic to the extent that an operatic orchestra's crescendo is comic. Crescendo! . . . Crescendo! CRRRRRESC. . . . The Hero *must* be coming! He didn't!

> Still like Shakespeare contemplating the creation of, say, Cordelia, Tietjens leaned against his shelf. From time to time he pulled the trigger of the horse-pistol; from time to time he rested the butt on his ledge and rammed a charge home. When one jammed he took another. He found himself keeping up a fairly steady illumination.

The Hero arrived. Naturally, he was a Hun. He

came over, all legs and arms going, like a cata-mount; struck the face of the parados, fell into the trench on the dead body, with his hands to his eyes, sprang up again and danced. With heavy deliberation Tietjens drew his great trench-knife rather than his revolver. Why? The butcher instinct? . . . The man's shoulders had come heavily on him as he had rebounded from the parados-face. He felt outraged. Watching that performing Hun he held the knife pointed and tried to think of the German for *Hands Up.* He imagined it to be *Hoch die Haende!* He looked for a nice spot in the Hun's side.

His excursion into a foreign tongue proved su-perogatory. The German threw his arm abroad, his—considerably mashed!—face to the sky.

Always dramatic, Cousin Fritz! Too dramatic, really.

He fell, crumbling, into his untidy boot. Nasty boots, all crumpled too, up the calves! But he didn't say *Hoch der Kaiser,* or *Deutschland über alles,* or anything valedictory.

Or in the more restrained image of no-man's land which Christopher sees from an observation post:

There were still the three wheels, a-tilt, attached to slanting axles, in a haze of disintegrated wire, that, be-dewed, made profuse patterns like frost on a window. There was their own apron—a perfect village!—of wire over which he looked. Fairly intact. The Germans had put up some of their own in front of the lost trenches, a quarter of a mile off, over the reposing untidinesses. In between there was a perfect maze: their own of the night before last. How the deuce had it not been *all* mashed to pieces by the last Hun bar-rage? Yet there were three frosty erections—like fairy sheds, halfway between the two lines. And, suspended in them, as there would have to be, three bundles of rags and what appeared to be a very large, squashed crow. How the devil had that fellow managed to get smashed into that shape? It was improbable. There was also—suspended, too, a tall melodramatic object, the head cast back to the sky. One arm raised in the attitude of, say, a Walter Scott Highland officer waving his men on. Waving a sword that wasn't there. . . . That was what wire did for you.

But passages like these are few. Ford's picture of the lines is, for the most part, a muted compound of reflections, re-lationships, and details. A listing may suggest its quality. It is made up of such matters as the anxiety of the troops about the wind: when it comes from the east, the Germans can use their poison gas, and will resume their offensive; and the Tommies' underlying fear of being driven into the North Sea. Of the sound of subterranean digging, and the voice that Christopher once hears from below his camp-bed: *"Bringt dem Hauptmann eine Kerze."* Of the spiritu-ally broken commanding officer (whom Tietjens has re-placed), the victim of a war which has lasted too long and destroyed too many of his friends. Of Christopher's con-cern, as he foresees the breaking up of trench warfare, that the men of his battalion know how to keep in communica-tion with their neighboring units. Of such mundane but interesting matters as the variance in the nature of the trenches themselves, as the soil changes from red gravel to marl to pure alluvial soil and even bog; and what to do with the springs they traverse (Christopher has devised a unique siphon-drain). And such lyric details as the clear, sweet sound of a bugler in the near distance, playing: "I know a lady fair and kind / Was never face so pleased my mind." Or the astonishing fact of skylarks nesting on the battlefield. Or such touches of class comedy as Christo-pher's promise, in a moment of strong affection, to give each of his men a ticket for Drury Lane next Boxing Day, and the cheery reply: "Mike it the old Shoreditch Empire, sir, n we'll thenk you!"

The strengths of *The Last Post,* set in the post-war world, are of a different sort: mainly pastoral and domestic. The writing is imbued with Ford's love of country things: the pleased detailing of the great view of four counties from Mark's outdoor bed; the haygrass, and the raspberry canes by the hedgerows; the careful bottling of the cider; the ducks on the pond; the hedge-sparrow at the dripping set out for the tomtits; the collecting of the eggs in the hen-house. Attractive also is the detailed portrait of Marie-Léonie, her daily routine and verbal meanderings, which always end on the theme with which she has begun. And, unusual for Ford, but engaging, are the monologues in di-alect form, of the peasant Gunning and the cabinet-maker Cramp. Thus, the "country reaction" to Marie-Léonie:

She was 'Er Ladyship, a good mark, a foreign Frenchy. That was bad. She was extraordinarily efficient about the house and garden and poul-try-yard, a matter for mixed feelings. She was fair, not black-avised, a good mark; she was buxom, not skinny, like the real Quality. A bad mark because she was, then, not real Quality; but a qualifiedly good mark because if you 'as to 'ave Quality all about you in the 'ouse tis better not to 'ave real Quality. . . . But on the whole the general feeling was favourable because like themselves she was floridly blond. It made 'er 'uman like. Never you trust a dark woman and if she marries a dark man 'e will treat you bad. In the English countryside it is like that.

Beyond these quieter elements, there are several intense, if somewhat theatrical, confrontations between various characters, particularly Sylvia's with the pregnant Valen-tine. But most fascinating in *The Last Post* is the very con-ception of Mark's willed retreat from the world, and those two stunning moments at the end when he speaks aloud.

The decline of the later Tietjens novels is clear enough. Yet a provocative question remains: why? Such explana-tion is the task primarily of the biographer, of course, rather than the critic, whose business is to say whether the art-work is achieved or not. We may venture to guess, however, that between the completion of *Some Do Not* and the publication of *No More Parades,* some event oc-curred to crucially undermine Ford's self-confidence. To set oneself to write a great novel is to be, above all, auda-cious and supremely assured. Ford, as we know, always felt uncertain of his own great powers, and Stella Bowen and others have written of how setbacks could easily drain his self-belief. And for such a confidence-sapping event we do not need to look far, for in this period Ford was dealt not one but two hard personal blows. The first was Jessie Conrad's assault on him (in the December 4, 1924, issue of the *Times Literary Supplement*) for his book on her husband, in which Mrs. Conrad unjustly condemned him before the world (the account being quickly picked up in New York) as being, in effect, a liar and false pretender. This assault alone would have battered Ford's ego but it was not all. Earlier in the same year (January 19, 1924), Violet Hunt had reopened the whole unhappy past by writing a letter to the weekly *Westminster* referring to Ford as her husband and signing herself "Violet Hunt Hueffer"; and once again Mrs. Elsie Hueffer brought suit against Violet, the case coming up on February 10, 1925, two months after Mrs. Conrad's letter. If this were not enough, in the following year Violet Hunt published *The Flurried Years* (1926), an intimate account of her relation with Ford, the divorce scandal, and the several court hearings. The book was no doubt an act of aggression on Violet's part, who was almost surely stung at being identified with the vindictive Sylvia, as she writes in the memoir that people had done. So that at these various hostile acts, Ford, a reserved person who dreaded the exposure of his private life, may well have felt the heart go out of him. He himself, as we have seen, has ascribed the deterioration of his work to writer's cramp, but such an explanation inevitably must seem superficial. The influence of work conditions is subtle, but to the artist functioning as artist they are scarcely likely to be crushing unless there is a deeper cause. Surely it is not unreasonable to speculate that Ford's suddenly intensified physical difficulty after *Some Do Not* was a psychosomatic manifestation resulting from the jolts administered to his personal pride, that it was a symptom of the artistic abdication evident in the pages of the last three books rather than its cause.

One cannot but feel the loss to modern literature in the decline of the Tietjens books. Had they been continued on the scale and with the care and imagination with which they were begun, they would be among the largest, most impressive productions of twentieth-century fiction. As it is, they have the unfortunate tendency to leak away in the mind of the reader the impact of the characters who live with such vitality and excitement in the first volume. The world of letters and the arts, however, is full of such accidents, splendid conceptions well begun but left in fragment. Art, like every other human enterprise, is beset by chance, and the critic's task is to value not what might have been, but what has flowered. Regret, in short, should not blind us to the very real achievement of *Some Do Not.* And by itself the first novel goes very far toward fulfilling the ends of the larger conception. Of the vital incidents of the later books, it lacks only the picture of the Armistice night closing, which ultimately images Ford's theme of "Parade's End." The base-depot episode and Christopher's concern for his men are, in fact, very largely suggested in *Some Do Not* by his reflections during his visit to the War Office. And the theme that a man of disturbed private life cannot be a satisfactory officer and trustworthy member of society, which Campion impresses on Christopher in the later books, is actually dealt with in the first— in the conversation in which Campion calls him "a regular Dreyfus": "fellows like that *unsettle* society. You don't

know where you are. You can't judge. They make you uncomfortable." A man like Dreyfus is worse than guilty— "the sort of fellow you couldn't believe in and yet couldn't prove anything against. The curse of the world. . . . " (To which, Christopher replies, as if in self-revelation: "Ah.") And the motif of the hard, frugal life of Christopher's desire, although developed more fully afterwards, also is introduced in the first volume. In a very real sense, in *Some Do Not* Ford has said all that he had to say— about his people and his theme.

The true achievement of Ford's Tietjens creations is the first volume, *Some Do Not*. The succeeding books will not last. Where *Some Do Not* is a magnificent and rich work of the novelist's imagination in almost all aspects—characterization, narrative suspense, authoritative atmosphere, and emotional power—the rest are thin productions which peter out the vein.

—John A. Meixner

A work of fiction distinguished by the breadth, richness, and variety of the world it has created and by the great emotional poignancy and power it has caught and expressed, *Some Do Not* can only be described as a masterpiece of the novel, excellent in each of the multitudinously demanding aspects of the form. And in the following pages, an attempt will be made to articulate something of the nature of its art and craft.

The theme of England lies at the roots of nearly all Ford's fictional works, but none of his other novels approaches *Some Do Not* in the range or depth with which the life of his native country is portrayed. Since Ford's intention was to show the impact on the nation of the Great War, its Englishness is hardly accidental: the British milieu required elaboration. It needed to be given the thick, complex feel of actuality—had, in James's phrase, to be "done." Thus the novel is rich with the peculiar motifs, amply developed, of English life: the role and character of the governing classes; the class structure and the demarcation between those "born" and those of undistinguished lineage; political struggles between Conservatives and Liberals; the pervasive dominance of Victorian sexual morality, and the diversity of English types: military man (Campion), banker (Lord Port Scatho), country squire and landowner (Christopher's father), politician (Waterhouse), industrialist (Paul Sandbach), arbiters of society (Lady Claudine and Glorvina), fashion leaders (Sylvia), and the presiders over aesthetic salons (Edith Ethel). Touched upon as well are such motifs as the typical Englishman's distrust of abstract thought; his fondness for his countryside, its birds and flowers; his love of cricket, golf, and animals; his poorly prepared food (*Das Pillen-land,* as Christopher reflects); and, particularly, his historical and literary heritage. Far more than any other novel of Ford's, too, its vocabulary draws on indigenously English words, including dialect and slang: *higgler, coulter, lurcher, haulm, whin, hop oasts, horse-coper, tweeney, quiff, snaffle, squits,* to cite a few.

This world of England is, however, undergoing radical change. Signs of the ferment are present in various cries for social reform: Waterhouse wants economic revisions, Port Scatho seeks to liberalize divorce laws, Valentine campaigns for the female vote, and her brother is ardently a Marxist. Yet these agitations are only symptoms of still deeper shifts in the arrangements of society. The fundamental change is, as it was in ***The Good Soldier,*** from a basically feudal order, which is rooted in agriculture and the life of the country, to the modern industrial system, founded on capital and centering itself in the giant city. And this movement by which one way of life in England is supplanted by another is, in the ultimate sense, the subject of ***Some Do Not.***

It is through the careers of his principal characters that Ford chiefly gives expression to his theme. The richness and vitality with which he has endowed them, imaginatively and credibly uniting complex desire, particular personality and mythic type, has already been described in detail. We may now examine how, set in the context of the larger world, they also, in what happens to them, serve Ford as symbols of that world and give the novel its emotional power.

At the dramatic heart of ***Some Do Not*** is a deeply poignant love story, that of Christopher and Valentine; and the chief action of the novel is their affair, from first meeting through the growth of their passion to its final outcome. Paralleling their relationship, however, is another, in significant contrast, between Macmaster and Edith Ethel. In depicting the private worlds of both pairs of lovers, Ford has been remarkably successful, sensitively rendering their emotions at all stages with depth and imagination. He has also understood that in reality a love story never exists apart. Being social as well as private and physical, the relation between the sexes is inevitably implicated in the larger world of which the lovers are members—its values, wise and foolish, its habits and rituals, its fears and taboos. What men esteem in society abstractly, they desire concretely in their mates, for our lovers objectify what we love or lust after. So it is with these two couples, minor and major

The Macmasters live according to appearances, skillfully adapting to the requirements of a corrupt, superficial society—climbers aiming to make successful, publicly honored careers, and ready in the process to discard acquaintances who are no longer useful, Valentine and Christopher among them. While their fellow countrymen at the front die by the thousands, their own concern is to increase their influence and prestige at home and to be the preservers, as Edith Ethel tremulously puts it, of what beauty remains. The hypocrisy of their lives is especially made clear by the course of their relationship. Although both prate of a higher, more delicate sensibility and morality, and Vincent approvingly quotes poetic lines by Rossetti urging the separation of lovers who may not love, ironically it is

they, not the other couple, who are adulterous. When by chance their liaison is revealed, they are terrified, and the romantic Edith Ethel lashes savagely out at her lover in the manner and language of Billingsgate.

Christopher and Valentine, on the other hand, are unselfseeking personalities, direct, courageous, and loyal. Often critical of the state of society they find themselves in, they possess sufficient fortitude to persist in their course despite society's sanctions. Both are deeply affected by the carnage and stupidities of the war. Christopher, though a good soldier, is infuriated by the condition of the enlisted men and the treacherous self-aggrandizement of the authorities. Valentine, a pacifist, is simply moved by the mutilations piled on mutilations, deaths piled on deaths. In the working out of their own relationship, they are in ironic contrast with the Macmasters: "I stand for monogamy and chastity. And no talking about it," Christopher had said, scoffing at the "polysyllabic" mouthings of Rossetti and aesthetes like him. "Of course if a man who's a man wants to have a woman he has her. And again, no talking about it." Long acting on his principle of monogamy and chastity, Christopher decides, however, the day before his return to France, to ask Valentine to be his mistress, and wins her consent. But the fates decree otherwise. Between the afternoon of their compact and the night of their consummation, circumstances arising directly out of the social disorder of wartime conditions prevent it. And in the end, each is unwilling to mar the ideal of their mutual love and regard. Some, like the Macmasters, "do"; and some, like Christopher and Valentine, "do not."

The ultimate symbolic act occurs when Macmaster, wanting to impress his superiors, presents as his own one of Christopher's brilliant and prodigal mathematical formulations and is richly rewarded for his treachery by important promotions and illustrious honors. The incident and society's bounty comprise the final irony of the novel, dramatizing its larger meaning of social deterioration.

The effectiveness of the central action and the expressiveness of Ford's theme are still further enhanced by the elegant simplicity of the design in which he has embodied them—the classic form which E. M. Forster has likened to an hourglass. The characteristic shape of the hourglass comes, of course, from the manner in which the lines of its two equal and separate halves flow together at the center, cross, and seem to exchange their relative positions. Thus it is with the form of ***Some Do Not.***

At the beginning, the shining star in the social firmament is Christopher Tietjens, well-born, secure, admired, and deferred to; and toward him Macmaster looks upward, ruefully acknowledging the truth of the words, "The Gods to each ascribe a differing lot: Some enter by the portals: Some do not!" By the middle of the book the lines of relationship have begun to converge; and at the end they are reversed. Dishonored, vilified, and self-denied, Christopher wearily goes to his bed, prepared to leave in the morning for Waterloo Station and the war. Macmaster, on the other hand, is celebrating as reward for his statistical coup the bestowal of the knighthood he has long coveted.

Like the hourglass also, the novel is separated into two

equal (142 and 144 pages respectively) and thoroughly demarcated halves, which in their contrast of time and setting splendidly serve to dramatize Ford's theme. Part One takes place in an England still undisrupted by the national disaster fate has in store for it. Although an impending war is hinted, the country is securely at peace. Its traditions, its values of honor and uprightness, and its social structure are still intact. It is England under the old dispensation. Appropriately, the scene of the action is almost completely rural, in the southeastern English countryside. Part Two, on the other hand, is set entirely in London in the midst of the war. The closely woven social fabric has been rent and frayed in numberless places. The youth of the nation are being bled abroad, and at home schemers press their selfish game. Backbiting, malicious gossip, and character assassination thrive. Rectitude and honesty in the military corps (Campion) and in finance (Port Scatho) have turned into the vindictive unscrupulousness of Major Drake and of Brownlie, Port Scatho's nephew, who covets Tietjens' wife and exploits the bank to ruin him. It is the new dispensation. To it from the old, time has flowed in the hourglass. The contrast between the two parts is thus the analogue of that between the two couples: where the Macmasters move in drawing rooms, the major pair find their most congenial home in pastoral England.

Although the society and atmosphere of each part are dominated by the ethos appropriate to it, the two worlds of the novel are not, of course, completely homogeneous. Signs of the rising forces intrude into Part One, for example, when two "city men" from London disrupt with raucous vulgarity the even tenor of the golf-course club house. The progress of the "unborn" Macmaster and the overly civilized, unrooted spirit of Sylvia also are indications of the emerging conditions. And the bold suffragettes' raid on the golf-playing cabinet minister is still another example.

The most striking invasion into the old order by the new occurs, however, at the close of Part One. In the first half of *Some Do Not,* the horse is, significantly, the means by which the characters are transported. In London, it is a hansom cab—"the only conveyance fit for a gentleman," says Christopher, who loves horses and is marvelously skilled with them; in the country, it is a fly and, notably, a horse-drawn dog-cart. A motor car never appears. Suddenly, however, at the end of the part, an uncontrolled automobile roars out of the dawn mist and mortally wounds the horse that is pulling Christopher and Valentine. Excitingly dramatic, the action also is intensely symbolic. The death blow is triple: physically to the animal by its supplanter, the motor car; and figuratively by the industrial order, of which the automobile is fact and sign, to the world in which the horse thrived, and also to the kind of men it produced. (The very name of chivalry, we should be reminded, derives from the horse.) At the very end, Christopher, sobbing with grief, waits beside the injured beast and, in the last line, the cart of the knacker—the merchant who trades in the carcasses of horses—lumbers into sight. The symbols are simple, natural, and fundamental, as valid in the real world as in the imaginative. The episode is the crux of the novel—the connecting place between the two bell-like compartments of the hourglass.

In one exciting moment and image is summed up the theme and foreshadowed the new world which will dominate the second part about to open.

The form of the novel and the conflict between the two orders are, of course, not as sharply drawn as analysis here makes them. *Some Do Not* is a novel about human beings first of all, not an allegory of black and white. Nor does Ford line up his characters with deadly neatness on contrasting sides. Valentine, for example, is a suffragette and socialist; and the driver of the car which destroys the horse is, in fact, a figure of the old order, General Campion. (The fact that Campion, a man in a position of national leadership, is thoroughly incapable of controlling the machine, though he refuses to admit it, has no doubt its own point, however.) Nor are the major figures mere machined products of the cultures that produced them. Complex human beings, they share in other systems of triumph and defeat than those of a society they may or may not be in tune with. The lines of the hourglass, which form the basic pattern of development and meaning, are therefore counterpointed, and the novel enriched, by other conflicts. Thus, although Macmaster comes to a dominating social position, he is not free from shame before Christopher at the means of his triumph, or from the reader's contempt. Nor does Christopher as a man decline merely because the world that created him is deteriorating. That world may be gone, and his own position in it have become isolated and extreme, with stoicism as the only valid philosophy. But Christopher himself is not destroyed. Having an insides and will, he affirms his values despite the altered circumstances of society. Principles are necessary, he declares as he waits for the knacker's cart, for "Principles are like a skeleton map of a country—you know whether you're going east or north." Christopher's moral superiority, of clarity and principle, is symbolized in the final chapter of Part One. The mist which shrouds the dark countryside in vagueness is a rich symbol of the confusion in which all of England wanders, including the radical Valentine who moves on foot immersed in it. Only Christopher, perched up on the dog-cart, the mist extending level from his neck, his head (like Neptune's in the *Aeneid*) in the clear—only he has a view of objects in the distance and of the stars and the moon above.

Nor, in the end, is Christopher content merely to sit waiting for the knacker's cart. Living in a world which he dislikes and which is hostile to him, he yet must choose a course of action in it. Although this choice is not overtly dramatized in *Some Do Not* (as it is in the later volumes), it is symbolized, however, in the progress of his walk, in Part Two, with Mark and later with Valentine through the streets of London. Christopher's argosy starts at his rooms in Gray's Inn, which are dominated by the persecuting figure of Sylvia; proceeds through the urban, industrialized city; and ends with Valentine in the pastoral environs of St. James Park. The course of his walk takes him past the symbols of power and of careers in twentieth-century London: Fleet Street (the press), the Middle Temple (the law), Whitehall (government and the military). Only as he moves along the Embankment does his way leave the city masonry, and then the Thames is described as looking like "dirty silver" and the prospect called a "grim effect of landscape," as though Ford were accenting the dominance over the river of the industrial city. Firmly implied in the journey is Tietjens' rejection of the urban world and his decision to carve out a life with Valentine in a place of greenery and naturalness of growth.

The theme of **Some Do Not** and the characters and form which help give it expression have been considered; we now need to examine more closely the manner in which Ford has told his story. How, more specifically, has he given to it its qualities of richness and variety, of narrative excitement, and emotional force? What, in short, are his highly effective tools of composition?

The chief technical means which Ford has employed in **Some Do Not** are particularly appropriate for a work which combines in one both the novel of society and the novel of character. For the first, the public, a broad canvas is needed; for the second, the private analysis in depth. Within his design Ford has handsomely achieved his diverse ends. Through the over-all organization, the selection of point of view, and the use of the time-shift, he has knit together Space—of historical time, social types and milieu, and diverse settings—with Depth—of personality and rendered emotion. It is a work at the same time both extensive and concentrated.

The keystone of Ford's achievement is his arrangement of the action. Although exploring a large and various social world, he very skillfully has brought his material into tight dramatic unity by framing the action of each of the two halves into brief periods of time. Part One covers less than two days, while part Two, which takes place roughly ten years later, occurs within three hours (excluding the final epilogue-like chapter set ten hours afterward).

The first element which makes this flexibility possible is the point of view—the third person (an angle of vision all but inevitable for any large-canvased novel) and which Ford has not employed with such technical variety and richness of effect since the **Fifth Queen** books. As earlier, he does not restrict himself to any single mode of the third person. Sometimes he writes as the disengaged "omniscient" observer, placing his characters in their social time and place, and striking his "public" note; but this novelist's voice is mainly informational, without any Thackerayan "dear-reader" tone or moral comment. Chiefly it enables him to speed his narrative, setting a scene quickly and avoiding a disproportionate expository machinery. The novel thus begins: "The two young men—they were of the English public official class—sat in the perfectly appointed railway carriage." And "omnisciently" the theme is elaborated:

> Their class administered the world, not merely the newly created Imperial Department of Statistics under Sir Reginald Ingleby. If they saw policemen misbehave, railway porters lack civility, an insufficiency of street lamps, defects in public services or foreign countries, they saw to it, either with nonchalant Balliol voices, or with letters to the *Times*, asking in regretful indignation: "Has the British This or That come to *this!*" Or they wrote, in the serious reviews of which so many still survived, articles taking

> under their care, manners, the Arts, diplomacy, inter-Imperial trade, or the personal reputations of deceased statesmen and men of letters.

At other times, he will become the detached observer, reporting the external behavior of his actors, their speeches, gestures, and deeds—an angle of vision usually reserved for high dramatic moments. On occasion Ford moves in the other direction, completely entering the consciousness of a character in order to present his inward reflections.

> This, Tietjens thought, is England! A man and a maid walk through Kentish grass fields: the grass ripe for the scythe. The man honourable, clean, upright; the maid virtuous, clean, vigorous; he of good birth; she of birth quite as good; each filled with a too good breakfast that each could yet capably digest . . . Each knew the names of birds that piped and grasses that bowed: chaffinch, greenfinch, yellow-ammer (*not,* my dear, hammer! *ammer* from the Middle High German for "finch"), garden warbler, Dartford warbler, pied-wagtail, known as "dishwasher." (These *charming* local dialect names.) . . .

Passages of interior monologue, however, are comparatively rare.

Most often Ford blends the public and private, simultaneously presenting objective event and the subjective reflection of a particular character, the perspective being as though partly within and partly behind its focal character. Very appropriately to his "public" aims, Ford's focus changes frequently, and includes Valentine, Sylvia, Macmaster, Edith Ethel, Mark, and, of course, Christopher.

Ford's variable use of third-person modes thus greatly helps him in creating a universe that is both broadly social and intensely personal. The remarkable depth and richness of personality of his main characters is clearly made possible by his entrance into their awarenesses. The method enables Ford—in fact, requires him—to explore and objectify in detail their inner rationales, ambitions, motivations, temperaments, and longings; and the reader, in consequence, observes them intimately in their deepest selves. At the same time, and as importantly, the reader also sees them externally, through the eyes of the omniscient and observant author and of the other characters. The impressive reality, for example, with which Christopher and Macmaster are introduced in the opening chapter owes its success particularly to the shift in focus between the two men. Not being the prisoner of their own consciousness (or, even for that matter, of the author's), Ford's people thus take on a remarkably rounded, solid dimension and an enhanced independent life.

Similarly, Ford's method increases the actuality of his public, objective milieu. Seen variously, the world grows impressionistically richer. And since most of the external events of the novel are transmitted to the reader not objectively alone but also colored by a single consciousness which is deeply engrossed in them, they gain enormously in interest, urgency, and drama.

One of the most striking illustrations of the dramatic effects made possible by Ford's shift of focus from character to character is in the opening chapter of Part Two—the stunning revelation to the reader that the immensely learned, intellectually arrogant Christopher has lost his memory from shell-shock. Instead of presenting the information from the focal point of view of Christopher, as in the two preceding chapters, Ford chooses to render the scene through Sylvia's eyes. By sealing off Christopher's consciousness from the reader and presenting him from the outside, he thus wins the full impact of surprise when the condition is revealed. And by showing the effect of the news on the consciousness of Sylvia, the person least sympathetic to him, the episode is doubly enhanced. Her shock and pity are all the more effective a medium for transmitting a kindred shock and pity to the reader.

The second major tool of composition, the time-shift, is made possible by the first and is probably even more fundamental. By the very fact of entering into the consciousness of a character, the author may freely range wherever he wishes within it—including its roomiest domain, the memory. (As Ford himself has said: "we are almost always in one place with our minds somewhere quite other.") More than any other element, the time-shift is the source of the technical originality and freshness of the novel, making possible in large measure its broad and deep social picture, its exciting narration, and its remarkable verisimilitude.

Although the action of *Some Do Not* is concentrated, as we have seen, into two brief periods, the use of the time-shift, in which Ford switches between the present and the past, allows him to extend far beyond these confines. The opening chapter provides an excellent example: the immediate scene is aboard a train carrying Christopher and Macmaster southward from London to Rye. During the journey Macmaster works on the proofs of his monograph and at one point the pair heatedly dispute the merits of its subject. But in the course of the chapter the scene and the time often change. The reader observes Macmaster effectively moving in cultivated drawing rooms; both men dealing with the head of their department; Christopher in a scene with his mother and in another with his father. The two friends are also observed in several past conversations, in different London rooms, and in a hansom cab which that morning had taken them to their office. Ford's canvas plainly is stretched spatially no less than chronologically. Like his variable point of view, the time-shift thus enables him, if in another way, to combine space and depth.

A fictional method which frequently turns backward risks the serious hazard of becoming static and dull. But in Ford's management of the time-shift in *Some Do Not*—however it might be with a number of his other novels—the narrative is made only more exciting. . . .

The success of the novel depends, however, on the masterful handling of tools other than point of view and time-shift. Of these, the most important involve the process by which the work moves through time—the relentlessness of its advance and the modulation of its effect. Principles of composition rather than devices, they cut across and in part draw on the other methods. Let us examine each in turn.

Like his other fine novels, *Some Do Not* beautifully illustrates the theory of *progression d'effet*. The novel moves purposefully forward in every word, growing faster and more intense as it proceeds. Every device or effect serves to advance the story and to develop the over-all plan. The movement of the mist chapter, for example, is not dictated principally by the requirements of exposition, as engrossing as that may be presented. The chief drama develops rather from the conflict within Christopher between his Yorkshireman's stolid observance of the proprieties and his desire to take a holiday from them. Although chronologically the action moves backward, emotionally it intensifies, bringing the lovers closer and closer together in feeling. Similarly in the opening chapter, Ford's division of the points of view between Christopher and Macmaster is not a mere tour de force of character presentation, the simple revelation of their different qualities through their contrasting responses to the same circumstances. Although the subject of their reflections overlaps, the progress of the action from the focus of Christopher to that of Macmaster is not in the slightest repetitive. Macmaster's thoughts further advance the situation. Even the division of the book into two separate parts enables Ford to satisfy the doctrine of *progression d'effet* that the narrative accelerate in speed and intensity as it advances. The very nature of the world of Part One is slower—an agrarian society at peace, while the world of Part Two is intrinsically faster and more agitated—urban, industrial, and torn by the emotions of war. Characteristically, Ford rounds out this onward, intensifying progress of his narrative with a quieter final chapter. A richly complex coda, it weaves together, by means of time-shift in the mind of Tietjens, all the various emotional strands of the book—its places, persons, and evocative lines of poetry, the social atmosphere of England and London, Macmaster's shamed betrayal, Christopher's love for Valentine and his self-denial—and so produces an understated, summatory close which is at once remarkably moving and aesthetically satisfying.

But the most fascinating example of Ford's sheer narrative finesse is his handling of the opening and closing of a tandem pair of chapters (Three and Four) in Part One. "At the slight creaking made by Macmaster in pushing open his door," Chapter Three begins abruptly, "Tietjens started violently." In the ensuing conversation we learn only that it is night and that as a result of the day's events General Campion is indignant at Christopher. The rest of the chapter and of Four develops what had happened, the former concentrating on Macmaster and his remembrance of the day and the latter, through an adroit transition, focusing on Christopher within that day. Throughout the second chapter, Christopher is shown as intently trying not to reflect upon his impending reunion with Sylvia, seeking to lose himself in mathematical calculations and a game of solitaire; and the opening of its final paragraph returns to Macmaster's sudden entrance into the room and Tietjens' violent start—which is described as giving Christopher "a really terrible physical shock." "He nearly vomited; his brain reeled and the room fell about," and the paragraph continues to the chapter's end:

> He drank a great quantity of whisky in front of

Macmaster's goggling eyes; but even at that he couldn't talk, and he dropped into his bed faintly aware of his friend's efforts to loosen his clothes. He had, he knew, carried the suppression of thought in his conscious mind so far that his unconscious self had taken command and had, for the time, paralysed both his body and his mind.

The extremity of Christopher's reaction plainly is at variance with his behavior described earlier at the opening of Chapter Three, for then Christopher had only been discomforted at being seen to start and immediately had entered into a long conversation with Macmaster. The inconsistency, however, is far from being a flaw; rather it is a remarkable stroke of narrative economy. The reader, as Ford knew, never feels any discrepancy. Not only do forty pages intervene between the two moments, but the very nature of the method of the time-shift does not require strict factual consistency. Less bound in its mode, closer to poetry, its aesthetic principle is much less "scientific" than the chronological novel; the consistency it demands is emotional. Thus, with masterly assurance Ford has made one instance of startle achieve two dramatic purposes—to launch with interest his backward-turning account of the day's events and to enforce emotionally upon the reader the intensity of the burdens pressing upon Christopher.

No less important than *progression d'effet* in **Some Do Not** is the principle of variety. Ford's continual modulation of the unfolding experience of the novel perpetually requickens its life by preventing a dulling sameness of effect. Variety, in short, serves to make the temporal movement of the narrative constantly new, fresh, and engaging. The elements of the novel which Ford varies for this purpose are many and are almost as complex in relation to one another as the variations of sound—pitch, volume, timbre, tempo—available to the musician. They include point of view; mood; personality; time: past and present, objective and subjective; modes of rendering experience: dramatic and novelistic, realist and impressionist; and rhythm and surprise, both of language and action.

The virtuoso powers with which Ford has modulated and renewed the life of **Some Do Not** may be understood more clearly through a closer look at a single section, which of necessity must be more than usually technical and detailed. The intense fifth chapter which presents the Duchemin breakfast episode, one of the big scenes of the novel, constitutes the crux of Part One, bringing together for the first time all four lovers. Its chief narrative end is to dramatize the growth and crystallization of the passion between Macmaster and Edith Ethel. Wishing to help Macmaster in his literary research, Mrs. Duchemin had arranged the meeting in the hope that her husband's insane state might pass unnoticed. Instead the Reverend Duchemin violently disrupts the social occasion by provocatively uttering sexually charged phrases, even attempting to reveal intimacies between himself and his wife. On discovering the conditions under which Mrs. Duchemin must live, Macmaster's sympathy for her grows still stronger and, after her husband is led away, the pair exchange pledges of devotion.

The action of the chapter is divided into four parts or "movements," formally separated from each other by the particular angle of vision adopted. The first movement (six pages), which sets the scene and presents a revealing conversation between the two old friends, Valentine and Edith Ethel, is told strictly from the objective point of view. The chief purposes of the section are to set the scene and to characterize, and objectify, the two women who have been presented up to this point only through the eyes of their respective lovers. The second movement (nine pages), which groups the various guests, seats them at the breakfast table, and introduces the explosion of the Reverend Duchemin's obscene words, is more complex in its handling of point of view. Omniscient and objective at the outset, it soon slides into Valentine's consciousness, for a longer time into Christopher's, and then by way of an adroit objective transition, enters the key awareness of Edith Ethel, where the focus remains, except for a brief but important return to Christopher, until the end of the unit. The third movement (five and a half pages) which begins a few minutes in time before the close of the second, concentrates on a single awareness, Macmaster's, as he seeks to manage the unruly Duchemin. The fourth movement (four pages), in which the lovers pledge their troth, combines the objective and focal points of view, alternating between the detached author and the separate inner reflections of the impassioned pair, who agree to meet again at dusk.

This continual shifting of the angle of vision within the chapter is of key importance in achieving the variety of effect, but other elements are also significantly varied. Fundamental are the shifts between realism and impressionism and the contrasts of mood and dramatic intensity. The opening movement, the conversation between Valentine and Edith Ethel, is itself markedly different in method from the pages preceding it—which had depicted the aftermath of Christopher's golfing day and his violent upset at Macmaster's sudden entrance. The method of the earlier episode was impressionistic in character (telescoping several hours and tending toward vaguely outlined detail); the new section, on the other hand, is realistic and dramatic (objective, following clock time, and with sharply defined particularity). The earlier mood had been tense and, in the end, profoundly disturbing; the beginning of the new chapter is relaxed, conversational and decorative in atmosphere, with the interest deriving mainly from a simple contrasting of two very different women. The turmoil to come is only slightly hinted: no more than Macmaster or Christopher has the reader been let in on the true condition of the husband.

As the first section of the chapter contrasts with the pages before, so it does also with those that follow. The opening of the second movement returns to the impressionistic, but this time from the omniscient, not focal, point of view. It is a method, as managed, highly appropriate to presenting the atmosphere of a situation in which various people are politely and superficially meeting each other for the first time. By combining omniscience and impressionism, Ford is able to create the illusion of the quick elapse of time in which nothing vital is happening. But soon, as Ford enters the minds of Valentine and Christopher and then moves toward Edith Ethel, the method changes again, becoming more objective and realistic. (With these alterations, it should be pointed out, the reader's sense of the movement of time also varies: having hurried along impressionistically, it slows to the stretched-out subjective time of consciousness; then, when completely objective, it quickens to regular clock time; soon, however, it will slow again to agitated consciousness, only to change tempo once more—a process which continues, giving life to the experience, throughout the chapter, and, in fact, the book.) Essentially social comedy, the first half of the second movement continues, like the first movement, with comparative quiet. Its drama and interest derive largely from the characters' underlying evaluation of each other revealed as the internal focus changes.

But the second half of the movement, which shifts into Edith Ethel's consciousness, marks a decided change—not only from realism to impressionism but, even more strikingly, in tension and mood. Part of the dramatic conflict in the episode is provided by the various obstacles, such as Mrs. Wannop and Christopher, that stand in the way of Mrs. Duchemin's having Macmaster for herself. More intensely dramatic, however, is her desperate wish that her new guests will not discover her husband's condition. Her fearful panic as the polite structure begins to collapse dominates the mood of this half and is the more frightening and disturbing because, although permitted within her mind, the reader does not know the source of her terror. The knowledge is finally acquired through an entry into Christopher's consciousness, shortly before the end of the section, at the same time that he himself perceives the truth. Not only has Ford varied his method again from realism to impressionism, but he has also varied the kind of impressionism itself. Unlike the earlier passage in which the gathering of the guests was presented vaguely, this instance in Edith Ethel's mind is personal and well chosen to intensify the experience.

Thoroughly different again are the mood, method, and dramatic tension of the third movement. From the blurred sensibility of an emotionally distraught personality, the focus shifts to an individual, Macmaster, in whom the cool, rational principle is uppermost. The method thus turns realistic again. At the very entrance of the Reverend Duchemin—who now for the first time is presented clearly to the reader (having been before a voice speaking from behind table flowers)—Macmaster had become suspicious and alerted. Only disciplined intellect, he recognized, could save the situation. The intense drama of the third part springs, therefore, from Macmaster's determination to enforce his will on the demented man, which he does through the adoption of a donnish tone and a scholarly challenging of the accuracy of the clergyman's Latin. At one point, when for the moment Macmaster turns aside to exchange passionate confidences with Edith Ethel, Duchemin slips from check and becomes disruptive again. Only physical violence—a discreet jab to the kidney by the clergyman's attendant upon Macmaster's orders—ends the disturbance.

The mood and tension of the final movement alters again, is quieter and more romantic. From coolly resourceful manager, Macmaster becomes the tremulous poetic lover.

And the section ends impressionistically, in still another change of method, on a rococo wave of delicate sensibility between him and Edith Ethel which spiritually echoes the description of the exquisite decor with which the chapter began.

Thus by modulating these various elements, and still others (such as prose rhythm which would here require too elaborate an analysis), Ford perpetually enlivens his action. At times, two or more of these separate elements may operate in conjunction, as we have seen, but the particular combinations are continually altering.

Not only is Ford's skill in varying his experience masterful within his chapters but also from chapter to chapter. Consider as example the splendid modulation of Part One. The opening chapter, divided in focus between two key characters, Christopher and Macmaster, begins leisurely and operates mainly on the principle of time-shift. But Chapter Two, which moves to Sylvia, her mother, and Father Consett in Germany, is dramatic and strictly chronological. The third chapter, on the other hand, returns to the time-shift, almost entirely in the mind of Macmaster, and its beginning (Christopher's startle) is not leisurely but abrupt. The next change, to the objective and public, begins before the section ends and continues into the next, but in time Ford enters Christopher's consciousness—not in retrospect but *during* the day. The method thus becomes chronologically impressionistic. Only at the end of Chapter Four, when the startle incident is rounded out, is the time-shift employed. The contrasting organization of Chapter Five, the breakfast episode, we have already seen in detail: the time-shift is not used at all; the focus is on at least four characters, not one; and the experience is more social or public in nature than personal or private. (Still another variation is its leisurely beginning.) The management of Chapter Six is again modulated: Ford focuses on the consciousness of a single character throughout (except for a brief entry into Valentine's awareness) and returns, though not *in medias res,* to the time-shift. For the first time in such a case, the action is divided in the middle by a change of scene and time. As important is the variance of mood between Chapters Five and Six, the first being extremely intense and exciting, the second, for much of the way, pastoral, lyric, and relaxed. In the final Chapter Seven, the mist episode, the form changes once more. Although Christopher continues as focus, this time the action is launched abruptly in the midst of things. And again Ford's principle of organization is fresh: unlike the earlier abrupt ("startle") opening of Chapter Three, in which the action that followed took place entirely in the past, this time the narrative not only looks back but also dramatically moves forward at the same time.

The richness and variety of **Some Do Not** derives also from its diverse, thick texture and atmosphere. Its surface is vigorous with splendid detail. . . . Consider, as example, the revealing particularity of the quoted opening sentence of Macmaster's monograph—so rounded, judicious, and formally authoritative in tone, so calculated to impress:

> Whether we consider him as the imaginer of
> mysterious, sensuous and exact plastic beauty;

as the manipulator of sonorous, rolling and full-mouthed lines; of words as full of colour as were his canvases; or whether we regard him as the deep philosopher, elucidating and drawing his illumination from the arcana of a mystic hardly greater than himself, to Gabriel Charles Dante Rossetti, the subject of this little monograph, must be accorded the name of one who has profoundly influenced the outward aspects, the human contacts, and all those things that go to make up the life of our higher civilisation as we live it to-day. . . .

Or Christopher's long telegram to Sylvia, which is given an extra touch of reality—beyond its biting opening words, *accept resumption yoke*—by its real misprint in transmission, *esoecially*. Or again in the prose, which (though essentially "simple" in style) is given atmospheric effectiveness not only by the already mentioned anglicisms, but also by the occasional use of uncommon, richly suggestive words like *tantalus, capercailzies, epergne, galantine, spikenard, glaucous, matutinal, pawkiness, tendential, fane, cockerel, dockleaf.*

One of Ford's two unmistakable masterpieces, *Some Do Not* inevitably demands comparison with his other, *The Good Soldier.* Written by the same novelist and sharing certain basic attitudes and themes, they are yet extraordinarily different works—in method, spirit, and the intensity and configuration of their emotion. Something of this contrast may perhaps be conveyed by observing that where *The Good Soldier* derives from the French tradition—it has, in fact, been called "the greatest French novel in English"—*Some Do Not* is, surprisingly, in the line of the English novel. Such classification should not, of course, be applied too strictly. It does not mean, as analysis makes clear, that the later work is wanting in the gallic concern with form which justifiably earned the earlier book John Rodker's description. What is indicated, rather, is that the pattern and experience of the novel has not been drawn with the excruciating tightness of *The Good Soldier.* Spacious and leisurely, the book is more easily accessible. It does not demand of the reader the very close attention required for the full understanding of *The Good Soldier.* Rather than the novel as poem, *Some Do Not* is the novel as novel. But the book also belongs in the native tradition because of its peculiarly English character and spirit—especially, its humor. For *Some Do Not* is a richly comic work—not in the ironic vein of *The Good Soldier,* which is a mordant, intellectual, French form of comedy, but in the warm English tradition of Fielding and Dickens. . . .

Which of Ford's two finest novels, we must ask finally, is the greater? Critical judgment will vary with varying criteria, and it will be further made uncertain by the thoroughly different natures of the two works. But ultimately the greater achievement does seem to be *The Good Soldier. Some Do Not,* for all its high art, is not an unflawed work. The second chapter of Part Two, dealing with the dishonoring of Tietjens' checks, is, for example, inferior to the rest of the novel—the one place where the persecution Christopher suffers seems unconvincing, its details excessively piled on and unobjectified. On occasion, too, Ford is carelessly inconsistent: Valentine's brother changes name from Edward to Gilbert; Christopher's

brothers, Ernest and James, become Curly and Longshanks; and the day of the action in Part Two shifts in mid-course from Friday to Monday. (None of these inconsistencies is particularly obvious, however). A fastidious critic might observe also that the technical management of the second half is a trifle less subtle and various than the supremely artistic accomplishment of Part One—a value which only begins to assume aesthetic significance, however, after several readings. This novel, finally, is not quite as intensely piercing, intellectually or emotionally, as the earlier book. Meanings often lie deep in *Some Do Not* but the novel cannot equal *The Good Soldier* in its power to fascinate—to create the sense that the ultimate has not yet been reached, that meaning still lies beckoning within meaning to lure us on.

Readers who invoke other criteria than these no doubt will disagree. They may hold perhaps that no work of fiction should require more than one reading. Or, more seriously, that a novel should be a novel, not a poem. Or that character creation is nine tenths of the novelist's genius and that *Some Do Not* is filled with the more full-bodied cast. But however any individual verdict may go between this pair of superb works, one conclusion is clear: Ford has written two masterpieces which are successful, abundantly, in the two great traditions of the novel. He more than earned the right of being addressed as "Cher Maître."

Carol Ohmann   (essay date 1964)

SOURCE: "*Parade's End,*" in *Ford Madox Ford: From Apprentice to Craftsman,* Wesleyan University Press, 1964, pp. 112-74.

[*In the following excerpt, Ohmann compares* Parade's End *with* The Good Soldier.]

More obviously than *The Good Soldier,* the four novels *Some Do Not . . .* (1924), *No More Parades* (1925), *A Man Could Stand Up—* (1926) and *The Last Post* (1928)—all republished in the United States in 1950 as *Parade's End*—are the culmination of Ford's efforts to record and to evaluate the life of his times. In their breadth of scene and their length, these novels are reminiscent of Victorian and Edwardian social realism. They present a picture of England, particularly of upper-class England, on the brink of World War I, in the trenches of the Western Front, and in the uneasy peace that followed the Treaty of Versailles.

Parade's End covers a more ambitious range of affairs than *The Good Soldier,* and it is a frankly intellectual work. It offers numerous passages of reflection, of discussion, of argument not only about men and women—the relationship which Dowell calls "the first thing in the world"—but also about English finance, politics, social reform, and the conduct of the war in Westminster and in Flanders and France. And where *The Good Soldier* works by implication, *Parade's End* is often explicit. Dowell, for example, questions the ideals and the actions of the Ashburnhams. But Valentine Wannop concludes that Edith Ethel Duchemin sincerely aspires to the virtues she can only imitate. "Valentine knew that Edith Ethel really loved beauty, circumspection, urbanity. It was no hypocrisy that made her advocate the Atalanta race of chastity."

This same shift from the implicit toward the explicit, from question toward conclusion, is evident in the whole thematic movement of the tetralogy. In the opening chapter of *Some Do Not . . . ,* Christopher Tietjens, in a comically one-sided dispute with Vincent Macmaster, sets forth a scale of moral values: "I stand for monogamy and chastity. And for no talking about it. Of course if a man who's a man wants to have a woman he has her. And again, no talking about it. He'd no doubt be in the end better, and better off, if he didn't. Just as it would probably be better for him if he didn't have the second glass of whisky and soda." The ethical contrast, of course, is typically Fordian. Tietjens stands for a scrupulous fidelity to Christian morality or, as he terms it on other occasions, "saintliness" or "Anglican sainthood." But next to that ideal he prizes direct self-expression. Both of these standards of conduct he terms "clean," and he opposes them to the absolute bottom of his scale, "lachrymose polygamy," whose practitioners disguise fornication with "polysyllabic Justification by Love" and attempt to "creep" into "heaven." Such self-deceit and pretentious virtue are "filthy" and "loathsome." And Tietjens measures more than private life with his scale of values: making a success of a public career is also a "dirty business."

Tietjens' apparently incidental argument—it arises from Macmaster's casual quotation of Rossetti—prepares for all that follows. The ethical attitudes Tietjens describes are echoed and re-echoed in the course of the tetralogy and spring, again in typical Fordian fashion, from a psychological basis. Tietjens thinks, "Stoic or Epicurean; Caliph in the harem or Dervish desiccating in the sand; one or the other you must be." The tetralogy qualifies his thought to one *and* the other you must be—for the impulse toward goodness lives in the human personality side by side with the impulse toward evil. Repression of passion, more likely than not, leads to its lawless expression. The Reverend Mr. Duchemin "acquired the craving for drink when fasting, from finishing the sacramental wine after communion services." Tietjens' promiscuous wife Sylvia knows the "stimulation to be got out of parsimonious living." Valentine, after a wartime term of service in a public girls' school, "a sort of nonconformist cloister," longs for "the sea of Tibullus, of the Anthologists, of Sappho, even." Even Tietjens, whose wish has always been for relentless self-control, has married Sylvia because he made love to her in a railway carriage.

Like these of its members, at once individual and representative, English society as Ford presents it is impelled both to goodness and evil, both to control and to express its pride, anger, jealousy, sexual passion. It subscribes officially to the Christian code of conduct. But it lives according to an intricate system of moral shifts and compromises. It pretends to virtue; it deceives itself; it goes on talking with "polite animation" as if it had never heard Mr. Duchemin's voice insistent with alcohol.

To introduce the particular compromises of his society, or rather, to expose them, is one of Ford's principal aims in *Parade's End.* Indeed, in *Some Do Not . . .* his charac-

ters so frequently take up and expand the title, the principal leitmotiv, that they virtually compose an ethical primer for gentlemen and women, witness the following quotations on love and marriage:

> No gentleman thinks such things of his wife [as that she may have seduced him].

> Such calamities [as a wife's infidelity] are the will of God. A gentleman accepts them.

> A woman who has been let down by one man has the right—has the duty for the sake of her child—to let down a man.

> If a man who's a gentleman suffers the begetting of his child he must, in decency, take the consequences.

> No one but a blackguard would ever submit a woman to the ordeal of divorce.

> There's no reason why a man shouldn't have a girl [a shopgirl, not a lady], and if he has he ought to keep her decently.

The confrontation of human nature is obviously oblique, and the license allowed sexual passion arbitrary. The English "tradition," to choose one of the many words with which Ford describes society's *de facto* moral code, is a system of checks and balances; gentlemen and women may err with impunity—in certain prescribed ways.

So many rules of conduct should at least render men secure. But from the opening chapters of *Some Do Not . . . ,* it is apparent that the class that "administered the world" in "nonchalant Balliol voices" is uneasy and fearful. Its order is threatened by the clamorous voices of those who share neither its responsibilities nor its privileges. In a hitherto circumspect golf club at Rye, for example, prosperous and overfed city men frankly compare the merits of Gertie and the Gitana girls, and suffragettes disturb the rituals of the game on the links. The two groups of interlopers clash with such violence that even gentlemen become involved. Tietjens hears himself threaten to knock the head off one of the city men and, "exhausted, beyond thinking or shouting," trips the policeman who reluctantly tries to arrest the girls. The final result is conflict, albeit verbal rather than physical, among gentlemen themselves:

> Mr. Sandbach refused to continue his match with Tietjens. He said that Tietjens was the sort of fellow who was the ruin of England. He said he had a good mind to issue a warrant for the arrest of Tietjens—for obstructing the course of justice. Tietjens pointed out that Sandbach wasn't a borough magistrate and so couldn't. And Sandbach went off, dot and carry one, and began a furious row with the two city men who had retreated to a distance. He said they were the sort of men who were the ruin of England.

While this treatment of the disruption of tradition is primarily comic, the scene has its sinister implications.

Even when they are undisturbed by the impertinences of *nouveaux riches* and radicals, gentlemen scarcely live in amity. Their polite animation often gives way to dissent, direct contradiction, expressions of grievance, insults, or simply inattention to one another's remarks. Macmaster, Sandbach, and Tietjens are already at odds before the suffragettes and city men antagonize them. (I quote only the spoken discourse from the text):

> (Macmaster to Sandbach): "Don't you know that you don't shout while a man is driving? Or haven't you played golf?"
>
> (Sandbach to Tietjens): "Golly! That chap's got a temper!"
>
> (Tietjens): "Only over this game. You deserved what you got."
>
> (Sandbach): "I did. . . . But I didn't spoil his shot. He's out-driven the General twenty yards."
>
> (Tietjens): "It would have been sixty but for you."
>
> (Sandbach, after a pause): "By Jove, your friend is on with his second . . . You wouldn't believe it of such a *little* beggar! He's not much class, is he?"
>
> (Tietjens): "Oh, about *our* class! He wouldn't take a bet about driving into the couple ahead."
>
> (Sandbach): "Ah, I suppose he gets you out of scrapes with girls and the Treasury, and you take him about in return. It's a practical combination."

Often Ford's gentlemen and women reveal their hostility to one another even more directly—in such phrases as "look here," "listen here," "damn it all," and "oh no you don't."

While traditional morals and manners permit a considerable exercise of aggressive impulses, human nature is continually tempted to take still greater license. The city men—the "little competition wallah head clerks" of the government and the "beastly squits" of commerce—are, after all, merely exaggerations of the Tietjens, Macmasters, and Sandbachs, different in degree of self-expression rather than kind. As Valentine in the confines of her nonconformist cloister sums up the motivations of the ruling class, "You had to keep them—the Girls, the Populace, everybody!—in hand now, for once you let go there was no knowing where They, like waters parted from the seas, mightn't carry You." If tradition is obviously menaced from without, it also clearly has enemies within. Order itself is always tempted to anarchy. Hence the insistence, the fervor, with which society continually voices its ethical premises and the panic with which it conceals infractions even of its own imperfect code.

Each of the novels of the tetralogy develops a major thematic movement. In *Some Do Not . . . ,* Tietjens vacillates between saintliness and tradition. His wife's beauty and her recklessness, for the present, no longer tempt him. But his hopeless love for Valentine Wannop, which develops in counterpoint to Macmaster's illicit passion for Mrs. Duchemin, brings him to the edge of a clandestine affair. After the war begins, Tietjens and Valentine decide to indulge their love secretly, like Macmaster and Mrs. Du-

chemin, with due arrangement for the preservation of appearances, of propriety; but at the last instant they both change their minds. Tietjens, who has since left the civil service for the army, goes to France rejecting both his own initial premise of lawlessness and society's proposition of permissible vice: "If then a man who's a man wants to have a woman. . . . Damn it, he doesn't!" In his personal life, Tietjens decides for saintliness.

No More Parades, however, discovers him still a public man of tradition. In a base camp outside Rouen he trains and equips his men for the front as if he were a "Chelsea adjutant getting off a draft of the Second Coldstreams." Just as there are rules for love and marriage, so there are regulations for the proper conduct of violence. Yet when Sylvia appears in Rouen, her passion whetted by her husband's indifference, Tietjens very nearly succumbs to her attractions and hence to lawlessness. Because of his involvement with his wife, he does, in fact, strike a superior officer; and when his godfather, General Campion, puts him informally on trial and asks him why he does not rid himself of Sylvia for good, by divorce, he cannot answer. After a strained discussion in which even the General—the most stalwart defender of tradition in *Parade's End*—is "in disorder," both men take refuge from their personal difficulties in the performance, at once comic and pathetic, of army duty: they inspect Tietjens' cook-houses. Saintliness is a remote possibility. And tradition, a slim bulwark against anarchy.

In *A Man Could Stand Up—,* as psychological drama and historical event continue to interact, both Tietjens and Valentine pass beyond even the limited protection of tradition. Each of them confronts a world bereft of order and each experiences a mental strain so severe that it borders on insanity. On the morning of the Armistice, against the background of all London celebrating, Valentine controls her thoughts with difficulty and quarrels to the point of insult with Miss Wanostrocht, the prudent and prudish head of her school. Tietjens, a member now of the ragtag army at the weakest sector of the front, saves his sanity only by the memory of Valentine. They meet again, on Armistice Day, determined to live together in spite of both the old dictates of tradition and the chaos that now surrounds them. They choose to effect a new compromise between self-denial and self-expression; and *The Last Post,* carrying them into peace-time, confirms and elaborates the nature of their choice. The main thematic movement of *Parade's End,* reminiscent of *A Call* and *The Good Soldier,* is dialectical.

Ford's art is almost always equal to his ambitious purposes in *Parade's End.* Yet it should be remarked that the tetralogy is a less perfect work than *The Good Soldier.* The last two volumes, particularly, show momentary lapses in artistic control. Some flaws—for example, an awkward explanation of a time shift in Part One of *A Man Could Stand Up—* and a few pages of sing-song prose in *The Last Post*—seem to be due simply to carelessness. Some, like a mock-heroic digression on Chantecler and Madame Partlet, apparently proceed from an enthusiastic but inappropriate sense of whimsy. Other yieldings to old temptations, however, are more extensive and more serious. At the end of Part Two of *A Man Could Stand Up—,* Tietjens suffers two heavy strokes of sheer bad fortune. He receives a virtually unmotivated and wholly unjustifiable reproof from General Campion, and he learns that one of his junior officers was shot as he carried him to apparent safety. For the moment, Tietjens appears to be simply the innocent victim of a malevolent universe. A somewhat similar kind of simplification occurs in *The Last Post* when, at the very end, Ford sentimentalizes Sylvia. Momentary kindness, particularly kindness that springs from defiance, is typical of Sylvia. Thus when Tietjens' hired man accuses her of trying to make Valentine miscarry and she calls him a "damn fool" in reply and canters down the hill to announce her decision to divorce Tietjens, Sylvia is convincing. But when she says to Valentine, "I have a fine [child] but I wanted another," she ceases to be the Sylvia of familiar acquaintance. Here, as in Part Two of *A Man Could Stand Up—,* Ford may be misled by excessive sympathy for his character, or he may be overstating the resolution of his forces of conflict. (Certainly *The Last Post* shows other unmistakable signs of thematic insistence, notably in the pagan and Christian symbolism with which Ford rather awkwardly overlays his narrative.) All of these moments of carelessness, of whimsy, of sentimentality, and of overstatement are, admittedly, very uncomfortable ones. But though they detract from they certainly do not destroy an otherwise impressive performance.

For all its frank intellectuality, for all its plain social and moral concerns, *Parade's End* does not read like a Fabian tract or a paper in ethics. Just as Ford's impressionism in *The Good Soldier* achieves more than a gradual, hence lifelike, introduction to a complex set of characters, so his very similar methods in the tetralogy offer more than a record of a particular period of English life. His detached and superior narrative voice speaks intermittently throughout the series; in *Some Do Not . . . ,* which primarily introduces the principal characters and their social milieu, it speaks at length. To forget the tone of this voice, to fail to note the absurd human behavior in many of the scenes it presents, and to overlook the fact that Ford's juxtapositions of episode are often funny as well as thematically significant, is to forget, as some critics have done, one of the most engaging and characteristic features of the Tietjens series. From beginning to end, *Parade's End* is, in part, social comedy. In *Some Do Not . . . ,* for example, Mrs. Duchemin gives a traditionally elegant breakfast to Macmaster, Valentine, Tietjens, and a handful of other guests. In its setting of Turner paintings, old woodwork, expensive tableware, and caviar ordered from Bond Street, the scene is historically and socially accurate. But it is also broadly comic. Mrs. Duchemin's position at her own table is "strategic" and her silver chafing dishes, épergnes, and rosebowls form a "fortification"—behind which the Reverend Mr. Duchemin will presently rise to shout obscenities in his "Oxford Movement voice."

Of course, despite Ford's disposition to be explicit in *Parade's End,* he nonetheless involves us intellectually in his fiction. We need not work our way through such intricate deceits as Dowell's self-defense, but we are induced to participate, to organize the discrete, and to make complex moral judgments.

In his treatment of the recurrent themes of saintliness, self-expression, and tradition, Ford favors none of his characters with consistent sympathy or approval. As he insists in his preface to *A Man Could Stand Up—,* even Tietjens is "not, *not, NOT*" the author's spokesman. Tietjens criticizes tradition, but he belongs to it all the same; and Ford arranges many of the incidents in *Some Do Not . . .* in order to contrast what Tietjens says with what he does. Immediately after he rudely sets his scale of values before Macmaster, Tietjens descends from the train at Ashford to confront the "extraordinarily blue, innocent eyes" of General Campion. When the General asks, "How's your mother-in-law?" Tietjens answers, "I believe she's much better. Quite restored." With these words, Tietjens supports a fiction invented to save traditional appearances. In reality, his mother-in-law has not been ill; she has gone to the Continent to disguise the fact that Sylvia has fled there with a lover. Tietjens also conceals Macmaster's affair with Mrs. Duchemin and fails to expose a fraudulently low report of French war losses that Macmaster submits to His Majesty's Ministry of Imperial Statistics.

Tietjens is neither a hypocrite nor a coward. His actions are influenced by personal loyalty—to his wife, to his friend, to his godfather. They are also influenced by a genuine attraction to the very tradition he criticizes. Like most men, in Ford's world and the real one, Tietjens is morally inconsistent. As Sylvia sums up his dilemma: "I tell you he's so formal he can't do without all the conventions there are and so truthful he can't use half of them." His inconsistency alone accounts for many of the *contretemps* he suffers.

All the principal characters of *Parade's End* may be aligned on Tietjens' moral scale. But, like Tietjens, they too are inconstant, sometimes saintly, sometimes rebellious, sometimes traditional. Indeed, since Ford's attitude transcends those of his characters, the points of the scale themselves frequently change their relative positions. And, as a summary of the dialectic movement of the tetralogy has already suggested, the entire scale is finally superseded by a further definition of goodness. While the characters are in the process of living, they are also learning. Each of them at times speaks truthfully about himself, about others, about the way they all act, and about the way they should act. But their statements and their actions must always be judged by the immediate context in which they occur and by the context of the whole tetralogy.

Tietjens, Sylvia, Valentine, Mr. and Mrs. Duchemin, and Macmaster all live lives larger than their various thematic roles. They carry their ethical burdens easily, even incidentally, because they are strong in their fidelity to human nature. They compel our belief—and also our sympathy. Ford involves us emotionally as well as intellectually in the moral dilemmas of his characters; and just as in *The Good Soldier* he elicits an indulgent response to the longing for innocence, so in *Parade's End* he forces us to recognize the attractions not only of saintliness, but also of tradition and even of anarchy.

Bernard Bergonzi (essay date 1965)

SOURCE: "Retrospect II: Fiction," in *Heroes' Twilight*, second edition, The Macmillan Press Ltd., 1980, pp. 171-97.

[*In the following excerpt Bergonzi discusses the effects of World War I as presented in* Parade's End.]

Parade's End is a trilogy or a tetralogy, depending on whether one accepts the final volume, *Last Post,* as an integral part of the total design. The first section, *Some Do Not,* came out in 1924, *No More Parades* in 1925, and *A Man Could Stand Up* in 1926. *Last Post* appeared in 1928; it seems that Ford wrote it because of the importunate desire of a woman friend to know what happened to his characters, and a few years later he virtually disowned it, saying that if the work was ever to appear in a single volume he would like it to do so as a trilogy. In fact, the one-volume American edition of 1950 included all four volumes; the recent Bodley Head reprint was restricted to three. *Last Post* is, indisputably, very different in tone and technique from the first three volumes of the sequence: it represents a certain desire on Ford's part to tie up loose ends, and at the same time to adopt a radically different mode of narration. Ford's critics are very much at variance about the place of *Last Post* in the sequence: Robie Macauley and Richard Cassell believe that it is essential to round off the work; whereas John Meixner has argued vehemently against this opinion, claiming that *Parade's End* forms an artistic whole only as a trilogy, and he is supported in this by Graham Greene in his introduction to the Bodley Head edition. My own view inclines towards the latter opinion; *Last Post* seems to be so loosely connected as to form a sequel rather than an integral part of the novel. As Meixner says, the trilogy, beginning with Ford's hero, Christopher Tietjens, travelling in a luxuriously appointed railway compartment, and ending, in the last paragraph of *A Man Could Stand Up,* with Tietjens celebrating Armistice Day in the empty flat from which his vindictive wife has stripped all the furniture, does have a distinct unity and symmetry.

Parade's End deals, in essentials, with the long martyrdom of Christopher Tietjens, officer and gentleman, who is subject to constant persecution, above all from his wife, the beautiful sexual terrorist, Sylvia, and, during the war, from his military superiors and from powerful civilians at home. *Parade's End* is, it seems to me, the finest novel by an Englishman to have been produced by the Great War; but at the same time, it can hardly be regarded simply as a 'war novel'. . . . Indeed, the whole of the magnificent opening section of *Some Do Not* takes place some years before the outbreak of war. Nevertheless, *Parade's End* does offer a profound imaginative grasp of the effect of the war on the traditional patterns of English life. In this novel we see a bringing together of the several dominant themes which . . . characterized the literature of the Great War: the supersession of the Hero as a tangible ideal; a nostalgic love of rural England, combined with an anguished sense that centuries of English tradition were being overthrown; the alienation of the soldier from the civilians. Ford embodies all these themes in Christopher Tietjens, a deeply and intensely realized figure whose presence provides the

necessary unity of the first three volumes (he is largely absent from the scene in *Last Post*), and who is at the same time made to bear an unusually wide range of significance: he is the last true Tory, the final anachronistic embodiment of the virtues of the eighteenth-century English gentleman, an Anglican saint, even something of a Christ-figure, turning the other cheek to his persecutors. And yet Tietjens is always recognizable as a living human being: fair, red-faced, large, slow-moving.

In the opening paragraph of *Some Do Not,* Ford brilliantly places Tietjens, and his friend Macmaster, in their appropriate context in the pre-war ruling class:

> The two young men—they were of the English public official class—sat in the perfectly appointed railway carriage. The leather straps to the windows were of virgin newness; the mirrors beneath the new luggage racks immaculate as if they had reflected very little; the bulging upholstery in its luxuriant, regulated curves was scarlet and yellow in an intricate, minute dragon pattern, the design of a geometrician in Cologne. The compartment smelt faintly, hygienically of admirable varnish; the train ran as smoothly—Tietjens remembered thinking—as British gilt-edged securities. It travelled fast; yet had it swayed or jolted over the rail joints, except at the curve before Tonbridge or over the points at Ashford where these eccentricities are expected and allowed for, Macmaster, Tietjens felt certain, would have written to the company. Perhaps he would even have written to *The Times.*

They live in a world which is ordered, controlled, predictable (even the railway upholstery's curves are both luxuriant and regulated); a world, too, of security and conspicuous consumption. And yet it is not entirely Tietjens's world, as the clear note of distancing irony in this description suggests; the succeeding paragraphs show that it is the young Scottish *arriviste,* Macmaster, who is the conscious upholder of Edwardian ruling-class attitudes. Tietjens, on the other hand, moves through this world with considerable indifference to the refinement of its *mœurs.* He is in but not of it—a brilliant mathematician working in the Imperial Department of Statistics—and his real allegiances are rooted in an older England, symbolized by the family home, Groby, in the North Riding.

Unquestionably, Tietjens, and what he stands for, is heavily romanticized by Ford. Half-German by birth, and the precocious child of a cosmopolitan, artistic household, Ford had had little opportunity to make extensive observations of the English gentry. There is both a simplicity and a glamour in his picture of Tietjens's Tory ideals that suggests a foreigner's romantic image of England; hence, perhaps, the high reputation of *Parade's End* in America (William Carlos Williams claimed that the four novels 'constitute the English prose masterpiece of their time'). Yet Ford's image is exaggerated rather than false: he shows us a familiar subject in an unfamiliar light, which may distort but also illuminates. Tietjens, the Yorkshire squire, stands for a more remote England than the Liberal England, centred on the week-end cottage in the Home Counties, of Forster and the Georgian poets; he preserves something of the feudal manner. In *A Man Could Stand*

Up, Tietjens reflects in the trenches: 'The Feudal Spirit was broken. Perhaps it would therefore be harmful to Trench Warfare. It used to be comfortable and cosy. You fought beside men from your own hamlet under the leadership of the parson's son.'

One finds, too, an almost Gothic romanticism in Tietjens's conviction that there is a curse on Groby because the house was once dispossessed from its Catholic owners (the Tietjens family came over from Holland with William and Mary), and that the curse will not be lifted until Groby is once more in Catholic hands (as will happen when it is inherited by Tietjens's son, whom Sylvia is having brought up as a Catholic). Yet his visions of England have affinities with those entertained during the war years by writers of very different temperament. The following extract from one of Tietjens's reveries in the front line, evoked by hearing a cornet player practising an air by Purcell, recalls [passages from Lawrence's wartime letters] . . . :

> The only satisfactory age in England! . . . Yet what chance had it today? Or, still more, tomorrow? In the sense that the age of, say, Shakespeare had a chance. Or Pericles! or Augustus!
>
> Heaven knew, we did not want a preposterous drum-beating such as the Elizabethans produced—and received. Like lions at a fair. . . . But what chance had quiet fields, Anglican sainthood, accuracy of thought, heavy-leaved, timbered hedgerows, slowly creeping ploughlands moving up the slopes? . . . Still, the land remains. . . .
>
> The land remains. . . . It remains! . . . At that same moment the dawn was wetly revealing; over there in George Herbert's parish. . . . What was it called? . . . What the devil was its name? Oh, Hell! . . . Between Salisbury and Wilton. . . . The tiny church. . . . But he refused to consider the ploughlands, the heavy groves, the slow high-road above the church that the dawn was at that moment wetly revealing—until he could remember that name. . . . He refused to consider that, probably even to-day, that land ran to . . . produced the stock of . . . Anglican sainthood. The quiet thing!

In part, the random, fragmentary quality of the writing here may be regarded as expressive of Tietjens's disordered consciousness, still not properly recovered from shell-shock and amnesia. But at the same time, these stylistic devices occur with uncomfortable frequency in the later volumes of *Parade's End*; compared with the mastery writing of *Some Do Not,* their prose is often uncontrolled and fluid, and the use of dots as punctuation becomes obsessive.

Like Lawrence, Ford was very conscious of living in a doomed society, though some of the reflections by which Tietjens expresses this conviction read a little oddly. As when, in *Some Do Not,* Tietjens is in earnest conversation with his brother Mark, and glances at the fountain of the Inner Temple by which they are standing: 'He considered the base of the fountain that was half full of leaves. This civilization had contrived a state of things in which leaves rotted by August.' Unlike Lawrence, Ford dramatizes

rather than describes his conviction of social decay; there is nothing equivalent to the retrospective diatribes of *Kangaroo.* Tietjens is constantly shown as the honourable man harried by the low, unworthy forces that manifest themselves when the opulent Edwardian upper-class world, so vividly evoked in the novel's opening paragraphs, becomes corrupt in the atmosphere of war. Macmaster, the energetic social climber whom Tietjens had befriended and helped, picks his friend's brains and rises to a pinnacle of bureaucratic eminence, whilst Tietjens remains an obscure infantry officer. Tietjens is disgraced when his bank unjustly refuses to meet his cheques. We learn that the banker responsible is one of Sylvia's admirers. She explains to Tietjens:

> 'But of course he hates you for being in the army. All the men who aren't hate all the men that are. And, of course, when there's a woman between them, the men who aren't do all they can to do the others in. When they're bankers they have a pretty good pull. . . .'

And from Sylvia, Tietjens suffers unspeakable humiliations; in his study of their relationship Ford shows unsurpassed psychological insight. For several years they have sustained a marriage without mutual love; indeed, Sylvia has actively despised Tietjens. But when he falls in love with the young suffragette, Valentine Wannop, Sylvia's jealousy turns into a violent sexual passion for her husband, and when he fails to respond she turns to extremes of cruelty. Sylvia, though a monster, never entirely alienates the reader's sympathy. As V. S. Pritchett has shrewdly commented: 'One has a sneaking sympathy for his wife who at one moment complains that her husband is trying to be Jesus Christ as well as the misunderstood son of a great landowner. Her cruelties are an attempt to turn a martyr into a man.'

The word 'martyr' is, indeed, significant. Ford is trying to write a novel about a particular kind of hero; not the towering martial heroes of the Renaissance whose insufficiencies for the life of the Western Front had been sardonically glanced at by Barbusse; nor the ardent young votaries of the early months of the war, whose spirit was summed up in Julian Grenfell's 'Into Battle'. In so far as Tietjens is intended by his creator to be more than a private man, to embody certain national traditions and habits of mind, he has remote affinities with the ancient heroes of epic, though he reflects a Virgilian *pietas* rather than an Homeric *virtù*. More specifically, Tietjens is a passive and suffering hero, whose triumphs arise, not from violent action, but from *patience* (derived, ultimately, from *patior,* to suffer). The most famous example in English of this kind of hero is the Christ of *Paradise Regained.* Yet Ford, working without Milton's theological frame of reference, is less able to convince us of Tietjens's ultimate triumph. The novel (as opposed to such sharply generic forms as the thriller and the western) is not an easy form in which to accommodate heroic figures; its natural bias is so much to the realistic, the typical, the ordinary, that the presence of any figure of conspicuous stature and virtue is liable to set up ironic tensions. The drama remains, still, a more convincing vehicle for such types. In our final glimpse of Tietjens in *Last Post,* he has retired into quiet country life with

Valentine, as a small-holder and antique-dealer; Sylvia has at least abated her hostility, and this perhaps represents a triumph for Tietjens, but he is now purely a private man and not a representative figure. His ancestral home, Groby, is leased to a crazy and destructive American woman; the symbolism is unmistakable.

In those scenes of *Parade's End* that deal specifically with the war in France, Tietjens's role as a suffering figure is underlined. In the opening chapter of *No More Parades,* Tietjens refuses—for very good reason—to give compassionate leave to a Welsh private called O Nine Morgan. A few minutes later the man is killed by a shell splinter. Tietjens bends over the body:

> The heat from the brazier was overpowering on his bent face. He hoped he would not get his hands all over blood, because blood is very sticky. It makes your fingers stick together impotently. But there might not be any blood in the darkness under the fellow's back where he was putting his hand. There was, however: it was very wet.

Tietjens associates Morgan's death with his refusal of leave, and assumes a corresponding burden of guilt. Again, in the sustained section set in the trenches in *A Man Could Stand Up,* Tietjens rescues the young subaltern, Aranjuez, after he had been partly buried by a falling shell; he is carrying Aranjuez to safety when the boy suddenly runs off screaming, with his hands to his face. Tietjens thinks, disapprovingly, that Aranjuez has lost his nerve. Only later does he hear that he had been hit by a sniper and has lost an eye. Tietjens, already tormented beyond endurance by his private life, has to bear the infantry officer's common load of compassion and guilt for the sufferings of his men. He is also subjected to the animus of his new commanding officer, General Campion, a friend of Sylvia's, who transfers Tietjens to the ignominious task of guarding prisoners of war.

These trench scenes frequently manifest the fluidity of writing that is one of the major faults of the later sections of *Parade's End.* And Henry Williamson has attacked them, in 'Reality in War Literature', for inaccuracy of military detail and a general air of inauthenticity. Nevertheless, to an uninitiated reader, and despite their stylistic weaknesses, they convey a compelling impression of frontline life; more vividly, in fact, than many exact documentary descriptions. Ford was invariably an impressionistic artist rather than a reporter.

This discussion of *Parade's End* has only glanced at a few of its salient features, and has not done justice to its outstanding literary qualities. A full analysis, for instance, would trace Ford's virtuoso use of the time-shift technique in the first part of *Some Do Not,* and would examine in detail the superbly sensitive effects he could achieve by his characteristically impressionist prose. One could also dwell on the breadth and richness of his characters; in which, although an avowed disciple of Flaubert and James, Ford showed himself a possibly unconscious follower of the great Victorians. Tietjens himself, Sylvia, Valentine, General Campion, Edith Ethel Duchemin, all have an instinctive vitality. At the same time, one must admit

the work's unevenness: effects which were triumphant in the first volumes become weakly repetitive in later ones. In particular, some of Ford's uses of the time-shift seem like devices for evading a possibly tricky narrative climax. The great expanse of the three—or four—volumes makes it clear that Ford was weak at sustaining the architectonics of a large fictional structure; his numerous successes are all local rather than large-scale, and *Parade's End* is, *in toto,* rather less than the sum of its distinguished parts.

Yet the work's traditional novelistic virtues do, in my view, undoubtedly transcend its failures of technique. In contrast to other prose works produced by the Great War, *Parade's End* offers little concrete documentation but a great deal of brilliant insight into the effects of that war. Tietjens's romantic Tory England was, no doubt, an extravagant concept; but its affinities with the more modest visions of the poets in uniform are sufficient to produce a recognizable picture. As I have suggested, *Parade's End,* more than any other work, succeeds in combining the dominant literary preoccupations of the war.

In the course of discussing *Parade's End,* V. S. Pritchett has observed, 'As a character Tietjens escapes from the cliché of almost all the war novels of that time in which the hero conveys that the whole war has been declared against him personally'.

Frank MacShane (essay date 1965)

SOURCE: "*Parade's End,*" in *The Life and Work of Ford Madox Ford,* Routledge & Kegan Paul, 1965, pp. 170-90.

[*An American author and educator whose publications include well-received biographies of Ford, Raymond Chandler, James Jones, and John O'Hara, MacShane has specialized in studies of the so-called "stepchildren of literature." MacShane's works combine narrative and critical insight in an effort to rescue some relatively forgotten authors from what he considers their undeserved obscurity. In the following excerpt, he examines form and technique in* Parade's End.]

Parade's End is an immensely suggestive panoramic novel that at the same time provides a profound psychological analysis of a small number of human beings. Superficially, it has much in common with *Vanity Fair* and, in so far as it presents a study of the war between the sexes against a background of rising and falling social classes, it resembles Proust's *A la Recherche du Temps Perdu.* Yet comparison with these books or even with Joyce's *Ulysses* succeeds only in placing it in a class of literature. The success of *Parade's End* depends on Ford's skill in combining the intimate psychological techniques of James with a large social framework. This milieu is itself original in the sense that while the ordinary nineteenth-century novel seems to present an apparently static society with only an undercurrent of dissatisfaction and turmoil, and the twentieth-century novel shows a society whose institutions are wholly disrupted and discredited, *Parade's End,* standing halfway between these two, portrays the actual disruption as it took place during the war. Yet even in its psychological aspects, this tetralogy is not merely the sort of book James might have written had he attempted the 'big subject' of a Galsworthy or Balzac. For, as Granville Hicks remarked, Ford 'has done certain sorts of things that James could never have done and would not have attempted.'

The substance of *Parade's End* would never have come through without the technical skill with which Ford treated his subject, and here the two are perfectly suited to each other. Hitherto, with the exception of *The Good Soldier,* Ford's work was uneven and his conception of his subject rarely lived up to the technical brilliance of his writing. Often his heroes were too extraordinary for belief, and sometimes, as Arnold Bennett wrote in a review of *A Call,* Ford endowed his characters 'with a comprehensive fineness of perception, and a skill in verbal expression which it is absolutely impossible that they, living the life they do live, could possess.' Other faults like an excessive reliance on coincidence or an overpopulation of characters come from Ford's avowed notion that it mattered little what a man's subject was so long as the treatment was admirable. In his letters to other writers and during the long hours of conversation with Conrad, Ford had been concerned solely with the way in which a writer could best get his effects. For a novelist like H. G. Wells, this preoccupation was meaningless, and it is true that whatever may be the faults of Wells's work, it is strong where Ford's early work was weak: Wells's characters and situations were real; Ford's were not. Ford's devotion to technique, however, paid its dividends in such works as *The Good Soldier* and *Parade's End,* whereas much of Wells's later work suffers from the very sloppiness Ford was endeavouring to avoid.

In conceiving the characters of the Tietjens tetralogy, what Ford has done, as Melvin Seiden has pointed out, is to make Christopher into an anti-hero who has affinities with Dostoievsky's *Idiot,* and to make his heroine the precise opposite of the typical British heroine. As the world has turned upside down, he seems to be saying, so also have people, so that a modern version of Pamela would necessarily have to be different from Richardson's. But the real point Ford makes is that Sylvia is neither extremely virtuous in the tradition of the British heroine of romance, nor fiendish in the manner of Lady Macbeth. Rather, she is merely a decent enough woman of the world. In an early essay, **'The Woman of the Novelists',** Ford criticized the English fictional heroine for always being an extreme—either a representative of the 'fair sex' or some sort of monster. Recognizing the falsehood of this notion, he tried in Sylvia Tietjens to create a real woman rather than a 'super-woman' of the type of Desdemona, Juliet or Sophia Western.

Thus in all his work Ford was a self-conscious writer who was always able to say, 'I know exactly how I get my effects as far as those effects go. Brought up in Victorian times when literature was more a matter of morality than of art, he found relief in the works of foreign writers lent him by his grandfather, Ford Madox Brown. And after reading such books as *Madame Bovary, Le Rouge et le Noir* and the *Lettres de Mon Moulin* of Daudet, along with all the usual classics of nineteenth-century English fiction, he perceived that the modern French novel was less amateurish than the English. He therefore strove to learn as much as he could from such Continental writers as Sten-

dhal, Maupassant, Turgenev and Flaubert and from such writers in English as Marryat and Henry James who followed the same path. In the years of his apprenticeship, both alone and with Conrad, he gradually consolidated his method. The first product of it is *The Good Soldier*; the first detailed exposition of it occurs in his book on Joseph Conrad. The job of writing *The Good Soldier* was doubtless hard enough, but for a psychological novelist like Ford, the effort of maintaining tension and interest for the eight hundred pages of *Parade's End* must have been extremely difficult.

In an article on Ford [in *National Review,* August 1948], Edward Crankshaw pointed out that both he and Conrad were rebelling against the traditional panoramic novel, preferring instead to limit their subject to an 'affaire'. In *Parade's End,* however, Ford goes beyond this limitation and adds what Crankshaw calls a 'mirror of society'. The result is a work that 'combines the intensiveness of the new school with the extensiveness of the old masters.'

What made this achievement possible was Ford's attention to over-all form: every individual element of the book is subordinated to the central issue. The difficulty of achieving what Poe called 'unity of effect' is, of course, increased when the writer thinks not in terms of short stories but in sequels. But even in his first trilogy, *The Fifth Queen* series, he took care to plan the work in terms of three books. The result, he found, was that the second volume was better than the first, as it was intended to be, because he had already got in his setting and descriptions in the earlier book. In his later work, Ford's planning was necessarily more complex than simply deciding where to put descriptions and where to put action. He had, for example, to consider the rôle particular scenes would play in the book as a whole. The use of a strong scene is often tempting for a writer, since climactic moments are dramatic and exciting. They are sometimes also very false, however, and tend to stick out from the surface so that the reader remembers one particular scene, but not the book itself. The writer who considers his work as a progression in which motives and actions will be made clear only at the very end, must therefore suppress strong scenes. For however attractive they may be in themselves, they will interfere with his final effect.

Ford's willingness to obey this rigorous code so as to protect the architecture of his whole book is made clear in the suppression of the scene with which *Some Do Not* was to have ended. This scene, which now exists only in manuscript, depicts the last dramatic interview that takes place between Christopher and Sylvia before Tietjens leaves for the front; it stresses the sexual antagonism that has grown up between them and it contains a good deal of violence. Had *Some Do Not* been designed to stand alone, this ending would have been satisfactory, but as it was only a part of a tetralogy, it was suppressed, and Ford put its substance in the next novel in the form of Tietjens' reminiscences.

Mention of form brings up the question of the final book of the series, *The Last Post.* It is clear from a letter Ford wrote in 1930, in which he said that he did not like this book and 'always intended the series to end with *A Man*

Could Stand Up,' that *Parade's End* was intended as a trilogy. In recent years, however, it has been twice published as a tetralogy. *The Last Post* differs from the preceding three novels in so far as the focus turns from Christopher Tietjens to his brother, Mark. Compared to the others, *The Last Post* is static and involves a certain amount of recapitulation of previously narrated events. Yet, as Robie Macauley points out, without this novel, the work as a whole would be 'sadly truncated,' for not only does one find out, as Ford wrote in his preface, 'what became of Tietjens,' one also finds in this denouement that Tietjens is perpetuated as a symbol, thus making him not merely one man who walked a stage and was heard of no more, but a representative of a whole class. Those who live at Groby—Mark Tietjens and his retinue—constitute a kind of Greek chorus that serves to connect Tietjens with the Yorkshire soil, and indeed, with present reality. Artistically, it was also essential that the focus be changed; the Christopher-centred novel was designed for three novels, and to stretch it would have spoiled its form. A coda, then, was the only possible solution.

With regard to the various techniques Ford employed in this book—the time-shift, the purposed longueur, *progression d'effet* and the others—enough has been said of them as they were applied to the collaborated works and to *The Good Soldier.* In a sense, it is remarkable that Ford knew for so long what Impressionism was supposed to do. Thus what he wrote in 1914 was wholly applicable to the Tietjens books of the 1920's. Not for a long time, however, did he succeed in doing himself what he had for so long set up as a model.

The statement [from **"On Impressionism—I,"** by Ford Madox Hueffer, in *Poetry and Drama,* June 1914] that appears below was the intention, but it was not really fulfilled until he wrote *Parade's End.*

> For the first business of Impressionism is to produce an impression, and the only way in literature to produce an impression is to awaken interest. And, in a sustained argument, you can only keep interest awakened by keeping alive, by whatever means you may have at your disposal, the surprise of your reader. You must state your argument; you must illustrate it, and then you must stick in something that appears to have nothing whatever to do with either subject or illustration, so that the reader will exclaim: 'What the devil is the fellow driving at?' And then you must go on in the same way arguing, illustrating and startling and illustrating—until at the very end your contentions will appear like a ravelled skein.

> And then, in the last few lines, you will draw towards you the master-string of that seeming confusion, and the whole pattern of the carpet, the whole design of the net-work will be apparent.

> This method, you observe, founds itself upon analysis of the human mind. For no human being likes listening to long and sustained arguments. Such listening is an effort, and no artist has the right to call for any effort from his audience. A picture should come out of its frame and seize the spectator.

One technical change in *Parade's End* which increased the accessibility of Ford's prose is here worth noticing. Whereas much of the success of *The Good Soldier* had depended on Ford's use of a narrator whose very mannerisms contributed to the point of the book, in the tetralogy he returned to his own voice and emphasized dialogue. While this method may owe something to Hemingway, it differs from Hemingway in being far less abrupt and telegraphic, for Ford's greatest gift, as distinct from an acquired technique, was his mastery of flowing prose rhythms. Coupled with this new directness of manner is Ford's abandonment of the endlessly modified sentence of James and the highly coloured phraseology of Conrad. The result therefore is a novel that is at once complex in its over-all form and extraordinarily lucid in its language. The work as a whole has an individuality of style that makes it an original contribution to the world's literature. As Caroline Gordon said, in writing it Ford 'succeeded in doing the thing that Poe said could not be done. He produced a long work whose tensions are so nicely adjusted, whose tone is sustained as that of a short tale or lyric poem.'

Alan Kennedy (essay date 1970)

SOURCE: "Tietjens' Travels: *Parade's End* as Comedy," in *Twentieth Century Literature,* Vol. 16, No. 2, April, 1970, pp. 85-95.

[*In the following essay, Kennedy identifies comedic elements in* Parade's End.]

One can easily see Tietjens as a model of integrity, of morality, of pre-Edwardian honour and Christian long-suffering; as an innocent who is the victim of "an old bitch gone in the teeth." The ease of such a vision may be an indication that it is the best, most correct reaction to *Parade's End.* One need not, certainly, be always looking for complications. Tietjens' story does appear to have a direct simplicity, and one cannot be too far wrong in saying that Ford approved more of Tietjens' integrity than he did of the "lachrymose polygamy" of such moderns as Rossetti and McMaster.

In contrast, though, to a view which sees Tietjens as a tragic victim of a decaying society, one must remember the immense comic spirit which informs the whole of the work. I do not disagree that *Parade's End* sounds a note of regret for the passing of a way of life which so emphasized public virtue. But surely, Ford's regret for Victorianism-Edwardianism is of the same type as Swift's "lament" over the fact that we cannot all be as reasonable as Houyhnhnms. Swift seems to say that it would of course be desirable if we could establish the reign of reason in the affairs of men. But, after all, look what happens to a man, Gulliver, when he attempts to become all reason and no body. He declines into misanthropy, avoiding his wife and cultivating his relationship with his horses. Ford seems to be saying something similar about the values summed up by the word "parade." Of course it would be nice if we could all be at "moral attention forever," but my dear fellow, it is just not in the nature of human beings to torment themselves that way.

To make a fetish of reason or to make a fetish of a code of honour, then, is contrary to the nature of man. If Ford looks with a touch of regret at the passing of a particular code, he looks much more actively towards the proper fulfilling of the passionate needs of men. In saying this I imply that *Parade's End* is ultimately comic and not tragic; that we are not meant to grieve at the protracted suffering caused Tietjens by a corrupt society. Rather we should laugh at and ultimately with him. We should also revel in those other feelings of release, freedom and clear vision that come with the best of comedy.

Of course, most readers have long since recognized that the "easy" view outlined above is not wholly correct and that there is much that is funny in *Parade's End.* No one fails to find Sir Vincent McMaster and his Egeria anything but funny, and there are the two famous scenes, breakfast with the mad divine, Duchemin, and the dinner during which Sylvia decorates Tietjens' dress tunic with her two chops and aspic. Writers like Carol Ohmann remind us that there is an element of the comic in *Parade's End:*

> To forget the tone of his voice, to fail to note the absurd human behavior in many of the scenes it presents, and to overlook the fact that Ford's juxtapositions of episode are often funny as well as thematically significant, is to forget, as some critics have done, one of the most engaging and characteristic features of the Tietjens series. From beginning to end *Parade's End* is, in part, social comedy.

It may be inconsistent to suggest that the tone of voice of the novel is consistently comic while the tale itself is comic only in places and therefore, supposedly, tragic overall. There is an implication that Ford was not completely in control of his technique. But at least Mrs. Ohmann gives us a needed reminder about comedy in *Parade's End,* even though she sees comedy as merely relief from the more serious aspects of the book. We find a similar point of view in John A. Meixner's comment that *Parade's End* is "full of comic surprise." However, "Christopher is tragic, of course, but he is decidedly amusing, particularly when he is being very much the Yorkshireman as in Part One." Here one becomes even more suspicious; can a tragic hero be "decidedly amusing?" It is my belief that not only the voice and isolated incidents are comic, but that the very structure of *Parade's End* suggests that Ford was consciously employing the comic mode in his great novel about the shift from one world into another.

To be able to see *Parade's End* as comic, one must first see that the novel is not primarily a cry of pain about the end of "parade." In essence it is rather a celebration of the passing of a way of life no longer possible. If "parade" sums up the qualities and values of Victorian-Edwardian society, then Ford's point must be that that particular parade has ended in World War. Parade is a term used for the state of being on duty in military service. So the title directs our attention to the time when duty is over, when the war is ended, and new life can begin. Parade also implies an overt code of behaviour which one displays to indicate culture, cultivation. The noble, feudal atmosphere evoked by "parade" may indeed be one that had much appeal for Ford. One need not conclude, however, that this

appealing atmosphere made Ford incapable of seeing that the parade of high manners, of social distinctions, had become so extreme, so much a hollow sham of one-upmanship, that it led to slaughter. So *Parade's End* plays the Last Post for parade, hope, glory, honour; but it also indicts the parade of a misdirected society and indicates a method by which a new hope can be realized. With "oppressions, inaccuracies, gossip, backbiting, lying, corruptions and vileness, you had the combination of wolf, tiger, weasel and louse-covered ape that was human society."

During the course of the tetralogy, Tietjens is able to extricate himself from the demands of a society turned so bestial and from a code which is revealed to be inhuman in its application. He goes "underground" and attains enough personal freedom to permit his establishing a "marriage" with Valentine and the pastoral resolution of the fourth novel. Mark Tietjens holds on to the old dignities, to the old values and refuses to accept the new world with its new ways. In so doing, he wills his own paralysis and spends the whole of *The Last Post* mute before his lover. By the end of the tetralogy, "parade" has been thoroughly exploded.

Parade's End then, is not necessarily a tragic story about loss of the Golden Age. Tietjens periodically hungers for the comfort of the past, for Bemerton, Herbert's parsonage, but in this he is very similar to the absurd McMaster who "was in search of the inspiration of the past." Tietjens learns to accept and to live in the present, even though he is still tormented by Mrs. de Bray Pape and her entourage. Tietjens is freed from what Northrop Frye would call "ritual bondage," and this release from bondage is one of the essentials of comedy. Frye says that the normal comic pattern is the movement from one type of society to another. The society in control at the beginning of the action is restrictive, repressive and humoristic. It must be overthrown by the young generation of lovers, by the representatives of Eros. The society in control at the beginning of *Parade's End* is obviously ripe for overthrow; its central representatives are Sir Vincent McMaster and Lord Edward Campion, K.C.M.G. Campion's relationship to Tietjens suggests the Oedipal situation common to comedy. Campion acts *in loco parentis* to Tietjens, advising him to set up some girl in a tobacco shop (advice which Tietjens has already given McMaster), but his real interest would seem to be in Tietjens' wife Sylvia. In the fourth novel we see Sylvia and Campion poised on the verge of elopement to India.

At first glance then, Tietjens and Valentine are the youthful lovers, who are thwarted in their attempt at an affair because of the strict Victorian code of behaviour. The point of interest here, though, is that Tietjens is both the young lover and the *senex,* the member of the repressive old order of society. He is both the promoter and the inhibitor of the comic action. As comic hero and comic villain he portrays the same inner conflict that troubles Edwardian society in its time of transition. Tietjens applies to himself a code of behaviour which he does not demand of his friends (witness his toleration of McMaster's erotic peccadilloes) and this inconsistency indicates his readiness for change. Tietjens' morality is an unimaginative version of dogmatic Tory-Christian correct behaviour for a gentleman, summed up best by his pronouncement that, "No one but a blackguard would ever submit a woman to the ordeal of divorce."

It is in the first of the novels that Christopher announces his decision to take a holiday from principles, and at the end of Part I of *Some Do Not . . .* we find him in a characteristic quandary over principles:

> A long long time afterwards he said:
>
> "Damn all principles!" And then;
>
> "But one has to keep on going. . . . Principles are like a skeleton map of a country—you know whether you're going east or north."
>
> The knacker's cart lumbered round the corner.

Tietjens' little holiday from principles allows him to go comfortably for a ride in the horse cart with Valentine, finally to collide with the carelessly driven car of General Campion. The question of inconsistent or inadequate values is here tied closely to an incident of physical violence and the knacker's cart lumbers around the corner to collect the injured horse. The knacker's cart is also coming for the whole world in the form of war, as the inevitable concomitant of inconsistency and inadequacy of moral vision.

For Tietjens before the War, morality is a simple thing; it is a matter of opposing desire and restraint:

> I stand for monogamy and chastity. And for no talking about it. Of course if a man who's a man wants to have a woman he has her. And again, no talking about it. He'd no doubt be in the end better, and better off, if he didn't. Just as it would probably be better for him if he didn't have the second glass of whisky and soda. . . .

McMaster quite rightly objects to the equating of this mathematical self-restraint with morality. In fact, Tietjens' morality is not much different in kind from the "lachrymose polygamy," the "fumbling in placket-holes," the "sham sexual morality" of McMaster *et al.* Both are inadequate guides to the evaluation of human experience. McMaster and the rest of Edwardian society take a holiday from principles by slipping into hypocrisy about sexuality, all the while mumbling about honour. This holiday from principles is one of the motives for the explosion of society into violence and destruction. The other is the discovery that Tietjens' ethic of repression is inadequate and that the attempt to deny the animal in man results in a perverted release of human energy. When the natural man is denied, he becomes the wolf, tiger or louse-covered ape mentioned above.

The wound that Tietjens suffers in the War is highly appropriate for a man who has been repressing his instincts. Immediately that he and Valentine come to their mutual conclusion that they are the sort who do not, Tietjens rushes off into uniform and is blown up on the battlefield to return home in a state of semi-amnesia. His brain is half dead, "Without a proper blood supply. . . . So a great portion of it, in the shape of memory, has gone." This event is part of the destruction in Tietjens of the repressive

habit; it is part of the process which will refine out of him the dogmatic Tory and free in him the erotically successful comic hero. That he loses his mind, his most prized asset, should not be regarded as tragic or pathetic. Of course, any suffering looked at too closely becomes unbearable. But we are not asked to look closely at Tietjens' private loss. Instead we are given the very funny picture of Tietjens laboriously trying to memorize the *Encyclopaedia Britannica* and being unable at one point to answer a question about Metternich because he had not yet reached the "M's." Suffering of this sort seems to be so deserved that it cannot be tragic.

For the early Tietjens, human relationships are practical, rational, predictable, diplomatic, functional, but never personal. When he decides to take Sylvia back after her affair with Perowne, he says, " 'Yes, in principle I'm determined to. But I shall take three days to think out the details.' He seemed to have no feelings about the matter." His attitude here recalls the Houyhnhnms whose care for their children "proceedeth entirely from the Dictates of Reason" because they have no natural "Fondness for Their Colts or Foles." For Tietjens, while wearing his Tory mask, the upper mind must always control the lower; there must be, above all, no scenes; there must be no disruptions:

> For the basis of Tietjens' emotional existence was a complete taciturnity—at any rate as to his emotions. As Tietjens saw the world, you didn't "talk." Perhaps you didn't even think about how you felt.

As strictly as Tietjens denies his emotional self, however, it continues to build up subterranean pressures. During the golf-course incident, Tietjens is supremely cool in dealing with the disreputable golfers who chase Valentine and Gertie yelling, "Strip the bitch naked! . . . Uhg . . . Strip the bitch stark naked!". Tietjens stops the primitive emotions of the "city man" who stands "as if the bottom of his assured world, where all men desire in their hearts to bash women, had fallen out." The punishment envisioned for the two girls, to be stripped naked for having invaded the golf-course, could be suggested only in a work of comedy. As it turns out, Tietjens shares this primitive desire to "bash" women, but is completely unaware of it. There is a long passage which occurs when Tietjens is walking with Valentine in the country after Duchemin's breakfast, which is worth quoting at length. Tietjens is describing the "perfect" England:

> "God's England!" Tietjens exclaimed to himself in high good humour. " 'Land of Hope and Glory!'—F natural descending to tonic, C major: chord of 6-4, suspension over dominant seventh to common chord of C major. . . . All absolutely correct! Double basses, 'cellos, all violins, all woodwind, all brass. Full grand organ, all stops, special *vox humana* and key-bugle effect. . . . Across the counties came the sound of bugles that his father knew. . . . Pipe exactly right. It must be: pipe of Englishman of good birth; ditto tobacco. Attractive young woman's back. English midday midsummer. Best climate in the world! No day on which man may not go abroad!" Tietjens paused and aimed with his

hazel stick an immense blow at a tall spike of yellow mullein with its undecided, furry, glaucous leaves and its undecided, buttony, unripe lemon-coloured flower. The structure collapsed, gracefully, like a woman killed among crinolines!

"Now I'm a bloody murderer!" Tietjens said. "Not gory! Green stained with vital fluid of innocent plant . . . And by God! Not a woman in the country who won't let you rape her after an hour's acquaintance!" He slew two more mulleins and a sow-thistle! A shadow, but not from the sun, a gloom, lay across the sixty acres of purple grass bloom and marguerites, white: like petticoats of lace over the grass!

Tietjens is certainly here being held up to the light of comic revelation. The perfect world that he crows about, is pushing him more and more into the extremes of violent self-expression indicated by the symbolic rape of the flowers. Ford declares the flowers female, but their phallic appearance might suggest what Tietjens is doing to his own sexuality by adhering to his repressive morality.

By the time we reach *No More Parades,* Tietjens would seem to have gained enough insight into himself to be able to judge his own sexual inaction. O Nine Morgan has just died in his arms and Tietjens muses:

But, damn it, he had never kissed her. So how did he know how she smelt! She was a little tranquil, golden spot. He himself must be a— eunuch. By temperament. That dead fellow down there must be one, physically. It was probably indecent to think of a corpse as impotent. But he was, very likely.

One function of this passage is to make the association of sexual impotence and abstinence, with death. This association becomes a central theme of *No More Parades* as Tietjens discovers the meaning of death and as a correlative, discovers the necessity of sexuality and love for life. The passage also presents Tietjens' own value judgment, that the chivalric code by which he has attempted to live, has made him virtually a eunuch. His self-awareness is another step towards his deliverance.

It has long been noted that Ford makes much use of animal imagery. The particular use of images of animals in *Parade's End* is to express the psychological problems encountered by Victorian modes of behaviour which attempt to curb the animal nature of man. Valentine imagines her "fainting mind; her consenting limbs," only to be brought sharply back to "reality" by Tietjens' taciturn: "Certainly not. I imagined you knew me better." Valentine tries to recapture her sense of an aroused Tietjens and recalls him as a "raging stallion then!" But Tietjens' brushing her aside transforms him into a being "of crystal purity." The vitality of the stallion has been immobilized into the stasis of crystal.

We have another example of sexual paralysis in the figure of the Rev. Mr. Duchemin, who at one point seems to be dreaming of the freedom he could have as a stallion:

"Chaste!" He shouted. "Chaste, you observe! What a world of suggestion in the word . . ." He surveyed the opulent broadness of his table-

cloth; it spread out before his eyes as if it had been a great expanse of meadow in which he could gallop, relaxing his limbs after long captivity. He shouted three obscene words and went on in his Oxford Movement voice: "But chastity. . . ."

For Duchemin, sexual release can come only in obscenity, or in the sad ramblings on the theory of *post coitum tristis,* or in his references to Petronius' highly homosexual *Satyricon.* He is a gelding that will never gallop again.

Sylvia's situation is also seen in terms of imagery of horses:

"*You* know what it is to ride a horse for miles with too tight a curb-chain and its tongue cut almost in half. . . . Well! Think of *this* mare's mouth sometimes! You've ridden me like that for seven years. . . ."

Because Tietjens rides Sylvia too hard, keeps too tight a rein on her passions, we might justifiably see him as a villain who has very little of the comic about him. In fact, it is in the story of Sylvia that the novel comes closest to tragedy, and perhaps closest also to pathos and sentimentality. One must remember, however, that it is not necessary for all events in a novel to be happy or funny for the whole to be comic in essence and structure. Ford can convey the pain of Sylvia's life within the context of a novel which does not lose sight of that which might bring a better world.

Having made that consideration, one can perhaps go further to show that Sylvia's suffering is not wholly Tietjens' responsibility. We know that she has had some liaison before their marriage and that Tietjens is tormented by the thought that he may not be the father of his son. Sylvia's response to sexuality and love has been dictated by an experience in her life before she met Tietjens. Sylvia had "been taken advantage of, after champagne, by a married man called Drake." Frightened by her mother (about the possibility of pregnancy) she seduced Tietjens in a railway car and "married him in Paris to be out of the way." After marriage she continued to have visions of the "distorted face of Drake" and she "knew that she had been very near death. She had wanted death." Sylvia's sexual paralysis is an event, then, in which Tietjens is involved only after the fact.

The miserable memory would come, ghost-like, at any time, anywhere. She would see Drake's face, dark against the white things; she would feel the thin night-gown ripping off her shoulder; but most of all she would seem, in darkness that excluded the light of any room in which she might be, to be transfused by the mental agony that there she had felt: the longing for the brute who had mangled her, the dreadful pain of the mind. The odd thing was that the sight of Drake himself, whom she had seen several times since the outbreak of the war, left her completely without emotion. She had no aversion, but no longing for him. . . . She had, nevertheless, longing, but she knew it was longing merely to experience again that dreadful feeling. And not with Drake. . . .

Sylvia's particular sexual disaster is that she has been

forced into the rigidity of a "rape mentality." We can see Sylvia's castigations of Tietjens in light of the passage quoted above. Her charges against him are part of her need to be attacked again and again.

She says that Tietjens might have done something to bring them together if only he had "once in our lives said to me: 'You whore! You bitch! You killed my mother. May you rot in hell for it. . . . ' " Tietjens refuses to take part in an emotional scene and replies, "That's, of course, true!" And when he says that, one must almost take back any defence of him. Sylvia goes on to indicate that she may be capable of developing genuine human responses:

> "Oh, Christopher," she said, "don't carry on that old play acting. I shall never see you again, very likely, to speak to. You'll sleep with the Wannop girl to-night; you're going out to be killed tomorrow. *Let's* be straight for the next ten minutes or so."

Sylvia here breaks through her shell, while Tietjens does not; he continues to wear his mask of insane reserve and he does not sleep with the Wannop girl. If he is not directly responsible for Sylvia's plight, he is responsible for accentuating it. It is because, as we noted above, that he is a member of the old way, that he is one of the inhibitors of the comic action, that Tietjens can, in the early parts of the tetralogy, restrict the freeing of Eros.

The presence of Sylvia, then, need not be seen as detracting from the comic nature of **Parade's End**. Although her story does add to the melancholic effect of the record of the passing of a way of life, she also contributes to the comic action by her "pulling the strings of shower baths." In the dinner scene referred to earlier, she is a character in slapstick comedy, attempting to break through the armour of one of the enemies of Eros. The irony of her life is that she succeeds, at least partially. She keeps up the pressure on Tietjens which will eventually turn him into the successful lover of Valentine Wannop.

The freeing of Tietjens occurs primarily in the two middle novels, and it occurs as a physical discovery on Tietjens' part. Whereas in **Some Do Not . . .** our impression of him is that of a man of great intellect, we see him in **No More Parades** and **A Man Could Stand Up,** forcibly being reminded of the physical realities of a man's life. We have noted already the scene in which O Nine Morgan dies in Tietjens' arms. The sight of Morgan's blood becomes almost an obsession of Tietjens: "It astonished Tietjens to see that a human body could be so lavish of blood." It is at the same time that he begins to reject the concept of honour expressed in his regimental motto: "Anguish is better than dishonour. The devil it is!" The passage recalls an earlier one which presented to us the terms of Valentine's desire for Tietjens: "Great waves of blood rushed across her being as if physical forces as yet undiscovered or invented attracted the very fluid itself. The moon so draws the tides."

As physical death becomes a reality for Tietjens, he moves from correct passivity into passionate activity. He begins to overcome his paralyzing complexes:

> Now what the Hell was he? A sort of Hamlet of

the Trenches! No, by God he was not. . . . He was perfectly ready for action. Ready to command a battalion. He was presumably a lover. They did things like commanding battalions. And worse!

That "And worse!" reminds us that there is no escaping the tone of comic irony, even here, or perhaps particularly here, where Tietjens begins to show signs of looking dangerously like a hero. Even with the smiling intelligence of Ford in the background, Tietjens does achieve his independence by declaring that he and Valentine "would do what they wanted and take what they got for it!" Tietjens makes a claim for the freedom of the passionate individual as opposed to the dried-out dictates of misused authority, and a misconception of the nature of man:

> What distinguished man from the brutes was his freedom. When, then, a man was deprived of freedom he became like a brute. To exist in his society was to live with brutes, like Gulliver amongst the Houyhnhnms!

The modernity of Tietjens' reflection can be seen by considering what Sartre and existentialism say about the nature of man: man is the free animal. But the comment about Gulliver is perhaps much more important. It is the Houyhnhnms that are equated with brutes. Those pretenders to reason and Augustan aloofness have become the brutes and therefore Gulliver's, and Tietjens', greatest error must be their denial of Yahoo characteristics; that is, the denial of the physical body and the passions. It is Gulliver who becomes misanthropic to the point of insanity, and Swift and Ford both seem to understand why.

Tietjens enters his new life in a scene which has overtones of a rebirth, indeed it is like the mythic birth of the hero. He emerges from the ground, having been buried by an explosion. The first explosion Tietjens experiences is an attack on his mind. The second explosion again serves to emphasize the body:

> It assimilated his calves, his thighs. It imprisoned him above the waist. His arms being free, he resembled a man in a life-buoy. The earth moved him slowly. It was solidish.

The young Aranjuez is buried simultaneously and cries out: "Save me, Captain!" Tietjens replies: "I've got to save myself first!" This reply is in marked contrast to the statement made earlier about Tietjens: "He saved others; himself he could not save!" Tietjens has given up the sacrificial ideal embodied in his desire to be an Anglican Saint or even Christ. He is born into a world which recognizes the need for self-salvation, a world in which the needs of the body are as real as those of the soul: "It was a condemnation of a civilization that he, Tietjens, possessed of enormous physical strength, should never have needed to use it before."

The process of release for Tietjens takes place primarily in the second part of the third novel, **A Man Could Stand Up.** This novel is finely structured (as are the other three), the relatively short sections, Part I and Part III, which occur in London during and immediately after the marking of armistice, flank the last of the battle scenes at the front which we have just been considering. The emergence of the new man of passion is framed by the celebration of the beginning of a new world on the one hand, and on the other, the beginning of a new type of human relationship for Tietjens and Valentine.

Valentine feels herself to be in a "World Turned Upside Down." She seems to have made the same discovery of the physical world that Tietjens has: "The military physical developments of the last four years had been responsible for a real exaggeration of physical values."

She joins in the spirit of physical and erotic liberation that informs Armistice Day:

> Undoubtedly what the Mistresses with the Head at their head had feared was that if they, Head-mistresses, Mistresses, Masters, Pastors—by whom I was made etcetera!—should cease to be respected because saturnalia broke out on the sounding of a maroon the world would go to pieces! An awful thought! The Girls no longer sitting silent in the nonconformist hall while the Head addressed repressive speeches to them. . . .

Very clearly, the Head will no longer rule the Heart, and we begin to see the saturnalian world that is the end of the writer of comedy.

A Man Could Stand Up is quite properly concluded with a dance and with the "wedding" of Tietjens and Valentine. The couple is at the centre of a vast ritual dance:

> They were prancing. The whole world round them was yelling and prancing round. They were the centre of unending roaring circles.

Tietjens, although at the centre of the circle, does not remain motionless as he used to do, but takes an active part. For Valentine he is no longer a threatening, raging stallion, nor is he the other type of horse, the cold, reasonable Houyhnhnm. He has instead become a helpful, friendly beast:

> Tietjens was stretching out his two hands from the waist. It was incomprehensible. His right hand was behind her back, his left in her right hand. She was frightened. She was amazed. Did you ever! He was swaying slowly. The elephant! They were dancing! . . . On an elephant. A dear, meal-sack elephant. She was setting out on. . .

It is probably no accident that Ford chose the elephant, traditionally the animal with the enormous memory, as an emblem for the renewed Tietjens. *Parade's End* works towards a balance of desire and intellect and not towards the death of the mind.

The discussion thus far has been concerned only with the first three of the novels, and not extensively with *The Last Post.* My purpose is not to pass judgment on the quality of the last novel, although I would agree that it does seem a bit of a maverick given the tight structure of the first three. I am concerned only to show what were the structural and thematic preoccupations that Ford was working with. It is sufficient to say that in *The Last Post* we do not find that he abandons the comic mode. *The Last Post* is an extension of the comic argument of the first three books. It is certainly an entertaining and interesting book, which serves, at least, to show what happens to Mark Tietjens, who holds on to the old values. He is a "tired horse" who spends the space of the novel in paralysis and silence except for the last few pages in which he, in effect, gives his blessing to the new menage of Valentine and Christopher. He even becomes capable of a brief moment of genuine human feeling: "Never thou let thy barnie weep for they sharp tongue to thy goodman. . . ."

The death of Mark Tietjens dramatically points out for us the wrong way to respond to the flux of reality. His defeat counterpoints the comic achievement of Christopher. One must be wary, however, of reading *Parade's End* as some sort of recipe book for the good life. Ford was strict in his doctrine that the novel must not descend into propaganda. He said that it is "obviously best if you can contrive to be without views at all; your business with the world is rendering, not alteration." It was with such a comment in mind that I undertook to write of the comic structure of *Parade's End,* for it is in consideration of form, of total vision, that one can find the paradoxical justification for another claim of Ford's, that he wanted to write a book "that should have for its purpose the obviating of all future wars." Certainly *Parade's End,* could not end war by evoking in us a horror of battle. We are given almost no scenes of physical torment in war. The greatest suffering we witness is the pain of private lives gone wrong, and there the villain is a society which does not recognize the nature and needs of man. By watching the comic action, by seeing the effects of one way of life which enforces repression, and by seeing the gradual freeing of one worthy individual from his ritual bondage to worn out dogma, we are surely meant to follow the same process ourselves; that is, to undergo a freeing of human feelings and understanding which would ultimately build a better, more human world. It is by means of his comic vision of things that Ford hoped to make us see what the world could be. Tietjens sets out on his rickety bicycle, on the road towards a better life, and his name may remind us of another Christopher, the patron saint of all travellers.

James M. Heldman   (essay date 1972)

SOURCE: "The Last Victorian Novel: Technique and Theme in *Parade's End,*" in *Twentieth Century Literature* Vol. 18, No. 4, October, 1972, pp. 271-84.

[*In the following essay, Heldman contends that the progression of the fiction techniques used in the four novels in* Parade's End *represents the transition from Victorian to modern writing.*]

In a letter to Percival Hinton in 1931, Ford Madox Ford wrote: "I think the *Good Soldier* is my best book technically unless you read the Tietjens books as one novel in which case the whole design appears." The most complete description of that "whole design" had appeared in his 1925 dedication of *No More Parades* to William Bird: "*Some Do Not*—of which this one is not so much a continuation as a reinforcement—showed you the Tory at home during war-time; this shows you the Tory going up the line. If I am vouchsafed health and intelligence for long enough I propose to show you the same man in the line and in the process of being reconstructed." Though Ford himself was later contradictory and inconsistent about whether *Parade's End* should be a trilogy or a tetralogy, critics now generally agree that it should be seen as a four-novel sequence and that *The Last Post,* the final novel, is a necessary and appropriate conclusion to it.

Ford's version of the conception of the Tietjens novels suggests that he began with two distinct ideas. On the one hand, he wanted to take as his subject "the world as it culminated in the war." The subject was in fact to be the end of the Victorian age—that is, it was to be historical, social, and cultural. He wanted to see something done "on an immense scale," and in undertaking this project he wanted the novelist "in fact to appear in his really proud position as historian of his own time." Set against this broad conception, however, was a distinctly modern concern—Ford's interest in how his late friend Arthur Marwood might have responded to witnessing the death of one civilization and the birth of another. Thus, the genesis of the series embodies two markedly different perspectives—the broadly public and the intensely personal—and the tension between the two suggests the general theme of the tetralogy as well as a broad range of fictional possibilities involving both the novelist's relationship to his characters and the particular methods by which the characters and their stories may be presented. Like Ford himself, *Parade's End* stands in two ages—the Victorian and the modern—and partakes of both; and, also like Ford, it moves from one to the other. Thematically the tetralogy dramatizes an historical and social movement, but it also reflects a literary movement as well. As has generally been noted, the technique of the tetralogy modulates as the series progresses. But what might be thought of as inconsistency in this regard seems to me to be more accurately seen as a technical complement to the substance and theme of the series as a whole. As the progression of the novels dramatizes the end of the Victorian age, so the changing technique of the series dramatizes the end of the Victorian novel and points toward the fictional techniques of the twentieth century.

Read as one novel, *Parade's End* is very much the Victorian large fiction. Its size, scope, and comprehensiveness in presenting a picture of an entire society is strikingly similar to the panorama of the Victorian world depicted in *The Last Chronicle of Barset, Bleak House,* or *Middlemarch.* The Victorian sense of the past is reflected in Christopher Tietjens' preoccupation with established tradition and his responsibilities within that tradition. At the same time, Tietjens' acute awareness of what is happening to his world—of the disparity between traditional values and the values practiced by his peers—is analogous to the Victorian collective self-consciousness about the present which led Trollope, Dickens, and George Eliot to "study" society in their novels. And the impulse of these Victorian novelists to depict the tension between the present and the past and to write their novels as histories of sweeping change is literally carried to its conclusion in Ford's interest in dramatizing the culmination of the Victorian world. Perhaps the most Victorian feature of *Parade's End* is the

emphasis Ford places on the extent to which individual identity is or can be defined in relation to a community. As J. Hillis Miller observes [in *The Form of Victorian Fiction,* 1968], a character in a typical Victorian novel could not say, "I think, therefore I am." Instead, such a character would say, "I am related to others, therefore I am," or "I know myself in relation to others," or "I am conscious of myself as conscious of others." He finally comes to see himself in relation to the community which surrounds him. Integration with the community is at least possible. And whatever stability the character achieves at the end of the novel depends in part on his willingness to define his identity in terms of his relationship to the community of "others" who are the means of his self-knowledge.

More significantly, however, in *Parade's End* Christopher Tietjens moves from a vestigal sense of community to isolation. The process and the result make it an epitome of the experience of modern man and an archetypal modern novel. The tetralogy begins with Tietjens' assuming that identification with a community is still possible, proceeds to describe his growing awareness of the community's disappearance, and ends with his attempts to make a life for himself on his own terms rather than on out-moded loyalties. In *Some Do Not . . .* Tietjens remains doggedly committed to his obligations and responsibilities as an English gentleman. In *No More Parades* he comes to realize that the traditional and established English community no longer exists except in what has become the hollow sham of ritual and empty ceremony. *A Man Could Stand Up—* culminates in Tietjens' decision to break with his allegiance to what is clearly now the dead past, and *The Last Post* leaves him standing alone with his private and personal values. The progression in *Parade's End* thus dramatizes the final decay and disappearance of a discernible community that an individual can identify with. This thematic movement in the tetralogy is informed and restated in the gradual modulation of the technique by which that movement is presented—particularly in the shifting points of view that Ford employs. *Parade's End* may be viewed as being written in four distinct points of view. The most public of these is the conventional omniscience in which the narrator comments, judges, evaluates, and speaks as a version of the community voice which characterizes the typical Victorian novel. A second distinctive point of view in *Parade's End* may be described as "dramatic" or "objective" narrative in which the narrator speaks in a relatively impersonal and descriptive voice. He is essentially a presenter of scenes, and though he is of course present, as a personality he is essentially silent. In addition, Ford also employs a third-person narrative of the thoughts of individual characters that may be thought of as "focused" narrative. This narrative is internal rather than external or detached, and primary emphasis is placed on the contents of characters' thoughts, presented either in coherent sentences or in fragmentary, associational patterns and usually in language approximating the language of the character. The sense of focused narrative is more descriptive than evaluative, and there is in it less of the impression of a commentator as such. It conveys the sense that we are being told about a mind, and the mind and not the telling is the focus of interest. The final major point of view in *Parade's End* is the most internalized, most intensely personal of the four and may be thought of as "interior" narrative. In this case the narrator as presenter has disappeared entirely, and characters' thoughts are presented directly in the first person. More often than in focused narrative, interior narrative is presented in fragmentary and associational patterns. But in both, when the mind is occupied with responses to immediate sense perceptions, the narrative comes closest to a kind of pure impressionism which reflects the character's consciousness of the moment. Omniscient narrative is given widest and most frequent play in *Some Do Not. . . .* It is still very much evident, though somewhat less so, in *No More Parades.* It is used even less frequently in *A Man Could Stand Up*—and only in rare instances and for essentially specialized purposes in *The Last Post.* Thus, the over-all movement of the tetralogy in placing less emphasis on omniscient narrative and more emphasis on dramatic, focused, and interior narrative is to move away from the broad, detached, public view of the Victorian novel and to throw increasingly more emphasis on the interaction between event and individual response. And in *The Last Post,* in which relatively few events take place (the novel covers a period of only about an hour on a single afternoon), the overwhelming bulk of emphasis is placed on the subjective responses of a few characters to the complex influences from both past and present which impinge upon them. In this inward movement, thematically and technically, *Parade's End* takes us not only into the twentieth century but into the twentieth-century novel as well.

In length and scope *Parade's End* is very much the comprehensive fiction that is the Victorian novel. It ranges over all classes—poor, rich, intellectual, official, military, commercial, sophisticated, and simple.

—*James M. Heldman*

Some Do Not . . . is the most technically complex of the four novels and serves not only as a model of the variety of narrative techniques Ford draws on throughout the tetralogy but also, in its over-all movement, foreshadows the gradual shift in perspective which takes place in the series as a whole. The novel opens with Tietjens and his friend Macmaster, public servants in the Imperial Department of Statistics, riding in a well-appointed railway car on their way to a weekend of golf at Rye. In the context of the tetralogy, they are in fact official public England riding comfortably and smoothly toward the chaos and disaster of World War I. This scene is the purest example of conventional omniscient narrative to be found in all of *Parade's End.* The narrator provides information about both Tietjens and Macmaster, looks into the character of each, tells us about the world they inhabit, and furnishes lengthy passages of dialogue to make the scene dramatically immediate. Except for the tone of the narrator's comments, the

chapter might well have been lifted from George Eliot. But these comments establish Ford's presence throughout the scene as informed but detached and mildly ironic. When the narrator tells us that their "class administered the world," his overstatement emphasizes the complacent superiority of public England in 1912. Ford's voice reflects simultaneously a public attitude and an interpretation of that attitude. The narrator directs his attention alternately on Tietjens and Macmaster, and though much of his description is informational, it is liberally sprinkled with the kind of commentary which frequently reminds us that the judgments reflected are not likely to be the judgments of the characters themselves. When describing Macmaster's reaction to the experience of correcting the proofs of his first book, the narrator tells us: "He had expected a wallowing of pleasure—almost the only sensuous pleasure he had allowed himself for many months. Keeping up the appearances of an English gentleman on an exiguous income was no mean task. But to wallow in your own phrases, to be rejoiced by the savour of your own shrewd pawkinesses, to feel your rhythm balanced and yet sober—that is a pleasure beyond most, and an inexpensive one at that." The passage reflects Ford's ingenuity in juxtaposing the right word, for accuracy, and the wrong word, for irony. Since Macmaster is Scottish and lower class, he might well think privately of his own cleverness in the Scottish dialect word "pawkinesses," but he would hardly think of his indulgence in self-satisfaction as "a wallowing of pleasure." Similarly, when the narrator's attention is directed at Tietjens, he gives us what first appears to be an essentially objective description (or perhaps a description of Tietjens' awareness of himself) and then concludes with a touch to remind us of the judging presence different from the character. With regard to Tietjens the narrator says: "He was a Tory—and as he disliked changing his clothes, there he sat, on the journey, already in large, brown, hugely welted and nailed golf boots, leaning forward on the edge of the cushion, his legs apart, on each knee an immense white hand—and thinking vaguely." Tietjens has enough self-awareness to recognize the logical disjunction between being a Tory and not caring to change clothes, but at this stage of his life he is too confident of his intellectual power to be able to consider himself capable of thinking vaguely. Though much of the chapter is presented in dialogue between Tietjens and Macmaster which suggests dramatic rather than omniscient narrative, comments such as these frequently remind us of the pervasive, though often silent, omniscient presence. The scene at Lobscheid in the following chapter, which introduces Sylvia, Mrs. Satterthwaite, and Father Consett, is presented in much the same technique as Chapter I, except that the omniscient narrative is limited principally to the first few pages, after which Ford shifts to an almost exclusively dramatic point of view limited to dialogue and the sparest, most objective kind of stage directions. The narrator introduces noticeably only once, when Sylvia enters, but his description of her includes just enough interpretation to indicate the omniscient and commenting voice rather than the objective one. In the middle of an otherwise routine description of Sylvia, we are told: "Her very oval, regular face had an expression of virginal lack of interest such as used to be worn by fashionable Paris courtesans a decade before that time." The judgment and temperament conveyed might be similar to Sylvia's, but the terms in which they are rendered are clearly not hers. As in Chapter I, the brief intrusion reminds us of an evaluating presence other than the character. Otherwise, the chapter moves cleanly and distinctly from the omniscient to the dramatic.

In Chapters III and IV of Part One, which concern Tietjens' and Macmaster's first day at Rye, Ford moves into the first of a number of time-shifts which he employs with increasing frequency in the tetralogy. Though it begins with the narrator's attention directed to Macmaster, the shift remains the narrator's rather than Macmaster's as evidenced by the occurrence of the narrator's comments within it. For example, the narrator's presence is suggested in the irony implicit in Macmaster's reaction to the location of Mr. Duchemin's church: "It was, in short, an ideal cure of souls for a wealthy clergyman of cultured tastes, for there was not so much as a peasant's cottage within a mile of it." And Macmaster's response to Mrs. Duchemin is almost a parody of Pre-Raphaelite sentiment: "Mrs. Duchemin bore the sunlight! Her dark complexion was clear; there was, over the cheekbones, a delicate suffusion of light carmine. Her jawbone was singularly clear-cut, to the pointed chin—like an alabaster, mediaeval saint's." Such instances as this illustrate the narrator's irony even when he appears to be presenting directly the thoughts of a character. And the fact that the attention shifts from Macmaster to Tietjens in the middle of the time-shift also points clearly to the control of perspective being retained by the narrator. The mild distortion of time in these chapters suggests perhaps the beginning of a disorientation in the community. Macmaster is almost a burlesque of sensibility. And the world of the gentleman golfer is being assaulted by vulgarity in the club house and suffragettes on the fairway. But at this point sufficient vestiges of order and decorum remain in the society for such departures to be viewed with the sanity and wit of the narrator's detached, public perspective.

The Duchemin breakfast scene gives Ford the opportunity to explore even more fully the possibilities of manipulation and flexibility he has tentatively investigated up to this point. After brief dramatic and omniscient passages, the chapter moves to the first significant occurrence of what I have called "focused" narrative, in which Valentine Wannop's and Tietjens' thoughts about each other are presented without the intervention of a commenting narrator. Tietjens is musing on the implications of his involvement on the golf course the day before with Valentine—a girl who is both a suffragette and a domestic servant:

> It was all very well for his surface mind to say
> that the girl was not by birth a tweeny maid; she
> was the daughter of Professor Wannop and she
> could jump! For Tietjens held very strongly the
> theory that what finally separated the classes
> was that the upper could lift its feet from the
> ground whilst common people couldn't. . . .
> But the strong impression remained. Miss Wan-
> nop was a tweeny maid. Say a lady's help, by na-
> ture. She was of good family, for the Wannops
> were first heard of at Birdlip in Gloucestershire
> in the year 1417—no doubt enriched after Agin-
> court. But even brilliant men of good family will

> now and then throw daughters who are lady
> helps by nature. That was one of the queernesses
> of heredity.

This is obviously an instance of Tietjens' mind being mirrored rather than filtered through a mediating consciousness. The sympathy for the establishment, the concern for propriety and class, the sense of history, the awareness of some of the less heroic consequences of the Battle of Agincourt, the recollection of the experience of the previous day, and even the expert horseman's use of the word "throw" to describe birth—all are what we have been conditioned to expect as the products of Tietjens' personality. After the entrance of Mr. Duchemin, Ford as narrator emerges again, and though he stays away from noticeable intrusive comment, the quick shifts of focus from one character to another interspersed with dramatic narrative serve to point up the comedy in the nearly catastrophic breakfast and indicate that the narrator is clearly present, selecting and controlling the narrative focus. The effect is that Ford maintains a public perspective—in this case, a comic one reminiscent of Trollope—and at the same time anticipates his subsequent movement to an almost exclusively private vision.

The two final chapters of Part One of *Some Do Not . . .* foreshadow more clearly than the previous chapters the direction in which Ford moves in the tetralogy. Chapter VI opens with the omniscient narrator's presentation of the scene, but after the first paragraph the chapter moves directly into a focused narrative of Tietjens' responses. And almost immediately Ford shifts into the first real instance of interior narrative in the novel. Tietjens' mind is rendered directly: " 'Land of Hope and Glory!'—F natural descending to tonic, C major: chord of 6-4, suspension over dominant seventh to common chord of C major. . . . All absolutely correct! Double basses, 'cellos, all violins, all woodwind, all brass. Full grand organ, all stops, special *vox humana*." And the narrative continues in this manner for three pages, with brief intrusions devoted to external interruptions, as Tietjens' mind ranges associationally over music, England, Tories, Valentine, and Macmaster, among other things. The musical metaphor is appropriate for the state of Tietjens' mind at the time. He privately rejoices with enthusiasm at his image of the England he still believes in, though events have already suggested that the foundations of the structure are disintegrating. The orderly chord progression, fully orchestrated and including the human voice, ending in a full resolution, reflects Tietjens' positive and even joyous loyalty to the community. And his reference to "Land of Hope and Glory" of course prefigures his subsequent reflections on the same song, in a different context and with strikingly different conclusions, in *No More Parades.* In the "dog-cart" episode which ends Part One Ford restricts the narrative to third- and first-person focus on Tietjens—that is, to focused or interior narrative—combined with fragmentary dramatic narrative of external details to create an essentially impressionistic treatment of the interplay between event and individual response which culminates in the description of Tietjens' version of the dog-cart's collision with General Campion's car:

> Not ten yards ahead Tietjens saw a tea-tray, the

Ford and Janice Biala (foreground) with American writers Caroline Gordon and Allen Tate, in Clarksville, Tennessee, circa 1935.

underneath of a black-lacquered tea-tray, gliding towards them, mathematically straight, just rising from the mist. He shouted, mad, the blood in his head. His shout was drowned by the scream of the horse; he had swung it to the left. The cart turned up, the horse emerged from the mist, head and shoulders, pawing. A stone seahorse from the fountain of Versailles! Exactly that! Hanging in air for an eternity; the girl looking at it, leaning slightly forward.

The incident dramatizes the larger situation in the society. Tietjens, the man of principle, emerges from the fog of his own present confusions and clashes head-on with the actual establishment represented by General Campion, who insists on driving his own car though he is manifestly incompetent to do so. And it foreshadows the conscious conflict that is later to develop in Tietjens' mind regarding his commitment to an essentially Victorian world view. Significantly, the scene is rendered as Tietjens' impressions. Thus the technique of the final chapter of Part One of *Some Do Not . . . ,* with its nearly exclusive focus on interior experience, anticipates in miniature the technique of *The Last Post.*

Part Two of *Some Do Not . . .* in effect repeats the vari-

ety and complexity of Part One in that it combines omniscient, dramatic, and focused narrative. The omniscient, commenting narrator is still very much present intermittently—for example, when Sylvia considers her relationship with Tietjens and when Valentine recalls the history of her involvement with Tietjens, Macmaster, and Mrs. Duchemin. As in Part One, however, Ford refrains from moving into interior narrative until the final chapter of Part Two when Tietjens recalls the moment in which he and Valentine had decided that they were the kind of people who did not become lover and mistress. Although the chapter opens with omniscient narrative, Ford shifts quickly into focus on Tietjens and then almost immediately into interior narrative.

> If then a man who's a man wants to have a woman. . . . Damn it, he doesn't! In ten years he had learnt that a Tommie who's a decent fellow. . . . His mind said at one and the same moment, the two lines running one over the other like the two subjects of a fugue:

> "Some beguiling virgins with the broken seals of perjury," and "Since when we stand side by side, only hands may meet!"

He said [the context clearly indicates to himself]:

"But damn it; damn it again! The beastly fellow was wrong! Our hands didn't meet. . . . I don't believe I've shaken hands. . . . I don't believe I've touched the girl . . . in my life. . . . Never once! . . . Not the hand-shaking sort . . . A nod! . . . A meeting and parting! . . . English, you know . . . "

The passage reflects the continuing debate in Tietjens' mindbetween what he wants and what he thinks he ought to do. At this point, however, the disparity between personal and public values is still a matter of private indecision. The remainder of the chapter records Tietjens' recollection of the parting. The episode appears to be conventional omniscient narrative, complete with comments and judgments, but in fact it occurs within the framework of Tietjens' reflections. In a subtle but significant and prophetic way, Tietjens has temporarily replaced the narrator. As in Part One, the movement is from the public to the private, and the thematic development is mirrored in the technical one.

No More Parades takes Tietjens to France and, more importantly, to the conscious realization that the community to which he has been committed no longer exists. For the first time Tietjens can admit this openly. In a conversation with MacKechnie he says:

"At the beginning of the war, I had to look in on the War Office, and in a room I found a fellow. . . . What do you think he was doing . . . what the hell do you think he was doing? He was divising the ceremonial for the disbanding of a Kitchener battalion. You can't say we were not prepared in one matter at least. . . . Well, the end of the show was to be: the adjutant would stand the battalion at ease: the band would play 'Land of Hope and Glory,' and then the adjutant would say: *There will be no more parades.* . . . Don't you see how symbolical it was: the band playing 'Land of Hope and Glory,' and then the adjutant saying *There will be no more parades*? . . . For there won't. There won't, there damn well won't. . . . No more Hope, no more Glory, no more parades for you and me any more. Nor for the country . . . Nor for the world, I dare say . . . None . . . Gone . . . No . . . more . . . parades!"

The novel itself dramatizes the fact that meaningful parades are gone. It is comparable to *Some Do Not . . .* in complexity, but the terms of that complexity are somewhat different. Tietjens is the focal point of Part One, Sylvia of Part Two, and Tietjens of Part Three. Ford still resorts to omniscient narrative from time to time throughout, but his principal emphasis is on the interplay between event and individual response reflected in the novel's reliance on dramatic, focused, or interior narrative. For example, the death of O Nine Morgan in Part One is presented initially as an event: "A man, brown, stiff, with a haughty parade step, burst into the light. He said with a high wooden voice: 'Ere's another bloomin' casualty'." But then Ford moves into a focused narrative rendering Tietjens' actions, impressions, and associations interspersed with his perceptions of the comments of others in

the scene. The emphasis is predominantly internal rather than external. A few pages later, the interplay between event and response is reflected still more markedly in a scene in which two thought processes are going on at once. Tietjens is interviewing Lieutenant Hotchkiss, the veterinarian.

The old lieutenant said:

"Hotchkiss . . . " And Tietjens exclaimed:

"Of course it's Hotchkiss . . . I've seen your name signing a testimonial to Pigg's Horse Embrocation. . . . Then if you don't want to take this draft up the line . . . Though I'd advise you to . . . It's merely a Cook's Tour to Hazebrouck . . . No, Bailleul . . . and the sergeant-major will march the men for you . . . And you will have been in the First Army Lines and able to tell all your friends you've been on active service at the real front. . . . "

His mind said to himself while his words went on . . .

"Then, good God, if Sylvia is actively paying attention to my career I shall be the laughing-stock of the whole army. I was thinking that ten minutes ago! . . . What's to be done? What in God's name is to be done?" A black crape veil seemed to drop across his vision. . . . Liver . . .

A bit later a soldier's request for an overnight pass is juxtaposed against Tietjens' simultaneous preoccupation with Valentine, and in Part Two a similar combination of dramatic, focused, and interior narrative is used in the scene with Ex-Sergeant-Major Cowley, Tietjens, and Sylvia, this time with the interior focus on Sylvia. The scene of Lady Sachse's reception recalls the Duchemin breakfast in *Some Do Not. . . .* In this instance, however, instead of being presented and controlled by an omniscient narrator, the scene occurs as Sylvia's recollection of it in a time-shift in which hers is the controlling mind and consists of events juxtaposed against her internal responses to them. The dramatic impact of such scenes is not in the event or the thought process but rather in their occurring simultaneously. The juxtapositions reflect the tension between the outer and inner life that continues throughout the novel and indicate not only the characters' growing sense of the disparity between the two but the force and validity of their private sense of reality. Part Three is presented almost completely in dramatic or focused narrative with only brief and occasional narrator's comments. But at the end of the final chapter Ford reemphasizes the tension between the public and private by returning abruptly to omniscient narrative. The confrontation between Tietjens and Campion culminating in the announcement of Tietjens' impending transfer to the front has been presented in a combination of dramatic, focused, and interior narrative, and it has been a deeply disturbing experience for both men. But when Campion, accompanied by Tietjens, conducts his traditional inspection of the cook-house, when he asks his traditional questions, and when he discovers the traditionally placed dirty jacket, Ford resumes his role as an omniscient narrator. In a striking demonstration of ironic power, he concludes *No More Parades* in his public voice with a description of men "on parade."

A Man Could Stand Up— dramatizes the separate decisions of Valentine and Tietjens to turn their back on traditional values, to commit themselves to each other regardless of the codes they had formerly subscribed to, and reunites them on Armistice Day. Both decide that they are now individuals who *do*. Technically, *A Man Could Stand Up—* is the simplest of the four novels, though it is intellectually and emotionally as complex as the others. Part One is focused entirely on Valentine and is presented entirely in a combination of focused and interior narrative. Though external events occur—the telephone conversation with Lady Macmaster, for example, and the interview with Miss Wanostrocht, the headmistress of the school where Valentine teaches—they are presented as perceptions of events rather than as externalized events themselves. Lady Macmaster's remarks on the phone are loaded with sibilant blasts which suggest the grotesqueness of public conduct when seen from the private perspective: " 'His brothers.s.s got pneumonia, so his mistress.ss.ss even is unavailable to look after . . . ,' " and when Valentine asks who is speaking, "She got back a title. . . . Lady someone or other. . . . It might have been Blastus." Furthermore, the passage of time in Part One is retarded and associational rather than chronological; thus, while Valentine is listening to Miss Wanostrocht, her mind is preoccupied with the telephone conversation she finished ten minutes earlier. At this stage in the tetralogy Ford has moved completely into the private world. The same kind of close focus continues in Part Two, though here it is on Tietjens in the trenches. After he returns from observing the enemy lines before an expected offensive, his sergeant says to him: " 'Then a man could stand hup on an 'ill. . . . You really mean to say, sir, that you think a man will be able to stand up on a bleedin' 'ill . . . You sir . . . You're a law hunto yourself '." As Tietjens mulls these ideas over, he slowly comes to realize that this is what peace means—to be able to stand up on a hill, to be a law unto himself, to live simply, privately, independently. He no longer feels the compulsion to live his life in conformity with the publicly, culturally sanctioned standards that were once valid, desirable, and even necessary for an ordered and responsible life. The public order that was once nurtured by those standards no longer exists. Indeed, there is no public order, no community with which a man can identify himself. All that remains is individual conscience, individual integrity, individual fulfillment, individual peace. Though the quantity of action and dialogue in Part Two suggests a partially dramatic presentation combined with focused and interior narrative, the emphasis is decidedly in the direction of the inner response rather than the action itself. The real drama, even in combat, now lies within the man. The intensely personal quality of the reunion between Tietjens and Valentine in Part Three is reflected in the fact that the experience is presented entirely in focused third-person narrative. External events are presented in what seems to be dramatic narrative, but the recurring emphasis on individual response suggests rather strongly that what we see is not an objective drama but a perceived one. And since this is a reunion, the focus on Valentine in Part One and on Tietjens in Part Two alternates from one to the other in Part Three.

The Last Post brings the increasing tension between public and private to a final disjunction. The central character of the novel is not Christopher Tietjens but his older brother Mark, who has determined that he will never speak and never move again. In his self-induced paralysis, he is the representative of the dying era, unwilling and unable to begin a new epoch with a fresh start. Christopher appears only briefly in the final pages. Mark is a mute; Christopher is in eclipse. The two men of principle and integrity who were once vital members of the old community order have consciously and deliberately turned away from the sham that community has become. Christopher, however, is trying to make a new life—to stand up on his private hill and be a law unto himself. Though he is physically absent, he is very much in the minds of those few characters whose thoughts make up the bulk of the novel. The public community in terms of which his character was defined in *Some Do Not . . .* has all but disappeared and has been replaced by the small domestic circle of his home in the Sussex hills. It would perhaps be most satisfying to be able to claim that the omniscient narrator does not appear at all in *The Last Post,* but such is not the case. Little in Ford and nothing in *Parade's End* is quite that simple. The narrator does appear, but only in limited ways and for limited purposes. He is used to introduce the new characters who appear for the first time in the series—Marie-Léonie, Gunning, Mrs. de Bray Pape, and Fittleworth. He is used briefly to set scenes and to describe limited actions. And he indulges in omniscient commentary about Sylvia alone or about Sylvia and Campion together. It is perhaps only chance but also perhaps significant that the only omniscient commentary as such in *The Last Post* is devoted to the only two major characters who still subscribe to and represent the public world on which Tietjens, Mark, Valentine, and Marie-Léonie have now turned their backs—the only two characters who are still trying to ride in the "perfectly appointed railway carriage." Otherwise the novel is devoted in separate parts to the thoughts and reflections of Marie-Léonie, Valentine, Sylvia (though only briefly), and Mark Tietjens. Outside of a few bits of action described objectively, whatever events transpire are seen through their eyes—the arrival of Sylvia's party, Sylvia's confrontation with Valentine, the return of Christopher. The bulk of the novel is presented in focused narrative—focused on one or the other of these four characters—in language, thought patterns, and tones that are appropriate to each character—Mark's Yorkshire independence, Marie-Léonie's preoccupations with domestic matters, Sylvia's bitterness, and Valentine's emotionalism. The content of each character's thoughts is equally fitting. Mark is primarily concerned with reconciling the inconsistencies of the past. Marie-Léonie assures herself that her choices in the past had been the right ones. Sylvia finally can admit to herself that her years-long struggle with Tietjens has been foolish and futile. And Valentine is concerned only with the present and the future—with her life with Tietjens and the life of the child she carries in her womb. The predominant emphasis in *The Last Post* then rests with individual needs, individual responses, and individual values. And Ford relies primarily on the technique

which reflects those values. At the last post of one civilization and the beginning of another, the only reality is the
reality of individual consciousness.

In length and scope *Parade's End* is very much the comprehensive fiction that is the Victorian novel. It ranges
over all classes—poor, rich, intellectual, official, military,
commercial, sophisticated, and simple. It moves from the
golf links of Rye to the salons of London to the trenches
of France. More important, it dramatizes the final decay
and the disappearance of any discernible public community that an individual can identify with and leaves him trying to stand up on his private hill. As Christopher Tietjens
becomes a twentieth-century man, *Parade's End* is a Victorian novel which becomes a modern novel, and in this
becoming lies its essential modernity. The modulation of
techniques by which Ford dramatizes this process effectively informs and supports the process itself. And the predominant technique of *The Last Post* seems a logical and
necessary conclusion of this movement. In the shift of values from public to private and in his increasing reliance
on focused and interior narrative, Ford may be seen as
dramatizing both an historical phenomenon and a literary
one—the movement of both society and the novel from the
nineteenth to the twentieth century.

Malcolm Bradbury   (essay date 1976)

SOURCE: "The Denuded Place: War and Form in *Pa-
rade's End* and *U.S.A.*" in *The First World War in Fiction:
A Collection of Critical Essays,* edited by Holger Klein,
The Macmillan Press Ltd., 1976, pp. 193-209.

[*An English man of letters, Bradbury is best known as the
author of such satiric novels as* Eating People Is Wrong
(1959) and Stepping Westward *(1965). In the following excerpt from his comparative examination of post–World
War I epic novels, Bradbury suggests that Ford juxtaposed
in* Parade's End *Edwardian realism with Modernist experimental techniques to demonstrate the passing of Tietjens'
way of life.*]

Parade's End is the culmination of Ford Madox Ford's
achievement, rivalled only by his novel of 1915, *The Good
Soldier,* not directly about the war. But it came late in a
long, mixed career; Ford—then Ford Madox Hueffer—
had been writing since the turn of the century. An exemplary Edwardian novelist, he had steadily oscillated between the claims of liberal realism and experimentalism.
He collaborated with Conrad, wrote historical novels, like
The Fifth Queen, and novels of contemporary political
and social life (*The Inheritors, A Call,* etc.): novels in different ways devoted to the 'Condition of England' question central to the fiction of the day, and to its predominant theme, of the movement from the older, caring world
to the new world of mechanism, atomism, indifference.
Like Forster, in *Howards End* (1910), Ford was preoccupied with the ideal polity, the connected society, unifying
reason with emotion, commerce with art. But his conser-
vative-liberal politics and his avant-garde tastes were hard
to reconcile; art, he felt, transcended issues, required an
ultimate technical expertise, a Flaubertian perfection of
form, which set the writer outside and beyond purposes,

political commitments. In 1908 he tried to reconcile his interests in *The English Review,* the journal he edited; it was
a valiant effort to merge the old-fashioned socio-political
'great review' with the modern 'little magazine'. But in the
following years, perhaps because of increasing social tension and international stress, the avant-garde movement
peaked in London. Ford moved excitedly with this, seeing
a new experimental age. He intensified his commitment to
'impressionism'; he wrote *The Good Soldier,* just before
the war; part of it appeared in the Vorticist magazine ominously called *Blast. The Good Soldier* intersects his social
and aesthetic concerns. On the one hand, he sees society
redeemed from its present crass materialism by the acceptance of social responsibility and duty; on the other, he
sees it lost by virtue of the fact that society withholds and
represses, especially in the sexual realm. From that ironic
contrast, Hueffer gained a technical position, a detachment, the possibility of a rendered vision; the novel would
be a 'hard', 'flawless' object of the modern Vorticist type,
like 'a polished helmet', and it would interseam the causal,
progressive, realistic novel, which sustained society in its
substance and significance, with an oblique, fragmentary
method of association and juxtaposition, which would
question it.

Like many writers in England just before the war, then,
Hueffer was experiencing a growing social disillusion coupled with a deepening interest in modernist technique. The
war was to drive that process much further. In 1915,
Hueffer published two propaganda books on behalf of the
war effort. They attack German imperialist materialism,
the threat of the new nation-state; they also attack the
emergence of the same processes of materialism and statism in England. Ford confessed his own old-fashioned
ideals, and realised the war was a general threat to them.
Nonetheless, though over military age, he got a commission in the Welsh Regiment, and served for a time on the
Western Front, an experience that produced in him a 'profound moral change'. Certainly he came back from the
war with a vastly greater suspicion of vested interests and
materialist forces, a strong identification with the men at
the front, and a deep conviction that England was sinking
back into negativism, commercialism, and anti-art. It was
now that he changed his name from Hueffer to Ford, and,
after various attempts at post-war pamphleteering, left
London for Paris. This was partly because he felt London
was betraying the effort of the war, partly because of personal and financial problems that made it unlikely he
could live by writing at home; also in part because he had
conceived an allegiance to the post-war international republic of letters, of which Paris now seemed the Anglo-
American centre. There he joined the modernist expatri-
ates, edited *transatlantic review,* associated with Pound,
Stein, Joyce and Hemingway, and began *Parade's End.*
An habitual, if not always an accurate, memoirist, he records much of this story in his novel-memoir *It Was the
Nightingale.* His justifications for the sequence are partly
modernist-aesthetic—he wanted to write a great cosmopolitan work—and partly socio-historical: 'I wanted the
Novelist in fact to appear in his really proud position as
historian of his own time.' He saw himself as taking up the
vacancy left by the death of Proust, as the creator of the
'ponderous novel'; yet the subject of the novel would be

'the public events of the decade' and 'the world as it culmi-nated in the war'. It would be a work of 'rendering', but also a novel with a purpose: 'I sinned against my gods to the extent of saying that I was going . . . to write a work that should have for its purpose the obviating of all future wars.'

Ford wished, then, to write a book about large social ten-dencies and forces, and considered using the method whereby 'all the characters should be great masses of peo-ple—or interests.' In this notion, he came close to the method of Dos Passos's *U.S.A.,* which sustains its mas-siveness by following the story of many characters, some fictional, some historical, and certain systems of interest through an historical process. But Ford felt this method was not for him; it was too large, and also risked inhuman-ity, the turning of men into statistics; and, wanting a great-er humanism, he resolved to focus his sequence around one central character who experiences the tribulations of peace *and* war. He also noted that observation of active warfare had led him to 'a singular conclusion', that what preyed most on the minds of non-professional soldiers were not the horrors—'you either endure them or you do not'—but 'what was happening at home'. In particular, what was happening at home was a massive change in mores, in the dispositions of political and class power, and in men-women relationships. This, of course, is Dos Pas-sos's concern too; but Ford's resolved method is not to amass a large society behind the events of war, rather to a create a central character who has a place in peace and war, and is capable both of suffering and critically observ-ing change: a character based, in fact, on an old, dead friend, Arthur Marwood, a Yorkshire Tory. His central character, then, would be a man torn both in public and private life by the pressure of the times, 'a poor fellow whose body is tied in one place, but whose mind and per-sonality brood eternally over another distant locality'. To give his hero the right kind of intersection with history and with public life, he would be an officer and a gentle-man, but, more, a member of the Ruling Classes—a land-owner with Westminster connections. In all this, then, Ford went in the classic direction of the realist historical novel, the Lukáczian prescription, the novel about the rep-resentative historical agent who carries the forces of the time with him, who is the man of history. And in this, one might say, Ford is opting for a very English possibility, the novel of social and historical life in which individuals can clearly represent their class, can function as a primary so-cial focus.

However, Christopher Tietjens is more than the embodi-ment of his class; he is, indeed, at odds with it. For Tietjens is also 'the last Tory', the 'Christian gentleman', the wit-ness to the chivalric view of life, a man whose roots go down into English society and life; but who is already lost and suffering amid the new dispositions of power, the new sexual mores, the new habits and standards of Georgian England. Tietjens' world has, indeed, already newly disap-peared before the War starts; he has already become ab-surd in his chivalry, his code of honour, monogamy and chastity. From the start a certain comic absurdity attaches to him; he is a mealsack elephant. His enduring values are already part-displaced; misfortunes accumulate around

his ideas and ideals, around his house, Groby, around his attempts to establish his standards in life. He is in fact a comic character, and *Parade's End* is indeed a certain sort of war comedy, in a species that was to reappear in fresh form in the parallel English trilogy for the Second World War, Evelyn Waugh's *Sword of Honour.* Like Waugh's Guy Crouchback, Tietjens retains ancient, hereditary no-tions of chivalry; he quests for just causes and true wars. He is a man of 'clear Eighteenth-Century mind,' passion-ate yet constrained, agonised yet expressionless, living out the contradictions of the old code to their last possible conclusion, hoping to take 'the last train to the old Heav-en'. He is a romantic figure caught at the point of extinc-tion, a man of parades in a new world in which, socially as well as militarily, there are no more parades. And like Guy (or Don Quixote) he is thrust into a world of chaotic and lowered history. So, comically, he has to be taken along the path of disillusionment; the bleak and terrible events of the war are that path, and he follows it, with ele-phantine blundering, to base reality. At the same time his ideals function as an essential criticism of that lowered world, and subtract political significance from most of the events that take place. His war thus starts long before the outbreak of hostilities, in the strange, chivalric marriage he makes to a deceitful wife, pregnant by another man, and in his growing, but chaste, emotional relationship with the new woman, Valentine Wannop.

W. H. Auden once noted that the sequence 'makes it quite clear that World War I was a retribution visited upon Western Europe for the sins and omissions of its ruling class, for which not only they, but also the innocent con-scripted millions on both sides, must suffer'. It is true that Ford is much concerned in these novels with the debase-ment of the ruling class, the selfish corruptions and false motives, 'the swine in the corridors' of Whitehall, the bun-gled political issue of the Single Command, with the hor-ror and boredom of the battlefield. Yet *Parade's End* is not primarily a sequence about the system, nor about the hor-rors of trench warfare and bombardment. Ford saw the battlefield as part of a larger experience, as a place always intruded on by 'money, women, testamentary bothers'; hence the social war and the sex war move to the lines, with Tietjens' bitch-wife Sylvia and the malicious General Campion, who wants her as his mistress and who misuses Tietjens in his pursuit, always in the background. War is thus always connected in the book with political and social events, but those events are themselves part of the larger victimisation of Tietjens and his ancient values. It is Tiet-jens' purgatory, a version of the great, pressing machine of modern life. And through it Tietjens is pressed into ad-aptation. He suffers, is buried, wounded, persecuted, forced into action and heroism, split away from the past. If he recognises the flaws in his own class, and the de-manding democracy of the front, he is also insistently de-prived of his more chivalric hopes; it is a gross, modern, material, selfish war. The war in fact deprives him of many of the social meanings that have made him the potential hero of the story in the first place; he loses his old values, his old heaven, his world of parades and moral prohibi-tions. But he gains his new woman and a new life, becom-ing, ironically, an antique dealer in the new, paradeless world: 'The war had made a man of him! It had coarsened him and hardened him . . . It had made him reach a point at which he could no longer stand unbearable things.' The world too has changed accordingly:

> Feudalism was finished; its last vestiges were gone. It held no place for him. He was going—he was damn well going!—to make a place in it for . . . A man could now stand up on a hill, so he and she could surely get into some hole together!

But the point is that Ford does not tell this as a simple fable of moral growth; indeed so detached in his method, so ironically placed his narrator, that the book can be, and has been, read in several ways: as a tragedy of Tietjens' accumulated suffering, or a comedy of his emergence into a new life, as a conservative assault on the decline of English society, its cold, bureaucratic mechanism exposed by the war, or a celebration of the greater democracy and justice of the post-war world. The peculiarity of the tone arises in part because Ford is always trying to merge a coherent structure, a historical fable, with an impressionistic technique; the technique qualifies the structure. The problem of relating an intense impressionism with a 'hidden long logic' is one Ford must have known from Crane's *Red Badge of Courage,* that ambiguous novel set on another battlefield, in the American Civil War. But Crane was above all concerned with the consciousness of his central character; hence his impressionism. Ford's is a less interior technique; he uses impressionism for private and public purposes at the same time, to relate inward motions of consciousness with compounded exterior circumstances. Moreover Ford was dealing not with a brief set of incidents but a long historical span, embodying a logic and an evolution, indeed an extended Spenglerian cycle from feudalism to modern class war and materialist democracy. His task was more broadly spread; he was using impressionist modes not to suggest the freedom or independence or even the mechanisation of consciousness, but the motion of mind amid historical coercions; men are subject to historical facts and historical change. Likewise the war itself is a reality prior to any aesthetic intervention in it. What the novelist is responsible for creating is therefore not the facts, which are historically predetermined objects of representation, but the 'treatment'. Thus far Ford himself saw impressionism as a heightened realism, a mode of dealing with the reality of life; his war is not, like Crane's, a metaphor. But he also saw it as a technique for coping with the perceptual chaos of the times, with the novelist's incapacity to intervene; it was a mode of detachment and irony. And it was also a way of representing the subjective motions of consciousness moving not only parallel with, but atemporally against, the significant motion of history, the insistent realities of war. In any case, those realities were in part a dislocation *of* reality; as he said in *It Was the Nightingale,* war damaged confidence in substance: 'it had been revealed to you that beneath Ordered Life itself was stretched, the merest film with, beneath it, the abysses of Chaos.'

Thus, if one part of Ford's effort went into substantiating the historical novel as a form for dealing with the times, another part went into taking it away again. The first book, *Some Do Not . . . ,* begins on a prose of apparent solidity, realistic weight:

> The two young men—they were of the English public official class—sat in the perfectly appointed railway carriage. The leather straps to the windows were of virgin newness; the mirrors beneath the new luggage racks immaculate as if they had reflected very little; the bulging upholstery in its luxuriant regulated curves was scarlet and yellow in an intricate, minute dragon pattern, the design of a geometrician in Cologne. The compartment smelt faintly, hygienically of admirable varnish; the train ran as smoothly—Tietjens remembered thinking—as British gilt-edged securities . . .

This is England in 1912, given with weighty realism. But it is of course a very hard-edge realism, which does not so much humanise as render things stark and abstract. The train has a glossy brittle newness; the two young men are at a temporal distance; the language, like the upholstery, has an abstract foreign geometry. Ford is opening up an aloof space between the material and the novelist, an indirect, angular form of presentation, and it is into this space that technique comes. History and form alike will tell against this solid world; the desubstantiation of this reality will be manifested both by the novelist and the war. Using the method he calls *progression d'effect,* Ford accumulates, by juxtaposition, a sequence that establishes this world of 1912 as one of already breaking principles, muddled history, colliding forces. Harsh machinery intersects with organic life; subjective consciousness struggles with public responsibility; sexual instincts subvert moral codes. In this increasingly chaotic world Tietjens attempts to stabilise life by asserting the need for principle, 'a skeleton map of a country'; but his mind wanders, the knacker's cart comes round the corner, and—in using a larger structural irony he will make into a basic device of the sequence—Ford shifts the action in time directly to 1917, to a war-wounded Tietjens, socially absurd, publicly unpopular, lost in the chaos he has attempted to control. Impressionism thus becomes a technique for dematerialising the solid world, partly in order to extend its historical significance, relating one part of life to another, partly in order to move the action inward into consciousness and allow for its anguish and disordered movement, the movement that itself mirrors a decomposing world.

It is this double motion that allows Ford to make impressionism into an effective technique for coping with the war, for creating a significant historiography. It allowed Ford to merge realism with technical modernism, treating a disjunctive history but granting it historical significance. In *No More Parades,* the next volume, the impressionistic mode can dominate as a method for representing the contingency and fragmentation of the battlefield itself, the chaos of conduct, the loss of rule and order, the massing of perceptual and mental chaos. Historical solidity and substance are shattered.

Now, in the next volume, *A Man Could Stand Up,* which passes between the battlefield and the Armistice, between the consciousness of Tietjens and that of Valentine Wannop, a painful, disorderly new coherence can start to emerge. With *The Last Post,* Ford faced his most difficult problem, that of dealing with a post-war world in which both chaos and a new economy of order exist. The technique is fragmentary, as is Tietjens' past and the present form of his social being; but, as with [D. H. Lawrence's *Lady Chatterley's Lover,* 1928], the book gestures toward the need for a new life and a new language amid the ruins. Ford settles for a modernist technique with vague organic overtones, a tentative and ironic resolution. It was an answer he seems to have been uneasy with himself; he proposed on occasion dropping the book from the sequence. In fact it has stylistic validity, and enforces the ironic meaning of the whole; what it lacks is the urgent strength the war sections gave to Ford's entire technique. It is indeed the war part of the novel that makes it Ford's most triumphant work, an extraordinary probe into a culture, wherein the double inheritance of technique he carried with him—part realistic, part modernistic—fuses itself into a historical meaning. In his fable of Tietjens entering a lowered history, a world of reduced substance and solidity, Ford led the way for many subsequent English novelists who found the world of the twenties and thirties, or indeed the sixties and seventies, capable of acquiring meaning only if treated with something of Ford's comic and modernistic indifference.

Sondra J. Stang   (essay date 1977)

SOURCE: "*Parade's End,*" in *Ford Madox Ford,* Frederick Ungar Publishing Co., 1977, pp. 94-123.

[*Stang is an American writer and editor specializing in the study and criticism of the works of Ford Madox Ford. In the following excerpt, she provides an overview of* Parade's End, *focusing particularly on the symbolism of the main characters and their interactions with one another.*]

Parade's End is, of course, a "war novel"—really an anti-war novel, Ford called it, for he intended to show "what war was like" without overstating its physical horrors. W. H. Auden called *Parade's End* a "four-volume study of Retribution and Expiation"; Graham Greene read it as a book about the power of a lie. These themes are present, but they are lesser themes. As Robie Macauley has pointed out, Ford's book is really "more about our own world than his"; Ford wrote prophetically about the world he saw and understood. *Parade's End* is about historical change; its theme, most inclusively stated, is the great and irreversible change in human consciousness that took place when the shift from the civilization of the nineteenth century to that of the modern world as we know it occurred under the stress of World War I.

The complicated story of *Parade's End* tells itself in a series of images. At the center is the triangle composed of Christopher Tietjens, the main character; his estranged wife, Sylvia, who pursues him and would destroy him, if she could, and prevent another woman from having him; and Valentine Wannop, the other woman, whom Christopher loves, finally acknowledges to himself that he loves, and lives with after the war.

The secondary yet overlapping story, which takes the form of a seesaw, is of the rise of Vincent Macmaster, son of a poor shipping clerk, and Christopher's corresponding "fall" in the great world of English government and society. The war, with Christopher at the front, is imaged by Ford in explosions, trenches, huts. And after the war, Christopher and Valentine retreat to the English countryside, in *Last Post,* to live their own lives and raise their child.

Parade's End consists of four novels, published as separate volumes (1924–1928) exactly a decade after the war (1914–1918): *Some Do Not . . .* (1924), *No More Parades* (1925), *A Man Could Stand Up—* (1926), and *Last Post* (1928). The books were not published in one volume until 1950 in the United States, nor were they known in England as *Parade's End.* The American title is merciful: even the best-intentioned readers have difficulty remembering and keeping in order the first three teasing, low-keyed, and unwieldy titles. Oddly, Ford was emphatic on two points: it is clear from his correspondence in 1930 (1) that he intended the novels as a trilogy rather than a tetralogy ("I strong wish to omit *Last Post* from the edition. I do not like the book and have never liked it. . . .") and (2) that if the novels were to have one general title, it should not be *The Tietjens Saga,* though Ford had often referred to them as the Tietjens novels. ("I do not like the title *Tietjens Saga*—because in the first place 'Tietjens' is a difficult name for purchasers to pronounce and booksellers would almost inevitably persuade readers that they mean the Forsyte [sic] Saga with great damage to my sales.")

The title *Parade's End* was originally Ford's own suggestion in 1930 and picks up the note of the second volume, emphasizing its title. The words "no more parades" meant, of course, that given the kind of war being waged and the social changes taking place, there would be no more pomp, no more ceremony, no more public processions, no more posturing. Not that the idea of ceremony is contemptible, but by itself, with nothing behind it, it is the outward show of nothing. Having no meaning, it has no reason for being.

> "At the beginning of the war," Tietjens said, "I had to look in on the War Office, and in a room I found a fellow. . . . What do you think he was doing . . . what the hell do you think he was doing? He was devising the ceremonial for the disbanding of a Kitchener battalion. You can't say we were not prepared in one matter at least. . . . Well, the end of the show was to be: the adjutant would stand the battalion at ease: the band would play 'Land of Hope and Glory,' and then the adjutant would say: There will be no more parades. . . . Don't you see how symbolical it was: the band playing 'Land of Hope and Glory,' and then the adjutant saying *There will be no more parades*? . . . For there won't. There won't, there damn well won't. . . . No more Hope, no more Glory, no more parades for you and me any more. Nor for the country . . . Nor for the world, I dare say . . . None . . . Gone . . . Napoo finny No . . . more . . . parades!"

Professor Fussell, in *The Great War and Modern Memory* has spoken of "the collision . . . between events and the public language used for over a century to celebrate the idea of progress." World War I was a breaking point in European culture, and Ford was marking the break not only in public events but in language. By "no more parades" he meant, in addition to the more obvious sense of the phrase, no more hollow rhetoric, no more heroic abstractions like hope and glory and honor—an end of traditional moral language, those words that, compared to the concrete names of villages, indeed seemed obscene to Hemingway in *A Farewell to Arms*.

To Ford those words seemed extinct, and in *Parade's End* his achievement was to render the experience of the war in a language adequate to it and more accurate than the language inherited from another era. Of the great modernist writers—Joyce, Eliot, Pound, Yeats, Lawrence—Ford was the only one to have been involved directly in the war, and he was alone in bringing to that experience the great technical innovations of twentieth century literature. Aside from its other merits, *Parade's End* is, for this reason, historically the most important English novel to come out of World War I.

Ford's reasons for disliking *Last Post* were never clear. He tells us that he had originally intended to deal with the period before the war and the war itself, not with the lives of his characters in the years following it. But it may be that his natural preference for the three-part form more than anything else made him regret the actual necessity for the fourth part as it came upon him. In his introductory letter to *A Man Could Stand Up—*, he referred to that volume as "penultimate": obviously, he could not, much as he wanted to, do without *Last Post* and keep to his original three-part idea. The *aba* song form was as inevitable and right for him in the design of his novels as it was in his life: how else account for the curious name he constructed for himself after the war?

No More Parades and *A Man Could Stand Up—* have a clear three-part structure, and *Some Do Not . . .*, while divided into two parts, illustrates the characteristic Fordian return to the opening theme. *Some Do Not . . .* opens—and the first paragraph has been justly celebrated as one of the great openings in the English novel—with two young men, Christopher Tietjens and Vincent Macmaster, riding in the pre-war railway carriage, the leather straps on the windows "of virgin newness," the upholstery "luxuriant" and "regulated" in "an intricate pattern, the design of a geometrician in Cologne," the smooth-running train smelling "hygienically" of varnish—every detail contributing to an image of design, order, opulence, and perfection of surface, all a metaphor for the civilization about to be changed irrevocably.

The end of the novel returns to this scene: Tietjens's mind counterpoises it with the party celebrating Macmaster's knighthood. The two men are once more together. The war has intervened, Macmaster has profited from it (his knighthood is conferred for statistical calculations Christopher had made), and Christopher is about to leave for the fighting in France again.

The title of *Some Do Not . . .*, like all the other titles of the tetralogy, recurs throughout the novel, turning up in different contexts, emerging in variations ("Gentlemen don't," "women didn't," "some girls have") and wandering into the other books, there acquiring unexpected, witty, and poignant resonances. "Some do not" is part of a line from Ford's poem **"Mr. Bosphorus and the Muses"** (1923). In the title of the novel Ford quotes himself:

> The gods to each ascribe a differing lot:
> Some rest on snowy bosoms! Some do not!

And Macmaster, who, at the opening of the novel misreads the times (he believes a war is impossible) and misreads Rossetti (yet will build his career on his monograph on Rossetti), misquotes the lines, changing them to

> The gods to each ascribe a differing lot:
> Some enter at the portal. Some do not!

A careerist of the most determined kind, Macmaster characteristically changes the verb and the image, so that the categories refer to success and failure rather than luck. The snowy bosoms are replaced by portals: Macmaster's sexuality, always circumspect, and his well-managed affair with Edith Ethel Duchemin, the wife of the Reverend Duchemin, form the second story of the book, parallel to Christopher's; and each of the stories comments on the other.

Ford could not see the issue of sexual morality apart from that of the war, nor could Christopher.

> Macmaster said loftily:
>
> "You're extraordinarily old-fashioned at times, Chrissie. You ought to know as well as I do that a war is impossible—at any rate with this country in it. Simply because . . . " He hesitated and then emboldened himself: "*We*—the circumspect—yes, the circumspect classes, will pilot the nation through the tight places."

And Christopher answers:

> "War, my good fellow" . . . —the train was slowing down preparatorily to running into Ashford—"is inevitable, and with this country plumb centre in the middle of it. Simply because you fellows are such damn hypocrites. There's not a country in the world that trusts us. We're always, as it were, committing adultery—like your fellow [Dante Gabriel Rossetti]!—with the name of Heaven on our lips." He was jibing again at the subject of Macmaster's monograph.

In the figures of Macmaster and Edith Ethel—as well as Christopher's wife, Sylvia, Ford connects the two issues, the sexual conduct of men and women and the world at war. Edith Ethel, "passionately cultured," with the "elegance and portentousness of a funeral horse," and her lover, Macmaster, make a show of Pre-Raphaelite sensibility and English respectability, camouflaging their eroticism elaborately and affectedly with an aesthetic they exploit for their mutual profit—though the sexual antagonism Edith Ethel harbors but will not acknowledge is as immense as her essential vulgarity.

It is this mixture, and not the fact of fornication, that Christopher sees as filthy. Both at the beginning of the story and ten years later, at the end of *Some Do Not . . .*, he declares, with his characteristic preference for clarity in thought and conduct:

> I stand for monogamy and chastity. And for no talking about it. Of course if a man who's a man wants to have a woman he has her. And again no talking about it. . . .

And Christopher in fact suffers for monogamy and chastity; the Macmasters pretend to. It is their way of having what they want and not taking the consequences that seems unprincipled to Christopher. "Principles are like a skeleton map of a country—you know whether you're going east or north." Having no principles, only instincts for self-advancement, they become expert social climbers, appropriately representing a government that, in the same way, has deserted the idea of virtue. The Office of Statistics, to which Christopher will not go back, falsifies official figures; England's political strategy in respect to its allies is exploitative and treacherous; the men at Whitehall betray the men at the front and nullify all sacrifice. No more truth and honor: Ford saw a government run by sycophants and cowards feathering their nests in the middle of the war.

In the famous breakfast scene early in *Some Do Not . . .* the Reverend Duchemin's obscenities explode, appalling and testing the excellent manners of the guests, who almost succeed in appearing to ignore what is so unseemly. The scene is a brilliant image of violence erupting that anticipates the larger violence of the coming war and probes with great subtlety the relationship between sexuality, madness, and culture.

Professor Steven Marcus's conclusion to *The Other Victorians* connects the treatment of sexual life with the social criticism of the modern novel. His comment applies strikingly to *Parade's End.*

> In the work of the great late nineteenth-century and early twentieth-century avant-garde artists, and in particular among the novelists, the entire fabric of modern society came in for attack. The focus of their assault was the sexual life of the bourgeois or middle classes, as those classes and the style of life they conducted had come to be the prevailing social powers. The difficulties, agonies, contradictions, double-dealings, hypocrisies, inequities, guilts, and confusions of the sexual life of the middle classes were for these novelists not only bad in themselves; they were symbolic of general circumstances of injustice, unpleasantness, demoralization, and malaise which for these artists characterized the world they inhabited. They endorsed a freer sexual life as a good in itself; and they depicted the sexual anguish of modern persons and the sexual hypocrisies and contradictions of modern society not merely for the sake of exposure and sensationalism (although there was that too), but in order to outrage and awaken the society which had imposed upon itself such hideous conditions of servitude. Society being what it is, they were often punished for their efforts, but the work of awakening had been furthered, the work of bringing back into the central discourse of civilization

that sexual life upon which it is built and through which it is perpetuated.

". . . You must have a pattern to interpret things by. You can't really get your mind to work without. The blacksmith said: By Hammer and hand all art doth stand!" Toward the end of the fourth novel, *Last Post,* Christopher's dying brother Mark applies the rules of art of life: coherence is necessary, he means, and it must be wrought; it will not come by itself. His words take us back across the four novels to the opening theme, the "intricate, minute" pattern of the upholstery in the railway car, a pattern that will be dissolved by the events of history.

"I think *The Good Soldier* is my best book technically unless you read the Tietjens books as one novel in which case the whole design appears," Ford had written in a letter. The care with which he—and the other great twentieth-century novelists, notably Conrad, Joyce, and Virginia Woolf—approached questions of pattern and technique, was, as it has been pointed out, a response to the disorder presented by the external world. "The most general common characteristic" of modernist writers was "the inverse relation between the rendered aesthetic order and the represented chaos":

> The more disordered the world represented, the more ordered the rendering of the work. . . . The very techniques used to represent a world of dissolving appearances and discontinuous selves, of crumbling institutions and discredited authorities . . . are also the techniques that bind part to part and part to whole with an unprecedented adhesive force.

Ford's impressionism, the literary theory comprising the whole set of artistic assumptions that enabled him to write his novels, provided the "rules" for working into coherence the raw material the world presents. But rather than deal with the raw facts themselves—that is, the phenomena of the external world—he tried to get at the very nature of experience, to study the impact of the external world upon human consciousness. In other words, he was interested not in "realism" but in psychological reality.

And in rendering the experience of each of his characters—Tietjens, Sylvia, their son Mark, Valentine, Christopher's brother Mark, Mark's wife, Marie Léonie—Ford was as much interested in the individual way each mind experienced as in what it experienced. The characteristic sound of its thoughts, the psychological rhythms of perception and speech, the special syntax of each separate consciousness—through these the reader can grasp each character's unique psychological experience as well as the facts to which he responds. The reader is forced to stand, with each of the characters, "at different angles" to the perceived world and to experience twice every act of perception: once with the character, and once for himself, reassembling all that he has learned from the implications of the text. In getting the facts, the reader simultaneously experiences the whole range of the characters' responses to them.

**Perhaps the greatest critical problem
Parade's End offers is the character of
Sylvia Tietjens. How are we to understand
her and her relationship to Christopher?
What, by inference, are we to make of
Christopher, who married her?**

— *Sondra J. Stang*

In *Parade's End,* the point of view is not confined to any
one character (as it is in *The Good Soldier*), though, as
Ford tells us in *It Was the Nightingale,* there was to be
a central observer whose attitudes affect the way in which
we read the whole story. But *Parade's End* is not *told* by
Tietjens, as *The Good Soldier* is by Dowell: rather, Tietjens's story is told through a far-ranging, "authorial,"
"omniscient" presence who puts together for us a complicated tissue of the consciousness of each of the many characters. The principal relationships are examined by every
character, each aware of the other's awareness. The technique provides a set of reflecting mirrors.

Like the French impressionist painters, writers espousing
literary impressionism were forced to make a set of quite
revolutionary technical innovations. The most far-
reaching and dramatic was the breaking up of chronological time or, as it has come to be known, the time shift. Behind the time shift is the principle of juxtaposition. Chronological time is broken up and rearranged so that we are
presented with disparate moments, recalled either voluntarily or involuntarily—because two spots of time, two impressions taken together, like two spots of color, acquire
more emotional vibrancy and meaning than they have separately. It is really the old and universal principle of contrast—the two stories in a Shakespearean play coloring
one another—applied to the surface of time.

In *Parade's End,* Ford created an elaborate design out of
the tension between the actual chronology of the many
events that take place before, during, and after World War
I, and the activity of the perceiving mind of each of the
characters experiencing the events. Two kinds of time
therefore make themselves felt throughout the story—
chronological and experienced time, and their mingling
produces what has been described as a kind of keyboard
of all the tenses of memory. Ford himself develops the
analogy with music: "The motives mingled fugally," he
wrote in *No More Parades.* What we have is a fluid succession of present moments—or, to use another of Ford's
metaphors, a surgical cutting and stitching.

She said:

"If we *could* wash out . . . "

He said, and for the first moment felt grand, tender, protective:

"Yes, you *can*," he said. "You cut out from this
afternoon, just before 4.58 it was when I said
that to you and you consented. . . . I heard the

Horse Guards clock. . . . To now. . . . Cut it
out; and join time up. . . . It *can* be done. . . .
You know they do it surgically; for some illness. . . . "

The actual prototype for Christopher, as we know from
It Was the Nightingale, was Arthur Marwood, Ford's
good friend who had been long dead when Ford began *Parade's End.* Marwood had "the widest and most serene intelligence of any human being I have yet met." Ford
could, he claimed, "set" his mind by him. So haunted was
Ford by the power of Marwood's intelligence and personality that he listed him among the "revenants": the ghosts
of the past who had for him more reality than the men and
women he saw every day. Tietjens was to be a recreation
of Marwood, and Ford's intention was "to project how
this world would have appeared to him today."

The emphasis of the novel is on Christopher's observation
and understanding of the world—and consequently on his
suffering, the "human tribulations" that, as Ford noted in
It Was the Nightingale, "are the only things worth writing
about," and that came to him as the original material of
the book; the character was to carry "a permanent shackle
and ball on his leg . . . something of a moral order and
something inscrutable." "He was to go through the public
affairs of distracted Europe" with a "private cannonball."
The two themes—public and private life—are clearly connected here in Ford's account of the genesis of *Parade's
End.* The world war and the private battlefield are inseparable from one another, or, as Ford put it, the war was the
"outward sign of inward and spiritual disarray": two related wars and their two resolutions, one central figure to
bear the double pressure, and two women.

Remarkably unlucky and hard-pressed, in fact overtested
by his misfortunes and the strain and anxiety of going
through the war, Christopher bears his trials with such
"strength of mind and composure" that Ford counted on
his stoicism and his "power of cool observation in tremendous crises" to excite the reader's sympathy—as the heroes of other novelists might excite sympathy by their
weakness. Christopher is a strong central character, but
not a "hero." Ford deliberately avoided the term in his
comments on the book: "I was in no mood for the heroic."

> My character would be deprived of any
> glory. . . . He was to be too essentially critical
> to initiate any daring sorties. Indeed his activi-
> ties were most markedly to be in the realm of
> criticism.
>
> . . . When it seemed to be his duty he would
> criticise. That would get him, even at the Front,
> into many and elaborate messes. . . . So I
> should get my "intrigue" screwed up tighter and
> always tighter.

The critical spirit would replace the heroic—would indeed
become the only form of heroism untainted by anachronism. Tietjens was to be a "sort of lonely buffalo. . . . An
exact observer." The novel would show the chasm between the critical attitude (a phrase Ford liked and used
as the title of a book of essays in 1911) and the way the
world is really run. In *Parade's End,* knowledge and
power move unalterably apart.

Perhaps the greatest critical problem the book offers is the character of Sylvia Tietjens. How are we to understand her and her relationship to Christopher? What, by inference, are we to make of Christopher, who married her? She has often been taken to be the embodiment of evil, an allegorical figure, and one of the great *femmes fatales* in literature. How can we square such an image with Ford's novelistic method, which rests upon the idea that the sympathetic imagination can enlarge the reader's capacity for identification with other people and understanding of them?

Ford's idea of the art of the novel derived largely from Flaubert's principle "ne pas conclure." Ford would often quote that phrase, intended for the practicing novelist, and it meant do not sum up a character; do not draw the reader's conclusions for him; allow him to see and understand for himself. Like Flaubert, Ford seldom gives us a complete physical description of a character. Instead, the character—even the way he looks—emerges from different contexts, always freshly to be perceived, and never totally grasped. In this respect Ford's men and women are like human beings outside the novel, at every meeting needing to be reinterpreted and never finally to be wholly understood. More than any character in Ford's novels—that is to say, more than any of the hundreds of characters he created, Sylvia is the most problematic and difficult to understand.

She had first presented herself to Ford's imagination as a pagan goddess. As he tells us in *It Was the Nightingale,* he once saw a woman in the railway station at Amiens:

> She was in a golden sheath-gown and her golden hair was done in bandeaux, extraordinarily brilliant in the dimness. Like a goddess come in from the forest of Amiens!
>
> I exclaimed:
>
> "Sylvia!" So I didn't have to cast about for a name.

Sylvan, of the woods: the original shining figure became, before Ford was done with her, a character of tantalizing complexity. "Who is Silvia? What is she?" Shakespeare's song may have had as much to do with Ford's naming her as did the fresh and arrestingly pagan quality of the actual woman he once saw in Amiens.

Early in *Some Do Not . . . ,* Sylvia is compared to the mythological Astarte, Phoenician goddess of love and fertility, and Lamia, in Greek stories the witch who sucked human blood. Though the mythic dimension is certainly implied, and at times implied very strongly, Sylvia *is* neither of these. What is significant is her many-facetedness, and it was present in Ford's original inspiration as a quality of light—coruscating, brilliant, flashing different images at different times, now a goddess, at other times a woman, never reducible to a single fixed aspect.

Virgin and courtesan, devil as well as "a picture of Our Lady by Fra Angelico," she is presented in paradoxes, with each quality calling up its opposite. Perverse, unpredictable, her character is "a matter of contrariety." "To be seductive and to be chaste" is the condition she aspires

to. To do wickedness and not be wicked: it is a theological distinction she makes, and perhaps it is the ultimate paradox of her nature. Ford repeatedly uses the verb *coil* in connection with Sylvia to suggest a snake, yet the imagery of writhing is, as often as not, connected with her suffering. And she speaks of the "almost painful emotion of joyful hatred." "Coldly passionate," she goes to the front to torment and allure Christopher in the hope of a *rapprochement.* She loves him for his mind, she says, but she hates his ideas. "There was no end to the contradiction in men's characters"—or women's. That she loves him as she does is, of course, "the impossible complication." The character of Sylvia needs four books to unfold itself, and Ford is at great pains to present her point of view with scrupulous fairness.

The Tietjens books have been described by Graham Greene as "almost the only adult novels dealing with the sexual life that have been written in English." In the story of Sylvia and Tietjens, the relation between the sexes is seen as a condition of warfare. Christopher's problem *is* "the whole problem of the relation of the sexes." Sylvia's "sex viciousness," her "sex ferocity," her "sex cruelty" are plain. But that repeated note cannot obscure the fact that the struggle between them is neither simple nor one-sided and that they are two antagonists of considerable subtlety, whose antagonism is made all the more subtle by the similarities between them. Their story is a study in obstinacies—two strong wills engaged in a war. On the one side Sylvia acts out of a strongly instinctual nature; on the other side Christopher distrusts his instincts and acts from a set of principles which, as he comes to recognize, can no longer serve. In order to use them, he is forced to reexamine them.

Curiously, the novel insists on how similar Christopher and Sylvia are. They are both *hallucinés* (Pound's word for Ford), given to actual hallucination. They are both venerators of the ideal of chastity as a state of physical and moral purity. And their sensitivity to one another's psychological processes is expressed by Christopher's compulsion (his "obsession") to shield Sylvia against gossip and slander, and on her side, by her pity and revulsion at how far she has succeeded in destroying him. There are moments when they meet and fight with the "friendly weariness of old enemies." Even their child—the young Mark—speculates about the basis of their enmity.

> Questions of . . . sex-attraction, in spite of all the efforts of scientists, remained fairly mysterious. The best way to look at it . . . the safest way, was that sex attraction occurred as a rule between temperamental and physical opposites because Nature desired to correct extremes. No one in fact could be more different than his father and mother—the one [Sylvia] so graceful, athletic and . . . oh, charming. And the other [Christopher] so . . . oh, let us say perfectly honourable but lawless. Because, of course, you can break certain laws and remain the soul of honour.

It is Sylvia who is generally regarded as lawless, but as she sees Christopher, it is he who is immoral. His principles are so baffling—for example, his systematic refusal to stand up for himself—that they make no sense, and they are so outmoded that she cannot even identify them. He "unsettles" society. As Christopher explains to General Campion:

> . . . I've no politics that did not disappear in the eighteenth century. . . . I'm a Tory of such an extinct type that she might take me for anything. The last megatherium. She's absolutely to be excused.

Christopher understands her difficulties.

Their relationship began as a "courtship of spiders," with the female enticing the male. Having married Sylvia "on the hop when he was only a kid," as his brother Mark puts it, Christopher forgives her her "sin." (She believed herself to be pregnant after an affair with a man named Drake.) As Sylvia perceives her marriage to Christopher, she is perpetually the woman taken in adultery. Though she grants that Christopher is more Christian than any man she knows, she finds it unbearable that with her he should play the part of Christ. "But our Lord was never married. He never touched on topics of sex."

Christopher is, in his remarkable selflessness and detachment from the world, correctly regarded as a saint, and his wish for saintliness is one of the repeated themes of the book. But Sylvia's view is to be considered. Christopher cherishes forgiveness (and, as Mark realizes in *Last Post*, Christopher cherishes unforgiveness as well), but Sylvia wants neither his forgiveness nor his saintliness. "How could any woman live beside you . . . and be forever forgiven?" If he had denounced her or cursed her, he "might have done something to bring us together." But his aloofness and self-containment—she complains that he closes himself in "invisible bonds"—make him seem merely cold and feelingless, though he is neither.

Everything in his training as an Englishman and a Yorkshireman (a point Ford makes much of) has worked against the ready and spontaneous show of feeling. To make a display of one's deepest emotions is against the rules. His "calculatedly wooden" expression, his "terrifying expressionlessness," make him as much an enigma to Sylvia as she is to him. Intellectual, abstract, he has a monolithic quality she cannot deal with, except to attack it. She perceives him as a rock, a frozen marble statue. His extraordinary self-control, which puts him beyond her reach as he accepts the consequences of her wildest efforts to humiliate and slander him, is, as she understands it, a form of aggression against her, a way of refusing to acknowledge that she can touch him. It is a tacit statement that she is excluded from his life.

Christopher's brother Mark, who is Sylvia's most implacable enemy, understands this: that she is unable to attract her man is the mainspring of her behavior. It is a case of thwarted love become destructive. A woman unused to frustration or failure with men, she is "sappily in love" with him; that she is "forgiven" but not loved by him is the basic fact of their relationship. Jealous even of Christopher's battalion because he cares about his men so deeply, she says to one of them: "I'm glad the captain . . . did not leave you in the cold camp . . . For punishment, you know."

There is something anarchic about Sylvia; her jealousy and destructive passion resist containment. It is not evil as an absolute that she represents, even at her worst, so much as chaos, irrationality, impulse gone berserk. She is an unhappy, even masochistic woman who must have weak things to torture. She sees Christopher "with a mixture of pity and hatred" as a "tired, silent beast" whom she takes pleasure in lashing, as she once thrashed a white bulldog. On the other hand, "Tietjens' words cut her as if she had been lashed with a dog-whip." Ford is suggesting a mysterious identification here.

All the plumb lines are so entangled, as Ford liked to say about human relations and motives, that human behavior seems incapable of simplicity. Though the marriage is improbable from the start, and Sylvia's adultery makes it even more so, Christopher refuses, out of his sense of honor as a gentleman, to divorce her—a refusal that keeps them connected, and at the same time, alienated. The perversities of her nature make it impossible for her to leave him alone, and the game she plays is to torment him, to provoke him into intimacy. Tietjens understands this side of her and calls it "pulling the strings of the shower-bath." Her game is impulsive rather than systematic. She wants to see where and how and whether Christopher is exposed, and she stops only when he seems to have nothing more to lose, having lost money, property, position, and reputation. Her sense of decency makes an attack on Valentine and her baby unthinkable. Besides, by the time of *Last Post*, it seems to her that "God has changed sides."

Christopher's strength inheres in the fundamental principle of his being, his certainty about his own autonomy, his own outlines. Sylvia's sense of herself is a good deal weaker. She wants to possess him, but possession, as she comes to see, is meaningless without self-possession. And rather than fight back, Christopher merely waits for her ("anguish is better than dishonour" is his battalion's motto) to expend herself, as she finally does.

Christopher's metaphor of the shower bath is, in its understatement, intended to deflate Sylvia's effectiveness. But not even his clearness of mind and temperamental affinity with eighteenth-century rationalism can dissipate the sense of evil that hovers around Sylvia. We first see her in Lobscheid, the "last place in Europe" to be Christianized. There, Father Consett, her "saintly" confessor, hears "the claws of evil things scratching on the shutters" and tries to attribute Sylvia's "evil thoughts" to the "evil place" they are in. But the suggestion remains, no matter how much we understand Sylvia's psychology, that Christopher is under her spell and that she herself may be under a spell. The possibility of magic in Sylvia's capacity for destructiveness inheres in the book, emerging often enough to demand interpretation.

Magic has been defined by the late Hannah Arendt [in *Rahel Varnhagen*, 1974] as an "intensification of the world to such a pitch of extraordinariness that reality would necessarily fail to come up to its expectations." Sylvia lives in such an intensified world, but not consistently.

Standing away from it long enough to try to understand it, she asks:

> How was it possible that the most honourable man she knew should be so overwhelmed by foul and baseless rumours? It made you suspect that honour had, in itself, a quality of the evil eye. . . .

No matter how farfetched her charge or inaccurate her aim, her success in hurting Christopher is uncanny and not to be wholly explained in terms of cause and effect. "I have always been superstitious myself and so remain—impenitently," Ford wrote in 1932. "The most rationalist of human beings does not pass his life without saying: 'I am in luck today!' " In *No Enemy* he had spoken of the "type of feeling" that men engaged in agriculture often have and that makes them "so often passionately disagreeable and apparently unreasonable"—the sense of "wrestling with a personal devil," of an "intelligent, malignant . . . being with a will for evil directed against you in person." "I think that, whilst it lasts," he wrote, "it is the worst feeling in the world."

Ford's belief in a kind of animism—really more significant than his nominal Catholicism for an understanding of his novels—that is, his sense of a universe full of unknown and living forces creating "an atmosphere of loaded dice"—is surely at work in his conception of the Catholic Sylvia. Insofar as she suggests Astarte or Lamia, Sylvia is, in spite of her Catholicism, a creature from the world of romance. Throughout his long career, the pendulum of Ford's imagination swung back and forth between two kinds of fictional reality—the subjective and the objective: which is to say that he wrote two kinds of fiction—those he called romances and those he referred to as novels, and he was usually careful to designate by a subtitle which was which. Roughly half of his works of fiction bear the subtitle *A Romance* (*Romance,* which he wrote with Conrad, surely needed no subtitle) or some equivalent like *An Extravagant Story* or *A Just Possible Story* or *A Sheer Comedy.* And the historical novels are often, though not consistently, designated as romances. What *Parade's End* represents is a merging of the two genres—the combination of psychological reality and fantasy in the same framework, a conjunction that offers an interesting critical problem.

Tietjens has, as in a fairy tale, incurred the malignity of a dangerous woman. In putting himself beyond her influence, he moves from the world of romance, where cause and effect are incommensurate, to a small corner of the real world. In Ford's early fairy tales and romances, metamorphoses occur and miracles heal and bring back to life. The natural law of cause and effect is suspended, and we are in the realm of magic and divine intervention, in "that sacred and beautiful thing Romance," Ford called it. In *Parade's End,* Tietjens must face the tangled consequences of every small action—his own or Sylvia's—and live them down, as Ford put it when he discussed the genesis of the novel in *It Was the Nightingale.* If Tietjens is to have a new life, he must make it for himself. Ford is clear about keeping Tietjens in this imperfect world: the resolution of the book is coincident with Christopher's growing

sense of reality. And *Parade's End,* unlike *The Good Soldier,* is about learning how to live rather than how to die.

As Ford wrote in another context [*When Blood Is Their Argument,* 1915] the purpose of philosophy was "to teach a man how to bear himself during, and what to expect from, life. All else is stamp-collecting."

Christopher can make a new life ("a man could stand up") because of Valentine.

> But, positively, she and Sylvia were the only two human beings he had met for years whom he could respect: the one for sheer efficiency in killing; the other for having the constructive desire and knowing how to set about it. Kill or cure! The two functions of man. If you wanted something killed you'd go to Sylvia Tietjens in the sure faith that she would kill it; emotion: hope: ideal: kill it quick and sure. If you wanted something kept alive you'd go to Valentine: she'd find something to do for it. . . . The two types of mind: remorseless enemy: sure screen: dagger . . . sheath!

He can respect both women for their opposite perfections. Sylvia kills; Valentine cures. And he asks: "Perhaps the future of the world then was to women?"

Valentine is a militant suffragette. When we first see her, she is on a golf course where she has been demonstrating for the vote. She is exercising one of the suffragette movement's characteristic tactics—to invade the traditionally male preserve. Ford himself had helped the suffragettes by writing for Mrs. Emmeline Pankhurst, leader of the Women's Social and Political Union, a pamphlet entitled *This Monstrous Regiment of Women* (1913), published by the Women's Freedom League, and he had a strong sense of the women's movement as the beginning of a new consciousness.

Valentine, whose name suggests love, health, and strength, is a fitting heroine for a novel that is as turned toward the future as *The Good Soldier* was turned toward the past. "She would have to be a militant if my book ever came to anything," Ford wrote later. But Valentine is also the daughter of Professor Wannop, the classical scholar, and from him she has received a sound classical education. Her intellectual roots are in the past, and she longs to read Euripides by the Mediterranean. Christopher admires not only her Latin, which is superior to his, but the fact that her head "is screwed on right." Having worked as a "slavey" to support herself and her mother, Mrs. Wannop, the aging and neglected novelist whose work Christopher so much admires, Valentine has a larger firsthand experience of the English class system than Christopher, and a grasp of reality he admires.

> I daresay you're a heroine all right. *Not* because you persevere in actions the consequences of which you fear. But I daresay you can touch pitch and not be defiled.

Although Valentine is as unlike Sylvia as to be her mythical opposite (healer vs. destroyer), Ford has not created a simple antithesis. Instead, he deals with a "civilized ambiguity": in many ways they are similar—and unlike

Christopher. For example, neither woman can bear the thought of war: both are pacifists, and though Christopher does not share their views, he understands them.

> Not three hours ago my wife used to me almost the exact words you have just used. Almost the exact words. She talked of her inability to sleep at night for thinking of immense spaces full of pain that was worse at night. . . . And she, too, said that she could not respect me. . . .

Both are blonde, both are athletes (unlike the slow and heavy Tietjens). Sylvia is strikingly tall and calls Valentine, who is small, a miniature of herself. Both women are presented along with their mothers, so that we see them as daughters. Both express the same irritation with Christopher in the same language. Valentine feels "something devouring" and "overwhelming" in him that "pushed you and your own problems out of the road." She notes his "calculatedly wooden expression and his omniscience" and his "blasted complacent perfections." Like Sylvia, she feels he has insulted her by not making love to her. When they first meet, Valentine says: "I pity your wife . . . The English country male! . . . The feudal system all complete. . . ."

> Tietjens winced. The young woman had come a little too near the knuckle of his wife's frequent denunciations of himself.

Ironically, although Sylvia was conceived as a pagan, it is Valentine whose outlook is more authentically pagan. She is free of the burden of sin and the sense of dualism (body and soul leading separate lives) that Sylvia's Catholic upbringing has given her. In Valentine, body and mind work together. She can be as critical as Sylvia of Christopher's faults. But free of Sylvia's conflicts and morbid engrossment in her own capacity to sin, she has no wish to destroy. Harmony, discipline, "bread-and-butter sense": with these qualities she offers Christopher a "little, tranquil, golden spot" in an unstrung world.

In *The Education of Henry Adams,* Adams had asked: "What could become of such a child of the seventeenth and eighteenth centuries, when he should wake up to find himself required to play the game of the twentieth?" As if in answer, Christopher says:

> . . . It is not a good thing to belong to the seventeenth or eighteenth centuries in the twentieth. Or really, because it is not good to have taken one's public-school's ethical system seriously. I am really, sir, the English public schoolboy. That's an eighteenth-century product. . . . Other men get over their schooling. I never have. I remained adolescent. These things are obsessions with me.

Christopher suffers from the defects of his qualities, and the scrupulousness with which he has adopted this code of behavior makes him slow to know his own feelings, which are often in conflict with his principles. Sitting on his mind as if it were a horse, "a coffin-headed, leather-jawed charger," he is at the same time aware of and aloof from the claims and needs of his "under mind," with all its repressed impulses. "He occupied himself with his mind. What was it going to do?" He is a man "in need of

a vacation from himself," as he realizes. Under the double stress of the war and Sylvia's harassment, his mind becomes more and more detached until he sees his own dissociation as a danger signal, a portent of the madness he fears.

His decision to live with Valentine is a way of freeing himself and healing himself so that he can adapt to a new set of conditions. "Today's today," he tells himself. "The world was changing and there was no particular reason why he should not change with it." His brother Mark refuses to change; his muteness is a refusal to speak in a world he has come to loathe and despair of, and he wills his own death. In his book on Henry James, Ford had spoken of "the journey towards an entire despair or towards a possible happiness." It is toward the possible happiness that *Parade's End* moves.

> . . . He would no longer stand unbearable things. . . . And what he wanted he was prepared to take. . . . What he had been before, God alone knew. A Younger Son? A Perpetual Second-in-Command? Who knew? But to-day the world changed. Feudalism was finished; its last vestiges were gone. It held no place for him. He was going—he was damn well going!—to make a place in it for . . . A man could now stand up on a hill, so he and she could surely get into some hole together!

Christopher has inherited, through the deaths of his older brothers, the vast ("between forty and sixty rooms") Yorkshire estate of Groby that his family had acquired at the time of William of Orange. He renounces Groby because his disaffection with his own class makes it impossible for him honestly to accept its privileges, not the least of them being the immense income the estate yields. But more importantly, by giving it up, Christopher divests himself of the whole unwieldy feudal structure he has inherited. In exchange, he can, for the first time, recognize the legitimacy of personal happiness; "noblesse oblige" comes to include the obligation to oneself.

Christopher has learned that his sanity and his life depend on knowing what to preserve from the past and what to discard. He would like to keep "the old goodnesses"—without their old trappings and parade. And he reinterprets—by the spirit rather than the letter—the laws that have kept him second-in-command of his own life. Salvaging himself from the wreckage, he trims and consolidates his world, selling what is left of his beautiful old furniture, withdrawing from public life to a private life of "infinite conversations," a life of frugality, self-sufficiency, and comparative serenity. He will live his own life, rather than a predetermined model of it—and it will have order and meaning.

"In contentment live obscurely the inner life," Ford wrote later in *Provence.* In *Last Post,* we see Christopher mislaying some precious old prints and Valentine ashamed of the condition of her underthings and Sylvia and her entourage invading the landscape: Ford cannot offer an ideal solution for Christopher and Valentine, and that is the point. He makes it clear in his dedicatory letter to *Last Post*: "And so he will go jogging along with ups and downs and plenty of worries and some satisfactions, the Tory Englishman, running his head perhaps against fewer walls, perhaps against more. . . . " His descendants will carry on the country "without swank."

Christopher has to rethink his connection with the life he has been born to, and for that way of life Ford created one of the memorable symbols in modern literature, that of Groby Great Tree. The tallest cedar in Yorkshire, the fantastic tree was planted to commemorate the birth of Christopher's great-grandfather who "had died in a whoreshop." The tree was said never to forgive the Tietjens family for transplanting it from Sardinia, and it was connected with the family's bad luck, darkening the windows of the house and tearing chunks out of its foundations.

> . . . Groby Great Tree overshadowed the house. You could not look out of the schoolroom windows at all for its great, ragged trunk and all the children's wing was darkened by its branches. Black . . . funeral plumes. The Hapsburgs were said to hate their palaces—that was no doubt why so many of them . . . had come muckers. At any rate they had chucked the royalty business.

Though the tree "did not like the house," Mark knows how much Christopher loved the tree. He would "pull the house down if he thought it incommoded the tree. . . . The thought that the tree was under the guardianship of unsympathetic people would be enough to drive Christopher almost dotty."

The spell is broken through Sylvia's agency, as a final act of revenge on Christopher for the peace he and Valentine share. Sylvia allows the tenant who was renting the ancestral house "furnished" to have the tree cut down—"to suit the sanitary ideas of the day." It is cut down before Christopher can intervene. The act cannot be undone, and Sylvia, recognizing this, assigns the part to an American. But the curse is removed, as she realizes: "God was lifting the ban." And ironically, Sylvia is the agent by whom the curse of the past is removed.

The ancestors against whom she sins had taken Groby from its rightful owners when the first Tietjens had come over from Holland with William III. The tree, with its great roots and yet its baleful influence, is an ambiguous symbol of the past. In any case, the tree will not darken the house for the generations to come.

Just before Mark dies, Valentine asks him "How are we to live? How are we ever to live?" Her question too is ambiguous, and at last breaking his silence, he answers indirectly, in the old Yorkshire dialect.

He whispered:

"'Twas the mid o' the night and the barnies grat
And the mither beneath the mauld heard that."

. . . "An old song. My nurse sang it. . . . Never thou let thy barnie weep for thy sharp tongue to thy goodman. . . . A good man! . . . Groby Great Tree is down. . . . "

Thinking of the future—Valentine's unborn child—Mark reverts to the oldest words he knows. They express the wisdom of the past, the wisdom of the folk. Having heard them as a child from his nurse, Mark uses them to express the continuity of the generations. To Valentine's question "How are we to live?" he answers—in harmony with Christopher, for the sake of the child. The message is for the future, and since he and Marie Léonie have no children, it is clear to Valentine why she should not tell Lady Tietjens of his last words.

> She would have liked to have had his last words. . . .
> But she did not need them as much as I.

Alfred Kazin (essay date 1979)

SOURCE: "Ford's Modern Romance," in *The New York Review of Books,* Vol. XXVI, No. 18, November 22, 1979, pp. 31-2.

[*A highly respected American literary critic, Kazin is best known for his essay collections* The Inmost Leaf *(1955) and* Contemporaries *(1962), and particularly for* On Native Grounds *(1942), a study of American prose writing since the era of William Dean Howells. In the following review of the first paperback edition of* Parade's End, *which appeared more than fifty years after the four novels of the tetralogy were originally published, Kazin examines Romantic elements in* Parade's End.]

Parade's End, Ford Madox Ford's tetralogy, revolves around Christopher Tietjens, "the last British Tory," a Yorkshire gentleman of ancient family and impeccable instincts whose dazzling, promiscuous wife is so enraged by his perfection that she tries for almost nine hundred pages to destroy him. It is a prodigiously fluent and inventive fiction that is no less captivating for being such a vibrant representation of Ford Madox Ford's absurd mind. (It is now being published for the first time in a single paperback.)

Obviously there is less difficulty in creating a subtle, very long, and even exemplary *social* novel out of characters and situations that are often comically unbelievable if you live deeply enough in your own myth, your favorite fancy of yourself. Ford was a notoriously unreliable witness. He had a genius for getting lied about, for being on the wrong side of people he liked and worked with, and you can see from his long record of mishaps and disasters, farcically the same even as you droop at coming on still another one, why *everything* he wrote turned, as he said, into a novel. He could not stop writing and he could not tell the "truth" to himself about anything. The capacity to dream on paper, and to demand rewards for it from a distracted world, never had a more undismayed example over a hundred books than Ford Madox Ford. Occasionally, as in *Parade's End,* he and his dream meshed—if not unobtrusively—altogether delightfully.

The four volumes of *Parade's End* were published between 1924 and 1928. Ford regretted the concluding volume, *The Last Post,* in which the still-married Tietjens, after having been in love with Valentine Wannop since the opening volume, *Some Do Not,* finally consents to live with her on Armistice Day. As Ford uneasily made clear, this was possible only because his parfit gentle knight had virtually been unhinged from his principles by the corruption of wartime England and the beastliness of the trenches. But Ford could not have done without this totally romantic conclusion to what is essentially a knightly romance about a sordid modern world. In **The Last Post** the firstborn of the Tietjens family, Sir Mark, dies under a thatched roof, not in his great house at Groby, much as the virtuous or chastened characters in *As You Like It* and *The Tempest* signal their final reconciliation with life far from their proper palaces. Christopher has until now refused to accept his rightful share of the estate because Mark has seemed to credit the lies of Christopher's terrible wife Sylvia. Mark, by making a good death at last, and marrying his French mistress of many years, regularizes all things at Groby in preparation for the accession of his long-exiled and slandered youngest brother Christopher.

As in a classic fairy tale or romance, Christopher the supposedly "errant" brother who is secretly virtuous must undergo many trials and adventures before entering into his inheritance. And at the end the wicked Sylvia (who of course *loves* her wickedness and discourses on it) gives up trying to destroy her husband only because Valentine is bearing his child. She will not harm a pregnant woman. Without Mark's marrying, Valentine's childbearing, Sylvia's contrition, there would not be the final justification that Christopher's stoic patience calls for. Ford was writing a romance about a wicked world; in a romance, that literary shadow of the medieval church, the world is justified because we are reconciled with it.

But what has our hero not had to suffer from his wife's delirious hatred, and her industrious spreading of calumnies? His reputation has in fact suffered through the whole of upper-class English society and even the high command of the British Army in France. At the opening, in **Some Do Not . . .** , we meet a blond, thickset Christopher Tietjens (as oversized and immovable as the Ford whom Hemingway in *A Moveable Feast* with all possible malice prepense described as looking like a hogshead) whose gifts and virtues are equally oversize. He is a superlative mathematician in the central government bureau of statistics who can *from memory* recall all the mistakes in the *Encyclopaedia Britannica,* despises people who consult books of reference, lends money carelessly to a "friend" who palms off Tietjens's most brilliant work as his own and is knighted for it. Of Ford's endless fantasies, one of my favorites is that Tietjens is so pure a mathematician that he disrespects astronomy. He is so principled that he refuses to doctor some statistics at the behest of the government. To cap it all, Sylvia Tietjens contemptuously asks him to take her back after she has gone off with another man. Of course Tietjens does; a gentleman does not divorce his wife if she has a child—not even when he is quite sure, and Sylvia is happy to encourage him in thinking this, that the child is not his.

Sylvia's hatred of her husband, a fire that burns throughout the book—you can positively hear it crackling, she is so determined on the subject—*seems* to be based on the unavailing sexual heat that he rouses in her. She is uncontrollably exasperated with his patient constancy and con-

sideration for her. While he looks at her "attentively, as if with magpie anguish," Sylvia "went on with her denunciation. 'If you had once in our lives said to me, "You whore! You bitch! You killed my mother. May you rot in hell for it . . .," you might have done something to bring us together.' " To which he replies: "That's, of course, true." "Don't you know, Christopher Tietjens, that there is only one man from whom a woman could take *'Neither I condemn thee'* and not hate him more than she hates the fiend!" Sylvia is tireless only because, like Milton's Satan, she is bored by heaven. Still, " . . . taking up with a man was like reading a book you had read when you had forgotten that you had read it." There is no satisfaction anywhere. And that *is* wickedness.

Although "some do not," Sylvia circulates rumors from the beginning that Valentine has had a child by Christopher. Somehow news gets around that Christopher's father committed suicide in shame at Christopher's seducing Valentine, the daughter of the father's closest friend. Christopher is also in trouble because of his careless loans to a colleague, Macmaster, who was knighted for work that he stole from Christopher. Macmaster's wife defames Christopher rather than repay him. And when we come to the second volume, **No More Parades,** we find that rumors are circulating around the British Army that Christopher "sold" his wife to General Lord Campion. That credulous man (supposedly the best military brain among the slow-thinking English) believes Sylvia's accusations that Christopher has a bastard somewhere, is a "Socialist," . . . and went off to war with Sylvia's two best sheets. The delicious absurdity of such details is a credit to Ford's fluent storytelling, since you get too absorbed to protest that the British Army has more to worry about than one captain's back-home fornications or his estranged wife's sheets.

The more these many defamations mount up against our Christopher, "so appallingly competent, so appallingly always in the center of his own picture," the more stony and unconcerned he seems. But by this time he is so *nervously* (never morally!) disordered by the killing and dying that he is exhausted by the tribulations of his men and the dottiness of his fellow officers. In one pyrotechnical section of **No More Parades,** Sylvia arrogantly wangles her way to wartime France and makes elaborate preparations for seducing her husband. Of this he seems only vaguely conscious. Tietjens's problem is that he has refused a Welsh soldier leave to go home, for the man's wife is living with a prizefighter who would kill the husband. But the soldier is now shot and dies, horribly bleeding, in Tietjens's arms.

> A man, brown, stiff, with a haughty parade step, burst into the light. He said with a high wooden voice:
>
> "'Ere's another bloomin' casualty." In the shadow he appeared to have draped half his face and the right side of his breast with crape. He gave a high, rattling laugh. He bent, as if in a stiff bow, woodenly at his thighs. He pitched, still bent, on to the iron sheet that covered the brazier, rolled off that and lay on his back across the legs of the other runner, who had been crouched beside the brazier. In the bright light it was as

if a whole pail of scarlet paint had been dashed
across the man's face on the left and his chest.
It glistened in the firelight—just like fresh paint,
moving!

Ford's accomplishment is very subtle in war scenes ironically dominated by the endless ripples of Sylvia's false-
hoods. He works with a narrative line so rapid and fluent
as to seem continuous, which fits in with the noise of the
battlefield seething like a "pot." There is a casual, unset-
tlingly chatty interweaving of battle sounds and soldier
fright, of killing, domestic anxiety, English gamesman-
ship. Ford's tone is almost one of banter. There is a low-
keyed surface of tone necessary to the complicated counterpoint of Sylvia and war. Tietjens, who as we know can
do anything, writes a sonnet, from some catchwords set
for him, in two minutes. Captain Mackenzie (who mysteriously becomes McKechnie) is going off his head, hates
Tietjens for not going off his, and as a prize Latinist offers
in rivalry with Tietjens to turn the sonnet into Latin hex-
ameters.

What Ford handles particularly well in the war novels—
No More Parades and *A Man Could Stand Up*—is the
modernist magic show of separating thought from action
so as to dramatize the powerlessness of the modern conscience. The clipped, vaguely derisory shuttling back and
forth of time frames has been a feature of the movement
of *Parade's End* from the opening, where we see Tietjens
and the untrustworthy Macmaster on a train that moves
into the past and out again on the slightest word from
Ford. But in the two middle novels, *No More Parades* and
A Man Could Stand Up, it is the necessary *unreality* of
war to the frightened crowded eye that gives these sections
Ford's characteristically hallucinated but casual quality.

This unforced and even breezy fluency is all the more remarkable because of the social yearning for archaic England, legendary England, that bursts out in *A Man Could
Stand Up.* Tietjens recalls with rapture the opening of
George Herbert's "Virtue"—"Sweet day, so cool, so calm,
so bright. . . . " In the trenches a man has to stoop. In
the ideal dream world of George Herbert's parsonage, a
man could stand up on a hill. . . .

Ford was such a dreamer that he once agreed to help drive
Shaw and the Webbs from the leadership of the Fabians,
but described himself as "a member of a [political] party
that never was on land or sea but that may rule the world
when Arthur shall rule again." *Parade's End* is a dazzling
modernist performance based, like so much of Eliot,
Pound, Yeats, Céline, on yearning for a world that existed
only in the literature of romance. But we are very far here
from the "mysticism" of *Little Gidding* or the addiction
to religion-as-culture in *Mont St. Michel and Chartres.*
Offhand I can think of no other fully accomplished modernist work in which a wholly symbolic and visionary figure like George Herbert enters—and leaves—so casually.
Herbert is another of Ford's passing fancies, one of his
many dream creations that evoke a genuine longing for a
principled world. But the legend of Herbert, the pure Anglican genius, flits through the book like so many other figures and details in *Parade's End.* How right Ford was to
say in *It was the Nightingale—* "My brain, I think, is a

sort of dovecote. The thoughts from it fly round and
round, seem about to settle and circle even further than
before and more and more swiftly." He added: "I try in
the end to let them come home with the velocity and precision of swifts that fly at sixty miles an hour into their aper-
tures that you would say could not let them through. I
hope thus to attain a precision of effect as startling as any
Frenchman."

Ford in his too many books before and after never did as
well as he did in *Parade's End.* For once, he captured neatly, almost curtly, on an impressive scale, his besetting
dream of himself as a man misunderstood by everyone but
finally, as in great romance, *justified.* In the marvelous
way of fiction, which gives its real prizes not to the clever-
est but to the *possessed*—those enraptured by a particular
time and place—Ford was a virtuoso, not much of a thinker, above all, a writer bemused, caught up, who did not always know his dream from "reality." Christopher Tietjens
somehow shrinks from 1912 to 1918 only because the
world can no longer support his knightly vision of perfect
faith and rectitude. In *The Last Post* we see that Christopher will accept the house at Groby and all its perquisites
because Valentine, pregnant with his child, cries out, How
will we live? Christopher will not go back on anything that
demands self-sacrifice; he cannot sacrifice a woman and
their child. And to tell the truth, his stiff upper lip in the
face of Sylvia's hate—born of her disgust that her "wood-
en faced" husband will reject life's sensual gifts—has become rather trying to us too. It is the fact that life finally
takes him over, forces him to adjust to another's needs,
that makes *The Last Post,* sentimental as it is, necessary
to the tetralogy.

But by taking him over, and making him a little more ame-
nable to the world he has scorned, we see the force of the
compulsion behind Ford's book, the myth of a perfect English knight—in our time!—that has rooted this strange,
laughable, but forceful book in such a vision of human
perfection as the current novel hardly understands. "Modernism" and "experimentation" are the rarest notes struck
by fiction just now. It is all documentation and has no perspective but individual psychology, our favorite tautology.
Ford's "absurdity" in seeing so far behind the modern
world has made this book last.

Norman Page   (essay date 1980)

SOURCE: "Living as Ritual in *Parade's End,*" in *Studies
in the Literary Imagination,* Vol. XIII, No. 1, Spring,
1980, pp. 43-50.

*[Page is an English author, editor, and educator whose
works include studies of Thomas Hardy, Henry James, and
D. H. Lawrence. In the following essay, he examines Ford's
treatment of ritual and conformity as hallmarks of social
stability in* Parade's End.*]*

Certain novelists, in common with many of us who are not
novelists, betray an addiction, usually unconscious, to certain words or turns of phrase; and in them, as in us, the
reiteration may be more than a trivial mannerism—may,
indeed, offer an insight, through a tiny verbal crack in the
fence, into central preoccupations or obsessions. I do not

think, for example, that any of Arnold Bennett's critics has pointed to his fondness for two words, one of them very unusual and the two of them in conjunction highly suggestive as to his individual vision and method as a writer of fiction. *Dailiness* seems to convey a sense of boring but reassuring routine, of the pattern or ritual of repeated actions which make up an individual life; *mystical* (somewhat loosely used by Bennett), a contrasting and complementary sense of life's unpredictability, of the unguessed-at lurking just behind the humdrum. Less readily accounted for, but no less striking, is D. H. Lawrence's repeated use of *vague, vaguely, vagueness,* and (what seems to be related) the adverb *rather.* From a small verbal fulcrum of this kind we may venture to weigh the novelist's world.

With Ford Madox Ford, such a word is *convention,* and I shall try to show in this essay how the word and the idea dominate his tetralogy **Parade's End** without being at all confined to that work. But we may note first that some of his critics have been infected by Ford's fondness for the word and its near-synonyms. Mark Schorer tells us [in *his The World We Imagine: Selected Essays,* 1968] that **The Good Soldier** "is about the difference between convention and fact" and that the narrator discovers he has "mistaken the conventions of social behaviour for the actual human fact"; whilst Arthur Mizener [in his *The Saddest Story: A Biography of Ford Madox Ford,* 1971] sees the same novel as depicting "a society in which the life of men's feelings no longer flows into the beautiful, refined *ritual* of the society's most cultivated life" (italics mine). The antitheses suggested here are also fruitful in relation to **Parade's End. The Good Soldier** may be allowed to detain us a little longer, however, in order to show that Ford's concern with the place of convention or ritual in individual and social life antedates the tetralogy, in which nevertheless this theme was to receive much more extensive treatment. In the earlier novel Ashburnham is introduced in terms which imply an extreme, even caricatural conventionality in the sense of unquestioning adherence to the traditional way of life of a particular social class and an almost religious absorption in the material details of its prescribed life-style:

> His hair was fair, extraordinarily ordered in a wave, running from the left temple to the right; his face was a light brick-red, perfectly uniform in tint up to the roots of the hair itself; his yellow moustache was as stiff as a toothbrush and I verily believe that he had his black smoking jacket thickened a little over the shoulder-blades so as to give himself the air of the slightest possible stoop. It would be like him to do that; that was the sort of thing he thought about. Martingales, Chiffney bits, boots; where you got the best soap, the best brandy, the name of the chap who rode a plater down the Khyber cliffs; the spreading power of number three shot before a charge of number four powder . . . by heavens, I hardly ever heard him talk of anything else.

This is very skilfully done: the tone is casual, but every detail tells, and the suggestion of simulation and calculation is not accidental (the "perfectly uniform" face, mask-like rather than of human flesh; the moustache resembling a toothbrush rather than hair). Not only Ashburnham's clothes and habits but his physical features and complexion imply a self-conscious deference to a mode of life acknowledged as appropriate to a member of the British upper classes. And what at first appears to be a genuine concern with quality ("where you got the best soap . . .") is quickly shown to be a limitation of human freedom:

> The given proposition was, that we were all 'good people.' We took for granted that we all liked beef underdone but not too underdone; that both men preferred a good liqueur brandy after lunch; that both women drank a very light Rhine wine qualified with Fachingen water— that sort of thing.

"That sort of thing" is seen, in a moment of ironic rebellion or humorous disillusion on the part of the narrator, to be:

> . . . an almost unreasonably high standard. For it is really nauseating, when you detest it, to have to eat every day several slices of thin, tepid, pink india rubber, and it is disagreeable to have to drink brandy when you would prefer to be cheered up by a warm, sweet Kümmel. And it is nasty to have to take a cold bath in the morning when what you want is really a hot one at night. And it stirs a little of the faith of your fathers that is deep down within you to have to have it taken for granted that you are an Episcopalian when really you are an old-fashioned Philadelphia Quaker.

> But these things have to be done: it is the cock that the whole of this society owes to Aesculapius.

"These things have to be done": the class which appears to enjoy the greatest freedom, an enviable leisure and privilege and affluence, is constrained in matters great and small by the exactly ordained rituals of tradition. As we shall see, the subject of **Parade's End** is the death—throes of that tradition. In **The Good Soldier,** the antithesis of the conformity that is unquestioned by everyone except the narrator (who is in every sense an outsider) is Ashburnham's helpless infatuations: his romantic and sexual impulses constitute a rebellion against the demands of a society shown as tyrannically working through conventions at all levels from food and drink to morality and religion in order to restrict personal liberty. Much later in the book, when Nancy Rufford is "exported to India," we are told:

> It was the conventional line; it was in tune with the tradition of Edward's house. I daresay it worked out for the greatest good of the body politic. Conventions and traditions, I suppose, work blindly but surely for the preservation of the normal type; for the extinction of proud, resolute, and unusual individuals.

At a moment of moral crisis, convention and tradition are the substitutes for individual judgement and decision, and they work in the interests of a social Darwinism with the elimination of individuality as its goal. The struggle in **The Good Soldier** is between passion and convention, but the big battalions are on the side of the latter.

This antithesis is developed further in *Parade's End.* In *The Good Soldier,* convention is tyrannical but makes for social cohesion: stability is purchased at the price of variety, spontaneity, eccentricity, unpredictability. Within the limits of this short novel the drama can only be shown as operating in the arena of private lives. In the tetralogy, the cohesion and stability of society are devastated by the upheaval of the Great War, and much of the action takes place on or near the battlefield; yet the historical cataclysm only dramatizes on a vast scale the upheaval in the Tietjens family caused by the unconventionality of Christopher. That quality is shown in the opening scene of the first novel, *Some Do Not,* the very title of which hints, of course, in one of its meanings at Christopher Tietjens' nonconformity. Almost every detail of the description of Tietjens and Macmaster in the "perfectly appointed railway carriage" works to convey the profound antithesis beneath their superficial similarity—the one man's eager obedience to society's rules (conformity being the price of worldly success), the other's disregard for them. Both belong to "the English public official class," a common educational background (as a fact of social history) going far to neutralize the difference in their social origins. It is the class that "administered the world," yet very quickly the point is made that Macmaster is readier than Tietjens to operate the machinery of ruling-class influence, to resort to the "nonchalant" yet authoritative Balliol voice or a letter to *The Times.* Macmaster's appearance recalls the conscious conformity of Ashburnham's, but Tietjens "could not remember what coloured tie he had on." As the first-class carriage runs smoothly and symbolically along the tracks, Macmaster reads the proofs of his belletristic efforts (for man of letters is one of the roles he plays)—and the detection of errors and lapses and their firm rectification is an entirely appropriate activity: his ambition, to pursue the metaphor, is to live his life as if it were a text beyond criticism. This long chapter ends with the first appearance of the title-phrase; it has begun with a suggestion of resemblance, almost uniformity, between the two men, but now it ambiguously foreshadows Tietjens' experience which is to be traced through four novels; for it is Macmaster, starting out with considerably less than Tietjens' advantages of birth, who becomes a "squire," acquires a title, and is accorded the public respect that eludes his friend. Tietjens' failure in worldly terms must in large part be laid at the door of his scant regard for convention; yet the antithesis between the man indifferent to society's dictates and the man enslaved by them is not over-simplified, for Tietjens himself is shown as cased in conventional reactions—in responses determined, that is to say, by what is prescribed and expected in a given case rather than by what proceeds from the special pleading of the mind or heart. Thus at the outset he is prepared to take back Sylvia, knowing her infidelity and suspecting that her child is not his, whereas Macmaster urges him to "drag the woman through the mud." That a gentleman does not initiate divorce proceedings is an article of faith with Tietjens; he is concerned with honour, Macmaster with honours. And this provides a solution to the apparent paradox: Tietjens, unlike Macmaster in both respects, is indifferent to conventionalities of surface but deeply conventional, even against his own interests, where honour is at stake. I borrow that last phrase from the lines of Hamlet's that come to mind as apposite:

> Rightly to be great
> Is not to stir without great argument,
> But greatly to find quarrel in a straw
> When honour's at the stake.

This reading of the two characters is confirmed by the similar contrast to be found (more dramatically heightened, however) between the two major women characters of the tetralogy. Sylvia's conventionality—she is a woman who is photographed for the society magazines, with all that this implies of conformity of appearance and social conduct—is a cloak for destructive malignity; Valentine Wannop is as unconventional as she can well be in her time, a sort of latter-day Sue Bridehead in her epicene appearance and her militant feminism, only much more attractive than Hardy's exasperating heroine and much more clearly enjoying the author's moral assent. Christopher and Valentine meet for the first time on a golf course, the scene, scrupulously kept as to appearances, of a highly ritualized and mainly masculine and upper-class game (the early Auden was to use "The golf-house quick one" as shorthand for a whole way of life); Valentine's behaviour there is intrusive, maverick, rocking the boat of complacent privilege, and she is abetted by Christopher.

If there is something *voulu* in Valentine's defiance of convention, however, Christopher's unconventionality sometimes has the air of innocence, a total absence of calculation of effects. This does not prevent the conventional world from thinking the worst of him, and one of the most powerful elements in the whole work is the appalling sense of society's readiness to believe evil of a good man who has proved unwilling to respect its conventions far enough to play the hypocrite.

The word "convention" makes a significant multiple appearance in the important scene which ends Part One of *Some Do Not:*

> "Are you all right?" The cart might have knocked her down. He had, however, broken the convention. Her voice came from a great distance. . . .
>
> His last thought came back to him. He had broken their convention: he had exhibited concern: like any other man. . . . He said to himself:
>
> "By God! Why not take a holiday: why not break all conventions?"
>
> They erected themselves intangibly and irrefragably. He had not known this young woman twenty-four hours: not to speak to: and already the convention existed between them that he must play stiff and cold, she warm and clinging. . . .
>
> A convention of the most imbecile type . . . Then break all conventions: with the young woman: with himself above all. For forty-eight hours. . . .

Note the delicate mirroring of Tietjens' shifting responses through slight linguistic variations: "the convention," "their convention," "all conventions." The escapade—escape from convention—ends in detection by the General "In full tog," feathered and bemedalled. The grotesquely elaborate uniform ("something like a scarlet and white cockatoo") epitomizes convention at its most strikingly visual; like any uniform, it announces the submission of the individual to the group and reproves Tietjens' impulsive behaviour. Indeed, the whole episode seems stage-managed by providence to instruct him in the perils of defying convention. Yet he is not, or not yet, an instinctively unconventional man: he accepts the unwritten rules of his class, later accepting the inevitability of his ruin when his cheques are dishonoured (the banker's term is felicitous), even though the fault is not his: not inner motive but public event is decisive in accomplishing his dishonour. In this context, membership of his club becomes not just a matter of convenience but a badge of his own sense of his social acceptability: he resigns, withdraws the resignation, and then in an assertion of his own dignity resigns again the next day. To an outsider (the American narrator of *The Good Soldier,* for instance) such actions might seem to constitute an absurd charade; to Tietjens they are a profound moral drama.

Before the end of *Some Do Not,* Mark Tietjens, Christopher's brother, is presented in terms which make plain his role: if Christopher vacillates between conformity and rebellion at this stage, Mark is a paragon of conformity for whom outward forms, however apparently trivial, are everything:

> Mark was considering that one of the folds of his umbrella was disarranged. He seriously debated with himself whether he should unfold it at once and refold it—which was a great deal of trouble to take!—or whether he should leave it till he got to his club, where he would tell the porter to have it done at once. That would mean that he would have to walk for a mile and a quarter through London with a disarranged umbrella, which was disagreeable.

As we shall see, Mark's role becomes a major one in *The Last Post* and the representative quality of the two brothers then becomes fully explicit. But *The Last Post* is set in the postwar period, its predecessor having ended with the Armistice; and the two inside novels of the tetralogy are novels of the war that went far towards shattering for ever the social order depicted in *Some Do Not. No More Parades* echoes in its title that of the whole tetralogy, *Parade's End,* and Ford surely intended the word to evoke not only (more obviously) the secondary, military sense of *parade* but the primary meaning (from *parare,* to adorn) of "show, display, ostentation," which both as noun and as verb has a close semantic relationship to his use of "convention." The sweep of the tetralogy—its action brief in years, profound in irrevocable change to a whole civilization—records the death-throes of that world in which "parade," whether manifested in dress, in social behaviour, or in public morality, had been erected into a principle of existence by a tiny but enormously powerful minority. (Not that the extinction was complete, of course, as any observer of the contemporary British scene can confirm: forty years after Ford's death the Eton and

Harrow match, mentioned in *Some Do Not,* is still an annual ritual; certain shops in Piccadilly are devoted to furnishing the expensive and improbable impedimenta of an Edwardian lifestyle; and London clubs like the one Mark Tietjens belonged to still exist in order to persuade their members that the nineteenth century has not ended. But the exception in these cases proves the rule.)

The Last Post, variously viewed as an integral part of the work and a superfluous afterthought, is of considerable interest in relation to the persisting theme of conformity and its decline as the century advances. Mark Tietjens has been shown as an almost parodically conventional creature, dressed like a foreigner's or cartoonist's stereotype of the English gentleman, even his vices regularized into unvarying and unquestioned habits: he visits his French mistress twice a week (with an equally regular interruption for his annual holiday), and for twenty years she has cooked him the same dinner. In *The Last Post* bowler and umbrella are abandoned, and he no longer sits down to his prescribed dinner of two mutton chops and two floury potatoes, for he has become an invalid who refuses to speak: the abandonment of the rituals which have hitherto composed his life represents his symbolic protest against the dishonour of public life in the period in which he now finds himself living. Before the war he had consciously incorporated ritual into his life: Mark's response to the loss of this ritual (manifested, for example, in the brotherhood of the trenches) is to abdicate from life in as thoroughgoing a way as is possible, short of suicide. By a more abrupt and dramatic route, a more patently symbolic gesture, he has reached a conclusion not unlike his brother's.

Groby, the ancestral home in the north of England, dominates *The Last Post* not as a dramatic setting but as a constant point of reference. Its existence is coextensive with that of the Tietjens family and of Groby Great Tree, which has overshadowed the house and darkened the schoolroom and the children's wing. The fate of tree and house in this final novel gives us, by a kind of shorthand, a version of the fate of the family. The American tenant-usurper, Mrs. de Bray Pape, essays to preserve the rituals of the past: she has a sentimental-snobbish fondness for powdered footmen and forelock-tugging peasants, but of course these rituals are empty and meaningless. The tree is uprooted, as a contribution to progress and modern improvement, and brings down with it part of the building, including the rooms associated with Christopher's childhood. The symbolism is, to modern tastes, a little crude, and in any case superfluous, for the end of the Tietjens tradition has already been rendered, more subtly, through the postwar fates of Christopher and Mark.

Like Forster's *Howards End, The Last Post* has an epilogue which asserts renewal and continuity after destruction. The child of Christopher and Valentine embarks on a life freed from the heavy hand of tradition and its limitations on personal freedom (of the self and of others). Convention and artifice have been dissolved—a point neatly made in a final image. *Some Do Not* has opened in a railway compartment in an atmosphere of newly varnished wood, and for Ford, as for Dickens in *Little Dorrit,* the varnish may well carry a metaphorical meaning. At the end of *The Last Post* Christopher holds in his hand a piece of wood from Groby Great Tree, as plain and unvarnished as Ford's symbolism, one is tempted to say. He has travelled from the first-class carriage to a rural retreat in which he will pursue a William Morrissy simple life (again, the path traced resembles that of Forster's remarkable prewar novel). It is a way of life in which convention and ritual will have no place.

FURTHER READING

Criticism

Braybrooke, Neville. "The Walrus and the Windmill: A Study of Ford Madox Ford." *The Sewanee Review* 74 (1966): 810-31.
   Considers the marital and extra-marital relationships of Ford's protagonists within the context of the sexual mores and political climate of late Victorian England.

Gordon, Ambrose, Jr. *The Invisible Tent: The War Novels of Ford Madox Ford.* Austin: University of Texas Press, 1964, 153 p.
   Study of *Parade's End* and three other novels Ford wrote.

Gose, Elliott B., Jr. "Reality to Romance: A Study of Ford's *Parade's End*." *College English* 17, No. 8 (May 1956): 445-50.
   Traces the biographical origins of Christopher Tietjens in the lives of Ford and his friend Arthur Marwood.

Griffiths, Marlene. "A Double Reading of *Parade's End*." *Modern Fiction Studies* 9, No. 1 (Spring 1963): 25-38.
   Analysis of *Parade's End* focusing on what the critic calls the novel's balanced treatment of "the world of social experience (external reality) and the world of personal sensibility (internal reality)."

Henighan, T. J. "Tietjens Transformed: A Reading of *Parade's End*." *English Literature in Transition* 15, No. 2 (1972): 144-57.
   Comprehensive reading of the novel focusing on Ford's dramatization of Christopher Tietjens' emotional and mental transformation.

Hynes, Samuel. "Ford Madox Ford: 'Three Dedicatory Letters to *Parade's End*' with Commentary and Notes." *Modern Fiction Studies* XVI, No. 4 (Winter 1970-71): 515-28.
   Text and discussion of Ford's dedicatory letters to the first three novels of his Tietjens series.

Kashner, Rita J. "Tietjens' Education: Ford Madox Ford's Tetralogy." *Critical Quarterly* 8 (Summer 1966): 150-63.
   Argues that *The Last Post* is "thematically congruous, and even necessary" yet "technically . . . unequal" to the preceding three novels of *Parade's End*.

Kenner, Hugh. "Remember That I Have Remembered." *The Hudson Review* III, No. 4 (Winter 1951): 602-11.
   Discusses origins and context of critical interest in Ford's World War I novels during the early 1950s.

Levin, Gerald. "Character and Myth in Ford's *Parade's End*." *Journal of Modern Literature* I, No. 2 (1970-71): 183-96.
   Consideration of the novel's central characters and their reflection of figures from classical literature and mythology.

Lid, R. W. "Modern Chronicle." In his *Ford Madox Ford: The Essence of His Art*, pp. 137-85. Berkeley and Los Angeles: University of California Press, 1964.
   Detailed analysis of *Parade's End* described by the author as an "examination of the sources and development of Ford's narrative style, which is the essence of his art."

Meyer, Eric. "Ford's War and (Post)Modern Memory: *Parade's End* and National Allegory." *Criticism* XXXII, No. 1 (Winter 1990): 81-99.
   Focuses on *Parade's End* as a "national narrative" which reconstructs the British experience of World War I through the story of Christopher Tietjens.

Mizener, Arthur. "A Large Fiction." In *The Kenyon Review* 13, No. 1 (Winter 1951): 142-47.
   Addresses Ford's use of interior monologue and time-shift as narrative techniques in *Parade's End*.

Moser, Thomas C. "*Parade's End* as Christmas Pantomime." In *The Life in the Fiction of Ford Madox Ford*, pp. 214-53. Princeton, N.J.: Princeton University Press, 1980.
   Traces similarities between Ford's personal life and the characters and events of *Parade's End*.

Seiden, Melvin. "The Living Dead—VI: Ford Madox Ford and His Tetralogy." *The London Magazine* 6, No. 8 (August 1959): 45-55.
   Discusses the paradoxical personalities of Ford's characters in *Parade's End* and expresses hope for a revival of interest in Ford's novels.

Else Lasker-Schüler

1869-1945

(Born Elisabeth Schüler) German poet, novelist, short story writer, playwright, and essayist.

INTRODUCTION

A noted Expressionist poet and playwright, Lasker-Schüler is best known for works in which she presents a fictionalized version of her life. The subject of critical controversy, these works have been alternately viewed as enigmatic masterpieces and as the failed experiments of a highly egocentric talent. Lasker-Schüler's books were burned by the Third Reich and were not republished until the 1950s, when they were read and admired by many postwar German poets and critics. The obscurity of her works and the confusion surrounding the facts of her life have made her both an alluring and a puzzling subject for literary critics and biographers.

Biographical Information

The daughter of a cultured and prosperous German Jewish family, Lasker-Schüler was born in Eberfeld, Germany. She married Dr. Jonathan Berthold Lasker, a Berlin physician, in 1894 and gave birth to a son, Paul, in 1900. In 1899 Lasker-Schüler published her first poems, some of which she had written as a teenager, in various literary journals. At this time she also began to act out the personality traits and the lifestyle of characters in her poems, such as "Prinz von Theben" ("Prince of Thebes") and "Tino of Baghdad." She wore colorful, unusual clothing and pursued an itinerant existence, occupying various furnished rooms and hotels and often sleeping on park benches. She frequented the cafés where Expressionist artists and writers gathered, and became acquainted with such prominent figures as painter Franz Marc, poet Gottfried Benn, critic Karl Kraus, and film director Friedrich Wilhelm Murnau. During this period, Lasker-Schüler also met poet Peter Hille, who became her close friend and mentor. In 1903 she divorced Lasker and married Georg Levin, a noted Expressionist writer who used the pseudonym Herwarth Walden. Walden published a great many of Lasker-Schüler's poems in his Expressionist periodical *Der Sturm* and was an avid promoter of her works. The two divorced for unknown reasons in 1911. In 1933, when the political climate became hostile for German Jews, Lasker-Schüler fled the country and traveled through Europe before settling in Palestine in 1937. Refusing all offers of assistance from friends, Lasker-Schüler lived in poverty until her death in 1945.

Major Works

Lasker-Schüler's works reflect a fictionalized version of the realities of her life and portray actual people as extrav-

agant characters in fantastic settings and imaginary circumstances. For example, she portrays her relationship with Hille in *Das Peter Hille-Buch*, which comprises forty-six short scenes in which the Apostle Peter and his female follower Tino travel through forests and mountains, encountering other characters with whom they attempt, unsuccessfully, to establish an isolated community in order to escape what they perceive as a hostile world. When Peter dies, Tino becomes grief-stricken and lives out the rest of her life in the mountains in a state of solitary, self-imposed exile. The character Tino returns later in the collection of short stories *Die Nächte der Tino von Baghdad*. Other examples of Lasker-Schüler's use of autobiographical material include her depictions in her poetry of her mother, her brother, and her son as idealized, saintly figures. Several of the literary figures with whom Lasker-Schüler was acquainted, including Benn and the poet Jakob van Hoddis, serve as the models for such characters as The Slav, The Bishop, The Dalai-Lama, and The Son of the Sultan of Morocco in her epistolary novel *Mein Herz*. In her last collection of poetry, *Mein blaues Klavier*, Lasker-Schüler expresses her readiness for death and the pain and loneliness of living as an exile in Palestine, where she feels she has lost her will to live and her ability to write. In the title poem, she states: "I have a blue piano at home, / But I don't know a single note. / It is standing in the dark of the cellar door / Since the world turned savage."

Critical Reception

Lasker-Schüler's poetry has often been faulted for its egocentrism and obscurity. In a letter to philosopher Martin Buber, she defended her highly personal imagery and subject matter by stating that since she knew only her own life, this subject was the only one about which she could write with authority. G. Guder asserted: "Else Lasker-Schüler . . . wrote her poems in the first person singular, but she is not subjective in the worst sense of the word. . . . Even at a time when the motif of her poems was increasingly homelessness, uprootedness and dread of life, she the ageing, ailing woman, remained concerned with the efficiency of her poetic voice as mediator, so that her last poems, too, with the same subjective tone transcend all that is purely individual and are timeless symbols of the fate of man and of the artist in an age of increasing inhumanity."

PRINCIPAL WORKS

Styx (poetry) 1902
Der siebente Tag (poetry) 1905
Das Peter Hille-Buch (short stories) 1906
Die Nächte der Tino von Bagdad (short stories) 1907
Die Wupper: Schauspiel in fünf Aufzügen (drama) 1909
Meine Wunder (poetry) 1911
Meine Herz: Ein Liebesroman mit Bildern und wirklich lebenden Menschen (novel) 1912
Gesichte: Essays und andere Geschichten (essays and poetry) 1913
Hebräische Balladen (poetry) 1913
Der Prinz von Theben: Ein Geschichtenbuch (short stories) 1914
Die gesammelten Gedichte (poetry) 1917
Der Malik: Eine Kaisergeschichte mit Bildern und Zeichnungen (novel) 1919
Die Kuppel: Der Gedichte zweiter Teil (poetry) 1920
Theben: Gedichte und Lithographien (poetry) 1923
Ich räume auf! Meine Anklage gegen meine Verleger (essays and poetry) 1925
Arthur Aronymus: Die Geschichte meines Vaters (drama) 1932
Konzert (essays and poetry) 1932
Das Hebräerland (poetry) 1937
Mein blaues Klavier: Neue Gedichte (poetry) 1943
Dichtungen und Dokumente: Gedichte, Prosa, Schauspiele, Briefe, Zeugnis und Erinnerung (poetry, short stories, letters, and essays) 1951
Gedichte, 1902-1943 (poetry) 1959
Gesammelte Werke. 3 vols. (poetry) 1959-1962
Verse und Prosa aus dem Nachlaß (poetry and short stories) 1961

Sämtliche Gedichte (poetry and short stories) 1966
*Hebrew Ballads, and Other Poems (poetry) 1980
†Your Diamond Dreams Cut Open My Arteries (poetry) 1982

*This collection contains selected poems from *Styx, Meine Wunder, Hebräische Balladen,* and *Mein blaues Klavier.*

†This collection contains selected poems from *Gesammelte Werke,* vol. 1.

CRITICISM

Heinz Politzer (essay date 1950)

SOURCE: "The Blue Piano of Else Lasker-Schueler," translated by Ralph Manheim, in *Commentary*, Vol. 9, No. 4, April, 1950, pp. 335-44.

[*Politzer was an Austrian-born American educator, editor, and critic who became personally acquainted with Lasker-Schüler in Palestine, and has written a number of scholarly works on the role of Jewish writers in German literature. In the following excerpt, he surveys Lasker-Schüler's career, noting especially her wordplay, and her role in the evolution of Jewish-German literature.*]

On a cold winter's day at the end of 1944, as the war was drawing to its close, we buried Else Lasker-Schueler. Services were held in the mortuary of the Hadassah Hospital in Jerusalem, under the merciless sun of Palestine, on a vitreous clear noonday, in view of the desert which descends in dunes to the Dead Sea.

The sextons busied themselves with a little bundle smaller than the body of a child. The last words were spoken by a friend of the dead woman who had feared her and cared for her, smiled and worried over her, like almost everyone who had befriended her here in Palestine. The portly rabbi with the face of an actor suffering because he had to play-act and because his sufferings were also play-acting, did something unheard of in view of the vast hatred that prevailed in Jewish Palestine for all things German: he recited a poem in German, a poem by Else Lasker-Schueler:

> Ich weiss, dass ich bald sterben muss.
> Es leuchten doch alle Bäume
> Nach langersehntem Julikuss—
>
> Fahl werden meine Träume—
> Nie dichtete ich einen trübern Schluss
> In den Büchern meiner Reime.
>
> Eine Blume brichst du mir zum Gruss—
> Ich liebte sie schon im Keime.
> Doch ich weiss, dass ich bald sterben muss.
>
> Mein Odem schwebt über Gottes Fluss—
> Ich setze leise meinen Fuss
> Auf dem Pfad zum ewigen Heime.
>
> (I know that I must die soon.
> Yet all the trees are radiant
> After summer's long-awaited kiss—

My dreams grow gray—
Never have I written a sadder ending
In my books of rhymes.

You pluck a flower for me—
I loved it in the bud.
Yet I know that I must die soon.

My breath hovers over the river of God—
Softly I set my foot
On the path to my long home.)

But there was an inner rightness in reciting this German poem in Palestine instead of the Hebrew prayer for the dead, which should traditionally have been said. For this poetess had written Hebrew poetry in German. . . .

Her life and work place her in the last generation of German Jews, whose origins were, in a way, less of a problem for them than they had been for Heine and Boerne. There was no conflict between her Jewishness and the language she spoke, and she did not, like her contemporary Jakob Wassermann, look upon her "road as a German and as a Jew" as a Calvary. From this she was saved by her boundless spontaneity of expression. More than almost any other poet, she was voice and nothing but voice; with a candor bordering on sadism she expressed what poured from the depth of a soul which she herself, as she said, often did not understand. If ever a poet has embodied in his work C. G. Jung's concept of the collective unconscious—the sum of the experience of our fathers that lies dormant in the mind of the individual—it was Else Lasker-Schueler. This experience, inherited with her blood, consisted in the wild and tender images of the Biblical world or rather, in memories of the pre-Biblical era of the Jews, which she came to identify with names and places that she found in Scripture. She dreamt Hebrew visions, but the only words she could clothe them in were German.

And it is the grotesque tragedy of Else Lasker-Schueler and of the best of her generation that they never learned to speak the language of their dreams and that the language that was the source of her songs sounded weird and unfamiliar in her ears when she first went to Palestine. In Germany she called herself "Prince Yussuf" and was proud to be a foreigner; when she went to her homeland she remained Else Lasker-Schueler, and a foreigner.

She knew of this foreignness and bore it with a dignity which gave her witchlike presence a ludicrous human dignity. In 1925, she wrote: "I composed the poems of my first book between the ages of 15 and 17. At that time I found my way back to my primal language, derived from the era of Saul, the royal wild Jew. Today I can still speak this language, which probably came to me in my dreams. Among others, my poem **'Weltflucht' ('Flight from the World')** is written in this 'mystical Asiatic.'"

Here, first of all, is the poem as it was written in German:

Ich will in das Grenzenlose
Zu mir zurück,
Schon blüht die Herbstzeitlose—
Vielleicht ist es zu spät—zurück
Ob ich sterbe zwischen euch
Die ihr mich erstickt mit euch.

Fäden möchte ich um mich ziehen
Wirrwarr endend,
Verwirrend,
Zu entfliehen
Meinwärts.

(Into the boundless
Let me go back to myself,
The autumn crocus is flowering—
Perhaps it is too late—let me go back
Even though I die among you
Who smother me with your selves.
I would draw threads around me
To end confusion
And confuse,
To escape
Me-wards.)

And now the same poem in "mystical Asiatic":

Min salihi wali kinahu
Rahi hatiman
fi is bahi lahi fassun—
Min hagas assama anadir,
Wakan liachad abtal,
Latina almu lijádina binassre.
Wa min tab ihi
Anahu jatelahu
Wanu bilahum.
Assama ja saruh
fi es supi bila uni
El fidda alba hire
Wa wisuri—elbanaff!

This of course was a game, but a meaningful game. Amid the childish euphony of this wishful dream language, we note intimations of Hebrew roots ("liachad," "lijádina," etc.) and Hebrew endings. But this language sounds both more primitive and more beautiful than any idiom of historic growth.

It is an old dream of the poets to find a language in which feeling and vision can express themselves without subservience to the rules of linguistic logic. The creative imagination has long yearned to soar free, without regard for the social obligation to communicate; an understandable desire, though dangerous in its undisciplined manifestations.

Most poets have rejected this desire as a sin of youth. But we do know that the hieratic German, Stefan George, invented such a language of his own, in which the Romance element was predominant—as was the Hebraic in Else Lasker-Schueler's "mystical Asiatic."

The country of which the Rhinelander Stefan George dreamed was strangely compounded of Dante's Italy and Mallarmé's Parnasse. But the compulsive, infantile repetition of Gertrude Stein and the cryptically lulling and compelling measures of *Finnegans Wake* embody a similar longing for a language that is autonomous and free from communication, that carries its own fulfillment. And in Gertrude Stein, as well as in the late Joyce, we clearly discern the tendency to return by way of a magical, unintelligible idiom into the magical labyrinth of the poet's own childhood.

But Else Lasker-Schueler did not go back to her childhood

or past, but to the myth, the prehistoric past. She who in her life was so entirely individualistic and so filled with herself that, with lucid self-knowledge, she could entitle her last play **Ich und Ich**, was, in the best of her poems, absolutely anonymous. She saw the patriarchs: Jacob, the "buffalo of his flock," Abraham and Isaac and the sacrifice of Isaac, the women of the Old Testament, Esther, "slender as a palm tree," or Ruth:

> Am Brunnen meiner Heimat
> Steht ein Engel,
> Der singt das Lied meiner Liebe,
> Der singt das Lied Ruths.
>
> (At the well of my native place
> Stands an angel,
> He sings the song of my love,
> He sings the song of Ruth.)

And in her late years, in her last poems, she saw Jerusalem ("Out of his spine God built Palestine; out of a single bone, Jerusalem"), and she captured the moonlight landscape of the hills of Judea in visions upon which she was able to set the stamp of authenticity not because, but although, she lived among them. There is in her verses an inhuman, primeval tone, a sobriety of image that combines with the drunken, melodic intertwining of her rhymes to produce an effect that is unique. Her visions have the bareness of Biblical imagery, while her melodies carry the lyric richness of Oriental poetry.

She was, in her self-willed way, as un-German as Franz Kafka. And like him, she does not fit into the tradition of German Jewish literature, let alone of German literature proper. Asia is in her and the myth of Asia, as it was also in Kafka and his work. She wrote the main body of her work during the rise and fall of German Expressionism.

From Expressionism she took certain mannerisms, some of them unfortunate, but essentially her work is primordial, alien to Europe and Germany. She has had no disciples except for the German Jewish poetess Nelly Sachs, who more than a generation later [in *Stern verdunkelung*, 1949] wrote of her experience of Hitler's pogroms and the concentration camps in verses which echo the style of Else Lasker-Schueler but lack her depth. And there is a profound irony in the circumstance that figures like Franz Kafka and Else Lasker-Schueler, in whom for the first time German Jewish writing achieved originality and legitimacy, belonged essentially to a realm outside German culture.

For this reason the history of German Jewish literature is, properly speaking, a history of disassimilation. There was Richard Beer-Hofmann, who cast his Biblical dramas and his feelings for the blood bond between the generations in Goethean verses (*Miriams Schlaflied*). There was Karl Wolfskehl, disciple, herald, and in certain critical respects also preceptor of Stefan George, whom the persecutions of 1933, of which he had long had a foreboding, threw back on a Judaism whose substance is the dialogue of man with God. There was Rudolph Borchardt, the lie of whose existence, the lie that he was a German, was at the heart of his creative impulse—and also of the grotesque doom that befell him when the Nazis deported him, the German

officer, the self-styled German national poet. There was Alfred Mombert, who built himself a world-removed dream realm of art and myth, and Karl Kraus who purified the German language until in his hands it became a lifeless, sterile organism, and then revived it with his anger, his prophetic Jewish anger.

Richard Beer-Hofmann attempted to advance the process of disassimilation by combining a pseudo-Biblical Judaism with a pseudo-classical Germanism; Karl Kraus, an Austrian Nietzschean, vaingloriously placed himself outside both the Jewish and the German frame, and searched the *past* for succor in a conflict that was *present* within him. For the others, disassimilation, the eruption of the Jewish through the German, came as a negative reaction to the historical shock of 1933. All of them were, in many masks, epigones of the German tradition, and since they were late epigones, they knew their dilemma and sought their primal source in dreams.

Amid all her confusion, Else Lasker-Schueler experienced this process of disassimilation organically, in her own skin, and bore witness to it in her best poems. For her the German language was little more than a vehicle—and sometimes an inadequate one. Consequently she was without masters and without emulators, indefinable, a stumbling block for literary history.

Essentially, however, the problem of the Jews in German writing should not be viewed historically, but phenomenologically. Not the German, not even the German-Jewish context is decisive, but solely to what extent these various writers left Germanism behind them, in what direction they left it, and with how much honesty. And more is involved than the process of "homegathering" demanded by Bialik. It is not only a question of gathering these broken spikes of grain and storing them in the granary of the Jewish tradition. For, from a historical point of view, this Jewish tradition is itself heterogeneous and broken, contradictory and paradoxical. The history of the Jews in almost two centuries of German literature is a striving of individuals for self-portrayal and self-realization, a tragic striving, whose aim is to be sought in the moral as well as the aesthetic sphere.

The moral, to be sure, inevitably determined the aesthetic. The closer these poets came to themselves, i.e., not only the more Jewish they became, but the more marked the existential conflict between their Jewishness and their Germanness became, the deeper their search for individual authenticity, the better poems they wrote.

So long as the German Jews were struggling for the possession of their language, they remained its debtors. The linguistic jokes and original locutions with which the generation of Heine and Boerne and the generations afterwards amused themselves are, as is so often the case with jokes, merely confessions of a deep-seated insecurity. Only when the German Jews began to attach more importance to what they said than to *how* they said it, only when they began to rise above the language, and sovereignly master it, i.e., only when they began to deal in German with their own un-German, necessarily un-German themes, and above all with their German-Jewish conflict, did they give the language a new face, new possibilities of expression and a strange new beauty, which could already be surmised in the later Jewish poems of Heine.

Ever since Goethe's *Westoestlicher Diwan*, German poets had striven to assimilate oriental sounds and oriental metaphors to German poetry. Platen's *Ghaselen* and Rueckert's *Makamen* were attempts also to reproduce the specific verse forms of the East. But it was Else Lasker-Schueler who first effected that complete fusion of West and East with which Goethe had autobiographically played. It was only when the German language had become incidental to the Jewish poet, when it had become natural and almost a matter of indifference to him, that he was able to make a significant addition to it. Like many great cultural works, the significant achievement of German Jewish literature was made unintentionally, and as though unconsciously. The price of this achievement was, to be sure, estrangement, estrangement from German as well as Jewish culture.

Nowhere in the work of Else Lasker-Schueler is this estrangement so perceptible as in her play **Die Wupper**, in which she attempts to depict the people and landscape of her childhood. It is a thoroughly Expressionistic play, a phantasmagoria full of frantic eloquence and incoherent visions. Its structure was disrupted by the same utter lack of responsibility toward reality that drove Lasker-Schueler aimlessly through her own life. Her contempt for psychology, her self-obsession, which allowed her fellow-man to be no more than the thankful and passive receiver of the beauty which she bestowed upon him, deprived her "Wuppers" of all plasticity and verisimilitude. Although they bear German names, these figures do not belong to the German landscape. They are nothing but the un-German "I" of the poetess divided up among puppets.

In Berlin she became habituated to the heterogeneous society that made its home in the cafés, particularly the one called Romanische Café. She led the life of the true bohemian, who suffers from his uprootedness but draws creative strength from this very suffering. "Of course, we all look on the café as the devil. But without this devil, there's nothing at all."

It was in Berlin that she met Oskar Goldberg, who in his *Wirklichkeit der Hebräer* (*Reality of the Hebrews*) had elucidated the myth content of the Old Testament and fitted it into the religious history of the Orient as a whole. (Though Goldberg has exerted a profound influence upon the Jewish religious scholarship of our time, though his ideas and discoveries play, directly or indirectly, a prominent part in the Biblical novels of Thomas Mann, his work has today been well-nigh forgotten.)

Else Lasker-Schueler boasted of having read nothing since her school days, and there is no doubt that at least in her later years she was utterly indifferent to the work of other writers. She needed no books. She took from people what was useful to her, and she learned to understand the work through her contact with the man who had created it. For her, present and past were totally blurred. She judged and condemned Goethe as though he had just been walking down the street with her, and sometimes she honored her contemporaries with words that carried the weight of posthumous fame. Her judgments always had reference to herself and were based solely on the benefit that she and her poetry might draw from the person she was judging. Her judgments were always mad. But since madness nearly always weaves its fabric around a core of authentic experience, Else Lasker-Schueler's wildest opinion often carried the thorn of an apt insight.

Thus it is unlikely that she had ever read *Die Wirklichkeit der Hebräer*. But she understood that here, in the midst of Western civilization, the myth of the Old Testament had been freshly unearthed, and that the stubborn density, the wildness and beauty of this primeval world, bore a kinship to the dreams that she herself harbored. Oskar Goldberg, whose name she never mentioned, was more closely akin to her than any of the writers to whom she dedicated poems. And while the Hebrew literature of her time sang in mournful tones of the exile and persecution of her people, as in Bialik, or yearned for the gods of Greece and a beauty less laden with suffering, as in Tschernichowsky, or devoted a Gogolesque humor to the little people of Galicia and the great faith that kept them alive, as in S. J. Agnon—Else Lasker-Schueler, the German, the "*Zivilisationsliteratin*" (Thomas Mann), penetrated deep into prehistory and there gathered a sense of her people that was more cruel, more authentic, and at the same time more visionary than the ephemeral cliché which awakening Jewish nationalism was just beginning to create.

> Der Fels wird morsch
> Dem ich entspringe
> Und meine Gotteslieder singe. . . .
> Jäh stürz ich vom Weg
> Und riesele ganz in mir
> Fernab, allein über Klagegestein
> Dem Meer zu.
>
> Hab mich so abgeströmt
> Von meines Blutes
> Mostvergorenheit.
> Und immer, immer noch der Widerhall
> In mir,
> Wenn schauerlich gen Ost
> Das morsche Felsgebein,
> Mein Volk,
> Zu Gott schreit.
>
> (The rock crumbles
> From which I spring
> Singing my songs to the Lord. . . .
> Steep from the path I fall
> And all within me I flow
> Down, slowly down, alone over rocks of lamentation,
> To the sea.
>
> I have poured myself so far
> From the seething
> New wine of my blood.
> And still, still the echo always
> Within me,
> When terribly eastward
> The crumbling bones of rock,
> My people,
> Cry out to God.)

Else Lasker-Schueler loved much, easily, unselectively,

and always unhappily. Nearly every one of her poems bears a dedication, and nearly every dedication is to a man she loved. In her love poems she hid her face behind masks, and when she spoke of herself, it was a self in the mask of a man, just as she sometimes appeared on the platform in trousers, to recite her verses. After "Yussuf, Prince of Thebes," came "Malik"—Hebrew: *melech*—another royal mask, but there was also the girl, "Tino of Bagdad." She also conferred the title of king or cardinal upon others, and fell in love with the phantasms that she herself had conjured up. She loved Peter Hille, a German Tolstoyan and mediocre muddlehead, whom she looked on quite simply as a saint ("To the great prophet St. Peter Hille, in veneration"), and Herwarth Walden who in his magazine *Der Sturm* carried German Expressionism to the extreme ("I should have become a clown, Herwarth, if that wouldn't have been an insult to you"), and the "dear half-brother," the "blue, blue knight," Franz Marc, who, with his "Tower of Blue Horses," had helped to free German painting from the mists of impressionism, and then had fallen in the First World War. All this, it is certain, was no more than a charming, lively game, but on each occasion she thought she was bleeding to death, and then she wrote poems like **"Der alte Tibetteppich" ("The Old Tibetan Carpet")**, in which love and rhetoric were woven into an artificial fabric that had however something of the intensity and rich imagery of the *Song of Songs*. And even her last work includes love poems full of girlish reticence and hesitant restrained passion.

A Jewish trait spoke in Else Lasker-Schueler insofar as love ceased to be a game with her only when she turned to her mother or her child. As soon as she saw herself situated in the chain of the generations, the feeling she otherwise squandered so heedlessly became solemn earnest. In her songs of mourning for her lost mother and her son who died while still a boy, she revealed herself unmasked, a poor lonely woman, shivering in the cold wind.

> Immer wieder wirst du mir
> Im scheidenden Jahr sterben, mein Kind,
>
> Wenn das Laub zerfliesst
> Und die Zweige schmal werden. . . .
>
> Die Liebe zu dir ist das Bildnis
> Das man sich von Gott machen darf . . .
>
> Nie ahnte ich den Tod—
> Spüren um dich, mein Kind—
>
> Und ich liebe des Zimmers Wände,
> Die ich bemale mit deinem Knabenantlitz.
>
> Die Sterne, die in diesem Monat
> So viele sprühend ins Leben fallen,
> Tropfen schwer auf mein Herz.
>
> (Always in the parting year
> You will die to me, my child,
>
> When the leaves scatter
> And the branches grow thin . . .
>
> My love for you is the image
> Which it is given us to form of God . . .
>
> I never thought to feel death

> For your sake, my child—
>
> And I love the walls of the room
> That I paint with your boyish face.
>
> So many stars in this month
> Fall showering into life,
> Drop heavy on my heart.)

It is characteristic of the great woman poets of all ages and languages, that they dare, almost innocently, to express what men conceal behind the form of their poems. Where a man turns his passion into a metaphor or a riddle, a woman—be she Louise Labé of Lyon or Elizabeth Barrett Browning—frankly gives herself in her poetry. Similarly, Else Lasker-Schueler was without shame in her lyrical confessions of love, and doubly so, because she performed her love before the random, promiscuous audience of the Berlin literary cafés, and because it was from behind a mask, and often a male mask, that she loved. Only when pain came to her, not in the form of longing or disillusionment, but as death, the death of one she loved, only when her grief forbade her to be anyone but herself, no longer a prince or a king, but a suffering, aging woman, motherless and bereft of her child, only when she ceased to play charming games of make-believe amid the demi-monde of the cafés, does her poetry become human and take on human dignity. Not in yearning or fulfillment, but in grief over the life that had given her life and the life that owed its life to her, was she, the Jewess, entirely herself, and a great creative poet.

Her hunger for life was insatiable and she let no occasion pass on which to appease it. In her eyes there was always hunger and her fingers, which in old age resembled the talons of a hawk, were forever twitching. She hated all those who were satiated, those who possessed and defended their possessions. She found friends enough who admired what was extraordinary in her and her work. It is astonishing how much help was offered her in a Palestine menaced by war and trembling with inner unrest, though she made no secret of her hostility, though she openly spoke and wrote German, the language of the murderer. But she rejected, or wasted, all the help that was offered her with a contempt that was an admission of her own fear of life. She lived in a bare hovel, shivering and sleepless.

She took refuge in dreams of angels who resembled heavenly gardeners, in dreams of her mother and child, or in madness. But she still possessed sufficient sense of reality to know that her madness was half escape and half pretense. Often she allowed false counselors to edit her finest, most self-willed lines into commonplaces. And as though she knew that she herself was often not entirely serious about her poetry, that her poetry was not adequate to the visions which still poured in upon her, she complemented her songs with drawings. . . .

The central problem of Jewish writing in our time is that of truthfulness. Exposed to foreign influences, in rivalry with foreign writers, striving to outdo them and yet to be himself, the Jewish writer can be judged only by the authenticity with which he represents the situation of the Jew. In all other present-day literatures, the lie is no more than an illegitimate child of the imagination: the critic exposes it, smilingly. The Jew, however, who has always been a symbol to the Western world, is in process of becoming a new mythical figure, the last perhaps, and assuredly one of the profoundest which the Western imagination is capable of creating, the myth of the modern man, homeless but at home in his homelessness. Only by complete self-identification, by complete honesty, can the Jewish writer avoid disappointing the hopes which the perceptive reader, himself a sufferer from the crisis of our times, places in him. If the Israeli is to emerge as a new variety of the species Jew, he will have to legitimize his appearance in a Palestinian literature that, as far as we can see, does not yet exist. Only then will it be possible to enter in any discussion of the contribution Palestinian civilization is making to the context of Jewish literature the world over.

Else Lasker-Schueler, however, was a Hebrew poetess in the German tongue. This paradox embodies her tragedy and the imperfection of that tragedy. Her poems are dominated by the madness of the enthusiast, the seer, the prophetess, which served her contact with the profane world. But she was wise enough to know that she was mad, and shrewd enough to play with the abyss separating her from reality, to use it in her search for the "I" that she never discovered, because she never found the Other, who would have disclosed her identity. And so her passion was artifical and her hatred was a defense mechanism, a mimicry, and not organic. But she was authentic in her mythical visions, and since she was authentic there, the contradiction between Hebraic vision and German word annulled itself in them. She was authentic in her lament for mother and child, and authentic in those songs in which she saw herself as a fugitive, as the singer of the old mysterious, magical song, who was persecuted because the song was no longer understood.

> Ich habe zu Hause ein blaues Klavier
> Und kenne doch keine Note.
>
> Es steht im Dunkel der Kellertür,
> Seitdem die Welt verrohte.
>
> Es spielen Sternenhände vier
> —Die Mondfrau sang im Boote—
> Nun tanzen Ratten im Geklirr.
>
> Zerbrochen ist die Klaviatür . . .
> Ich beweine die blaue Tote.
>
> Ach, liebe Engel, öffnet mir
> —Ich ass vom bittern Brote—
> Mir lebend schon die Himmelstür—
> Auch wider dem Verbote.
>
> (I have a blue piano at home,
> Yet I don't know a single note.
>
> It stands in the dark by the cellar door,
> Since the coarsening of the world.
>
> Four starry hands are playing
> —The moon woman sang in the bark—
> Now rats are dancing to the din.
>
> Broken is the keyboard . . .
> I weep for the blue dead.
> Ah, dear angels, open

> —I have eaten the bitter bread—
>
> Heaven's gate to me while I live—
> Forbidden though it is.)

This is the plaint of Orpheus, the plaint for the song that has been lost in an un-musical, songless, mute age. Yeats in his old age took up this plaint, and Rainer Maria Rilke was filled with it. Else Lasker-Schueler enriched it with the realization that song had become estranged, removed even from herself. " . . . Yet I don't know a single note. . . . " an insight which embraces much of the forlornness and metaphysical irony of Franz Kafka. We shall make no mistake if we designate as Jewish, if not Hebrew, this specific contribution of Else Lasker-Schueler to the self-portrait of the poet in our time.

She was seldom so authentic and wise as in this poem. When she was honest, her wisdom was that of a child, emerging suddenly, unexpectedly, in strange forms. At such times her love was also the love of a child, recognizing no limit or barrier, an endless yearning for tenderness and requited trust. The best among the poems of Else Lasker-Schueler will endure.

G. Guder   (essay date 1962)

SOURCE: "The Poetry of Else Lasker-Schüler," in *Modern Languages,* Vol. XLIII, No. 2, June, 1962, pp. 53-60.

[*In the following essay, Guder surveys the major themes of Lasker-Schüler's poetry.*]

Examining the whole body of [Lasker-Schüler's] poetry from the publication of her first volume of verse, *Styx*, in Berlin, 1902, to *Mein Blaues Klavier*, written in exile and published in 1943 in Jerusalem, two years before the poet's death, one realizes that throughout her whole life her poetry was the expression of one unchanging experience. This experience was the outcome of an aim which was deeply rooted in Else Lasker-Schüler's thought and feeling, and of which a clear definition is given by the poet herself in her essay 'Meine Andacht':

> Ich habe mich stets befleissight, nicht nach Gold
> aber nach Gott zu graben; manchmal stiess ich
> auf Himmel [*Gedichte 1902-1943*, 1959].

When Else Lasker-Schüler is classified as one of the German Expressionists, with whom she has, no doubt, stylistic characteristics in common (her second husband was Herwarth Walden, the editor of *Der Sturm*), it is too readily overlooked that for Else Lasker-Schüler God is not 'die grosse, nur mit unerhörter Ekstase zu erreichende Spitze des Gefühls' (Edschmid) [quoted by Arno Schirokauer, 'Expressionismus der Lyrik,' in *Germanistische Studien,* 1957] but the God of her fathers. Werner Kraft, a close friend of the poet, bears this out when he writes 'die montheistische jüdische Glaubenskraft gab ihren Dichtungen eine Grundlage, die sie in ihren besten Schöpfungen vor jeder mythischen Selbstzersprühung bewahrte' [*Wort and Gedanke,* 1959]. Floundering in cosmic mysticism, exaggerated eruption of feeling, purely rhetorical pathos— these weaknesses which became more and more obvious in the expressionistic lyric, are practically non-existent in the poetry of Else Lasker-Schüler. With the exception of the ***Hebräische Balladen,*** Else Lasker-Schüler, too, wrote her poems in the first person singular, but she is not subjective in the worst sense of the word, i.e. 'ich-besessen'. Her early poem **'Mein Volk'** (1902) embodies her consciousness that the I of a great poet is a functional I, as distinguished from the purely biographical I:

> Und immer, immer noch der Widerhall
> In mir,
> Wenn schauerlich gen Ost
> Das morsche Felsegebein
> Mein Volk zu Gott schreit.

Even at a time when the motif of her poems was increasingly homelessness, uprootedness and dread of life, she, the ageing, ailing woman, remained concerned with the efficiency of her poetic voice as mediator, so that her last poems, too, with the same subjective tone transcend all that is purely individual and are timeless symbols of the fate of man and of the artist in an age of increasing inhumanity. The poet's sense of responsibility, as she explains in her religious reflections in the essay **'Das Gebet'**, links him with the prophet. In particular the poem **'Mein Blaues Klavier'** with its subjective tone, which gives its title to her last volume, is not only the personal lament of Else Lasker-Schüler but also the expression of the tragic situation of the poet-prophet in a world which no longer heeds his warning:

> Ich habe zu Hause ein blaues Klavier
> Und kenne doch keine Note.
>
> Es steht im Dunkel der Kellertür,
> Seitdem die Welt verrohte.

The second line especially implies that in the present situation the poet's inspiration has failed.

The most dominant stylistic characteristic of Else Lasker-Schüler's poetry is her tendency towards pictographic expression. She, who herself could draw with no little skill, experienced life 'tableaumässig', as she describes it in a letter to Herwarth Walden, adding 'ich sterbe am Leben und atme im Bilde wieder auf'. These words confirm the affinity of her poetry with painting and indicate that she knew how to contain even the most subjective anguish in imagery. This is especially noticeable in poems which she addressed to Gottfried Benn, the expression of the purely personal experience of her great love which Benn did not return. The pictorial presentation of this most painful emotion prevents it from becoming obtrusively sentimental. The poem **'Lauter Diamant'**, beginning

> Ich hab in deinem Antlitz
> Meinen Sternenhimmel ausgeträumt,

is a suitable illustration of how the purely subjective is objectified into a common human situation as expressed in the last stanza

> Dunkel ist es—
> Es flackert nur noch
> Das Licht meiner Seele.

But Else Lasker-Schüler is by no means always so successful in this, often not when she gives herself up completely to an experience of ecstatic bliss, especially when this experience is more imagined than real. In one of her 'Mönch' poems she says:

> Und mein Herz wird ein Weihbecken,
> Besterne dich mit meinem Blut;

This is an image drawn from the Roman Church, and although the figure of Christ attracted Else Lasker-Schüler, it was not as Christ the Son of God, but as the One who was persecuted but did not retaliate. Some of her poems, if only in occasional verses, come near to the folk-song, and this brings with it a soulful tone. 'Der Sturz kopfüber in den Kitsch, in gemachte Süsslichkeit, ist oft unvermeidbar', states Georges Schlocker, [in *Expressionismus,* 1956], and quotes as example **'An den Gralprinzen'**:

> Wenn wir uns ansehn,
> Blühn unsere Augen
>
> Und wir staunen
> Vor unseren Wundern—nicht?
> Und alles wird so süss.

It is the wonder of the awakening of love which transfigures earthly existence—'Ich glaube wir sind Engel' the poem ends. Whilst the lines expressing the effect of love, which to Else Lasker-Schüler is something of a miracle, have some artistic merit, the line 'Und alles wird so süss' shows how small the distance is between genuine bliss and sentimentality. Within the whole body of her poetry, however, such lines are rather the exception than the rule; they need therefore not tip the scale too heavily in the final assessment. As well as those quoted from **'Der Mönch'**, the line 'Blühn unsere Augen' is noteworthy in so far as it shows a feature of expressionistic style—to invest objects and their purpose with qualities and meanings which are not usually attributed to them. The same principle applies to the way in which Else Lasker-Schüler uses colour in her poetry. Colours are ascribed to objects to which they normally do not belong—'blaues Klavier,' 'blaue Tote,' 'schwarze Sterne,' 'schwarze Taube'—or to abstracts which are beyond visual perception—'blaue Allmacht,' 'blaue Seele'. At the same time Else Lasker-Schüler often uses colours with their more traditional meaning. Her tribute to Karl Sonnenschein, 'Dem grossen Armenapostel und Dichter' contains a description which is typical of this usage in her poetry as well:

> Er war ja heilig. Seine Seele, eine fromme dreifarbige
> Fahne; ihr weisses Linnen, ein Symbol seines makellosen
> Wandels; der rote Streif hielt sein Leben wach und lebendig
> Für den aufopfernden Dienst an der Menschheit; doch das zarte
> Blau führte ihn ungehemmt in die höhere Welt.

Blue for her, as it was for her friend Franz Marc, is the colour with greatest significance. In what is probably her best-known poem, **'Gebet'**, which belongs to the mid-period of her work, the second stanza may be interpreted as one of Else Lasker-Schüler's many avowals of her poetic mission:

> Und wandle immer tiefer in die Nacht . . .
> Ich habe Liebe in die Welt gebracht—

> Dass blau zu blühen jedes Herz vermag,—
> Und hab ein Leben müde mich gewacht,
> In Gott gehüllt den dunklen Atemschlag.

Blue signifies untiring striving towards God, and for Else Lasker-Schüler becomes the symbol of her poetry and of the manifestation of divine power. Even in moments of deepest anguish, as after the death of her only son, who died of tuberculosis in his teens, she remained aware of that power. In her essay **'Meine Andacht'** she writes:

> . . . und man vermag nur zu knien, sein Kind
> im Sterben zu erreichen. Der Himmel ist es eben,
> die blaue Verklräung, die den Sterbenden von
> dem Zurückgebliebenen trennt.

Thus her believing trust in God prevented her from yielding to the temptation of making her own Ego the measure of all things. In the poem **'An mein Kind,'** which she wrote after this blow of fate, stating that her eyes will no longer turn towards the world because even the green of the leaves—for Else Lasker-Schüler the life-giving colour—hurts them, she continues:

> —Aber der Ewige wohnt in mir.
> Die Liebe zu dir ist das Bildnis,
> Das man sich von Gott machen darf.

Obedience is for her the bridge to God. It is with this same obedience that she accepts God's curse on the world. The world before and the world after the Fall are ever present in her poetry. Grey represents the turning away of man from God or man's doubt of God, which Else Lasker-Schüler, too, is not spared. Her early poem **'Weltende'** is typical of man's existential dread in a time of which [Friedrich] Nietzsche proclaimed 'Gott ist tot'.

> Es ist ein Weinen in der Welt,
> Als ob der liebe Gott gestorben wär,
> Und der bleierne Schatten, der niederfällt,
> Lastet grabesschwer.

And even in her late poem **'Hingabe'** Else Lasker-Schüler confesses:

> Mit einem Kleid aus Zweifel war ich angetan,
> Das greises Leid geweight für mich am Zeitrad
> spann.
> Und jedes Bild, das ich von dieser Welt gewann,
> Verlor ich doppelt, und auch das, was ich er-
> sann.

What she imaged to herself was the re-creation of a world without conflict.

Since the Hebraic Ballads appeared in 1913, Else Lasker-Schüler's poems have been viewed too one-sidedly as the manifestation of Oriental myths, a view which was aided by the fact that she referred to herself as Prinz Jussuf von Theben (Egypt). Consequently the influence on her poetry of Else Lasker-Schüler's encounter with life has not been sufficiently recognized. The *one* myth which characterizes her work as a whole is that of the lost Paradise. In the poems in which she regains Paradise, even if only momentarily, she creates a reciprocating love-relation. The love aspect is hardly ever missing from any poem even though it be a love remembered. In the power of love she believes firmly, or rather clings to it desperately, because for her

love is literally identical with Heaven. In her essay **'Freundschaft und Liebe'** she defines love as a state 'in den man durch himmlische Geschebnisse versetzt wird. Ein Zustand vor oder nach dem Tode.' Poems which illustrate this state place man once more in the proximity of God, in the midst of a shining world full of vigour and energy, in which the law of gravity does not exist and man is therefore free from the fetters of earthly existence. A typical example of this is the early poem **'Frühling,'** one of those poems with an abundance of detail which appears to transpose a painted picture into words. The experience is summed up in the last stanza:

> Der liebe Gott träumt seinen Kindertraum
> Vom Paradies—von seinen zwei Gespielen,
> Und grosse Blumen sehn uns an von Dorn-
> enstielen . . .
> Die düstre Erde hing noch grün am Baum.

The erotic tone which is sometimes noticeable in poems of similar content will be more easily understood if it is remembered that in poems which conjure up an idyllic existence, as in her conception of love in general, Else Lasker-Schüler goes beyond the purely human plane. The poem **'Ein Liebeslied'** from *Mein Blaues Klavier* comes to mind. It begins

> Komm zu mir in der Nacht—wir schlafen eng-
> verschlungen.
> Müde bin ich sehr, vom Wachen einsam.

and ends

> Wir wollen wie zwei seltene Tiere liebesruhen
> Im hohen Rohre hinter dieser Welt.

Between lies a picture which is best illustrated by the lines

> Es öffnen Blumen sich vor allen Quellen
> Und färben sich mit deiner Augen Im-
> mortellen . . .

The link between Else Lasker-Schüler and Franz Marc was strengthened through a common conception of animal life. Having stated in a letter to him that she dares anybody to say anything against birds, she continues 'es sind die höchsten Menschen, sie leben zwischen Luft und Gott, wir leben zwischen Erde und Grab'. Even if this remark was called forth by the narrowness and poverty of her Berlin lodgings at the time, it reveals something of that deeper sense which sees the animal in unbroken harmony with the original Creation. Franz Marc's aim was, as he himself defined it, 'Ein unirdisches Sein zu zeigen, das hinter allem wohnt, den Spiegel des Lebens zu zerbrechen, dass wir in das Sein schauen [quoted by Walter Hess in *Dokumente zum Verständis der modernen Malerei,* 1958]. He is attracted by the mystery of the idea of how nature presents itself to the eye of the animal. 'Wie armselig seelenlos ist unsere Konvention, Tiere in eine Landschaft zu setzen, die unseren Augen zugehört, statt uns in die Seele des Tiers zu versenken, um dessen Bildkreis zu erraten.' The inner bond between man and animal is there, even though the attempt must remain incomplete as long as the artist is earthbound. The bond consists in the fact that they both originate from the same act of creation. From this angle many of Else Lasker-Schüler's love poems embody a myth, and move, not on the level of this world but in the sphere of the original harmony of Creation (hence 'hinter dieser Welt'). This experience finds symbolic expression in her poetry in the colour gold, as, for instance, in an earlier poem, also entitled **'Ein Liebeslied,'** where gold carries a sacred meaning:

> Aus goldnem Odem
> Erschufen uns Himmel.
> O, wie wir uns lieben . . .

In the light of this it is understandable that in her poetry there is no conflict between sensuality and the spirit. For her man's guilt manifests itself in 'man's inhumanity to man' as a result of his disobedience to God. The necessity that man should realize that he must find his way back to God is a recurring motif in many of her longer poems. Her meditation at the end of the year, in one of the last poems that she wrote in Germany, **'Letzter Abend im Jahr,'** culminates in her concern for the metaphysical fate of man:

> O Gott, wie kann der Mensch verstehen,
> Warum der Mensch haltlos vom Menschen
>   bricht,
> Sich wieder sammeln muss im höheren Geschehen.

In addition to this anxiety comes the fear that God must have turned His face away from man.

The possibility of feeling herself secure in a transfigured world even at a time when her poems written in exile increasingly reflect her despair of this world and preparation for death, is one of the most striking features of her poetry. This can be partly explained by the fact that love for her continued to signify Heaven and the power that ultimately would transform the world. Whether as a young girl or as an aged, banished woman, she writes of love with the same magic. One of her last poems, **'Ich säume liebentlang'** (a word of her own coinage) recalling the memory of past love, ends

> Es lächelten die Immortellen hold in deinem
>   Angesicht,
> Als du im Liebespsalme unserer Melodie
> Die Völker tauchtest und erhobest sie.

It is equally remarkable that Else Lasker-Schüler never yielded to the temptation of escapism (one of her early poems bears the title **'Weltflucht'**). This is due to the high conception she had of the poet's role to lead man, estranged from God, back to his Creator. In his essay 'Goethe und Heine' [in *Der Dichter und die Zeit,* 1947] Fritz Strich states 'Nur der Schmerz macht den Juden Schöpferisch. Heine musste ihn sich einbilden, wenn er ihn nicht empfand.' Else Lasker-Schüler did not invent a kind of romantic 'Weltschmerz' for herself; she really felt her deep anguish, felt it as man in a loveless world, and felt it as a poet who had no 'Volk'. She created for herself the solace of a mythical world, but one in which God and love are always the centre. Her love poems are therefore basically religious poems. Her legacy to our times is summed up in a verse from her late poem **'Herbst'**:

> Das ewige Leben dem, der viel von Liebe weiss
>   zu sagen.
> Ein Mensch der Liebe kann nur auferstehen!

> Hass schachtelt ein, wie hoch die Fackel auch
>   mag schlagen.

Kurt Schümann has given one of the most sensitive appreciations of Else Lasker-Schüler, but here, too, there is a tendency to see in her a typical representative of Expressionism. Nowadays it can act as an obstacle to the appreciation of a poet's work if the impression is created that it is typical of a largely time-conditioned movement which reached its climax in the last few years before the First World War. The question is whether her poems are those of a genuine poet who has created timeless works of art. In her travel journal **Das Hebräerland,** written after her first stay in Palestine, Else Lasker-Schüler says of herself:

> Ich bin nicht Hebräerin der Hebräer willen, aber
> Gottes willen! Doch dieses Bekenntnis schliesst
> die Liebe und Treue unerschütterlicher Erge-
> benheit zu Seinem Volke ein.

The religious aspect therefore remains the most genuine element in her verse. Her description of the outer world is significant for the expression of her inner religious experience. Her late poem **'An Apollon,'** for instance, is typical of her technique. In the first stanza she perceives in the impressionistic manner a fleeting stir of life:

> Es ist am Abend im April.
> Der Käfer kriecht ins dichte Moos.
> Er hat so Angst—die Welt so gross!

This expression of fear leads in the second stanza to the image of the whirlwinds wrangling with God, an image from which arises her expression of her submission to God:

> Ich halte meine Hände still ergeben
> Auf meinem frommbezwungnen Schoss.

The three stanzas that follow are her reflection on the poet's experience in this world, a reflection which is in some ways a parallel to the experience of the natural object in the first stanza. The imagery in this reflection, the stream of consciousness in the poem, as it were, though emancipated from a logical connexion with the description in the first and the image in the second stanza, contributes nevertheless to the psychological continuity of the poem by the poet's adherence to the same consciousness throughout. An insecure human being experiences a reality which is under constant threat. Else Lasker-Schüler's insecurity was overcome by her faith. Her submission to God prevented her from developing an expressionistic problematic nature which projects its own problems constantly into outer reality. In one of her major poems written in exile, **'Jerusalem,'** she begins by comparing the Holy City to a graveyard, and then in the second stanza continues

> Es starren Gründe hart den Wanderer an—
> Und er versinkt in ihre starren Nächte.
> Ich habe Angst, die ich nicht überwältigen kann.

Thus Jerusalem has become symptomatic of change and decay. But as the epigraph anticipates 'Gott baute aus Seinem Rückgrat: Palästina; aus einem einzigen Knochen: Jerusalem,' Jerusalem is at the same time symbolically the spiritual backbone of the world, and thus becomes a symbol of regeneration. The spiritual rebirth is envisaged as completed in the prophecy with which the poem ends:

> Es grüssen uns
> Des 'Einzigen Gottes' lebendige Fahnen,
> Grünende Hände, die des Lebens Odem säen.

Furthermore, this poem is a good example of Else Lasker-Schüler's ability to express her doubts and fears, and also her religious trust, without exaggerating either her disillusionment or her exultation. This gives her poetry not only convincing substance but also the power of language reminiscent of the prophets. Her diction is especially direct when she uses Old Testament stories as parables. The events serve as symbols of inner experience. The biblical story, as in the ballad of **'Abraham und Isaak'** with its addition of the sea and an altar decorated with sponges and shells, may be altered by the poet's imagination:

> Und Gott ermahnte: Abraham!!
> Er brach vom Kamm des Meeres Muscheln ab
>   und Schwamm
> Hoch auf den Blöcken den Altar zu schmücken,

but the biblical spirit, Abraham's obedience, is kept as a timeless symbol:

> Und trug den einzigen Sohn gebunden auf den
>   Rücken
> Zu werden seinem grossen Herrn gerecht—
> Der aber liebte seinen Knecht.

Already forty years ago these Hebraic Ballads were adequately described by Meir Wiener [in *Juden in der Deutschen Literatur,* 1922] as 'Kleine althebräische Hoheliedlein'. When Else Lasker-Schüler uses biblical tropes it is by no means necessary to know the corresponding biblical passages. For instance, a poem which neither in time nor content belongs to the Hebraic Ballads, **'Ein Lied,'** begins with the lament,

> Hinter meinen Augen stehen Wasser,
> Die muss ich alle weinen,

which is as likely to be a spontaneous expression of her own feeling as a conscious recall of the prophet's lament in Jeremiah ix. i.

With this a criterion is given by which Else Lasker-Schüler's poetry may be judged: true art must have an independent life, and the reader should not need explanations of the poet's subjective angle. Else Lasker-Schüler combines self-expression with communication, and thus her poetry is valid at the particular as well as at the universal level. Hers is a lyric verse which does not employ rhyme or word-music as ends in themselves. Whether she writes in free verse, as she generally does in poems addressed to particular persons, or in rhyme, in poems containing moments of revelation—a revelation of the state of the world, of her position in the world, or of transcendence—her poems are always carried by a rhythm adequate to their meaning.

Robert P. Newton on Lasker-Schüler's poetic talent:

Undoubtedly there are many unresolved problems of critical evaluation which await resolution for Else Lasker-Schüler's work. Despite some exquisitely finished poems, she leans to stylistic carelessness and is not immune to rashes of saccharine sentimentality. No one would claim that all her poems are guided by a coherent logic (but, then, what about [Georg] Trakl and [Gottfried] Benn?). Nevertheless, a good deal of her imagery is original and symbolically well-founded, and many of her poems dynamically cohere through verbal and psychological association, in a way unrecognized by hasty and condescending critics. In particular, her visual imagination—which is emotionally driven, concrete and often subtle in its correspondences—has very fruitfully, and more fully than other poets, exploited some traditional aspects of the age-old symbolism of the eye—namely its power—and has expanded in the symbolic mode of eye = spirit (as opposed to knowledge or light) the German language's metaphoric scope, far beyond what any previous poet has accomplished. In this and other respects Lasker-Schüler's poetic gift deserves to be treated with greater attention and seriousness, should we not be inclined to approach it thus already because of the jewel-like brilliance of rhythm and epigrammatic phrase which is attained in many of her best poems.

Robert P. Newton, in his "Eye Imagery in Else Lasker-Schüler," MLN, April, 1982.

G. Guder   (essay date 1965)

SOURCE: "The Significance of Love in the Poetry of Else Lasker-Schüler," in *German Life & Letters,* Vol. XVIII, 1964-65, pp. 177-88.

[In the following essay, Guder compares Lasker-Schüler's concept of love to that of the German Expressionists, and examines the effect of her personal experiences on the emotional outlook of her poetry.]

Much has been left to conjecture about the meaning of love for Else Lasker-Schüler herself and about its significance in her poetry. This is chiefly due to her habit of shrouding her life in mystery and making obscure statements, often contradictory, about herself. There is also a tendency among her critics to see her poetry mainly as a mirror of personal experience, which, indeed, it is; but at the same time these experiences form the background against which a problem of general human significance is presented. W. H. Sokel, [in *The Writer in Extremis,* 1959], sums up Else Lasker-Schüler's conception of love as 'a luxury, a refined poetic system of sensations which could never be grasped by the *vulgus profanum*'. Else Lasker-Schüler was married twice, at twenty-four to Dr Berthold Lasker, and at the age of thirty-two to Herwarth Walden. Both marriages ended in divorce. K. J. Höltgen in his valuable dissertation, [*Untersuchungen zur Lyrik Else Lasker-Schülers,* 1955], referring to the metaphysical aspects of her melancholy, states: 'Aus dem gleichen metaphysischen Ungenügen an jedem menschlichen Du kam es um 1911 zur Scheidung von Herwarth Walden.' Hölt-gen bases his argument largely on the passage from **Mein Herz** in which Else Lasker-Schüler says of herself and Herwarth Walden: 'Ich kenne Dich und Du kennst mich, wir können uns nicht mehr überraschen, und ich kann nur leben von Wundern.' This statement, as Astrid Gehlhoff-Claes points out, [in *Else Lasker-Schüler, Briefe an Karl Kraus*], has been used like a chemical formula, as it were, to explain the poet's relation to the human 'Thou'. This is true. Gehlhoff-Claes quotes as an example George Schlocker's opinion '—doch ihrem masslosen Anspruch konnten Menschen nicht Genüge leisten' [in *Expressionismus,* 1956]. To this may be added the statement in [*Untersuchung der Lyrik Else Lasker-Schülers,* 1956] by Eldeltrud Aker: 'Doch auf diesen Wegen dämonischer Leidenschaft konnte ihr niemand folgen.' Of the biographical accounts available, that compiled by Gehlhoff-Claes is the most complete and reliable, since it is based upon evidence obtained from people who knew both Else Lasker-Schüler and Herwarth Walden well. Thus it is now known that, in fact, Herwarth Walden left Else Lasker-Schüler for another woman. If Schlocker's statement is applied to Else Lasker-Schüler's poetry instead of purely to her person, and is taken in its context, viz. that her emotion constantly strives towards the infinite, it does, in fact, describe the crux of her love poems. This is not to say that her conception of love is identical with that of Expressionists. As with her orthodox belief in the monotheistic God of the Jews, she is a figure apart in this respect. The Expressionists' emphasis on the brotherhood of all men could not resolve her sense of isolation. For her, love is personal and particular, a feeling of the heart that reaches its ultimate fulfilment only in giving itself to, and finding its response in, a beloved individual.

The poems **'Trieb,'** **'Nervus Erotis'** and **'Sinnenrausch'** from **Styx,** published in 1902, contain an element which is characteristic of this first collection and which recurs throughout the entire body of her poetry. These poems are the dynamic expression of burning passion as an unbridled force:

> Es treiben mich brennende Lebensgewalten,
> Gefühle, die ich nicht zügeln kann,

the first poem begins. The particular characteristic of these poems is that they are unmistakably erotic, but that, at the same time, the first does not mention an object towards which the feeling is directed, and the 'Du' of the other two is an unnamed dream figure. This latter aspect can be seen even more clearly in other poems of the same period; the two-stanza poem **'Dann'** in its opening line recalls a dream which in the second stanza leads to a yearning for a revelation of love by the dream-object, culminating in the desire:

> Möchte an Deinem Munde brennen
> Eine Traumzeit von tausend Jahren.

This is eroticism which has welled up from the depths of the soul and now seeks in the world an object which can respond to this feeling. In the poem **'Ein alter Tibetteppich,'** written about 1910, addressed to Karl Kraus, the 'Du' has now become real. [C.] Heselhaus [in *Deutsche*

Lyrik der Moderne, 1961], raising the question whether this is a love poem or a dream vision, states that for the three first stanzas it appears to be a love poem, and in the last stanza turns into a dream-poem:

> Süsser Lamasohn auf Moschuspflanzenthron,
> Wie lange küsst dein Mund den meinen wohl
> Und Wang die Wange buntgeknüpfte Zeiten
>   schon?

With the words 'buntgeknüpfte Zeiten' the dream points to a design in the carpet and to a mythical past. In this poem two spheres are interwoven. The first stanza begins with the situation as it exists in the present:

> Deine Seele, die die meine liebet,
> Ist verwirkt mit ihr im Teppichtibet

This situation is the manifestation in an individual of an objective and eternal principle. With the beginning of the third stanza the two souls, now become one, merge with the sensuous. Both the present relationship of 'I' and 'Thou' and the timeless eternal phenomenon of love are united and made visible in the symbol of the Tibetan carpet. This poem is a manifestation of love itself, an eternal force which is revealed through individual human feeling. It is true, in the temporal world love often dies, but it nevertheless continues to exist as the Eternal; especially through joining the present with a mythical past, the eternal nature of love which cannot be lost—and this, for Else Lasker-Schüler, is the criterion—is emphasized. Its earthly manifestation is the 'Du' without which man is doomed. How basic this need was for her can be seen if the early poem **'Weltende'** (1905) is brought in for comparison. The grief pervading this poem is so deep that it can be expressed only by the assumption that God himself must be dead:

> Es ist ein Weinen in der Welt,
> Als ob der liebe Gott gestorben wär.

These opening lines state a general condition, but the chief cause for the feeling of doom may be said to be the poet's own grief at the decline of the world. It is because of the darkness of the times that the poet seeks refuge with a loving human 'Thou'. The personal call in the second stanza to another being is repeated in an intensified form at the beginning of the third and last stanza. But in this poem there is no response. Life in all hearts lies dead as in a coffin. God being dead, Love is dead, and that means that Life itself is dead. All that remains is the unfulfilled longing:

> Es pocht eine Sehnsucht an die Welt,
> An der wir sterben müssen.

Even if this poem, dedicated to Herwarth Walden, is partly determined by a very personal grief and by Else Lasker-Schüler's own feeling of remoteness from God, it nevertheless gives expression to a general human dilemma. The poem **'Das Lied des Gesalbten'** opens up a wider and more personal perspective. It is the first poem in **Styx** with an obviously biblical strain. The first lines:

> Zebaoth spricht aus dem Abend:
> Verschwenden sollst Du mit Liebe

are the commandment which gives the key to the poem. In images reminiscent of the *Song of Solomon* the poet's gifts are promised. The second line, 'Verschwenden sollst Du mit Liebe', is repeated. This command, for Else Lasker-Schüler, is inseparable from her conception of her poetic mission as she affirms it in **'Gebet,'** published in 1920:

> Ich habe Liebe in die Welt gebracht
> Dass blau zu blühen jedes Herz vermag.

Love brings participation in a perfect existence which throughout her poetry is characterized by a vitality of burgeoning life. **'Das Lied des Gesalbten'** introduces the basis upon which she experiences reality, and form which, for her, the demands of her poetic calling arise. It is a mythical speculation in which an originally pure divine creation has fallen victim to the sinfulness of man, a creation which the poet is called upon to re-establish; hence the further commandment:

> Und die Schwermut, die über Jerusalem trübt,
> Mit singenden Blütendolden umkeimen.

Its aim is to bring man closer to God and thus transform him into a more perfect being. This process has as a prerequisite complete surrender of the self, for only through surrender does love reach the stage in which it is the opposite of the preservation of the self, i.e. of an existence limited to and by this earth. Thus, for Else Lasker-Schüler, the lavishing of love, together with the expression of it in her poetry, has a religious significance. Such a love in its depth cannot be satisfied even through the most intense sensual intoxication. Indeed, the enslavement of a love bound to the senses is the very obstacle to its fulfilment as a transcendental force. Its intensity, however, is the means whereby it is raised to a purified form—a yearning for union with something higher. This desire, inborn in the spiritual part of man, the poet in the last line calls nostalgia for Paradise. This perfect life, as Else Lasker-Schüler knows, cannot be attained in this world; it can be experienced only in moments of transcendence. In the love poem **'Sulamith'** which follows immediately after **'Das Lied des Gesalbten'** the resulting exaltation makes the soul oblivious of earthly existence. The lines:

> Und verwehe im Weltraum,
> In Zeit,
> In Ewigkeit

illustrate how the extension of time and place has been swallowed up, as it were, by the intensity of emotion. As the transfiguration of reality resulting from this experience remains throughout her life a striking feature of her poetry, it is essential to examine whether the eternity of Paradise is, as in the poem **'Sulamith,'** a religious concept of time, or whether it is, as in the poems dedicated to named individuals, merely a concept of quality **'Sulamith'** ends:

> Und meine Seele verglüht in den Abendfarben
> Jerusalems.

This poem also ends her prose work *Das Hebräerland,* an impression of Palestine seen through a poet's eye, written in 1937. If the last line of **'Sulamith'** is brought into relation with her statement:

> Von Gott abgelöst, bewegt sich unsere Welt; nur

> Jerusalem hängt noch an des Schöpfers Heiligen
> Traumes Schnur. Sein Jerusalem, das nicht von
> dieser Welt! . . . [*Dichtungen und Dokumente*]

the full significance that Jerusalem had for her is revealed, and it can be seen that the colour metaphor suggests the merging of the soul with God.

In her poetry there is nearly always the moment when she goes back to the Beginning. **'Im Anfang,'** the last poem in *Styx,* gives a picture of her imaginary existence soon after the Creation. The childlike playfulness in this lighthearted poem is a feature the full significance of which may easily escape the reader. The poem appears to be no more than a game, a prank the poet played on God and the Devil, were it not for the last four lines:

> Würde 10 000 Erdglück geben,
> Noch einmal so gottgeboren zu leben,
> So gottgeborgen, so offenbar.
>   Ja! Ja!
> Als ich noch Gottes Schlingel war!

This wish to go back to the relationship of a child to its father, for a life in the closest proximity to God, indicates that earthly love was not always able to give her the anchor she sought. It is one of the extraordinary features of her poetry that her search for love is closely bound up with her search for God, and that when earthly love is missing, God's face is hidden. **'Ein Lied an Gott'** (1932), longer than most of her poems, shows her basic attitudes in their interdependence. The poet's concern in the first stanza is whether, when spring comes, she will love again. From this thought she goes on to state that she has searched for God with every fibre of her being, but as love is missing, she cannot recognize Him. Since she is God's child, as she states in the fourth stanza, she is not ashamed, in her trusting attitude to God, to unfold her heart completely to Him and to pray:

> Schenk mir ein Lichtchen von dem ewigen
>   Licht!—
> Zwei Hände, die mich lieben, sollen es mir hal-
>   ten.

The spark of the eternal life is love, but it must come to her through a human medium. This search for love is accompanied by a mental picture from the realm of play and the world of the child:

> Ich und die Erde wurden wie zwei Spielgefähr-
>   ten gross!
> Und dürfen 'du' dich beide, Gott der Welten,
>   nennen.

It is from the viewpoint of her own heart that she sees that the times are gloomy:

> So trübe aber scheint mir gerade heut die Zeit
> Von meines Herzens Warte aus gesehen.

The emotional content of the poem culminates in an expression of lostness, that existential experience in fact, which in 1914 found expression in [Ranier Maria] Rilke's famous line 'Ungeborgen, hier auf den Bergen des Herzens'. As in the case of a child, her feeling of insecurity could be overcome only by a human relationship of love. In the consciousness of loving and the belief that she was loved she came to a greater awareness of God; when she realized that the love she felt was not returned, there was nothing left for her but the direct committal of her soul to God. If at the end of the poem **'Im Anfang,'** no amount of earthly happiness was worth as much as living 'gottgeborgen,' to use her own word, it may be concluded that the humorous spirit of that poem served the same purpose as her longing for union with God, i.e. to integrate her world. Right to the end of her life the contrivance of playful situations, the evocation of childhood play, and the re-creation of a poetic paradise remained her means of compassing in her poetry a more comprehensive reality than that in which she lived. Beside the ecstatic transmutation of reality as part of the unconscious creative act, there exists in her poetry as part of her own nature a deliberate play with emotions and persons. In a letter to Karl Kraus who apparently had criticized this tendency, she maintains 'Jedenfalls liebe ich *nach meiner Sehnsucht* die Leute alle zu kleiden, damit ein Spiel zu Stande kommt .. *Spielen ist alles*'. To what extent she endows her friends with imaginary personalities and then plays with them as figures of fancy, can be seen in practically any poem dedicated to an individual person. A poem **'Laurencis',** dedicated in the Collected Poems of 1917 to 'Hans Siemsen dem lieben Heiligen' begins:

> Ich gab dir einen Namen
> Wie eine fromme Guirlande.

Having given him this name, the poet says she will always use it in love (i.e. as in love one conjures up the vision of the beloved), and immediately ascribes her own feeling to Laurencis who is to see her in the golden light shimmering through her heart, and no longer in the dim mist of love-lessness. In the fifth verse she speaks of the effect on her that the bestowal of the name produced (as can be seen in the use of the past tense):

> Meine Seele spielte Auferstehn.

The new reality has raised her to life again, and by the end of the poem she speaks of them both as in complete accord. The next poem she wrote is called **'Abschied,'** and although the chart of ecstasy and disappointment is not always perfectly regular, the sequence of bliss and despair repeats itself again and again. In **'Abschied'** the first and last stanzas begin with the lament:

> Aber du kamst nie mit dem Abend—

Between lies the picture of a broken heart and a withered garland. When she pictures her heart as hanging at every doorpost, also at the door of the beloved, the suspicion is justified that with all the symbolic meaning of the heart, there is nevertheless, even in her disillusionment, an indulgence in playfulness.

Her tendency to believe that the love she felt for another was reciprocated, and consequently her ability to enhance his personality by fantasy, reaches its climax in the seventeen poems dedicated to Gottfried Benn (*Gesammelte Gedichte,* 1917) to whom she dedicated more poems than to any other person. Her love for Gottfried Benn was probably the deepest she ever felt. **'Das Lied des Spielprinzen'**

is typical of the feeling that is built up through the five previous poems:

> Wie kann ich dich mehr noch lieben?
> Ich sehe den Tieren und Blumen
> Bei der Liebe zu.
>
> Küssen sich zwei Sterne,
> Oder bilden Wolken ein Bild—
> Wir spielten es schon zarter.

This feeling does not wholly depend on a series of intensifying images. They are there, of course, and play their part; and some of them as in stanza four:

> Und in deines Kinnes Grube
> Bau ich mir ein Raubnest—
> Bis—du mich aufgefressen hast.

show of what artistic lapses she was capable. As participation in the divine in her love poems is only possible through heightened ecstasy, so with the dawning realization of the onesidedness of her love for Gottfried Benn, her world becomes one in which she is no longer able to perceive the presence of God. The poem **'O Gott'** is the first in which she is completely thrown back upon reality without love, where therefore God is perceptible neither in nature, the elements nor man:

> Jeder kehrt in sein totes Herz heim.

The restraint and the starkness of the imagery in this poem, and the directness of the final cry:

> O Gott, o Gott, wie weit bin ich von dir!

—standing as a verse by itself—transmutes the poet's own personal despair into a common human situation. There is a tendency to put too much emphasis upon her flight from the harshness of reality into Mythos. Kurt Pinthus in his Anthology [*Menschheitsdämmerung,* 1959] introduces his paragraph on Else Lasker-Schüler with one of her early statements about herself:

> Ich bin in Theben (Ägypten) geboren, wenn ich auch in Elberfeld zur Welt kam im Rheinland. Ich ging bis elf Jahre zur Schule, wurde Robinson, lebte fünf Jahre im Morgenlande, und seitdem vegetiere ich.

A. Gehlhoff-Claes commenting upon this statement says 'es beleuchtet den Versuch, aus der Situation äusserer Heimat-und innerer Halt-losigkeit in den Traum, in den Mythos zu flüchten und in ihm die Heimat zu suchen, die ihr die Welt versagte.' True, in the figures of identification which she created for herself, especially that of Prinz Jussuf von Theben, Else Lasker-Schüler tried to maintain herself against the contradictions of her existence in this world, and in moments of despair she falls back on her oriental metaphors: but these are more based upon the Old Testament than on Mythos, as in the *Hebraic Ballads,* written in 1913; and after her shattering disillusionment with Gottfried Benn, the anchor she had to find was God. Thus in the poem immediately after **'Das Lied des Spielprinzen,'** with a title which is its opening line, her grief is reminiscent of the prophet's lament in Jeremiah IX, I:

> Hinter Bäumen berg ich mich
> Bis meine Augen ausgeregnet haben.

and whilst the second last poem of the Benn cycle sees her again as Joseph of Egypt, in the last **'O ich möcht aus der Welt'** her grief is that of a despairing human being in such darkness as suggests that even God is dead.

Yearning for God in a world in which man has abandoned God, and which at times appears to have been abandoned by Him, was for her the basic motif of her poetry, and all her life her need for love remained closely connected with her search for God. The more the tragedy of her own life deepened, the more indispensable did love become. There is, however, one difference noticeable, viz. that love comes more frequently to be experienced as a memory; but its significance remains unchanged. The poem **'Die Verscheuchte,'** written in exile, is filled with the same feeling of dread which thirty years earlier produced the poem **'Weltende.'** Its opening lines:

> Es ist der Tag im Nebel völlig eingehüllt,
> Entseelt begegnen alle Welten sich—

evoke the same atmosphere of deadness which in the earlier poem was described in the lines:

> Das Leben liegt in aller Herzen
> Wie in Särgen.

But whereas in **'Weltende'** the presentiment of disaster is general, in **'Die Verscheuchte'** it is immediate and personal. In both poems there is the call for a 'Thou'. If it is said, as Heselhaus says, that in **'Die Verscheuchte'** prayer and God take the place of love, it must also be stated that the step before prayer is the linking up with another being: '—Komm bete mit mir—denn Gott tröstet mich', and this then evokes a memory of love: '—ja ich liebte dich . . .'. As these words end the stanza which begins with the question 'Wo weilt der Odem, der aus meinem Leben wich?', and in which the poet sees herself as homeless as the hunted game, it may be concluded that here the memory of love has the same function as love itself, to restore once more something of the *élan vital* which love produces. Again it is evident how interfused love and God are in the poet's emotions. Her 'Song of the Exile' becomes a lament of love which passes into prayer. Concerned with the metaphysical fate of man, and at the same time overcome by her own isolation, she needed human love as the mediator between herself and God, and between God and man. It is therefore not so extraordinary as it may appear that Else Lasker-Schüler, the ageing, uprooted woman, still wrote such ecstatic poems as the late poem **'Ich liebe dich.'** The third stanza with its thrice repeated exclamation 'Ich liebe dich' expresses passionate love, the transcendental effect of which is obvious in the next two stanzas:

> Es öffnen deine Lippen sich . . .
> Die Welt ist taub,
> Die Welt ist blind
>
> Und auch die Wolke
> Und das Laub—
> —Nur wir, der goldene Staub
> Aus dem wir zwei bereitet:
> —Sind!

The state of being thus reached is attained through earthly love but goes beyond it, i.e. from sense to soul. Poems of this kind in the work of Else Lasker-Schüler are perhaps better understood if her earlier poem **'An mein Kind,'** published in 1932 and incorporated again in her last collection of poems *Mein Blaues Klavier,* published in Jerusalem in 1943, is recalled. In it the nature of her love for her son is summed up in the lines:

> Die Liebe zu dir ist das Bildnis,
> Das man sich von Gott machen darf.

As the love of a mother for her son is free from passion, so the transcendental effect of love, in Else Lasker-Schüler's conception of it, leads to that stage beyond passion where love gives a promise of eternal life. In the poem **'Herbst'** in the collection *Mein Blaues Klavier* this stage is the central theme:

> Das ewige Leben *dem,* der viel von Liebe weiss
> zu sagen.
>   Ein Mensch der *Liebe* kann nur auferstehen!

Love here is more embracing than that between two people. It is a basic attitude towards the world, love as the regenerating power leading to a spiritual rebirth in this world and with a promise of eternal life. If the poems in which she expresses her expectation of death are in the first instance the outcome of her hopeless situation in exile, her longing for death is nevertheless as strongly determined by the realization that man can look upon the true reality of God and the soul only after death. Both the beginning and the end of the poem **'Abendzeit,'** a poetic summary of her view of her own life, express her weariness of life. In the third stanza the poet speaks as a mystic who, already freed from the husk of this world, experiences once more the original Creation:

> Und so erlebe ich die Schöpfung dieser Welt,
> Auf Erden schon entkommen ihrer Schale.

Interspersed in some of her prose writings are brief references to the *Cabbala.* As the body ties man to the finite world, so it also tends for her to come between her and her approach to the Infinite God. About this she states:

> Es ist gewiss nicht leicht, mit der ganzen Hingebung seines Herzens zum 'Unsichtbaren Gott' zu beten. . . . Vom Star der Körperhülle erlöst, erkennt aus himmlischer Perspektive, nach dem Erdenleben, die Seele die Seele und—die Weltseele des Herrn [*Dichtungen und Dokumente*].

In moments of inspiration the poet, however, is able to strip the husk from his soul: 'Diesen Zustand nennt man: Inspiration: Platzmachen für Gott!' In such mystic exaltation her soul embraces infinite spheres both in space and time:

> Ich bin der Hieroglyph,
> Der unter der Schöpfung steht
>
> Und mein Auge
> Ist der Gipfel der Zeit;
>
> Sein Leuchten küsst Gottes Saum.
>   **('Mein stilles Lied')**

Here again the influence of the *Cabbala* is traceable, for it teaches that our human world of time and space has come into being by means of emanations descending in diminishing degrees from the highest to the lowest. Considered as gradations of light the worlds of these diminishing degrees comprise the Creator's inner and outer garment, the hem of which is the outer sphere of God. In the soaring-up of love the soul is able to reach this hem, as it were. The three last lines become even clearer if the Cabbalistic conception of Adam Kadmon is recalled. He is the Being made of light, the *radius primus,* who existed before this world and who anticipated the whole Creation. Else Lasker-Schüler states: 'Die Kabbala sagt; "Der erste Mensch lag ein Schein über die Welt gebreitet." ' In the same context she expresses her view that it is the tragedy of the soul that it is endangered by the body. In the most general sense one can take this to mean that the body blinds the soul so that it cannot perceive the light of God, and ties it to this world. Viewed from this angle, the meaning of love in her poetry has to be based upon the idea of Eros as the power which loosens the chains that bind the soul to the body, an ecstatic love lifting the lovers out of Time, a love which stirs visions of an earlier world and which reaches its culminations in union with the Divine. Therefore it is not so extraordinary as it may appear that the love poems of the closing period of her life still contain an erotic element.

There is no doubt that Else Lasker-Schüler's poems are coloured by her own actual experiences. Werner Kraft who was a close friend right to the end of her life says [in *Verse und Prosa aus dem Nachlass,* 1961]: 'Sie ging ihren Weg auch in der Liebe zuende. Es ist kaum glaubhaft und doch wahr, dass diese Frau am Ende ihres Lebens noch einmal geliebt und die ganze Hölle einer hoffnungslosen Leidenschaft durchlitten hat.' This falling in love, with its subsequent disillusionment and ensuing grief, subjectively speaking, may appear as a 'mania'; but objectively considered as an integral part of the whole body of her poetry, it is the result of life in this world. For living without love means living in Time and being exposed to the onslaughts of the world against which most human beings are defenceless. If it is extraordinary that this love sequence persisted to the end, it is equally extraordinary that right up to the end Else Lasker-Schüler felt the loss of her mother acutely, and in the last prose-poem of *Mein Blaues Klavier* comforts herself with the thought that her mother will come and take her to Heaven. Set beside this, the first of her poems on her mother, the dirge with the dedication 'Dem heiligsten Stern über meinem Leben', shows that the loss of her mother produced an awareness of rootlessness, so acute as if her own life had withered away:

So nackt war nie mein Leben,

Page from Der Malik, *with one of Lasker-Schüler's illustrations.*

So in die Zeit gegeben,
Als ob ich abgeblüht

                                              ('Mutter')

As the star is symbolic of nearness to God, and in subsequent poems, e.g. **'Heimlich zur Nacht,'** the beloved is identified with the star, it can be seen that the love Else Lasker-Schüler had to find from another fulfilled the same function as the mother-love she missed, i.e. to give her protection against the vicissitudes of the world. In such a state of vulnerability in Time, the poet increasingly looks forward to existence after death:

Ich träume so fern dieser Erde
Als ob ich gestorben wär
Und nicht mehr verkörpert werde.
                          (**'So lange ist es her. . . . '**)

a state which is, in fact, a return of the soul to timeless pre-existence in God. The three ecstatic states which could lift the poet beyond the temporal world—dream, love, and nearness to God—run as constant possibilities through Else Lasker-Schüler's poetry: either dream alone or dream and love, or love alone—but love was not enough without God. When poetry itself had become alien to her in this world, as the poem which gave her last collection its title shows:

Ich habe zu Hause ein blauses Klavier
Und kenne doch keine Note

and she was no longer able to resolve the dichotomy of her life in terms of transcendental visions, direct acceptance of reality and submission to God take precedence of both love and prayer for love. Her last poem, **'An Apollon,'** gives expression to this, her final attitude:

Die Wirbelwinde hadern mit dem Leben,
Ich halte meine Hände still ergeben
Auf meinem frommbezwungenen Schoss.

Bernhardt G. Blumenthal   (essay date 1970)

SOURCE: "The Play Element in the Poetry of Else Lasker-Schüler," in *The German Quarterly*, Vol. XLIII, September, 1970, pp. 571-76.

[*In the following essay, Blumenthal discusses Lasker-Schüler's use of childhood and play imagery in her love poetry.*]

The poetry of Else Lasker-Schüler is distinguished by its rich and deceptively simple imagery and by the fact that almost all of it consists of love poems. Her poetic acts of love are at once ritual, entertainment, artistry, riddle-making, doctrine, persuasion, sorcery, soothsaying, prophecy, and competition: in short—play. Gottfried Benn knew this and dedicated his volume of verse, *Söhne*, to her playfully: "Ich grüsse Else Lasker-Schüler: ziellose Hand aus Spiel und Blut." The poetess was herself aware of the central position which play occupies in her work and frequently defined her poetic mission in terms of it: "Spielen ist alles," she states simply, for "die Spielsachen sind wohl die Hauptsachen der Welt, die fassbaren und die unberührbaren."

The literature on Else Lasker-Schüler gives, however, very sparse treatment to the play motif in her work. Nowhere is the topic developed beyond a few sentences, and where reference is made to it, play appears only as a mechanism of escape. The poetess' toying with the world, however, constitutes no retreat from life, for she was very much involved with the affairs of everyday life and suffered greatly as a result of this involvement. Her forward thrust to paradise does not pass the world by. Rather, she makes it the object of very profound jesting. With play the poetess strives to overcome obstacles, to unite the disparate elements of life. Play is the product of a special freedom—the freedom of the poetess to express her love for life—in spite of all suffering.

The poetess' games of love recall the spirited play of children who build castles in the sand and fashion worlds from the accustomed things of everyday experience. With fascination she lingers on the hands of the beloved, for these hands still recall the things which they have fondled in childhood: "O, deine Hände / Sind meine Kinder. / Alle meine Spielsachen / Liegen in ihren Gruben." Hands are the vehicles of a special revelation. They fill an essentially sad life with the laughter of games played in forgotten innocence. They imprint forever the landscape of yesterday's wild abandon on the countenance of the beloved: "Niemand kann so schön / Mit deinen Händen spielen, Schlösser bauen, wie ich / Aus Goldfinger; / Burgen mit hohen Türmen! / Strandräuber sind wir dann."

God is but one of the many companions at play that inhabit Lasker-Schüler's world. Despite the great volume of literature on the poetess which attributes her every act to a mythical attachment to Jewish tradition, the playful, loving God of her verse is decidedly not the God of the Old Testament but one of her own creation. She formulates it this way:

Ich habe Gott nie wie einen Lehrer betrachtet, nie wie einen Strafenden oder Starren. Ich konnte ihn mir nur so wie einen innigen Menschen denken, der auch geliebt sein will weich und ohne Nebengedanken, dass er nicht vereinsame unter seinen so vielen Figuren. Manchmal glaubte ich sogar, er helfe mir bei meinen Streichen.

She plays out with God in the game-world what she hopes he will effect in reality. Her creative toying with the world involves participation in divine acts. It is a question of playing out cosmic events in poetry, of elevating the game's designer to assume a role as co-creator with God. The game, therefore, becomes sacred; its moves save and sanctify. The one condition for salvation in the game is faith, a willingness to play along.

The dialogue which Else Lasker-Schüler maintains with God in her verse is childlike and playful, for she hopes in a naive attachment to Him to find favor and gain grace for herself and her loved ones. She encourages a Creator, frustrated by His own creation, to take heart: "Gott weine nicht" and reestablish faith in men. Her conversations of innocence are those both of a bereaved woman and a happy, irresponsible child. Often, indeed, her writing is too coy. There is at times an embarrassing affectation about her work, a willful naiveté, as though she were determined to be not only a child in the eyes of God, but to be a spoiled one. Her love affair with God, however, uniquely blends whimsicality and wisdom, so that what seems at first to be idle play suddenly turns to revelation. The teasing is a prelude to love. The entire process of flirtation and wooing, as an introduction to love, is, as Huizinga points out, a matter of play. It involves in Else Lasker-Schüler's case the creation of obstacles, surprise, pretense, and tension.

In play Else Lasker-Schüler gains distance from prosaic reality and tries to give authentic existence to the despiritualized things of the external world that she so loves. "Es giebt nur eine Rettung," she notes, "mein Spiel." She sought sanctuary in play, although she knew that the poet—even as player—could not triumph over the powers of darkness in life. The player-protagonist of her poems lacks the physical and spiritual strength to assert himself in the world and can not drive the forces of destruction from life. Her early verse, written during her years in Berlin in association with Peter Hille, is especially playful. The personal tragedies of her middle and later years, however, introduce sadness into her verse and occasion the loss of her naive faith in the world. She found her own postwar world barren: democracy was without splendor; fascism was without humanity, and she abhorred both. She substituted monarchy, a play-world of kings and princes that recalls Biblical times and preserves a link with the past. The increasing melancholy of her later work is, however, not without its playfulness. Even in old age she regarded herself as a child: "Ich sitze noch heute sitzengeblieben auf der untersten Bank der Schulklasse, wie einst . . . Doch mit spätem versunkenem Herzen: 1000 und 2-jährig, dem Märchen über den Kopf gewachsen." The spirit of playfulness never left her, not even in moments of great despair. Rejected and abandoned in her love, she chides her fickle lover: "O du falscher Gaukler, / Du spanntest ein loses Seil." The "Gaukler" has broken faith with the principal player and must be ejected from the game-world.

The poetess' unusually creative handling of poetic language and style is a product both of her uninhibited verbal playfulness and her search for more authentic expression. She has a naive affinity for the word and a special talent for producing new vocabulary items from combinations of existing ones: for example, "hindusanft," "Mostvergorenheit," and "Stiefkönigin." Some words are especially appealing to her, and she employs them in frequent and novel combinations: *"alt"*: "gott*alt*," "pharaonen*alt*," "schöpfungs*alt*," "sinai*alt*," "zeder*alt*," and "alt*alt*;" *"jung"*: "adam*jung*," "blüten*jung*," and "blutmut*jung*;" and *"bunt"*: "*bunt*gebenedeit," "*bunt*geknüpft," "*bunt*umschlungen," and "teppich*bunt*gestickt."

She frequently brings the contents of an entire sentence playfully into one word: for example, "blauvertausendfacht," "gottgelichtet," and "liebesruhen"; or she appends to a word the prefix or, more frequently, the suffix of some other vocabulary item, like *"ge*mondet," "betu*sam*," "bl-au*erlei*," and "mein*wärts*." Here too the poetess has a predilection for toying with word-parts, which recur in frequent and different combinations in her work: "*-ab*": "er-

den*ab*," "fern*ab*," "grau*ab*," "herz*ab*," and "kugel*ab*"; *"-auf"*: "herz*auf*," "Räum*auf*-Träum*auf*," and "rund*auf*"; *"-her"*: "damals*her*," "düster*her*," and "taumel-*her*," *"-hin"*: "gott*hin*," "hell*hin*," "herz*hin*pochend," "heute*hin*," "leise*hin*," "nacht*hin*," "schwarz*hin*," "traum*hin*," and "wandel*hin*"; and *"-weise"*: "gold*weise*" and "traum*weise*." At times the poetess would devaluate her own rational powers and express herself in the singsong rhythms, alliterative devices, diminutives, onomatopoetic sounds, and naively constructed rhymes of children's speech. Two of her poems, **"Weltflucht"** and **"Marie von Nazareth,"** are reworkings of earlier versions written in "mystical Asiatic," a language drawn from Hebrew roots, but decidedly of her own creation. This is the mystical dream language of her childhood and age of innocence.

Love in her poetry is associated again and again with play. The poetess refers to her heart as "mein spielendes Herz" and describes its activities as: "Mein Herz spielt mit dem jungen Morgenrot" and "Um deinen süssesten Brunnen / Gaukelte mein Herz." Play is an artful imitation of reality; it designs its own actuality by toying creatively with the world. Play, excited by love, is the springboard for Lasker-Schüler's extralogical, quasi-mystical experiences. Playfully she clothes the personages of her verse in the imagery of childhood. Each of her lovers and friends receives a new name; this is a title of nobility with which they can gain entrance into the unbroken world of her dreams. She explains it this way: "Jedenfalls liebe ich nach meiner Sehnsucht die Leute alle zu kleiden, damit ein Spiel zu Stande kommt." Her father, the banker Aron Schüler, for example, appears in the accounts of her youth as "Arthur Schüler," town architect (in view of the regal position of authority which her father occupied in her private world, possibly a playful allusion to King Arthur of the Round Table and an expression of her belief that her father as king and architect would construct castles for her in life, where she could dream the dream of a better world for herself and her loved ones); Peter Hille, the rock upon which she founded her temple of verse, becomes the apostle "Petrus"; and Franz Marc, her "blauer Reiter." She dubbed Karl Kraus as a high priest of language and as an arbiter of good taste in literature, "der Dalai-Lama" and "der Cardinal" and Gottfried Benn, her minstrel, "Giselheer," and her fickle lover, "Barbar." She assumes oriental titles for herself, which play on themes from *The Thousand and One Nights* and Bible stories, and refers to herself as "dein spielender Herzschelm," "dein spielerischer Bibelprinz," and as a "spielendes Sternenmädchen." Those others who act out the drama of her playful heart appear in her verse as "Süssgeliebter," "der kleine Süsskönig," "kleiner Spielkönig," "Spielgefährte" and "Spielgenosse." In the play-sphere her make-believe princes and kings become real; they acquire a spiritual dimension that they would not ordinarily possess.

The poetess' desire for total possession of the beloved, however, threatens to take the fun out of the game and destroy it. Sexual union is a religious act for her, and the erotic play of her early verse is but an intense form of love mysticism. The cabala, the great collection of Jewish mysticism, teaches that the intellect resides in the senses; Eros is truth. Else Lasker-Schüler, who was familiar with the cabala, sought in the uninhibited expression of love that perfect physical and spiritual union which a man and a woman must attain to gain deliverance. She is, therefore, unashamed in the declaration of her love. She offers herself to the beloved in the most unrestrained fashion; her love partners never satisfy her demand; only the designer of the game is proficient at it.

Else Lasker-Schüler's game of love is her grand design for life. Her playful verse, a product of what Hermann Hesse in *Das Glasperlenspiel* terms "die freispielende Plastizität der Spielsprache," attempts to restore lost vigor to sterile reality, warmth and charm to a language which has become a mass of clichés, and love to depersonalized human relationships. Her game-world recalls childhood; it is her vision of paradise; it is her world of freedom. The rules of the game define the limits of her world and the specific spheres of influence for each of her protagonists. They guarantee her loved ones protection from life's harm and exclude from the protective circle of her private world those who have transgressed the rules.

Hans W. Cohn (essay date 1974)

SOURCE: "The Swing of the Pendulum: The Backward Movement, Withdrawal," in *Else Lasker-Schüler: The Broken World,* Cambridge University Press, 1974, pp. 37-79.

[*In the following excerpt, Cohn examines several of Lasker-Schüler's works, demonstrating the departure from reality evidenced in her poetry.*]

It is my intention to show the bipolar structure of Else Lasker-Schüler's mode of being, as it manifests itself in her poetry. I have chosen to start with an examination of the various manifestations of her tendency to withdraw from reality, and to follow this with a consideration of the opposite tendency, her outgoing search for contact.

This order of examination is not immediately given by the bipolar structure of withdrawal and outgoing. Using the image of the swinging pendulum, it is clear that, to some extent, it is arbitrary at what point we start to describe its movement. Throughout Else Lasker-Schüler's life, outgoing and withdrawal impulses alternated, often in quick succession. If, nevertheless, I have chosen to examine her search for contact *after* her tendency to withdraw, it is because I believe that in the highest manifestation of this search, her search for God, she came closest to reconciling the opposing forces, and that she came increasingly closer to this point of reconciliation—the point where the pendulum comes to rest in a centre—as she grew older.

The constant alternation of outgoing and withdrawal impulses is also reflected in her poetry. This fact poses a special problem in the development of my theme: for I find myself under the necessity of having to consider apart what, in reality, belongs together. In most of her poems outgoing and withdrawal elements can be found side by side, though emphasis may lie on one or the other. Similarly, the various forms of withdrawal shade into each other: thus, disappointment, resentment, despair, isolation and

fantasies cannot always be clearly separated. In the same way, the longing for human contact, for the more specific erotic encounter and the search for God tend to merge. I have, nevertheless, attempted to find a number of poems which show a particular tendency sufficiently strongly to serve as illustrations, and I have added stanzas, or lines from other poems, for further elucidation.

Another difficulty must here be mentioned. An outgoing element can be coloured or distorted by an underlying withdrawal impulse, and vice versa; thus, the image of God can take on an infantile shape, while a concern with death will appear, at times, not as the extreme of self-destructiveness, but as a transition pointing towards acceptance and reconciliation. We are here faced with the basic problem which a necessarily 'linear' treatment of a 'polyphonic' theme presents: the limitations of any classification must constantly be borne in mind lest it turn into a straitjacket for the living phenomena which we are trying to observe.

Finally, I wish to say something about the way in which I have subdivided the two main parts of my work. The principle which I adopted in order to describe the various forms of withdrawal and outgoing we meet in Else Lasker-Schüler's poetry is that of intensification. Thus, in the section on withdrawal, disappointment is the awareness of a failure of contact, to which resentment is the aggressive reaction. Despair enlarges the area of resentment, turning it against the world as well as against oneself, while isolation is the resulting state of lack of contact. From this state, escape is sought in wishes for loss of life (concern with death) or loss of identity (flight into fantasies).

Similarly, the categories of outgoing present an intensification of the outgoing impulse: from the longing for contact in general through the specific wish for contact with another person in the erotic encounter to the search for the highest 'person', God.

THE BACKWARD MOVEMENT: WITHDRAWAL

(I) *Disappointment and Resentment*

'Abschied'

Aber du kamst nie mit dem Abend—
Ich saß im Sternenmantel.

. . . Wenn es an mein Haus pochte,
War es mein eigenes Herz.

Das hängt nun an jedem Türpfosten,
Auch an deiner Tür;

Zwischen Farren verlöschende Feuerrose
Im Braun der Guirlande.

Ich färbte dir den Himmel brombeer
Mit meinem Herzblut.

Aber du kamst nie mit dem Abend—
. . . Ich stand in goldenen Schuhen.

The poem **'Abschied'** is found in the collection *Meine Wunder* and is included in the section dedicated to Hans Adalbert von Maltzahn. It is, therefore, possible that the poem is addressed to him, though love poems explicitly addressed to other men are included in this section. The factual circumstances under which Else Lasker-Schüler's poems were written are often very difficult, if not impossible, to ascertain. What matters here is that this is one of the numerous poems expressing her disappointment in someone's failure to return her love: the mere number of such poems indicates that the involvement was more often imaginary than actual.

The first and last stanzas describe the situation of disappointment: she was ready for the beloved, he did not come. Her readiness is expressed by the way in which she has adorned herself for him: 'Ich saß im Sternenmantel.'... 'Ich stand in goldenen Schuhen.'

In 'Sternenmantel' we meet one of Else Lasker-Schüler's most important, though also most elusive, symbols. In the context of this poem, 'Stern' probably signified, in [W.] Muschg's words, 'das Wunder schlechthin, die Gnade der Liebe' ['Else Lasker-Schüler,' *Von Trakl zu Brecht,* 1961]. But Muschg proceeds to enumerate many other meanings, and we will come to see that the star is perhaps best understood as a symbol of transcendence.

She uses colour symbolically, as it was used by most German Expressionist writers and painters, particularly by her friend Franz Marc. Once more, we can follow Muschg, who suggests that 'das mythische Bild des Goldes' expresses in this poet's work 'vor allem die erotische Erfüllung'. ([G.] Guder's interpretation [in *Else Lasker-Schüler,* 1966] of the colour gold as either indicating nobility or being just used for decoration seems to me insufficient.) Muschg adds that 'die Goldfarbe erzeugt bei ihr unfehlbar Märchenstimmung', and certainly a legendary feeling is created in this poem that removes the event from reality.

The second stanza depicts the sensation of futile waiting simply and realistically, but this is followed, in the following stanzas, by a sudden switch-over to fantastic elaboration, reminding one of the 'conceits' of seventeenth-century poetry. The heart is another fundamental symbol of Else Lasker-Schüler's, a 'Grundwort', as Muschg calls it. Her use of it is essentially straightforward and traditional: it is the seat of feeling, and therefore, at the same time, the core of being. This basic meaning undergoes, however, a great many variations. The third stanza shows the heart exposed in all its vulnerability, and there is a characteristic tendency to turn the personal into the universal ('an jedem Türpfosten'). The fourth, with a sudden change of imagery, introduces the death theme, never far away in these poems of 'withdrawal': the heart has become a 'verlöschende Feuerrose'. In the fifth stanza, the depth of her love is expressed by a hyperbolic image which, again, is significant for her need to draw the whole world, here the sky, into the whirl of her feeling. This refusal to distinguish between objective reality and subjective experience, this 'romantische Ichbezogenheit' (Muschg), is a fundamental aspect of Else Lasker-Schüler's life, as the outline of her biography has shown, and we meet it here as an important element in her poetry.

The emphasis in this poem is on the poet's disappointment in a love situation. No open resentment against the lover is expressed, though a faint note of reproach can perhaps be felt throughout which becomes audible in 'auch an deiner Tür' and 'Ich färbte dir den Himmel brombeer'. Such restraint is rare. In the following poem which belongs to the same collection, and forms part of a cycle reflecting her relationship with Gottfried Benn, her resentment of the lover's rejection breaks through:

'Hinter Bäumen berg ich mich'

Bis meine Augen ausgeregnet haben,

Und halte sie tief verschlossen,
Daß niemand dein Bild schaut.

Ich schlang meine Arme um dich
Wie Gerank.

Bin doch mit dir verwachsen,
Warum reißt du mich von dir?

Ich schenkte dir die Blüte
Meines Leibes,

Alle meine Schmetterlinge
Scheuchte ich in deinen Garten.

Immer ging ich durch Granaten,
Sah durch dein Blut

Die Welt überall brennen
Vor Liebe.

Nun aber schlage ich mit meiner Stirn
Meine Tempelwände düster.

O du falscher Gaukler,
Du spanntest ein loses Seil.

Wie kalt mir alle Grüße sind,
Mein Herz liegt bloß,

Mein rot Fahrzeug
pocht grausig.

Bin immer auf See
Und lande nicht mehr.

The title of this poem which forms, at the same time, the first line states the theme of withdrawal: her reaction to her lover's rejection is to hide herself, and a state of isolation is already implied in this. (It can here be seen how impossible it is to separate the various 'categories' of withdrawal.) The next lines develop her conception of love as a complete fusion of the lovers, a conception which carries the seed of disappointment in itself: she has taken the image of the beloved, preserved in her eyes, with her into hiding, guarding it jealously (stanzas 1 and 2)—as they had grown into one ('bin doch mit dir verwachsen'), how did he dare to destroy this one-ness (stanzas 3 and 4)? At this point, her resentment breaks into the open. It is interesting to see how clearly, though probably unintentionally, she expresses the suffocating effect which her total demand must have had on those she loved: 'Ich schlang meine Arme um dich / Wie Gerank.' It was this aspect of her approach to others which alienated many of her friends, and provoked the attacks of her enemies.

The next four stanzas further elaborate her vision of love: she has given herself totally, and has seen the whole world in terms of this fusion ('durch dein Blut'). Again, the equation between the world and herself is more than a metaphor: it is an expression of her way of being. In the lover's refusal the whole world seems to deny her. Stanzas 9 and 11-13 depict the poet's 'world' after the lover's refusal. Stanza 9 is elliptical; I suggest this paraphrase: her love has now become a prison, darkened by her self-destructive protest. The last three stanzas show in greater details the effect the lover's rejection has had on the poet's 'world'. All(!) greetings have become cold (stanza 11). Her heart, the vehicle that conveys her through life, is damaged and no longer able to bring her back to safety (stanzas 12 and 13). In these lines themes that go beyond disappointment and resentment are sounded: the image of the injured heart implies a threat to life itself, and the concluding lines conjure up the Flying Dutchman, a potent symbol of isolation.

This depiction of the way in which the poet's 'world' is affected by her disappointment is interrupted by two lines (stanza 10) which are a vehement expression of her resentment, taking the form of an accusation: the lover has tricked her. The image of the betrayer luring his victim on to a loose rope points at another aspect of Else Lasker-Schüler's view of her love relationships: she sees herself completely at the mercy of the other, balanced in a state of utter precariousness.

It is thus her own heart whose vulnerability she describes in a variety of images, while the heart of the lover, in its stony coldness, represents the threat:

> Ich baute uns ein Himmelreich, dir unantastbar
>   zu gehören
> —Das an den Riffen deiner Herzensnacht zerbrach.
>
> Als an deinem steinernen Herzen
> Meine Flügel brachen,
>
> Fielen die Amseln wie Trauerrosen
> Hoch vom blauen Gebüsch.

But the longing for the erotic encounter is only a particular instance of her longing for contact; and disappointment and resentment are experienced and expressed equally strongly on a more general plane. In the early poem **'Mein Drama'**, there is a sudden transition from the expression of frustration in a private love situation to a total rejection of 'Mann und Weib':

> . . . Mit allen duftsüssen Scharlachblumen
>   Hat er mich gelockt,
> Es regt sich wieder weh in meiner Seele
> Und leitet mich durch all' Erinnern weit.
> Sei still, mein wilder Engel mein,
>   Gott weine nicht
>   Und schweige von dem Leid,
> Mein Schmerzen soll sich nicht entladen,
> Keinen Glauben hab' ich mehr an Weib und
>   Mann,
> Den Faden, der mich hielt mit allem Leben,
> Hab' ich der Welt zurückgegeben
>   Freiwillig!

This rejection leads again to a withdrawal from 'allem Leben', a withdrawal which gives the title to another early poem, **'Weltflucht'**, which I wish to examine more closely:

> Ich will in das Grenzenlose

> Zu mir zurück,
> Schon blüht die Herbstzeitlose
>   Meiner Seele,
> Vielleicht—ist's schon zu spät zurück!
> O, ich sterbe unter Euch!
> Da Ihr mich erstickt mit Euch.
> Fäden möchte ich um mich ziehn—
> Wirrwarr endend!
>   Beirrend,
> Euch verwirrend,
>   Um zu entfliehn
>   Meinwärts!

Though this poem is not divided into stanzas, three parts can be clearly distinguished. The first (lines 1-5) expresses the wish to withdraw, the second (lines 6 and 7) says something about what provokes this withdrawal, the third (lines 8-13) elaborates the form which the withdrawal takes.

The first five lines work out the theme stated by the title: the poet wishes to withdraw 'in das Grenzenlose / Zu mir zurück'—the form of the escape from reality is that of a withdrawal to herself and beyond that into an undifferentiated realm which, I think, we would be justified in calling the unconscious. The use of another Freudian term seems equally appropriate, that of 'regression': the meeting with others is felt as too difficult, and a retreat into a more self-related ('narcissistic'), less conscious position is the result. The anxiety which such a situation generates is expressed in lines 3-5 where the 'autumn crocus of the soul' hints at the closeness of winter which here is probably an allusion to death. 'Vielleicht—ist's schon zu spät zurück!' is the voice of naked panic.

The next two lines give strong expression to the poet's resentment: other people are felt as a threat to her life, they suffocate her, it seems, by their very existence; no concrete reason is given. We meet such apparently unmotivated outbursts against 'die Menschen' also in her letters to [Karl] Kraus; thus, she writes in a letter dated 20.4.11: 'Aber die Menschen sind mir über; ich bin müde.' Perhaps the occurrence of the word 'Wirrwarr' in line 9 throws some light on the nature of her feeling of suffocation: being with others inevitably causes 'confusion', reality is muddled and lacks the clear-cut, simple outlines of her image of paradise, and this 'confusion' can only be ended by separation.

The remainder of the poem shows how this separation comes about: the poet spins a web in order to cover her retreat 'meinwärts'. [C.] Heselhaus' comments on these lines are relevant:

> Dahinter steht das alte Dichter-Emblem: der Seidenwurm, der sich mit dem eigenen Gespinst sein Grab spinnt. Goethe hat dieses Bild, das schon bei Petrarca auftaucht, seinem Tasso in den Mund gelegt ['Else Lasker-Schülers literarisches Traumspiel,' *Deutsche Lyrik der Moderne*, 1961].

In this poem, resentment of the others' existence is expressed without any disappointment being brought out. In the long poem **'Mein stilles Lied'** her disappointment in men as well as her desperate need for contact are displayed:

Meine Lieder trugen des Sommers Bläue
Und kehrten düster heim.

Verhöhnt habt ihr mir meine Lippe
Und redet mit ihr.

Doch ich griff nach euren Händen,
Denn meine Liebe ist ein Kind und wollte
    spielen.

Here it is the rejection of her poetry, in which she quite naively saw a gift to the world, which throws her into disillusionment. The second of the three stanzas quoted here is rather enigmatic: what does 'Und redet mit ihr' mean? Perhaps an answer can be found in a sentence from a letter addressed to Kraus: '(. . .) aber alle lieben wohl meine Gedichte—Niemand mein Herz.' It seems to me as if the two lines in **'Mein stilles Lied'** echo this—a complaint that people try to dissociate her from her work, appreciating the poetry without acknowledging the poet.

Also the third stanza quoted here is worth looking at: it brings in two more key-words of Else Lasker-Schüler— 'Kind' and 'spielen'. Childhood meant to her a kind of paradise before the Fall, a return to it a way out of the 'Wirrwarr' of adult life. We shall have to concern ourselves with this aspect of her impulse to withdraw when we turn to her flight into fantasies. At this point, it seems to me important to observe that the image of love as a child arises at the very moment when she most passionately expresses her longing for contact. But where a grown-up person's love wants to 'play', disappointment is inevitable. The outgoing impulse is distorted by a regressive tendency.

Sometimes, the resentment of the other is balanced by a feeling of her own failure. Thus, in **'Abschied'**, she says: 'Ich hab' die Welt, die Welt hat mich betrogen,' and similarly in **'Dämmerung'**, a poem published posthumously: 'Mich hat das Leben, ich hab es verstoßen.' Something of a realization of her own withdrawal from life which is seen as a betrayal and a rejection breaks through. In **'Abschied'** this is followed by a question which will be seen to be her principal question: where, in all this, is God? Has he withdrawn from his creature in anger and dismay?

Warum hat Gott im Osten wetterleuchtend sich
    verzogen,
Vom Ebenbilde Seines Menschen übermannt?

The question remains here unanswered, and the poem ends on a note of desolation:

Und was mich je mit Seiner Schöpfung Ruhetag
    verband,
Ist wie ein spätes Adlerheer unstät in diese Dun-
    kelheit geflogen.

In **'Dämmerung'** the recognition of her own rejection of life is followed by what seems to be a half-awareness of the precariousness of her flight into fantasy:

Und lebe angstvoll nun im Übergroßen
Im irdischen Leibe schon im Himmelreich.

The withdrawal to an imaginary paradise, which is here seen as a state of life-in-death, is experienced as 'angstvoll'.

In **'Letzter Abend im Jahr'**, she is able to express loneliness without resentment:

Mein Herz blieb ganz für sich
Und fand auf Erden keinen Trost.

The tone of this poem is one of sadness rather than anger, and out of this more accepting mood, a different kind of question arises, a question not about, but to, God:

O Gott, wie kann der Mensch verstehen,
Warum der Mensch haltlos vom Menschtum
    bricht,
Sich wieder sammeln muß im höheren Gesche-
hen.

Another stage of her experience of loneliness is reached: she does not fight it, nor does she put all the blame on the behaviour of others—she simply asks for the ability to understand the limitations of man.

In her love poetry, too, she achieves at times a quieter, more accepting note, particularly in the cycle **'An Ihn'** which appeared two years before her death as the last section of her last collection of poetry. Here contact with the beloved remains unattainable, but resentment has given way to longing. The following poem conveys the theme of rejection with a quiet simplicity which she did not often command. Once again, the heart is the central symbol, but the imagery is here much less baroque:

'Und'

Und hast mein Herz verschmäht—
In die Himmel wärs geschwebt
Selig aus dem engen Zimmer!

Wenn der Mond spazieren geht,
Hör ichs pochen immer
Oft bis spät.

Aus Silberfäden zart gedreht
Mein weiß Gerät—
Trüb nun sein Schimmer.

In the same cycle, however, we find also more discordant poems. In **'Apollo'** a number of different modes of reaction can be found side by side. There is the element of acceptance:

Ich halte meine Hände still ergeben
Auf meinem frommbezwungenen Schoß

but also the escape into fantasy and the past:

Ein Engel spielte sanft auf blauen Tasten,
Langher verklungene Phantasie.

There is the extravagantly phrased outburst of despair:

Jäh tut mein sehr verwaistes Herz mir weh—
Blutige Fäden spalten seine Stille.
Zwei Augen blicken wund durch ihre Mar-
morhülle
In meines pochenden Granates See.

And there is the note of resentment against the unfaithful lover, characteristically transformed into the God Apollo:

Nicht mal sein Götterlächeln
Ließ er mir zum Pfande.

Even at the end of her life, when she often came much closer to acceptance and reconciliation, the split was never quite healed.

(2) *Despair and Isolation*

'Ich liege wo am Wegrand'

Ich liege wo am Wegrand übermattet—
Und über mir die finstere kalte Nacht—
Und zähl schon zu den Toten längst bestattet.

Wo soll ich auch noch hin—von Grauen über-
schattet—
Die ich vom Monde euch mit Liedern still bedacht
Und weite Himmel blauvertausendfacht.

Die heilige Liebe, die ihr blind zertratet,
Ist Gottes Ebenbild . . . !
Fahrlässig umbebracht.

Darum auch lebten du und ich in einem Schacht!
Und—doch im Paradiese trunken blumumblattet.

With this text we move one step further on the path of withdrawal—from disappointment and resentment to despair and isolation. The first stanza of the poem conjures up the image of the aimless wanderer, a symbol of isolation like that of the never-landing sailor. . . . Night, as often in Else Lasker-Schüler's poetry, is experienced as cold and hostile, and the third line introduces the death-in-life theme to be examined at a later point. The next stanza elaborates the picture of the outcast: there is an element of resentment against those to whom she has given her songs and who have not accepted her, reminding us of the lines from **'Mein stilles Lied'** . . . :

Meine Lieder trugen des Sommers Bläue
Und kehrten düster heim.

Verhöhnt habt ihr mir meine Lippe
Und redet mit ihr.

In the corresponding lines 'Die ich vom Monde euch mit Liedern still bedacht / Und weite Himmel blauvertausendfacht' there is a note of superiority which can be found also in other poems, as for instance in **'Ankunft'**, another poem depicting extreme isolation, which ends with the line 'Aber meine Schultern heben sich, hochmütige Kuppeln'. By this superiority the outcast seems to take a revenge on a world that has rejected her, a revenge which in Else Lasker-Schüler's case we can assume to have been unconscious.

In this stanza we also meet an important example of Else Lasker-Schüler's colour symbolism. In her essay on Carl Sonnenschein, she herself commented on what some of the primary colours meant to her:

Seine Seele, eine fromme dreifarbige Fahne; ihr weißes Linnen, ein Symbol seines makellosen Wandels, der rote Streif hielt sein Leben wach und lebendig für den aufopfernden Dienst an der Menschheit; doch das zarte Blau führte ihn ungehemmt in die höhere Welt.

It is this meaning of the colour blue that is carried by her neologism 'blauvertausendfacht'. Blue is for her the colour of the spirit, as it had been for the Middle Ages, not always simply 'Gottesfarbe', 'die Farbe der göttlichen Offenbarung', but always pointing beyond the conflicts and confusion of worldly existence, like the star a transcending symbol. In this poem, she sees herself as a kind of divine messenger, and this gives special weight to the world's rejection.

The accusation becomes more vehement in the following stanza: the world has not only refused the divine message, it has killed love itself, and as love is 'Gottes Ebenbild', it has killed God. Here is one of the approximations to Christian ideas to which we shall return. The consequences of the world's murder of love (=God) are expressed in the first line of the last stanza, and again we observe that romantic fusion of the universal and the personal characteristic of this poet: because 'ihr' (i.e. the world) have destroyed love, 'du und ich' (i.e. the poet and her lover) are imprisoned in darkness, 'in einem Schacht'.

The last line brings a sudden break-through of the opposite: the dark pit is also paradise. However, I am not certain whether this line expresses a genuine acceptance of the reality of human love, which, whatever its limitations, can still be 'blumumblattet', or whether the use of the word 'trunken' indicates a state less real and closer to a fantasy which drowns despair in forgetfulness.

The image of the eternal wanderer which dominates this poem recurs throughout Else Lasker-Schüler's poetry. Thus, **'Lied meines Lebens'** starts with the (twice-repeated) line 'Sieh in mein verwandertes Gesicht,' and one of the poems published in *Nachlaß* brings another variation on the theme of the sailor 'immer auf See':

Wir treiben durch den Ozean der Luft,
Und jedem Wind weiht jede Blume ihren Duft,
Und immer landet nur der Tod (. . .)

In **'Mein Tanzlied'** the eternal dancer joins the eternal wanderer and the eternal sailor as an incarnation of rest- and rootlessness:

So tanz' ich schon seit tausend Jahr,
Seit meiner ersten Ewigkeiten.

Despair is here experienced as an infinite state, as also in the poem that takes as its title and theme a line in which Richard Dehmel is said to have summed up his impression of the poet, 'Täubchen, das in seinem eigenen Blute schwimmt':

Als ich also diese Worte an mich las,
Erinnerte ich mich
Tausend Jahre meiner.

Eisige Zeiten verschollen—Leben vom Leben,
Wo liegt mein Leben—
Und träumt nach meinem Leben.

Ich lag allen Tälern im Schoß,
Umklammerte alle Berge,
Aber nie meine Seele wärmte mich (. . .)

This experience of being 'verschollen' we found condensed into the two words 'wurde Robinson' in the biographical sketch which she wrote for [the first Expressionist anthology], *Menschheitsdämmerung* [1920]. In one of her essays, after remembering a family scene which spelt warmth and security, she writes:

> Das ist lange her, ich weiß auch nicht, warum ich daran so oft denke, zumal ich doch Robinson wurde, durchbrannte in die Welt, weil ich dem Robinson auf dem Deckel seiner Geschichte so ähnlich sah.

But there was also the fear of the crippling narrowness of such security, hinted at in the next sentence of this passage:

> Und ich liebte das Abenteuer, das hat nichts mit der Stube zu tun, und wenn es auch eine herrliche ist.

In a letter to Ludwig von Ficker, the editor of *Der Brenner* and friend of [Georg] Trakl, this longing for the sea as an embodiment of creative freedom, and the dread of the inhibiting heaviness of 'das Schwarze der Erde', finds vivid expression:

> Lauter Wasser, manchmal hängen Muscheln an mir, Seetiere; ich erschrecke nur, wenn Erde an mir hängt. Ich finde das Schwarze der Erde nicht abzuschütteln. Ich bin so herunter, sitz ich und will dichten, bin ich wie Welle, muß zurück, so aber ohne Strand und Hand.

The last sentence points to the ambiguity of her experience: she feels the threat of 'Erde', of security; but the insecurity of 'lauter Wasser', of being 'ohne Strand', leaves her also 'ohne Hand', that is paralysed, without creative impulse.

In **'Ich liege wo am Wegrand'** we find the elements of disappointment and resentment intensified to despair and isolation. But there is still a reference to a specific love relationship. The following poem conveys the state of despair as such, in all its nakedness:

'Chaos'

Die Sterne fliehen schreckensbleich
Vom Himmel meiner Einsamkeit,
Und das schwarze Auge der Mitternacht
Starrt näher und näher.

Ich finde mich nicht wieder
In dieser Todverlassenheit!
Mir ist: ich lieg' von mir weltenweit
Zwischen grauer Nacht der Urangst . . .

Ich wollte, ein Schmerzen rege sich
Und stürze mich grausam nieder
Und riß mich jäh an mich!
Und es lege eine Schöpferlust
Mich wieder in meine Heimat Unter der Mutterbrust.

Meine Mutterheimat ist seeleleer,
Es blühen dort keine Rosen
Im warmen Odem mehr.—
. . . Möcht einen Herzallerliebsten haben!
Und mich in seinem Fleisch vergraben.

As so often, the first stanza presents the theme as an image. The stars, symbols of the grace of love, are in flight from what she calls, with characteristic ambiguity, the 'Himmel meiner Einsamkeit'. Again, night is experienced

as a threat. In the next stanza, the poet describes a state of extreme abandonment: this is felt in the first two lines, once more, as 'Todverlassenheit', in the following two as an estrangement from herself in 'grauer Nacht der Urangst'. It is interesting to observe how here, as in other places, the extreme emotional pressure destroys the grammatical structure: 'zwischen' is, of course, grammatically incorrect here, but it conveys the feeling of being caught more precisely than any other preposition.

The beginning of the third stanza shows her intuitive psychological awareness: if only she could feel pain, she would come to herself again. The deadness which is at the core of despair is this very inability to feel the pain that is nevertheless there, though cut off from conscious experience. The poet's intuition expresses a truth which is the psychotherapist's daily experience. In these lines there is an opening towards reality from which, however, she turns away in the remainder of the stanza: there is a regressive movement towards childhood, towards the 'Heimat unter der Mutterbrust'.

The impossibility of such a 'return' is seen at the beginning of the last stanza, but in regret, not in acceptance. The end of the poem brings the image of sexual union as an alternative out of the 'chaos' of despair. But this is seen as a means to forget, a kind of death ('Und mich in seinem Fleisch vergraben') rather than a forward movement towards contact and meeting.

All concrete references have disappeared from this poem. A fundamental state of mind is revealed which is perhaps best understood through the keyword 'Urangst'. Anxiety is the emotional experience which, above all, characterizes the state of rootlessness and isolation. F. J. Schneider points to Else Lasker-Schüler's great gift for expressing this experience:

> Kein Moderner hat ergreifender wie sie die beklemmenden Angstgefühle eines einsam, steuer- und kompasslos gewordenen Menschenherzen ausgesprochen. [*Der expressive Menschund die deutsche Lyrik der Geggenwart*, 1927]

The poet herself, in *Ich räume auf,* has linked the feeling of not belonging anywhere with the experience of 'Angst':

> (. . .) überall blicke ich nach einem heimatlichen Boden aus, wer von uns hätte den gefunden und nicht erlitten des Heimwehs qualvollste Angst. . . .

The experience of 'existential anxiety' is always also an opportunity for change. It is the point where the pendulum may swing in the opposite direction. In this poem, as we have seen, this does not happen: in sexual and childhood fantasies the opportunity is lost.

But there are poems which show such a turning point. In such poems, questions again occur, carrying the poet's search for meaning. They are usually questions to God:

> Ich suchte Gott auf innerlichsten Wegen
> Und kräuselte die Lippe nie zum Spott.
> In meinem Herzen fällt ein Tränenregen;
> Wie soll ich dich erkennen lieber Gott . . .
>
> O mein Gott mein, nur alleine,

Lasker-Schüler circa 1912. Dressed in her customary exotic garb, she often played the flute during her poetry readings.

> Ich verdurste und verweine
> In dem Segen (. . .)
>
> Und ich kann es nicht verstehen,
> Da ich unter seinem Dach
> Oft so traurig erwach.

There are attempts to understand her despair as a kind of atonement for her neglect of the task which God has given her:

> Es lehren Flügelmenschen, die des Wegs ein
>   Stück
> Mich, meines Amtes wegen, stärken und
>   begießen—
> Und wieder jenseits in die Lüfte fließen:
> Daß ich für—unerfüllte Gottesweisung—büße.

We have seen before how much she saw her writing of poetry as a divine 'office', and that she considered the rejection of her poems by the world as a rejection of something larger than herself. In this stanza she takes upon herself the responsibility which such an 'office' carries.

In **'Aus der Ferne'** she sees exile itself as a condition for a closer contact with God:

> Es wachsen auch die Seelen der verpflanzten
>   Bäume
> Auf Erden schon in Gottes blaue Räume,
> Um inniger von Seiner Herrlichkeit zu träumen.

In this, as in many others of her poems, the appearance of God is like a break in the wall of isolation, the possibility of contact enters like a shaft of light, and despair turns into sadness and longing.

In these poems, the pendulum swings out of despair forward into a search for meaning—in **'Ankunft,'** by contrast, the pendulum, swinging back into complete withdrawal, has reached a point of isolation where despair is no longer felt:

> Ich bin am Ziel meines Herzens angelangt.
> Weiter führt kein Strahl.
> Hinter mir laß ich die Welt,
> Fliegen die Sterne auf: Goldene Vögel.
> Hißt der Mondturm die Dunkelheit—
>   . . . O, wie mich leise eine süße Weise
>   betönt . . .
> Aber meine Schultern heben sich, hochmütige
>   Kuppeln.

Title and first line show to what extent the poet has here given in to the impulse of withdrawal: isolation is described as her destination, the 'Ziel meines Herzens'. The following line emphasizes this affirmation of a reversal of the forward movement: for a ray is usually imagined as radiating outwards rather than inwards. In the third line, the withdrawal from the world is unambiguously stated, and the last line of this stanza echoes the beginning of **'Chaos':** the stars, symbols of a transcending love, are moving away.

The first line of the second stanza, in a bold metaphor, introduces once again night as a symbol of isolation, but this time not as a threat, but welcoming the poet's 'arrival' like a flag. The magic powers conjured up by 'Mondturm' become potent in the following line depicting the drug-like quality of this state of mind: we are reminded of the song of the Sirens. The poem ends, as we saw before . . . , on a note of superiority characteristic for the illusionary happiness which a state of complete isolation can create.

One other way in which Else Lasker-Schüler expresses despair and isolation in her poetry remains to be considered—that of 'objectification'. Many, perhaps the majority, of her poems embody the inner reality of her state of mind in images which, for all their vividness, have little relation to the objective world around her. They are, predominantly, 'I-poems'.

But there came the moment when the outcast in mind became the outcast in fact: when she had to leave Germany as a refugee. Suddenly, inner and outer reality fused, and the shock was overwhelming. . . .

The poem **'Die Verscheuchte'**, in which the experience and the suffering of sudden exile is crystallized, shows the poet's imagination anchored, as it were, in a concrete situation. Heselhaus, in his analysis of the poem, compares it with **'Weltflucht'**, and rightly stresses its greater immediacy, its increased 'Naturanschauung'. He quotes a passage from a letter to Hulda Pankok in which she describes how she spent the first days in exile 'am See unter einem Baum versteckt' and links it with the line 'Ich streife heimatlos zusammen mit dem Wild'. But I suggest that it is the fact that the 'eternal wanderer' has ceased to be a metaphor and has become a deeply suffered reality which gives the poem its immediacy and keeps it free from the hyperbolic excesses found in some of her more 'subjective' poetry. When we compare

> Ich will in das Grenzenlose
>   Zu mir zurück,
> Schon blüht die Herbstzeitlose
>   Meiner Seele,
> Vielleicht—ist's schon zu spät zurück!

with

> Wo soll ich hin, wenn kalt der Nordsturm
>   brüllt?
> Die scheuen Tiere aus der Landschaft wagen
>   sich
> Und ich vor deine Tür, ein Bündel Wegerich.

the gain in precision and poignancy is striking.

The poet herself refers to this correspondence between inner and outer exile in another letter to Professor Rose, written five years later (I quote the passage from the typewritten letter without change):

> I am so tired from all thinks in the World and
> from my live. 6 Years auf Wanderschaft allways,
> sir, also in heart I mean.

But she achieved an even greater degree of 'objectification' already twenty years before **'Die Verscheuchte'** was written. (Again, we see that no straight-line 'development' can be traced in this poet's work.) **'Die Verscheuchte'** remains an 'I-poem', though the experience it expresses is rooted in objective fact. But in 1913 a collection of Else Lasker-Schüler's poetry appeared under the title of **Hebräische Balladen** which to a great extent consisted of re-interpretations of Old Testament events and where the 'I' of the poet has withdrawn behind the stories she interprets. The stories of Abel, Joseph, Moses, Saul and other biblical figures served as 'objective correlatives', to use T. S. Eliot's phrase, for the emotions which the poet wished to express. Thus, in the following poem the experience of separation, exile and despair is made concrete through the highly original re-telling of an ancient story:

'Hagar und Ismael'

> Mit Muscheln spielten Abrahams kleine Söhne
> Und ließen schwimmen die Perlmutterkähne;
> Dann lehnte Isaak bang sich an den Ismael
>
> Und traurig sangen die zwei schwarzen Schwäne
> Um ihre bunte Welt ganz dunkle Töne,
> Und die verstoßne Hagar raubte ihren Sohn sich
>   schnell.
>
> Vergoß in seine kleine ihre große Träne,

> Und ihre Herzen rauschten wie der heilige
>   Quell,
> Und übereilten noch die Straußenhähne.
>
> Die Sonne aber brannte auf die Wüste grell
> Und Hagar und ihr Knäblein sanken in das
>   gelbe Fell
> Und bissen in den heißen Sand die weißen
>   Negerzähne.

We meet here familiar themes: the vision of a childhood paradise, Isaac's and Ishmael's 'bunte Welt' which is 'blackened' by rejection and the breaking-up of relationship, and in consequence the painful departure into the 'desert' of desolation. We know these experiences to be very specifically Else Lasker-Schüler's own: but here she has distanced herself from them, is no longer identified with them, and through this has, I think, heightened their impact and the degree of their universal validity.

(3) Escape into Fantasy

(a) Childhood; Lost Paradise. In our biographical outline, we have met Else Lasker-Schüler's need to mythify her life, particularly to re-think and re-feel her childhood into a kind of paradise, inhabited by the legendary figures of father, mother and brother. This myth she created as a sanctuary for herself where she could feel safe from the 'Tatsächlichkeiten des empirischen Neben- und Nacheinander'. Heinz Politzer's statement [in "The Blue Piano of Else Lasker-Schüler," *Commentary*, 1950] that 'Else Lasker-Schüler did not go back to her childhood or past, but to the myth, the prehistoric past' is not quite correct: there are, in fact, many poems in which actual childhood figures and events are referred to, though they appear remoulded into images of myth. But there are also others in which the concrete past has been left behind, and only the 'feel' of childhood as a lost and ever-longed-for paradise is conveyed, as in **'Im Anfang'**:

> Hing an einer goldenen Lenzwolke,
> Als die Welt noch Kind war,
> Und Gott noch junger Vater war.
>   Schaukelte, hei!
>   Auf dem Ätherei,
>   Und meine Wollhärchen flitterten ringelrei.
> Neckte den wackelnden Mondgroßpapa,
> Naschte Goldstaub der Sonnenmama,
> In den Himmel sperrte ich Satan ein
> Und Gott in die rauchende Hölle ein.
> Die drohten mit ihrem größten Finger
> Und haben 'klumbumm! klumbumm!' gemacht
> Und es sausten die Peitschenwinde!
> Doch Gott hat nachher zwei Donner gelacht
> Mit dem Teufel über meine Todsünde.
> Würde 10 000 Erdglück geben,
> Noch einmal so gottgeboren zu leben,
> So gottgeborgen, so offenbar.
>   Ja! Ja!
> Als ich noch Gottes Schlingel war!

This poem is the last in her first collection. It conjures up the vision of paradise seen through the eyes of a child, describes playfully (as the subtitle of its first version, 'Weltscherzo', which the poet later dropped, announces), almost in the manner of a nursery rhyme.

The poem has no strophic structure; but for the sake of

analysis three sections can be distinguished. Lines 1-6 show the world 'in the beginning' with God as its 'young father', and the poet herself as a child in it, swinging on the 'there-egg' (from which the world, or herself, has hatched?), with her curly hair dancing a ring-a-ring-a-roses.

The central part describes the child's misbehaviour: she teases grandfather Moon, nibbles from grandmother Sun's gold-dust, and even locks Satan up in Heaven, and God in Hell—but this 'Todsünde' has no serious consequences: for this is a world entirely beyond Good and Evil.

The last five lines express the poet's longing for such a world: she is ready to give all earthly happiness for this state of 'Gottgeborgenheit'—for the idyllic security of being 'Gottes Schlingel'. This expression which might be translated, not quite precisely, as 'God's naughty boy' is something of a key-word. The longing for God is here expressed as a longing for irresponsibility, for a withdrawal into a world of playfulness and unreality. The image of God is carried by the backward swing of the pendulum into the realm of fairy-tale.

This longing for a time long ago when all was play and harmony is, of course, not only an individual experience, but is also met as a collective phenomenon in the Greek myth of the 'Golden Age' where people 'lived without cares or labour, eating only acorns, wild fruit, and honey that dripped from the trees . . . never growing old, dancing and laughing much . . .'. Robert Graves's comments on this myth [in his *Greek Myths,* 1958] are of some interest in our context, though they do, in accordance with his exclusively historical approach, overlook the universality of the experience: he interprets the myth as an idealization of 'pre-agricultural times' whose 'savagery . . . had been forgotten by Hesiod's day'. Her childhood also is unlikely to have been as idyllic as she makes it appear. When she writes to a twelve-year-old girl 'Und wie gefällt Dir die Schule? Ich saß nämlich immer untenan und lauter Tadel bekam ich eingeschrieben. Machs auch so!', a less paradisical picture seems to emerge from between the lines, in spite of 'Machs auch so!'.

But on the whole, a view of childhood as an ideal state of being pervades her writing. 'Tatsächlich, ein anständiger Mensch hat sein lebenlang Primaner zu bleiben,' she exclaims in one of her essays, and the first paragraph of the prose poem which closes her last collection of poetry echoes the letter to her twelve-year-old friend, but with a romantic transfiguration of the difficulties of school life:

> Ich sitze noch heute sitzengeblieben auf der untersten Bank der Schulklasse, wie einst . . .
> Doch mit spätem versunkenem Herzen: 1000 und 2-jährig, dem Märchen über den Kopf gewachsen. . . .

In some poems, childhood is presented very specifically as the state of innocence, a mode of being without sin, and growing up then appears as a kind of 'fall'. In **'Der gefallene Engel,'** the poet addresses her friend, the vagabond-poet Peter Hille, as 'St. Petrus Hille', and seeing in him the redeeming power of Christ ('Des Nazareners Lächeln strahlt aus deinen Mienen'), she asks for his help.

> Darf ich mit Dir auf weiten Höhen schreiten!
> Hand in Hand, Du und ich, wie Kinder . . .
> Wenn aus dem Abendhimmel wilde Sterne gleiten
> Durch's tiefe Blauschwarz, wie verstoss'ne Sünder,
> Und scheu in Gärten fallen, die voll Orchideen
> Und stummen Blüten steh'n
> In gold'nen Hüllen.
>
> Und in den Kronen schlanker Märchenbäume
> Harrt meine Unschuld unter Wolkenflor,
> Und meine ersten, holden Kinderträume
> Erwachen vor dem gold'nen Himmelsthor.
> Und wenn wir einst ins Land des Schweigens gehen,
> Der schönste Engel wird mein Heil erfleh'n
> Um Deiner Liebe willen.

The condition for 'salvation' is the re-awakening of the poet's 'ersten, holden Kinderträume'. Once more we meet the symbol of the stars, but here they have become 'wild', 'verstoß'ne Sünder', have fallen from grace. The state of sin is symbolized by gardens 'full of orchids'—probably an image of sexual involvement: we have already met the erotic connotation of the colour 'golden', and the orchid is a common sexual symbol. Other lines, occurring earlier in the poem, also suggest such an interpretation:

> (. . .) Und meine Lippen öffnen sich mit Zagen,
> Wie gift'ge Blüten, die dem Satan dienen
> (. . .)
>
> (. . .) Und meine Träume tränkt ein blut'ger Regen
> Und reizt mit seinem Schein zum Laster meine Nerven (. . .)
>
> (. . .) Und diese roten, feurigen Granaten
> Gab mir ein Königgreis für meine Nächte,
> (. . .)

From this poem, an image emerges of childhood as a paradise which is lost through 'Satan's' sexual temptation, and can be regained with the help of a child-like saint.

In **'Hundstage,'** the poet, in despair over the uncertain intentions of her lover ('Von der Tollwut der Zweifel zerbissen'), again recalls childhood as a time of peace and security.

> . . . Wie friedvoll die Malvenblüten starben
> Unter süssen Himmeln der Lenznacht—
> Ich war noch ein Kind, als sie starben.
>
> Hab' so still in der Seele Gottes geruht—
> (. . .)

In some her poems, her fantasy withdraws, so to speak, behind and beyond childhood, into what we could rightly call, with Politzer, a 'prehistoric past':

> Es ist so dunkel heut am Heiligen Himmel . . .
> Ich und die Abendwolken suchen nach dem Mond—
> Wo beide wir einst vor dem Erdenleben,
> Schon nahe seiner Leuchtewelt gewohnt.

Once, 'vor dem Erdenleben', the lovers were united. The

darkness of today is contrasted with the 'Leuchtewelt' of some 'prehistoric' existence.

This theme recurs, though with an essential difference, in **'Ich schlafe in der Nacht,'** published after her death:

> Ich schlafe in der Nacht an fremden Wänden
> Und wache in der Frühe auf an fremder Wand.
> Ich legte mein Geschick in harten Händen
> Und reihe Tränen auf, so dunkle Perlen ich nie
>   fand.
>
> Ich habe einmal einen blauen Pfad gekannt
> Doch weiß ich nicht mehr wo ich mich vor
>   dieser Welt befand.
> Und—meine Sehnsucht will nicht enden! . . .
>
> Vom Himmel her sind beide wir verwandt
> Und unsere Seelen schweben übers Heilige Land
> In *einem* Sternenkleide leuchtend um die Len-
>   den.

The first stanza calls up, once more, the lonely, uprooted life of the outcast which at the time this poem was written was no doubt already a hard reality for the poet. In the second stanza, the poet's longing for 'einen blauen Pfad' reminds us of the German romantic's search for the 'blue Blume'. But we have seen that for her the colour blue leads 'in die höhere Welt', that it indicates a transcendence of worldly confusion, and in thus hinting at a possibility of reconciliation, it points not only backwards but also forwards.

The last stanza of the poem brings this out: here the 'path' to union lies no longer in the past, 'vor dieser Welt'—the lovers' separation is overcome in the here-and-now, transcendence has become reality through reconciliation ('in *einem* Sternenkleide') and the lovers' union is itself a symbol of a more universal, transcendental state of being which appears here crystallized in the image of the 'Heilige Stadt', Jerusalem.

Mother. We have previously seen how great a part Else Lasker-Schüler's mother played in her life. Sigrid Bauschinger has interpreted the meaning of this poet's work in terms of her relationship with mother ('Ein Kind sucht in diesem Werke nach der Mutter, im Bereich der Nature, im Wasser, in der Erde, unter den Bäumen, im Schutz der Nacht und im Schein der Sterne') [*Die Symbolik des Mütterlichen im Werke Else Lasker-Schülers,* 1960], and though such a monistic approach seems to me to sacrifice a wealth of phenomena to one single idea, the role of the mother as unrivalled queen of the poet's childhood paradise nevertheless deserves special consideration in our study.

In **'Chaos'** we met her longing for a return to the infant's intimate relationship with mother ('Ich wollte (. . .) / (. . .) es lege eine Schöpferlust / Mich wieder in meine Heimat / Unter der Mutterbrust'). The poem **'Mutter,'** written very much later, expresses the same longing.

'Mutter'

> O Mutter, wenn du leben würdest,
> Dann möcht ich spielen in deinem Schoß.

> Mir ist bang und mein Herz schmerzt
> Von der vielen Pein.
> Überall sprießt Blutlaub.
>
> Wo soll mein Kind hin?
> Ich baute keinen Pfad froh,
> Alle Erde ist aufgewühlt.
>
> Liebe, liebe Mutter.

This is a simple poem which needs little comment. 'Überall sprießt Blutlaub' is another example of the poet's tendency to turn private loss into cosmic catastrophe. The third stanza is important for the light it throws on her own experience of motherhood, by linking her inability to build a 'Pfad' for her son, to create a secure basis for his life, with her never-accepted loss of her own mother.

Sigrid Bauschinger rightly points to the fact that Else Lasker-Schüler does not seem to have written any poem 'das von der lebenden Mutter spricht', and raises the question whether she did not perhaps only start writing after her mother's death. Against this, we have the poet's own statement: 'die Gedichte meines ersten Buches dichtete ich zwischen 15 und 17.' But we have also seen that at times she made herself seven years younger than she was. All this lies in the realm of speculation, but it is possible that the following poem, which appeared in her first collection, was written under the immediate impact of her mother's death:

'Mutter'

> Ein weisser Stern singt ein Totenlied
>   In der Julinacht,
> Wie Sterbegeläut in der Julinacht.
> Und auf dem Dach die Wolkenhand,
> Die streifende, feuchte Schattenhand
> Sucht nach meiner Mutter.
> Ich fühle mein nacktes Leben,
> Es stößt sich ab vom Mutterland,
> So nackt war nie mein Leben,
> So in die Zeit gegeben,
> Als ob ich abgeblüht
> Hinter des Tages Ende,
>   Versunken
> Zwischen weiten Nächten stände,
> Von Einsamkeiten gefangen.
> Ach Gott! Mein wildes Kindesweh!
>   . . . Meine Mutter ist heimgegangen.

The first six lines once more make the cosmos the carrier of the poet's private loss—it is the star that mourns, the cloud that searches for the dead mother. The impression here, however, is not so much one of romantic exaggeration as almost of objectification: the poet distances herself from her grief. But with the seventh line, the poet enters, so to speak, the poem with an image that expresses the ambiguity of the situation: for it indicates birth as well as deprivation. From the eleventh line on, however, there is nothing left but a feeling of utter desolation. 'Ich fühle mein nacktes Leben / Es stößt sich ab vom Mutterland' still means a new beginning, the need to live without the dominating influence of mother which, with all its painfulness, is yet an opportunity. But '(. . .) abgeblüht / Hinter des Tages Ende' seems to deny the possibility of any further life at all.

'Als ob ich (. . .) / (. . .) / Zwischen weiten Nächten stände' anticipates lines in **'Chaos'** which have been considered earlier: 'Mir ist: ich lieg' von mir weltenweit / Zwischen grauer Nacht der Urangst': again, night becomes the symbol of extreme isolation. Sigrid Bauschinger's insistence that for Else Lasker-Schüler night is 'ihrer Natur nach das Bild der gütigen Mutter' with the qualification 'Überall wo sie nicht in dieser Gestalt erscheint, hat sie sich durch schreckliche Ereignisse gewandelt . . .' shows, I think, again the limitations of the reductive approach which loses the weight of the actual phenomenon, here the experience of night as a desolate vastness in which the poet is utterly lost.

She omitted the last two lines in a later version of the poem, probably because she felt—rightly, I think—that in them raw emotion was insufficiently transformed into poetry. Whether the other change she made, the substitution of 'Alleine' for 'Von Einsamkeiten gefangen', is equally successful seems to me questionable.

There is yet another version of this poem, textually not different from the second (1917), but showing a division into four three-line stanzas, which appeared in her prose book *Das Hebräerland* as late as 1937. That it was possible for her to reprint this poem as part of a new work thirty-five years after it was first written, conveys something of her unchanged feeling throughout her life about her mother's death. In *Das Hebräerland* she also wrote:

> Eines Morgens neigte sich meine unvergeßliche Mutter über mich Erwachende und lächelte . . . Nach diesem Lächeln habe ich mich seit ihrem Heimgang zu Gott gesehnt. Es erwärmte und kräftigte mich als Kind schon, und seitdem ich dieses Wunderlächeln hier in Jerusalem erleben durfte, begann ich eine niegekannte Freude und ein tiefes Verständnis zum Heiligen Lande zu empfinden, zu unserem lieben Heiligen Lande.

Throughout her life, she saw in her mother a kind of guiding spirit, a guardian angel:

> War sie der große Engel,
> Der neben mir ging? [. . .]
>
> Und weiß es nicht, ob meine Mutter
>   mein . . .
> Es war, die mir erschien im lichten
>   Engelkleid . . .
>
> (. . .) Sterb ich am Wegrand wo, liebe Mutter,
> kommst du und trägst mich hinauf zum blauen
> Himmel.

In the prose extract from *Das Hebräerland,* the awareness of her mother's presence leads to a deeper experience of Jerusalem; the image of her mother does not lure the poet back into the past, but helps to a 'niegekannte Freude und ein tiefes Verständnis' of the Holy Land, here and now. On the other hand, in **'Resignation'** which starts

> Umarm' mich mütterlich und weich,
> Und zeige mir das Himmelreich,
> Du träumerische Nacht; (. . .)

and ends

> Und sehne mich nach ew'ger Nacht.

> Zu schmelzen still im Abendrot,
> In deinem Heilandarme, Tod.

the 'motherly' arms of the night become the 'Heilandarm' of death. Once more we see the point from where the pendulum can swing in either direction.

Play. One important aspect of her nostalgic view of childhood is her passionate 'Spiellust' which she felt she had inherited from her father. Her poetry abounds with references to 'Spiel', 'spielen' and 'Spielsachen', and she repeatedly compared the process of writing with that of playing:

> Ob man mit grünen, lila und blauen Steinen
> spielt oder ob man dichtet, das ist ganz dasselbe,
> man hat dasselbe Glücksgefühl denn bunter
> kann man die Welt auch nicht durch den
> Rausch als durch die Gläser sehen. . . .
>
> Ich gebe mir Müh, aber ich kann nur spielen,
> auch in der Schreiberei.

In another letter to Kraus, she defends her habit of turning her friends into mythical figures and letting them appear in her books (she thinks that Kraus has expressed himself critically about this in a letter to Walden):

> Ich kann mir ja nur denken, daß Sie nicht gegen
> meine Dichtung etwa schrieben, [sondern] nur
> [dagegen] daß ich allerlei Figur mitspielen lasse.
> (. . .) Jedenfalls liebe ich nach meiner Sehn-
> sucht die Leute alle zu kleiden, damit ein Spiel
> zu Stande kommt. (. . .) Spielen ist alles. Sie,
> Minister, der Sie am aller entzücktesten wären,
> würden Sie wirklich mal die Spiele erleben, die
> ich noch spielen könnte, beklagen sich über end-
> lich, endlichen Frühling in der Dichtung.

Without entering too deeply into the various theories of play, we must, I think, distinguish between play as a creative activity, and play as withdrawal from a reality which seems too difficult to master. Else Lasker-Schüler's 'Spiellust' is rooted in both aspects, and it must once more be stressed that it is not always possible to sustain the theoretical distinction in studying the phenomenon.

By calling art a 'play', she wished to emphasize how seriously she took it:

> Kunst ist kein Gewerbe, wie auch der Mensch
> oder ein Tier oder gar ein Gott kein Gewerbe ist.
> (. . .) Kunst ist keine Beschäftigung, (. . .)
> Spiel keine Spielerei. Liebelt das Kunstgewerbli-
> che mit der Zierlichkeit des Goldpantöffelchens
> seiner Stoffpuppen, so ist es mir doch sympathi-
> scher, malt der Künstler mal frech und gesch-
> macklos dem Weib des Amenophis einen Sch-
> nurrbart an.

This is a defence of childlike fantasy against childish artiness. Her poetry is particularly rich in such fantasy, the manifestation of creative freedom. Bold metaphors, successful neologism and delightful nonsense verse anticipating dadaist experiments bear witness to the resourcefulness of her 'Spielsprache'. But at this moment we are more concerned with the other side of her 'Spiellust', her attempts 'die Menschheit zu verkindlichen' in which we saw a refusal to accept the claims of a grown-up world.

In **'Mein stilles Lied'** we have met one example of such

a 'Verkindlichung'—'Denn meine Liebe ist ein Kind und wollte spielen.' This longing for a love relationship that has the quality of 'child's play' is expressed also in **'Nebel.'** The poem starts on a note of hopelessness:

> Wir sitzen traurig Hand in Hand,
> Die gelbe Sonnenrose,
> Die strahlende Braut Gottes,
> Leuchtet erdenabgewandt.

It ends, however, in highspirited playfulness:

> Und was werden wir beide spielen . . .
> Wir halten uns fest umschlungen
> Und kugeln uns über die Erde,
> Über die Erde.

The intervening stanzas show the process of change from desolation to idyllic contentment: the lovers in their longing become like children ('Und unsere Augen weiten / Sich fragend wie Kinderaugen'), fantasy creates a childhood paradise ('(. . .) du, wir wollen / Wie junge Himmel uns lieben'), despair dissolves into 'rauschende Süße', and love, in the end, becomes play.

In the cycle of poems entitled **'Gottfried Benn,'** the play imagery is striking. The following poem shows the 'Verkindlichung' in an extreme form:

'O, Deine Hände'

> Sind meine Kinder.
> Alle meine Spielsachen
> Liegen in ihren Gruben.
>
> Immer spiel ich Soldaten
> Mit deinen Fingern, kleine Reiter,
> Bis sie umfallen.
>
> Wie ich sie liebe
> Deine Bubenhände, die zwei.

One of these poems bears the title **'Giselheer dem Knaben,'** another **'Das Lied des Spielprinzen.'** In **'Giselheer dem Tiger,'** she calls the beloved one

> Du mein Indianerbuch,
> Wild West,
> Siouxhäuptling!
>
> Im Zwielicht schmachte ich
> Gebunden am Buxbaumstamm—
>
> Ich kann nicht mehr sein
> Ohne das Skalpspiel.

In the characteristically entitled **'Klein Sterbelied,'** she turns her pain over the lover's rejection into a kind of children's prayer:

> Mein Herz noch klein
> Starb leis an Pein.
>
> War blau und fromm!
> O Himmel, komm.

In **'Abschied,'** a poem from a cycle dedicated to Hans Adalbert von Maltzahn, marriage can only be seen in a child's setting:

> Aber wenn meine Spieluhren spielen
> Feiern wir Hochzeit.

But this longing for a 'Verkindlichung' of existence goes beyond the wish for playful love relationships. The ideal relation to the world, even to God, is sometimes seen as one between playmates:

> Ich und die Erde wurden wie zwei Spielgefährten groß! . . .
>
> Kinder waren unsere Seelen,
> Als sie mit dem Leben spielten,
> Wie die Märchen sich erzählen. . . .
>
> Meine erste Blüte Blut sehnte sich nach dir,
> So komme doch,
> Du süßer Gott,
> Du Gespiele Gott,
> Deines Tores Gold schmilzt an meiner Sehnsucht.

The first stanza of **'Letzter Abend im Jahr'** shows, I think, that Else Lasker-Schüler was not altogether aware of the evasive aspect of her 'Spiellust':

> Es ist so dunkel heut,
> Man kann kaum in den Abend sehen.
> Ein Lichtchen loht,
> Verspieltes Himmelchen spielt Abendrot
> Und weigert sich, in seine Seligkeit zu gehen.
> —So alt wird jedes Jahr die Zeit—
> Und die vorangegangene verwandelte der Tod.

Her own fear of the reality of time seems here projected on to the sky which, by playing 'Abendrot', refuses, so to speak, to grow up. This poem ends, as we have seen, in great seriousness with a question to God:

> O Gott, wie kann der Mensch verstehen,
> Warum der Mensch haltlos vom Menschtum bricht,
> Sich wieder sammeln muß im höheren Geschehen.

At this point, there is no evasion, but a readiness to ask fundamental questions, more moving even for its simplicity. 'Verspieltes Himmelchen' has turned into the 'blausten Himmel in Gottost'.

Jakob Hessing   (essay date 1976)

SOURCE: "Else Lasker-Schüler and Her People," in *Ariel*, Jerusalem, No. 41, 1976, pp. 61-76.

[*In the following excerpt, Hessing discusses Lasker-Schüler's regard for her Jewish heritage and its influence on her works.*]

> I am not a Hebrew for the sake of the Hebrews, but—for God's sake! This confession, however, includes the love and the faith of an unshakeable devotion to His people. To my smallest nation amongst the nations, to which I belong with heart and soul.
>
> Else Lasker-Schüler, *Das Hebräerland* (*The Land of the Hebrews*)

She was born in 1869, into a pious Jewish family of Wuppertal-Elberfeld, Germany; between the years 1894 and 1911, she was married twice, and twice divorced; by 1933, when she had to leave Germany, her poetry had established her as one of the leading figures in the literary world of her country; she spent her last years in Switzerland and, after 1939, in Jerusalem, where she died in 1945. Her outward life falls into the all-too familiar pattern. There does not seem to be anything very particular about it.

Except, perhaps, for one little fact. She was " . . . the greatest lyrical poetess Germany ever had": this is the verdict of the famous German poet Gottfried Benn about Else Lasker-Schüler.

Almost inevitably, Gottfried Benn's dictum accounts for the fact that she is not known outside her language. Else Lasker-Schüler *is* her language. Hardly anything has been written about her in English, and the one notable exception, Hans W. Cohn's book *Else Lasker-Schüler, The Broken World* (1974), quotes all her poetry and prose in German.

Anyone who remembers her—in Jerusalem, or elsewhere—recalls her German which was entirely her own. To relate some of her meaning in a foreign tongue will be the most difficult task of this essay.

Else Lasker-Schüler did not shape only her art into symbols, but her personal life as well: hers was a world of fantasy. "Prince Yussuf" she called herself, "She-Star," "Tiger," "Tino of Baghdad." She also gave fancy names to her friends, to Gottfried Benn, Georg Trakl, Franz Werfel, and, because she decided to call him so, her second husband, Georg Lewin, became famous as Herwarth Walden. For some, this double symbolism establishes an organic relationship between her art and her life. Others, bent on the destruction of a myth, recognize it as her failure to come to terms with reality.

Above all, however, there was her peculiar fate. In the land of the Hebrews, to which she had dedicated one of her most beautiful books of prose, she found her final rest, perhaps her only rest; in the City of which she had said in her book: "Jerusalem is the observatory of the beyond, the heaven before heaven."

But when Else Lasker-Schüler was buried on the Mount of Olives on January 23, 1945, it had nothing to do with symbolism. It was not a messianic feeling that had made her spend her final years in Jerusalem, but harsh reality: World War II made it impossible for her to return to Europe.

This reality may indeed be a partial explanation for her flight into fantasy. "In our biographical outline," Hans W. Cohn writes, "we have met Else Lasker-Schüler's need to mythify her life, particularly to re-think and re-feel her childhood into a kind of paradise, inhabited by the legendary figures of father, mother and brother. This myth she created as a sanctuary for herself where she could feel safe from the 'Tatsächlichkeiten des empirischen Neben- und Nacheinanders'."

Tatsächlichkeiten—the facts of the empirical one-by-one and one-after-the-other. The process of internalization has often been noted in her poetic language. In it she found the means to cut herself off from the outer world that was oppressing her. Nothing expresses her withdrawal more clearly than the early poem, **"Flight from the World"**:

> Into the boundless
> Let me go back to myself,
> The autumn crocus is flowering—
> Perhaps it is too late—let me go back,
> Even though I die among you
> Who smother me with your selves.
> I would draw threads around me
> To end confusion
> And confuse,
> To escape
> Me-wards.

(translated by Ralph Manheim)

"Perhaps it is too late—." In the life of Else Lasker-Schüler, one cannot help feeling, something was taking place that she could not control. Somehow, she seemed to know it, and she erected her fantasy world in defence against her inexplicable fate. In her book ***I'm Putting Things in Order!*** (1925) we find a strange allusion to the "Me-wards" at the end of the poem:

"I had recovered my original language then, stemming from the time of Saul, the savage Jew of royal blood. I can speak it even today, this language which I have probably inhaled in my dreams . . . Among others, I have written my poem **'Flight from the World'** in this mystical Asiatic."

And then, as though she wanted to make the "And confuse" come true, she gives us this "Asiatic," of which two lines may suffice as an example:

> Min salihihi wali kinahu
> Rahi hatiman

According to Cohn, she escaped from reality into her childhood. In passages like the one quoted above, however, Heinz Politzer finds evidence that she went back much further, "not . . . to her childhood or past, but to the myth, the prehistoric past." ("The Blue Piano of Else Lasker-Schüler," *Commentary* IX, 1950).

But here, too, defence seems to be the mainspring of her expression. Her book ***I'm Putting Things in Order!*** bears the subtitle "My accusation of my publishers," and the "Times of Saul" may well be played off against an unbearable present.

Yet, when she finally came to Jerusalem and was overwhelmed by what she experienced as its "biblical" quality, she soon wanted to replace this reality also—by an "earth" which she now believed to be far away. In 1934, after two months in Jerusalem, she returned to Switzerland. There she was asked for the reason for her departure. In *The Land of the Hebrews* she has recorded an answer:

> I say drily: I am returning to Europe for—
> geographical reasons; to find out whether one
> can reach Earth from the Bible Star.

She never wanted to go from Germany to Jerusalem, and she certainly did not choose her way consciously. Her phrase about the Bible Star recalls the "observatory of the beyond," but her drily geographical answer reveals its irony now: it seems as though she had enough of this Bible Star already, and her sudden departure seems like another flight.

Even as late as 1939, during her third visit to this country, she wished to leave it again. But this time, as may be gathered from her letters of the period, her reasons were rather more prosaic. "I depart August 17," she wrote her niece on July 30, "I am done for. The poverty is shocking."

She was not unfamiliar with material poverty. As early as 1913, Karl Kraus had had to raise financial support for the poetess, in the pages of his influential publication, *Die Fackel.* But, in the culturally rather backward *Yishuv* "poverty" acquired a spiritual dimension for her. At one point she called her Land of the Hebrews "Misraël," and the dedication of her last volume of lyrics has become famous: "To my unforgettable friends, men and women, in German cities—and to those who, like me, have been driven out and are now scattered in the world, in fidelity!"

My Blue Piano, her last volume of poetry, was printed by Dr. Moshe Spitzer in Jerusalem, in 1943. By a strange inversion of terms she speaks of Jerusalem as though it were the Diaspora: "scattered in the world." Once again, as often before in Else Lasker-Schüler's life, fantasy and reality are revealed in clashing dissonance. Zion, the gathering-place of a persecuted people, is transformed into another symbol of the eternal exile which was her life, and from which she wanted to escape into her poetry.

Perhaps the feeling underlying this dedication has contributed no little to the fact that German critics refer to Else Lasker-Schüler's life after 1933 as her "years of exile." Conveniently, it makes her a part of the "emigrant literature" of Germany's "unmastered past."

But for her own people, also, Else Lasker-Schüler is part of an unmastered past. Remembering her in Jerusalem, one does not think of her as a pioneer who has finally come home. The blue piano of her last volume sounds a very different chord for a German Jew, a chord both confused and tragic.

> I have a blue piano at home,
> Yet I don't know a single note.
>
> It stands in the dark by the cellar door,
> Since the coarsening of the world.
>
> Four starry hands are playing
> —The moon woman sang in the bark—
> Now rats are dancing to the din,
>
> Broken is the keyboard . . .
> I weep for the blue dead.
>
> Ah, dear angels, open
> —I have eaten the bitter bread—
> Heaven's gate to me while I live—
> Forbidden though it is.

(Translated by Ralph Manheim)

Since the coarsening of the world, Else Lasker-Schüler has gained a new meaning in Jerusalem. And this, too, is part of her curious fate: she did not live to learn of this new meaning. A short time after her death, all over Europe the survivors of her people emerged from the dark through the cellar doors and came to the country where she had written of her blue piano.

And yet, the rats are dancing to the din. "The black swan

of Israel," Peter Hille had called her, "a Sappho whose world had broken apart." These are famous words about her, and Hans W. Cohn has taken the title of his book, *The Broken World,* from them. They point to a central quality in Else Lasker-Schüler's work, to the deep rupture which runs through her poetry.

This rupture may be traced as far back as to her early Hebrew Ballads. These were written at a better time in her life, when her blue piano was not yet dead. "Through the poetry of my Hebrew Ballads, I have contributed to the building of Palestine; I have not been idle in God's work," she says in *The Land of the Hebrews.*

Better than anything else, perhaps, her "God's work" bears witness to the broken world which she inhabited. **"My People,"** the most famous of her early poems, is a graphic expression of this rupture. In it two people identify themselves: the one in the emigrant who did not want to leave, the other in the woman whom fate had turned into an immigrant against her will.

> The rock grows brittle
> From which I spring
> To which my canticles I sing . . .
> Down I rush from the track
>
> And inwardly only ripple
> Far off, alone over wailing stones
> Toward the sea.
>
> Have flowed so much away
> From the wine ferment
> Of my blood.
> And yet for ever, endlessly the echo
> In me,
> When eastward, awesomely,
> The brittle rock of bone,
> My people,
> Cries out to God.

(Translated by Michael Hamburger)

Not only in Jerusalem may this extraordinary poem be considered as a central piece of her work. The strong effect it had on Germans is confirmed by Gottfried Benn: "In its perfection it is a complete fusion of the Jewish and the German," he said in 1952, "The expression of an existential communion of the highest order. Had art been what it should have been among us, it could have had political consequences as well."

It was written very early, in 1905, and the poetess herself was always attracted by its haunting power. Never altering a word, she incorporated the poem in all five collections of lyrics which she published before 1920. Its magic effect on her may be inferred from an article by Schalom Ben-Chorin. He describes a reading she gave in 1937, during her second visit to Jerusalem: "She began her recitation with the unforgettable poem 'My People' . . . The large audience listened raptly to the powerful visions of this true granddaughter of the psalmists. After half an hour she broke off for a short intermission . . . Again the lights dimmed, again the poetess sat down at the lectern, and once more she read: The rock grows brittle, from which I spring . . . "

The metaphor of the rock may express the "existential

communion" referred to by Gottfried Benn. Although in its later repetition it clearly refers to the Jewish people, the Christian reader, too, may recognize it as an image from his own faith: "Thou art Peter," said Jesus, "And on this rock I will build my church," in the Gospel according to Matthew. The brittle rock, then, symbolizes the lack of faith in the Christian world which was deeply felt by Else Lasker-Schüler's contemporaries, the German Expressionists.

The association is not irrelevant. A quotation from *The Land of the Hebrews* shows that Else Lasker-Schüler thought also in Christian terms. At the same time it takes us closer to the essence of her very personal expression. The poetess describes a Sabbath Eve which she spent at the house of the Hebrew writer S. J. Agnon:

"The poet's dear children were already asleep when their loving mother—for I was so afraid—put me to bed like one of her children. For I felt—the fear of God on the naked land behind our house. And was ashamed to admit it to the *geveret.* 'Isn't it cozy in the room,' the dear one consoled me. But there it was, you see! The enormous contrast of inside and outside created the impetuous emotion. I thought of the words of the last prophet-poet *(Prophetendichter)* Peter Hille, whose name, Petron, had also meant a rock to us, his friends and disciples. It is written in his psalmodies: 'God is the genius of the world—He is, however, not genial'." These lines, moreover, probe a greater depth: her "fear of God."

Her poetic language internalizes everything external, and critics have often noticed that her inner self never changes. Thirty years later we partially recognize something of this fear of God in her poem **"My People."**

God, if we read the text literally, is "on the naked land behind our house." "Inside," then, is the sheltered room. And yet the poetess is afraid although she is "inside."

A highly significant detail: it is a Sabbath Eve being described, celebrated in a pious home in Jerusalem. One thinks of *My Blue Piano,* of Else Lasker-Schüler's being "scattered in the world," of her sudden departure from the Bible Star, Jerusalem.

The feeling of exile runs very deep in her work. ". . . their loving mother—for I was so afraid—put me to bed like one of her children." Compare this motif with her poem "Mother," which was written as early as 1902:

> A white star is singing a song of death
>   in the nights of July,
> Like a knell in the night of July,
> And on the roof the cloudy hand,
> The grazing humid shadow-hand,
> Is searching for my Mother.
>
> I feel my naked life,
> It breaks away from Motherland,
> Never was my life so naked,
> So exposed to time,
> As though I stood withered
> Behind the end of day
> Between sweeping nights
>   Alone.

The mother who cannot help any longer; naked life and naked land; alone between sweeping nights, and fear of God between inside and outside—the composite image which Else Lasker-Schüler creates of herself in two such different contexts, and across a span of thirty-five years, is repeated almost to the detail. The loss of her only son, Paul, who died of consumption in his twenties, deepened the break with the "coarsening world." And perhaps she identified with the mother, no less than with the children in the "cozy room," the double loss making her even more defenceless.

Thus, through a substantiation of the Christian element in the rock motif in the Hebrew Ballad **"My People,"** and through her fear of God, the prose text in *The Land of the Hebrews* leads us to the basic rupture in the poem. In her fear, she turns away from God, but at the same time she turns towards Him. In the thrust and the withdrawal of **"My People"** we discover her secret, the cardinal point of her being upon which she performs a constant double movement (a movement which is very carefully traced by Cohn in his book). To understand the poem properly we must realize that she is turning *towards* God, as well.

Also in *The Land of the Hebrews,* Else Lasker-Schüler speaks the *Shema,* as a direct invocation of God, at Agnon's Sabbath table. "The most reverential prayer of the Jews, the *Shema*—for a good reason it is not incorporated at the table of the Shabbat—suddenly broke forth and in high intervals it foamed over the dune of my mouth, a stream which had left its bed."

A pious Jew, whom she ironically cells "Talmude," speaks up against "The way in which I, his neighbour at table, have dared to say the most respectful prayer to the Lord, it vexes, nay, it offends His Holiness through all His Heavens."

As mentioned in the beginning, she shaped not only her art into symbols, but her own life as well. In the answer with which she defends herself against her neighbour at table, the poetess expresses her fundamental creed:

> I took the occasion, once again, to defend myself in a parable: Once upon a time there was a shepherdess amongst the people of Israel, who, when she was not busy tending her lambs, made poems for the Lord. One morning she was very thirsty and bent low over the edge of a well in order to drink: When, over the spring, a drop of the water-of-innumerable-drops welled forth, in which the entire creation was reflected, *the Creator Himself.* And the shepherdess went to search for a cup, to shelter the ineffable gem; but she did not find a single one worthy of the beauty of the tiny sparkling water, neither in the niches of the Temple nor in the gardens of the palaces. So she spun the red threads of her transparent pure heart into a chalice of crystal sound and lovely darkness; and she put the trembling eternity, sheltered in a tiny drop, *the diamond* of prayers, the *Shema*—between the spun walls of her God-offered heart. The *Shema,* the holy hieroglyphic on the canvas of creation, survives the world.

The scene at the Sabbath table immediately precedes the

one in the cozy room, and it may serve as a psychological explanation for the fear of God which takes hold of her there. Her invocation of God in the *Schema,* has brought her face to face with her Creator, and she is afraid. At the same time, however, in the shepherdess who "made poems for the Lord," Else Lasker-Schüler gives us her conception of the true poet: he locks God into his heart, and in the holy language of the *Shema* survives the world.

By this true vocation of the poet Else Lasker-Schüler measured her existence. It is the duty which she has undertaken. Lines from her early and late poems show how seriously she took this duty, and how much she suffered under its burden.

"My Quiet Song" was written very early in her career and exists in two versions. The later version ends with the lines:

> I am the hieroglyphic
> Standing under the creation
>
> And my eye
> Is the summit of time;
>
> Its shining light kisses God's hem.

These lines give the impression that she has mastered her task; here, clearly, the poetess is turning towards God. But how difficult it was may be seen from the earlier version of the poem:

> I am the hieroglyphic standing under the cre-
>   ation.
> And I have shaped myself after you
> Because of the longing for Man.
>
> I tore the eternal glances from my eyes,
> The victorious light from my lips—
>
> Do you know of a captive more captive,
> Of a magician more evil than I.
>
> And my arms which want to rise
> Are sinking . . .

The "hieroglyphic" in the parable, then, is she herself. But, nevertheless, the *Shema* could not really take the fear of God from her; she could never share the purity of belief of the shepherdess in her parable. In *My Blue Piano,* in the late poem **"The Banished,"** we come across the motifs of the heart and the chalice once more:

> For how long has no heart been kind to
>   mine . . .
>
> The world's grown cold, Man has grown pale.
>
> —Come pray with me—for God consoles me.
>
>   . . . . .
>
> Soon will the tears have washed away all heav-
>   ens,
>
> The chalices at which the poets quenched their
>   thirst—
>
> You too, and I.

Compare this with the latter poem about herself: there is a consoling God here, too. Eyes seem to bend over "all heavens" and here, too, water wells forth. But creation is not reflected in it. It has turned into tears, and all heaven, all the chalices are washed away.

This is a bare sample of Else Lasker-Schüler's language. Returning now to **"My People,"** one marvels at what it is able to achieve: the poem is carried by a double movement, by a twofold relationship of the "I" and the "people," it performs a "turning towards" and a "turning away." Only the "canticles" at the beginning (in the German it is "songs of God"), and in the end the crying out to God, hold these two opposed movements together and concentrate, rather than waste, their energy.

Suddenly, one understands her language and many of its connotations.

> The rock grows brittle
> From which I spring
> To which my canticles I sing . . .

The canticles, one feels, are very much like the *Shema* which the shepherdess had locked into her heart at the edge of the well. But how shall we read the words "From which I spring"? Do they mean, "from which I stem," do they reflect an essential bond between the I and its brittle rock? Or do they mean, "from which I jump" and does the I leave the rock?

The rhythm of the first stanza seems to suggest a parting. The turning away is carried out in a threefold movement. The I "springs" from the rock, jumps from it, "rushes from the track" and cuts itself off in the inwardness of its canticles: it " . . . inwardly only ripples, Far off, alone."

The I turns away to the sea. One remembers the *Shema* in *The Land of the Hebrews,* and again one marvels at the consistency of her language: it "suddenly broke forth and in high intervals it foamed over the dune of my mouth, a stream which had left its bed." In jumping, rushing, rippling waves, very much like a stream—the first stanza of this poem, too, is moving towards its sea.

Then, at the beginning of the second stanza, the rhythm calms down.

> Have flowed so much away
> From the wine ferment
> Of my blood.

One pauses. All movement has suddenly stopped. There is silence now.

What does "the wine ferment of my blood" mean? Again, as always, Else Lasker-Schüler refers us back to herself, to her own personal use of words. The task of the poet is the singing of canticles, of songs to God. This is what she says about it in *The Land of the Hebrews:* "Man too, taking example from God, should give time to art; mostly, however,—the artist *to himself.* He who feels responsible for his gifts. Art is wine. It wants to ferment, to filter; the longer the precious wine ferment rests in the heart of the dreaming, foaming artist, the incomparably sweeter becomes his poetry's bouquet."

"Have flowed so much away . . ." Has the I renounced its art, has the parting with the rock been carried over into a parting with the canticles as well? Or does the poetess here, at the beginning of her second stanza, give time to her canticles, time to ferment and to filter?

Must we, then, revise our impression of the first stanza? Does it not really tell us of a flight from the rock? It seems to be so. The first stanza was full of movement: here, suddenly, all action ceases.

> And yet for ever, endlessly the echo
> In me,

"And yet": an enormous change takes place in these two lines. The "for ever, endlessly" stretches the moment of rest at the beginning of the second stanza into long long time again. The "echo" recovers all space which the fleeing I, by now, may have put between itself and the rock. "In me": the outside—the rock, the track, the sea—is suddenly transformed into the inner self of the poetess again, into the "brittle rock of bone." The rock which seemed so far away has turned into the brittle skeleton which the I carries within, as "My people" from which it springs—stems, not jumps. All attempts to part with the rock have suddenly become futile, and the canticles which we expected break forth in a single cry.

Something very curious takes place in the two stanzas of the poem: the driving force of the first lines is not only stopped, but imperceptibly, without a single verb between "Have flowed" and "Cries," the second stanza reverses its movement. It seems as though the sea, which had drawn the I away from the rock at first, suddenly rushes back in a wave and throws the I onto the rock again.

Who cries? A distant people, or the bones which are flung against the rock? And where did the flight lead to in the first place? "Over wailing stones," it says in the poem, and later, about the people's cry to God: "eastward, awesomely." Is it the Western Wall in Jerusalem, the symbol of the Jewish exile, where the echo of the brittle rock reverberates?

With a Christian association of the rock motif we made our first step into the world of the poem. In conclusion, let us mention a Jewish association as well. Fifty years before Else Lasker-Schüler wrote **"My People,"** in 1854, another Jewish poet who had made some contribution to German literature re-formulated his relationship with his own people: "May the Lord forgive me my sin, but sometimes I feel as though this Mosaic God were nothing but the reflected light of Moses himself, whom he resembles so much, in wrath and in love—It would be a great sin, it would be anthropomorphism, if one were to assume such an identity of the God and His prophet—but the resemblance is striking," Heinrich Heine writes in his *Confessions*. At the end of his life, he recognizes the great artist in Moses:

> I failed to perceive that Moses, notwithstanding his enmity to art, was nevertheless himself a great artist, and possessed the true artistic spirit. Only, this artistic spirit with him, as with his Egyptian countrymen, was applied to the colossal and the imperishable. But, unlike the Egyptians, he did not construct his works of art from bricks and granite; he built human pyramids and carved human obelisks. He took a poor shepherd

tribe and from it created a nation which should defy centuries; a great, an immortal, a consecrated race, a God-serving people, who should serve as a model and prototype for all other nations: he created Israel. [Hugo Bieber (ed.) *Heinrich Heine, A Biographical Anthology,* 1956]

Heinrich Heine's anthropomorphism and Else Lasker-Schüler's canticles each mark a tremendous and painful chapter in the history of Jewish emancipation. Moses, she would have answered, created nothing. Moses pronounced—God created. The pathos of her poems—how much more modest it sounds than Heinrich Heine's! Once he was asked at a customs barrier if he had anything to declare. "Only my genius," was his famous answer.

But has Else Lasker-Schüler, therefore, come closer to her goal? Has she managed to approach the true *Tsur Yisrael,* the Rock of Israel, the Refuge of Israel? *Tzur Yisrael,* in the original biblical image was God Himself.

There is something strange—and looking back one should almost like to use her own word: awesome—about Else Lasker-Schüler. In everything her mythical language expressed a part of her own personal fate was foreshadowed. Much in her early poem **"My People"** can later be recognized in her curiously confused, voluntary-involuntary return to Jerusalem.

Even the motif of the rock.

In *The Land of the Hebrews* she speaks of the "weight of the stones surrounding Palestine, 'felt from far away' by its breathing of old-old breath. Many a newcomer feels nightmarishly oppressed and threatened by these huge stony giants; by this world of calcified encrusted landscapes of primeval times. And yet, again and again, the biblical People finds a ready soil in which to strike its roots into this earth of clotted blood."

And in this book, in words which again express a "turning towards" and a "turning away," she speaks of her fear of the cemeteries in Jerusalem:

> Between stony heights—they almost reach into the clouds—there slumbers a cemetery, heroically between God and His earth. I am afraid of this death watched by spying peaks; although its peace wears an invisible image of the Godhead around its neck.

And in a third place in *The Land of the Hebrews,* she speaks of her search for a house:

> Man's final skin ought to be his house in which he incarnates himself . . . I may certainly say from experience: since I have left the home of my childhood no (skin) ever really fitted me . . . Never since, living as a tenant in foreign stone buildings outside my parent's house, have my body and my soul found rest. Finally, therefore, I have preferred to move into *freedom;* its wallpapers, at least, have always been to my taste. But not everybody can maintain himself without a coat. This is the advantage of the poetess. I am a devil of a fellow, says the artistic masterbuilder, [Leopold] Krakauer. A Viennese by birth. Philistines are afraid, some of them, to have him build their houses; for they know that

only the artistic architect is capable of breathing life into the building. The houses Krakauer builds are *alive*.

Yehuda Amichai on Lasker-Schüler's enduring image:

When I was a boy in Jerusalem in the thirties I used to see [Else Lasker-Schuler] sometimes. Her strange figure made us laugh and jest. She was the first hippie I ever saw, long before it became a fashion. . . .

Her image has often revisited me—as have her poems. In Jerusalem in 1967, as I wrote,

> Poets come with evening into the Old City
> and leave it loaded with images
> and metaphors and little maxims
> and twilight similes between vaults and rims.
> Darkening fruits
> and wrought-iron filigree of the heart.

> I lifted my hand to my forehead
> to wipe the sweat
> and brought up Else Lasker-Schüler
> by chance. Light and small as she was in her life
> how much more so in her death. But her poems!

Yehuda Amichai, in his preface to Hebrew Ballads and Other Poems, *by Else Lasker-Schüler, edited and translated by Audri Durchslag and Jeanette Litman-Demeestère, 1980.*

Audri Durchslag and Jeanette Litman-Demeestère (essay date 1980)

SOURCE: An introduction to *Hebrew Ballads and Other Poems* by Else Lasker-Schüler, edited and translated by Audri Durchslag and Jeanette Litman-Demeestère, The Jewish Publication Society, 1980, pp. xi-xxii.

[*In the following excerpt, Durchslag and Litman-Demeestère survey Lasker-Schüler's career and discuss major images and themes in her poetry.*]

[In 1902, Lasker-Schüler's first book of poetry], *Styx*, appeared. Certain general themes and characteristics which appear in this early volume were to recur—though in different guises and styles—throughout Lasker-Schüler's poetic career. Like a mystical Ovid, Lasker-Schüler saw the world as a tribute to and an embodiment of passion and unfolding life. With her, however, the runic replaces the metamorphic. Nature, like almost everything else in Lasker-Schüler's world, reveals a dynamism beyond itself, possessing special power as a hieroglyph (a word which recurs in both her poetry and prose) of yet another, magical realm. Although images of real flowers appear in her poems, generally the names of her flowers resonate with other meanings, for example, the *"Immortelle"* of **"A Lovesong" ("Ein Liebeslied")** (the English translation, "strawflower," cannot, unfortunately, capture the symbolic dimension of the word play). More characteristic are such fabulated flowers as "fireroses" (*"Feurrose"*) in the poem **"Parting" ("Abschied")** or the "glitterflowers" (*"Schimmerblumen"*) in **"Mary of Nazareth" ("Marie von Nazareth")**. Just as the poet's intense internal life colors and discovers new forms in creation, so it colors her language. Unable to find an exact German word to serve as counter for the nuance or intensity she needs, the poet simply extends the givens of language, either by playing on words, such as the "me-wards" of **"Flight"** (*"Meinwärts"* instead of *"einwärts"* or "inwards") or by devising neologisms through combination, as with the *"liebesruhen"* (literally, to rest after / from love) of **"A Lovesong."**

So, too, with love. Its centrality in Lasker-Schüler's life and poetry was bound to a deep conviction that passion, true child of innocence, constituted the essential encounter joining human beings to one another and to God's world. The powerful sensuality in both tone and subject matter of much of Lasker-Schüler's poetry is often wed to an intensely spiritual yearning. Not surprisingly, so exacting an ideal could find little accommodation in what Lasker-Schüler saw as the rigid and loveless actuality of most of the world around her.

Lasker-Schüler's poem **"Flight" ("Weltflucht")** reveals the poet's need to escape the suffocation of so sterile—and therefore so devastating—a world. The poem rhythmically captures the diastole-systole of the poet's being, maintaining a fine tension between outer and inner. The "whirring" and restless movement seeking an end is simultaneously echoed and reflected on the levels of sound, morphology, and meaning by the words themselves:

> Fäden möchte ich um mich ziehen
> Wirrwarr endend!
> Beirrend,
> Euch verwirrend,
> Zu entfliehn
> Meinwärts.

> (O, to draw threads around me,
> Ending confusion!
> Misleading,
> Confusing you,
> To escape
> Me-wards.)

Yet Lasker-Schüler's deepening estrangement was matched by an equally ardent desire for the passionate communication that alone could sustain her in a coarsening world. She was to love many, but her loves most often ended in disillusionment and loneliness rather than in the oneness of which she dreamed. **"My Drama" ("Mein Drama")** exposes the pain and the vulnerability of a personal love relationship and ends in a mood of total disaffection with male/female relationships, while **"Chaos"** expresses the poet's distance from her deepest self.

That longing for communion with the Other was, even during this early period of the poet's life, also frequently directed toward God, and we can recognize its echoes in the early poem **"Shulamite" ("Sulamith")**. Unlike the other loss of self which the poet suffers in her intercourse with the world, here the poet describes a sensuous dissolution of self that is experienced as a deep mystical consummation:

And I dissolve
With blossoming heartbreak
And I drift away in the universe
Into time,
To forever . . .

An important influence during this early agitated period in Lasker-Schüler's life was her friendship with the poet Peter Hille. She felt a deep affinity with this poet-prophet's spiritual and dreamlike qualities. After Hille's death in 1902, Lasker-Schüler canonized him as Saint Peter in her first prose work, *The Peter Hille Book* (*Das Peter Hille-Buch,* 1906), a series of legendary episodes. In this work, Hille is mythicized as a kind of sage, a fairy-tale figure with whom the poet wanders through many lands.

The legendary and mythical character of *The Peter Hille Book* was but the first example of Lasker-Schüler's tendency to mythicize; soon thereafter she was to create her own mythical world, a pageantry of eclectic figures, such as the Eastern princess Tino of Baghdad (*Die Nächte Tino von Bagdads,* 1907)—the first of Lasker-Schüler's masks—Prince Jussuf of Thebes, who later becomes associated with the biblical Joseph, King David, and others.

Nor was this mythicizing penchant restricted to her art alone. She similarly rejected the primacy of mundane reality in her relationships with her friends and fellow artists. Those in whom she recognized a certain spark she would rename—for example, King Giselheer (Gottfried Benn), the Blue Rider (Franz Marc), Saint Peter (Peter Hille), the Prince of Prague (Franz Werfel), the Cardinal or Dalai Lama (Karl Kraus). For the poet, these persons were possessed of a special nobility; they represented for her an aristocracy of the spirit which set them apart from most people.

One of these "elect" was George Levin, an art critic and composer several years younger than herself, whom Else Lasker-Schüler married in 1901. As Herwarth Walden, a name bestowed upon him by the poet, he became well known as one of the leading promoters and theoreticians of the German Expressionist movement. In 1904 in Berlin, he founded the art society "Verein für Kunst" and in 1910 started publishing *Der Sturm,* which soon became a major Expressionist journal. Lasker-Schüler's poems began to appear in *Der Sturm* (a name she also provided) as well as in such other important journals of the time as *Die Aktion* and *Die Fackel.* After 1911, however, her poems appeared less frequently in Walden's journal. One reason given for this was that her originality and strong will could not tolerate the programmed Expressionist art which Walden was promoting; the second was that in 1911 the marriage between Else Lasker-Schüler and Herwarth Walden came to an end.

With the dissolution of this second marriage, Lasker-Schüler's life became even more unstable. Never again was she to have a permanent home or financial security. She moved from furnished rooms to cellars, but wherever she was, she surrounded herself with playthings, dolls, stuffed animals, and knickknacks. Most of her days and nights were spent at the same Berlin café which she described as "our nocturnal home . . . our oasis, our gypsy caravan, our tent in which we can rest after the painful battles of the day."

It was in this Berlin café atmosphere that Lasker-Schüler wrote the poems which were to comprise her Expressionist volume, *My Wonder* (*Meine Wunder*), published in 1911. In these seemingly dialogical poems, the heart's cry—the poet's confessions of ecstasy as well as raw pain—is powerfully intoned in a charged collage of end-stopped couplets. The "new freedom of association," the disengagement of the image from a mimetic grounding in external reality, characteristic of so much Expressionist art, is evident in *My Wonder.* The striking color symbolism found in many of the Expressionist artists was but a logical extension of this liberation. Like many of her fellow artists, Lasker-Schüler experienced the world in particular colors and translated that experience into her poetry. The most frequently encountered and possibly the most important color in Lasker-Schüler's palette is blue, the color which for her expresses all that is pure and godlike in the thoughts and feelings of mankind. Although Lasker-Schüler did adopt such Expressionist techniques—and she has frequently been categorized as an Expressionist poet—she did so primarily because she found in Expressionism a congenial reflection of her own particular imagination where limitations of time, space, and logic found little place.

It was also in the Berlin cafés that Lasker-Schüler became intimately acquainted with many of the great Expressionist artists of the period: Georg Trakl, who dedicated some of his most beautiful poems to her as did Gottfried Benn, with whom she had a tempestuous love affair; Franz Marc; Karl Kraus; Oscar Kokoschka; George Grosz; Franz Werfel; and others. Many of the poems in *My Wonder* are about, or are dedicated to, these and other artists. . . .

Many of the poet's earlier concerns and images recur in [*My Blue Piano,* her last volume of poetry], but with a density and, frequently, a calm largely absent in her early writings. The images of petrifaction and decay, which earlier had been associated with the quality of human responses, return in some of the last poems, but with a difference. In both "My Blue Piano" ("Mein blaues Klavier") and "Over Glistening Gravel" ("Über glitzernden Kies"), there occurs the new realization that there is something in the texture of the universe that is now out of tune with pristine harmony. "Over Glistening Gravel" speaks of the "downfall of the world" and of the consequent freeze and death that have stilled "all songs of love." Reminiscent of a Blakean song of experience, Lasker-Schüler's famous poem "My Blue Piano" similarly laments the loss of melody "since the world's decay." Heinz Politzer has called this the plaint of Orpheus [in "The Blue Piano of Else Lasker-Schüler, *Commentary,* 1950], and he is surely correct when he sees Lasker-Schüler as enriching the plaint with the desolate realization that even song had become estranged from herself:

> At home I have a blue piano
> But have no note to play.
>
> It stands in the shadow of the cellar door,
> There since the world's decay.

In the poem **"Jerusalem,"** the stony landscape of the holy city becomes a fitting counter for a larger spiritual paralysis indistinguishable from the poet's own inertia. Characteristically, it is only a meeting with the "you"—the ardently sought-after Other—that can bring both the poet and Jerusalem back to life again. Even though only part of a conditional wish fulfillment ("Were you to come . . ."), the poem ends in a present tense replete with process and promise:

> We are greeted by
> Living banners of the One God,
> Greening hands, sowing the breath of life.

Ever more aware of the progress of death in the world around her, Else Lasker-Schüler never surrendered her visions. They had caused her much anguish in her contact with the world; they also inspired moments of ecstasy and profound calm. In **"I Know" ("Ich weiss")**, a poem which speaks of her approaching death, Lasker-Schüler is still able to see the world in sensuous terms, a vision which is deepened by a resonant serenity:

> My breath hovers over God's river—
> Softly I set my foot
> On the path to my eternal home.

That note of peace, distant echo of the imagined harmonies that once sounded from her blue piano, was one of the few that Else Lasker-Schüler ever knew. . . .

Robert P. Newton   (essay date 1982)

SOURCE: An introduction to *Your Diamond Dreams Cut Open My Arteries* by Else Lasker-Schüler, translated by Robert P. Newton, The University of North Carolina Press, 1982, pp. 3-50.

[*Newton is an American educator, translator, and noted scholar of German poetry. In the following excerpt, he provides an overview of Lasker-Schüler's career and the criticism on her works.*]

Though the basic themes of Lasker-Schüler's art persist through all of her books, lines of thematic and formal development do exist. . . . Her first-born (*Styx,* 1902) contains, if we may believe the poetess, some poems that had been written in her adolescent years, from the age of fifteen to seventeen. In this volume she had not yet developed her most characteristic metrical style—the two- and three-line, free-verse strophes—but her rhymed forms are often handled freely in terms of meter and stanzaic structure. The use of extravagant, grotesque, intensifying metaphor is already her own. The main themes—love, dejection, religious feeling, her child—are all convoked, but verses astir with a candid erotic passion are more prominent than in her settled years, and, on the whole, the taste of the times shows through. But despite its reflection of literary fashion, the volume contains some fine lyrics.

Echoes of neoromanticism, decadence, and art nouveau can be heard in the titles: **"Jealousy," "Instinct," "My Blush," "Nervus Erotis," "Vagabonds," "Old Spring," "Orgy," "Fever," "Eros," "Sensual Ecstasy"**; or, in the fashion of romantic demonism: **"Damnation," "Chaos,"** **"Weltschmerz," "The Fallen Angel," "Suicide," "Guilt," "Unhappy Hate," "After-Pain," "Revenge," "The Fear Deep in My Blood."**

The desire for love is there, and for union, both sexual and spiritual. Complete union is the goal, a spiritual state that rejects real circumstances and exists at a perpetually high pitch. It cannot, like simple friendship, be induced or cultivated; it either takes place between two people or it does not. Lasker-Schüler deprecates mere "love," which is bourgeois, compared with her own overpowering "falling in love" (*verliebt sein*), a faculty in which she knows that few can match her, for, in the same breath she goes on to say, "Or somebody must have loved me. Did you love me, Herwarth? Who loved me?"

She herself did not hesitate to give the answer: she herself. For the love that remained true after the disappointment of unresponsive and unfaithful lovers was narcissistic; "I am my only immortal love," she said at one time, with obvious pleasure in her aphorism, however painful the fact. A friend, Grete Fischer, opines, "She was in love with love. I hardly believe that she was in love with the men about whom she speaks with such enthusiasm" [*Else Lasker-Schüler: Ein Buch zum 100. Geburtstag,* 1969]. The poetess confided to Karl Kraus, "I know so many people I write a love poem for six people together"; and "The only important thing is how I give expression to the models. I have nothing further to do with them"; and "I only need people to furnish my stars." She wrote to Walden, "I never perceived people other than as a frame in which I put myself."

But it would be a mistake to press this psychological catechizing to an extreme. Unquestionably she had known real love—for Peter Hille, Gottfried Benn, Johannes Holzmann, her son, her mother. And despite the professional cynicism of the artist in her *bons mots* to Karl Kraus, her friends and Lasker-Schüler herself record repeated infatuations on her part until advanced age; the beautiful **"A Love Song"** appeared in her last book. Shades of Goethe! (And was Goethe always "really" in love?)

She may have been well aware that these fleeting enchantments were a game, but it was *her* vital game, the talent, along with her gift for language, that gave meaning to her life as a homeless transient. Love was for her a source of vitality and a resurrection of the spirit, the counteractive to hate and violence, as we read in the poem **"Autumn,"** where her memories of National Socialist torchlight parades may also be invoked: "Eternal life to *him* who can say much of love. / A being of *love* will rise most certainly! / Hate boxes in! High though the torch may flare above."

It is less clear what we are to think of Lasker-Schüler's personal erotic propensities. There are some torridly beautiful verses in *Styx,* for example in **"Sensual Ecstasy"** or in these lines from **"Fortissimo":** "And our desire came breaking loose / And hunted us in blood-storm swells: / We sank into the Smyrna moss / Gone wild and screaming like gazelles." The arsenal of images in the early poems is bristling with fires, conflagrations, glowings, pourings, sinkings, plungings. Curiously enough, we have no way of verifying to what extent these poetic visions record actual desires or erotic adventures. Other than her possible but puzzling affair with the father of her child, the nebulous Alcibiades de Rouan, it is difficult to pin down a specifically sexual encounter, although it is sometimes assumed her relationship with Benn was such. To be sure, Kurt Hiller accused her of seducing young poets to win their loyalty "in a base way"; but this unchivalrous charge aroused her intense and apparently honest indignation. Here, offended honor was involved, but, in addition, a kind of aesthetic prudishness can be detected in what she allegedly said to Sigismund von Radecki: "The physical act by which a human being is created is something so impossible that it is only justified when two people, because of their love, simply can't do otherwise" [*Dichtungen und Dokumente,* 1951]. Nevertheless, in her own prose writings, more reliable than Radecki's report, what we find is a balanced view of spiritual and physical love, not at all Victorian or Wilhelminian: "I am thence at least capable of understanding man's body, which God created after his primordial image. And I wonder why one should despise this image, the flesh, the covering of the soul, especially since we enjoy the foliage of the forest, luxuriantly dense, and of each individual tree; why not the beauty of the bodily temple, which preserves in itself a treasure, the most holy, the soul" [*Gesammelte Werke,* Vol. 2, 1962]. The imagery here is itself probably sexual. The body, i.e., sexuality, was for her in her later essayistic writings a pathway to and for the soul. Lasker-Schüler sees even the prostitute's profession as just a pretext; even she is only looking for a residue of paradise: "Love is always a psychic possession, sexuality its chalice. To reject sexuality thus would mean not to respect the body that hosts the soul. This often occurs erroneously. But I think sexuality is to be condemned which isn't seeking love's paradise. I praise the Don Juan, who, through all the hearts, is only seeking the paradisical one. Naturally there is a love, prepared in the love-light of God's East, which needs no chalice" [*Gesammelte Werke,* Vol. 1].

[Hans W.] Cohn maintains that this latter, unchaliced love is given pride of place by Lasker-Schüler [*Else Lasker-Schüler: The Broken World,* 1974]. This does not necessarily emerge from the passage or the context, although it is true that platonic relationships such as hers to Johannes Holzmann ("Senna Hoy") were important occasions of her life, almost parareligious experiences. Yet the above passage was written from the viewpoint of a woman in later years and need not express the attitude of the author of the *Styx.* Actually, only the poems themselves tell us about the force of eros in Lasker-Schüler's youth, and if we believe them—even discounting a bit of literary pose—it was a drive of which she was much aware, whether or not (very likely not) it was promiscuously indulged. Cohn himself points out the candor and mature psychological self-observation of poems like **"Instinct,"** where "the expression of sexual need does not betray any feeling of guilt."

Both specific and oblique sexual imagery abounds in the poetry. In contrast to the body-soul harmony promulgated in her later prose writings, the sexual drive may be depicted as an uncontrollable force or attack to which she submits will-lessly (**"Instinct"**), or as a torture (**"In-**stinct"**) or narcotic (**"Sensual Ecstasy"**), while in another mood it is felt as a joyful, inseparable union of rushing cataracts (**"Viva!"**) or the wild rapture of gazelles (**"Fortissimo"**). In **"Knowledge,"** she celebrates the "primal cry, the song of Eve," whose "longing was the snake"; and in **"Flight of Love"** (from *The Seventh Day,* her second book of lyrics) a lover "leaped with me on the winds, / Godwards, until our breath gave way." The whole spectrum of the sex drive's sometimes alien, sometimes exultant, but always overmastering force is clearly projected from: "Let's whet our lusts in hellish heats" (**"Vagabonds"**) to "Now like two children let us play" (**"Spring"**).

Yet there are also indications of resentment at the power of this instinctive drive. In **"Karma"** the speaker mutters morosely, "In a night of stars all blazing free / I killed the man who was next to me"; and in **"His Blood,"** the tormented blood (read "natural instinct") of the lover would "really prefer to pluck my joy's / Last rose in Maytime / And throw it in the gutter slime." In the poem **"My Drama"** the poetess seems to resent being "lured" and thinks her beloved is, if the truth were told, "afraid" of her; she is miserable, longs for her loneliness and has learned "hate for my body, my heart's blood and him." In the uncharacteristically Gothic **"Ballad from the Mountains of the Sauerland,"** it is the woman figure who exercises a demonic domination destructive to the man, and in **"Elegy,"** a love "which had died young" drives her "exhausted into Satan's arms."

It has frequently been noted that there was a distinct masculine component in Lasker-Schüler's nature. She wore short hair and sometimes pants, before these became customary feminine attributes. Her mythical masks (in the prose) were often male—the Prince of Thebes, Jussuf of Egypt—although in her poems she normally speaks in her own woman's voice. Perhaps close identification with father, brother, son, and platonic lovers reinforced this tendency, though certainly her mother was a primary guiding figure in her life. However, the poems themselves only infrequently hint at any homoerotic tendencies, e.g., in **"Old Spring."** More often the relation of two ostensible males (**"Pharaoh and Joseph"** or **"David and Jonathan"**) is really more like that of male and female, with the poetess speaking from the female point of view. Most of the imagery presupposes a feminine self-conception of freely chosen devotedness, along with the unquestioned acceptance of an emotionally strong sexual role, both experienced within the limits of an absolute personal independence. In this respect, despite some turn-of-the-century arabesques of sentiment and literary allusion, she seems to me quite modern in her realization of an autonomous femininity, with all the open potentials for gratification and disaster that any extreme autonomy of character imports.

The Seventh Day (1905), the next volume of lyrics, was dedicated to her mother as *Styx* had been to both "dear parents." It was published by a different house, as indeed almost each of her books was; she was convinced of the exploitative intent of her successive publishers and compared their enterprises to the "bordellos of soul-merchants." This book, about half the size of the previous one, contains several poems considerably longer than preceding efforts (**"Knowledge," "My Quiet Song"**)—a departure that was soon abandoned. Here also appeared some early unrhymed triadic stanzas (**"Dove That Swims in Its Own Blood," "My Love Song"**) and the unrhymed two-line stanzas (**"My Quiet Song"**) that proved to be Lasker-Schüler's most unique and fruitful formal innovations, later perfected into the hymnic earmark of her work. (Two brief rhymed two-liners, **"Weltschmerz"** and **"Karma,"** had been published in *Styx*.)

Thematically, the *Seventh Day* is familiar, although several humorous poems open new territory (**"School Days," "Grotesque"**), but the best examples of her irony and grotesque humor are naturally in the prose. **"The End of the World,"** adopting a favorite motif of the expressionists, implies the death of God, while other poems are preoccupied with human mortality, her fear of which was undoubtedly sharpened by perceiving the transitoriness of her own feelings. The poet is obviously well on the way to her personal imaginative and metric style, though literary echoes still can be heard—for example, of Stefan George in **"Fighters"** (**"Streiter"** . . .). The best attempts are in the new rhymeless forms.

In *My Miracles* (1911) we witness the ripening mastery of poems written in two- or three-line strophes or in a mixture of various verse-group lengths. Among these stand the first of the biblical poems, such as the fine **"Pharaoh and Joseph,"** as well as her perhaps most famous lyric, **"An Old Tibetan Rug."**

This signatory style of Lasker-Schüler has often been compared to the metric of paralleled members (*parallelismus membrorum*) employed by Hebrew poetry, as in the *Psalms,* but parallelism in the sense of repeated syntactical structures or of the pairing of synonymous or substantively related (or contrasted) images is not present. Lasker-Schüler claimed to have read frequently in the Bible, but her familiarity with it has been questioned. Nevertheless, in her verses as in biblical poetry we experience a comparable series of brief paratactic statements, heavy with imagery but without metrical regularity.

It may be significant, regarding the question of influence, that the poetess once claimed in her half-serious, half-ironic way that her poems were written in Hebrew. Because of this affinity her characteristic form has been called by [Fritz] Martini "mythically old and at the same time very modern. . . . Modernity was ready for the forms of the archaic," [*Der deutsche Expressionismus: Formen und Gestalten,* 1965] an idea recalling Thomas Mann's theory of modern art in *Doctor Faustus* as an intellectualized reversion to primitive forms. But in Lasker-Schüler's poetry there is no trace of the "bloodless intellectuality" allied with "bloody barbarism" that is found in Adrian Leverkühn's music. Her poems give voice to the "soul" that Leverkühn lacked.

These short strophes in free verse are by no means without rhythmic principles, but they are mainly principles of proportion. There are, for example, usually limits to the number of emphatic stresses grouped in a strophe; in **"Pharaoh and Joseph,"** in the German original, this number varies from five to nine. Strophes may show the same number of emphases in each verse or may contain both longer and shorter lines, variations in this point enlivening the rhythm. Most frequently, syntax and strophe proceed in congruence—each verse group comprises a single sentence; sometimes, however, the syntax is allowed to enjamb. Verse-end pauses may coincide with any phrasal juncture but will not intervene within a prepositional or noun phrase. More than in regular metrical poetry there is a strong interaction between breath grouping and the endings of verse and stanza. A rhythmic factor hardly to be overestimated in its importance is the overlapping enchainment of inner assonance, which does so much to provide continuity to the rhythmic flow. In this, Lasker-Schüler is a master. A grasp of the dynamic relationship of repeated sounds is a vital compositional skill in the euphony of free verse, and we have been told that even as a child Lasker-Schüler was sensitive to the disharmony of off-rhymes (though they litter her poems and were thus probably consciously accepted as a means of expressive freedom).

The phenomenological correlative of these devices, in concord, has been described as "dreamspun music," / "magical monotony," / or a "proclamatory tone" such as that in Old Testament poetry. At its best, it mildly hypnotizes and creates the same hyperaesthesia as meter, but more than regular meter it alerts the listener to the palpable objective silence that the poet's words must dominate. The images are strung in luminous isolation, each suspended in a moment of unique tension, each subject to time's immediate decay. Psychologically, the representations proceed more as in memory or in dream than as in conscious reflection or in direct reality. Lasker-Schüler has in this way realized the necessary aesthetic distance from her emotions, which tend to be unrestrained or sentimentalized. Ceremonious attention, even solemnity, reins the affections; a reposeful measuredness is insinuated by the strophic rhythm.

This dream-speech can, of course, also lapse into mere routine, a mechanical mannerism, but that is true in the same degree of regular metrical poetry; we are simply more attuned to, and thus unaware of, the strictures of the latter. One specific source of potential monotony in this particular form, however, is the lack of interaction between a rhythmic norm and the norm's incomplete realization in concrete language. Since there is no fixed standard, we lose the sense of variety. This is a debility in all free verse, but particularly in Lasker-Schüler's short verses and sentences (as opposed to long rhapsodic lines of free verse), which arouse an expectation of proportional rhythmic form but lack a firm norm that could underline moments of expressive change. At times they may fail to escape repetitiveness and may become a "flowing into boundlessness," which never reaches the intended end of movement in fulfilled repose. Actually, from the viewpoint of both logic and thematic development, Lasker-Schüler has occasional trouble in gathering her poems to an effective conclusion, a weakness consequent in part on her effusive, imagistic style.

A traditional topos employed by tone-deaf critics is the supposedly crushing announcement that free verse sounds no different than prose, a charge supported by typographical resetting of the poem in question in a prose format. Dieter Bänsch, [in *Else Lasker-Schüler: Zur Kritik eines, etablierten Bildes,* 1971], does just this with Lasker-Schüler, and *mirabile dictu*—at the magic swish of a scholar's pointer-wand—the poem indeed then sounds like prose. But, naturally, one has destroyed the whole structure of rhythm in the process and should not be proud of the results. The reverse transformation is just as astonishing (if not more so); real prose reset in short lines that introduce rhythmic proportions and recurrent pauses, thus focusing attention on the sounds themselves, will lead a reader to assume the heightened ethos of poetic performance.

We have every reason to believe that the finely tuned rhythm we hear in these poems was the music heard by Lasker-Schüler herself. In her recitations she was credited [in *Else Lasker-Schüler: Ein Buch zum 100. Geburtstag*] with a "masterful" delivery, carried by a "dark, melodic, expressive voice," however odd her other sound effects (bells, flutes) and her exorbitant garb may have appeared. Her conscious theory concerning the relationship between breathing and poetry led her to report that she felt "bodily injury from a vowel or consonant that causes undefined disturbances in measure or hearing" (meter or sound harmony is what she probably meant.) Not infrequently her *regular* metrical forms show deviations from their given schemes. One cannot be sure that she consciously scanned her verses (I rather imagine she would have thought that pedantry), but it is precisely in the nature of free verse that one dare spurn such Philistine niceties as scansion, and the poet's inner rhythm can hold sway.

In *My Miracles* we first take note of recurring motifs that acquire symbolic value. These verbal counters seem to be extremely important for the poetess, even if in their later persistence they at times begin to ring hollow.

Foremost among these hieroglyphs is certainly the "star." Even visually, Lasker-Schüler was fascinated by the star as conventionally drawn; her sketches frequently imprint it on the cheek or brow of human faces, on buildings, even show it, as Philistines might expect, in the sky. Such drawings come to mind then when we read: "I am a star / In the blue cloud of your face" (from **"But Your Brows Are a Storm"**), where the image also bears a symbolic meaning. Her letters, too, are full of pictorial doodlings and ideographs, including frequent stars.

But the meaning of "star" as a metaphor is somewhat elusive. The poem **"Say It Softly"** begins "You took for yourself all the stars / Above my heart," and in **"Reconciliation"** we are informed, "There will be a giant star fall in my womb," and in **"Evening"** . . . , "A weeping angel carves the inscription / On the pillar of my body in stars." The natural and conventional symbolism of stars includes the semantic features: brilliance, distance, fateful significance, order, everlastingness. Such meanings may often be applied in Lasker-Schüler's poems; the "star" there may suggest a high, incandescent moment of feeling, or something or someone of unchanging brilliance, a lodestar inaccessible to the lower creatures of the earth. Cohn sees the image simply as a symbol of transcendence, which perhaps lacks in precision because it ignores the suggestions of radiance and significance. For [Walter] Muschg the star is the "absolutely miraculous, the grace of love"; to bear it on one's face is a sign of the elect [*Von Trakl zu Brecht: Dichter des Expressionismus,* 1961]. In Georges Schlocker's view the star becomes a token of the "miraculous worlds" to which the poetess aspires out of her constitutional ennui [*Expressionismus*].

In a little noted essay titled **"Astrology,"** in the volume *Visions (Gesichte),* Lasker-Schüler contrasts the original chaos in the self, which is palpable and the source of suffering, with the "star system" in the same self, which is untouchable and regulatory: "I speak of your most invisible, of your highest part, which you cannot grasp, like the stars above you." The descent of God's son to earth, for example, is a "transformation from star into chaos." (Lasker-Schüler speaks figuratively here to express God's entry into the earthly being of Jesus.)

An "undisturbed astral course" is what determines the greatness of human figures, like St. Peter Hille, whereas human ills stem from the collision of "stars strayed from their paths." One dies of "burst stars or the chilling of your sun or from darkness." In this "astrological" context, we can understand the stars as the vital determinant forces of each human fate, whose harmonious constellation and unabating energy light up the chaos of the unconscious life and whose clear radiance attracts other souls charismatically. A star as a person is a kind of spiritual guardian: "O she was a staress— / Strewed shimmering light around her" (**"Alice Trübner"**); or "All of my dreams hang from your gold; / I have chosen you among all stars" (**"Secretly at Night"**). Lasker-Schüler was not versed in conventional symbolism, but it is interesting to note in conjunction with the **"Astrology"** essay that J. E. Cirlot's *Dictionary of Symbols,* based on a multicultural survey, finds that the star "stands for the forces of the spirit struggling against the forces of darkness," a meaning that, [J. E. Cirlot claims in *A Dictionary of Symbols,* 1962], appears worldwide in emblematic art.

The poetess's astral views help to explain such otherwise abstruse verses as: "See my colors / Black and star" (**"To Giselheer the Heathen"**), where black represents material chaos and the curious adjective "star" suggests the transcendent light, both of which poles she recognizes in herself and others. In **"Reconciliation,"** with its initial line "There will be a giant star fall in my womb," she expects a miraculous regenerative force to accompany her reconciliation with the person addressed; life will be renewed; "Whenever we embrace we do not die." The ambiguity of the word *Schoß* in the original of this poem, meaning either "lap" or "womb," imports a subliminally erotic image that also suggests the renewal of life through procreation. The common interpretation of this poem sees it as referring primarily to the Day of Atonement. This view is supported in the text by the prayer in a harp-shaped alphabet, i.e., Hebrew, by the overflow of God, and by the word "Versöhnung," which in German also occurs in the translation of Yom Kippur. This theory, however, overlooks the obviously given situation that a lover is addressing her beloved and the fact that the word "versöhnen" in the original appears as a reflexive ("Wir wollen uns versöhnen die Nacht"), almost certainly indicating a personal reconciliation rather than a ritual of atonement.

A closely related symbol is the color *blue,* which Cohn terms the "color of the spirit" or of "spiritual peace." Blue, Schlocker contends, is the "covering of the divine," a cue that opens vast "spiritual spaces" for Lasker-Schüler. Blue is in fact often associated with an immaterial realm of purity by natural symbolism; Cirlot lists thinking, truth, equilibrium, religious feeling, heaven, devotion, and innocence as correlatives of blue in various cultures. In **"Say It Softly"** the blueness of the eyes of her lover has been stolen from an archangel, and in **"I Am Sad"** the lover appears "Blue from [caused by] Paradise," suggesting heavenliness, calm, integrity, and innocence. The same qualities make sense of her claim in **"Prayer":** "I brought love to the world, and light— / So every heart can blossom forth in blue."

Gold, say Muschg and Cohn, has an erotic connotation for the poetess; they have in mind, perhaps, lines such as "And like the moon of gold—your body" in **"From Afar".** . . . For Guder it implies nobility or is mere decoration [*The Broken World*]. In Cirlot's broader cultural view it is the color of superiority and glory, correspondent to the sun. It is indeed true in Lasker-Schüler's work that *gold* most commonly appears in the physical description of people, often to glorify the color of skin or hair, or generally to exalt the feature described. Erotic overtones are perhaps intended in **"A Love Song":** "A night of gold; / Stars made of night . . . / Nobody sees us"; but these are less likely in a metaphor such as "Golden icons / Are your eyes," in the poem **"When I Met Tristan".** . . .

Other motifs, such as the *angel, wing, flower, sea, night, mother,* and *heart,* would reward an effort at more exact definition, but they often adhere to the natural, conventional, or figurative implications of the words. Nevertheless, reference to Lasker-Schüler's prose is sometimes helpful. When she writes in *Concert,* in the essay **"Friendship and Love,"** that unrequited love is a case of the wings of love's angel being broken, we immediately recall the first stanza of **"Prayer":**

> I'm searching for a city in these lands
> Before whose gate a mighty angel stands;
> For, broken at the shoulder blade,
> I bear his wings' gigantic spans,
> And on my brow his star as seal is laid.

The dejected and forlorn poetess searches for the angel of love, love that is not returned but whose broken wing (the power of love's flight) she possesses and whose star (symbol of a guiding light) is imprinted on her brow—as in the sketches she never tired of drawing.

Hebrew Ballads (1913) enjoys a greater degree of thematic unity than any of its predecessors. Its topics are all religious, mainly profiles of biblical figures or episodes, hardly ballads at all, but reinterpretations or original legends with a powerful immediacy of their own. This biblical involvement presages, but does not as yet fulfill, the later turn to a more personal religious lyricism. In this volume—not constricted by fidelity to the letter of the Testament—she conjures up her own visions of Abraham,

Jacob, Joseph, and others, setting them in a poetic world that, as Bänsch correctly notes, is as characteristic of the turn-of-the-century scene as it is of early Hebraic history. The portrait of **"Jacob,"** for example, bears little resemblance to its subject, but its titanism and narcissistic smile of defeat (or victory) would seem quite in order for a hero of the decadence.

These historical motifs produce an effect of objectivity, because the poems, even when spoken in the first person, are constrained in part by the factual model and hence mask to some extent the poet's subjectivity. This quality makes the *Hebrew Ballads,* for Hans Cohn, "the most evenly excellent of all her collections," and Fritz Martini affirms that with this book she became the greatest poet of Jewish faith writing in German in the twentieth century.

From the aesthetic point of view, these poems are indeed more consistently harmonious structures than those of the earlier creative periods. Compared with Rilke's biblical poetry, Bänsch states, they may seem "more Old Testament-like, more inelegant, more naïve." "Like in an edifying book for children," Bänsch remarks, "little stories are unfolded." But there are moments of terse drama in Lasker-Schüler's language, the repertoire of images is refreshed, and a chiseled, archaic quality is achieved in poems like **"Abraham and Isaac"** or **"Moses and Joshua,"** which is more robust than Rilke's suave rhythms and subtle perceptions.

Lasker-Schüler's relationship to Judaism was personally and culturally deep but not theologically exclusive. She called herself a "most fervent Herbrew" and was, as Cohn says, "profoundly conscious of being a Jew"—even as a child she had been exposed to anti-Semitism—but her religious piety toward life encompassed everyone of comparable good faith, be it a Catholic Hille or a Protestant-born Benn. The Bible strongly influenced her themes and style; certain Judaic conceptions, such as paradise and the fall, she grasped in terms of her loss of childhood's security, and Eve became a symbol of her womanhood as did Jerusalem of the final homeland. She knew a bit about Jewish mysticism; what she was familiar with in the Jewish literary tradition is unclear. Yet all of these circumstances, as significant as they are, do not add up to a doctrinal faith but rather more to a tradition of religious culture. She identified with the Jewish people (see **"My People"**) but actually more, according to Sigismund von Radecki, with the "wild, Maccabean Jews." In her own words, "It's fine to be a Jew . . . if one has remained true to it, grown part of it, not misled by any external triviality, but washed by the Jordan. Who can tear me away from the old skeleton of Jehovah, the unshakable rock."

Yet she did not countenance the fractioning of religion by a sectarian spirit. Lack of theological rigor is evident in her ambiguous attitude toward the figure of Jesus. She was not beyond calling him the Messiah or God's son, and she could even say, perhaps in a mood to flabbergast the middle classes, that "the Jew who rejects the Heavenly One [Jesus] proves that he is a bourgeois." She wrote a poem to Mary and often refers to the Nazarene, but it was as human figures that she was devoted to them, as part of her heritage of Jewish religious paragons like the characters of the Old Testament, "the people of the primordial stories who laid the roots of mankind." Her love for Jesus and his mission, for his apostles, and for early Christianity extends only through the time of the early Christians' persecution. In later years she wrote, "Today I am sympathetic only to individual persons, whatever their religion may be." Ernst Ginsberg [in *Else Lasker-Schüler: Zur Kritik eines etablierten Bildes*] claims that in the early thirties Lasker-Schüler was on the point of converting to Catholicism, but, even should that be the case (and it is not hinted at elsewhere), one should not assume it would have basically changed her eclectic religious views or her loyalty to her mythical Joseph, to **"My People"** or to Jerusalem. For her there was only "one faith, one God, one creation, one heaven." In exile in the real Jerusalem of strife and tension, she hoped in vain to find a "reconciliation" realized and in the end, Cohn notes, found her refuge to be spiritually dead, a sentiment underlying the poem **"Jerusalem."** But not even that could mar her spirit's mythical city.

No genre of the lyric is so uniquely Lasker-Schüler's as the pointillistic portraits of her beloved ones and friends, those of the former largely hymnic, those of the latter sometimes chatty and informal. Both come to the fore in the **Collected Poems** (1917), which adds to the reprinted earlier works those new series of poems dedicated several-

ly to Senna Hoy, Hans Ehrenbaum-Degele, Gottfried Benn, Hans Adalbert von Maltzahn, and to **"My Beautiful Mother."** In the first four series are gathered some of her finest love poems in two- and three-line stanzas, works that are usually eulogistic but containing a few, particularly among those to Benn, that express the dejection of disappointed love and reproach the beloved, usually mildly. The last two series unite sketches of her numerous friends with poems to her sister and child, some of them drawn from earlier books. In **"My Beautiful Mother"** rhyme schemes reappear, and love poetry is absent. The portraits of friends in the Maltzahn group share the situational objectivity of the **Hebrew Ballads** and, like them, expand the previous range of motifs and feelings, thus breaking the spell of a style that tended increasingly toward automatism. These works vividly recreate for us the atmosphere of the poetess's activities and companionship in Berlin during the most youthfully vigorous and outgoing years of her life, and they add a certain ballast of social reality to the solitary, burning elevations in which the poetess confronts her beloved. Whether or not these vignettes of admiring friendship truthfully reproduce their subjects, they are at least poetic artifacts in their own right, sharply limned mosaics in bright pinpointed colors.

The late poems of Else Lasker-Schüler, harvest of the sor-

The dedication of a memorial in the summer of 1989 to Lasker-Schüler in her birthplace, Wuppertal-Elberfeld.

rows of penurious years and endless loneliness, of her son's death and the terror of her flight and exile, spread a mood of resignation sometimes succumbing to hopelessness; yet they also speak the language of an increasingly humble personal piety in some of her best religious lyrics such as **"God Hear . . ."** in *Concert* (1932), **"Prayer"** in *My Blue Piano* (1943), the movingly dignified elegy to her dead son (**"To My Child"**), and her apotheosis of love in **"Autumn."** The poetess returns to a contemplation of her own experience within now accepted limits of reality and in a less mannered style. The love poems, no longer in the majority, are less imperative, more modest, more touching in their honest respect for the otherness of the beloved.

Lasker-Schüler's relationship to God began in childish fantasy and ended in childlike faith. The God of her earlier poems may at one moment be a playful young father, wagging a finger with forced jollity at an even younger rascal of a poet (**"In the Beginning"**), while only shortly later it appears that God has precipitately aged and died (**"End of the World"**) or at least absconded. "God, where are you?" she asks in **"To God"**. . . . Bänsch quips that she treats God as one more poetic figure among others, almost as a painted decoration. But there is also a real and lasting skepticism in her soul. We have previously quoted her letter to Karl Kraus in 1914, when she was already forty-five years of age: "Waves are always beating on my heart; I always have to go over God's grave; I almost believe he's dead and the Bible is his tombstone. For human feelings it can only seem like willfulness—if he lives and has turned away." True to decadent rhetoric, Satan plays in the early poems a more reliably present role than God (**"Damnation," "Elegy"**).

Her feelings are marked by a vacillation between skepticism and a picture-book image of God the Father, between fear of his disappearance and the devotion of the mystical bride. She admits, "It is so easy to assert that there is no God" but confesses too, "I was always busy digging, not for gold but for God. I didn't dig for the eternal out of bold arrogance but from religious adventure-lust." The tone of her late poems is caught in an essay entitled **"My Devotion,"** from *Concert:* "I rely on God, because how often I have put my pain and joy into his hands." At this point she has apparently overcome the doubt that is prompted by the perennial problem of theodicy: how it is that God's omnipotence can tolerate evil, in particular the suffering of her soul, which longs to be devout? The world of the suffering body is here seen as an illusion, a mere "crystallization of the soul's homeward longing for protection in God the Father's hands," and it is thus of lesser reality. Perhaps she should have said, "God the Mother," because God's protectiveness toward the world is seen as the relation of mother and child. In any event, in her last poems a child's trustful submission to the parent's will is the experiential ground of her faith. God has become an imperative and not just a poetic image with which to convey charming beliefs or resentful desolations.

The propensity toward faith was a lifelong implication of her divided character: her constitutional commingling of sharp anxiety and dulled feeling, her sense of being a lonely outcast in society and yet suffocated by its grip, this lat-

ter an impression that in several respects—culminating in her persecution and forced exile—was only too close to the truth. God's was then the only reassuring love that would never reject or disappoint.

Her letters, real and fictional, repeatedly report that she is alone, even though she knows nice people, even in the Café of the West. She cannot find a bridge to anyone's soul. "Nobody can get to me, I can't get to anybody." She loves no one, and no one loves her. Life is purposeless; one takes refuge in one's self: "We're only on the way; life is just a way, has no arrival, because it isn't coming from anywhere. Where should one go anyway? Take refuge in yourself! That's why people are so poor, their hearts are asylums; they feel themselves secure in their sociable homesteads." She is driven to "flee mewards," in her **"Flight from the World."**

"I could never be compared with other people," she opined in a letter to Herwarth Walden, and she thought of herself as an Indian, a Robinson Crusoe, a Theban prince, Joseph the Egyptian, anybody but a mere Frau Else Lasker-Schüler, put down like a million others with their inexorable birth dates in a file in an archive in a swarming city somewhere on the Brandenburger flats. Her fantasy worlds were theatrically cozy homesteads envisioned by a homeless wanderer, who also, repeatedly and to great effect, burned bridges she had not yet built across the human stream.

But the stage behind these fantastic props stood empty again as soon as the poetess's audience had left. She was bored, benumbed, but apprehensive and afraid of death:

> I cannot find myself again
> In this dead abandonment!
> It's as if: I lie world-far from me
> Among gray night of old anxiety. (**"Chaos"**)

Urangst, "old anxiety," is for Cohn a key word, expressing the mood of her "rootlessness and isolation." It is the pathos of self-abandonment and helplessness, draining away the essential elán of life. In **"Spring Sorrow"** this "repose of death" is to be revivified by an infusion of her lover's warming "spring-like blood," for probably, as in **"Revenge"** . . . , "Death spent the night in my soul / And ate my springtimes." This ebbing of vitality is the victory of death's forces (**"The Fear Deep in My Blood"**), which, on more manic occasion (**"Youth"**), is roundly defied: "Why *me* in the City of the Dead, / Me, whose rejoicing's just begun." Symptomatically, a condition of listless dread and paralysis of feeling gives way to a spell of rebelliousness: "And my soul lies there like a pale, wide plain / And hears life grinding in the mill, / Dissolving in a heavy chill, / And gathering hot for battle once again" (in **"Fighters"** . . .). With the passing of youth, however, the resistance of sheer animal vitality had to give way to courage or to faith.

In the prose works Lasker-Schüler's depressive ennui is plainly described. She is "restless with fearful boredom." She is tired of life and wants to die adventuresomely: "I'm fed up with everything, even the leaves on the trees. Always green and always green. If only I'd meet some magical people, I mean some who had grand wishes, but they are all serious, only I am in earnest. I'm so lonely—whoever looks at me for a long time will fall into a dark—heaven." "I'm through; I hate to wake up in the morning because I hate the world; I don't want to sleep because I dream of the world." She clearly recognizes that this spiritual vastation is the obverse of her spiritual freedom: "I no longer have anything to hold on to. . . . I never made a system for myself like smart women do, never fortified a world-view like still smarter men, I haven't built myself an ark. I am unattached." Because she was unattached personally (especially after the death of Paul) and to an extent also socially (especially in exile), and because she served no ideology other than her art and found it to be unrecognized even in her Promised Land, she in the end turned back to her happier beginning and saw the power of love in herself not as hers to be requited—as such it had overpowered both others and herself—but as a divine presence: "Holy love which you blindly trampled / Is God's image." (**"I Lie Somewhere by the Side of the Road"** . . .). Love is the completed bridge between herself and God, to whom she could now proffer her soul with the modesty of a woman returning a lost possession to its rightful owner: "Oh God, though it of fault be full— / Take it quietly in your hand. . . . / That, in you, it may gleam—and end" (**"Prayer"**).

The potency of love is the immanence of God. This conviction becomes not only a religious principle but an aesthetic one as well, in the form: creativity is divine inspiration, hence a revelation, a belief that leads Bänsch to speak of Lasker-Schüler's "undaunted romantic definition of art and the founding of religion" as one and the same. She says, "I even assert that the artist who has overcome ambition is concerned only with the Nirvana of inspiration, drifting off into sleep, the streaming away of the heart, making room for God." A true work of art proceeds from a state of enthusiasm (*Schwärmerei;* the English word literally means to have God in oneself); and it is this state of the soul that is to be sought, not the poet's probably faulty record of the experience: "It is not the poem that is important, but the poetic state in which one creates it." Put thus, it sounds quite like the expressionist poetics, which extols the poet's intensity, ethical or aesthetic, rather than the technical perfection of his actual poems. The poetic state transcends the inadequacies of life as it sadly is; it is a resurrection: "I die from life and catch my breath again in images." So, despite her poverty, her writing made her rich: "I've been composing poetry now for two days and two nights; I'm actually a person who has many palaces. I can enter my poetdom, as wide as a thousand mornings and nights—and I cannot lose it, and the very fact that one must pay his taxes with his blood—that is possession."

We might be led to think that for Lasker-Schüler the poet's office is austerely sacerdotal, as it was for Stefan George. But we know already that it was also a kind of delightful game: "Whether one plays with green, lilac, and blue stones or whether one writes poetry, it's all the same, one has the same feeling of happiness, because one can't see the world any more vividly through ecstasy than through bits of [colored] glass." She metaphorized her writing habits like this: "I write for myself primarily, let everything I've written get hard like an earth, like a star that becomes earth. Then I take the earth in my hand and play ball with it." Translated into everyday reality, this suggests that the poetess, after an initial flow of associations, put her creations aside and later perhaps rearranged the parts—phrases, sentences, or strophes. In many poems the array of images is conceivably commutable; the pieces could be "played" in a different sequence; but, of course, each arrangement results in differently felt emphases in the experience. Very likely the composition is not by chance. We know that Lasker-Schüler worked over and revised her poems continuously, often long after their original publication. Compare, for example, the two versions of **"My Quiet Song."**

Lasker-Schüler rejected the intrusion of external "purpose" into art: "I almost slapped [Stefan] George on the street"—although on an earlier occasion she had approached and wordlessly given him a flower—"I was so disappointed. Affected people! Art shouldn't educate but crown with garlands." She was also distrustful of Hugo von Hofmannsthal's gracefully perfect form, especially of his *Jedermann's* didactic intent. Her own poetic labors were mainly in praise of others or were lamentations on the sorrows of the self.

Art was reception of God; it was a game with colored stones; but certainly it was not to be an exercise in intellectual or spiritual vanity, a public preening of one's feathers. Schalom Ben-Chorin reports [in *Else Lasker-Schüler: Ein Buch zum 100. Geburtstag*] that she did not like self-conscious talk about artistic matters, preferring to discuss—it sounds quite curious—politics. She once exclaimed, "You wouldn't believe how literary topics revolt me, that pluck to pieces and plunder the game, the charms of the soul. I am so alone, so barren inwardly that I scorn every sensation, every immodesty." A café friend whom she dubbed Cajus-Majus, Caesar of Rome, provoked her to the outburst: "If he only weren't always talking about literature! As long as it's my verses it's okay, but when he begins to blather about Aristophanes, let Dante's Inferno fetch him."

Some of her critics wish that she had been less reluctant to think about questions of taste. In the end we must also face those critical doubts that even sympathy never spared her. The most frequent charges are: kitsch, monotony, defective workmanship—all of them true to a degree.

Marianne Lienau, one of Else Lasker-Schüler's most unforgiving detractors, but not the only one, decries her "cutesy kitsch" (*neckischer Kitsch*), deplores her lack of self-criticism, and deprecates her "calamitous teen-ager tone" (*fataler Backfischton*). Apparently on political grounds, Lienau denies a gifted artist the right to say, "I don't know myself "; to do so is an asocial self-indulgence. Lasker-Schüler makes a cult of her Self without examining how this Self reflects her social being. She should have learned to distinguish between kitsch and real sweetness, gaiety and silliness, originality of language and buffoonery.

Perhaps Lasker-Schüler was herself regretting a certain sentimental indecisiveness of mind when she noted, "The teeth have fallen out of my thoughts, I think too sweetly," yet this very image shows how her uncontrolled associations can forge incisive language. The boundary between sentimentality and rapture is a fine one, as Schlocker admits, and not only the poet but also the reader may misjudge it subjectively. One might contend that it is best to avoid these swampy borderlands of feeling. For good or ill, however, poets tend to wander quite heedlessly through all the territory they inhabit. Lasker-Schüler's realm verged on the marshes of sentiment, that much is clear, and she inevitably sometimes crossed the line. Most readers will recognize this wavering boundary *within* her work, even within particular poems, without confining her finally to either side.

Her images, rhythms, and sentiments are sometimes repetitive. Bänsch detects a "wearying stereotypy," and for Schlocker she fails to escape the "danger of playing with the worn-out coins of words." Particularly in the two- and three-line stanzas, Lasker-Schüler's rhythmic style can ring repetitive because of the predominant conjoining of brief rhythmic and syntactic periods, their brevity being the (negative) operative factor. When, in addition, the images are picked from her staple stock of favorite "stones" or "buttons"—words like *star, blue, gold*—an individual poem may not come alive, especially if read in company with others that use the same repertoire. Of course, countless other poets have cultivated personal mannerisms or rethreshed empty grain—one thinks of Trakl immediately or even Heine—but what poet has not? The greatest poets will be the most continuous fountains of innovation; the merely good ones will be graced with a score of poems in which their genius springs to life, while the rest of their works may be respectfully shelved like significant scraps from the atelier, clues to the designs perfected in the best.

Her critics have begrudged the embattled poetess even these few perfected poems, though this is surely less easy to understand. Pörtner judges himself as a critic, rather than her as a poet, when he concludes: "I don't know any perfect poem by her. . . . When I seek in my memory I find words, series of words, verses of poems, but no poems." And Schlocker: "It is not given to the poem to reach ripeness" under Lasker-Schüler's hand. Or Heselhaus: "The literary significance of Lasker-Schüler lies in the individual pearls of the metaphors." It has become a repetitive cliché in its own right to describe Lasker-Schüler's poems as fragmentary and without logical development. Yet, although some poems may be circular "garlands of praise," the best progressively evoke their subject and build to a rhetorical climax. It is difficult to see how this simple fact can be overlooked.

Beginning with **"Spring,"** one can go on to name **"Old Spring," "Then," "Weltschmerz," "Viva!," "Fortissimo,"** and **"Youth,"** in *Styx* alone, as not necessarily great poems, but yet as developed, rounded, in their own way unflawed works. And who could carelessly deny the truly completed beauty of **"Reconciliation," "Pharaoh and Joseph," "A Song of Love," "To the Barbarian," "A Song," "George Trakl," "My Quiet Song"** (second version), **"Prayer," "Abraham and Isaac," "Moses and Joshua," "David and Jonathan," "Esther," "Genesis," "To My Child," "My Blue Piano," "Chased Away,"** or **"A Love Song"**?

The thematic range of these songs is narrow, if the forces of love and dejection can be thought of as limited, but the sentiments ring true, and the music is haunting and original. Solipsistic Lasker-Schüler may have been—eccentric, careless, paranoid, in some respects selfish. Yet the powerful glow of her eros holds transfixed for us in its beam the figures of long-forgotten people—people more practical than she, more selfless, less distracted, less anxious, less afraid of death, who did not jingle their cheap jewelry in others' faces, and who did not die with little left so far from home.

Where are they now, though?

In these few poems.

FURTHER READING

Biography

Hirshberg, Jehoash. "Joseph Tal's Homage to Else." *Ariel*, Jerusalem, No. 41 (1976): 83-93.

> Discusses Tal's opera based on Lasker-Schüler's life and works.

Criticism

Guder, G. "Else Lasker-Schüler's Conception of Herself as a Poet." *Orbis Litterarum* 25, No. 1 (1960): 184-99.

> Analyzes Lasker-Schüler's depiction of the poet as prophet in her poetry.

———. "The Meaning of Colour in Else Lasker-Schüler's Poetry." *German Life & Letters* XIV (1960-61): 175-87.

> Explores the symbolic use of color in Lasker-Schüler's poetry.

Zohn, Harry. "Poet and Scarecrow." *Times Literary Supplement*, No. 4,098 (16 October 1981): 1207.

> Briefly examines Lasker-Schüler's personal life and provides a mixed assessment of *Hebrew Ballads, and Other Poems*.

Additional coverage of Lasker-Schüler's life and works is contained in the following sources published by Gale Research: *Dictionary of Literary Biography*, Vols. 66 and 124.

Wilhelm Reich

1897-1957

Austrian-born American psychoanalyst.

INTRODUCTION

A major contributor to the early development of psycho-analysis, Reich is remembered primarily for his pioneering theories about human sexuality. Initially accepted as a legitimate theorist, Reich fell into disfavor with the scientific community as he advanced his later, more controversial, ideas and was for the most part dismissed at the time of his death as little more than a fraud with messianic delusions.

Biographical Information

Reich was born in Galicia and grew up in Bukowina, two provinces attached to Austria prior to the collapse of the Hapsburg empire in 1918. When Reich was fourteen his parents' turbulent relationship ended with the suicide of his mother after Reich informed his father of her affair with a tutor. Some scholars speculate that Reich was haunted by this incident for the remainder of his life, and that some of his psychosexual theories may have arisen from guilt over his mother's suicide. In 1916 Reich joined the Austrian army and served in Italy during World War I. After the war Reich went to Vienna to study medicine, becoming a practicing psychologist at the age of twenty-two. As a member of the Vienna Psychoanalytical Society, he encountered Freud's libido theory, which held that repressed sexual energy engendered most human neuroses. Reich accepted this idea and published his first major study of sexuality, *Die Funktion des Orgasmus* (*The Function of the Orgasm*), in 1927. He broke with Freud, however, over the role of society in the development of sexuality and neuroses. While Freud maintained that the sexual repression imposed by society was necessary to forestall anarchy, Reich argued that healthy sexual experiences would prevent both neuroses and social disintegration. In 1928 Reich joined the Austrian Communist Party and co-founded the Socialist Society for Sex Consultation and Sexological Research, setting up health and counseling clinics for the working classes. Two years later Reich moved to Berlin, where he helped establish a sex education program called Verlag für Sexualpolitik. In the early 1930s he was expelled from both the Communist Party and the International Psychoanalytic Association because of his advocacy of sex-oriented politics. Reich left Germany in 1938 to escape the Nazis, settling first in Denmark, then in Norway. By this time Reich had severed his ties with most of his scientific and political associates. He was driven from Scandinavia by a massive newspaper campaign against his increasingly narrow focus on the importance of sexuality, and in 1939 he emigrated to the United States. There he claimed to have discovered "orgone ener-

gy," a cosmic life force that could be captured in boxes Reich called orgone accumulators and used to cleanse the body and cure disease. In the 1940s Reich moved to Oregon, Maine, and built a laboratory to further study orgone energy. Reportedly becoming delusional, he believed he was being persecuted and developed a strong identification with Jesus Christ. He also began experiments with weather control and believed himself to be an alien. In the 1950s, in what is now considered by many scholars to be the result of McCarthyist hysteria and gross misunderstanding of Reich's essentially harmless experiments, the Food and Drug Administration brought charges of fraud against Reich, stating that he alleged his orgone accumulators could cure cancer. Arguing that the court did not possess the scientific understanding to judge his work, Reich refused to comply with orders banning the use of all orgone accumulators and all references to orgone energy in his writings. He was charged with contempt of court and sentenced to two years in the Federal Penitentiary in Lewisburg, Pennsylvania. His orgone accumulators and most of his books were seized by authorities and burned in New York in 1956. Reich died in prison in 1957.

Major Works

Several of Reich's early works are considered standards of psychoanalytic study. *The Function of the Orgasm* is a Freudian examination in which Reich argued that healthy orgasm releases pent-up energy that, unreleased, will stagnate and cause neurosis. In *Charakteranalyse (Character Analysis)* Reich posited that individual character is an ego-defense mechanism, or "character armor," designed to protect people from threatening emotional situations. He maintained that the analyst's function was to break down character armor and thereby enable patients to undergo effective psychotherapy. Reich's reaction to nazism resulted in *Massenpsychologie des Faschismus (The Mass Psychology of Fascism)*, which contends that fascism is an expression of sexual repression. Much of Reich's later work evidences his fear of persecution and his frustration over the dismissal of his ideas. *Listen, Little Man!*, for example, is an inflammatory condemnation of the "common man." Other later works focus on his study of orgone energy and its alleged ability to cure emotional and physical illness.

Critical Reception

A controversial figure from the start, Reich first incurred strong disapproval from his colleagues when he differed from Freud on the issue of sex and society. His assertion that children should be allowed freedom for sexual experimentation led to further ostracism, and by the end of his life Reich was fully discredited as a doctor. Today critics consider his early writings, particularly *The Function of the Orgasm* and *Character Analysis*, to be seminal works in the field of psychoanalysis. Most critics maintain that although *The Mass Psychology of Fascism* is simplistic in its reasoning and development, its fundamental argument is valid. The existence of orgone energy has never been proven, although some commentators believe Reich's theory to be the forerunner to what is now known as alternative medicine.

*PRINCIPAL WORKS

Der triebhafte Charakter (nonfiction) 1925
Die Funktion des Orgasmus (nonfiction) 1927
  [*The Function of the Orgasm*, 1948]
Der Einbruch der Sexualmoral (nonfiction) 1932
  [*The Invasion of Compulsory Sex-Morality*, 1971]
Der Sexuelle Kampf der Jugend (nonfiction) 1932
Charakteranalyse (nonfiction) 1933
  [*Character Analysis*, 1945]
Massenpsychologie des Faschismus (nonfiction) 1933
  [*The Mass Psychology of Fascism*, 1946]
Dialektischer Materialismus und Psychoanalyse (nonfiction) 1934
Psychischer Kontakt und Vegetative Strömung (nonfiction) 1935
Die Sexualität im Kulturkampf (nonfiction) 1936
  [*The Sexual Revolution*, 1945]

Experimentelle Ergebnisse über die Elektrische Funktion von Sexualität und Angst (nonfiction) 1937
Die Bione (nonfiction) 1938
The Cancer Biopathy (nonfiction) 1948
Listen, Little Man! (nonfiction) 1948
Cosmic Superimposition (nonfiction) 1951
Ether, God, and Devil (nonfiction) 1951
The Orgone Energy Accumulator (nonfiction) 1951
The Emotional Plague of Mankind. 2 vols. (nonfiction) 1953
Sex-Pol: Essays 1929-1934 (essays) 1972

*Reich's early works were originally published in German, his later works in English.

CRITICISM

Paul Goodman   (essay date 1960)

SOURCE: "Dr. Reich's Banned Books," in *Utopian Essays and Practical Proposals,* Random House, 1962, pp. 138-44.

[*Goodman was an American writer and educator whose works include* Growing Up Absurd: Problems of Youth in the Organized System *(1960) and* People or Personnel: Decentralizing and the Mixed System *(1965). In the following essay, which was first published in 1960, he defends Reich's books at a time when they were banned by the Food and Drug Administration.*]

We are here concerned with the fate of Dr. Reich's books, banned by the Food and Drug Administration. The relation of theory and practice, of a scientific theory and its applications, is a thorny one; but it *must* in every case be decided in the direction of absolute freedom of speculation and publication, otherwise it is impossible to live and breathe. The practical policing of therapies is not an author's responsibility. The Administrator's reasoning in Section 5 of his injunction is intolerable; if it cannot be struck down, it must be flouted—we must applaud the republication (by Farrar, Straus) of some of the banned passages, and the forthcoming publication of *The Function of the Orgasm.*

The forbidding of "statements pertaining to the *existence* of orgone energy" is simply ludicrous. The Administrator of the drug law is not the Creator of the heavens and the earth; he is not even the Pope in Rome. Is he quite sane, to write such a proposition?

His notion of the books as "constituting labeling" is more interesting; for no one can candidly read *The Function of the Orgasm; The Cancer Biopathy; The Sexual Revolution; The Mass-Psychology of Fascism; Listen, Little Man;* or *Character Analysis* in any edition, and regard them as labels or advertisements. In the first place, the very vulgarity of such a conception makes one smile—and wince. The Administrator has been moving too much in the racketeering circles of the drug companies, the medical journals, and certain members of the A.M.A. who were recently under Congressional investigation for their plugging and pricing. But my guess is that the Administrator's lack of candor betrays a different intent. The real objection to Dr. Reich's work has little to do with orgone energy, but is to its whole drift as pedagogy, social science, and perhaps medical science; and *therefore* his books are banned and any convenient pretext is seized on to impede their circulation. Dealing with strong universal drives and terrible real situations, Dr. Reich's theories cannot easily be disregarded or explained away. They generate their own propaganda. Therefore it has been convenient to try to silence them altogether by treating them as commercial plugs for a contraband commodity. How American!

Consider a fair analogy to the Administrator's high-handed procedure in banning the books with the box. Let us compare Reich and Volta. At the end of the eighteenth century, Volta was able to make available electrical energy of any potential by wrapping some metal sticks in wet rags, a device as primitive as Reich's box. Now suppose that—inspired by his colleague Galvani's jumping dead frogs, and perhaps by Mesmer's "animal magnetism" (which we here analogize to Freud's "libido")—Volta or somebody else hit on the electro-shock therapy for "lunacy." (This therapy was highly esteemed among us ten years ago, is still in use, and has certainly done more damage than all the orgone accumulators, though nobody has gone to jail.) And suppose again that, like mesmerism in France, this electro-shock therapy was banned.

According to the logic of the Administrator of the drug law, all traces of Volta's battery, his equipment, his reports, his theory of differential potentials, should then be expunged from the face of the earth. They are labels for the illegal therapy. And the *existence* of flowing electricity must henceforth never be mentioned.

Whether or not Reich was a Volta, I don't know; but how in the devil is a bureaucrat to decide the question? It is the kind of thing that must be determined by generations of scholars and their experiments, with free publication and no holds barred. Naturally, as a human being, I hope that Reich was right and that we have discovered something new and wonderful, whatever the applications.

Let me say something about a few of these banned books. (I am writing from memory, if the reader will pardon me.)

The Function of the Orgasm is a classic almost by definition, from its title. For here Reich seized on a phenomenon of universal occurrence and obvious importance, definite, observable, and experimentable, which had nevertheless never been seriously studied. Simply making the obvious metabolic, electrical, and muscular observations and experiments, and fitting the findings into standard modern psychology and his own character-analytic methods, the doctor produced a great book. Why should not such a book exist? To answer this question I submit to the philosophical reader the following puzzle: How is it possible that this subject had to wait until the second quarter of the twentieth century to get a halfway adequate treatment? Indeed, the puzzle is still with us. E.g., in the Kinsey reports, although Reich's relevant studies are mentioned in

the bibliography, the statistics are nevertheless collected by counting undifferentiated and unstructured "climaxes," as though Reich's careful anatomy and physiology did not exist. Naturally Kinsey says many absurd things.

Quite apart from its ingenious cancer theory, *The Cancer Biopathy* is a remarkable work. For what Reich does again is to seize on problems and approaches that are important but are precisely swept under the rug or frowned on by modern medical orthodoxy: e.g., biogenesis, the frequent embarrassments of the germ-infection hypothesis, and especially the factors of susceptibility and resistance of various patients to various diseases. It is the hallmark of genius to pay attention to such dark and *suppressed* areas, and to find connections among entities that tend to be neglected. But it is not to be expected that the orthodox will shout for joy about it; nor that they will much respect the simple-mindedness and dumb-bunny apparatus of a primary researcher. At the same time, Reich's work is full in the stream of important cancer problems, e.g., the virus or nonvirus etiology, and the puzzling relevance of sexual organs and sexual types. It is a pity that the research reported never seems to be informed about Reich's hypotheses. It is not a field in which we can afford to burn books.

Listen, Little Man I remember as the anguished and somewhat frenzied outcry of a high-aspiring and inwardly oppressed strong soul caught in a petty and apathetic world. Not unlike a chapter out of Dostoevski, and exactly the kind of thing that should be reprinted in anthologies like the recent *Identity and Anxiety: Survival of the Person in Mass Society.* Why it should be banned and burned is beyond me, unless with the spiteful aim of blotting out a man's memory.

Character Analysis is a universally admired text, powerfully influential in modern clinical practice; and I am told that it is now legal "for professional use." It deals with character resistance, the muscular defensive "armor," and methods of active therapy.

The Sexual Revolution and *The Mass-Psychology of Fascism,* finally, are excellent studies in the application of psychoanalysis to politics and history, in the wake of Freud's *Mass-Psychology and the Analysis of the Ego* and *Totem and Taboo,* and no more exceptionable than the similar attempts of Fromm, Kardiner, etc. Like the others, Reich is concerned with the authoritarian character and especially, as an ex-Marxist, with the psychology of cultural lag. *The Sexual Revolution* contains a beautiful history of the reaction in the Soviet Union under Stalin and is, to my mind, invaluable for the understanding of that country. Both books, however, are practical in intent and prescribe, among other things, the sexual freedom of children and adolescents as absolutely essential for the restoration of social health. I am convinced that this is the explanation of the antagonism to them. (E.g., the liberal *New Republic* commissioned and then banned as scandalous a review of them that summarized their arguments.)

Such, roughly, are the actual contents of the books which have been banned and burned as "labels" for orgone accumulators! All six books are interesting; a couple are perhaps great. (I am not acquainted with the other, shorter, pamphlets on the banned list.)

I feel impelled to make a further remark to the Americans on this issue. We are living in a precarious time. Let me mention two aspects of it.

During the last months before the execution of Caryl Chessman, there were several polls of public opinion. By and large throughout the country, opinion ran more than 70 per cent against him. (The pacifist *Catholic Worker* reported with astonishment that *its* readers were 75 per cent for immediate execution!) But the significant thing was the tone of this opinion, as expressed in very many letters. It was violently, sickeningly sadistic, pornographic, and vindictive; and this on an issue not of momentary indignation, but after several years of discussion and debate. Now, the justice meted out to one individual is important; the question of capital punishment is important; but the tone of such a majority was, to my mind, the frightening and portentous fact about that case. It means that when I walk down the street, I am not safe, for these are the thoughts and feelings that seethe just beneath the civil surface in the majority of my fellow citizens. My friends and I, who want to live productively and sexually, must live here; and it is in this insane asylum that I have to bring up my children.

It was to the terrible reality of this "emotional plague," as he called it, that Dr. Reich directed his efforts, according to his lights. I do not know if he had the cure for it; but he accurately named the disease; and certainly no less radical prescription than his can possibly be of any avail. Our government jailed him and burned his books; but if he is not allowed to speak out, none of us will be allowed.

Secondly, on a world-wide scale many human beings are manufacturing bombs that can blow up the world; they are poisoning the atmosphere testing them; they are impressing the best brains of mankind in the study of how to develop them and best launch them. Meantime, the rest of the human beings, in the "advanced" nations, are acquiescing in this, paying for it, and de facto approving it. All this may explode any day. Such lunatic behavior and catatonic paralysis are not new things among us, but there has never been a time when the behavior was so dangerous and so universally admitted to be universally catastrophic, and when, therefore, the paralysis of people was so evidently irrational.

It was against this trend toward mass suicide that Dr. Reich evolved and, rather desperately, tried to apply his theory of primary masochism. Just as Freud spoke in despair of the need for Eros, and others of us are willing to risk other desperate alternatives like anarchy, ahimsa, and wooing the creator spirit. It is not a good time for Administrators to put obstacles in the way of freedom of the spirit. Get them out of the way.

Walter Briehl (essay date 1966)

SOURCE: "Wilhelm Reich: Character Analysis," in *Psychoanalytic Pioneers,* Franz Alexander, Samuel Eisenstein, Martin Grotjahn, eds., Basic Books, Inc., Publishers, 1966, pp. 430-38.

[*In the following essay, Briehl provides an overview of Reich's career as a psychoanalyst.*]

Of the many psychoanalysts who have contributed to the theoretical and technical aspects of the science, Wilhelm Reich stands out because of his overwhelming preoccupation with the problems of technique.

Reich was born in 1897 in Austria, where his father was a farmer. He became interested in biology early in life and, prior to his military service during World War I, maintained plant and insect collections and his own breeding laboratory. In 1918, at the age of twenty-one, he matriculated at the University of Vienna School of Medicine where he was awarded the Doctor of Medicine degree "with distinction." His post-graduate work was carried on at the Vienna Neuropsychiatric Institute under Julius von Wagner-Jauregg and Paul Schilder. At the age of twenty-three, while still a medical student, he attained membership in the Vienna Psychoanalytic Society, a recognition that could only be bestowed on one who showed promise in this field. The position of older members in the society—Federn, Hitschmann, Nunberg, and others—had already been firmly established by virtue of maturity and talent. Nevertheless, Reich's driving energy (expended in analysis, teaching, lecturing, writing, and administration) advanced his prestige rapidly. Temperamental clashes between Reich and other members of the group and differences of opinion concerning some of his ideas and technical procedures at times required the dispassionate intercession of Dr. Federn for the re-establishment of objectivity and soberness.

A basis for Reich's work seems to have been laid by Ferenczi of Budapest. Having been Freud's closest friend, Ferenczi was highly regarded in Vienna, even though his technique varied so sharply later in his from even the bold therapeutic innovations embodied in his "active therapy" that he and Freud parted psychoanalytic company. As Ferenczi had developed his active therapeutic procedures for use when and where a long trial of classical analysis is unable to penetrate ego structures, so Reich developed his theory and practice of character analysis after he discovered that all too frequently the therapeutic efforts of analysts had been thwarted, but because of countertransference this outcome had ended in a blind alley (*Sackgasse*) rationalized as the patient's resistance against getting well.

Reich was director of the Seminar for Psychoanalytic Therapy in Vienna from 1924 to 1930. This seminar was designed to work exclusively with case histories of stalemates and analytic failures; by its nature it proved a most stimulating and provocative undertaking. Contributions from this seminar and from his analyses furnished the material for his most important paper, **"Über Charakteranalyse,"** 1928, although before this publication numerous forerunners had appeared that had already created American interest in Reich as the representative of a more active psychoanalytic therapy in Vienna. Because of the inaccessibility of Freud (whose time and energy were reserved for such older and established colleagues as Clarence Oberndorf, Abram Kardiner, George Amsden, Smiley Blanton, Monroe Meyer, and Ruth Mack Brunswick), analysands who wished to go abroad to the psychoanalytic mecca, Vienna, were advised by training analysts in New York and by Ferenczi (who was lecturing in New York during 1926-1927) to go to Reich for their personal analyses. Accordingly, a number of persons who became prominent were brought into close contact with the personality and theories of Reich.

One of Reich's early papers lays down several rather categorical standards for successful or unsuccessful treatment. One, perhaps of greatest validity at that time, is this: "If the genital period is not reached either by genital masturbation, or genital exhibitionism or genital incestuous wishes, such cases have a bad prognosis" (1924). Reich supplemented some of the hypotheses of this paper with some technical principles in a report given before the Eighth International Association Congress in Salzburg in 1924:

> As a criterion of the genital or pregenital organization of adult patients, it is advisable to observe the specific form which onanism may assume in them. Here one must not hesitate to forbid absolutely every extra-genital form of onanism, but to encourage the genital form. And an analysis cannot be accounted complete until the patient has freed his genitality from the sense of guilt and withdrawn it from the incestuous object and also has finally risen above his prepregenital level of organization. The criteria of this change are to be found in the phantasies and dreams of the transference.

In 1926 Reich delivered a paper before the Vienna Seminar for Psychoanalytic Therapy that was the forerunner of his most distinguished work, *Character Analysis* (1945). This earlier presentation, which also appeared in the *Zeitschrift* (1927), was titled **"The Technique of Interpretation and of Resistance Analysis."** It is strange that this excellent paper never has been translated into English, dealing as it does with one of the most significant aspects of analytic therapy, the transference neurosis in its repressed and disguised manifestations—particularly in its negative aspects. In this paper, Reich laid special emphasis on, in essence, "no interpretation of content without first interpreting the resistance to the process of free association." (During this period of psychoanalysis the term "resistance" was used, later giving way to the broader term, "defense.")

Many of the ideas of technique that Reich was formulating in the later twenties accrued not only from his own experience but from the suggestions of members of the therapy seminar. He may not have been the originator of such ideas, but it must be said that in Vienna he was the dynamic power behind their organization. Freud often expressed regret that the teaching of psychoanalysis precludes the presence of an observer, as is possible in hospital bedside teaching. To reduce this inadequacy to a minimum, Reich conducted his seminar with informality and spontaneity. He placed emphasis on two main themes: the study of individualized resistance problems and the study of the reasons for analytic failures, which up to this time had been considered due to individual inexperience or errors, rather than to limitations of technique.

From these studies Reich published several books: *Der*

Triebhafte Charakter, in 1925, *Die Funktion des Orgasmus,* in 1927, and in 1933 his most important work, *Charakteranalyse,* which appeared in an English edition (1945). In later editions, so much material of a nonpsychoanalytic nature is interspersed and admixed that one reviewer has stated: "It is not the translation of the German book which Reich published in 1928 and which became a marking stone in psychoanalysis as a scientific technique, deeply influencing almost the entire generations of English psychoanalysts." An abstract or reading would only detract from the prestige that was Reich's during the period of his psychoanalytic accreditation, a prestige well-earned by his work.

Although Karl Abraham's *Psycho-Analytic Studies on Character Development* preceded Reich's papers on character analysis, Abraham's studies are primarily restricted to what might be called the phenomenological aspects of character formation, that is, character formation as an outgrowth and development of oral, anal, and genital ego types. Nevertheless, one of Abraham's papers deserves mention at this point. Here Abraham writes of encountering marked narcissistic resistance in some patients and not being able to proceed analytically until he had made known to them the nature of such narcissistic resistance at the very beginning of treatment (1919). In brief, Abraham's approach regards the character of narcissistic resistance as a transient one, whereas in Reich's approach such resistance is considered as a more or less chronic, structured ego function, the dissolution of which becomes the focal point of therapy.

Freud, as is known, modified his technique from that of direct interpretation of symptoms to that of analyzing and overcoming resistances and defenses. Reich would not have changed the term "resistance analysis" to that of "character analysis" had not particular circumstances made the latter term preferable to him. Of the various types of resistance encountered in practice, Reich noted a particular group to which he gave the name "character resistance." To quote:

> These acquire their specific imprint, not from their content, but from the patient's individual mode of behavior. . . . The form taken by the reactions of the ego—a form which in the face of similarity of experiential content differs according to the character—is just as much determined by infantile experiences as is the content of the symptoms and phantasies.

Although other psychoanalysts, Edward Glover and Franz Alexander foremost among them, have differentiated character and symptom neurosis as nosological entities, Reich was of the opinion that a neurotic character is invariably the underlying basis of a symptom neurosis, that is, that, rather than being separate and somewhat unrelated entities, they have a direct, causal relationship.

> The difference between character neuroses and symptom neuroses is simply that in the latter the neurotic character has produced symptoms as well—that the neurotic symptoms are, so to speak, a concentrate of the neurotic character . . . the more deeply we penetrate into its [the symptom's] determinants, the further we

get from the field of symptomatology proper and the more does the characterological substratum come to the fore.

Coming to the fore, this characterological substratum serves as a compact defense mechanism against therapeutic efforts, a phenomenon to which Reich gave the name "character armor."

How did Reich put his theories of character analysis into a system of technique? This problem involves the therapeutic viewpoint, that is, does the therapist interpret the id striving, or, without touching upon the id striving, does he preferably approach the aspect of resistance, which is more closely related to the conscious ego, the ego defense, the rejection? From the latter aspect of therapy, Reich postulated that every defense ultimately must end in a negative transference and the character, the armor of the ego likewise, revealed and uncovered.

The turning point necessary for a successful analysis is the emotional outburst or activated aggressiveness in the sense of a negative transference. Observing in a patient a major "character armor" trait, for example, affectlessness and indifference, Reich would continually belabor him with it—practically to the exclusion of all other interpretations. The patient would then have the choice of either discontinuing therapy or of mobilizing a reaction—aggression or hostility—against the repetitive therapeutic provocation aimed at his characterological armor. When such a situation has been brought about, the blocking of affect has been broken down, and the patient becomes analyzable. Whether the armor be of the nature of affectlessness or some mannerism of speech or motility, the technique remains the same.

Reich followed the publication of his work **"Über Characteranalyse"** in 1928 with another significant contribution, **"The Genital and the Neurotic Character"** (1929), devoted mainly to the psychoanalytic theory of character. This he defined as the typical mode of reaction of the ego toward the id and the outer world. "Character resistance" is not to be confused with Freud's "ego resistance," which is resistance with a specific content offered by the ego. Character resistance refers to the typical form of resistance adopted in defense and remains the same whether of id or superego origin. Thus there is a close relationship between repression of instinctual demands and character that, once formed, makes a great deal of repression needless, since the instinctual energies that float freely in ordinary repression are consumed by the character formation in rigid ego-syntonic reactions and behavior. Repressions that have resulted in well-established character traits are more difficult to eliminate than those at the basis of a symptom.

In this paper, Reich places much emphasis on sublimation and reaction formation. Reaction formation and reactive achievement are largely responsible for increased damming up of the libido.

Reich's third important contribution, *Character Formation and the Phobias of Childhood* (1930), is an attempt to develop further the theoretical aspects of the two above-mentioned papers. Reich's acceptable contributions to psychoanalytic literature came to an end shortly thereafter. In 1934, he officially resigned from membership in the psychoanalytic movement, and from that time on he became further and further removed from analytic associations.

What relationship and attitudes might have existed between Freud and Reich? What previous set of circumstances might have effected such a resignation? What was the dramatic last link in the association? In his biography of Freud, Jones wrote that Freud thought highly of Reich in the early days, but, "Reich's political fanaticism has led to both personal and scientific estrangement." Although Reich was considered an alarmist and a political fanatic, the fact remains that his conjecture on the course of events and the dangers of the Nazi regime, as elucidated in his book on Fascism, were realistic and correct—though too premature for current acceptance. However, when he blended his political ideology and psychoanalytic theory, he raised a storm of conflict. A paper in this vein was published in the *Zeitschrift* and, according to Freud, "culminated in the nonsensical statement that what we have called the death instinct is a product of the capitalistic system."

But perhaps other and subtle factors of a personal nature were operative. Reich was still esteemed for his work in the late twenties and early thirties, yet there was an aura of misgiving about his future. Perhaps Freud sensed the presence of an intrapsychic conflict, and, as a result, Reich's resignation met with no great opposition. Alienated from psychoanalysis, Reich also fell into disfavor with Marxist groups as he sought to introduce ideas of sexual reform and enlightenment to them.

Reich left Vienna in 1930 and worked in Berlin, Copenhagen, and, finally, Oslo, from whence he had to flee following the threat of the Nazi occupation of Norway. At these places, he won adherents who shared his thinking and activity and who, under the name *Sexpol,* issued a *Journal of Political Psychology and Sexual Economy,* as well as pamphlets on related themes. He also practiced a form of psychotherapy to which he gave the name "vegetotherapy," which he considered an extension of character analysis to its deepest repository of resistance, the autonomic system. Here, he believed, dammed-up libido and orgastic impotence cause the tensions and malfunctioning of psyche and soma alike. Related to this and with the aid of a well-equipped laboratory in Oslo, he carried on extensive experimentation that I shall not discuss in detail, but which can be pinpointed from a pamphlet title, *Electric Function of Sexuality and Anxiety* (1937). It is worthy of mention that, according to Reich's own judgment, he had never repudiated basic psychoanalytic principles. Rather, he believed that all he had accomplished—however unacceptable to analysts—was but of the nature of profoundest penetration into hitherto unknown areas.

In 1939, during the years of the Hitler nightmare in Europe, Reich came to the United States through the efforts of American colleagues who, with funds and affidavits, brought as many European analysts as possible to our shores, to spare them the concentration camp or to save their lives.

Shortly after his arrival here, friendly overtures were made to Reich, but he avoided them. He established himself on Long Island with the extensive laboratory equipment he had brought from Oslo and attracted about himself a group of friends and interested persons. At the first, I was a member of this group, but it was obvious that personality changes had occurred and that he was not the Reich of old, of the psychoanalytic therapy seminars in Vienna. Finally, he began to react with increasing irritability and projected hostility to helpful advice offered in various categories (for example, whether to avoid conflict, how to effect adjustment, or suggestions pertaining to medical licensure); with this state of affairs—offering no basis for personal or professional understanding—further association became impossible and our relationship was terminated.

Reich finally settled in Maine, where he obtained a large estate to carry on the experimentation on "biones" that he had begun in Oslo. He claimed that his discovery of biones had fundamentally advanced a theory concerning the origin of life, and that it was also related to the cancer problem. Going beyond his theory of biones, Reich claimed that he had discovered a method for gathering cosmic radiation that, with a device he used on patients, had therapeutic value. But these claims brought him into legal difficulty with the U.S. Food and Drug Administration. When Reich took the position that the Court had no jurisdiction to render opinions or judgment on truth and error in matters of natural science, he was held guilty of contempt of court. Subsequently, he was fined and given a two-year sentence, and by court order his devices and the printed matter pertaining thereto were destroyed. He had served several months of this sentence when, in 1957, death intervened. Reich left behind a sealed legacy to be opened fifty years after his death. Does this legacy contain the answer to the question: What ego identity did he seek that motivated him to change from one object relationship to another, to establish through his scientific experimentation a world of his own, only to destroy himself in the process?

Notwithstanding the opinion of practically all of Reich's colleagues that he had disassociated himself from acceptable psychoanalytic theory and practice, there is unanimity of opinion that his thinking and earlier works have earned a permanent place in the archives of psychoanalytic literature.

Michel Cattier   (essay date 1969)

SOURCE: "Irrational Mass Behavior," in *The Life and Work of Wilhelm Reich,* translated by Ghislaine Boulanger, Horizon Press, 1971, pp. 114-37.

[*In the following excerpt, which was originally published in French in 1969, Cattier explains how Reich combined concepts from Marxism and psychoanalysis to create a "social psychology."*]

Marx and Engels formulated a principle of sociological definition which contemporary social scientists still use— the way of assessing a group of people is determined by their living conditions. For example, the political attitudes, moral values, and artistic tastes of a social class reflect its material situation.

A distinction can be drawn between the ruling classes and the oppressed by the way in which they conduct themselves in society. The ruling classes cannot picture the state of the world as it stands because this would require them to recognize that their supremacy is contingent upon the whole society. Their ideology has always been to justify the established order by assuming that it is a constant factor. The bourgeoisie, for example, has a fixed vision of the world which denies historical evolution, putting forward its own values as the accepted values of society. No ruling class can, in effect, allow itself to recognize that one day its reign must end.

On the other hand, one could expect that once the proletariat becomes aware of its condition it will fight to gain supremacy. A glance at the history of the workers' movement shows that this theory is not borne out by reality.

The theory that the working classes clearly understand their own interests, and act in consequence, is inherited from the old rationalist psychology of the eighteenth century. We see this psychology repeated by the liberals who believe that the citizens' political choices are dictated by rational motives. The liberals hold that when an individual arrives at the voting booth, he knows the programs of each party on the ballot and votes according to this knowledge.

These theories are belied by the facts. Today we know that neither the behavior of the electorate, nor the behavior of the consumer, nor the behavior of the oppressed classes is rational. Advertising men are well aware that for the most part unconscious factors determine the consumer's choice. That is to say that when one asks a housewife why she chose one brand of soap over another, the reasons she gives are not the true ones (even if she gives them in good faith).

The advertising agencies' success has led the bourgeois parties to profit from their services in organizing electoral campaigns.

If a linear relation did exist between the proletariat's consciousness and its economic exploitation it would mean, all other things being equal, that a rise in the cost of living would trigger pressure for a wage rise, and in turn, that the higher wages would be reflected by a lessening of the working classes' militancy. This plan is simplistic because it lays the blame for the living conditions of working classes squarely on economic oppression and assumes that the working classes are conscious of the oppression. Engels had already exploded this myth. Everything that spurs man into action must come from his brains, he said, but the form this impulse takes in the brain varies according to the circumstances.

Reich reasoned that there must be some factor barring the working classes' awareness of the fact that they are being exploited. He advanced the theory that the working class is steeped in the bourgeois cultural environment. Radio, newspapers, and television are all in the hands of the bourgeoisie and help spread its ideology to all levels of society.

It is thus exposed to the daily contamination of the dominant ideology. But he knew that this does not explain why it submits on a long-term basis without throwing off the bourgeois yoke. If one believed that this is the only reason, one would fall into voluntarist ideology, which holds that intellect has the power to govern material situations by annulling the effect of the economic variables. A closer examination is necessary to see what factor in the proletariat's life style paralyzes its will to protest.

In the first chapter of his book *The Mass Psychology of Fascism,* Reich outlines the broad facts of the problem of class consciousness and shows that psychoanalysis can help to resolve it. He begins by stating that the Fascist success in highly industrialized countries has cast doubt on the validity of the fundamental concepts of Marxist sociology. In effect, once the economic situation in Europe was ripe for a revolution, the worker's movement broke down. Instead of revolution there was Fascism, that most virulent expression of reactionary politics, which corrupted Europe. The defeat of the worker movement was preceded by the failure of the Second International, by the downfall of the Spartakist Revolution, and the crushing of the Hungarian commune of Bela Kun. Reich blamed the vulgar Marxists who had drained Marxism of its scientific content. It is sufficient to compare one page of Marx or Engels with a book written by a Communist to see that Marxism had degenerated into a sterile theory, dependent upon economic determinism. (Economic determinism is a doctrine which reduces the concrete existence of man to its economic components, like buying power, the fluctuations of salaries, the rate of unemployment, etc.)

To these "Marxists," the Fascist victory was incomprehensible:

> This vulgar Marxism contended that an economic crisis of the magnitude of that between 1929 and 1933 must of necessity lead to the development of a Leftist ideology in the masses. Even after the defeat in January 1933, its representatives continued to talk of a "revolutionary upsurge." In reality, the economic crisis had—contrary to their expectations—led to an extreme development of a reactionary ideology in the masses. [*The Mass Psychology of Fascism*]

The discrepancy between the economic infrastructure of advanced capitalism and the impotence of the proletariat to fulfill its historic mission to overthrow capitalism must be explained. All the economic conditions were ripe for a Socialist takeover; the capital was concentrated in monopolies; the development of the world economy was hampered by customs regulations and national frontiers. In Reich's time capitalism had just suffered an enormous economic crisis which had pointed up the system's inability to resolve its internal contradictions. The economic machine was turning at fifty percent of its production capacity. Coffee was burned; the crops were destroyed; and thousands of pigs butchered to raise world prices; while in Europe and the U.S.A. millions were out of work, and the other workers were living in poverty. We were, says Reich, at the crossroads between socialism and barbarianism, and the working class chose barbarianism. From a rational point of view, one could have expected a revolutionary response from the impoverished masses. Instead of that they put Hitler in the saddle. Thus we come to the existing discrepancy between the condition of the working classes and their conservative ideology. When the masses are politically conscious of their condition, they act in a rational way which needs no psychological explanation. For example, when a starving man steals a loaf of bread, or when workers living in poverty decide to call a wildcat strike, their behavior is rational and self-explanatory. On the other hand, what social psychology must explain is not

> . . . why the starving individual steals or why the exploited individual strikes, but why the majority of starving individuals do *not* steal and the majority of exploited individuals do *not* strike. Socio-economics, then, can satisfactorily explain a social phenomenon when human thinking and acting serve a rational purpose, when they serve the satisfaction of needs and directly express the economic situation. It fails, however, when human thinking and acting *contradict* the economic situation, when, in other words, they are *irrational*.

Reich then tackles the problem of the reaction of ideology on its economic base. According to Marxist doctrine, ideological superstructures react upon the social infrastructure which gave birth to them. This shows that economic factors determine the social conditions in which people live; that these conditions are reflected by their brains in the form of ideas; and that men then act in accordance with these ideas to change their lives. Reich attacks the vulgar Marxists who underestimate the action in exchange for the ideology on its material base. The Communists, for example, repeat in parrot fashion that economic infrastructures and ideological super-structures interact, but they have never tried to explain precisely, with the help of scientific psychology, how a political doctrine spreads through a whole nation. The eruption of Nazism on the German political scene and its rapid spread to all social classes has shown that a reactionary ideology can set a large industrial country in motion. The retroaction of the ideology on the economic base can then prevail, at least temporarily, over the action of the economic factors. By ignoring the role of the "subjective factor" in history, the Communists believe themselves to be very materialist, but they are in fact falling into superficial ideology. Each time the working classes behave in a manner which belies their social oppression, the Communists say that the class has been deceived, that it lacks class consciousness, etc., or they deny the failure of the workers' movement by saying that all is going well, and that they are going from victory to victory. In brief, vulgar Marxists are incapable of explaining the contradiction between the economic frustrations endured by the proletariat and its lack of aggression.

Daniel Geurin, author of the best historical and economic study of Fascism [*Fascism and Big Business,* 1939], arrived at exactly the same conclusion:

> The degenerate Marxists, however, believe it is very "marxist" and "materialist" to disdain human factors and be interested only in the material and economic factors. They accumulate figures, statistics, and percentages; they study

with great accuracy the profound causes of social phenomena. But by failing to study with the
same care the way in which these causes *are reflected in the consciousness* of man, they miss the
living reality of these phenomena.

Hence, if they are interested only in the material
factors, they understand absolutely nothing of
the way in which the privations suffered by the
masses are transmuted into a religious aspiration.

To fill in this gap (that is to say, illustrate the role and the
nature of the subjective factor in history), Reich created
a social psychology, based on Marxism and psychoanalysis, which explains how an ideology takes shape in people's minds as a result of their social conditions, and how
this ideology influences the masses. We have already seen
that the psychological explanation is superfluous when the
behavior of the exploited masses is rational, that is, when
they respond to their poverty by riots and uprisings. Thus,
says Reich, "collective psychology must begin when the
immediate socio-economic explanation proves abortive."

When he says that an ideology has a retroactive effect on
its material base, Reich means that this ideology takes
hold of men and makes them act in an unexpected fashion.
And that once it becomes part of mass behavior, it is a material force. Reich asked himself how a reactionary doctrine could spread through a social class or through a
whole society: the doctrine must fit in with a certain collective mentality, what Reich calls the "character structure of the masses." Let us take the example of the 1914-18
War. It involved a confrontation between French, English, and German Imperialism. Yet it was necessary that
the masses be prepared to fight. They were. Those who
fought on the front were fighting to conquer industrial
zones and to ensure the European hegemony of their national bourgeoisie. But they did not know it. If one had
asked a French worker why he had been mobilized, he
would have replied that it was to defend France against
the German barbarians or to save civilization. The problem is to understand how the proletariat could have been
carried away by nationalist fervor and entered with enthusiasm into an affair that was no concern of theirs. Idealistic
reasons are always put forward—the failure of the Second
International, for instance. But, as Reich remarked, we
should ask ourselves why the proletariat allowed itself to
be betrayed.

Reich demonstrates that reactionary ideologies take hold
of the proletariat easily because they fall on fertile character terrain. The collective character structure represents
the subjective factor in history, and thus irrational mass
behavior can be explained. We cannot take Marx and Engels to task for not having recognized it because the only
way to understand it is through psychoanalysis, which did
not exist in their time:

The character structure of acting man, the so-
called "subjective factor in history" in the sense
of Marx, remained unexplored: Marx was a soci-
ologist and not a psychologist, and there was, in
his day, no scientific psychology. Thus the question remained unanswered as to why people, for

thousands of years, have tolerated exploitation
and moral degradation, in brief, slavery.

The vulgar Marxists consider the workers as adults who
hire out their labor to a capitalist and who are exploited.
Reich agrees with this definition but says that one must
take into account the social conditions of the worker if one
wishes to understand his political attitudes. Among other
things this means that he has had a childhood, that he has
been educated by his parents, that he has a wife and children of his own, sexual needs, and family conflicts. Why
should these factors be overlooked when the behavior of
the working classes is in question?

The unity of the family cell depends upon the children
being obedient to their parents. . . . [In] learning to obey
their parents, the children also learn obedience per se. The
results obtained during the family training are carried
over to all situations where the adult finds himself faced
with an official superior. In punishing their children who
masturbate and controlling the time their daughter returns home each evening, parents make sexual repression
part of this family training. In order to adapt to the family
environment, young people must then repress their sexuality. (Conversely, if their sexual needs are fulfilled, the
young people appear to be in revolt against the parents.
When a young girl returns home at six o'clock in the
morning, she is defying her parents.)

Punishment teaches children to obey and forces them to
give up sexual pleasure. Each time that the child is caught
playing with his sexual organs, he is hit or threatened;
when he is impertinent, he is reprimanded. In this way
punishment succeeds in associating feelings of anxiety
with the forbidden behavior. The anxiety which accompanies the expression of sexual needs comes from the same
source as the anxiety which is aroused by rebellious impulses because sexuality and rebelliousness were indis-
criminately repressed by the educators. To escape this
anxiety, the child represses all those needs whose expression leads to punishment. In other words, the repression
of sexuality is confused with the repression of all rebellious
inclinations. In the end, the child is frightened by his sexual desires and by his tendency to revolt, and he stops the
instincts from revealing themselves.

Reich then turned to an examination of the effects of these
repressions. It is an established fact that repression is a
psychological process which suppresses the perception of
a need, an idea, etc. If the repression is total, the individual
loses all consciousness of what he is repressing. But he has
to use up a great deal of energy to arrive at this point. For
repression is a costly process; the repressed impulses do
not cease to exist; they lose none of their dynamism, and
continue to lead an underground life in the unconscious.
This means that the individual must constantly be defending himself against them by draining his psychological potential. Beyond the obvious neuroses and psychoses, this
results in a narrowing of consciousness, a weakening of the
mental faculties, and a lessening of the ability to concentrate. The consciousness atrophies and becomes a mere
flicker.

Reich places all this in its sociological context:

Suppression of the natural sexuality in the child, particularly of its genital sexuality, makes the child apprehensive, shy, obedient, afraid of authority, "good," and "adjusted" in the authoritarian sense; it paralyzes the rebellious forces because any rebellion is laden with anxiety; it produces, by inhibiting sexual curiosity and sexual thinking in the child, a general inhibition of thinking and of critical faculties. In brief, the goal of sexual suppression is that of producing an individual who is adjusted to the authoritarian order and who will submit to it in spite of misery and degradation.

In this passage Reich establishes:

1. That sexual repression creates individuals who are terrorized by authority, and

2. That sexual repression, which results from the interiorization of sexual needs, weakens the ego because the individual who must constantly invest energy in stopping the conscious expression of his sexual desires is not allowing himself to realize his full potential.

Reich tirelessly emphasized the social function of sexual repression. It trains the character to submit to authority and to fear liberty; resulting in the conditions which allow the enslavement of the masses to continue from generation to generation.

The child adapts, then, by trial and error to his family environment. When he masturbates he is punished, and he stops playing with his sexual organs. When he differs with his parents, he is chastised again and no longer dares stand up to them. And thus sexual repression is identified with the fear of authority. When the child appears gentle and obedient, he is rewarded. Little by little his personality builds itself through these exchanges. Character traits emerge, consolidate and will remain for the whole of his life. The first imprints that society leaves on the organism are indelible. The character represents, as it were, the history of the childhood which has been crystallized into the individual's behavior. In order to adapt to the family environment, the child represses his sexual needs and the hatred of his parents. Little boys achieve these repressions partly by identifying with the paternal image, foreshadowing the time when, as adults, they will identify with the authority of the state, of the firm where they work, etc. In effect, the father is the state's representative within his family. Identification with the paternal image and the attitude of servility which the son adopts toward his father heralds an ulterior identification with all forms of authority.

In order to neutralize his sexual needs and hatred of his parents, the child overcompensates for these attitudes. Therefore, by the time he has reached adulthood, the unconscious revolt against his father is masked by extreme submission to all forms of authority; and the fear of expressing his sexual needs has given rise to prudishness. Everyone is familiar with the frustrated old women and dried-up curates who passionately seek out the least sign of sexual excitement in children. They are so busy not thinking of sexual matters in themselves that they attack anything that evokes sexuality in others. . . .

[The character armor that Reich had discovered in his patients] is the totality of the defenses built up by the individual against his repressed needs. It is reflected in his behavior and helps diminish his psychological tensions by damming up in the unconscious anything that might arouse anxiety. Basically, the individual is a machine that functions in such a way as to keep anxiety at its lowest possible level.

The result of this process is fear of freedom, and a conservative, reactionary mentality. Sexual repression aids political reaction not only through this process which makes the mass individual passive and unpolitical but also by creating in his structure an interest in actively supporting the authoritarian order.

The character armor, already formed by the end of infancy, will only grow harder in the course of time. In order to endure his existence within the family, this state in miniature, the child has had to repress his sexuality and rebellious instincts against his parents. Since adult life similarly demands that the individual give way to authority and renounce sexual pleasure, it is, in a way, prolonging the infantile condition. To tolerate all the worries and privations of our everyday life, we must be protected against the world and against everything in ourselves which kicks against the life we know. Otherwise existence would be unbearable.

Some animals have adapted themselves to their surroundings by forming a hard shell that protects them at the same time as it imprisons them. The human being has used a similar method to adapt himself to his social environment.

The results of an inquiry conducted several years ago in the United States by T. W. Adorno on the authoritarian personality confirm Reich's conclusions. According to some sources, Adorno knew Reich in Germany during his Association for Sexual Politics period.

Adorno's team used five criteria to define what it called the "authoritarian personality":

1. The individual has a hierarchic view of human relations and exhibits great deference toward his superiors.

2. He depersonalizes human relations. He puts people "in their place" and expects similar treatment.

3. He is very conventional about correct behavior. Conformity is, in fact, one of his dominant character traits.

4. He exercises strict control over his impulses.

5. He is intolerant, morally rigid, and lacks the ability to adapt.

In studying the family histories of their subjects, Adorno's team of researchers discovered that they had the following points in common: their parents were strict, intolerant and showed a marked moral rigidity. They expected strict obedience from their children. They held themselves up to be ideal models (which can be interpreted partly as hostility toward the child and partly as a need for justification). The child submits to this system of injunctions and orders, represses his aggression toward authority, and becomes a servile little being who grovels before all bearers of authority. Later, he will project on to his subordinates the hate that is boiling up inside him; he is suspicious of others, repeats continually that people must be kept in hand, etc.

What Reich calls an authoritarian character structure tallies with the above description. He established that this character type is frequently found in the middle classes. Small tradesmen and employees often have a rigid moral code based on honor and duty to justify their colorless existence. They make a virtue of necessity. Depending on the political/cultural context, these people will either make good noncommissioned officers, become Fascists, or bureaucratic Communists.

The atmosphere in working-class families is generally less obsessive, and the parents tolerate their children's sexuality more easily. But it is only a difference in degree. The major obstacle preventing the development of revolutionary movements in the USSR, the U.S.A., and in Europe is the authoritarian family manufacturing slaves through the perpetuation of sexual repression. If there were no slaves there would be no slave drivers.

An individual's neurotic character structure will hinder his consciousness of class interests. The fear of freedom, the anxiety of being without a leader, the guilt provoked by enjoying oneself, ruin any attempts at social emancipation.

> Now we understand a basic element of the reaction of ideology on the economic base. *Sexual inhibition alters the structure of the economically suppressed individual in such a manner that he thinks, feels, and acts against his own material interests.*

When Reich was treating patients he realized that they were mobilizing all their defense mechanisms against him. They clung to their neurotic balance and were afraid when the psychiatrist touched upon the repressed impulses. Similarly, revolutionary proposals slide off the character armor of the masses because they recall all the impulses that the people have had to smother in order to endure their brutalization.

It would be a mistake to believe that the masses do not revolt because of a lack of information on the mechanics of economic exploitation. In reality, revolutionary propaganda, explaining the social injustices and irrationality of the economic system to the masses, falls on deaf ears. People who get up at five in the morning to go to work in a factory and who must also spend two hours a day in a subway or suburban train, can adapt to this existence only by refusing to consider anything that is likely to cast doubt on their way of life. If they realized they were wasting their lives in the service of an absurd system, they would commit suicide or they would go mad. To avoid facing this painful truth, they justify their existence and rationalize it. They repress everything which could upset them and develop a character structure adapted to the conditions in which they live. At this point, the idealist approach of explaining to people that they are oppressed serves no purpose because they have had to suppress the realization of

this oppression in order to be able to live with it. Revolutionary propagandists often say that they want to enlighten the people; experience shows their efforts are rarely crowned with success because they are going against all the unconscious defense mechanisms and various rationalizations that the people have made so as not to become aware of their exploitation and of the emptiness of their lives.

When did antisexual morality first make its appearance in history? Reich wrote a large book, ***Der Einbruch der Sexualmoral,*** in answer to this question. Today this book is unavailable in any language. It was never translated into English.

Reich referred to Engels, Morgan, Bachofen, and Malinowski in establishing the social and economic conditions which gave rise to sexual repression.

He adapted two of Engels' fundamental theses on the social life of primitive peoples: first, the existence of a mode of production based on the collective ownership of the working tools (which Engels calls "primitive Communism"); and second, the preponderance of women over men, which is seen in matriarchal societies. Let us examine briefly how primitive Communism and mother right came about. Engels maintained that meager profits which did not allow the establishment of a permanent surplus of riches that could be appropriated by a nonproductive class gave rise to primitive Communism. Since the tribe produced just enough to subsist on, no overproduction existed that a fraction of the community could have turned to its own advantage. When barbarianism came to an end and man began to find uses for iron, to domesticate and breed animals, and to cultivate the land, the work returns increased considerably. From the moment that "two arms produced more than one mouth could consume," the creation of a social overproduction became possible. This permanent surplus of food and material goods upset the balance of primitive Communism, giving way to a system of production based on the exploitation of slaves.

The sexual life in primitive Communist societies was characterized by a very great freedom and by the superior position women held in the tribe. Given this free sexual commerce, the facility with which couples formed and broke up, there was no way of determining the paternity of a child. On the other hand, the mother was always known; the line of descent could therefore be passed only through the maternal side. Bachofen coined the phrase "mother right" to designate the matrilineal system.

According to the division of labor, the men were expected to furnish food and the necessary tools while the women took care of the household. The development of husbandry and slavery put a new source of wealth into the men's hands, bringing them additional importance within the matriarchal society. Little by little the women's place was reduced and the men benefited from this reversal of power. According to Engels, the men wanted their own children to profit from their increased wealth, and therefore matrilineal descent was invalidated. The end of mother right, which Engels calls "the great historical defeat of the female sex," was, then, the result of technical progress which, because of the division of labor, brought additional economic power to the men, and this was found to be incompatible with the social supremacy of women. The contradiction between production methods based on the use of slaves and agriculture on the one hand, and a matrilineal society on the other, shattered this latter which was replaced by the patriarchal family where women were dominated by men. In summary, primitive Communism was dissolved for economic reasons, destroying mother right and establishing masculine sovereignty.

The advent of masculine domination (the patriarchy) radically transformed society. A class of polygamous chiefs was formed; their wives were kept cloistered to be used as instruments of pleasure and reproduction. From now on women were confined to secondary roles; their debasement and their subjugation to men began at this time. Reich has shown that antisexual morality rose with patriarchy. His argument may be summarized as follows: The leaders of primitive communities were in possession of the political power, and a large part of the society's wealth was concentrated in their hands. Since these leaders bequeathed to their children the riches they had accumulated, they had to be sure their wives were faithful. Patrilineal filiation requires the chastity of women. Thus sexual life within ruling class families was strictly regulated.

Reich was surprised to discover a fine example of the effects of material interests on sexual life among the Trobriand Islanders. The example corroborated his theory that sexual repression first appeared in ruling-class families when they were in the process of formation. The Trobriand Islanders have two forms of marriage: If a girl marries her first cousin, her mother's brother's child, it is considered to be a good match. All other marriages are more or less disparaged.

This custom appears bizarre and contrasts deeply with the very great sexual freedom that the Trobriand Islanders enjoy. (They still have a matriarchal system.)

Thanks to the custom of paying dowries, the chiefs add to their wealth by accumulating those paid by their wives' brothers, and recovering others they themselves paid to their sisters if their sons make a good marriage—that is, if they marry their cousins. A good marriage thus succeeds in bringing back to the family the riches that went out of it in the form of dowries.

Children destined for good marriages are subjected to unaccustomed sexual restrictions. They are not allowed to indulge in sexual games like all the other little Trobrianders, and their sexual education resembles that taught in Western societies—Europe, USSR, U.S.A. As a result of this obsessive morality, which prepares them for good marriages resulting in the accumulation of dowries by the polygamous leader's family, they fall prey to neuroses. There is, then, an apparent correlation between the economic power of the ruling class and the sex life of its members. They may no longer marry whom they wish, for fear of squandering their heritage. Only profitable unions, from the material point of view, are permitted. In other words, economic interests—the growth of riches within the ruling class—become confused with sexuality and cause sexual freedom within the class to be restricted.

In addition, the patriarchal system demands that women be faithful to their husbands because this is the only guarantee the men have that their children are really theirs. This is to say that a moral code condemning extramarital relations for women necessarily accompanies a patriarchy. (Even today, society tolerates a husband's infidelity far more readily than a wife's, and turns a complacent eye on the male Don Juan, while it severely condemns female adultery).

In brief, according to Reich, sexual repression arose with private ownership and the setting up of a patriarchal system. It, therefore, has a well-defined historical origin and did not simply fall out of the heavens. Reich had already arrived at these conclusions when he heard of Malinowski's studies on the sex life of the Trobrianders.

Since Malinowski's work confirmed what Reich had already discovered, he was delighted by it.

The first thing that strikes the European observer is the great sexual liberty enjoyed in the Trobriand Islands:

> Every man and woman in the Trobriands settles down eventually to matrimony, after a period of sexual play in childhood, followed by general license in adolescence, and later by a time when the lovers live together in a more permanent intrigue, sharing with two or three other couples a communal "bachelor's house." [Bronislaw Malinowski, *Sex and Repression in Savage Society*]

Malinowski was equally struck by the almost total absence of psychological troubles. He says he never once encountered a nervous tic, a neurosis, or a sexual perversion. Homosexuality in particular was almost nonexistent. He was familiar with psychoanalysis and understood the relationship between their sexual liberty and the rarity of neuroses:

> Another point which might be interpreted in favor of the Freudian solution to this problem is the correlation of sexual perversions with sexual repression. Freud has shown that there is a deep connection between the course of infantile sexuality and the occurrence of perversion in later life. On the basis of his theory, an entirely lax community like that of the Trobrianders, who do not interfere with the free development of infantile sexuality, should show a minimum of perversions. This is fully confirmed in the Trobriands. [*The Sexual Struggle of Youth*]

Since then, missionaries have wrought havoc with this state of affairs. They have separated the boys from the girls, confining them in boarding schools, and are teaching them the Christian religion, giving them a little general instruction, and, naturally, imposing Western principles and discipline upon them. As Reich said, missionaries are the forerunners of the colonial system.

The contrast between matriarchal societies where there is no central authority and where sexual liberty goes hand in hand with well-balanced, healthy, and spontaneously friendly human beings, on the one hand, and patriarchal societies which produce nervous wrecks as a result of sexual repression, on the other, is striking.

The reinstatement of antisexual morality in the USSR illustrates the tie which exists between dictatorships and the authoritarian family. By abolishing private ownership, the Russian Revolution brought a sexual revolution in its wake. The family and established morality disappeared in the immense social upheaval. The new Soviet legislation reflected this evolution—marriage and divorce became simple formalities; sexual relationships between young people were allowed and took place; abortion was legal and free; and everyone could buy contraceptives for a few kopecks.

When the bureaucratic Stalinist rule began, they hastened to put an end to the sexual revolution. Puritan concepts had always prevailed in the heart of the Bolshevik party (Lenin was very conservative in this regard). At first, voices were raised against the young people's "abandon" and the "dissolute life" they led. Bourgeois influences were held responsible for their "unrestrained sensuality." Toward the middle of the thirties, laws punishing homosexuality and forbidding abortion were passed. The cult of the family made its appearance in the USSR and enjoyed a vogue which in no way differed from that instituted by the Nazis. The official moral code could have been confused with middle-class morality in capitalist countries, and a burdensome conformity finally colored everyday life.

In *The Sexual Revolution,* Reich offers a brilliant study of the decline of sexual freedom in the USSR, where the reappearance of sexual repression and of the patriarchal family confirmed his theories on the social role and historical origin of sexual repression.

An excerpt from *The Function of the Orgasm*

"Morality" is dictatorial when it lumps natural feelings of life together with pornography. In doing so, it perpetuates sexual smut and blights natural happiness in love, whether this is what it intends or not. It is necessary to raise a strong protest when those who determine their social behavior on the basis of inner laws instead of external compulsive codes are labeled immoral. A man and a woman are husband and wife not because they have received the sacrament, but because they feel themselves to be husband and wife. The inner and not the external law is the yardstick of genuine freedom. Moralistic bigotry cannot be fought with another form of compulsive morality, but only with knowledge of the natural law of the sexual process. Natural moral behavior presupposes that the natural life process can develop freely. On the other hand, compulsive morality and pathological sexuality go hand in hand.

Wilhelm Reich, in his The Function of the Orgasm, *translated by Vincent R. Carfagno, Farrar, Straus and Giroux, 1973.*

Bertell Ollman   (essay date 1972)

SOURCE: An introduction to *Sex-Pol: Essays 1929-1934* by Wilhelm Reich, edited by Lee Baxandall, translated by Anna Bostock, Tom DuBose, and Lee Baxandall, Vintage Books, 1972, pp. xi-xxviii.

[*Ollman is an American writer and educator whose works include* Alienation: Marx's Conception of Man in Capitalist Society *(1971) and* Social and Sexual Revolution *(1978). In the following essay, he discusses Marxist elements in Reich's writings.*]

Marx claimed that from the sexual relationship "one can . . . judge man's whole level of development . . . the relationship of man to woman is the most natural relation of human being to human being. It therefore reveals the extent to which man's natural behavior has become human" [*Economic and Philosophic Manuscripts of 1884*]. The women's liberation movement has provided ample evidence to show that in our society this relationship is one of inequality, one in which the woman is used as an object, and one which does not bring much satisfaction to either party. As predicted, these same qualities can be observed throughout capitalist life. Inequality, people treating each other as objects, as instances of a kind (not taking another's unique, personalizing characteristics into account), and the general frustration that results are major features in the alienation described by Marx.

Yet Marx himself never tried to explain what we may now call "sexual alienation." Pointing to the fact of exploitation and indicating that this is typical of what goes on throughout capitalist society is clearly insufficient. We also want to know how the capitalist system operates on the sexual lives and attitudes of people, and conversely, what role such practices and thinking plays in promoting the ends of the system. What is missing from this dialectical equation is the psychological dimension which, given the state of knowledge in his time, Marx was ill equipped to provide.

Half a century after Marx's death, the task of accounting for sexual alienation was taken up by Wilhelm Reich. Born in Austrian Galicia in 1897, Reich came to Vienna after World War I to study medicine, and in 1920, while still a student, became a practicing psychoanalyst. By 1924, he was director of the Viennese Psychoanalytic Society's prestigious seminar in psychoanalytic technique and highly regarded for his contributions in this field. Almost from the start of his career as an analyst, however, Reich was troubled by Freud's neglect of social factors. His work in the free psychoanalytic clinic of Vienna (1922-30) showed him how often poverty and its concomitants—inadequate housing, lack of time, ignorance, etc.—contribute to neuroses. He soon became convinced that the problems treated by psychoanalysis are at their roots social problems demanding a social cure. Further investigation brought him to Marxism and eventually, in 1927, to membership in the Austrian Social Democratic Party.

Reich's voluminous writings in his Marxist period (roughly 1927-1936) sought, on the one hand, to integrate basic psychoanalytic findings with Marxist theory and, on the other, to develop a revolutionary strategy for the working class based on this expansion of Marxism. The chief of these writings are **"Dialectical Materialism and Psychoanalysis,"** 1929 (in opposition to the Communist-inspired caricature, Reich argues that Freud's psychology is both dialectical and materialist); ***Sexual Maturity, Abstinence and Conjugal Morality,*** 1930 (a critique of bourgeois sexual morality); ***The Imposition of Sexual Morality,*** 1932 (a study of the origins of sexual repression); ***The Sexual Struggle of Youth,*** 1932 (a popularistic attempt to link the sexual interests of young people with the need for a socialist revolution); ***The Mass Psychology of Fascism,*** 1933 (an investigation of the character mechanisms that underlie the appeal of fascism); ***What Is Class Consciousness?,*** 1934 (a redefinition of class consciousness that emphasizes the importance of everyday life); and ***The Sexual Revolution,*** 1936 (along with a revised edition of ***Sexual Maturity, Abstinence and Conjugal Morality,*** a history of the sexual reforms and subsequent reaction in the Soviet Union).

The social revolution is only a prerequisite (and not a sufficient condition) for the sexual revolution, but Reich believed that recognition of their close relationship, particularly among the young, helped to develop consciousness of the need for both revolutions. With the exception of ***Character Analysis*** (1934), which psychoanalysts still regard as a classic in their field, and a few related articles, Reich's early work was devoted almost entirely to the attainment of such a consciousness.

Not content to debate his ideas, in 1929 Reich organized the Socialist Society for Sexual Advice and Sexual Research. A half dozen clinics were set up in poor sections of Vienna, where working-class people were not only helped with their emotional problems but urged to draw the political lessons which come from recognizing the social roots of these problems. Moving to Berlin in 1930, Reich joined the German Communist Party and persuaded its leadership to unite several sexual-reform movements into a sex-political organization under the aegis of the party. With Reich, the chief spokesman on sexual questions, lecturing to working-class and student audiences throughout the country, membership in the new organization grew quickly to about forty thousand.

By the end of 1932, however, the Communist Party decided—whether to placate potential allies against fascism or because of the general reaction that was then overtaking the Soviet Union—that Reich's attempt to link sexual and political revolution was a political liability. Interpretations which were previously considered "sufficiently" Marxist were now declared un-Marxist, and party organs were prohibited from distributing Reich's books. In February 1933, despite the support of his co-workers in Sex-Pol, Reich was formally expelled from the party.

If the Communist leaders found Reich's stress on sexuality intolerable, his psychoanalytic colleagues were no more appreciative of his Communist politics. Badly frightened by the import of Reich's ***Mass Psychology of Fascism*** (1933)—and, as difficult as it is to believe today, still hoping to make their peace with fascism—the International Psychoanalytic Association expelled Reich the following year.

First from Denmark, then from Sweden and Norway, Reich continued his efforts to influence the course of working-class protest against fascism. Most of his writings of this time appear in the *Zeitschrift für politische Psychologie und Sexualökonomie,* a journal he edited from 1934 to 1938. From about 1935 on, however, Reich's interest in politics was gradually giving way to a growing interest in biology, spurred by the belief that he had discovered the physical basis of sexual energy (libido). From being a psychoanalyst and Marxist social philosopher, Reich became a natural scientist, a metamorphosis that was to have drastic effects on both his psychoanalysis and social philosophy. Reich emigrated to America in 1939. Each year added to his spiritual distance from Marx and Freud. After a new round of persecution by the authorities, this time in connection with his scientific research, he died in an American prison in 1957.

Reich's later work, as fascinating and controversial as it is, lies outside the bounds of this [essay] which is concerned solely with his Marxist period. What does concern us is that the break with his Marxist past led him to dilute much of the class analysis and politically radical content of whatever works of this period he chose to republish. Consequently, ***The Sexual Revolution*** (1945) and ***The Mass Psychology of Fascism*** (1946), until recently the only "Marxist" works available in English, give a very misleading picture of Reich's Marxism. Two recent pirate editions of ***The Mass Psychology of Fascism,*** both taken from the 1946 English version, and a new translation of the third German edition, exhibit the same fault, as does ***The Invasion of Compulsory Sex Morality,*** which takes account of textual revisions Reich undertook in 1952. Only **"Dialectical Materialism and Psychoanalysis"** (*Studies on the Left,* July-August 1966) and **"What Is Class Consciousness?"** (*Liberation,* October 1971) are exempt from this criticism, but besides being difficult to obtain, these essays in themselves are hardly adequate as an introduction to Reich's Marxism. [*Sex-Pol: Essays 1929-1934*], then, offers the English-speaking reader his first real opportunity to become acquainted with Reich's contribution to Marxist theory.

As indicated above, I believe Reich's main efforts as a Marxist were directed to filling in the theory of alienation as it applies to the sexual realm. Reich himself would have been surprised by such a judgment, since he was only partially familiar with this theory and seldom employed the vocabulary associated with it. *The German Ideology* and *1844 Manuscripts,* which contain Marx's clearest treatment of alienation, became available only in 1928 and 1931 respectively, and it seems as if Reich never read the latter work. Still, fitting rather neatly into this Marxian matrix is his discussion of the split between the individual and his natural sexual activity, reflected in part by the split between spiritual and physical love (likewise between tenderness and eroticism); the fact that sexuality comes under the control of another (repression and manipulation); of its objectification in repressive structures (symptoms as well as social forms); of the reification (neurotic attachment) connected with each; of people's treatment of one another as sexual objects and the dissatisfaction this breeds; of the role money plays in purchasing sexual favors (which is only possible because they are no longer an integral part of the personality); and of the incipient conflict between repressors and repressed. Moreover, by using the theory of alienation Marx tried to show—in keeping with his dialectical conception—that people were not only prisoners of their conditions but of themselves, of what they had been made by their conditions. It is perhaps in marking the toll of sexual repression on people's ability to come to grips with their life situation (and, in particular, on the working class's ability to recognize its interests and become class-conscious) that Reich makes his most important contribution to Marx's theory of alienation.

In his investigation of sexual alienation, Reich was greatly aided by Freud's four major discoveries: 1) man's psychic life is largely under the control of his unconscious (this shows itself in dreams, slips of the tongue, forgetting and misplacing things—all have a "meaning"); 2) small children have a lively sexuality (sex and procreation are not identical); 3) when repressed, infantile sexuality is forgotten but doesn't lose its strength, its energy (this only gets diverted into various psychic disturbances which are beyond conscious control); 4) human morality is not of supernatural origins but is the result of repressive measures taken against children, particularly against expressions of natural sexuality.

To these basic discoveries Reich soon added two of his own. Psychoanalysts of the time were puzzled by the fact that many severely disturbed people had a "healthy" sex life, i.e., in the case of men, had erections and experienced orgasm. Reich began to question his patients more closely about the quality of their sexual activity, and found that none of them had great pleasure in the sexual act and that none experienced a complete release of tension in orgasm. Reich concluded that erective and ejaculative potency (the only types then recognized by psychoanalysis) did not necessarily lead to "orgastic potency" which he defined as "the capacity for complete surrender to the flow of biological energy without any inhibition, the capacity for complete discharge of all dammed-up sexual excitation." Without orgastic potency much of the sexual energy generated by the body remains blocked and available for neuroses and other kinds of irrational behavior.

Reich also noted that orgastic impotence in his patients was always coupled with distinctive ways—including both beliefs and bodily attitudes—of warding off instinctual impulses. He labeled these defensive behavior patterns "character structure." Reich believed that character structure originates in the conflicts of the oedipal period as ways of responding to external pressures and threats. Both its form and strength reflect the repression to which the individual was subjected at this time. The motive for developing such mechanisms is conscious or unconscious fear of punishment.

While protection against the outside world is the chief objective in the formation of character structure, this is not its main function in the adult individual. After maturation, it is mainly against internal dangers, against unruly impulses, that character mechanisms guard. In this case, character structure blocks the impulse and redirects the energy, acting both as repressing agent and controller of the resulting anxiety.

Achieving impulse control in this manner, however, has serious side effects on a person's overall motility and sensibility. According to Reich, it makes "an orderly sexual life and full sexual experience impossible." All the manifestations of character structure—the inhibition and the fears, the tense and awkward mannerisms, the stiffness and the deadness—work against the capacity to surrender in the sexual act, and thus limit both the pleasure and the discharge of tension attained in orgasm. Character structure also deadens people sufficiently for them to do the boring, mechanical work which is the lot of most people in capitalist society. The same dulling insulates people from outside stimuli, reducing the impact on them of further education and of life itself. Finally, the increased sexual blockage which results from damming up the libido is responsible for various reaction formations, chief of which is an ascetic ideology, which in turn increases the blockage.

Drawing upon his clinical experience, Freud had already noted a number of disturbing personality traits and problems that result from sexual repression. Among these are the "actual" neuroses, tension and anxiety ("modern nervousness"), attenuated curiosity, increased guilt and hypocrisy, and reduced sexual potency and pleasure. On one occasion, he goes so far as to claim that repressed people are "good weaklings who later become lost in the crowd that tends to follow painfully the initiative of strong characters" [" 'Civilized' Sexual Morality and Modern Nervousness," *Collected Papers,* vol. II, 1948]. This provocative remark is never developed. Reich, on the other hand, emphasizes those aspects of submissiveness and irrationality that we now associate with the notion of the authoritarian personality. For him, the most important effect of sexual repression is that it "paralyzes the rebellious forces because any rebellion is laden with anxiety" and "produces, by inhibiting sexual curiosity and thinking in the child, a general inhibition of thinking and critical faculties." And Reich is unique in rooting these qualities in the very defense mechanisms (character structure) responsible for self-repression.

But if the human cost of repression is so great, the question arises: Why does society repress sexuality? Freud's answer is that it is the *sine qua non* of civilized life. Reich replies that sexual repression's chief social function is to secure the *existing* class structure. The criticism which is curtailed by such repression is criticism of *today's* society, just as the rebellion which is inhibited is rebellion against the status quo.

Closely following Marx, Reich declares, "every social order creates those character forms which it needs for its preservation. In class society, the ruling class secures its position with the aid of education and the institution of the family, by making its ideology the ruling ideology of all members of the society." To this Reich adds the following: "it is not merely a matter of imposing ideologies, attitudes and concepts . . . Rather it is a matter of a deep-reaching process in each new generation, of the formation of a psychic structure which corresponds to the existing social order in all strata of the population."

In short, life in capitalism is not only responsible for our beliefs, the ideas of which we are conscious, but also for related unconscious attitudes, for all those spontaneous reactions which proceed from our character structure. Reich can be viewed as adding a psychological dimension to Marx's notion of ideology: emotions as well as ideas are socially determined. By helping to consolidate the economic situation responsible for their formation, each serves equally the interests of the ruling class.

Within the theory of alienation, character structure stands forth as the major product of alienated sexual activity. It is an objectification of human existence that has acquired power over the individual through its formation in inhuman conditions. Its various forms, the precise attitudes taken, are reified as moral sense, strength of character, sense of duty, etc., further disguising its true nature. Under the control of the ruling class and its agents in the family, church and school who use the fears created to manipulate the individual, character structure provides the necessary psychological support within the oppressed for those very external practices and institutions (themselves products of alienated activity in other spheres) which daily oppress them. In light of the socially reactionary role of character structure, Reich's political strategy aims at weakening its influence in adults and obstructing its formation in the young, where the contradiction between self-assertiveness and social restraint is most volatile. The repressive features of family, church and school join economic exploitation as major targets of his criticism.

To avoid the kind of misunderstanding that has bedeviled most discussion of Reich's ideas, I would like to emphasize that Reich's strategy is not a matter of "advocating" sexual intercourse. Rather, by exhibiting the devastating effects of sexual repression on the personality and on society generally, he wants people to overturn those conditions which make a satisfactory love life (and—through its connection to character structure—happiness and fulfillment) impossible. In a similar vein, Reich never held that a full orgasm is the *summum bonum* of human existence. Rather, because of the psychological ills associated with orgastic impotence, the full orgasm serves as an important criterion by which emotional well-being can be judged. Furthermore, with the relaxation of repression, Reich does not expect everybody to be "screwing" everybody all the time (a fear Freud shares with the Pope), though such relaxation would undoubtedly lead—as it already has in part—to people making love more frequently with others whom they find attractive.

Many of Reich's critics make it a point of honor never to engage him in intelligent debate, simply assuming that any position which is so "extreme" must be erroneous. Among those from whom we deserve better are Herbert Marcuse, who remarks [in *Eros and Civilization,* 1962], "sexual liberation *per se* becomes for Reich a panacea for individual and social ills," and Norman Brown who says of Reich, "This appearance of finding the solution to the world's problems in the genital has done much to discredit psychoanalysis; mankind, from history and from personal experience, knows better" [*Life against Death,* 1961]. Reich's masterly analysis of the social function of sexual repression is duly lost sight of behind these unsupported caricatures.

Another related misinterpretation, which is widespread among Marxists and must be taken more seriously, holds that Reich replaces "economic determinism" with "sexual determinism." At the time of his expulsion from the Communist Party, a spokesman for the party declared, "You begin with consumption, we with production; you are no Marxist." It is only fitting in an Introduction to a collection of Reich's Marxist essays that special attention be given to an objection which calls into question his entire enterprise.

Marxist theory offers Reich two complementary ways of responding: either the notion of production can be differently defined to include sexuality (which his Communist Party critic restricted to a form of consumption), or the interaction between the "base" and such elements of the "superstructure" as sexuality can be emphasized to bring out the hitherto neglected importance of the latter. Reich's strategy, as found in several of his works, takes advantage of both possibilities. On the one hand, he points out that Marx's materialism logically precedes his stress on economic factors, such as production, and that sex is a "material want." On the other hand, while willingly declaring even for sexual practices the primacy "in the last instance" of economic factors (work, housing, leisure, etc.), he argues that the social effects of sexual repression are far greater than have previously been recognized.

Marx's materialism is first and foremost a matter of beginning his study of society with the "real individual," who may be viewed strictly as a producer but is just as often seen as both producer and consumer. In his only methodological essay, Marx is at pains to show that production and consumption are internally related as aspects of the individual's material existence and that information which generally appears under one heading may be shifted—in order to satisfy some requirement of inquiry or exposition—to the other with no loss of meaning. Likewise, the "real individual" has both subjective and objective aspects—he feels as well as does—and again, because of this interrelatedness his life situation can be brought into focus by emphasizing either feelings or actions. Based essentially on methodological considerations, this choice simply subsumes those aspects not directly named under those which are.

Perfectly in keeping with this broader notion of materialism is Reich's claim that "Mankind exists with two basic psychological needs, the need for nourishment and the sexual need, which, for purposes of gratification, exist in a state of mutual interaction." Stressing the active component, Engels had said as much: "According to the materialist conception, the determining factor in history is, in the final instance, the production and reproduction of the immediate essentials of life. This, again, is of a twofold character. On the one side, the production of the means of existence . . . on the other side, the production of human beings themselves, the propagation of the species." The social organization of each epoch, according to Engels, is determined by both kinds of "production."

So little is this dual basis of Marx's conception of history appreciated—not least by Marx's followers—that the editor of the Moscow edition of *Origins of the Family, Private Property and the State,* where this remark appears, accuses Engels of "inexactitude," a serious admission for any Communist editor to make in 1948.

Reich, too, is not altogether satisfied with Engels' formulation. The parallel Engels draws between production and procreation as determining forces in history requires some emendation. For if people produce in order to satisfy the need for food, shelter, etc., they do not engage in sex in order to propagate the species. Goods are not only the result of production but its aim. Sex, however, is almost always engaged in for pleasure or to relieve bodily tension. For the greater part of human history the link between sexual intercourse and paternity was not even known. Beyond this, sexual desire, which makes its appearance in early childhood, precedes the possibility of procreation in the life of everyone. Consequently, as a material need, as a subjective aspect of the "real individual," sex is essentially the drive for sexual pleasure. It is, therefore, how society responds to the individual's attempt to satisfy his hunger and obtain sexual pleasure that determines the social organization of each epoch.

Besides accepting Marx's notion of "material forces" (however extended), Reich, as I have indicated, also accepted the primacy "in the last instance" of economic factors (narrowly understood). To grasp the latter admission in the proper perspective one must replace the causal model into which it is often forced with a dialectical one. On the basis of the dialectic, mutual interaction (or reciprocal effect) exists between all elements in reality. This basic assumption does not rule out the possibility that some elements exert a proportionately greater effect on others or on the whole as such. As Marx discovered, this was generally the case for economic factors. His claim regarding the primacy of economic factors is an empirical generalization based on a study of real societies, and not an a priori truth about the world. Consequently, Marx himself could call attention to the predominant role that war and conquest seem to have played in the development of ancient societies, and Engels could say that before the division of labor reached a certain point, kinship groups bore the chief responsibility for determining social forms. Reich, who made a special study of primitive societies, concurs with Engels' judgment, though his qualification shows him to be even more of an "economic determinist" in this matter than Engels. Basing himself primarily on the anthropology of Malinowski, Reich emphasizes the importance of the marriage dowry (arranged as a form of tribute between previously warring primal hordes) in establishing both clan exogamy and the incest taboo; whereas Engels, under the influence of Morgan and Darwin, attributes both developments to natural selection.

If Reich's research into the social origins of neuroses, beginning with his work in the free psychoanalytic clinic of Vienna, led him to accept the primacy in the last instance of economic factors, the same research made him want to alter the weight Marx attached to at least one of the elements in this interaction. Marx had mentioned sex as a natural and human power, as a way of relating to nature, along with eating, seeing, working and many other human conditions and functions. He did declare, as we saw, that the quality of the sexual relationship offers the clearest insight into the degree to which man the animal has become a human being. Yet, the only power whose influence is examined in any detail is work.

Reich does not by any means seek to belittle the importance Marx attributes to work, but he does wish to accord greater importance to sexuality, particularly in affecting people's capacity for rational action. For very different reasons, Marx and Freud had underestimated the influence on character and social development of the area of life investigated by the other. The result was that "In Marx's system, the sexual process led a Cinderella existence under the misnomer 'development of the family.' The work process, on the other hand, suffered the same fate in Freud's psychology under such misnomers as 'sublimation,' 'hunger instinct' or 'ego instincts.' " For Reich, synthesizing Marx and Freud meant breaking out of the prison imposed by such categories to redistribute causal influence in line with the basic discoveries of both men.

Sartre has recently remarked that most Marxists treat man as if he were born at the time of applying for his first job. Writing as a Marxist psychoanalyst, it is chiefly this distortion that Reich sought to correct.

The attack on Reich as a sexual determinist has led most Marxist critics to overlook the real differences that exist between Marx's materialist conception of history and Reich's. The chief of these has to do with the different time periods brought into focus. Whereas Marx concentrated on the social-economic forms that have come into existence in the West in the last two to three thousand years (slavery, feudalism, capitalism), Reich—while accepting Marx's divisions—generally operates with a periodization based on social-sexual developments, whose three main stages are matriarchy, patriarchy (covering the whole of recorded history) and communism. Though they overlap, these two ways of dividing time are not fully integrated, either conceptually—so that one is forced to think of one or the other—or practically—so that followers of Marx and Reich often dismiss economic or psychological factors (depending on the school) in accounting for social change.

This contrast between the two thinkers is nowhere so clearly drawn as in their treatment of contradictions. At the core of Marx's materialist conception of history, insofar as it passes beyond methodology (how best to study social change) to a set of generalizations on how such changes occur, is his stress on the reproduction of the conditions of social existence which at a certain point begins to transform the old order into a qualitatively new one. So it is that attracting more and more workers into towns to reproduce the conditions necessary for the production of capital results eventually, through social activity and combination, in the abolition of competition between workers which is a necessary condition for the production of capital. For Marx, the content of contradictions is always provided by the particular society in which their resolution takes place.

As a kindred thinker to Marx, Reich too is particularly attuned to contradictory tendencies in the material he examines. Yet, with few exceptions, the contradictions he believes will be resolved in capitalism possess a content that is derived from patriarchal society as such. This is the case with the contradiction between repression strengthening marriage and the family and, in virtue of the sexual misery caused, undermining them; and likewise of the contradiction he sees between repression producing a character structure which inclines youth to accept parental authority (and by extension all forms of authority) and simultaneously provoking sexual rebellion against parents (and by extension all forms of authority).

Without roots in the particular society in which they are found (capitalism), it is not altogether clear how these contradictions contribute to the demise of this society, nor why its demise will necessarily lead to the resolution of these contradictions. And adding that repression is greater in the capitalist era does not solve the problem. Even sexual alienation is affected, for to the extent that its peculiarly capitalist features are overshadowed by patriarchal ones it becomes, for the time span with which Marx is concerned, an ahistorical phenomenon. Thus, a form of sexual alienation, as Reich was forced to admit, could exist even in the Soviet Union, still a patriarchal society.

Reich's error—for all the use he made of Marx's analysis—lies in conceptualizing his findings apart from the findings of Marxist sociology, rather than integrating the two within the same social contradictions. He himself offers a good example of the alternative when he speaks of the capitalist economy fostering family ideology while simultaneously undermining it through inner family tensions caused by unemployment and forcing women to go to work. In this way, that is, through the operation of typical capitalist trends, the family whose ideological function is necessary to capitalism is rendered increasingly dysfunctional. Such examples in Reich's work, however, remain the exception.

Marxists have always managed better to explain the transition from slavery to feudalism and from feudalism to capitalism than to explain the onset of class society and, as events show, its eventual replacement by communism. It is just such developments, however, that Reich's work does most to illuminate. Yet, while Reich's contradictions occur in patriarchal times and the main contradictions Marx uncovered take place in capitalism, Reich's contribution to Marx's analysis can only be peripheral and suggestive. If Reich's "sexual economy" is ever to become an integral part of Marxism, the peculiarly capitalist qualities of sexual repression, including its distinctive forms and results within each social class (making allowances for racial, national and religious differences), must be brought out in greater detail. And, conceptually, from a patriarchal social relation, sexual repression must be broken down into slave, feudal, capitalist and even "socialist" social relations, in order to capture its special contribution to each period as well as the opportunities available in each period for its transcendence. Most of this research and work of reformulation is still to be done.

Aside from the accusation that Reich's theory is of sexual

determinism, another potentially telling criticism raised by many radicals today has to do with the relevance of his ideas in light of all the changes in sexual behavior that have occurred since he wrote. Have Reich's teachings missed their revolutionary moment? Reimut Reiche, in his book *Sexuality and the Class Struggle,* argues that the spread of sexual education, the availability of birth control pills and abortions, the easy access to cars (if not rooms) in which to make love, etc., have made it impossible to link the denial of a satisfactory sex life with the requirements of the capitalist system. The market has been able to absorb even these needs, turning their satisfaction into a profitable business venture for some section of the capitalist class. For him, the focus of interest has changed from finding out why sexuality is being denied to discovering how in the very means of its satisfaction it is being manipulated to serve the ends of the capitalist system.

Neither Reimut Reiche's optimism regarding the extent to which repression has diminished nor his pessimism as to the extent capitalism is able to exploit whatever new freedom exists seems fully justified. A recent poll of eighteen-year-old college students in the United States, for example, shows that 44 percent of the women and 23 percent of the men are still virgins, and one expects that a far greater percentage have known only one or a few encounters. Radicals tend to believe that on sexual matters, at least, their generally liberated attitudes and practices are shared by most of their age peers. This is a serious mistake.

As for capitalist reforms blunting the revolutionary edge of sexual protest, it must be admitted that this can happen. What remains to be seen, however, is whether the new contradictions embodied in these reforms simply make the old situation more explosive. How long can the pill be easily obtainable, venereal diseases curable, etc., and youth still frightened by the dangers of sexual intercourse? At what point in making marriage unnecessary for sex will young people stop getting married in order to have sex? When will the rebellion that has known some success in sexual matters be directed against intolerable conditions elsewhere? Put in Reichian terms, how long could capitalism survive with a working class whose authoritarian character structures have been eroded through modifications in their sexual lives?

The revolutionary potential of Reich's teachings is as great as ever—perhaps greater, now that sex is accepted as a subject for serious discussion and complaint virtually everywhere. The origins of the March Twenty-second Movement in France illustrate this point well. In February 1967, the French Trotskyist, Boris Frankel, spoke on Reich and the social function of sexual repression to a crowd of several hundred students at the Nanterre branch of the University of Paris. I can personally attest to the enthusiastic response of the audience, for I was there. In the week following the talk, Reich's booklet, *The Sexual Struggle of Youth,* was sold door to door in all the residence halls. This led to a widespread sex-educational campaign based—as Danny Cohn-Bendit tells us—on Reich's revolutionary ideas, and resulted in the occupation by men and women students of the women's dorms to protest against their restrictive rules. Other struggles over other issues followed, but the consciousness which culminated in the events of May 1968 was first awakened in a great number of Nanterre students in the struggle against their sexual repression.

The same struggle is being repeated with local variations at universities and even high schools throughout the capitalist world. Generally lacking, however, is the clear consciousness of the link between restrictions on sexual liberty and the capitalist order that one found at Nanterre. Reich's teachings, whatever their shortcomings, are the indispensable critical arm in forging these links.

Charles Rycroft   (essay date 1972)

SOURCE: "Energy, Character, and Orgasm," in *Wilhelm Reich,* The Viking Press, 1972, pp. 13-32.

[*An English psychoanalyst, Rycroft is noted for his dream theory, which differs significantly from the dream theories of both Sigmund Freud and Carl Jung. Rycroft maintains that dreams are "the sleeping form of creative imagination," rather than expressions of latent desires. In the following essay, he examines the influence of Freud's psychoanalytic theory on Reich's concepts of energy, character, and orgasm.*]

Reich's ideas about energy, character, and orgasm can only be understood in the light of their origin in the kind of psychoanalysis that he encountered in Vienna in the 1920s. At that time psychoanalysis was still under the unquestioned influence of Freud's ideal of a psychological theory that would satisfy all the criteria of a natural science.

As a young man Freud had worked as a physiologist under Ernst Brücke, who was a leading member of a crusading antivitalist scientific movement usually known as the Helmholtz School of Medicine. The aims of this school are epitomized by a "solemn oath" pledged in 1842 by Brücke and his fellow physiologist Du Bois-Reymond.

> No other forces than the common physical and chemical ones are active within the organism. In those cases which cannot at present be explained by these forces one either has to find the specific way or form of their action by means of the physical-mathematical method or to assume new forces equal in dignity to the chemical-physical forces inherent in matter, reducible to the force of attraction and repulsion.

The Helmholtz school was reductionist and both antiidealist and antireligious. It was concerned to ensure that religious and vitalist concepts such as "spirit," "*élan vital*," "life force" were excluded from the biological sciences and to demonstrate that the structure and behavior of living organisms were explicable solely in terms of the concepts of physics and chemistry. Its standpoint was strictly determinist and assumed that all explanations are in terms of causation; it seems to have been strangely untroubled by the possibility that the emergence of consciousness, and in man of reflective self-awareness, might pose awkward problems when it came to applying causal-

deterministic modes of thought to the behavior of man and the higher animals.

Inspired by this ideal, Freud's lifelong ambition was to construct a scientific psychology in which mental phenomena could be shown to be subject to the laws of causation and to be reducible to a number of simple statements about the forces of attraction and repulsion operating within a system or structure consisting of mental units or "ideas." He assumed that there exists some form of mental energy which, as he wrote in 1894, "possesses all the characteristics of quantity (though we have no means of measuring it), which is capable of increase, diminution, displacement, and discharge, and which is spread over the memory traces of ideas somewhat as an electric charge is spread over the surface of a body." He assumed further that this mental energy circulated within a mental apparatus, which was conceived to have structure. In Freud's original formulations this structure consisted of a conscious and an unconscious, but in 1923, with the publication of *The Ego and the Id,* the mental apparatus became tripartite, consisting of an id, an ego, and a superego. Ideas, impulses, emotions, etc., were conceived to be located at specific points in this apparatus; changes in feeling, desire, and thought were explained as the result of movements of quanta of energy from one part of the mental apparatus to another; while actions were conceived to be accompanied by discharge of energy.

Despite the fact that Freud's "scientific psychology" is patently a form of science fiction, with its quanta of unquantifiable energy and its transposition of temporal relationships into spatial ones (in the mental apparatus, the past is underneath the present and ideas move upward as they became conscious), in Freud's own writings it sounds very scientific and objective and Freud's followers in the 1920s seem, with the possible exceptions of Lou Andreas-Salomé and Oscar Pfister, to have been entirely oblivious of the complications produced by the fact that the data that it purported to explain were subjective phenomena derived from introspection and reminiscence. They seem to have accepted without question Freud's assumption that the translation of human experience into the language of the natural sciences was a worthwhile activity and not, as many analysts now believe, an unprofitable if sometimes amusing game.

Since Reich's later researches were primarily concerned with the nature of biological energy, two of Freud's ideas about mental energy must be mentioned briefly. First, he held that it existed in two forms, one mobile and the other "bound," mobile energy being characteristic of unconscious mental processes, which were regarded as "chaotic" and unstructured, bound energy being characteristic of conscious mental processes, which were regarded as having structure and organization. Since Freud also held that mental energy has its origin in bodily processes, this idea that mind consists of energy existing in two forms bears a remarkable resemblance to Blake's statement that "energy is the only life and is from the body; and reason is the bound and outward circumference of energy."

Second, Freud usually, though not quite always, equated general mental energy and erotic energy, "libido." Here again his thinking is curiously similar to Blake's "energy is eternal delight." However, despite the similarities between Freud's and Blake's views on the nature of mental energy, they differ fundamentally in respect of their origins and credentials. Blake reached his insight by an admitted act of poetic imagination, while Freud claimed to have reached his by scientific observation and reasoning.

Although Freud's first theories about mental energy and structure, which are described in his *Project for a Scientific Psychology,* written in 1895 but only published posthumously, were formulated in the hope that they would prove to correspond precisely with the way the brain works, he later saw clearly that his mental apparatus was a fiction, a metaphorical system that did not necessarily bear any real relation to the physiological and neurological processes accompanying and underlying mental activity. However, like all analogies, it could and often was taken literally by the philosophically unwary, and I think that there can be little doubt that Reich believed in the objective reality of Freud's mental apparatus.

However, despite his acceptance of the mechanist assumptions underlying the idea of the mental apparatus, Reich was also a vitalist, both by temperament and conviction. In the early 1920s he read a lot of Bergson, acquiring indeed the reputation of being a "crazy Bergsonian," and in the biographical chapter of the 1942 version of *The Function of the Orgasm* there is a revealing passage which shows that he always wanted to replace ideas by things and to resolve the vitalist-mechanist antithesis by discovering some "tangible" *thing* in which the life force could be located.

As we shall see, Reich eventually persuaded himself that he had succeeded in reconciling the vitalist intuitive perception of a life force with the mechanist appeal to the intellect by discovering a substance, which could be touched and "practically handled," in which the life force was embodied.

Just as Reich's ideas on life energy derive from Freud's ideas on mental energy and libido, so too his ideas on "character" can be traced back to Freud's concept of "defense."

According to Freud, unconscious ideas and wishes do not just happen to be unconscious. On the contrary, they strive energetically to become conscious but are prevented from becoming so by the action of "defense mechanisms," the best known and first described of these mechanisms being repression. In other words, the mind, the mental apparatus, is assumed to be divided into two parts, an instinctual part which strives for self-expression and for recurrent discharge of its accumulating energies, and another "reasonable" part which is concerned to maintain its equilibrium and to avoid tension, stress, and anxiety. If the wishes of the former part, the id, are felt to threaten the latter part's equilibrium or to endanger its relation to the outside world (by instigating actions that will be met by frustration, opposition, or social and moral disapproval), this latter part, the ego, will attempt to protect itself from the anticipated distress and to ensure itself against disap-

pointment and disapproval by activating defenses that prevent the disturbing impulse from becoming conscious.

There is, it will be noted, something ambiguous about this conception of the mind as a structure inherently divided against itself. The equilibrium-seeking part, the ego, is conceived to suffer from divided loyalties. On one hand, it wishes to experience the joys and pleasures of self-expression, of "instinctual satisfaction"; on the other hand, it seeks to accommodate itself to the limitations of the environment it finds itself in and to the moral values of the society of which it is a member. Moreover, since the ego is held to internalize (or identify with) these moral values and to construct within itself a third structure, the superego, whose inner commands it feels impelled to obey, the unfortunate ego is conceived to have the unenviable task of trying to reconcile three often incompatible sets of demands—those of the id, those of the superego, and those of the environment.

Now, although this theory purports to be scientific and morally neutral, and although too it can be used to describe and classify neurotic states in terms of such concepts as "the strength of the instincts," "the severity of the superego," "the strength of the ego," etc., the practical conclusions drawn from it are likely to depend to a considerable extent on the personality and temperament of the person using it. If he is an optimist who holds that man is basically good and if he sets a high value on self-expressive activity, he is likely to be pro-id and will tend to regard the superego and social morality as the villains of the piece; while if he is a pessimist convinced of man's evil and destructiveness, he will tend to side with the ego's struggle to master and control its unruly instinctual endowment.

It would be convenient and dramatically satisfying if it were possible to maintain that Freud was basically a pessimist opposed to the instincts and Reich an optimist wholeheartedly on the side of instinctual self-expression. This opposition is indeed sometimes assumed by Reich's followers, but it is, I think, unfair to both Freud and Reich.

Freud did, it is true, sometimes write very negatively about the id, which he once described as a "cauldron of seething excitations," while in *Civilization and Its Discontents* he developed the thesis that the development of all culture and civilization is unavoidably based on instinctual renunciation. However, he seems also to have held that instinctual renunciation involves a real and regrettable loss—i.e., his theory of culture is ironical and tragic and not ascetic—and in his paper "Civilized Sexual Morality and Modern Nervousness" he stated unequivocally his conviction that our own (or rather his, since this paper was written in 1908) civilization demands more renunciation of its members than is necessary for its preservation. As Ernest Jones said of this paper, "It was in essence a protest against the exorbitant demands of society, especially in the sexual sphere, on the life of the individual. The grounds of this protest are as valid now as then, but in some respects the paper has an interest as a period piece. It depicts a civilization in many ways different from our present one, and it can be said that some of the important changes in the past half-century are the direct result of

Freud's own work" [*The Life and Work of Sigmund Freud,* 1955].

Nor, although Reich certainly was an optimist who believed that inside every corrupted, civilized man there was a Rousseauan Noble Savage trying to escape, is it true that he believed in instinctual freedom in the sense of supposing that each and every desire should be acted upon immediately. Although he held that sexual deprivation produced states of "sexual stasis" that provided the energy with which neuroses are engendered and perpetuated, his conceptions of sexual potency and satisfaction included the necessity of total involvement of the personality in sexual relationships. He also maintained that the truly healthy man, the so-called "genital character," possessed a natural internal regulating function that makes socially enforced "compulsive morality" unnecessary.

> The healthy individual has no compulsive morality because he has no impulses which call for moral inhibition. . . . Intercourse with a prostitute becomes impossible. Sadistic phantasies disappear. To expect love as a right or even to rape a sexual partner becomes inconceivable, as do ideas of seducing children. Anal, exhibitionistic or other perversions disappear, and with these the social anxiety and guilt feelings. The incestuous fixation to parents and siblings loses its interest; this liberates the energy which was bound up in such fixations. In brief, all these phenomena point to the fact that the organism is capable of *self-regulation.* [***The Sexual Revolution***]

In this connection it is amusing to note that in one passage in ***The Function of the Orgasm*** Reich expresses with such definiteness his conviction that "genital characters" are moral that his American translator found it necessary to insert a footnote designed to reassure readers that Reich did not believe in lifelong monogamy; but only that sexual relationships, while they last, constitute a bond to which neither partner wishes to be unfaithful.

Freud's idea that the ego defends itself against impulses arising in the id leads naturally to the idea that a person's "character" may be a defense, and to the clinical concept that in addition to psychoneurotics whose symptoms are the result of conflict between repressed and repressing aspects of their personality, there are also "character neurotics" whose habitual stances and attitudes are interpretable as defenses against unwelcome, unconscious instinctual tendencies. In such people character traits are the equivalents of symptoms, since they are compulsive, involuntary patterns of behavior whose function it is to prevent the emergence of repressed impulses. Examples of such character defenses are habitual submissiveness and obsequiousness preventing the emergence of envy and hostility, habitual solicitousness covering cruelty, and habitual assertiveness acting as a defense against unconscious wishes to be passive and dependent.

This idea that a person's "character," in the sense of his habitual, stereotyped attitudes and responses to situations, is a defense has become an essential part of every analyst's intellectual equipment, but Reich cannot be credited with it, since it can be traced back in the psychoanalytical literature at least as far as 1908, when Freud published his *Character and Anal Erotism.* Reich does, however, seem to have been the first analyst to appreciate that it might be possible and indeed necessary to treat patients by interpreting the nature and functions of their character rather than by analyzing their dreams and free associations. Even when he was a conventional analyst he took the view that it was a waste of time listening to a patient's free association or interpreting his dreams unless the analyst had previously made him aware of his habitual attitude of, say, submissiveness or rudeness toward the analyst and had succeeded in getting him to understand why he found it necessary to relate to him in such a stereotyped way. Only after this had been made clear to the patient could he, in Reich's view, become at ease and spontaneous with his analyst and open up sincerely to him in a way that made his free associations valid communications.

Reich's advocacy of character analysis in addition or in preference to symptom analysis and dream interpretation also contributed to the realization that the therapeutic effect of psychotherapy derives not from the unearthing of traumatic memories or from the correct interpretation of dreams and symptoms but from the nature of the relationship which develops between analyst and patient. By insisting on the importance of analyzing the patient's defenses against spontaneous rapport between himself and the analyst, Reich opened up the possibility of discovering what really goes on between them and contributed significantly to the idea that psychotherapy consists in a confrontation or encounter between two real, live people. As a result his work constitutes a formative though not always acknowledged influence, not only on contemporary psychoanalysis with its emphasis on the importance of transference and countertransference interactions, but also on the existentialist, contractual, and "encounter" schools of psychotherapy.

However, Reich was not content to stop here. He soon went further, maintaining that character was *the* essential defense in *all* cases and that civilized Western man was imprisoned in a character armor that prevented him from expressing his spontaneous feelings of love and hatred in general, and from experiencing orgasm in particular. This character armor represented the precipitation within his personality of society's antiemotional, antilibidinal "compulsive morality," the origins of which Reich explained in terms of his social and political theories. . . .

Reich's theory of orgasm also has its roots in Freud's thinking. According to Freud (1894) the neuroses could be divided into two groups, actual neuroses and psychoneuroses; the former being the direct, physiological result of present-day (*aktuel*) disturbances of sexual function, the latter being complicated, psychological consequences of past experiences. Actual neuroses, being of physiological origin, were incapable of psychological interpretation and did not require it; they were cured automatically if the patient abandoned unhealthy sexual habits such as excessive masturbation, coitus interruptus, or abstinence. On the other hand the psychoneuroses, being complex psychological formations, could only be explained and cured by psychoanalytical investigation and interpretation of the patient's Oedipus complex and infantile sexual phantasies and by the recovery of repressed traumatic experiences.

Although this distinction between actual and psychoneuroses was in theory simple and straightforward, in practice matters were more complicated. If one sought to explain why any particular patient allowed himself to develop an actual neurosis, it often became necessary to postulate the simultaneous presence of a psychoneurosis that prevented him from organizing for himself a satisfactory sex life; while, since psychoneuroses lead to sexual inhibitions, they were bound to be compounded by a superimposed actual neurosis.

As a result some analysts denied the usefulness of the distinction, while even more denied the existence of the actual neuroses and sought to explain all neuroses and all neurotic anxiety in purely psychological terms. Reich, however, took the opposite stance, maintaining that an actual neurosis formed the core of every psychoneurosis, and that actual neuroses had a psychoneurotic superstructure. Furthermore, he argued, it was the inability of psychoneurotics to discharge sexual energy completely and with satisfaction during orgasm that created the damming up of energy (the "sexual stasis" in his terminology) that kept the psychoneurosis alive. In other words, he thought that neurotics were caught in a vicious circle. Their actual neurosis provided the energy to create and maintain their psychoneurosis, which then perpetuated their actual neurosis.

This view of the relationship between actual and psychoneuroses has not been absorbed into psychoanalytical thinking, but it has two great merits. It retains a connection between psychopathology and physiology—in the last resort the neuroses are not purely mental formations but arise from and affect the body—and it provides an explanation of why neuroses do not disappear spontaneously. So far as I know Reich is the only analyst to offer any sort of explanation as to why the childhood pathogenic experiences that according to psychoanalysis cause neuroses do not gradually lose their impact when neurotics move away from their childhood environment.

Now, since, as Reich himself readily admitted, many psychoneurotics appeared or claimed to be living normal and satisfactory sex lives, his position compelled him to call into question the normality and authenticity of much that passes for normal sex. In particular, he challenged the idea that orgastic potency could be defined simply in terms of the capacity for erection, penetration, and ejaculation (and *mutatis mutandis* for women). These capacities were, he maintained, only "the indispensable prerequisites" for orgastic potency. True orgastic potency involved much more and excluded much that passed for normal. It involved, *inter alia,* the capacities for uninhibited surrender to the flow of biological energy and discharge of dammed-up sexual excitation through involuntary contractions of the body (not just the genitals). It excluded the presence of any trace of sadism in the male or masochism in the female, or any sense of prowess or smugness in the male. Furthermore, the surrender is silent, or nearly so. Orgastically potent individuals never talk or laugh during the sexual act—with the exception of uttering words of tender-

ness. Both talking and laughing indicate a serious lack of the capacity for surrender, which requires an undivided absorption in the sensations of pleasure. Men to whom surrender means being "feminine" are always orgastically "disturbed."

With such high criteria in mind Reich was surely right in asserting that no neurotics are orgastically potent and that the great majority of human beings suffer from a character neurosis. His theories of character armor and orgasm constitute, therefore, a sweeping indictment of the sexual life of civilized man, an indictment similar in many ways to that made by D. H. Lawrence, whom indeed he resembled in combining an intense, almost mystical belief in the prime importance of sex with a puritanical insistence that it should always be treated with high if not dead seriousness. He and Lawrence also had in common the conviction that orgastic potency is a virtue to be found more commonly among working-class men than among aristocrats, bourgeois, and intellectuals, an idea for which no evidence exists.

In working out his theory of the function of the orgasm in preserving and maintaining health, Reich was led to make a minute analysis of the "orgastically satisfying sexual act." This is described, complete with a graph, in Chapter IV, Section 3, of the 1942 version of *The Function of the Orgasm*—which was written after he had persuaded himself that libido (bio-energy) is a "tangible" substance whose movements in the body can be traced and recorded electrically.

Reich's account of the ideal sexual act is remarkable both for its explicitness, which must have required courage in the pre-Kinsey, pre-Masters and Johnson era in which it was written, and for its omission of the one word "love." And yet it is clear that it is love he is talking about. Orgastic potency as formulated by Reich is the capacity to love body and soul, psychosomatically—in Pauline terminology it is a matter of the Body and not only of the Spirit or the Flesh—but at this stage in his development his adherence to the natural-scientific approach prevented his saying so.

Another remarkable feature of this account of the sexual act is Reich's insistence that in genital characters it differs physically as well as psychologically from that experienced by the orgastically immature. Whereas the typical civilized man with his inhibiting character armor only experiences "partial releases of tension which are *similar* to orgasm," the genital character experiences an "ultimate vegetatively involuntary surrender" of which lesser mortals have no inkling. Even if one succeeds in attaching some meaning to this phrase and is prepared to accept the idea that there may exist people, presumably either untreated industrial workers or ex-patients of Reich's, who are familiar with this ultimate vegetatively involuntary surrender, one is still left wondering how Reich knew, from what experiences of his own or his patients he derived this insight—or even more how he reached by natural-scientific means the conclusion that "all feelings about nature derive from this function or from the longing for it."

Reich's conviction that all neurotics and indeed most civilized men and women lack full orgastic potency, coupled with his belief in the existence of sexual energies requiring recurrent orgastic discharge, raised for him the question of what happened to these energies when they were not effectively discharged. One answer was, as already mentioned, that they were expended in neurotic symptoms and systems of thought, and provided the energy which activated and maintained infantile sexual phantasies. Another answer was that they were experienced as anxiety. Undischarged energy, which would have been experienced as pleasure if it had been discharged orgastically, is experienced as anxiety if it is discharged through other bodily systems. Here again Reich was following a line of thought begun by Freud, whose original theory of anxiety was that undischarged libido is "converted" into anxiety. This theory, which Freud himself abandoned in the 1920s, assumed that anxiety is a direct physiological result of repressed sexual tension, but the precise nature of the process designated "conversion" was admitted to be mysterious. Reich, in line with his general tendency to remain loyal to Freud's early ideas and to reject his later reformulations, sought to retain Freud's idea of the intimate physiological connection between libido and anxiety by solving the mystery of conversion. This he did by maintaining that anxiety is simply libidinal discharge occurring through the cardiovascular system. Whereas sexual pleasure is experienced in the genitals, anxiety is experienced in the cardiac and diaphragmatic region.

Reich's third answer to the question of the fate of undischarged libido was that it was transformed into sadism; the repressed wish for true orgasm continues to strive for discharge, and the resulting aggression, which in healthy persons is only a means to an end, becomes an end in itself. Love turns into hate, aggression into sadism, all destructive activity being the organism's reaction to the frustration of vital needs.

This view of sadism forms the basis and rationale for the contemporary slogan Make Love Not War, which contains Reich in a nutshell. It appeals immediately to all that is warm, generous, and spontaneous in human nature. It assumes an extraordinarily direct and simple connection between orgastic deprivation and destructiveness—according to Reich, even genital characters become sadists if confronted with a sudden obstacle to their accustomed gratification. And yet it is naïve by its omissions. Just as Reich's confident assertions about the natural placidity and peacefulness of bulls and dogs completely ignore the aggressiveness associated with territoriality (see the writings of Lorenz, Storr, and Ardrey) and the establishment of hierarchical "pecking orders" within animal communities, so the Make Love Not War philosophy completely ignores the psychology of power—and in practical terms such complications as the fact that those who decide to make wars are not, under modern conditions, the people who fight in them and that there is no evidence that the majority of those who do the fighting get any sadistic gratification out of it.

Finally, it must be emphasized that all Reich's ideas about the effects of orgastic frustration derive from psychoana-lytical ways of thinking—and were in his own view a defense of Freud's original position against a retrogressive development in psychoanalysis emanating from Freud himself. In the mid-1920s both Freud and Reich, presumably for the same social and historical reasons, became impressed by man's tendency to behave destructively, but whereas Freud sought to explain this by postulating a death instinct, an innate drive toward destructiveness and self-destruction, Reich adopted the explanation that it was due to a much greater and more widespread repression of sexuality than Freud had ever envisaged. And in taking up this position Reich conceived himself to be defending Freud's original revolutionary insights against a loss of nerve and hope on Freud's part.

Both explanations, however, raised as many problems as they solved. Freud's raised problems about the evolutionary status of an instinct that appeared to run counter to evolution, while Reich's raised problems about the origin of man's tendency to construct a character armor against his own nature. Freud's biological justification of the death-instinct concept is singularly unconvincing, since, as Jones, a loyal Freudian if ever there was one, says, "No biological observation can be found to support the idea of a death instinct, one which contradicts all biological principles," and it has been accepted by only a minority even of psychoanalysts. It has, however, contributed to the widespread belief that psychoanalysis is the modern dismal science that sets limits on human progress. Reich . . . produced at different phases of his life two different and incompatible explanations of the origin of the tendency to construct character armor, the first sociological and the second "religious." Both are still with us; the second indeed always has been, since it resembles closely the account of the Fall of Man given in Genesis.

Paul Edwards   (essay date 1974)

SOURCE: "The Greatness of Wilhelm Reich," in *The Humanist*, Vol. XXXIV, No. 2, March-April, 1974, pp. 32-5.

[*Edwards is an Austrian-born American philosopher and educator. In the following essay, he addresses what he considers misconceptions about Reich's life and works.*]

When I came to New York in the fall of 1947, Wilhelm Reich was the talk of the town. Reich had at that time a large and enthusiastic following, especially among young intellectuals and people whose sympathies were clearly on the left but who, like Reich himself, had become totally disenchanted with communism as it had developed in Russia.

The main source of Reich's attractiveness was not the orgone theory, which was received with a good deal of skepticism even by many of his warmest admirers. It was first and foremost Reich's new therapy that seemed an exciting advance over the techniques of establishment psychiatry of the Freudian and other schools. There was also a widespread feeling that Reich had an original and penetrating insight into the troubles of the human race—that he had the answers to such questions as why children become neurotic, why marriages so rarely produce any lasting happiness, why masses of people again and again turn to demagogues who preach the most irrational ideologies, why the best-intentioned political reform movements frequently end in disaster, and, not least of all, why there is a hunger for some kind of dogmatic religion even among highly critical and intelligent people. All of these questions were discussed in great detail in Reich's four major books—*The Function of the Orgasm, Character Analysis, The Mass Psychology of Fascism,* and *The Sexual Revolution*—which appeared in English translation in the early 1940s. I never saw sales figures, but the circulation of these books must have been immense, although they were published by Reich's own tiny press, which never did any kind of advertising. About a week after I came to New York, A. S. Neill (a friend and former patient of Reich's) gave a lecture in the packed auditorium of the New School for Social Research. He talked mostly about Summerhill, but there were frequent references to Reichian therapy. Every mention of Reich was greeted with thunderous applause.

Although Reich had a large following, the people who derided and denounced him were far more numerous. The opposition came from Stalinists and their fellow-travelers, of whom there were a great many in those days, but above all from the psychiatric establishment and from the many people who were patients in some form of psychoanalysis. There was a peculiar venom to the attacks on Reich, which I was never again to encounter in disputations on other topics. I had the impression, which subsequent experiences confirmed, that the people denouncing Reich were defending their very existence, that they would regard it as a personal calamity if Reich's teachings about orgastic potency were correct or if his new therapy was really superior to the "accepted" forms of psychoanalysis. I was repeatedly assured that Reich had been institutionalized during his stay in Scandinavia. I was often told that he was in fact right then in a mental institution. At other times I was treated to the story that Reich masturbated his patients, and it was widely believed, even by people who were not particularly hostile, that women patients in Reichian therapy had to have sexual intercourse with their therapists.

I had started corresponding with Reich while still living in Australia and his letters were not only sane but warm and helpful. I had a session with him shortly after my arrival in New York. He did not seem the slightest bit mad. On the contrary, he was quite wonderful, and the one session was enough to show me that he had hit on a remarkable new approach to the treatment of neurosis. When I would firmly deny that Reich was insane or that he was doing any of the evil things he was alleged to be doing, the people who made these accusations often became greatly upset. They assured me that, even though Reich might not be insane, the new therapy was nothing but "phrenology," that it was worthless, and that it had been rejected as such by all psychoanalysts in good standing. The virulence of the opposition to Reich only intensified my attachment, and for some years many of my friends and I regarded him as something akin to a messiah.

By the late 1940s more and more psychiatrists came to Reich for their training. At that time it was not unreason-

able to expect that Reichian therapy would before long become a major force in psychiatry. For some time Reich had been spending several months every year at his estate in Rangeley, Maine, and in 1950 he left New York permanently. From that time on he was almost exclusively concerned with the development of his orgone theory. His claims became ever wilder and more fantastic. Ilse Reich, his third wife, has published a moving account of Reich's life during these years. Her biography presents compelling evidence that, from 1951 on, Reich was subject to increasingly severe paranoid delusions. In 1954 the Food and Drug Administration obtained an injunction ordering the destruction of all orgone accumulators and the burning of practically all of Reich's publications. Reich refused to appeal, declaring that a court of law was not the appropriate place for adjudicating scientific questions. For some months Reich obeyed the injunction, but in October 1954 he notified the authorities that he was about to resume all of the activities of his institute, including the sale of books and periodicals. In 1956 he was tried for contempt of court and given maximum sentence of two years. He died in Lewisburg penitentiary in 1957. The books were burned in several separate actions in 1956 and 1960. Reich was present at one of these burnings and, according to the FDA inspector, he was quite affable. He commented that his books had been burned once before, in Germany, and that he was surprised that such a thing could happen in America.

The injunction against Reich was an unbelievable document. It in effect legislated orgone energy out of existence and made the very use of the word "orgone" (at least by Reich and his associates) a crime. Paul Goodman said at the time that the FDA commissioner was confusing himself with the Deity. Included among the banned writings were not only all the works describing the experiments on which Reich based his orgone theory but also books such as *Character Analysis* and *The Mass Psychology of Fascism,* which do not even mention the theory. Burning or banning of books is not a practice most Americans approve, but apparently in Reich's case it suddenly became justifiable. Although copies of the injunction were sent to various psychiatric journals, not a single spokesman of the psychiatric establishment protested against the book burning. At the request of Elsworth Baker, a psychiatrist close to Reich, I tried to enter the case on the ground that the banning of Reich's books interfered with my work as a university teacher. Throughout the summer of 1956 I worked with Roland Watts, who was then the general counsel of the American Civil Liberties Union, trying to prevent the destruction of Reich's books. Reich himself would not collaborate with us and it was found that I had no legal standing in the case. The ACLU finally issued a statement condemning the injunction as "a serious challenge to the freedom of scientific inquiry and to the freedom of the press," but this did not prevent the book burning. It is interesting to note that, in a recent study devoted to the many sins of commission and omission of the FDA (James S. Turner, *The Chemical Feast*, 1970), the Ralph Nader Study Group singles out the Reich case as one of the worst infamies in the inglorious history of the agency. The study details the many distortions perpetrated by the FDA and concludes that its case against Reich amounted to "a vicious campaign" carried out with "frightening vigor."

I have no doubt that many of the pronouncements of Reich's last years were little more than fantasies, and I am sorry that there are intelligent people who feel obliged to defend everything Reich said and did. I now regard his teachings as a mixture of truth and error, but I still think that he was a singularly bold thinker who made some momentous discoveries that are not yet sufficiently understood. I should like to say a few words about the one that has meant most to me personally—Reich's insight that neuroses are not just "mental" disturbances but are, on the contrary, anchored in certain chronic muscular rigidities. This idea, and the therapy based on it, is such a drastic departure from all forms of psychoanalysis that people who are accustomed to think of neurosis as a purely psychological phenomenon have great difficulty in comprehending Reich's approach.

Reich's work on the physiological anchoring of neurosis is best explained if we first examine the concept of the "character armor," which Reich developed in the years preceding his expulsion from the Psychoanalytic Association in 1934. Neurotic character attitudes, according to Reich, are developed in order to protect the individual against external injury (such as being hurt or rejected by other human beings) and to protect him against feeling his own repressed emotions, especially (though not exclusively) various kinds of destructiveness. Reich introduced the term "character armor" to refer to the totality of chronic attitudes of this kind characterizing a given individual. It is, writes Reich, "as if the affective personality put on an armor, a rigid shell on which the knocks from the outer world as well as the inner demands rebound." The armor is most rigid in severe compulsion neuroses and chronic depressions, but it is present in all patients and indeed in most people who grow up in a repressive environment. The armor makes the individual less sensitive to pain but it also reduces his emotional motility and thereby his capacity for pleasure and achievement. It was the object of Reich's technique of "character analysis" to break down the neurotic attitudes and thus bring the repressed emotions to the surface. Reich totally abandoned the psychoanalytic technique current in his day, which he came to call "symptom analysis." He questioned the existence of "monosymptomatic neuroses"—neuroses with only one serious symptom. "There are no neurotic symptoms," he later observed, "without a disturbance of the total character. Neurotic symptoms are, as it were, nothing but peaks of a mountain chain representing the neurotic character." Unless the characterological basis of a symptom has been eliminated, it or some equally troublesome symptom is likely to reappear.

Reich's interest in character attitudes led him to emphasize the "how" of a patient's communications. The infantile structure, he argued, is "conserved" not only in *what* an individual does but also in the *way* in which he acts, talks, and thinks. Reich gradually abandoned free association, especially since many patients sooner or later would not give any associations. The main point of attack became the *manner* of a patient's communications or of his

silence. Patients who kept silent were also communicating something, and what they were expressing could gradually be understood. In a posthumously published letter, written from Scandinavia to a disciple who had stayed in Berlin, Reich describes the first session of a young girl who had previously been treated by three well-known analysts—Kempner, Pfister and Fenichel:

> I immediately noticed what three or four years ago I probably would not have seen till much later: rigid body attitude, stiff as a board, arms stretched out, hands folded, head practically nailed down. In speaking, the lips hardly moved, the voice without resonance, high-pitched, nearly inaudible. In previous analyses she had always insisted that she could not, and would not, speak: for three and a half years. The more she was urged to talk, the less she could do so . . . the first thing I tell her is: "You're behaving as if you were facing an operation—completely stiff." Her reply: "I've never been afraid of operations; on the contrary, I've always wanted them." I slowly began to describe her attitude, feature by feature: mouth, voice, posture, masklike face, head virtually nailed down. After about fifteen minutes she starts speaking softly and urgently, and suddenly remembers the *anxiety* she felt as a child about operations. That she was always stretched out so expectantly; that at one time she was very angry with her mother because under some pretext she took her to a doctor without telling her the truth. It had hurt a great deal. The posture stiffened even more. I have an idea: "Corpse." I tell her that a single word seems to me to describe her attitude, but that I will not mention it because she would have to begin to feel it herself. Her reply: "Were you thinking of a corpse?" Then come memories: once her hair got stuck in a crate while she was playing; she would go wild if someone suddenly grasped her from behind. The "nailed down" head gradually acquired meaning, but I said nothing and merely continued describing her attitude. At the end of the hour she said: "I don't like my back. I'm lying here as if it were glued down, as if I had no back, as if I'd been cut in two lengthwise," etc. Now what do you say to that? Not once in three years of analysis did she remember that she was afraid of surgery. Her very *attitude* communicated this. I confess I was shaken.

Special attention to the "how" of a patient's behavior naturally led to close observation of physical changes during and after the release of repressed emotions. Such releases were generally accompanied by a change in muscular behavior: chronic tensions loosened up, habitual postures changed, movements became less rigid and more supple. Reich was on the verge of making what seems to me one of the most exciting discoveries in the history of psychiatry. I should like to quote a paragraph from another early case history which illustrates particularly well what Reich meant by the "physiological anchoring" of emotions:

> In Copenhagen in 1933, I treated a man who put up especially strong resistances against the uncovering of his passive-homosexual phantasies. This resistance was manifested in an extreme at-

titude of stiffness of the neck . . . After an energetic attack upon his resistance, he suddenly gave in, but in a rather alarming manner. For three days, he presented severe manifestations of vegetative shock. The color of his face kept changing rapidly from white to yellow or blue; the skin was mottled and of various tints; he had severe pains in the neck and the occiput; the heartbeat was rapid; he had diarrhea, felt worn out, and seemed to have lost hold . . . *Affects had broken through somatically after the patient had yielded in a psychic defense attitude.* The stiff neck, expressing an attitude of tense masculinity, apparently had bound vegetative energies which now broke loose in an uncontrolled and disordered fashion . . . It was the musculature that served this inhibitory function. When the muscles of the neck relaxed, powerful impulses broke through, as if propelled by a spring.

This and other cases led to a systematic study of chronic muscular rigidities and their relation to neurotic character attitudes. Reich found chronic muscular rigidities and spasms in many different parts of the body: in the forehead, around the mouth and in the chin, in the throat, the shoulders, the chest, the abdomen, the pelvis and thighs, and many other places. The fixed expression in the eyes of many patients, their habitual "stare," is the result of a chronic rigidity in the lid muscles. The breathing of neurotic individuals is disturbed in comparison with the natural and free respiration of emotionally healthy people. Reich emphasized that it is muscle groups rather than individual muscles that become spastic—muscle groups that jointly serve a certain function, for example, to suppress the impulse to cry. Not only do the lower lips become tense but also "the whole musculature of the mouth, the jaw, and the throat, that is, all the muscles that, as a functional unit, become active in the process of crying." Reich referred to the totality of the chronic muscular rigidities as the individual's "muscular armor" and the goal of therapy became the dissolution of this armor.

The next natural step was to inquire whether the liberation of repressed emotions could be achieved by a direct "attack" on the muscular rigidities. I cannot discuss here the details of such direct physiological dissolutions of the muscular armor, but I would like to testify to the great ingenuity of Reich's new method. In my one session with him he worked for a few minutes on the muscles of my face and neck. This at once triggered an outburst of crying. He asked me, "What does it mean?" At that time the crying did not have any content; but later, when I regularly saw a Reichian psychiatrist, I cried through many sessions and for many hours outside the therapy; and then the crying was accompanied by the most vivid memories of disappointing and frustrating experiences.

Several writers, who obviously lack any firsthand knowledge, have referred to Reichian therapy as a kind of Yoga or chiropractic. Such a comparison is most misleading. I have myself taken Yoga classes (and greatly enjoyed them) and I have on occasions consulted an osteopath. Any similarities with Reichian therapy are quite superficial. There are no exercises in Reichian therapy. Furthermore, many of the muscle groups on which a Reichian

therapist is likely to concentrate do not figure at all in Yoga exercises or in chiropractic manipulations. To give just one example: by suitable work on the chin, enormous amounts of anger can be set free. Again—and here there is usually no manipulation at all—by encouraging the movement of certain muscles around the mouth, suppressed feelings of disgust can be liberated. Above all, verbal communication remains an essential part of the therapy. Reich himself was very emphatic on this point. As a result of direct work on the muscular armor, the breakthrough of repressed emotions becomes more complete, more forceful, more thoroughly experienced, and it also occurs more rapidly. However, it is impossible to dispense with work on character attitudes. With some patients, work on the muscular rigidities will predominate from the beginning; with others, work on the character attitudes; but in all cases work on the muscular armor becomes more important in the later stages of the treatment.

One of the most interesting features of Reichian therapy is that the patient's body will not "give," that the muscular rigidities cannot be dissolved unless the relationship between the patient and the therapist is undisturbed. In his earlier work Reich had emphasized the crucial importance of the negative transference—the patient's anxieties and suspicions about the therapy and his hostility to the therapist as the person who is threatening his neurotic equilibrium. The patient must feel free to criticize the psychiatrist and any attitudes that mask his hostility have to be broken down. All of this remains true in the new therapy. The very verbal articulation of objections to the therapy and to the therapist's personability will sometimes bring about releases of suppressed emotions, such as sadistic glee or anxiety, in the form of trembling; but in any event work on the body cannot proceed unless the hostility has been brought into the open. Moreover, as in all other forms of therapy, the patient must feel that the psychiatrist has an intuitive understanding of his personality and problems. Once, when my own psychiatrist was unavailable, I had a session with another therapist. After some talking he worked on my body, but nothing at all happened. I experienced no relief of any kind. In retrospect I realized that throughout the session I felt that this man did not really understand what troubled me and hence my body refused to cooperate.

The very sketchy outline presented here cannot do justice to the richness and power of Reichian therapy, but I hope I have explained some of its underlying principles and removed certain widespread misconceptions. In closing, I would like to mention briefly the orgone theory, which was the basis of Reich's legal troubles. I am sure that many of my readers would like me to dismiss it as nothing but a fantasy hatched in Reich's brain as he was going mad. This is in fact the view of many who are quite prepared to grant Reich's genius as a psychiatrist. I do not think that the truth is as neat and simple as this. I concede that Reich had no real competence as a physicist and that he probably made many errors that a professional would have avoided. At the same time I am quite convinced that the orgone theory cannot be complete nonsense. For a number of years, largely out of curiosity, I sat in an orgone accumulator once a day. I never experienced any benefit, but on several occasions when I stayed in the box for an extended period I suffered attacks of acute conjunctivitis. Eventually, for this reason, I stopped using the box. Similar experiences have been reported by other people. A friend of mine, a psychiatrist who was closely connected with Reich's work in the late 1940s and early 1950s, but who broke with Reich for a variety of reasons, experienced the same kind of thing much more intensely. He could not even be in the same room with an orgone accumulator without suffering a severe attack of conjunctivitis. He consulted many ophthalmologists, who were mystified. After several such attacks he was strongly urged to avoid exposing himself to whatever conditions caused the conjunctivitis, since his eyes were liable to suffer permanent damage. These and other facts make it impossible to dismiss the orgone theory. I should add that I have never seen convincing evidence that the orgone accumulator has any therapeutic value and I have no confidence in the objectivity of writers in Reichian journals who claim to have confirmed Reich's claims on this subject. Equally, however, I am not impressed by the kind of a priori dismissal of the theory found in Charles Rycroft's recent book on Reich (*Wilhelm Reich,* 1972). Perhaps one day competent and genuinely unprejudiced scientists will investigate Reich's claims. Until then it would be the better part of wisdom to suspend judgment on this subject.

An excerpt from *Passion of Youth*

The fact that my Mother had died, as sad as it was in itself, and under such circumstances, overwhelmed me less with grief than with fascination at a novel situation. Mother was the first person I had seen die. Yes, I must admit that I felt a certain pride in having the right to be called an orphan. Later on, when I began to ponder life and death, mankind and its lot, I reached the conclusion that the religious ceremonies which automatically ensue when a person dies run their strict course perhaps for the very purpose of suppressing feelings of mourning (if not directly, then indirectly). By this, I mean the genuine mourning which forces one to turn away and be alone and which I experienced only once, later in life, at the death of a friend. As a rule, it is suppressed, or rather masked by all that convention requires, the handshaking, the thanking for sympathy shown, arranging for the burial, etc. This can have a therapeutic effect if it relieves one of the necessity of feigning grief before *oneself.* But I would not like the task of deciding whether the other necessity, namely of exhibiting grief to the outside world, is any easier, especially when that grief is the genuine expression of an inner loss.

Wilhelm Reich, in his Passion of Youth, *Farrar, Straus and Giroux, 1988.*

Frederick Crews (essay date 1974)

SOURCE: "Anxious Energetics," in *Out of My System: Psychoanalysis, Ideology, and Critical Method,* Oxford University Press, 1975, pp. 145-64.

[*Crews is an American writer and educator. In the following essay, which was originally published in* Partisan Review *in 1974, he surveys the writings of Reich's followers and questions the validity of orgonomy in the treatment of psychological disorders.*]

Until fairly recently it seemed apparent that Wilhelm Reich, though a persistent presence in "left" or "advanced" circles since the 1940's, was fated eventually to be dismissed as a minor curiosity of American cultural history. The founder of character analysis and orgonomy, who died in 1957 after being imprisoned as a cancer quack, has never been entirely forgotten, either as a therapeutic innovator or as a prophet of sexual freedom. But the most prominent and sophisticated Reichians of the postwar period either gradually lost interest in his ideas or felt required to hedge them with major reservations, and Reich became a remote and implausible figure whose zealous advocacy of the orgasm seemed more quaint that courageous.

Now, however, in a distinctly altered cultural atmosphere, Reich has begun to find something like the broad following he always expected. Political radicals and ex-radicals, whose hopes for a better society have become increasingly focused on an end to neurosis, admire him not only for his stand against capitalism and patriarchy, but for his rejection of "adjustment" as a therapeutic goal. Orgonomy and its offshoot "activity therapies" are attracting favorable notice from psychiatrists and psychologists who feel that psychoanalysis has proved itself too cumbersome and cautious for purposes of broad social hygiene. Reich's scientific propositions, once generally ridiculed, are the subject of numerous conferences and seminars. His major writings have been reissued in hardcover and paper editions, and he is himself the topic of other books, one of which implicitly ranks him in influence, if not in merit, among the "Modern Masters." Reich's particular version of antinomianism seems well suited to what one conference brochure calls "today's emphasis on sexual, political, and spiritual liberation."

To some extent it might be said that Reich's own ideas helped to bring about the climate in which he is now being rehabilitated. Some of the radical intellectuals who had been drawn to his work in the forties became themselves propagators of body-centered therapy, uncoercive education, anti-authoritarian politics, and an ideology of dionysiac individualism. In England, A. S. Neill welcomed Reich as a philosophical ally in his efforts to promote the self-regulation and free development of children. In America, Paul Goodman and Frederick Perls used Reich, not Freud, as their point of departure when they fashioned Gestalt therapy; and Goodman, Dwight MacDonald, and others, accepting the Reichian insight that "a coercive society depends upon instinctual repression" [Paul Goodman, *Drawing the Line,* 1946], invoked Reich as the patron of a sensuous and decentralized new politics. In addition, Reich was admired for diverse reasons by Saul Bellow, Isaac Rosenfeld, Norman Mailer, Allen Ginsberg, Jack Kerouac, and William Burroughs. Although none of these writers forwarded the more practical aspects of orgonomy, all of them can be presumed to have influenced the development of a "Reichian" cultural atmosphere.

If the early phase of Reichianism can teach us anything about the present one, it is that ideological and temperamental affinities are likely to be more important than intellectual agreement with Reich's ideas. In the forties and fifties those ideas were largely untested and only vaguely understood by many of Reich's most ardent followers. Psychological and political radicals turned to Reich not because they found him a more careful student of the world than Marx and Freud, but because they felt historically disinherited and stymied. By the forties Freudian doctrine, which had once seemed so exhilaratingly resistant to every form of authority, was suspected of conformist tendencies, and so in a grimmer sense was Marxism in its Stalinist guise. In the gloom of the Cold War years, intellectuals whose historicism had been shaken faced the choice of either accommodating themselves to a prosperous anti-Communist society or taking a stand directly on what Mailer, citing Reich, called "the rebellious imperatives of the self " ["The White Negro: Superficial Reflections on the Hipster," *Advertisements for Myself*]. It was evidently Reich's irrefutably vague optimism, rather than his specific notions about orgasm or work democracy or orgone energy, that answered the embattled radicals' mood. As Theodore Solotaroff has said of Isaac Rosenfeld, "The very extremism of Reich's system—as over against the Freudian—must have commended it in this time of extremity . . ." [introduction to Isaac Rosenfeld, *An Age of Enormity: Life and Writing in the Forties and Fifties*]. To be a Reichian, with or without acceptance of Reich's claim to have discovered the life force in Cosmic Orgone Energy, was to seek contact with Mailer's "God . . . located in the senses of [one's] body, that trapped, mutilated and nonetheless megalomaniacal God who is It, who is energy, life, sex, force, the Yoga's *prana,* the Reichian's orgone, Lawrence's 'blood,' Hemingway's 'good' . . .". In Mailer's hands the orgasmic principle became a license to hurl oneself against "every social restraint and category," to break "those mutually contradictory inhibitions against violence and love which civilization has exacted of us."

This same diffuse rebelliousness still animates many Reichians, especially those political activists of the sixties who, like their thwarted counterparts after World War II, have been regrouping around the banner of "radical psychiatry." They too, it seems, respond more to Reich's mood of visionary defiance than to the fine points of orgonomy. So do radical feminists like Kate Millett and Juliet Mitchell, who value Reich (with stern qualifications) for prefiguring their own stance against patriarchal oppression.

Yet we can no longer be so certain that Reich's current appeal is entirely ideological. In contrast to the early admirers who had only an approximate sense of his scientific claims, many now argue in detail that he was primarily a great investigator of nature. Instead of observing the once-customary practice of distinguishing between "constructive" and "wild" phases in Reich's career, they tend to embrace it in its entirety, excepting only the last four or five years in which Reich, by then unquestionably paranoid,

fancied himself a messenger from outer space and a veteran of interplanetary war. Even the most moderate of Reich's recent exegetes, such as W. Edward Mann and David Boadella, are ready to defend not only the relatively accessible ideas about character armor and the orgasm reflex, but the whole chain of Reich's subsequent assertions about electrophysiology, plasma flow, radiation, cancer pathology, weather control, and so forth.

By far the best case for this new assessment is the one made by Boadella, who, by tracing Reich's career from each hypothesis to the next and recapitulating the conditions and results of his major experiments—meanwhile documenting the often shameful tactics of his opponents—shows the logical and evidential basis of ideas that might otherwise look like sheer science fiction. Reich, Boadella maintains, was drawn reluctantly to his conclusions by unanticipated, unanswerable findings. Those conclusions, he says, may have been only approximate first efforts, but the findings remain and must be dealt with by anyone who would challenge Reich's credibility. Where the original reports and case studies are missing, blame must be laid on the American government for the indiscriminate book-burning that was inflicted on Reich in 1956. And as for the prima facie implausibility of one man's making major breakthroughs in psychiatry, physiology, chemistry, biology, medicine, meteorology, physics, and astronomy, we must suspend judgment and grant Reich the synthetic nature of his enterprise. As an "energetic functionalist" Reich looked for unifying principles that would characterize life in all its forms. There is every reason to suppose that such principles exist, and no reason to doubt that they could be at least roughly sketched by a genius who devoted thirty years to isolating them. The clinching argument, for Mann as well as Boadella, is that later, independent researches in ionization, cosmic rays, geomagnetic forces, pollution, body auras, and psychosomatic medicine have turned up hard facts that Reich had been getting at in his idiosyncratic way.

My own ignorance of laboratory procedures, combined with my sense that normal science is moving rapidly toward integrative understanding of life processes and even toward rapprochement with elements of "the occult," makes me hesitate to criticize this reasoning. Reich has at least been vindicated in overriding the conventional borders between mind and body and in depicting all creatures as energy fields interacting with energy streams of cosmic origin. Some Reichian ideas that were dismissed as primitivism by Philip Rieff and Charles Rycroft now seem much less outlandish than they did just a few years ago. Nor do I wish to deny that many of the effects Reich observed may have been real. On the contrary, the one incontestable fact about Reich is that he was a charismatic person in whose presence odd things tended to happen, not just to himself but to experimental subjects and witnesses. (Whether he made sufficient allowance for this exceptional influence in drawing laws from his experience is another question.) It seems fair to think of Reich as a figure comparable to Franz Mesmer, who, in another century dominated by mechanistic physics, correctly emphasized the importance of energy transactions which neither he nor anyone else could reconcile with existing knowledge.

To see Reich in these terms, however, is not at all to settle the issue of his cultural or ideological meaning. Like Mesmer himself, Reich owes his popularity not to the approval of scientific colleagues, but to the charm his ideas exert on people who are generally sympathetic to life-affirming and unitary theories—in a word, to romantics. Efforts like Boadella's to assimilate Reich's work to the perspective of normal science may obscure the fact that Reichianism has been in several ways an *anti*-scientific movement, holding out promises that are seductive precisely because of the contrast they make with the austerity and fragmented awareness of science as usually practiced. As a structure of postulates orgonomy is open to the charge of tautology, but this apparent defect can be an advantage to people who want their revolutionary certitude kept secure from intrusion.

Reich was remarkably candid about the unorthodox relation between his findings and his presuppositions. He observed that his experiments were directed, not merely toward testing his hypotheses, but above all toward suppressing his misgivings about them. He mustered the courage "to go on in spite of disturbing and apparently negative findings in control experiments; not to invalidate new facts with superficial controls; *always to check negative control findings personally*; and, finally, not to give in to the temptation of saying, 'It was just an illusion'." When traditional methods and devices failed to detect the phenomena Reich believed in, he resorted to "special, hitherto unknown, methods and research procedures" that would yield the desired results. Believing that *"man cannot feel or imagine anything that has no real, objective existence in one form or another,"* he found his proofs in such subjective impressions as his subordinates' headaches, the appearance of spots before his closed eyes, otherwise unaccountable feelings of rage, and an absence of "sparkle" in the landscape. Even allowing for the handicaps of exile and persecution under which Reich operated, we have to notice a strong element of wishfulness in these practices.

Then, too, there was Reich's eccentric way of shielding his supposed discoveries from criticism. As Ola Raknes naïvely states [in *Wilhelm Reich and Orgonomy*],

> One of the common criticisms against Reich was that, instead of repeating and varying an experiment so as to detect any possible source of error, "as scientists should do," he would trust his findings, as soon as he had been able to place them in some rational connection, and go on to new discoveries. What his critics did not know was that in most cases he would keep his discoveries to himself, sometimes for years, until they led him to new discoveries, which was his criterion for the validity of a finding.

Reich, in other words, hid his experimental results from the scientific community while using them as a basis for further inferences, then taking the latter as confirmation of the former. This combination of secretiveness and dogmatism constituted a fundamental break with the empirical spirit—a spirit, we should note, whose cardinal point isn't the forming of hypotheses based on observation, but the submitting of those hypotheses to the fullest scrutiny according to agreed-upon criteria of adequacy.

The keystone of Reich's science is an unwillingness to be judged by rational skepticism. That skepticism, because it remains unmoved by "subjective organ sensations," is itself condemned as a debility of overcivilization. "It is those who feel only very little or nothing at all," says Boadella, "who need most desperately to deny the existence of an energy which, once accepted, would make obvious the fact that their organ sensations were seriously disturbed" [*Wilhelm Reich*]. Hence no one outside Reich's purified circle of believers can be trusted as a critic of orgonomy. When such intruders do presume to attack Reich, they are merely displaying their own orgastic deficiency. Only those whose "own organismic energy can function freely" (Raknes) deserve to be heard, and this free functioning—reachable by inhibited moderns through the one avenue of orgone treatment—produces a new style of sensuous knowing. Instead of abstractly investigating the world, the adept lives with the truth as a practical mystic, listening to the "objectively expressive language" of orgonotic streamings.

This is not to say, however, that orgonomy makes its claims on a forthrightly mystical basis. Reich always insisted that he was a strict materialist who had, to his own satisfaction at least, demonstrated his propositions. No one ever maintained more adamantly that all phenomena are physical and that all philosophy is illusion; the Blakean rules Reich detected in the universe were presented as mere inferences from meter readings. This double emphasis, at once hortatory and positivistic, gave Reich a rhetorical advantage over avowedly antiscientific thinkers. Orgonomy amounts to what Michael Polanyi, thinking of Marxism, defined as a dynamo-objective coupling, in which "Alleged scientific assertions, which are accepted as such because they satisfy moral passions, will excite these passions further, and thus lend increased convincing power to the scientific affirmations in question—and so on, indefinitely." As Polanyi adds, "such a dynamo-objective coupling is also potent in its own defence. Any criticism of its scientific part is rebutted by the moral passion behind it, while any moral objections to it are coldly brushed aside by invoking the inexorable verdict of its scientific findings" [*Personal Knowledge: Towards a Post-Critical Philosophy*, 1964].

The analogy with Marxism is not a casual one. Reich was among other things a theorist of dialectical materialism who, for a while at least, reflected all the sanguine historicism of the original Marxist vision. Like his old Berlin comrade Arthur Koestler, he didn't simply evolve into a fervent anti-Communist when history failed to obey the script, but also sublimated his transcendent expectations into "revolutionary" scientific doctrine. The exit from history that Marx had posited in temporal terms as the proletariat's eventual triumph was transposed into a repeal of the laws of physical necessity, and the now-dubious power of the masses became the power—sexual, perceptual, even mystical—of the sufficient self. Unlike Koestler, however, Reich continued to present himself as an explicitly political revolutionary, thus sparing his followers the necessity of choosing between Tamburlaine and Faust. Somehow the spread of erotic freedom and the harnessing of orgone energy would result in an end to capitalism and patriarchy—the very outcome that seemed unreachable through traditional means of struggle. Meanwhile the secondary benefits of revolutionism, such as elite membership, privileged insight, a sense of evangelical mission, and faith in the future, could be found in a movement organized around supposed truths about nature.

The rallying point of Reich's new creed was the orgasm, an eloquent choice on several counts. In the first place, the experience is a private one, in marked contrast to the proletariat's assumption of state power. In a time of shattered public expectations, local orgastic success or the illusion of it can be taken as proof that the revolution is going forward after all. Again, as an immediate and total release of tension, the orgasm is an ideal vehicle for a drastically compressed historicism: the fulfillment that was to have worked itself out through decades of class struggle becomes a matter of personal ecstasy. The orgasm, furthermore, is defined in part as a blotting-out of consciousness—inevitably including consciousness of setbacks in more orthodox political ventures. We have already seen how Reich's subjectivist posture insulates his whole system from criticism. Within that system the mute and obliterative orgasm serves as a refuge from unwelcome surprises, pessimistic reflections, fruitless calculation—even from language itself, the medium of thinking too precisely on the event.

The flight from language and intellection becomes especially pertinent when we consider the centrality of Reich's quarrel with Freud. Orgonomy was devised as an inversion not of Marxism but of psychoanalysis, the talking cure, in which "making the unconscious conscious" is the therapeutic aim. That aim obviously depends on a broader consensus that rationality and control are worth striving for. By putting the orgasm in the place of self-knowledge, Reich addresses not only thwarted radicals and scarred veterans of psychoanalysis, but many others who now feel that rational consciousness and inhibition are synonymous. The fortunes of orgonomy seem tied to the currency of this sentiment more than any other.

Thus Reich has become the posthumous beneficiary of a widespread demoralization in our culture, a weakening of the once-axiomatic belief that conduct should be guided by reason. In a subtle and paradoxical way, that belief had already been eroded by Freud, who honored it with such apparent tenacity. It was Reich's destiny to expose the ethical ambiguity of Freud's psychology and to resolve it on the side of irrationalism. For people who want to forsake neither their insurrectionary sentiments nor their yearning for transcendent meaning, Reich held out desublimation as a quasi-religious goal.

Modern psychologies in general, as the successors to a moribund faith, have tried not simply to describe how mental equilibrium is maintained, but to put forward that equilibrium as an ethical ideal, persuading a restless, doctrinally confused public that sanity in this world, though more problematical than anyone once supposed, is in itself a worthy goal of striving. The full difficulty of this project can be observed in the stoic Freud, who urged us to restrain our impulses but denied that we possess a native conscience; who made self-knowledge his ideal but characterized the mind as a self-deceiving organ; and who plunged us into the chthonian unconscious while steadfastly maintaining the humdrum secular norm of healthy functioning. In his role as ironic physician Freud refused to set his sights beyond what he called ordinary human unhappiness, but as a Nietzschean *conquistador,* challenging the whole basis of Western conscious rationality, he encouraged utopian speculations about abolishing repression. In retrospect it seems inevitable that ideologies such as Reich's would rush in to satisfy the appetite for catharsis that Freud had both whetted and disdained.

When Reich described himself as the one faithful interpreter of libido theory he was making a perfectly cogent claim. What he did was to pick up the mechanistic side of Freud's thought and accept its consequences unreservedly. It was Freud, not Reich, who first supposed that all mental acts were theoretically traceable to missed gratification, and who posited the idea of "actual neuroses" stemming from dammed-up libido. It was also Freud who extended psychoanalytic speculation to prehistory and the cellular level; whose notion of the superego implied that social compliance comes about through the internalization of paternal castration threats; and whose account of culture depicted every gain for order as stolen from sexuality. Reich's instinctual demonology is recognizably Freud's own, set loose from the misgivings that prompted Freud to superimpose a vocabulary of motives on his vocabulary of cathexes. It merely remained for Reich to ideologize tension release as a *summum bonum* which, in the light of Freud's own energy hydraulics, could be attained through removal of every social demand upon the individual.

Thus Reich's disagreement with Freud can be understood as an endorsement of extremist implications in Freud's own thought. Freud's retraction, in the 1920's, of the idea that all anxiety was blocked libido signified a retreat from an exclusively sexual etiology of the neuroses—a retreat that Reich interpreted in political terms as an accommodation to a repressive society. Whether or not he was correct in this inference, Reich himself assuredly had extrascientific reasons for insisting that the original "quantitative factor" be retained. Libido, after all, was a metaphorical concept, not a physical substance that could be observed by either Freud or Reich. When Freud downplayed libido he was making room for an ego psychology of motives, defenses, and adaptations; when Reich championed libido he was rejecting all such mentalistic categories so as to retain a determinism with eschatological implications. If neuroses were caused by sexual deprivation alone, then one could lay all blame for unhappiness on the (paternal) inhibitors of sexuality, speak confidently about a single, real human nature behind the twisted masks of character, and justify the peremptory removal of those masks in the patients' best interest. Libido was Reich's revolutionary leverage, the promised manna that would be plentiful after the social and intrapsychic overthrow of the superego.

This conceptual sparring acquires concrete and far-reaching import when translated into clinical practice. From the beginning of his association with psychoanalysis

Reich felt galled by the length of treatment, by the analyst's supposed neutrality and inconspicuousness, and by the patient's seemingly endless dodges and deceptions. What he wanted was to make the patient over into the free and open person that he, Reich, knew was trapped beneath the character armor. His Pygmalion impulse found its earliest outlet in a critique of Freudian method—a critique which was trenchant and shrewd, for Reich in his restlessness was able to see that the apparent compliance of patients was likely to be a pseudocompliance masking a continued hostility to the analysis. No one should suppose, however, that the Reich of *Character Analysis* (1933) was simply repairing a weakness in analytical procedure. Rather, he was revoking the whole Freudian therapeutic alliance and putting in its place a relationship more congenial to his hectoring disposition. Now the analyst would be a hero, daring to thwart the patient's resistances at every point, to take the full fury of his aggression, and then to crush his defensive system so that an ideal "genital character" could emerge.

Whatever the merits of this approach, it constituted a reversal of psychoanalytic ethics, whereby the therapist must try to refrain from passing judgment on the patient's conscious values. "Full orgastic potency" as Reich conceived it was not something his patients had hoped to attain when they came to him, but a distant ideal which *he* told *them* was the proper object of human striving, and which he regarded as beyond the reach of civilized man under capitalism. Only by joining Reich's worldwide crusade could the patient hope to bring about the preconditions of complete mental health for himself and others. Submitting not just to the therapist's manipulations but to Reich's social vision as well, the patient was evidently meant to undergo a conversion experience and become a disciple—with or without "cure" in the conventional sense.

It is no secret, of course, that discipleship can be curative, offering as it does a resurgence of faith in a guiding parent figure and a meaningful life. As one case history may illustrate, the "religious" aspect of orgonomy is paramount for people who are not so much sick as confused and starved for purpose. In his book-length narrative of a Reichian treatment at the hands of Dr. Elsworth Baker, the actor Orson Bean patently accepts Reich as a savior. Bean never tells us what, if anything, was wrong with his biosystem before Dr. Baker began pushing and pedalling it, but he does say that simply by reading one of Reich's books he discovered the meaning of existence. For someone who has experienced one true orgasm, he then realized, "the question of what life is all about never has to be asked again." His own "messianic fervor" to convert others seems to have resulted chiefly from his empathy with the martyred leader. Reich, Bean tells us, was hounded by "the little character assassins of the world," who falsely accused him of having been a Communist and of pretending to cure cancer. In reality he was "one of the greatest men in the history of the human race." Thus, "Reich was one of the few true revolutionaries who ever lived and I had decided to join the revolution." Now filled with a Reichian sense of license, Bean and his new wife can "look up into the sky to see the little units of orgone energy tum-

bling and popping around in the atmosphere"; and he draws strength from knowing that those orgones "don't care about any of it, do they?" He has become, as it were, homeopathically delusional, light-heartedly believing himself the beneficiary of special powers and therefore feeling lively enough to carry out ordinary Christian ideas about marriage and service in a fallen world.

When a therapy of total conversion produces such a benign outcome, we must give some credit to the convert's inherent stability. With less secure patients the effect may be altogether different. Bean himself remarks that the cracking of character armor causes severe "orgasm anxiety," an ultimate terror of letting go, and that "The only cure for it is to learn to tolerate it and hope that it will diminish." But suppose it doesn't diminish? "It is especially in the last phases of treatment," says Ola Raknes, "when the patient feels the orgonotic streamings as irresistible but dares not surrender to them, that the danger of suicide may be imminent and that all the skill of the therapist is needed to avert it." One of Reich's own patients, Nic Waal, felt personally helped by the therapy but recalled that Reich's "cruel and penetrating technique" had tragic effects on some people, who "became either crushed or obsessively oppositional or projective . . .". And Reich himself, in a temporarily recanting mood, confessed to Kurt Eissler in 1952 that the whole idea of trying to dissolve character

> is very dangerous. You see, the armor, thick as it is and as bad as it is, is a protective device, and it is good for the individual under present social and psychological circumstances to have it. He couldn't live otherwise. That is what I try to teach my doctors today. I tell them I am glad they don't succeed in breaking down that armor because people, who have grown up with such structures, are used to living with them. If you take that away, they break down. They can't, they just can't live any longer. . . . if you would break down all of the armoring in the world today, there would be chaos. Perfect chaos! Murder everywhere!

Even this negative statement, which has evidently had no deterrent effect on Reich's movement, clearly indicates that the scope of orgonomic treatment is nothing less than the removal of the individual's adaptive apparatus. That apparatus stands under indictment as the product of unwanted (i.e., societal) influences. Whether or not he retains his sanity, the patient will at least have been purged of evil. And what is sanity, after all? As Reich learned more of nature's secrets he began to value the wisdom of psychotics, whose ideas so amazingly resembled his own. Without denying his original aim of securing orgastic potency, he came to treasure the emergence of the buried self in vatic form. Thus, in a halting and inconsistent way, Reich foreshadowed the fully inverted value system of his admirer R. D. Laing, who has decreed that "True sanity entails in one way or another the dissolution of the normal ego, that false self competently adjusted to our alienated social reality; the emergence of the 'inner' archetypal mediators of divine power, and through this death a rebirth, and the eventual re-establishment of a new kind of ego-functioning, the ego now being the servant of the divine, no longer its betrayer" [*The Politics of Experience,* 1967].

We needn't be surprised, then, to learn that Reich's fanatically materialistic system gradually acquired all the superficial features of a religion. Orgonomy as finally elaborated possesses a pantheistic deity (the Cosmic Orgone Energy Ocean), a devil of sorts (Deadly Orgone Energy), an earthly heaven (the elusive but ever-beckoning perfect orgasm), a lost paradise (our matriarchal prehistory), an original sin (the imposition of patriarchy and sexual denial), a righteous animus toward evil (Reich's fulmination against every detumescent influence), and a body of disciples trained to evoke and bestow a holy substance that is invisible to unbelievers. And it has Reich himself explicitly playing Christ, a role he could not refuse after perceiving that the seemingly ascetic Jesus had been an ideal genital character who was crucified for anticipating orgonomy. These parallels suggest, not that Reichianism is a religion, but that by virtue of its *contemptus mundi* it is structurally and rhetorically akin to one. Materialism such as Reich's elides into religious prophecy because its intent is to negate the Actual and make way for the Real, the suppressed inner kingdom.

No doubt a similar need for purgative negation informs all revolutionary dialectic, whatever its manifest goals; the more successful a movement is in pursuing those goals, the more easily the revolutionist can bury his negativity in practical work. What makes Reich a typical figure for our time is precisely the unmediated, insatiable quality of his apocalyptic drive, which finds nothing in reality to pause over for long. By casting himself as Christ, Reich at once confesses his worldly failure and makes a virtue of it, setting himself off from an ever wider conspiracy of persecutors who are blamed for his bad moods and lost opportunities. And paranoid though it may be, this strategy has a resonant effect on others who feel cheated by history, disillusioned with the customary radical mottoes, and therefore all the more goaded by iconoclastic passion.

It may be, indeed, that Reichianism chiefly provides its supporters with "scientific" validation of defenses against a loss of boundary between oneself and a menacing outer world. Sensations of emptiness and vulnerability flourish in an age when secure adversary identities (the revolutionist, the radical intellectual, the avant-garde artist) appear to be swallowed within an all-assimilating, all-cheapening sociopolitical system. The scarcity of recognizable *others,* whose differentness would permit a clear and purposeful self-definition on one's own part, may be an underrated factor contributing to modern anxiety. Norman Mailer felt it in the fifties when he was drawn toward Reichian energetics because he feared being "jailed in the prison air of other people's habits, other people's defeats, boredom, quiet desperation, and muted icy self-destroying rage," and the same sensation is again common today, after the interlude of polarization and activism provided by the Vietnam war. Quite ordinary citizens as well as romantic anarchists now feel themselves to be rebuffed by standardized surroundings, enmeshed in automated procedures, assailed by motivational conditioning, awash in trivia, merged with their neighbors—and at a loss to know whom

to blame or how the nets of dependency can be undone. Such a time is bound to be auspicious for purveyors of happiness, and doubly so for those who can stir up the old conviction that there is a simple battle to be won after all, a cause that lends historical consequence to one's own oppositional drive.

Although it may seem perverse to argue that a radically optimistic vision such as Reich's succeeds largely by mobilizing feelings of inadequacy and desperation, those feelings are just what we might expect to find undergirding any structure of manic affirmation. In Reich's case they are plainly apparent. The essence of orgonomy is that one's vital currents are always being either enhanced or drained away, and that hence one can never be too careful about one's contacts. Despite his rhetoric of comradeship and cooperation, Reich can only be understood as sponsoring a jealous guarding of the self against a suspect world. Thus the ostensible aim of a loving mutuality is pursued through emphasis on one's own pelvic unblocking, one's own libido, one's own orgasm; and thus there is a hysterical urgency in Reich's proclamations that life need *not* be utterly oppressive, that children *can and must* break the death-grip of their parents, that heterosexual genitality *is* approachable despite society's concerted and sinister opposition to it. Reich's declaration that life energy is everywhere denies that it is nowhere. That denial was personally necessary to Reich, I gather, in order to abate his fear of being contaminated by others, but it is also received as a blessing by people who, for good historical reasons, experience themselves as manipulated, depleted, and swept toward a paralytic apathy.

That the blessing is genuinely beneficial for most of those who accept it cannot be doubted. The preponderant testimony of Reichian patients is that they have come to feel more at home with their bodies and more capable of useful action. Yet the prevalence in our society of Reichianism and related doctrines may be evidence of a reduced tolerance, in the dual sense of a diminished willingness to allow others to be themselves and a reduced capacity to withstand stress.

Whatever its successes, orgonomy is a therapy of imposition in which the patient's value system is forcibly assailed and replaced by the doctor's, which is presumed superior because it comes straight from the inspired teachings of Reich. Americans like to consider themselves resistant to such authoritarianism, but in a time of identity diffusion many people become at once more restive and more credulous, demanding that their minds be ravished by an infallible guru. Perhaps they stop short of commitment to overtly dictatorial schemes, such as Reich's proposal that anxiety-free sexuality be enforced by state decree. But they are caught up by the general notion that freedom consists in the overthrow of customs, institutions, family ties, even the canons of scientific objectivity, all of which are thought to violate the supreme right of the inner self to find expression. Such a belief illustrates and hastens the shrinkage of horizons toward an anxious personal narcissism, with a consequent readiness to embrace any propositions that shore up that narcissism. A sense of exposure resulting in part from a loss of cultural sustenance causes the remaining fragments of tradition to be mistaken for the real source of unhappiness, and the process of deracination is then accelerated into a euphoric ideological program.

If this development is due in part to irreversible processes at work in the modern world, it is also traceable to an ethical assumption that can be consciously reconsidered. The assumption was originally Freud's, not Reich's: it was the belief, founded on positivistic nineteenth-century science, that "normal functioning" should be pursued as the highest end of existence. Once that belief leaves the hands of an ironic humanist like Freud, all conventional aspects of life, all bonds between generations, all disciplines whose mastery requires postponement of gratification can be made to appear as intolerable threats to somatic fulfillment. It is a short step, as we have seen, from Freud's distinctly horrific conception of the superego to Reich's decision that the superego must be smashed. And it is just another step, one that happens to span the arc of Reich's own career, to the compensatory idea of control over divine energies, for the new antagonism to "society" requires that the self find its guardian in higher circles.

In the end, for Reich and many others who have tried to use psychology as an all-sufficient ethical guide, the world can be made safe for genitality only through cultic delusion, and perhaps not even then. Such examples ought to remind us that man truly "functions normally" when his attention is directed beyond his immediate well-being—when he is involved with people and places, institutions and principles, that sustain him even as they shape and limit him. To those who accept this point at all, it is a truism; but it is one that casts a devastating light on much romantic radicalism of the past quarter-century.

Ira H. Cohen   (essay date 1982)

SOURCE: "Character Structure, Ideology, and the Internalization of Social Relationships," in *Ideology and Unconsciousness: Reich, Freud, and Marx,* New York University Press, 1982, pp. 137-69.

[*In the following essay, Cohen outlines the major social and psychological principles in Reich's works.*]

Freud's great contribution was to develop the concepts and techniques which theorists have applied to try to reveal the influence of social forces on the individual psyche. Yet Freud himself failed to recognize the historical nature of the relationship between, on the one hand, the development of our civilization and, on the other, the repression and distortion of human needs and desires . . . . [His] social theory was based on the ideological presupposition that manifest behavior reflected certain universals of human nature which have been retained throughout history. Thus Freud could conclude that the conflict between the demands of civilization and the needs of the individual was inevitable and that the mature individual would be able to accept the limitations that are imposed on his activity. Many of Freud's followers became even more conformist in their theory and therapy. Lacking a critical perspective on the relationship between the individual and society, many psychoanalysts focused their research on the thera-

peutic aim of psychic accommodation to social conditions. Reich's early work was the first attempt to develop a critical perspective on Freud; it remains the most significant.

Reich argued that Freud's work was an invaluable contribution to the study of human consciousness. While Marxian theory explored the conditioning of consciousness by social factors, it could not explain how this takes place, "what happens in man's brain in this process" [Reich, *The Mass Psychology of Fascism*]. Consequently it was more adequate for explaining beliefs and activities that were consistent with one's social position than those which were not. Since psychoanalysis revealed the irrational forces which underlie conscious thought, Reich believed that it was essential for understanding beliefs and activities that were inconsistent with the interests of one's social class.

Reich emphasized four findings of psychoanalysis which could be used to explain how social factors conditioned conscious thought. First, consciousness is conditioned by unconscious processes that are not accessible to conscious control. Second, the small child develops a lively sexuality that has nothing to do with procreation. Third, the child's sexual activity is repressed by the fear of punishment. Though the repression withdraws his sexuality from the influence of consciousness, repression also intensifies sexuality's force. This intensification is manifested in various disturbances of the mind. Finally, the moral code which inhibits instinctual gratification is derived from the suppression of childhood sexuality. Reich claimed that

> Just as Marxism was sociologically the expression of man becoming conscious of the laws of economics and the exploitation of a majority by a minority, so psychoanalysis is the expression of man becoming conscious of the social repression of sex. Such is the principal social meaning of Freudian psychoanalysis.

Freud originally distinguished two main groups of instincts, which could not be reduced further in psychological terms. These are the self-preservation instincts and the sexual instincts. Whereas the self-preservation instincts have to be satisfied directly, the sexual instincts can also be satisfied indirectly. Reich observed that the frustration of the self-preservation instincts leads to rebelliousness, while the repression of sexuality leads to an unconscious inhibition of rebelliousness. The repression of sexuality results in a psychological structure which submits to rather than resists the social restraints imposed upon it. This psychological structure mediates the process of the conditioning of consciousness by social conditions, so that even the self-preservation instincts can subsequently be influenced. In contrast, the psychology implicit in the traditional Marxian theory of class consciousness assumes a more immediate relationship between the frustration of the self-preservation instincts and its manifestations in consciousness.

Freud revealed how the psychic structure of the individual develops in conformity with the social order. Yet, although Freud ably described the psychology of the fragmented psyche and partial consciousness, he considered them to be necessary consequences of the instinctual repression required by human civilization. By legitimizing the repression of instinctual pleasure seeking in the interest of social interaction, Freud obscured the critical potential of psychoanalytic theory. Reich sought to demonstrate that it was not social interaction in general which is being preserved by the socially demanded repression but the exploitative relationships of a class society. The psychic structure that Freud described is native to a particular form of social organization.

In response to Freud's conformist views, Reich suggested that political psychology seek "to determine, as completely as possible, the myriad intermediate links in the transforming of the 'material basis' into the 'ideologic superstructure.' " This requires analyses of both the immediate and mediated effects of social conditions on our impulses and psychic processes.

Reich's psychology emphasized the historical flexibility of the instincts and the social specificity of the frustrations they encounter. The reality principle, the concept with which Freud refers to all limitations and social necessities which diminish fundamental needs or defer their satisfaction, may require varying types and degrees of modification of the pleasure principle. Accordingly social conditions impinge upon and transform human impulses and needs before these impulses and needs can be socially expressed.

Reich contended that the limitations imposed by the reality principle upon the human organism in its attempts to discharge tension are greater than those necessary for social existence or the development of human culture; they are necessary only for the maintenance of a class society. Rigorously conceived, the reality principle embodies the demands of the existing society with its specific institutions and social relationships. To conceive it as the demands of "society" or "reality" in general or as an absolute, is to lapse into abstraction. In a society in which the owners of capital accumulate surplus value produced or actualized through surplus and detailed labor, the reality principle must reflect the contradiction between the needs of the workers and material interests of capital. The reality principle and the consequent psychic modification is an essential component of capitalist hegemony. Reich claimed that the reality principle of the capitalist era imposed "upon the proletarian a maximum limitation of his needs." Economic exploitation and authoritarian institutions interact to effect a severe frustration of material and sexual needs and desires. The result is widespread anxiety, pain, and psychic conflict.

The idea that psychic processes function to avoid painful conflict with the outer world is basic to psychoanalytic theory. Reich believed that what remained to be explained was the way in which the individual characteristically absorbed and diffused anxiety and filtered disturbing internal and external stimuli. Reich referred to these characteristic processes as the individual's character structure. Reich argued that character structure develops as a response to the demands and prohibitions confronted by the individual and constitutes the individual's general pattern of responses to internal and external dangers. . . .

Reich developed his theory of character structure through clinical practice. As a clinician, Reich emphasized problems of technique: How could the analyst best effect a cure for the psychological disturbances which troubled the individual. In 1922, at Reich's suggestion and with Freud's enthusiastic approval, a psychoanalytic "technical seminar" for the study of therapeutic problems was established. Reich was to lead this seminar from 1924 to 1930. In the course of this seminar he began to develop his theories on the psychological function of the orgasm and character analysis. Also in 1924 Reich formally introduced the concept of orgastic potency. These ideas marked the beginning of Reich's work on the human capacity for sexual self-regulation. His conceptualization of mental health as the ability to overcome repression and to establish a social life based on the satisfaction of instincts contrasted sharply with Freud's adaptationist criterion. Even as a clinician, Reich stressed the importance of social conditions in the formation of psychic structures and processes.

In his work on character structure, Reich attempted to make the psychoanalytic theory of neuroses more systematic. In psychoanalytic theory, anxiety stemming from sexual stasis is manifested in and absorbed by neurotic symptoms. The person's resistances prevent him from becoming conscious of the causes of the anxiety. Very often the resistances also block awareness of the anxiety as anxiety. The resistance is made up of the repressed libidinal impulse and an ego defense which represses it. Both the impulse and the defense operate unconsciously. Reich reached the conclusion that the economic function of absorbing anxiety is not a function of isolated symptoms and resistances but of the character of the individual's entire pattern of interacting with his environment. Hence underlying pathologies can be expressed in character traits no less than in symptoms.

The person's character begins to develop as soon as he attempts to adjust in infancy to the demands of his environment. Reich dissected character into three levels. The most obvious is that of personality, the conscious sense of self that we present in our social interactions. Personality is the most rational and cultivated level of character and the area on which cognitive psychologists and social scientists focus. Reich saw personality as a mask which can be dropped to expose the second layer of character, which is comprised of all the "cruel, sadistic, lascivious, rapacious, and envious impulses" that led Freud to posit a primary death instinct. However, Reich argued that these antisocial impulses are secondary drives, perverted expressions of more fundamental drives, the expression of which is repressed. These fundamental or primary drives constitute the third level of character which Reich called the biological core. "In this core, under favorable social conditions, man is an essentially honest, industrious, cooperative, loving, and if motivated, rationally hating animal."

Character structure represents "an armoring against the stimuli of the outer world and the repressed inner drives. The external form of this armoring, however, is always historically determined." Although this "character armor" is essentially formed in infancy and early childhood, the ego continues to mold character throughout life.

Since the ego represents the more-or-less conscious sense of self that the individual forms in the context of a specific social structure, character is conditioned by the existing social institutions. Character structure "represents an expression of the person's entire past" and "is the congealed sociological process of a given epoch." Reich claimed that, "every social organization produces those character structures which it needs to exist." This is not to suggest that social institutions explicitly aim at producing a particular character or are even invariably successful in accomplishing this, but only that the infant's ego always develops character in response to the prevailing social order and its prohibitions.

The specific structure of the individual's character is a result of the opposition of an aggregate of repressed drives which are directed toward the outer world and an aggregate of defense forces which maintain the repression. "The two formed a functional unity within the person's specific character." What is to be repressed and how severely is always socially determined. The conflict between the primary drives and the organism's environment produces the antisocial drives that Reich situated in the second character layer.

Reich's theory of character structure is a theory of psychological development and the social expression of physiological impulses. The cooperative and otherwise positive potential of the inner core of character can only be realized in "favorable social conditions." Reich's formulation of character structure, in opposition to Freud's formulation of the psyche, suggests that there need not be a severe conflict between the needs of the individual and the demands of civilization; the latter rather than the former might require modification. For Reich, as for Marx, human nature "is no abstraction in each single individual . . . it is the ensemble of social relations." Indeed, Reich developed the implications of Marx's insight. Through the reality principle the structure of social relationships fundamentally transforms human needs and impulses. These transformed needs and impulses become active elements in the individual's character. The contradiction which Freud observed is not inherent in human existence. It is contradiction between the socially distorted secondary drives and the social structure which produces them.

Reich carefully differentiated several character types on the basis of the infantile conditions of impulse frustration. These are important clinical distinctions. In terms of political psychology however, the crucial distinction is that between the genital character and the neurotic character. The genital character binds anxiety through genital sexuality and sublimation; the neurotic, through symptoms and reaction formations. Reich compared these two ways of binding anxiety as follows:

> What strikes us about these phenomena is that the reaction formation is spasmodic and compulsive, whereas the sublimation flows freely. In the latter case, the id, in harmony with the ego and ego-ideal, seems to have a direct contact with reality; in the former case, all achievements seem to be imposed upon a rebelling id by a strict superego.

The harmony of the genital character referred to by Reich is by no means free of tension. The sexually healthy person still may experience tension, but he or she will avoid the severe conflict that results when an internalized compulsive morality confronts the pleasure-seeking strivings of the organism. Stasis anxiety, which results from the repressive self-restriction of the primary impulses, may be avoided. But real anxiety, which results from the inevitable clash between a pleasure-seeking organism and a repressive social order, cannot be; "the more real anxiety is avoided, the stronger stasis anxiety becomes, and vice versa." The healthy character, because it is in contact with its environment, realizes it must resist its environment's repressive demands; the pathological character avoids at all costs conflict with its environment. Consequently it is overwhelmed by its own internal conflicts.

The sound libido of the genital character can provide the individual with the capacity for self-regulation. The gratification of primary drives allows the genital character to minimize the expression of antisocial secondary drives. Its capacity for the orgastic discharge of libidinal tensions makes it capable of sublimating energy in socially constructive uses.

The potential of the human organism for self-regulation is the central theme of the theory of character structure. Socially responsible people will not tolerate authoritarian institutions and excessive regulation of life. Yet some social regulation is necessary, although it inhibits social responsibility, for the socially distorted secondary drives must be regulated in the interest of social interaction. More fundamental than the contradiction between the individual and his civilization is a historical cycle of social repression—psychological repression. Social repression results in psychological processes which reproduce and reinforce the need for social repression. But the cycle need not be a vicious one. The way out, according to Reich, is to change the social conditions which demand the excessive repression:

> To the extent that society makes possible the gratification of needs and the transformation of the corresponding human structures, the moral regulation of social life will fall away. The final decision lies not in the sphere of psychology but in the sphere of the sociological processes.

Reich's conception of character structure is a critical description of human psychology as it has been formed through the history of a particular society. For Reich social processes and psychological processes are interpenetrating components of the process of human development. Social repression results in the formation of antisocial secondary drives. Once produced, these secondary drives become deeply ingrained in the individual's character and hence must be regulated socially. Yet social regulation may exacerbate the problem and may make necessary more regulation in the future. The potential for self-regulation, stunted by social repression, can be actualized through collective activity aimed at abolishing the source of social repression.

Reich's theory of character structure is meant to describe the conditioning of character through the interaction between basic needs and social relationships. Like Freud, Reich defined mental health as an appropriate response to social conditions. In contrast to Freud, Reich sharply distinguished appropriateness from adaptation. Furthermore Reich could not follow Freud in seeing as inevitable the conflict between the impulse and social institutions. Reich believed very strongly that the antisocial expressions of instincts results from their repression and that the instincts can become socialized under less-repressive institutions.

In a well-known work on social character, Erich Fromm, arguing against Freud and implicitly Fromm's own earlier theory on character, claimed that we must move beyond the categories of the libido theory to describe more adequately the connections between character and social relationships. Utilizing such terms as productive, hoarding, receptive, exploitative, and marketing orientations, Fromm appeared to be presenting a characterology which developed the psychological insights implicit to Marx's writings. Fromm explained character types in terms of market relationships. In contrast, Reich traced the development of character to the institutions and authority figures confronted in childhood and examined the processes through which the individual internalizes the authority of a class society long before participating in the relationships of commodity production and exchange. Rather than grounding character directly in class relationships, Reich examined the extent to which capitalist social hegemony affected the individual's psychological development. Furthermore, Reich's exploration of the social and psychological processes through which character develops was concerned with more than categorizing character types. Reich sought to make explicit the psychological and social sources of repression in order to raise the possibility of overcoming repression. By comparing Reich's characterology with Fromm's, I will make these aspects of Reich's theory of character more explicit.

Fromm differentiated character types on the basis of their orientation toward social production. He differentiated the productive character from various types of unproductive characters and claimed that

> The whole personality of the average individual is molded by the way people relate to each other, and it is determined by the socio-economic and political structure of society to such an extent that, in principle, one can infer from the analysis of one individual the totality of the social structure in which he lives.

> The receptive orientation is often to be found in societies in which the right of one group to exploit another is firmly established. Since the exploited group has no power to change or any idea of changing its situation, it will tend to look up to its masters as to its providers, as to those from whom one receives everything life can give. [*Man for Himself,* 1947]

Although this passage seems to be a straightforward attempt to describe the effects of capitalist social relationships on psychological orientations, it nevertheless reveals succinctly the most fundamental problem of Fromm's position. That is, Fromm fails to distinguish the surface layer of personality from the deeper character layers. In a class

society, the totality of social structure can be inferred from the analysis of one individual only by analyzing the deeply rooted contradictions within the individual as manifestations of the contradictions of the social order. In Reich's categorization of libidinal types, social contradictions are mediated through unconsciousness before being expressed in consciousness; in Fromm's categorization of productive types, social contradictions are expressed more immediately in consciousness.

For example, Fromm's description of the "receptive orientation" fails to differentiate the actual helplessness of the exploited class from the psychological "feelings of helplessness which prevent it from engaging in meaningful collective action." As Theodor Adorno has claimed, actual helplessness "might be expected to prompt resistance to the social system rather than further assimilation to it," whereas feelings of helplessness are associated with the psychological inability of individuals to "experience or confront their helplessness" ["Sociology and Psychology, Part II," *New Left Review,* January-February 1968]. This feeling of helplessness can be understood as an active defense against social responsibility. Workers socially produce the products necessary for life; they do not receive them from an outside source. Yet they evade the responsibility that control over the process of production would entail. As in neurotic symptoms such as anxiety, this evasion is a futile effort to avoid pain by avoiding conflict with a repressive environment. Reich explained the fundamental role of the social frustration of libidinal impulses in producing this type of defense. The passivity of the working class does not result directly from its exploitation. Rather, passivity is a defense against the frustration of basic impulses, a frustration which occurs when the impulses are expressed within exploitative social relationships.

In addition, Fromm bemoans the fact that psychoanalytic thought has been so little concerned with the healthy human character or the productive orientation. Yet Fromm's description of the productive orientation suggests the same behavior in social interaction as Reich's self-regulating character. For example, both the self-regulating and productive individual can relate meaningfully to other persons as more than mere objects for the gratification of his needs. He can participate without coercion in life-supporting social activity when the social relationships of the labor process do not fragment his role and alienate him from control of the process. The difference is that Fromm conceived of the healthy character in terms of ethical ideals; Reich conceived of it as the potential of a pleasure-seeking yet self-preserving organism within the context of "favorable social conditions." However, within a repressive and exploitative social structure, this self-regulating potential is extremely difficult if not impossible to actualize. Social repression brings about the psychic processes which distort and transform human needs. The potential for self-regulation can be achieved only when the individual becomes conscious of these psychic processes and resists the repressive social conditions which underlie them. In Reichian theory, the way the individual relates to the world is a function of his libidinal organization. Yet the libido develops only in the context of the institutions and relationships which define society. It is only by maintaining a dichotomy between libido and social relations that Fromm can claim that "the character system can be considered the human substitute for the instinctive apparatus of the animal." Character is no substitute for the instincts. Rather, as Reich has shown, it is the outgrowth of the necessary interaction between primary drives (self-preservation and the release of tension) and the outer world.

While the primary impulses require participation in social relationships for their satisfaction, the institutional structure of these relationships conditions the impulses themselves, thereby modifying or distorting them. By forming relationships, we act as the agents of the social process. But we become objects of the very same process when we confront these relationships as institutions beyond our control. These reified institutions then reproduce themselves within us by molding corresponding psychic structures.

Fromm may have described a more direct relationship between consciousness and social position than Reich, but in doing so he lost much of the richness of both psychoanalytic and Marxian modes of explanation. This richness is preserved in Reich's theory of character which attempts both to make the unconscious conscious and to suggest how change in character can result from social activity. To accomplish these aims, Reich emphasized the psychic mediations involved in the development of a character structure.

Yet Reich did not emphasize the psychic mediations at the expense of the social antecedents of character structure. He sought to make explicit the institutional framework within which character develops. The most effective institution for the molding of the prevailing character structures was, for Reich, the nuclear family. In the family the social structure reproduces itself within the child, leaving him susceptible to later influences by an authoritarian social system. In his analysis of family relationships, Reich sought to make the connection between psychoanalytic and critical Marxist theory more explicit. . . .

Reich saw the family as the institution through which the complementary social processes of economic and social repression interacted and mediated one another. For this reason the family has been a concern of both psychoanalytic and Marxian research. Freud examined the role played by family relationships in the transmission of social values. Engels was concerned with the connection between family relationships and the social forces of production. In Reich's analysis, the family is at once an economic unit, a transmitter of social ideologies, and an agent in the development of a submissive character structure. Let us consider each in turn.

In his classic study of the family, Engels, even while describing the decline of the family as a mode of social production, refers to the family as the basic economic unit of capitalist society. The division of labor between the sexes places the man and woman in an asymmetrical economic relationship and effects the position of each on the labor market. The man's task generally is considered to be to earn a living and to support his family. According to Engels, "that in itself gives him a position of supremacy without any need for special legal titles and privileges." In contrast, the wife is charged with the private service of household management and, to the extent that she performs this service, is unable to participate fully in the labor market and unable, therefore, to earn wages. She can participate in the process of social production and earn independently only to the detriment of her domestic function. Engels claimed that "The modern individual family is founded on the open or concealed domestic slavery of the wife, and modern society is a mass composed of these individual families as its molecules." [*The Origin of the Family, Private Property, and the State,* edited by Eleanor Burke Leacock, 1972].

Reich, like Engels, recognized the exploitation of women within the nuclear family. He described the connection between the domestic and social division of labor. The family as a social institution directly supported the dominant social relationships of a class society. Although the wife provided comfort for her husband, the main beneficiary of the domestic exploitation of women was the employing class:

> The women's economic dependence on the man and the lower value placed on her participation in the productive process transforms marriage into a protective institution for her, even though she is doubly exploited in this "protective set-up." Not only is she the sexual object of her husband and the birth apparatus of the state, but her unpaid work in the household indirectly raises the profits of the employer. For the man can produce surplus value at current low wages only if a certain amount of work is taken off his shoulders at home.

Reich's analysis of the economic significance of the family assumed a society with a rigid domestic division of labor. In fact, he assumed that the division of labor is more rigid in regard to the division of domestic chores between the sexes than in regard to the exclusion of women from the labor market. Both Reich and Engels observed that in working-class families it is not at all uncommon for the wife to perform wage work as well as her domestic chores. Yet her job is generally of secondary importance. Engels claimed that she participates in social production only as "proletarian wife." Reich observed that the working woman continues to perform "additional, unpaid work to keep her house in order."

Here we begin to confront a contradiction between the woman's domestic and social positions. While women's position in the household continues to be subordinate, women are being increasingly integrated into the work force. Yet, whether or not the woman makes a significant contribution to the financial support of the household, the man continues to assume the position of authority that Engels attributed to his role in the process of social production, a role which made him the major provider. Accordingly, the persistence of domestic roles cannot be explained entirely in terms of economic dependency; the nuclear family persists ideologically even while its economic determinants are changing. Nevertheless even as an ideological rather than economic arrangement, the family reinforces class relationships. That is, Reich argued that the family had an ideological as well as economic function.

The ideological function of the family is experienced by its members as feelings of family responsibility. For example, the man, as head of the household, is held to his job not only by economic necessity. If he lost his job, the hardship caused might be alleviated by having his wife and children enter the labor market, at least temporarily. The fear of losing a job is also the fear of the stigma of having failed in his responsibility as family provider. Thus the wage earner accepts the conditions of employment imposed by the employer and represses the anger provoked by his exploitation. This ideologically reconciles the worker to his subordinate position in the labor market. The woman, also reconciled ideologically by family responsibility, continues to serve as the domestic servant of the household.

Reich claimed that what is being served by the domestic arrangement is not as much the economic interests of the family members as the structure of capitalist relationships. The family is that social institution through which a compliant working class, necessary for the maintenance of capitalist production, is reproduced both biologically and ideologically. In this regard the domestic division of labor reinforces capitalist ideological hegemony and its repression of social criticism. The patriarchal nuclear family breeds conservatism by ideologically reconciling its members to capitalist relationships and repressing the articulation of anger and frustration in the interest of family responsibility.

Reich added to Engels' analysis of the economic interrelationship of the social and domestic divisions of labor a description of their ideological interrelationship. For Reich the family is the factory for the reproduction of social ideologies and the germ cell of political reaction. The parents, who are ideologically reconciled to the existing social order, communicate their reconciliation and acceptance to their off-spring. But the family's ideological role is neither exclusively nor primarily a matter of conscious thought. Reich believed that the ideological hegemony of the exploiting class requires a particular character structure among the exploited, for conscious reconciliation is too susceptible to conscious criticism. In Reich's analysis the nuclear family was the major agency for reproducing social ideologies by molding a compatible character structure.

The influence of the family on character development is to condition its members to submit to social authority. The family performs this function by providing an effective framework for the lifelong repression of sexuality. The repression of sexuality results in the association of unconscious feelings of guilt with sexual desires. Consequently, sexuality is inhibited by ego conflicts and the increasing inability of the ego to resist sexual prohibitions. This same psychological disposition is the basis of mass acceptance of class authority and exploitation. From the very time that the child surrenders a part of his own interest by assimilating internally the external authority he so fears, the individual is predisposed to submit to and internalize the authority he confronts.

Reich analyzed the role of the family in the repression of sexuality through three major stages of the individual's life: childhood, adolescence, and adulthood. By outlining this process of repressing sexuality, the role of the family in conditioning character will be made evident.

In psychoanalytic theory, the family is the setting within which the child learns to introject and identify with the authority figures upon whom he depends for his well-being. The relationships of the nuclear family are the child's most immediate social interactions. The structure of the nuclear family and its effects on the child's sexual and hence psychological development brings about that crucial situation—the Oedipus complex and its mode of dissolution—by which the child is initiated into the culture within which he will live. In the process of resolving the Oedipus complex and internalizing the oedipal prohibitions, the general pattern for the individual's reaction to authority is established. Reich claimed that

> Translated into the language of sociology, Freud's central thesis concerning the importance of the oedipus complex in the development of the individual means precisely that social being determines that development. The child's instincts and disposition—empty molds ready to receive their social contents—go through the social processes of relationships with father, mother, and teacher, and only then acquire their final form and content.

Reich sought to make Freud's theory more specific by examining the interconnections between the patriarchal structure of authority in the family and the class structure of authority in society. He claimed that the fact that "an oedipus complex occurs at all must be ascribed to the socially determined structure of the family." Reich found support for his historical understanding of the Oedipus complex in the anthropology of Bronislaw Malinowski. Malinowski's work on the Trobriand Islanders convinced Reich that the social repression of the incest desire need not lead to neurotic formations if direct erotic gratification were a real possibility. Furthermore, since the relationship between parent and child defined by the family structure is different for the Trobrianders and ourselves, the way in which the incest desire was repressed would also be different with qualitatively different consequences. Reich interpreted Malinowski as saying "that the oedipus complex is a sociologically conditioned fact which changes its form with the structure of society." For Reich, the obvious conclusion of Malinowski's work was that the nuclear family is the primary cause of the neurotic disturbances which are so pervasive in modern societies.

Reich's views contrast sharply with Freud's. For Freud, as his choice of mythic terms suggested, the Oedipus complex was a "universal event of childhood." For Reich it was a product of the patriarchal nuclear family, which was itself historically conditioned and the methods of child-rearing peculiar to it. What was important to Reich was not just the development and repression within the nuclear family of the sensuous and tender feelings of the child for the parent, but the additional repression of alternative means of satisfaction. If the child is allowed to interact erotically with his playmates, Reich argued, the repression of the oedipal feelings would not be so damaging. The child's simultaneously contrived isolation within the nuclear family and forced repression of libidinal drives directed toward family members are what make the effects of the oedipal situation so severe. "A child who might be raised from the third year on in the company of other children, uninfluenced by ties to his parents, would develop a quite different sexuality."

Reich insisted on the importance of understanding sexual repression as a lifelong process. Sexual repression is a process initiated in childhood and reinforced throughout the individual's life. It is a process in which psychological and sociological factors interact with, modify, complement, and contradict one another. The Oedipus complex and its mode of resolution in particular have a twofold influence in later life. On the one hand, they are retained as unconscious memory traces which influence conscious thought and behavior. On the other, they are retained as integral components of the individual's character structure. However, character structure is the result not only of infantile conflicts but of later conflicts and repressions as well. That is, the influence of the Oedipus complex on character is modified by subsequent social conditions.

The Oedipus complex is the culmination of childhood sexuality and ushers in a period of sexual latency. The Oedipus complex develops from the phallic stage during which the child's eroticism becomes directed at people who are also the object of the child's emotional attachments. Yet the Oedipus complex results in the repression of phallic sexuality and is resolved in the establishment of the superego. Until this point the libidinal impulse was directed toward the parents. Now it is repressed until the emergence of genital sexuality, when libidinal desires are aimed at people outside the family.

Puberty, then, marks the physiological sexual maturity of the individual and becomes a crucial stage in characterological development. The pubescent youth is physically capable of developing mature sexual relationships, but faces tremendous social restraints on the gratification of sexuality. The adolescent living in the parental home experiences a severe conflict between his or her emerging sexuality and the antisexual inhibitions acquired from parents and later other adults, such as teachers. Even if he can resolve this conflict adequately and overcome the guilt associated with sexuality, various social factors actively discourage the adolescent from satisfying his sexual desires. For instance, pregnancy is a real danger associated with sexual intercourse. Only infrequently does the family or school help the adolescent to solve the problem of contraception. The less-inhibited girl may secretively seek help from a birth-control clinic, and the boy may have his responsibility in this regard impressed upon him. But there still will remain the problem of privacy. Without a home of their own, the erotic encounters of adolescents usually assume a tense and clandestine character which can aggravate the unconscious guilt associated with the act.

Reich believed that the ability of the youth to overcome these social barriers depends on the extent to which infantile fixations are overcome, that is, the extent to which the youth is successful in transforming infantile narcissism into emotional attachments and exchanging the infantile objects of erotic impulses for more appropriate objects. If the fixations are not overcome, the expression of sexuality will involve unconscious conflicts provoked by infantile fears. However, social obstacles to the expression of sexuality still may effect a regression to infantile modes of satisfaction even in a youth that has developed normally to puberty. Once again, the expression of sexuality will involve unconscious conflicts. The individual will repress erotic impulses and will seek relief in substitutes or symptoms. Nevertheless, the psychic costs of these processes notwithstanding, regression and fixation prepare the adolescent for later life by accommodating his or her sexuality to the demands of a socially imposed morality.

As an adult the individual confronts this morality as the compulsive monogamy of marriage. The moralistic confinement of sexuality to the family intensifies emotionally the relationships of the family and separates the members of the family from the outside world. That is "sexual inhibition is the basis of the familial encapsulation of the individual . . . the tie to the authoritarian family is established by sexual repression." The affection and support that members of the family may provide for one another is not the issue here. Rather, the issue is the way in which instinctual satisfaction is made to conform to institutional arrangements which require a great deal of repression to maintain. The adult is conditioned to accept this repression in childhood and adolescence. The emotional intensification of family ties that results from this repression is a precondition for the adult's acceptance of family ideology with its notions of family responsibility.

Reich's description of the repression of sexuality in childhood, adolescence, and adulthood supported his belief that the compulsive and authoritarian features of family life are in severe conflict with human sexuality. On the basis of the role of the family in repressing sexuality and the connection between sexual and political repression, Reich attributed to the family a dual political function:

> 1. It reproduces itself by crippling people sexually. . . .
>
> 2. It produces the authority-fearing, life-fearing vassal, and thus constantly creates new possibilities whereby a handful of men in power can rule the masses.

Hence, Reich claimed that his theory of character structure can help to explain the lack of opposition to exploitation and domination. The demands of social institutions, particularly the family, condition the individual to respond to conflict by surrendering a part of his own interest and internalizing the authority he confronts. He is unlikely to resist the sources of the prohibitions and limitations imposed upon him. Reich argued that his theory added a psychological dimension to Marx's theory of ideology, which explained this compliance in terms of the dominance of the ideas of the ruling class. Ideologies are produced socially as the ideas of the ruling class and the expression of its dominance; ideologies are reproduced within individuals through an unconscious association with repressed impulses and emotions. The social conditions which force people to repress basic needs and emotions help to bring about a character structure which readily submits to the relationships of authority that are taken for granted in the dominant ideologies. . . .

Like the theory of ideology, Reich's theory of character structure is meant to explain not only the systematic distortion involved in the prevailing ways of understanding social life, but also the ability of the exploited classes to overcome that distorted understanding. The material conditions of life among the exploited can lead to a new understanding of social conditions, an understanding in opposition to that of the dominant class. . . .

Reich believed that the character structure molded by the patriarchal family and its ideology was susceptible to excitement and motivation by the ideologies of the dominant class. This is not to suggest that patriarchal authority is the form or basis of all social authority. "From the point of view of social development, the family cannot be regarded as the basis of the authoritarian state, but only as one of the most important institutions that supports it." I believe Reich's thought in this regard can be made clearer by making explicit the psychoanalytic formulations which underlie it.

Freud observed that the child's superego was constructed on the model of his parents' superego rather than the parents themselves. In the course of its development the superego is influenced by the figures of authority appropriate to the individual's stage of development. Freud mentions educators and teachers but we can include work supervisors and political figures as well. Freud concluded from this that the superego becomes "the vehicle of tradition and of all time-resisting judgments of value," and that the ideologies of the superego are formed by the traditions of the race "independently of economic conditions." The patriarchal tradition of the species, which is embedded in the superego via the Oedipus complex, creates the general pattern for the individual's interaction with authority.

Implicit in Reich's analysis is a critical revision of Freud's conclusions. Patriarchy, as both a structure of social relationships and its ideological expression, exerts an influence on human activity which is not reducible to material preconditions. Yet while the ideological significance of the superego may explain the submissiveness of the adult to the authority figures he encounters, it does not explain why, in the first place, the authority figures come to be constituted as such. The authority of the educator, supervisor, or politician derives from the social relationships of particular institutions. Their authority is primarily material and only secondarily psychological. Their influence on the development of the superego represents the conditioning of psychic structures by social structures. It is a materially defined authority that the superego comes to represent. Since the child's superego is based on his parents' superego, the child's superego is influenced indirectly by the social institutions outside the family which condition his parents' superegos. Accordingly, Reich claimed that the authoritarian position of the father is a political role which represents within the family the authoritarianism of the state and the dominant class.

The harsh superego internalizes the authority it confronts.

The individual then comes to experience his conflicts with the outer world as internal or psychological conflicts. For example, the internalization of parental authority leads to the repression from consciousness of the conflict between the child's primary impulses and the parental prohibitions. The internalization of political and economic authority activates the mechanisms which repress the consciousness of conflict between the individual's needs and desires and the limitations socially imposed upon them. This pattern of internalization can be overcome by the conscious intervention of the ego, which has the capacity to evaluate the social prohibitions and to resist them when appropriate, as it does with the impulses of the id. But generally the ego succumbs to the severity of the pressures it encounters and begins to identify with the authority that has been internalized in the superego. The ego becomes the agent of repression for the internalized authority and constructs an elaborate system of defenses to maintain the repression. The social structure, from which the internalized authority is derived, thus becomes embedded in the individual's very sense of self.

Identification with the dominant authority impedes recognition among the exploited of a conflict between the dominant and subordinant classes. The individual is psychologically susceptible to ideologies which obscure class structure and mystify class conflict into a symbolic unity, such as the unity of a "nation" or "people" and the ahistorical absolutes of kinship and religion. The individual resists attempts to expose the class structure and the mystifications since any exposure would force him to confront the exploitation and repression he suffers, thereby disturbing the tenuous psychic equilibrium between repressed impulses and characterological defenses.

Reich saw identification as "the psychological basis of national narcissism, i.e., the self-confidence that individual man derives from the 'greatness of the nation.' " Clearly, one does not resist or challenge an authority with which one identifies. It may appear then as if Freud was correct: Social collectivities are formed through the identification with a common leader or symbols of authority.

Yet the leader is the object of identification because he is the leader; he is not the leader because he is the object of identification. The psychological processes of internalization and identification may explain the consensus of the led, or, as the other side of this, the hegemony of the leaders, but it does not explain the derivation of social authority. Reich recognized that social authority cannot be explained with psychological concepts. It derives from the structure of social relationships.

In class societies, social authority embodies the domination of one class over another. The hegemony of the ruling class is expressed in the dominant institutions and ideologies; it permeates society and its classes. Yet along with the hegemonic influence there is the influence of the conditions of life of the particular class. There may be various degrees of contradiction between the influences of hegemony and class position on consciousness and activity. These contradictory influences, in turn, condition the extent of identification with or resistance to the dominant authority. In other words, as we shall see, there is a class differential in the process of the reproduction of the social structure as character structure.

Reich emphasized that character structure develops in response to the specific social conditions that the individual confronts. Although he held that social institutions such as the family, church, and government were conditioned by the social relationships of productive activity, he did not posit an immediate relationship between character structure and productive relationships. Instead, the family provided the crucial mediation between the social relations of production and the development of character.

In capitalist societies the patriarchal nuclear family is the prevailing form of family. However, although the patriarchal family permeates all classes, the influence of patriarchal institutions and ideologies varies according to class. Reich identified the source of this variation as the position of the class in the process of production.

Reich believed that the position of the middle class in the labor process resulted in a rigidly patriarchal family structure. This, in turn, conditioned a character structure predisposed to identify with socially defined authority. Actually, when Reich speaks of the middle class he is speaking of three different factions: the rural middle class, the owners of small businesses, and white-collar workers and civil servants. Reich observed that although these individuals were not directly subject to the regimentation of the capitalist production process in the same way as industrial workers, their economic conditions were hardly better than that of the industrial worker. The rural and business middle class worked long and hard for the modicum of comfort they achieved and had little security against the expansion of big business. The white-collar workers and civil servants, especially the lower echelons which comprised 70 percent of this category, often received a smaller paycheck than the skilled industrial worker. Yet these workers were reluctant to organize and to act collectively in pursuit of their interests.

According to Reich, the atomism and individualism of the middle class proceeded from the social conditions of their work, both directly and as mediated through the family. In the rural and business middle class, the family was involved in the individual business enterprise. The economic competition between small enterprises directly impeded both recognition of class interests and their organized articulation. Furthermore, the control exercised by the father in the family enterprise results in a rigidly patriarchal family structure, which in term molds the character structure from which is derived the individual's later attitudes toward authority.

In the other segment of the middle class, the civil servants and white-collar workers, the conditions of work are somewhat different. They are not individual entrepreneurs but workers within a corporate or government division of labor. Yet they work in greater isolation from one another and seem to have more autonomy in their roles than do industrial workers. Socioeconomically, what differentiates them from the workers is not a higher standard of living but the prospect of a career. Since the middle-class employee is dependent upon his employer for the realization

of this prospect, "a competitive bearing towards one's colleagues prevails in this class, which counteracts the development of solidarity." The social consciousness of this faction is characterized not by recognition of common interests with coworkers, but by identification with the government or company. This identification is the primary compensation of the lower-middle-class worker for the sacrifice required to pursue his career. Since his living standard is not much better, he differentiates himself from the working class in a sexually moralistic way. He forms notions of honor and duty based upon the dominant ideology, such as the value of hard (alienated) work, self-sacrifice (exploitation), and morality (sexual repression). These notions are what he believes to be necessary to make the most out of life. He imposes them upon his family for what he believes to be their own good. For this reason, Reich believed that the role of the father as the representative of socially defined authority was most rigid among middle-class employees. As in the other factions of the middle class, family structure and material conditions combine to alienate the individual from those in a similar position, whom he looks upon as competitors, and leads him to identify with the socially defined authority.

To claim that patriarchy is most rigid among the middle class is not to neglect its significance in the working class. Religion and conventional morality, the subordination of women, the restriction of the father's role to disciplinarian, and identification with the firm can produce working-class as well as middle-class authoritarianism. Furthermore, Reich believed that the living standard of the working class also had a detrimental effect on sexual development. He emphasized the excessive restrictions imposed upon the sexual activity of working-class individuals, for instance, by the housing shortage. Crowded housing makes it difficult for lovers, especially young people, to be together privately. Couples are often partially dressed while making love, and concerned about being discovered. Also, insofar as working-class people, especially young people, have less access to birth-control information and service, the sex act has to be interrupted to avoid unwanted pregnancy and dangerous abortions. However, the influences on character structure and ideology are not as homogeneous in the working class as in the middle class. So although patriarchy permeates the working class, it is not as rigid there. Working-class relationships exert an influence in contradiction to the hegemonic influences.

The capitalist division of labor necessitates cooperation and interdependence among workers. Workers crowded, impoverished, and segregated neighborhoods encourages cooperation and friendliness among their families. That is, working-class families are not as isolated from one another as their middle-class counterparts. So, while the relationships of patriarchy promote an identification with authority, the relationships between workers at work and in their neighborhoods favor a mutual identification with one another. Of course, other Marxist theorists . . . have described in more detail than Reich the influences of political and social, as well as economic, relationships on the development of the working class. Reich's contribution was to make explicit the implications of at least some of these relationships on the character and hence ideological orientation of workers. He argued that the way in which workers and their families work and live together results in a less-rigid character structure. Psychologically, as well as socially, workers are more likely than middle-class employees to resist the authority of their exploiters.

Reich found support for his comparison of working-class and middle-class character structures in the success that the German National Socialists had in mobilizing the middle class. Nazi propaganda focused on the idealized middle class, stressing the tradition of the family and the virtues of the independent peasant and businessman. The rural, business, and employee middle class formed the largest core of the fascists' followers. Reich explained the Nazis' successful mobilization of the middle class in terms of the characterological rigidity and authoritarian moralism of the middle class.

Admittedly, fascism is an extreme form of authoritarian ideology. However Reich saw it as a continuation of class authority rather than a different type of authority. "Fascism's lower middle class is the same as liberal democracy's lower middle class, only in a different historical epoch of capitalism." Reich saw fascism as, in part, a revolt of the middle class prompted by the economic crisis and deteriorating conditions of middle-class life. But it was a distorted and ineffective revolt which actually strengthened the dominance and hegemony of corporate capital by supporting its militaristic, imperialistic policies.

A warning is in order here. Political psychology cannot be used to analyze the emergence of fascist states in a Europe that was economically depressed and scarred by war. That analysis requires attention to the historical dynamics of capitalist world economy and, in particular, the struggle for markets among huge international cartels. Reich focused on a corollary problem: How did fascism become a mass movement; why were large numbers of people mobilized by it? Reich sought an answer at a level of explanation general enough to apply to fascism as an international rather than distinctly German problem.

Reich believed that the strength of the fascist movement resulted from its appeal to the authoritarian character structure molded by the middle-class family. The greatness of the nation and the Fuhrer was a greatness that the fascist masses, being predisposed as a result of their character development, could share via identification. The race theory clearly identified who could participate in this greatness and defined the enemy as impure influences within the nation. The enemy was responsible for compromising the morality of the folk and thereby the greatness of the nation. The enemy was the cause of the deterioration in living conditions; the emergence of a new order was predicated on the elimination of inferior races.

Reich thought it hopeless to argue against the racists and their notion of racial inferiority. "The race theory can be refuted only by exposing its irrational function." Reich interpreted the creed of a "racial soul" and its "purity" as the creed of asexuality or sexual repression. It was the mystical-political expression of a moralism too stern to practice consistently.

Fascism appealed to the secondary character drives and

sexual fears which resulted from the effects of a strict moralism on sexual development. It appealed to the secondary drives by the violence and hatred it expressed through its ideology, the spontaneous outbursts of its mobilized adherents, and its aggressive and brutal state policies. The Nazi theory of blood purity and blood poisoning was an example of the appeal to fear. Reich associated the Nazi claim that the pure Aryan blood was poisoned by miscegenation with the fear of syphilis, which Freud considered to be a manifestation of the castration complex. Infantile fixations underlied the irrational fears of racism. This fear is directed at the so-called inferior races thereby isolating them from the fascist mass.

Reich's analysis of Naziism explained how ideology can become the distorted expression of the dissatisfaction experienced in a class society. The extremism of Naziism was a response to the exploitation, domination, and repression that the people endured. Yet fascism could not alleviate these problems, for it never addressed their determinants in the class relationships of society. In fact, it functioned to maintain capitalist hegemony, despite severe economic crisis, through the identification with Aryan greatness and the cathexis of racism. Reich's analysis suggested that extreme nationalism and racism can politically motivate a socially frustrated people whenever a rigid patriarchy and an extreme frustration of impulses molds the requisite character structure. As Gad Horowitz claimed, in his work on the psychoanalytic theory of repression, "Reich's great insight into fascism was that it was the first modern counterrevolutionary strategy able to mobilize the rebellious as well as the submissive impulses of the authoritarian personality" [*Repression,* 1977]. But, in doing so, it became an ideological force more devastating than the material forces it appeared to be challenging.

In Reich's analysis of the psychology of both fascism and capitalist hegemony, the family is the central social institution in the process of the introjection of the social structure. In general, a pattern of submissive reaction to authority is established through the patriarchal relationships of the family. In the fascist, a character structure which expresses its submissiveness through aggressive identification with violent authority is molded by a rigid patriarchy and extreme instinctual frustration. It is only the character of the submissive response that is molded by the family, not the characteristics of the authority or the ideology.

This last distinction is important because Reich has been misinterpreted often. In particular he has been accused of proposing a simplistic relationship between sexual repression and fascism or, conversely between sexual liberation and political freedom. Marcuse, for example, characterized the relationship in Reich's work between sexuality and authoritarianism as follows:

> Wilhelm Reich was right in emphasizing the roots of fascism in instinctual repression; he was wrong when he saw the mainsprings for the defeat of fascism in sexual liberation. The latter can proceed quite far without endangering the capitalist system at the advanced stage. . . . [*Counterrevolution and Revolt,* 1972]

Marcuse argued that advanced capitalism can accommodate some forms of sexual liberation. However, Reich saw fascism not as a typical consequence of advanced capitalism but as an ideological movement which embodied the *contradiction* of capitalist economic crisis and capitalist cultural hegemony. Nor did Reich consider instinctual repression to be the root of fascism. Rather it was the precondition for the individual's identification with fascism. Reich believed that an understanding of this momentous mass movement required a political and economic analysis of the conditions which led to the emergence and rise of the Fuhrer and his party. It also required a political and psychological analysis of the condition which produced the secondary drives to which Naziism appealed. Reich saw sexual repression as responsible for those drives. By alleviating sexual misery Reich hoped that the distortions of character necessary for fascist support could be prevented.

Furthermore, there is a looseness of terminology in Marcuse's statement which distorts Reich's meaning. By "sexual liberation" Reich meant something quite different than Marcuse's interpretation. Elsewhere Marcuse claimed that in Reich's work, "Progress in freedom appears as a mere release in sexuality" [*Eros and Civilization,* 1974]. This is hardly the case. Rather, for Reich progress in freedom was the development of the capacity for self-regulation in work and pleasure. Reich knew well that the mere release of sexuality could occur within compulsively repetitive patterns of interaction and could be associated with infantile conflicts which evoked guilt and anxiety. Reich had ample opportunity to observe allegedly liberalized sexual activity which did not fulfill his criteria of self-regulation.

In fact, Reich could not help but notice that German nationalism and racism developed in a social milieu which was libertine as well as repressive. Postwar Berlin (and prewar Vienna, which has been described as the birthplace of German nationalism) was a city marked by a relatively permissive and promiscuous social life. Prostitution and erotic entertainment were commonplace. The economic strain of inflation made marriage an unlikely prospect for working women who were unable to provide the expected dowries. Consequently premarital chastity was devalued as a social norm. In fact, psychoanalysis itself, with its emphasis on the repression of sexuality in the etiology of neurosis, was better received in Berlin than elsewhere.

Ironically, the very moral liberalization that increased the popularity of psychoanalysis is itself at least perverse and perhaps even pathological by psychoanalytic standards. The cathexis of pornography required a "flight into fantasy" which psychoanalytic theory associates with infantile fixation. Prostitution and promiscuity may somatically engage the individual genitally. However, they lack an important characteristic attributed to the genitally organized libido: the occurrence simultaneously of aim-inhibited, emotional attachment and erotic desire for the same person. Freud attributed the separation of the emotional impulse from the erotic impulse to the fixation of the emotional impulse on the incestuous object of infantile eroticism, the mother, and the redirection of sexuality in relationships that lack emotional attachment. Such sexuality

only reinforces the infantile fixations on which this fragmentation is based.

Reich, who lived and practiced in both Vienna and Berlin, maintained that what he meant by sexual liberation was significantly different from the sexual activity that was rampant in those cities. Compulsively repetitive promiscuity and "Don Juanism," which Reich described as "emotionally degrading and sex-economically worthless," is hardly self-regulating sexuality. He polemicized against prostitution as a sexual practice which resulted from women's socially and psychically subordinate position. These activities were hardly self-regulating. Reich associated the potential for self-regulation with orgastic potency, or "the full ability to relate to the partner without blockages to emotional contact caused by neurotic problems." Orgastic potency required the occurrence of both emotional and erotic impulses toward the sexual partner. Yet the relationships of the family as they are economically and ideologically conditioned promote fixations at and regressions to infantile modes of satisfaction and infantile choices of objects. Hence, sexual encounters evoke the guilt and anxiety associated with the infantile fixations. This guilt and anxiety can be expressed in such diverse patterns of behavior as strict repression or the compulsive pursuit of sexual encounters. That is, Reich distinguished sexual activity in terms of human relationships.

Reich's orgastic potency was something quite different than the "pansexualism" or sexual panacea with which Marcuse and other critics have charged him. Typical of the criticism made of Reich was Marcuse's interpretation of Reich's emphasis on sexual liberation as a "sweeping primitivism" which arrested the critical insights of Reich's early works and foreshadowed "the wild and fantastic hobbies of Reich's later years." This criticism misses the mark. True, the critical insights are somewhat arrested and the latter work is foreshadowed in the early. Yet it is a more subtle methodological contradiction, rather than a "sweeping primitivism" or "pansexualism," which is responsible for this.

The methodological contradiction in Reich's work is this. After distinguishing such activity as promiscuity and self-regulating sexuality in terms of emotional contact, Reich attempted to measure the quantity of libidinal release involved in each. First he reduced all types of libidinal impulses (partial, genital, incestuous, aim-inhibited, and sublimated impulses) to the abstraction of quantity, then determined that genital sexuality involves a quantitatively greater release than the others. Therefore, he concluded, as long as the genital impulse is satisfied, the other impulses can be sublimated in production. On the basis of this distinction, Reich posited genital primacy as the natural organization of the libido which we achieve automatically as long as society does not impede our development. The partial impulses correspond to different stages of biological development. But once the biological stage passes, the corresponding psychic impulse becomes pathological if it is not sublimated. The repression of genital sexuality does not facilitate this development but rather impedes it by cathecting the partial drives with more energy than can be sublimated effectively. However, if the genital impulse is satisfied, the others can be sublimated in productive activity. Consequently, the conflict between genital sexuality and social activity is not necessary; sexual repression results only from class domination.

In the minds of many of his critics, Reich's belief in the biologically self-generated development of the libido lessened the significance of all his work. This is unfortunate, for his theory of character structure remains the most systematic framework for the examination of the effects of social structures on the expression of human needs. Indeed, Reich argued that our impulses could not even be expressed without social organization. What he failed to recognize is that the interpenetration of needs and means of satisfying them which is fundamental to his description of the social conditioning of character, does not allow for the absolute libido he sought to measure.

In other words, there are two different conceptions of libido in Reich's work: a psychological and a physiological. The psychological conception describes the development, change, redirection, and repression of impulses as the individual makes his way through the institutions he confronts; the physiological describes the natural growth of the instincts as the body matures.

An excerpt from *The Mass Psychology of Fascism*

Identification with authority, firm, state, nation, etc., which can be formulated "*I* am the state, the authority, the firm, the nation," constitutes a psychic reality and is one of the best illustrations of an ideology that has become a material force. At first it is only the idea of being like one's superior that stirs the mind of the employee or the official, but gradually, owing to his pressing material dependence, his whole person is refashioned in line with the ruling class. Always ready to accommodate himself to authority, the lower middle-class man develops *a cleavage between his economic situation and his ideology.* He lives in materially restricted circumstances, but assumes gentlemanly postures on the surface, often to a ridiculous degree. He eats poorly and insufficiently, but attaches great importance to a "decent suit of clothes." A silk hat and dress coat become the material symbol of this character structure. And nothing is more suited for a first-impression appraisal of the mass psychology of a people than its dress. It is its accommodating attitude that specifically distinguishes the structure of the lower middle-class man from the structure of the industrial worker.

Wilhelm Reich, in his The Mass Psychology of Fascism, *translated by Vincent R. Carfagno, Farrar, Straus and Giroux, 1970.*

Mark Shechner   (essay date 1987)

SOURCE: "From Socialism to Therapy, II: Wilhelm Reich," in *After the Revolution: Studies in the Contemporary Jewish American Imagination,* Indiana University Press, 1987, pp. 91-101.

[*In the following essay, Shechner examines the influence of Reich's works on Jewish American writers.*]

The most affirmative of the doctrines to make headway among writers during and after the war were those of Wilhelm Reich, whose system of character analysis (or vegetotherapy or, as it grew metaphysical, orgonomy) pinpointed the source of recent political disaster in the armored character of Western Man and prescribed an arduous program of action therapy as the key to individual salvation and social renewal. Reich's theories of sex economy and character armoring plausibly accounted for certain observed universals of political behavior: the weakness for authoritarianism in the democratic nations and the rule of what political philosopher Robert Michels had called the "iron law of oligarchy" in political systems everywhere, including the most revolutionary and "democratic" parties [*Political Parties: A Sociological Study of the Oligarchical Tendencies of Modern Democracy,* 1915]. Unlike Freud, whose politics were tinged with skepticism, Reich was nothing if not righteous and impassioned, and his political credentials were, on the face of them, impeccably radical. He fancied himself a democrat and a feminist and propounded something he called "work democracy," which he defined in terms reminiscent of the young, "humanist" Karl Marx as the "sum total of all naturally developed and developing life functions which organically govern rational human relationships" [*The Mass Psychology of Fascism*]. Fascism, then, which Reich abominated, was the political expression of an organic maladjustment, the epidemic severence of men from their life functions, rendering them susceptible to demagogic promises of fulfillment through submission to authority and explosive outbursts of violence. (Some of his followers, however, including Norman Mailer and Paul Goodman, would regard such outbursts as tonic.) And despite an early affection for Marxism and membership in the German Communist party, from which he was expelled, Reich was, by the postwar era, bitterly opposed to Stalinism. He called it "red fascism" and "Modju" [the critic adds in a footnote: " 'Modju' was a term Reich constructed from the initial letters of Mocenigo, the man who denounced Giordano Bruno, and Dzhugashvili, Stalin's original, Georgian name."], and saw it as a retreat from the ideals of Marx, Engels, and Lenin toward dictatorship, a retreat abetted, not incidentally, by the Russian masses themselves. Substitute Stalinism for fascism in the following typical explanation of the latter in *The Mass Psychology of Fascism,* and you have Reich's essential explanation of it.

> My medical experience with individuals from all kinds of social strata, races, nationalities and religions showed me that "fascism" is only the politically organized expression of the average human character structure, a character structure which has nothing to do with this or that race, nation or party but which is general and international. In this characterological sense, *"fascism" is the basic emotional attitude of man in authoritarian society, with its machine civilization and its mechanistic-mystical view of life.*

Such views are consistent with those of Freud, who also took politics for an expression of the universals in the character of man, and with those of Erich Fromm, who read in fascism the human desire to escape from freedom and submit to the mass and the dictates of authority. But where Reich distinguished himself from Freud and the neo-Freudians was in exalting the sexual principle as the key determinant of the social will. "In brief, the goal of sexual suppression," he urged in *Mass Psychology,* "is that of producing an individual who is adjusted to the authoritarian order and who will submit to it in spite of all misery and degradation."

> At first, the child has to adjust to the structure of the authoritarian miniature state, the family; this makes it capable of later subordination to the general authoritarian system. *The formation of the authoritarian structure takes place through the anchoring of sexual inhibition and sexual anxiety.*

Neither the death instinct nor the superego nor the innate aggression of the species nor alienation but "the social suppression of genital love" is the bacillus of totalitarianism. But like a bacillus and unlike a genetic defect, it is susceptible to countermeasures. In narrowing down the problem of alienation to the sexual sphere, Reich rescued political psychology from tragic biology and delivered it into the hands of medicine—not, to be sure, conventional medicine, as the American Medical Association and the Federal [Food and] Drug Administration understood it, but medicine as premodern naturalists imagined it, as a branch of moral philosophy. Notwithstanding the bold sweep of his analyses, Reich was the most resolutely biologistic of Freud's renegade disciples, and there is ample reason to look upon his system as a political neurobiology and *not* as a psychology.

Reich's attraction for intellectuals in the 1940s lay partly in his reduction of the field of battle from society to the body, where gains might be more easily registered, and partly in his gospel of the orgasm as the sine qua non of psychological and social hygiene. In part also it lay in his putative ability to account for the failures of the Russian revolution and of leftism everywhere by fastening upon the sexual sphere as the missing variable in prior revolutionary calculations, and therefore, in effect, keeping revolutionary hopes alive. Sex, for Reich, *was* politics, and the contentious language of his manifestoes, with its military metaphors of blocks and breakthroughs, made his system sound less like a retreat from the blows of history than a regrouping for a war of liberation against the residual puritanism and production-oriented austerities of American life. His rejection of adjustment in favor of revolutionary assault upon all superegos, personal and social, and his clinical methods for relaxing muscular rigidity, dissolving psychic resistance, and storming the barricades of sexual pleasure appealed to stymied radicals as adjustments downward of the campaign against Wall Street that more conventional strategies had failed to carry through.

"In the gloom of the Cold War years," Frederick Crews has observed, "intellectuals whose historicism had been shaken faced the choice of either accommodating themselves to a prosperous anti-Communist society or taking a stand directly on what Mailer, citing Reich, called 'the rebellious imperatives of the self'" ["Anxious Energet-

ics," in *Out of My System: Psychoanalysis, Ideology, and Critical Method,* 1975]. Crews poses the alternatives perhaps too starkly. One could be Dwight Macdonald and cling to an undefined anarcho-pacifism, risking the isolation and impotence of anarcho-pacifists everywhere. Still, Crews rightly points out that Reich's ideas had a special cachet for revolutionists without a revolution, for whom the field of battle had dwindled to the self. It was as a sanction for individual desublimation that Reich's orgonomy rendered its appeal as an insurrectionary code, as hostile to the fetishes of party and doctrine in Russia as it was to those of achievement and production in America. Paul Goodman, in touting the political superiority of Reich's psychology in the 1940s, spoke contemptuously of the counterrevolutionary social adjustments demanded by the New Deal and Stalinism alike ["The Political Meaning of Some Recent Revisions of Freud," *Politics,* July, 1945]. Such a cavalier linking of Roosevelt and Stalin seems sheer madness to us now that the nature of the Soviet state is so plain and so appalling (though it was anything but a secret in 1945), though it seemed perfectly plausible to some radicals after the war who saw little more in the struggle between East and West than shadowboxing between Gog and Magog, variants on the same predatory imperialism. Some, like Goodman and Dwight Macdonald, were anarchists; others, certainly Norman Mailer in the forties, were lingering Leninists who still smarted, ten years after the fact, from the Comintern's scuttling of all-out class warfare for a meliorist "people's front" in 1935. But anarchists and class warriors alike, they held fast to their old dreams of striking deep, disclosing the basic laws of human conduct, and drawing up blueprints for the liberation of man wherever he was oppressed, in Russia or America.

In fact, once the question of Russia was settled for all but a handful of popular front loyalists, America became the great conundrum. For homeless radicals of the 1940s, some of whom found a home in Dwight Macdonald's *Politics* during its brief existence, Moscow and Levittown enjoyed a certain parity as centers of the emotional plague. America's wartime alliance with Russia was either the lull before Armageddon or a treacherous reconciliation of opposites into a repressive global imperium—the end of history by bang or by whimper. "It is a war fought by two different exploitative systems," instructs McLeod, Norman Mailer's spokesman for the Trotskyist analysis in his novel *Barbary Shore,* "a system vigorous in the fever of death, and another monstrous in the swelling of anemia. One doesn't predict the time precisely, but regardless of the temporary flux of the military situation, it is a war which ends as a conflict between two virtually identical forms of exploitation." The prospect of peace between the new superpowers was scarcely more cheering than the threat of war. For the work of liberating mankind, hands across the sea loomed as ominous as guns along the shore. The state of tension, even were it not to erupt into shooting, could only strengthen the machinery of domination in both societies, fostering permanent garrison states in which the regimentation of populaces, sustained by their citizens' anxious flights from freedom, would effectively destroy all social distinctions between the two. Indeed, the advent of McCarthyism would be taken by some as proof

positive of the Stalinization of America. And yet, while
Trotskyists and anarchists alike might concur on such theses as these, few had any heart for spirited calls to arms.
To whom would they be issued? To the rank and file of
America's "proletarians," employed as never before in a
dynamic, expanding economy and organized into labor
unions that were skilled at converting surly impulses into
wage and hour demands? To the restive petite bourgeoisie
who were so busy turning their candy stores into super-
markets that calls to revolution never got past their answering services? To the legions of white negros (and some
black ones too) gathering nightly at the San Remo or the
White Horse in anticipation of the Great Revolt or a fistfight between rival poets? To the comic armies of the night
that, two decades later, would endeavor to levitate the
Pentagon by mantra power alone? Who were the toiling
masses anyway?

It was altogether reasonable, then, that stymied intellectuals, drugged by the daily crisis, downcast over their isolation, and weary of signing up for Cold War conferences
sponsored by Moscow or Washington, would respond to
a political biology that appealed to their most anarchic ap-
petites while promising comprehensive social benefits
from their indulgence. "Unrepressed people," declared
Paul Goodman in the pages of *Politics* in 1945, citing
Reich, "will provide for themselves a society that is peace-
able and orderly enough." Saul Bellow's Moses Herzog
says it more bluntly later on, musing that "to get laid is
actually socially constructive and useful, an act of citizenship." Would that Reich had Herzog's concision, for the
latter's aphorism speaks tedious volumes. Reich could be
as literal-minded about sex and salvation as any bachelor
on the loose and just as monotonous. Dispensing with the
tedium of organization and theory, of party caucuses and
Marxist study groups, he envisioned a revolutionary spirit
disburdened of wearisome politics. The revolution could
be forwarded at home, in bed, in the revolutionist's spare
time, saving him the agonies of canvassing and cajoling,
factional rivalries and power struggles, conflicting doctrines and hairsplitting interpretations, and, most grateful-
ly, painful appeals to a working class that was fundamentally hostile to revolutionism. In the Reichian utopia, the
party would be abolished and the new revolutionary
movement organized along the lines of the clinic or research institute. (Indeed, as social redemption became a
function of personal prophylaxis, doctrine took a back seat
to counselling.) Man's compulsive escape from freedom
would now reverse itself spontaneously as his treatment
took effect.

The flow of consciousness envisioned by Reich was spontaneous and ineluctable, carrying the analysand from private desublimation to public vigilance. The lineaments of
gratified desire had the curious feature of bringing to life
one's social dissatisfactions. The "little man" made whole
and sexually vital would not stand for a corrupt, armored,
or fascist world. As he gained harmony with his own nature, his militancy would spread in ripples from the body
to the body politic, which Reich imagined in almost Platonic terms as the individual writ large. Man and state, microcosm and macrocosm, were joined by the life force it-

self, and whatever impinged upon the one would quickly
be registered upon the other.

Of itself that vision hardly distinguished Reich from
Marx; after all, a metaphysic of correspondences is not
very different in its working details from a dialectic of man
and society. What distinguished Reich is the literalness
with which he imagined the metaphor of the body politic
and the vectors of revolutionary potential. Reich's revolutionary equations always began with the private, sexual
self and flowed outward toward the public, political self.
(Late in his career, his erotics of redemption stretched all
the way from the genitals to the heavens.) Such a meta-
physics of bodily revolt ("the gonad theory of revolution,"
sneered C. Wright Mills) not only played down questions
of institutional, impersonal power, it happily cancelled the
tragic conflict of self and civilization that Freud took to
be irreducible. At its most extreme, orgonomy turned
against the Freudian virtues of sublimation, strength of
character, and self-knowledge, abominating them as toxic
substances, literally carcinogens. In his later years, Reich
would complain—or was it a boast?—that *Civilization and
Its Discontents* was written in response to one of his,
Reich's, lectures in Freud's home in 1929: "I was the one
who was 'unbehaglich in der Kultur' " [*Reich Speaks of
Freud*, 1967]. Not only were the tragic vistas of the later
Freud washed over by the orgonomic streams of Eros, so
was the sole ground of optimism on which a younger
Freud had established his own therapeutic discipline: the
potential for self-correction through self-awareness.
Under the Reichian dispensation, self-inquiry became just
another layer of suppressive armor, a clinically fashionable way of blocking the flow of natural vegetative juices.
If the hero of Freud's old age was Moses, that of Reich's
was the segmented earthworm. The modern therapeutic
offshoots of the Reichian ethos such as est have maintained this hostility to reasoned self-interrogation which,
according to them, merely reinforces the inhibitions that
afflict the neurotic. Viewing modern man as Hamlet, they
see the native hue of resolution everywhere sicklied o'er
with the pale cast of thought.

How American this sounds, and how profitable it has become to Reich's spiritual heirs, from Fritz Perls and Ida
Rolf to Arthur Janov and Werner Erhard, who recognized
the growth potential of spiritual relief and were wary
enough not to rouse the Federal [Food and] Drug Administration on the way to the bank. And thus how strange
it is to ponder the FDA's persecution of Reich for so naive
a contraption as the orgone accumulator, which posed neither a political nor a sexual challenge to American society
and was so transparently useless that the taste for it would
shortly have proven as perishable as the rage for T'ai Ch'i
or the Last Chance Diet had not the FDA confirmed
Reich's paranoia by tacking an earthly martyrdom onto
his intergalactic trials. That too, Reich's final episode of
arrogant hucksterism—which he conducted, naturally, as
a crusade—was American to the core. The orgone accumulator was as harmless as Hadacol and as innocent as
snake oil. Reich's bioenergetic revivalism, despite its origin in German dialectics and the thought-tormented arena
of Jewish modernity, was surprisingly in tune with the up-
beat mood of postwar suburbia. Its promises of psychic re-

birth, moral reawakening, and a magical reintegration of the alienated self had an American zest to them. Reich didn't put the ailing into analysis; he sent them into training, and there is a quality in his demeanor—the crackpot boosterism—and a note in his voice—a boozy collegiate vivacity—that recalls not Freud or Marx or Trotsky but Woody Hayes. Had the FDA not prosecuted him as a cancer quack and banned the sale of his orgone accumulators—those upright plywood coffins, their walls packed with rockwool and steelwool to catch and focus the fluxions of eternity—they would surely have found their way into dens and rumpus rooms all over America, alongside the barbells and the exercycle, to become bioenergetic supplements to aerobic dancing and tantric yoga. In the orgone box, as on the exercycle, one enjoys the grateful illusion of moving forward without having to leave the house.

Reich was a revivalist for the post-Bible belt, and what he offered was nothing so much as a secular, erotic baptism into a life beyond conflict and neurosis. Such an appeal, the appeal of ecstatic rebirth, had implications far beyond the intellectual circles in which they initially took root. When one peels away the layers of militancy that were properties of Reich's own abrasive character but not necessarily of his therapy, one discovers a revolutionism for the depressed suburbanite, fearful of conforming and just as fearful of taking any drastic step that might expose his imaginary independence. We see him on bike paths everywhere as the man in the gray flannel warm-ups, jogging away the blues, lonely as a long-distance runner in the evening, solid as a Rotarian from nine to five. Holding the therapies of "adjustment" in contempt, Reichianism and its spin-offs from Gestalt to est have cleared a path to social adjustment by inducing regular, convulsive fits of rage in the therapeutic session, creating a purely synaptic equilibrium and permitting the troubled individual to get on with the loathesome job at hand. In orgonomy, Freud's reflex arc becomes Reich's guide to the perplexed.

Even among intellectuals, who are less inclined to equipoise and appreciate the use of imbalance, it does seem to be the case that they, in their Reichian phases, while striking anti-American postures were always profoundly patriotic in their deeper intuitions. "America," announced Allen Ginsberg in a famous early poem, "I'm putting my queer shoulder to the wheel." Certainly, the self-reliant brand of radicalism they advanced appealed to the same American love of tinkering and weekend projects that spawned the do-it-yourself craze in home improvement and auto repair. Reichianism was pragmatic and self-applied, and like capitalism it envisioned the transformation of private labors into public benefits. Yet it was not just the convenience of mounting a revolution by simply mounting a friend or the authorization of the orgasm as a blow against repression or even the opportunity to join erotic forces with the hedonists of Peyton Place that made the appeal to intellectuals so seductive. Another factor was bound to register with artists and writers: the promise that sexual desublimation would also free the imagination. Artists and writers, after all, are patrons of the unconscious and know better than anyone how painful the daily solicitation can be. The deeper life on which the artist must draw is not always on tap, and artists are always on the lookout for ways to allure it, stalk it, beguile and tame it. Philip Reiff charges in *The Triumph of the Therapeutic* that artists in the forties and fifties found the Reichian doctrine that identifies the artists with the "genital character" flattering and therefore flocked to it from a grateful sense of being the erotic elect. Yet common sense and some available evidence urge a different view: that it was misery, not self-congratulation, that drew artists and writers to orgonomy, the misery of not being able to strike deep at will. Orgonomy promised baptism in the waters of the imagination as they raced through the canyons of the mind.

And yet, one wants also to observe the degree to which Reichianism *did* elevate the free-lance intellectual into the role of moral and cultural leader who could exercise a salubrious influence on the culture by the example of transcending it. As Paul Goodman, as Norman Mailer, as Allen Ginsberg all understood in the sixties, it was not only their ideas that elevated them to positions of moral eminence but their examples, the lives of free eroticism they *seemed* to be living. Goodman, chagrined by the prospect of sainthood before death, endeavored mightily to keep all that was raw and tormented in his character on show. It did little good, as the cachet attached to his spokesmanship for desublimation overshadowed the more unsavory aspects of his compulsive cruising. Reichianism is indeed, as Rieff has complained, an antipolitics, though a more precise term might be counterpolitics, since it seeks to revolutionize the social order by transforming the individual, rather than organizing and deploying power. In Reichian thought—and the politics of Goodman's Gestalt were essentially Reichian—personal culture, rather than being a superstructure, is the very engine of the social order and therefore the key to social change. It is the magnetic field that binds the politics of the body to the body politic and the crucible in which the liberated intellectual, not the politician or the minister or even the soldier, is the indispensable catalyst of change. Yet, in a counterpolitics as in any other, the rebel has his eye on power; he simply approaches it in new ways and looks for new windows of vulnerability. The hero of a counterpolitics confronts power without a sword, armed only with the moral example of his being, an example which the isolate, the martyr, and the poet are best equipped to furnish. In a counterpolitics, the only slingshot David permits himself is his superior moral character. Where Gandhi, modern history's outstanding counterpolitician, took that superiority from an exemplary abstinence, Reich supposed it to derive from an exemplary indulgence. If Freud, then, was the social philosopher for intellectuals who saw in the agony of Europe a picture of man's fate, Reich supplied the program for those who saw in America—an eroticised, Whitmanized America to be sure—a picture of man's hope.

Thus it was Reich more than Freud who captured the imagination of a handful of stranded ex-Trotskyists in the 1940s and provided the program that, for a brief moment, was the implicit script for efforts to confirm a new literary radicalism. Jew, exile, and finally martyr, he was the Trotsky of mental revolutionism, a romantic hero for homeless radicals in search of a rallying point during and just after the war. Like revolutionary Marxism, Reichianism was an ideology of liberation with uncompromising values, a world-integrative view of reality that armed its adherents with basic interpretations, and rigid internal dialects that pointed the way to freedom through submission to a stern agenda of treatment. It was both a dogma and a discipline. Among the literary Reichians, Isaac Rosenfeld recast his entire life into a bioenergetic mold, becoming for his contemporaries the spirit of Greenwich Village incarnate as he conducted his life with the aim of breaking through to his "animal nature." His fiction and literary essays incorporated major elements of Reich's moralized energetics, and they can still be read as illustrations of the power and the limits of a moral criticism that portrays life as a flux of vital substances. Saul Bellow absorbed the Reichian system intact into his own scheme of character analysis in two novels, *Seize the Day* and *Henderson the Rain King,* and two plays, *The Last Analysis* and *The Wrecker.* But in all this writing Bellow's typically ironic handling of ideas makes it hard to tell where he is appealing to their explanatory powers and where exploiting their amusement value. Paul Goodman, the only therapist among the New York intellectuals, fashioned his own system of Gestalt therapy on a Reichian base and would later become the most influential spokesman for Reich's ideas. And Norman Mailer would, in his *Village Voice* columns and *Advertisements for Myself,* conduct a stunning public demonstration of therapy that would eventually make him famous and rich.

Conversions affected under such auspices were not so much changes of mind as upheavals of *will,* violent purges of all that was routine and stagnant in existence. Sometimes the violence was physical. In the therapeutic session the patient was urged to smash his character armor with spontaneous screams or "clonisms," involuntary spasms of the "orgasm reflex" that replicated, as Reich believed, the lusty thrashings of the segmented earthworm. Outside the clinic, he could look forward to the apocalyptic orgasm, the party to end all parties, the fistfight, even the stabbing. In the fifties, a certain romance of violence affected writers who were up on the latest calisthenics of self-renewal and denounced composure as not only self-destroying but counterrevolutionary. The artist entered therapy to shake loose the mind-forged manacles of surplus culture and disburden himself of craft, of caution, of history, of tradition, of guilt, of the superego—of the Jew in himself. The superego, that Nobodaddy of the mind to which Freud had assigned the task of keeping the instincts in line, was now assigned the role in the morality play of revolution formerly held by the bourgeoisie. Bellow, in recalling the temper of revolt in which he wrote *The Adventures of Augie March,* would reflect years later:

> A writer should be able to express himself easily, naturally, copiously in a form which frees his mind, his energies. Why should he hobble himself with formalities? With a borrowed sensibility? With the desire to be "correct"? Why should I force myself to write like an Englishman or a contributor to *The New Yorker*?

Mailer, in a more violent idiom, would speak in *Advertisements for Myself* of "blowing up the logjam of accumulated timidities and restraints" and of becoming "a psychic outlaw." Allen Ginsberg would howl to Carl Solomon, "I'm with you in Rockland / Where you're madder than I am," and Philip Roth, roughly a decade later, would agitate for putting the id back into Yid. All courted exposure—even sought humiliation—in order to reclaim their spontaneity and their genius. Propelled by an energy of self-rejection, such conversions were normally convulsive, reckless, and a little hysterical.

It was in the writing of Goodman, Mailer, and Allen Ginsberg in the 1950s that Reich's revivalism was most faithfully recorded and the ideology of the redemptive orgasm most consistently promoted as a comprehensive plan of social renewal. These three were the most political of the literary Reichians and, not surprisingly, the most influential in an intensely political decade. It was they who made the romantic ferment of the late 1940s available to the counterculture of the 1960s, who joined hands between kindred decades across the great divide of the fifties. They were the conduits for that current of revivalism that looked to the body as the redeeming agent in a corrupt world. They were the instructors in breaking through.

Joel Kovel   (essay date 1988)

SOURCE: "Why Freud or Reich?" in *The Radical Spirit: Essays on Psychoanalysis and Society,* Free Association Books, 1988, pp. 251-69.

[*An American psychoanalyst and writer, Kovel is the author of* White Racism: A Psychohistory *(1970),* A Complete Guide to Therapy: From Psychoanalysis to Behavior Modification *(1976), and* The Age of Desire: Case Histories of a Radical Psychoanalyst *(1981). In the following essay, he critiques conceptions about Reich advanced by Janine Chasseguet-Smirgel and Béla Grunberger in their book* Freud or Reich? *(1986), and explicates the principal differences between Freudian and Reichian psychotherapy.*]

Janine Chasseguet-Smirgel and Béla Grunberger's *Freud or Reich?* (1986) demands that anyone who comments upon it declare himself in relation to the subject-matter. Let me say then that I first encountered Reich by reading of his ignominious death in the *New York Times.* Although my initial reaction was little more than a vague curiosity, a number of personal matters led me soon after to seek therapy with a well-known Reichian, Simeon Tropp. Tropp, who had been one of Reich's principal lieutenants in the last phase of his life, made a powerful impression on me, so much so that I eventually undertook clandestine Reichian training. I was then a medical student and in those days Reich's works, with the exception of **Character Analysis,** were banned in the USA and had to be smuggled in by friends returning from Europe—a feature that undoubtedly enhanced their appeal. Indeed, I was for a while rather inclined to accept the whole package.

After a few years of Reichianism, I began to sour on the idea, for reasons to be discussed presently, and turned to Freud and classical psychoanalytic training. Although I am still deeply involved with psychoanalysis, I have not remained within the psychoanalytic movement. Instead I complicated things further by adding a figure 'gone through' by Reich, namely Marx, not to mention that of a contemporary of Reich's cordially disliked by Chasseguet-Smirgel and Grunberger: Marcuse (and a few others besides). Worse yet, I have even made some efforts to do what the authors claim cannot be done—to try to encounter Freud and Marx with something of the spirit of a Reich and something of the spirit of a Marcuse. And since the motive for this, according to Chasseguet-Smirgel and Grunberger, is fundamentally one of destroying both founding fathers of modern discourse, it can be seen right away that my vantage point on *Freud or Reich?* is scarcely a neutral one.

So be it, for this is a book that demands engagement. There is nothing neutral about it, and nothing to be gained by passive appreciation. As the authors correctly assert, whether or not Reichianism flourishes as a movement is not the main point. It is rather what Reich stood for, epitomized in his relation to Freud, that counts. Chasseguet-Smirgel and Grunberger care passionately about this, and their combative tract keeps the subject heated until the last page. And for all that Freud wins the contest hands down, their book may be read as a genuine, if backhanded, tribute to Reich.

Here I must express another distinction between my view of Freud and Reich and that of the authors. Chasseguet-Smirgel and Grunberger evidently write from a context—the France of the early seventies—in which the *gauchisme* of the previous decade had spilled over into a number of flirtations with the perennially revolutionizing spirit of Reich. At the same time, they seem to have felt themselves politically marginalized as Freudians.

By contrast, I write from the centre of psychoanalytic culture in a time of general retreat for the Left as a whole. From where I sit, Reichianism is a minuscule and indeed negligible movement in itself, while Freudian psychoanalysis plays a dynamic role in the intellectual life of modern urban society. Despite the fitful yet inexorable decline of clinical psychoanalysis amidst a welter of competing therapies, the prestige and influence of Freud as culture-hero continues to grow. On the surface, then, there would seem to be no contest at all, and scarcely anything to bother writing about. Freud is installed in our pantheon as a kind of Prometheus, while Reich died in prison, mocked and, one might even say, despised. And unlike the Jesus with whom he so palpably identified, no significant move towards resurrection and deification occurs as we come to the end of the third decade after his death. An occasional biography (the latest, by Myron Sharaf [1983], is probably definitive), scattered outcroppings of followers, periodic calls to investigate seriously his innumerable scientific claims—this is all that stands. Reich, in short, remains marginal when he is remembered at all. Why beat, as they say, a dead horse?

Precisely because, as our authors clearly recognize, no matter how low Reich may have fallen he remains the quintessential, complete and perennial revolutionary. Or shall we say, a man of extreme tendencies? Or as the authors insist, a man of illusion, a man who began close to Freud, who traversed the psychoanalytic path and came out facing in the opposite direction from the founding fa-

ther of psychoanalysis. Reich, the revolutionary, is seen as a threat to Freud, the anti-revolutionary, and since it is Freud who must be apotheosized it is Reich who must be demolished.

As with Edward Glover's *Freud or Jung?* of a half-century ago, Chasseguet-Smirgel and Grunberger are out to show that there is but one legitimate spirit of psychoanalytic discourse, that of its sire. This superiority of Freud extends far beyond the consulting room; to the authors of this book, Freud is nothing less than the peerless philosopher of our time. With respect to Reich, Freud is doubly right—in the sense of being scientifically true and in the sense of being morally as well as politically superior. And if this implies yet a third sense of the term, that of being politically right-wing, so much the better. For in the eyes of our authors, it is the illusionist revolutionary who, given the power, turns bloodthirsty ('Every time an illusion is activated, a bloodbath follows close behind . . .'); while Freud, the quietly heroic dis-illusionist, represents the best, perhaps the sole hope of saving the human race from its destructive tendencies. And of course it must be added—in line with the observation that Reich himself may be less important than the kind of heresy he represents—that all revolutionaries, all people who think they can change the world by radically altering existing institutions, are essentially in the same boat with Wilhelm Reich, even if they may not show his peculiarities.

I shall have more to say about these matters below. First, however, a brief sketch of Chasseguet-Smirgel and Grunberger's main case against Reich—and for Freud—may be helpful here. The theme cuts to the core of psychoanalysis—its reading of desire, and the relation of desire to reality.

Essentially, the difference between Freud and Reich comes down to this: for the former, desire exists in opposition to nature, that is, as fantasy, while for the latter, desire can be realized only in nature. This basic belief of Reich's, which he followed to its catastrophic end, defines his primary illusion for Chasseguet-Smirgel and Grunberger. More, in following his conviction to the breaking point, Reich, who was always paranoid by virtue of his character structure, became frankly psychotic. The customary reading of Reich's relation to psychoanalytic orthodoxy is that he was all right up until the writing of **Character Analysis** in the early thirties but fell apart after being expelled from the psychoanalytic movement in 1934. Chasseguet-Smirgel and Grunberger argue rather that Reich's paranoia infected his thinking from the outset, and turned it steadily from illusion to delusion.

As is well known, Reich took over a branch in the path of psychoanalysis that Freud had himself turned away from, and stayed with it until the end. At issue was the significance of sexuality and the relative roles of the real and imaginary. At first, Freud had argued for the primacy of the 'actual neurosis' (*Aktualneurose*)—neurotic formation on the basis of real, traumatic experience—and for a programme of sexual reform as necessary for the general health of the population. His emphasis on the noxious effects of coitus interruptus is but one example of this tendency, which continued at least until the writing of 'Civilized sexual morality and modern nervous illness' in 1908. However such notions may have hung about somewhere in Freud's thinking throughout his life, it cannot be doubted that they became increasingly marginal to psychoanalytic discourse, which became ever more centred on the dimension of fantasy. The decline of the seduction theory as an explanation for neurosogenesis, the supplementation of 'actual neurosis' by psychoneurosis, the theory of dreaming and its interpretation—all of this testified to the fact that the locus of psychoanalysis had shifted to the realm of the imaginary: psychic reality. Above all, the theory of infantile sexuality established the shift, by claiming sexuality itself for the sphere of fantasy. Not altogether—for drives still had to have their source in the real body—but essentially, for the object of the drive, a specifically subjective phenomenon became the ultimate determiner of sexual deployment.

More fundamental still, the fantastic nature of sexuality is a consequence of existential givens: dependency, prolonged immaturity, the wishful, that is, illusory character of psychic activity as such. Thus it inscribes a more basic proposition than physical sexuality, or, to put the matter slightly differently, fantasy and illusion determine infantile sexuality, and infantile sexuality determines life in its essentials. We are, according to Chasseguet-Smirgel and Grunberger's reading of Freud, primarily determined by the exigencies of infantile sexuality: by the great facts of the difference between the generations and between the sexes, by our passionate and doomed desire for parents, by the inherent state of mental castration which flows from these foundations—by, ultimately, that which is internal and subjective instead of external and objective.

The image of human nature which emerges from this discourse is positively Calvinist in its remorselessness. Freud was a sceptic and a stoic, but his view was almost cheerful compared to these Freudians. For them, it is not enough to have a castration complex: one must also recognize that one is really, inevitably *castrated*. As they freely admit, this fact implies another which enables them to deal in advance with all criticism as a manifestation of the congenital human inability to accept unpleasure and the lack of narcissistic fulfilment.

For we do not want to believe what the tough-minded Freudian tells us, because we cannot bear the painful truth about ourselves. We live by illusion instead, projecting our dream world outwards, giving it the name of objective reality, and dreaming that we can save ourselves from the subjective castration which is our human fate, by changing the external world. We all become paranoid to some degree or other, although some are worse paranoids than others, and cannot abandon their delusory ideas. And of them all, Reich was the worst paranoid, because he attempted to subvert this most basic position of Freud's in the name of psychoanalysis and science.

It is possible to say that Reich's entire course was defined by his refusal to accept, as Freud had, the limited importance of real sexual gratification. Despite Reich's early eminence in the psychoanalytic movement, deep differences with the mainstream of Freudian thought can be traced to his earliest writings. These surfaced with the or-

gasm theory of 1927 and never ceased widening for the rest of his spectacular career. The authors provide a more or less accurate account of the main relevant ideas of Reich and of the points that distinguish him from Freud. Since Reich was nothing if not consistent (in thought but not in life), these can be readily summarized as a rejection of the imaginary basis of infantile sexuality, or, to be more exact, a rendering of it as epiphenomenal. What mattered was not the ineradicable inscription of a fundamentally tragic situation on the infantile mind, but how one actually functioned sexually. Sexual stasis (later, in an entirely logical development, that of the orgone energy itself) caused the occlusions of neurotic subjectivity, and not the other way around, as the later Freud held.

Associated with this was a thoroughgoing ontological difference. Subjectivity was to be subordinated to the physical and biological, so much so that it can be said that Reich, for all his contributions to psychoanalysis, was never really a psychologically minded person at all. In this light, his later orgonomic developments seem to be the unfolding of an inner essence. However bizarre they may have been in themselves, the orgone theories were a more authentic expression of Reich than his psychoanalytic phase.

Finally, it should be added that the differences between Reich and Freud were expressed in the remarkable optimism of the former and the pessimism of the latter. Those who put their faith in changing the world, whether of the body or society, can generally look forward to brighter prospects than those who insist that the fault lies in ourselves. Freud's generally bleak prospect for the human species was compounded from a twofold conviction: that we were saddled with ineluctable aggressivity and, perhaps more fundamental, that the pleasure principle prevented us from being truthful about ourselves. As for Reich, even as he was being crushed under the heels of the state, he held out hope for the future triumph of the life force. Indeed, the worse Reich's personal fortunes, the more messianic became his outlook, pulled beyond the mundane on the wings of a cosmic energy.

How is one to decide between these drastically different world-views? Certainly not by Reich's disastrous end and Freud's relative triumph. To die in ignominy does not prove the worthlessness of what one lived for; it only indicates that one did not get along with the world. Neither does Reich's obvious—and obviously worsening—psychosis invalidate what he held. Reich was no more a lunatic than Newton; and nobody disputes Newtonian physics on account of the madness of its progenitor. Moreover, as mad as Reich was towards the end (he believed, for example, that a race of spacemen were involved in changing about the structure of orgone energy, and that the US Air Force was secretly on his side), Sharaf's detailed biography makes it clear that Reich's delusions were of the loculated kind, so that he could be quite capable of not simply normal, but highly rational and indeed brilliant behaviour at the same time as he harboured utterly fantastic beliefs.

There is no reason, therefore, for not assuming that it was the rational Reich who formulated his principal ideas—

almost all of which were presented in the regalia of full-scale scientific discourse—to a much greater extent, by the way, than Freud ever bothered to do. Chasseguet-Smirgel and Grunberger believe that Freud was 'scientific' because he was not a victim of Reich's illusory tendencies, but this is slippery ground indeed for deciding on the superiority of one over the other. Anybody who advances Freudian psychoanalysis as scientific these days is asking for a lot of trouble. In fact, one could argue that Freud, who dealt in the extremely problematic world of intersubjective discourse as a 'data base', would fare much worse epistemologically from the standpoint of normal science than Reich, who ultimately appealed to something 'out there', even if only the orgonomically healthy could perceive it accurately.

And yet a critical distinction needs to be drawn. Either one disregards both Freud and Reich as trivial and deluded, or one gives them both the credit of recognizing that a serious contradiction exists, which must be carefully assessed. I think it should be obvious that passive observation of this matter will not do. One neither can nor should be personally absent from any judgement drawn. Certainly Chasseguet-Smirgel and Grunberger's impassioned polemic against Reich and for Freud is determined in some measure by concern for the integrity and value of their life's work as psychoanalysts.

In my case the same basic considerations hold, even if the trajectory taken is a different one. I shifted from Reich to Freud, and though I have grown critical of the latter, I have not swung back to the former. Why? Because, essentially, I encountered things in my experience with Reichianism which disappointed me, first with the practice and then the theory. Indeed, my experience confirmed to some degree what is said in *Freud or Reich?* I found, in brief, that the abolition of subjectivity did not suit me; it did not make for the kind of therapy I wanted, and it presented a foreshortened and, ultimately, repressive view of human life.

For the Reichian, the key thing is 'to get the energy moving'. Everything else will take care of itself if, and only if, orgastic potency can be achieved. It matters not what the orgone therapist *means* to the patient—for example, whether he behaves in a domineering or repulsive way—so long as he permits the energy to move. Or rather, there is no way of connecting these things within the theory. This extreme naturalism more or less puts any serious reflection upon either psychological or social relations into a deep shade. It is not hard to imagine the degree of mischief and incompetence that can proceed under the cover of this ultimately technocratic approach. If the energy is outside ordinary ken, and the therapist-expert has special access to it, then the therapist can more or less get away with anything so long as some effect is achieved. This is all the more so given the fact that the therapy clearly taps into powerful and 'moving' feelings, often in a consciously anti-intellectual, or at least markedly uncritical, framework.

From another angle, Reich's extreme naturalism made for repressiveness in the very sexuality he was seeking to liberate. If 'energy' is all, and energy is contained in orgastic

potency, then a fixed regimen of sexual hygiene is mandated as a prescription for well-being. Gone was the space for playfulness and the special madness of sexuality that makes human existence unique. In its place stood a tyranny of genitality that could rival that of fundamentalist religious sects in its subordination of Eros to 'higher' ends, and its rigid, doctrinaire rejection of homosexuality.

Perhaps the greatest damage wrought by Reich's naturalism was political, both within and outside of the movement he founded. The orgonomy movement exceeded even that of psychoanalysis in the lack of freedom, its domination by one powerful man. Nothing is handier than an appeal to suprahuman influence as a buttress to charisma and authoritarianism. There was scarcely any dialogue to speak of, much less a free flow of ideas, within Reich's entourage. Orgonomy was strictly a one-man operation. Able minds were now and then drawn to Reichianism, but they either stayed as passive recipients of the genius's insights, or withdrew. As a result, the movement showed no real growth after Reich's death, lapsing instead into a kind of mechanistic formalism.

As for Reich's external politics, while he remained attached to a semi-anarchistic vision of 'work democracy' as a social goal, his lack of interest in, and indeed frank contempt for, larger-scale social structures rendered the politics of orgonomy puerile when they were not frankly reactionary. It was a long descent that led the author of the **Sex-Pol Essays** (which seem not to have been available in their entirety to Chasseguet-Smirgel and Grunberger) to form a favourable judgement of President Eisenhower because he seemed to be a 'genital character'—long and doleful, but not inconsistent with the fundamental inclination of Reich's thought. Note, however, that the political direction taken by Reich was itself sharply rightward. Although it does not square with the authors' linkage of Reichianism and left-wing politics as equivalent illusions, this is what one might expect from such a pure naturalism as he developed. By the end Reich was more than conservative and more than anti-Communist: he actively believed in plots by 'red fascists' to get him.

Whether Reich's naturalism was cause or effect of his paranoia is an interesting problem to which the authors devote considerable attention. I shall not address myself to the substantive matters of this question, but rather to another aspect raised by their treatment of it. And here I must sharply take issue with *Freud or Reich?* For it is hard to avoid the conclusion that Chasseguet-Smirgel and Grunberger, despite admitting that mental disturbance does not *per se* invalidate the work, have in these pages carried the psychoanalysing of Reich to unseemly proportions.

This is unfortunate, and in more than one sense. To psychoanalyse someone when you are engaged in an ideological struggle with him strikes me as a bad practice both clinically and intellectually. It becomes a particularly unhappy strategy in view of the decision to exempt Freud from the same treatment. To claim that psychoanalysing Freud is 'a sterile enterprise', and meanwhile to declare open season on Reich, down to reducing the orgone to the paternal phallus, must be one of the least effective ways imaginable to secure rational assent to an argument.

We may also be reminded here of the injunction against the throwing of stones by those who reside in glasshouses. Despite the authors' hagiographic treatment of Freud and reduction of Reich to a mass of psychopathology, the reader might recall that the founder of psychoanalysis was himself prone to serious 'work-related' lapses (the cocaine phase, the unconscionable ganging up with Fliess against Emma Eckstein, the peccadilloes concerning the relationship with Jung, and so on), while the founder of orgonomy was capable, despite obvious mental disturbance, of great moral courage and fidelity to principle. If Chasseguet-Smirgel and Grunberger were to hear somebody reduce Freud's life-work to various attempts at overcoming his hostility to women, they would be justifiably outraged. Why do the same sort of thing to Reich?

Matters are only made worse by the authors' efforts at self-justification. At the end of chapter 6, they anticipate criticism for psychoanalysing Reich with such a free hand. Observing quite correctly that they do not, after all, know their subject except through his writings and second-hand accounts, they excuse themselves on the grounds, first, that Reich, being paranoid, wouldn't have tolerated the analytic context anyway; and second, that Freud successfully analysed the paranoiac Schreber strictly through the latter's writings. This assumes that Reich would have had to be 'paranoid'—that is irrational—to refuse an analysis in such a spirit as is evinced here; and it overlooks the fact that Freud studied Schreber to understand him and not to pass judgement. Can one imagine a person who would agree to an 'analysis' for the purpose of being compared with Freud?

At issue here is the spirit of sectarianism—surely as great a contributor to human misery as all other foibles combined. To put the problem at the level of 'illusion' and paranoia seems to me to miss the point by not carrying the analysis far enough. What is destructive is not illusion or paranoia as such, but *socially organized* paranoid illusions, expressed as sectarianism—and backed up, to be sure, by violence against the Other who is deemed to represent evil. Reich was severely subject to the sectarian plague— though the only violence he brought about was to himself. But Freud was no stranger to the bug, either, and I am afraid that Chasseguet-Smirgel and Grunberger have gone one better than him in their attempt to demolish Reich, or, for that matter, as they briskly go about purging the impure from psychoanalysis, namely:

> It is surprising, then, that some analysts are being carried away by fashion and popular consensus, and are trying to explain female sexuality in terms of social and economic conditions. The most basic concern for consistency and integrity would require them to stop practising a profession in which they no longer believe (unless they are victims of an astonishingly split personality).

In sum, we can reframe the question: why must it be Freud *or* Reich? I am not proposing an alternative which flaccidly accepts any and everything. Differences are real, and both Freud and Reich cannot be right. But there is another approach to take, which seems to me to be preferable altogether. Once one abandons the urge to elevate either figure to the ranks of the superhuman, the possibility opens up that it could be neither Freud nor Reich who had the exclusive lock on the truth. . . .

A critical judgement negates its object without destroying it. Its goal is transcendence, and it recognizes the partiality of all human endeavour—Freud's and Reich's included. Tolerance is not the issue. It is rather to recognize the impossibility of either Freud or Reich solving the dialectical problem before him—that of being human under the conditions of contemporary civilization. To be critical is to recognize this, and to grant each his greatness and his limitation.

Such recognition expresses the whole emancipatory motion of psychoanalytic revolution, viewed as the undoing of repression. Freud discovered that sexuality and infantility were repressed in modern civilization, and since the common term of sexuality and childhood was closeness to nature, that nature was repressed as well. His genius was to raise this dialectic, otherwise blind, into consciousness, whence it could re-enter the history that was transforming subjectivity and the conditions of sexuality and childhood.

But we need to remind ourselves that the real Freud was not necessarily equal to the dialectical power of his own genius. In what I would consider his greatest moments, for example when, in the *New Introductory Lectures,* he expressed *Wo es war, soll ich werden* (literally, 'where it was, there shall I become'), Freud identified the psychoanalytic project with the formation of the conscious subject out of the primordium, not as rejection but as appropriation of desire. For the ego, or 'I', to appropriate the id, or 'it', the subject must dissolve, become open to nature, the unspeakable, and the erotic infantile body. All of this is the domain of the negative, which is both subversive and, to some essential degree, illusory with respect to the socially constructed world. The psychoanalytic recovery of the self requires, therefore, a degree of acceptance of this negative dimension, coupled with an intellectual judgement concerning its unreality. It is a subtle, dialectical balance, which can in no way be encompassed in a simple-minded discourse of triumph over illusion; or rather, psychoanalysis cannot be a gendarme over illusion and remain true to its emancipatory and transcendent potential.

There is nothing, of course, which says that psychoanalysis must remain emancipatory—a measure requiring both an affirmation of Eros and a critique of the socially constructed world. Certainly Freud waffled a good bit on the point. The same Freud who relentlessly attacked social repressiveness and hypocrisy could, with an absolute lack of critical insight, endorse the existing set of repressive social regulations as if they had been inscribed by Moses in stone. In the words of Adorno, for Freud, '[t]he fatality was that, in the teeth of bourgeois ideology, he tracked down conscious actions materialistically to their unconscious instinctual basis, but at the same time concurred with the bourgeois contempt of instinct which is itself a product of precisely the rationalizations that he dismantled'.

The same could be said for *Freud or Reich?* except that in dealing with Reich, of whom the last thing that could be said was that he held a contempt for instinct, the authors seem impelled to press their rejection of nature past the bounds of Freud, and indeed, what prudent people would deem a reasonable balance. For example, by more or less consigning the orgasm theory to a fantasy of bowel evacuation, they are led actually to reject, or at least minimize, the value of sexual gratification itself. One does not have to be an ardent Reichian or a victim of illusion to take exception to a statement such as:

> In reality, orgasm, in itself, has no particular value or merit in our view. True, it is a discharge of tension, and this is, inherently, a kind of evacuation (Alexander writes of 'drainage'), but the tension in question is of a more complex nature than the purely anal.

This is, I am sure, cheering news to those who have had clitoridectomy, not to mention the rest of us who have to bear up under the common human fate of mental castration. It is touching to have such consolation.

Chasseguet-Smirgel and Grunberger are good at flailing away. But they are locked into Manichean dualism and, for all their pretensions, incapable of critical thought. Critique requires a dialectical attitude, which demands the holding together of opposites, as well as a view of the whole, and not a fixation on 'inner' or 'outer'. Freud was a great, if lapsed, master at this, while Reich can be said to be less dialectical than Freud. But Reich also set his sights higher and was not afraid to hurl himself into the void. He believed that opposites could be unified, and differentiation abolished. Reich's lapses in his search for a monistic view of the universe were greater than Freud's— worse philosophically, and perhaps the weaker for it; but grander, too, in insisting that human beings were entitled to more gratification than their civilization was affording. We should remember, too, that Reich's views on pleasure could in no way be reduced to any purely sensual calculus. As we have already observed, his views on sexuality had a crypto-Puritanism to them. But beyond this, he so expanded the idea of sexuality as to make it identical with participation in nature and the extrahuman itself.

Reich was, then, a kind of religious visionary. One can take him as such—although not as a way of neglecting his scientific claim, and not as a sign of his psychopathology. His lapse was to absorb the human into an extreme naturalism. Reich's severe naturalism signifies his own abandonment of—or was it an inability to sustain?—the dialectic of being human. Swallowed by nature, negativity vanishes and subjectivity returns as epiphenomenon. The results become mechanistic, even disastrous; we have seen their deleterious effects, and would share to this extent in the critique of Reich.

But let us affirm as well the magnificence of his tragic and doomed life. And let us take Reich seriously enough to wonder whether the savage fate handed to him by the authorities—psychoanalytic, Communist and of the US state apparatus—was more than a reaction to his difficult personality. Instead, could the repression of Reich have been also a sign of the seriousness of the forces his insights unleashed? If it can be said that Freud and Reich each slid off the perhaps impossible point of the dialectic, it can also be said that Freud slid in the safer direction, that of 'bourgeois contempt for instinct', leaving for Reich the direction of hell.

Why should we give any credence to Reich, considering all that is manifestly unreliable in his life's work? Because there is much more than a philosophical interest in what he achieved. Set aside the haste, the grandiosity, the gross overreach, and what remains is remarkable. Or better, do not set aside the derelictions, but consider their effects upon Reich's discourse, and see what lies there nevertheless. A major problem with Reich was that he so personalized his thought as to lose track of the dialogue which forms the fabric of normal scientific activity. He spoke *at* science, not *to* scientists, who understandably turned away. It thus becomes exceedingly difficult to engage the truth-value of what he is saying. The mode of his presentation was so self-referential, so sealed away in a cocoon of internal logic, so alien to everyday discourse and, above all, so repudiative of everything else that anybody had done in the way of science, that out-of-hand rejection was virtually automatic.

It is true, then, that Reich's work has never been put to an adequate test, having been subjected instead to the partisanship of either true believers or true unbelievers, and essentially remaining outside of rational inquiry for methodological reasons. Whether this limit can ever be overcome is arguable. One would have thought so—but one has thought so for decades now, with little change in the situation.

If, however, we bracket the science and concentrate instead on the *prescience,* then a different picture emerges. Reich's vision led him to the edge of the known, where he touched upon many things that suggest an emergent truth. Nor should we overlook the fact that he seems to have anticipated much which has by now become routine. I would share the authors' opinion that Reich's views on the sexual liberties to be offered to children were deeply flawed. I would also claim, however, that his role in promoting an atmosphere of spontaneity in early childhood education (principally through his lifelong friendship with A. S. Neill) should be appreciated. To do less than this is to admit the wish to turn back the clock to the days of the authoritarian classroom. When we examine the sphere of more immediate interest to him, a case could be made for Reich having contributed to more movements in contemporary psychotherapy than anyone with the exception of Freud. Family therapy, sex therapy, Gestalt therapy, aside from the more obviously 'Reichian' body treatments—all these owe more to Reich than is generally admitted. In addition, the powerful 'holistic' tendencies in contemporary health care derive as much, if not more, from Reich as from any other individual.

I am not interested here in delineating Reich's precise relationship to these movements, or in weighing their entire value, about much of which I would have reservations. The point is only that Reich seems to have been able to sense some basic things about the organism. What yielded to a repressive naturalism or floated off into grandiose speculation could also recapture a primitive, even Taoist respect for the integrity of life.

Given the fact that Reich operated—as we still do today—in the context of rampant technological domination, we should not be surprised that this most eccentric of geniuses could also enunciate some good, plain—and protective—sense. It should not be forgotten that, with the aid of his much-maligned and indeed ridiculed theory of the orgone, Reich was able courageously to call attention to the severe biological dangers posed by even very low doses of ionizing radiation many years before the mainstream of scientific medicine woke up to the threat. A lucky stroke induced by paranoia, or a prescient insight into the life process? In any case, not a simple matter of illusion.

If Reich was driven by paranoia, then we should develop more respect for paranoia. Kirilian auras, the recent reopening of the problem of biogenesis, the expansion of our conception of viruses and other intermediate forms of life . . . these and other lines of contemporary scientific investigation, anticipated in one way or another by Reich, tell us that the man is neither to be ignored nor to be reduced to the sum of his psychopathology. Perhaps we can say that, within the social context of modern science, it took a certain madness to achieve certain fundamental insights. The same madness could distort the insight and pull it outside of constructive dialogue. This is, however, no reason to despise the madness. It rather demands that we criticize the social context in greater measure than its victim.

And so Wilhelm Reich cannot be critically appreciated unless his society is critically measured as well. Much as he attempted to deny the social—a denial that led to his tragic downfall when he refused the US government's jurisdiction over his case—Reich's whole life and work remains defined by social forces. The dualism he rejected with his radical monism was a historical product. Who is Reich, after all, but the most extreme anti-Cartesian of our time? And since the Cartesian split between psyche and nature defines the rationality of the modern age, Reich was necessarily mad. His madness cannot be reduced, however, to the psychopathological because he poses for us in the sharpest terms imaginable the unbearable price extracted by society for its domination of nature. It is ironic, then, that a man who so violently rejected the significance of the social needs to be judged ultimately according to one's assessment of civilization.

All this is of no matter to Chasseguet-Smirgel and Grunberger, who have no difficulty in consigning Reich to the trashcan of history precisely because they have no interest in, or to be more exact, they have a fear of and active hostility towards, any assessment of civilization which calls into question the existing order of things. Hence their warning against the 'bloodbath' which is sure to ensue after any fulfilment of revolutionary ideals. Hence, too, their hatred for Marcuse along with Reich, their blanket condemnation of the Freudo-Marxist project, and their dismissal of Marx, or indeed, all political radicalism. And they bend psychoanalysis to this purpose. No paraphrase or summary could convey the spirit in which this is undertaken better than a sampling of their remarks on the subject (some of these are meant as a gloss on *Civilization and its Discontents,* but they express also what might be called the authors' enhancement of Freud's attitude, their Calvinist rendition of his scepticism):

> Freud's work is a repudiation of illusion, especially the illusion of alternative societies, and the illusion of the overthrow of the process of civilization . . . We have no choice. The alternative to civilization is not the pastoral idyll, but barbarism . . .

> Psychoanalytic theory . . . considers that primary drives—aggressivity and the hunger for love—determine the economic conditions themselves. This theory tends to see social institutions as the exosmosis of the unconscious, a projection of the drives and the defences against the drives . . . [This] accounts for the resistances which this kind of work inevitably encounters.

> The aim of political ideologies seems to be to ascribe the source of human suffering to external factors. This usually entails blaming a system (private property, capitalism, patriarchy, the 'consumer society'), or a group of people (Jews, the bourgeoisie, 'armoured characters', *homo normalis,* or Oedipalists), or even society in general, for human suffering. Ideologies never seek to explain these miseries as the effect of the drives, or of the human condition itself, but they try, instead, to escape this suffering. And this, no doubt, is their main function. Furthermore, they extend the promise of a reconciliation between man and his lost unity; be it Marx's 'complete man', or the purified Aryan race, the non-armoured genital character enjoying his full orgasmic capacity, or the neo-Rousseauist return to nature. All these ideologies are based on a denial of castration: a castration which psychoanalysis stresses and which religions deny.

> These explanatory models of political ideologies are very much like the 'influencing machine' fantasy that is so characteristic of paranoid-schizophrenics, which has been brilliantly described and analysed by Tausk (1919).

> Human beings can only act and create on the basis of their internal psychosexual model. We project this model out on to the world when creating political systems, institutions and economic structures, thus making them in our own image . . . political ideologies . . . foster the illusion of the possibility of escaping from castration . . . At the heart of all ideologies lies the romantic and fashionable idea of 'changing the world'. Psychoanalytic understanding tends to act against the idea.

This is miserable, mean-spirited stuff. It makes me ashamed as an analyst to see it so used. It is not that there is no truth to what they say. There is actually an important truth embedded here, a truth of the critique of messianic and objectivizing doctrines. However, this truth, which is specifically psychoanalytic, is perverted by the mean-spirited and, yes, grossly *ideological* temper in which it is expressed. I have referred already to the hopelessly undialectical character of the authors' thought. If there were any questions on this score, these quotes, lost in blinkered single vision, should settle them.

Interestingly, the authors themselves give the lie to their uncritical dichotomization when they admit, as if unaware of the implications, that 'every psychic manifestation, all human behaviour . . . is related, *although sometimes at great distance,* to the primary drives' (my italics). Who could disagree with this sensible statement, which substitutes 'related to' for 'caused by', and admits that there may be something else, some mediation, just possibly having to do with the real practical world, substantially between the drives and at least some behaviour? Evidently Janine Chasseguet-Smirgel and Béla Grunberger, for it flies in the face of their subjectivization of reality and their inability to deal with multiple causation.

But these flaws are perhaps the less interesting side of our authors' defence of psychoanalytic hegemony. I am more taken with its ideological basis. To be blunt, which side are the authors on? For whom are these reflections into the human condition written? Ostensibly, everyone; that is, there is a clear universalizing attempt, evinced, if by nothing else, in the ubiquitous reference to 'Man'. Yet (setting aside the sexism) consider how ethnocentric, how utterly parochial, are the thoughts expressed here. Who else but a late-capitalist professional élite would be the least interested in these notions, and who other than the bourgeoisie can be served by them? From where else could they have come but Europe—a Europe, now North America as well, preaching of civilization to the barbarians, baffled by the barbarous turn of its own civilization.

Imagine our analysts attempting to convince, say, Black Africans in Soweto of the need to accept their 'castration', or to give up on the hope of changing the world because the *real* problems are within. Or the Filipinos who are waiting to overthrow the US-imposed Marcos dictatorship. Or lecturing Nicaragua's Sandinistas on the inevitable bloodbath to which their search for the ideal—that is, a free and self-determining society—must lead. The latter would tell them, by the way, that there were no executions of the hated dictator Somoza's bloodthirsty National Guard after the triumph in 1979—perhaps because none of the Sandinistas read this book—but that there has been quite a bloodbath since, 8,000-9,000 lives more or less, instigated by a bourgeois counter-revolution bent on revenge. Or they might point out that Salvador Allende in Chile tried to change the world, refused to kill anyone or even to arm the people, and for his pains got butchered, along with more than 20,000 of his people, by another bourgeoisie bent on revenge. So if there is a psychohistorical problem worth investigating, it is that of the boundless savagery of the bourgeoisie (or any ruling group threatened from below)—a phenomenon that takes us, once again, into the domain of the repression of desire.

It may of course well be that there is no way radically to improve this civilization, although I must add that the prospect makes me shudder. But if so, it is because the forces on the ruling side are, taken all in all, the stronger. Never let it be said, however, that this makes what they are saying true. And so long as this is the case, we will need divinely inspired paranoids, who will not be thanked for their services, to point a way out. I happen to think, though, that there will be a better day. I know it may be an illusion to think so, but it is not entirely an illusion, and in the difference, everything may reside. The paranoid visionary Rousseau helped point the way to a French Revolution that gave us a bourgeois society for the likes of Janine Chasseguet-Smirgel and Béla Grunberger to defend. Can we say what the visionary paranoid Reich was prefiguring?

FURTHER READING

Biography

Cattier, Michel. *The Life and Work of Wilhelm Reich.* Translated by Ghislaine Boulanger. New York: Horizon Press, 1971, 224 p.
    Examines major milestones in Reich's career.

Placzek, Beverley R., ed. *Record of a Friendship: The Correspondence between Wilhelm Reich and A. S. Neill, 1936-1957.* New York: Farrar, Straus and Giroux, 1981, 429 p.
    Collects letters written between Reich and the noted child psychologist A. S. Neill.

Sharaf, Myron. *Fury on Earth: A Biography of Wilhelm Reich.* New York: St. Martin's Press/Marek, 1983, 550 p.
    Discussion of Reich's life and career by one of his former patients.

Criticism

Boadella, David. *Wilhelm Reich: The Evolution of His Work.* London: Vision Press, 1973, 400 p.
    Traces Reich's career.

Chasseguet-Smirgel, Janine, and Grunberger, Béla. *Freud or Reich? Psychoanalysis and Illusion.* Translated by Claire Pajaczkowska. New Haven and London: Yale University Press, 1986, 252 p.
    Freudian critique of Reich that attempts to discredit his theories by psychoanalyzing him.

Chesser, Eustace. *Salvation through Sex: The Life and Work of Wilhelm Reich.* New York: William Morrow & Co., 1973, 114 p.
    Comprehensive examination of Reich's work in human sexuality.

Cohen, Ira H. *Ideology and Unconsciousness: Reich, Freud, and Marx.* New York and London: New York University Press, 1982, 235 p.
    Concentrates on the social and political writings of the three thinkers.

Gardner, Martin. "Orgonomy." In his *Fads and Fallacies in the Name of Science,* pp. 250-62. New York: Dover Publications, 1952.
    Early evaluation of Reich's claims about orgone energy.

Higgins, Mary, and Raphael, Chester, M.D., eds. *Reich Speaks of Freud.* New York: Farrar, Straus and Giroux, 1967, 296 p.
    Contains an interview with Reich conducted by Kurt R. Eissler in 1952, as well as Reich's letters to friends and

colleagues, in which Reich discusses his personal and
professional relationship with Sigmund Freud.

Mann, W. Edward, and Hoffmann, Edward. *Wilhelm Reich:
The Man Who Dreamed of Tomorrow*. Northamptonshire,
England: Crucible, 295 p.
    Concentrates on Reich's ideas about orgone energy.

Ollman, Bertell. *Social and Sexual Revolution: Essays on
Marx and Reich*. Montreal: Black Rose Books, 1978, 228 p.
    Examines Reich's theories about Marxism and the social
    function of sexual repression.

Robinson, Paul A. "Wilhelm Reich." In his *The Freudian
Left: Wilhelm Reich, Geza Roheim, Herbert Marcuse*, pp.
9-73. New York, Evanston, and London: Harper and Row,
1969.
    Places Reich, Geza Roheim, and Herbert Marcuse in
    the "radical tradition in psychoanalysis" in an attempt
    to reevaluate Freud's alleged conservatism. Robinson
    argues that through the work of these psychoanalysts,
    Freud "emerges as the architect of a more erotic and
    more humane organization of man's communal life."

Rycroft, Charles. *Wilhelm Reich*. Edited by Frank Kermode.
New York: Viking Press, 1969, 115 p.
    Critical discussion of Reich's major theses.

Wilson, Colin. "Wilhelm Reich's Sex and Psychology."
Books and Bookmen 17, No. 203 (August 1972): 18-21.
    Reviews *Reich Speaks of Freud, The Mass Psychology of
    Fascism, The Invasion of Compulsory Sex Morality*, and
    Listen, Little Man!

Edgar Wallace
1875-1932

(Full name Richard Horatio Edgar Wallace) English novelist, playwright, journalist, screenwriter, and short story writer.

INTRODUCTION

Wallace was a prolific writer of crime thrillers, detective stories, and stage plays based on his books. His works are noted for their fast-paced narratives and accurate depiction of English working-class life.

Biographical Information

Born in Greenwich to an unmarried actor and actress, Wallace was adopted and raised by foster parents in the town of Billingsgate. As a teenager he worked at a succession of factories and unskilled jobs before enlisting in the British army in 1893. Wallace spent six years in the military, the last three of which he served as a member of the Medical Staff Corps in South Africa. While stationed there, he began writing poetry and made the acquaintance of Rudyard Kipling, who, after reading some of Wallace's early work, encouraged him to pursue writing as a career. Wallace bought his army discharge in 1899, but remained in South Africa as a news correspondent during the Boer War. He continued his journalistic career upon returning to England, and worked as a reporter and editor for most of his adult life. It was not until the age of forty that Wallace became known as a writer of fiction. In the last decade of his life he wrote books that sold millions of copies. At one point during his prolific career it was estimated that one out of every four books sold in England was written by Edgar Wallace. He died in 1932.

Major Works

During his lifetime Wallace wrote numerous plays and film scripts and produced over one hundred seventy novels. His first novel, *The Four Just Men*, a thriller published at his own expense in 1906, marked the beginning of his career as a popular writer. Though he wrote in a wide variety of genres, Wallace is best known for his thrillers and detective stories, including *The Crimson Circle, The Clue of the New Pin, The Fellowship of the Frog,* and *The Mind of Mr. J. G. Reeder.* He was also well known for a series of short stories set in colonial Africa featuring the fictional Commissioner Sanders. In addition, Wallace wrote science fiction and social satire, and completed a ten-volume history of World War I. At the time of his death he was working on the script for the film *King Kong.*

Critical Reception

During his lifetime, Wallace was widely read and generally well-received by critics as a provider of entertainment. In addition to selling well in England and America, his books were extremely popular in translation in Germany. While some modern critics dismiss Wallace as a producer of mere pulp, others credit him with helping to create an audience for the modern thriller. Many commentators praise Wallace's gift for fast-paced plots, accurate depictions of the British working class, and authentic portrayals of criminals. Commentators also continue to praise his Commissioner Sanders stories for their evocations of colonial Africa.

PRINCIPAL WORKS

The Mission That Failed! A Tale of the Raid, and Other Poems (poetry) 1898
Writ in Barracks (poetry) 1900
The Four Just Men (novel) 1906
Sanders of the River (short stories) 1911
The Melody of Death (novel) 1915
The Tomb of T'sin (novel) 1916
Lieutenant Bones (short stories) 1918
Captains of Souls (novel) 1922
The Crimson Circle (novel) 1922
The Clue of the New Pin (novel) 1923
Double Dan (novel) 1924; also published as *Diana of Kara-Kara*, 1924
Educated Evans (short stories) 1924
The Fellowship of the Frog (novel) 1925
The Mind of Mr. J. G. Reeder (short stories) 1925; also published as *The Murder Book of Mr. J. G. Reeder*, 1929
The Door with Seven Locks (novel) 1926
*The Ringer (drama) 1926
The Man Who Was Nobody (novel) 1927
The Squeaker (novel) 1927; also published as *The Squealer*, 1928
The India-Rubber Men (novel) 1929
Planetoid 127 (novel) 1929
Red Aces (screenplay) 1929
On the Spot (drama) 1930
The Frightened Lady (novel) 1932
**King Kong (screenplay) 1933

*This drama is an adaptation of the novel *The Gaunt Stranger.*

**This work was completed by James Creelman and Ruth Rose.

CRITICISM

The New York Times Book Review   (essay date 1922)

SOURCE: A review of *The Angel of Terror,* in *The New York Times Book Review,* April 12, 1922, p. 11.

[*In the following review, the critic praises Wallace's inventiveness in portraying a female villain in* The Angel of Terror.]

The author of [*The Angel of Terror*] has devised something new in fiction. He has reversed all the conventional methods of dealing with pretty girls and presents us with a heroine—or, to be accurate, a co-heroine—who is something very different in the heroine line. She is exquisitely beautiful, but her beauty is, indeed, only skin deep and it camouflages more sublimated essence of Satan than could be condensed out of a thousand ordinary heroines. Mr. Wallace's originality has gone even further than the usual endeavors of fiction writers to provide something a bit wicked in their feminine creations, for they are usually content to allow their wicked women to be bad merely in the way of getting what they want by exploiting their sex. But Mr. Wallace's Jean Briggerland is very proper in her behavior toward men. She is a thoroughgoing criminal, well endowed with intelligence and using it all for criminal purposes. She is quite devoid of all ethical sense and her standard of judgment for her actions is whether they enable her to succeed in some criminal enterprise.

At the beginning of the story a man who has been somewhat attentive to her is shot and killed at her doorway and another man, her cousin and fiancé, is arrested for the crime. Her testimony at the trial convicts him, although he denies the truth of what she says. His lawyers succeed in a hazardous scheme of getting him out of custody long enough to marry him to a very nice girl who sees him only through the few moments of the wedding ceremony. Almost immediately afterward he is found dead in the garden, supposedly a suicide, but clutching the revolver in his right hand, while the shot is in his left temple. It develops that the lovely devil and her father would have inherited his fortune if he had not married and would still be his heirs if his widowed bride should die. As the lovely devil has won the widowed bride's confidence and sympathy, her lawyers, who know the beautiful girl's real character, have need for all their resources and ingenuity to prevent her from cutting short the earthly career of the unsuspecting young woman. Mr. Wallace has endowed his Jean Briggerland with a fertile imagination in contriving unusual and natural-looking means of death and he leads the reader through an exciting maze of events wherein Jean concocts one scheme after another, only to find herself foiled in the outcome. The story, of course, is of the wholly artificial variety, with no pretense of presenting a mirror of life, but it is well made and well told, it is ingenious in its freshening up of the materials which go into most stories of crime, and for people who like novels of that kind it will provide a very entertaining hour.

The New York Times Book Review   (essay date 1923)

SOURCE: A review of *The Clue of the New Pin,* in *The New York Times Book Review,* April 15, 1923, pp. 22, 24.

[*In the following review, the critic notes Wallace's flair for plotting, suspense, and humor in* The Clue of the New Pin.]

Fiction mystery stories have a marked advantage over those of real life. The reader knows that eventually the criminal will be found out, the tangled skein unraveled. No matter how exciting the opening columns of a newspaper murder report or great gem robbery may be, it profiteth little if in a few days the perplexed police give out the statement that "the department is still working on the crime, but does not expect to have anything further to report for some time." Disillusioned by the fact, the reader may well turn to fiction, with its always obliging last chapters. To meet such a presumed contingency, Edgar Wallace has written *The Clue of the New Pin.*

Germs and robbery, murder and sudden death, all play their part in this intricate story. Mr. Wallace's recipe for plotmaking includes many of the most delectable ingredients. The story has its roots in an Oriental past. Once bring in the "heathen Chinee" and anything may happen. Then there is a house with a subterranean and secret vault, to which there is but one key.

True to form, likewise, are some of the persons involved. Meet the miser, Jesse Trasmere. He hoards his lucre without the assistance of any bank. He has had sinister relations with the Far East in which he was born, and whose hieroglyphics he manipulates with the same ease as the A B C's. Meet also his valet, Walters, alias Walter Felling, an ex-jailbird with a record as long as his arm, and Wellington Brown, an unwelcome visitor from Chel-Feu.

Then there is "Tab" Holland, a likable and likely young reporter, a former collegiate football star, and so fortunate financially as to possess "innumerable maiden aunts," so that "he received on an average one legacy a year." Why "Tab"? Because the boys at the office had discovered his passion for making his exit on a good line. He lives with his pal, Rex Lander, nephew and presumably heir to Miser Trasmere, unless that erratic gentleman should decide, as Rex put it, to leave all his riches to "the Dog's Home or the Cat's Crèche." Of course there is a detective, Carver by name, who possesses, "Tab" explains, the conventional detective "sixty-nine-inch brain."

> A sixty-nine-inch brain is the brain of a man who is chosen for the subtle business of criminal investigation, not because he is clever or shrewd or has a knowledge of the world, but because he stands 69 inches in his stockings and has a chest expansion of 38. Napoleon and Caesar, to mention only two bright lads, could never have got into the police force.

And then there is Ursula Ardfern, an actress, beautiful, clever and popular, yet with a trait unique among members of her profession—a distaste for publicity. All have their parts to play in the murder in the subterranean vault.

But *The Clue of the New Pin*? That is Mr. Wallace's task to tell, and the reader will find him well equipped for the work. Mystery story thrills are, after all, much of a muchness, but *The Clue of the New Pin* has the advantage of being told by an author who possesses a flair for satire and a certain amount of dry humor.

The New York Times Book Review (essay date 1925)

SOURCE: "The Head Hunter," in *The New York Times Book Review*, July 19, 1925, p. 13.

[*In the following review, the critic finds Wallace's* The Hairy Arm *to be an entertaining suspense novel.*]

In *The Hairy Arm,* Edgar Wallace, one of England's most prolific writers of mystery stories, has added another to his already long list of thrillers. Edgar Allan Poe's most famous murder tale undoubtedly supplied the germ idea of the book, but the story has its own ingenious complications. The dénouement is totally unexpected when it does come, though all the while the master clue was as prominently displayed as is the warning semaphore arm over a railroad track.

The Hairy Arm deals with murders committed by a sort of Jack the Ripper, who has peculiarities all his own. He neatly slices off his victim's head, packs it in a cardboard box, sends a typewritten message to the police, signing it "The Head Hunter," and tells where the grewsome parcel is to be found.

In twelve years the Head Hunter has decapitated seven men. In each case the murdered man has been a fugitive from justice. In a sense, therefore, the killer might be considered a social benefactor, since he rids the world of some of its undesirables. His latest victim is Francis Elmer, a middle-aged clerk who was about to be arrested for embezzlement.

Captain Michael Brixan, free-lance detective, in the employ of the British Government and of Scotland Yard, is the man chosen to clear up the murder. Brixan discovers that Elmer had a niece, Adele Leamington. Thinking the girl may have valuable information about her late uncle, Brixan goes down to Chichester, where she is working as an "extra" in a moving picture company. Her employer, Jack Knebworth, is an American producer engaged in filming a picture.

In books, the unknown actress invariably leaps into fame at a moment's notice. So, too, Adele, given her chance to replace the temperamental "star," Stella Mendoza, instantly proves that Mary Pickford's laurels are in danger. Of course, Michael falls in love with Adele and their romance furnishes the heart interest of the book. A foil to this perfect couple are Stella Mendoza and Sir Geoffrey Penne of Griff Towers.

Sir Geoffrey, who has passed much of his life in Borneo, has a passion for Eastern customs and things. He is a thick-set, sinister person, with a skin which the sun of Borneo and an unrestricted appetite have dyed a color between purple and brown. His face is crossed with innumerable ridges, while his small, pale eyes look out at the world through two narrow slits. No wonder Adele repulses his

amorous advances, even though her captiousness gets her into all manner of trouble.

Sir Geoffrey is the owner of an enormous orang-outang, with huge hairy chest and arms as thick as an average man's thigh. Bhag has been trained to do his master's bidding, even to the carrying off of lovely maidens who happen to strike his fancy. Another of the eccentric baronet's hobbies is collecting swords. Hundreds of them hang in his armory—poignards, scimitars, ancient swords of Japan, basket-hilted hangers, two-handled swords that once have felt the grip of long-dead Crusaders. But his choicest possessions are two great Sumatran swords, so sharp that they can split a hair in half or cut a man in two so swiftly that he would never know what had happened.

In pleasant contrast to Sir Geoffrey Penne is Sampson Longvale of Dower House. This benevolent old gentleman indulges in the harmless idiosyncracy of wearing clothes of a past period. Sampson Longvale's personal peculiarities, though apparently extraneous to the story, have the deepest bearing on the mystery of "The Hairy Arm." He is the owner of Dower House, the dilapidated old mansion which, with Griff Towers, Knebworth has rented as settings for some of his outdoor scenes.

In the midst of all sorts of turmoil and tangles comes another murder. This time the Head Hunter has decapitated Lawley Foss, Knebworth's rascally scenario writer, who has just been discharged because of financial irregularities. By this time the clues have narrowed down to one particular person and the reader feels sure that the murderer is about to be cornered. But, not at all. It is only when Michael Brixan, whose suspicions have never included the apparent murderer, accidentally stumbles upon the lair of the Head Hunter, that the secret is disclosed.

The Hairy Arm, because of its author's virile, vigorous style makes most entertaining reading. It goes along at a

---

Wallace's finances:

[Wallace's] views on finance were unorthodox and unsuccessful. His idea of a balance sheet was a list of his debts set against probable future earnings. His economics were no match for his generosity. The books were written; the books were sold; the money rolled in—and out: spent on the maisonette in London's fashionable Portland Place; on the country house on the Thames at Bourne End; on winter holidays in Switzerland; on his family—Bryan, Pat and Michael from his first marriage and myself from the second; on his friends—weekends at Chalklands, Christmas at Caux in Switzerland; on the needy and often on the not-so-needy. Mean-minded people refer to his "reckless extravagance" but those who knew him remember how little was spent on himself. And surely there are many who would be just as generous if they had the necessary income.

*Penelope Wallace, in "A Man and His Books," * The Mystery and Detection Annual, *1972.*

smart pace from the first page; but the last quarter of the book carries the reader along at terrific speed until he comes upon the unexpected and unique climax.

The New York Times Book Review (essay date 1926)

SOURCE: "London Dope Runners," in *The New York Times Book Review,* January 24, 1926, p. 9.

[In the following review, the critic notes Wallace's skill as a craftsman of the suspense novel.]

One of the most remarkable aspects of the writers of the modern American popular fiction is their amazing fruitfulness. These facile craftsmen turn out countless novels year after year without ever seeming to run dry. For a month or two their books are displayed on the shelves and in the windows of the Booksellers and then are seen no more. In theme these pleasant ephemers of the fiction world cover a wide variety of subjects. They include tales of the sea, the Far West, murder mysteries, divorce and society scandal. And each of these, it would seem, has its own coterie of readers, for the books sell and make money for the author and publisher alike.

Edgar Wallace's latest opus, **The Sinister Man,** is of this stamp. This prolific writer's seventeenth novel does not differ appreciably from his first either in contents or in form. It is an interesting story about dope smuggling in England and is done in the usual style of such tales. In so far as technique and style are concerned **The Sinister Man** is the work of an exceedingly competent craftsman. Mr. Wallace's novel is unmarred by bad phrasing, obvious heroics or objectionable platitudes. It will, in all likelihood, prove a temporary diversion for the average reader of modern-day fiction.

The background of the novel is laid in modern-day London. Scotland Yard has been exerting all its cunning in an endeavor to run to earth the principals of two powerful opium gangs which are flooding the city with illicit drugs. These are engaged in a death struggle between themselves for the supremacy of the dope-smuggling field in Great Britain. Every effort has been made by the detectives to break up this sordid trade and to apprehend the ringleaders. None of these attempts, however, has been successful. The detectives have at last resigned themselves to passive watchfulness and the shadowing of the several persons suspected of having connections with either of the nefarious organizations.

The man most suspected by the opium squad is a certain Major Amery, President of a well-known firm of importers. Rumor has it that this sinister figure is the mythical Soyoka, the head of the larger and more powerful of the two gangs. Lean, dark, grim, forbidding, this character is the hub around which the interest and action of the story revolve. Ostensibly the villain of the piece, Major Amery is in the end neatly turned by the author from the role of potential villain to that of the avenging hero. Mr. Wallace shows himself a very capable craftsman in this transformation. The change is made cleverly and without any obvious break.

There is a girl in the story, of course. Elsa Marlowe is rather a conventional type. Her role as Major Amery's secretary consists largely of a series of inward rebellings against that ruthless person's impersonal and somewhat tyrannical manner of ordering her about, and although she tells herself vehemently that she hates Major Amery Elsa really loves him. When his enemies plant contraband narcotics in his office and inform the police of their presence the girl rises nobly to the occasion and saves her employer from arrest, though she is not at all certain of his innocence. And after all the shooting is over, Soyoka killed, and the dope-smuggling gangs dispersed the cold and indifferent Major suddenly becomes aware that he—but surely you can guess the rest.

A far more interesting character is that of Soyoka. The author presents this conscienceless murderer as Mr. Tupperwill, President of a private bank in London. Mr. Tupperwill is comfortably stout, extremely regular in his personal habits, and quite mild and inoffensive in manner. Unfortunately, this character is not developed along with the story, and his introduction at the end as the infamous Soyoka is far too abrupt to be convincing.

Louis J. McQuilland (essay date 1926)

SOURCE: "The Bookman Gallery: Edgar Wallace," in *The Bookman,* London, Vol. LXIX, No. 414, March, 1926, pp. 301-04.

[In the following essay, McQuilland discusses Wallace's writing process and gives an overall assessment of his books.]

Big sales in novels are viewed with contempt by many writers and readers outside the range of the lucky publisher and the almost equally lucky author and his personal friends. So far has this contempt progressed that it is now generally assumed that because a novel sells in considerable quantities, it must be a piece of bad art. I recently heard a clever woman, herself a novelist of capacity, declare that *The Constant Nymph,* because of its general popularity, placed Miss Margaret Kennedy amongst the Philistines of fiction.

Of course this is complete nonsense. Dickens and Thackeray had, and still have, enormous sales. Joseph Conrad in his later years was a best-seller. There are quite a number of good novelists to-day who sell three to five editions.

I am sure my friend Mr. Edgar Wallace would disclaim any pretence of being an æsthete, and would say frankly that he wrote for all and sundry, without any literary pretensions; but he is a case of the really good story-teller who appeals to hundreds of thousands of readers, not because he is inferior, or vulgar, or cheap, but simply because he has that quality of invention which carries one from page to page and from chapter to chapter without any thought as to the passage of the night hours.

Mr. Wallace is a great serial writer, and practically all his serials appear later as novels. When he is well at work he turns out 5,000 words a day, and he has written the stuff of an entire novel in a week. He has been keeping this up for many years without the least trace of failing invention.

Each novel that he writes has strong vitality; and he has never any need to indulge in padding. He speaks his stories into the dictaphone. His secretary sets the first draft down on paper, and then Mr. Wallace revises the typescript very completely.

One of his main lines (as they say of a railway system) is the mystery story—the crime and crook and detective story.

Two of these have just appeared. *The Three Just Men* and *The Door with Seven Locks.* When, a number of years back, Mr. Wallace wrote *The Four Just Men,* he accomplished the best "shocker" since Fergus Hume's *The Mystery of a Hansom Cab,* Hugh Conway's *Called Back* and Mr. E. C. Bentley's *Trent's Last Case.* The sequel is just as full of thrills. George Manfred, Leon Gonsalez and their colleague Poiccart, rich men who take the law into their hands when the law is powerless, are an amazing trio, with an amazing task before them. All over London people are dropping dead, the cause of death being certified as snake-bite. But there are no snakes in evidence. When the Three Men take up the disappearance of Mirabelle Leicester, and come face to face with Dr. Eruc Obserzohn, an evil old man with evil agents, they get on the first trail of the serpent.

The Door With Seven Locks concerns a tomb, built like a treasure-house which can only be opened by the simultaneous use of seven keys which are in widely disparate hands. Mr. Wallace's hero is Dick Martin, a young man of means, who has joined Scotland Yard because he has a turn for criminology. As the book opens he is about to retire, but is furnished with a private case, concerning the missing Lord Selford. Havelock the lawyer, who gives Martin his instructions, is distrusted by Martin from the start. Through an accident and a pretty girl Martin happens on Dr. Stalletti, another agent of conspiracy. The story is singularly ingenious and, like all Mr. Wallace's work, has humour in addition to drama. He has the faculty of keeping his reader on the stretch from his opening sentence.

It will be of interest to recall the beginnings of this famous sensational writer. He had very little education and entered the Army before the Boer War as a private soldier. He had always a feeling for the use of words, and he had written verse as a schoolboy. As a Tommy he issued a book of poems, *Writ in Barracks.* He was then in Simonstown, South Africa. There was something promising in the little book, and it got a fair press—with one exception. Mr. Jerome K. Jerome wrote a column of ridicule which made Wallace feel entirely foolish and humiliated. He feels that humiliation to the present day, which should be a warning to critics not to hit young authors too hard.

"I could just read and write when I went into the Army," he said to me. "Every book of my own has been an education. The advice I would give all neophytes is to write verse and keep on writing verse (I say this in spite of my own mortification). Secondly, I would recommend a close study of the Book of Job, which as pure literature is to me the finest thing in the Bible. I am immensely taken with its simplicity. It abounds in one- and two-syllable words

expressing the most poignant thought—straight, stark English written in old English words.

"I encountered a simplicity without any literary value in the vocabulary of the African natives. The Swahili and the Mobongo have a limitation of words. Getting on to lying—which is a form of literature—the native has no subtlety. He will say to you, 'I lied to you because it was difficult to tell the truth,' and you wouldn't have believed it."

Of course everyone knows—or ought to know—that Mr. Wallace's African stories dealing with Sanders, Bones, Bosambo, the lying chief, and other choice characters, are entirely different from his crime stories. They have infinite humour, and display a surprising knowledge of native life. Mr. Wallace has just written his tenth book in that vein, called *Sanders,* and has also undertaken a Sanders play. Mr. Wallace has had as much success with these novels as with the others, though they are in an entirely different genre. His knowledge of Africa is obtained at first hand, as he has been through the Dark Continent twice.

Of late years Wallace is giving freer play to his sense of fun. His series of stories about "Educated Evans," a little racing tipster, are extremely diverting. Wallace knows all about the turf. He has a zest for racing, and is the possessor of one of those precious animals which are as delicate as fine ladies—and as a rule much more costly. He admits a moderate passion for gambling, and has certainly done very rash things at Monte Carlo, but he says he is learning some sense with regard to the tables there. He has made very good use of his experiences as sportsman and a gambler, in local colour for his books, which represents compensation for any bad days on the Turf or at the Casino. Two of his racing stories are *The Flying Fifty-Fifty* and *Down Under Donovan.*

Mr. Wallace believes a writer should be equipped for life from all possible points, and he holds that the most thorough way of doing this is in being a journalist. In fact he is much prouder of the title of journalist than novelist. He says he owes his whole success as a writer to Mr. Thomas Marlowe, who gave him his first start on the *Daily Mail* and thereafter appointed him War Correspondent and Special Correspondent all over the world. His first important work was in connection with the South African War. He finished the war for the *Mail.* He knows the United States and Europe better than most men know their native county. Morocco was a happy hunting ground for him as regards future fiction. He prophesied the big trouble with the Riffs twenty years back.

Wallace is a man with an extraordinary news-sense. He can go into Bukarest or Madrid, two very difficult towns for the stranger, as they are both anti-social, and can get in a single night, at an hotel or café, the whole social and political situation without having to speak a word. That is a special gift, which has much more to do with instinct than with intellect.

In the United States he has travelled right through from the Atlantic to the Pacific. He made the courageous admission: "I love the States; I love the people. You cannot meet real Americans in New York or Southampton, however. You have to get them where they live outside the range of their Smart Set and their tourists. England stands higher than ever she did in the esteem of the good American who stays at home."

Edgar Wallace is popular with the big American public through his stories in the *Saturday Evening Post,* the *Chicago News* and the *Cosmopolitan.* His novels, too, are beginning to boom there.

As a writer Wallace's output on a hard working day is 10,000 words. In writing up a short history of the war, which had to be turned out at top speed, he managed to do 36,000 words between 9 a.m. and midnight. The customary thing to say of such an output is "it looks just like that"—but it doesn't. Edgar Wallace is, as he himself so often declares, first and foremost a journalist, and the first-class journalist can and does, under emergency, write good English at top speed. Wallace's secretary-typist, Mr. R. G. Curtis, holds a world's record. He can type at high speed and carry on a conversation at the same time; but seldom indulges in that dual trick. This explains why Mr. Wallace turned out a novel of 75,000 words (which sold 20,000 copies) between a Thursday and a Monday afternoon.

"I am proud of my big output," said Wallace, "and I write hot-foot. High class novelists make up their serials from day to day, and they seem to lose interest in them. As a rule when these are turned into books they have lost even literary value. The only way to write a story is to believe in it tremendously at any rate when you are engaged on it. I think every new story I do is my best, and go ahead with it, and furthermore I write serials as books. In doing so I endeavour to preserve unity and proportion. If I find a character getting too prominent, I cut him down. I should not describe myself as a novelist. I am a tale-teller, one of the old confraternity that roamed the roads of early England or sauntered in the streets of ancient Bagdad. After all, the story is the thing. It will endure after all experimental forms of fiction have been tried, and most of them found wanting."

How does Mr. Wallace get his infinitely varied plots? He dreams them! And he governs these dreams! They do not come in real sleep, but when he is sitting before his writing-table for hours. First of all he thinks what a man would, or could do, if he fell into a fortune of a million pounds, or he had a palace into which he wanted to admit only the people he cared for; or if he were an innocent man pursued by the law on the strongest possible charge of murder. The second dream subject resulted in *The Door with Seven Locks.*

The genesis of *The Three Just Men* was the image of a gentleman coming into the vestibule of an hotel and suddenly dropping dead. It occurred to the waking-dreamer that he could be killed in a certain mysterious way—and he kept that way for the *dénouement* of his book. Then he had another day-dream about a mountain of gold, and that supplied a further hint.

For *The Clue of the New Pin* he imagined a steel room in which there was only a door and a number of little air-holes above it. That door could only be locked from the

outside. He pictured a man dead at a table with a knife in him. The door was locked. Beside the head of the dead man was the key. How did the key get there? Wallace thought of a murderer who fixed a pin to the table and attached to it a thread to come out through an air hole. To that thread was attached the key with which the assassin had locked the door. With a jerk from the thread he could switch back the key on to the table, and with another jerk dislodge the pin. The pin on the floor, which might have escaped even close attention, was the only clue. It sounds very simple, but that is only because it is explained.

The idea of *The Green Archer*—his thoughts of course are not all dream ones—came to Edgar Wallace when he was waiting in the Savoy Grill Room for a host who was inconsiderately late. He sent out a boy for an early edition of an evening paper, and read therein of a murderous shooting affray. "Why always revolvers?" he pondered. "Why not have a shot back at times when gunpowder was not in use, and apply that method to modern crime?" The result was the thrilling story of the stern figure who disposed of disagreeable people, like the sparrow of nursery fame, "with his bow-and-arrow."

In *The Black Avons* Mr. Wallace sketched out four periods of English history—Tudor, Cavalier-and-Roundhead, the period between 1800 and 1860, and again from 1912 to the present time, and let the same family appear through them. The result has been a volume which is being used in schools as a textbook for the young. They will feel no dullness, those young people, in their study of the historic past of their country.

I have written that a forthcoming story of Wallace's is one of the famous River series, called *Sanders.* This is the first time that this leading figure had had his name on the title page. He is going to follow this by a big mystery story— the best he has ever done. I have hinted that Wallace believes this of all his books. It is, like most of his novels, to be a mystery story with a current of humour through it. He is of opinion that the man who writes a mystery story without the light relief of fun is a bore.

Mr. Frank Curzon is going to produce a drama of Wallace's, *The Ringer.* The suggestion of the title is a man who rings the changes. *Double Dan* was originally a play. Wallace has extraordinary dexterity as editor and sub-editor of his own work. He turned the play into a book, and now he is turning it into a play again. He can take three of his stories and make them into one consecutive whole. On a previous occasion when I talked to Wallace about the theatre, he had great hopes of *My Lady* as a play. I asked him why he thought it had not made good. "I will make a curious confession," he said gravely; "it did not make good because it was one of the worst ever."

Edgar Wallace's books are read by all and sundry. At least two people have made a complete collection of them. One is Lord St. Davids, and the other a butcher in Smithfield Market. Wallace holds that one book sells another. The old theory was that the market could only absorb two books a year from any writer. Last year he had seven books issued, and he therefore holds that the market will absorb anything that it fancies. The interest is in the story, not the author. A famous author will attract his following, but he must not alone give it what it expects, he must advance with the changes of time.

Mr. Wallace has his own ideas about style. He believes in what he calls "colour-words," and says they should be used sparingly. For him "morbid" is a colour-word, and he would only use it once in the course of the same story. He thinks Michael Arlen is a spendthrift in the use of colour-words, and remarks curiously that Arlen owes a good deal of his manner to Laurence Sterne and a lot of his atmosphere to "The Arabian Nights."

The New York Times Book Review (essay date 1927)

SOURCE: "A Girl Detective," in *The New York Times Book Review*, June 19, 1927, p. 24.

[*In the following essay, the critic gives a favorable review of Wallace's* The Girl from Scotland Yard, *but faults Wallace for using "questionable" plot devices.*]

A past master of the mystery novel, with some thirty-odd volumes to his credit, has assembled in his latest thriller [*A Girl Detective*] a collection of characters precisely like those of many another yarn except for the fact that they are practically all women. Leslie Maughan the sleuth who solves the riddle, is the only girl detective at Scotland Yard. The villain—a very evil and sinister villain—is also a woman—the Princess Anita Bellini. And, finally, Druze, the murdered butler, is revealed to be a woman in disguise.

It is quite possible that Mr. Wallace has sprinkled the fair sex so liberally through his pages in order to win over a host of feminine readers to his clientele. Whatever his intention, he has turned out a puzzle that should baffle even the most skilled of those who pride themselves upon being able to guess the guilty party in the first chapter or two. All the elements of a dozen mystery tales are here, thrown together into a veritable Gordian knot, the solution of which must be reached by blind cutting rather than careful untangling. Further confusion is added by the somewhat questionable device of imparting to the characters at frequent intervals information which is withheld from the reader, who is left to blunder along after Miss Maughan and her assistants as best he may.

The deluge of personages is no less remarkable than the flood of events that follow one another before Anita is safe in jail and Leslie and Dawlish in each other's arms. Druze, the lady butler, is shot; Peter Dawlish is half strangled in an alley, and the girl detective is spirited off to the Bellini house and is about to be tortured when the bobbies arrive. After the excitement has subsided, Leslie holds an "at home" and tells her bewildered entourage just how she achieved her results.

Desmond MacCarthy (essay date 1930)

SOURCE: "Very Much *On the Spot*" in *New Statesman*, Vol. XXXV, No. 890, May 17, 1930, pp. 180-82.

[*MacCarthy was one of the foremost English literary and drama critics of the twentieth century. He served for many years on the staff of the* New Statesman *and edited* Life and Letters. *A member of the Bloomsbury group, which also included Leonard and Virginia Woolf, John Maynard Keynes, E. M. Forster, and Lytton Strachey among its number, MacCarthy was guided by their primary tenet that "one's prime objects in life were love, the creation and enjoyment of aesthetic experience, and the pursuit of knowledge." MacCarthy brought to his work a wide range of reading, serious and sensitive judgement, an interest in the works of new writers, and high critical standards. In the following excerpt, he praises Wallace's play* On the Spot.]

With a little more industry Mr. Edgar Wallace might provide all the light reading the inhabitants of this island require. He already provides a considerable part of it. Nor do I see why he should not also write most of the plays. I am sure they would be different from each other. **On the Spot,** for instance, is by no means in the key of **The Ringer.** Indeed, I can imagine many of his devoted readers being not a little taken aback by it. It is thrilling but decidedly grim. There are three murders and a suicide in it, and a fine tension of suspense sustains the plot. It is exciting, sensational, surprising, and it is also a serious study of contemporary though fortunately distant aspects of modern life—life in the Chicago gangland. "If," says Mr. Wallace on the programme, "a play were a proper and suitable vehicle for such a complimentary gesture, I would dedicate this drama to my good friends William Russell, Chief Commissioner, and John Stege, Deputy Commissioner of the Chicago Police Department, who daily and hourly are dealing effectively with situations more incredible and fantastical than any I have depicted in **On the Spot.**" Well, in a sense, Mr. Wallace has made that gesture, and it proves that he has not been interested in his subject as copy for a " 'tec versus crook" play, but interested in it in a thorough and high-brow manner. A "high-brow" is essentially one who respects his subject. Mr. Wallace's interest in racing, for instance, is so intensely high-brow that only "racing high-brows" can read him, just as no ordinary reader of poetry can read Robert Bridges on prosody. It is not the theme but the treatment which marks the high-brow author. As a high-brow dramatic critic I recognise in Mr. Wallace a high-brow dramatist. His dialogue is excellent, and in spite of having splendid opportunities of engaging the sympathy of his audiences for his cool, unscrupulous crooks, he shows up the paragon of audacity among them, who in the first act has fascinated half the women in the audience, as, after all, a dirty "bit of yellow mud," bottomless in his treachery and squalidly infantile in his megalomania. But the "world" he has to exhibit is so fantastic that the public greedily swallows his high-browism. Mr. Wallace does not gloss over the fact that his master boot-legger, who does "not want any tr-rouble" and to placate a rival is ready to place any of his comrades "on the spot" (this means sending them to a place where they can be conveniently shot), is also a brothel keeper and white-slave dealer on a huge scale, and in the habit of sending off his discarded mistresses, however devoted, to serve in those lust-shops—and all for money. In fact, Tony Perelli is not romanticised at all; and he is such an amazing figure that if we had not heard of Al Capone he would be incredible.

Tony flourishes throughout like a forest of green bay-trees—till the end, by which time the audience has seen through his sordidly emotional nature and can enjoy watching Tony grovel in handcuffs, destined to "The Chair" at last for a murder of which, for once, he is innocent.

The curtain goes up on a short death-scene: a crook of the O'Hara gang has been "bumped off " by two of the Perelli gang. We are at his bedside; he refuses to say who did it, which is characteristic of modern brigands. When all is up they remember that, although they murder each other freely and with every circumstance of treachery, society is their common enemy. When, in February last year, seven "big shots" of the Bugs Moran gang were "bumped off " with machine guns, probably by orders of "Scarface" Capone, one of the victims, Frank Gunstenberg, was found still breathing. "They never gave you a chance, Frank. Who shot you?" asked the sergeant. True to the gangland code he whispered, "Nobody," and died. I mention this to show how closely Mr. Wallace follows facts. We find ourselves in a huge fantastic room, decorated with Byzantine extravagance. Every foot of wall-space not covered with gilded carvings is plastered with luscious frescoes. On one side stands a golden organ; on the other a statuette of the Virgin, and the back of the room opens on a great balcony beyond which the many-windowed towers of Chicago rise into the warm, pale-blue sky. On a corner of a long antique table is spread a delicate breakfast. There is also something about the room which a later reference to it as "an ecclesiastical bawdy house" describes. The view from the balcony of the clustered skyscrapers reminds one vaguely of the fortified silhouette of San Gimignano, where, too, once the hand of every man was against his neighbour and the ruffian ruled the roost while he lived—which was not long. Indeed, though we are in a world of automatic pistols, dope, police and telephones, the moral atmosphere is not at all unlike the Italian Renaissance (only there is no taste, no art), when as an alternative to the anarchy of ruthless individualism the suggestions of Machiavelli appeared statesmanlike and moderate to those who longed for order. Seated at the organ, a large, plump, exuberant man, obviously of Italian origin, is seen revelling in the lush melodies of Gounod, while in the foreground a Chinese woman dressed in imperial yellow, her arms glittering with modern bracelets, is quietly embroidering a dragon on a tambourine. This is the apartment, on Michigan Avenue, of Tony Perelli, or of Al Capone if you like, who makes about two million dollars a year by providing the city with drink and brothels, of which he has to spend about a million in bribing police, law officers and municipal electors. Still, that leaves a nice margin, and he "wants no tr-rouble." When it arises, he deals with it promptly. He has the self-confidence of a baron-brigand and the vulgarity of a modern swindler. The Chinese woman, Minn Lee, has been his chief mistress for some years. Trouble is going to arise out of that little matter of "bumping off " the fellow whom we saw upon his death-bed, not from the police but from that man's gang. He happens also to have been a lover of the sister of its leader, an unfortunate woman who, as her brother touchingly remarks when he interviews Tony on the subject, apparently had "sex attraction" only for the dead man. It made the case a hard one. Now, apart from "hi-jacking" each other's liquor supplies, that is to say, intercepting them or robbing stores—which, of course, is a shooting matter—the Chicago gangs seem to get on comfortably together by dividing the city into "spheres of influence." Sometimes an ambitious leader will, of course, poach on another's preserves; then there may be, if not a street battle, a good deal of wholesale murdering. (The Bugs Moran gang were guilty of aggression of this kind.) O'Hara demands satisfaction for the shooting, and Tony consents to put the two men who did it "on the spot." One of these is an imported "big shot" from New York; the other a youth expelled from a University for theft to whom this murder was not quite the trifle it should have been. This youth adores Minn Lee, and she, though she has no passion for anyone but Tony, is touched by him. She overhears enough of Tony's talk with O'Hara to guess what is in the wind, in spite of the former's declaration that the youth is dearer to him than a brother. All this happens during the first act, which is first-rate and without blemish. The curtain descends upon Tony standing, hushed into sudden reverence, beside a magnificent floral tribute to the murdered man.

This tableau leaves us in a state of thrilling suspense. Will Minn Lee save the unfortunate youth? Will the detective who has called round informally to convey to Tony that he knows all about the murder, but can't bring the charge home yet, succeed in involving the Perelli gang?

The second act contains a surprise for us. It is the night of Tony's party. Minn Lee has given herself to the uneasy, conscience-stricken youth, but she has not saved him from his fate. She thought he would be happier dead, and although we soon see the point of her strange ecstasy at the moment when she knows he will be "on the spot," we do not catch its significance at the moment. Here, then, there is a slight weakness in Mr. Wallace's stage-craft. The New York "big-shot" was too old a hand to be taken in even by Tony's perfect lying, and he has avoided the rendezvous with the murderers of the rival gang, but he will return for his girl who is spending the night in Tony's arms. Perelli knows that a dangerous man is now loose. He instantly dispatches his machine-gunners to pick him off, but the victim gets past them, and is neatly shot by Tony and popped into a specially constructed ottoman which is wheeled out as expeditiously as an ambulance slipper. The body is deposited far from the scene. This second act is again admirable, though not quite up to the first. In the last, Minn Lee—finding that the detective's warnings are coming true, namely, that Tony will ask her to give him her jewels to reset (the detective has seen them on other women of Tony's) and then pack her off to a brothel—quietly cuts her own throat while Tony is playing the organ. At the sight of her blood he loses his nerve. While the wet knife actually is in his hand, the detective—who has guessed the nature of the bargain struck between Perelli and O'Hara, and therefore the cause of the two last murders—suddenly comes in. Perelli swears Minn Lee killed herself, and points to the note which she scribbled before she died. The detective sees his chance. He slips on the handcuffs and burns the paper. At last he has got the murderer of twenty men; for, as he remarked previously,

"Our juries may be yellow but, thank God, they're sentimental." Cowards though they are and corrupt, they will not acquit a man who has killed a woman.

Golly, what a world!

What impresses one about it is not the graft, its utter contempt for law, or the bloodshed, but the almost childlike cynicism and the *good-natured* ruthlessness of it, the business-like air of its atrocities, the innocently casual brutality of its love affairs, the heartiness which covers depths of treachery, and the extraordinary amoral light-mindedness—moral idiocy really—and love of excitement which infects even the relations of the Detective Commission himself with the gangsters. Everything, however horrible, is only part of a boy's game. *On the Spot* is certainly a remarkable study of a real enough state of things. But the last act is thin compared with the others—too much talk; though the easy, comforting cynicism with which Angelo, Perelli's lieutenant, lies to Maria about the fate of her ex-lover the New Yorker, and the blandishments with which Tony prepares Minn Lee for her fate, are worth listening to.

H. Douglas Thomson   (essay date 1931)

SOURCE: "The Thriller," in his *Masters of Mystery: A Study of the Detective Story,* W. Collins & Co. Ltd., 1931, pp. 212-37.

[*In the following excerpt, Thomson analyzes the themes and patterns that recur in Wallace's novels.*]

To many people detective fiction is nowadays synonymous with the novels of Mr. Edgar Wallace. Born in 1875, Mr. Wallace has had a varied career. He has served as a private soldier, been a miner, war correspondent, journalist on the staff of at least two London daily papers, and has experimented in numerous other occupations. Then three or four years ago his detective stories suddenly became popular; now he is one of the world's celebrities. If my memory does not play me false, it was only a few years ago that he was enlivening the columns of the less dignified Sunday papers with the adventures of an *Aberdeen Annie*: but he has put on his three-league boots since then. His international popularity is probably greatest in America and then Germany. He edits a German magazine of detective stories, and the enterprising bookseller of even the small German provincial town dresses his windows with an attractive display of *Romanen von Edgar Wallace.* Germans will smile at you when you inform them that of their contemporary writers you read only Ludwig, Feuchtwanger and Remarque. But you cannot afford to smile in return when they tell you they read Shaw, Galsworthy, and Edgar Wallace.

Mr. Wallace's output is the wonder of our age. Over two years ago, the *Daily Mail* published the following statistics of "returns":

140 novels (though he might have forgotten ten or a dozen).

Half a dozen plays (at least).

Two hundred (or it might be four hundred) short stories.

About 9,000,000 words.

Recent figures are not to hand, but although there has been a slight falling off in output, the figures quoted have been very considerably increased. This mass production means an uncanny precipitancy in execution, and no doubt Mr. Wallace's experience on the staff of the *Daily News* (1900) and the *Daily Mail* (1901-02) stood him in good stead. Mr. Wallace gives the following as his record speed:

A firm of publishers asked me on a Thursday for a novel of 70,000 words by noon on Monday. Working seventeen hours a day, dictating it all to a typist, with my wife doing the corrections, I delivered **The Strange Countess** on Monday morning.

One remembers, too, "The Midday Wallace" joke in *Punch,* and Mr. Wallace's favourite excerpt from the *Wabash Monitor:*

Edgar Wallace, world's most prolific writer, was called on the long-distance at the Marquery Hotel, Park Avenue, "Sorry," said his secretary. "Mr. Wallace has just started a new novel." "Great!" said the voice from Cincinnati, O. "I'll hold the wire till he's through."

Let us take a peep into the Wallace *phrontisterion.* We must be careful not to enter in the D. B. Wyndham Lewis spirit, or we may rouse Mr. Wallace to biting sarcasm. The Wallace Collection is run on strictly business lines. Which is a pity, for the very introduction of the business element is tantamount to a sacrifice of quality. But Mr. Wallace prefers quantity to quality, and the critic *will* have him follow in the steps of Dumas. "The Wallace library is extensive, especially on crime subjects." Yes, decidedly that is a selling-point. Apparently, if Mr. Wallace cannot lay his fingers on certain details, reference works in public libraries needs must be consulted. Better still! A dictaphone stands in the corner. Of course it may not actually occupy that position: but there *is* a dictaphone, and in detective stories the corner is always the position allocated. It is rumoured that there are innumerable files with cross references and subsections which play a not inconspicuous part in the great fight against time. Mr. Wallace has a stenographer: now and then he calls him a typist, but he will probably hear about that. This stenographer is one of the champions of Great Britain—and he would need to be. In and out and round about the sanctum creep strange men. "It is no new experience for me," Mrs. Wallace has admitted, "to come face to face with a criminal on the staircase. Down-and-outs, hoboes, people-with-stories-to-tell, and others keep calling on Edgar, and the result of their visits is sometimes manifest in articles, sometimes books, and occasionally in plays." Does it not seem *infra dig.* that criminals who can always turn a dishonest penny should have preferred this labour exchange?

Mrs. Wallace is the lady with the blue pencil. She sins on the side of the angels. Work for the day usually begins at seven in the morning: during the rush season at four or even at midnight. It is alleged that all Mr. Wallace's plots are thought out before the dictaphone is used: and that he does not write on the spur of the moment.

Mr. Wallace's work is curiously varied, both in theme and in style. He is a most unequal writer. "When he is good, he is very very good, but when he is bad he is horrid." On the credit side he has these virtues:

(1) His narrative is straightforward, and there is no padding, and no nonsense.

(2) He is genuinely exciting, and relies on no artifices for his creation of atmosphere. He follows the old saw, *Ars est celare artem.*

(3) His humour is never strained. "The Sparrow" and "J. G. Reeder" are inimitable characters, naturally humorous.

(4) He has an inside knowledge of Scotland Yard and police methods.

(5) He is familiar with the lingo of crooks.

On the other hand:

(1) He is too fond of "the most-unlikely-person" theme.

(2) Impossibilities and improbabilities occur too frequently.

(3) He is by no means word-perfect. He calls a napkin a serviette, and is guilty of a phrase like "she shrugged milky shoulders." His grammar, also, is not unimpeachable.

(4) His sensationalism is often extremely crude, and not in perfect taste.

Mr. Arnold Bennett finds one very grave defect in Edgar Wallace:

> He is content with society as it is. He parades no subversive opinions. He is "correct." Now, it is very well known that all novelists who have depicted contemporary society, and who have lived, abound in subversive opinions. Look at Defoe, Swift and Fielding. Feel their lash. Remember the whips and scorpions of Dickens, and the effort of even the Agag-footed Thackeray to destroy utterly the popular convention of the romantical hero. And Hardy's terrible rough-hewing of the divinity that shapes our ends. . . . It may be counted a maxim that good modern literature is never made out of correct sentiments. If there are exceptions to this rule they must be extremely few. . . . Perhaps I am unfair to Edgar Wallace. Perhaps in earlier years he has chastised society with intent to be immortal.

This criticism seems to be very wide of the mark. It is absurd to require the detective novelist to be a social reformer. Besides, Mr. Bennett starts from the assumption that society in Mr. Wallace's novels is his idea of actual Society! If Mr. Bennett does not make this assumption, one asks whether he can force us to attach any substantial meaning whatsoever to his objection. For if he does not, it would seem he finds fault with Mr. Wallace for not being in his writing a social reformer as well as a writer of detec-

tive stories—a conclusion which cannot cast any reflection, whether for good or ill, on his detective stories as such. As it is, the joyous absence of any subversive opinions might well be considered a merit instead of a defect.

For convenience' sake we might classify the Wallace novels in five main groups. Perhaps I should admit that, as I cannot claim to be a member of any Edgar Wallace Club, I have read only a fraction of the grand total.

(1) *The Four Just Men Series.* (**The Four Just Men, The Four Just Men of Cordova, The Law of the Four Just Men, The Three Just Men.**) In these stories murder is regularly committed from the highest motives. The Four Just Men form a Crusade to rid the world of its most noxious members. They are the champions of moral as opposed to legal justice. Thus the police, as the upholders of an inadequate system, become the villains. The Four Just Men began badly, for they put to sleep a "fairly harmless Secretary of State." Of course, it cannot be said they did not warn him, but the unfortunate politician had to think of the Press. The quartet improved fortunately with experience, and ran a highly successful Co-operative Murder Campaign. One notes the close affinity of this series to the Arsène Lupin stories.

(2) The Police novels, such as **The Crimson Circle, The Ringer, The Squeaker, The Terror,** etc. It is here that Mr. Wallace overdoes "the most unlikely person" theme, the detective finally emerging as the villain or *vice versa.* Gaston Leroux's *Le Mystère de la Chambre Jaune* is parent to this engaging family.

(3) Just thrillers, which need no further comment. **The Green Archer, The Avenger, The Black Abbot, The India Rubber Men, The Sinister Man, The Yellow Snake, Room 13, The Clue of the New Pin,** etc.

(4) The J. G. Reeder stories—**The Mind of J. G. Reeder, The Orator.**

(5) *The Sanders of the River stories—***Sanders of the River, Bosambo of the River, Bones, Lieutenant Bones, Bones in London,** etc. . . .

Mr. Wallace's detective dramas such as **The Ringer, The Terror,** and **The Flying Squad,** caught the public favour; and the West-End, thereupon, suffered from a spate of police plays. (**On the Spot** was more an amusing satire on Chicago than an honest detective play.) Then followed a tendency to substitute for sheer excitement social propaganda, as in Mr. Vosper's *People Like Us,* or humour, as in *Sorry You've Been Troubled!* . . .

The detective play may be either a thriller pure and simple like **The Flying Fool, The House of Danger,** etc., or it may make some pretence of containing a problem, in which latter case only one *motif* is virtually possible, that of the most unlikely person. Mr. Wallace again shows his preference for the latter, as in **The Ringer.**

Francis D. Grierson   (essay date 1932)

SOURCE: "Edgar Wallace: The Passing of a Great Personality," in *The Bookman,* London, Vol. LXXXI, No. 486, March, 1932, pp. 3101.

[*Grierson was an English-born author best known for his crime novels and nonfiction works on crime detection. In the following excerpt, he praises Wallace as a pioneer of the thriller genre and highlights the novelist's accurate depiction of the London underworld.*]

Edgar Wallace is dead.

The world has lost a great man.

For Wallace *was* great—not merely because he wrote some one hundred and fifty novels and thirty plays, and film scenarios, pen-pictures and newspaper articles by the score; but because of the indomitable spirit that made a little newsboy into one of the most amazing figures of his generation, and a very fine gentleman withal.

Fifty-six years ago Wallace came into the world, a workhouse child, and his first job was to sell newspapers in the Fleet Street in which he was to become a power.

He enlisted in the Army and went to South Africa, and it was there that he wrote a poem which made Kipling, then visiting Cape Town, advise him to beat his bayonet into a fountain-pen.

Wallace saved money and bought his discharge, and in the following years made his name as a brilliant war correspondent, descriptive writer and all-round journalist.

So much for his early days.

It is with his books that I am more concerned. He determined to make a reputation as a writer of fiction. Those people who do not realise the accuracy a modern newspaper demands from its reporters might hint that his early training singularly fitted him for such a sphere; they would be more right than they realised.

Wallace's "thrillers" were indeed thrilling, but they were not the fiction of guess-work. His knowledge of what is popularly called the "underworld" was astonishing. His criminals, his "narks" and his policemen were genuine types.

It is unfortunately true that when, after the War, his vogue became so great that even his rapid output could not exhaust the public demand, he sometimes allowed his stories to contain errors which annoyed his readers. It was a pity; but it was due to haste, not to ignorance of his subject.

His highest level of writing, perhaps—apart from the clever dialogue of some of his plays—was reached in his early African series, in which ***Sanders of the River*** impressed one as a particularly convincing character.

In the realm of criminology, his first effort—an immediate success—was ***The Four Just Men,*** put out in 1906, which placed him at once in the front ranks of authors of that genre.

It is amusing to remember that not so many years ago an educated man blushed to be found reading a "thriller." To-day the scientist, the philosopher, the politician, as well as the Man in the Street, applies to the crime of which he reads in his newspaper the methods of his favourite character in detective fiction. With that revolution Wallace had much to do.

He possessed an exceptionally rapid mind. To those who knew him, the suggestion that he employed a "ghost" was as absurd as it was unjust. A man who could turn out an eighty thousand word serial in three days needed no such aid.

Wallace was a great soul. He lived quickly and he died quickly. Let us be glad at least that death came to him at the height of his success, before the inevitable hour when every man must say to himself: "My day is over."

E. C. Bentley   (essay date 1932)

SOURCE: "Edgar Wallace: The Great Storyteller," in *The English Review,* Vol. LIV, March, 1932, pp. 3114.

[*Bentley was an English-born journalist and author best known for his detective novel* Trent's Last Case *(1913). In the following essay, Bentley praises Wallace's storytelling techniques, rendering of dialect, and knowledge of the British working classes.*]

When Edgar Wallace died last month, it was not only the obituary-men and the social diarists who told and annotated the story of his amazing life. The leader-writers, from the *Times* downwards, swelled the chorus. The chorus of what? Hardly of pure admiration for his literary talent—though that, and nothing else, had made his name. Very few of the choristers, I should think, were thoroughgoing Edgar Wallace "fans." Most of them allowed it, in all delicacy, to appear that they were not. But they wrote in emphatic, and sincere, and kindly appreciation of a literary success that is without a parallel; a success honestly won by incredible powers of hard work, and by appeal to that love of a thrilling and entertaining story that is shared by ambassadors and office boys and all between. Not that all ambassadors, or even all office boys, have retained that simple taste in all its keenness. There are highbrows everywhere, and a genuine highbrow obtains far more satisfaction from the things of the mind than the best of Edgar Wallace thrillers could give to his most devoted reader. That, at least, is the idea of being a highbrow; and I hope the idea is a correct one, since there is little other honourable satisfaction to be got by that unpopular and despised type of being. But the mass of mankind are either lowbrows pure and simple, or else dwell in that happy borderland where the level of brows can be raised or depressed at will, as necessity or inclination may require. And that mass was Edgar Wallace's public—the greatest ever gathered to the standard of any author.

It was not confined to the English-speaking peoples. He was known by translation, I am told, to all the civilized world. And that is a remarkable fact; for if there ever was a writer racy of the English soil—and especially that of the least distinguished parts of London—that man was Edgar Wallace. If it is true that Dickens, who was translated in every country, was really untranslatable, it is true that Edgar Wallace was much more so. Nine-tenths of his dialogue simply would not go into any other tongue than that of Cockney London. Will anyone who knows the ***Educat-***

ed Evans stories pretend that a single page of them could be rendered into any foreign speech? The very incidents are totally unintelligible to anyone not acquainted with the complicated underworld of the English Turf. Perhaps no one really had the temerity to attempt translating *Evans*; but for his straight mystery-stories his public was as wide as the world. And that is the proof of his most solid gift—the gift of the story-teller. He was the great *improvisatore* of our time; for he actually could invent and plan and complete a new story, and an excellent one, in a week if he tried.

That was the granite foundation; and the same gift in a less degree, and without addition, has been the making of many lesser favourites of the novel-reading public. But in Edgar Wallace there was added to it a great deal. He had humour of the robust, cheerful, knockabout sort which practically everyone loves. And the dialogue which was the vehicle of most of his humour was always a delight—fresh and vivid, with a rapid fire of sally and repartee that came naturally to one who had been, as Edgar Wallace had been, a London street-boy. The excellence of it was one-half the secret of the success of the plays which, late in his career, he suddenly began to turn out with the ease of an old theatrical hand; some of them bad, some very good, indeed. How some of his "lines" dwell in the memory! There is the heart-broken exclamation of the wife of the Chicago gangster on hearing that he has been murdered: "Oh! And I look like hell in black!" And the affecting farewell between a thief, who has just been sentenced to a term of imprisonment, and the wife of his bosom: "I'll come and see you every fortnight, Bill." "Never you mind about coming to see me. You keep away from the milkman!"

That sort of thing was, of course, another vital element in the fascination of Edgar Wallace's work for his countrymen. Many authors have written much and successfully about criminals, costermongers, betting-touts, public-house loafers, fish-porters, and the poor of London in general, both honest and dishonest. But none, as far as my reading extends, has ever done them so well as Edgar Wallace. Dickens did them—those of his day—to the universal admiration; and his leading characters of that sort are greater by far than anything in Edgar Wallace's work. But that was because they were created by Dickens; not because he knew their world better. Edgar Wallace, during the whole of his life before he enlisted in the army, lived in that world and knew nothing of any other—and the fact that it produced him is one of the best proofs of the soundness of our national character. Dickens knew that world in a sense; but there was about his up-bringing, even when his parents' fortunes were at the lowest, an atmosphere of gentility that nothing could disperse. They were never "frankly common"—very far from it, indeed; and the young Charles did but observe narrowly from outside a world into which Edgar Wallace was born—as a child of unknown parents, too—and in which he passed the whole formative period of his life. This is the explanation of the quality in Edgar Wallace's work which leads a friend of mine—a profound student of both life and letters—to maintain that the *Educated Evans* tales are the best things he ever did.

It is an opinion I do not share. I know that farcical odyssey of a little Camden Town racing tipster as well as another man; but my own taste tells me that in the Chicago gangster play, *On the Spot,* and the racing melodrama, *The Calendar,* we have the best of Edgar Wallace. And another will insist that the best is to be found in his West African stories, the least popular of all his writings.

I do not believe that Edgar Wallace's powers of industry have ever been equalled by any writer. Arnold Bennett used to declare that literary composition was the hardest of all hard work. Perhaps the kind in which Edgar Wallace specialized was not so hard; but consider the mere volume of his output! The elder Dumas used to be regarded as the wonder of literary history in this respect. He once told Louis Napoleon that he had produced 1,200 works—a statement of which I take the same view that, probably, the Emperor took. Dumas' achievements never lost anything in his accounts of them. But he began writing in his teens, and he lived twelve years longer than Edgar Wallace; nor is there any doubt at all that in the matter of "ghosts" he was what is called a large employer. There is no sound basis of comparison, but I suspect that if all the immense mass of Edgar Wallace's journalism and other fugitive work were brought into account—as, no doubt, was that of Dumas—the Englishman would win. One explanation, I suppose, was that his brain was the only active part of him. He was, he once declared, "physically the laziest man in the world"; and on the same occasion (a few years ago) he said: "For twenty-five years I have walked, on an average, three or four miles a year."

His death will be regretted as long as some millions of us live. He will always be spoken of as Edgar Wallace; for he was held in affection. Who ever speaks of Charles Lamb as Lamb?

George Jean Nathan   (essay date 1935)

SOURCE: "Several Writers for the Theatre—and Miss Stein" in his *Passing Judgements,* Alfred A. Knopf, 1935, pp. 140-76.

[*Nathan has been called the most learned and influential drama critic the United States has yet produced. During the early decades of the twentieth century, he was greatly responsible for shifting the emphasis of the American theatre from light entertainment to serious drama and for introducing audiences and producers to the work of Eugene O'Neill, Henrik Ibsen, and Bernard Shaw, among others. Nathan was a contributing editor to H. L. Mencken's magazine the* American Mercury *and coeditor of the* Smart Set. *With Mencken, Nathan belonged to an iconoclastic school of American critics who attacked the vulgarity of accepted ideas and sought to bring a new level of sophistication to American culture, which they found provincial and backward. Nathan shared with Mencken a gift for stinging invective and verbal adroitness, as well as total confidence in his own judgements. In the following excerpt, Nathan asserts that Wallace's work, while popular, was vulgar and insignificant.*]

There are just two reasons, or justifications, for a writing man doing a prodigious amount of work. One is to achieve something eventually beautiful and, with it, a deserved glory. The other is to make a pot of money. If a man doesn't achieve one or the other, his life may be put down—by himself as well as by others—as a failure.

The late Edgar Wallace did an enormous amount of work, producing plays, novels, short stories and what not by the train-load. Much of this work was popular, but none of it had the slightest artistic reason for being. What is more, according to the published reports of his estate after his recent death, it made him, considering its bulk, only a fair-ish amount of money. Hence, in the way the world looks at such things—and looks at it soundly—he was a dud. True enough, he was, as has been noted, popular, which is to say that thousands of inferior persons admired what he wrote. But no man worth his salt, even in his own secret estimation, takes pride in any such jitney *kudos*. It is, indeed, down in his better and more ambitious heart, just a little disgusting to him. True enough, again, Wallace liked the superficial luxuries of life and his income, while it lasted, was sufficient to allow him to gratify his tastes in that direction. But the gratification of such tastes is a transient thing, as even the fellow of most gala impulses only too well knows, and is a sorry makeshift and but a momentary opiate for wishes closer and deeper and infinitely more thrilling.

There are dolts who imagine that hard work is its own reward and these will accordingly say that Wallace doubtless got a sufficient excitement out of it, whatever else it may or may not subsequently have brought him. But hard work is exciting only if it is followed by a worthy recompense of one kind or another: fame founded upon the quality of what one has done, or fortune, or, at least, personal satisfaction grounded upon the firm conviction that what one has written is grand stuff. As I have said, Wallace did not win such fame; he did not win such fortune; and I doubt if, in his innards, he ever for a moment believed that

his work touched even remotely the borders of quality. He was a "successful" writer in a relative sense—he didn't make one-tenth the money that such a ten-thousand times superior writer as Shaw, say, has made—and he gained only a tawdry renown. His career should be an inspiration, in an opposite direction, to all young and aspiring writers.

Colin Watson (essay date 1971)

SOURCE: "King Edgar, and How He Got His Crown," in his *Snobbery with Violence: Crime Stories and Their Audience,* Eyre & Spottiswoode, 1971, pp. 73-84.

[*Watson was an English journalist and novelist who was known for his detective novels. In the following essay, he speculates that the wide popularity of Wallace's novels was due to predictable plots and characters, as well as the author's refusal to question middle-class tastes and morality.*]

From the analysis of the method and content of Wallace's work which Margaret Lane has offered in her book, *Edgar Wallace: Biography of a Phenomenon,* the picture emerges of a writer supremely adept in an 'off-the-cuff' technique but observant all the time of a set of strict conventions. The nature of these conventions cannot be unrelated to what must have been the mental and emotional climate of forty years ago, for Wallace came nearer to being universally read by his generation than did any other author.

The first of the Wallace rules, as listed by Miss Lane, was subordination of everything to action. Nothing was to be what it seemed; confusion and suspense were to be maintained to the end, with none of the two-dimensional characters allowed a static moment. There was not a floor, not a wall, that might not suddenly go into motion. Even in the realm of crime fiction, there have been very few writers so constantly suggestive of restlessness.

All this, however, had to be resolved to satisfy the second convention: that the world be seen as an essentially safe place, a sunny garden at the end of the secret passage. No serious harm could be allowed to befall any of the 'good' characters, however horrifying the means of dispatch that the 'bad' ones might prepare for them. It was permissible for criminals temporarily to thwart the law, but never in a way that might shake the reader's confidence in it. (Wallace's policemen were sometimes baffled; they were never ridiculous).

The third convention was the banishment of anything that might produce genuine emotional reaction, anything capable of upsetting standard assumptions. Margaret Lane defined the objects of this rule as 'excitement without anxiety, suspense without fear, violence without pain and horror without disgust'. She could have added crime without sin and sentiment without sex.

Trying to assess Wallace's work in literary terms would be as pointless as applying sculptural evaluation to a load of gravel. He wrote as well as he needed to write in satisfaction of a voracious but uninstructed public appetite. At least he spared his readers the pages of portentous padding which less brisk operators saw fit to inflict upon theirs, while here and there, one even detects a spark of original

---

Wallace on his writing process:

I cannot prepare a synopsis of any book I intend writing. I have done so, but the story I eventually wrote bore no relationship whatever to the sketch I had prepared in advance. A story must tell itself, and so often the big situation, or the chief characterization grows out of some accidental development of the plot. The blind man, who figures in *The Dark Eyes of London,* came quite by accident into the story, and with him the main theme. I rarely give a book its title until it is written. *The Ringer* and *The Squeaker* were exceptions, and the title of *The Crimson Circle* was chosen to meet the demands of an editor who wanted to have a simple device which he could print on a contents bill. I do not consciously write for any public. I try to write clean adventure stories, entirely free from sex interest, because I hold pretty definite views on sex stories.

Edgar Wallace, in "What Interviewers Miss," The Bookman, *January, 1930.*

---

and lively characterization. It is a pleasant surprise, for instance, to receive this piece of information about his detective, Mr J. G. Reeder:

> All his life he had had a suspicion of milk. He had calculated that a nimble homicide, working on systematic lines, could decimate London in a month.

For most of the time, though, Wallace's story-telling was fast, facile and careless. A man who habitually planned six and more novels simultaneously and who once completed a book of 80,000 words in a single week-end could not afford to linger over the fashioning of phrases. He had to snatch them out of stock. The following are but a few of those he used in one typical sequence of events in the story of *Terror Keep* (1927):

> She had hardly done so when she heard a sound which brought her heart to her mouth . . . slipping off her shoes, she sped along in the darkness . . . plucking up courage, after a few minutes she retraced her steps . . . when, to her horror, she felt it moving aways from her and had just time to shrink back when . . . hoping and praying that she would find a niche into which she could shrink . . . with a gasp of horror she realized that in the confusion of the moment she had taken the wrong direction . . . as she stood motionless with fear . . . for a second he stared at her as though she were some ghastly apparition of his mad dreams . . . in a second she was flying up the awful staircase . . . not for a fortune would she have looked behind . . . her breath was coming in long sobs; her heart beat as though it would burst . . . and then there came a sound which froze the marrow of his bones . . . the scream of a human soul in agony . . . suddenly Margaret saw something which made her breath come faster . . . in terror she struggled madly, but the man held her in a grip of iron, and then her senses left her and she sank limply into his arms . . . it seemed almost an eternity before she came to the surface. Fortunately, she was a good swimmer . . .

The plots of the Wallace books were simply hastily contrived vessels into which could be poured a stream of cliché of the above order. Here, by way of general illustration, is that of the *Three Oak Mystery.*

Detective Socrates Smith, retired from Scotland Yard with the help of a legacy of £6,000 a year, is invited to stay with a former colleague, John Mandle, at his country house near London. Mandle has a pretty step-daughter, Molly Templeton, and two near neighbours. One is Bob Stone, yet another ex-Yard man; the other is a Mr Jetheroe, soon to be identified as a former convict. Smith's fellow guest at Mandle's house is his brother, Lexington Smith, who falls in love with Molly.

One morning the brothers find Mandle shot dead. Stone is discovered trussed up at his home. The police are informed but they hand over the entire investigation to Smith. Smith hopes that a clue to the reason for the murder may be found in a secret drawer of the dead man's desk. Before he can search, somebody fires the house and it burns to the ground. Undeterred, Smith buys a hatchet in the nearest village and chops up the charred remnants of the desk. He finds two keys, labelled 'Pool-in-the . . .' and succeeds in connecting this partial address with a deserted house on Dartmoor. Meanwhile Jetheroe has been shot and his body has disappeared.

Smith travels with his brother to Devon, finds 'Pool-in-the-Moor' and cuts his way through the overgrown garden with another hatchet, this one bought at Exeter. Inside the house, which no one has entered for twenty years, Smith finds bloodstains and a spent bullet. A scorched fragment of a thousand-franc bank-note lies in the fireplace. It looks to Smith as though he has discovered the scene of the murder of Deveroux, the Lyons Bank robber, who was supposed to have escaped abroad in 1902 after eluding Mandle and Stone, both at that time policemen officially on his trail.

The brothers return to the house of Bob Stone, where they had left Molly Templeton after the fire. She has disappeared. False messages send them to London in search of her. On their return, Socrates confronts Stone and accuses him of Mandle's murder and the abduction of Molly. Stone admits his guilt, produces a gun and locks Smith in a cupboard.

At the house of mystery, 'Pool-in-the-Moor', Molly is in the custody of a woman with a criminal record earned while she kept a private lunatic asylum. During the night, Molly descends to the cellar and with a pick that has been left lying about she demolishes a brick wall, disclosing the skeleton of Deveroux, the Lyons bank robber. This upsets her, as does the sight of the face of a mysterious stranger at an attic window.

The stranger proves to be a policeman, assigned on Smith's instructions to keep an eye on Molly. When Stone arrives and tries to extort from Molly a promise of marriage, the policeman appears in the doorway and announces: 'My name is Sub-Inspector Frank Weldon from Scotland Yard. I shall take you into custody on a charge . . .' A shot rings out and Weldon pitches forward. Stone has fired from the hip. He bundles the body into a car and dumps it in a nearby lake. He then enters the cellar armed with two automatic pistols and awaits developments.

Socrates and his brother are not long in making an appearance. Another arrival is Mr Jetheroe, recovered from his wound so fully that he has been able to scale the fourteen-feet-high garden wall, set with broken glass. He proves to be none other than Molly's father, who has been awaiting a chance to clear his name. Sub-Inspector Weldon also has revived, thanks to the coldness of the water in the lake, and reports for further duty.

Stone dies in the shooting that ensues. Molly accepts Lexington Smith's offer of marriage. She says she cannot take a penny of Mandle's ill-gotten fortune (his share of the loot of Deveroux, the Lyons bank robber). Socrates says: 'Anyway, Lex has got quite a lot.' Jetheroe adds, fondly: 'And so has Lexington's future father-in-law.'

Lexington's eyes meet the girl's. 'Money!' he says, contemptuously.

It may readily be judged that the readers of the 150 or so novels which Edgar Wallace turned out on essentially similar lines to *The Three Oak Mystery* were in no great danger of philosophical, moral or political derangement. They were treated to nothing worse (provided they were not stylistically sensitive) than a vicarious dash from one unlikely situation to another. How exciting this was felt to be depended on the individual reader's degree of ignorance of real life; alternatively, on the extent to which he was ready and able to disregard the voice of experience and reason in the interest of his own entertainment. Practice, it seems, can make the suspension of intelligence a progressively easier matter. Wallace's books would never have achieved the astonishing sales that ultimately they did if they had been rejected by all sensible and educated people. The author Clemence Dane wrote in 1933: 'There is a joyous crowd of story-tellers which frankly accepts the fact that good stories and money-making go together. Edgar Wallace is their king . . . And though he may sneer, the highbrow generally reads the low-brow's *Blood-stained Cabbage-stalk* avidly . . .' She was right: in or around that year, it was estimated that of every four books being read in Britain one was an Edgar Wallace.

Such a situation indicated something more than casual, undiscriminating acceptance. Wallace was demanded. Censorious critics of the time used the word 'drug' repeatedly in connection with his work. The epithet was appropriate enough, no doubt, but it did not explain *why* this deluge of superficial, silly, slipshod fiction found addicts at every social level. Clemence Dane's reference was to 'good' stories but if by that she meant to connote convincing characterization, ingenuity of plot, credible conflict and logically satisfying resolution, Wallace was a nonstarter. Orwell accused Wallace of intellectual sadism. It seems unlikely, though, that anything so subtle would have won readers by the million. Wallace never created a scene of cruelty comparable with those that were to be commonplaces of crime fiction twenty years after his death. Nor did any of his novels portray sexual behaviour beyond the stage of chaste enfoldment in arms. He himself declared more than once that there was 'too much nastiness in modern literature'.

From these facts emerges the strong possibility that Wallace's success was, in large measure if not completely, due to those very characteristics of his writing which a critic believing himself to be sophisticated would consider deficiencies.

Taking his last-mentioned attribute first—the disinclination to treat of sex save in the most perfunctory, unreal terms—might not this in fact have matched a widespread public attitude? Britain in the 1920s was not populated exclusively by Bright Young Things, nor had Suffragettism and the Black Bottom seduced a war-sickened generation to the delights of free love. The solid majority was still bound by Victorian inhibition, the result of sexual ignorance and fear. It was tolerant of titillation at the level of 'bathing belle' pictures in newspapers and the regimented leg waving of revue choruses, but regarded Marie Stopes as a filthy-minded eccentric and poor D. H. Lawrence as a menace to society. To these people's self-defensive puri-

tanism, Edgar Wallace offered nothing offensive, nothing disquieting. Negative virtues commend themselves to negatory minds.

Perhaps it also holds true that there is a quality in the contrivances of a lazy mind that appeals to people whose mood is one of reluctance to think. A Wallace book, like any other piece of escapist literature, was bought or borrowed as a means of temporary withdrawal from the demanding, worrying, disappointing world in which the reader normally lived. In that world, there were as many three-dimensional characters as he could cope with; it was a welcome change to be among a two-dimensional variety that required no effort to understand. All the cardboard figures were labelled—hero, heroine, villain, comic manservant, policeman—and so sympathy could be simply and accurately apportioned until the time came at the book's end for it to be collected up again like so much play-money.

As for silliness of plot: its heavy reliance on coincidence, pseudo-scientific devices, unidentified foreign powers, miraculous survival, intuition, and all the other intelligence-defying tricks of the pot-boiling trade—here again, it may be that Wallace offered not an affront but solace of a kind. People were aware in their hearts that the 1914-18 war had solved nothing and that the public optimism of the politicians masked their impotence and perplexity. There was as yet no question of impending catastrophe, but something seemed to have gone sadly wrong with the process of perpetual improvement that had been assumed to be natural law not only by the Victorians but by many of their successors. To read of events reaching a happy conclusion by manifestly *un*natural and illogical means provided relief from the unpleasant feeling of having been let down.

Armin Arnold   (essay date 1976)

SOURCE: "Friedrich Dürrenmatt and Edgar Wallace," in *The International Fiction Review*, Vol. 3, No. 2, July, 1976, pp. 142–44.

[*In the following essay, Arnold compares the plot elements of Wallace's* The Four Just Men *to those in a novel by German writer Friedrich Dürrenmatt.*]

In 1959, Siegfried M. Pistorius interviewed Friedrich Dürrenmatt in the latter's home above Neuchâtel and found that Dürrenmatt had complete sets of the novels by Edgar Wallace, Georges Simenon, and Agatha Christie on the shelves. In his book on Dürrenmatt's prose works, Peter Spycher mentions this fact, but says nothing concrete about influences from these authors on Dürrenmatt's detective stories. I intend to show elsewhere that Simenon's inspector Maigret has contributed certain traits to the figure of Inspektor Bärlach (*Der Richter und sein Henker*, 1952; *Der Verdacht*, 1953), and that Dürrenmatt's novel *Das Versprechen* (1958, based on his filmscript *Es geschah am hellichten Tag*) is a clever transformation of Simenon's novel *Maigret tend un piège* (1955). Here I wish to point out the influence of some works by Edgar Wallace on Dürrenmatt's short novel *Die Panne* (1956).

In 1905, Edgar Wallace published a novel entitled *The Four Just Men.* It was followed by two related novels, *The Council of Justice* (1908) and *The Three Just Men* (1925), and by a collection of short stories, *Again the Three* (1928). The heroes in all four books are the same: a trio of friends named Leon Gonsalez, George Manfred, and Raymond Poiccart. A fourth friend had been killed before 1905 in Bordeaux. These men, all extremely rich, have made it the purpose of their lives to find out and punish all those criminals against whom the present laws provide no protection, or who are too clever or too powerful to be caught by those responsible for enforcing existing laws. Gonsalez, Poiccart, and Manfred are known in the world as "the four Just Men"—although, in fact, only three Just Men ar still alive to carry out the actions recorded in the four books mentioned above.

In Wallace's novel of 1905, Gonsalez, Poiccart and Manfred hire an expert murderer to help them kill the British Secretary of State for Foreign Affairs. This politician wants to pass a Bill which would force foreign politicians who have sought—and found—refuge in England to go back to their countries—where certain death is awaiting them. The Just Men first try everything in their power to get the Foreign Secretary to withdraw this Bill—to no purpose. They have to kill him in order to stop the Bill from passing parliament and to save the lives of idealists like Manuel Garcia. Aren't the Just Men murderers? No. Manfred says: " . . . we kill for justice, which lifts us out of the ruck of professional slayers. When we see an unjust man oppressing his fellows; when we see an evil thing done against the good God . . . and against man—and know that by the laws of man this evildoer may escape punishment—we punish."

Before 1905, the Just Men had killed at least sixteen persons, among them "General Trelovitch, the leader of the Servian Regicides," a French army contractor named Conrad, and the philosopher Hermon le Blois "for corrupting the youth of the world with his reasoning." They have killed bribers of juries, suborners of witnesses, swindlers; they have attacked "systems which defied correction, corporations beyond punishment." It is only natural that the Just Men are hunted by the police forces of the entire world; 1000 pounds is offered as a reward for their capture.

Why this instinct for justice? Manfred explains: " . . . we kill and we will kill because we are each sufferers through acts of injustice, for which the law gave us no remedy." But this had been one motive only; later, the Just Men felt that they were "indispensable instruments of a divine providence," "I am judge, jury, hangman," says Manfred. By 1925 (*The Three Just Men*), Gonsalez, Poiccart, and Manfred have become reconciled to the world. They are friends with some London police officers. In 1928 (*Again the Three*), they run a sort of detective agency and amuse themselves by solving smaller problems—in the style of Sherlock Holmes.

One of the main motives in most of Dürrenmatt's works is the idea of justice. In the early works, Dürrenmatt's is upset about the injustice of God: God is a sadist, he loves torturing humans, he does not reward the good or punish the bad. Inspector Bärlach, like Manfred, is his own judge, jury, and hangman (*Der Richter und sein Henker*), and Claire Zachanassian manages to get justice because—like Wallace's Just Men—she is enormously rich (*Der Besuch der alten Dame,* 1956). After Peter Schneider had written a study on *Die Fragwürdigkeit des Rechts im Werk von Friedrich Dürrenmatt* (1967), Dürrenmatt wrote down some variations on his own theory of justice: *Monstervortrag über Gerechtigkeit und Recht* (1969).

It is clear that the ideas propagated by Wallace in *The Four Just Men* and some later books must have appealed to Dürrenmatt. They had appealed to Agatha Christie before—who used them in her book *And Then There Were None* (1940) where a judge kills a collection of criminals who are "all quite untouchable by the law."

In Dürrenmatt's *Die Panne,* the traveling salesman Traps walks into the trap of four just men. They are: an attorney, a judge, a defense lawyer and a hangman. They are not enormously rich like Wallace's men, but they have no financial worries either: they are pensioned. The word "trap" is used prominently in the "Prologue" to Wallace's *The Four Just Men*: the criminal "traps" a girl; then Manfred "traps" the criminal—and kills him. This is what happens to Dürrenmatt's criminal named Traps: he has murdered his boss—by seducing the latter's wife and by letting the boss know about it. The boss who had had a heart condition, had promptly died. Traps cannot be prosecuted; nobody considers him to be a killer; he is not even conscious of the fact that he is responsible for the death of his boss. But Dürrenmatt's four just men find out: they question Traps, trap him, establish the truth, and condemn him to death. There is considerable fun in Wallace's novel of 1905; Dürrenmatt's tale also bristles with irony. In the prose version, Trap hangs himself; in the radio play version (also 1956) he continues to live—and to kill.

The theory of Dürrenmatt's four just men is exactly the same as Wallace's. The judge explains to Traps: "Unsere Art, Gericht zu halten, scheint Ihnen fremd . . . Doch, Wertgeschätzter, wir vier an diesem Tisch sind pensioniert und haben uns vom unnötigen Wust der Formeln, Protokolle, Schreibereien, Gesetze und was für Kram sonst noch unsere Gerichtssäle belasten, befreit. Wir richten ohne Rücksicht auf die lumpigen Gesetzbücher und Paragraphen." Like the Just Men in Wallace's books the just men in Dürrenmatt's story use the death penalty. Dürrenmatt's men have reintroduced it privately after it had been abolished by the government.

In 1960, Dürrenmatt told Jean-Paul Weber that a short story by Maupassant (he had forgotten which one) had inspired him to write *Die Panne*. Peter Spycher has tried to identify the story and suggests that "Le Voleur" in the volume *Mademoiselle Fifi* might be the tale Dürrenmatt had in mind. There are, in fact, some striking parallels—but there seems to be no doubt that *The Four Just Men* are at the root of *Die Panne*.

It is only to be expected that Dürrenmatt's story is, in many ways, a parody of Wallace's novel. Wallace's Just Men are comparatively young and work hard to keep up with the most glaring crimes which would—without their intervention—go unpunished. Dürrenmatt's just men are old and pensioned. Although every interview turns up some crime (". . . ein Verbrechen lasse sich immer finden"), they are overjoyed when they are confronted by a juicy murder: "Glück, wir haben Glück. Ein Toter ist aufgestöbert . . ." exclaims Dürrenmatt's prosecuting attorney. He and his friends deeply regret that the sort of crimes committed before the advent of the atomic age and formerly punished by Wallace's Just Men are no longer fashionable. Governments and multinational corporations cannot be punished, not even by millionaire gentlemen detectives; today's fans of justice have to be satisfied with trapping unimportant people like Traps. Wallace's criminals die at the hands of the Just Men; the peak of Dürrenmatt's irony is reached when his criminal commits suicide and when Dürrenmatt's just men profoundly regret the death of their victim. [The critic adds in a footnote: "We have since learned that Dürrenmatt wrote the radio play and the novel, both entitled *Die Panne,* in 1955. *The Four Just Men* had appeared in 1954 in a German translation as a pocket book, published by Goldmann Verlag, Munich. It must be this text which Dürrenmatt had read. It is quite obvious that Dürrenmatt parodies *The Four Just Men* who, in 1905, had been between 25 and 40 years old. In 1955 they would have been between 75 and 90, and, in fact, Dürrenmatt's heroes are aged as follows: Pilet: 77; Kummer: 82; Zorn: 86; the judge: 87."]

FURTHER READING

Bibliography

Sampson, Robert. In his *Yesterday's Faces, Volume V: Dangerous Horizons*, pp. 188-89. Bowling Green: Bowling Green State University, 1991.

    Checklist of works by and about Wallace.

Biography

Lane, Margaret. *Edgar Wallace: The Biography of a Phenomenon.* Rev. ed. London: Hamish Hamilton, 1965, 338 p.

    Biography that includes analysis of Wallace's fiction and attempts to account for its popular appeal.

Wallace, Penelope. "A Man and His Books." *The Mystery and Detection Annual* (1972): 93-97.

    Remembrance of Wallace's life, written by his daughter.

Criticism

Chesterton, G. K. "On Detective Story Writers." In his *Come to Think of It . . .* , pp. 29-33. London: Methuen, 1930.

    Compares Wallace's work to that of other popular mystery writers.

Twentieth-Century
Literary Criticism

Cumulative Indexes
Volumes 1-57

How to Use This Index

The main references

> Calvino, Italo
> 1923-1985.....CLC 5, 8, 11, 22, 33, 39,
> 73; SSC 3

list all author entries in the following Gale Literary Criticism series:

BLC = *Black Literature Criticism*
CLC = *Contemporary Literary Criticism*
CLR = *Children's Literature Review*
CMLC = *Classical and Medieval Literature Criticism*
DA = *DISCovering Authors*
DC = *Drama Criticism*
HLC = *Hispanic Literature Criticism*
LC = *Literature Criticism from 1400 to 1800*
NCLC = *Nineteenth-Century Literature Criticism*
PC = *Poetry Criticism*
SSC = *Short Story Criticism*
TCLC = *Twentieth-Century Literary Criticism*
WLC = *World Literature Criticism, 1500 to the Present*

The cross-references

> See also CANR 23; CA 85-88;
> obituary CA 116

list all author entries in the following Gale biographical and literary sources:

AAYA = *Authors & Artists for Young Adults*
AITN = *Authors in the News*
BEST = *Bestsellers*
BW = *Black Writers*
CA = *Contemporary Authors*
CAAS = *Contemporary Authors Autobiography Series*
CABS = *Contemporary Authors Bibliographical Series*
CANR = *Contemporary Authors New Revision Series*
CAP = *Contemporary Authors Permanent Series*
CDALB = *Concise Dictionary of American Literary Biography*
CDBLB = *Concise Dictionary of British Literary Biography*
DLB = *Dictionary of Literary Biography*
DLBD = *Dictionary of Literary Biography Documentary Series*
DLBY = *Dictionary of Literary Biography Yearbook*
HW = *Hispanic Writers*
JRDA = *Junior DISCovering Authors*
MAICYA = *Major Authors and Illustrators for Children and Young Adults*
MTCW = *Major 20th-Century Writers*
NNAL = *Native North American Literature*
SAAS = *Something about the Author Autobiography Series*
SATA = *Something about the Author*
YABC = *Yesterday's Authors of Books for Children*

Aldiss, Brian W(ilson)
1925- .... **CLC 5, 14, 40**
See also CA 5-8R; CAAS 2; CANR 5, 28;
DLB 14; MTCW; SATA 34

Alegria, Claribel 1924-............ **CLC 75**
See also CA 131; CAAS 15; HW

Alegria, Fernando 1918-........... **CLC 57**
See also CA 9-12R; CANR 5, 32; HW

Aleichem, Sholom .... **TCLC 1, 35**
See also Rabinovitch, Sholem

Aleixandre, Vicente 1898-1984 ... **CLC 9, 36**
See also CA 85-88; 114; CANR 26;
DLB 108; HW; MTCW

Alepoudelis, Odysseus
See Elytis, Odysseus

Aleshkovsky, Joseph 1929-
See Aleshkovsky, Yuz
See also CA 121; 128

Aleshkovsky, Yuz .... **CLC 44**
See also Aleshkovsky, Joseph

Alexander, Lloyd (Chudley) 1924- .. **CLC 35**
See also AAYA 1; CA 1-4R; CANR 1, 24,
38; CLR 1, 5; DLB 52; JRDA; MAICYA;
MTCW; SATA 3, 49

Alfau, Felipe 1902-.............. **CLC 66**
See also CA 137

Alger, Horatio, Jr. 1832-1899 ..... **NCLC 8**
See also DLB 42; SATA 16

Algren, Nelson 1909-1981 .... **CLC 4, 10, 33**
See also CA 13-16R; 103; CANR 20;
CDALB 1941-1968; DLB 9; DLBY 81,
82; MTCW

Ali, Ahmed 1910- .... **CLC 69**
See also CA 25-28R; CANR 15, 34

Alighieri, Dante 1265-1321 .... **CMLC 3**

Allan, John B.
See Westlake, Donald E(dwin)

Allen, Edward 1948-.............. **CLC 59**

Allen, Paula Gunn 1939-.......... **CLC 84**
See also CA 112; 143; NNAL

Allen, Roland
See Ayckbourn, Alan

Allen, Sarah A.
See Hopkins, Pauline Elizabeth

Allen, Woody 1935- .... **CLC 16, 52**
See also AAYA 10; CA 33-36R; CANR 27,
38; DLB 44; MTCW

Allende, Isabel 1942- .... **CLC 39, 57; HLC**
See also CA 125; 130; HW; MTCW

Alleyn, Ellen
See Rossetti, Christina (Georgina)

Allingham, Margery (Louise)
1904-1966 .... **CLC 19**
See also CA 5-8R; 25-28R; CANR 4;
DLB 77; MTCW

Allingham, William 1824-1889 ... **NCLC 25**
See also DLB 35

Allison, Dorothy E. 1949- .... **CLC 78**
See also CA 140

Allston, Washington 1779-1843 .... **NCLC 2**
See also DLB 1

Almedingen, E. M. .... **CLC 12**
See also Almedingen, Martha Edith von
See also SATA 3

Almedingen, Martha Edith von 1898-1971
See Almedingen, E. M.
See also CA 1-4R; CANR 1

Almqvist, Carl Jonas Love
1793-1866 .... **NCLC 42**

Alonso, Damaso 1898-1990 .... **CLC 14**
See also CA 110; 131; 130; DLB 108; HW

Alov
See Gogol, Nikolai (Vasilyevich)

Alta 1942-...................... **CLC 19**
See also CA 57-60

Alter, Robert B(ernard) 1935-...... **CLC 34**
See also CA 49-52; CANR 1

Alther, Lisa 1944-.............. **CLC 7, 41**
See also CA 65-68; CANR 12, 30; MTCW

Altman, Robert 1925-............. **CLC 16**
See also CA 73-76; CANR 43

Alvarez, A(lfred) 1929-......... **CLC 5, 13**
See also CA 1-4R; CANR 3, 33; DLB 14,
40

Alvarez, Alejandro Rodriguez 1903-1965
See Casona, Alejandro
See also CA 131; 93-96; HW

Amado, Jorge 1912-..... **CLC 13, 40; HLC**
See also CA 77-80; CANR 35; DLB 113;
MTCW

Ambler, Eric 1909-............ **CLC 4, 6, 9**
See also CA 9-12R; CANR 7, 38; DLB 77;
MTCW

Amichai, Yehuda 1924- ...... **CLC 9, 22, 57**
See also CA 85-88; MTCW

Amiel, Henri Frederic 1821-1881 .. **NCLC 4**

Amis, Kingsley (William)
1922- .. **CLC 1, 2, 3, 5, 8, 13, 40, 44; DA**
See also AITN 2; CA 9-12R; CANR 8, 28;
CDBLB 1945-1960; DLB 15, 27, 100, 139;
MTCW

Amis, Martin (Louis)
1949- .... **CLC 4, 9, 38, 62**
See also BEST 90:3; CA 65-68; CANR 8,
27; DLB 14

Ammons, A(rchie) R(andolph)
1926- .... **CLC 2, 3, 5, 8, 9, 25, 57**
See also AITN 1; CA 9-12R; CANR 6, 36;
DLB 5; MTCW

Amo, Tauraatua i
See Adams, Henry (Brooks)

Anand, Mulk Raj 1905-........... **CLC 23**
See also CA 65-68; CANR 32; MTCW

Anatol
See Schnitzler, Arthur

Anaya, Rudolfo A(lfonso)
1937- .... **CLC 23; HLC**
See also CA 45-48; CAAS 4; CANR 1, 32;
DLB 82; HW 1; MTCW

Andersen, Hans Christian
1805-1875 .. **NCLC 7; DA; SSC 6; WLC**
See also CLR 6; MAICYA; YABC 1

Anderson, C. Farley
See Mencken, H(enry) L(ouis); Nathan,
George Jean

Anderson, Jessica (Margaret) Queale
.... **CLC 37**
See also CA 9-12R; CANR 4

Anderson, Jon (Victor) 1940- .... **CLC 9**
See also CA 25-28R; CANR 20

Anderson, Lindsay (Gordon)
1923-..................... **CLC 20**
See also CA 125; 128

Anderson, Maxwell 1888-1959 ..... **TCLC 2**
See also CA 105; DLB 7

Anderson, Poul (William) 1926- .... **CLC 15**
See also AAYA 5; CA 1-4R; CAAS 2;
CANR 2, 15, 34; DLB 8; MTCW;
SATA 39

Anderson, Robert (Woodruff)
1917-..................... **CLC 23**
See also AITN 1; CA 21-24R; CANR 32;
DLB 7

Anderson, Sherwood
1876-1941 .... **TCLC 1, 10, 24; DA;
SSC 1; WLC**
See also CA 104; 121; CDALB 1917-1929;
DLB 4, 9, 86; DLBD 1; MTCW

Andouard
See Giraudoux, (Hippolyte) Jean

Andrade, Carlos Drummond de ...... **CLC 18**
See also Drummond de Andrade, Carlos

Andrade, Mario de 1893-1945..... **TCLC 43**

Andreas-Salome, Lou 1861-1937... **TCLC 56**
See also DLB 66

Andrewes, Lancelot 1555-1626 .... **LC 5**

Andrews, Cicily Fairfield
See West, Rebecca

Andrews, Elton V.
See Pohl, Frederik

Andreyev, Leonid (Nikolaevich)
1871-1919 .... **TCLC 3**
See also CA 104

Andric, Ivo 1892-1975 .... **CLC 8**
See also CA 81-84; 57-60; CANR 43;
MTCW

Angelique, Pierre
See Bataille, Georges

Angell, Roger 1920-.............. **CLC 26**
See also CA 57-60; CANR 13, 44

Angelou, Maya
1928- .... **CLC 12, 35, 64, 77; BLC; DA**
See also AAYA 7; BW 2; CA 65-68;
CANR 19, 42; DLB 38; MTCW;
SATA 49

Annensky, Innokenty Fyodorovich
1856-1909 .... **TCLC 14**
See also CA 110

Anon, Charles Robert
See Pessoa, Fernando (Antonio Nogueira)

Anouilh, Jean (Marie Lucien Pierre)
1910-1987 ...... **CLC 1, 3, 8, 13, 40, 50**
See also CA 17-20R; 123; CANR 32;
MTCW

Anthony, Florence
See Ai

Anthony, John
See Ciardi, John (Anthony)

Anthony, Peter
See Shaffer, Anthony (Joshua); Shaffer,
Peter (Levin)

Anthony, Piers 1934-............ **CLC 35**
See also AAYA 11; CA 21-24R; CANR 28;
DLB 8; MTCW

Antoine, Marc
See Proust, (Valentin-Louis-George-Eugene-)
Marcel

Antoninus, Brother
See Everson, William (Oliver)

Antonioni, Michelangelo 1912-..... **CLC 20**
See also CA 73-76; CANR 45

Antschel, Paul 1920-1970
See Celan, Paul
See also CA 85-88; CANR 33; MTCW

Anwar, Chairil 1922-1949 .... **TCLC 22**
See also CA 121

Apollinaire, Guillaume .. **TCLC 3, 8, 51; PC 7**
See also Kostrowitzki, Wilhelm Apollinaris
de

Appelfeld, Aharon 1932-....... **CLC 23, 47**
See also CA 112; 133

Apple, Max (Isaac) 1941-........ **CLC 9, 33**
See also CA 81-84; CANR 19; DLB 130

Appleman, Philip (Dean) 1926-..... **CLC 51**
See also CA 13-16R; CAAS 18; CANR 6,
29

Appleton, Lawrence
See Lovecraft, H(oward) P(hillips)

Apteryx
See Eliot, T(homas) S(tearns)

Apuleius, (Lucius Madaurensis)
125(?)-175(?)................ **CMLC 1**

Aquin, Hubert 1929-1977......... **CLC 15**
See also CA 105; DLB 53

Aragon, Louis 1897-1982........ **CLC 3, 22**
See also CA 69-72; 108; CANR 28;
DLB 72; MTCW

Arany, Janos 1817-1882........ **NCLC 34**

Arbuthnot, John 1667-1735.......... **LC 1**
See also DLB 101

Archer, Herbert Winslow
See Mencken, H(enry) L(ouis)

Archer, Jeffrey (Howard) 1940-.... **CLC 28**
See also BEST 89:3; CA 77-80; CANR 22

Archer, Jules 1915-.............. **CLC 12**
See also CA 9-12R; CANR 6; SAAS 5;
SATA 4

Archer, Lee
See Ellison, Harlan

Arden, John 1930-.......... **CLC 6, 13, 15**
See also CA 13-16R; CAAS 4; CANR 31;
DLB 13; MTCW

Arenas, Reinaldo
1943-1990 .... **CLC 41; HLC**
See also CA 124; 128; 133; HW

Arendt, Hannah 1906-1975 .... **CLC 66**
See also CA 17-20R; 61-64; CANR 26;
MTCW

Aretino, Pietro 1492-1556.......... **LC 12**

Arghezi, Tudor. .... **CLC 80**
See also Theodorescu, Ion N.

Arguedas, Jose Maria
1911-1969 .... **CLC 10, 18**
See also CA 89-92; DLB 113; HW

Argueta, Manlio 1936-............ **CLC 31**
See also CA 131; HW

Ariosto, Ludovico 1474-1533........ **LC 6**

Aristides
See Epstein, Joseph

Aristophanes
450B.C.-385B.C.... **CMLC 4; DA; DC 2**

Arlt, Roberto (Godofredo Christophersen)
1900-1942 .... **TCLC 29; HLC**
See also CA 123; 131; HW

Armah, Ayi Kwei 1939-.... **CLC 5, 33; BLC**
See also BW 1; CA 61-64; CANR 21;
DLB 117; MTCW

Armatrading, Joan 1950-.......... **CLC 17**
See also CA 114

Arnette, Robert
See Silverberg, Robert

Arnim, Achim von (Ludwig Joachim von
Arnim) 1781-1831 .... **NCLC 5**
See also DLB 90

Arnim, Bettina von 1785-1859.... **NCLC 38**
See also DLB 90

Arnold, Matthew
1822-1888 ..... **NCLC 6, 29; DA; PC 5;**
WLC
See also CDBLB 1832-1890; DLB 32, 57

Arnold, Thomas 1795-1842 ..... **NCLC 18**
See also DLB 55

Arnow, Harriette (Louisa) Simpson
1908-1986 .... **CLC 2, 7, 18**
See also CA 9-12R; 118; CANR 14; DLB 6;
MTCW; SATA 42, 47

Arp, Hans
See Arp, Jean

Arp, Jean 1887-1966.............. **CLC 5**
See also CA 81-84; 25-28R; CANR 42

Arrabal
See Arrabal, Fernando

Arrabal, Fernando 1932-... **CLC 2, 9, 18, 58**
See also CA 9-12R; CANR 15

Arrick, Fran...................... **CLC 30**

Artaud, Antonin 1896-1948 ..... **TCLC 3, 36**
See also CA 104

Arthur, Ruth M(abel) 1905-1979.... **CLC 12**
See also CA 9-12R; 85-88; CANR 4;
SATA 7, 26

Artsybashev, Mikhail (Petrovich)
1878-1927 .... **TCLC 31**

Arundel, Honor (Morfydd)
1919-1973 .... **CLC 17**
See also CA 21-22; 41-44R; CAP 2;
CLR 35; SATA 4, 24

Asch, Sholem 1880-1957 .... **TCLC 3**
See also CA 105

Ash, Shalom
See Asch, Sholem

Ashbery, John (Lawrence)
1927-......**CLC 2, 3, 4, 6, 9, 13, 15, 25,**
41, 77
See also CA 5-8R; CANR 9, 37; DLB 5;
DLBY 81; MTCW

Ashdown, Clifford
See Freeman, R(ichard) Austin

Ashe, Gordon
See Creasey, John

Ashton-Warner, Sylvia (Constance)
1908-1984 .... **CLC 19**
See also CA 69-72; 112; CANR 29; MTCW

Asimov, Isaac
1920-1992 ...... **CLC 1, 3, 9, 19, 26, 76**
See also BEST 90:2; CA 1-4R; 137;
CANR 2, 19, 36; CLR 12; DLB 8;
DLBY 92; JRDA; MAICYA; MTCW;
SATA 1, 26, 74

Astley, Thea (Beatrice May)
1925-....................... **CLC 41**
See also CA 65-68; CANR 11, 43

Aston, James
See White, T(erence) H(anbury)

Asturias, Miguel Angel
1899-1974 .... **CLC 3, 8, 13; HLC**
See also CA 25-28; 49-52; CANR 32;
CAP 2; DLB 113; HW; MTCW

Atares, Carlos Saura
See Saura (Atares), Carlos

Atheling, William
See Pound, Ezra (Weston Loomis)

Atheling, William, Jr.
See Blish, James (Benjamin)

Atherton, Gertrude (Franklin Horn)
1857-1948 .... **TCLC 2**
See also CA 104; DLB 9, 78

Atherton, Lucius
See Masters, Edgar Lee

Atkins, Jack
See Harris, Mark

Atticus
See Fleming, Ian (Lancaster)

Atwood, Margaret (Eleanor)
1939- ..... **CLC 2, 3, 4, 8, 13, 15, 25, 44,**
84; DA; PC 8; SSC 2; WLC
See also AAYA 12; BEST 89:2; CA 49-52;
CANR 3, 24, 33; DLB 53; MTCW;
SATA 50

Aubigny, Pierre d'
See Mencken, H(enry) L(ouis)

Aubin, Penelope 1685-1731(?)........ **LC 9**
See also DLB 39

Auchincloss, Louis (Stanton)
1917-.............. **CLC 4, 6, 9, 18, 45**
See also CA 1-4R; CANR 6, 29; DLB 2;
DLBY 80; MTCW

Auden, W(ystan) H(ugh)
1907-1973 ...... **CLC 1, 2, 3, 4, 6, 9, 11,**
14, 43; DA; PC 1; WLC
See also CA 9-12R; 45-48; CANR 5;
CDBLB 1914-1945; DLB 10, 20; MTCW

Audiberti, Jacques 1900-1965 ...... **CLC 38**
See also CA 25-28R

Audubon, John James
1785-1851 .... **NCLC 47**

Auel, Jean M(arie) 1936-........... **CLC 31**
See also AAYA 7; BEST 90:4; CA 103;
CANR 21

Auerbach, Erich 1892-1957 .... **TCLC 43**
See also CA 118

Augier, Emile 1820-1889 .... **NCLC 31**

LITERARY CRITICISM SERIES   **BOGAN**

Author Index

Besant, Annie (Wood) 1847-1933 . . . **TCLC 9**
See also CA 105

Bessie, Alvah 1904-1985. . . . . **CLC 23**
See also CA 5-8R; 116; CANR 2; DLB 26

Bethlen, T. D.
See Silverberg, Robert

Beti, Mongo. . . . . **CLC 27; BLC**
See also Biyidi, Alexandre

Betjeman, John
1906-1984 . . . . **CLC 2, 6, 10, 34, 43**
See also CA 9-12R; 112; CANR 33;
CDBLB 1945-1960; DLB 20; DLBY 84;
MTCW

Bettelheim, Bruno 1903-1990 . . . . . . **CLC 79**
See also CA 81-84; 131; CANR 23; MTCW

Betti, Ugo 1892-1953 . . . . **TCLC 5**
See also CA 104

Betts, Doris (Waugh) 1932-. . . . **CLC 3, 6, 28**
See also CA 13-16R; CANR 9; DLBY 82

Bevan, Alistair
See Roberts, Keith (John Kingston)

Bialik, Chaim Nachman
1873-1934 . . . . **TCLC 25**

Bickerstaff, Isaac
See Swift, Jonathan

Bidart, Frank 1939- . . . . **CLC 33**
See also CA 140

Bienek, Horst 1930-. . . . . **CLC 7, 11**
See also CA 73-76; DLB 75

Bierce, Ambrose (Gwinett)
1842-1914(?) . . . . **TCLC 1, 7, 44; DA;
SSC 9; WLC**
See also CA 104; 139; CDALB 1865-1917;
DLB 11, 12, 23, 71, 74

Billings, Josh
See Shaw, Henry Wheeler

Billington, (Lady) Rachel (Mary)
1942- . . . . **CLC 43**
See also AITN 2; CA 33-36R; CANR 44

Binyon, T(imothy) J(ohn) 1936- . . . . **CLC 34**
See also CA 111; CANR 28

Bioy Casares, Adolfo
1914- . . . . . . **CLC 4, 8, 13; HLC; SSC 17**
See also CA 29-32R; CANR 19, 43;
DLB 113; HW; MTCW

Bird, C.
See Ellison, Harlan

Bird, Cordwainer
See Ellison, Harlan

Bird, Robert Montgomery
1806-1854 . . . . **NCLC 1**

Birney, (Alfred) Earle
1904- . . . . **CLC 1, 4, 6, 11**
See also CA 1-4R; CANR 5, 20; DLB 88;
MTCW

Bishop, Elizabeth
1911-1979 . . . . . . **CLC 1, 4, 9, 13, 15, 32;
DA; PC 3**
See also CA 5-8R; 89-92; CABS 2;
CANR 26; CDALB 1968-1988; DLB 5;
MTCW; SATA 24

Bishop, John 1935-. . . . . **CLC 10**
See also CA 105

Bissett, Bill 1939-. . . . . **CLC 18**
See also CA 69-72; CAAS 19; CANR 15;
DLB 53; MTCW

Bitov, Andrei (Georgievich) 1937-. . . **CLC 57**
See also CA 142

Biyidi, Alexandre 1932-
See Beti, Mongo
See also BW 1; CA 114; 124; MTCW

Bjarme, Brynjolf
See Ibsen, Henrik (Johan)

Bjornson, Bjornstjerne (Martinius)
1832-1910 . . . . **TCLC 7, 37**
See also CA 104

Black, Robert
See Holdstock, Robert P.

Blackburn, Paul 1926-1971 . . . . . . **CLC 9, 43**
See also CA 81-84; 33-36R; CANR 34;
DLB 16; DLBY 81

Black Elk 1863-1950 . . . . **TCLC 33**
See also CA 144

Black Hobart
See Sanders, (James) Ed(ward)

Blacklin, Malcolm
See Chambers, Aidan

Blackmore, R(ichard) D(oddridge)
1825-1900 . . . . **TCLC 27**
See also CA 120; DLB 18

Blackmur, R(ichard) P(almer)
1904-1965 . . . . **CLC 2, 24**
See also CA 11-12; 25-28R; CAP 1; DLB 63

Black Tarantula, The
See Acker, Kathy

Blackwood, Algernon (Henry)
1869-1951 . . . . **TCLC 5**
See also CA 105

Blackwood, Caroline 1931- . . . . **CLC 6, 9**
See also CA 85-88; CANR 32; DLB 14;
MTCW

Blade, Alexander
See Hamilton, Edmond; Silverberg, Robert

Blaga, Lucian 1895-1961 . . . . **CLC 75**

Blair, Eric (Arthur) 1903-1950
See Orwell, George
See also CA 104; 132; DA; MTCW;
SATA 29

Blais, Marie-Claire
1939- . . . . **CLC 2, 4, 6, 13, 22**
See also CA 21-24R; CAAS 4; CANR 38;
DLB 53; MTCW

Blaise, Clark 1940-. . . . . **CLC 29**
See also AITN 2; CA 53-56; CAAS 3;
CANR 5; DLB 53

Blake, Nicholas
See Day Lewis, C(ecil)
See also DLB 77

Blake, William
1757-1827 . . . . . **NCLC 13, 37; DA; WLC**
See also CDBLB 1789-1832; DLB 93;
MAICYA; SATA 30

Blasco Ibanez, Vicente
1867-1928 . . . . **TCLC 12**
See also CA 110; 131; HW; MTCW

Blatty, William Peter 1928-. . . . . **CLC 2**
See also CA 5-8R; CANR 9

Bleeck, Oliver
See Thomas, Ross (Elmore)

Blessing, Lee 1949-. . . . . **CLC 54**

Blish, James (Benjamin)
1921-1975 . . . . **CLC 14**
See also CA 1-4R; 57-60; CANR 3; DLB 8;
MTCW; SATA 66

Bliss, Reginald
See Wells, H(erbert) G(eorge)

Blixen, Karen (Christentze Dinesen)
1885-1962
See Dinesen, Isak
See also CA 25-28; CANR 22; CAP 2;
MTCW; SATA 44

Bloch, Robert (Albert) 1917-. . . . . . . **CLC 33**
See also CA 5-8R; CANR 5; DLB 44;
SATA 12

Blok, Alexander (Alexandrovich)
1880-1921 . . . . **TCLC 5**
See also CA 104

Blom, Jan
See Breytenbach, Breyten

Bloom, Harold 1930- . . . . **CLC 24**
See also CA 13-16R; CANR 39; DLB 67

Bloomfield, Aurelius
See Bourne, Randolph S(illiman)

Blount, Roy (Alton), Jr. 1941- . . . . . **CLC 38**
See also CA 53-56; CANR 10, 28; MTCW

Bloy, Leon 1846-1917. . . . . **TCLC 22**
See also CA 121; DLB 123

Blume, Judy (Sussman) 1938-. . . **CLC 12, 30**
See also AAYA 3; CA 29-32R; CANR 13,
37; CLR 2, 15; DLB 52; JRDA;
MAICYA; MTCW; SATA 2, 31, 79

Blunden, Edmund (Charles)
1896-1974 . . . . **CLC 2, 56**
See also CA 17-18; 45-48; CAP 2; DLB 20,
100; MTCW

Bly, Robert (Elwood)
1926- . . . . **CLC 1, 2, 5, 10, 15, 38**
See also CA 5-8R; CANR 41; DLB 5;
MTCW

Boas, Franz 1858-1942. . . . . **TCLC 56**
See also CA 115

Bobette
See Simenon, Georges (Jacques Christian)

Boccaccio, Giovanni
1313-1375 . . . . **CMLC 13; SSC 10**

Bochco, Steven 1943-. . . . . **CLC 35**
See also AAYA 11; CA 124; 138

Bodenheim, Maxwell 1892-1954 . . . **TCLC 44**
See also CA 110; DLB 9, 45

Bodker, Cecil 1927- . . . . **CLC 21**
See also CA 73-76; CANR 13, 44; CLR 23;
MAICYA; SATA 14

Boell, Heinrich (Theodor)
1917-1985 . . . . **CLC 2, 3, 6, 9, 11, 15, 27,
32, 72; DA; WLC**
See also CA 21-24R; 116; CANR 24;
DLB 69; DLBY 85; MTCW

Boerne, Alfred
See Doeblin, Alfred

Bogan, Louise 1897-1970. . . . . **CLC 4, 39, 46**
See also CA 73-76; 25-28R; CANR 33;
DLB 45; MTCW

Bogarde, Dirk .... **CLC 19**
See also Van Den Bogarde, Derek Jules
    Gaspard Ulric Niven
See also DLB 14

Bogosian, Eric 1953- .... **CLC 45**
See also CA 138

Bograd, Larry 1953-.............. **CLC 35**
See also CA 93-96; SATA 33

Boiardo, Matteo Maria 1441-1494 .... **LC 6**

Boileau-Despreaux, Nicolas
    1636-1711 .... **LC 3**

Boland, Eavan (Aisling) 1944-... **CLC 40, 67**
See also CA 143; DLB 40

Bolt, Lee
See Faust, Frederick (Schiller)

Bolt, Robert (Oxton) 1924-........ **CLC 14**
See also CA 17-20R; CANR 35; DLB 13;
    MTCW

Bombet, Louis-Alexandre-Cesar
See Stendhal

Bomkauf
See Kaufman, Bob (Garnell)

Bonaventura.................... **NCLC 35**
See also DLB 90

Bond, Edward 1934-....... **CLC 4, 6, 13, 23**
See also CA 25-28R; CANR 38; DLB 13;
    MTCW

Bonham, Frank 1914-1989......... **CLC 12**
See also AAYA 1; CA 9-12R; CANR 4, 36;
    JRDA; MAICYA; SAAS 3; SATA 1, 49,
    62

Bonnefoy, Yves 1923-........ **CLC 9, 15, 58**
See also CA 85-88; CANR 33; MTCW

Bontemps, Arna(ud Wendell)
    1902-1973 .... **CLC 1, 18; BLC**
See also BW 1; CA 1-4R; 41-44R; CANR 4,
    35; CLR 6; DLB 48, 51; JRDA;
    MAICYA; MTCW; SATA 2, 24, 44

Booth, Martin 1944-.............. **CLC 13**
See also CA 93-96; CAAS 2

Booth, Philip 1925-............... **CLC 23**
See also CA 5-8R; CANR 5; DLBY 82

Booth, Wayne C(layson) 1921- ..... **CLC 24**
See also CA 1-4R; CAAS 5; CANR 3, 43;
    DLB 67

Borchert, Wolfgang 1921-1947 ..... **TCLC 5**
See also CA 104; DLB 69, 124

Borel, Petrus 1809-1859......... **NCLC 41**

Borges, Jorge Luis
    1899-1986 ... **CLC 1, 2, 3, 4, 6, 8, 9, 10,
        13, 19, 44, 48, 83; DA; HLC; SSC 4;
                                            WLC**
See also CA 21-24R; CANR 19, 33;
    DLB 113; DLBY 86; HW; MTCW

Borowski, Tadeusz 1922-1951...... **TCLC 9**
See also CA 106

Borrow, George (Henry)
    1803-1881 .... **NCLC 9**
See also DLB 21, 55

Bosman, Herman Charles
    1905-1951 .... **TCLC 49**

Bosschere, Jean de 1878(?)-1953... **TCLC 19**
See also CA 115

Boswell, James
    1740-1795 .... **LC 4; DA; WLC**
See also CDBLB 1660-1789; DLB 104, 142

Bottoms, David 1949-............ **CLC 53**
See also CA 105; CANR 22; DLB 120;
    DLBY 83

Boucicault, Dion 1820-1890...... **NCLC 41**

Boucolon, Maryse 1937-
See Conde, Maryse
See also CA 110; CANR 30

Bourget, Paul (Charles Joseph)
    1852-1935 ....**TCLC 12**
See also CA 107; DLB 123

Bourjaily, Vance (Nye) 1922- .... **CLC 8, 62**
See also CA 1-4R; CAAS 1; CANR 2;
    DLB 2, 143

Bourne, Randolph S(illiman)
    1886-1918 ....**TCLC 16**
See also CA 117; DLB 63

Bova, Ben(jamin William) 1932-.... **CLC 45**
See also CA 5-8R; CAAS 18; CANR 11;
    CLR 3; DLBY 81; MAICYA; MTCW;
    SATA 6, 68

Bowen, Elizabeth (Dorothea Cole)
    1899-1973 ...... **CLC 1, 3, 6, 11, 15, 22;
                                            SSC 3**
See also CA 17-18; 41-44R; CANR 35;
    CAP 2; CDBLB 1945-1960; DLB 15;
    MTCW

Bowering, George 1935-........ **CLC 15, 47**
See also CA 21-24R; CAAS 16; CANR 10;
    DLB 53

Bowering, Marilyn R(uthe) 1949-... **CLC 32**
See also CA 101

Bowers, Edgar 1924- .... **CLC 9**
See also CA 5-8R; CANR 24; DLB 5

Bowie, David.................... **CLC 17**
See also Jones, David Robert

Bowles, Jane (Sydney)
    1917-1973 .... **CLC 3, 68**
See also CA 19-20; 41-44R; CAP 2

Bowles, Paul (Frederick)
    1910- .... **CLC 1, 2, 19, 53; SSC 3**
See also CA 1-4R; CAAS 1; CANR 1, 19;
    DLB 5, 6; MTCW

Box, Edgar
See Vidal, Gore

Boyd, Nancy
See Millay, Edna St. Vincent

Boyd, William 1952-........ **CLC 28, 53, 70**
See also CA 114; 120

Boyle, Kay
    1902-1992 ..... **CLC 1, 5, 19, 58; SSC 5**
See also CA 13-16R; 140; CAAS 1;
    CANR 29; DLB 4, 9, 48, 86; DLBY 93;
    MTCW

Boyle, Mark
See Kienzle, William X(avier)

Boyle, Patrick 1905-1982......... **CLC 19**
See also CA 127

Boyle, T. C.
See Boyle, T(homas) Coraghessan

Boyle, T(homas) Coraghessan
    1948- .... **CLC 36, 55; SSC 16**
See also BEST 90:4; CA 120; CANR 44;
    DLBY 86

Boz
See Dickens, Charles (John Huffam)

Brackenridge, Hugh Henry
    1748-1816 .... **NCLC 7**
See also DLB 11, 37

Bradbury, Edward P.
See Moorcock, Michael (John)

Bradbury, Malcolm (Stanley)
    1932-.................... **CLC 32, 61**
See also CA 1-4R; CANR 1, 33; DLB 14;
    MTCW

Bradbury, Ray (Douglas)
    1920- ... **CLC 1, 3, 10, 15, 42; DA; WLC**
See also AITN 1, 2; CA 1-4R; CANR 2, 30;
    CDALB 1968-1988; DLB 2, 8; MTCW;
    SATA 11, 64

Bradford, Gamaliel 1863-1932..... **TCLC 36**
See also DLB 17

Bradley, David (Henry, Jr.)
    1950- .... **CLC 23; BLC**
See also BW 1; CA 104; CANR 26; DLB 33

Bradley, John Ed(mund, Jr.)
    1958- .... **CLC 55**
See also CA 139

Bradley, Marion Zimmer 1930-..... **CLC 30**
See also AAYA 9; CA 57-60; CAAS 10;
    CANR 7, 31; DLB 8; MTCW

Bradstreet, Anne
    1612(?)-1672 .... **LC 4; DA; PC 10**
See also CDALB 1640-1865; DLB 24

Bragg, Melvyn 1939- .... **CLC 10**
See also BEST 89:3; CA 57-60; CANR 10;
    DLB 14

Braine, John (Gerard)
    1922-1986 .... **CLC 1, 3, 41**
See also CA 1-4R; 120; CANR 1, 33;
    CDBLB 1945-1960; DLB 15; DLBY 86;
    MTCW

Brammer, William 1930(?)-1978 .... **CLC 31**
See also CA 77-80

Brancati, Vitaliano 1907-1954..... **TCLC 12**
See also CA 109

Brancato, Robin F(idler) 1936-..... **CLC 35**
See also AAYA 9; CA 69-72; CANR 11,
    45; CLR 32; JRDA; SAAS 9; SATA 23

Brand, Max
See Faust, Frederick (Schiller)

Brand, Millen 1906-1980.......... **CLC 7**
See also CA 21-24R; 97-100

Branden, Barbara .... **CLC 44**

Brandes, Georg (Morris Cohen)
    1842-1927 .... **TCLC 10**
See also CA 105

Brandys, Kazimierz 1916-........ **CLC 62**

Branley, Franklyn M(ansfield)
    1915-...................... **CLC 21**
See also CA 33-36R; CANR 14, 39;
    CLR 13; MAICYA; SAAS 16; SATA 4,
    68

Author Index

Brathwaite, Edward (Kamau)
1930- . . . . **CLC 11**
See also BW 2; CA 25-28R; CANR 11, 26;
DLB 125

Brautigan, Richard (Gary)
1935-1984 . . . . **CLC 1, 3, 5, 9, 12, 34, 42**
See also CA 53-56; 113; CANR 34; DLB 2,
5; DLBY 80, 84; MTCW; SATA 56

Braverman, Kate 1950- . . . . **CLC 67**
See also CA 89-92

Brecht, Bertolt
1898-1956 . . . . . . **TCLC 1, 6, 13, 35; DA;
DC 3; WLC**
See also CA 104; 133; DLB 56, 124; MTCW

Brecht, Eugen Berthold Friedrich
See Brecht, Bertolt

Bremer, Fredrika 1801-1865 . . . . . **NCLC 11**

Brennan, Christopher John
1870-1932 . . . . **TCLC 17**
See also CA 117

Brennan, Maeve 1917- . . . . **CLC 5**
See also CA 81-84

Brentano, Clemens (Maria)
1778-1842 . . . . **NCLC 1**

Brent of Bin Bin
See Franklin, (Stella Maraia Sarah) Miles

Brenton, Howard 1942- . . . . **CLC 31**
See also CA 69-72; CANR 33; DLB 13;
MTCW

Breslin, James 1930-
See Breslin, Jimmy
See also CA 73-76; CANR 31; MTCW

Breslin, Jimmy . . . . **CLC 4, 43**
See also Breslin, James
See also AITN 1

Bresson, Robert 1907- . . . . **CLC 16**
See also CA 110

Breton, Andre 1896-1966 . . . **CLC 2, 9, 15, 54**
See also CA 19-20; 25-28R; CANR 40;
CAP 2; DLB 65; MTCW

Breytenbach, Breyten 1939(?)- . . **CLC 23, 37**
See also CA 113; 129

Bridgers, Sue Ellen 1942- . . . . **CLC 26**
See also AAYA 8; CA 65-68; CANR 11,
36; CLR 18; DLB 52; JRDA; MAICYA;
SAAS 1; SATA 22

Bridges, Robert (Seymour)
1844-1930 . . . . **TCLC 1**
See also CA 104; CDDLD 1890-1914,
DLB 19, 98

Bridie, James . . . . **TCLC 3**
See also Mavor, Osborne Henry
See also DLB 10

Brin, David 1950- . . . . **CLC 34**
See also CA 102; CANR 24; SATA 65

Brink, Andre (Philippus)
1935- . . . . **CLC 18, 36**
See also CA 104; CANR 39; MTCW

Brinsmead, H(esba) F(ay) 1922- . . . . **CLC 21**
See also CA 21-24R; CANR 10; MAICYA;
SAAS 5; SATA 18, 78

Brittain, Vera (Mary)
1893(?)-1970 . . . . **CLC 23**
See also CA 13-16; 25-28R; CAP 1; MTCW

Broch, Hermann 1886-1951 . . . . . . **TCLC 20**
See also CA 117; DLB 85, 124

Brock, Rose
See Hansen, Joseph

Brodkey, Harold 1930- . . . . **CLC 56**
See also CA 111; DLB 130

Brodsky, Iosif Alexandrovich 1940-
See Brodsky, Joseph
See also AITN 1; CA 41-44R; CANR 37;
MTCW

Brodsky, Joseph . . **CLC 4, 6, 13, 36, 50; PC 9**
See also Brodsky, Iosif Alexandrovich

Brodsky, Michael Mark 1948- . . . . . **CLC 19**
See also CA 102; CANR 18, 41

Bromell, Henry 1947- . . . . **CLC 5**
See also CA 53-56; CANR 9

Bromfield, Louis (Brucker)
1896-1956 . . . . **TCLC 11**
See also CA 107; DLB 4, 9, 86

Broner, E(sther) M(asserman)
1930- . . . . **CLC 19**
See also CA 17-20R; CANR 8, 25; DLB 28

Bronk, William 1918- . . . . **CLC 10**
See also CA 89-92; CANR 23

Bronstein, Lev Davidovich
See Trotsky, Leon

Bronte, Anne 1820-1849 . . . . **NCLC 4**
See also DLB 21

Bronte, Charlotte
1816-1855 . . . **NCLC 3, 8, 33; DA; WLC**
See also CDBLB 1832-1890; DLB 21

Bronte, (Jane) Emily
1818-1848 . . . . **NCLC 16, 35; DA; PC 8;
WLC**
See also CDBLB 1832-1890; DLB 21, 32

Brooke, Frances 1724-1789 . . . . **LC 6**
See also DLB 39, 99

Brooke, Henry 1703(?)-1783 . . . . **LC 1**
See also DLB 39

Brooke, Rupert (Chawner)
1887-1915 . . . . **TCLC 2, 7; DA; WLC**
See also CA 104; 132; CDBLB 1914-1945;
DLB 19; MTCW

Brooke-Haven, P.
See Wodehouse, P(elham) G(renville)

Brooke-Rose, Christine 1926- . . . . . . **CLC 40**
See also CA 13-16R; DLB 14

Brookner, Anita 1928- . . . . . . **CLC 32, 34, 51**
See also CA 114; 120; CANR 37; DLBY 87;
MTCW

Brooks, Cleanth 1906-1994 . . . . **CLC 24**
See also CA 17-20R; 145; CANR 33, 35;
DLB 63; MTCW

Brooks, George
See Baum, L(yman) Frank

Brooks, Gwendolyn
1917- . . . . . . **CLC 1, 2, 4, 5, 15, 49; BLC;
DA; PC 7; WLC**
See also AITN 1; BW 2; CA 1-4R;
CANR 1, 27; CDALB 1941-1968;
CLR 27; DLB 5, 76; MTCW; SATA 6

Brooks, Mel . . . . **CLC 12**
See also Kaminsky, Melvin
See also DLB 26

Brooks, Peter 1938- . . . . **CLC 34**
See also CA 45-48; CANR 1

Brooks, Van Wyck 1886-1963 . . . . . **CLC 29**
See also CA 1-4R; CANR 6; DLB 45, 63,
103

Brophy, Brigid (Antonia)
1929- . . . . **CLC 6, 11, 29**
See also CA 5-8R; CAAS 4; CANR 25;
DLB 14; MTCW

Brosman, Catharine Savage 1934- . . . . **CLC 9**
See also CA 61-64; CANR 21

Brother Antoninus
See Everson, William (Oliver)

Broughton, T(homas) Alan 1936- . . . **CLC 19**
See also CA 45-48; CANR 2, 23

Broumas, Olga 1949- . . . . **CLC 10, 73**
See also CA 85-88; CANR 20

Brown, Charles Brockden
1771-1810 . . . . **NCLC 22**
See also CDALB 1640-1865; DLB 37, 59,
73

Brown, Christy 1932-1981 . . . . **CLC 63**
See also CA 105; 104; DLB 14

Brown, Claude 1937- . . . . **CLC 30; BLC**
See also AAYA 7; BW 1; CA 73-76

Brown, Dee (Alexander) 1908- . . **CLC 18, 47**
See also CA 13-16R; CAAS 6; CANR 11,
45; DLBY 80; MTCW; SATA 5

Brown, George
See Wertmueller, Lina

Brown, George Douglas
1869-1902 . . . . **TCLC 28**

Brown, George Mackay 1921- . . . . **CLC 5, 48**
See also CA 21-24R; CAAS 6; CANR 12,
37; DLB 14, 27, 139; MTCW; SATA 35

Brown, (William) Larry 1951- . . . . . . **CLC 73**
See also CA 130; 134

Brown, Moses
See Barrett, William (Christopher)

Brown, Rita Mae 1944- . . . . . **CLC 18, 43, 79**
See also CA 45-48; CANR 2, 11, 35;
MTCW

Brown, Roderick (Langmere) Haig-
See Haig-Brown, Roderick (Langmere)

Brown, Rosellen 1939- . . . . **CLC 32**
See also CA 77-80; CAAS 10; CANR 14, 44

Brown, Sterling Allen
1901-1989 . . . . **CLC 1, 23, 59; BLC**
See also BW 1; CA 85-88; 127; CANR 26;
DLB 48, 51, 63; MTCW

Brown, Will
See Ainsworth, William Harrison

Brown, William Wells
1813-1884 . . . . **NCLC 2; BLC; DC 1**
See also DLB 3, 50

Browne, (Clyde) Jackson 1948(?)- . . . **CLC 21**
See also CA 120

Browning, Elizabeth Barrett
1806-1861 . . . . . **NCLC 1, 16; DA; PC 6;
WLC**
See also CDBLB 1832-1890; DLB 32

Browning, Robert
　　1812-1889 .... **NCLC 19; DA; PC 2**
　　See also CDBLB 1832-1890; DLB 32;
　　YABC 1

Browning, Tod 1882-1962 .... **CLC 16**
　　See also CA 141; 117

Bruccoli, Matthew J(oseph) 1931- .. **CLC 34**
　　See also CA 9-12R; CANR 7; DLB 103

Bruce, Lenny..................... **CLC 21**
　　See also Schneider, Leonard Alfred

Bruin, John
　　See Brutus, Dennis

Brulard, Henri
　　See Stendhal

Brulls, Christian
　　See Simenon, Georges (Jacques Christian)

Brunner, John (Kilian Houston)
　　1934- .... **CLC 8, 10**
　　See also CA 1-4R; CAAS 8; CANR 2, 37;
　　MTCW

Bruno, Giordano 1548-1600........ **LC 27**

Brutus, Dennis 1924- .... **CLC 43; BLC**
　　See also BW 2; CA 49-52; CAAS 14;
　　CANR 2, 27, 42; DLB 117

Bryan, C(ourtlandt) D(ixon) B(arnes)
　　1936- .... **CLC 29**
　　See also CA 73-76; CANR 13

Bryan, Michael
　　See Moore, Brian

Bryant, William Cullen
　　1794-1878 .... **NCLC 6, 46; DA**
　　See also CDALB 1640-1865; DLB 3, 43, 59

Bryusov, Valery Yakovlevich
　　1873-1924 .... **TCLC 10**
　　See also CA 107

Buchan, John 1875-1940 .... **TCLC 41**
　　See also CA 108; 145; DLB 34, 70; YABC 2

Buchanan, George 1506-1582 .... **LC 4**

Buchheim, Lothar-Guenther 1918- ... **CLC 6**
　　See also CA 85-88

Buchner, (Karl) Georg
　　1813-1837 .... **NCLC 26**

Buchwald, Art(hur) 1925-.......... **CLC 33**
　　See also AITN 1; CA 5-8R; CANR 21;
　　MTCW; SATA 10

Buck, Pearl S(ydenstricker)
　　1892-1973 .... **CLC 7, 11, 18; DA**
　　See also AITN 1; CA 1-4R; 41-44R;
　　CANR 1, 34; DLB 9, 102; MTCW;
　　SATA 1, 25

Buckler, Ernest 1908-1984......... **CLC 13**
　　See also CA 11-12; 114; CAP 1; DLB 68;
　　SATA 47

Buckley, Vincent (Thomas)
　　1925-1988 .... **CLC 57**
　　See also CA 101

Buckley, William F(rank), Jr.
　　1925- .... **CLC 7, 18, 37**
　　See also AITN 1; CA 1-4R; CANR 1, 24;
　　DLB 137; DLBY 80; MTCW

Buechner, (Carl) Frederick
　　1926- .... **CLC 2, 4, 6, 9**
　　See also CA 13-16R; CANR 11, 39;
　　DLBY 80; MTCW

Buell, John (Edward) 1927-........ **CLC 10**
　　See also CA 1-4R; DLB 53

Buero Vallejo, Antonio 1916- ... **CLC 15, 46**
　　See also CA 106; CANR 24; HW; MTCW

Bufalino, Gesualdo 1920(?)-........ **CLC 74**

Bugayev, Boris Nikolayevich 1880-1934
　　See Bely, Andrey
　　See also CA 104

Bukowski, Charles
　　1920-1994 .... **CLC 2, 5, 9, 41, 82**
　　See also CA 17-20R; 144; CANR 40;
　　DLB 5, 130; MTCW

Bulgakov, Mikhail (Afanas'evich)
　　1891-1940 .... **TCLC 2, 16**
　　See also CA 105

Bulgya, Alexander Alexandrovich
　　1901-1956 .... **TCLC 53**
　　See also Fadeyev, Alexander
　　See also CA 117

Bullins, Ed 1935- .... **CLC 1, 5, 7; BLC**
　　See also BW 2; CA 49-52; CAAS 16;
　　CANR 24; DLB 7, 38; MTCW

Bulwer-Lytton, Edward (George Earle Lytton)
　　1803-1873 .... **NCLC 1, 45**
　　See also DLB 21

Bunin, Ivan Alexeyevich
　　1870-1953 .... **TCLC 6; SSC 5**
　　See also CA 104

Bunting, Basil 1900-1985.... **CLC 10, 39, 47**
　　See also CA 53-56; 115; CANR 7; DLB 20

Bunuel, Luis 1900-1983 .. **CLC 16, 80; HLC**
　　See also CA 101; 110; CANR 32; HW

Bunyan, John 1628-1688 .. **LC 4; DA; WLC**
　　See also CDBLB 1660-1789; DLB 39

Burford, Eleanor
　　See Hibbert, Eleanor Alice Burford

Burgess, Anthony
　　. **CLC 1, 2, 4, 5, 8, 10, 13, 15, 22, 40, 62,
　　81**
　　See also Wilson, John (Anthony) Burgess
　　See also AITN 1; CDBLB 1960 to Present;
　　DLB 14

Burke, Edmund
　　1729(?)-1797 .... **LC 7; DA; WLC**
　　See also DLB 104

Burke, Kenneth (Duva)
　　1897-1993 .... **CLC 2, 24**
　　See also CA 5-8R; 143; CANR 39; DLB 45,
　　63; MTCW

Burke, Leda
　　See Garnett, David

Burke, Ralph
　　See Silverberg, Robert

Burney, Fanny 1752-1840 .... **NCLC 12**
　　See also DLB 39

Burns, Robert
　　1759-1796 ...... **LC 3; DA; PC 6; WLC**
　　See also CDBLB 1789-1832; DLB 109

Burns, Tex
　　See L'Amour, Louis (Dearborn)

Burnshaw, Stanley 1906- ..... **CLC 3, 13, 44**
　　See also CA 9-12R; DLB 48

Burr, Anne 1937- .... **CLC 6**
　　See also CA 25-28R

Burroughs, Edgar Rice
　　1875-1950 .... **TCLC 2, 32**
　　See also AAYA 11; CA 104; 132; DLB 8;
　　MTCW; SATA 41

Burroughs, William S(eward)
　　1914- .... **CLC 1, 2, 5, 15, 22, 42, 75;
　　DA; WLC**
　　See also AITN 2; CA 9-12R; CANR 20;
　　DLB 2, 8, 16; DLBY 81; MTCW

Burton, Richard F. 1821-1890.... **NCLC 42**
　　See also DLB 55

Busch, Frederick 1941- ... **CLC 7, 10, 18, 47**
　　See also CA 33-36R; CAAS 1; CANR 45;
　　DLB 6

Bush, Ronald 1946- .... **CLC 34**
　　See also CA 136

Bustos, F(rancisco)
　　See Borges, Jorge Luis

Bustos Domecq, H(onorio)
　　See Bioy Casares, Adolfo; Borges, Jorge
　　Luis

Butler, Octavia E(stelle) 1947- ..... **CLC 38**
　　See also BW 2; CA 73-76; CANR 12, 24,
　　38; DLB 33; MTCW

Butler, Robert Olen (Jr.) 1945-..... **CLC 81**
　　See also CA 112

Butler, Samuel 1612-1680 .... **LC 16**
　　See also DLB 101, 126

Butler, Samuel
　　1835-1902 ...... **TCLC 1, 33; DA; WLC**
　　See also CA 143; CDBLB 1890-1914;
　　DLB 18, 57

Butler, Walter C.
　　See Faust, Frederick (Schiller)

Butor, Michel (Marie Francois)
　　1926- .... **CLC 1, 3, 8, 11, 15**
　　See also CA 9-12R; CANR 33; DLB 83;
　　MTCW

Buzo, Alexander (John) 1944-...... **CLC 61**
　　See also CA 97-100; CANR 17, 39

Buzzati, Dino 1906-1972 .... **CLC 36**
　　See also CA 33-36R

Byars, Betsy (Cromer) 1928-....... **CLC 35**
　　See also CA 33-36R; CANR 18, 36; CLR 1,
　　16; DLB 52; JRDA; MAICYA; MTCW;
　　SAAS 1; SATA 4, 46

Byatt, A(ntonia) S(usan Drabble)
　　1936- .... **CLC 19, 65**
　　See also CA 13-16R; CANR 13, 33;
　　DLB 14; MTCW

Byrne, David 1952-............... **CLC 26**
　　See also CA 127

Byrne, John Keyes 1926-
　　See Leonard, Hugh
　　See also CA 102

Byron, George Gordon (Noel)
　　1788-1824 ...... **NCLC 2, 12; DA; WLC**
　　See also CDBLB 1789-1832; DLB 96, 110

C. 3. 3.
　　See Wilde, Oscar (Fingal O'Flahertie Wills)

Caballero, Fernan 1796-1877..... **NCLC 10**

Cabell, James Branch 1879-1958 ... **TCLC 6**
　　See also CA 105; DLB 9, 78

Cary, (Arthur) Joyce (Lunel)
1888-1957 . . . . TCLC 1, 29
See also CA 104; CDBLB 1914-1945;
DLB 15, 100

Casanova de Seingalt, Giovanni Jacopo
1725-1798 . . . . LC 13

Casares, Adolfo Bioy
See Bioy Casares, Adolfo

Casely-Hayford, J(oseph) E(phraim)
1866-1930 . . . . TCLC 24; BLC
See also BW 2; CA 123

Casey, John (Dudley) 1939- . . . . CLC 59
See also BEST 90:2; CA 69-72; CANR 23

Casey, Michael 1947- . . . . CLC 2
See also CA 65-68; DLB 5

Casey, Patrick
See Thurman, Wallace (Henry)

Casey, Warren (Peter) 1935-1988 . . . CLC 12
See also CA 101; 127

Casona, Alejandro . . . . CLC 49
See also Alvarez, Alejandro Rodriguez

Cassavetes, John 1929-1989 . . . . CLC 20
See also CA 85-88; 127

Cassill, R(onald) V(erlin) 1919- . . . CLC 4, 23
See also CA 9-12R; CAAS 1; CANR 7, 45;
DLB 6

Cassity, (Allen) Turner 1929- . . . . CLC 6, 42
See also CA 17-20R; CAAS 8; CANR 11;
DLB 105

Castaneda, Carlos 1931(?)- . . . . CLC 12
See also CA 25-28R; CANR 32; HW;
MTCW

Castedo, Elena 1937- . . . . CLC 65
See also CA 132

Castedo-Ellerman, Elena
See Castedo, Elena

Castellanos, Rosario
1925-1974 . . . . CLC 66; HLC
See also CA 131; 53-56; DLB 113; HW

Castelvetro, Lodovico 1505-1571 . . . . . LC 12

Castiglione, Baldassare 1478-1529 . . . LC 12

Castle, Robert
See Hamilton, Edmond

Castro, Guillen de 1569-1631 . . . . LC 19

Castro, Rosalia de 1837-1885 . . . . . NCLC 3

Cather, Willa
See Cather, Willa Sibert

Cather, Willa Sibert
1873-1947 . . . . TCLC 1, 11, 31; DA;
SSC 2; WLC
See also CA 104; 128; CDALB 1865-1917;
DLB 9, 54, 78; DLBD 1; MTCW;
SATA 30

Catton, (Charles) Bruce
1899-1978 . . . . CLC 35
See also AITN 1; CA 5-8R; 81-84;
CANR 7; DLB 17; SATA 2, 24

Cauldwell, Frank
See King, Francis (Henry)

Caunitz, William J. 1933- . . . . CLC 34
See also BEST 89:3; CA 125; 130

Causley, Charles (Stanley) 1917- . . . . . CLC 7
See also CA 9-12R; CANR 5, 35; CLR 30;
DLB 27; MTCW; SATA 3, 66

Caute, David 1936- . . . . CLC 29
See also CA 1-4R; CAAS 4; CANR 1, 33;
DLB 14

Cavafy, C(onstantine) P(eter) . . . . . . TCLC 2, 7
See also Kavafis, Konstantinos Petrou

Cavallo, Evelyn
See Spark, Muriel (Sarah)

Cavanna, Betty . . . . CLC 12
See also Harrison, Elizabeth Cavanna
See also JRDA; MAICYA; SAAS 4;
SATA 1, 30

Caxton, William 1421(?)-1491(?) . . . . . LC 17

Cayrol, Jean 1911- . . . . CLC 11
See also CA 89-92; DLB 83

Cela, Camilo Jose
1916- . . . . CLC 4, 13, 59; HLC
See also BEST 90:2; CA 21-24R; CAAS 10;
CANR 21, 32; DLBY 89; HW; MTCW

Celan, Paul . . . . . . CLC 10, 19, 53, 82; PC 10
See also Antschel, Paul
See also DLB 69

Celine, Louis-Ferdinand
. . . . CLC 1, 3, 4, 7, 9, 15, 47
See also Destouches, Louis-Ferdinand
See also DLB 72

Cellini, Benvenuto 1500-1571 . . . . LC 7

Cendrars, Blaise
See Sauser-Hall, Frederic

Cernuda (y Bidon), Luis
1902-1963 . . . . CLC 54
See also CA 131; 89-92; DLB 134; HW

Cervantes (Saavedra), Miguel de
1547-1616 . . . . . . LC 6, 23; DA; SSC 12;
WLC

Cesaire, Aime (Fernand)
1913- . . . . CLC 19, 32; BLC
See also BW 2; CA 65-68; CANR 24, 43;
MTCW

Chabon, Michael 1965(?)- . . . . CLC 55
See also CA 139

Chabrol, Claude 1930- . . . . CLC 16
See also CA 110

Challans, Mary 1905-1983
See Renault, Mary
See also CA 81-84; 111; SATA 23, 36

Challis, George
See Faust, Frederick (Schiller)

Chambers, Aidan 1934- . . . . CLC 35
See also CA 25-28R; CANR 12, 31; JRDA;
MAICYA; SAAS 12; SATA 1, 69

Chambers, James 1948-
See Cliff, Jimmy
See also CA 124

Chambers, Jessie
See Lawrence, D(avid) H(erbert Richards)

Chambers, Robert W. 1865-1933 . . . TCLC 41

Chandler, Raymond (Thornton)
1888-1959 . . . . TCLC 1, 7
See also CA 104; 129; CDALB 1929-1941;
DLBD 6; MTCW

Chang, Jung 1952- . . . . CLC 71
See also CA 142

Channing, William Ellery
1780-1842 . . . . NCLC 17
See also DLB 1, 59

Chaplin, Charles Spencer
1889-1977 . . . . CLC 16
See also Chaplin, Charlie
See also CA 81-84; 73-76

Chaplin, Charlie
See Chaplin, Charles Spencer
See also DLB 44

Chapman, George 1559(?)-1634 . . . . . . LC 22
See also DLB 62, 121

Chapman, Graham 1941-1989 . . . . . CLC 21
See also Monty Python
See also CA 116; 129; CANR 35

Chapman, John Jay 1862-1933 . . . . . TCLC 7
See also CA 104

Chapman, Walker
See Silverberg, Robert

Chappell, Fred (Davis) 1936- . . . . CLC 40, 78
See also CA 5-8R; CAAS 4; CANR 8, 33;
DLB 6, 105

Char, Rene(-Emile)
1907-1988 . . . . CLC 9, 11, 14, 55
See also CA 13-16R; 124; CANR 32;
MTCW

Charby, Jay
See Ellison, Harlan

Chardin, Pierre Teilhard de
See Teilhard de Chardin, (Marie Joseph)
Pierre

Charles I 1600-1649 . . . . LC 13

Charyn, Jerome 1937- . . . . CLC 5, 8, 18
See also CA 5-8R; CAAS 1; CANR 7;
DLBY 83; MTCW

Chase, Mary (Coyle) 1907-1981 . . . . . . DC 1
See also CA 77-80; 105; SATA 17, 29

Chase, Mary Ellen 1887-1973 . . . . CLC 2
See also CA 13-16; 41-44R; CAP 1;
SATA 10

Chase, Nicholas
See Hyde, Anthony

Chateaubriand, Francois Rene de
1768-1848 . . . . NCLC 3
See also DLB 119

Chatterje, Sarat Chandra 1876-1936(?)
See Chatterji, Saratchandra
See also CA 109

Chatterji, Bankim Chandra
1838-1894 . . . . NCLC 19

Chatterji, Saratchandra . . . . TCLC 13
See also Chatterje, Sarat Chandra

Chatterton, Thomas 1752-1770 . . . . LC 3
See also DLB 109

Chatwin, (Charles) Bruce
1940-1989 . . . . CLC 28, 57, 59
See also AAYA 4; BEST 90:1; CA 85-88;
127

Chaucer, Daniel
See Ford, Ford Madox

Chaucer, Geoffrey
1340(?)-1400 . . . . LC 17; DA
See also CDBLB Before 1660

Chaviaras, Strates 1935-
See Haviaras, Stratis
See also CA 105

Chayefsky, Paddy .... CLC 23
See also Chayefsky, Sidney
See also DLB 7, 44; DLBY 81

Chayefsky, Sidney 1923-1981
See Chayefsky, Paddy
See also CA 9-12R; 104; CANR 18

Chedid, Andree 1920- .... CLC 47
See also CA 145

Cheever, John
1912-1982 ...... CLC 3, 7, 8, 11, 15, 25,
64; DA; SSC 1; WLC
See also CA 5-8R; 106; CABS 1; CANR 5,
27; CDALB 1941-1968; DLB 2, 102;
DLBY 80, 82; MTCW

Cheever, Susan 1943- .... CLC 18, 48
See also CA 103; CANR 27; DLBY 82

Chekhonte, Antosha
See Chekhov, Anton (Pavlovich)

Chekhov, Anton (Pavlovich)
1860-1904 ..... TCLC 3, 10, 31, 55; DA;
SSC 2; WLC
See also CA 104; 124

Chernyshevsky, Nikolay Gavrilovich
1828-1889 .... NCLC 1

Cherry, Carolyn Janice 1942-
See Cherryh, C. J.
See also CA 65-68; CANR 10

Cherryh, C. J. .... CLC 35
See also Cherry, Carolyn Janice
See also DLBY 80

Chesnutt, Charles W(addell)
1858-1932 .... TCLC 5, 39; BLC; SSC 7
See also BW 1; CA 106; 125; DLB 12, 50,
78; MTCW

Chester, Alfred 1929(?)-1971 .... CLC 49
See also CA 33-36R; DLB 130

Chesterton, G(ilbert) K(eith)
1874-1936 .... TCLC 1, 6; SSC 1
See also CA 104; 132; CDBLB 1914-1945;
DLB 10, 19, 34, 70, 98; MTCW;
SATA 27

Chiang Pin-chin 1904-1986
See Ding Ling
See also CA 118

Ch'ien Chung-shu 1910- .... CLC 22
See also CA 130; MTCW

Child, L. Maria
See Child, Lydia Maria

Child, Lydia Maria 1802-1880 .... NCLC 6
See also DLB 1, 74; SATA 67

Child, Mrs.
See Child, Lydia Maria

Child, Philip 1898-1978 .... CLC 19, 68
See also CA 13-14; CAP 1; SATA 47

Childress, Alice
1920- .... CLC 12, 15; BLC; DC 4
See also AAYA 8; BW 2; CA 45-48;
CANR 3, 27; CLR 14; DLB 7, 38; JRDA;
MAICYA; MTCW; SATA 7, 48

Chislett, (Margaret) Anne 1943- .... CLC 34

Chitty, Thomas Willes 1926- .... CLC 11
See also Hinde, Thomas
See also CA 5-8R

Chomette, Rene Lucien 1898-1981
See Clair, Rene
See also CA 103

Chopin, Kate .... TCLC 5, 14; DA; SSC 8
See also Chopin, Katherine
See also CDALB 1865-1917; DLB 12, 78

Chopin, Katherine 1851-1904
See Chopin, Kate
See also CA 104; 122

Chretien de Troyes
c. 12th cent. - .... CMLC 10

Christie
See Ichikawa, Kon

Christie, Agatha (Mary Clarissa)
1890-1976 ...... CLC 1, 6, 8, 12, 39, 48
See also AAYA 9; AITN 1, 2; CA 17-20R;
61-64; CANR 10, 37; CDBLB 1914-1945;
DLB 13, 77; MTCW; SATA 36

Christie, (Ann) Philippa
See Pearce, Philippa
See also CA 5-8R; CANR 4

Christine de Pizan 1365(?)-1431(?) .... LC 9

Chubb, Elmer
See Masters, Edgar Lee

Chulkov, Mikhail Dmitrievich
1743-1792 .... LC 2

Churchill, Caryl 1938- .... CLC 31, 55
See also CA 102; CANR 22; DLB 13;
MTCW

Churchill, Charles 1731-1764 .... LC 3
See also DLB 109

Chute, Carolyn 1947- .... CLC 39
See also CA 123

Ciardi, John (Anthony)
1916-1986 .... CLC 10, 40, 44
See also CA 5-8R; 118; CAAS 2; CANR 5,
33; CLR 19; DLB 5; DLBY 86;
MAICYA; MTCW; SATA 1, 46, 65

Cicero, Marcus Tullius
106B.C.-43B.C. .... CMLC 3

Cimino, Michael 1943- .... CLC 16
See also CA 105

Cioran, E(mil) M. 1911- .... CLC 64
See also CA 25-28R

Cisneros, Sandra 1954- ...... CLC 69; HLC
See also AAYA 9; CA 131; DLB 122; HW

Clair, Rene .... CLC 20
See also Chomette, Rene Lucien

Clampitt, Amy 1920- .... CLC 32
See also CA 110; CANR 29; DLB 105

Clancy, Thomas L., Jr. 1947-
See Clancy, Tom
See also CA 125; 131; MTCW

Clancy, Tom .... CLC 45
See also Clancy, Thomas L., Jr.
See also AAYA 9; BEST 89:1, 90:1

Clare, John 1793-1864 .... NCLC 9
See also DLB 55, 96

Clarin
See Alas (y Urena), Leopoldo (Enrique
Garcia)

Clark, Al C.
See Goines, Donald

Clark, (Robert) Brian 1932- .... CLC 29
See also CA 41-44R

Clark, Curt
See Westlake, Donald E(dwin)

Clark, Eleanor 1913- .... CLC 5, 19
See also CA 9-12R; CANR 41; DLB 6

Clark, J. P.
See Clark, John Pepper
See also DLB 117

Clark, John Pepper 1935- .... CLC 38; BLC
See also Clark, J. P.
See also BW 1; CA 65-68; CANR 16

Clark, M. R.
See Clark, Mavis Thorpe

Clark, Mavis Thorpe 1909- .... CLC 12
See also CA 57-60; CANR 8, 37; CLR 30;
MAICYA; SAAS 5; SATA 8, 74

Clark, Walter Van Tilburg
1909-1971 .... CLC 28
See also CA 9-12R; 33-36R; DLB 9;
SATA 8

Clarke, Arthur C(harles)
1917- ...... CLC 1, 4, 13, 18, 35; SSC 3
See also AAYA 4; CA 1-4R; CANR 2, 28;
JRDA; MAICYA; MTCW; SATA 13, 70

Clarke, Austin 1896-1974 .... CLC 6, 9
See also CA 29-32; 49-52; CAP 2; DLB 10,
20

Clarke, Austin C(hesterfield)
1934- .... CLC 8, 53; BLC
See also BW 1; CA 25-28R; CAAS 16;
CANR 14, 32; DLB 53, 125

Clarke, Gillian 1937- .... CLC 61
See also CA 106; DLB 40

Clarke, Marcus (Andrew Hislop)
1846-1881 .... NCLC 19

Clarke, Shirley 1925- .... CLC 16

Clash, The
See Headon, (Nicky) Topper; Jones, Mick;
Simonon, Paul; Strummer, Joe

Claudel, Paul (Louis Charles Marie)
1868-1955 .... TCLC 2, 10
See also CA 104

Clavell, James (duMaresq)
1925- .... CLC 6, 25
See also CA 25-28R; CANR 26; MTCW

Cleaver, (Leroy) Eldridge
1935- .... CLC 30; BLC
See also BW 1; CA 21-24R; CANR 16

Cleese, John (Marwood) 1939- ..... CLC 21
See also Monty Python
See also CA 112; 116; CANR 35; MTCW

Cleishbotham, Jebediah
See Scott, Walter

Cleland, John 1710-1789 .... LC 2
See also DLB 39

Clemens, Samuel Langhorne 1835-1910
See Twain, Mark
See also CA 104; 135; CDALB 1865-1917;
DA; DLB 11, 12, 23, 64, 74; JRDA;
MAICYA; YABC 2

Cleophil
See Congreve, William

Clerihew, E.
See Bentley, E(dmund) C(lerihew)

Clerk, N. W.
See Lewis, C(live) S(taples)

Cliff, Jimmy....................... CLC 21
See also Chambers, James

Clifton, (Thelma) Lucille
1936- .... CLC 19, 66; BLC
See also BW 2; CA 49-52; CANR 2, 24, 42;
CLR 5; DLB 5, 41; MAICYA; MTCW;
SATA 20, 69

Clinton, Dirk
See Silverberg, Robert

Clough, Arthur Hugh 1819-1861.. NCLC 27
See also DLB 32

Clutha, Janet Paterson Frame 1924-
See Frame, Janet
See also CA 1-4R; CANR 2, 36; MTCW

Clyne, Terence
See Blatty, William Peter

Cobalt, Martin
See Mayne, William (James Carter)

Coburn, D(onald) L(ee) 1938- ...... CLC 10
See also CA 89-92

Cocteau, Jean (Maurice Eugene Clement)
1889-1963 .... CLC 1, 8, 15, 16, 43; DA;
WLC
See also CA 25-28; CANR 40; CAP 2;
DLB 65; MTCW

Codrescu, Andrei 1946- .... CLC 46
See also CA 33-36R; CAAS 19; CANR 13,
34

Coe, Max
See Bourne, Randolph S(illiman)

Coe, Tucker
See Westlake, Donald E(dwin)

Coetzee, J(ohn) M(ichael)
1940- .... CLC 23, 33, 66
See also CA 77-80; CANR 41; MTCW

Coffey, Brian
See Koontz, Dean R(ay)

Cohen, Arthur A(llen)
1928-1986 .... CLC 7, 31
See also CA 1-4R; 120; CANR 1, 17, 42;
DLB 28

Cohen, Leonard (Norman)
1934- .... CLC 3, 38
See also CA 21-24R; CANR 14; DLB 53;
MTCW

Cohen, Matt 1942- .... CLC 19
See also CA 61-64; CAAS 18; CANR 40;
DLB 53

Cohen-Solal, Annie 19(?)- .... CLC 50

Colegate, Isabel 1931- .... CLC 36
See also CA 17-20R; CANR 8, 22; DLB 14;
MTCW

Coleman, Emmett
See Reed, Ishmael

Coleridge, Samuel Taylor
1772-1834 .... NCLC 9; DA; WLC
See also CDBLB 1789-1832; DLB 93, 107

Coleridge, Sara 1802-1852....... NCLC 31

Coles, Don 1928- .... CLC 46
See also CA 115; CANR 38

Colette, (Sidonie-Gabrielle)
1873-1954 ...... TCLC 1, 5, 16; SSC 10
See also CA 104; 131; DLB 65; MTCW

Collett, (Jacobine) Camilla (Wergeland)
1813-1895 .... NCLC 22

Collier, Christopher 1930-......... CLC 30
See also CA 33-36R; CANR 13, 33; JRDA;
MAICYA; SATA 16, 70

Collier, James L(incoln) 1928- ..... CLC 30
See also CA 9-12R; CANR 4, 33; CLR 3;
JRDA; MAICYA; SATA 8, 70

Collier, Jeremy 1650-1726.......... LC 6

Collins, Hunt
See Hunter, Evan

Collins, Linda 1931-.............. CLC 44
See also CA 125

Collins, (William) Wilkie
1824-1889 .... NCLC 1, 18
See also CDBLB 1832-1890; DLB 18, 70

Collins, William 1721-1759 .... LC 4
See also DLB 109

Colman, George
See Glassco, John

Colt, Winchester Remington
See Hubbard, L(afayette) Ron(ald)

Colter, Cyrus 1910- .... CLC 58
See also BW 1; CA 65-68; CANR 10;
DLB 33

Colton, James
See Hansen, Joseph

Colum, Padraic 1881-1972......... CLC 28
See also CA 73-76; 33-36R; CANR 35;
MAICYA; MTCW; SATA 15

Colvin, James
See Moorcock, Michael (John)

Colwin, Laurie (E.)
1944-1992 .... CLC 5, 13, 23, 84
See also CA 89-92; 139; CANR 20;
DLBY 80; MTCW

Comfort, Alex(ander) 1920-........ CLC 7
See also CA 1-4R; CANR 1, 45

Comfort, Montgomery
See Campbell, (John) Ramsey

Compton-Burnett, I(vy)
1884(?)-1969 ...... CLC 1, 3, 10, 15, 34
See also CA 1-4R; 25-28R; CANR 4;
DLB 36; MTCW

Comstock, Anthony 1844-1915 .... TCLC 13
See also CA 110

Conan Doyle, Arthur
See Doyle, Arthur Conan

Conde, Maryse 1937-............. CLC 52
See also Boucolon, Maryse
See also BW 2

Condillac, Etienne Bonnot de
1714-1780 .... LC 26

Condon, Richard (Thomas)
1915- .... CLC 4, 6, 8, 10, 45
See also BEST 90:3; CA 1-4R; CAAS 1;
CANR 2, 23; MTCW

Congreve, William
1670-1729 ... LC 5, 21; DA; DC 2; WLC
See also CDBLB 1660-1789; DLB 39, 84

Connell, Evan S(helby), Jr.
1924- .... CLC 4, 6, 45
See also AAYA 7; CA 1-4R; CAAS 2;
CANR 2, 39; DLB 2; DLBY 81; MTCW

Connelly, Marc(us Cook)
1890-1980 .... CLC 7
See also CA 85-88; 102; CANR 30; DLB 7;
DLBY 80; SATA 25

Connor, Ralph .... TCLC 31
See also Gordon, Charles William
See also DLB 92

Conrad, Joseph
1857-1924 .... TCLC 1, 6, 13, 25, 43, 57;
DA; SSC 9; WLC
See also CA 104; 131; CDBLB 1890-1914;
DLB 10, 34, 98; MTCW; SATA 27

Conrad, Robert Arnold
See Hart, Moss

Conroy, Pat 1945-............. CLC 30, 74
See also AAYA 8; AITN 1; CA 85-88;
CANR 24; DLB 6; MTCW

Constant (de Rebecque), (Henri) Benjamin
1767-1830 .... NCLC 6
See also DLB 119

Conybeare, Charles Augustus
See Eliot, T(homas) S(tearns)

Cook, Michael 1933- .... CLC 58
See also CA 93-96; DLB 53

Cook, Robin 1940- .... CLC 14
See also BEST 90:2; CA 108; 111;
CANR 41

Cook, Roy
See Silverberg, Robert

Cooke, Elizabeth 1948- .... CLC 55
See also CA 129

Cooke, John Esten 1830-1886..... NCLC 5
See also DLB 3

Cooke, John Estes
See Baum, L(yman) Frank

Cooke, M. E.
See Creasey, John

Cooke, Margaret
See Creasey, John

Cooney, Ray .... CLC 62

Cooper, Henry St. John
See Creasey, John

Cooper, J. California............... CLC 56
See also AAYA 12; BW 1; CA 125

Cooper, James Fenimore
1789-1851 .... NCLC 1, 27
See also CDALB 1640-1865; DLB 3;
SATA 19

Coover, Robert (Lowell)
1932- ..... CLC 3, 7, 15, 32, 46; SSC 15
See also CA 45-48; CANR 3, 37; DLB 2;
DLBY 81; MTCW

Copeland, Stewart (Armstrong)
1952- .... CLC 26

Coppard, A(lfred) E(dgar)
1878-1957 .... TCLC 5
See also CA 114; YABC 1

Coppee, Francois 1842-1908 ...... TCLC 25

Coppola, Francis Ford 1939-....... CLC 16
See also CA 77-80; CANR 40; DLB 44

Author Index

Dickinson, Emily (Elizabeth)
1830-1886 .. NCLC 21; DA; PC 1; WLC
See also CDALB 1865-1917; DLB 1;
SATA 29

Dickinson, Peter (Malcolm)
1927- .... CLC 12, 35
See also AAYA 9; CA 41-44R; CANR 31;
CLR 29; DLB 87; JRDA; MAICYA;
SATA 5, 62

Dickson, Carr
See Carr, John Dickson

Dickson, Carter
See Carr, John Dickson

Diderot, Denis 1713-1784 .... LC 26

Didion, Joan 1934-..... CLC 1, 3, 8, 14, 32
See also AITN 1; CA 5-8R; CANR 14;
CDALB 1968-1988; DLB 2; DLBY 81,
86; MTCW

Dietrich, Robert
See Hunt, E(verette) Howard, Jr.

Dillard, Annie 1945-........... CLC 9, 60
See also AAYA 6; CA 49-52; CANR 3, 43;
DLBY 80; MTCW; SATA 10

Dillard, R(ichard) H(enry) W(ilde)
1937- .... CLC 5
See also CA 21-24R; CAAS 7; CANR 10;
DLB 5

Dillon, Eilis 1920-............... CLC 17
See also CA 9-12R; CAAS 3; CANR 4, 38;
CLR 26; MAICYA; SATA 2, 74

Dimont, Penelope
See Mortimer, Penelope (Ruth)

Dinesen, Isak........... CLC 10, 29; SSC 7
See also Blixen, Karen (Christentze
Dinesen)

Ding Ling........................ CLC 68
See also Chiang Pin-chin

Disch, Thomas M(ichael) 1940-... CLC 7, 36
See also CA 21-24R; CAAS 4; CANR 17,
36; CLR 18; DLB 8; MAICYA; MTCW;
SAAS 15; SATA 54

Disch, Tom
See Disch, Thomas M(ichael)

d'Isly, Georges
See Simenon, Georges (Jacques Christian)

Disraeli, Benjamin 1804-1881 .. NCLC 2, 39
See also DLB 21, 55

Ditcum, Steve
See Crumb, R(obert)

Dixon, Paige
See Corcoran, Barbara

Dixon, Stephen 1936-..... CLC 52; SSC 16
See also CA 89-92; CANR 17, 40; DLB 130

Dobell, Sydney Thompson
1824-1874 .... NCLC 43
See also DLB 32

Doblin, Alfred .... TCLC 13
See also Doeblin, Alfred

Dobrolyubov, Nikolai Alexandrovich
1836-1861 .... NCLC 5

Dobyns, Stephen 1941-........... CLC 37
See also CA 45-48; CANR 2, 18

Doctorow, E(dgar) L(aurence)
1931-...... CLC 6, 11, 15, 18, 37, 44, 65
See also AITN 2; BEST 89:3; CA 45-48;
CANR 2, 33; CDALB 1968-1988; DLB 2,
28; DLBY 80; MTCW

Dodgson, Charles Lutwidge 1832-1898
See Carroll, Lewis
See also CLR 2; DA; MAICYA; YABC 2

Dodson, Owen (Vincent)
1914-1983 .... CLC 79; BLC
See also BW 1; CA 65-68; 110; CANR 24;
DLB 76

Doeblin, Alfred 1878-1957........ TCLC 13
See also Doblin, Alfred
See also CA 110; 141; DLB 66

Doerr, Harriet 1910- .... CLC 34
See also CA 117; 122

Domecq, H(onorio) Bustos
See Bioy Casares, Adolfo; Borges, Jorge
Luis

Domini, Rey
See Lorde, Audre (Geraldine)

Dominique
See Proust, (Valentin-Louis-George-Eugene-)
Marcel

Don, A
See Stephen, Leslie

Donaldson, Stephen R. 1947-....... CLC 46
See also CA 89-92; CANR 13

Donleavy, J(ames) P(atrick)
1926- .... CLC 1, 4, 6, 10, 45
See also AITN 2; CA 9-12R; CANR 24;
DLB 6; MTCW

Donne, John
1572-1631 .... LC 10, 24; DA; PC 1
See also CDBLB Before 1660; DLB 121

Donnell, David 1939(?)-........... CLC 34

Donoso (Yanez), Jose
1924- .... CLC 4, 8, 11, 32; HLC
See also CA 81-84; CANR 32; DLB 113;
HW; MTCW

Donovan, John 1928-1992 .... CLC 35
See also CA 97-100; 137; CLR 3;
MAICYA; SATA 29

Don Roberto
See Cunninghame Graham, R(obert)
B(ontine)

Doolittle, Hilda
1886-1961 ..... CLC 3, 8, 14, 31, 34, 73;
DA; PC 5; WLC
See also H. D.
See also CA 97-100; CANR 35; DLB 4, 45;
MTCW

Dorfman, Ariel 1942-.... CLC 48, 77; HLC
See also CA 124; 130; HW

Dorn, Edward (Merton) 1929-... CLC 10, 18
See also CA 93-96; CANR 42; DLB 5

Dorsan, Luc
See Simenon, Georges (Jacques Christian)

Dorsange, Jean
See Simenon, Georges (Jacques Christian)

Dos Passos, John (Roderigo)
1896-1970 ..... CLC 1, 4, 8, 11, 15, 25,
34, 82; DA; WLC
See also CA 1-4R; 29-32R; CANR 3;
CDALB 1929-1941; DLB 4, 9; DLBD 1;
MTCW

Dossage, Jean
See Simenon, Georges (Jacques Christian)

Dostoevsky, Fedor Mikhailovich
1821-1881 ...... NCLC 2, 7, 21, 33, 43;
DA; SSC 2; WLC

Doughty, Charles M(ontagu)
1843-1926 .... TCLC 27
See also CA 115; DLB 19, 57

Douglas, Ellen .... CLC 73
See also Haxton, Josephine Ayres;
Williamson, Ellen Douglas

Douglas, Gavin 1475(?)-1522....... LC 20

Douglas, Keith 1920-1944 .... TCLC 40
See also DLB 27

Douglas, Leonard
See Bradbury, Ray (Douglas)

Douglas, Michael
See Crichton, (John) Michael

Douglass, Frederick
1817(?)-1895 .... NCLC 7; BLC; DA;
WLC
See also CDALB 1640-1865; DLB 1, 43, 50,
79; SATA 29

Dourado, (Waldomiro Freitas) Autran
1926- .... CLC 23, 60
See also CA 25-28R; CANR 34

Dourado, Waldomiro Autran
See Dourado, (Waldomiro Freitas) Autran

Dove, Rita (Frances)
1952- .... CLC 50, 81; PC 6
See also BW 2; CA 109; CAAS 19;
CANR 27, 42; DLB 120

Dowell, Coleman 1925-1985........ CLC 60
See also CA 25-28R; 117; CANR 10;
DLB 130

Dowson, Ernest Christopher
1867-1900 .... TCLC 4
See also CA 105; DLB 19, 135

Doyle, A. Conan
See Doyle, Arthur Conan

Doyle, Arthur Conan
1859-1930 .... TCLC 7; DA; SSC 12;
WLC
See also CA 104; 122; CDBLB 1890-1914;
DLB 18, 70; MTCW; SATA 24

Doyle, Conan
See Doyle, Arthur Conan

Doyle, John
See Graves, Robert (von Ranke)

Doyle, Roddy 1958(?)-............ CLC 81
See also CA 143

Doyle, Sir A. Conan
See Doyle, Arthur Conan

Doyle, Sir Arthur Conan
See Doyle, Arthur Conan

Dr. A
See Asimov, Isaac; Silverstein, Alvin

Drabble, Margaret
  1939- . . . . **CLC 2, 3, 5, 8, 10, 22, 53**
  See also CA 13-16R; CANR 18, 35;
  CDBLB 1960 to Present; DLB 14;
  MTCW; SATA 48

Drapier, M. B.
  See Swift, Jonathan

Drayham, James
  See Mencken, H(enry) L(ouis)

Drayton, Michael   1563-1631 . . . . **LC 8**

Dreadstone, Carl
  See Campbell, (John) Ramsey

Dreiser, Theodore (Herman Albert)
  1871-1945 . . . . . . **TCLC 10, 18, 35; DA;
                                                    WLC**
  See also CA 106; 132; CDALB 1865-1917;
  DLB 9, 12, 102, 137; DLBD 1; MTCW

Drexler, Rosalyn   1926- . . . . **CLC 2, 6**
  See also CA 81-84

Dreyer, Carl Theodor   1889-1968. . . . **CLC 16**
  See also CA 116

Drieu la Rochelle, Pierre(-Eugene)
  1893-1945 . . . . **TCLC 21**
  See also CA 117; DLB 72

Drinkwater, John   1882-1937 . . . . . . **TCLC 57**
  See also CA 109; DLB 10, 19

Drop Shot
  See Cable, George Washington

Droste-Hulshoff, Annette Freiin von
  1797-1848 . . . . **NCLC 3**
  See also DLB 133

Drummond, Walter
  See Silverberg, Robert

Drummond, William Henry
  1854-1907 . . . . **TCLC 25**
  See also DLB 92

Drummond de Andrade, Carlos
  1902-1987 . . . . **CLC 18**
  See also Andrade, Carlos Drummond de
  See also CA 132; 123

Drury, Allen (Stuart)   1918- . . . . **CLC 37**
  See also CA 57-60; CANR 18

Dryden, John
  1631-1700 . . . **LC 3, 21; DA; DC 3; WLC**
  See also CDBLB 1660-1789; DLB 80, 101,
  131

Duberman, Martin   1930- . . . . **CLC 8**
  See also CA 1-4R; CANR 2

Dubie, Norman (Evans)   1945- . . . . . . **CLC 36**
  See also CA 69-72; CANR 12; DLB 120

Du Bois, W(illiam) E(dward) B(urghardt)
  1868-1963 . . . . . . **CLC 1, 2, 13, 64; BLC;
                                                    DA; WLC**
  See also BW 1; CA 85-88; CANR 34;
  CDALB 1865-1917; DLB 47, 50, 91;
  MTCW; SATA 42

Dubus, Andre   1936- . . . **CLC 13, 36; SSC 15**
  See also CA 21-24R; CANR 17; DLB 130

Duca Minimo
  See D'Annunzio, Gabriele

Ducharme, Rejean   1941- . . . . **CLC 74**
  See also DLB 60

Duclos, Charles Pinot   1704-1772 . . . . . **LC 1**

Dudek, Louis   1918- . . . . **CLC 11, 19**
  See also CA 45-48; CAAS 14; CANR 1;
  DLB 88

Duerrenmatt, Friedrich
  1921-1990 . . . . . . **CLC 1, 4, 8, 11, 15, 43**
  See also CA 17-20R; CANR 33; DLB 69,
  124; MTCW

Duffy, Bruce   (?)- . . . . **CLC 50**

Duffy, Maureen   1933- . . . . **CLC 37**
  See also CA 25-28R; CANR 33; DLB 14;
  MTCW

Dugan, Alan   1923- . . . . **CLC 2, 6**
  See also CA 81-84; DLB 5

du Gard, Roger Martin
  See Martin du Gard, Roger

Duhamel, Georges   1884-1966 . . . . **CLC 8**
  See also CA 81-84; 25-28R; CANR 35;
  DLB 65; MTCW

Dujardin, Edouard (Emile Louis)
  1861-1949 . . . . **TCLC 13**
  See also CA 109; DLB 123

Dumas, Alexandre (Davy de la Pailleterie)
  1802-1870 . . . . **NCLC 11; DA; WLC**
  See also DLB 119; SATA 18

Dumas, Alexandre
  1824-1895 . . . . **NCLC 9; DC 1**

Dumas, Claudine
  See Malzberg, Barry N(athaniel)

Dumas, Henry L.   1934-1968 . . . . . **CLC 6, 62**
  See also BW 1; CA 85-88; DLB 41

du Maurier, Daphne
  1907-1989 . . . . **CLC 6, 11, 59**
  See also CA 5-8R; 128; CANR 6; MTCW;
  SATA 27, 60

Dunbar, Paul Laurence
  1872-1906 . . . . . . **TCLC 2, 12; BLC; DA;
                                                    PC 5; SSC 8; WLC**
  See also BW 1; CA 104; 124;
  CDALB 1865-1917; DLB 50, 54, 78;
  SATA 34

Dunbar, William   1460(?)-1530(?) . . . . **LC 20**

Duncan, Lois   1934- . . . . **CLC 26**
  See also AAYA 4; CA 1-4R; CANR 2, 23,
  36; CLR 29; JRDA; MAICYA; SAAS 2;
  SATA 1, 36, 75

Duncan, Robert (Edward)
  1919-1988 . . . . **CLC 1, 2, 4, 7, 15, 41, 55;
                                                    PC 2**
  See also CA 9-12R; 124; CANR 28; DLB 5,
  16; MTCW

Dunlap, William   1766-1839 . . . . **NCLC 2**
  See also DLB 30, 37, 59

Dunn, Douglas (Eaglesham)
  1942- . . . . **CLC 6, 40**
  See also CA 45-48; CANR 2, 33; DLB 40;
  MTCW

Dunn, Katherine (Karen)   1945- . . . . . **CLC 71**
  See also CA 33-36R

Dunn, Stephen   1939- . . . . **CLC 36**
  See also CA 33-36R; CANR 12; DLB 105

Dunne, Finley Peter   1867-1936 . . . . **TCLC 28**
  See also CA 108; DLB 11, 23

Dunne, John Gregory   1932- . . . . **CLC 28**
  See also CA 25-28R; CANR 14; DLBY 80

Dunsany, Edward John Moreton Drax
  Plunkett   1878-1957
  See Dunsany, Lord
  See also CA 104; DLB 10

Dunsany, Lord . . . . **TCLC 2**
  See also Dunsany, Edward John Moreton
  Drax Plunkett
  See also DLB 77

du Perry, Jean
  See Simenon, Georges (Jacques Christian)

Durang, Christopher (Ferdinand)
  1949- . . . . **CLC 27, 38**
  See also CA 105

Duras, Marguerite
  1914- . . . . **CLC 3, 6, 11, 20, 34, 40, 68**
  See also CA 25-28R; DLB 83; MTCW

Durban, (Rosa) Pam   1947- . . . . **CLC 39**
  See also CA 123

Durcan, Paul   1944- . . . . **CLC 43, 70**
  See also CA 134

Durkheim, Emile   1858-1917 . . . . . . **TCLC 55**

Durrell, Lawrence (George)
  1912-1990 . . . . **CLC 1, 4, 6, 8, 13, 27, 41**
  See also CA 9-12R; 132; CANR 40;
  CDBLB 1945-1960; DLB 15, 27;
  DLBY 90; MTCW

Durrenmatt, Friedrich
  See Duerrenmatt, Friedrich

Dutt, Toru   1856-1877 . . . . **NCLC 29**

Dwight, Timothy   1752-1817 . . . . . . **NCLC 13**
  See also DLB 37

Dworkin, Andrea   1946- . . . . **CLC 43**
  See also CA 77-80; CANR 16, 39; MTCW

Dwyer, Deanna
  See Koontz, Dean R(ay)

Dwyer, K. R.
  See Koontz, Dean R(ay)

Dylan, Bob   1941- . . . . . . **CLC 3, 4, 6, 12, 77**
  See also CA 41-44R; DLB 16

Eagleton, Terence (Francis)   1943-
  See Eagleton, Terry
  See also CA 57-60; CANR 7, 23; MTCW

Eagleton, Terry . . . . **CLC 63**
  See also Eagleton, Terence (Francis)

Early, Jack
  See Scoppettone, Sandra

East, Michael
  See West, Morris L(anglo)

Eastaway, Edward
  See Thomas, (Philip) Edward

Eastlake, William (Derry)   1917- . . . . . **CLC 8**
  See also CA 5-8R; CAAS 1; CANR 5;
  DLB 6

Eastman, Charles A(lexander)
  1858-1939 . . . . **TCLC 55**
  See also YABC 1

Eberhart, Richard (Ghormley)
  1904- . . . . **CLC 3, 11, 19, 56**
  See also CA 1-4R; CANR 2;
  CDALB 1941-1968; DLB 48; MTCW

Eberstadt, Fernanda   1960- . . . . **CLC 39**
  See also CA 136

Echegaray (y Eizaguirre), Jose (Maria Waldo)
1832-1916 . . . . TCLC 4
See also CA 104; CANR 32; HW; MTCW

Echeverria, (Jose) Esteban (Antonino)
1805-1851 . . . . NCLC 18

Echo
See Proust, (Valentin-Louis-George-Eugene-)
Marcel

Eckert, Allan W.   1931- . . . . CLC 17
See also CA 13-16R; CANR 14, 45;
SATA 27, 29

Eckhart, Meister   1260(?)-1328(?) . . CMLC 9
See also DLB 115

Eckmar, F. R.
See de Hartog, Jan

Eco, Umberto   1932- . . . . CLC 28, 60
See also BEST 90:1; CA 77-80; CANR 12,
33; MTCW

Eddison, E(ric) R(ucker)
1882-1945 . . . . TCLC 15
See also CA 109

Edel, (Joseph) Leon   1907- . . . . . . CLC 29, 34
See also CA 1-4R; CANR 1, 22; DLB 103

Eden, Emily   1797-1869 . . . . NCLC 10

Edgar, David   1948- . . . . CLC 42
See also CA 57-60; CANR 12; DLB 13;
MTCW

Edgerton, Clyde (Carlyle)   1944- . . . . CLC 39
See also CA 118; 134

Edgeworth, Maria   1767-1849 . . . . . . NCLC 1
See also DLB 116; SATA 21

Edmonds, Paul
See Kuttner, Henry

Edmonds, Walter D(umaux)   1903- . . CLC 35
See also CA 5-8R; CANR 2; DLB 9;
MAICYA; SAAS 4; SATA 1, 27

Edmondson, Wallace
See Ellison, Harlan

Edson, Russell . . . . CLC 13
See also CA 33-36R

Edwards, Bronwen Elizabeth
See Rose, Wendy

Edwards, G(erald) B(asil)
1899-1976 . . . . CLC 25
See also CA 110

Edwards, Gus   1939- . . . . CLC 43
See also CA 108

Edwards, Jonathan   1703-1758 . . . . LC 7; DA
See also DLB 24

Efron, Marina Ivanovna Tsvetaeva
See Tsvetaeva (Efron), Marina (Ivanovna)

Ehle, John (Marsden, Jr.)   1925- . . . . CLC 27
See also CA 9-12R

Ehrenbourg, Ilya (Grigoryevich)
See Ehrenburg, Ilya (Grigoryevich)

Ehrenburg, Ilya (Grigoryevich)
1891-1967 . . . . CLC 18, 34, 62
See also CA 102; 25-28R

Ehrenburg, Ilyo (Grigoryevich)
See Ehrenburg, Ilya (Grigoryevich)

Eich, Guenter   1907-1972 . . . . CLC 15
See also CA 111; 93-96; DLB 69, 124

Eichendorff, Joseph Freiherr von
1788-1857 . . . . NCLC 8
See also DLB 90

Eigner, Larry . . . . CLC 9
See also Eigner, Laurence (Joel)
See also DLB 5

Eigner, Laurence (Joel)   1927-
See Eigner, Larry
See also CA 9-12R; CANR 6

Eiseley, Loren Corey   1907-1977 . . . . . CLC 7
See also AAYA 5; CA 1-4R; 73-76;
CANR 6

Eisenstadt, Jill   1963- . . . . CLC 50
See also CA 140

Eisenstein, Sergei (Mikhailovich)
1898-1948 . . . . TCLC 57
See also CA 114

Eisner, Simon
See Kornbluth, C(yril) M.

Ekeloef, (Bengt) Gunnar
1907-1968 . . . . CLC 27
See also Ekelof, (Bengt) Gunnar
See also CA 123; 25-28R

Ekelof, (Bengt) Gunnar . . . . CLC 27
See also Ekeloef, (Bengt) Gunnar

Ekwensi, C. O. D.
See Ekwensi, Cyprian (Odiatu Duaka)

Ekwensi, Cyprian (Odiatu Duaka)
1921- . . . . CLC 4; BLC
See also BW 2; CA 29-32R; CANR 18, 42;
DLB 117; MTCW; SATA 66

Elaine . . . . TCLC 18
See also Leverson, Ada

El Crummo
See Crumb, R(obert)

Elia
See Lamb, Charles

Eliade, Mircea   1907-1986 . . . . CLC 19
See also CA 65-68; 119; CANR 30; MTCW

Eliot, A. D.
See Jewett, (Theodora) Sarah Orne

Eliot, Alice
See Jewett, (Theodora) Sarah Orne

Eliot, Dan
See Silverberg, Robert

Eliot, George
1819-1880 . . . . NCLC 4, 13, 23, 41; DA;
WLC
See also CDBLB 1832-1890; DLB 21, 35, 55

Eliot, John   1604-1690 . . . . LC 5
See also DLB 24

Eliot, T(homas) S(tearns)
1888-1965 . . . . . CLC 1, 2, 3, 6, 9, 10, 13,
15, 24, 34, 41, 55, 57; DA; PC 5; WLC 2
See also CA 5-8R; 25-28R; CANR 41;
CDALB 1929-1941; DLB 7, 10, 45, 63;
DLBY 88; MTCW

Elizabeth   1866-1941 . . . . TCLC 41

Elkin, Stanley L(awrence)
1930- . . CLC 4, 6, 9, 14, 27, 51; SSC 12
See also CA 9-12R; CANR 8; DLB 2, 28;
DLBY 80; MTCW

Elledge, Scott . . . . CLC 34

Elliott, Don
See Silverberg, Robert

Elliott, George P(aul)   1918-1980 . . . . . CLC 2
See also CA 1-4R; 97-100; CANR 2

Elliott, Janice   1931- . . . . CLC 47
See also CA 13-16R; CANR 8, 29; DLB 14

Elliott, Sumner Locke   1917-1991 . . . CLC 38
See also CA 5-8R; 134; CANR 2, 21

Elliott, William
See Bradbury, Ray (Douglas)

Ellis, A. E. . . . . CLC 7

Ellis, Alice Thomas . . . . CLC 40
See also Haycraft, Anna

Ellis, Bret Easton   1964- . . . . CLC 39, 71
See also AAYA 2; CA 118; 123

Ellis, (Henry) Havelock
1859-1939 . . . . TCLC 14
See also CA 109

Ellis, Landon
See Ellison, Harlan

Ellis, Trey   1962- . . . . CLC 55

Ellison, Harlan
1934- . . . . CLC 1, 13, 42; SSC 14
See also CA 5-8R; CANR 5; DLB 8;
MTCW

Ellison, Ralph (Waldo)
1914-1994 . . . . . . CLC 1, 3, 11, 54; BLC;
DA; WLC
See also BW 1; CA 9-12R; 145; CANR 24;
CDALB 1941-1968; DLB 2, 76; MTCW

Ellmann, Lucy (Elizabeth)   1956- . . . . CLC 61
See also CA 128

Ellmann, Richard (David)
1918-1987 . . . . CLC 50
See also BEST 89:2; CA 1-4R; 122;
CANR 2, 28; DLB 103; DLBY 87;
MTCW

Elman, Richard   1934- . . . . CLC 19
See also CA 17-20R; CAAS 3

Elron
See Hubbard, L(afayette) Ron(ald)

Eluard, Paul . . . . TCLC 7, 41
See also Grindel, Eugene

Elyot, Sir Thomas   1490(?)-1546 . . . . . LC 11

Elytis, Odysseus   1911- . . . . CLC 15, 49
See also CA 102; MTCW

Emecheta, (Florence Onye) Buchi
1944- . . . . CLC 14, 48; BLC
See also BW 2; CA 81-84; CANR 27;
DLB 117; MTCW; SATA 66

Emerson, Ralph Waldo
1803-1882 . . . . . . NCLC 1, 38; DA; WLC
See also CDALB 1640-1865; DLB 1, 59, 73

Eminescu, Mihail   1850-1889 . . . . . NCLC 33

Empson, William
1906-1984 . . . . CLC 3, 8, 19, 33, 34
See also CA 17-20R; 112; CANR 31;
DLB 20; MTCW

Enchi Fumiko (Ueda)   1905-1986 . . . . CLC 31
See also CA 129; 121

Ende, Michael (Andreas Helmuth)
1929- . . . . CLC 31
See also CA 118; 124; CANR 36; CLR 14;
DLB 75; MAICYA; SATA 42, 61

Endo, Shusaku 1923- ..... **CLC 7, 14, 19, 54**
See also CA 29-32R; CANR 21; MTCW

Engel, Marian 1933-1985 .... **CLC 36**
See also CA 25-28R; CANR 12; DLB 53

Engelhardt, Frederick
See Hubbard, L(afayette) Ron(ald)

Enright, D(ennis) J(oseph)
1920- .... **CLC 4, 8, 31**
See also CA 1-4R; CANR 1, 42; DLB 27;
SATA 25

Enzensberger, Hans Magnus
1929- .... **CLC 43**
See also CA 116; 119

Ephron, Nora 1941- .... **CLC 17, 31**
See also AITN 2; CA 65-68; CANR 12, 39

Epsilon
See Betjeman, John

Epstein, Daniel Mark 1948- .... **CLC 7**
See also CA 49-52; CANR 2

Epstein, Jacob 1956- .... **CLC 19**
See also CA 114

Epstein, Joseph 1937-............. **CLC 39**
See also CA 112; 119

Epstein, Leslie 1938- .... **CLC 27**
See also CA 73-76; CAAS 12; CANR 23

Equiano, Olaudah
1745(?)-1797 .... **LC 16; BLC**
See also DLB 37, 50

Erasmus, Desiderius 1469(?)-1536.... **LC 16**

Erdman, Paul E(mil) 1932- .... **CLC 25**
See also AITN 1; CA 61-64; CANR 13, 43

Erdrich, Louise 1954-......... **CLC 39, 54**
See also AAYA 10; BEST 89:1; CA 114;
CANR 41; MTCW

Erenburg, Ilya (Grigoryevich)
See Ehrenburg, Ilya (Grigoryevich)

Erickson, Stephen Michael 1950-
See Erickson, Steve
See also CA 129

Erickson, Steve .... **CLC 64**
See also Erickson, Stephen Michael

Ericson, Walter
See Fast, Howard (Melvin)

Eriksson, Buntel
See Bergman, (Ernst) Ingmar

Eschenbach, Wolfram von
See Wolfram von Eschenbach

Eseki, Bruno
See Mphahlele, Ezekiel

Esenin, Sergei (Alexandrovich)
1895-1925 .... **TCLC 4**
See also CA 104

Eshleman, Clayton 1935-........... **CLC 7**
See also CA 33-36R; CAAS 6; DLB 5

Espriella, Don Manuel Alvarez
See Southey, Robert

Espriu, Salvador 1913-1985 .... **CLC 9**
See also CA 115; DLB 134

Espronceda, Jose de 1808-1842... **NCLC 39**

Esse, James
See Stephens, James

Esterbrook, Tom
See Hubbard, L(afayette) Ron(ald)

Estleman, Loren D. 1952- .... **CLC 48**
See also CA 85-88; CANR 27; MTCW

Eugenides, Jeffrey 1960(?)- .... **CLC 81**
See also CA 144

Euripides c. 485B.C.-406B.C. .... **DC 4**
See also DA

Evan, Evin
See Faust, Frederick (Schiller)

Evans, Evan
See Faust, Frederick (Schiller)

Evans, Marian
See Eliot, George

Evans, Mary Ann
See Eliot, George

Evarts, Esther
See Benson, Sally

Everett, Percival L. 1956- .... **CLC 57**
See also BW 2; CA 129

Everson, R(onald) G(ilmour)
1903- .... **CLC 27**
See also CA 17-20R; DLB 88

Everson, William (Oliver)
1912-1994 .... **CLC 1, 5, 14**
See also CA 9-12R; 145; CANR 20; DLB 5,
16; MTCW

Evtushenko, Evgenii Aleksandrovich
See Yevtushenko, Yevgeny (Alexandrovich)

Ewart, Gavin (Buchanan)
1916- .... **CLC 13, 46**
See also CA 89-92; CANR 17; DLB 40;
MTCW

Ewers, Hanns Heinz 1871-1943 ... **TCLC 12**
See also CA 109

Ewing, Frederick R.
See Sturgeon, Theodore (Hamilton)

Exley, Frederick (Earl)
1929-1992 .... **CLC 6, 11**
See also AITN 2; CA 81-84; 138; DLB 143;
DLBY 81

Eynhardt, Guillermo
See Quiroga, Horacio (Sylvestre)

Ezekiel, Nissim 1924-............. **CLC 61**
See also CA 61-64

Ezekiel, Tish O'Dowd 1943-....... **CLC 34**
See also CA 129

Fadeyev, A.
See Bulgya, Alexander Alexandrovich

Fadeyev, Alexander .... **TCLC 53**
See also Bulgya, Alexander Alexandrovich

Fagen, Donald 1948-............. **CLC 26**

Fainzilberg, Ilya Arnoldovich 1897-1937
See Ilf, Ilya
See also CA 120

Fair, Ronald L. 1932-............. **CLC 18**
See also BW 1; CA 69-72; CANR 25;
DLB 33

Fairbairns, Zoe (Ann) 1948- .... **CLC 32**
See also CA 103; CANR 21

Falco, Gian
See Papini, Giovanni

Falconer, James
See Kirkup, James

Falconer, Kenneth
See Kornbluth, C(yril) M.

Falkland, Samuel
See Heijermans, Herman

Fallaci, Oriana 1930-............. **CLC 11**
See also CA 77-80; CANR 15; MTCW

Faludy, George 1913-............. **CLC 42**
See also CA 21-24R

Faludy, Gyoergy
See Faludy, George

Fanon, Frantz 1925-1961..... **CLC 74; BLC**
See also BW 1; CA 116; 89-92

Fanshawe, Ann 1625-1680 .... **LC 11**

Fante, John (Thomas) 1911-1983 ... **CLC 60**
See also CA 69-72; 109; CANR 23;
DLB 130; DLBY 83

Farah, Nuruddin 1945-....... **CLC 53; BLC**
See also BW 2; CA 106; DLB 125

Fargue, Leon-Paul 1876(?)-1947 ... **TCLC 11**
See also CA 109

Farigoule, Louis
See Romains, Jules

Farina, Richard 1936(?)-1966 .... **CLC 9**
See also CA 81-84; 25-28R

Farley, Walter (Lorimer)
1915-1989 .... **CLC 17**
See also CA 17-20R; CANR 8, 29; DLB 22;
JRDA; MAICYA; SATA 2, 43

Farmer, Philip Jose 1918-....... **CLC 1, 19**
See also CA 1-4R; CANR 4, 35; DLB 8;
MTCW

Farquhar, George 1677-1707 .... **LC 21**
See also DLB 84

Farrell, J(ames) G(ordon)
1935-1979 .... **CLC 6**
See also CA 73-76; 89-92; CANR 36;
DLB 14; MTCW

Farrell, James T(homas)
1904-1979 ...... **CLC 1, 4, 8, 11, 66**
See also CA 5-8R; 89-92; CANR 9; DLB 4,
9, 86; DLBD 2; MTCW

Farren, Richard J.
See Betjeman, John

Farren, Richard M.
See Betjeman, John

Fassbinder, Rainer Werner
1946-1982 .... **CLC 20**
See also CA 93-96; 106; CANR 31

Fast, Howard (Melvin) 1914- ...... **CLC 23**
See also CA 1-4R; CAAS 18; CANR 1, 33;
DLB 9; SATA 7

Faulcon, Robert
See Holdstock, Robert P.

Faulkner, William (Cuthbert)
1897-1962 ..... **CLC 1, 3, 6, 8, 9, 11, 14,
18, 28, 52, 68; DA; SSC 1; WLC**
See also AAYA 7; CA 81-84; CANR 33;
CDALB 1929-1941; DLB 9, 11, 44, 102;
DLBD 2; DLBY 86; MTCW

Fauset, Jessie Redmon
1884(?)-1961 .... **CLC 19, 54; BLC**
See also BW 1; CA 109; DLB 51

Faust, Frederick (Schiller)
1892-1944(?) .... **TCLC 49**
See also CA 108

Faust, Irvin 1924-................. **CLC 8**
See also CA 33-36R; CANR 28; DLB 2, 28;
DLBY 80

Fawkes, Guy
See Benchley, Robert (Charles)

Fearing, Kenneth (Flexner)
1902-1961 .... **CLC 51**
See also CA 93-96; DLB 9

Fecamps, Elise
See Creasey, John

Federman, Raymond 1928- ...... **CLC 6, 47**
See also CA 17-20R; CAAS 8; CANR 10,
43; DLBY 80

Federspiel, J(uerg) F. 1931-........ **CLC 42**

Feiffer, Jules (Ralph) 1929-.... **CLC 2, 8, 64**
See also AAYA 3; CA 17-20R; CANR 30;
DLB 7, 44; MTCW; SATA 8, 61

Feige, Hermann Albert Otto Maximilian
See Traven, B.

Feinberg, David B. 1956-.......... **CLC 59**
See also CA 135

Feinstein, Elaine 1930-............ **CLC 36**
See also CA 69-72; CAAS 1; CANR 31;
DLB 14, 40; MTCW

Feldman, Irving (Mordecai) 1928-.... **CLC 7**
See also CA 1-4R; CANR 1

Fellini, Federico 1920-1993 ..... **CLC 16, 85**
See also CA 65-68; 143; CANR 33

Felsen, Henry Gregor 1916- .... **CLC 17**
See also CA 1-4R; CANR 1; SAAS 2;
SATA 1

Fenton, James Martin 1949-....... **CLC 32**
See also CA 102; DLB 40

Ferber, Edna 1887-1968........... **CLC 18**
See also AITN 1; CA 5-8R; 25-28R; DLB 9,
28, 86; MTCW; SATA 7

Ferguson, Helen
See Kavan, Anna

Ferguson, Samuel 1810-1886..... **NCLC 33**
See also DLB 32

Ferling, Lawrence
See Ferlinghetti, Lawrence (Monsanto)

Ferlinghetti, Lawrence (Monsanto)
1919(?)-........ **CLC 2, 6, 10, 27; PC 1**
See also CA 5-8R; CANR 3, 41;
CDALB 1941-1968; DLB 5, 16; MTCW

Fernandez, Vicente Garcia Huidobro
See Huidobro Fernandez, Vicente Garcia

Ferrer, Gabriel (Francisco Victor) Miro
See Miro (Ferrer), Gabriel (Francisco
Victor)

Ferrier, Susan (Edmonstone)
1782-1854 .... **NCLC 8**
See also DLB 116

Ferrigno, Robert 1948(?)-.......... **CLC 65**
See also CA 140

Feuchtwanger, Lion 1884-1958 ..... **TCLC 3**
See also CA 104; DLB 66

Feuillet, Octave 1821-1890 ...... **NCLC 45**

Feydeau, Georges (Leon Jules Marie)
1862-1921 .... **TCLC 22**
See also CA 113

Ficino, Marsilio 1433-1499 .... **LC 12**

Fiedeler, Hans
See Doeblin, Alfred

Fiedler, Leslie A(aron)
1917- .... **CLC 4, 13, 24**
See also CA 9-12R; CANR 7; DLB 28, 67;
MTCW

Field, Andrew 1938-................ **CLC 44**
See also CA 97-100; CANR 25

Field, Eugene 1850-1895 .... **NCLC 3**
See also DLB 23, 42, 140; MAICYA;
SATA 16

Field, Gans T.
See Wellman, Manly Wade

Field, Michael .... **TCLC 43**

Field, Peter
See Hobson, Laura Z(ametkin)

Fielding, Henry
1707-1754 .... **LC 1; DA; WLC**
See also CDBLB 1660-1789; DLB 39, 84,
101

Fielding, Sarah 1710-1768 .... **LC 1**
See also DLB 39

Fierstein, Harvey (Forbes) 1954- ... **CLC 33**
See also CA 123; 129

Figes, Eva 1932-................. **CLC 31**
See also CA 53-56; CANR 4, 44; DLB 14

Finch, Robert (Duer Claydon)
1900- .... **CLC 18**
See also CA 57-60; CANR 9, 24; DLB 88

Findley, Timothy 1930- .... **CLC 27**
See also CA 25-28R; CANR 12, 42;
DLB 53

Fink, William
See Mencken, H(enry) L(ouis)

Firbank, Louis 1942-
See Reed, Lou
See also CA 117

Firbank, (Arthur Annesley) Ronald
1886-1926 .... **TCLC 1**
See also CA 104; DLB 36

Fisher, M(ary) F(rances) K(ennedy)
1908-1992 .... **CLC 76**
See also CA 77-80; 138; CANR 44

Fisher, Roy 1930-................. **CLC 25**
See also CA 81-84; CAAS 10; CANR 16;
DLB 40

Fisher, Rudolph
1897-1934 .... **TCLC 11; BLC**
See also BW 1; CA 107; 124; DLB 51, 102

Fisher, Vardis (Alvero) 1895-1968.... **CLC 7**
See also CA 5-8R; 25-28R; DLB 9

Fiske, Tarleton
See Bloch, Robert (Albert)

Fitch, Clarke
See Sinclair, Upton (Beall)

Fitch, John IV
See Cormier, Robert (Edmund)

Fitzgerald, Captain Hugh
See Baum, L(yman) Frank

FitzGerald, Edward 1809-1883 .... **NCLC 9**
See also DLB 32

Fitzgerald, F(rancis) Scott (Key)
1896-1940 .... **TCLC 1, 6, 14, 28, 55;
DA; SSC 6; WLC**
See also AITN 1; CA 110; 123;
CDALB 1917-1929; DLB 4, 9, 86;
DLBD 1; DLBY 81; MTCW

Fitzgerald, Penelope 1916-... **CLC 19, 51, 61**
See also CA 85-88; CAAS 10; DLB 14

Fitzgerald, Robert (Stuart)
1910-1985 .... **CLC 39**
See also CA 1-4R; 114; CANR 1; DLBY 80

FitzGerald, Robert D(avid)
1902-1987 .... **CLC 19**
See also CA 17-20R

Fitzgerald, Zelda (Sayre)
1900-1948 .... **TCLC 52**
See also CA 117; 126; DLBY 84

Flanagan, Thomas (James Bonner)
1923-.................... **CLC 25, 52**
See also CA 108; DLBY 80; MTCW

Flaubert, Gustave
1821-1880 .... **NCLC 2, 10, 19; DA;
SSC 11; WLC**
See also DLB 119

Flecker, (Herman) James Elroy
1884-1915 .... **TCLC 43**
See also CA 109; DLB 10, 19

Fleming, Ian (Lancaster)
1908-1964 .... **CLC 3, 30**
See also CA 5-8R; CDBLB 1945-1960;
DLB 87; MTCW; SATA 9

Fleming, Thomas (James) 1927- .... **CLC 37**
See also CA 5-8R; CANR 10; SATA 8

Fletcher, John Gould 1886-1950... **TCLC 35**
See also CA 107; DLB 4, 45

Fleur, Paul
See Pohl, Frederik

Flooglebuckle, Al
See Spiegelman, Art

Flying Officer X
See Bates, H(erbert) E(rnest)

Fo, Dario 1926-................. **CLC 32**
See also CA 116; 128; MTCW

Fogarty, Jonathan Titulescu Esq.
See Farrell, James T(homas)

Folke, Will
See Bloch, Robert (Albert)

Follett, Ken(neth Martin) 1949- .... **CLC 18**
See also AAYA 6; BEST 89:4; CA 81-84;
CANR 13, 33; DLB 87; DLBY 81;
MTCW

Fontane, Theodor 1819-1898 ..... **NCLC 26**
See also DLB 129

Foote, Horton 1916-............. **CLC 51**
See also CA 73-76; CANR 34; DLB 26

Foote, Shelby 1916- .... **CLC 75**
See also CA 5-8R; CANR 3, 45; DLB 2, 17

Forbes, Esther 1891-1967......... **CLC 12**
See also CA 13-14; 25-28R; CAP 1;
CLR 27; DLB 22; JRDA; MAICYA;
SATA 2

Forche, Carolyn (Louise)
1950- . . . . **CLC 25, 83; PC 10**
See also CA 109; 117; DLB 5

Ford, Elbur
See Hibbert, Eleanor Alice Burford

Ford, Ford Madox
1873-1939 . . . . **TCLC 1, 15, 39, 57**
See also CA 104; 132; CDBLB 1914-1945;
DLB 34, 98; MTCW

Ford, John 1895-1973. . . . . **CLC 16**
See also CA 45-48

Ford, Richard 1944- . . . . **CLC 46**
See also CA 69-72; CANR 11

Ford, Webster
See Masters, Edgar Lee

Foreman, Richard 1937- . . . . **CLC 50**
See also CA 65-68; CANR 32

Forester, C(ecil) S(cott)
1899-1966 . . . . **CLC 35**
See also CA 73-76; 25-28R; SATA 13

Forez
See Mauriac, Francois (Charles)

Forman, James Douglas 1932- . . . . . . **CLC 21**
See also CA 9-12R; CANR 4, 19, 42;
JRDA; MAICYA; SATA 8, 70

Fornes, Maria Irene 1930- . . . . . . **CLC 39, 61**
See also CA 25-28R; CANR 28; DLB 7;
HW; MTCW

Forrest, Leon 1937- . . . . **CLC 4**
See also BW 2; CA 89-92; CAAS 7;
CANR 25; DLB 33

Forster, E(dward) M(organ)
1879-1970 . . . . . **CLC 1, 2, 3, 4, 9, 10, 13,
15, 22, 45, 77; DA; WLC**
See also AAYA 2; CA 13-14; 25-28R;
CANR 45; CAP 1; CDBLB 1914-1945;
DLB 34, 98; DLBD 10; MTCW;
SATA 57

Forster, John 1812-1876 . . . . **NCLC 11**
See also DLB 144

Forsyth, Frederick 1938- . . . . . . **CLC 2, 5, 36**
See also BEST 89:4; CA 85-88; CANR 38;
DLB 87; MTCW

Forten, Charlotte L. . . . . **TCLC 16; BLC**
See also Grimke, Charlotte L(ottie) Forten
See also DLB 50

Foscolo, Ugo 1778-1827 . . . . **NCLC 8**

Fosse, Bob . . . . **CLC 20**
See also Fosse, Robert Louis

Fosse, Robert Louis 1927-1987
See Fosse, Bob
See also CA 110; 123

Foster, Stephen Collins
1826-1864 . . . . **NCLC 26**

Foucault, Michel
1926-1984 . . . . **CLC 31, 34, 69**
See also CA 105; 113; CANR 34; MTCW

Fouque, Friedrich (Heinrich Karl) de la Motte
1777-1843 . . . . **NCLC 2**
See also DLB 90

Fournier, Henri Alban 1886-1914
See Alain-Fournier
See also CA 104

Fournier, Pierre 1916- . . . . **CLC 11**
See also Gascar, Pierre
See also CA 89-92; CANR 16, 40

Fowles, John
1926- . . . . **CLC 1, 2, 3, 4, 6, 9, 10, 15, 33**
See also CA 5-8R; CANR 25; CDBLB 1960
to Present; DLB 14, 139; MTCW;
SATA 22

Fox, Paula 1923-. . . . . **CLC 2, 8**
See also AAYA 3; CA 73-76; CANR 20,
36; CLR 1; DLB 52; JRDA; MAICYA;
MTCW; SATA 17, 60

Fox, William Price (Jr.) 1926- . . . . . **CLC 22**
See also CA 17-20R; CAAS 19; CANR 11;
DLB 2; DLBY 81

Foxe, John 1516(?)-1587 . . . . **LC 14**

Frame, Janet . . . . **CLC 2, 3, 6, 22, 66**
See also Clutha, Janet Paterson Frame

France, Anatole . . . . **TCLC 9**
See also Thibault, Jacques Anatole Francois
See also DLB 123

Francis, Claude 19(?)- . . . . **CLC 50**

Francis, Dick 1920- . . . . **CLC 2, 22, 42**
See also AAYA 5; BEST 89:3; CA 5-8R;
CANR 9, 42; CDBLB 1960 to Present;
DLB 87; MTCW

Francis, Robert (Churchill)
1901-1987 . . . . **CLC 15**
See also CA 1-4R; 123; CANR 1

Frank, Anne(lies Marie)
1929-1945 . . . . **TCLC 17; DA; WLC**
See also AAYA 12; CA 113; 133; MTCW;
SATA 42

Frank, Elizabeth 1945- . . . . **CLC 39**
See also CA 121; 126

Franklin, Benjamin
See Hasek, Jaroslav (Matej Frantisek)

Franklin, Benjamin 1706-1790. . . **LC 25; DA**
See also CDALB 1640-1865; DLB 24, 43,
73

Franklin, (Stella Maraia Sarah) Miles
1879-1954 . . . . **TCLC 7**
See also CA 104

Fraser, (Lady) Antonia (Pakenham)
1932- . . . . **CLC 32**
See also CA 85-88; CANR 44; MTCW;
SATA 32

Fraser, George MacDonald 1925- . . . . **CLC 7**
See also CA 45-48; CANR 2

Fraser, Sylvia 1935- . . . . **CLC 64**
See also CA 45-48; CANR 1, 16

Frayn, Michael 1933- . . . . . . **CLC 3, 7, 31, 47**
See also CA 5-8R; CANR 30; DLB 13, 14;
MTCW

Fraze, Candida (Merrill) 1945- . . . . . **CLC 50**
See also CA 126

Frazer, J(ames) G(eorge)
1854-1941 . . . . **TCLC 32**
See also CA 118

Frazer, Robert Caine
See Creasey, John

Frazer, Sir James George
See Frazer, J(ames) G(eorge)

Frazier, Ian 1951-. . . . . **CLC 46**
See also CA 130

Frederic, Harold 1856-1898 . . . . . . **NCLC 10**
See also DLB 12, 23

Frederick, John
See Faust, Frederick (Schiller)

Frederick the Great 1712-1786 . . . . . . **LC 14**

Fredro, Aleksander 1793-1876 . . . . . **NCLC 8**

Freeling, Nicolas 1927- . . . . **CLC 38**
See also CA 49-52; CAAS 12; CANR 1, 17;
DLB 87

Freeman, Douglas Southall
1886-1953 . . . . **TCLC 11**
See also CA 109; DLB 17

Freeman, Judith 1946- . . . . **CLC 55**

Freeman, Mary Eleanor Wilkins
1852-1930 . . . . **TCLC 9; SSC 1**
See also CA 106; DLB 12, 78

Freeman, R(ichard) Austin
1862-1943 . . . . **TCLC 21**
See also CA 113; DLB 70

French, Marilyn 1929- . . . . . . **CLC 10, 18, 60**
See also CA 69-72; CANR 3, 31; MTCW

French, Paul
See Asimov, Isaac

Freneau, Philip Morin 1752-1832. . **NCLC 1**
See also DLB 37, 43

Freud, Sigmund 1856-1939 . . . . **TCLC 52**
See also CA 115; 133; MTCW

Friedan, Betty (Naomi) 1921- . . . . . . **CLC 74**
See also CA 65-68; CANR 18, 45; MTCW

Friedman, B(ernard) H(arper)
1926- . . . . **CLC 7**
See also CA 1-4R; CANR 3

Friedman, Bruce Jay 1930- . . . . **CLC 3, 5, 56**
See also CA 9-12R; CANR 25; DLB 2, 28

Friel, Brian 1929- . . . . **CLC 5, 42, 59**
See also CA 21-24R; CANR 33; DLB 13;
MTCW

Friis-Baastad, Babbis Ellinor
1921-1970 . . . . **CLC 12**
See also CA 17-20R; 134; SATA 7

Frisch, Max (Rudolf)
1911-1991 . . . . . **CLC 3, 9, 14, 18, 32, 44**
See also CA 85-88; 134; CANR 32;
DLB 69, 124; MTCW

Fromentin, Eugene (Samuel Auguste)
1820-1876 . . . . **NCLC 10**
See also DLB 123

Frost, Frederick
See Faust, Frederick (Schiller)

Frost, Robert (Lee)
1874-1963 . . . . **CLC 1, 3, 4, 9, 10, 13, 15,
26, 34, 44; DA; PC 1; WLC**
See also CA 89-92; CANR 33;
CDALB 1917-1929; DLB 54; DLBD 7;
MTCW; SATA 14

Froude, James Anthony
1818-1894 . . . . **NCLC 43**
See also DLB 18, 57, 144

Froy, Herald
See Waterhouse, Keith (Spencer)

Fry, Christopher 1907- . . . . . . **CLC 2, 10, 14**
See also CA 17-20R; CANR 9, 30; DLB 13;
MTCW; SATA 66

Gelber, Jack 1932- .... CLC **1, 6, 14, 79**
See also CA 1-4R; CANR 2; DLB 7

Gellhorn, Martha (Ellis) 1908- .. CLC **14, 60**
See also CA 77-80; CANR 44; DLBY 82

Genet, Jean
1910-1986 ... CLC **1, 2, 5, 10, 14, 44, 46**
See also CA 13-16R; CANR 18; DLB 72;
DLBY 86; MTCW

Gent, Peter 1942- .... CLC **29**
See also AITN 1; CA 89-92; DLBY 82

Gentlewoman in New England, A
See Bradstreet, Anne

Gentlewoman in Those Parts, A
See Bradstreet, Anne

George, Jean Craighead 1919- ...... CLC **35**
See also AAYA 8; CA 5-8R; CANR 25;
CLR 1; DLB 52; JRDA; MAICYA;
SATA 2, 68

George, Stefan (Anton)
1868-1933 .... TCLC **2, 14**
See also CA 104

Georges, Georges Martin
See Simenon, Georges (Jacques Christian)

Gerhardi, William Alexander
See Gerhardie, William Alexander

Gerhardie, William Alexander
1895-1977 .... CLC **5**
See also CA 25-28R; 73-76; CANR 18;
DLB 36

Gerstler, Amy 1956- .... CLC **70**

Gertler, T. .... CLC **34**
See also CA 116; 121

Ghalib 1797-1869 .... NCLC **39**

Ghelderode, Michel de
1898-1962 .... CLC **6, 11**
See also CA 85-88; CANR 40

Ghiselin, Brewster 1903- .... CLC **23**
See also CA 13-16R; CAAS 10; CANR 13

Ghose, Zulfikar 1935- .... CLC **42**
See also CA 65-68

Ghosh, Amitav 1956- .... CLC **44**

Giacosa, Giuseppe 1847-1906 ...... TCLC **7**
See also CA 104

Gibb, Lee
See Waterhouse, Keith (Spencer)

Gibbon, Lewis Grassic .... TCLC **4**
See also Mitchell, James Leslie

Gibbons, Kaye 1960- .... CLC **50**

Gibran, Kahlil
1883-1931 .... TCLC **1, 9; PC 9**
See also CA 104

Gibson, William 1914- .... CLC **23; DA**
See also CA 9-12R; CANR 9, 42; DLB 7;
SATA 66

Gibson, William (Ford) 1948- ... CLC **39, 63**
See also AAYA 12; CA 126; 133

Gide, Andre (Paul Guillaume)
1869-1951 .... TCLC **5, 12, 36; DA;**
SSC **13; WLC**
See also CA 104; 124; DLB 65; MTCW

Gifford, Barry (Colby) 1946- .... CLC **34**
See also CA 65-68; CANR 9, 30, 40

Gilbert, W(illiam) S(chwenck)
1836-1911 .... TCLC **3**
See also CA 104; SATA 36

Gilbreth, Frank B., Jr. 1911- .... CLC **17**
See also CA 9-12R; SATA 2

Gilchrist, Ellen 1935- .. CLC **34, 48; SSC 14**
See also CA 113; 116; CANR 41; DLB 130;
MTCW

Giles, Molly 1942- .... CLC **39**
See also CA 126

Gill, Patrick
See Creasey, John

Gilliam, Terry (Vance) 1940- .... CLC **21**
See also Monty Python
See also CA 108; 113; CANR 35

Gillian, Jerry
See Gilliam, Terry (Vance)

Gilliatt, Penelope (Ann Douglass)
1932-1993 .... CLC **2, 10, 13, 53**
See also AITN 2; CA 13-16R; 141; DLB 14

Gilman, Charlotte (Anna) Perkins (Stetson)
1860-1935 .... TCLC **9, 37; SSC 13**
See also CA 106

Gilmour, David 1949- .... CLC **35**
See also CA 138

Gilpin, William 1724-1804 .... NCLC **30**

Gilray, J. D.
See Mencken, H(enry) L(ouis)

Gilroy, Frank D(aniel) 1925- .... CLC **2**
See also CA 81-84; CANR 32; DLB 7

Ginsberg, Allen
1926- ...... CLC **1, 2, 3, 4, 6, 13, 36, 69;**
DA; PC **4; WLC 3**
See also AITN 1; CA 1-4R; CANR 2, 41;
CDALB 1941-1968; DLB 5, 16; MTCW

Ginzburg, Natalia
1916-1991 .... CLC **5, 11, 54, 70**
See also CA 85-88; 135; CANR 33; MTCW

Giono, Jean 1895-1970 .... CLC **4, 11**
See also CA 45-48; 29-32R; CANR 2, 35;
DLB 72; MTCW

Giovanni, Nikki
1943- ...... CLC **2, 4, 19, 64; BLC; DA**
See also AITN 1; BW 2; CA 29-32R;
CAAS 6; CANR 18, 41; CLR 6; DLB 5,
41; MAICYA; MTCW; SATA 24

Giovene, Andrea 1904- .... CLC **7**
See also CA 85-88

Gippius, Zinaida (Nikolayevna) 1869-1945
See Hippius, Zinaida
See also CA 106

Giraudoux, (Hippolyte) Jean
1882-1944 ....TCLC **2, 7**
See also CA 104; DLB 65

Gironella, Jose Maria 1917- .... CLC **11**
See also CA 101

Gissing, George (Robert)
1857-1903 .... TCLC **3, 24, 47**
See also CA 105; DLB 18, 135

Giurlani, Aldo
See Palazzeschi, Aldo

Gladkov, Fyodor (Vasilyevich)
1883-1958 .... TCLC **27**

Glanville, Brian (Lester) 1931- ...... CLC **6**
See also CA 5-8R; CAAS 9; CANR 3;
DLB 15, 139; SATA 42

Glasgow, Ellen (Anderson Gholson)
1873(?)-1945 ....TCLC **2, 7**
See also CA 104; DLB 9, 12

Glaspell, Susan (Keating)
1882(?)-1948 .... TCLC **55**
See also CA 110; DLB 7, 9, 78; YABC 2

Glassco, John 1909-1981 .... CLC **9**
See also CA 13-16R; 102; CANR 15;
DLB 68

Glasscock, Amnesia
See Steinbeck, John (Ernst)

Glasser, Ronald J. 1940(?)- .... CLC **37**

Glassman, Joyce
See Johnson, Joyce

Glendinning, Victoria 1937- .... CLC **50**
See also CA 120; 127

Glissant, Edouard 1928- .... CLC **10, 68**

Gloag, Julian 1930- .... CLC **40**
See also AITN 1; CA 65-68; CANR 10

Glowacki, Aleksander
See Prus, Boleslaw

Glueck, Louise (Elisabeth)
1943- .... CLC **7, 22, 44, 81**
See also CA 33-36R; CANR 40; DLB 5

Gobineau, Joseph Arthur (Comte) de
1816-1882 .... NCLC **17**
See also DLB 123

Godard, Jean-Luc 1930- .... CLC **20**
See also CA 93-96

Godden, (Margaret) Rumer 1907- ... CLC **53**
See also AAYA 6; CA 5-8R; CANR 4, 27,
36; CLR 20; MAICYA; SAAS 12;
SATA 3, 36

Godoy Alcayaga, Lucila 1889-1957
See Mistral, Gabriela
See also BW 2; CA 104; 131; HW; MTCW

Godwin, Gail (Kathleen)
1937- .... CLC **5, 8, 22, 31, 69**
See also CA 29-32R; CANR 15, 43; DLB 6;
MTCW

Godwin, William 1756-1836 ...... NCLC **14**
See also CDBLB 1789-1832; DLB 39, 104,
142

Goethe, Johann Wolfgang von
1749-1832 .... NCLC **4, 22, 34; DA;**
PC **5; WLC 3**
See also DLB 94

Gogarty, Oliver St. John
1878-1957 .... TCLC **15**
See also CA 109; DLB 15, 19

Gogol, Nikolai (Vasilyevich)
1809-1852 .... NCLC **5, 15, 31; DA;**
DC **1; SSC 4; WLC**

Goines, Donald
1937(?)-1974 .... CLC **80; BLC**
See also AITN 1; BW 1; CA 124; 114;
DLB 33

Gold, Herbert 1924- .... CLC **4, 7, 14, 42**
See also CA 9-12R; CANR 17, 45; DLB 2;
DLBY 81

Goldbarth, Albert 1948- .... CLC **5, 38**
See also CA 53-56; CANR 6, 40; DLB 120

Goldberg, Anatol 1910-1982 .... **CLC 34**
See also CA 131; 117

Goldemberg, Isaac 1945- .... **CLC 52**
See also CA 69-72; CAAS 12; CANR 11, 32; HW

Golding, William (Gerald)
1911-1993 .... **CLC 1, 2, 3, 8, 10, 17, 27, 58, 81; DA; WLC**
See also AAYA 5; CA 5-8R; 141; CANR 13, 33; CDBLB 1945-1960; DLB 15, 100; MTCW

Goldman, Emma 1869-1940 ...... **TCLC 13**
See also CA 110

Goldman, Francisco 1955- .... **CLC 76**

Goldman, William (W.) 1931- .... **CLC 1, 48**
See also CA 9-12R; CANR 29; DLB 44

Goldmann, Lucien 1913-1970 ...... **CLC 24**
See also CA 25-28; CAP 2

Goldoni, Carlo 1707-1793 .... **LC 4**

Goldsberry, Steven 1949- .... **CLC 34**
See also CA 131

Goldsmith, Oliver
1728-1774 .... **LC 2; DA; WLC**
See also CDBLB 1660-1789; DLB 39, 89, 104, 109, 142; SATA 26

Goldsmith, Peter
See Priestley, J(ohn) B(oynton)

Gombrowicz, Witold
1904-1969 .... **CLC 4, 7, 11, 49**
See also CA 19-20; 25-28R; CAP 2

Gomez de la Serna, Ramon
1888-1963 .... **CLC 9**
See also CA 116; HW

Goncharov, Ivan Alexandrovich
1812-1891 .... **NCLC 1**

Goncourt, Edmond (Louis Antoine Huot) de
1822-1896 .... **NCLC 7**
See also DLB 123

Goncourt, Jules (Alfred Huot) de
1830-1870 .... **NCLC 7**
See also DLB 123

Gontier, Fernande 19(?)- .... **CLC 50**

Goodman, Paul 1911-1972.... **CLC 1, 2, 4, 7**
See also CA 19-20; 37-40R; CANR 34; CAP 2; DLB 130; MTCW

Gordimer, Nadine
1923- .... **CLC 3, 5, 7, 10, 18, 33, 51, 70; DA; SSC 17**
See also CA 5-8R; CANR 3, 28; MTCW

Gordon, Adam Lindsay
1833-1870 .... **NCLC 21**

Gordon, Caroline
1895-1981 ... **CLC 6, 13, 29, 83; SSC 15**
See also CA 11-12; 103; CANR 36; CAP 1; DLB 4, 9, 102; DLBY 81; MTCW

Gordon, Charles William 1860-1937
See Connor, Ralph
See also CA 109

Gordon, Mary (Catherine)
1949- .... **CLC 13, 22**
See also CA 102; CANR 44; DLB 6; DLBY 81; MTCW

Gordon, Sol 1923- .... **CLC 26**
See also CA 53-56; CANR 4; SATA 11

Gordone, Charles 1925- .... **CLC 1, 4**
See also BW 1; CA 93-96; DLB 7; MTCW

Gorenko, Anna Andreevna
See Akhmatova, Anna

Gorky, Maxim .... **TCLC 8; WLC**
See also Peshkov, Alexei Maximovich

Goryan, Sirak
See Saroyan, William

Gosse, Edmund (William)
1849-1928 .... **TCLC 28**
See also CA 117; DLB 57, 144

Gotlieb, Phyllis Fay (Bloom)
1926- .... **CLC 18**
See also CA 13-16R; CANR 7; DLB 88

Gottesman, S. D.
See Kornbluth, C(yril) M.; Pohl, Frederik

Gottfried von Strassburg
fl. c. 1210- .... **CMLC 10**
See also DLB 138

Gould, Lois .... **CLC 4, 10**
See also CA 77-80; CANR 29; MTCW

Gourmont, Remy de 1858-1915.... **TCLC 17**
See also CA 109

Govier, Katherine 1948- .... **CLC 51**
See also CA 101; CANR 18, 40

Goyen, (Charles) William
1915-1983 .... **CLC 5, 8, 14, 40**
See also AITN 2; CA 5-8R; 110; CANR 6; DLB 2; DLBY 83

Goytisolo, Juan
1931- .... **CLC 5, 10, 23; HLC**
See also CA 85-88; CANR 32; HW; MTCW

Gozzano, Guido 1883-1916 .... **PC 10**
See also DLB 114

Gozzi, (Conte) Carlo 1720-1806 .. **NCLC 23**

Grabbe, Christian Dietrich
1801-1836 .... **NCLC 2**
See also DLB 133

Grace, Patricia 1937- .... **CLC 56**

Gracian y Morales, Baltasar
1601-1658 .... **LC 15**

Gracq, Julien .... **CLC 11, 48**
See also Poirier, Louis
See also DLB 83

Grade, Chaim 1910-1982 .... **CLC 10**
See also CA 93-96; 107

Graduate of Oxford, A
See Ruskin, John

Graham, John
See Phillips, David Graham

Graham, Jorie 1951- .... **CLC 48**
See also CA 111; DLB 120

Graham, R(obert) B(ontine) Cunninghame
See Cunninghame Graham, R(obert) B(ontine)
See also DLB 98, 135

Graham, Robert
See Haldeman, Joe (William)

Graham, Tom
See Lewis, (Harry) Sinclair

Graham, W(illiam) S(ydney)
1918-1986 .... **CLC 29**
See also CA 73-76; 118; DLB 20

Graham, Winston (Mawdsley)
1910- .... **CLC 23**
See also CA 49-52; CANR 2, 22, 45; DLB 77

Grant, Skeeter
See Spiegelman, Art

Granville-Barker, Harley
1877-1946 .... **TCLC 2**
See also Barker, Harley Granville
See also CA 104

Grass, Guenter (Wilhelm)
1927- ..... **CLC 1, 2, 4, 6, 11, 15, 22, 32, 49; DA; WLC**
See also CA 13-16R; CANR 20; DLB 75, 124; MTCW

Gratton, Thomas
See Hulme, T(homas) E(rnest)

Grau, Shirley Ann
1929- .... **CLC 4, 9; SSC 15**
See also CA 89-92; CANR 22; DLB 2; MTCW

Gravel, Fern
See Hall, James Norman

Graver, Elizabeth 1964- .... **CLC 70**
See also CA 135

Graves, Richard Perceval 1945- .... **CLC 44**
See also CA 65-68; CANR 9, 26

Graves, Robert (von Ranke)
1895-1985 ...... **CLC 1, 2, 6, 11, 39, 44, 45; PC 6**
See also CA 5-8R; 117; CANR 5, 36; CDBLB 1914-1945; DLB 20, 100; DLBY 85; MTCW; SATA 45

Gray, Alasdair 1934- .... **CLC 41**
See also CA 126; MTCW

Gray, Amlin 1946- .... **CLC 29**
See also CA 138

Gray, Francine du Plessix 1930- .... **CLC 22**
See also BEST 90:3; CA 61-64; CAAS 2; CANR 11, 33; MTCW

Gray, John (Henry) 1866-1934 .... **TCLC 19**
See also CA 119

Gray, Simon (James Holliday)
1936- .... **CLC 9, 14, 36**
See also AITN 1; CA 21-24R; CAAS 3; CANR 32; DLB 13; MTCW

Gray, Spalding 1941- .... **CLC 49**
See also CA 128

Gray, Thomas
1716-1771 ...... **LC 4; DA; PC 2; WLC**
See also CDBLB 1660-1789; DLB 109

Grayson, David
See Baker, Ray Stannard

Grayson, Richard (A.) 1951- .... **CLC 38**
See also CA 85-88; CANR 14, 31

Greeley, Andrew M(oran) 1928- .... **CLC 28**
See also CA 5-8R; CAAS 7; CANR 7, 43; MTCW

Green, Brian
See Card, Orson Scott

Green, Hannah
See Greenberg, Joanne (Goldenberg)

Green, Hannah .... **CLC 3**
See also CA 73-76

Harrison, Elizabeth Cavanna 1909-
See Cavanna, Betty
See also CA 9-12R; CANR 6, 27

Harrison, Harry (Max) 1925- . . . . . . CLC 42
See also CA 1-4R; CANR 5, 21; DLB 8;
SATA 4

Harrison, James (Thomas)
1937- . . . . CLC 6, 14, 33, 66
See also CA 13-16R; CANR 8; DLBY 82

Harrison, Jim
See Harrison, James (Thomas)

Harrison, Kathryn 1961- . . . . CLC 70
See also CA 144

Harrison, Tony 1937- . . . . CLC 43
See also CA 65-68; CANR 44; DLB 40;
MTCW

Harriss, Will(ard Irvin) 1922- . . . . . . CLC 34
See also CA 111

Harson, Sley
See Ellison, Harlan

Hart, Ellis
See Ellison, Harlan

Hart, Josephine 1942(?)- . . . . CLC 70
See also CA 138

Hart, Moss 1904-1961 . . . . CLC 66
See also CA 109; 89-92; DLB 7

Harte, (Francis) Bret(t)
1836(?)-1902 . . . . TCLC 1, 25; DA;
SSC 8; WLC
See also CA 104; 140; CDALB 1865-1917;
DLB 12, 64, 74, 79; SATA 26

Hartley, L(eslie) P(oles)
1895-1972 . . . . CLC 2, 22
See also CA 45-48; 37-40R; CANR 33;
DLB 15, 139; MTCW

Hartman, Geoffrey H. 1929- . . . . CLC 27
See also CA 117; 125; DLB 67

Haruf, Kent 19(?)- . . . . CLC 34

Harwood, Ronald 1934- . . . . CLC 32
See also CA 1-4R; CANR 4; DLB 13

Hasek, Jaroslav (Matej Frantisek)
1883-1923 . . . . TCLC 4
See also CA 104; 129; MTCW

Hass, Robert 1941- . . . . CLC 18, 39
See also CA 111; CANR 30; DLB 105

Hastings, Hudson
See Kuttner, Henry

Hastings, Selina . . . . CLC 44

Hatteras, Amelia
See Mencken, H(enry) L(ouis)

Hatteras, Owen . . . . TCLC 18
See also Mencken, H(enry) L(ouis); Nathan,
George Jean

Hauptmann, Gerhart (Johann Robert)
1862-1946 . . . . TCLC 4
See also CA 104; DLB 66, 118

Havel, Vaclav 1936- . . . . CLC 25, 58, 65
See also CA 104; CANR 36; MTCW

Haviaras, Stratis . . . . CLC 33
See also Chaviaras, Strates

Hawes, Stephen 1475(?)-1523(?) . . . . . LC 17

Hawkes, John (Clendennin Burne, Jr.)
1925- . . . . . . CLC 1, 2, 3, 4, 7, 9, 14, 15,
27, 49
See also CA 1-4R; CANR 2; DLB 2, 7;
DLBY 80; MTCW

Hawking, S. W.
See Hawking, Stephen W(illiam)

Hawking, Stephen W(illiam)
1942- . . . . CLC 63
See also BEST 89:1; CA 126; 129

Hawthorne, Julian 1846-1934 . . . . . TCLC 25

Hawthorne, Nathaniel
1804-1864 . . . . . . NCLC 39; DA; SSC 3;
WLC
See also CDALB 1640-1865; DLB 1, 74;
YABC 2

Haxton, Josephine Ayres 1921-
See Douglas, Ellen
See also CA 115; CANR 41

Hayaseca y Eizaguirre, Jorge
See Echegaray (y Eizaguirre), Jose (Maria
Waldo)

Hayashi Fumiko 1904-1951 . . . . TCLC 27

Haycraft, Anna
See Ellis, Alice Thomas
See also CA 122

Hayden, Robert E(arl)
1913-1980 . . . . . . CLC 5, 9, 14, 37; BLC;
DA; PC 6
See also BW 1; CA 69-72; 97-100; CABS 2;
CANR 24; CDALB 1941-1968; DLB 5,
76; MTCW; SATA 19, 26

Hayford, J(oseph) E(phraim) Casely
See Casely-Hayford, J(oseph) E(phraim)

Hayman, Ronald 1932- . . . . CLC 44
See also CA 25-28R; CANR 18

Haywood, Eliza (Fowler)
1693(?)-1756 . . . . LC 1

Hazlitt, William 1778-1830 . . . . . . NCLC 29
See also DLB 110

Hazzard, Shirley 1931- . . . . CLC 18
See also CA 9-12R; CANR 4; DLBY 82;
MTCW

Head, Bessie 1937-1986 . . . CLC 25, 67; BLC
See also BW 2; CA 29-32R; 119; CANR 25;
DLB 117; MTCW

Headon, (Nicky) Topper 1956(?)- . . . CLC 30

Heaney, Seamus (Justin)
1939- . . . . CLC 5, 7, 14, 25, 37, 74
See also CA 85-88; CANR 25;
CDBLB 1960 to Present; DLB 40;
MTCW

Hearn, (Patricio) Lafcadio (Tessima Carlos)
1850-1904 . . . . TCLC 9
See also CA 105; DLB 12, 78

Hearne, Vicki 1946- . . . . CLC 56
See also CA 139

Hearon, Shelby 1931- . . . . CLC 63
See also AITN 2; CA 25-28R; CANR 18

Heat-Moon, William Least . . . . CLC 29
See also Trogdon, William (Lewis)
See also AAYA 9

Hebbel, Friedrich 1813-1863 . . . . . NCLC 43
See also DLB 129

Hebert, Anne 1916- . . . . CLC 4, 13, 29
See also CA 85-88; DLB 68; MTCW

Hecht, Anthony (Evan)
1923- . . . . CLC 8, 13, 19
See also CA 9-12R; CANR 6; DLB 5

Hecht, Ben 1894-1964 . . . . CLC 8
See also CA 85-88; DLB 7, 9, 25, 26, 28, 86

Hedayat, Sadeq 1903-1951 . . . . TCLC 21
See also CA 120

Hegel, Georg Wilhelm Friedrich
1770-1831 . . . . NCLC 46
See also DLB 90

Heidegger, Martin 1889-1976 . . . . . . CLC 24
See also CA 81-84; 65-68; CANR 34;
MTCW

Heidenstam, (Carl Gustaf) Verner von
1859-1940 . . . . TCLC 5
See also CA 104

Heifner, Jack 1946- . . . . CLC 11
See also CA 105

Heijermans, Herman 1864-1924 . . . TCLC 24
See also CA 123

Heilbrun, Carolyn G(old) 1926- . . . . . CLC 25
See also CA 45-48; CANR 1, 28

Heine, Heinrich 1797-1856 . . . . NCLC 4
See also DLB 90

Heinemann, Larry (Curtiss) 1944- . . CLC 50
See also CA 110; CANR 31; DLBD 9

Heiney, Donald (William) 1921-1993
See Harris, MacDonald
See also CA 1-4R; 142; CANR 3

Heinlein, Robert A(nson)
1907-1988 . . . . . . CLC 1, 3, 8, 14, 26, 55
See also CA 1-4R; 125; CANR 1, 20;
DLB 8; JRDA; MAICYA; MTCW;
SATA 9, 56, 69

Helforth, John
See Doolittle, Hilda

Hellenhofferu, Vojtech Kapristian z
See Hasek, Jaroslav (Matej Frantisek)

Heller, Joseph
1923- . . . . CLC 1, 3, 5, 8, 11, 36, 63; DA;
WLC
See also AITN 1; CA 5-8R; CABS 1;
CANR 8, 42; DLB 2, 28; DLBY 80;
MTCW

Hellman, Lillian (Florence)
1906-1984 . . . . . . CLC 2, 4, 8, 14, 18, 34,
44, 52; DC 1
See also AITN 1, 2; CA 13-16R; 112;
CANR 33; DLB 7; DLBY 84; MTCW

Helprin, Mark 1947- . . . . . CLC 7, 10, 22, 32
See also CA 81-84; DLBY 85; MTCW

Helvetius, Claude-Adrien
1715-1771 . . . . LC 26

Helyar, Jane Penelope Josephine 1933-
See Poole, Josephine
See also CA 21-24R; CANR 10, 26

Hemans, Felicia 1793-1835 . . . . . . NCLC 29
See also DLB 96

Hoban, Russell (Conwell) 1925- . . CLC 7, 25
See also CA 5-8R; CANR 23, 37; CLR 3;
DLB 52; MAICYA; MTCW; SATA 1,
40, 78

Hobbs, Perry
See Blackmur, R(ichard) P(almer)

Hobson, Laura Z(ametkin)
1900-1986 . . . . CLC 7, 25
See also CA 17-20R; 118; DLB 28;
SATA 52

Hochhuth, Rolf 1931- . . . . CLC 4, 11, 18
See also CA 5-8R; CANR 33; DLB 124;
MTCW

Hochman, Sandra 1936- . . . . CLC 3, 8
See also CA 5-8R; DLB 5

Hochwaelder, Fritz 1911-1986 . . . . . . CLC 36
See also CA 29-32R; 120; CANR 42;
MTCW

Hochwalder, Fritz
See Hochwaelder, Fritz

Hocking, Mary (Eunice) 1921- . . . . . CLC 13
See also CA 101; CANR 18, 40

Hodgins, Jack 1938- . . . . CLC 23
See also CA 93-96; DLB 60

Hodgson, William Hope
1877(?)-1918 . . . . TCLC 13
See also CA 111; DLB 70

Hoffman, Alice 1952- . . . . CLC 51
See also CA 77-80; CANR 34; MTCW

Hoffman, Daniel (Gerard)
1923- . . . . CLC 6, 13, 23
See also CA 1-4R; CANR 4; DLB 5

Hoffman, Stanley 1944- . . . . CLC 5
See also CA 77-80

Hoffman, William M(oses) 1939- . . . CLC 40
See also CA 57-60; CANR 11

Hoffmann, E(rnst) T(heodor) A(madeus)
1776-1822 . . . . NCLC 2; SSC 13
See also DLB 90; SATA 27

Hofmann, Gert 1931- . . . . CLC 54
See also CA 128

Hofmannsthal, Hugo von
1874-1929 . . . . TCLC 11; DC 4
See also CA 106; DLB 81, 118

Hogan, Linda 1947- . . . . CLC 73
See also CA 120; CANR 45

Hogarth, Charles
See Creasey, John

Hogg, James 1770-1835 . . . . NCLC 4
See also DLB 93, 116

Holbach, Paul Henri Thiry Baron
1723-1789 . . . . LC 14

Holberg, Ludvig 1684-1754 . . . . LC 6

Holden, Ursula 1921- . . . . CLC 18
See also CA 101; CAAS 8; CANR 22

Holderlin, (Johann Christian) Friedrich
1770-1843 . . . . NCLC 16; PC 4

Holdstock, Robert
See Holdstock, Robert P.

Holdstock, Robert P. 1948- . . . . CLC 39
See also CA 131

Holland, Isabelle 1920- . . . . CLC 21
See also AAYA 11; CA 21-24R; CANR 10,
25; JRDA; MAICYA; SATA 8, 70

Holland, Marcus
See Caldwell, (Janet Miriam) Taylor
(Holland)

Hollander, John 1929- . . . . . . CLC 2, 5, 8, 14
See also CA 1-4R; CANR 1; DLB 5;
SATA 13

Hollander, Paul
See Silverberg, Robert

Holleran, Andrew 1943(?)- . . . . CLC 38
See also CA 144

Hollinghurst, Alan 1954- . . . . CLC 55
See also CA 114

Hollis, Jim
See Summers, Hollis (Spurgeon, Jr.)

Holmes, John
See Souster, (Holmes) Raymond

Holmes, John Clellon 1926-1988 . . . . CLC 56
See also CA 9-12R; 125; CANR 4; DLB 16

Holmes, Oliver Wendell
1809-1894 . . . . NCLC 14
See also CDALB 1640-1865; DLB 1;
SATA 34

Holmes, Raymond
See Souster, (Holmes) Raymond

Holt, Victoria
See Hibbert, Eleanor Alice Burford

Holub, Miroslav 1923- . . . . CLC 4
See also CA 21-24R; CANR 10

Homer c. 8th cent. B.C.- . . . . . CMLC 1; DA

Honig, Edwin 1919- . . . . CLC 33
See also CA 5-8R; CAAS 8; CANR 4, 45;
DLB 5

Hood, Hugh (John Blagdon)
1928- . . . . CLC 15, 28
See also CA 49-52; CAAS 17; CANR 1, 33;
DLB 53

Hood, Thomas 1799-1845 . . . . NCLC 16
See also DLB 96

Hooker, (Peter) Jeremy 1941- . . . . . . CLC 43
See also CA 77-80; CANR 22; DLB 40

Hope, A(lec) D(erwent) 1907- . . . . CLC 3, 51
See also CA 21-24R; CANR 33; MTCW

Hope, Brian
See Creasey, John

Hope, Christopher (David Tully)
1944- . . . . CLC 52
See also CA 106; SATA 62

Hopkins, Gerard Manley
1844-1889 . . . . NCLC 17; DA; WLC
See also CDBLB 1890-1914; DLB 35, 57

Hopkins, John (Richard) 1931- . . . . . . CLC 4
See also CA 85-88

Hopkins, Pauline Elizabeth
1859-1930 . . . . TCLC 28; BLC
See also BW 2; CA 141; DLB 50

Hopkinson, Francis 1737-1791 . . . . . . LC 25
See also DLB 31

Hopley-Woolrich, Cornell George 1903-1968
See Woolrich, Cornell
See also CA 13-14; CAP 1

Horatio
See Proust, (Valentin-Louis-George-Eugene-)
Marcel

Horgan, Paul 1903- . . . . CLC 9, 53
See also CA 13-16R; CANR 9, 35;
DLB 102; DLBY 85; MTCW; SATA 13

Horn, Peter
See Kuttner, Henry

Hornem, Horace Esq.
See Byron, George Gordon (Noel)

Horovitz, Israel 1939- . . . . CLC 56
See also CA 33-36R; DLB 7

Horvath, Odon von
See Horvath, Oedoen von
See also DLB 85, 124

Horvath, Oedoen von 1901-1938 . . . TCLC 45
See also Horvath, Odon von
See also CA 118

Horwitz, Julius 1920-1986 . . . . CLC 14
See also CA 9-12R; 119; CANR 12

Hospital, Janette Turner 1942- . . . . . CLC 42
See also CA 108

Hostos, E. M. de
See Hostos (y Bonilla), Eugenio Maria de

Hostos, Eugenio M. de
See Hostos (y Bonilla), Eugenio Maria de

Hostos, Eugenio Maria
See Hostos (y Bonilla), Eugenio Maria de

Hostos (y Bonilla), Eugenio Maria de
1839-1903 . . . . TCLC 24
See also CA 123; 131; HW

Houdini
See Lovecraft, H(oward) P(hillips)

Hougan, Carolyn 1943- . . . . CLC 34
See also CA 139

Household, Geoffrey (Edward West)
1900-1988 . . . . CLC 11
See also CA 77-80; 126; DLB 87; SATA 14,
59

Housman, A(lfred) E(dward)
1859-1936 . . . . . . TCLC 1, 10; DA; PC 2
See also CA 104; 125; DLB 19; MTCW

Housman, Laurence 1865-1959 . . . . . TCLC 7
See also CA 106; DLB 10; SATA 25

Howard, Elizabeth Jane 1923- . . . CLC 7, 29
See also CA 5-8R; CANR 8

Howard, Maureen 1930- . . . . . CLC 5, 14, 46
See also CA 53-56; CANR 31; DLBY 83;
MTCW

Howard, Richard 1929- . . . . . . CLC 7, 10, 47
See also AITN 1; CA 85-88; CANR 25;
DLB 5

Howard, Robert Ervin 1906-1936 . . . TCLC 8
See also CA 105

Howard, Warren F.
See Pohl, Frederik

Howe, Fanny 1940- . . . . CLC 47
See also CA 117; SATA 52

Howe, Irving 1920-1993 . . . . CLC 85
See also CA 9-12R; 141; CANR 21;
DLB 67; MTCW

Howe, Julia Ward 1819-1910 . . . . . TCLC 21
See also CA 117; DLB 1

Howe, Susan 1937- . . . . CLC 72
See also DLB 120

Howe, Tina 1937- . . . . CLC 48
See also CA 109

Howell, James   1594(?)-1666 . . . . LC 13

Howells, W. D.
See Howells, William Dean

Howells, William D.
See Howells, William Dean

Howells, William Dean
  1837-1920 . . . . **TCLC 7, 17, 41**
  See also CA 104; 134; CDALB 1865-1917;
  DLB 12, 64, 74, 79

Howes, Barbara   1914- . . . . CLC 15
  See also CA 9-12R; CAAS 3; SATA 5

Hrabal, Bohumil   1914- . . . . CLC 13, 67
  See also CA 106; CAAS 12

Hsun, Lu . . . . TCLC 3
  See also Shu-Jen, Chou

Hubbard, L(afayette) Ron(ald)
  1911-1986 . . . . CLC 43
  See also CA 77-80; 118; CANR 22

Huch, Ricarda (Octavia)
  1864-1947 . . . . TCLC 13
  See also CA 111; DLB 66

Huddle, David   1942- . . . . CLC 49
  See also CA 57-60; DLB 130

Hudson, Jeffrey
  See Crichton, (John) Michael

Hudson, W(illiam) H(enry)
  1841-1922 . . . . TCLC 29
  See also CA 115; DLB 98; SATA 35

Hueffer, Ford Madox
  See Ford, Ford Madox

Hughart, Barry   1934- . . . . CLC 39
  See also CA 137

Hughes, Colin
  See Creasey, John

Hughes, David (John)   1930- . . . . CLC 48
  See also CA 116; 129; DLB 14

Hughes, (James) Langston
  1902-1967 . . . . . CLC 1, 5, 10, 15, 35, 44;
              BLC; DA; DC 3; PC 1; SSC 6; WLC
  See also AAYA 12; BW 1; CA 1-4R;
  25-28R; CANR 1, 34; CDALB 1929-1941;
  CLR 17; DLB 4, 7, 48, 51, 86; JRDA;
  MAICYA; MTCW; SATA 4, 33

Hughes, Richard (Arthur Warren)
  1900-1976 . . . . CLC 1, 11
  See also CA 5-8R; 65-68; CANR 4;
  DLB 15; MTCW; SATA 8, 25

Hughes, Ted
  1930- . . . . CLC 2, 4, 9, 14, 37; PC 7
  See also CA 1-4R; CANR 1, 33; CLR 3;
  DLB 40; MAICYA; MTCW; SATA 27,
  49

Hugo, Richard F(ranklin)
  1923-1982 . . . . CLC 6, 18, 32
  See also CA 49-52; 108; CANR 3; DLB 5

Hugo, Victor (Marie)
  1802-1885 . . NCLC 3, 10, 21; DA; WLC
  See also DLB 119; SATA 47

Huidobro, Vicente
  See Huidobro Fernandez, Vicente Garcia

Huidobro Fernandez, Vicente Garcia
  1893-1948 . . . . TCLC 31
  See also CA 131; HW

Hulme, Keri   1947- . . . . CLC 39
  See also CA 125

Hulme, T(homas) E(rnest)
  1883-1917 . . . . TCLC 21
  See also CA 117; DLB 19

Hume, David   1711-1776 . . . . LC 7
  See also DLB 104

Humphrey, William   1924- . . . . CLC 45
  See also CA 77-80; DLB 6

Humphreys, Emyr Owen   1919- . . . . . CLC 47
  See also CA 5-8R; CANR 3, 24; DLB 15

Humphreys, Josephine   1945- . . . . CLC 34, 57
  See also CA 121; 127

Hungerford, Pixie
  See Brinsmead, H(esba) F(ay)

Hunt, E(verette) Howard, Jr.
  1918- . . . . CLC 3
  See also AITN 1; CA 45-48; CANR 2

Hunt, Kyle
  See Creasey, John

Hunt, (James Henry) Leigh
  1784-1859 . . . . NCLC 1

Hunt, Marsha   1946- . . . . CLC 70
  See also BW 2; CA 143

Hunt, Violet   1866-1942 . . . . TCLC 53

Hunter, E. Waldo
  See Sturgeon, Theodore (Hamilton)

Hunter, Evan   1926- . . . . CLC 11, 31
  See also CA 5-8R; CANR 5, 38; DLBY 82;
  MTCW; SATA 25

Hunter, Kristin (Eggleston)   1931- . . . CLC 35
  See also AITN 1; BW 1; CA 13-16R;
  CANR 13; CLR 3; DLB 33; MAICYA;
  SAAS 10; SATA 12

Hunter, Mollie   1922- . . . . CLC 21
  See also McIlwraith, Maureen Mollie
  Hunter
  See also CANR 37; CLR 25; JRDA;
  MAICYA; SAAS 7; SATA 54

Hunter, Robert   (?)-1734 . . . . LC 7

Hurston, Zora Neale
  1903-1960 . . . . CLC 7, 30, 61; BLC; DA;
                                              SSC 4
  See also BW 1; CA 85-88; DLB 51, 86;
  MTCW

Huston, John (Marcellus)
  1906-1987 . . . . CLC 20
  See also CA 73-76; 123; CANR 34; DLB 26

Hustvedt, Siri   1955- . . . . CLC 76
  See also CA 137

Hutten, Ulrich von   1488-1523 . . . . LC 16

Huxley, Aldous (Leonard)
  1894-1963 . . . . . CLC 1, 3, 4, 5, 8, 11, 18,
                              35, 79; DA; WLC
  See also AAYA 11; CA 85-88; CANR 44;
  CDBLB 1914-1945; DLB 36, 100;
  MTCW; SATA 63

Huysmans, Charles Marie Georges
  1848-1907
  See Huysmans, Joris-Karl
  See also CA 104

Huysmans, Joris-Karl . . . . TCLC 7
  See also Huysmans, Charles Marie Georges
  See also DLB 123

Hwang, David Henry
  1957- . . . . CLC 55; DC 4
  See also CA 127; 132

Hyde, Anthony   1946- . . . . CLC 42
  See also CA 136

Hyde, Margaret O(ldroyd)   1917- . . . CLC 21
  See also CA 1-4R; CANR 1, 36; CLR 23;
  JRDA; MAICYA; SAAS 8; SATA 1, 42,
  76

Hynes, James   1956(?)- . . . . CLC 65

Ian, Janis   1951- . . . . CLC 21
  See also CA 105

Ibanez, Vicente Blasco
  See Blasco Ibanez, Vicente

Ibarguengoitia, Jorge   1928-1983 . . . . CLC 37
  See also CA 124; 113; HW

Ibsen, Henrik (Johan)
  1828-1906 . . . . TCLC 2, 8, 16, 37, 52;
                              DA; DC 2; WLC
  See also CA 104; 141

Ibuse Masuji   1898-1993 . . . . CLC 22
  See also CA 127; 141

Ichikawa, Kon   1915- . . . . CLC 20
  See also CA 121

Idle, Eric   1943- . . . . CLC 21
  See also Monty Python
  See also CA 116; CANR 35

Ignatow, David   1914- . . . . . . CLC 4, 7, 14, 40
  See also CA 9-12R; CAAS 3; CANR 31;
  DLB 5

Ihimaera, Witi   1944- . . . . CLC 46
  See also CA 77-80

Ilf, Ilya . . . . TCLC 21
  See also Fainzilberg, Ilya Arnoldovich

Immermann, Karl (Lebrecht)
  1796-1840 . . . . NCLC 4
  See also DLB 133

Inclan, Ramon (Maria) del Valle
  See Valle-Inclan, Ramon (Maria) del

Infante, G(uillermo) Cabrera
  See Cabrera Infante, G(uillermo)

Ingalls, Rachel (Holmes)   1940- . . . . . CLC 42
  See also CA 123; 127

Ingamells, Rex   1913-1955 . . . . TCLC 35

Inge, William Motter
  1913-1973 . . . . CLC 1, 8, 19
  See also CA 9-12R; CDALB 1941-1968;
  DLB 7; MTCW

Ingelow, Jean   1820-1897 . . . . NCLC 39
  See also DLB 35; SATA 33

Ingram, Willis J.
  See Harris, Mark

Innaurato, Albert (F.)   1948(?)- . . CLC 21, 60
  See also CA 115; 122

Innes, Michael
  See Stewart, J(ohn) I(nnes) M(ackintosh)

Ionesco, Eugene
  1912-1994 . . . . CLC 1, 4, 6, 9, 11, 15, 41;
                              DA; WLC
  See also CA 9-12R; 144; MTCW; SATA 7;
  SATA-Obit 79

Iqbal, Muhammad   1873-1938 . . . . . TCLC 28

Ireland, Patrick
  See O'Doherty, Brian

Iron, Ralph
  See Schreiner, Olive (Emilie Albertina)

Irving, John (Winslow)
1942- .... **CLC 13, 23, 38**
See also AAYA 8; BEST 89:3; CA 25-28R;
CANR 28; DLB 6; DLBY 82; MTCW

Irving, Washington
1783-1859 .... **NCLC 2, 19; DA; SSC 2;
WLC**
See also CDALB 1640-1865; DLB 3, 11, 30,
59, 73, 74; YABC 2

Irwin, P. K.
See Page, P(atricia) K(athleen)

Isaacs, Susan 1943- .... **CLC 32**
See also BEST 89:1; CA 89-92; CANR 20,
41; MTCW

Isherwood, Christopher (William Bradshaw)
1904-1986 .... **CLC 1, 9, 11, 14, 44**
See also CA 13-16R; 117; CANR 35;
DLB 15; DLBY 86; MTCW

Ishiguro, Kazuo 1954- ...... **CLC 27, 56, 59**
See also BEST 90:2; CA 120; MTCW

Ishikawa Takuboku
1886(?)-1912 .... **TCLC 15; PC 10**
See also CA 113

Iskander, Fazil 1929- .... **CLC 47**
See also CA 102

Ivan IV 1530-1584 .... **LC 17**

Ivanov, Vyacheslav Ivanovich
1866-1949 .... **TCLC 33**
See also CA 122

Ivask, Ivar Vidrik 1927-1992....... **CLC 14**
See also CA 37-40R; 139; CANR 24

Jackson, Daniel
See Wingrove, David (John)

Jackson, Jesse 1908-1983 .... **CLC 12**
See also BW 1; CA 25-28R; 109; CANR 27;
CLR 28; MAICYA; SATA 2, 29, 48

Jackson, Laura (Riding) 1901-1991
See Riding, Laura
See also CA 65-68; 135; CANR 28; DLB 48

Jackson, Sam
See Trumbo, Dalton

Jackson, Sara
See Wingrove, David (John)

Jackson, Shirley
1919-1965 ..... **CLC 11, 60; DA; SSC 9;
WLC**
See also AAYA 9; CA 1-4R; 25-28R;
CANR 4; CDALB 1941-1968; DLB 6;
SATA 2

Jacob, (Cyprien-)Max 1876-1944 ... **TCLC 6**
See also CA 104

Jacobs, Jim 1942- .... **CLC 12**
See also CA 97-100

Jacobs, W(illiam) W(ymark)
1863-1943 .... **TCLC 22**
See also CA 121; DLB 135

Jacobsen, Jens Peter 1847-1885 .. **NCLC 34**

Jacobsen, Josephine 1908-......... **CLC 48**
See also CA 33-36R; CAAS 18; CANR 23

Jacobson, Dan 1929- .... **CLC 4, 14**
See also CA 1-4R; CANR 2, 25; DLB 14;
MTCW

Jacqueline
See Carpentier (y Valmont), Alejo

Jagger, Mick 1944-............... **CLC 17**

Jakes, John (William) 1932- .... **CLC 29**
See also BEST 89:4; CA 57-60; CANR 10,
43; DLBY 83; MTCW; SATA 62

James, Andrew
See Kirkup, James

James, C(yril) L(ionel) R(obert)
1901-1989 .... **CLC 33**
See also BW 2; CA 117; 125; 128; DLB 125;
MTCW

James, Daniel (Lewis) 1911-1988
See Santiago, Danny
See also CA 125

James, Dynely
See Mayne, William (James Carter)

James, Henry
1843-1916 ...... **TCLC 2, 11, 24, 40, 47;
DA; SSC 8; WLC**
See also CA 104; 132; CDALB 1865-1917;
DLB 12, 71, 74; MTCW

James, M. R.
See James, Montague (Rhodes)

James, Montague (Rhodes)
1862-1936 .... **TCLC 6; SSC 16**
See also CA 104

James, P. D. .... **CLC 18, 46**
See also White, Phyllis Dorothy James
See also BEST 90:2; CDBLB 1960 to
Present; DLB 87

James, Philip
See Moorcock, Michael (John)

James, William 1842-1910..... **TCLC 15, 32**
See also CA 109

James I 1394-1437 .... **LC 20**

Jameson, Anna 1794-1860 .... **NCLC 43**
See also DLB 99

Jami, Nur al-Din 'Abd al-Rahman
1414-1492 .... **LC 9**

Jandl, Ernst 1925- .... **CLC 34**

Janowitz, Tama 1957- .... **CLC 43**
See also CA 106

Jarrell, Randall
1914-1965 .... **CLC 1, 2, 6, 9, 13, 49**
See also CA 5-8R; 25-28R; CABS 2;
CANR 6, 34; CDALB 1941-1968; CLR 6;
DLB 48, 52; MAICYA; MTCW; SATA 7

Jarry, Alfred 1873-1907........ **TCLC 2, 14**
See also CA 104

Jarvis, E. K.
See Bloch, Robert (Albert); Ellison, Harlan;
Silverberg, Robert

Jeake, Samuel, Jr.
See Aiken, Conrad (Potter)

Jean Paul 1763-1825 .... **NCLC 7**

Jefferies, (John) Richard
1848-1887 .... **NCLC 47**
See also DLB 98, 141; SATA 16

Jeffers, (John) Robinson
1887-1962 .... **CLC 2, 3, 11, 15, 54; DA;
WLC**
See also CA 85-88; CANR 35;
CDALB 1917-1929; DLB 45; MTCW

Jefferson, Janet
See Mencken, H(enry) L(ouis)

Jefferson, Thomas 1743-1826 .... **NCLC 11**
See also CDALB 1640-1865; DLB 31

Jeffrey, Francis 1773-1850....... **NCLC 33**
See also DLB 107

Jelakowitch, Ivan
See Heijermans, Herman

Jellicoe, (Patricia) Ann 1927- ...... **CLC 27**
See also CA 85-88; DLB 13

Jen, Gish .... **CLC 70**
See also Jen, Lillian

Jen, Lillian 1956(?)-
See Jen, Gish
See also CA 135

Jenkins, (John) Robin 1912- .... **CLC 52**
See also CA 1-4R; CANR 1; DLB 14

Jennings, Elizabeth (Joan)
1926- .... **CLC 5, 14**
See also CA 61-64; CAAS 5; CANR 8, 39;
DLB 27; MTCW; SATA 66

Jennings, Waylon 1937-........... **CLC 21**

Jensen, Johannes V. 1873-1950.... **TCLC 41**

Jensen, Laura (Linnea) 1948- ...... **CLC 37**
See also CA 103

Jerome, Jerome K(lapka)
1859-1927 .... **TCLC 23**
See also CA 119; DLB 10, 34, 135

Jerrold, Douglas William
1803-1857 .... **NCLC 2**

Jewett, (Theodora) Sarah Orne
1849-1909 .... **TCLC 1, 22; SSC 6**
See also CA 108; 127; DLB 12, 74;
SATA 15

Jewsbury, Geraldine (Endsor)
1812-1880 .... **NCLC 22**
See also DLB 21

Jhabvala, Ruth Prawer
1927- .... **CLC 4, 8, 29**
See also CA 1-4R; CANR 2, 29; DLB 139;
MTCW

Jiles, Paulette 1943-........... **CLC 13, 58**
See also CA 101

Jimenez (Mantecon), Juan Ramon
1881-1958 .... **TCLC 4; HLC; PC 7**
See also CA 104; 131; DLB 134; HW;
MTCW

Jimenez, Ramon
See Jimenez (Mantecon), Juan Ramon

Jimenez Mantecon, Juan
See Jimenez (Mantecon), Juan Ramon

Joel, Billy .... **CLC 26**
See also Joel, William Martin

Joel, William Martin 1949-
See Joel, Billy
See also CA 108

John of the Cross, St. 1542-1591 .... **LC 18**

Johnson, B(ryan) S(tanley William)
1933-1973 .... **CLC 6, 9**
See also CA 9-12R; 53-56; CANR 9;
DLB 14, 40

Johnson, Benj. F. of Boo
See Riley, James Whitcomb

Johnson, Benjamin F. of Boo
See Riley, James Whitcomb

Johnson, Charles (Richard)
1948- . . . . CLC 7, 51, 65; BLC
See also BW 2; CA 116; CAAS 18;
CANR 42; DLB 33

Johnson, Denis 1949- . . . . CLC 52
See also CA 117; 121; DLB 120

Johnson, Diane 1934- . . . . CLC 5, 13, 48
See also CA 41-44R; CANR 17, 40;
DLBY 80; MTCW

Johnson, Eyvind (Olof Verner)
1900-1976 . . . . CLC 14
See also CA 73-76; 69-72; CANR 34

Johnson, J. R.
See James, C(yril) L(ionel) R(obert)

Johnson, James Weldon
1871-1938 . . . . TCLC 3, 19; BLC
See also BW 1; CA 104; 125;
CDALB 1917-1929; CLR 32; DLB 51;
MTCW; SATA 31

Johnson, Joyce 1935- . . . . CLC 58
See also CA 125; 129

Johnson, Lionel (Pigot)
1867-1902 . . . . TCLC 19
See also CA 117; DLB 19

Johnson, Mel
See Malzberg, Barry N(athaniel)

Johnson, Pamela Hansford
1912-1981 . . . . CLC 1, 7, 27
See also CA 1-4R; 104; CANR 2, 28;
DLB 15; MTCW

Johnson, Samuel
1709-1784 . . . . LC 15; DA; WLC
See also CDBLB 1660-1789; DLB 39, 95,
104, 142

Johnson, Uwe
1934-1984 . . . . CLC 5, 10, 15, 40
See also CA 1-4R; 112; CANR 1, 39;
DLB 75; MTCW

Johnston, George (Benson) 1913- . . . CLC 51
See also CA 1-4R; CANR 5, 20; DLB 88

Johnston, Jennifer 1930- . . . . CLC 7
See also CA 85-88; DLB 14

Jolley, (Monica) Elizabeth 1923- . . . CLC 46
See also CA 127; CAAS 13

Jones, Arthur Llewellyn 1863-1947
See Machen, Arthur
See also CA 104

Jones, D(ouglas) G(ordon) 1929- . . . . CLC 10
See also CA 29-32R; CANR 13; DLB 53

Jones, David (Michael)
1895-1974 . . . . CLC 2, 4, 7, 13, 42
See also CA 9-12R; 53-56; CANR 28;
CDBLB 1945-1960; DLB 20, 100; MTCW

Jones, David Robert 1947-
See Bowie, David
See also CA 103

Jones, Diana Wynne 1934- . . . . CLC 26
See also AAYA 12; CA 49-52; CANR 4,
26; CLR 23; JRDA; MAICYA; SAAS 7;
SATA 9, 70

Jones, Edward P. 1950- . . . . CLC 76
See also BW 2; CA 142

Jones, Gayl 1949- . . . . CLC 6, 9; BLC
See also BW 2; CA 77-80; CANR 27;
DLB 33; MTCW

Jones, James 1921-1977. . . . CLC 1, 3, 10, 39
See also AITN 1, 2; CA 1-4R; 69-72;
CANR 6; DLB 2, 143; MTCW

Jones, John J.
See Lovecraft, H(oward) P(hillips)

Jones, LeRoi . . . . CLC 1, 2, 3, 5, 10, 14
See also Baraka, Amiri

Jones, Louis B. . . . . CLC 65
See also CA 141

Jones, Madison (Percy, Jr.) 1925- . . . CLC 4
See also CA 13-16R; CAAS 11; CANR 7

Jones, Mervyn 1922- . . . . CLC 10, 52
See also CA 45-48; CAAS 5; CANR 1;
MTCW

Jones, Mick 1956(?)- . . . . CLC 30

Jones, Nettie (Pearl) 1941- . . . . CLC 34
See also BW 2; CA 137

Jones, Preston 1936-1979 . . . . CLC 10
See also CA 73-76; 89-92; DLB 7

Jones, Robert F(rancis) 1934- . . . . . . CLC 7
See also CA 49-52; CANR 2

Jones, Rod 1953- . . . . CLC 50
See also CA 128

Jones, Terence Graham Parry
1942- . . . . CLC 21
See also Jones, Terry; Monty Python
See also CA 112; 116; CANR 35; SATA 51

Jones, Terry
See Jones, Terence Graham Parry
See also SATA 67

Jones, Thom 1945(?)- . . . . CLC 81

Jong, Erica 1942- . . . . . . CLC 4, 6, 8, 18, 83
See also AITN 1; BEST 90:2; CA 73-76;
CANR 26; DLB 2, 5, 28; MTCW

Jonson, Ben(jamin)
1572(?)-1637 . . . . LC 6; DA; DC 4; WLC
See also CDBLB Before 1660; DLB 62, 121

Jordan, June 1936- . . . . CLC 5, 11, 23
See also AAYA 2; BW 2; CA 33-36R;
CANR 25; CLR 10; DLB 38; MAICYA;
MTCW; SATA 4

Jordan, Pat(rick M.) 1941- . . . . CLC 37
See also CA 33-36R

Jorgensen, Ivar
See Ellison, Harlan

Jorgenson, Ivar
See Silverberg, Robert

Josephus, Flavius c. 37-100 . . . . . . CMLC 13

Josipovici, Gabriel 1940- . . . . CLC 6, 43
See also CA 37-40R; CAAS 8; DLB 14

Joubert, Joseph 1754-1824 . . . . NCLC 9

Jouve, Pierre Jean 1887-1976 . . . . . . CLC 47
See also CA 65-68

Joyce, James (Augustine Aloysius)
1882-1941 . . . . . . TCLC 3, 8, 16, 35; DA;
SSC 3; WLC
See also CA 104; 126; CDBLB 1914-1945;
DLB 10, 19, 36; MTCW

Jozsef, Attila 1905-1937. . . . . TCLC 22
See also CA 116

Juana Ines de la Cruz 1651(?)-1695 . . . LC 5

Judd, Cyril
See Kornbluth, C(yril) M.; Pohl, Frederik

Julian of Norwich 1342(?)-1416(?) . . . . LC 6

Just, Ward (Swift) 1935- . . . . CLC 4, 27
See also CA 25-28R; CANR 32

Justice, Donald (Rodney) 1925- . . CLC 6, 19
See also CA 5-8R; CANR 26; DLBY 83

Juvenal c. 55-c. 127 . . . . CMLC 8

Juvenis
See Bourne, Randolph S(illiman)

Kacew, Romain 1914-1980
See Gary, Romain
See also CA 108; 102

Kadare, Ismail 1936- . . . . CLC 52

Kadohata, Cynthia. . . . . CLC 59
See also CA 140

Kafka, Franz
1883-1924 . . . . TCLC 2, 6, 13, 29, 47, 53;
DA; SSC 5; WLC
See also CA 105; 126; DLB 81; MTCW

Kahanovitsch, Pinkhes
See Der Nister

Kahn, Roger 1927- . . . . CLC 30
See also CA 25-28R; CANR 44; SATA 37

Kain, Saul
See Sassoon, Siegfried (Lorraine)

Kaiser, Georg 1878-1945 . . . . TCLC 9
See also CA 106; DLB 124

Kaletski, Alexander 1946- . . . . CLC 39
See also CA 118; 143

Kalidasa fl. c. 400- . . . . CMLC 9

Kallman, Chester (Simon)
1921-1975 . . . . CLC 2
See also CA 45-48; 53-56; CANR 3

Kaminsky, Melvin 1926-
See Brooks, Mel
See also CA 65-68; CANR 16

Kaminsky, Stuart M(elvin) 1934- . . . CLC 59
See also CA 73-76; CANR 29

Kane, Paul
See Simon, Paul

Kane, Wilson
See Bloch, Robert (Albert)

Kanin, Garson 1912- . . . . CLC 22
See also AITN 1; CA 5-8R; CANR 7;
DLB 7

Kaniuk, Yoram 1930- . . . . CLC 19
See also CA 134

Kant, Immanuel 1724-1804 . . . . . . NCLC 27
See also DLB 94

Kantor, MacKinlay 1904-1977 . . . . . . CLC 7
See also CA 61-64; 73-76; DLB 9, 102

Kaplan, David Michael 1946- . . . . . . CLC 50

Kaplan, James 1951- . . . . CLC 59
See also CA 135

Karageorge, Michael
See Anderson, Poul (William)

Karamzin, Nikolai Mikhailovich
1766-1826 . . . . NCLC 3

Karapanou, Margarita 1946- . . . . CLC 13
See also CA 101

Karinthy, Frigyes 1887-1938 . . . . . . TCLC 47

Karl, Frederick R(obert) 1927- . . . . . CLC 34
See also CA 5-8R; CANR 3, 44

Laredo, Betty
See Codrescu, Andrei

Larkin, Maia
See Wojciechowska, Maia (Teresa)

Larkin, Philip (Arthur)
1922-1985 .... CLC 3, 5, 8, 9, 13, 18, 33,
39, 64
See also CA 5-8R; 117; CANR 24;
CDBLB 1960 to Present; DLB 27;
MTCW

Larra (y Sanchez de Castro), Mariano Jose de
1809-1837 .... NCLC 17

Larsen, Eric 1941- .... CLC 55
See also CA 132

Larsen, Nella 1891-1964 ..... CLC 37; BLC
See also BW 1; CA 125; DLB 51

Larson, Charles R(aymond) 1938-... CLC 31
See also CA 53-56; CANR 4

Lasker-Schueler, Else 1869-1945 .. TCLC 57
See also DLB 66, 124

Latham, Jean Lee 1902-............ CLC 12
See also AITN 1; CA 5-8R; CANR 7;
MAICYA; SATA 2, 68

Latham, Mavis
See Clark, Mavis Thorpe

Lathen, Emma.................... CLC 2
See also Hennissart, Martha; Latsis, Mary
J(ane)

Lathrop, Francis
See Leiber, Fritz (Reuter, Jr.)

Latsis, Mary J(ane)
See Lathen, Emma
See also CA 85-88

Lattimore, Richmond (Alexander)
1906-1984 .... CLC 3
See also CA 1-4R; 112; CANR 1

Laughlin, James 1914-............ CLC 49
See also CA 21-24R; CANR 9; DLB 48

Laurence, (Jean) Margaret (Wemyss)
1926-1987 .. CLC 3, 6, 13, 50, 62; SSC 7
See also CA 5-8R; 121; CANR 33; DLB 53;
MTCW; SATA 50

Laurent, Antoine 1952- .... CLC 50

Lauscher, Hermann
See Hesse, Hermann

Lautreamont, Comte de
1846-1870 .... NCLC 12; SSC 14

Laverty, Donald
See Blish, James (Benjamin)

Lavin, Mary 1912-...... CLC 4, 18; SSC 4
See also CA 9-12R; CANR 33; DLB 15;
MTCW

Lavond, Paul Dennis
See Kornbluth, C(yril) M.; Pohl, Frederik

Lawler, Raymond Evenor 1922- .... CLC 58
See also CA 103

Lawrence, D(avid) H(erbert Richards)
1885-1930 .... TCLC 2, 9, 16, 33, 48;
DA; SSC 4; WLC
See also CA 104; 121; CDBLB 1914-1945;
DLB 10, 19, 36, 98; MTCW

Lawrence, T(homas) E(dward)
1888-1935 .... TCLC 18
See also Dale, Colin
See also CA 115

Lawrence of Arabia
See Lawrence, T(homas) E(dward)

Lawson, Henry (Archibald Hertzberg)
1867-1922 .... TCLC 27
See also CA 120

Lawton, Dennis
See Faust, Frederick (Schiller)

Laxness, Halldor................. CLC 25
See also Gudjonsson, Halldor Kiljan

Layamon fl. c. 1200-........... CMLC 10

Laye, Camara 1928-1980 ... CLC 4, 38; BLC
See also BW 1; CA 85-88; 97-100;
CANR 25; MTCW

Layton, Irving (Peter) 1912-..... CLC 2, 15
See also CA 1-4R; CANR 2, 33, 43;
DLB 88; MTCW

Lazarus, Emma 1849-1887....... NCLC 8

Lazarus, Felix
See Cable, George Washington

Lazarus, Henry
See Slavitt, David R(ytman)

Lea, Joan
See Neufeld, John (Arthur)

Leacock, Stephen (Butler)
1869-1944 .... TCLC 2
See also CA 104; 141; DLB 92

Lear, Edward 1812-1888 .... NCLC 3
See also CLR 1; DLB 32; MAICYA;
SATA 18

Lear, Norman (Milton) 1922- ...... CLC 12
See also CA 73-76

Leavis, F(rank) R(aymond)
1895-1978 .... CLC 24
See also CA 21-24R; 77-80; CANR 44;
MTCW

Leavitt, David 1961-.............. CLC 34
See also CA 116; 122; DLB 130

Leblanc, Maurice (Marie Emile)
1864-1941 .... TCLC 49
See also CA 110

Lebowitz, Fran(ces Ann)
1951(?)-.................. CLC 11, 36
See also CA 81-84; CANR 14; MTCW

Lebrecht, Peter
See Tieck, (Johann) Ludwig

le Carre, John .... CLC 3, 5, 9, 15, 28
See also Cornwell, David (John Moore)
See also BEST 89:4; CDBLB 1960 to
Present; DLB 87

Le Clezio, J(ean) M(arie) G(ustave)
1940- .... CLC 31
See also CA 116; 128; DLB 83

Leconte de Lisle, Charles-Marie-Rene
1818-1894 .... NCLC 29

Le Coq, Monsieur
See Simenon, Georges (Jacques Christian)

Leduc, Violette 1907-1972........ CLC 22
See also CA 13-14; 33-36R; CAP 1

Ledwidge, Francis 1887(?)-1917 ... TCLC 23
See also CA 123; DLB 20

Lee, Andrea 1953- .... CLC 36; BLC
See also BW 1; CA 125

Lee, Andrew
See Auchincloss, Louis (Stanton)

Lee, Don L........................ CLC 2
See also Madhubuti, Haki R.

Lee, George W(ashington)
1894-1976 .... CLC 52; BLC
See also BW 1; CA 125; DLB 51

Lee, (Nelle) Harper
1926- .... CLC 12, 60; DA; WLC
See also CA 13-16R; CDALB 1941-1968;
DLB 6; MTCW; SATA 11

Lee, Julian
See Latham, Jean Lee

Lee, Larry
See Lee, Lawrence

Lee, Lawrence 1941-1990......... CLC 34
See also CA 131; CANR 43

Lee, Manfred B(ennington)
1905-1971 .... CLC 11
See also Queen, Ellery
See also CA 1-4R; 29-32R; CANR 2;
DLB 137

Lee, Stan 1922-.................. CLC 17
See also AAYA 5; CA 108; 111

Lee, Tanith 1947-................ CLC 46
See also CA 37-40R; SATA 8

Lee, Vernon...................... TCLC 5
See also Paget, Violet
See also DLB 57

Lee, William
See Burroughs, William S(eward)

Lee, Willy
See Burroughs, William S(eward)

Lee-Hamilton, Eugene (Jacob)
1845-1907 .... TCLC 22
See also CA 117

Leet, Judith 1935- .... CLC 11

Le Fanu, Joseph Sheridan
1814-1873 .... NCLC 9; SSC 14
See also DLB 21, 70

Leffland, Ella 1931- .... CLC 19
See also CA 29-32R; CANR 35; DLBY 84;
SATA 65

Leger, Alexis
See Leger, (Marie-Rene Auguste) Alexis
Saint-Leger

Leger, (Marie-Rene Auguste) Alexis
Saint-Leger 1887-1975........ CLC 11
See also Perse, St.-John
See also CA 13-16R; 61-64; CANR 43;
MTCW

Leger, Saintleger
See Leger, (Marie-Rene Auguste) Alexis
Saint-Leger

Le Guin, Ursula K(roeber)
1929- .... CLC 8, 13, 22, 45, 71; SSC 12
See also AAYA 9; AITN 1; CA 21-24R;
CANR 9, 32; CDALB 1968-1988; CLR 3,
28; DLB 8, 52; JRDA; MAICYA;
MTCW; SATA 4, 52

Lehmann, Rosamond (Nina)
1901-1990 .... CLC 5
See also CA 77-80; 131; CANR 8; DLB 15

Leiber, Fritz (Reuter, Jr.)
1910-1992 .... **CLC 25**
See also CA 45-48; 139; CANR 2, 40;
DLB 8; MTCW; SATA 45;
SATA-Obit 73

Leimbach, Martha 1963-
See Leimbach, Marti
See also CA 130

Leimbach, Marti .... **CLC 65**
See also Leimbach, Martha

Leino, Eino .... **TCLC 24**
See also Loennbohm, Armas Eino Leopold

Leiris, Michel (Julien) 1901-1990 ... **CLC 61**
See also CA 119; 128; 132

Leithauser, Brad 1953-........... **CLC 27**
See also CA 107; CANR 27; DLB 120

Lelchuk, Alan 1938-.............. **CLC 5**
See also CA 45-48; CANR 1

Lem, Stanislaw 1921-........ **CLC 8, 15, 40**
See also CA 105; CAAS 1; CANR 32;
MTCW

Lemann, Nancy 1956-............ **CLC 39**
See also CA 118; 136

Lemonnier, (Antoine Louis) Camille
1844-1913 .... **TCLC 22**
See also CA 121

Lenau, Nikolaus 1802-1850 ...... **NCLC 16**

L'Engle, Madeleine (Camp Franklin)
1918- .... **CLC 12**
See also AAYA 1; AITN 2; CA 1-4R;
CANR 3, 21, 39; CLR 1, 14; DLB 52;
JRDA; MAICYA; MTCW; SAAS 15;
SATA 1, 27, 75

Lengyel, Jozsef 1896-1975......... **CLC 7**
See also CA 85-88; 57-60

Lennon, John (Ono)
1940-1980 .... **CLC 12, 35**
See also CA 102

Lennox, Charlotte Ramsay
1729(?)-1804 .... **NCLC 23**
See also DLB 39

Lentricchia, Frank (Jr.) 1940-...... **CLC 34**
See also CA 25-28R; CANR 19

Lenz, Siegfried 1926-............. **CLC 27**
See also CA 89-92; DLB 75

Leonard, Elmore (John, Jr.)
1925- .... **CLC 28, 34, 71**
See also AITN 1; BEST 89:1, 90:4;
CA 81-84; CANR 12, 28; MTCW

Leonard, Hugh.................... **CLC 19**
See also Byrne, John Keyes
See also DLB 13

Leopardi, (Conte) Giacomo (Talegardo
Francesco di Sales Save
1798-1837 .... **NCLC 22**

Le Reveler
See Artaud, Antonin

Lerman, Eleanor 1952-............. **CLC 9**
See also CA 85-88

Lerman, Rhoda 1936-............ **CLC 56**
See also CA 49-52

Lermontov, Mikhail Yuryevich
1814-1841 .... **NCLC 47**

Leroux, Gaston 1868-1927........ **TCLC 25**
See also CA 108; 136; SATA 65

Lesage, Alain-Rene 1668-1747........ **LC 2**

Leskov, Nikolai (Semyonovich)
1831-1895 .... **NCLC 25**

Lessing, Doris (May)
1919- ..... **CLC 1, 2, 3, 6, 10, 15, 22, 40;**
DA; SSC 6
See also CA 9-12R; CAAS 14; CANR 33;
CDBLB 1960 to Present; DLB 15, 139;
DLBY 85; MTCW

Lessing, Gotthold Ephraim
1729-1781 .... **LC 8**
See also DLB 97

Lester, Richard 1932-............. **CLC 20**

Lever, Charles (James)
1806-1872 .... **NCLC 23**
See also DLB 21

Leverson, Ada 1865(?)-1936(?) .... **TCLC 18**
See also Elaine
See also CA 117

Levertov, Denise
1923- ...... **CLC 1, 2, 3, 5, 8, 15, 28, 66**
See also CA 1-4R; CAAS 19; CANR 3, 29;
DLB 5; MTCW

Levi, Jonathan.................... **CLC 76**

Levi, Peter (Chad Tigar) 1931-..... **CLC 41**
See also CA 5-8R; CANR 34; DLB 40

Levi, Primo
1919-1987 .... **CLC 37, 50; SSC 12**
See also CA 13-16R; 122; CANR 12, 33;
MTCW

Levin, Ira 1929- .... **CLC 3, 6**
See also CA 21-24R; CANR 17, 44;
MTCW; SATA 66

Levin, Meyer 1905-1981 .... **CLC 7**
See also AITN 1; CA 9-12R; 104;
CANR 15; DLB 9, 28; DLBY 81;
SATA 21, 27

Levine, Norman 1924-............ **CLC 54**
See also CA 73-76; CANR 14; DLB 88

Levine, Philip 1928-.. **CLC 2, 4, 5, 9, 14, 33**
See also CA 9-12R; CANR 9, 37; DLB 5

Levinson, Deirdre 1931-........... **CLC 49**
See also CA 73-76

Levi-Strauss, Claude 1908- .... **CLC 38**
See also CA 1-4R; CANR 6, 32; MTCW

Levitin, Sonia (Wolff) 1934- .... **CLC 17**
See also CA 29-32R; CANR 14, 32; JRDA;
MAICYA; SAAS 2; SATA 4, 68

Levon, O. U.
See Kesey, Ken (Elton)

Lewes, George Henry
1817-1878 .... **NCLC 25**
See also DLB 55, 144

Lewis, Alun 1915-1944............ **TCLC 3**
See also CA 104; DLB 20

Lewis, C. Day
See Day Lewis, C(ecil)

Lewis, C(live) S(taples)
1898-1963 ..... **CLC 1, 3, 6, 14, 27; DA;**
WLC
See also AAYA 3; CA 81-84; CANR 33;
CDBLB 1945-1960; CLR 3, 27; DLB 15,
100; JRDA; MAICYA; MTCW;
SATA 13

Lewis, Janet 1899-.............. **CLC 41**
See also Winters, Janet Lewis
See also CA 9-12R; CANR 29; CAP 1;
DLBY 87

Lewis, Matthew Gregory
1775-1818 .... **NCLC 11**
See also DLB 39

Lewis, (Harry) Sinclair
1885-1951 ..... **TCLC 4, 13, 23, 39; DA;**
WLC
See also CA 104; 133; CDALB 1917-1929;
DLB 9, 102; DLBD 1; MTCW

Lewis, (Percy) Wyndham
1884(?)-1957 ....**TCLC 2, 9**
See also CA 104; DLB 15

Lewisohn, Ludwig 1883-1955...... **TCLC 19**
See also CA 107; DLB 4, 9, 28, 102

Lezama Lima, Jose 1910-1976 ... **CLC 4, 10**
See also CA 77-80; DLB 113; HW

L'Heureux, John (Clarke) 1934-.... **CLC 52**
See also CA 13-16R; CANR 23, 45

Liddell, C. H.
See Kuttner, Henry

Lie, Jonas (Lauritz Idemil)
1833-1908(?) .... **TCLC 5**
See also CA 115

Lieber, Joel 1937-1971............. **CLC 6**
See also CA 73-76; 29-32R

Lieber, Stanley Martin
See Lee, Stan

Lieberman, Laurence (James)
1935- .... **CLC 4, 36**
See also CA 17-20R; CANR 8, 36

Lieksman, Anders
See Haavikko, Paavo Juhani

Li Fei-kan 1904-
See Pa Chin
See also CA 105

Lifton, Robert Jay 1926-.......... **CLC 67**
See also CA 17-20R; CANR 27; SATA 66

Lightfoot, Gordon 1938-.......... **CLC 26**
See also CA 109

Lightman, Alan P. 1948-.......... **CLC 81**
See also CA 141

Ligotti, Thomas 1953- .... **CLC 44; SSC 16**
See also CA 123

Liliencron, (Friedrich Adolf Axel) Detlev von
1844-1909 .... **TCLC 18**
See also CA 117

Lilly, William 1602-1681........... **LC 27**

Lima, Jose Lezama
See Lezama Lima, Jose

Lima Barreto, Afonso Henrique de
1881-1922 .... **TCLC 23**
See also CA 117

Limonov, Eduard................. **CLC 67**

Lin, Frank
See Atherton, Gertrude (Franklin Horn)

Lincoln, Abraham 1809-1865..... NCLC 18

Lind, Jakov .... CLC 1, 2, 4, 27, 82
See also Landwirth, Heinz
See also CAAS 4

Lindbergh, Anne (Spencer) Morrow
1906- .... CLC 82
See also CA 17-20R; CANR 16; MTCW;
SATA 33

Lindsay, David 1878-1945....... TCLC 15
See also CA 113

Lindsay, (Nicholas) Vachel
1879-1931 .... TCLC 17; DA; WLC
See also CA 114; 135; CDALB 1865-1917;
DLB 54; SATA 40

Linke-Poot
See Doeblin, Alfred

Linney, Romulus 1930- .... CLC 51
See also CA 1-4R; CANR 40, 44

Linton, Eliza Lynn 1822-1898.... NCLC 41
See also DLB 18

Li Po 701-763................. CMLC 2

Lipsius, Justus 1547-1606 .... LC 16

Lipsyte, Robert (Michael)
1938- .... CLC 21; DA
See also AAYA 7; CA 17-20R; CANR 8;
CLR 23; JRDA; MAICYA; SATA 5, 68

Lish, Gordon (Jay) 1934-......... CLC 45
See also CA 113; 117; DLB 130

Lispector, Clarice 1925-1977...... CLC 43
See also CA 139; 116; DLB 113

Littell, Robert 1935(?)- .... CLC 42
See also CA 109; 112

Little, Malcolm 1925-1965
See Malcolm X
See also BW 1; CA 125; 111; DA; MTCW

Littlewit, Humphrey Gent.
See Lovecraft, H(oward) P(hillips)

Litwos
See Sienkiewicz, Henryk (Adam Alexander
Pius)

Liu E 1857-1909............... TCLC 15
See also CA 115

Lively, Penelope (Margaret)
1933- .... CLC 32, 50
See also CA 41-44R; CANR 29; CLR 7;
DLB 14; JRDA; MAICYA; MTCW;
SATA 7, 60

Livesay, Dorothy (Kathleen)
1909- .... CLC 4, 15, 79
See also AITN 2; CA 25-28R; CAAS 8;
CANR 36; DLB 68; MTCW

Livy c. 59B.C.-c. 17 .... CMLC 11

Lizardi, Jose Joaquin Fernandez de
1776-1827 .... NCLC 30

Llewellyn, Richard
See Llewellyn Lloyd, Richard Dafydd
Vivian
See also DLB 15

Llewellyn Lloyd, Richard Dafydd Vivian
1906-1983 .... CLC 7, 80
See also Llewellyn, Richard
See also CA 53-56; 111; CANR 7;
SATA 11, 37

Llosa, (Jorge) Mario (Pedro) Vargas
See Vargas Llosa, (Jorge) Mario (Pedro)

Lloyd Webber, Andrew 1948-
See Webber, Andrew Lloyd
See also AAYA 1; CA 116; SATA 56

Llull, Ramon c. 1235-c. 1316..... CMLC 12

Locke, Alain (Le Roy)
1886-1954 .... TCLC 43
See also BW 1; CA 106; 124; DLB 51

Locke, John 1632-1704 .... LC 7
See also DLB 101

Locke-Elliott, Sumner
See Elliott, Sumner Locke

Lockhart, John Gibson
1794-1854 .... NCLC 6
See also DLB 110, 116, 144

Lodge, David (John) 1935-........ CLC 36
See also BEST 90:1; CA 17-20R; CANR 19;
DLB 14; MTCW

Loennbohm, Armas Eino Leopold 1878-1926
See Leino, Eino
See also CA 123

Loewinsohn, Ron(ald William)
1937- .... CLC 52
See also CA 25-28R

Logan, Jake
See Smith, Martin Cruz

Logan, John (Burton) 1923-1987..... CLC 5
See also CA 77-80; 124; CANR 45; DLB 5

Lo Kuan-chung 1330(?)-1400(?)...... LC 12

Lombard, Nap
See Johnson, Pamela Hansford

London, Jack.. TCLC 9, 15, 39; SSC 4; WLC
See also London, John Griffith
See also AITN 2; CDALB 1865-1917;
DLB 8, 12, 78; SATA 18

London, John Griffith 1876-1916
See London, Jack
See also CA 110; 119; DA; JRDA;
MAICYA; MTCW

Long, Emmett
See Leonard, Elmore (John, Jr.)

Longbaugh, Harry
See Goldman, William (W.)

Longfellow, Henry Wadsworth
1807-1882 .... NCLC 2, 45; DA
See also CDALB 1640-1865; DLB 1, 59;
SATA 19

Longley, Michael 1939-........... CLC 29
See also CA 102; DLB 40

Longus fl. c. 2nd cent. - .... CMLC 7

Longway, A. Hugh
See Lang, Andrew

Lopate, Phillip 1943-............. CLC 29
See also CA 97-100; DLBY 80

Lopez Portillo (y Pacheco), Jose
1920- .... CLC 46
See also CA 129; HW

Lopez y Fuentes, Gregorio
1897(?)-1966 .... CLC 32
See also CA 131; HW

Lorca, Federico Garcia
See Garcia Lorca, Federico

Lord, Bette Bao 1938-............. CLC 23
See also BEST 90:3; CA 107; CANR 41;
SATA 58

Lord Auch
See Bataille, Georges

Lord Byron
See Byron, George Gordon (Noel)

Lorde, Audre (Geraldine)
1934-1992 .... CLC 18, 71; BLC
See also BW 1; CA 25-28R; 142; CANR 16,
26; DLB 41; MTCW

Lord Jeffrey
See Jeffrey, Francis

Lorenzo, Heberto Padilla
See Padilla (Lorenzo), Heberto

Loris
See Hofmannsthal, Hugo von

Loti, Pierre .... TCLC 11
See also Viaud, (Louis Marie) Julien
See also DLB 123

Louie, David Wong 1954- .... CLC 70
See also CA 139

Louis, Father M.
See Merton, Thomas

Lovecraft, H(oward) P(hillips)
1890-1937 .... TCLC 4, 22; SSC 3
See also CA 104; 133; MTCW

Lovelace, Earl 1935-.............. CLC 51
See also BW 2; CA 77-80; CANR 41;
DLB 125; MTCW

Lovelace, Richard 1618-1657........ LC 24
See also DLB 131

Lowell, Amy 1874-1925......... TCLC 1, 8
See also CA 104; DLB 54, 140

Lowell, James Russell 1819-1891 .. NCLC 2
See also CDALB 1640-1865; DLB 1, 11, 64,
79

Lowell, Robert (Traill Spence, Jr.)
1917-1977 ... CLC 1, 2, 3, 4, 5, 8, 9, 11,
15, 37; DA; PC 3; WLC
See also CA 9-12R; 73-76; CABS 2;
CANR 26; DLB 5; MTCW

Lowndes, Marie Adelaide (Belloc)
1868-1947 .... TCLC 12
See also CA 107; DLB 70

Lowry, (Clarence) Malcolm
1909-1957 .... TCLC 6, 40
See also CA 105; 131; CDBLB 1945-1960;
DLB 15; MTCW

Lowry, Mina Gertrude 1882-1966
See Loy, Mina
See also CA 113

Loxsmith, John
See Brunner, John (Kilian Houston)

Loy, Mina .... CLC 28
See also Lowry, Mina Gertrude
See also DLB 4, 54

Loyson-Bridet
See Schwob, (Mayer Andre) Marcel

Mahfouz, Naguib (Abdel Aziz Al-Sabilgi)
   1911(?)-
   See Mahfuz, Najib
   See also BEST 89:2; CA 128; MTCW

Mahfuz, Najib................ **CLC 52, 55**
   See also Mahfouz, Naguib (Abdel Aziz
   Al-Sabilgi)
   See also DLBY 88

Mahon, Derek 1941-.............. **CLC 27**
   See also CA 113; 128; DLB 40

Mailer, Norman
   1923- ...... **CLC 1, 2, 3, 4, 5, 8, 11, 14,**
                  28, 39, 74; DA
   See also AITN 2; CA 9-12R; CABS 1;
     CANR 28; CDALB 1968-1988; DLB 2,
     16, 28; DLBD 3; DLBY 80, 83; MTCW

Maillet, Antonine 1929-........... **CLC 54**
   See also CA 115; 120; DLB 60

Mais, Roger 1905-1955 .... **TCLC 8**
   See also BW 1; CA 105; 124; DLB 125;
   MTCW

Maistre, Joseph de 1753-1821.... **NCLC 37**

Maitland, Sara (Louise) 1950-..... **CLC 49**
   See also CA 69-72; CANR 13

Major, Clarence
   1936-............. **CLC 3, 19, 48; BLC**
   See also BW 2; CA 21-24R; CAAS 6;
     CANR 13, 25; DLB 33

Major, Kevin (Gerald) 1949-....... **CLC 26**
   See also CA 97-100; CANR 21, 38;
     CLR 11; DLB 60; JRDA; MAICYA;
     SATA 32

Maki, James
   See Ozu, Yasujiro

Malabaila, Damiano
   See Levi, Primo

Malamud, Bernard
   1914-1986 ...... **CLC 1, 2, 3, 5, 8, 9, 11,**
        18, 27, 44, 78, 85; DA; SSC 15; WLC
   See also CA 5-8R; 118; CABS 1; CANR 28;
     CDALB 1941-1968; DLB 2, 28;
     DLBY 80, 86; MTCW

Malaparte, Curzio 1898-1957 ..... **TCLC 52**

Malcolm, Dan
   See Silverberg, Robert

Malcolm X.................. **CLC 82; BLC**
   See also Little, Malcolm

Malherbe, Francois de 1555-1628..... **LC 5**

Mallarme, Stephane
   1842-1898 .... **NCLC 4, 41; PC 4**

Mallet-Joris, Francoise 1930-...... **CLC 11**
   See also CA 65-68; CANR 17; DLB 83

Malley, Ern
   See McAuley, James Phillip

Mallowan, Agatha Christie
   See Christie, Agatha (Mary Clarissa)

Maloff, Saul 1922-................ **CLC 5**
   See also CA 33-36R

Malone, Louis
   See MacNeice, (Frederick) Louis

Malone, Michael (Christopher)
   1942-..................... **CLC 43**
   See also CA 77-80; CANR 14, 32

Malory, (Sir) Thomas
   1410(?)-1471(?) .... **LC 11; DA**
   See also CDBLB Before 1660; SATA 33, 59

Malouf, (George Joseph) David
   1934-...................... **CLC 28**
   See also CA 124

Malraux, (Georges-)Andre
   1901-1976 ...... **CLC 1, 4, 9, 13, 15, 57**
   See also CA 21-22; 69-72; CANR 34;
     CAP 2; DLB 72; MTCW

Malzberg, Barry N(athaniel) 1939-... **CLC 7**
   See also CA 61-64; CAAS 4; CANR 16;
     DLB 8

Mamet, David (Alan)
   1947-......... **CLC 9, 15, 34, 46; DC 4**
   See also AAYA 3; CA 81-84; CABS 3;
     CANR 15, 41; DLB 7; MTCW

Mamoulian, Rouben (Zachary)
   1897-1987 .... **CLC 16**
   See also CA 25-28R; 124

Mandelstam, Osip (Emilievich)
   1891(?)-1938(?) .... **TCLC 2, 6**
   See also CA 104

Mander, (Mary) Jane 1877-1949... **TCLC 31**

Mandiargues, Andre Pieyre de...... **CLC 41**
   See also Pieyre de Mandiargues, Andre
   See also DLB 83

Mandrake, Ethel Belle
   See Thurman, Wallace (Henry)

Mangan, James Clarence
   1803-1849 .... **NCLC 27**

Maniere, J.-E.
   See Giraudoux, (Hippolyte) Jean

Manley, (Mary) Delariviere
   1672(?)-1724 .... **LC 1**
   See also DLB 39, 80

Mann, Abel
   See Creasey, John

Mann, (Luiz) Heinrich 1871-1950... **TCLC 9**
   See also CA 106; DLB 66

Mann, (Paul) Thomas
   1875-1955 .... **TCLC 2, 8, 14, 21, 35, 44;**
              DA; SSC 5; WLC
   See also CA 104; 128; DLB 66; MTCW

Manning, David
   See Faust, Frederick (Schiller)

Manning, Frederic 1887(?)-1935 ... **TCLC 25**
   See also CA 124

Manning, Olivia 1915-1980 ...... **CLC 5, 19**
   See also CA 5-8R; 101; CANR 29; MTCW

Mano, D. Keith 1942- .... **CLC 2, 10**
   See also CA 25-28R; CAAS 6; CANR 26;
     DLB 6

Mansfield, Katherine
   .... **TCLC 2, 8, 39; SSC 9; WLC**
   See also Beauchamp, Kathleen Mansfield

Manso, Peter 1940- .... **CLC 39**
   See also CA 29-32R; CANR 44

Mantecon, Juan Jimenez
   See Jimenez (Mantecon), Juan Ramon

Manton, Peter
   See Creasey, John

Man Without a Spleen, A
   See Chekhov, Anton (Pavlovich)

Manzoni, Alessandro 1785-1873 .. **NCLC 29**

Mapu, Abraham (ben Jekutiel)
   1808-1867 .... **NCLC 18**

Mara, Sally
   See Queneau, Raymond

Marat, Jean Paul 1743-1793....... **LC 10**

Marcel, Gabriel Honore
   1889-1973 .... **CLC 15**
   See also CA 102; 45-48; MTCW

Marchbanks, Samuel
   See Davies, (William) Robertson

Marchi, Giacomo
   See Bassani, Giorgio

Margulies, Donald................. **CLC 76**

Marie de France c. 12th cent. -.... **CMLC 8**

Marie de l'Incarnation 1599-1672.... **LC 10**

Mariner, Scott
   See Pohl, Frederik

Marinetti, Filippo Tommaso
   1876-1944 .... **TCLC 10**
   See also CA 107; DLB 114

Marivaux, Pierre Carlet de Chamblain de
   1688-1763 .... **LC 4**

Markandaya, Kamala .... **CLC 8, 38**
   See also Taylor, Kamala (Purnaiya)

Markfield, Wallace 1926-.......... **CLC 8**
   See also CA 69-72; CAAS 3; DLB 2, 28

Markham, Edwin 1852-1940 ..... **TCLC 47**
   See also DLB 54

Markham, Robert
   See Amis, Kingsley (William)

Marks, J
   See Highwater, Jamake (Mamake)

Marks-Highwater, J
   See Highwater, Jamake (Mamake)

Markson, David M(errill) 1927-.... **CLC 67**
   See also CA 49-52; CANR 1

Marley, Bob..................... **CLC 17**
   See also Marley, Robert Nesta

Marley, Robert Nesta 1945-1981
   See Marley, Bob
   See also CA 107; 103

Marlowe, Christopher
   1564-1593 ..... **LC 22; DA; DC 1; WLC**
   See also CDBLB Before 1660; DLB 62

Marmontel, Jean-Francois
   1723-1799 .... **LC 2**

Marquand, John P(hillips)
   1893-1960 .... **CLC 2, 10**
   See also CA 85-88; DLB 9, 102

Marquez, Gabriel (Jose) Garcia
   See Garcia Marquez, Gabriel (Jose)

Marquis, Don(ald Robert Perry)
   1878-1937 .... **TCLC 7**
   See also CA 104; DLB 11, 25

Marric, J. J.
   See Creasey, John

Marrow, Bernard
   See Moore, Brian

Marryat, Frederick 1792-1848 .... **NCLC 3**
   See also DLB 21

Marsden, James
See Creasey, John

Marsh, (Edith) Ngaio
1899-1982 .... CLC **7, 53**
See also CA 9-12R; CANR 6; DLB 77;
MTCW

Marshall, Garry 1934-........... CLC **17**
See also AAYA 3; CA 111; SATA 60

Marshall, Paule
1929-........ CLC **27, 72; BLC; SSC 3**
See also BW 2; CA 77-80; CANR 25;
DLB 33; MTCW

Marsten, Richard
See Hunter, Evan

Martha, Henry
See Harris, Mark

Martial 40-104 .... PC **10**

Martin, Ken
See Hubbard, L(afayette) Ron(ald)

Martin, Richard
See Creasey, John

Martin, Steve 1945-.............. CLC **30**
See also CA 97-100; CANR 30; MTCW

Martin, Violet Florence
1862-1915 .... TCLC **51**

Martin, Webber
See Silverberg, Robert

Martindale, Patrick Victor
See White, Patrick (Victor Martindale)

Martin du Gard, Roger
1881-1958 .... TCLC **24**
See also CA 118; DLB 65

Martineau, Harriet 1802-1876.... NCLC **26**
See also DLB 21, 55; YABC 2

Martines, Julia
See O'Faolain, Julia

Martinez, Jacinto Benavente y
See Benavente (y Martinez), Jacinto

Martinez Ruiz, Jose 1873-1967
See Azorin; Ruiz, Jose Martinez
See also CA 93-96; HW

Martinez Sierra, Gregorio
1881-1947 .... TCLC **6**
See also CA 115

Martinez Sierra, Maria (de la O'LeJarraga)
1874-1974 .... TCLC **6**
See also CA 115

Martinsen, Martin
See Follett, Ken(neth Martin)

Martinson, Harry (Edmund)
1904-1978 .... CLC **14**
See also CA 77-80; CANR 34

Marut, Ret
See Traven, B.

Marut, Robert
See Traven, B.

Marvell, Andrew
1621-1678 ..... LC **4; DA; PC 10; WLC**
See also CDBLB 1660-1789; DLB 131

Marx, Karl (Heinrich)
1818-1883 .... NCLC **17**
See also DLB 129

Masaoka Shiki.................. TCLC 18
See also Masaoka Tsunenori

Masaoka Tsunenori 1867-1902
See Masaoka Shiki
See also CA 117

Masefield, John (Edward)
1878-1967 .... CLC **11, 47**
See also CA 19-20; 25-28R; CANR 33;
CAP 2; CDBLB 1890-1914; DLB 10;
MTCW; SATA 19

Maso, Carole 19(?)-.............. CLC **44**

Mason, Bobbie Ann
1940-.......... CLC **28, 43, 82; SSC 4**
See also AAYA 5; CA 53-56; CANR 11,
31; DLBY 87; MTCW

Mason, Ernst
See Pohl, Frederik

Mason, Lee W.
See Malzberg, Barry N(athaniel)

Mason, Nick 1945-.............. CLC **35**

Mason, Tally
See Derleth, August (William)

Mass, William
See Gibson, William

Masters, Edgar Lee
1868-1950 ...... TCLC **2, 25; DA; PC 1**
See also CA 104; 133; CDALB 1865-1917;
DLB 54; MTCW

Masters, Hilary 1928-........... CLC **48**
See also CA 25-28R; CANR 13

Mastrosimone, William 19(?)-...... CLC **36**

Mathe, Albert
See Camus, Albert

Matheson, Richard Burton 1926- ... CLC **37**
See also CA 97-100; DLB 8, 44

Mathews, Harry 1930-......... CLC **6, 52**
See also CA 21-24R; CAAS 6; CANR 18,
40

Mathews, John Joseph 1894-1979... CLC **84**
See also CA 19-20; 142; CANR 45; CAP 2

Mathias, Roland (Glyn) 1915-...... CLC **45**
See also CA 97-100; CANR 19, 41; DLB 27

Matsuo Basho 1644-1694........... PC **3**

Mattheson, Rodney
See Creasey, John

Matthews, Greg 1949-........... CLC **45**
See also CA 135

Matthews, William 1942-......... CLC **40**
See also CA 29-32R; CAAS 18; CANR 12;
DLB 5

Matthias, John (Edward) 1941-...... CLC **9**
See also CA 33-36R

Matthiessen, Peter
1927- .... CLC **5, 7, 11, 32, 64**
See also AAYA 6; BEST 90:4; CA 9-12R;
CANR 21; DLB 6; MTCW; SATA 27

Maturin, Charles Robert
1780(?)-1824 .... NCLC **6**

Matute (Ausejo), Ana Maria
1925- .... CLC **11**
See also CA 89-92; MTCW

Maugham, W. S.
See Maugham, W(illiam) Somerset

Maugham, W(illiam) Somerset
1874-1965 ...... CLC **1, 11, 15, 67; DA;**
SSC 8; WLC
See also CA 5-8R; 25-28R; CANR 40;
CDBLB 1914-1945; DLB 10, 36, 77, 100;
MTCW; SATA 54

Maugham, William Somerset
See Maugham, W(illiam) Somerset

Maupassant, (Henri Rene Albert) Guy de
1850-1893 .... NCLC **1, 42; DA; SSC 1;**
WLC
See also DLB 123

Maurhut, Richard
See Traven, B.

Mauriac, Claude 1914-............. CLC **9**
See also CA 89-92; DLB 83

Mauriac, Francois (Charles)
1885-1970 .... CLC **4, 9, 56**
See also CA 25-28; CAP 2; DLB 65;
MTCW

Mavor, Osborne Henry 1888-1951
See Bridie, James
See also CA 104

Maxwell, William (Keepers, Jr.)
1908- .... CLC **19**
See also CA 93-96; DLBY 80

May, Elaine 1932- .... CLC **16**
See also CA 124; 142; DLB 44

Mayakovski, Vladimir (Vladimirovich)
1893-1930 .... TCLC **4, 18**
See also CA 104

Mayhew, Henry 1812-1887 ...... NCLC **31**
See also DLB 18, 55

Maynard, Joyce 1953-............. CLC **23**
See also CA 111; 129

Mayne, William (James Carter)
1928- .... CLC **12**
See also CA 9-12R; CANR 37; CLR 25;
JRDA; MAICYA; SAAS 11; SATA 6, 68

Mayo, Jim
See L'Amour, Louis (Dearborn)

Maysles, Albert 1926- .... CLC **16**
See also CA 29-32R

Maysles, David 1932-............. CLC **16**

Mazer, Norma Fox 1931- .... CLC **26**
See also AAYA 5; CA 69-72; CANR 12,
32; CLR 23; JRDA; MAICYA; SAAS 1;
SATA 24, 67

Mazzini, Guiseppe 1805-1872 ...... NCLC **34**

McAuley, James Phillip
1917-1976 .... CLC **45**
See also CA 97-100

McBain, Ed
See Hunter, Evan

McBrien, William Augustine
1930- .... CLC **44**
See also CA 107

McCaffrey, Anne (Inez) 1926-...... CLC **17**
See also AAYA 6; AITN 2; BEST 89:2;
CA 25-28R; CANR 15, 35; DLB 8;
JRDA; MAICYA; MTCW; SAAS 11;
SATA 8, 70

McCann, Arthur
See Campbell, John W(ood, Jr.)

Merritt, E. B.
See Waddington, Miriam

Merton, Thomas
1915-1968 .. **CLC 1, 3, 11, 34, 83; PC 10**
See also CA 5-8R; 25-28R; CANR 22;
DLB 48; DLBY 81; MTCW

Merwin, W(illiam) S(tanley)
1927- ...... **CLC 1, 2, 3, 5, 8, 13, 18, 45**
See also CA 13-16R; CANR 15; DLB 5;
MTCW

Metcalf, John 1938- .... **CLC 37**
See also CA 113; DLB 60

Metcalf, Suzanne
See Baum, L(yman) Frank

Mew, Charlotte (Mary)
1870-1928 .... **TCLC 8**
See also CA 105; DLB 19, 135

Mewshaw, Michael 1943- .... **CLC 9**
See also CA 53-56; CANR 7; DLBY 80

Meyer, June
See Jordan, June

Meyer, Lynn
See Slavitt, David R(ytman)

Meyer-Meyrink, Gustav 1868-1932
See Meyrink, Gustav
See also CA 117

Meyers, Jeffrey 1939- .... **CLC 39**
See also CA 73-76; DLB 111

Meynell, Alice (Christina Gertrude Thompson)
1847-1922 .... **TCLC 6**
See also CA 104; DLB 19, 98

Meyrink, Gustav .... **TCLC 21**
See also Meyer-Meyrink, Gustav
See also DLB 81

Michaels, Leonard
1933- .... **CLC 6, 25; SSC 16**
See also CA 61-64; CANR 21; DLB 130;
MTCW

Michaux, Henri 1899-1984 ...... **CLC 8, 19**
See also CA 85-88; 114

Michelangelo 1475-1564........... **LC 12**

Michelet, Jules 1798-1874....... **NCLC 31**

Michener, James A(lbert)
1907(?)- .... **CLC 1, 5, 11, 29, 60**
See also AITN 1; BEST 90:1; CA 5-8R;
CANR 21, 45; DLB 6; MTCW

Mickiewicz, Adam 1798-1855 ..... **NCLC 3**

Middleton, Christopher 1926- ...... **CLC 13**
See also CA 13-16R; CANR 29; DLB 40

Middleton, Richard (Barham)
1882-1911 .... **TCLC 56**

Middleton, Stanley 1919-....... **CLC 7, 38**
See also CA 25-28R; CANR 21; DLB 14

Migueis, Jose Rodrigues 1901- ..... **CLC 10**

Mikszath, Kalman 1847-1910 ..... **TCLC 31**

Miles, Josephine
1911-1985 .... **CLC 1, 2, 14, 34, 39**
See also CA 1-4R; 116; CANR 2; DLB 48

Militant
See Sandburg, Carl (August)

Mill, John Stuart 1806-1873 ..... **NCLC 11**
See also CDBLB 1832-1890; DLB 55

Millar, Kenneth 1915-1983 .... **CLC 14**
See also Macdonald, Ross
See also CA 9-12R; 110; CANR 16; DLB 2;
DLBD 6; DLBY 83; MTCW

Millay, E. Vincent
See Millay, Edna St. Vincent

Millay, Edna St. Vincent
1892-1950 ...... **TCLC 4, 49; DA; PC 6**
See also CA 104; 130; CDALB 1917-1929;
DLB 45; MTCW

Miller, Arthur
1915- .... **CLC 1, 2, 6, 10, 15, 26, 47, 78;**
DA; DC 1; WLC
See also AITN 1; CA 1-4R; CABS 3;
CANR 2, 30; CDALB 1941-1968; DLB 7;
MTCW

Miller, Henry (Valentine)
1891-1980 .... **CLC 1, 2, 4, 9, 14, 43, 84;**
DA; WLC
See also CA 9-12R; 97-100; CANR 33;
CDALB 1929-1941; DLB 4, 9; DLBY 80;
MTCW

Miller, Jason 1939(?)- .... **CLC 2**
See also AITN 1; CA 73-76; DLB 7

Miller, Sue 1943- .... **CLC 44**
See also BEST 90:3; CA 139; DLB 143

Miller, Walter M(ichael, Jr.)
1923- .... **CLC 4, 30**
See also CA 85-88; DLB 8

Millett, Kate 1934- .... **CLC 67**
See also AITN 1; CA 73-76; CANR 32;
MTCW

Millhauser, Steven 1943- .... **CLC 21, 54**
See also CA 110; 111; DLB 2

Millin, Sarah Gertrude 1889-1968 .. **CLC 49**
See also CA 102; 93-96

Milne, A(lan) A(lexander)
1882-1956 .... **TCLC 6**
See also CA 104; 133; CLR 1, 26; DLB 10,
77, 100; MAICYA; MTCW; YABC 1

Milner, Ron(ald) 1938- .... **CLC 56; BLC**
See also AITN 1; BW 1; CA 73-76;
CANR 24; DLB 38; MTCW

Milosz, Czeslaw
1911- ... **CLC 5, 11, 22, 31, 56, 82; PC 8**
See also CA 81-84; CANR 23; MTCW

Milton, John 1608-1674... **LC 9; DA; WLC**
See also CDBLB 1660-1789; DLB 131

Minehaha, Cornelius
See Wedekind, (Benjamin) Frank(lin)

Miner, Valerie 1947- .... **CLC 40**
See also CA 97-100

Minimo, Duca
See D'Annunzio, Gabriele

Minot, Susan 1956- .... **CLC 44**
See also CA 134

Minus, Ed 1938- .... **CLC 39**

Miranda, Javier
See Bioy Casares, Adolfo

Mirbeau, Octave 1848-1917...... **TCLC 55**
See also DLB 123

Miro (Ferrer), Gabriel (Francisco Victor)
1879-1930 .... **TCLC 5**
See also CA 104

Mishima, Yukio
...... **CLC 2, 4, 6, 9, 27; DC 1; SSC 4**
See also Hiraoka, Kimitake

Mistral, Frederic 1830-1914 ...... **TCLC 51**
See also CA 122

Mistral, Gabriela............ **TCLC 2; HLC**
See also Godoy Alcayaga, Lucila

Mistry, Rohinton 1952-........... **CLC 71**
See also CA 141

Mitchell, Clyde
See Ellison, Harlan; Silverberg, Robert

Mitchell, James Leslie 1901-1935
See Gibbon, Lewis Grassic
See also CA 104; DLB 15

Mitchell, Joni 1943-.............. **CLC 12**
See also CA 112

Mitchell, Margaret (Munnerlyn)
1900-1949 .... **TCLC 11**
See also CA 109; 125; DLB 9; MTCW

Mitchell, Peggy
See Mitchell, Margaret (Munnerlyn)

Mitchell, S(ilas) Weir 1829-1914 .. **TCLC 36**

Mitchell, W(illiam) O(rmond)
1914- .... **CLC 25**
See also CA 77-80; CANR 15, 43; DLB 88

Mitford, Mary Russell 1787-1855.. **NCLC 4**
See also DLB 110, 116

Mitford, Nancy 1904-1973........ **CLC 44**
See also CA 9-12R

Miyamoto, Yuriko 1899-1951 ..... **TCLC 37**

Mo, Timothy (Peter) 1950(?)- ...... **CLC 46**
See also CA 117; MTCW

Modarressi, Taghi (M.) 1931-...... **CLC 44**
See also CA 121; 134

Modiano, Patrick (Jean) 1945-..... **CLC 18**
See also CA 85-88; CANR 17, 40; DLB 83

Moerck, Paal
See Roelvaag, O(le) E(dvart)

Mofolo, Thomas (Mokopu)
1875(?)-1948 .... **TCLC 22; BLC**
See also CA 121

Mohr, Nicholasa 1935-...... **CLC 12; HLC**
See also AAYA 8; CA 49-52; CANR 1, 32;
CLR 22; HW; JRDA; SAAS 8; SATA 8

Mojtabai, A(nn) G(race)
1938- .... **CLC 5, 9, 15, 29**
See also CA 85-88

Moliere 1622-1673 .... **LC 10; DA; WLC**

Molin, Charles
See Mayne, William (James Carter)

Molnar, Ferenc 1878-1952........ **TCLC 20**
See also CA 109

Momaday, N(avarre) Scott
1934- .... **CLC 2, 19, 85; DA**
See also AAYA 11; CA 25-28R; CANR 14,
34; DLB 143; MTCW; NNAL; SATA 30,
48

Monette, Paul 1945-.............. **CLC 82**
See also CA 139

Monroe, Harriet 1860-1936....... **TCLC 12**
See also CA 109; DLB 54, 91

Monroe, Lyle
See Heinlein, Robert A(nson)

Montagu, Elizabeth 1917- .... NCLC 7
See also CA 9-12R

Montagu, Mary (Pierrepont) Wortley
1689-1762 .... LC 9
See also DLB 95, 101

Montagu, W. H.
See Coleridge, Samuel Taylor

Montague, John (Patrick)
1929- .... CLC 13, 46
See also CA 9-12R; CANR 9; DLB 40;
MTCW

Montaigne, Michel (Eyquem) de
1533-1592 .... LC 8; DA; WLC

Montale, Eugenio 1896-1981... CLC 7, 9, 18
See also CA 17-20R; 104; CANR 30;
DLB 114; MTCW

Montesquieu, Charles-Louis de Secondat
1689-1755 .... LC 7

Montgomery, (Robert) Bruce 1921-1978
See Crispin, Edmund
See also CA 104

Montgomery, L(ucy) M(aud)
1874-1942 .... TCLC 51
See also AAYA 12; CA 108; 137; CLR 8;
DLB 92; JRDA; MAICYA; YABC 1

Montgomery, Marion H., Jr. 1925- .. CLC 7
See also AITN 1; CA 1-4R; CANR 3;
DLB 6

Montgomery, Max
See Davenport, Guy (Mattison, Jr.)

Montherlant, Henry (Milon) de
1896-1972 .... CLC 8, 19
See also CA 85-88; 37-40R; DLB 72;
MTCW

Monty Python
See Chapman, Graham; Cleese, John
(Marwood); Gilliam, Terry (Vance); Idle,
Eric; Jones, Terence Graham Parry; Palin,
Michael (Edward)
See also AAYA 7

Moodie, Susanna (Strickland)
1803-1885 .... NCLC 14
See also DLB 99

Mooney, Edward 1951-
See Mooney, Ted
See also CA 130

Mooney, Ted .... CLC 25
See also Mooney, Edward

Moorcock, Michael (John)
1939- .... CLC 5, 27, 58
See also CA 45-48; CAAS 5; CANR 2, 17,
38; DLB 14; MTCW

Moore, Brian
1921- .... CLC 1, 3, 5, 7, 8, 19, 32
See also CA 1-4R; CANR 1, 25, 42; MTCW

Moore, Edward
See Muir, Edwin

Moore, George Augustus
1852-1933 .... TCLC 7
See also CA 104; DLB 10, 18, 57, 135

Moore, Lorrie .... CLC 39, 45, 68
See also Moore, Marie Lorena

Moore, Marianne (Craig)
1887-1972 .... CLC 1, 2, 4, 8, 10, 13, 19,
47; DA; PC 4
See also CA 1-4R; 33-36R; CANR 3;
CDALB 1929-1941; DLB 45; DLBD 7;
MTCW; SATA 20

Moore, Marie Lorena 1957-
See Moore, Lorrie
See also CA 116; CANR 39

Moore, Thomas 1779-1852........ NCLC 6
See also DLB 96, 144

Morand, Paul 1888-1976 .... CLC 41
See also CA 69-72; DLB 65

Morante, Elsa 1918-1985........ CLC 8, 47
See also CA 85-88; 117; CANR 35; MTCW

Moravia, Alberto....... CLC 2, 7, 11, 27, 46
See also Pincherle, Alberto

More, Hannah 1745-1833 .... NCLC 27
See also DLB 107, 109, 116

More, Henry 1614-1687............. LC 9
See also DLB 126

More, Sir Thomas 1478-1535 .... LC 10

Moreas, Jean................... TCLC 18
See also Papadiamantopoulos, Johannes

Morgan, Berry 1919- .... CLC 6
See also CA 49-52; DLB 6

Morgan, Claire
See Highsmith, (Mary) Patricia

Morgan, Edwin (George) 1920-..... CLC 31
See also CA 5-8R; CANR 3, 43; DLB 27

Morgan, (George) Frederick
1922- .... CLC 23
See also CA 17-20R; CANR 21

Morgan, Harriet
See Mencken, H(enry) L(ouis)

Morgan, Jane
See Cooper, James Fenimore

Morgan, Janet 1945- .... CLC 39
See also CA 65-68

Morgan, Lady 1776(?)-1859...... NCLC 29
See also DLB 116

Morgan, Robin 1941-............. CLC 2
See also CA 69-72; CANR 29; MTCW

Morgan, Scott
See Kuttner, Henry

Morgan, Seth 1949(?)-1990 .... CLC 65
See also CA 132

Morgenstern, Christian
1871-1914 .... TCLC 8
See also CA 105

Morgenstern, S.
See Goldman, William (W.)

Moricz, Zsigmond 1879-1942 ..... TCLC 33

Morike, Eduard (Friedrich)
1804-1875 .... NCLC 10
See also DLB 133

Mori Ogai .... TCLC 14
See also Mori Rintaro

Mori Rintaro 1862-1922
See Mori Ogai
See also CA 110

Moritz, Karl Philipp 1756-1793 ...... LC 2
See also DLB 94

Morland, Peter Henry
See Faust, Frederick (Schiller)

Morren, Theophil
See Hofmannsthal, Hugo von

Morris, Bill 1952-............... CLC 76

Morris, Julian
See West, Morris L(anglo)

Morris, Steveland Judkins 1950(?)-
See Wonder, Stevie
See also CA 111

Morris, William 1834-1896 .... NCLC 4
See also CDBLB 1832-1890; DLB 18, 35, 57

Morris, Wright 1910-... CLC 1, 3, 7, 18, 37
See also CA 9-12R; CANR 21; DLB 2;
DLBY 81; MTCW

Morrison, Chloe Anthony Wofford
See Morrison, Toni

Morrison, James Douglas 1943-1971
See Morrison, Jim
See also CA 73-76; CANR 40

Morrison, Jim .... CLC 17
See also Morrison, James Douglas

Morrison, Toni
1931- .. CLC 4, 10, 22, 55, 81; BLC; DA
See also AAYA 1; BW 2; CA 29-32R;
CANR 27, 42; CDALB 1968-1988;
DLB 6, 33, 143; DLBY 81; MTCW;
SATA 57

Morrison, Van 1945- .... CLC 21
See also CA 116

Mortimer, John (Clifford)
1923- .... CLC 28, 43
See also CA 13-16R; CANR 21;
CDBLB 1960 to Present; DLB 13;
MTCW

Mortimer, Penelope (Ruth) 1918-.... CLC 5
See also CA 57-60; CANR 45

Morton, Anthony
See Creasey, John

Mosher, Howard Frank 1943-...... CLC 62
See also CA 139

Mosley, Nicholas 1923-........ CLC 43, 70
See also CA 69-72; CANR 41; DLB 14

Moss, Howard
1922-1987 .... CLC 7, 14, 45, 50
See also CA 1-4R; 123; CANR 1, 44;
DLB 5

Mossgiel, Rab
See Burns, Robert

Motion, Andrew 1952-........... CLC 47
See also DLB 40

Motley, Willard (Francis)
1909-1965 .... CLC 18
See also BW 1; CA 117; 106; DLB 76, 143

Motoori, Norinaga 1730-1801.... NCLC 45

Mott, Michael (Charles Alston)
1930- .... CLC 15, 34
See also CA 5-8R; CAAS 7; CANR 7, 29

Mowat, Farley (McGill) 1921- ..... CLC 26
See also AAYA 1; CA 1-4R; CANR 4, 24,
42; CLR 20; DLB 68; JRDA; MAICYA;
MTCW; SATA 3, 55

Moyers, Bill 1934-............... CLC 74
See also AITN 2; CA 61-64; CANR 31

Mphahlele, Es'kia
See Mphahlele, Ezekiel
See also DLB 125

Mphahlele, Ezekiel 1919-..... **CLC 25; BLC**
See also Mphahlele, Es'kia
See also BW 2; CA 81-84; CANR 26

Mqhayi, S(amuel) E(dward) K(rune Loliwe)
1875-1945 .... **TCLC 25; BLC**

Mr. Martin
See Burroughs, William S(eward)

Mrozek, Slawomir 1930-........ **CLC 3, 13**
See also CA 13-16R; CAAS 10; CANR 29;
MTCW

Mrs. Belloc-Lowndes
See Lowndes, Marie Adelaide (Belloc)

Mtwa, Percy (?)-................. **CLC 47**

Mueller, Lisel 1924-........... **CLC 13, 51**
See also CA 93-96; DLB 105

Muir, Edwin 1887-1959 .... **TCLC 2**
See also CA 104; DLB 20, 100

Muir, John 1838-1914 .... **TCLC 28**

Mujica Lainez, Manuel
1910-1984 .... **CLC 31**
See also Lainez, Manuel Mujica
See also CA 81-84; 112; CANR 32; HW

Mukherjee, Bharati 1940-......... **CLC 53**
See also BEST 89:2; CA 107; CANR 45;
DLB 60; MTCW

Muldoon, Paul 1951-.......... **CLC 32, 72**
See also CA 113; 129; DLB 40

Mulisch, Harry 1927-............. **CLC 42**
See also CA 9-12R; CANR 6, 26

Mull, Martin 1943-............... **CLC 17**
See also CA 105

Mulock, Dinah Maria
See Craik, Dinah Maria (Mulock)

Munford, Robert 1737(?)-1783 .... **LC 5**
See also DLB 31

Mungo, Raymond 1946-........... **CLC 72**
See also CA 49-52; CANR 2

Munro, Alice
1931- .... **CLC 6, 10, 19, 50; SSC 3**
See also AITN 2; CA 33-36R; CANR 33;
DLB 53; MTCW; SATA 29

Munro, H(ector) H(ugh) 1870-1916
See Saki
See also CA 104; 130; CDBLB 1890-1914;
DA; DLB 34; MTCW; WLC

Murasaki, Lady................. **CMLC 1**

Murdoch, (Jean) Iris
1919- ...... **CLC 1, 2, 3, 4, 6, 8, 11, 15,
22, 31, 51**
See also CA 13-16R; CANR 8, 43;
CDBLB 1960 to Present; DLB 14;
MTCW

Murnau, Friedrich Wilhelm
See Plumpe, Friedrich Wilhelm

Murphy, Richard 1927-........... **CLC 41**
See also CA 29-32R; DLB 40

Murphy, Sylvia 1937-............. **CLC 34**
See also CA 121

Murphy, Thomas (Bernard) 1935-... **CLC 51**
See also CA 101

Murray, Albert L. 1916- .... **CLC 73**
See also BW 2; CA 49-52; CANR 26;
DLB 38

Murray, Les(lie) A(llan) 1938- ..... **CLC 40**
See also CA 21-24R; CANR 11, 27

Murry, J. Middleton
See Murry, John Middleton

Murry, John Middleton
1889-1957 .... **TCLC 16**
See also CA 118

Musgrave, Susan 1951- .... **CLC 13, 54**
See also CA 69-72; CANR 45

Musil, Robert (Edler von)
1880-1942 .... **TCLC 12**
See also CA 109; DLB 81, 124

Musset, (Louis Charles) Alfred de
1810-1857 .... **NCLC 7**

My Brother's Brother
See Chekhov, Anton (Pavlovich)

Myers, Walter Dean 1937- ... **CLC 35; BLC**
See also AAYA 4; BW 2; CA 33-36R;
CANR 20, 42; CLR 4, 16, 35; DLB 33;
JRDA; MAICYA; SAAS 2; SATA 27, 41,
71

Myers, Walter M.
See Myers, Walter Dean

Myles, Symon
See Follett, Ken(neth Martin)

Nabokov, Vladimir (Vladimirovich)
1899-1977 ..... **CLC 1, 2, 3, 6, 8, 11, 15,
23, 44, 46, 64; DA; SSC 11; WLC**
See also CA 5-8R; 69-72; CANR 20;
CDALB 1941-1968; DLB 2; DLBD 3;
DLBY 80, 91; MTCW

Nagai Kafu..................... **TCLC 51**
See also Nagai Sokichi

Nagai Sokichi 1879-1959
See Nagai Kafu
See also CA 117

Nagy, Laszlo 1925-1978............ **CLC 7**
See also CA 129; 112

Naipaul, Shiva(dhar Srinivasa)
1945-1985 .... **CLC 32, 39**
See also CA 110; 112; 116; CANR 33;
DLBY 85; MTCW

Naipaul, V(idiadhar) S(urajprasad)
1932- .... **CLC 4, 7, 9, 13, 18, 37**
See also CA 1-4R; CANR 1, 33;
CDBLB 1960 to Present; DLB 125;
DLBY 85; MTCW

Nakos, Lilika 1899(?)-............ **CLC 29**

Narayan, R(asipuram) K(rishnaswami)
1906- .... **CLC 7, 28, 47**
See also CA 81-84; CANR 33; MTCW;
SATA 62

Nash, (Fredric) Ogden 1902-1971 .. **CLC 23**
See also CA 13-14; 29-32R; CANR 34;
CAP 1; DLB 11; MAICYA; MTCW;
SATA 2, 46

Nathan, Daniel
See Dannay, Frederic

Nathan, George Jean 1882-1958 ... **TCLC 18**
See also Hatteras, Owen
See also CA 114; DLB 137

Natsume, Kinnosuke 1867-1916
See Natsume, Soseki
See also CA 104

Natsume, Soseki .... **TCLC 2, 10**
See also Natsume, Kinnosuke

Natti, (Mary) Lee 1919-
See Kingman, Lee
See also CA 5-8R; CANR 2

Naylor, Gloria
1950- .... **CLC 28, 52; BLC; DA**
See also AAYA 6; BW 2; CA 107;
CANR 27; MTCW

Neihardt, John Gneisenau
1881-1973 .... **CLC 32**
See also CA 13-14; CAP 1; DLB 9, 54

Nekrasov, Nikolai Alekseevich
1821-1878 .... **NCLC 11**

Nelligan, Emile 1879-1941....... **TCLC 14**
See also CA 114; DLB 92

Nelson, Willie 1933-.............. **CLC 17**
See also CA 107

Nemerov, Howard (Stanley)
1920-1991 .... **CLC 2, 6, 9, 36**
See also CA 1-4R; 134; CABS 2; CANR 1,
27; DLB 6; DLBY 83; MTCW

Neruda, Pablo
1904-1973 ..... **CLC 1, 2, 5, 7, 9, 28, 62;
DA; HLC; PC 4; WLC**
See also CA 19-20; 45-48; CAP 2; HW;
MTCW

Nerval, Gerard de 1808-1855...... **NCLC 1**

Nervo, (Jose) Amado (Ruiz de)
1870-1919 .... **TCLC 11**
See also CA 109; 131; HW

Nessi, Pio Baroja y
See Baroja (y Nessi), Pio

Nestroy, Johann 1801-1862...... **NCLC 42**
See also DLB 133

Neufeld, John (Arthur) 1938- ...... **CLC 17**
See also AAYA 11; CA 25-28R; CANR 11,
37; MAICYA; SAAS 3; SATA 6

Neville, Emily Cheney 1919-....... **CLC 12**
See also CA 5-8R; CANR 3, 37; JRDA;
MAICYA; SAAS 2; SATA 1

Newbound, Bernard Slade 1930-
See Slade, Bernard
See also CA 81-84

Newby, P(ercy) H(oward)
1918- .... **CLC 2, 13**
See also CA 5-8R; CANR 32; DLB 15;
MTCW

Newlove, Donald 1928- .... **CLC 6**
See also CA 29-32R; CANR 25

Newlove, John (Herbert) 1938-..... **CLC 14**
See also CA 21-24R; CANR 9, 25

Newman, Charles 1938-.......... **CLC 2, 8**
See also CA 21-24R

Newman, Edwin (Harold) 1919- .... **CLC 14**
See also AITN 1; CA 69-72; CANR 5

Newman, John Henry
1801-1890 .... **NCLC 38**
See also DLB 18, 32, 55

Newton, Suzanne 1936-........... **CLC 35**
See also CA 41-44R; CANR 14; JRDA;
SATA 5, 77

Nexo, Martin Andersen
1869-1954 . . . . **TCLC 43**

Nezval, Vitezslav 1900-1958 . . . . . . **TCLC 44**
See also CA 123

Ng, Fae Myenne 1957(?)- . . . . **CLC 81**

Ngema, Mbongeni 1955- . . . . **CLC 57**
See also BW 2; CA 143

Ngugi, James T(hiong'o) . . . . **CLC 3, 7, 13**
See also Ngugi wa Thiong'o

Ngugi wa Thiong'o 1938- . . . . . **CLC 36; BLC**
See also Ngugi, James T(hiong'o)
See also BW 2; CA 81-84; CANR 27;
DLB 125; MTCW

Nichol, B(arrie) P(hillip)
1944-1988 . . . . **CLC 18**
See also CA 53-56; DLB 53; SATA 66

Nichols, John (Treadwell) 1940- . . . . **CLC 38**
See also CA 9-12R; CAAS 2; CANR 6;
DLBY 82

Nichols, Leigh
See Koontz, Dean R(ay)

Nichols, Peter (Richard)
1927- . . . . **CLC 5, 36, 65**
See also CA 104; CANR 33; DLB 13;
MTCW

Nicolas, F. R. E.
See Freeling, Nicolas

Niedecker, Lorine 1903-1970. . . . **CLC 10, 42**
See also CA 25-28; CAP 2; DLB 48

Nietzsche, Friedrich (Wilhelm)
1844-1900 . . . . **TCLC 10, 18, 55**
See also CA 107; 121; DLB 129

Nievo, Ippolito 1831-1861 . . . . **NCLC 22**

Nightingale, Anne Redmon 1943-
See Redmon, Anne
See also CA 103

Nik. T. O.
See Annensky, Innokenty Fyodorovich

Nin, Anais
1903-1977 . . . . . . **CLC 1, 4, 8, 11, 14, 60;
SSC 10**
See also AITN 2; CA 13-16R; 69-72;
CANR 22; DLB 2, 4; MTCW

Nissenson, Hugh 1933- . . . . **CLC 4, 9**
See also CA 17-20R; CANR 27; DLB 28

Niven, Larry . . . . **CLC 8**
See also Niven, Laurence Van Cott
See also DLB 8

Niven, Laurence Van Cott 1938-
See Niven, Larry
See also CA 21-24R; CAAS 12; CANR 14,
44; MTCW

Nixon, Agnes Eckhardt 1927- . . . . . . **CLC 21**
See also CA 110

Nizan, Paul 1905-1940. . . . . **TCLC 40**
See also DLB 72

Nkosi, Lewis 1936- . . . . **CLC 45; BLC**
See also BW 1; CA 65-68; CANR 27

Nodier, (Jean) Charles (Emmanuel)
1780-1844 . . . . **NCLC 19**
See also DLB 119

Nolan, Christopher 1965- . . . . **CLC 58**
See also CA 111

Norden, Charles
See Durrell, Lawrence (George)

Nordhoff, Charles (Bernard)
1887-1947 . . . . **TCLC 23**
See also CA 108; DLB 9; SATA 23

Norfolk, Lawrence 1963- . . . . **CLC 76**
See also CA 144

Norman, Marsha 1947- . . . . **CLC 28**
See also CA 105; CABS 3; CANR 41;
DLBY 84

Norris, Benjamin Franklin, Jr.
1870-1902 . . . . **TCLC 24**
See also Norris, Frank
See also CA 110

Norris, Frank
See Norris, Benjamin Franklin, Jr.
See also CDALB 1865-1917; DLB 12, 71

Norris, Leslie 1921- . . . . **CLC 14**
See also CA 11-12; CANR 14; CAP 1;
DLB 27

North, Andrew
See Norton, Andre

North, Anthony
See Koontz, Dean R(ay)

North, Captain George
See Stevenson, Robert Louis (Balfour)

North, Milou
See Erdrich, Louise

Northrup, B. A.
See Hubbard, L(afayette) Ron(ald)

North Staffs
See Hulme, T(homas) E(rnest)

Norton, Alice Mary
See Norton, Andre
See also MAICYA; SATA 1, 43

Norton, Andre 1912- . . . . **CLC 12**
See also Norton, Alice Mary
See also CA 1-4R; CANR 2, 31; DLB 8, 52;
JRDA; MTCW

Norton, Caroline 1808-1877 . . . . . . **NCLC 47**
See also DLB 21

Norway, Nevil Shute 1899-1960
See Shute, Nevil
See also CA 102; 93-96

Norwid, Cyprian Kamil
1821-1883 . . . . **NCLC 17**

Nosille, Nabrah
See Ellison, Harlan

Nossack, Hans Erich 1901-1978 . . . . . **CLC 6**
See also CA 93-96; 85-88; DLB 69

Nostradamus 1503-1566 . . . . **LC 27**

Nosu, Chuji
See Ozu, Yasujiro

Notenburg, Eleanora (Genrikhovna) von
See Guro, Elena

Nova, Craig 1945- . . . . **CLC 7, 31**
See also CA 45-48; CANR 2

Novak, Joseph
See Kosinski, Jerzy (Nikodem)

Novalis 1772-1801 . . . . **NCLC 13**
See also DLB 90

Nowlan, Alden (Albert) 1933-1983 . . **CLC 15**
See also CA 9-12R; CANR 5; DLB 53

Noyes, Alfred 1880-1958 . . . . **TCLC 7**
See also CA 104; DLB 20

Nunn, Kem 19(?)- . . . . **CLC 34**

Nye, Robert 1939- . . . . **CLC 13, 42**
See also CA 33-36R; CANR 29; DLB 14;
MTCW; SATA 6

Nyro, Laura 1947- . . . . **CLC 17**

Oates, Joyce Carol
1938- . . . . . . **CLC 1, 2, 3, 6, 9, 11, 15, 19,
33, 52; DA; SSC 6; WLC**
See also AITN 1; BEST 89:2; CA 5-8R;
CANR 25, 45; CDALB 1968-1988;
DLB 2, 5, 130; DLBY 81; MTCW

O'Brien, Darcy 1939- . . . . **CLC 11**
See also CA 21-24R; CANR 8

O'Brien, E. G.
See Clarke, Arthur C(harles)

O'Brien, Edna
1936- . . . **CLC 3, 5, 8, 13, 36, 65; SSC 10**
See also CA 1-4R; CANR 6, 41;
CDBLB 1960 to Present; DLB 14;
MTCW

O'Brien, Fitz-James 1828-1862 . . . **NCLC 21**
See also DLB 74

O'Brien, Flann . . . . **CLC 1, 4, 5, 7, 10, 47**
See also O Nuallain, Brian

O'Brien, Richard 1942- . . . . **CLC 17**
See also CA 124

O'Brien, Tim 1946- . . . . **CLC 7, 19, 40**
See also CA 85-88; CANR 40; DLBD 9;
DLBY 80

Obstfelder, Sigbjoern 1866-1900 . . . **TCLC 23**
See also CA 123

O'Casey, Sean
1880-1964 . . . . **CLC 1, 5, 9, 11, 15**
See also CA 89-92; CDBLB 1914-1945;
DLB 10; MTCW

O'Cathasaigh, Sean
See O'Casey, Sean

Ochs, Phil 1940-1976 . . . . **CLC 17**
See also CA 65-68

O'Connor, Edwin (Greene)
1918-1968 . . . . **CLC 14**
See also CA 93-96; 25-28R

O'Connor, (Mary) Flannery
1925-1964 . . . . **CLC 1, 2, 3, 6, 10, 13, 15,
21, 66; DA; SSC 1; WLC**
See also AAYA 7; CA 1-4R; CANR 3, 41;
CDALB 1941-1968; DLB 2; DLBY 80;
MTCW

O'Connor, Frank . . . . **CLC 23; SSC 5**
See also O'Donovan, Michael John

O'Dell, Scott 1898-1989 . . . . **CLC 30**
See also AAYA 3; CA 61-64; 129;
CANR 12, 30; CLR 1, 16; DLB 52;
JRDA; MAICYA; SATA 12, 60

Odets, Clifford 1906-1963 . . . . **CLC 2, 28**
See also CA 85-88; DLB 7, 26; MTCW

O'Doherty, Brian 1934- . . . . **CLC 76**
See also CA 105

O'Donnell, K. M.
See Malzberg, Barry N(athaniel)

O'Donnell, Lawrence
See Kuttner, Henry

O'Donovan, Michael John
    1903-1966 . . . . **CLC 14**
    See also O'Connor, Frank
    See also CA 93-96

Oe, Kenzaburo 1935- . . . . **CLC 10, 36**
    See also CA 97-100; CANR 36; MTCW

O'Faolain, Julia 1932- . . . . **CLC 6, 19, 47**
    See also CA 81-84; CAAS 2; CANR 12;
    DLB 14; MTCW

O'Faolain, Sean
    1900-1991 . . . . **CLC 1, 7, 14, 32, 70;**
                                                       SSC 13
    See also CA 61-64; 134; CANR 12;
    DLB 15; MTCW

O'Flaherty, Liam
    1896-1984 . . . . **CLC 5, 34; SSC 6**
    See also CA 101; 113; CANR 35; DLB 36;
    DLBY 84; MTCW

Ogilvy, Gavin
    See Barrie, J(ames) M(atthew)

O'Grady, Standish James
    1846-1928 . . . . **TCLC 5**
    See also CA 104

O'Grady, Timothy 1951- . . . . **CLC 59**
    See also CA 138

O'Hara, Frank
    1926-1966 . . . . **CLC 2, 5, 13, 78**
    See also CA 9-12R; 25-28R; CANR 33;
    DLB 5, 16; MTCW

O'Hara, John (Henry)
    1905-1970 . . . . **CLC 1, 2, 3, 6, 11, 42;**
                                                       SSC 15
    See also CA 5-8R; 25-28R; CANR 31;
    CDALB 1929-1941; DLB 9, 86; DLBD 2;
    MTCW

O Hehir, Diana 1922- . . . . **CLC 41**
    See also CA 93-96

Okigbo, Christopher (Ifenayichukwu)
    1932-1967 . . . . . **CLC 25, 84; BLC; PC 7**
    See also BW 1; CA 77-80; DLB 125;
    MTCW

Olds, Sharon 1942- . . . . **CLC 32, 39, 85**
    See also CA 101; CANR 18, 41; DLB 120

Oldstyle, Jonathan
    See Irving, Washington

Olesha, Yuri (Karlovich)
    1899-1960 . . . . **CLC 8**
    See also CA 85-88

Oliphant, Laurence
    1829(?)-1888 . . . . **NCLC 47**
    See also DLB 18

Oliphant, Margaret (Oliphant Wilson)
    1828-1897 . . . . **NCLC 11**
    See also DLB 18

Oliver, Mary 1935- . . . . **CLC 19, 34**
    See also CA 21-24R; CANR 9, 43; DLB 5

Olivier, Laurence (Kerr)
    1907-1989 . . . . **CLC 20**
    See also CA 111; 129

Olsen, Tillie
    1913- . . . . **CLC 4, 13; DA; SSC 11**
    See also CA 1-4R; CANR 1, 43; DLB 28;
    DLBY 80; MTCW

Olson, Charles (John)
    1910-1970 . . . . . **CLC 1, 2, 5, 6, 9, 11, 29**
    See also CA 13-16; 25-28R; CABS 2;
    CANR 35; CAP 1; DLB 5, 16; MTCW

Olson, Toby 1937- . . . . **CLC 28**
    See also CA 65-68; CANR 9, 31

Olyesha, Yuri
    See Olesha, Yuri (Karlovich)

Ondaatje, (Philip) Michael
    1943- . . . . **CLC 14, 29, 51, 76**
    See also CA 77-80; CANR 42; DLB 60

Oneal, Elizabeth 1934-
    See Oneal, Zibby
    See also CA 106; CANR 28; MAICYA;
    SATA 30

Oneal, Zibby . . . . **CLC 30**
    See also Oneal, Elizabeth
    See also AAYA 5; CLR 13; JRDA

O'Neill, Eugene (Gladstone)
    1888-1953 . . . . . . **TCLC 1, 6, 27, 49; DA;**
                                                       WLC
    See also AITN 1; CA 110; 132;
    CDALB 1929-1941; DLB 7; MTCW

Onetti, Juan Carlos 1909-1994 . . . **CLC 7, 10**
    See also CA 85-88; 145; CANR 32;
    DLB 113; HW; MTCW

O Nuallain, Brian 1911-1966
    See O'Brien, Flann
    See also CA 21-22; 25-28R; CAP 2

Oppen, George 1908-1984 . . . . **CLC 7, 13, 34**
    See also CA 13-16R; 113; CANR 8; DLB 5

Oppenheim, E(dward) Phillips
    1866-1946 . . . . **TCLC 45**
    See also CA 111; DLB 70

Orlovitz, Gil 1918-1973 . . . . **CLC 22**
    See also CA 77-80; 45-48; DLB 2, 5

Orris
    See Ingelow, Jean

Ortega y Gasset, Jose
    1883-1955 . . . . **TCLC 9; HLC**
    See also CA 106; 130; HW; MTCW

Ortiz, Simon J(oseph) 1941- . . . . **CLC 45**
    See also CA 134; DLB 120

Orton, Joe . . . . **CLC 4, 13, 43; DC 3**
    See also Orton, John Kingsley
    See also CDBLB 1960 to Present; DLB 13

Orton, John Kingsley 1933-1967
    See Orton, Joe
    See also CA 85-88; CANR 35; MTCW

Orwell, George
    . . . . **TCLC 2, 6, 15, 31, 51; WLC**
    See also Blair, Eric (Arthur)
    See also CDBLB 1945-1960; DLB 15, 98

Osborne, David
    See Silverberg, Robert

Osborne, George
    See Silverberg, Robert

Osborne, John (James)
    1929- . . . . **CLC 1, 2, 5, 11, 45; DA; WLC**
    See also CA 13-16R; CANR 21;
    CDBLB 1945-1960; DLB 13; MTCW

Osborne, Lawrence 1958- . . . . **CLC 50**

Oshima, Nagisa 1932- . . . . **CLC 20**
    See also CA 116; 121

Oskison, John Milton
    1874-1947 . . . . **TCLC 35**
    See also CA 144

Ossoli, Sarah Margaret (Fuller marchesa d')
    1810-1850
    See Fuller, Margaret
    See also SATA 25

Ostrovsky, Alexander
    1823-1886 . . . . **NCLC 30**

Otero, Blas de 1916-1979 . . . . **CLC 11**
    See also CA 89-92; DLB 134

Otto, Whitney 1955- . . . . **CLC 70**
    See also CA 140

Ouida . . . . **TCLC 43**
    See also De La Ramee, (Marie) Louise
    See also DLB 18

Ousmane, Sembene 1923- . . . . **CLC 66; BLC**
    See also BW 1; CA 117; 125; MTCW

Ovid 43B.C.-18(?) . . . . **CMLC 7; PC 2**

Owen, Hugh
    See Faust, Frederick (Schiller)

Owen, Wilfred (Edward Salter)
    1893-1918 . . . . . . **TCLC 5, 27; DA; WLC**
    See also CA 104; 141; CDBLB 1914-1945;
    DLB 20

Owens, Rochelle 1936- . . . . **CLC 8**
    See also CA 17-20R; CAAS 2; CANR 39

Oz, Amos 1939- . . . **CLC 5, 8, 11, 27, 33, 54**
    See also CA 53-56; CANR 27; MTCW

Ozick, Cynthia
    1928- . . . . **CLC 3, 7, 28, 62; SSC 15**
    See also BEST 90:1; CA 17-20R; CANR 23;
    DLB 28; DLBY 82; MTCW

Ozu, Yasujiro 1903-1963 . . . . **CLC 16**
    See also CA 112

Pacheco, C.
    See Pessoa, Fernando (Antonio Nogueira)

Pa Chin . . . . **CLC 18**
    See also Li Fei-kan

Pack, Robert 1929- . . . . **CLC 13**
    See also CA 1-4R; CANR 3, 44; DLB 5

Padgett, Lewis
    See Kuttner, Henry

Padilla (Lorenzo), Heberto 1932- . . . **CLC 38**
    See also AITN 1; CA 123; 131; HW

Page, Jimmy 1944- . . . . **CLC 12**

Page, Louise 1955- . . . . **CLC 40**
    See also CA 140

Page, P(atricia) K(athleen)
    1916- . . . . **CLC 7, 18**
    See also CA 53-56; CANR 4, 22; DLB 68;
    MTCW

Paget, Violet 1856-1935
    See Lee, Vernon
    See also CA 104

Paget-Lowe, Henry
    See Lovecraft, H(oward) P(hillips)

Paglia, Camille (Anna) 1947- . . . . **CLC 68**
    See also CA 140

Paige, Richard
    See Koontz, Dean R(ay)

Pakenham, Antonia
    See Fraser, (Lady) Antonia (Pakenham)

Palamas, Kostes 1859-1943 . . . . **TCLC 5**
See also CA 105

Palazzeschi, Aldo 1885-1974 . . . . . . **CLC 11**
See also CA 89-92; 53-56; DLB 114

Paley, Grace 1922- . . . . **CLC 4, 6, 37; SSC 8**
See also CA 25-28R; CANR 13; DLB 28;
MTCW

Palin, Michael (Edward) 1943- . . . . . **CLC 21**
See also Monty Python
See also CA 107; CANR 35; SATA 67

Palliser, Charles 1947- . . . . **CLC 65**
See also CA 136

Palma, Ricardo 1833-1919 . . . . **TCLC 29**

Pancake, Breece Dexter 1952-1979
See Pancake, Breece D'J
See also CA 123; 109

Pancake, Breece D'J . . . . **CLC 29**
See also Pancake, Breece Dexter
See also DLB 130

Panko, Rudy
See Gogol, Nikolai (Vasilyevich)

Papadiamantis, Alexandros
1851-1911 . . . . **TCLC 29**

Papadiamantopoulos, Johannes 1856-1910
See Moreas, Jean
See also CA 117

Papini, Giovanni 1881-1956 . . . . . . **TCLC 22**
See also CA 121

Paracelsus 1493-1541 . . . . **LC 14**

Parasol, Peter
See Stevens, Wallace

Parfenie, Maria
See Codrescu, Andrei

Parini, Jay (Lee) 1948- . . . . **CLC 54**
See also CA 97-100; CAAS 16; CANR 32

Park, Jordan
See Kornbluth, C(yril) M.; Pohl, Frederik

Parker, Bert
See Ellison, Harlan

Parker, Dorothy (Rothschild)
1893-1967 . . . . **CLC 15, 68; SSC 2**
See also CA 19-20; 25-28R; CAP 2;
DLB 11, 45, 86; MTCW

Parker, Robert B(rown) 1932- . . . . . . **CLC 27**
See also BEST 89:4; CA 49-52; CANR 1,
26; MTCW

Parkin, Frank 1940- . . . . **CLC 43**

Parkman, Francis, Jr.
1823-1893 . . . . **NCLC 12**
See also DLB 1, 30

Parks, Gordon (Alexander Buchanan)
1912- . . . . **CLC 1, 16; BLC**
See also AITN 2; BW 2; CA 41-44R;
CANR 26; DLB 33; SATA 8

Parnell, Thomas 1679-1718 . . . . **LC 3**
See also DLB 94

Parra, Nicanor 1914- . . . . **CLC 2; HLC**
See also CA 85-88; CANR 32; HW; MTCW

Parrish, Mary Frances
See Fisher, M(ary) F(rances) K(ennedy)

Parson
See Coleridge, Samuel Taylor

Parson Lot
See Kingsley, Charles

Partridge, Anthony
See Oppenheim, E(dward) Phillips

Pascoli, Giovanni 1855-1912 . . . . . **TCLC 45**

Pasolini, Pier Paolo
1922-1975 . . . . **CLC 20, 37**
See also CA 93-96; 61-64; DLB 128;
MTCW

Pasquini
See Silone, Ignazio

Pastan, Linda (Olenik) 1932- . . . . . . **CLC 27**
See also CA 61-64; CANR 18, 40; DLB 5

Pasternak, Boris (Leonidovich)
1890-1960 . . . . . . **CLC 7, 10, 18, 63; DA;
                                    PC 6; WLC**
See also CA 127; 116; MTCW

Patchen, Kenneth 1911-1972 . . . **CLC 1, 2, 18**
See also CA 1-4R; 33-36R; CANR 3, 35;
DLB 16, 48; MTCW

Pater, Walter (Horatio)
1839-1894 . . . . **NCLC 7**
See also CDBLB 1832-1890; DLB 57

Paterson, A(ndrew) B(arton)
1864-1941 . . . . **TCLC 32**

Paterson, Katherine (Womeldorf)
1932- . . . . **CLC 12, 30**
See also AAYA 1; CA 21-24R; CANR 28;
CLR 7; DLB 52; JRDA; MAICYA;
MTCW; SATA 13, 53

Patmore, Coventry Kersey Dighton
1823-1896 . . . . **NCLC 9**
See also DLB 35, 98

Paton, Alan (Stewart)
1903-1988 . . . . . . **CLC 4, 10, 25, 55; DA;
                                    WLC**
See also CA 13-16; 125; CANR 22; CAP 1;
MTCW; SATA 11, 56

Paton Walsh, Gillian 1937-
See Walsh, Jill Paton
See also CANR 38; JRDA; MAICYA;
SAAS 3; SATA 4, 72

Paulding, James Kirke 1778-1860 . . **NCLC 2**
See also DLB 3, 59, 74

Paulin, Thomas Neilson 1949-
See Paulin, Tom
See also CA 123; 128

Paulin, Tom . . . . **CLC 37**
See also Paulin, Thomas Neilson
See also DLB 40

Paustovsky, Konstantin (Georgievich)
1892-1968 . . . . **CLC 40**
See also CA 93-96; 25-28R

Pavese, Cesare 1908-1950 . . . . **TCLC 3**
See also CA 104; DLB 128

Pavic, Milorad 1929- . . . . **CLC 60**
See also CA 136

Payne, Alan
See Jakes, John (William)

Paz, Gil
See Lugones, Leopoldo

Paz, Octavio
1914- . . . . **CLC 3, 4, 6, 10, 19, 51, 65;
                            DA; HLC; PC 1; WLC**
See also CA 73-76; CANR 32; DLBY 90;
HW; MTCW

Peacock, Molly 1947- . . . . **CLC 60**
See also CA 103; DLB 120

Peacock, Thomas Love
1785-1866 . . . . **NCLC 22**
See also DLB 96, 116

Peake, Mervyn 1911-1968 . . . . **CLC 7, 54**
See also CA 5-8R; 25-28R; CANR 3;
DLB 15; MTCW; SATA 23

Pearce, Philippa . . . . **CLC 21**
See also Christie, (Ann) Philippa
See also CLR 9; MAICYA; SATA 1, 67

Pearl, Eric
See Elman, Richard

Pearson, T(homas) R(eid) 1956- . . . . **CLC 39**
See also CA 120; 130

Peck, Dale 1968(?)- . . . . **CLC 81**

Peck, John 1941- . . . . **CLC 3**
See also CA 49-52; CANR 3

Peck, Richard (Wayne) 1934- . . . . . **CLC 21**
See also AAYA 1; CA 85-88; CANR 19,
38; CLR 15; JRDA; MAICYA; SAAS 2;
SATA 18, 55

Peck, Robert Newton 1928- . . . . **CLC 17; DA**
See also AAYA 3; CA 81-84; CANR 31;
JRDA; MAICYA; SAAS 1; SATA 21, 62

Peckinpah, (David) Sam(uel)
1925-1984 . . . . **CLC 20**
See also CA 109; 114

Pedersen, Knut 1859-1952
See Hamsun, Knut
See also CA 104; 119; MTCW

Peeslake, Gaffer
See Durrell, Lawrence (George)

Peguy, Charles Pierre
1873-1914 . . . . **TCLC 10**
See also CA 107

Pena, Ramon del Valle y
See Valle-Inclan, Ramon (Maria) del

Pendennis, Arthur Esquir
See Thackeray, William Makepeace

Penn, William 1644-1718 . . . . **LC 25**
See also DLB 24

Pepys, Samuel
1633-1703 . . . . **LC 11; DA; WLC**
See also CDBLB 1660-1789; DLB 101

Percy, Walker
1916-1990 . . . . **CLC 2, 3, 6, 8, 14, 18, 47,
                                              65**
See also CA 1-4R; 131; CANR 1, 23;
DLB 2; DLBY 80, 90; MTCW

Perec, Georges 1936-1982 . . . . **CLC 56**
See also CA 141; DLB 83

Pereda (y Sanchez de Porrua), Jose Maria de
1833-1906 . . . . **TCLC 16**
See also CA 117

Pereda y Porrua, Jose Maria de
See Pereda (y Sanchez de Porrua), Jose
Maria de

Peregoy, George Weems
See Mencken, H(enry) L(ouis)

Perelman, S(idney) J(oseph)
1904-1979 ... **CLC 3, 5, 9, 15, 23, 44, 49**
See also AITN 1, 2; CA 73-76; 89-92;
CANR 18; DLB 11, 44; MTCW

Peret, Benjamin 1899-1959 .... **TCLC 20**
See also CA 117

Peretz, Isaac Loeb 1851(?)-1915... **TCLC 16**
See also CA 109

Peretz, Yitzkhok Leibush
See Peretz, Isaac Loeb

Perez Galdos, Benito 1843-1920 ... **TCLC 27**
See also CA 125; HW

Perrault, Charles 1628-1703 .... **LC 2**
See also MAICYA; SATA 25

Perry, Brighton
See Sherwood, Robert E(mmet)

Perse, St.-John .... **CLC 4, 11, 46**
See also Leger, (Marie-Rene Auguste) Alexis
Saint-Leger

Peseenz, Tulio F.
See Lopez y Fuentes, Gregorio

Pesetsky, Bette 1932-............. **CLC 28**
See also CA 133; DLB 130

Peshkov, Alexei Maximovich 1868-1936
See Gorky, Maxim
See also CA 105; 141; DA

Pessoa, Fernando (Antonio Nogueira)
1888-1935 .... **TCLC 27; HLC**
See also CA 125

Peterkin, Julia Mood 1880-1961.... **CLC 31**
See also CA 102; DLB 9

Peters, Joan K. 1945-............. **CLC 39**

Peters, Robert L(ouis) 1924-........ **CLC 7**
See also CA 13-16R; CAAS 8; DLB 105

Petofi, Sandor 1823-1849....... **NCLC 21**

Petrakis, Harry Mark 1923-........ **CLC 3**
See also CA 9-12R; CANR 4, 30

Petrarch 1304-1374................ **PC 8**

Petrov, Evgeny .... **TCLC 21**
See also Kataev, Evgeny Petrovich

Petry, Ann (Lane) 1908- ...... **CLC 1, 7, 18**
See also BW 1; CA 5-8R; CAAS 6;
CANR 4; CLR 12; DLB 76; JRDA;
MAICYA; MTCW; SATA 5

Petursson, Halligrimur 1614-1674 .... **LC 8**

Philipson, Morris H. 1926-........ **CLC 53**
See also CA 1-4R; CANR 4

Phillips, David Graham
1867-1911 .... **TCLC 44**
See also CA 108; DLB 9, 12

Phillips, Jack
See Sandburg, Carl (August)

Phillips, Jayne Anne
1952-............ **CLC 15, 33; SSC 16**
See also CA 101; CANR 24; DLBY 80;
MTCW

Phillips, Richard
See Dick, Philip K(indred)

Phillips, Robert (Schaeffer) 1938-... **CLC 28**
See also CA 17-20R; CAAS 13; CANR 8;
DLB 105

Phillips, Ward
See Lovecraft, H(oward) P(hillips)

Piccolo, Lucio 1901-1969......... **CLC 13**
See also CA 97-100; DLB 114

Pickthall, Marjorie L(owry) C(hristie)
1883-1922 .... **TCLC 21**
See also CA 107; DLB 92

Pico della Mirandola, Giovanni
1463-1494 .... **LC 15**

Piercy, Marge
1936- .... **CLC 3, 6, 14, 18, 27, 62**
See also CA 21-24R; CAAS 1; CANR 13,
43; DLB 120; MTCW

Piers, Robert
See Anthony, Piers

Pieyre de Mandiargues, Andre 1909-1991
See Mandiargues, Andre Pieyre de
See also CA 103; 136; CANR 22

Pilnyak, Boris .... **TCLC 23**
See also Vogau, Boris Andreyevich

Pincherle, Alberto 1907-1990 ... **CLC 11, 18**
See also Moravia, Alberto
See also CA 25-28R; 132; CANR 33;
MTCW

Pinckney, Darryl 1953-......... **CLC 76**
See also BW 2; CA 143

Pindar 518B.C.-446B.C......... **CMLC 12**

Pineda, Cecile 1942-............. **CLC 39**
See also CA 118

Pinero, Arthur Wing 1855-1934 ... **TCLC 32**
See also CA 110; DLB 10

Pinero, Miguel (Antonio Gomez)
1946-1988 .... **CLC 4, 55**
See also CA 61-64; 125; CANR 29; HW

Pinget, Robert 1919- .... **CLC 7, 13, 37**
See also CA 85-88; DLB 83

Pink Floyd
See Barrett, (Roger) Syd; Gilmour, David;
Mason, Nick; Waters, Roger; Wright,
Rick

Pinkney, Edward 1802-1828 ..... **NCLC 31**

Pinkwater, Daniel Manus 1941-.... **CLC 35**
See also Pinkwater, Manus
See also AAYA 1; CA 29-32R; CANR 12,
38; CLR 4; JRDA; MAICYA; SAAS 3;
SATA 46, 76

Pinkwater, Manus
See Pinkwater, Daniel Manus
See also SATA 8

Pinsky, Robert 1940-........ **CLC 9, 19, 38**
See also CA 29-32R; CAAS 4; DLBY 82

Pinta, Harold
See Pinter, Harold

Pinter, Harold
1930- ..... **CLC 1, 3, 6, 9, 11, 15, 27, 58,
73; DA; WLC**
See also CA 5-8R; CANR 33; CDBLB 1960
to Present; DLB 13; MTCW

Pirandello, Luigi
1867-1936 ...... **TCLC 4, 29; DA; WLC**
See also CA 104

Pirsig, Robert M(aynard)
1928-................... **CLC 4, 6, 73**
See also CA 53-56; CANR 42; MTCW;
SATA 39

Pisarev, Dmitry Ivanovich
1840-1868 .... **NCLC 25**

Pix, Mary (Griffith) 1666-1709....... **LC 8**
See also DLB 80

Pixerecourt, Guilbert de
1773-1844 .... **NCLC 39**

Plaidy, Jean
See Hibbert, Eleanor Alice Burford

Planche, James Robinson
1796-1880 .... **NCLC 42**

Plant, Robert 1948- .... **CLC 12**

Plante, David (Robert)
1940- .... **CLC 7, 23, 38**
See also CA 37-40R; CANR 12, 36;
DLBY 83; MTCW

Plath, Sylvia
1932-1963 ..... **CLC 1, 2, 3, 5, 9, 11, 14,
17, 50, 51, 62; DA; PC 1; WLC**
See also CA 19-20; CANR 34; CAP 2;
CDALB 1941-1968; DLB 5, 6; MTCW

Plato 428(?)B.C.-348(?)B.C.... **CMLC 8; DA**

Platonov, Andrei .... **TCLC 14**
See also Klimentov, Andrei Platonovich

Platt, Kin 1911- .... **CLC 26**
See also AAYA 11; CA 17-20R; CANR 11;
JRDA; SAAS 17; SATA 21

Plick et Plock
See Simenon, Georges (Jacques Christian)

Plimpton, George (Ames) 1927-..... **CLC 36**
See also AITN 1; CA 21-24R; CANR 32;
MTCW; SATA 10

Plomer, William Charles Franklin
1903-1973 .... **CLC 4, 8**
See also CA 21-22; CANR 34; CAP 2;
DLB 20; MTCW; SATA 24

Plowman, Piers
See Kavanagh, Patrick (Joseph)

Plum, J.
See Wodehouse, P(elham) G(renville)

Plumly, Stanley (Ross) 1939- ...... **CLC 33**
See also CA 108; 110; DLB 5

Plumpe, Friedrich Wilhelm
1888-1931 .... **TCLC 53**
See also CA 112

Poe, Edgar Allan
1809-1849 ..... **NCLC 1, 16; DA; PC 1;
SSC 1; WLC**
See also CDALB 1640-1865; DLB 3, 59, 73,
74; SATA 23

Poet of Titchfield Street, The
See Pound, Ezra (Weston Loomis)

Pohl, Frederik 1919- .... **CLC 18**
See also CA 61-64; CAAS 1; CANR 11, 37;
DLB 8; MTCW; SATA 24

Poirier, Louis 1910-
See Gracq, Julien
See also CA 122; 126

Poitier, Sidney 1927-.............. **CLC 26**
See also BW 1; CA 117

Polanski, Roman 1933- .... **CLC 16**
See also CA 77-80

Poliakoff, Stephen 1952-.......... **CLC 38**
See also CA 106; DLB 13

Pynchon, Thomas (Ruggles, Jr.)
1937- . . . . . CLC **2, 3, 6, 9, 11, 18, 33, 62,**
72; DA; SSC 14; WLC
See also BEST 90:2; CA 17-20R; CANR 22;
DLB 2; MTCW

Qian Zhongshu
See Ch'ien Chung-shu

Qroll
See Dagerman, Stig (Halvard)

Quarrington, Paul (Lewis) 1953- . . . . CLC **65**
See also CA 129

Quasimodo, Salvatore 1901-1968 . . . CLC **10**
See also CA 13-16; 25-28R; CAP 1;
DLB 114; MTCW

Queen, Ellery . . . . CLC **3, 11**
See also Dannay, Frederic; Davidson,
Avram; Lee, Manfred B(ennington);
Sturgeon, Theodore (Hamilton); Vance,
John Holbrook

Queen, Ellery, Jr.
See Dannay, Frederic; Lee, Manfred
B(ennington)

Queneau, Raymond
1903-1976 . . . . CLC **2, 5, 10, 42**
See also CA 77-80; 69-72; CANR 32;
DLB 72; MTCW

Quevedo, Francisco de 1580-1645 . . . . LC **23**

Quiller-Couch, Arthur Thomas
1863-1944 . . . . TCLC **53**
See also CA 118; DLB 135

Quin, Ann (Marie) 1936-1973 . . . . . . CLC **6**
See also CA 9-12R; 45-48; DLB 14

Quinn, Martin
See Smith, Martin Cruz

Quinn, Simon
See Smith, Martin Cruz

Quiroga, Horacio (Sylvestre)
1878-1937 . . . . TCLC **20; HLC**
See also CA 117; 131; HW; MTCW

Quoirez, Francoise 1935- . . . . CLC **9**
See also Sagan, Francoise
See also CA 49-52; CANR 6, 39; MTCW

Raabe, Wilhelm 1831-1910 . . . . TCLC **45**
See also DLB 129

Rabe, David (William) 1940- . . . CLC **4, 8, 33**
See also CA 85-88; CABS 3; DLB 7

Rabelais, Francois
1483-1553 . . . . LC **5; DA; WLC**

Rabinovitch, Sholem 1859-1916
See Aleichem, Sholom
See also CA 104

Radcliffe, Ann (Ward) 1764-1823 . . NCLC **6**
See also DLB 39

Radiguet, Raymond 1903-1923 . . . . TCLC **29**
See also DLB 65

Radnoti, Miklos 1909-1944 . . . . TCLC **16**
See also CA 118

Rado, James 1939- . . . . CLC **17**
See also CA 105

Radvanyi, Netty 1900-1983
See Seghers, Anna
See also CA 85-88; 110

Rae, Ben
See Griffiths, Trevor

Raeburn, John (Hay) 1941- . . . . CLC **34**
See also CA 57-60

Ragni, Gerome 1942-1991 . . . . CLC **17**
See also CA 105; 134

Rahv, Philip 1908-1973 . . . . CLC **24**
See also Greenberg, Ivan
See also DLB 137

Raine, Craig 1944- . . . . CLC **32**
See also CA 108; CANR 29; DLB 40

Raine, Kathleen (Jessie) 1908- . . . CLC **7, 45**
See also CA 85-88; DLB 20; MTCW

Rainis, Janis 1865-1929 . . . . TCLC **29**

Rakosi, Carl . . . . CLC **47**
See also Rawley, Callman
See also CAAS 5

Raleigh, Richard
See Lovecraft, H(oward) P(hillips)

Rallentando, H. P.
See Sayers, Dorothy L(eigh)

Ramal, Walter
See de la Mare, Walter (John)

Ramon, Juan
See Jimenez (Mantecon), Juan Ramon

Ramos, Graciliano 1892-1953 . . . . . TCLC **32**

Rampersad, Arnold 1941- . . . . CLC **44**
See also BW 2; CA 127; 133; DLB 111

Rampling, Anne
See Rice, Anne

Ramuz, Charles-Ferdinand
1878-1947 . . . . TCLC **33**

Rand, Ayn
1905-1982 . . . . . . CLC **3, 30, 44, 79; DA;**
WLC
See also AAYA 10; CA 13-16R; 105;
CANR 27; MTCW

Randall, Dudley (Felker)
1914- . . . . CLC **1; BLC**
See also BW 1; CA 25-28R; CANR 23;
DLB 41

Randall, Robert
See Silverberg, Robert

Ranger, Ken
See Creasey, John

Ransom, John Crowe
1888-1974 . . . . CLC **2, 4, 5, 11, 24**
See also CA 5-8R; 49-52; CANR 6, 34;
DLB 45, 63; MTCW

Rao, Raja 1909- . . . . CLC **25, 56**
See also CA 73-76; MTCW

Raphael, Frederic (Michael)
1931- . . . . CLC **2, 14**
See also CA 1-4R; CANR 1; DLB 14

Ratcliffe, James P.
See Mencken, H(enry) L(ouis)

Rathbone, Julian 1935- . . . . CLC **41**
See also CA 101; CANR 34

Rattigan, Terence (Mervyn)
1911-1977 . . . . CLC **7**
See also CA 85-88; 73-76;
CDBLB 1945-1960; DLB 13; MTCW

Ratushinskaya, Irina 1954- . . . . CLC **54**
See also CA 129

Raven, Simon (Arthur Noel)
1927- . . . . CLC **14**
See also CA 81-84

Rawley, Callman 1903-
See Rakosi, Carl
See also CA 21-24R; CANR 12, 32

Rawlings, Marjorie Kinnan
1896-1953 . . . . TCLC **4**
See also CA 104; 137; DLB 9, 22, 102;
JRDA; MAICYA; YABC 1

Ray, Satyajit 1921-1992 . . . . CLC **16, 76**
See also CA 114; 137

Read, Herbert Edward 1893-1968 . . . . CLC **4**
See also CA 85-88; 25-28R; DLB 20

Read, Piers Paul 1941- . . . . . . CLC **4, 10, 25**
See also CA 21-24R; CANR 38; DLB 14;
SATA 21

Reade, Charles 1814-1884 . . . . NCLC **2**
See also DLB 21

Reade, Hamish
See Gray, Simon (James Holliday)

Reading, Peter 1946- . . . . CLC **47**
See also CA 103; DLB 40

Reaney, James 1926- . . . . CLC **13**
See also CA 41-44R; CAAS 15; CANR 42;
DLB 68; SATA 43

Rebreanu, Liviu 1885-1944 . . . . TCLC **28**

Rechy, John (Francisco)
1934- . . . . CLC **1, 7, 14, 18; HLC**
See also CA 5-8R; CAAS 4; CANR 6, 32;
DLB 122; DLBY 82; HW

Redcam, Tom 1870-1933 . . . . TCLC **25**

Reddin, Keith . . . . CLC **67**

Redgrove, Peter (William)
1932- . . . . CLC **6, 41**
See also CA 1-4R; CANR 3, 39; DLB 40

Redmon, Anne . . . . CLC **22**
See also Nightingale, Anne Redmon
See also DLBY 86

Reed, Eliot
See Ambler, Eric

Reed, Ishmael
1938- . . . CLC **2, 3, 5, 6, 13, 32, 60; BLC**
See also BW 2; CA 21-24R; CANR 25;
DLB 2, 5, 33; DLBD 8; MTCW

Reed, John (Silas) 1887-1920 . . . . . . TCLC **9**
See also CA 106

Reed, Lou . . . . CLC **21**
See also Firbank, Louis

Reeve, Clara 1729-1807 . . . . NCLC **19**
See also DLB 39

Reich, Wilhelm 1897-1957 . . . . TCLC **57**

Reid, Christopher (John) 1949- . . . . . CLC **33**
See also CA 140; DLB 40

Reid, Desmond
See Moorcock, Michael (John)

Reid Banks, Lynne 1929-
See Banks, Lynne Reid
See also CA 1-4R; CANR 6, 22, 38;
CLR 24; JRDA; MAICYA; SATA 22, 75

Reilly, William K.
See Creasey, John

Reiner, Max
See Caldwell, (Janet Miriam) Taylor
(Holland)

Reis, Ricardo
See Pessoa, Fernando (Antonio Nogueira)

Remarque, Erich Maria
1898-1970 . . . . **CLC 21; DA**
See also CA 77-80; 29-32R; DLB 56;
MTCW

Remizov, A.
See Remizov, Aleksei (Mikhailovich)

Remizov, A. M.
See Remizov, Aleksei (Mikhailovich)

Remizov, Aleksei (Mikhailovich)
1877-1957 . . . . **TCLC 27**
See also CA 125; 133

Renan, Joseph Ernest
1823-1892 . . . . **NCLC 26**

Renard, Jules 1864-1910 . . . . **TCLC 17**
See also CA 117

Renault, Mary . . . . **CLC 3, 11, 17**
See also Challans, Mary
See also DLBY 83

Rendell, Ruth (Barbara) 1930- . . **CLC 28, 48**
See also Vine, Barbara
See also CA 109; CANR 32; DLB 87;
MTCW

Renoir, Jean 1894-1979 . . . . **CLC 20**
See also CA 129; 85-88

Resnais, Alain 1922- . . . . **CLC 16**

Reverdy, Pierre 1889-1960 . . . . **CLC 53**
See also CA 97-100; 89-92

Rexroth, Kenneth
1905-1982 . . . . . . **CLC 1, 2, 6, 11, 22, 49**
See also CA 5-8R; 107; CANR 14, 34;
CDALB 1941-1968; DLB 16, 48;
DLBY 82; MTCW

Reyes, Alfonso 1889-1959 . . . . **TCLC 33**
See also CA 131; HW

Reyes y Basoalto, Ricardo Eliecer Neftali
See Neruda, Pablo

Reymont, Wladyslaw (Stanislaw)
1868(?)-1925 . . . . **TCLC 5**
See also CA 104

Reynolds, Jonathan 1942- . . . . **CLC 6, 38**
See also CA 65-68; CANR 28

Reynolds, Joshua 1723-1792 . . . . **LC 15**
See also DLB 104

Reynolds, Michael Shane 1937- . . . . **CLC 44**
See also CA 65-68; CANR 9

Reznikoff, Charles 1894-1976 . . . . **CLC 9**
See also CA 33-36; 61-64; CAP 2; DLB 28,
45

Rezzori (d'Arezzo), Gregor von
1914- . . . . **CLC 25**
See also CA 122; 136

Rhine, Richard
See Silverstein, Alvin

Rhodes, Eugene Manlove
1869-1934 . . . . **TCLC 53**

R'hoone
See Balzac, Honore de

Rhys, Jean
1890(?)-1979 . . . . **CLC 2, 4, 6, 14, 19, 51**
See also CA 25-28R; 85-88; CANR 35;
CDBLB 1945-1960; DLB 36, 117; MTCW

Ribeiro, Darcy 1922- . . . . **CLC 34**
See also CA 33-36R

Ribeiro, Joao Ubaldo (Osorio Pimentel)
1941- . . . . **CLC 10, 67**
See also CA 81-84

Ribman, Ronald (Burt) 1932- . . . . **CLC 7**
See also CA 21-24R

Ricci, Nino 1959- . . . . **CLC 70**
See also CA 137

Rice, Anne 1941- . . . . **CLC 41**
See also AAYA 9; BEST 89:2; CA 65-68;
CANR 12, 36

Rice, Elmer (Leopold)
1892-1967 . . . . **CLC 7, 49**
See also CA 21-22; 25-28R; CAP 2; DLB 4,
7; MTCW

Rice, Tim 1944- . . . . **CLC 21**
See also CA 103

Rich, Adrienne (Cecile)
1929- . . . . **CLC 3, 6, 7, 11, 18, 36, 73, 76;**
PC 5
See also CA 9-12R; CANR 20; DLB 5, 67;
MTCW

Rich, Barbara
See Graves, Robert (von Ranke)

Rich, Robert
See Trumbo, Dalton

Richards, David Adams 1950- . . . . . . **CLC 59**
See also CA 93-96; DLB 53

Richards, I(vor) A(rmstrong)
1893-1979 . . . . **CLC 14, 24**
See also CA 41-44R; 89-92; CANR 34;
DLB 27

Richardson, Anne
See Roiphe, Anne (Richardson)

Richardson, Dorothy Miller
1873-1957 . . . . **TCLC 3**
See also CA 104; DLB 36

Richardson, Ethel Florence (Lindesay)
1870-1946
See Richardson, Henry Handel
See also CA 105

Richardson, Henry Handel . . . . **TCLC 4**
See also Richardson, Ethel Florence
(Lindesay)

Richardson, Samuel
1689-1761 . . . . **LC 1; DA; WLC**
See also CDBLB 1660-1789; DLB 39

Richler, Mordecai
1931- . . . . **CLC 3, 5, 9, 13, 18, 46, 70**
See also AITN 1; CA 65-68; CANR 31;
CLR 17; DLB 53; MAICYA; MTCW;
SATA 27, 44

Richter, Conrad (Michael)
1890-1968 . . . . **CLC 30**
See also CA 5-8R; 25-28R; CANR 23;
DLB 9; MTCW; SATA 3

Riddell, J. H. 1832-1906 . . . . **TCLC 40**

Riding, Laura . . . . **CLC 3, 7**
See also Jackson, Laura (Riding)

Riefenstahl, Berta Helene Amalia 1902-
See Riefenstahl, Leni
See also CA 108

Riefenstahl, Leni . . . . **CLC 16**
See also Riefenstahl, Berta Helene Amalia

Riffe, Ernest
See Bergman, (Ernst) Ingmar

Riggs, (Rolla) Lynn 1899-1954 . . . . **TCLC 56**
See also CA 144

Riley, James Whitcomb
1849-1916 . . . . **TCLC 51**
See also CA 118; 137; MAICYA; SATA 17

Riley, Tex
See Creasey, John

Rilke, Rainer Maria
1875-1926 . . . . **TCLC 1, 6, 19; PC 2**
See also CA 104; 132; DLB 81; MTCW

Rimbaud, (Jean Nicolas) Arthur
1854-1891 . . . . . **NCLC 4, 35; DA; PC 3;**
WLC

Rinehart, Mary Roberts
1876-1958 . . . . **TCLC 52**
See also CA 108

Ringmaster, The
See Mencken, H(enry) L(ouis)

Ringwood, Gwen(dolyn Margaret) Pharis
1910-1984 . . . . **CLC 48**
See also CA 112; DLB 88

Rio, Michel 19(?)- . . . . **CLC 43**

Ritsos, Giannes
See Ritsos, Yannis

Ritsos, Yannis 1909-1990 . . . . . **CLC 6, 13, 31**
See also CA 77-80; 133; CANR 39; MTCW

Ritter, Erika 1948(?)- . . . . **CLC 52**

Rivera, Jose Eustasio 1889-1928 . . . **TCLC 35**
See also HW

Rivers, Conrad Kent 1933-1968 . . . . . . **CLC 1**
See also BW 1; CA 85-88; DLB 41

Rivers, Elfrida
See Bradley, Marion Zimmer

Riverside, John
See Heinlein, Robert A(nson)

Rizal, Jose 1861-1896 . . . . **NCLC 27**

Roa Bastos, Augusto (Antonio)
1917- . . . . **CLC 45; HLC**
See also CA 131; DLB 113; HW

Robbe-Grillet, Alain
1922- . . . . . . **CLC 1, 2, 4, 6, 8, 10, 14, 43**
See also CA 9-12R; CANR 33; DLB 83;
MTCW

Robbins, Harold 1916- . . . . **CLC 5**
See also CA 73-76; CANR 26; MTCW

Robbins, Thomas Eugene 1936-
See Robbins, Tom
See also CA 81-84; CANR 29; MTCW

Robbins, Tom . . . . **CLC 9, 32, 64**
See also Robbins, Thomas Eugene
See also BEST 90:3; DLBY 80

Robbins, Trina 1938- . . . . **CLC 21**
See also CA 128

Roberts, Charles G(eorge) D(ouglas)
1860-1943 . . . . **TCLC 8**
See also CA 105; CLR 33; DLB 92;
SATA 29

Roberts, Kate 1891-1985 .... **CLC 15**
See also CA 107; 116

Roberts, Keith (John Kingston)
1935- .... **CLC 14**
See also CA 25-28R

Roberts, Kenneth (Lewis)
1885-1957 .... **TCLC 23**
See also CA 109; DLB 9

Roberts, Michele (B.) 1949-........ **CLC 48**
See also CA 115

Robertson, Ellis
See Ellison, Harlan; Silverberg, Robert

Robertson, Thomas William
1829-1871 .... **NCLC 35**

Robinson, Edwin Arlington
1869-1935 .... **TCLC 5; DA; PC 1**
See also CA 104; 133; CDALB 1865-1917;
DLB 54; MTCW

Robinson, Henry Crabb
1775-1867 .... **NCLC 15**
See also DLB 107

Robinson, Jill 1936-.............. **CLC 10**
See also CA 102

Robinson, Kim Stanley 1952- ...... **CLC 34**
See also CA 126

Robinson, Lloyd
See Silverberg, Robert

Robinson, Marilynne 1944-........ **CLC 25**
See also CA 116

Robinson, Smokey................ **CLC 21**
See also Robinson, William, Jr.

Robinson, William, Jr. 1940-
See Robinson, Smokey
See also CA 116

Robison, Mary 1949-............. **CLC 42**
See also CA 113; 116; DLB 130

Rod, Edouard 1857-1910 .... **TCLC 52**

Roddenberry, Eugene Wesley 1921-1991
See Roddenberry, Gene
See also CA 110; 135; CANR 37; SATA 45

Roddenberry, Gene .... **CLC 17**
See also Roddenberry, Eugene Wesley
See also AAYA 5; SATA-Obit 69

Rodgers, Mary 1931-............. **CLC 12**
See also CA 49-52; CANR 8; CLR 20;
JRDA; MAICYA; SATA 8

Rodgers, W(illiam) R(obert)
1909-1969 .... **CLC 7**
See also CA 85-88; DLB 20

Rodman, Eric
See Silverberg, Robert

Rodman, Howard 1920(?)-1985 ..... **CLC 65**
See also CA 118

Rodman, Maia
See Wojciechowska, Maia (Teresa)

Rodriguez, Claudio 1934-......... **CLC 10**
See also DLB 134

Roelvaag, O(le) E(dvart)
1876-1931 .... **TCLC 17**
See also CA 117; DLB 9

Roethke, Theodore (Huebner)
1908-1963 ...... **CLC 1, 3, 8, 11, 19, 46**
See also CA 81-84; CABS 2;
CDALB 1941-1968; DLB 5; MTCW

Rogers, Thomas Hunton 1927- ..... **CLC 57**
See also CA 89-92

Rogers, Will(iam Penn Adair)
1879-1935 .... **TCLC 8**
See also CA 105; 144; DLB 11

Rogin, Gilbert 1929-.............. **CLC 18**
See also CA 65-68; CANR 15

Rohan, Koda .... **TCLC 22**
See also Koda Shigeyuki

Rohmer, Eric.................... **CLC 16**
See also Scherer, Jean-Marie Maurice

Rohmer, Sax .... **TCLC 28**
See also Ward, Arthur Henry Sarsfield
See also DLB 70

Roiphe, Anne (Richardson)
1935- .... **CLC 3, 9**
See also CA 89-92; CANR 45; DLBY 80

Rojas, Fernando de 1465-1541 ...... **LC 23**

**Rolfe, Frederick (William Serafino Austin
Lewis Mary)** 1860-1913...... **TCLC 12**
See also CA 107; DLB 34

Rolland, Romain 1866-1944....... **TCLC 23**
See also CA 118; DLB 65

Rolvaag, O(le) E(dvart)
See Roelvaag, O(le) E(dvart)

Romain Arnaud, Saint
See Aragon, Louis

Romains, Jules 1885-1972.......... **CLC 7**
See also CA 85-88; CANR 34; DLB 65;
MTCW

Romero, Jose Ruben 1890-1952 ... **TCLC 14**
See also CA 114; 131; HW

Ronsard, Pierre de 1524-1585 .... **LC 6**

Rooke, Leon 1934-............ **CLC 25, 34**
See also CA 25-28R; CANR 23

Roper, William 1498-1578 .... **LC 10**

Roquelaure, A. N.
See Rice, Anne

Rosa, Joao Guimaraes 1908-1967 ... **CLC 23**
See also CA 89-92; DLB 113

Rose, Wendy 1948-................ **CLC 85**
See also CA 53-56; CANR 5; NNAL;
SATA 12

Rosen, Richard (Dean) 1949-....... **CLC 39**
See also CA 77-80

Rosenberg, Isaac 1890-1918....... **TCLC 12**
See also CA 107; DLB 20

Rosenblatt, Joe .... **CLC 15**
See also Rosenblatt, Joseph

Rosenblatt, Joseph 1933-
See Rosenblatt, Joe
See also CA 89-92

Rosenfeld, Samuel 1896-1963
See Tzara, Tristan
See also CA 89-92

Rosenthal, M(acha) L(ouis) 1917-... **CLC 28**
See also CA 1-4R; CAAS 6; CANR 4;
DLB 5; SATA 59

Ross, Barnaby
See Dannay, Frederic

Ross, Bernard L.
See Follett, Ken(neth Martin)

Ross, J. H.
See Lawrence, T(homas) E(dward)

Ross, Martin
See Martin, Violet Florence
See also DLB 135

Ross, (James) Sinclair 1908-....... **CLC 13**
See also CA 73-76; DLB 88

Rossetti, Christina (Georgina)
1830-1894 ... **NCLC 2; DA; PC 7; WLC**
See also DLB 35; MAICYA; SATA 20

Rossetti, Dante Gabriel
1828-1882 .... **NCLC 4; DA; WLC**
See also CDBLB 1832-1890; DLB 35

Rossner, Judith (Perelman)
1935-.................. **CLC 6, 9, 29**
See also AITN 2; BEST 90:3; CA 17-20R;
CANR 18; DLB 6; MTCW

Rostand, Edmond (Eugene Alexis)
1868-1918 .... **TCLC 6, 37; DA**
See also CA 104; 126; MTCW

Roth, Henry 1906-........... **CLC 2, 6, 11**
See also CA 11-12; CANR 38; CAP 1;
DLB 28; MTCW

Roth, Joseph 1894-1939.......... **TCLC 33**
See also DLB 85

Roth, Philip (Milton)
1933- ...... **CLC 1, 2, 3, 4, 6, 9, 15, 22,
31, 47, 66; DA; WLC**
See also BEST 90:3; CA 1-4R; CANR 1, 22,
36; CDALB 1968-1988; DLB 2, 28;
DLBY 82; MTCW

Rothenberg, Jerome 1931-....... **CLC 6, 57**
See also CA 45-48; CANR 1; DLB 5

Roumain, Jacques (Jean Baptiste)
1907-1944 .... **TCLC 19; BLC**
See also BW 1; CA 117; 125

Rourke, Constance (Mayfield)
1885-1941 .... **TCLC 12**
See also CA 107; YABC 1

Rousseau, Jean-Baptiste 1671-1741 ... **LC 9**

Rousseau, Jean-Jacques
1712-1778 .... **LC 14; DA; WLC**

Roussel, Raymond 1877-1933 ..... **TCLC 20**
See also CA 117

Rovit, Earl (Herbert) 1927-......... **CLC 7**
See also CA 5-8R; CANR 12

Rowe, Nicholas 1674-1718........... **LC 8**
See also DLB 84

Rowley, Ames Dorrance
See Lovecraft, H(oward) P(hillips)

Rowson, Susanna Haswell
1762(?)-1824 .... **NCLC 5**
See also DLB 37

Roy, Gabrielle 1909-1983....... **CLC 10, 14**
See also CA 53-56; 110; CANR 5; DLB 68;
MTCW

Rozewicz, Tadeusz 1921-........ **CLC 9, 23**
See also CA 108; CANR 36; MTCW

Ruark, Gibbons 1941- .... **CLC 3**
See also CA 33-36R; CANR 14, 31;
DLB 120

Rubens, Bernice (Ruth) 1923-... **CLC 19, 31**
See also CA 25-28R; CANR 33; DLB 14;
MTCW

Rudkin, (James) David 1936- ...... **CLC 14**
See also CA 89-92; DLB 13

Rudnik, Raphael 1933-............ **CLC 7**
See also CA 29-32R

Ruffian, M.
See Hasek, Jaroslav (Matej Frantisek)

Ruiz, Jose Martinez .... **CLC 11**
See also Martinez Ruiz, Jose

Rukeyser, Muriel
1913-1980 .... **CLC 6, 10, 15, 27**
See also CA 5-8R; 93-96; CANR 26;
DLB 48; MTCW; SATA 22

Rule, Jane (Vance) 1931-......... **CLC 27**
See also CA 25-28R; CAAS 18; CANR 12;
DLB 60

Rulfo, Juan 1918-1986.... **CLC 8, 80; HLC**
See also CA 85-88; 118; CANR 26;
DLB 113; HW; MTCW

Runeberg, Johan 1804-1877...... **NCLC 41**

Runyon, (Alfred) Damon
1884(?)-1946 .... **TCLC 10**
See also CA 107; DLB 11, 86

Rush, Norman 1933-.............. **CLC 44**
See also CA 121; 126

Rushdie, (Ahmed) Salman
1947- .... **CLC 23, 31, 55**
See also BEST 89:3; CA 108; 111;
CANR 33; MTCW

Rushforth, Peter (Scott) 1945- ..... **CLC 19**
See also CA 101

Ruskin, John 1819-1900......... **TCLC 20**
See also CA 114; 129; CDBLB 1832-1890;
DLB 55; SATA 24

Russ, Joanna 1937-.............. **CLC 15**
See also CA 25-28R; CANR 11, 31; DLB 8;
MTCW

Russell, (Henry) Ken(neth Alfred)
1927- .... **CLC 16**
See also CA 105

Russell, Willy 1947-.............. **CLC 60**

Rutherford, Mark .... **TCLC 25**
See also White, William Hale
See also DLB 18

Ryan, Cornelius (John) 1920-1974 ... **CLC 7**
See also CA 69-72; 53-56; CANR 38

Ryan, Michael 1946- .... **CLC 65**
See also CA 49-52; DLBY 82

Rybakov, Anatoli (Naumovich)
1911- .... **CLC 23, 53**
See also CA 126; 135; SATA 79

Ryder, Jonathan
See Ludlum, Robert

Ryga, George 1932-1987 .... **CLC 14**
See also CA 101; 124; CANR 43; DLB 60

S. S.
See Sassoon, Siegfried (Lorraine)

Saba, Umberto 1883-1957 .... **TCLC 33**
See also CA 144; DLB 114

Sabatini, Rafael 1875-1950 ...... **TCLC 47**

Sabato, Ernesto (R.)
1911- .... **CLC 10, 23; HLC**
See also CA 97-100; CANR 32; HW;
MTCW

Sacastru, Martin
See Bioy Casares, Adolfo

Sacher-Masoch, Leopold von
1836(?)-1895 .... **NCLC 31**

Sachs, Marilyn (Stickle) 1927- ..... **CLC 35**
See also AAYA 2; CA 17-20R; CANR 13;
CLR 2; JRDA; MAICYA; SAAS 2;
SATA 3, 68

Sachs, Nelly 1891-1970 .... **CLC 14**
See also CA 17-18; 25-28R; CAP 2

Sackler, Howard (Oliver)
1929-1982 .... **CLC 14**
See also CA 61-64; 108; CANR 30; DLB 7

Sacks, Oliver (Wolf) 1933- .... **CLC 67**
See also CA 53-56; CANR 28; MTCW

Sade, Donatien Alphonse Francois Comte
1740-1814 .... **NCLC 47**

Sadoff, Ira 1945-................ **CLC 9**
See also CA 53-56; CANR 5, 21; DLB 120

Saetone
See Camus, Albert

Safire, William 1929-............. **CLC 10**
See also CA 17-20R; CANR 31

Sagan, Carl (Edward) 1934-........ **CLC 30**
See also AAYA 2; CA 25-28R; CANR 11,
36; MTCW; SATA 58

Sagan, Francoise .... **CLC 3, 6, 9, 17, 36**
See also Quoirez, Francoise
See also DLB 83

Sahgal, Nayantara (Pandit) 1927-... **CLC 41**
See also CA 9-12R; CANR 11

Saint, H(arry) F. 1941- .... **CLC 50**
See also CA 127

St. Aubin de Teran, Lisa 1953-
See Teran, Lisa St. Aubin de
See also CA 118; 126

Sainte-Beuve, Charles Augustin
1804-1869 .... **NCLC 5**

Saint-Exupery, Antoine (Jean Baptiste Marie Roger) de
1900-1944 .... **TCLC 2, 56; WLC**
See also CA 108; 132; CLR 10; DLB 72;
MAICYA; MTCW; SATA 20

St. John, David
See Hunt, E(verette) Howard, Jr.

Saint-John Perse
See Leger, (Marie-Rene Auguste) Alexis
Saint-Leger

Saintsbury, George (Edward Bateman)
1845-1933 .... **TCLC 31**
See also DLB 57

Sait Faik .... **TCLC 23**
See also Abasiyanik, Sait Faik

Saki .... **TCLC 3; SSC 12**
See also Munro, H(ector) H(ugh)

Sala, George Augustus .... **NCLC 46**

Salama, Hannu 1936-............. **CLC 18**

Salamanca, J(ack) R(ichard)
1922- .... **CLC 4, 15**
See also CA 25-28R

Sale, J. Kirkpatrick
See Sale, Kirkpatrick

Sale, Kirkpatrick 1937-........... **CLC 68**
See also CA 13-16R; CANR 10

Salinas (y Serrano), Pedro
1891(?)-1951 .... **TCLC 17**
See also CA 117; DLB 134

Salinger, J(erome) D(avid)
1919- ...... **CLC 1, 3, 8, 12, 55, 56; DA; SSC 2; WLC**
See also AAYA 2; CA 5-8R; CANR 39;
CDALB 1941-1968; CLR 18; DLB 2, 102;
MAICYA; MTCW; SATA 67

Salisbury, John
See Caute, David

Salter, James 1925- .... **CLC 7, 52, 59**
See also CA 73-76; DLB 130

Saltus, Edgar (Everton)
1855-1921 .... **TCLC 8**
See also CA 105

Saltykov, Mikhail Evgrafovich
1826-1889 .... **NCLC 16**

Samarakis, Antonis 1919- .... **CLC 5**
See also CA 25-28R; CAAS 16; CANR 36

Sanchez, Florencio 1875-1910..... **TCLC 37**
See also HW

Sanchez, Luis Rafael 1936-........ **CLC 23**
See also CA 128; HW

Sanchez, Sonia 1934-... **CLC 5; BLC; PC 9**
See also BW 2; CA 33-36R; CANR 24;
CLR 18; DLB 41; DLBD 8; MAICYA;
MTCW; SATA 22

Sand, George
1804-1876 ...... **NCLC 2, 42; DA; WLC**
See also DLB 119

Sandburg, Carl (August)
1878-1967 .... **CLC 1, 4, 10, 15, 35; DA; PC 2; WLC**
See also CA 5-8R; 25-28R; CANR 35;
CDALB 1865-1917; DLB 17, 54;
MAICYA; MTCW; SATA 8

Sandburg, Charles
See Sandburg, Carl (August)

Sandburg, Charles A.
See Sandburg, Carl (August)

Sanders, (James) Ed(ward) 1939- ... **CLC 53**
See also CA 13-16R; CANR 13, 44;
DLB 16

Sanders, Lawrence 1920-.......... **CLC 41**
See also BEST 89:4; CA 81-84; CANR 33;
MTCW

Sanders, Noah
See Blount, Roy (Alton), Jr.

Sanders, Winston P.
See Anderson, Poul (William)

Sandoz, Mari(e Susette)
1896-1966 .... **CLC 28**
See also CA 1-4R; 25-28R; CANR 17;
DLB 9; MTCW; SATA 5

Saner, Reg(inald Anthony) 1931- .... **CLC 9**
See also CA 65-68

Sannazaro, Jacopo 1456(?)-1530...... **LC 8**

Sansom, William 1912-1976....... **CLC 2, 6**
See also CA 5-8R; 65-68; CANR 42;
DLB 139; MTCW

Santayana, George 1863-1952..... **TCLC 40**
See also CA 115; DLB 54, 71

Scott, Walter
1771-1832 .... **NCLC 15; DA; WLC**
See also CDBLB 1789-1832; DLB 93, 107,
116, 144; YABC 2

Scribe, (Augustin) Eugene
1791-1861 .... **NCLC 16**

Scrum, R.
See Crumb, R(obert)

Scudery, Madeleine de 1607-1701..... **LC 2**

Scum
See Crumb, R(obert)

Scumbag, Little Bobby
See Crumb, R(obert)

Seabrook, John
See Hubbard, L(afayette) Ron(ald)

Sealy, I. Allan 1951- .... **CLC 55**

Search, Alexander
See Pessoa, Fernando (Antonio Nogueira)

Sebastian, Lee
See Silverberg, Robert

Sebastian Owl
See Thompson, Hunter S(tockton)

Sebestyen, Ouida 1924- .... **CLC 30**
See also AAYA 8; CA 107; CANR 40;
CLR 17; JRDA; MAICYA; SAAS 10;
SATA 39

Secundus, H. Scriblerus
See Fielding, Henry

Sedges, John
See Buck, Pearl S(ydenstricker)

Sedgwick, Catharine Maria
1789-1867 .... **NCLC 19**
See also DLB 1, 74

Seelye, John 1931- .... **CLC 7**

Seferiades, Giorgos Stylianou 1900-1971
See Seferis, George
See also CA 5-8R; 33-36R; CANR 5, 36;
MTCW

Seferis, George .... **CLC 5, 11**
See also Seferiades, Giorgos Stylianou

Segal, Erich (Wolf) 1937- .... **CLC 3, 10**
See also BEST 89:1; CA 25-28R; CANR 20,
36; DLBY 86; MTCW

Seger, Bob 1945-................. **CLC 35**

Seghers, Anna .... **CLC 7**
See also Radvanyi, Netty
See also DLB 69

Seidel, Frederick (Lewis) 1936-..... **CLC 18**
See also CA 13-16R; CANR 8; DLBY 84

Seifert, Jaroslav 1901-1986..... **CLC 34, 44**
See also CA 127; MTCW

Sei Shonagon c. 966-1017(?) ...... **CMLC 6**

Selby, Hubert, Jr. 1928- ..... **CLC 1, 2, 4, 8**
See also CA 13-16R; CANR 33; DLB 2

Selzer, Richard 1928-............. **CLC 74**
See also CA 65-68; CANR 14

Sembene, Ousmane
See Ousmane, Sembene

Senancour, Etienne Pivert de
1770-1846 .... **NCLC 16**
See also DLB 119

Sender, Ramon (Jose)
1902-1982 .... **CLC 8; HLC**
See also CA 5-8R; 105; CANR 8; HW;
MTCW

Seneca, Lucius Annaeus
4B.C.-65.................... **CMLC 6**

Senghor, Leopold Sedar
1906- .... **CLC 54; BLC**
See also BW 2; CA 116; 125; MTCW

Serling, (Edward) Rod(man)
1924-1975 .... **CLC 30**
See also AITN 1; CA 65-68; 57-60; DLB 26

Serna, Ramon Gomez de la
See Gomez de la Serna, Ramon

Serpieres
See Guillevic, (Eugene)

Service, Robert
See Service, Robert W(illiam)
See also DLB 92

Service, Robert W(illiam)
1874(?)-1958 ...... **TCLC 15; DA; WLC**
See also Service, Robert
See also CA 115; 140; SATA 20

Seth, Vikram 1952-............... **CLC 43**
See also CA 121; 127; DLB 120

Seton, Cynthia Propper
1926-1982 .... **CLC 27**
See also CA 5-8R; 108; CANR 7

Seton, Ernest (Evan) Thompson
1860-1946 .... **TCLC 31**
See also CA 109; DLB 92; JRDA; SATA 18

Seton-Thompson, Ernest
See Seton, Ernest (Evan) Thompson

Settle, Mary Lee 1918- .... **CLC 19, 61**
See also CA 89-92; CAAS 1; CANR 44;
DLB 6

Seuphor, Michel
See Arp, Jean

Sevigne, Marie (de Rabutin-Chantal) Marquise
de 1626-1696 .... **LC 11**

Sexton, Anne (Harvey)
1928-1974 .... **CLC 2, 4, 6, 8, 10, 15, 53;
DA; PC 2; WLC**
See also CA 1-4R; 53-56; CABS 2;
CANR 3, 36; CDALB 1941-1968; DLB 5;
MTCW; SATA 10

Shaara, Michael (Joseph Jr.)
1929-1988 .... **CLC 15**
See also AITN 1; CA 102; DLBY 83

Shackleton, C. C.
See Aldiss, Brian W(ilson)

Shacochis, Bob .... **CLC 39**
See also Shacochis, Robert G.

Shacochis, Robert G. 1951-
See Shacochis, Bob
See also CA 119; 124

Shaffer, Anthony (Joshua) 1926-.... **CLC 19**
See also CA 110; 116; DLB 13

Shaffer, Peter (Levin)
1926- .... **CLC 5, 14, 18, 37, 60**
See also CA 25-28R; CANR 25;
CDBLB 1960 to Present; DLB 13;
MTCW

Shakey, Bernard
See Young, Neil

Shalamov, Varlam (Tikhonovich)
1907(?)-1982 .... **CLC 18**
See also CA 129; 105

Shamlu, Ahmad 1925- .... **CLC 10**

Shammas, Anton 1951-........... **CLC 55**

Shange, Ntozake
1948- .... **CLC 8, 25, 38, 74; BLC; DC 3**
See also AAYA 9; BW 2; CA 85-88;
CABS 3; CANR 27; DLB 38; MTCW

Shanley, John Patrick 1950-....... **CLC 75**
See also CA 128; 133

Shapcott, Thomas William 1935- ... **CLC 38**
See also CA 69-72

Shapiro, Jane.................... **CLC 76**

Shapiro, Karl (Jay) 1913- .. **CLC 4, 8, 15, 53**
See also CA 1-4R; CAAS 6; CANR 1, 36;
DLB 48; MTCW

Sharp, William 1855-1905 .... **TCLC 39**

Sharpe, Thomas Ridley 1928-
See Sharpe, Tom
See also CA 114; 122

Sharpe, Tom.................... **CLC 36**
See also Sharpe, Thomas Ridley
See also DLB 14

Shaw, Bernard.................... **TCLC 45**
See also Shaw, George Bernard
See also BW 1

Shaw, G. Bernard
See Shaw, George Bernard

Shaw, George Bernard
1856-1950 .... **TCLC 3, 9, 21; DA; WLC**
See also Shaw, Bernard
See also CA 104; 128; CDBLB 1914-1945;
DLB 10, 57; MTCW

Shaw, Henry Wheeler
1818-1885 .... **NCLC 15**
See also DLB 11

Shaw, Irwin 1913-1984....... **CLC 7, 23, 34**
See also AITN 1; CA 13-16R; 112;
CANR 21; CDALB 1941-1968; DLB 6,
102; DLBY 84; MTCW

Shaw, Robert 1927-1978 .... **CLC 5**
See also AITN 1; CA 1-4R; 81-84;
CANR 4; DLB 13, 14

Shaw, T. E.
See Lawrence, T(homas) E(dward)

Shawn, Wallace 1943- .... **CLC 41**
See also CA 112

Sheed, Wilfrid (John Joseph)
1930- .... **CLC 2, 4, 10, 53**
See also CA 65-68; CANR 30; DLB 6;
MTCW

Sheldon, Alice Hastings Bradley
1915(?)-1987
See Tiptree, James, Jr.
See also CA 108; 122; CANR 34; MTCW

Sheldon, John
See Bloch, Robert (Albert)

Shelley, Mary Wollstonecraft (Godwin)
1797-1851 .... **NCLC 14; DA; WLC**
See also CDBLB 1789-1832; DLB 110, 116;
SATA 29

Shelley, Percy Bysshe
1792-1822 .... **NCLC 18; DA; WLC**
See also CDBLB 1789-1832; DLB 96, 110

Author Index

Shepard, Jim 1956-.............. CLC 36
See also CA 137

Shepard, Lucius 1947-............ CLC 34
See also CA 128; 141

Shepard, Sam
1943-......... CLC 4, 6, 17, 34, 41, 44
See also AAYA 1; CA 69-72; CABS 3;
CANR 22; DLB 7; MTCW

Shepherd, Michael
See Ludlum, Robert

Sherburne, Zoa (Morin) 1912-...... CLC 30
See also CA 1-4R; CANR 3, 37; MAICYA;
SAAS 18; SATA 3

Sheridan, Frances 1724-1766........ LC 7
See also DLB 39, 84

Sheridan, Richard Brinsley
1751-1816 ... NCLC 5; DA; DC 1; WLC
See also CDBLB 1660-1789; DLB 89

Sherman, Jonathan Marc.......... CLC 55

Sherman, Martin 1941(?)-......... CLC 19
See also CA 116; 123

Sherwin, Judith Johnson 1936-... CLC 7, 15
See also CA 25-28R; CANR 34

Sherwood, Frances 1940-......... CLC 81

Sherwood, Robert E(mmet)
1896-1955 .... TCLC 3
See also CA 104; DLB 7, 26

Shestov, Lev 1866-1938 .... TCLC 56

Shiel, M(atthew) P(hipps)
1865-1947 .... TCLC 8
See also CA 106

Shiga, Naoya 1883-1971........... CLC 33
See also CA 101; 33-36R

Shilts, Randy 1951-1994 .... CLC 85
See also CA 115; 127; 144; CANR 45

Shimazaki Haruki 1872-1943
See Shimazaki Toson
See also CA 105; 134

Shimazaki Toson................. TCLC 5
See also Shimazaki Haruki

Sholokhov, Mikhail (Aleksandrovich)
1905-1984 .... CLC 7, 15
See also CA 101; 112; MTCW; SATA 36

Shone, Patric
See Hanley, James

Shreve, Susan Richards 1939-...... CLC 23
See also CA 49-52; CAAS 5; CANR 5, 38;
MAICYA; SATA 41, 46

Shue, Larry 1946-1985............ CLC 52
See also CA 145; 117

Shu-Jen, Chou 1881-1936
See Hsun, Lu
See also CA 104

Shulman, Alix Kates 1932-...... CLC 2, 10
See also CA 29-32R; CANR 43; SATA 7

Shuster, Joe 1914-.............. CLC 21

Shute, Nevil.................... CLC 30
See also Norway, Nevil Shute

Shuttle, Penelope (Diane) 1947-..... CLC 7
See also CA 93-96; CANR 39; DLB 14, 40

Sidney, Mary 1561-1621 .... LC 19

Sidney, Sir Philip 1554-1586.... LC 19; DA
See also CDBLB Before 1660

Siegel, Jerome 1914- .... CLC 21
See also CA 116

Siegel, Jerry
See Siegel, Jerome

Sienkiewicz, Henryk (Adam Alexander Pius)
1846-1916 .... TCLC 3
See also CA 104; 134

Sierra, Gregorio Martinez
See Martinez Sierra, Gregorio

Sierra, Maria (de la O'LeJarraga) Martinez
See Martinez Sierra, Maria (de la
O'LeJarraga)

Sigal, Clancy 1926-............... CLC 7
See also CA 1-4R

Sigourney, Lydia Howard (Huntley)
1791-1865 .... NCLC 21
See also DLB 1, 42, 73

Siguenza y Gongora, Carlos de
1645-1700 .... LC 8

Sigurjonsson, Johann 1880-1919... TCLC 27

Sikelianos, Angelos 1884-1951 .... TCLC 39

Silkin, Jon 1930- .... CLC 2, 6, 43
See also CA 5-8R; CAAS 5; DLB 27

Silko, Leslie (Marmon)
1948- .... CLC 23, 74; DA
See also CA 115; 122; CANR 45; DLB 143

Sillanpaa, Frans Eemil 1888-1964... CLC 19
See also CA 129; 93-96; MTCW

Sillitoe, Alan
1928-......... CLC 1, 3, 6, 10, 19, 57
See also AITN 1; CA 9-12R; CAAS 2;
CANR 8, 26; CDBLB 1960 to Present;
DLB 14, 139; MTCW; SATA 61

Silone, Ignazio 1900-1978 .... CLC 4
See also CA 25-28; 81-84; CANR 34;
CAP 2; MTCW

Silver, Joan Micklin 1935- .... CLC 20
See also CA 114; 121

Silver, Nicholas
See Faust, Frederick (Schiller)

Silverberg, Robert 1935- .... CLC 7
See also CA 1-4R; CAAS 3; CANR 1, 20,
36; DLB 8; MAICYA; MTCW; SATA 13

Silverstein, Alvin 1933- .... CLC 17
See also CA 49-52; CANR 2; CLR 25;
JRDA; MAICYA; SATA 8, 69

Silverstein, Virginia B(arbara Opshelor)
1937 .... CLC 17
See also CA 49-52; CANR 2; CLR 25;
JRDA; MAICYA; SATA 8, 69

Sim, Georges
See Simenon, Georges (Jacques Christian)

Simak, Clifford D(onald)
1904-1988 .... CLC 1, 55
See also CA 1-4R; 125; CANR 1, 35;
DLB 8; MTCW; SATA 56

Simenon, Georges (Jacques Christian)
1903-1989 .... CLC 1, 2, 3, 8, 18, 47
See also CA 85-88; 129; CANR 35;
DLB 72; DLBY 89; MTCW

Simic, Charles 1938-... CLC 6, 9, 22, 49, 68
See also CA 29-32R; CAAS 4; CANR 12,
33; DLB 105

Simmons, Charles (Paul) 1924-..... CLC 57
See also CA 89-92

Simmons, Dan 1948-.............. CLC 44
See also CA 138

Simmons, James (Stewart Alexander)
1933-...................... CLC 43
See also CA 105; DLB 40

Simms, William Gilmore
1806-1870 .... NCLC 3
See also DLB 3, 30, 59, 73

Simon, Carly 1945-.............. CLC 26
See also CA 105

Simon, Claude 1913-....... CLC 4, 9, 15, 39
See also CA 89-92; CANR 33; DLB 83;
MTCW

Simon, (Marvin) Neil
1927-........... CLC 6, 11, 31, 39, 70
See also AITN 1; CA 21-24R; CANR 26;
DLB 7; MTCW

Simon, Paul 1942(?)-............. CLC 17
See also CA 116

Simonon, Paul 1956(?)- .... CLC 30

Simpson, Harriette
See Arnow, Harriette (Louisa) Simpson

Simpson, Louis (Aston Marantz)
1923-................CLC 4, 7, 9, 32
See also CA 1-4R; CAAS 4; CANR 1;
DLB 5; MTCW

Simpson, Mona (Elizabeth) 1957-... CLC 44
See also CA 122; 135

Simpson, N(orman) F(rederick)
1919-...................... CLC 29
See also CA 13-16R; DLB 13

Sinclair, Andrew (Annandale)
1935-...................... CLC 2, 14
See also CA 9-12R; CAAS 5; CANR 14, 38;
DLB 14; MTCW

Sinclair, Emil
See Hesse, Hermann

Sinclair, Iain 1943-.............. CLC 76
See also CA 132

Sinclair, Iain MacGregor
See Sinclair, Iain

Sinclair, Mary Amelia St. Clair 1865(?)-1946
See Sinclair, May
See also CA 104

Sinclair, May.................. TCLC 3, 11
See also Sinclair, Mary Amelia St. Clair
See also DLB 36, 135

Sinclair, Upton (Beall)
1878-1968 ...... CLC 1, 11, 15, 63; DA;
WLC
See also CA 5-8R; 25-28R; CANR 7;
CDALB 1929-1941; DLB 9; MTCW;
SATA 9

Singer, Isaac
See Singer, Isaac Bashevis

Singer, Isaac Bashevis
1904-1991 .... CLC 1, 3, 6, 9, 11, 15, 23,
38, 69; DA; SSC 3; WLC
See also AITN 1, 2; CA 1-4R; 134;
CANR 1, 39; CDALB 1941-1968; CLR 1;
DLB 6, 28, 52; DLBY 91; JRDA;
MAICYA; MTCW; SATA 3, 27;
SATA-Obit 68

Sterne, Laurence
1713-1768 . . . . **LC 2; DA; WLC**
See also CDBLB 1660-1789; DLB 39

Sternheim, (William Adolf) Carl
1878-1942 . . . . **TCLC 8**
See also CA 105; DLB 56, 118

Stevens, Mark 1951- . . . . **CLC 34**
See also CA 122

Stevens, Wallace
1879-1955 . . . . **TCLC 3, 12, 45; DA;
PC 6; WLC**
See also CA 104; 124; CDALB 1929-1941;
DLB 54; MTCW

Stevenson, Anne (Katharine)
1933- . . . . **CLC 7, 33**
See also CA 17-20R; CAAS 9; CANR 9, 33;
DLB 40; MTCW

Stevenson, Robert Louis (Balfour)
1850-1894 . . . . **NCLC 5, 14; DA;
SSC 11; WLC**
See also CDBLB 1890-1914; CLR 10, 11;
DLB 18, 57, 141; JRDA; MAICYA;
YABC 2

Stewart, J(ohn) I(nnes) M(ackintosh)
1906- . . . . **CLC 7, 14, 32**
See also CA 85-88; CAAS 3; MTCW

Stewart, Mary (Florence Elinor)
1916- . . . . **CLC 7, 35**
See also CA 1-4R; CANR 1; SATA 12

Stewart, Mary Rainbow
See Stewart, Mary (Florence Elinor)

Stifle, June
See Campbell, Maria

Stifter, Adalbert 1805-1868 . . . . . . **NCLC 41**
See also DLB 133

Still, James 1906- . . . . **CLC 49**
See also CA 65-68; CAAS 17; CANR 10,
26; DLB 9; SATA 29

Sting
See Sumner, Gordon Matthew

Stirling, Arthur
See Sinclair, Upton (Beall)

Stitt, Milan 1941- . . . . **CLC 29**
See also CA 69-72

Stockton, Francis Richard 1834-1902
See Stockton, Frank R.
See also CA 108; 137; MAICYA; SATA 44

Stockton, Frank R. . . . . **TCLC 47**
See also Stockton, Francis Richard
See also DLB 42, 74; SATA 32

Stoddard, Charles
See Kuttner, Henry

Stoker, Abraham 1847-1912
See Stoker, Bram
See also CA 105; DA; SATA 29

Stoker, Bram . . . . **TCLC 8; WLC**
See also Stoker, Abraham
See also CDBLB 1890-1914; DLB 36, 70

Stolz, Mary (Slattery) 1920- . . . . **CLC 12**
See also AAYA 8; AITN 1; CA 5-8R;
CANR 13, 41; JRDA; MAICYA;
SAAS 3; SATA 10, 71

Stone, Irving 1903-1989 . . . . **CLC 7**
See also AITN 1; CA 1-4R; 129; CAAS 3;
CANR 1, 23; MTCW; SATA 3;
SATA-Obit 64

Stone, Oliver 1946- . . . . **CLC 73**
See also CA 110

Stone, Robert (Anthony)
1937- . . . . **CLC 5, 23, 42**
See also CA 85-88; CANR 23; MTCW

Stone, Zachary
See Follett, Ken(neth Martin)

Stoppard, Tom
1937- . . . . . . **CLC 1, 3, 4, 5, 8, 15, 29, 34,
63; DA; WLC**
See also CA 81-84; CANR 39;
CDBLB 1960 to Present; DLB 13;
DLBY 85; MTCW

Storey, David (Malcolm)
1933- . . . . **CLC 2, 4, 5, 8**
See also CA 81-84; CANR 36; DLB 13, 14;
MTCW

Storm, Hyemeyohsts 1935- . . . . **CLC 3**
See also CA 81-84; CANR 45

Storm, (Hans) Theodor (Woldsen)
1817-1888 . . . . **NCLC 1**

Storni, Alfonsina
1892-1938 . . . . **TCLC 5; HLC**
See also CA 104; 131; HW

Stout, Rex (Todhunter) 1886-1975 . . . **CLC 3**
See also AITN 2; CA 61-64

Stow, (Julian) Randolph 1935- . . **CLC 23, 48**
See also CA 13-16R; CANR 33; MTCW

Stowe, Harriet (Elizabeth) Beecher
1811-1896 . . . . **NCLC 3; DA; WLC**
See also CDALB 1865-1917; DLB 1, 12, 42,
74; JRDA; MAICYA; YABC 1

Strachey, (Giles) Lytton
1880-1932 . . . . **TCLC 12**
See also CA 110; DLBD 10

Strand, Mark 1934- . . . . . . **CLC 6, 18, 41, 71**
See also CA 21-24R; CANR 40; DLB 5;
SATA 41

Straub, Peter (Francis) 1943- . . . . . . **CLC 28**
See also BEST 89:1; CA 85-88; CANR 28;
DLBY 84; MTCW

Strauss, Botho 1944- . . . . **CLC 22**
See also DLB 124

Streatfeild, (Mary) Noel
1895(?)-1986 . . . . **CLC 21**
See also CA 81-84; 120; CANR 31;
CLR 17; MAICYA; SATA 20, 48

Stribling, T(homas) S(igismund)
1881-1965 . . . . **CLC 23**
See also CA 107; DLB 9

Strindberg, (Johan) August
1849-1912 . . . . . . **TCLC 1, 8, 21, 47; DA;
WLC**
See also CA 104; 135

Stringer, Arthur 1874-1950 . . . . . . **TCLC 37**
See also DLB 92

Stringer, David
See Roberts, Keith (John Kingston)

Strugatskii, Arkadii (Natanovich)
1925-1991 . . . . **CLC 27**
See also CA 106; 135

Strugatskii, Boris (Natanovich)
1933- . . . . **CLC 27**
See also CA 106

Strummer, Joe 1953(?)- . . . . **CLC 30**

Stuart, Don A.
See Campbell, John W(ood, Jr.)

Stuart, Ian
See MacLean, Alistair (Stuart)

Stuart, Jesse (Hilton)
1906-1984 . . . . **CLC 1, 8, 11, 14, 34**
See also CA 5-8R; 112; CANR 31; DLB 9,
48, 102; DLBY 84; SATA 2, 36

Sturgeon, Theodore (Hamilton)
1918-1985 . . . . **CLC 22, 39**
See also Queen, Ellery
See also CA 81-84; 116; CANR 32; DLB 8;
DLBY 85; MTCW

Sturges, Preston 1898-1959 . . . . **TCLC 48**
See also CA 114; DLB 26

Styron, William
1925- . . . . **CLC 1, 3, 5, 11, 15, 60**
See also BEST 90:4; CA 5-8R; CANR 6, 33;
CDALB 1968-1988; DLB 2, 143;
DLBY 80; MTCW

Suarez Lynch, B.
See Bioy Casares, Adolfo; Borges, Jorge
Luis

Su Chien 1884-1918
See Su Man-shu
See also CA 123

Sudermann, Hermann 1857-1928 . . **TCLC 15**
See also CA 107; DLB 118

Sue, Eugene 1804-1857 . . . . **NCLC 1**
See also DLB 119

Sueskind, Patrick 1949- . . . . **CLC 44**
See also Suskind, Patrick

Sukenick, Ronald 1932- . . . . . **CLC 3, 4, 6, 48**
See also CA 25-28R; CAAS 8; CANR 32;
DLBY 81

Suknaski, Andrew 1942- . . . . **CLC 19**
See also CA 101; DLB 53

Sullivan, Vernon
See Vian, Boris

Sully Prudhomme 1839-1907 . . . . . . **TCLC 31**

Su Man-shu . . . . **TCLC 24**
See also Su Chien

Summerforest, Ivy B.
See Kirkup, James

Summers, Andrew James 1942- . . . . . **CLC 26**

Summers, Andy
See Summers, Andrew James

Summers, Hollis (Spurgeon, Jr.)
1916- . . . . **CLC 10**
See also CA 5-8R; CANR 3; DLB 6

Summers, (Alphonsus Joseph-Mary Augustus)
Montague 1880-1948 . . . . **TCLC 16**
See also CA 118

Sumner, Gordon Matthew 1951- . . . **CLC 26**

Surtees, Robert Smith
1803-1864 . . . . **NCLC 14**
See also DLB 21

Susann, Jacqueline 1921-1974 . . . . . . **CLC 3**
See also AITN 1; CA 65-68; 53-56; MTCW

Suskind, Patrick
See Sueskind, Patrick
See also CA 145

Sutcliff, Rosemary 1920-1992 ...... **CLC 26**
See also AAYA 10; CA 5-8R; 139;
CANR 37; CLR 1; JRDA; MAICYA;
SATA 6, 44, 78; SATA-Obit 73

Sutro, Alfred 1863-1933.......... **TCLC 6**
See also CA 105; DLB 10

Sutton, Henry
See Slavitt, David R(ytman)

Svevo, Italo .... **TCLC 2, 35**
See also Schmitz, Aron Hector

Swados, Elizabeth 1951- .... **CLC 12**
See also CA 97-100

Swados, Harvey 1920-1972 .... **CLC 5**
See also CA 5-8R; 37-40R; CANR 6;
DLB 2

Swan, Gladys 1934- .... **CLC 69**
See also CA 101; CANR 17, 39

Swarthout, Glendon (Fred)
1918-1992 .... **CLC 35**
See also CA 1-4R; 139; CANR 1; SATA 26

Sweet, Sarah C.
See Jewett, (Theodora) Sarah Orne

Swenson, May
1919-1989 .... **CLC 4, 14, 61; DA**
See also CA 5-8R; 130; CANR 36; DLB 5;
MTCW; SATA 15

Swift, Augustus
See Lovecraft, H(oward) P(hillips)

Swift, Graham 1949- .... **CLC 41**
See also CA 117; 122

Swift, Jonathan
1667-1745 ...... **LC 1; DA; PC 9; WLC**
See also CDBLB 1660-1789; DLB 39, 95,
101; SATA 19

Swinburne, Algernon Charles
1837-1909 ...... **TCLC 8, 36; DA; WLC**
See also CA 105; 140; CDBLB 1832-1890;
DLB 35, 57

Swinfen, Ann .... **CLC 34**

Swinnerton, Frank Arthur
1884-1982 .... **CLC 31**
See also CA 108; DLB 34

Swithen, John
See King, Stephen (Edwin)

Sylvia
See Ashton-Warner, Sylvia (Constance)

Symmes, Robert Edward
See Duncan, Robert (Edward)

Symonds, John Addington
1840-1893 .... **NCLC 34**
See also DLB 57, 144

Symons, Arthur 1865-1945 .... **TCLC 11**
See also CA 107; DLB 19, 57

Symons, Julian (Gustave)
1912- .... **CLC 2, 14, 32**
See also CA 49-52; CAAS 3; CANR 3, 33;
DLB 87; DLBY 92; MTCW

Synge, (Edmund) J(ohn) M(illington)
1871-1909 .... **TCLC 6, 37; DC 2**
See also CA 104; 141; CDBLB 1890-1914;
DLB 10, 19

Syruc, J.
See Milosz, Czeslaw

Szirtes, George 1948-............. **CLC 46**
See also CA 109; CANR 27

Tabori, George 1914-............ **CLC 19**
See also CA 49-52; CANR 4

Tagore, Rabindranath
1861-1941 .... **TCLC 3, 53; PC 8**
See also CA 104; 120; MTCW

Taine, Hippolyte Adolphe
1828-1893 .... **NCLC 15**

Talese, Gay 1932-................ **CLC 37**
See also AITN 1; CA 1-4R; CANR 9;
MTCW

Tallent, Elizabeth (Ann) 1954- ..... **CLC 45**
See also CA 117; DLB 130

Tally, Ted 1952-................ **CLC 42**
See also CA 120; 124

Tamayo y Baus, Manuel
1829-1898 .... **NCLC 1**

Tammsaare, A(nton) H(ansen)
1878-1940 .... **TCLC 27**

Tan, Amy 1952- .... **CLC 59**
See also AAYA 9; BEST 89:3; CA 136;
SATA 75

Tandem, Felix
See Spitteler, Carl (Friedrich Georg)

Tanizaki, Jun'ichiro
1886-1965 .... **CLC 8, 14, 28**
See also CA 93-96; 25-28R

Tanner, William
See Amis, Kingsley (William)

Tao Lao
See Storni, Alfonsina

Tarassoff, Lev
See Troyat, Henri

Tarbell, Ida M(inerva)
1857-1944 .... **TCLC 40**
See also CA 122; DLB 47

Tarkington, (Newton) Booth
1869-1946 .... **TCLC 9**
See also CA 110; 143; DLB 9, 102;
SATA 17

Tarkovsky, Andrei (Arsenyevich)
1932-1986 .... **CLC 75**
See also CA 127

Tartt, Donna 1964(?)-............. **CLC 76**
See also CA 142

Tasso, Torquato 1544-1595 .... **LC 5**

Tate, (John Orley) Allen
1899-1979 .... **CLC 2, 4, 6, 9, 11, 14, 24**
See also CA 5-8R; 85-88; CANR 32;
DLB 4, 45, 63; MTCW

Tate, Ellalice
See Hibbert, Eleanor Alice Burford

Tate, James (Vincent) 1943- ... **CLC 2, 6, 25**
See also CA 21-24R; CANR 29; DLB 5

Tavel, Ronald 1940-.............. **CLC 6**
See also CA 21-24R; CANR 33

Taylor, Cecil Philip 1929-1981 ..... **CLC 27**
See also CA 25-28R; 105

Taylor, Edward 1642(?)-1729.... **LC 11; DA**
See also DLB 24

Taylor, Eleanor Ross 1920-........ **CLC 5**
See also CA 81-84

Taylor, Elizabeth 1912-1975 ... **CLC 2, 4, 29**
See also CA 13-16R; CANR 9; DLB 139;
MTCW; SATA 13

Taylor, Henry (Splawn) 1942-...... **CLC 44**
See also CA 33-36R; CAAS 7; CANR 31;
DLB 5

Taylor, Kamala (Purnaiya) 1924-
See Markandaya, Kamala
See also CA 77-80

Taylor, Mildred D. .... **CLC 21**
See also AAYA 10; BW 1; CA 85-88;
CANR 25; CLR 9; DLB 52; JRDA;
MAICYA; SAAS 5; SATA 15, 70

Taylor, Peter (Hillsman)
1917- ...... **CLC 1, 4, 18, 37, 44, 50, 71;
SSC 10**
See also CA 13-16R; CANR 9; DLBY 81;
MTCW

Taylor, Robert Lewis 1912-........ **CLC 14**
See also CA 1-4R; CANR 3; SATA 10

Tchekhov, Anton
See Chekhov, Anton (Pavlovich)

Teasdale, Sara 1884-1933......... **TCLC 4**
See also CA 104; DLB 45; SATA 32

Tegner, Esaias 1782-1846........ **NCLC 2**

Teilhard de Chardin, (Marie Joseph) Pierre
1881-1955 .... **TCLC 9**
See also CA 105

Temple, Ann
See Mortimer, Penelope (Ruth)

Tennant, Emma (Christina)
1937- .... **CLC 13, 52**
See also CA 65-68; CAAS 9; CANR 10, 38;
DLB 14

Tenneshaw, S. M.
See Silverberg, Robert

Tennyson, Alfred
1809-1892 .. **NCLC 30; DA; PC 6; WLC**
See also CDBLB 1832-1890; DLB 32

Teran, Lisa St. Aubin de .... **CLC 36**
See also St. Aubin de Teran, Lisa

Terence 195(?)B.C.-159B.C....... **CMLC 14**

Teresa de Jesus, St. 1515-1582...... **LC 18**

Terkel, Louis 1912-
See Terkel, Studs
See also CA 57-60; CANR 18, 45; MTCW

Terkel, Studs .... **CLC 38**
See also Terkel, Louis
See also AITN 1

Terry, C. V.
See Slaughter, Frank G(ill)

Terry, Megan 1932-.............. **CLC 19**
See also CA 77-80; CABS 3; CANR 43;
DLB 7

Tertz, Abram
See Sinyavsky, Andrei (Donatevich)

Tesich, Steve 1943(?)-.......... **CLC 40, 69**
See also CA 105; DLBY 83

Teternikov, Fyodor Kuzmich 1863-1927
See Sologub, Fyodor
See also CA 104

Tevis, Walter 1928-1984 . . . . **CLC 42**
See also CA 113

Tey, Josephine . . . . **TCLC 14**
See also Mackintosh, Elizabeth
See also DLB 77

Thackeray, William Makepeace
1811-1863 . . . . **NCLC 5, 14, 22, 43; DA;**
                                                    WLC
See also CDBLB 1832-1890; DLB 21, 55;
    SATA 23

Thakura, Ravindranatha
See Tagore, Rabindranath

Tharoor, Shashi 1956- . . . . **CLC 70**
See also CA 141

Thelwell, Michael Miles 1939- . . . . . **CLC 22**
See also BW 2; CA 101

Theobald, Lewis, Jr.
See Lovecraft, H(oward) P(hillips)

Theodorescu, Ion N. 1880-1967
See Arghezi, Tudor
See also CA 116

Theriault, Yves 1915-1983 . . . . **CLC 79**
See also CA 102; DLB 88

Theroux, Alexander (Louis)
1939- . . . . **CLC 2, 25**
See also CA 85-88; CANR 20

Theroux, Paul (Edward)
1941- . . . . **CLC 5, 8, 11, 15, 28, 46**
See also BEST 89:4; CA 33-36R; CANR 20,
    45; DLB 2; MTCW; SATA 44

Thesen, Sharon 1946- . . . . **CLC 56**

Thevenin, Denis
See Duhamel, Georges

Thibault, Jacques Anatole Francois
1844-1924
See France, Anatole
See also CA 106; 127; MTCW

Thiele, Colin (Milton) 1920- . . . . **CLC 17**
See also CA 29-32R; CANR 12, 28;
    CLR 27; MAICYA; SAAS 2; SATA 14,
    72

Thomas, Audrey (Callahan)
1935- . . . . **CLC 7, 13, 37**
See also AITN 2; CA 21-24R; CAAS 19;
    CANR 36; DLB 60; MTCW

Thomas, D(onald) M(ichael)
1935- . . . . **CLC 13, 22, 31**
See also CA 61-64; CAAS 11; CANR 17,
    45; CDBLB 1960 to Present; DLB 40;
    MTCW

Thomas, Dylan (Marlais)
1914-1953 . . . **TCLC 1, 8, 45; DA; PC 2;**
                                                    SSC 3; WLC
See also CA 104; 120; CDBLB 1945-1960;
    DLB 13, 20, 139; MTCW; SATA 60

Thomas, (Philip) Edward
1878-1917 . . . . **TCLC 10**
See also CA 106; DLB 19

Thomas, Joyce Carol 1938- . . . . **CLC 35**
See also AAYA 12; BW 2; CA 113; 116;
    CLR 19; DLB 33; JRDA; MAICYA;
    MTCW; SAAS 7; SATA 40, 78

Thomas, Lewis 1913-1993 . . . . **CLC 35**
See also CA 85-88; 143; CANR 38; MTCW

Thomas, Paul
See Mann, (Paul) Thomas

Thomas, Piri 1928- . . . . **CLC 17**
See also CA 73-76; HW

Thomas, R(onald) S(tuart)
1913- . . . . **CLC 6, 13, 48**
See also CA 89-92; CAAS 4; CANR 30;
    CDBLB 1960 to Present; DLB 27;
    MTCW

Thomas, Ross (Elmore) 1926- . . . . . . **CLC 39**
See also CA 33-36R; CANR 22

Thompson, Francis Clegg
See Mencken, H(enry) L(ouis)

Thompson, Francis Joseph
1859-1907 . . . . **TCLC 4**
See also CA 104; CDBLB 1890-1914;
    DLB 19

Thompson, Hunter S(tockton)
1939- . . . . **CLC 9, 17, 40**
See also BEST 89:1; CA 17-20R; CANR 23;
    MTCW

Thompson, James Myers
See Thompson, Jim (Myers)

Thompson, Jim (Myers)
1906-1977(?) . . . . **CLC 69**
See also CA 140

Thompson, Judith . . . . **CLC 39**

Thomson, James 1700-1748 . . . . **LC 16**

Thomson, James 1834-1882 . . . . . **NCLC 18**

Thoreau, Henry David
1817-1862 . . . . . . **NCLC 7, 21; DA; WLC**
See also CDALB 1640-1865; DLB 1

Thornton, Hall
See Silverberg, Robert

Thurber, James (Grover)
1894-1961 . . . **CLC 5, 11, 25; DA; SSC 1**
See also CA 73-76; CANR 17, 39;
    CDALB 1929-1941; DLB 4, 11, 22, 102;
    MAICYA; MTCW; SATA 13

Thurman, Wallace (Henry)
1902-1934 . . . . **TCLC 6; BLC**
See also BW 1; CA 104; 124; DLB 51

Ticheburn, Cheviot
See Ainsworth, William Harrison

Tieck, (Johann) Ludwig
1773-1853 . . . . **NCLC 5, 46**
See also DLB 90

Tiger, Derry
See Ellison, Harlan

Tilghman, Christopher 1948(?)- . . . . . **CLC 65**

Tillinghast, Richard (Williford)
1940- . . . . **CLC 29**
See also CA 29-32R; CANR 26

Timrod, Henry 1828-1867 . . . . **NCLC 25**
See also DLB 3

Tindall, Gillian 1938- . . . . **CLC 7**
See also CA 21-24R; CANR 11

Tiptree, James, Jr. . . . . **CLC 48, 50**
See also Sheldon, Alice Hastings Bradley
See also DLB 8

Titmarsh, Michael Angelo
See Thackeray, William Makepeace

**Tocqueville, Alexis (Charles Henri Maurice
    Clerel Comte)** 1805-1859 . . . . . **NCLC 7**

Tolkien, J(ohn) R(onald) R(euel)
1892-1973 . . . . **CLC 1, 2, 3, 8, 12, 38;**
                                                    DA; WLC
See also AAYA 10; AITN 1; CA 17-18;
    45-48; CANR 36; CAP 2;
    CDBLB 1914-1945; DLB 15; JRDA;
    MAICYA; MTCW; SATA 2, 24, 32

Toller, Ernst 1893-1939 . . . . **TCLC 10**
See also CA 107; DLB 124

Tolson, M. B.
See Tolson, Melvin B(eaunorus)

Tolson, Melvin B(eaunorus)
1898(?)-1966 . . . . **CLC 36; BLC**
See also BW 1; CA 124; 89-92; DLB 48, 76

Tolstoi, Aleksei Nikolaevich
See Tolstoy, Alexey Nikolaevich

Tolstoy, Alexey Nikolaevich
1882-1945 . . . . **TCLC 18**
See also CA 107

Tolstoy, Count Leo
See Tolstoy, Leo (Nikolaevich)

Tolstoy, Leo (Nikolaevich)
1828-1910 . . . . . . **TCLC 4, 11, 17, 28, 44;**
                                                    DA; SSC 9; WLC
See also CA 104; 123; SATA 26

Tomasi di Lampedusa, Giuseppe 1896-1957
See Lampedusa, Giuseppe (Tomasi) di
See also CA 111

Tomlin, Lily . . . . **CLC 17**
See also Tomlin, Mary Jean

Tomlin, Mary Jean 1939(?)-
See Tomlin, Lily
See also CA 117

Tomlinson, (Alfred) Charles
1927- . . . . **CLC 2, 4, 6, 13, 45**
See also CA 5-8R; CANR 33; DLB 40

Tonson, Jacob
See Bennett, (Enoch) Arnold

Toole, John Kennedy
1937-1969 . . . . **CLC 19, 64**
See also CA 104; DLBY 81

Toomer, Jean
1894-1967 . . . . . . **CLC 1, 4, 13, 22; BLC;**
                                                    PC 7; SSC 1
See also BW 1; CA 85-88;
    CDALB 1917-1929; DLB 45, 51; MTCW

Torley, Luke
See Blish, James (Benjamin)

Tornimparte, Alessandra
See Ginzburg, Natalia

Torre, Raoul della
See Mencken, H(enry) L(ouis)

Torrey, E(dwin) Fuller 1937- . . . . **CLC 34**
See also CA 119

Torsvan, Ben Traven
See Traven, B.

Torsvan, Benno Traven
See Traven, B.

Torsvan, Berick Traven
See Traven, B.

Torsvan, Berwick Traven
See Traven, B.

Torsvan, Bruno Traven
See Traven, B.

Torsvan, Traven
See Traven, B.

Tournier, Michel (Edouard)
1924- .... CLC 6, 23, 36
See also CA 49-52; CANR 3, 36; DLB 83; MTCW; SATA 23

Tournimparte, Alessandra
See Ginzburg, Natalia

Towers, Ivar
See Kornbluth, C(yril) M.

Townsend, Sue 1946- .... CLC 61
See also CA 119; 127; MTCW; SATA 48, 55

Townshend, Peter (Dennis Blandford)
1945- .... CLC 17, 42
See also CA 107

Tozzi, Federigo 1883-1920....... TCLC 31

Traill, Catharine Parr
1802-1899 .... NCLC 31
See also DLB 99

Trakl, Georg 1887-1914.......... TCLC 5
See also CA 104

Transtroemer, Tomas (Goesta)
1931- .... CLC 52, 65
See also CA 117; 129; CAAS 17

Transtromer, Tomas Gosta
See Transtroemer, Tomas (Goesta)

Traven, B. (?)-1969............. CLC 8, 11
See also CA 19-20; 25-28R; CAP 2; DLB 9, 56; MTCW

Treitel, Jonathan 1959- .... CLC 70

Tremain, Rose 1943-.............. CLC 42
See also CA 97-100; CANR 44; DLB 14

Tremblay, Michel 1942-........... CLC 29
See also CA 116; 128; DLB 60; MTCW

Trevanian...................... CLC 29
See also Whitaker, Rod(ney)

Trevor, Glen
See Hilton, James

Trevor, William
1928- .... CLC 7, 9, 14, 25, 71
See also Cox, William Trevor
See also DLB 14, 139

Trifonov, Yuri (Valentinovich)
1925-1981 .... CLC 45
See also CA 126; 103; MTCW

Trilling, Lionel 1905-1975 .... CLC 9, 11, 24
See also CA 9-12R; 61-64; CANR 10; DLB 28, 63; MTCW

Trimball, W. H.
See Mencken, H(enry) L(ouis)

Tristan
See Gomez de la Serna, Ramon

Tristram
See Housman, A(lfred) E(dward)

Trogdon, William (Lewis) 1939-
See Heat-Moon, William Least
See also CA 115; 119

Trollope, Anthony
1815-1882 ...... NCLC 6, 33; DA; WLC
See also CDBLB 1832-1890; DLB 21, 57; SATA 22

Trollope, Frances 1779-1863 ..... NCLC 30
See also DLB 21

Trotsky, Leon 1879-1940........ TCLC 22
See also CA 118

Trotter (Cockburn), Catharine
1679-1749 .... LC 8
See also DLB 84

Trout, Kilgore
See Farmer, Philip Jose

Trow, George W. S. 1943-........ CLC 52
See also CA 126

Troyat, Henri 1911-.............. CLC 23
See also CA 45-48; CANR 2, 33; MTCW

Trudeau, G(arretson) B(eekman) 1948-
See Trudeau, Garry B.
See also CA 81-84; CANR 31; SATA 35

Trudeau, Garry B.................. CLC 12
See also Trudeau, G(arretson) B(eekman)
See also AAYA 10; AITN 2

Truffaut, Francois 1932-1984....... CLC 20
See also CA 81-84; 113; CANR 34

Trumbo, Dalton 1905-1976 .... CLC 19
See also CA 21-24R; 69-72; CANR 10; DLB 26

Trumbull, John 1750-1831....... NCLC 30
See also DLB 31

Trundlett, Helen B.
See Eliot, T(homas) S(tearns)

Tryon, Thomas 1926-1991 ...... CLC 3, 11
See also AITN 1; CA 29-32R; 135; CANR 32; MTCW

Tryon, Tom
See Tryon, Thomas

Ts'ao Hsueh-ch'in 1715(?)-1763....... LC 1

Tsushima, Shuji 1909-1948
See Dazai, Osamu
See also CA 107

Tsvetaeva (Efron), Marina (Ivanovna)
1892-1941 .... TCLC 7, 35
See also CA 104; 128; MTCW

Tuck, Lily 1938-................. CLC 70
See also CA 139

Tu Fu 712-770..................... PC 9

Tunis, John R(oberts) 1889-1975 ... CLC 12
See also CA 61-64; DLB 22; JRDA; MAICYA; SATA 30, 37

Tuohy, Frank..................... CLC 37
See also Tuohy, John Francis
See also DLB 14, 139

Tuohy, John Francis 1925-
See Tuohy, Frank
See also CA 5-8R; CANR 3

Turco, Lewis (Putnam) 1934- ... CLC 11, 63
See also CA 13-16R; CANR 24; DLBY 84

Turgenev, Ivan
1818-1883 ...... NCLC 21; DA; SSC 7; WLC

Turgot, Anne-Robert-Jacques
1727-1781 .... LC 26

Turner, Frederick 1943-........... CLC 48
See also CA 73-76; CAAS 10; CANR 12, 30; DLB 40

Tutu, Desmond M(pilo)
1931- .... CLC 80; BLC
See also BW 1; CA 125

Tutuola, Amos 1920- ... CLC 5, 14, 29; BLC
See also BW 2; CA 9-12R; CANR 27; DLB 125; MTCW

Twain, Mark
... TCLC 6, 12, 19, 36, 48; SSC 6; WLC
See also Clemens, Samuel Langhorne
See also DLB 11, 12, 23, 64, 74

Tyler, Anne
1941- .... CLC 7, 11, 18, 28, 44, 59
See also BEST 89:1; CA 9-12R; CANR 11, 33; DLB 6, 143; DLBY 82; MTCW; SATA 7

Tyler, Royall 1757-1826.......... NCLC 3
See also DLB 37

Tynan, Katharine 1861-1931 .... TCLC 3
See also CA 104

Tyutchev, Fyodor 1803-1873..... NCLC 34

Tzara, Tristan .... CLC 47
See also Rosenfeld, Samuel

Uhry, Alfred 1936-................ CLC 55
See also CA 127; 133

Ulf, Haerved
See Strindberg, (Johan) August

Ulf, Harved
See Strindberg, (Johan) August

Ulibarri, Sabine R(eyes) 1919- ..... CLC 83
See also CA 131; DLB 82; HW

Unamuno (y Jugo), Miguel de
1864-1936 .... TCLC 2, 9; HLC; SSC 11
See also CA 104; 131; DLB 108; HW; MTCW

Undercliffe, Errol
See Campbell, (John) Ramsey

Underwood, Miles
See Glassco, John

Undset, Sigrid
1882-1949 .... TCLC 3; DA; WLC
See also CA 104; 129; MTCW

Ungaretti, Giuseppe
1888-1970 .... CLC 7, 11, 15
See also CA 19-20; 25-28R; CAP 2; DLB 114

Unger, Douglas 1952-............. CLC 34
See also CA 130

Unsworth, Barry (Forster) 1930-.... CLC 76
See also CA 25-28R; CANR 30

Updike, John (Hoyer)
1932- ...... CLC 1, 2, 3, 5, 7, 9, 13, 15, 23, 34, 43, 70; DA; SSC 13; WLC
See also CA 1-4R; CABS 1; CANR 4, 33; CDALB 1968-1988; DLB 2, 5, 143; DLBD 3; DLBY 80, 82; MTCW

Upshaw, Margaret Mitchell
See Mitchell, Margaret (Munnerlyn)

Upton, Mark
See Sanders, Lawrence

Urdang, Constance (Henriette)
1922- .... CLC 47
See also CA 21-24R; CANR 9, 24

Uriel, Henry
See Faust, Frederick (Schiller)

Uris, Leon (Marcus) 1924-....... CLC 7, 32
See also AITN 1, 2; BEST 89:2; CA 1-4R; CANR 1, 40; MTCW; SATA 49

Urmuz
See Codrescu, Andrei

Ustinov, Peter (Alexander) 1921- .... **CLC 1**
See also AITN 1; CA 13-16R; CANR 25;
DLB 13

Vaculik, Ludvik 1926- .... **CLC 7**
See also CA 53-56

Valdez, Luis (Miguel)
1940- .... **CLC 84; HLC**
See also CA 101; CANR 32; DLB 122; HW

Valenzuela, Luisa 1938-... **CLC 31; SSC 14**
See also CA 101; CANR 32; DLB 113; HW

Valera y Alcala-Galiano, Juan
1824-1905 .... **TCLC 10**
See also CA 106

Valery, (Ambroise) Paul (Toussaint Jules)
1871-1945 .... **TCLC 4, 15; PC 9**
See also CA 104; 122; MTCW

Valle-Inclan, Ramon (Maria) del
1866-1936 .... **TCLC 5; HLC**
See also CA 106; DLB 134

Vallejo, Antonio Buero
See Buero Vallejo, Antonio

Vallejo, Cesar (Abraham)
1892-1938 .... **TCLC 3, 56; HLC**
See also CA 105; HW

Valle Y Pena, Ramon del
See Valle-Inclan, Ramon (Maria) del

Van Ash, Cay 1918- .... **CLC 34**

Vanbrugh, Sir John 1664-1726 ...... **LC 21**
See also DLB 80

Van Campen, Karl
See Campbell, John W(ood, Jr.)

Vance, Gerald
See Silverberg, Robert

Vance, Jack .... **CLC 35**
See also Vance, John Holbrook
See also DLB 8

Vance, John Holbrook 1916-
See Queen, Ellery; Vance, Jack
See also CA 29-32R; CANR 17; MTCW

Van Den Bogarde, Derek Jules Gaspard Ulric
Niven 1921-
See Bogarde, Dirk
See also CA 77-80

Vandenburgh, Jane .... **CLC 59**

Vanderhaeghe, Guy 1951- .... **CLC 41**
See also CA 113

van der Post, Laurens (Jan) 1906- ... **CLC 5**
See also CA 5-8R; CANR 35

van de Wetering, Janwillem 1931- .. **CLC 47**
See also CA 49-52; CANR 4

Van Dine, S. S. .... **TCLC 23**
See also Wright, Willard Huntington

Van Doren, Carl (Clinton)
1885-1950 .... **TCLC 18**
See also CA 111

Van Doren, Mark 1894-1972..... **CLC 6, 10**
See also CA 1-4R; 37-40R; CANR 3;
DLB 45; MTCW

Van Druten, John (William)
1901-1957 .... **TCLC 2**
See also CA 104; DLB 10

Van Duyn, Mona (Jane)
1921- .... **CLC 3, 7, 63**
See also CA 9-12R; CANR 7, 38; DLB 5

Van Dyne, Edith
See Baum, L(yman) Frank

van Itallie, Jean-Claude 1936-....... **CLC 3**
See also CA 45-48; CAAS 2; CANR 1;
DLB 7

van Ostaijen, Paul 1896-1928 ..... **TCLC 33**

Van Peebles, Melvin 1932- ...... **CLC 2, 20**
See also BW 2; CA 85-88; CANR 27

Vansittart, Peter 1920-............ **CLC 42**
See also CA 1-4R; CANR 3

Van Vechten, Carl 1880-1964 ...... **CLC 33**
See also CA 89-92; DLB 4, 9, 51

Van Vogt, A(lfred) E(lton) 1912-..... **CLC 1**
See also CA 21-24R; CANR 28; DLB 8;
SATA 14

Varda, Agnes 1928- .... **CLC 16**
See also CA 116; 122

Vargas Llosa, (Jorge) Mario (Pedro)
1936- .... **CLC 3, 6, 9, 10, 15, 31, 42, 85;**
DA; HLC
See also CA 73-76; CANR 18, 32, 42; HW;
MTCW

Vasiliu, Gheorghe 1881-1957
See Bacovia, George
See also CA 123

Vassa, Gustavus
See Equiano, Olaudah

Vassilikos, Vassilis 1933-......... **CLC 4, 8**
See also CA 81-84

Vaughan, Henry 1621-1695........ **LC 27**
See also DLB 131

Vaughn, Stephanie................. **CLC 62**

Vazov, Ivan (Minchov)
1850-1921 .... **TCLC 25**
See also CA 121

Veblen, Thorstein (Bunde)
1857-1929 .... **TCLC 31**
See also CA 115

Vega, Lope de 1562-1635........... **LC 23**

Venison, Alfred
See Pound, Ezra (Weston Loomis)

Verdi, Marie de
See Mencken, H(enry) L(ouis)

Verdu, Matilde
See Cela, Camilo Jose

Verga, Giovanni (Carmelo)
1840-1922 .... **TCLC 3**
See also CA 104; 123

Vergil 70B.C.-19B.C. .... **CMLC 9; DA**

Verhaeren, Emile (Adolphe Gustave)
1855-1916 .... **TCLC 12**
See also CA 109

Verlaine, Paul (Marie)
1844-1896 .... **NCLC 2; PC 2**

Verne, Jules (Gabriel)
1828-1905 .... **TCLC 6, 52**
See also CA 110; 131; DLB 123; JRDA;
MAICYA; SATA 21

Very, Jones 1813-1880.......... **NCLC 9**
See also DLB 1

Vesaas, Tarjei 1897-1970......... **CLC 48**
See also CA 29-32R

Vialis, Gaston
See Simenon, Georges (Jacques Christian)

Vian, Boris 1920-1959 .... **TCLC 9**
See also CA 106; DLB 72

Viaud, (Louis Marie) Julien 1850-1923
See Loti, Pierre
See also CA 107

Vicar, Henry
See Felsen, Henry Gregor

Vicker, Angus
See Felsen, Henry Gregor

Vidal, Gore
1925- ..... **CLC 2, 4, 6, 8, 10, 22, 33, 72**
See also AITN 1; BEST 90:2; CA 5-8R;
CANR 13, 45; DLB 6; MTCW

Viereck, Peter (Robert Edwin)
1916- .... **CLC 4**
See also CA 1-4R; CANR 1; DLB 5

Vigny, Alfred (Victor) de
1797-1863 .... **NCLC 7**
See also DLB 119

Vilakazi, Benedict Wallet
1906-1947 .... **TCLC 37**

Villiers de l'Isle Adam, Jean Marie Mathias
Philippe Auguste Comte
1838-1889 .... **NCLC 3; SSC 14**
See also DLB 123

Vinci, Leonardo da 1452-1519....... **LC 12**

Vine, Barbara .... **CLC 50**
See also Rendell, Ruth (Barbara)
See also BEST 90:4

Vinge, Joan D(ennison) 1948-...... **CLC 30**
See also CA 93-96; SATA 36

Violis, G.
See Simenon, Georges (Jacques Christian)

Visconti, Luchino 1906-1976....... **CLC 16**
See also CA 81-84; 65-68; CANR 39

Vittorini, Elio 1908-1966...... **CLC 6, 9, 14**
See also CA 133; 25-28R

Vizinczey, Stephen 1933-.......... **CLC 40**
See also CA 128

Vliet, R(ussell) G(ordon)
1929-1984 .... **CLC 22**
See also CA 37-40R; 112; CANR 18

Vogau, Boris Andreyevich 1894-1937(?)
See Pilnyak, Boris
See also CA 123

Vogel, Paula A(nne) 1951-......... **CLC 76**
See also CA 108

Voight, Ellen Bryant 1943-........ **CLC 54**
See also CA 69-72; CANR 11, 29; DLB 120

Voigt, Cynthia 1942- .... **CLC 30**
See also AAYA 3; CA 106; CANR 18, 37,
40; CLR 13; JRDA; MAICYA;
SATA 33, 48, 79

Voinovich, Vladimir (Nikolaevich)
1932- .... **CLC 10, 49**
See also CA 81-84; CAAS 12; CANR 33;
MTCW

Voloshinov, V. N.
See Bakhtin, Mikhail Mikhailovich

Voltaire
    1694-1778 . . . **LC 14; DA; SSC 12; WLC**

von Daeniken, Erich 1935- . . . . **CLC 30**
    See also AITN 1; CA 37-40R; CANR 17,
    44

von Daniken, Erich
    See von Daeniken, Erich

von Heidenstam, (Carl Gustaf) Verner
    See Heidenstam, (Carl Gustaf) Verner von

von Heyse, Paul (Johann Ludwig)
    See Heyse, Paul (Johann Ludwig von)

von Hofmannsthal, Hugo
    See Hofmannsthal, Hugo von

von Horvath, Odon
    See Horvath, Oedoen von

von Horvath, Oedoen
    See Horvath, Oedoen von

von Liliencron, (Friedrich Adolf Axel) Detlev
    See Liliencron, (Friedrich Adolf Axel)
    Detlev von

Vonnegut, Kurt, Jr.
    1922- . . . . . . **CLC 1, 2, 3, 4, 5, 8, 12, 22,
                40, 60; DA; SSC 8; WLC**
    See also AAYA 6; AITN 1; BEST 90:4;
    CA 1-4R; CANR 1, 25;
    CDALB 1968-1988; DLB 2, 8; DLBD 3;
    DLBY 80; MTCW

Von Rachen, Kurt
    See Hubbard, L(afayette) Ron(ald)

von Rezzori (d'Arezzo), Gregor
    See Rezzori (d'Arezzo), Gregor von

von Sternberg, Josef
    See Sternberg, Josef von

Vorster, Gordon 1924- . . . . **CLC 34**
    See also CA 133

Vosce, Trudie
    See Ozick, Cynthia

Voznesensky, Andrei (Andreievich)
    1933- . . . . **CLC 1, 15, 57**
    See also CA 89-92; CANR 37; MTCW

Waddington, Miriam 1917- . . . . **CLC 28**
    See also CA 21-24R; CANR 12, 30;
    DLB 68

Wagman, Fredrica 1937- . . . . **CLC 7**
    See also CA 97-100

Wagner, Richard 1813-1883 . . . . **NCLC 9**
    See also DLB 129

Wagner-Martin, Linda 1936- . . . . **CLC 50**

Wagoner, David (Russell)
    1926- . . . . **CLC 3, 5, 15**
    See also CA 1-4R; CAAS 3; CANR 2;
    DLB 5; SATA 14

Wah, Fred(erick James) 1939- . . . . . . **CLC 44**
    See also CA 107; 141; DLB 60

Wahloo, Per 1926-1975 . . . . **CLC 7**
    See also CA 61-64

Wahloo, Peter
    See Wahloo, Per

Wain, John (Barrington)
    1925-1994 . . . . **CLC 2, 11, 15, 46**
    See also CA 5-8R; 145; CAAS 4; CANR 23;
    CDBLB 1960 to Present; DLB 15, 27,
    139; MTCW

Wajda, Andrzej 1926- . . . . **CLC 16**
    See also CA 102

Wakefield, Dan 1932- . . . . **CLC 7**
    See also CA 21-24R; CAAS 7

Wakoski, Diane
    1937- . . . . **CLC 2, 4, 7, 9, 11, 40**
    See also CA 13-16R; CAAS 1; CANR 9;
    DLB 5

Wakoski-Sherbell, Diane
    See Wakoski, Diane

Walcott, Derek (Alton)
    1930- . . . . **CLC 2, 4, 9, 14, 25, 42, 67, 76;
                                                BLC**
    See also BW 2; CA 89-92; CANR 26;
    DLB 117; DLBY 81; MTCW

Waldman, Anne 1945- . . . . **CLC 7**
    See also CA 37-40R; CAAS 17; CANR 34;
    DLB 16

Waldo, E. Hunter
    See Sturgeon, Theodore (Hamilton)

Waldo, Edward Hamilton
    See Sturgeon, Theodore (Hamilton)

Walker, Alice (Malsenior)
    1944- . . . . **CLC 5, 6, 9, 19, 27, 46, 58;
                                        BLC; DA; SSC 5**
    See also AAYA 3; BEST 89:4; BW 2;
    CA 37-40R; CANR 9, 27;
    CDALB 1968-1988; DLB 6, 33, 143;
    MTCW; SATA 31

Walker, David Harry 1911-1992 . . . . **CLC 14**
    See also CA 1-4R; 137; CANR 1; SATA 8;
    SATA-Obit 71

Walker, Edward Joseph 1934-
    See Walker, Ted
    See also CA 21-24R; CANR 12, 28

Walker, George F. 1947- . . . . **CLC 44, 61**
    See also CA 103; CANR 21, 43; DLB 60

Walker, Joseph A. 1935- . . . . **CLC 19**
    See also BW 1; CA 89-92; CANR 26;
    DLB 38

Walker, Margaret (Abigail)
    1915- . . . . **CLC 1, 6; BLC**
    See also BW 2; CA 73-76; CANR 26;
    DLB 76; MTCW

Walker, Ted. . . . . **CLC 13**
    See also Walker, Edward Joseph
    See also DLB 40

Wallace, David Foster 1962- . . . . **CLC 50**
    See also CA 132

Wallace, Dexter
    See Masters, Edgar Lee

Wallace, (Richard Horatio) Edgar
    1875-1932 . . . . **TCLC 57**
    See also CA 115; DLB 70

Wallace, Irving 1916-1990 . . . . **CLC 7, 13**
    See also AITN 1; CA 1-4R; 132; CAAS 1;
    CANR 1, 27; MTCW

Wallant, Edward Lewis
    1926-1962 . . . . **CLC 5, 10**
    See also CA 1-4R; CANR 22; DLB 2, 28,
    143; MTCW

Walpole, Horace 1717-1797 . . . . **LC 2**
    See also DLB 39, 104

Walpole, Hugh (Seymour)
    1884-1941 . . . . **TCLC 5**
    See also CA 104; DLB 34

Walser, Martin 1927- . . . . **CLC 27**
    See also CA 57-60; CANR 8; DLB 75, 124

Walser, Robert 1878-1956 . . . . **TCLC 18**
    See also CA 118; DLB 66

Walsh, Jill Paton. . . . . **CLC 35**
    See also Paton Walsh, Gillian
    See also AAYA 11; CLR 2; SAAS 3

Walter, Villiam Christian
    See Andersen, Hans Christian

Wambaugh, Joseph (Aloysius, Jr.)
    1937- . . . . **CLC 3, 18**
    See also AITN 1; BEST 89:3; CA 33-36R;
    CANR 42; DLB 6; DLBY 83; MTCW

Ward, Arthur Henry Sarsfield 1883-1959
    See Rohmer, Sax
    See also CA 108

Ward, Douglas Turner 1930- . . . . **CLC 19**
    See also BW 1; CA 81-84; CANR 27;
    DLB 7, 38

Ward, Mary Augusta
    See Ward, Mrs. Humphry

Ward, Mrs. Humphry
    1851-1920 . . . . **TCLC 55**
    See also DLB 18

Ward, Peter
    See Faust, Frederick (Schiller)

Warhol, Andy 1928(?)-1987 . . . . **CLC 20**
    See also AAYA 12; BEST 89:4; CA 89-92;
    121; CANR 34

Warner, Francis (Robert le Plastrier)
    1937- . . . . **CLC 14**
    See also CA 53-56; CANR 11

Warner, Marina 1946- . . . . **CLC 59**
    See also CA 65-68; CANR 21

Warner, Rex (Ernest) 1905-1986 . . . . **CLC 45**
    See also CA 89-92; 119; DLB 15

Warner, Susan (Bogert)
    1819-1885 . . . . **NCLC 31**
    See also DLB 3, 42

Warner, Sylvia (Constance) Ashton
    See Ashton-Warner, Sylvia (Constance)

Warner, Sylvia Townsend
    1893-1978 . . . . **CLC 7, 19**
    See also CA 61-64; 77-80; CANR 16;
    DLB 34, 139; MTCW

Warren, Mercy Otis 1728-1814 . . . **NCLC 13**
    See also DLB 31

Warren, Robert Penn
    1905-1989 . . . . **CLC 1, 4, 6, 8, 10, 13, 18,
                    39, 53, 59; DA; SSC 4; WLC**
    See also AITN 1; CA 13-16R; 129;
    CANR 10; CDALB 1968-1988; DLB 2,
    48; DLBY 80, 89; MTCW; SATA 46, 63

Warshofsky, Isaac
    See Singer, Isaac Bashevis

Warton, Thomas 1728-1790 . . . . **LC 15**
    See also DLB 104, 109

Waruk, Kona
    See Harris, (Theodore) Wilson

Warung, Price 1855-1911 . . . . **TCLC 45**

Warwick, Jarvis
See Garner, Hugh

Washington, Alex
See Harris, Mark

Washington, Booker T(aliaferro)
1856-1915 .... TCLC 10; BLC
See also BW 1; CA 114; 125; SATA 28

Washington, George   1732-1799 ...... LC 25
See also DLB 31

Wassermann, (Karl) Jakob
1873-1934 .... TCLC 6
See also CA 104; DLB 66

Wasserstein, Wendy
1950- .... CLC 32, 59; DC 4
See also CA 121; 129; CABS 3

Waterhouse, Keith (Spencer)
1929- .... CLC 47
See also CA 5-8R; CANR 38; DLB 13, 15;
MTCW

Waters, Roger   1944- .... CLC 35

Watkins, Frances Ellen
See Harper, Frances Ellen Watkins

Watkins, Gerrold
See Malzberg, Barry N(athaniel)

Watkins, Paul   1964- .... CLC 55
See also CA 132

Watkins, Vernon Phillips
1906-1967 .... CLC 43
See also CA 9-10; 25-28R; CAP 1; DLB 20

Watson, Irving S.
See Mencken, H(enry) L(ouis)

Watson, John H.
See Farmer, Philip Jose

Watson, Richard F.
See Silverberg, Robert

Waugh, Auberon (Alexander)   1939- .. CLC 7
See also CA 45-48; CANR 6, 22; DLB 14

Waugh, Evelyn (Arthur St. John)
1903-1966 ...... CLC 1, 3, 8, 13, 19, 27,
44; DA; WLC
See also CA 85-88; 25-28R; CANR 22;
CDBLB 1914-1945; DLB 15; MTCW

Waugh, Harriet   1944- .... CLC 6
See also CA 85-88; CANR 22

Ways, C. R.
See Blount, Roy (Alton), Jr.

Waystaff, Simon
See Swift, Jonathan

Webb, (Martha) Beatrice (Potter)
1858-1943 .... TCLC 22
See also Potter, Beatrice
See also CA 117

Webb, Charles (Richard)   1939- ...... CLC 7
See also CA 25-28R

Webb, James H(enry), Jr.   1946- .... CLC 22
See also CA 81-84

Webb, Mary (Gladys Meredith)
1881-1927 .... TCLC 24
See also CA 123; DLB 34

Webb, Mrs. Sidney
See Webb, (Martha) Beatrice (Potter)

Webb, Phyllis   1927- .... CLC 18
See also CA 104; CANR 23; DLB 53

Webb, Sidney (James)
1859-1947 .... TCLC 22
See also CA 117

Webber, Andrew Lloyd .... CLC 21
See also Lloyd Webber, Andrew

Weber, Lenora Mattingly
1895-1971 .... CLC 12
See also CA 19-20; 29-32R; CAP 1;
SATA 2, 26

Webster, John   1579(?)-1634(?) .... DC 2
See also CDBLB Before 1660; DA; DLB 58;
WLC

Webster, Noah   1758-1843 .... NCLC 30

Wedekind, (Benjamin) Frank(lin)
1864-1918 .... TCLC 7
See also CA 104; DLB 118

Weidman, Jerome   1913- .... CLC 7
See also AITN 2; CA 1-4R; CANR 1;
DLB 28

Weil, Simone (Adolphine)
1909-1943 .... TCLC 23
See also CA 117

Weinstein, Nathan
See West, Nathanael

Weinstein, Nathan von Wallenstein
See West, Nathanael

Weir, Peter (Lindsay)   1944- .... CLC 20
See also CA 113; 123

Weiss, Peter (Ulrich)
1916-1982 .... CLC 3, 15, 51
See also CA 45-48; 106; CANR 3; DLB 69,
124

Weiss, Theodore (Russell)
1916- .... CLC 3, 8, 14
See also CA 9-12R; CAAS 2; DLB 5

Welch, (Maurice) Denton
1915-1948 .... TCLC 22
See also CA 121

Welch, James   1940- .... CLC 6, 14, 52
See also CA 85-88; CANR 42

Weldon, Fay
1933(?)- .... CLC 6, 9, 11, 19, 36, 59
See also CA 21-24R; CANR 16;
CDBLB 1960 to Present; DLB 14;
MTCW

Wellek, Rene   1903- .... CLC 28
See also CA 5-8R; CAAS 7; CANR 8;
DLB 63

Weller, Michael   1942- .... CLC 10, 53
See also CA 85-88

Weller, Paul   1958- .... CLC 26

Wellershoff, Dieter   1925- .... CLC 46
See also CA 89-92; CANR 16, 37

Welles, (George) Orson
1915-1985 .... CLC 20, 80
See also CA 93-96; 117

Wellman, Mac   1945- .... CLC 65

Wellman, Manly Wade   1903-1986 .. CLC 49
See also CA 1-4R; 118; CANR 6, 16, 44;
SATA 6, 47

Wells, Carolyn   1869(?)-1942 ...... TCLC 35
See also CA 113; DLB 11

Wells, H(erbert) G(eorge)
1866-1946 .... TCLC 6, 12, 19; DA;
SSC 6; WLC
See also CA 110; 121; CDBLB 1914-1945;
DLB 34, 70; MTCW; SATA 20

Wells, Rosemary   1943- .... CLC 12
See also CA 85-88; CLR 16; MAICYA;
SAAS 1; SATA 18, 69

Welty, Eudora
1909- ...... CLC 1, 2, 5, 14, 22, 33; DA;
SSC 1; WLC
See also CA 9-12R; CABS 1; CANR 32;
CDALB 1941-1968; DLB 2, 102, 143;
DLBY 87; MTCW

Wen I-to   1899-1946 .... TCLC 28

Wentworth, Robert
See Hamilton, Edmond

Werfel, Franz (V.)   1890-1945 ...... TCLC 8
See also CA 104; DLB 81, 124

Wergeland, Henrik Arnold
1808-1845 .... NCLC 5

Wersba, Barbara   1932- .... CLC 30
See also AAYA 2; CA 29-32R; CANR 16,
38; CLR 3; DLB 52; JRDA; MAICYA;
SAAS 2; SATA 1, 58

Wertmueller, Lina   1928- .... CLC 16
See also CA 97-100; CANR 39

Wescott, Glenway   1901-1987 .... CLC 13
See also CA 13-16R; 121; CANR 23;
DLB 4, 9, 102

Wesker, Arnold   1932- .... CLC 3, 5, 42
See also CA 1-4R; CAAS 7; CANR 1, 33;
CDBLB 1960 to Present; DLB 13;
MTCW

Wesley, Richard (Errol)   1945- .... CLC 7
See also BW 1; CA 57-60; CANR 27;
DLB 38

Wessel, Johan Herman   1742-1785 .... LC 7

West, Anthony (Panther)
1914-1987 .... CLC 50
See also CA 45-48; 124; CANR 3, 19;
DLB 15

West, C. P.
See Wodehouse, P(elham) G(renville)

West, (Mary) Jessamyn
1902-1984 .... CLC 7, 17
See also CA 9-12R; 112; CANR 27; DLB 6;
DLBY 84; MTCW; SATA 37

West, Morris L(anglo)   1916- ..... CLC 6, 33
See also CA 5-8R; CANR 24; MTCW

West, Nathanael
1903-1940 ..... TCLC 1, 14, 44; SSC 16
See also CA 104; 125; CDALB 1929-1941;
DLB 4, 9, 28; MTCW

West, Owen
See Koontz, Dean R(ay)

West, Paul   1930- .... CLC 7, 14
See also CA 13-16R; CAAS 7; CANR 22;
DLB 14

West, Rebecca   1892-1983 .. CLC 7, 9, 31, 50
See also CA 5-8R; 109; CANR 19; DLB 36;
DLBY 83; MTCW

Westall, Robert (Atkinson)
1929-1993 . . . . **CLC 17**
See also AAYA 12; CA 69-72; 141;
CANR 18; CLR 13; JRDA; MAICYA;
SAAS 2; SATA 23, 69; SATA-Obit 75

Westlake, Donald E(dwin)
1933- . . . . **CLC 7, 33**
See also CA 17-20R; CAAS 13; CANR 16,
44

Westmacott, Mary
See Christie, Agatha (Mary Clarissa)

Weston, Allen
See Norton, Andre

Wetcheek, J. L.
See Feuchtwanger, Lion

Wetering, Janwillem van de
See van de Wetering, Janwillem

Wetherell, Elizabeth
See Warner, Susan (Bogert)

Whalen, Philip 1923- . . . . **CLC 6, 29**
See also CA 9-12R; CANR 5, 39; DLB 16

Wharton, Edith (Newbold Jones)
1862-1937 . . . . . . **TCLC 3, 9, 27, 53; DA;
SSC 6; WLC**
See also CA 104; 132; CDALB 1865-1917;
DLB 4, 9, 12, 78; MTCW

Wharton, James
See Mencken, H(enry) L(ouis)

Wharton, William (a pseudonym)
. . . . **CLC 18, 37**
See also CA 93-96; DLBY 80

Wheatley (Peters), Phillis
1754(?)-1784 . . . . **LC 3; BLC; DA; PC 3;
WLC**
See also CDALB 1640-1865; DLB 31, 50

Wheelock, John Hall 1886-1978 . . . . **CLC 14**
See also CA 13-16R; 77-80; CANR 14;
DLB 45

White, E(lwyn) B(rooks)
1899-1985 . . . . **CLC 10, 34, 39**
See also AITN 2; CA 13-16R; 116;
CANR 16, 37; CLR 1, 21; DLB 11, 22;
MAICYA; MTCW; SATA 2, 29, 44

White, Edmund (Valentine III)
1940- . . . . **CLC 27**
See also AAYA 7; CA 45-48; CANR 3, 19,
36; MTCW

White, Patrick (Victor Martindale)
1912 1990 . . **CLC 3, 4, 5, 7, 9, 18, 65, 69**
See also CA 81-84; 132; CANR 43; MTCW

White, Phyllis Dorothy James 1920-
See James, P. D.
See also CA 21-24R; CANR 17, 43; MTCW

White, T(erence) H(anbury)
1906-1964 . . . . **CLC 30**
See also CA 73-76; CANR 37; JRDA;
MAICYA; SATA 12

White, Terence de Vere
1912-1994 . . . . **CLC 49**
See also CA 49-52; 145; CANR 3

White, Walter F(rancis)
1893-1955 . . . . **TCLC 15**
See also White, Walter
See also BW 1; CA 115; 124; DLB 51

White, William Hale 1831-1913
See Rutherford, Mark
See also CA 121

Whitehead, E(dward) A(nthony)
1933- . . . . **CLC 5**
See also CA 65-68

Whitemore, Hugh (John) 1936- . . . . . **CLC 37**
See also CA 132

Whitman, Sarah Helen (Power)
1803-1878 . . . . **NCLC 19**
See also DLB 1

Whitman, Walt(er)
1819-1892 . . . . . **NCLC 4, 31; DA; PC 3;
WLC**
See also CDALB 1640-1865; DLB 3, 64;
SATA 20

Whitney, Phyllis A(yame) 1903- . . . . **CLC 42**
See also AITN 2; BEST 90:3; CA 1-4R;
CANR 3, 25, 38; JRDA; MAICYA;
SATA 1, 30

Whittemore, (Edward) Reed (Jr.)
1919- . . . . **CLC 4**
See also CA 9-12R; CAAS 8; CANR 4;
DLB 5

Whittier, John Greenleaf
1807-1892 . . . . **NCLC 8**
See also CDALB 1640-1865; DLB 1

Whittlebot, Hernia
See Coward, Noel (Peirce)

Wicker, Thomas Grey 1926-
See Wicker, Tom
See also CA 65-68; CANR 21

Wicker, Tom . . . . **CLC 7**
See also Wicker, Thomas Grey

Wideman, John Edgar
1941- . . . . **CLC 5, 34, 36, 67; BLC**
See also BW 2; CA 85-88; CANR 14, 42;
DLB 33, 143

Wiebe, Rudy (Henry) 1934- . . . **CLC 6, 11, 14**
See also CA 37-40R; CANR 42; DLB 60

Wieland, Christoph Martin
1733-1813 . . . . **NCLC 17**
See also DLB 97

Wiene, Robert 1881-1938 . . . . **TCLC 56**

Wieners, John 1934- . . . . **CLC 7**
See also CA 13-16R; DLB 16

Wiesel, Elie(zer)
1928- . . . . **CLC 3, 5, 11, 37; DA**
See also AAYA 7; AITN 1; CA 5-8R;
CAAS 4; CANR 8, 40; DLB 83;
DLBY 87; MTCW; SATA 56

Wiggins, Marianne 1947- . . . . **CLC 57**
See also BEST 89:3; CA 130

Wight, James Alfred 1916-
See Herriot, James
See also CA 77-80; SATA 44, 55

Wilbur, Richard (Purdy)
1921- . . . . **CLC 3, 6, 9, 14, 53; DA**
See also CA 1-4R; CABS 2; CANR 2, 29;
DLB 5; MTCW; SATA 9

Wild, Peter 1940- . . . . **CLC 14**
See also CA 37-40R; DLB 5

Wilde, Oscar (Fingal O'Flahertie Wills)
1854(?)-1900 . . . . **TCLC 1, 8, 23, 41; DA;
SSC 11; WLC**
See also CA 104; 119; CDBLB 1890-1914;
DLB 10, 19, 34, 57, 141; SATA 24

Wilder, Billy . . . . **CLC 20**
See also Wilder, Samuel
See also DLB 26

Wilder, Samuel 1906-
See Wilder, Billy
See also CA 89-92

Wilder, Thornton (Niven)
1897-1975 . . . . . . **CLC 1, 5, 6, 10, 15, 35,
82; DA; DC 1; WLC**
See also AITN 2; CA 13-16R; 61-64;
CANR 40; DLB 4, 7, 9; MTCW

Wilding, Michael 1942- . . . . **CLC 73**
See also CA 104; CANR 24

Wiley, Richard 1944- . . . . **CLC 44**
See also CA 121; 129

Wilhelm, Kate . . . . **CLC 7**
See also Wilhelm, Katie Gertrude
See also CAAS 5; DLB 8

Wilhelm, Katie Gertrude 1928-
See Wilhelm, Kate
See also CA 37-40R; CANR 17, 36; MTCW

Wilkins, Mary
See Freeman, Mary Eleanor Wilkins

Willard, Nancy 1936- . . . . **CLC 7, 37**
See also CA 89-92; CANR 10, 39; CLR 5;
DLB 5, 52; MAICYA; MTCW;
SATA 30, 37, 71

Williams, C(harles) K(enneth)
1936- . . . . **CLC 33, 56**
See also CA 37-40R; DLB 5

Williams, Charles
See Collier, James L(incoln)

Williams, Charles (Walter Stansby)
1886-1945 . . . . **TCLC 1, 11**
See also CA 104; DLB 100

Williams, (George) Emlyn
1905-1987 . . . . **CLC 15**
See also CA 104; 123; CANR 36; DLB 10,
77; MTCW

Williams, Hugo 1942- . . . . **CLC 42**
See also CA 17-20R; CANR 45; DLB 40

Williams, J. Walker
See Wodehouse, P(elham) G(renville)

Williams, John A(lfred)
1925- . . . . **CLC 5, 13; BLC**
See also BW 2; CA 53-56; CAAS 3;
CANR 6, 26; DLB 2, 33

Williams, Jonathan (Chamberlain)
1929- . . . . **CLC 13**
See also CA 9-12R; CAAS 12; CANR 8;
DLB 5

Williams, Joy 1944- . . . . **CLC 31**
See also CA 41-44R; CANR 22

Williams, Norman 1952- . . . . **CLC 39**
See also CA 118

Williams, Tennessee
1911-1983 . . . . . **CLC 1, 2, 5, 7, 8, 11, 15,
19, 30, 39, 45, 71; DA; DC 4; WLC**
See also AITN 1, 2; CA 5-8R; 108;
CABS 3; CANR 31; CDALB 1941-1968;
DLB 7; DLBD 4; DLBY 83; MTCW

Williams, Thomas (Alonzo)
    1926-1990 . . . . **CLC 14**
    See also CA 1-4R; 132; CANR 2

Williams, William C.
    See Williams, William Carlos

Williams, William Carlos
    1883-1963 . . . . **CLC 1, 2, 5, 9, 13, 22, 42,
                                        67; DA; PC 7**
    See also CA 89-92; CANR 34;
        CDALB 1917-1929; DLB 4, 16, 54, 86;
        MTCW

Williamson, David (Keith) 1942- . . . . **CLC 56**
    See also CA 103; CANR 41

Williamson, Ellen Douglas 1905-1984
    See Douglas, Ellen
    See also CA 17-20R; 114; CANR 39

Williamson, Jack . . . . **CLC 29**
    See also Williamson, John Stewart
    See also CAAS 8; DLB 8

Williamson, John Stewart 1908-
    See Williamson, Jack
    See also CA 17-20R; CANR 23

Willie, Frederick
    See Lovecraft, H(oward) P(hillips)

Willingham, Calder (Baynard, Jr.)
    1922- . . . . **CLC 5, 51**
    See also CA 5-8R; CANR 3; DLB 2, 44;
        MTCW

Willis, Charles
    See Clarke, Arthur C(harles)

Willy
    See Colette, (Sidonie-Gabrielle)

Willy, Colette
    See Colette, (Sidonie-Gabrielle)

Wilson, A(ndrew) N(orman) 1950- . . **CLC 33**
    See also CA 112; 122; DLB 14

Wilson, Angus (Frank Johnstone)
    1913-1991 . . . . **CLC 2, 3, 5, 25, 34**
    See also CA 5-8R; 134; CANR 21; DLB 15,
        139; MTCW

Wilson, August
    1945- . . **CLC 39, 50, 63; BLC; DA; DC 2**
    See also BW 2; CA 115; 122; CANR 42;
        MTCW

Wilson, Brian 1942- . . . . **CLC 12**

Wilson, Colin 1931- . . . . **CLC 3, 14**
    See also CA 1-4R; CAAS 5; CANR 1, 22,
        33; DLB 14; MTCW

Wilson, Dirk
    See Pohl, Frederik

Wilson, Edmund
    1895-1972 . . . . **CLC 1, 2, 3, 8, 24**
    See also CA 1-4R; 37-40R; CANR 1;
        DLB 63; MTCW

Wilson, Ethel Davis (Bryant)
    1888(?)-1980 . . . . **CLC 13**
    See also CA 102; DLB 68; MTCW

Wilson, John 1785-1854 . . . . **NCLC 5**

Wilson, John (Anthony) Burgess 1917-1993
    See Burgess, Anthony
    See also CA 1-4R; 143; CANR 2; MTCW

Wilson, Lanford 1937- . . . . **CLC 7, 14, 36**
    See also CA 17-20R; CABS 3; CANR 45;
        DLB 7

Wilson, Robert M. 1944- . . . . **CLC 7, 9**
    See also CA 49-52; CANR 2, 41; MTCW

Wilson, Robert McLiam 1964- . . . . . **CLC 59**
    See also CA 132

Wilson, Sloan 1920- . . . . **CLC 32**
    See also CA 1-4R; CANR 1, 44

Wilson, Snoo 1948- . . . . **CLC 33**
    See also CA 69-72

Wilson, William S(mith) 1932- . . . . . **CLC 49**
    See also CA 81-84

Winchilsea, Anne (Kingsmill) Finch Counte
    1661-1720 . . . . **LC 3**

Windham, Basil
    See Wodehouse, P(elham) G(renville)

Wingrove, David (John) 1954- . . . . . . **CLC 68**
    See also CA 133

Winters, Janet Lewis . . . . **CLC 41**
    See also Lewis, Janet
    See also DLBY 87

Winters, (Arthur) Yvor
    1900-1968 . . . . **CLC 4, 8, 32**
    See also CA 11-12; 25-28R; CAP 1;
        DLB 48; MTCW

Winterson, Jeanette 1959- . . . . **CLC 64**
    See also CA 136

Wiseman, Frederick 1930- . . . . **CLC 20**

Wister, Owen 1860-1938 . . . . **TCLC 21**
    See also CA 108; DLB 9, 78; SATA 62

Witkacy
    See Witkiewicz, Stanislaw Ignacy

Witkiewicz, Stanislaw Ignacy
    1885-1939 . . . . **TCLC 8**
    See also CA 105

Wittig, Monique 1935(?)- . . . . **CLC 22**
    See also CA 116; 135; DLB 83

Wittlin, Jozef 1896-1976 . . . . **CLC 25**
    See also CA 49-52; 65-68; CANR 3

Wodehouse, P(elham) G(renville)
    1881-1975 . . . **CLC 1, 2, 5, 10, 22; SSC 2**
    See also AITN 2; CA 45-48; 57-60;
        CANR 3, 33; CDBLB 1914-1945;
        DLB 34; MTCW; SATA 22

Woiwode, L.
    See Woiwode, Larry (Alfred)

Woiwode, Larry (Alfred) 1941- . . . **CLC 6, 10**
    See also CA 73-76; CANR 16; DLB 6

Wojciechowska, Maia (Teresa)
    1927- . . . . **CLC 26**
    See also AAYA 8; CA 9-12R; CANR 4, 41;
        CLR 1; JRDA; MAICYA; SAAS 1;
        SATA 1, 28

Wolf, Christa 1929- . . . . **CLC 14, 29, 58**
    See also CA 85-88; CANR 45; DLB 75;
        MTCW

Wolfe, Gene (Rodman) 1931- . . . . . . **CLC 25**
    See also CA 57-60; CAAS 9; CANR 6, 32;
        DLB 8

Wolfe, George C. 1954- . . . . **CLC 49**

Wolfe, Thomas (Clayton)
    1900-1938 . . . **TCLC 4, 13, 29; DA; WLC**
    See also CA 104; 132; CDALB 1929-1941;
        DLB 9, 102; DLBD 2; DLBY 85; MTCW

Wolfe, Thomas Kennerly, Jr. 1931-
    See Wolfe, Tom
    See also CA 13-16R; CANR 9, 33; MTCW

Wolfe, Tom . . . . **CLC 1, 2, 9, 15, 35, 51**
    See also Wolfe, Thomas Kennerly, Jr.
    See also AAYA 8; AITN 2; BEST 89:1

Wolff, Geoffrey (Ansell) 1937- . . . . . **CLC 41**
    See also CA 29-32R; CANR 29, 43

Wolff, Sonia
    See Levitin, Sonia (Wolff)

Wolff, Tobias (Jonathan Ansell)
    1945- . . . . **CLC 39, 64**
    See also BEST 90:2; CA 114; 117; DLB 130

Wolfram von Eschenbach
    c. 1170-c. 1220 . . . . **CMLC 5**
    See also DLB 138

Wolitzer, Hilma 1930- . . . . **CLC 17**
    See also CA 65-68; CANR 18, 40; SATA 31

Wollstonecraft, Mary 1759-1797 . . . . . . **LC 5**
    See also CDBLB 1789-1832; DLB 39, 104

Wonder, Stevie . . . . **CLC 12**
    See also Morris, Steveland Judkins

Wong, Jade Snow 1922- . . . . **CLC 17**
    See also CA 109

Woodcott, Keith
    See Brunner, John (Kilian Houston)

Woodruff, Robert W.
    See Mencken, H(enry) L(ouis)

Woolf, (Adeline) Virginia
    1882-1941 . . . . **TCLC 1, 5, 20, 43, 56;
                                        DA; SSC 7; WLC**
    See also CA 104; 130; CDBLB 1914-1945;
        DLB 36, 100; DLBD 10; MTCW

Woollcott, Alexander (Humphreys)
    1887-1943 . . . . **TCLC 5**
    See also CA 105; DLB 29

Woolrich, Cornell 1903-1968 . . . . **CLC 77**
    See also Hopley-Woolrich, Cornell George

Wordsworth, Dorothy
    1771-1855 . . . . **NCLC 25**
    See also DLB 107

Wordsworth, William
    1770-1850 . . . . **NCLC 12, 38; DA; PC 4;
                                        WLC**
    See also CDBLB 1789-1832; DLB 93, 107

Wouk, Herman 1915- . . . . **CLC 1, 9, 38**
    See also CA 5-8R; CANR 6, 33; DLBY 82;
        MTCW

Wright, Charles (Penzel, Jr.)
    1935- . . . . **CLC 6, 13, 28**
    See also CA 29-32R; CAAS 7; CANR 23,
        36; DLBY 82; MTCW

Wright, Charles Stevenson
    1932- . . . . **CLC 49; BLC 3**
    See also BW 1; CA 9-12R; CANR 26;
        DLB 33

Wright, Jack R.
    See Harris, Mark

Wright, James (Arlington)
    1927-1980 . . . . **CLC 3, 5, 10, 28**
    See also AITN 2; CA 49-52; 97-100;
        CANR 4, 34; DLB 5; MTCW

Wright, Judith (Arandell)
1915- . . . . CLC **11, 53**
See also CA 13-16R; CANR 31; MTCW;
SATA 14

Wright, L(aurali) R. 1939- . . . . CLC **44**
See also CA 138

Wright, Richard (Nathaniel)
1908-1960 . . . . CLC **1, 3, 4, 9, 14, 21, 48,
74; BLC; DA; SSC 2; WLC**
See also AAYA 5; BW 1; CA 108;
CDALB 1929-1941; DLB 76, 102;
DLBD 2; MTCW

Wright, Richard B(ruce) 1937- . . . . . . CLC **6**
See also CA 85-88; DLB 53

Wright, Rick 1945- . . . . CLC **35**

Wright, Rowland
See Wells, Carolyn

Wright, Stephen Caldwell 1946- . . . . CLC **33**
See also BW 2

Wright, Willard Huntington 1888-1939
See Van Dine, S. S.
See also CA 115

Wright, William 1930- . . . . CLC **44**
See also CA 53-56; CANR 7, 23

Wu Ch'eng-en 1500(?)-1582(?) . . . . LC **7**

Wu Ching-tzu 1701-1754 . . . . LC **2**

Wurlitzer, Rudolph 1938(?)- . . . CLC **2, 4, 15**
See also CA 85-88

Wycherley, William 1641-1715 . . . . LC **8, 21**
See also CDBLB 1660-1789; DLB 80

Wylie, Elinor (Morton Hoyt)
1885-1928 . . . . TCLC **8**
See also CA 105; DLB 9, 45

Wylie, Philip (Gordon) 1902-1971 . . . CLC **43**
See also CA 21-22; 33-36R; CAP 2; DLB 9

Wyndham, John . . . . CLC **19**
See also Harris, John (Wyndham Parkes
Lucas) Beynon

Wyss, Johann David Von
1743-1818 . . . . NCLC **10**
See also JRDA; MAICYA; SATA 27, 29

Yakumo Koizumi
See Hearn, (Patricio) Lafcadio (Tessima
Carlos)

Yanez, Jose Donoso
See Donoso (Yanez), Jose

Yanovsky, Dasile S.
See Yanovsky, V(assily) S(emenovich)

Yanovsky, V(assily) S(emenovich)
1906-1989 . . . . CLC **2, 18**
See also CA 97-100; 129

Yates, Richard 1926-1992 . . . . . CLC **7, 8, 23**
See also CA 5-8R; 139; CANR 10, 43;
DLB 2; DLBY 81, 92

Yeats, W. B.
See Yeats, William Butler

Yeats, William Butler
1865-1939 . . . . . TCLC **1, 11, 18, 31; DA;
WLC**
See also CA 104; 127; CANR 45;
CDBLB 1890-1914; DLB 10, 19, 98;
MTCW

Yehoshua, A(braham) B.
1936- . . . . CLC **13, 31**
See also CA 33-36R; CANR 43

Yep, Laurence Michael 1948- . . . . . . CLC **35**
See also AAYA 5; CA 49-52; CANR 1;
CLR 3, 17; DLB 52; JRDA; MAICYA;
SATA 7, 69

Yerby, Frank G(arvin)
1916-1991 . . . . CLC **1, 7, 22; BLC**
See also BW 1; CA 9-12R; 136; CANR 16;
DLB 76; MTCW

Yesenin, Sergei Alexandrovich
See Esenin, Sergei (Alexandrovich)

Yevtushenko, Yevgeny (Alexandrovich)
1933- . . . . CLC **1, 3, 13, 26, 51**
See also CA 81-84; CANR 33; MTCW

Yezierska, Anzia 1885(?)-1970 . . . . . CLC **46**
See also CA 126; 89-92; DLB 28; MTCW

Yglesias, Helen 1915- . . . . CLC **7, 22**
See also CA 37-40R; CANR 15; MTCW

Yokomitsu Riichi 1898-1947 . . . . . . TCLC **47**

Yonge, Charlotte (Mary)
1823-1901 . . . . TCLC **48**
See also CA 109; DLB 18; SATA 17

York, Jeremy
See Creasey, John

York, Simon
See Heinlein, Robert A(nson)

Yorke, Henry Vincent 1905-1974 . . . CLC **13**
See also Green, Henry
See also CA 85-88; 49-52

Yoshimoto, Banana . . . . CLC **84**
See also Yoshimoto, Mahoko

Yoshimoto, Mahoko 1964-
See Yoshimoto, Banana
See also CA 144

Young, Al(bert James)
1939- . . . . CLC **19; BLC**
See also BW 2; CA 29-32R; CANR 26;
DLB 33

Young, Andrew (John) 1885-1971 . . . . CLC **5**
See also CA 5-8R; CANR 7, 29

Young, Collier
See Bloch, Robert (Albert)

Young, Edward 1683-1765 . . . . LC **3**
See also DLB 95

Young, Marguerite 1909- . . . . CLC **82**
See also CA 13-16; CAP 1

Young, Neil 1945- . . . . CLC **17**
See also CA 110

Yourcenar, Marguerite
1903-1987 . . . . CLC **19, 38, 50**
See also CA 69-72; CANR 23; DLB 72;
DLBY 88; MTCW

Yurick, Sol 1925- . . . . CLC **6**
See also CA 13-16R; CANR 25

Zabolotskii, Nikolai Alekseevich
1903-1958 . . . . TCLC **52**
See also CA 116

Zamiatin, Yevgenii
See Zamyatin, Evgeny Ivanovich

Zamyatin, Evgeny Ivanovich
1884-1937 . . . . TCLC **8, 37**
See also CA 105

Zangwill, Israel 1864-1926 . . . . TCLC **16**
See also CA 109; DLB 10, 135

Zappa, Francis Vincent, Jr. 1940-1993
See Zappa, Frank
See also CA 108; 143

Zappa, Frank . . . . CLC **17**
See also Zappa, Francis Vincent, Jr.

Zaturenska, Marya 1902-1982 . . . . CLC **6, 11**
See also CA 13-16R; 105; CANR 22

Zelazny, Roger (Joseph) 1937- . . . . . CLC **21**
See also AAYA 7; CA 21-24R; CANR 26;
DLB 8; MTCW; SATA 39, 57

Zhdanov, Andrei A(lexandrovich)
1896-1948 . . . . TCLC **18**
See also CA 117

Zhukovsky, Vasily 1783-1852 . . . . NCLC **35**

Ziegenhagen, Eric . . . . CLC **55**

Zimmer, Jill Schary
See Robinson, Jill

Zimmerman, Robert
See Dylan, Bob

Zindel, Paul 1936- . . . . CLC **6, 26; DA**
See also AAYA 2; CA 73-76; CANR 31;
CLR 3; DLB 7, 52; JRDA; MAICYA;
MTCW; SATA 16, 58

Zinov'Ev, A. A.
See Zinoviev, Alexander (Aleksandrovich)

Zinoviev, Alexander (Aleksandrovich)
1922- . . . . CLC **19**
See also CA 116; 133; CAAS 10

Zoilus
See Lovecraft, H(oward) P(hillips)

Zola, Emile (Edouard Charles Antoine)
1840-1902 . . . . . . TCLC **1, 6, 21, 41; DA;
WLC**
See also CA 104; 138; DLB 123

Zoline, Pamela 1941- . . . . CLC **62**

Zorrilla y Moral, Jose 1817-1893 . . NCLC **6**

Zoshchenko, Mikhail (Mikhailovich)
1895-1958 . . . . TCLC **15; SSC 15**
See also CA 115

Zuckmayer, Carl 1896-1977 . . . . CLC **18**
See also CA 69-72; DLB 56, 124

Zuk, Georges
See Skelton, Robin

Zukofsky, Louis
1904-1978 . . . . CLC **1, 2, 4, 7, 11, 18**
See also CA 9-12R; 77-80; CANR 39;
DLB 5; MTCW

Zweig, Paul 1935-1984 . . . . CLC **34, 42**
See also CA 85-88; 113

Zweig, Stefan 1881-1942 . . . . TCLC **17**
See also CA 112; DLB 81, 118

Literary Criticism Series
Cumulative Topic Index

This index lists all topic entries in the Gale Literary Criticism Series *Classical and Medieval Literature Criticism, Contemporary Literary Criticism, Literature Criticism from 1400 to 1800, Nineteenth-Century Literature Criticism,* and *Twentieth-Century Literary Criticism.*

Symbolism, Russian TCLC 30: 266-333
doctrines and major figures, 267-92
theories, 293-98
and French Symbolism, 298-310
themes in poetry, 310-14
theater, 314-20
and the fine arts, 320-32

Symbolist Movement, French
NCLC 20: 169-249
background and characteristics, 170-86
principles, 186-91
attacked and defended, 191-97
influences and predecessors, 197-211
and Decadence, 211-16
theater, 216-26
prose, 226-33
decline and influence, 233-47

Theater of the Absurd TCLC 38: 339-415
"The Theater of the Absurd," 340-47
major plays and playwrights, 347-58
and the concept of the absurd, 358-86
theatrical techniques, 386-94
predecessors of, 394-402
influence of, 402-13

Tin Pan Alley
See **American Popular Song, Golden Age of**

Transcendentalism, American
NCLC 24: 1-99
overviews, 3-23
contemporary documents, 23-41
theological aspects of, 42-52
and social issues, 52-74
literature of, 74-96

Travel Writing in the Nineteenth Century NCLC 44: 274-392
the European grand tour, 275-303
the Orient, 303-47
North America, 347-91

Travel Writing in the Twentieth Century TCLC 30: 407-56
conventions and traditions, 407-27
and fiction writing, 427-43
comparative essays on travel writers, 443-54

Ulysses **and the Process of Textual Reconstruction** TCLC 26: 386-416
evaluations of the new *Ulysses,* 386-94

editorial principles and procedures, 394-401
theoretical issues, 401-16

Utopian Literature, Nineteenth-Century
NCLC 24: 353-473
definitions, 354-74
overviews, 374-88
theory, 388-408
communities, 409-26
fiction, 426-53
women and fiction, 454-71

Vampire in Literature TCLC 46: 391-454
origins and evolution, 392-412
social and psychological perspectives, 413-44
vampire fiction and science fiction, 445-53

Victorian Autobiography NCLC 40: 277-363
development and major characteristics, 278-88
themes and techniques, 289-313
the autobiographical tendency in Victorian prose and poetry, 313-47
Victorian women's autobiographies, 347-62

Victorian Novel NCLC 32: 288-454
development and major characteristics, 290-310
themes and techniques, 310-58
social criticism in the Victorian novel, 359-97
urban and rural life in the Victorian novel, 397-406
women in the Victorian novel, 406-25
Mudie's Circulating Library, 425-34
the late-Victorian novel, 434-51

World War I Literature TCLC 34: 392-486
overview, 393-403
English, 403-27
German, 427-50
American, 450-66
French, 466-74
and modern history, 474-82

Yellow Journalism NCLC 36: 383-456
overviews, 384-96
major figures, 396-413
the role of reporters, 413-28
the Spanish-American War, 428-48

Yellow Journalism and society, 448-54

Young Playwrights Festival
1988—CLC 55: 376-81
1989—CLC 59: 398-403
1990—CLC 65: 444-48

TCLC Cumulative Nationality Index

AMERICAN

Adams, Andy **56**
Adams, Henry (Brooks) **4, 52**
Agee, James (Rufus) **1, 19**
Anderson, Maxwell **2**
Anderson, Sherwood **1, 10, 24**
Atherton, Gertrude (Franklin Horn) **2**
Austin, Mary (Hunter) **25**
Baker, Ray Stannard **47**
Barry, Philip **11**
Baum, L(yman) Frank **7**
Beard, Charles A(ustin) **15**
Belasco, David **3**
Bell, James Madison **43**
Benchley, Robert (Charles) **1, 55**
Benet, Stephen Vincent **7**
Benet, William Rose **28**
Bierce, Ambrose (Gwinett) **1, 7, 44**
Black Elk **33**
Boas, Franz **56**
Bodenheim, Maxwell **44**
Bourne, Randolph S(illiman) **16**
Bradford, Gamaliel **36**
Brennan, Christopher John **17**
Bromfield, Louis (Brucker) **11**
Burroughs, Edgar Rice **2, 32**
Cabell, James Branch **6**
Cable, George Washington **4**
Carnegie, Dale **53**
Cather, Willa Sibert **1, 11, 31**
Chambers, Robert W. **41**
Chandler, Raymond (Thornton) **1, 7**
Chapman, John Jay **7**
Chesnutt, Charles W(addell) **5, 39**
Chopin, Kate **5, 14**
Comstock, Anthony **13**
Cotter, Joseph Seamon **28**
Cram, Ralph Adams **45**
Crane, (Harold) Hart **2, 5**

Crane, Stephen (Townley) **11, 17, 32**
Crawford, F(rancis) Marion **10**
Crothers, Rachel **19**
Cullen, Countee **4, 37**
Davis, Rebecca (Blaine) Harding **6**
Davis, Richard Harding **24**
Day, Clarence (Shepard) **25**
De Voto, Bernard (Augustine) **29**
Dreiser, Theodore (Herman Albert) **10, 18, 35**
Dunbar, Paul Laurence **2, 12**
Dunne, Finley Peter **28**
Eastman, Charles A(lexander) **55**
Faust, Frederick (Schiller) **49**
Fisher, Rudolph **11**
Fitzgerald, F(rancis) Scott (Key) **1, 6, 14, 28, 55**
Fitzgerald, Zelda (Sayre) **52**
Flecker, (Herman) James Elroy **43**
Fletcher, John Gould **35**
Forten, Charlotte L. **16**
Freeman, Douglas Southall **11**
Freeman, Mary Eleanor Wilkins **9**
Futrelle, Jacques **19**
Gale, Zona **7**
Garland, (Hannibal) Hamlin **3**
Gilman, Charlotte (Anna) Perkins (Stetson) **9, 37**
Glasgow, Ellen (Anderson Gholson) **2, 7**
Glaspell, Susan (Keating) **55**
Goldman, Emma **13**
Grey, Zane **6**
Guiney, Louise Imogen **41**
Hall, James Norman **23**
Harper, Frances Ellen Watkins **14**
Harris, Joel Chandler **2**
Harte, (Francis) Bret(t) **1, 25**
Hatteras, Owen **18**
Hawthorne, Julian **25**

Hearn, (Patricio) Lafcadio (Tessima Carlos) **9**
Henry, O. **1, 19**
Hergesheimer, Joseph **11**
Higginson, Thomas Wentworth **36**
Hopkins, Pauline Elizabeth **28**
Howard, Robert Ervin **8**
Howe, Julia Ward **21**
Howells, William Dean **7, 17, 41**
James, Henry **2, 11, 24, 40, 47**
James, William **15, 32**
Jewett, (Theodora) Sarah Orne **1, 22**
Johnson, James Weldon **3, 19**
Kornbluth, C(yril) M. **8**
Kuttner, Henry **10**
Lardner, Ring(gold) W(ilmer) **2, 14**
Lewis, (Harry) Sinclair **4, 13, 23, 39**
Lewisohn, Ludwig **19**
Lindsay, (Nicholas) Vachel **17**
Locke, Alain (Le Roy) **43**
London, Jack **9, 15, 39**
Lovecraft, H(oward) P(hillips) **4, 22**
Lowell, Amy **1, 8**
Markham, Edwin **47**
Marquis, Don(ald Robert Perry) **7**
Masters, Edgar Lee **2, 25**
McCoy, Horace (Stanley) **28**
McKay, Claude **7, 41**
Mencken, H(enry) L(ouis) **13**
Millay, Edna St. Vincent **4, 49**
Mitchell, Margaret (Munnerlyn) **11**
Mitchell, S(ilas) Weir **36**
Monroe, Harriet **12**
Muir, John **28**
Nathan, George Jean **18**
Nordhoff, Charles (Bernard) **23**
Norris, Benjamin Franklin **24**
O'Neill, Eugene (Gladstone) **1, 6, 27, 49**
Oskison, John Milton **35**

Phillips, David Graham **44**
Porter, Gene(va Grace) Stratton **21**
Post, Melville Davisson **39**
Rawlings, Marjorie Kinnan **4**
Reed, John (Silas) **9**
Reich, Wilhelm **57**
Rhodes, Eugene Manlove **53**
Riggs, (Rolla) Lynn **56**
Riley, James Whitcomb **51**
Rinehart, Mary Roberts **52**
Roberts, Kenneth (Lewis) **23**
Robinson, Edwin Arlington **5**
Roelvaag, O(le) E(dvart) **17**
Rogers, Will(iam Penn Adair) **8**
Rourke, Constance (Mayfield) **12**
Runyon, (Alfred) Damon **10**
Saltus, Edgar (Everton) **8**
Santayana, George **40**
Sherwood, Robert E(mmet) **3**
Slesinger, Tess **10**
Steffens, (Joseph) Lincoln **20**
Stein, Gertrude **1, 6, 28, 48**
Sterling, George **20**
Stevens, Wallace **3, 12, 45**
Stockton, Frank R. **47**
Sturges, Preston **48**
Tarbell, Ida M(inerva) **40**
Tarkington, (Newton) Booth **9**
Teasdale, Sara **4**
Thurman, Wallace (Henry) **6**
Twain, Mark **6, 12, 19, 36, 48**
Van Dine, S. S. **23**
Van Doren, Carl (Clinton) **18**
Veblen, Thorstein (Bunde) **31**
Washington, Booker T(aliaferro) **10**
Wells, Carolyn **35**
West, Nathanael **1, 14, 44**
Wharton, Edith (Newbold Jones) **3, 9, 27, 53**
White, Walter F(rancis) **15**
Wister, Owen **21**
Wolfe, Thomas (Clayton) **4, 13, 29**
Woollcott, Alexander (Humphreys) **5**
Wylie, Elinor (Morton Hoyt) **8**

ARGENTINIAN
Arlt, Roberto (Godofredo Christophersen) **29**
Guiraldes, Ricardo (Guillermo) **39**
Lugones, Leopoldo **15**
Storni, Alfonsina **5**

AUSTRALIAN
Baynton, Barbara **57**
Franklin, (Stella Maraia Sarah) Miles **7**
Furphy, Joseph **25**
Ingamells, Rex **35**
Lawson, Henry (Archibald Hertzberg) **27**
Paterson, A(ndrew) B(arton) **32**
Richardson, Henry Handel **4**

AUSTRIAN
Broch, Hermann **20**
Freud, Sigmund **52**
Hofmannsthal, Hugo von **11**
Kafka, Franz **2, 6, 13, 29, 47, 53**
Kraus, Karl **5**
Kubin, Alfred **23**
Meyrink, Gustav **21**
Musil, Robert (Edler von) **12**
Roth, Joseph **33**
Schnitzler, Arthur **4**

Steiner, Rudolf **13**
Trakl, Georg **5**
Werfel, Franz (V.) **8**
Zweig, Stefan **17**

BELGIAN
Bosschere, Jean de **19**
Lemonnier, (Antoine Louis) Camille **22**
Maeterlinck, Maurice **3**
van Ostaijen, Paul **33**
Verhaeren, Emile (Adolphe Gustave) **12**

BRAZILIAN
Andrade, Mario de **43**
Cunha, Euclides (Rodrigues Pimenta) da **24**
Lima Barreto, Afonso Henrique de **23**
Machado de Assis, Joaquim Maria **10**
Ramos, Graciliano **32**

BULGARIAN
Vazov, Ivan (Minchov) **25**

CANADIAN
Campbell, Wilfred **9**
Carman, (William) Bliss **7**
Carr, Emily **32**
Connor, Ralph **31**
Drummond, William Henry **25**
Garneau, (Hector de) Saint-Denys **13**
Grove, Frederick Philip **4**
Knister, Raymond **56**
Leacock, Stephen (Butler) **2**
McCrae, John **12**
Montgomery, L(ucy) M(aud) **51**
Nelligan, Emile **14**
Pickthall, Marjorie L(owry) C(hristie) **21**
Roberts, Charles G(eorge) D(ouglas) **8**
Scott, Duncan Campbell **6**
Service, Robert W(illiam) **15**
Seton, Ernest (Evan) Thompson **31**
Stringer, Arthur **37**

CHILEAN
Huidobro Fernandez, Vicente Garcia **31**
Mistral, Gabriela **2**

CHINESE
Hsun, Lu **3**
Liu E **15**
Lu Hsun **3**
Su Man-shu **24**
Wen I-to **28**

COLOMBIAN
Rivera, Jose Eustasio **35**

CZECH
Capek, Karel **6, 37**
Hasek, Jaroslav (Matej Frantisek) **4**
Nezval, Vitezslav **44**

DANISH
Brandes, Georg (Morris Cohen) **10**
Hansen, Martin A. **32**
Jensen, Johannes V. **41**
Nexo, Martin Andersen **43**
Pontoppidan, Henrik **29**

DUTCH
Couperus, Louis (Marie Anne) **15**
Frank, Anne(lies Marie) **17**

Heijermans, Herman **24**
Hillesum, Etty **49**
Schendel, Arthur van **56**

ENGLISH
Barbellion, W. N. P. **24**
Baring, Maurice **8**
Beerbohm, Henry Maximilian **1, 24**
Belloc, (Joseph) Hilaire (Pierre) **7, 18**
Bennett, (Enoch) Arnold **5, 20**
Benson, E(dward) F(rederic) **27**
Benson, Stella **17**
Bentley, E(dmund) C(lerihew) **12**
Besant, Annie (Wood) **9**
Blackmore, R(ichard) D(oddridge) **27**
Blackwood, Algernon (Henry) **5**
Bridges, Robert (Seymour) **1**
Brooke, Rupert (Chawner) **2, 7**
Butler, Samuel **1, 33**
Chesterton, G(ilbert) K(eith) **1, 6**
Conrad, Joseph **1, 6, 13, 25, 43, 57**
Coppard, A(lfred) E(dgar) **5**
Corelli, Marie **51**
Crofts, Freeman Wills **55**
Crowley, Aleister **7**
Dale, Colin **18**
de la Mare, Walter (John) **4, 53**
Doughty, Charles M(ontagu) **27**
Douglas, Keith **40**
Dowson, Ernest Christopher **4**
Doyle, Arthur Conan **7**
Drinkwater, John **57**
Eddison, E(ric) R(ucker) **15**
Elaine **18**
Elizabeth **41**
Ellis, (Henry) Havelock **14**
Field, Michael **43**
Firbank, (Arthur Annesley) Ronald **1**
Ford, Ford Madox **1, 15, 39, 57**
Freeman, R(ichard) Austin **21**
Galsworthy, John **1, 45**
Gilbert, W(illiam) S(chwenck) **3**
Gissing, George (Robert) **3, 24, 47**
Gosse, Edmund (William) **28**
Granville-Barker, Harley **2**
Gray, John (Henry) **19**
Gurney, Ivor (Bertie) **33**
Haggard, H(enry) Rider **11**
Hall, (Marguerite) Radclyffe **12**
Hardy, Thomas **4, 10, 18, 32, 48, 53**
Henley, William Ernest **8**
Hilton, James **21**
Hodgson, William Hope **13**
Housman, A(lfred) E(dward) **1, 10**
Housman, Laurence **7**
Hudson, W(illiam) H(enry) **29**
Hulme, T(homas) E(rnest) **21**
Hunt, Violet **53**
Jacobs, W(illiam) W(ymark) **22**
James, Montague (Rhodes) **6**
Jerome, Jerome K(lapka) **23**
Johnson, Lionel (Pigot) **19**
Kaye-Smith, Sheila **20**
Kipling, (Joseph) Rudyard **8, 17**
Lawrence, D(avid) H(erbert Richards) **2, 9, 16, 33, 48**
Lawrence, T(homas) E(dward) **18**
Lee, Vernon **5**
Lee-Hamilton, Eugene (Jacob) **22**
Leverson, Ada **18**
Lewis, (Percy) Wyndham **2, 9**
Lindsay, David **15**

Lowndes, Marie Adelaide (Belloc) 12
Lowry, (Clarence) Malcolm 6, 40
Macaulay, Rose 7, 44
MacCarthy, (Sir Charles Otto) Desmond
    36
Manning, Frederic 25
Meredith, George 17, 43
Mew, Charlotte (Mary) 8
Meynell, Alice (Christina Gertrude
    Thompson) 6
Middleton, Richard (Barham) 56
Milne, A(lan) A(lexander) 6
Murry, John Middleton 16
Noyes, Alfred 7
Oppenheim, E(dward) Phillips 45
Orwell, George 2, 6, 15, 31, 51
Ouida 43
Owen, Wilfred (Edward Salter) 5, 27
Pinero, Arthur Wing 32
Powys, T(heodore) F(rancis) 9
Quiller-Couch, Arthur Thomas 53
Richardson, Dorothy Miller 3
Rohmer, Sax 28
Rolfe, Frederick (William Serafino Austin
    Lewis Mary) 12
Rosenberg, Isaac 12
Ruskin, John 20
Rutherford, Mark 25
Sabatini, Rafael 47
Saintsbury, George (Edward Bateman) 31
Saki 3
Sapper 44
Sayers, Dorothy L(eigh) 2, 15
Shiel, M(atthew) P(hipps) 8
Sinclair, May 3, 11
Stapledon, (William) Olaf 22
Stead, William Thomas 48
Stephen, Leslie 23
Strachey, (Giles) Lytton 12
Summers, (Alphonsus Joseph-Mary
    Augustus) Montague 16
Sutro, Alfred 6
Swinburne, Algernon Charles 8, 36
Symons, Arthur 11
Thomas, (Philip) Edward 10
Thompson, Francis Joseph 4
Van Druten, John (William) 2
Wallace, (Richard Horatio) Edgar 57
Walpole, Hugh (Seymour) 5
Ward, Mrs. Humphry 55
Warung, Price 45
Webb, (Martha) Beatrice (Potter) 22
Webb, Mary (Gladys Meredith) 24
Webb, Sidney (James) 22
Welch, (Maurice) Denton 22
Wells, H(erbert) G(eorge) 6, 12, 19
Williams, Charles (Walter Stansby) 1, 11
Woolf, (Adeline) Virginia 1, 5, 20, 43, 56
Yonge, Charlotte (Mary) 48
Zangwill, Israel 16

ESTONIAN
Tammsaare, A(nton) H(ansen) 27

FINNISH
Leino, Eino 24
Soedergran, Edith (Irene) 31

FRENCH
Alain 41
Alain-Fournier 6
Apollinaire, Guillaume 3, 8, 51

Artaud, Antonin 3, 36
Barbusse, Henri 5
Barres, Maurice 47
Bergson, Henri 32
Bernanos, (Paul Louis) Georges 3
Bloy, Leon 22
Bourget, Paul (Charles Joseph) 12
Claudel, Paul (Louis Charles Marie) 2, 10
Colette, (Sidonie-Gabrielle) 1, 5, 16
Coppee, Francois 25
Daumal, Rene 14
Desnos, Robert 22
Drieu la Rochelle, Pierre(-Eugene) 21
Dujardin, Edouard (Emile Louis) 13
Durkheim, Emile 55
Eluard, Paul 7, 41
Fargue, Leon-Paul 11
Feydeau, Georges (Leon Jules Marie) 22
France, Anatole 9
Gide, Andre (Paul Guillaume) 5, 12, 36
Giraudoux, (Hippolyte) Jean 2, 7
Gourmont, Remy de 17
Huysmans, Joris-Karl 7
Jacob, (Cyprien-)Max 6
Jarry, Alfred 2, 14
Larbaud, Valery (Nicolas) 9
Leblanc, Maurice (Marie Emile) 49
Leroux, Gaston 25
Loti, Pierre 11
Martin du Gard, Roger 24
Mirbeau, Octave 55
Mistral, Frederic 51
Moreas, Jean 18
Nizan, Paul 40
Peguy, Charles Pierre 10
Peret, Benjamin 20
Proust, (Valentin-Louis-George-Eugene-)
    Marcel 7, 13, 33
Radiguet, Raymond 29
Renard, Jules 17
Rolland, Romain 23
Rostand, Edmond (Eugene Alexis) 6, 37
Roussel, Raymond 20
Saint-Exupery, Antoine (Jean Baptiste Marie
    Roger) de 2, 56
Schwob, (Mayer Andre) Marcel 20
Sully Prudhomme 31
Teilhard de Chardin, (Marie Joseph) Pierre
    9
Valery, (Ambroise) Paul (Toussaint Jules)
    4, 15
Verne, Jules (Gabriel) 6, 52
Vian, Boris 9
Weil, Simone (Adolphine) 23
Zola, Emile (Edouard Charles Antoine) 1,
    6, 21, 41

GERMAN
Andreas-Salome, Lou 56
Auerbach, Erich 43
Benjamin, Walter 39
Benn, Gottfried 3
Borchert, Wolfgang 5
Brecht, Bertolt 1, 6, 13, 35
Carossa, Hans 48
Doblin, Alfred 13
Ewers, Hanns Heinz 12
Feuchtwanger, Lion 3
George, Stefan (Anton) 2, 14
Hauptmann, Gerhart (Johann Robert) 4
Heym, Georg (Theodor Franz Arthur) 9

Heyse, Paul (Johann Ludwig von) 8
Hitler, Adolf 53
Huch, Ricarda (Octavia) 13
Kaiser, Georg 9
Klabund 44
Kolmar, Gertrud 40
Lasker-Schueler, Else 57
Liliencron, (Friedrich Adolf Axel) Detlev
    von 18
Mann, (Luiz) Heinrich 9
Mann, (Paul) Thomas 2, 8, 14, 21, 35, 44
Morgenstern, Christian 8
Nietzsche, Friedrich (Wilhelm) 10, 18, 55
Plumpe, Friedrich Wilhelm 53
Raabe, Wilhelm 45
Rilke, Rainer Maria 1, 6, 19
Spengler, Oswald (Arnold Gottfried) 25
Sternheim, (William Adolf) Carl 8
Sudermann, Hermann 15
Toller, Ernst 10
Wassermann, (Karl) Jakob 6
Wedekind, (Benjamin) Frank(lin) 7
Wiene, Robert 56

GHANIAN
Casely-Hayford, J(oseph) E(phraim) 24

GREEK
Cavafy, C(onstantine) P(eter) 2, 7
Kazantzakis, Nikos 2, 5, 33
Palamas, Kostes 5
Papadiamantis, Alexandros 29
Sikelianos, Angelos 39

HAITIAN
Roumain, Jacques (Jean Baptiste) 19

HUNGARIAN
Ady, Endre 11
Babits, Mihaly 14
Csath, Geza 13
Herzl, Theodor 36
Horvath, Oedoen von 45
Jozsef, Attila 22
Karinthy, Frigyes 47
Mikszath, Kalman 31
Molnar, Ferenc 20
Moricz, Zsigmond 33
Radnoti, Miklos 16

ICELANDIC
Sigurjonsson, Johann 27

INDIAN
Chatterji, Saratchandra 13
Premchand 21
Tagore, Rabindranath 3, 53

INDONESIAN
Anwar, Chairil 22

IRANIAN
Hedayat, Sadeq 21

IRISH
Cary, (Arthur) Joyce (Lunel) 1, 29
Dunsany, Lord 2
Gogarty, Oliver St. John 15
Gregory, Isabella Augusta (Persse) 1
Harris, Frank 24
Joyce, James (Augustine Aloysius) 3, 8, 16,
    35

Nationality Index

495

TCLC-57 Title Index

ISBN 0-8103-2439-3